THink
Pen Zen Diaries

Peter Magyar

This book is established to provide information and inspiration to all readers. It is designed with the understanding that the author is not engaged to render any psychological, legal, or any other kind of professional advice. The content is the sole expression of the author.

ISBN: 978-1-950303-16-8 (Paperback)
ISBN: 978-1-950303-17-5 (Ebook)

Contents

Amy Karolyi: Window

Translated from Hungarian by Peter Magyar

The window is important.
Connects with the is,
With the isn't,
With the in,
And with the out.

It allows millions of lightyears to be radiated
at the floor,
Like as if the end-intent
of the rays
Would be to reach you.

Think about it, hand,
While closing or opening the window,
What kind of cosmic gesture,
You forbid with,
or let in
the Universe.

Foreword

"Die Linie ist ein Punkt der spazieren geht" - Paul Klee

A line is a dot that went for a walk.

The reference to Zen is new, but for a long time I had the strong conviction that only the undefinable aspects of design can create the ephemeral richness and poetry of any projects! So walking through the tip of my fountain pen along the thousands of lines, I always felt, the architecture is the roots of Infinity!

Working at the boundaries of the known, the unknown and the unknowable, I prioritize the two latter notions. Intend to excavate the preconscious from the subconscious strata. My tools are my pen and lately the stylus or the Apple-Pen (for drawing on digital tablets). The material starting point is the epidermis of the place, but from there one as to ascend to the rarefied spheres of thoughts and even feelings. This floating in the domains of the unknown and unknowable, unfortunately, during the design process and as the straight consequence of the same, shifts more and more towards the sphere of the known, and in the constructed reality, every unknown must be excluded.

My process drawings aim to serve the prolongation of the floating phase, and interrogate that hope, whether the materialized reality could convey anything at all from the Icarusean gift, provided by the design-experience for its enthusiastic laborer

Chapter 1

BETWEEN BRIDGES

Pen Zen Diaries #1

Chapter 1

(P.Z.D.1)
Between Bridges / The Public Safety Building
Pittsburg, PA

Knowingly or unknowingly, we employ, analyze and practice the following cognitive processes in design:

Reflect on, establish and internalize the constellation of relevant attributes, both in general, overarching status, as well as in their particular, circumstantial mutations (= research)

Induce, recognize, enhance and apply targeted intuition, to bring forth the germ of the physical manifestation of an integrated universe, containing all the elements from the previous phase, ordered by the ethical, epistemological and ontological hierarchies (=design)

Apply the selected and relevant societal, environmental and technological restrictions, in order to communicate the conditions of singularity (=design development)

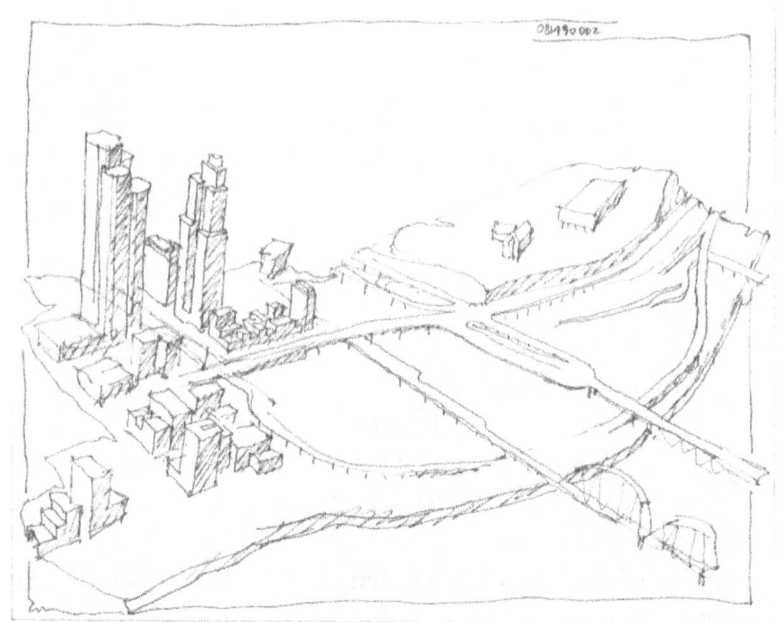

The case study of the design of the Pittsburgh Public Safety Building intends to illustrate the previously described issues. The drawings are excerpted from a much longer process, but they represent the changes and the major steps of the evolutional process. The ensemble on the shoreline of the Monongahela River, was to include -additionally to the Public Safety Building - a light-rail train station, a Federal Courthouse and parking for 2800 cars .

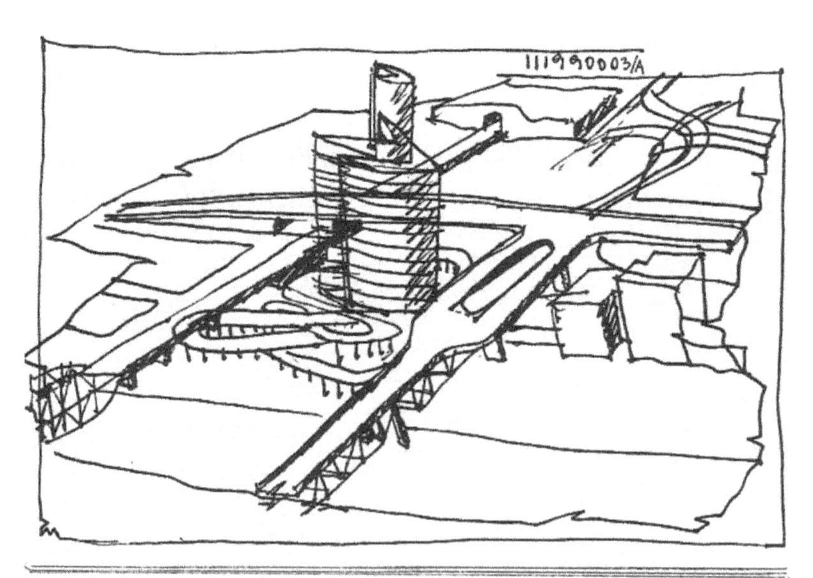

Barely inhibited by the existing elements, this image depicts a childlike interpretation of a tower, the labyrinth of roads, as the parking, and the adjoining volume of the jail. The Monongahela River is in the forefront

Another uninhibited drawing, breaking with the habit of repeated pancake-like floorplates.
To draw without much thinking is as important, as the opposite of it, to reflect for hours or more, then capture those thoughts with a form.
Thinking with our hand. I baptized this process as "think - ink", referring to the usual media of my drawings.

Another quick impression of the extended site. The Public Safety Building has to establish its identity against the forest of tall buildings.

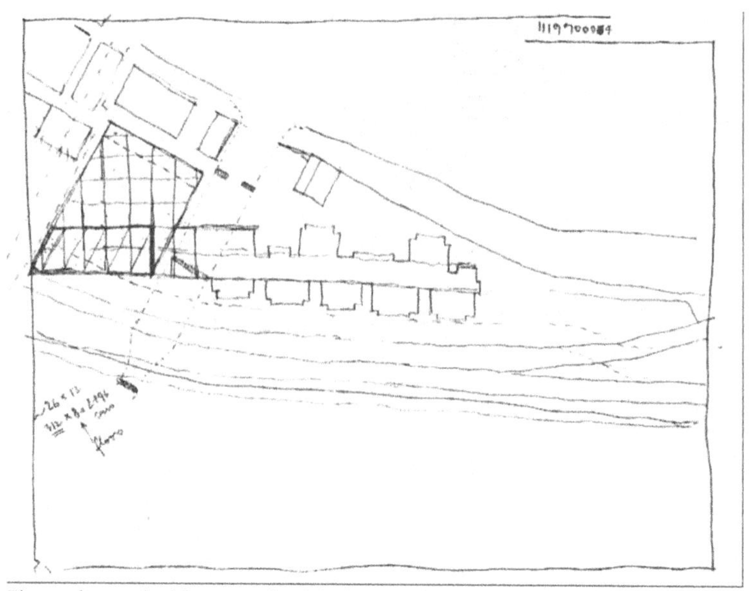

First and very significant result of the "targeted intuition" process. The close to scale drawing provides the potential to exploit the complexity gained from the rotated grids of the parking and the office building. At this stage it is as yet hidden, the office's directionality prevails.

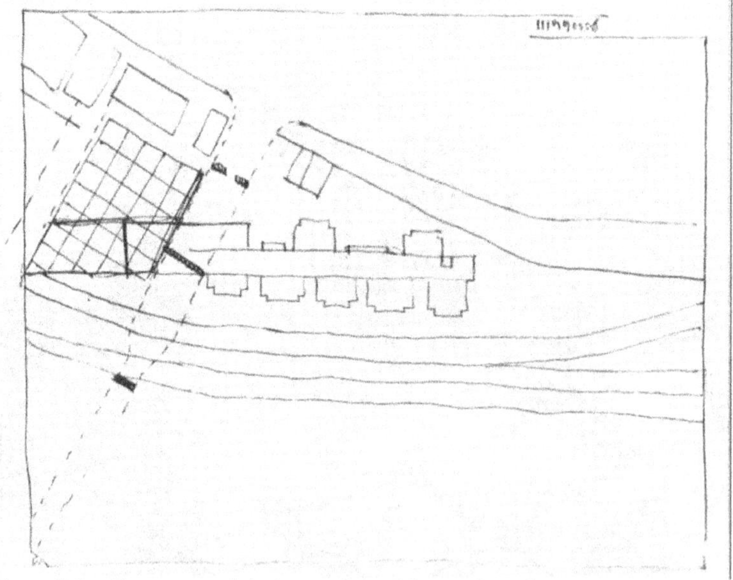

Just a little adjustment, and the known fact of the smaller office module superimposed on the sixty feet grid of the parking structure created thefeeling of the direction to explore.

Known and felt, two different appearances of wisdom one has to be aware of during the design. However strong the "known" part, and barely perceptiblthe"felt" one is, one has to listen! It is something, we receive from a greater receptacle of knowledge, maybe as a gift for our relentless toiling towards the "solution".

The bridges point to the jail, the hill, and the towers in the background, and we can see the new elements of the riverbank. The importance of the siluet- effect is clearly tangible, in order to gain a formal identity against the race of being the highest vertical prism, and so the most important member of the business district.

All present, the jail, the hill behind it, the two bridges, the volume of the parking and on top of it the PSB. Looming in the background we see some of the high-rise buildings of Downtown Pittsburgh.

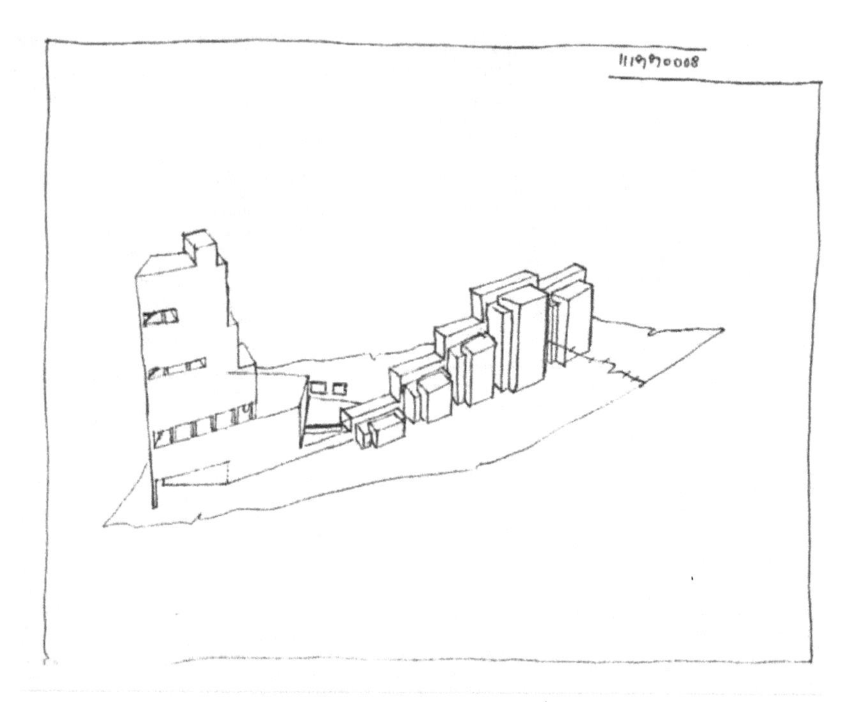

Bridges removed, this is the first three-dimensional image of the jail - court house - parking -office building ensemble. A triangular volume is carved out from the parking, in order to accommodate the bend of the Penn Lincoln Parkway, present already in the first two site plans, shown earlier.

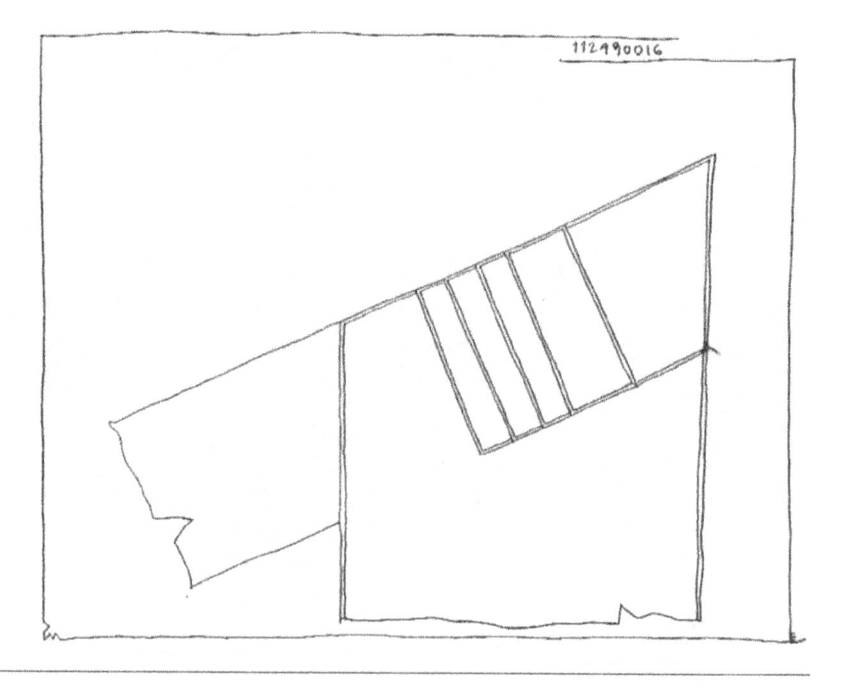

View of the roof.

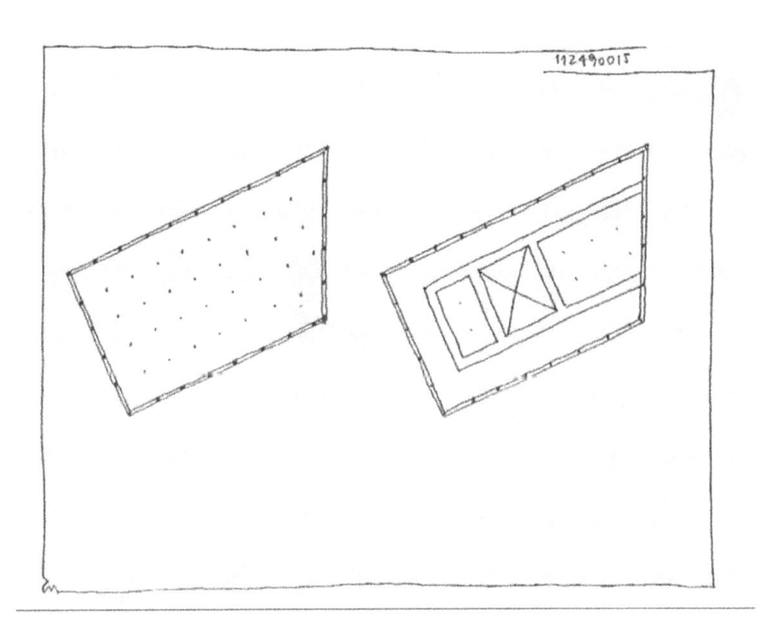

Office floor plan grid and circulation system discovery diagrams. The right one shows the smaller offices banded around the three perimeters of the block, surrounding so some internal service area, vertical circulation group (with the diagonal lines) and a large room, which borrowed its name from H. H. Richardson's Carnegie - Libraries, called "the living room of the city". This would be the interface between the Planning Authorities of the cityof Pittsburgh, and its interested population.

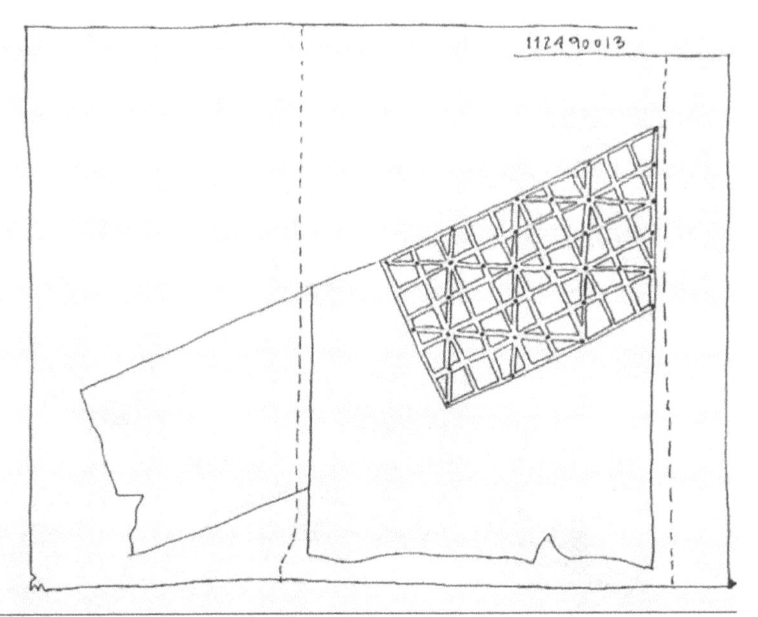

Superimposed grids of the office structure and the parking beneath of it.
The complexity of a double transfer-beam system is predicted by this overlap.

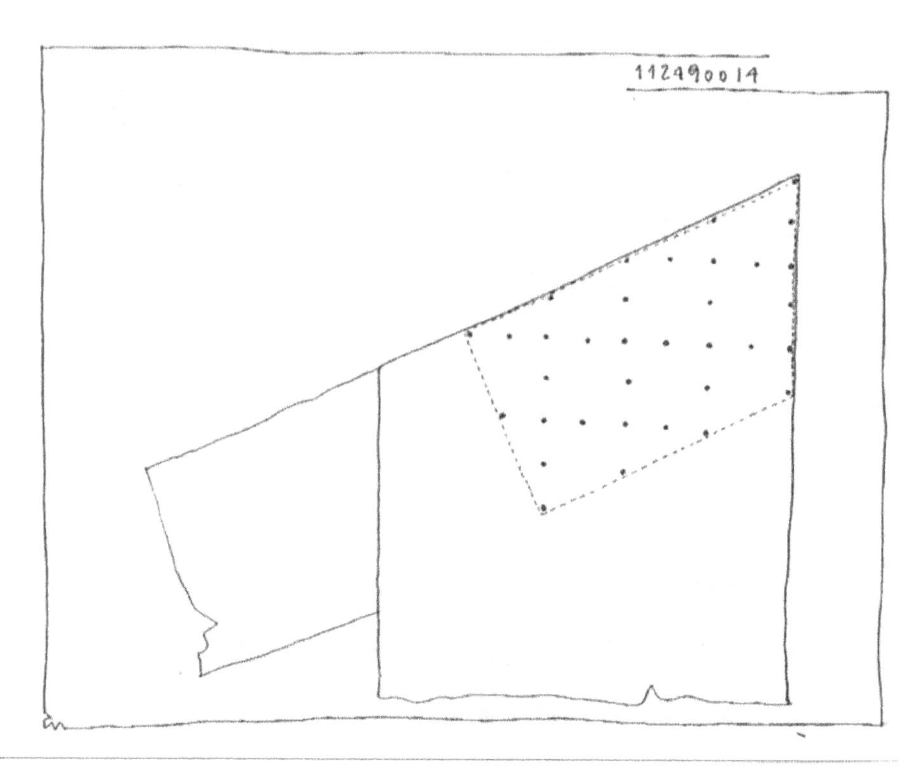

The outline of the office and the projected structural grid of the parking.

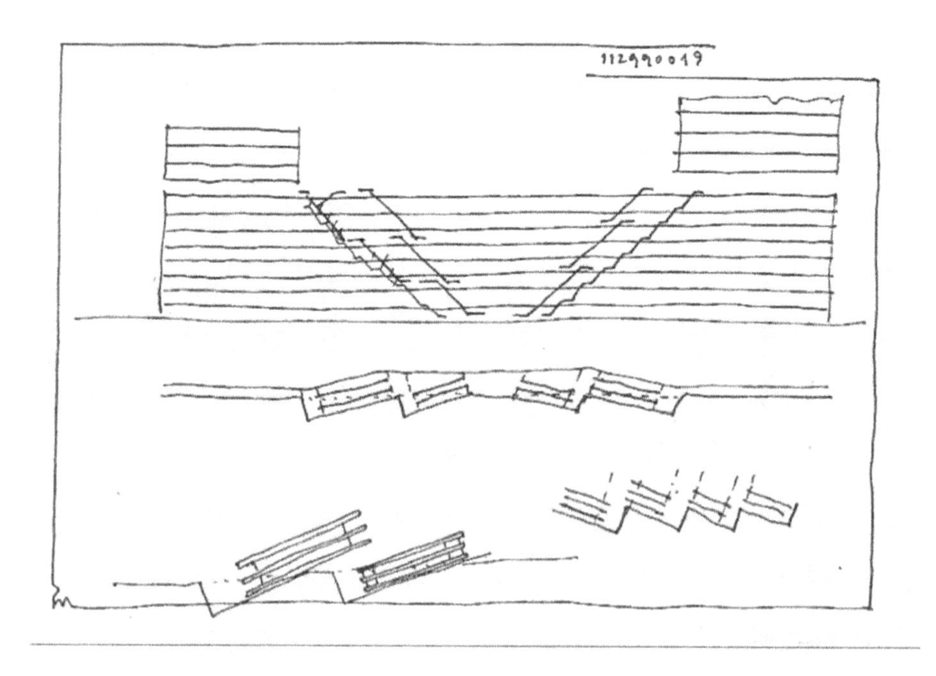

Graphic notes about the escalators leading from ground level to the elevated plaza.

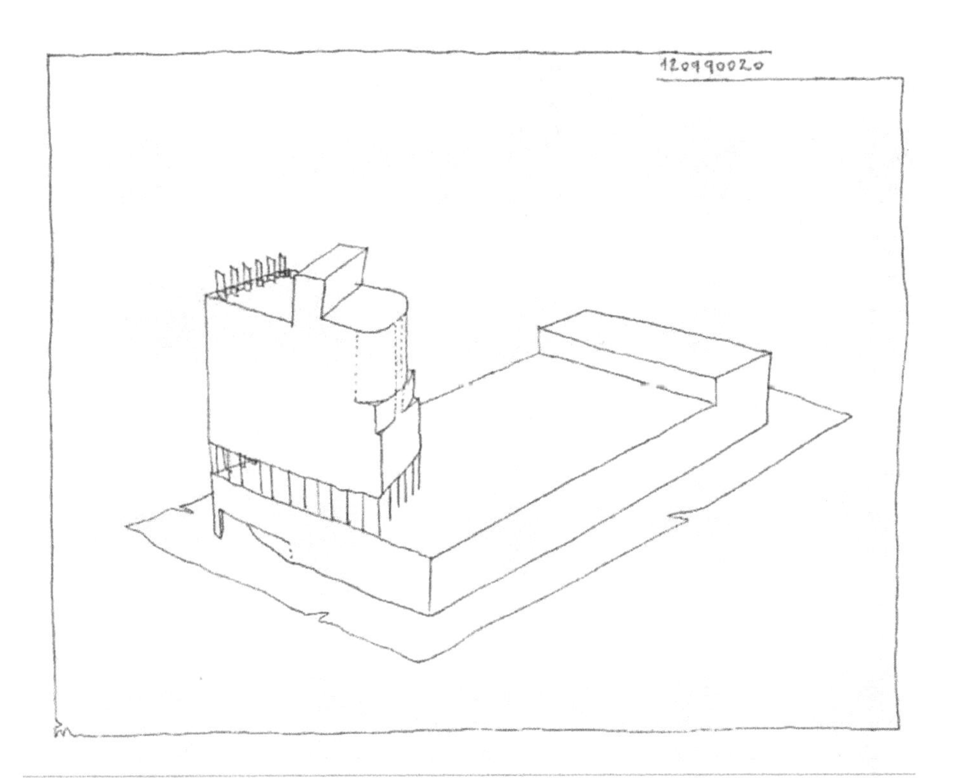

Articulated massing of the office tower.

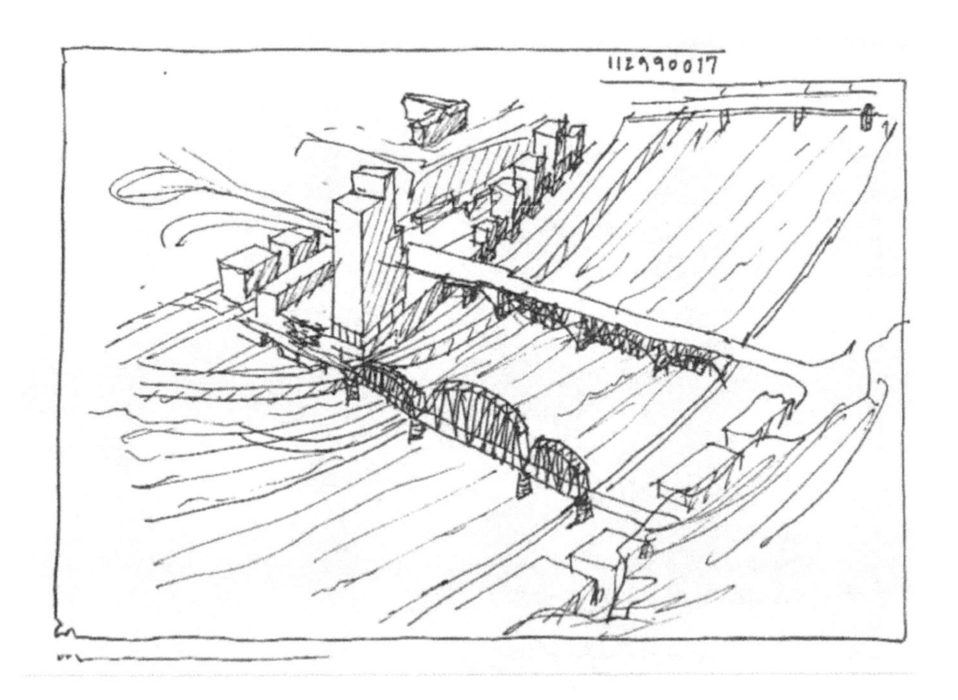

Same as before, put in the immediate context of its surrounding.

Watery view of the bridges and the PSB Complex.
These quick, but telling images test the design, because through them, the ambiance and character of the new situation can be evaluated, simultaneously weighing the "known" and the "felt" impulses.

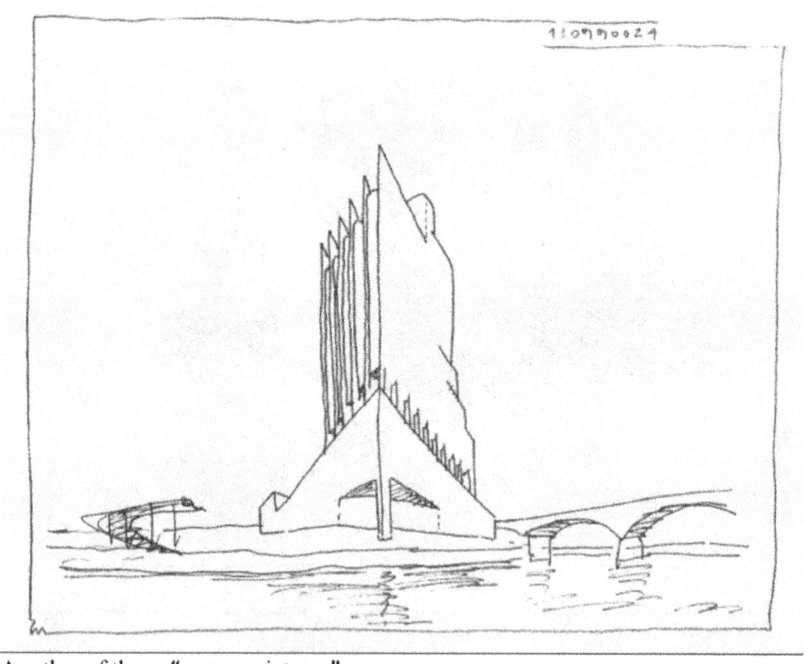

Another of those "money pictures".
Involuntary exaggeration sometimes is necessary, because it reveals the subconscious direction of the explorations.

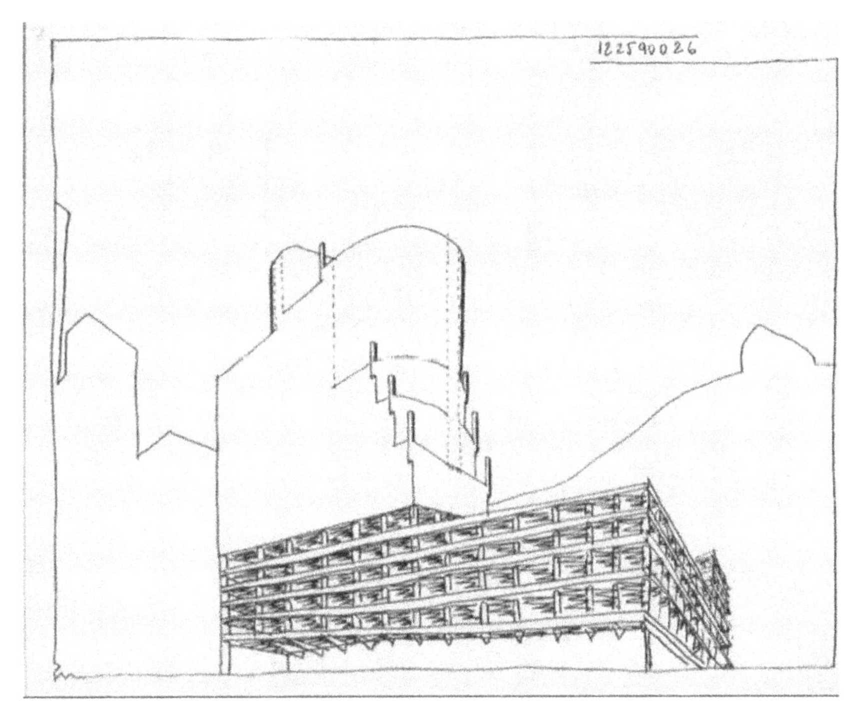

Most of the times the bottom of the structural slabs will be visible from street level, so to add Le Corbusier's fifth elevation, the roof, we have to think of the sixth one, the bottom of the plates.

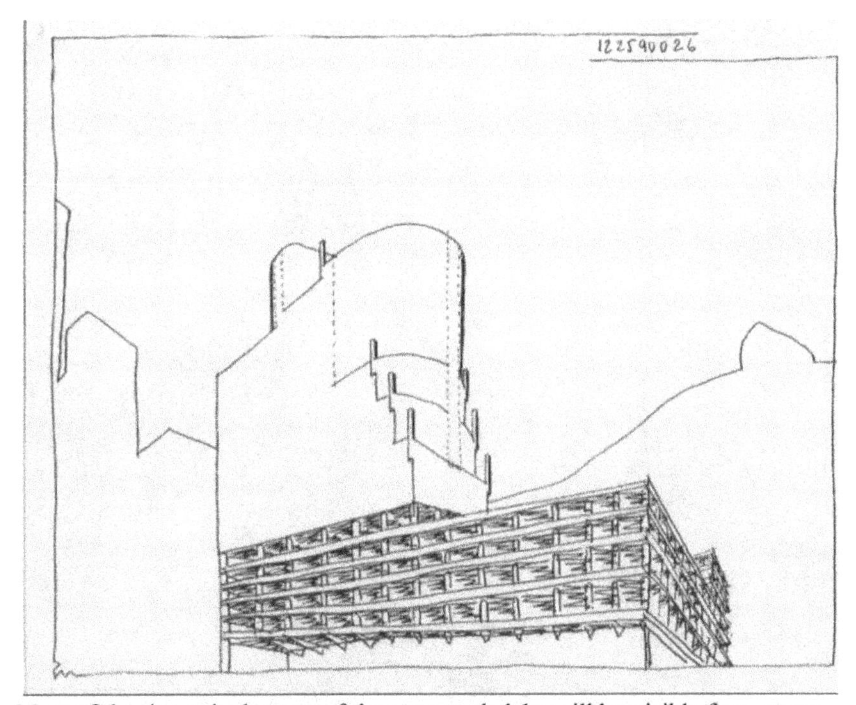

Most of the times the bottom of the structural slabs will be visible from street level, so to add Le Corbusier's fifth elevation, the roof, we have to think of the sixth one, the bottom of the plates.

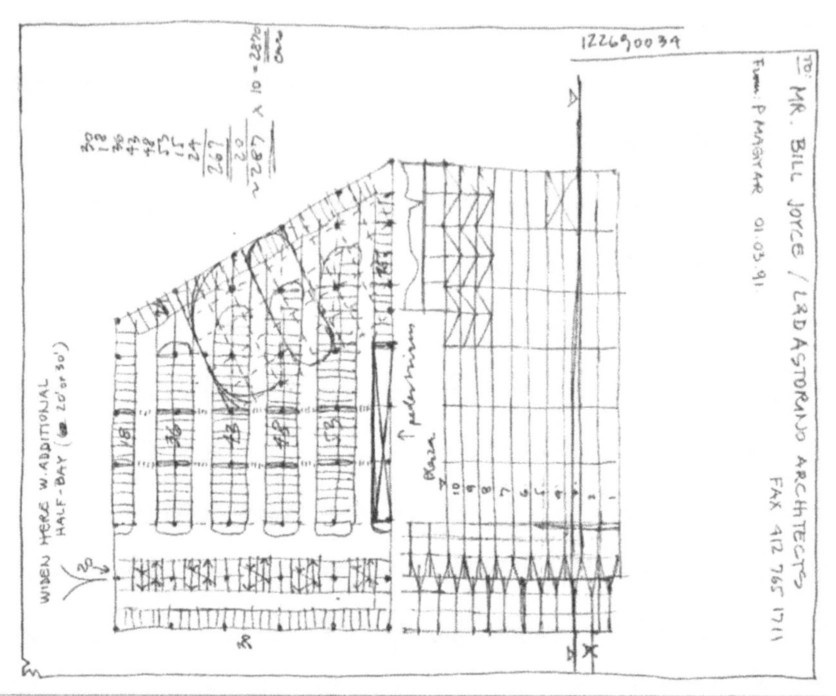

Outline of the section and general floor-plan of the parking. Available parking spaces are inventoried. Reference is being made to the locations of the transfer-structures.

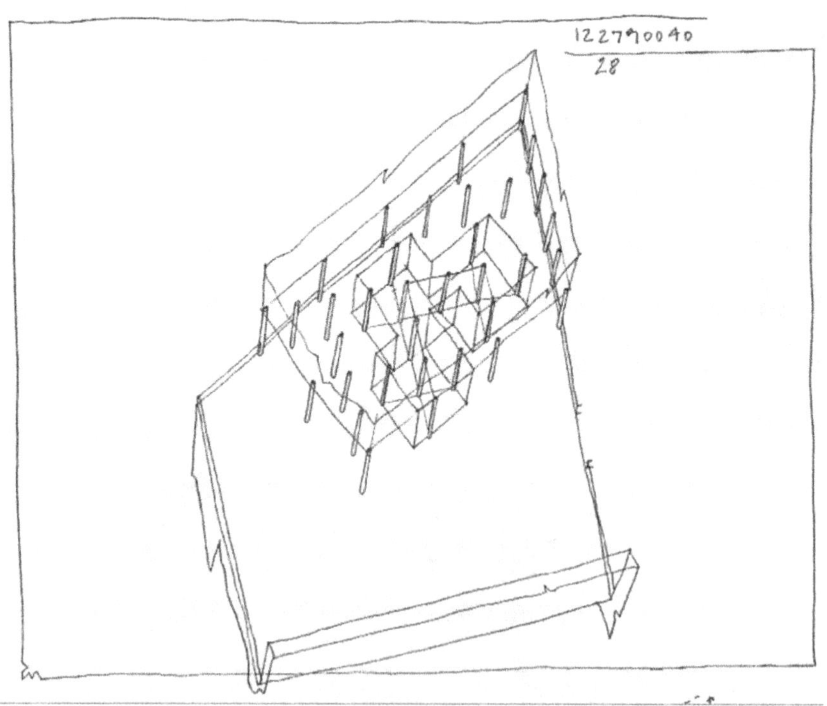

The previous structure, with the enclosed spaces of the plaza level, and the indication of the continuing vertical envelopes of the tower.

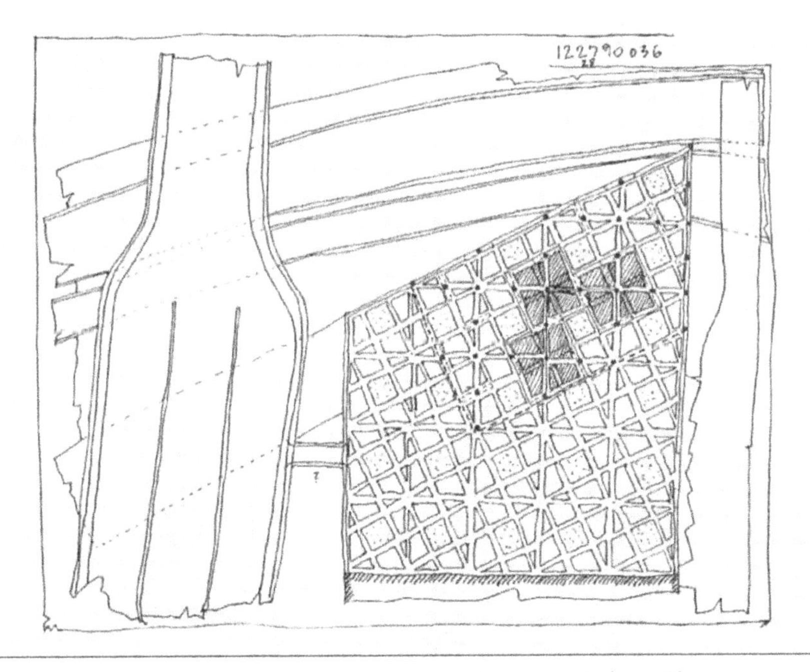

Partial view of the top of the parking structure, the elevated plaza. The pavement pattern is consistent with the dual grids of the larger and smaller structural elements. The darkened area indicates the enclosed spaces of the plaza level of the office tower.

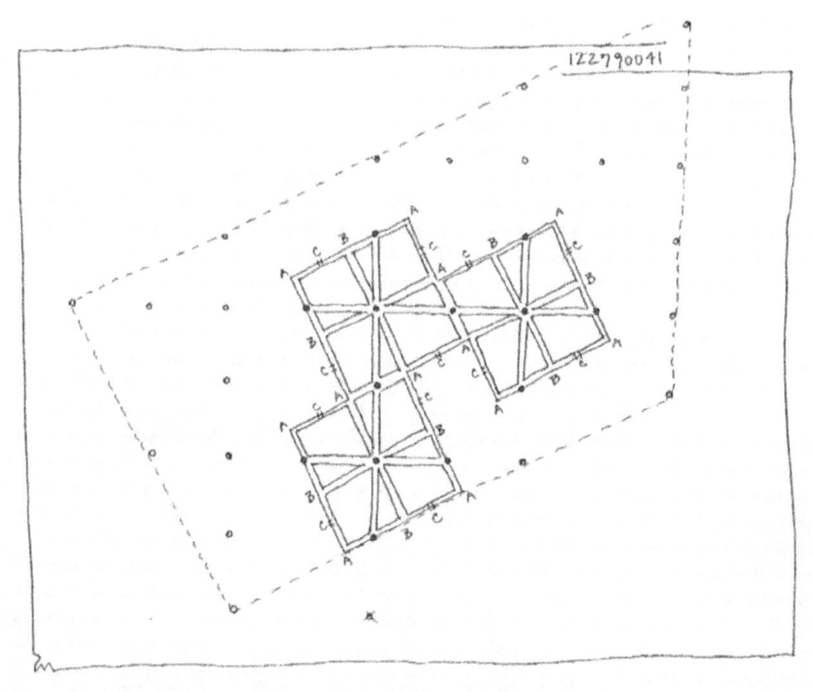

The superimposed grids, latently containing the structural distribution of the bottom of the tower, above the plaza level.

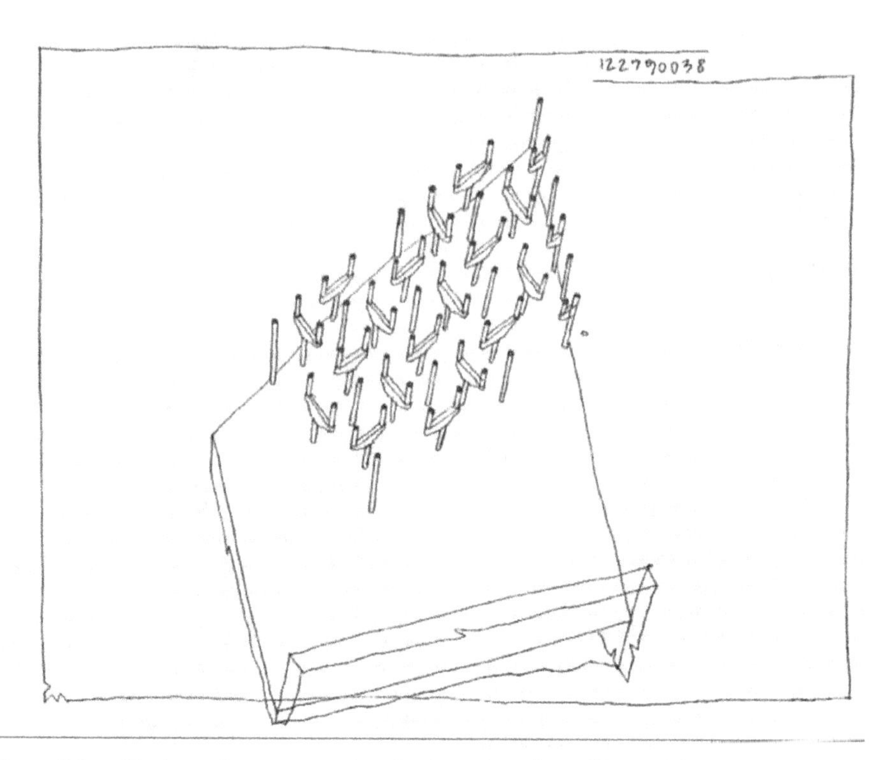

One of the eliminated systems, clearly denoting the office grid.

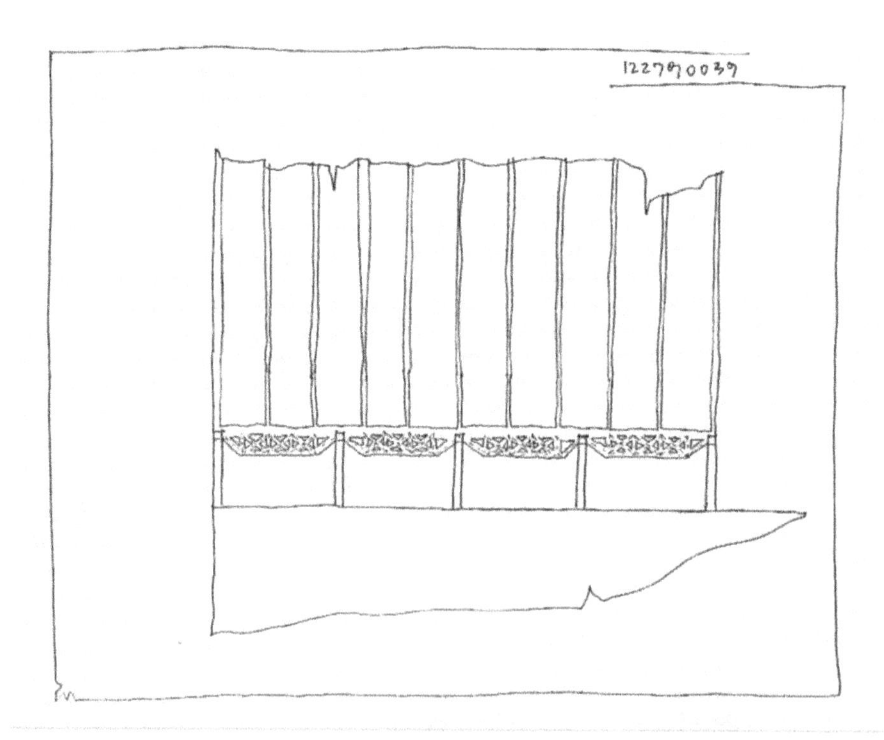

Sketch of the side elevation. The 2-2-1, 1-2-2 rhythm of the structural subdivision is clearly visible.

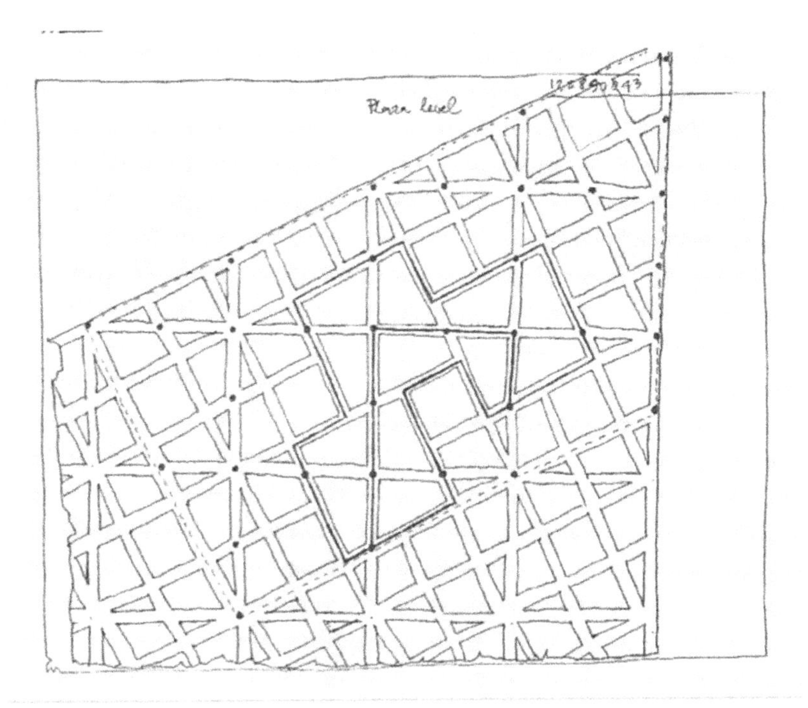

Partial view of the plaza, with the indication of the enclosed area on the plaza level. The load-transfer points are clearly visible, the pavement pattern contains the projected position of the trusses above.

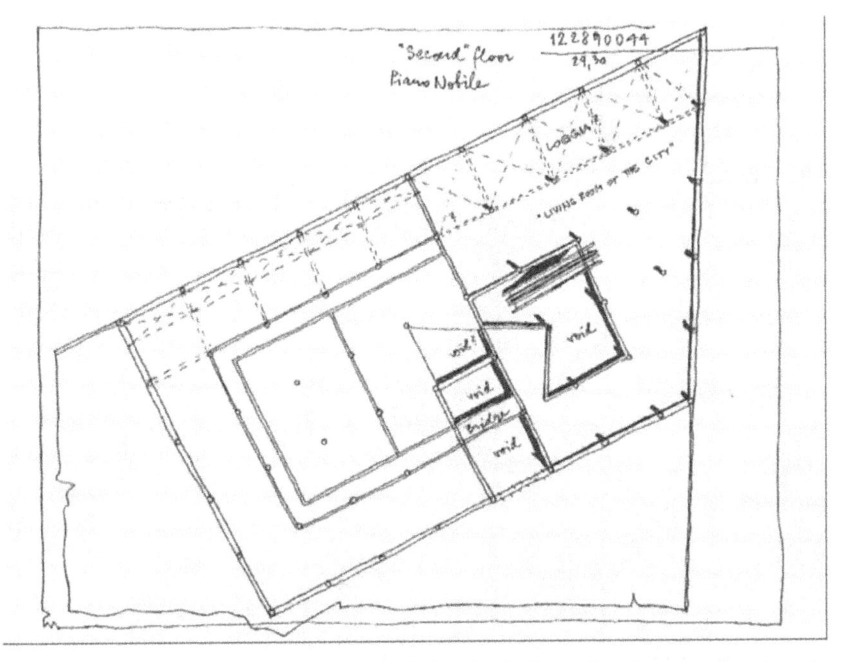

The previously addressed "living room of the city", above the plaza level. A loggia opens on the side of the river, and through a two-storey high portion, escalators come up from the plaza level to this "Piano Nobile" of the building.

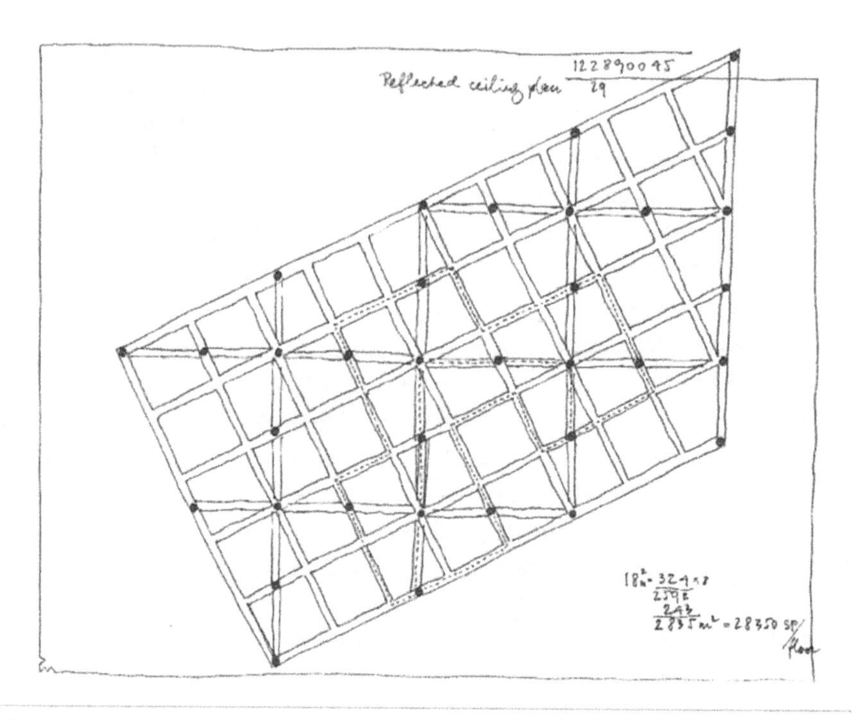

The formative superimposition of the two grids. The office structure's Vertical load-bearing elements are located at the intersections of the smaller grid.

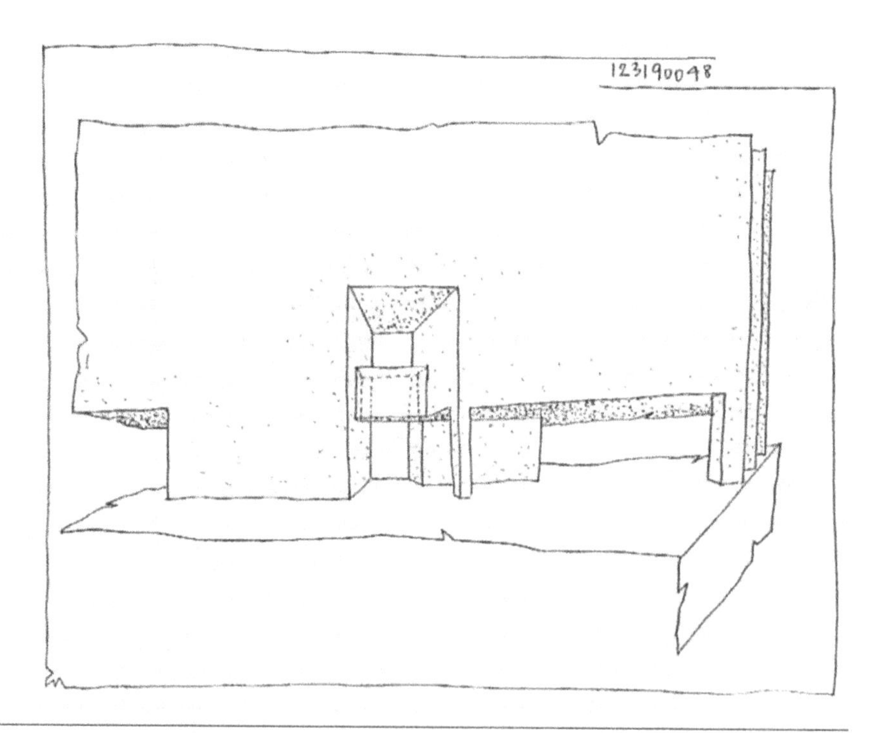

Massing detail of the office tower, with the clearly visible two storey high portion of the plaza level.

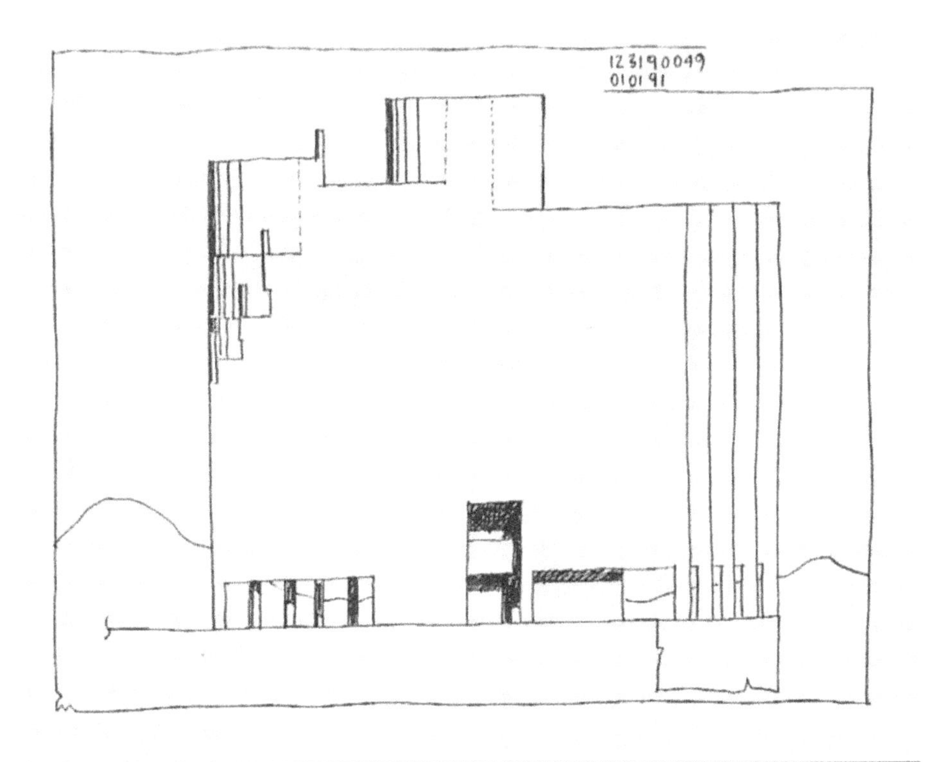

The "tower" above the plaza level.

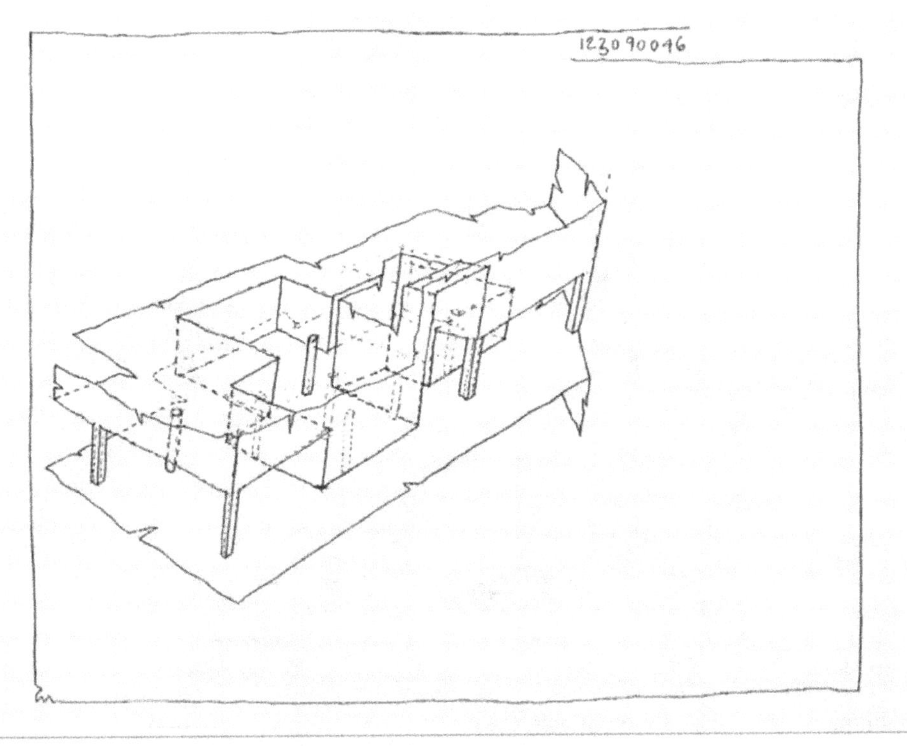

Detail of the entrance part above the plaza level.

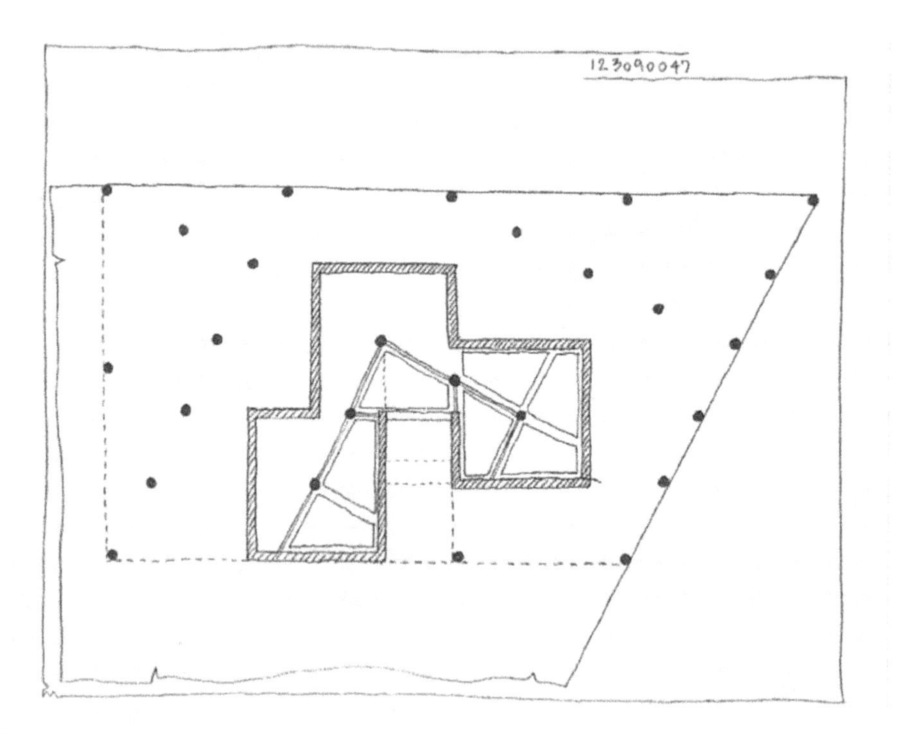

Vertical-structure elements of the plaza level. The dotted line indicates the volume above.

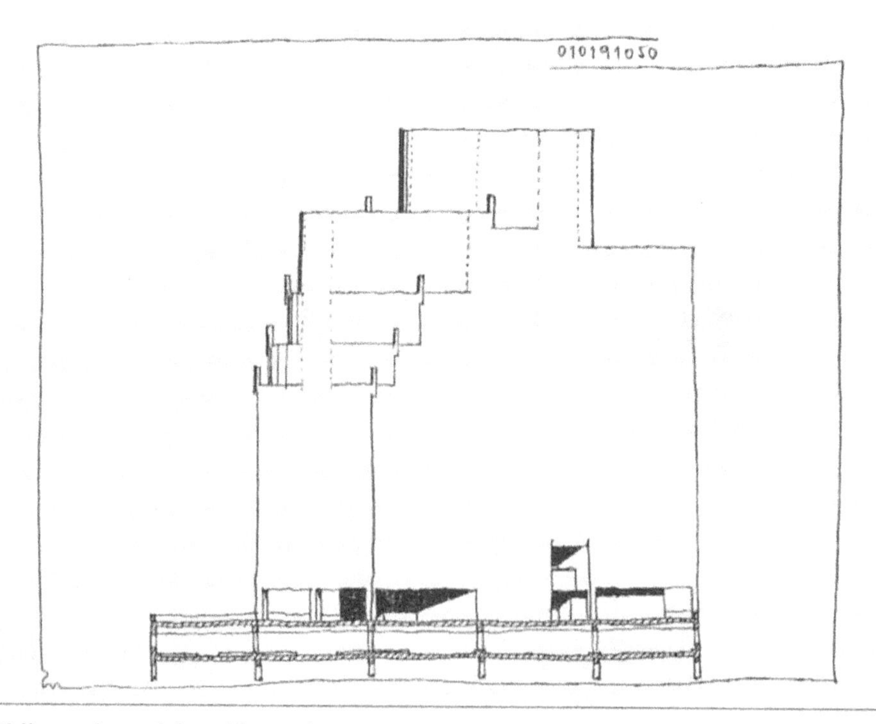

Oblique view of the office volume.

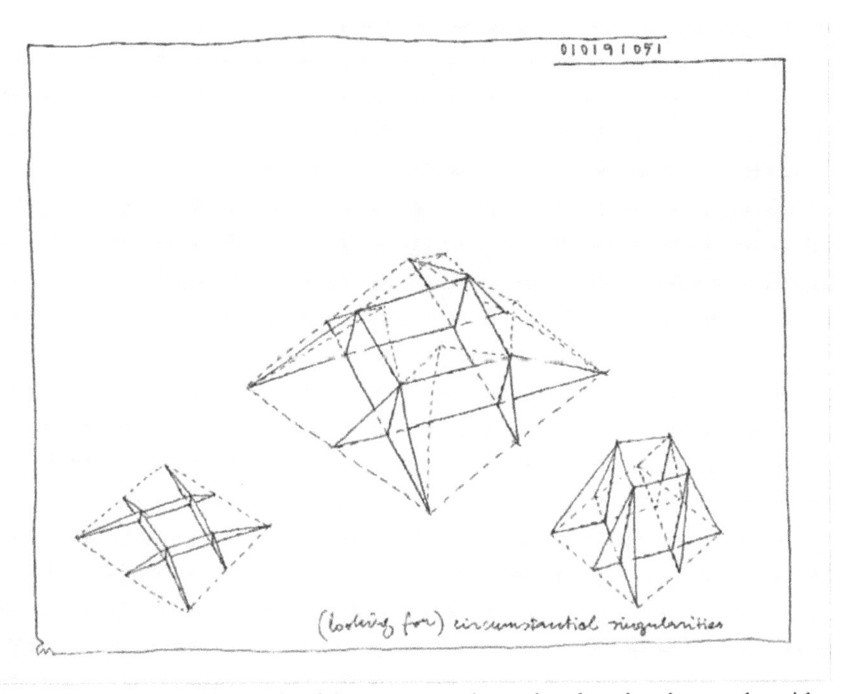

The first depiction of one unit of the structure above the plaza level, turned upside down.
The simple rotation of the end-points of the structure creates a surprising geometrical condition.

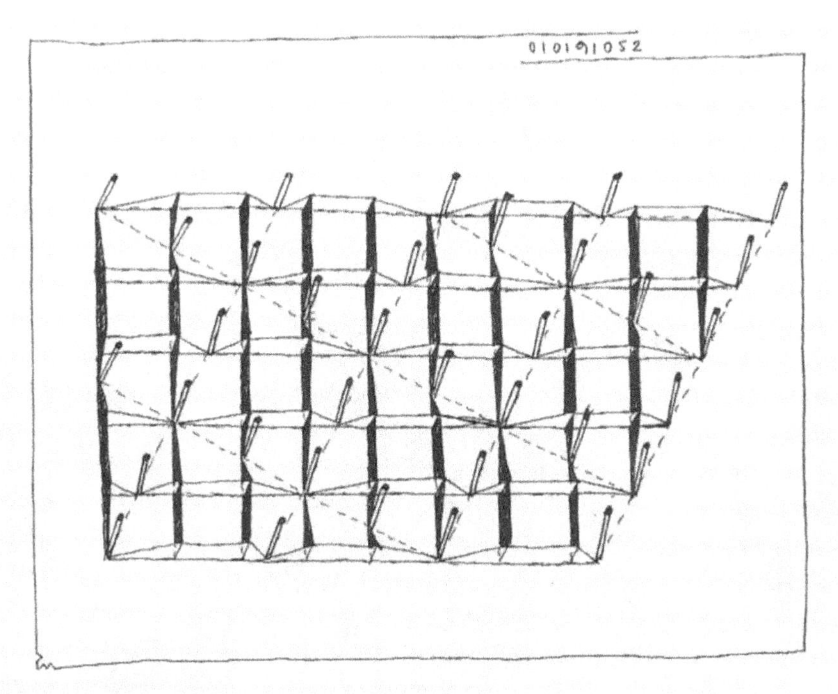

Connecting several of the units just shown, a very interesting, unusual system was discovered.

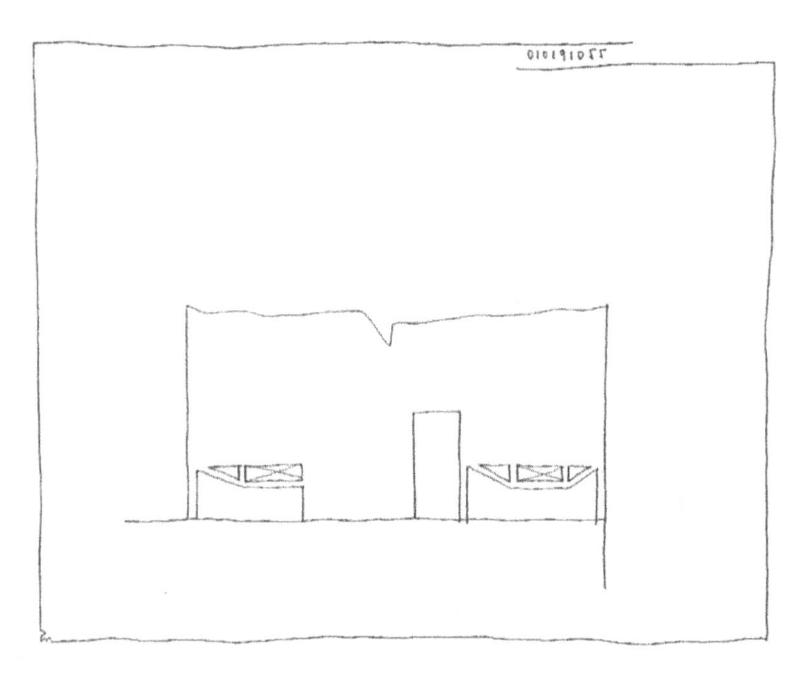

Partially solid, partially perforated structure on the side elevation.

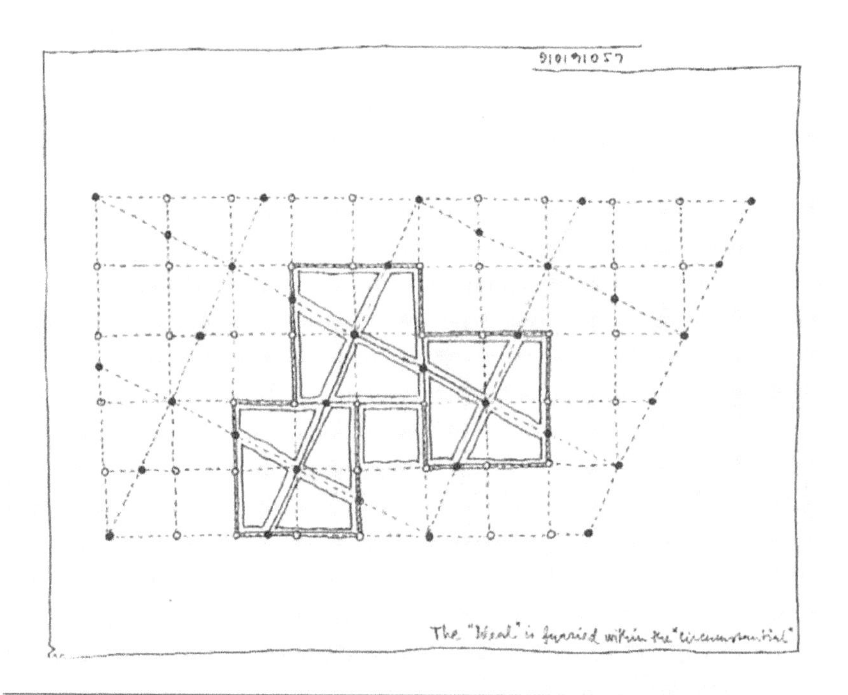

Some of the walls of the enclosed plaza level absorb the columns of the vertical load-bearing system, others are left free-standing, creating a somewhat enigmatic order. The dotted lines are representing the office-grid.

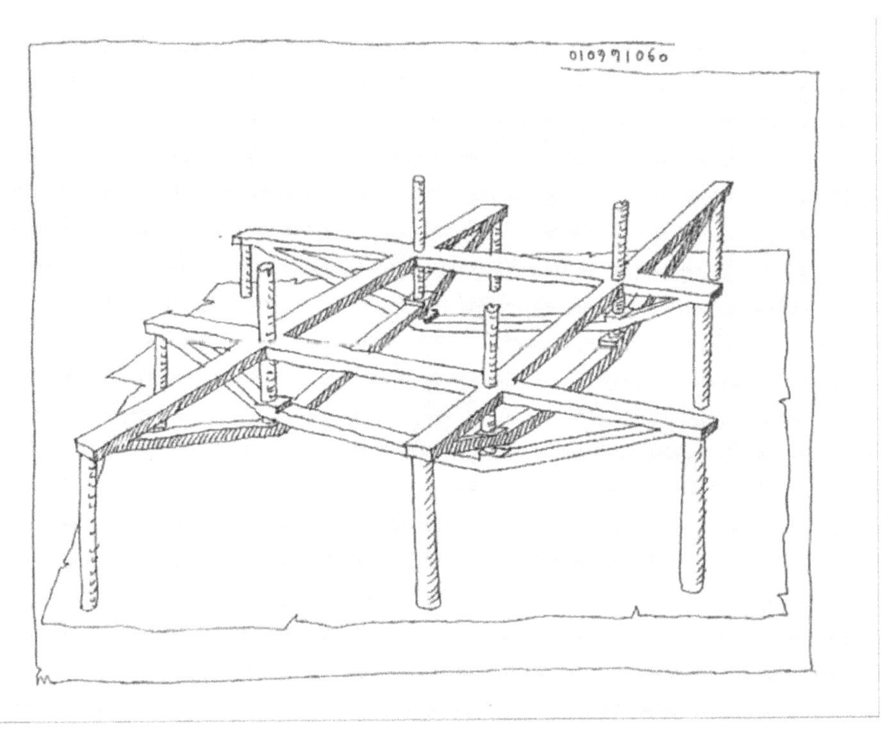

Again one unit of the transfer system above the plaza level, with straight tensional members.

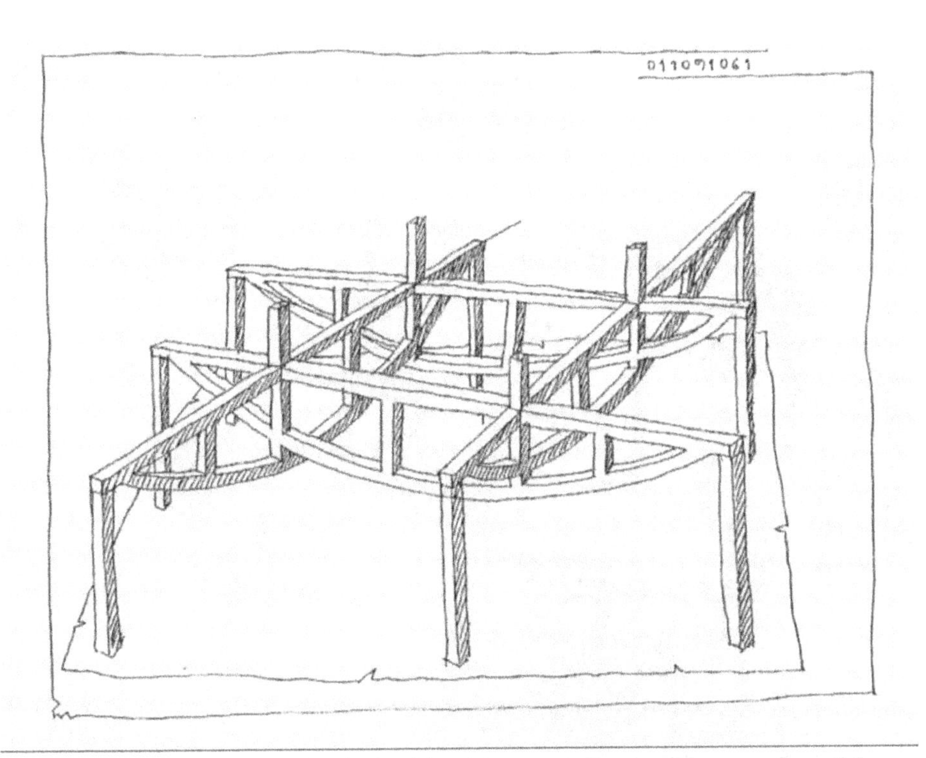

The same as the previous one, just with a bow-truss format. The crossing of the trusses happen at the 2/5th and 1/5th points, as a byproduct of the geometry.

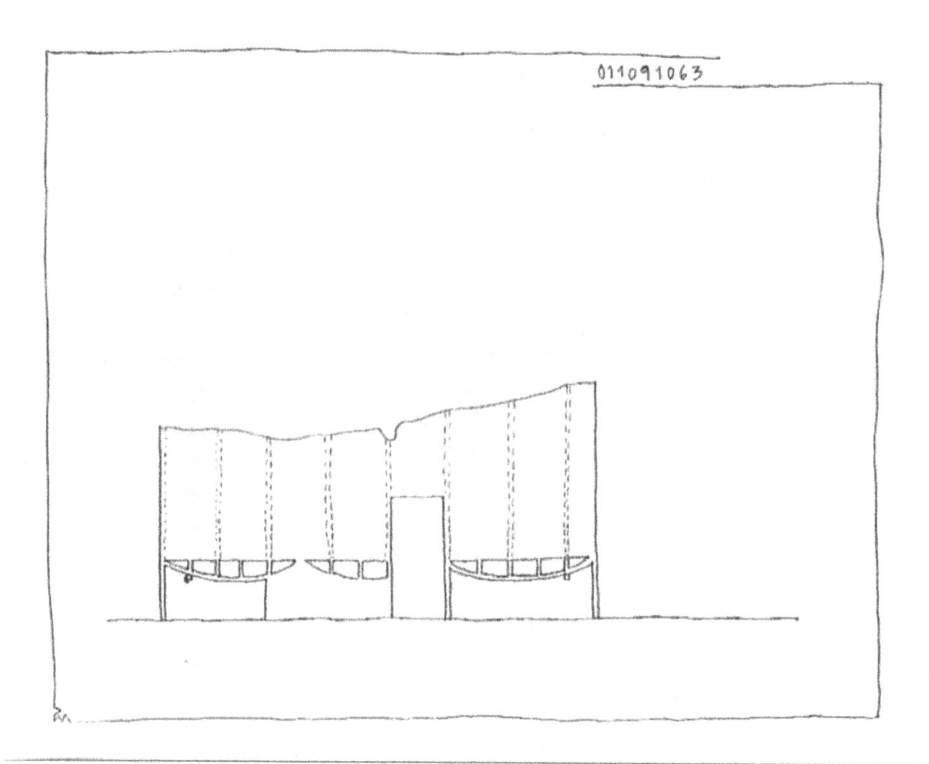

Elevation sketch, showing the open and enclosed areas of the plaza level.

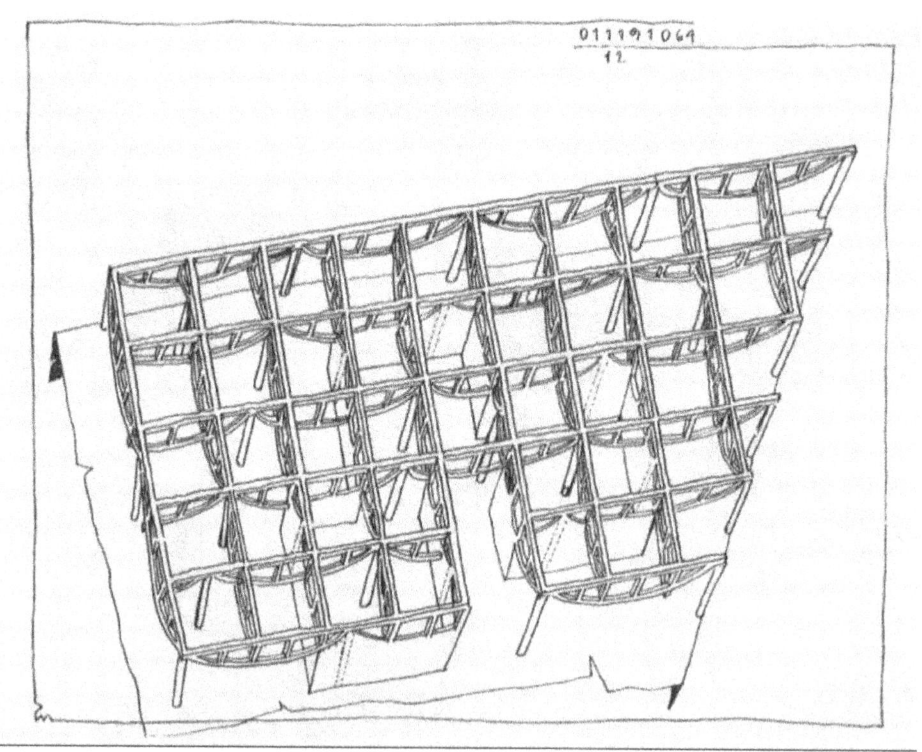

View of the transfer structure above the plaza level. This will be the "sixth elevation", mentioned before, looking at it from below.

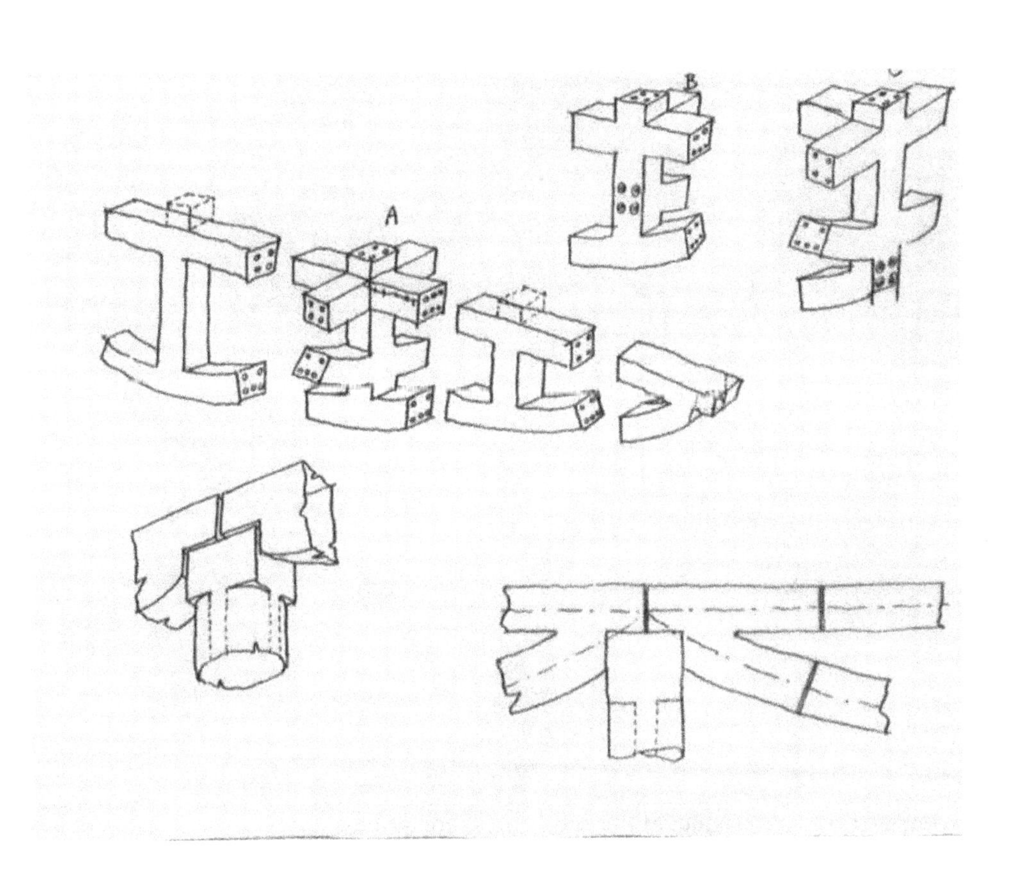

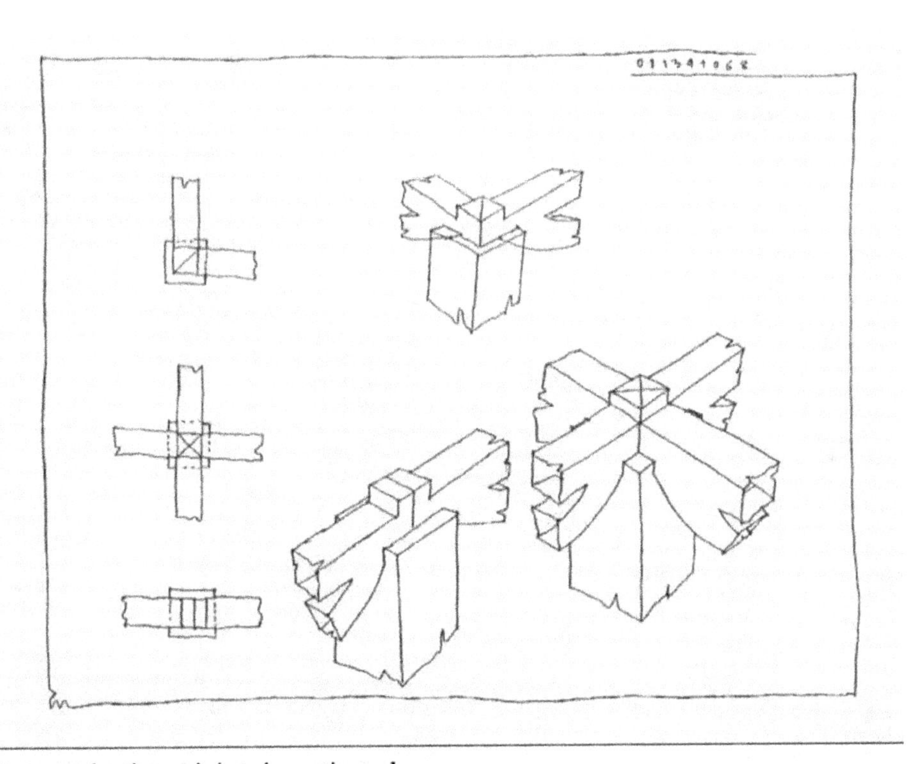

Truss and column joints investigated.

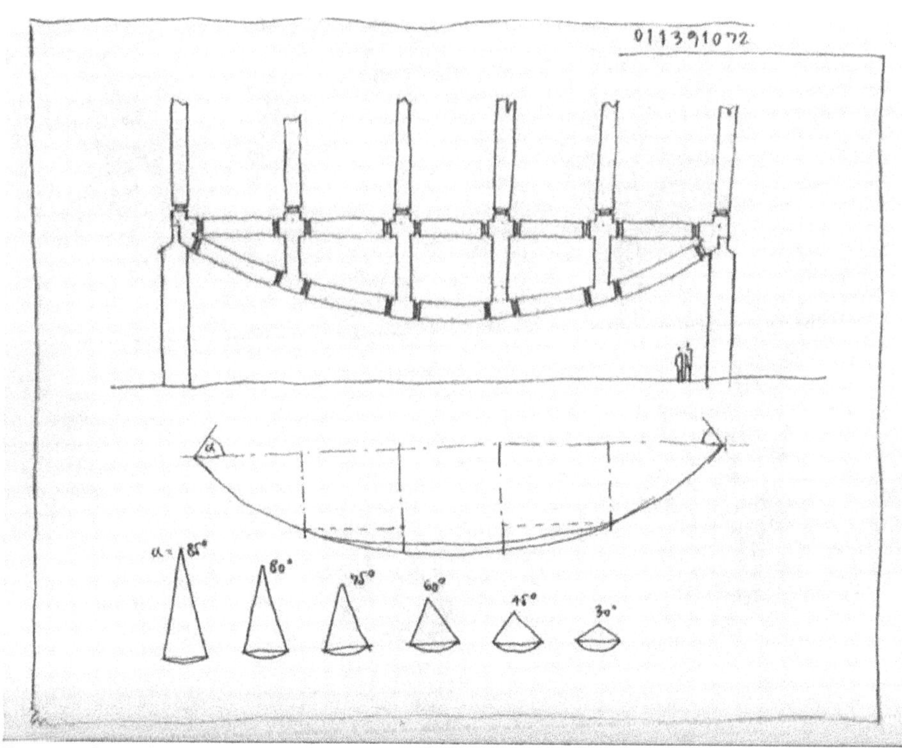

Bow and cord, as product of the geometrical conditions.

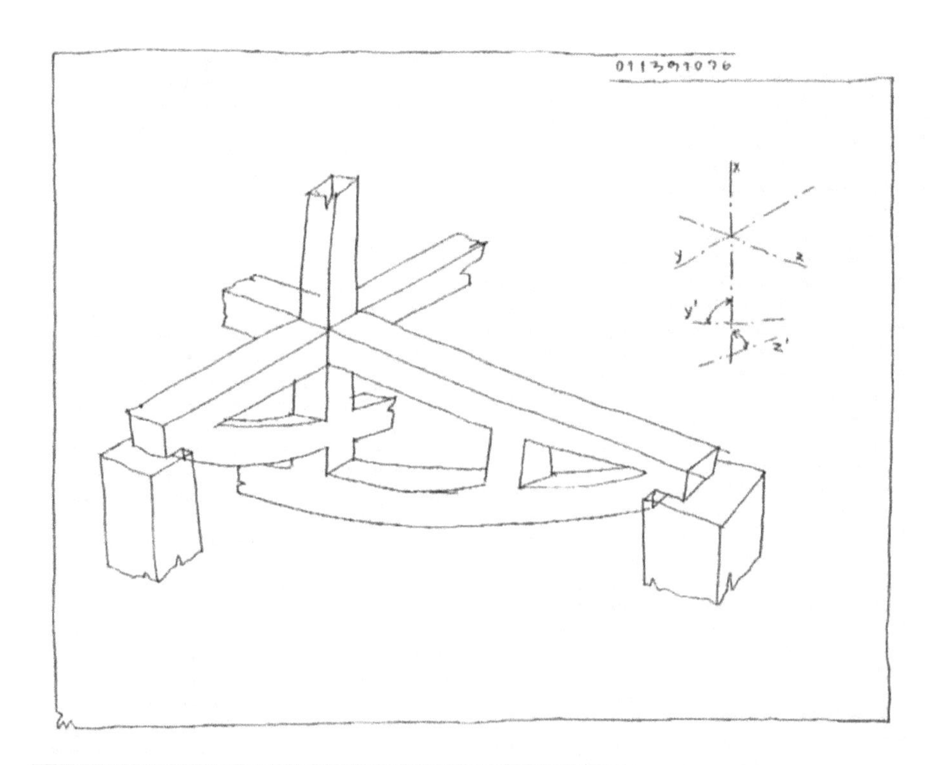

To understand clearly a detail, sometimes one has to be redundant.

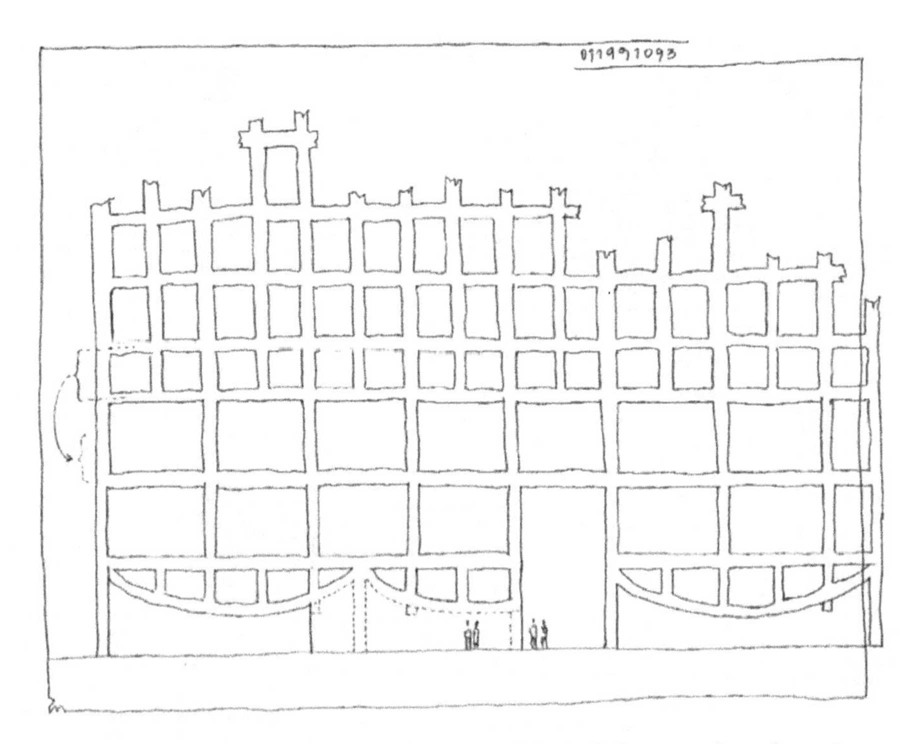

First attempt to generate the planar elements of the building envelope from the linear elements of the trusses.

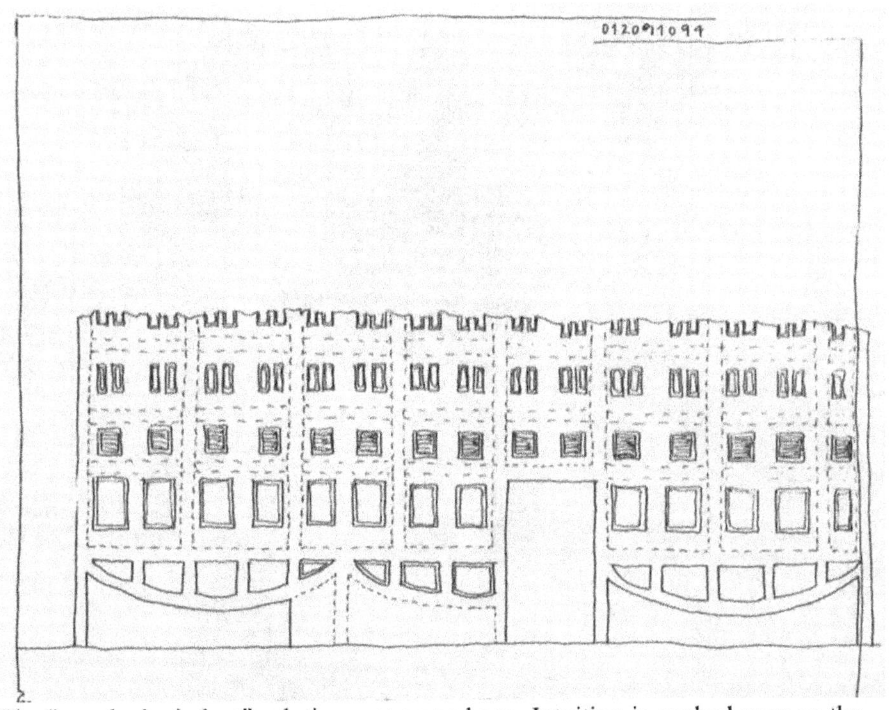

The "punched window" solution, not a good one. Intuition is evoked even on the detail level.

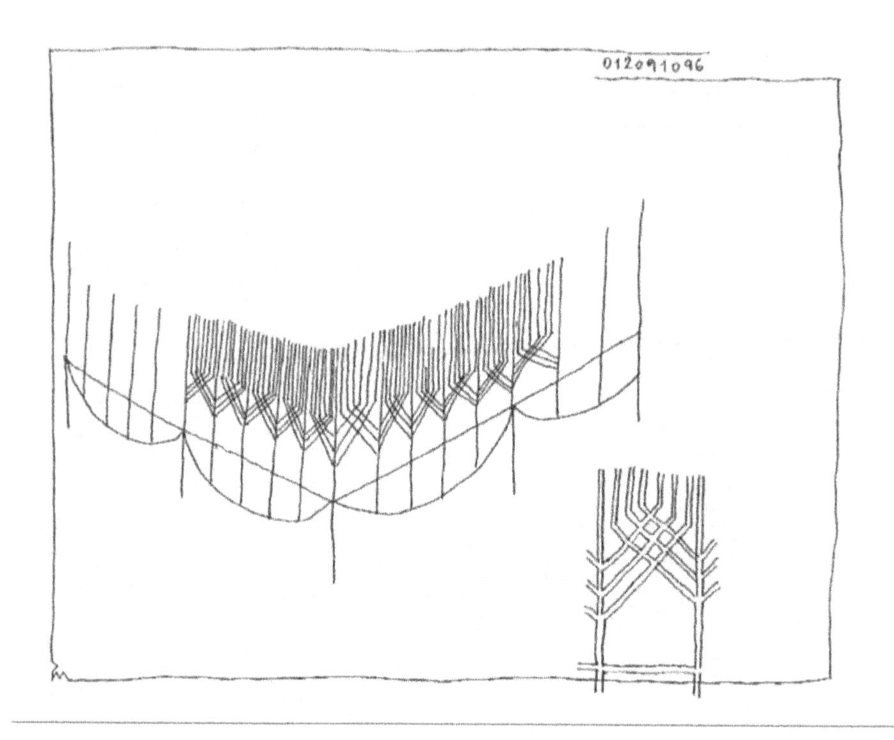

Lines are capable to create a "field".

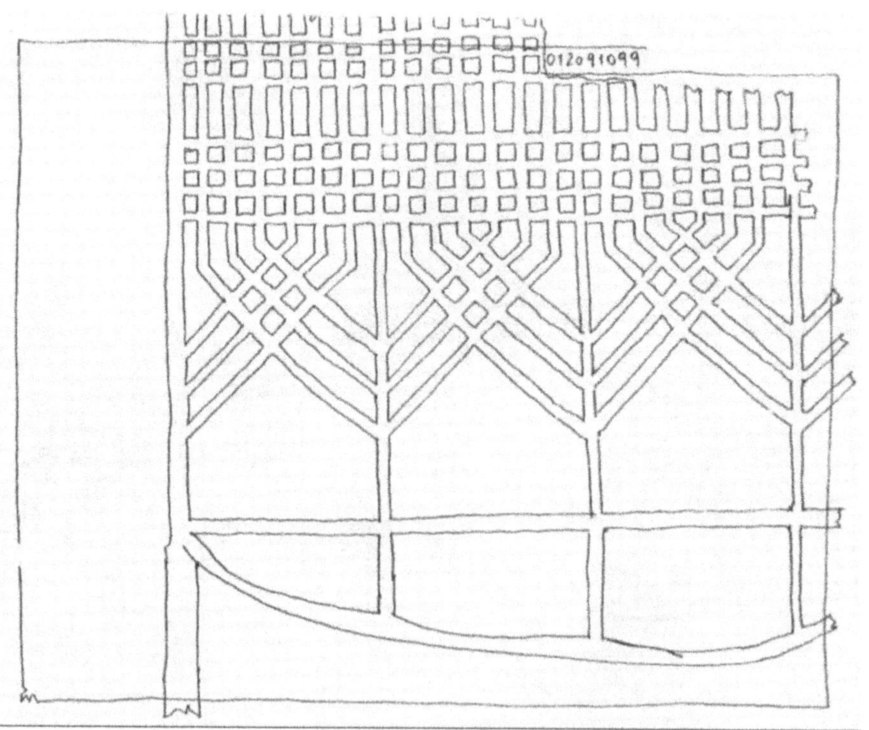

The "Piano Nobile" could be handled differently, than the other, more mundane parts of the envelope.

The "field-effect" produces different densities of the openings, which could be exploited to express the differences in the internal functions.

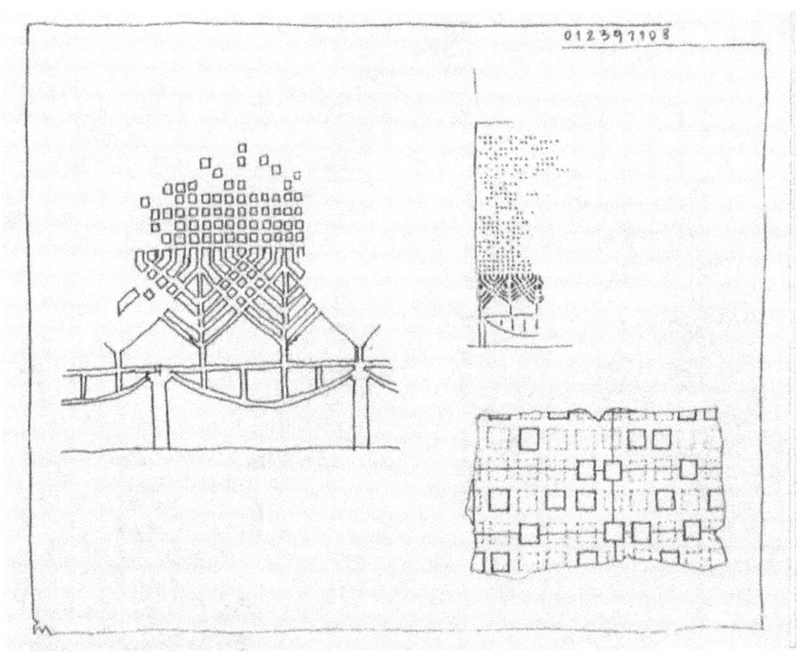

The three different zones of the elevation: the randomly distributed small openings of the offices (this project was conceived more than ten years earlier, and published well before Steven Holl's Cambridge Dormitory at the Massachusetts Institute of Technology), the crossing patterns at the main floor level, and the open trusses at the plaza level.

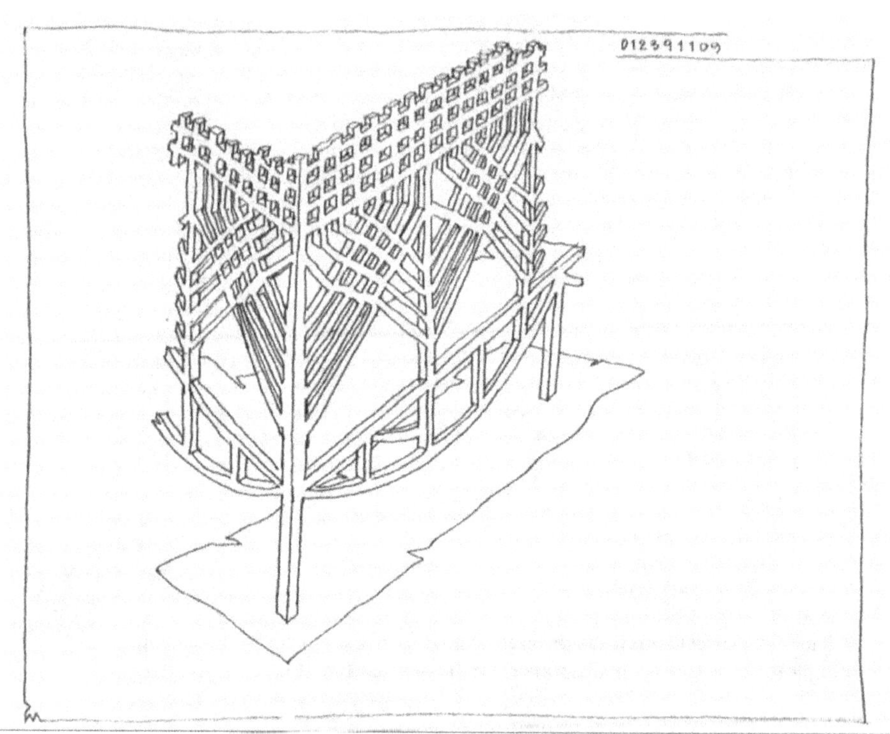

The corner at the "Piano Nobile".

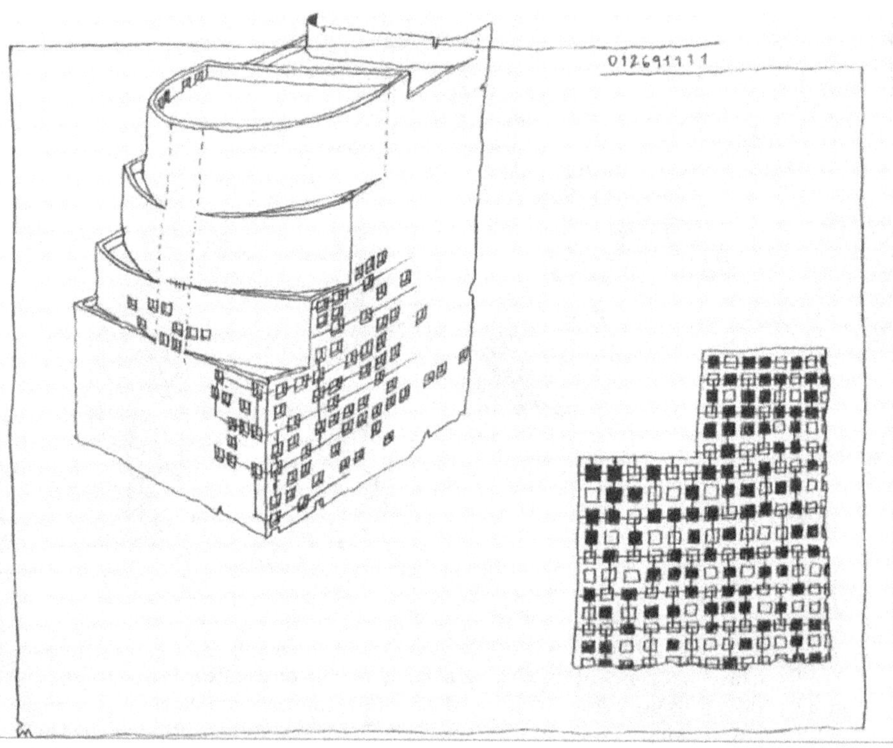

Partial image of the elevations, with the potential, but un-punched locations, and the random holes, indicated in black.

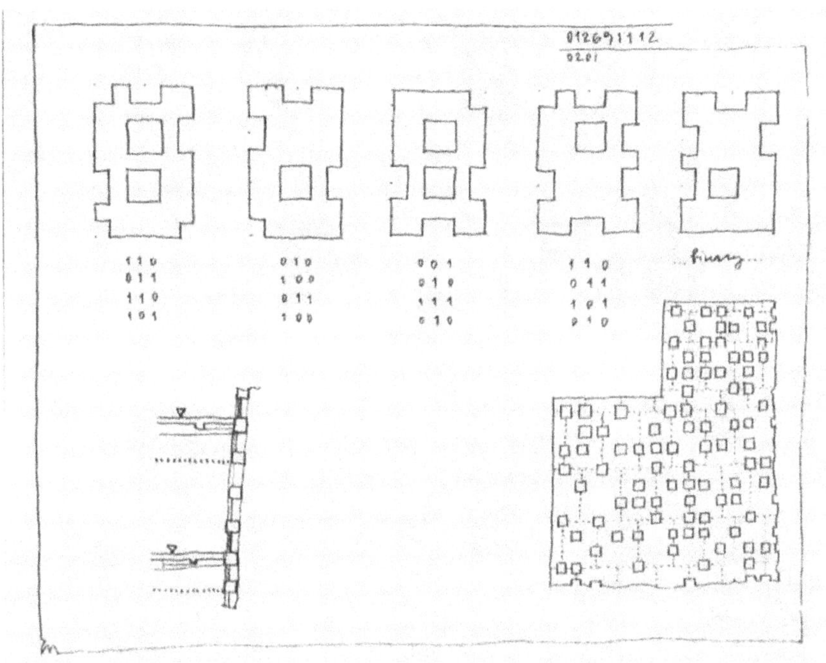

Binary random variations of the openings of the prefabricated wall-panels. "1" means opening, "0" means potential of opening, but not punched through.

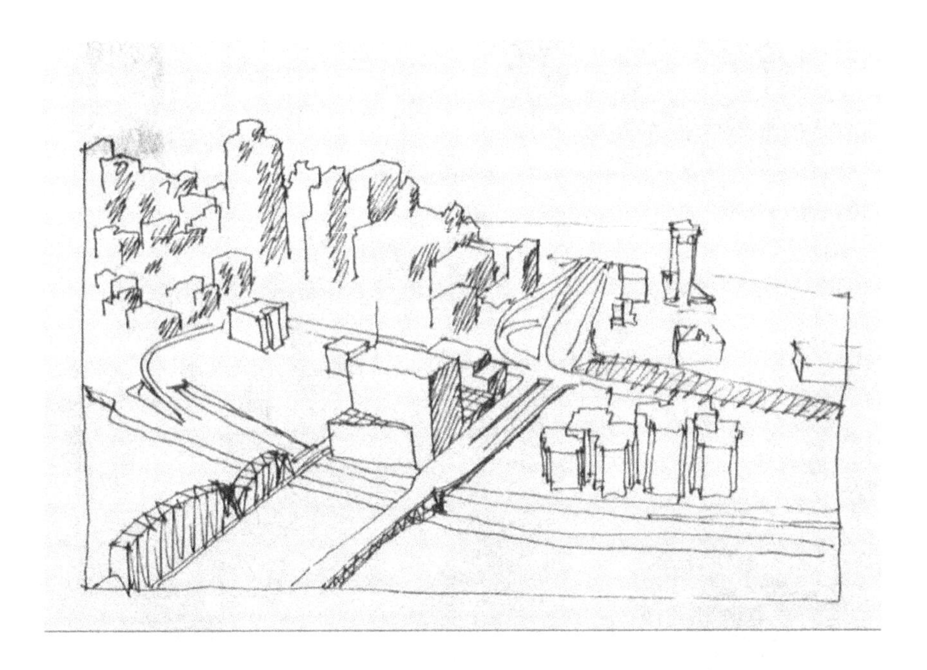

When the Partners of the Firm I was consulting for respond for the previously described process with "...and what would it happen, if we place the building to the other corner of the parking...", then you know, that a new beginning is on the horizon.

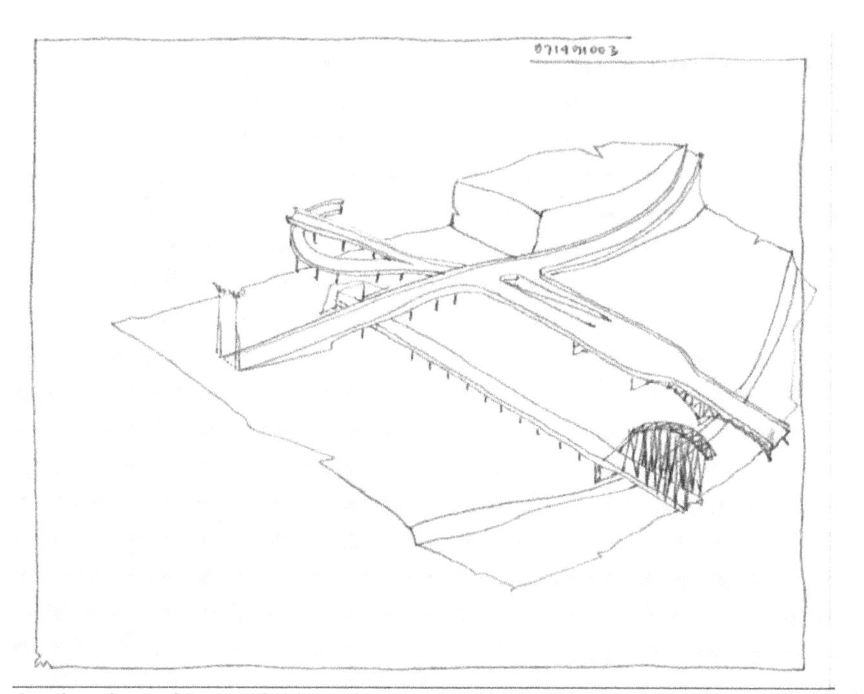

Continuations of the two bridges, the river and the Boulevard of the Allies enclose the site. This latter road connects to the downtown-network of roads with a gate element, two high columns with sculptures on their tops.

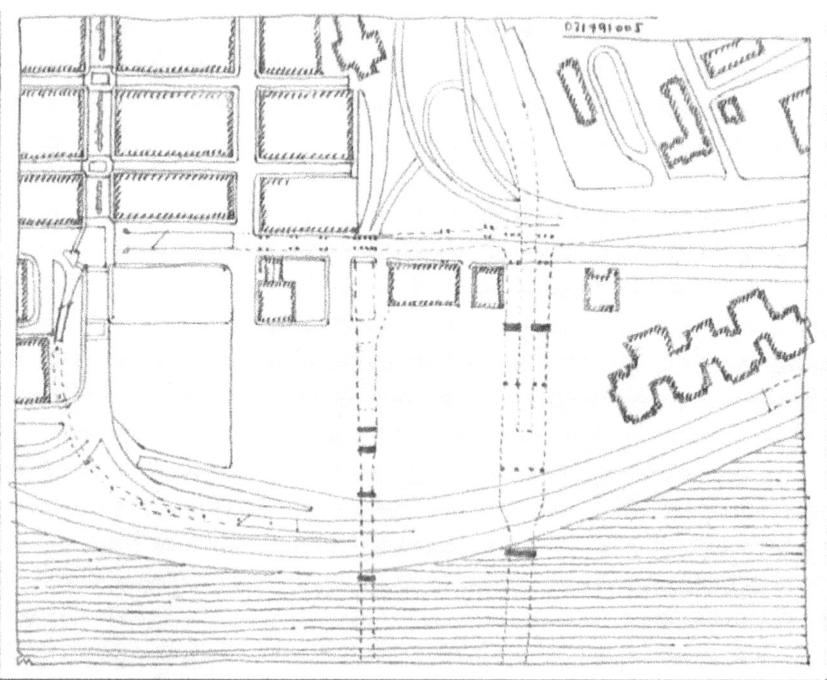

A master-site plan is drawn on the ground level, indicating the main players of the site.
This drawing has been used to investigate different variations of the possible occupancy of the area.

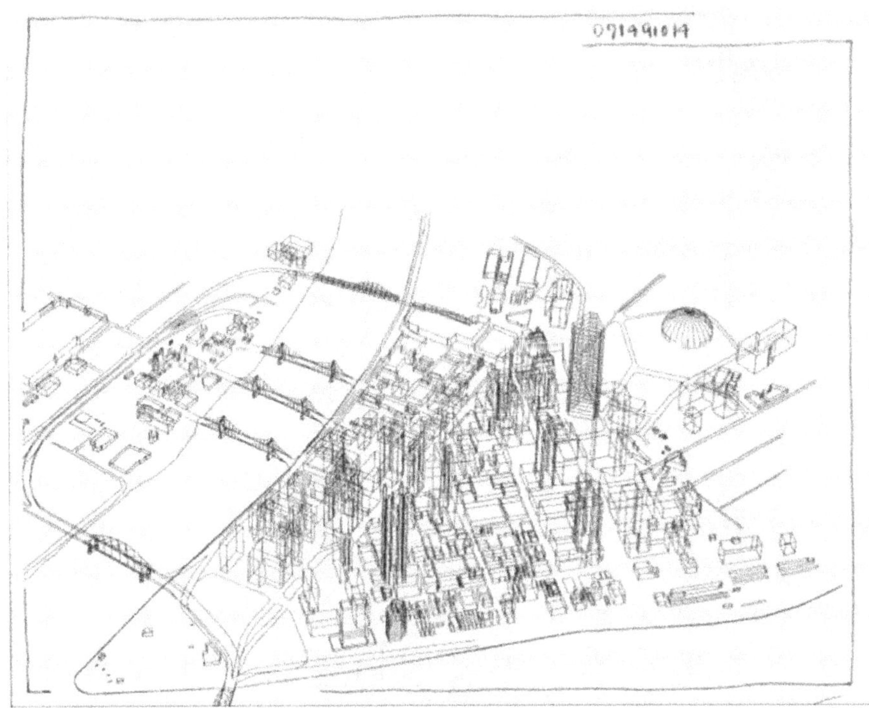

An early computer rendering of the area. The site is in the lower right corner of the image,

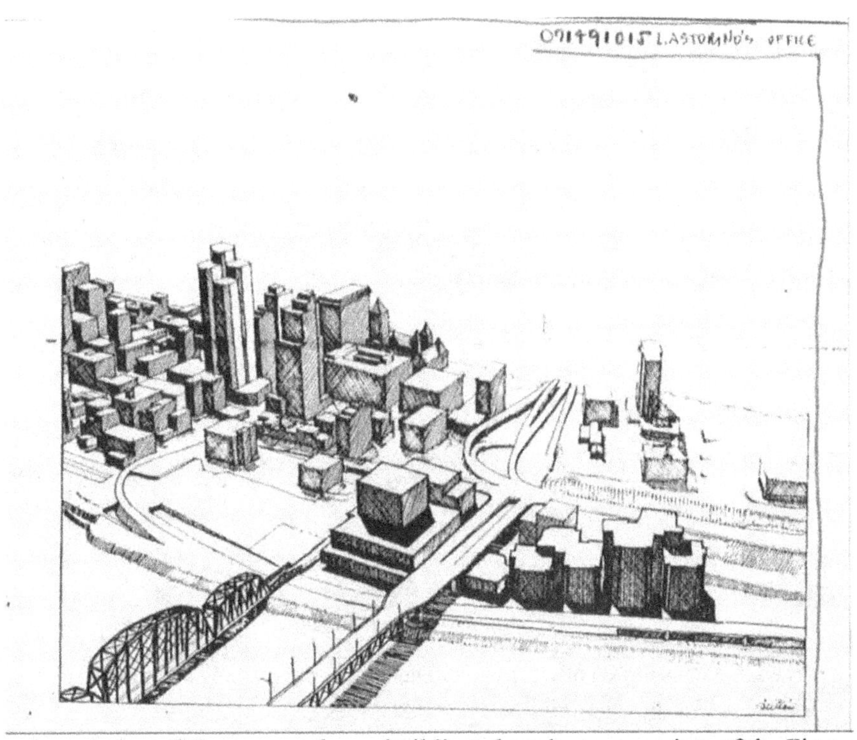

A hand-rendering of the proposed new building, done by an associate of the Firm.

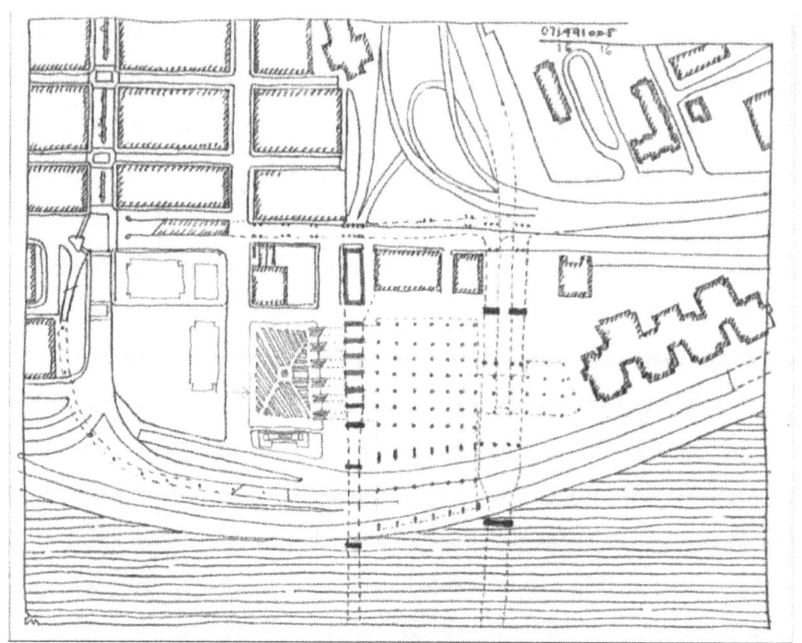

Ground-floor column grid for the parking , the light-rail train station, its connection to the plaza at the West from the site. Indications include a grid for the court house, adjoining the jail, and on the Southern side, between the bridges , a possible cover and terracing above the Penn Lincoln Parkway. This is an early attempt to incorporate the bridges into the design of the whole complex.

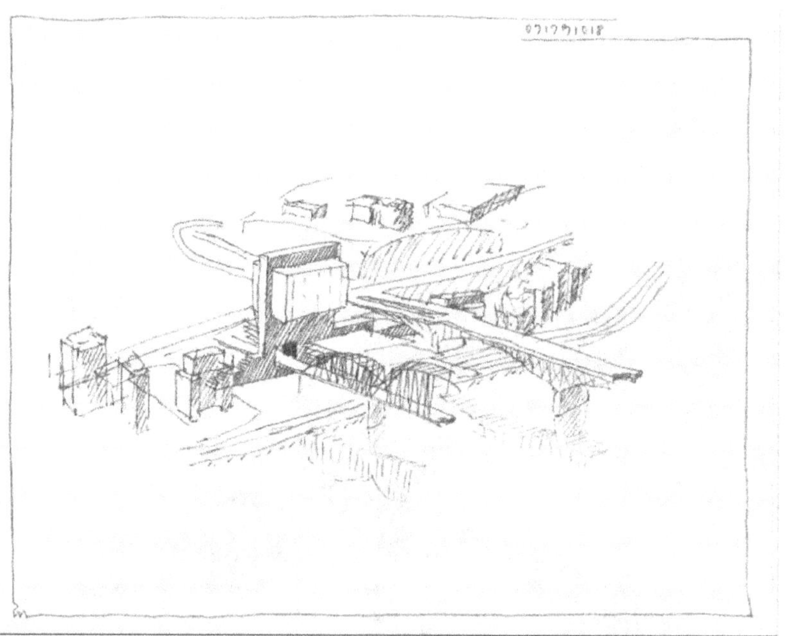

The same with clip-on office volume. The bridges are piercing and running above the core. No solution as yet for the parking.

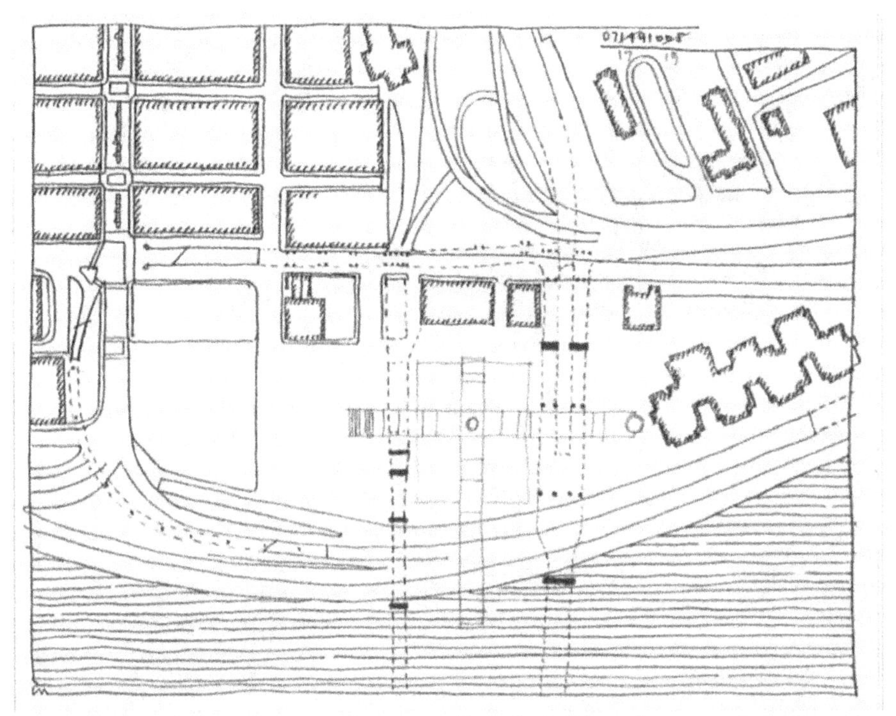

A two-core variation, the second one parallels the bridges, in approximately at the center of the space between them. It runs out above the water.

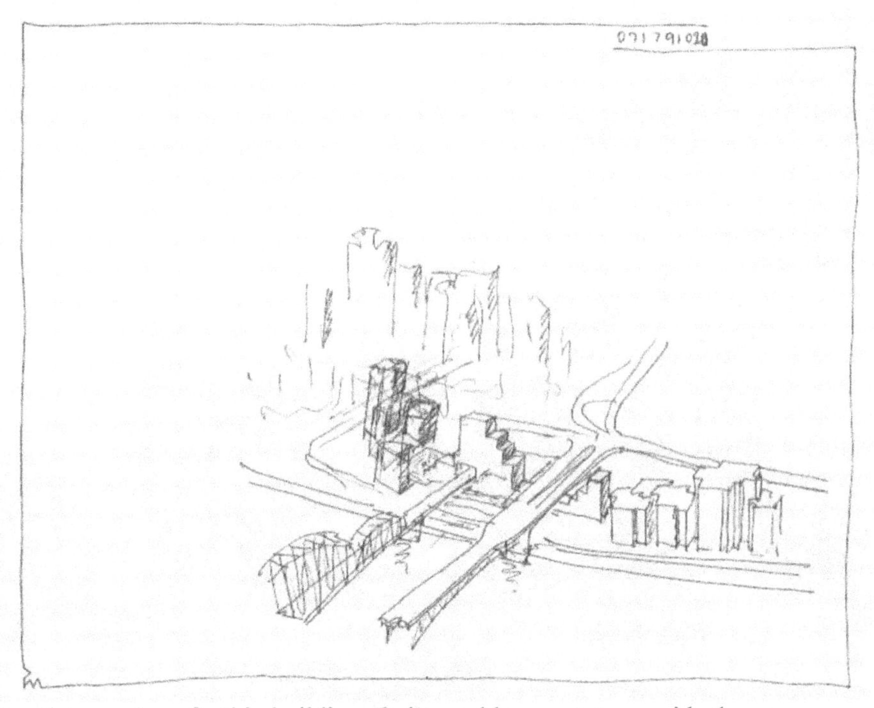

Another version of a thin building. Quite unable as yet, to provide the necessary areas.

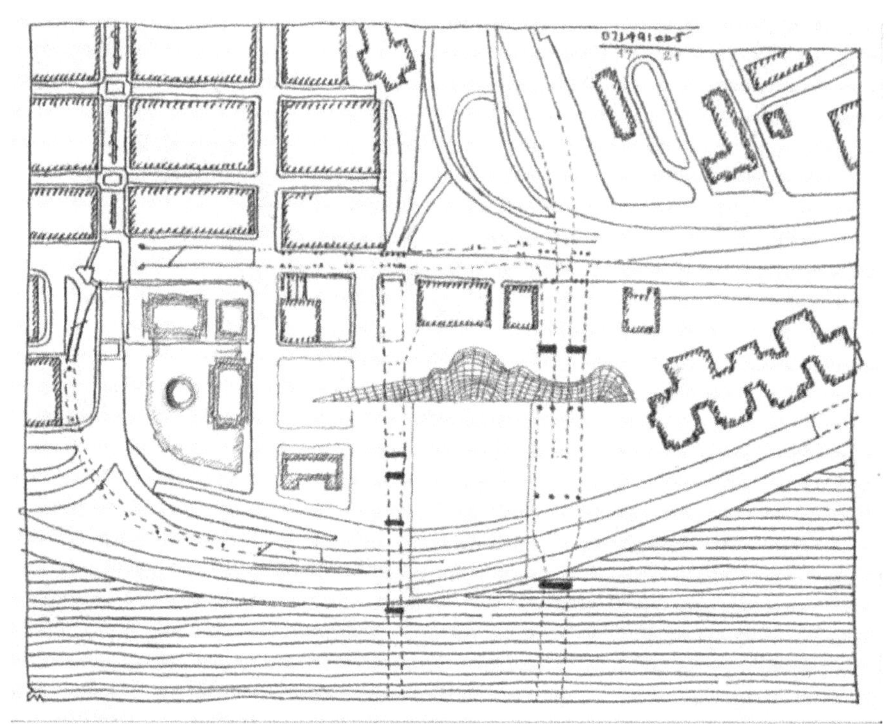

An idea-gram. The essence of it, to restrict the building at the river side to follow an ordering plane, while in the back it could extend as needed.

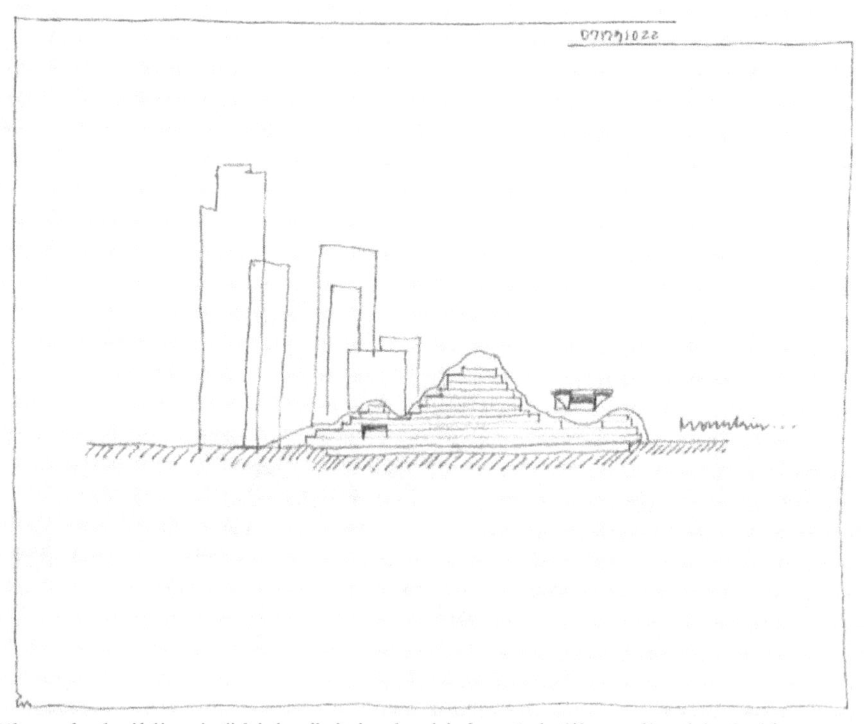

Where the building is "thicker", it is also higher. It is like a sliced-in-half mountain.

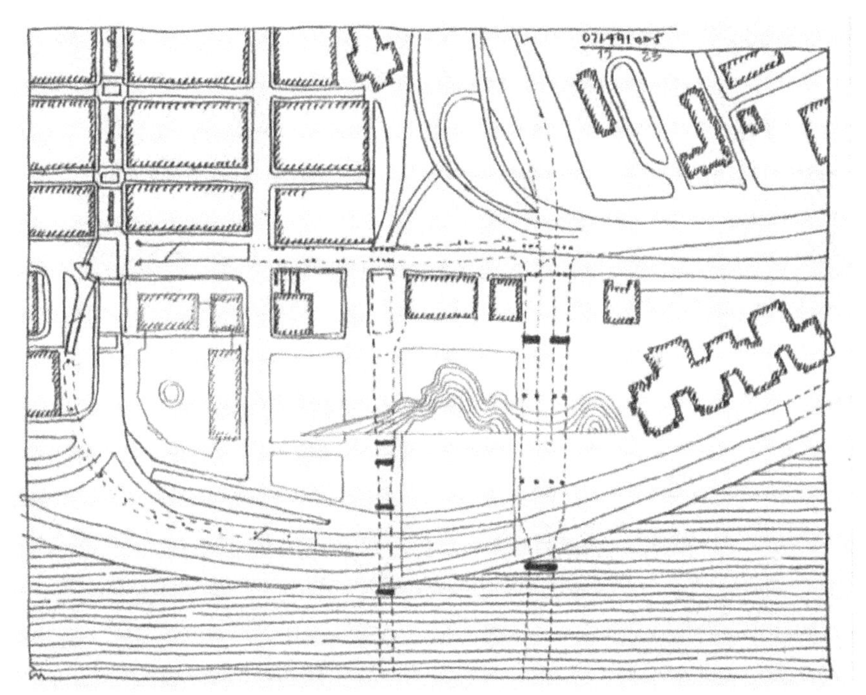

Variation on the previous idea, but it became the vehicle to recognize a very important urban connection: to align the new building with the existing row of offices and multi storey residences farther West from the site.

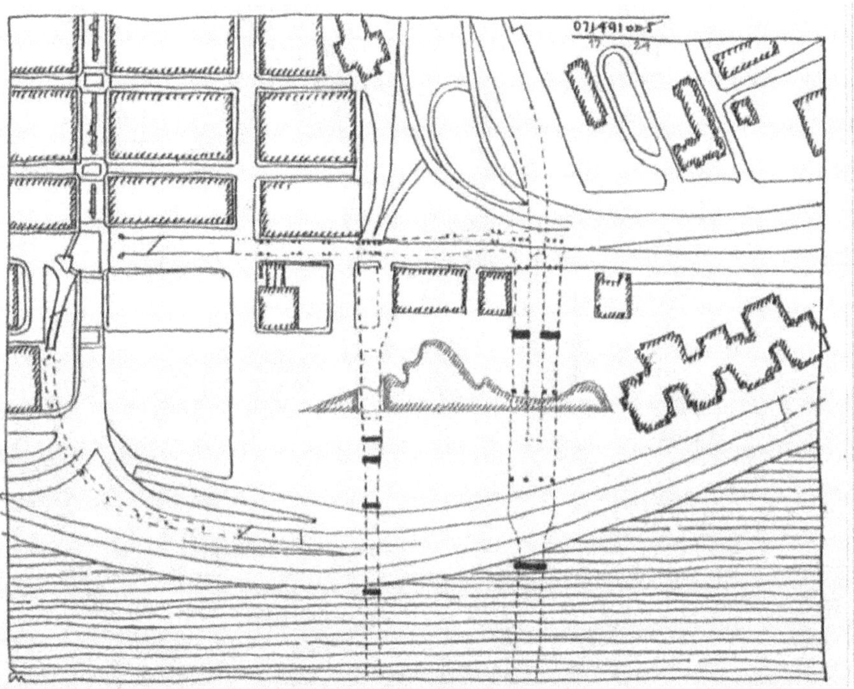

Adjusted to make the alignment. Aspects of some earlier drawings are reappearing here, with the face-plane intersecting with the rotated axis of the jail.

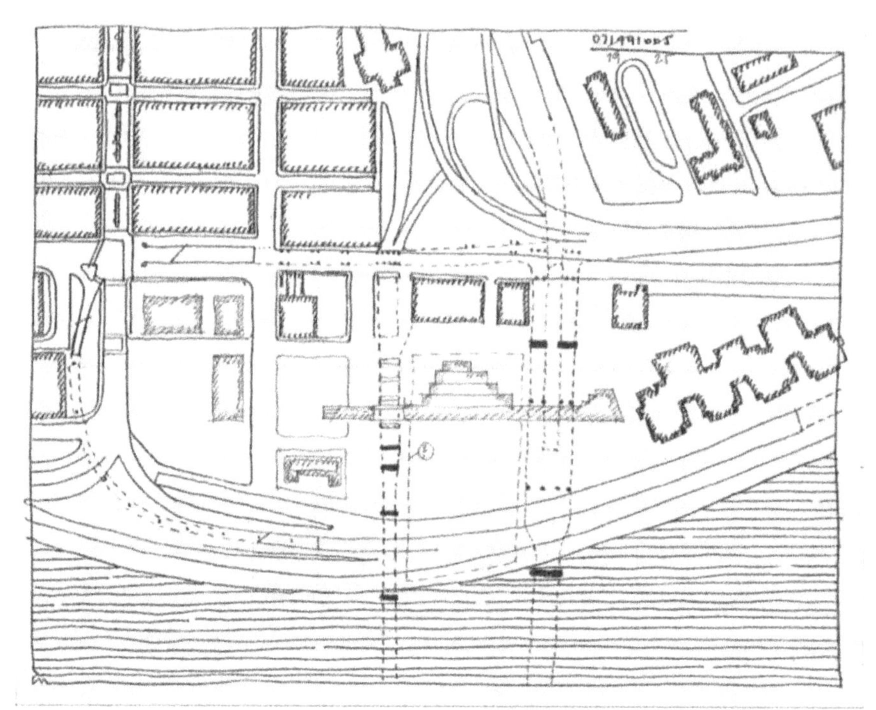

Sometimes a formal idea is insistent, to manifest itself in slight variations.

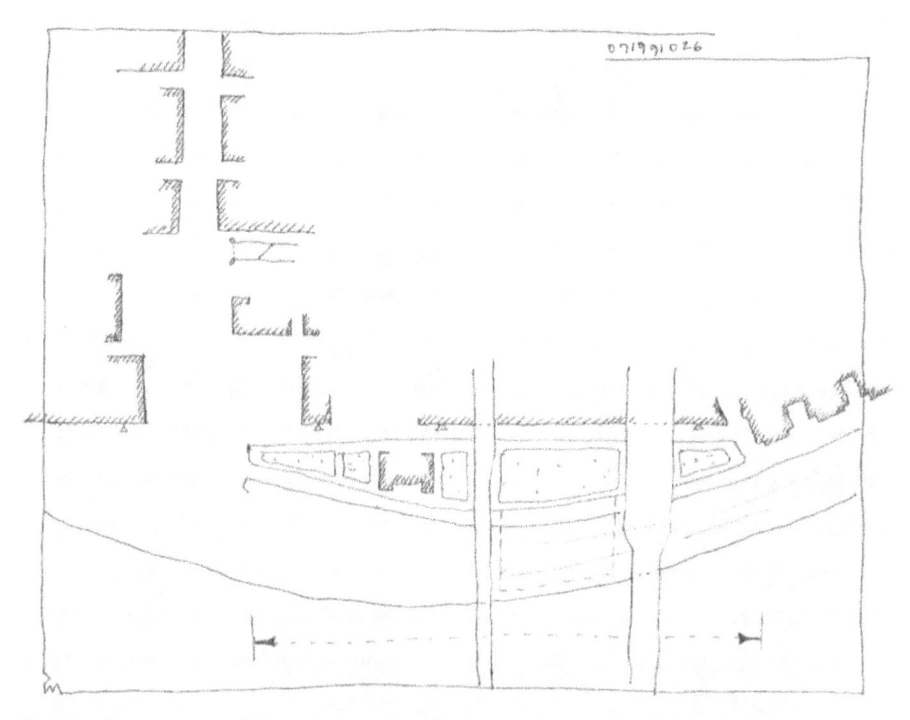

Finally the essence of the urban order. Between the new building and the Penn Lincoln Parkway, a park could act as a buffer. Its regulating ability exceeds the length of the site.

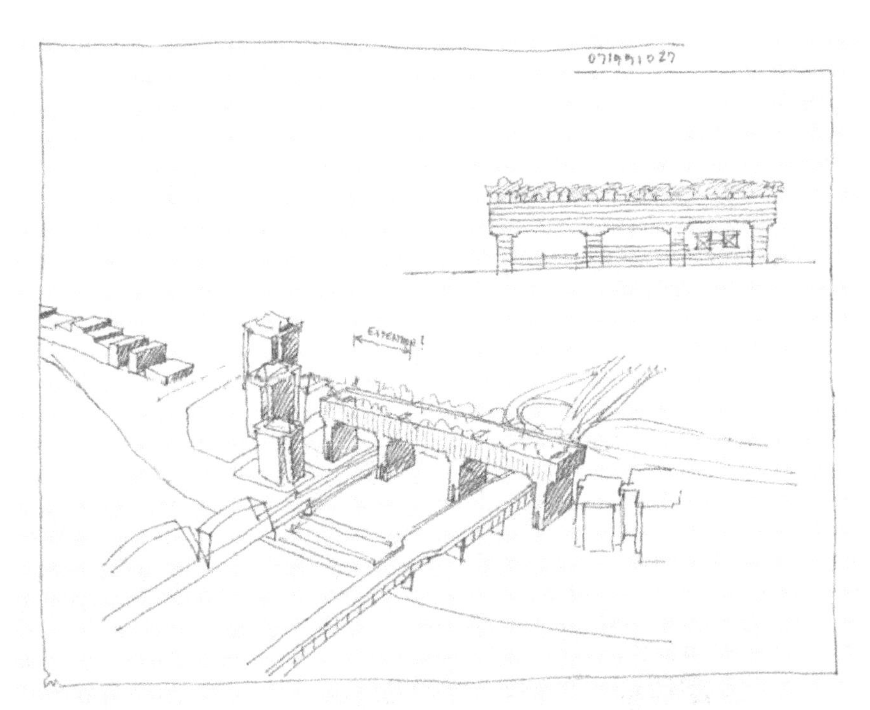

Some echo of the Finance Ministry in Paris, member of the Grand Projects of President Mitterrand. Has the same problem, as the earlier schemes: no parking yet.

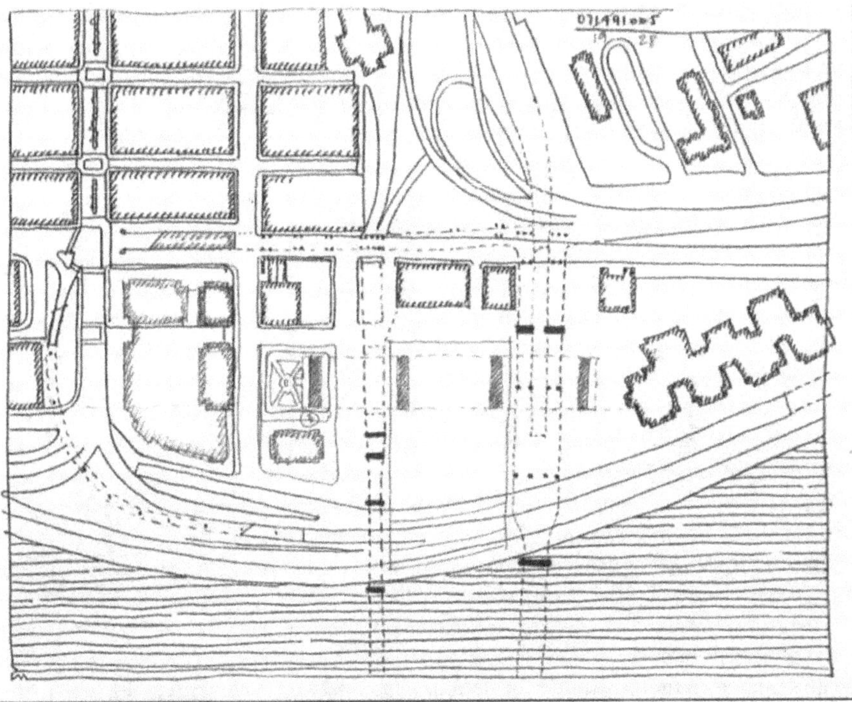

This proposal would have had its value, since it opens up the view of the river. Its consequence would have been the very expensive underground parking.

One has to have the courage, to try out obvious nonsensical proposals, like this one. With its curved body-shapes, the horizontal plateau of the top gains an almost symbolic quality, an offering to higher authority. The curved lines of the floor plates act as contour-lines, helping to interpret the form.

The same, even more extreme formation. Also one would have great difficulty to convince the City Council about its advantages, if it had any at all.

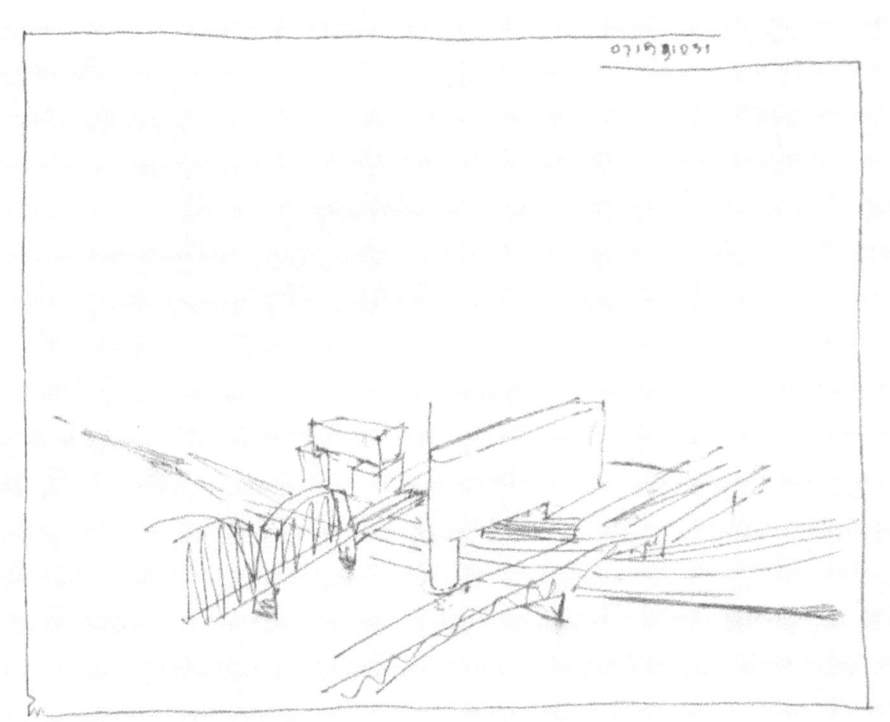

The building is positioned parallel with the bridges. Became the basis for some other proposal, related to the parking.

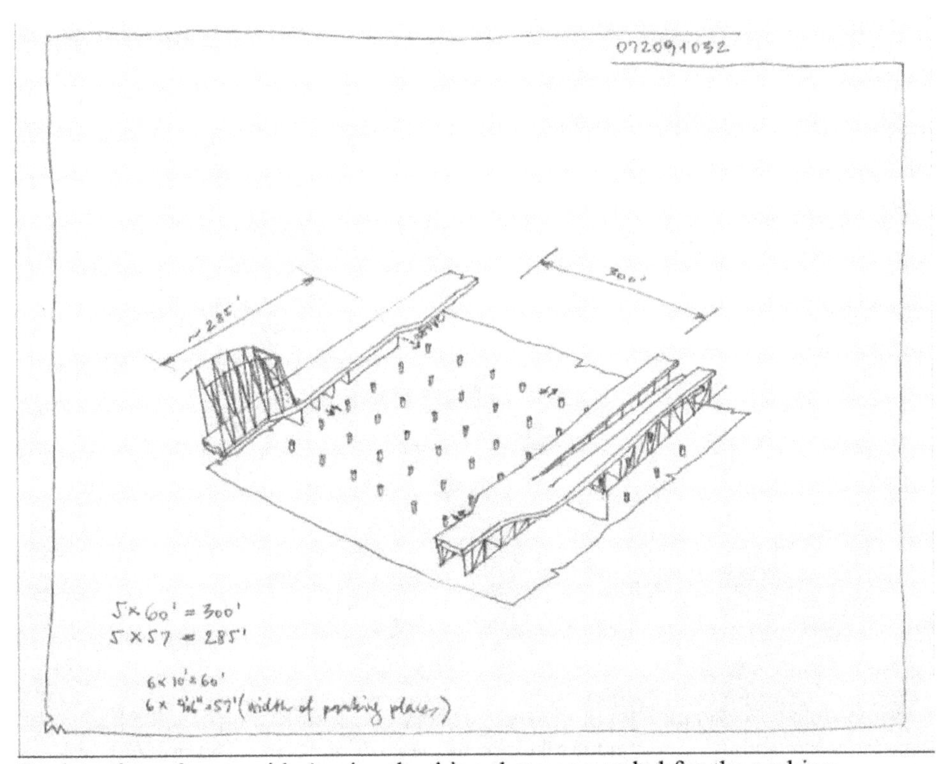

Back to the column-grid. Again, checking the area needed for the parking.

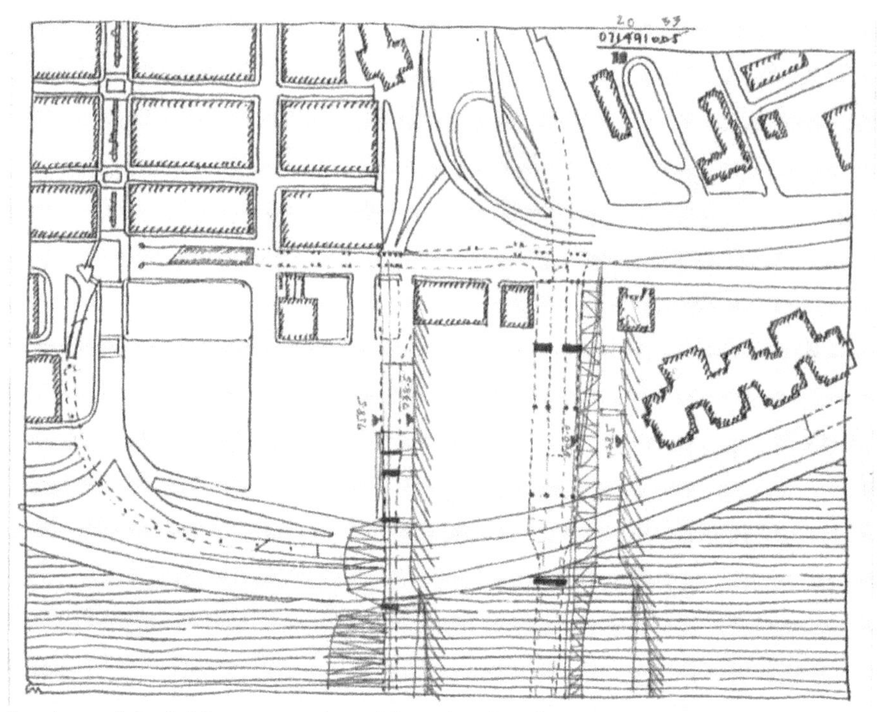

Sections of the bridges are projected into the site plan. There is a considerable difference in their landing elevations.

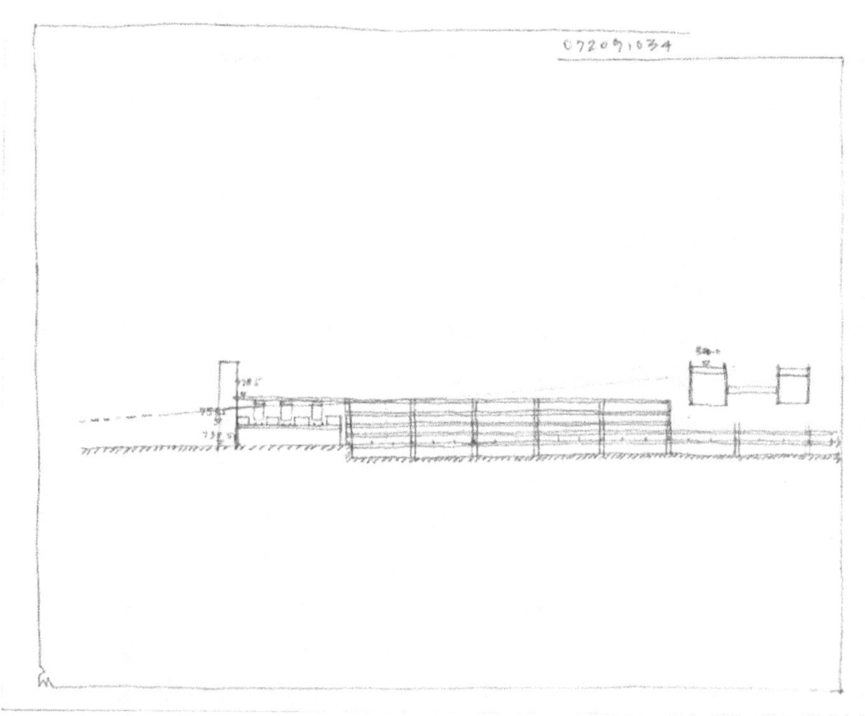

Proportional section parallel to the river. It very perceptibly indicates the height-differences, and the consequent relations to the parking levels. The dotted line denotes the slope of the Boulevard of the Allies.

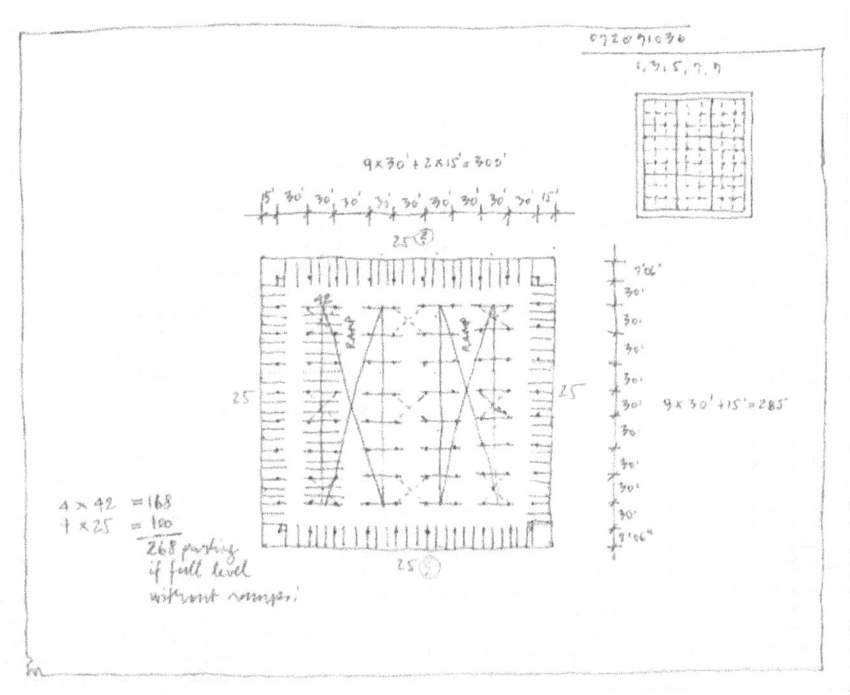

Parking distribution scheme. The diagonal lines indicate the ramps.

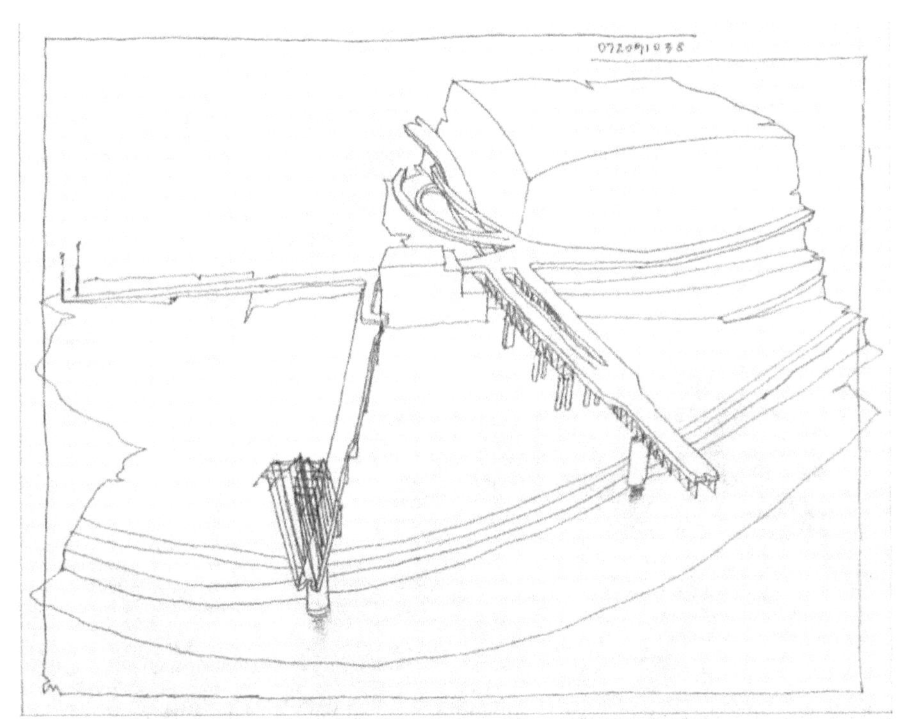

Major road connections depicted. The gate-posts at the joint of Grand Avenue and the Boulevard of the Allies are at the left edge of the image. Time to time, it is very useful to be reminded about the complexity of the terrain.

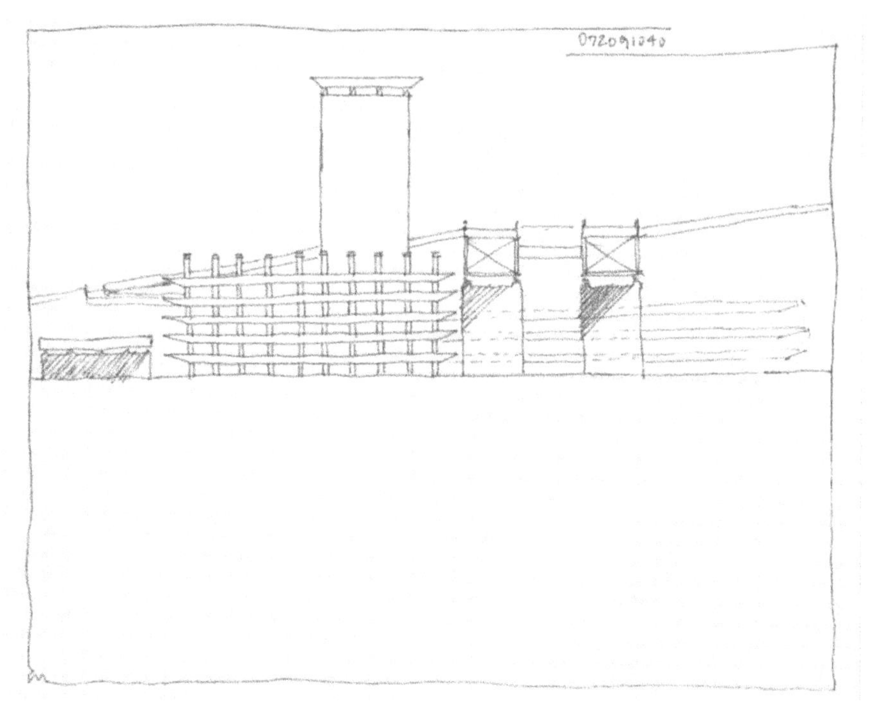

A new scheme emerged, emphasizing the raised plaza level with the vertical extension of the columns of the parking structure.

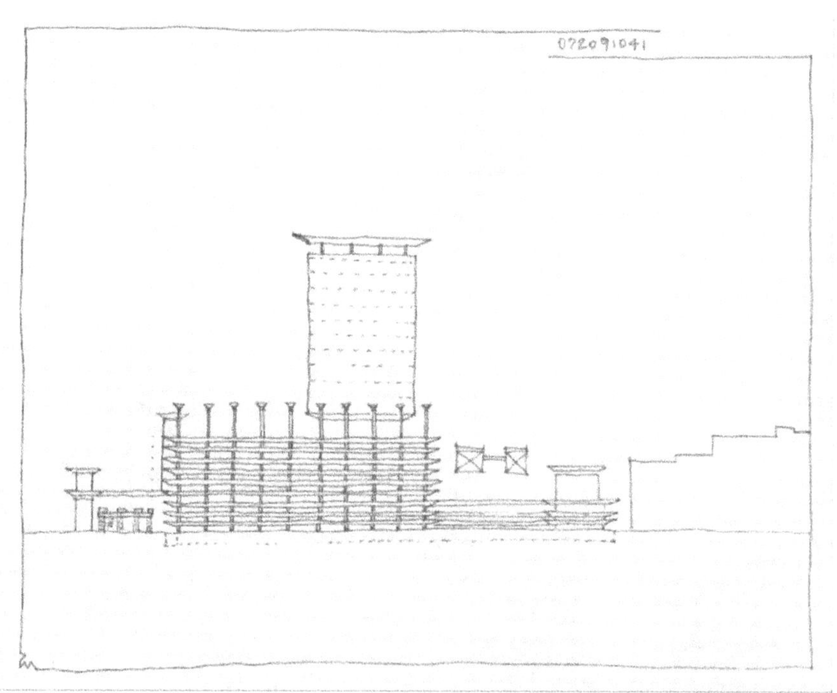

The same as on the previous page, but with increased height of the parking-structure.
The drawing contains references of the light-rail train station as well as of the Court, besides the jail.

Detail of the former arrangement, viewed from the plaza in front of the West side of the building. The tower-like element is the vertical connection to the railway station, and the first increment to connect the plaza on the ground and the one on top of the parking.

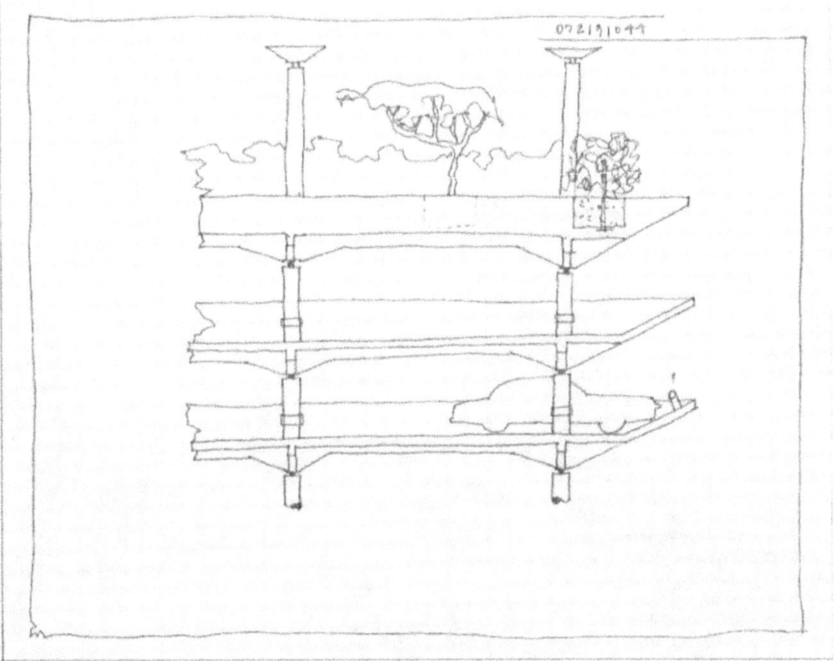

Section-detail of the parking. The intent was to hide the cars from viewing the parking from below. The upper level of the parking could have planters sunk in their structure, so shading trees could be planted there.

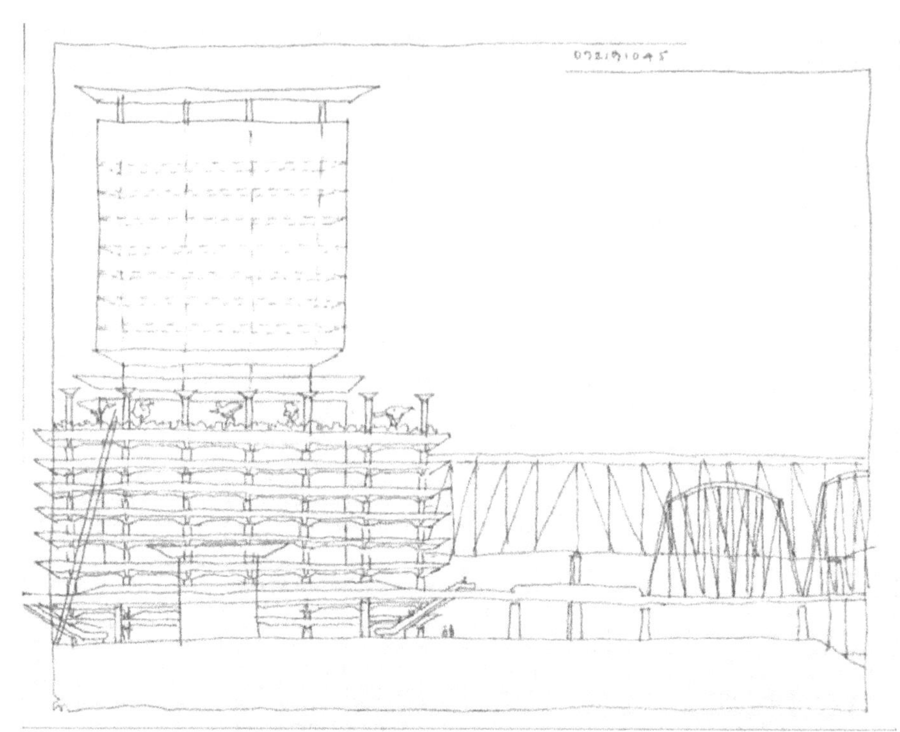

The western view of the complex. The office tower is indicated by its volume only. The structures of the bridges are quite important elements of the ensemble.

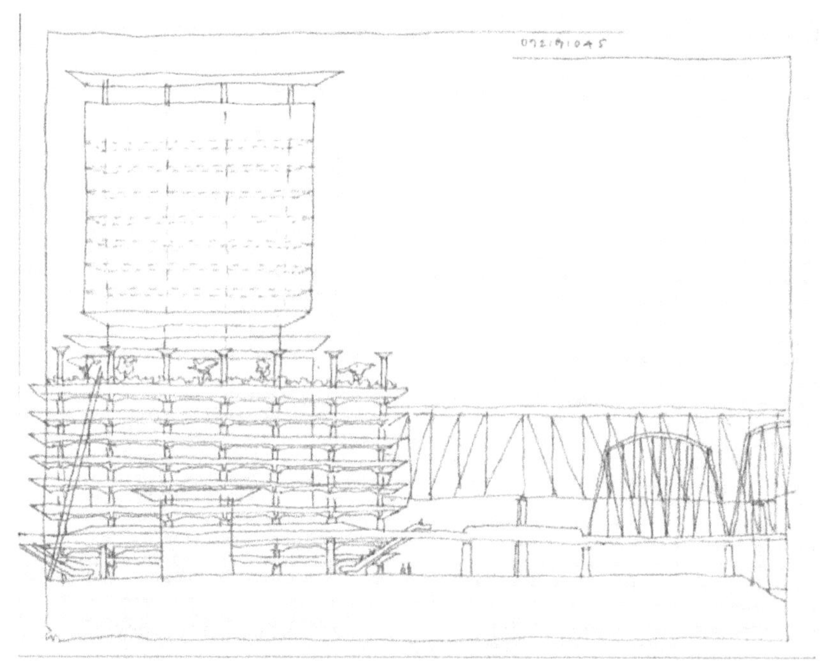

The western view of the complex. The office tower is indicated by its volume only. The structures of the bridges are quite important elements of the ensemble.

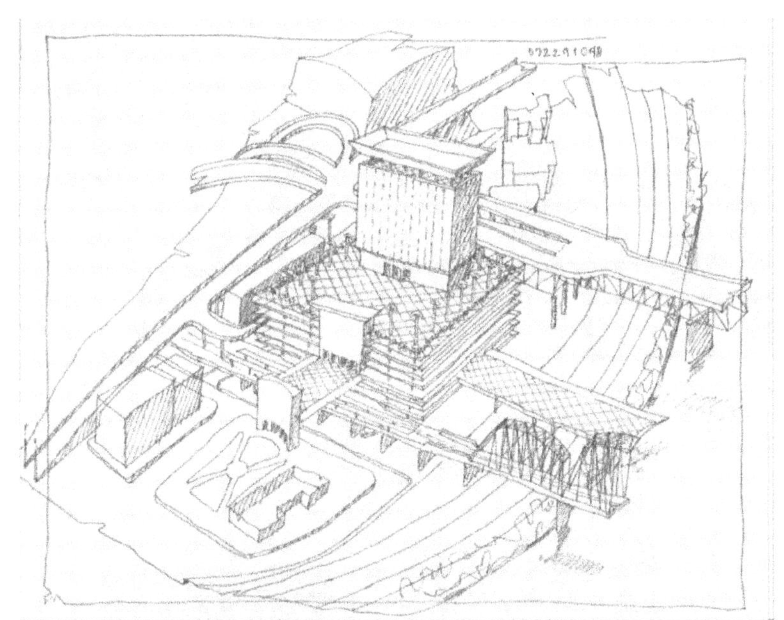

Sketch of the complex, as it would have appeared according to the previous site plan. One builds up drawings of this complexity progressing from the front of the image towards the rear of it, enhancing the three-dimensional deception by covering up, what is behind. With an acquired routine, one has to gather the whole complex in one's mind, and it just waits to be notated. Sometimes "writing" an image is the proper expression, for how it is made. All the drawings, by the way, are original ink drawings, without any pencil outlines in advance. The dependency of the whole from its parts is a very important issue one has to remember.

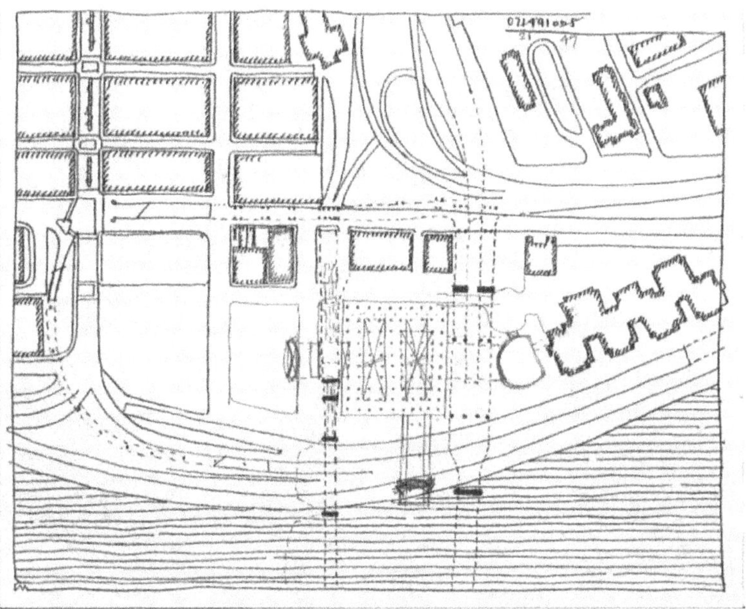

Site plan, indicating the connector-elements to the ground-level plaza, an extension to the river, and the link to the round court house.

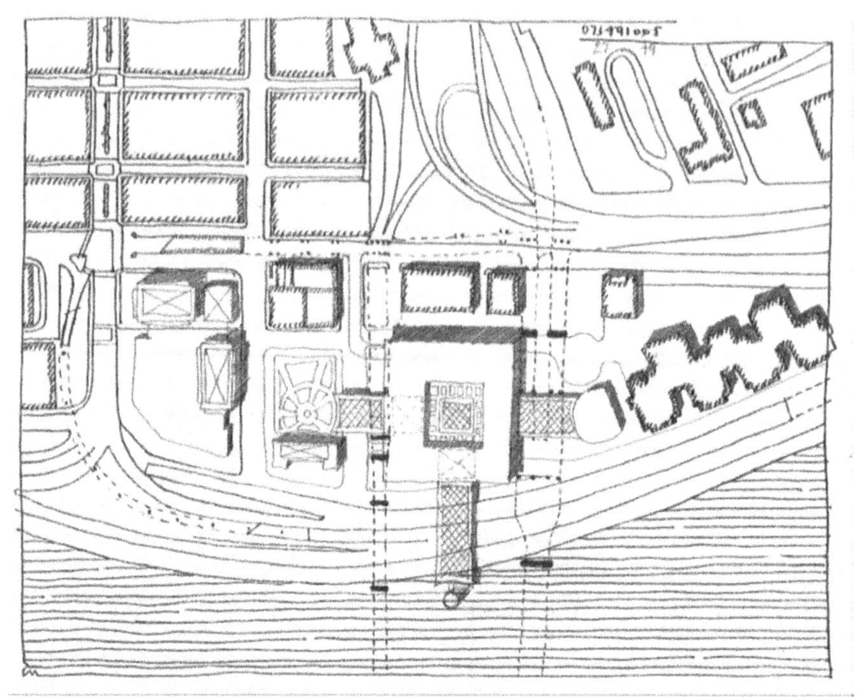

Another variation of the previous urban situation, with a lower building, enclosing a courtyard in the middle.

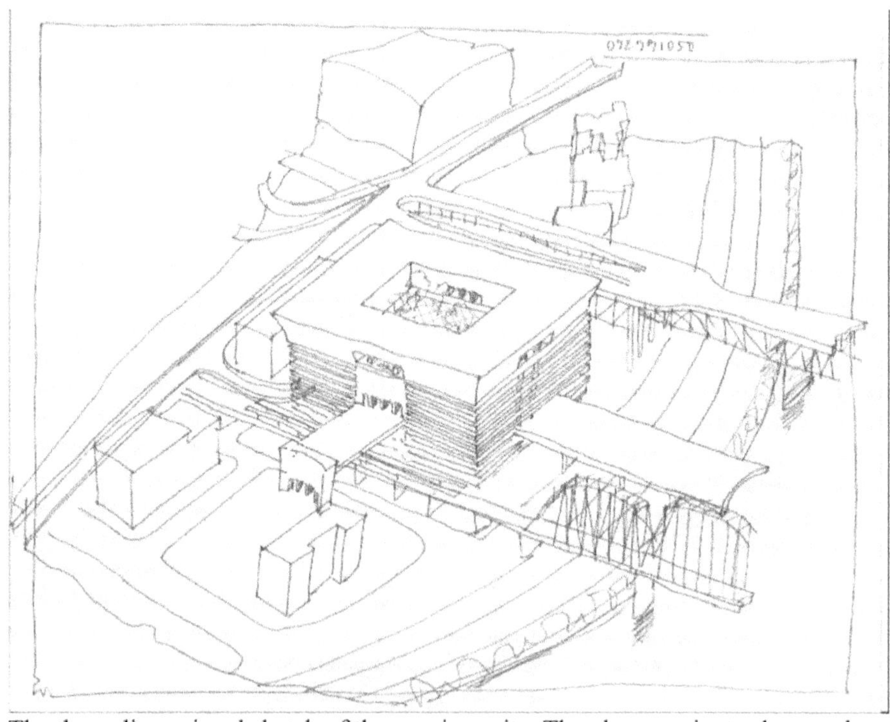

The three-dimensional sketch of the previous site. The close to ninety-thousand square feet sizes of the floor-plates of the parking would have overwhelmingly big relative to the surrounding elements.

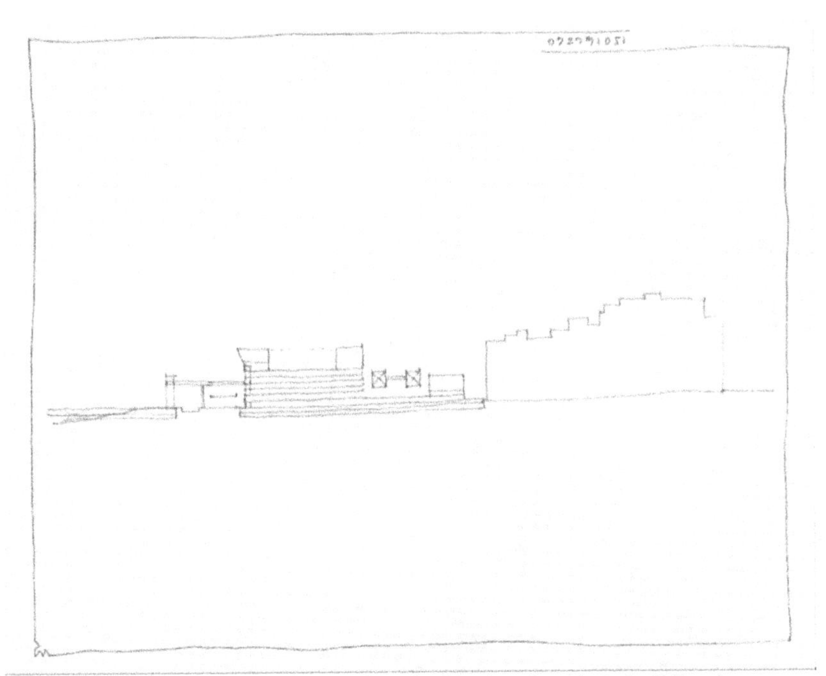

The bulk of the jail in vertical sense is quite big, but the whole building is relatively thin.

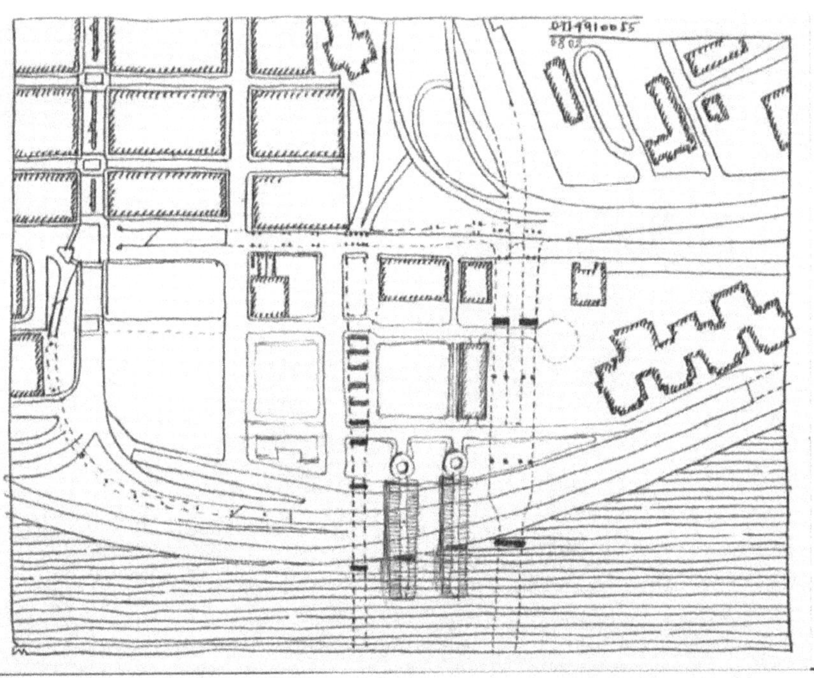

Recurrence of the previously depicted parallel bodies with the bridges. In this case the occupy the air-right of the Penn Lincoln Parkway as well as partially the river's. They would have relieved the site area from the parking, and would have made a ground level plaza possible, as the entrance to the Public Safety Building.

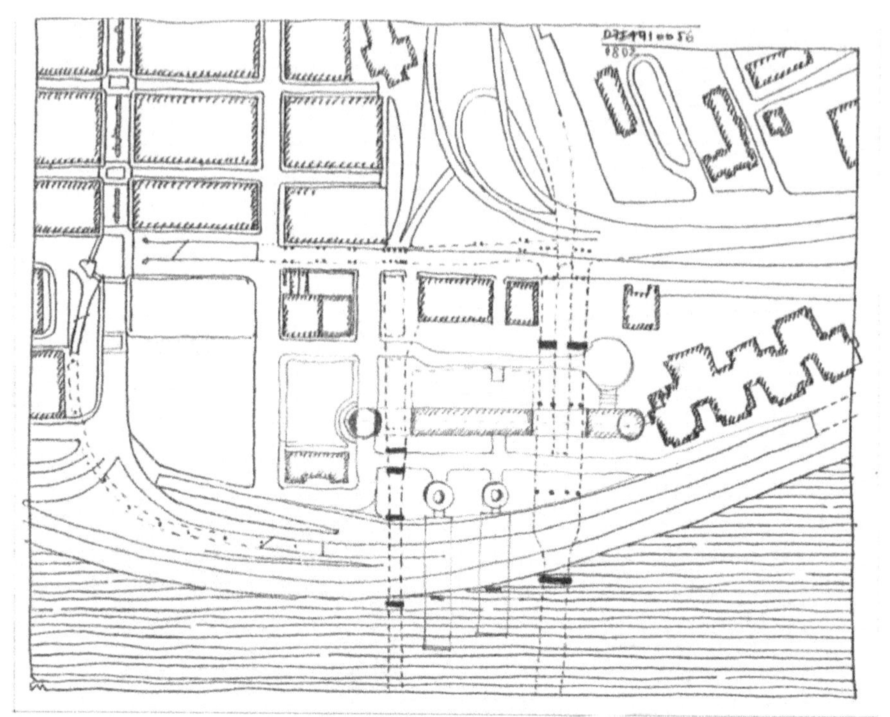

Apparently the linear solution had further temptations, here it is coupled to the parking on the river.

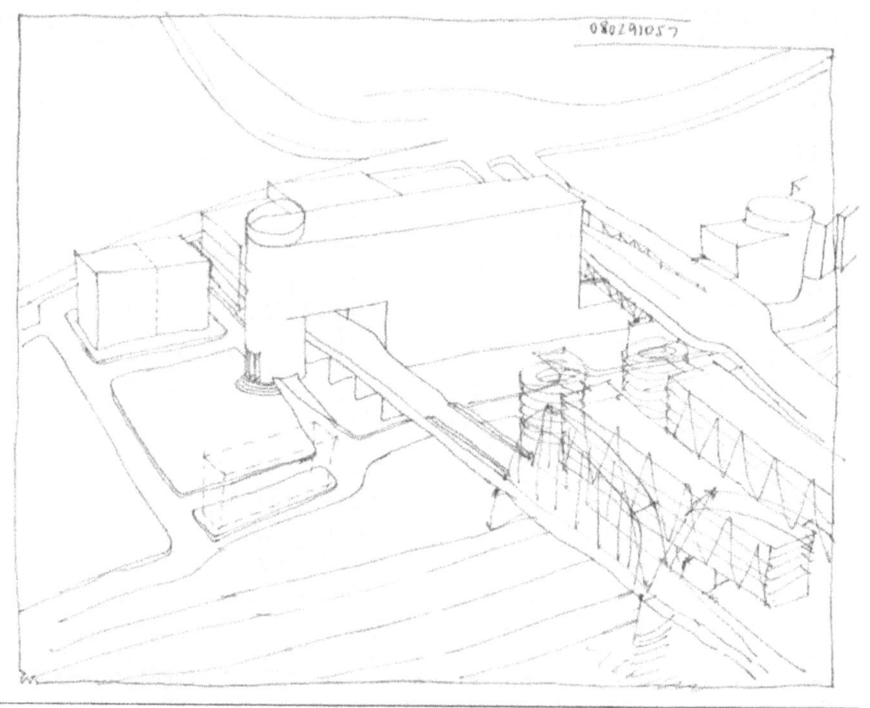

The sketch depicts the arrangement on the previous site plan.

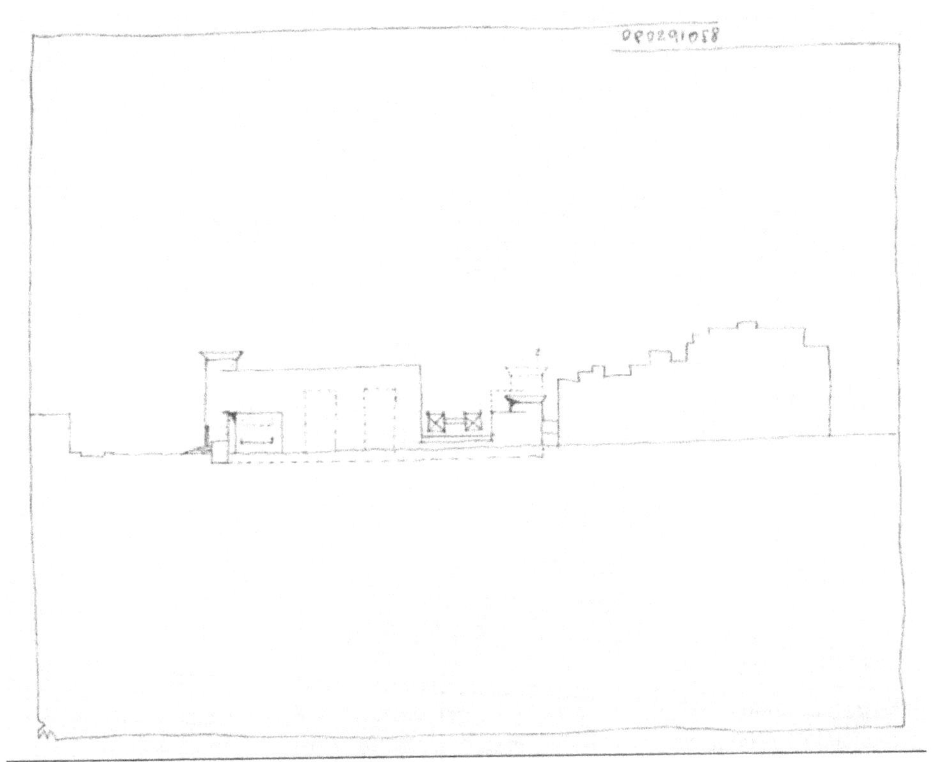

Massing of the previous drawings.

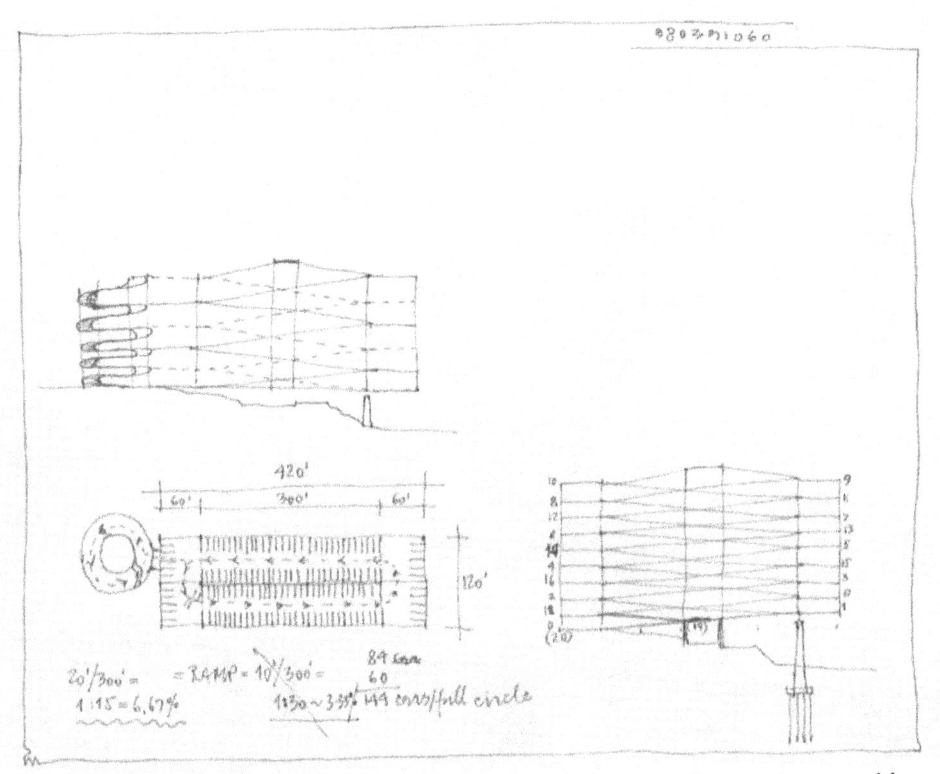

Some deliberations related to the parking structures. In this format they would

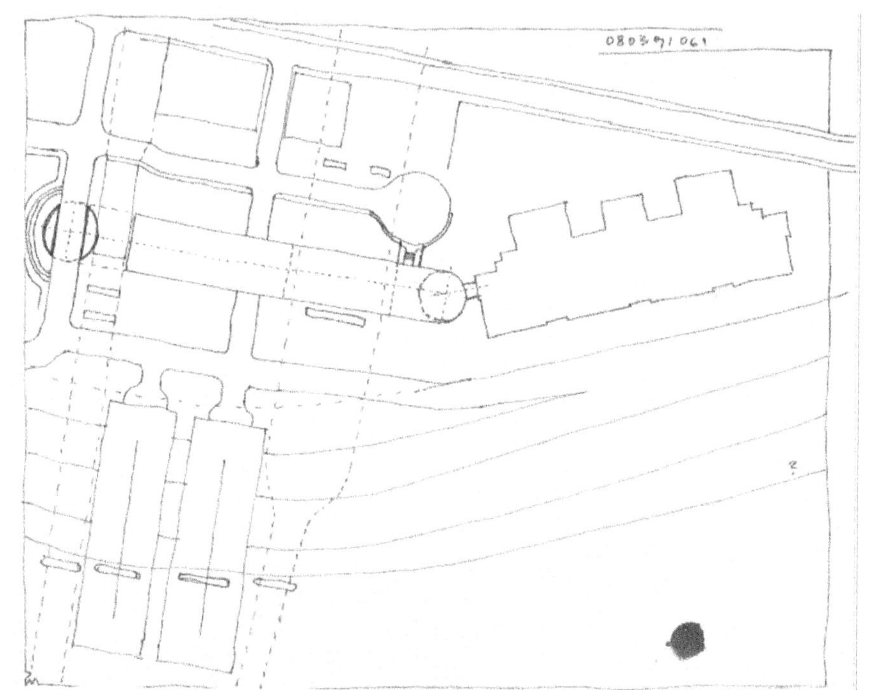

More site studies of the parking-bridge arrangement. Very rarely, but even the best fountain pens could leave their unwanted trace on the paper. Maybe my Mont Blanc didn't agree with this solution.

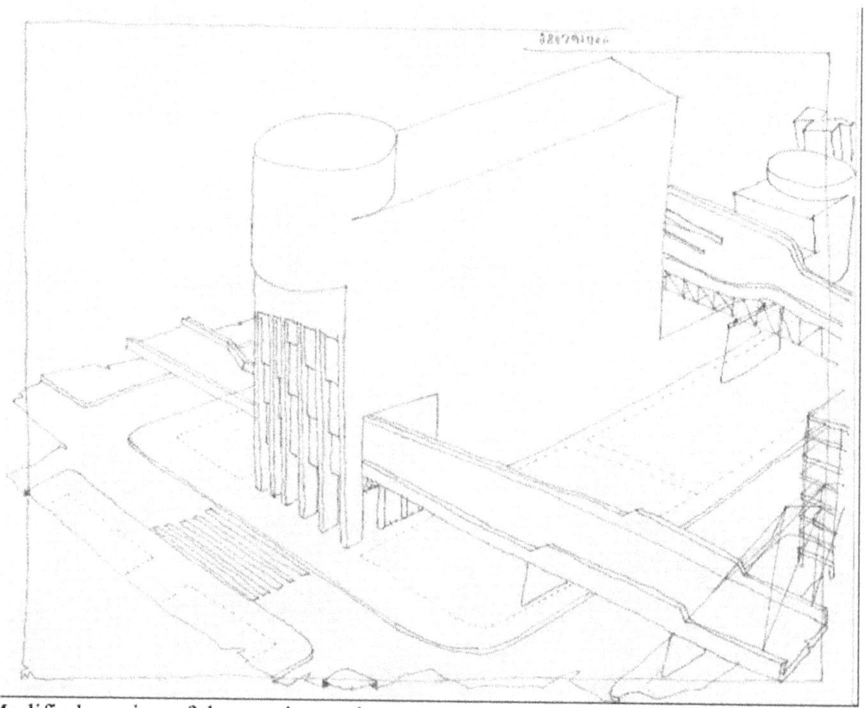

Modified version of the previous scheme.

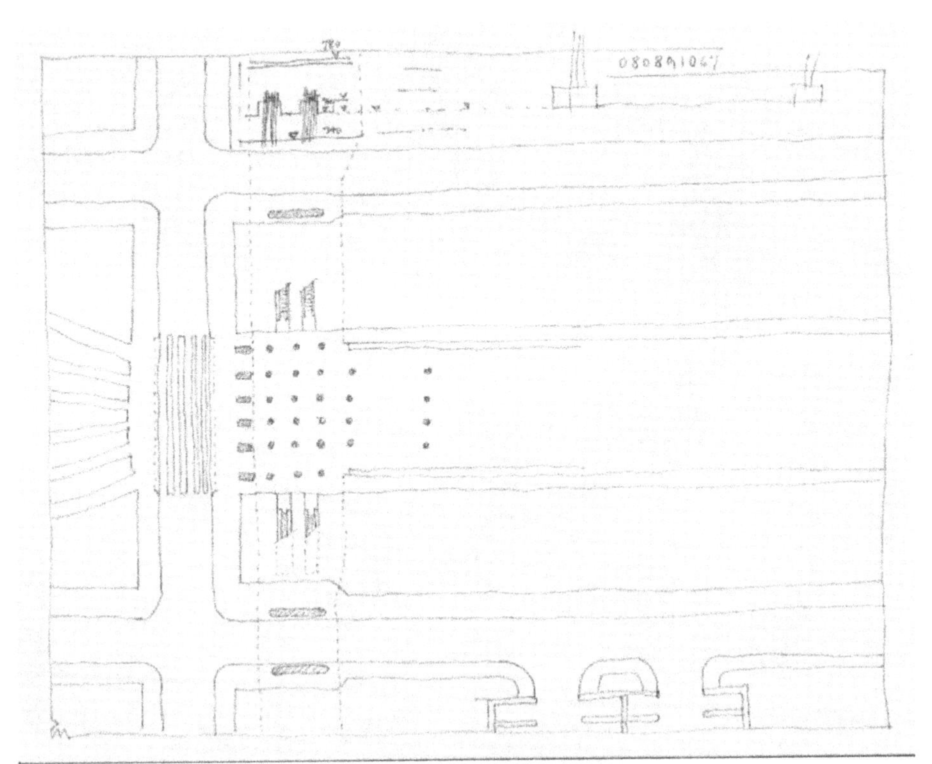

Site consequences of the previous drawing are studied here.

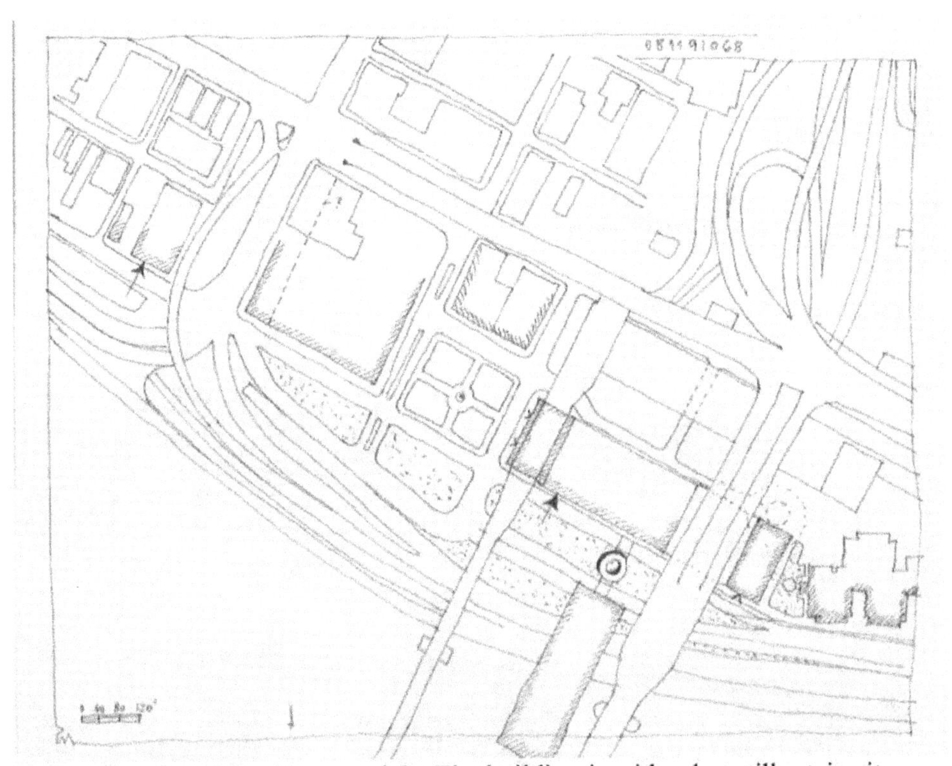

A new site plan, full with potentials. The building is wider, but still retains its linear character.

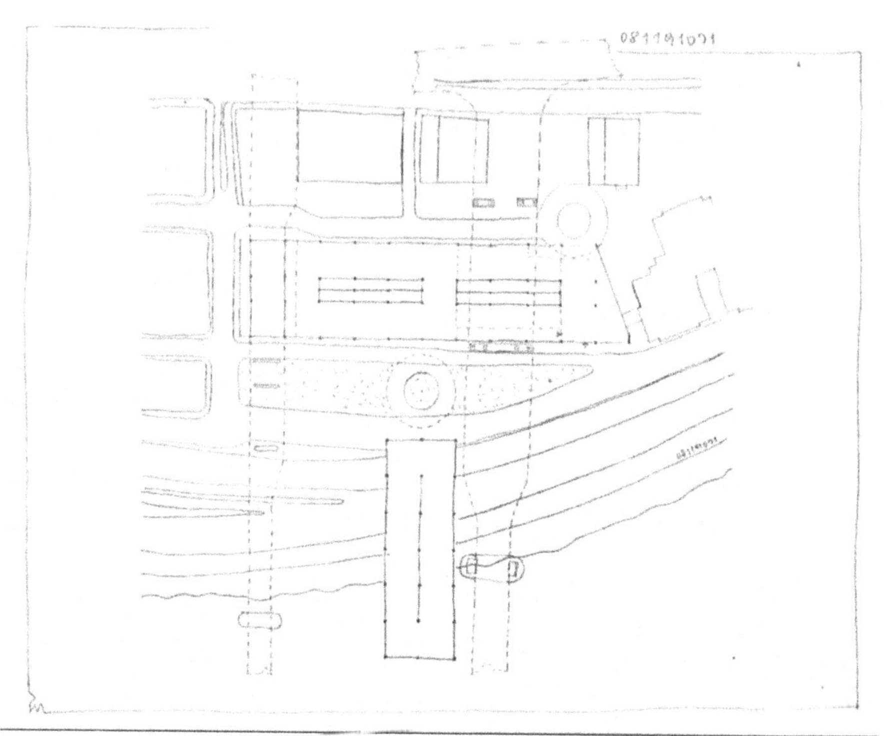

Enrichment and simplification processes follow each other repeatedly. This drawing was an early predecessor of the final solution.

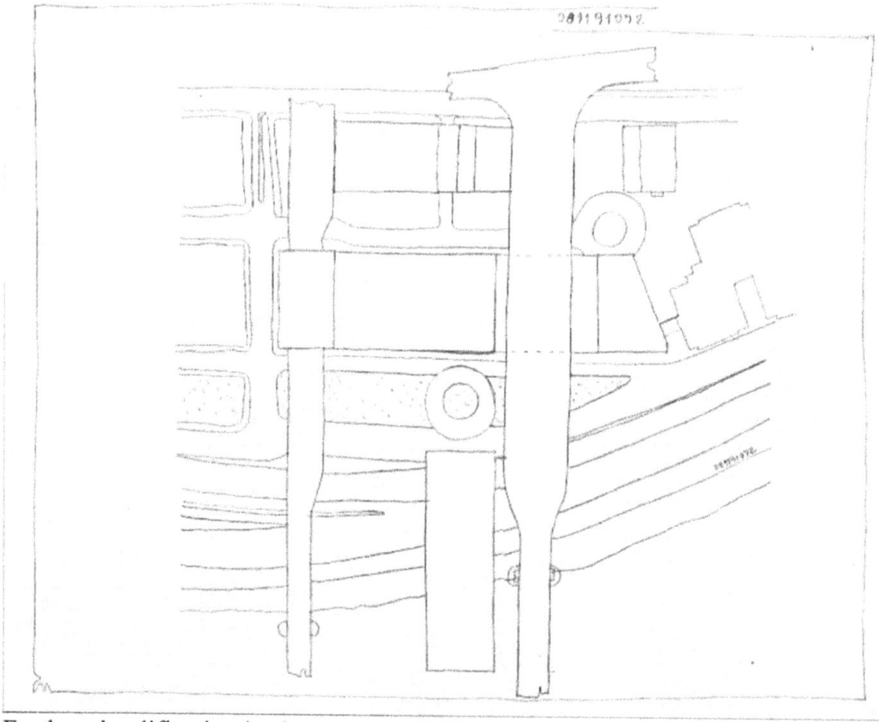

Further simplification is always a possibility.

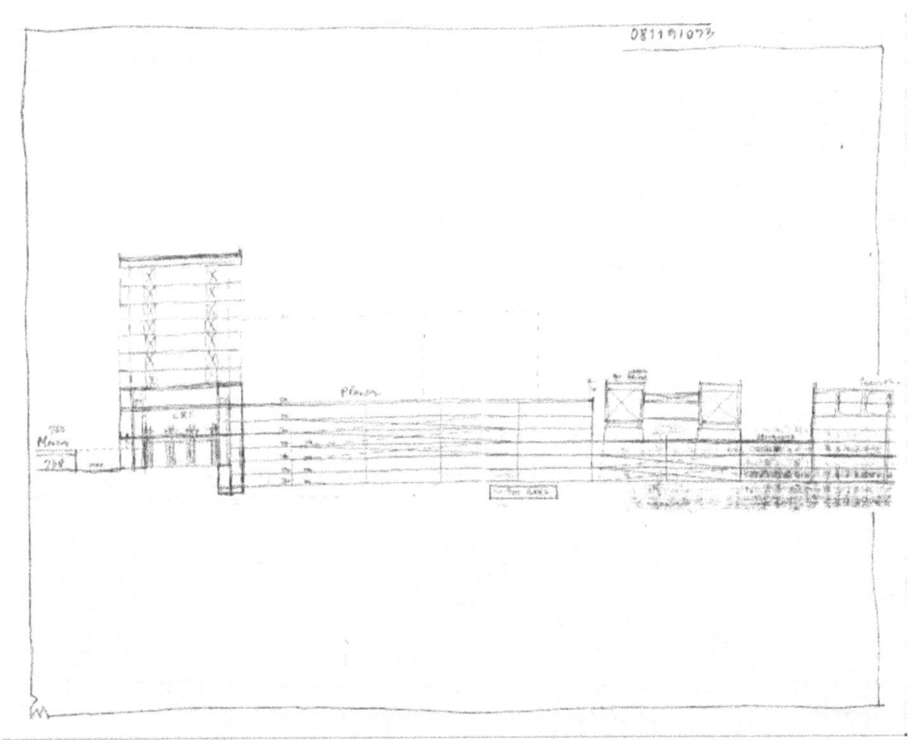

An almost viable scheme, unifying in itself many of the previous discoveries.

An almost viable scheme, unifying in itself many of the previous discoveries.

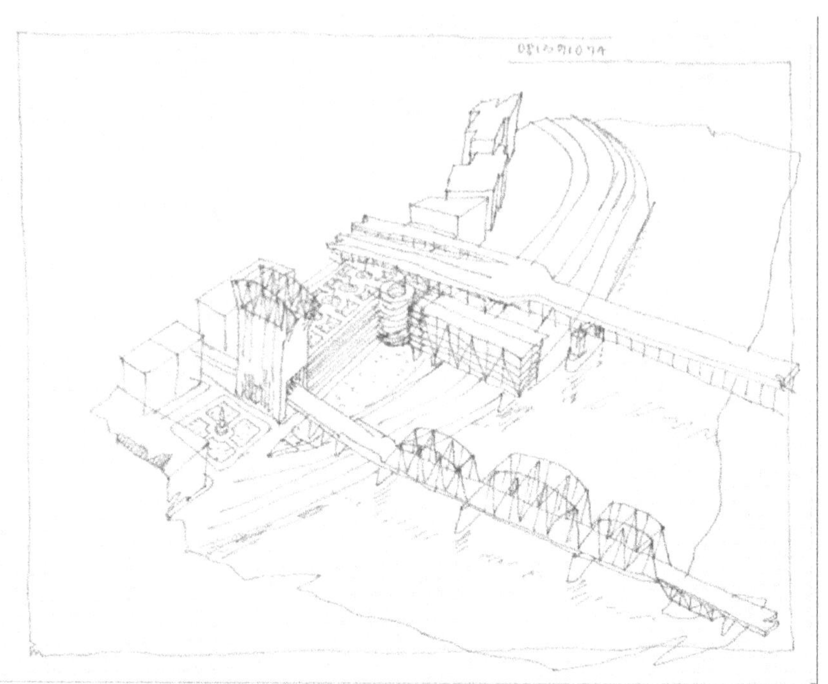

It would have been very easy to stop here, and develop this version. The somewhat formalistic "tiara" on the top of the office building intended to make formal connection with the railway-bridge, but it became a bit too literal. It could have even serve some function on the top of the building, to have a large room (the "living room of the City"), with a large-span suspended structure.

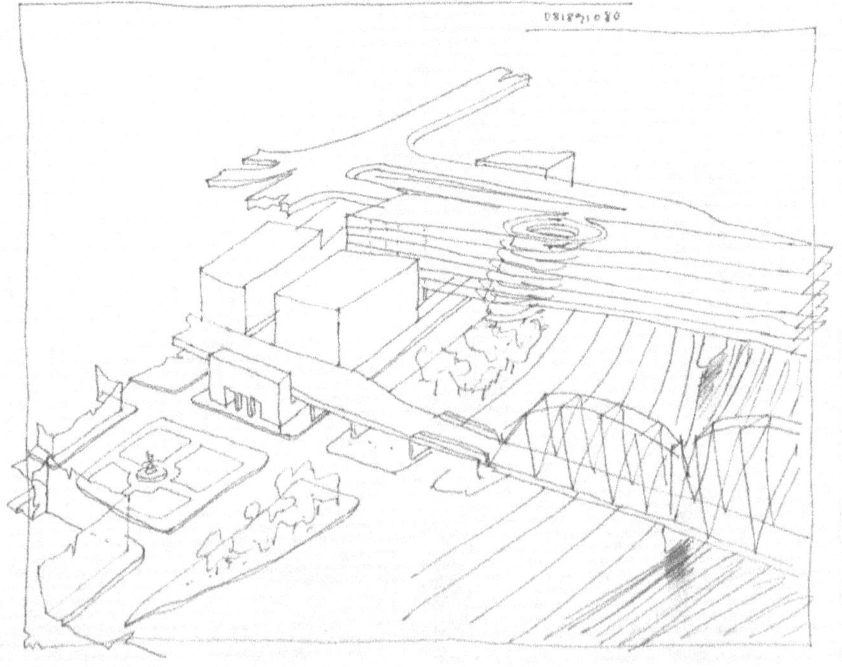

As it is visible from this sketch, it is not a successful solution.

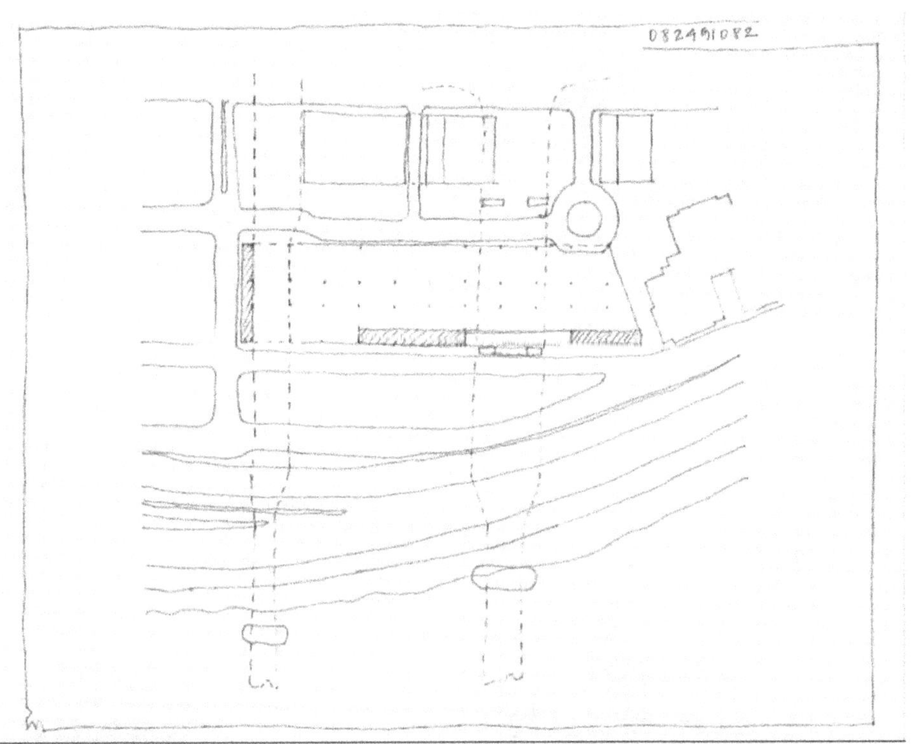

With this drawing a long process began, leading eventually to the schematic design. The hatched areas indicate entrance zones.

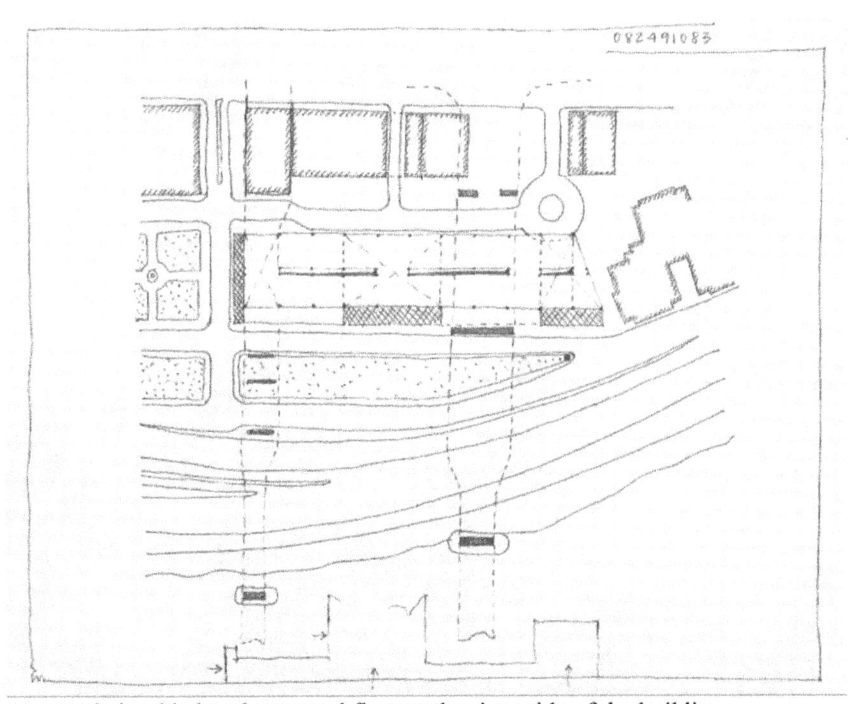

An arcade is added to the ground floor at the river side of the building.
The diagonals denote from West to East the railway station, the tower and the courthouse, respectively.

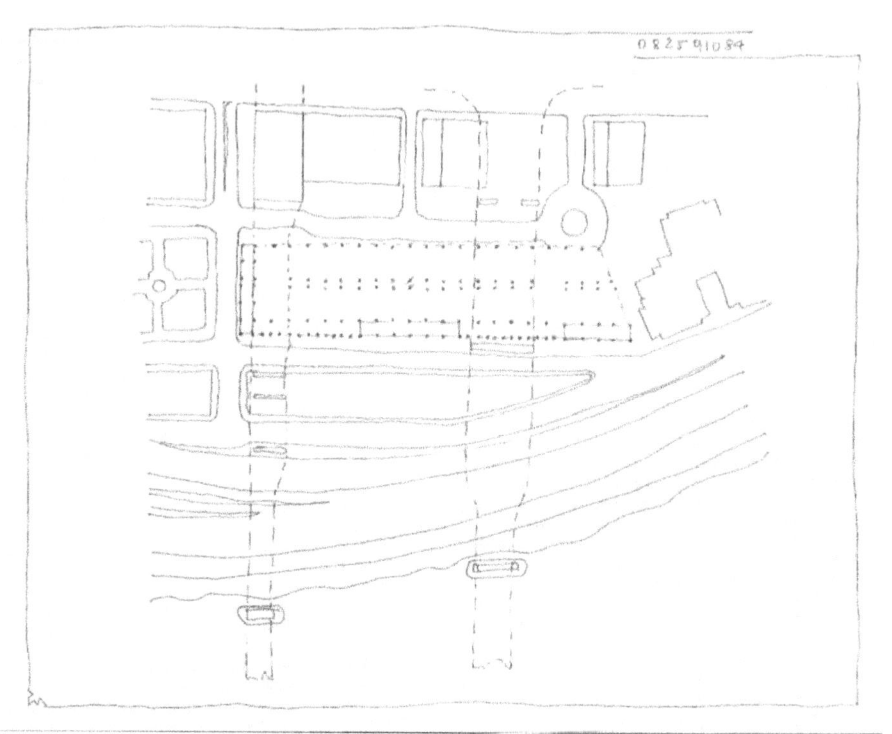

In the middle of the building, a double row of columns create a venting slit for the parking levels.

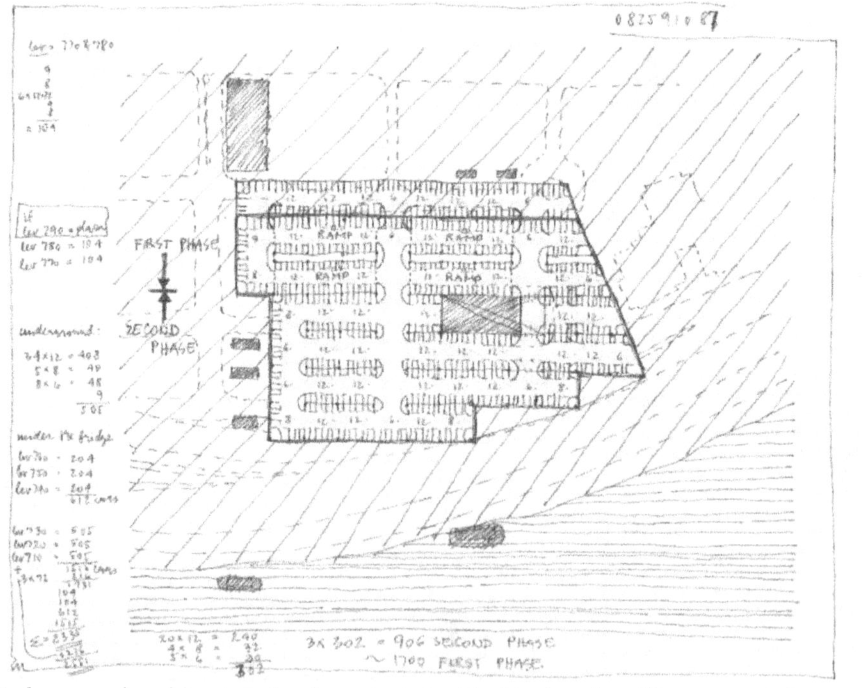

Underground parking is being inventoried with this drawing. The excavated area couldn't encroach the area of the Penn Lincoln Parkway.

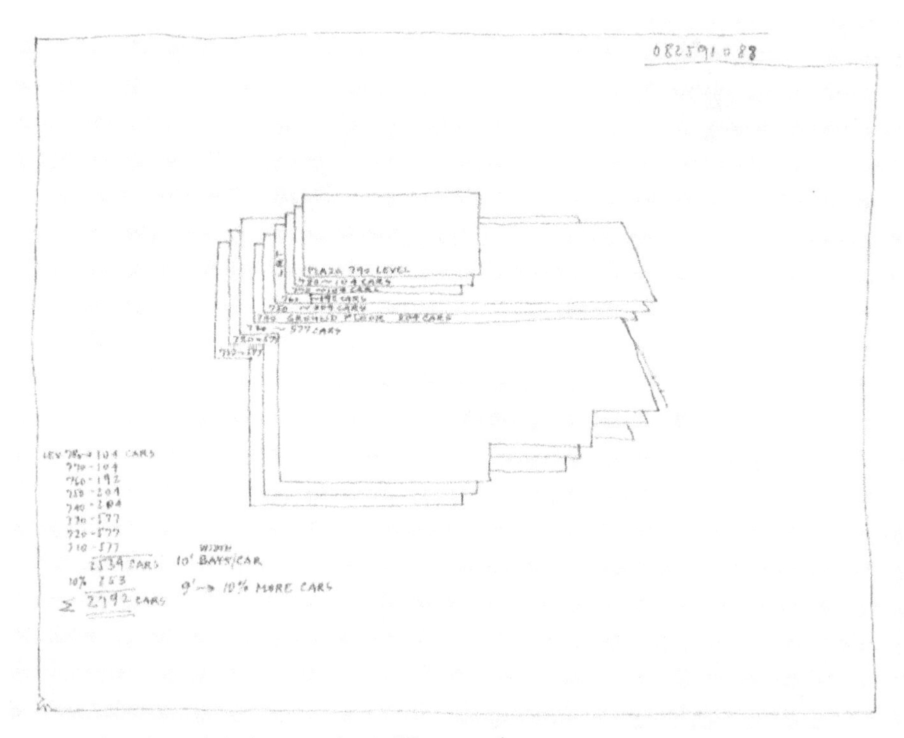

Parking levels and their capacity is illustrated.

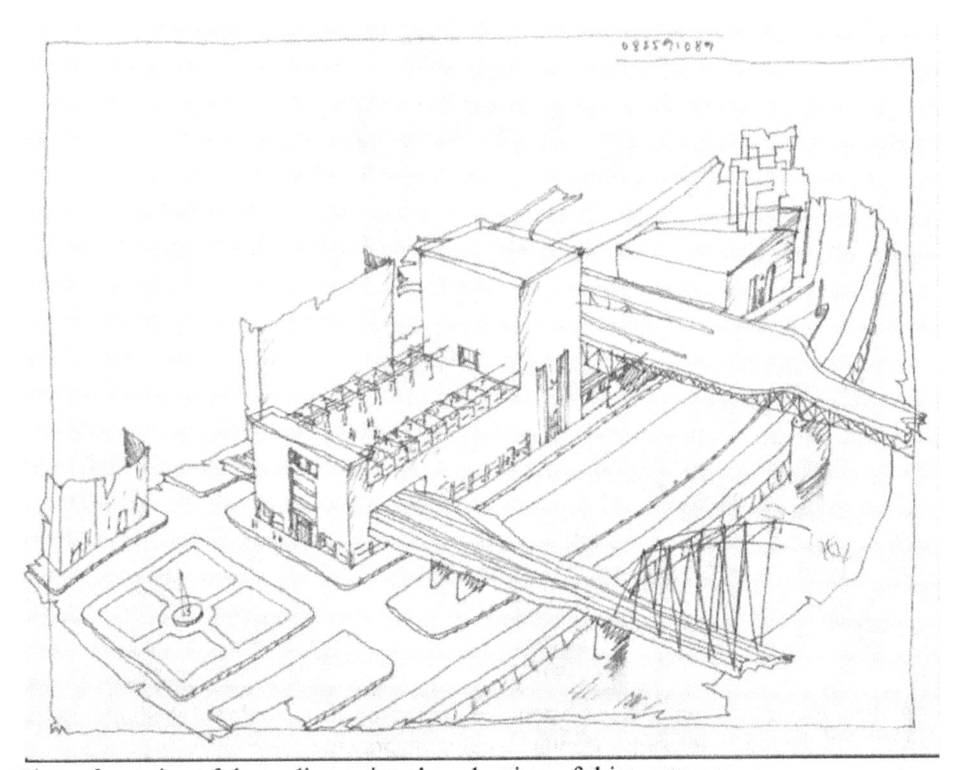

First of a series of three dimensional evaluation of this system.

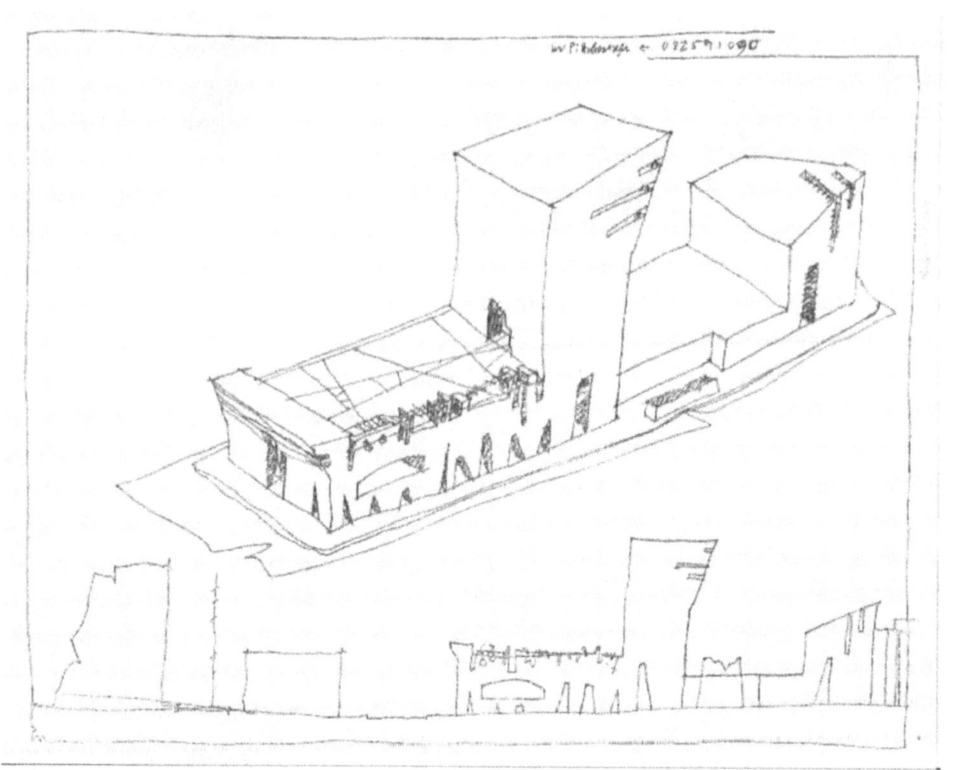

A further interpretation of the building.

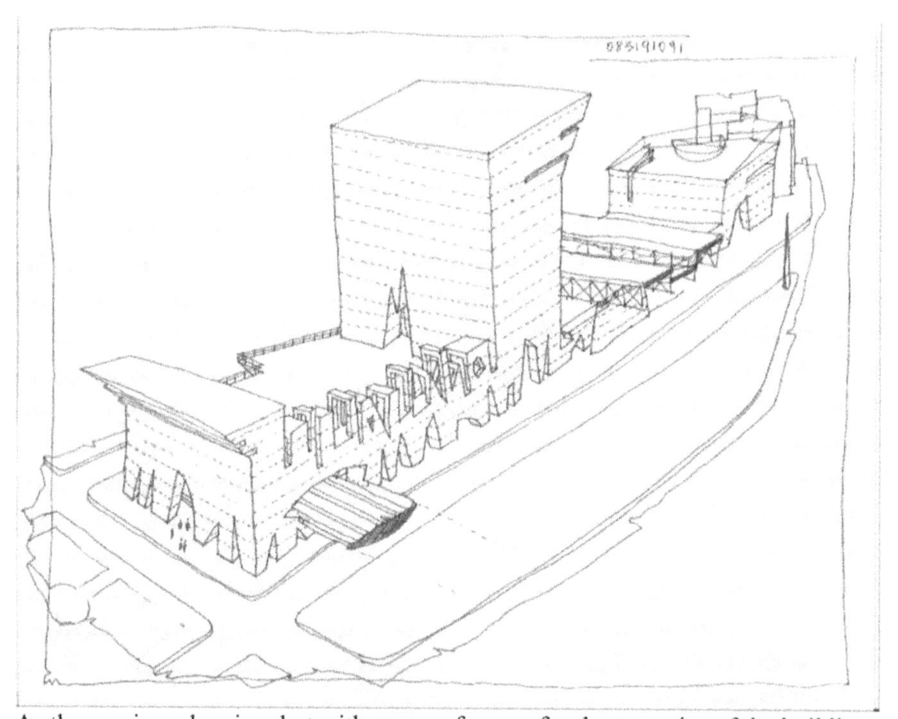

As the previous drawing, but with some reference for the tectonics of the building. Just with the indication of horizontal scoring, the drawing can convey an almost tactile reading of the elements.

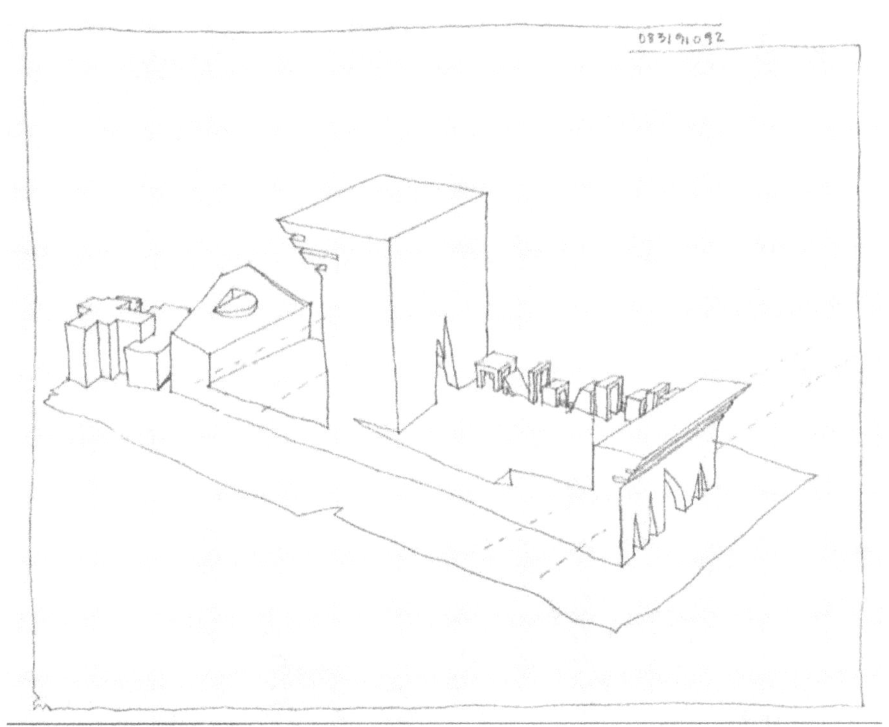

North-West view, without the bridges.

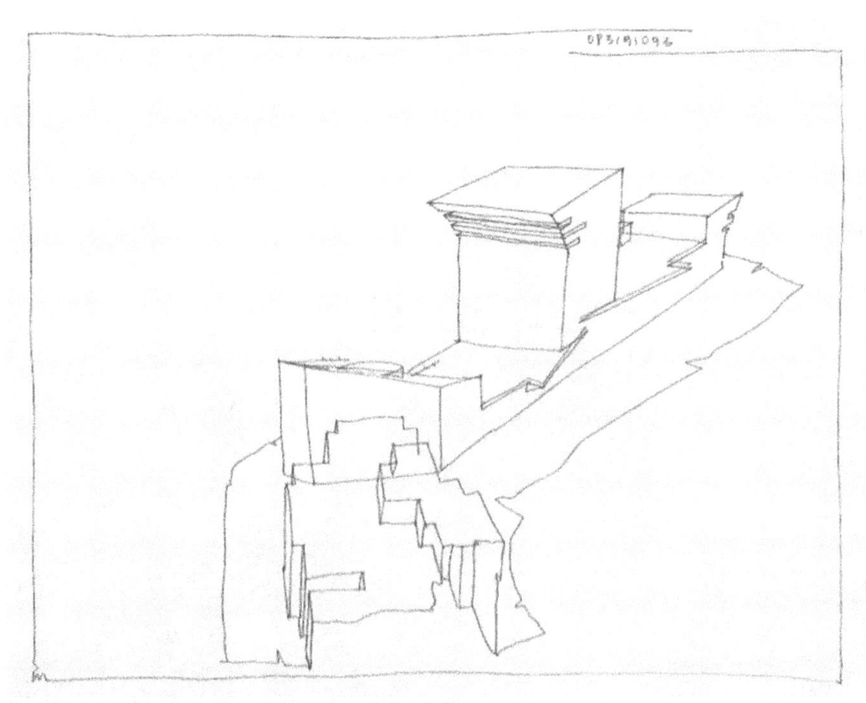

Looking at the massing from above the jail.
These last five drawings won an Award of the American Society of Architectural Perspectivists in the Sketch Category.

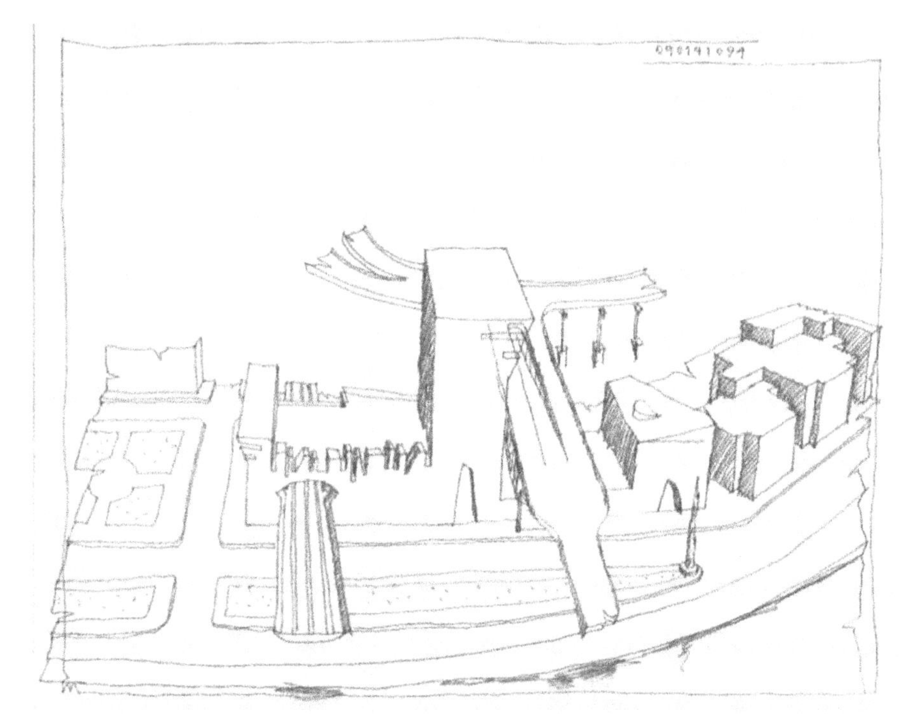

The last of the series again contains a view from the direction of the river.

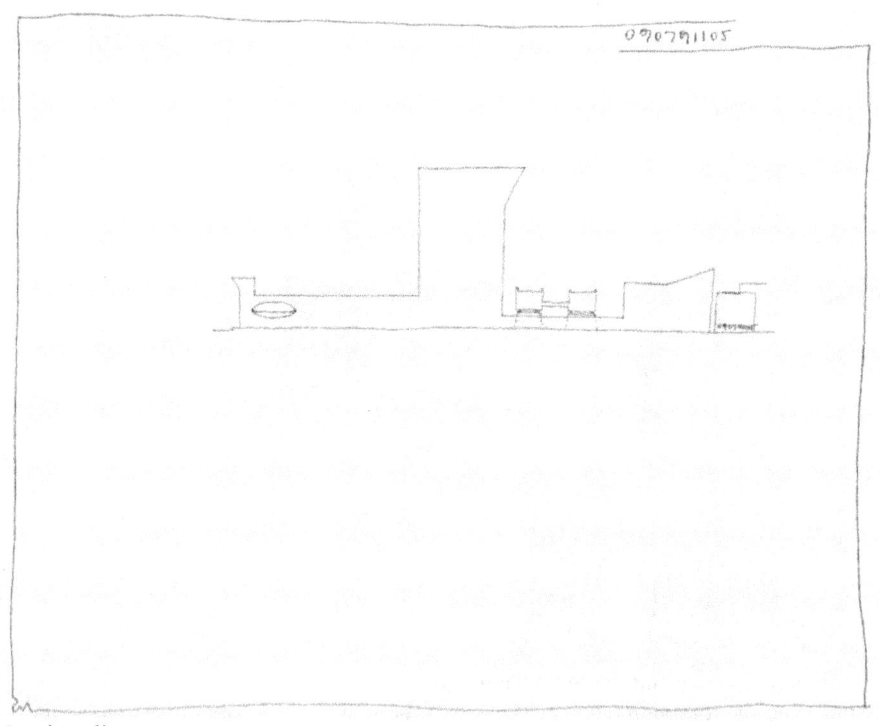

Massing diagram.

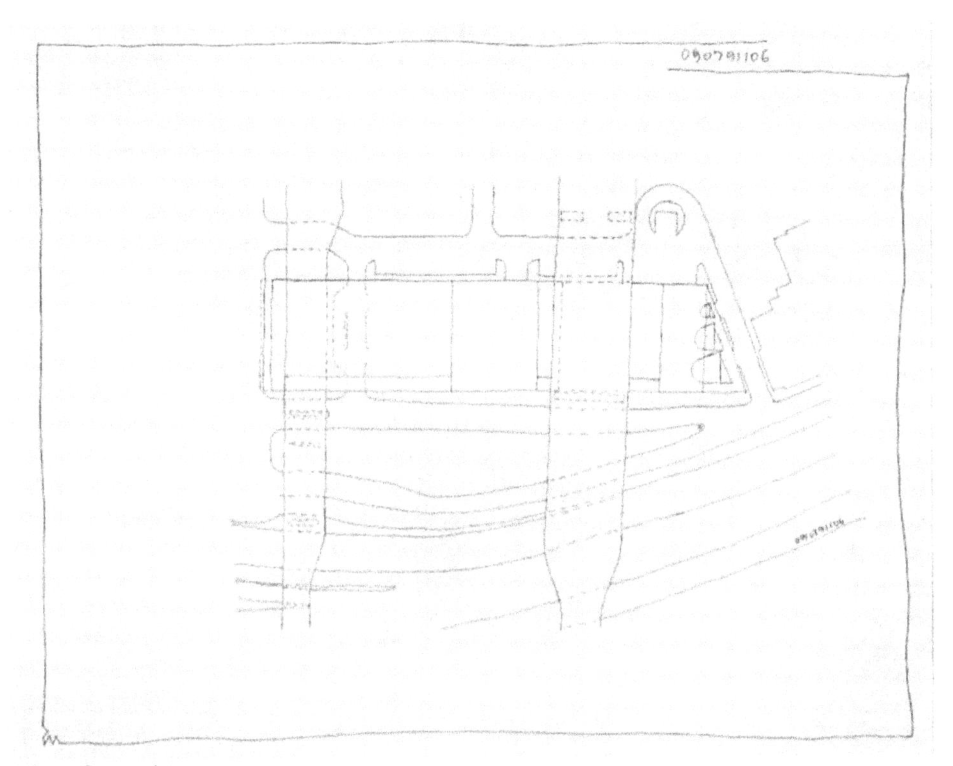

View from above.

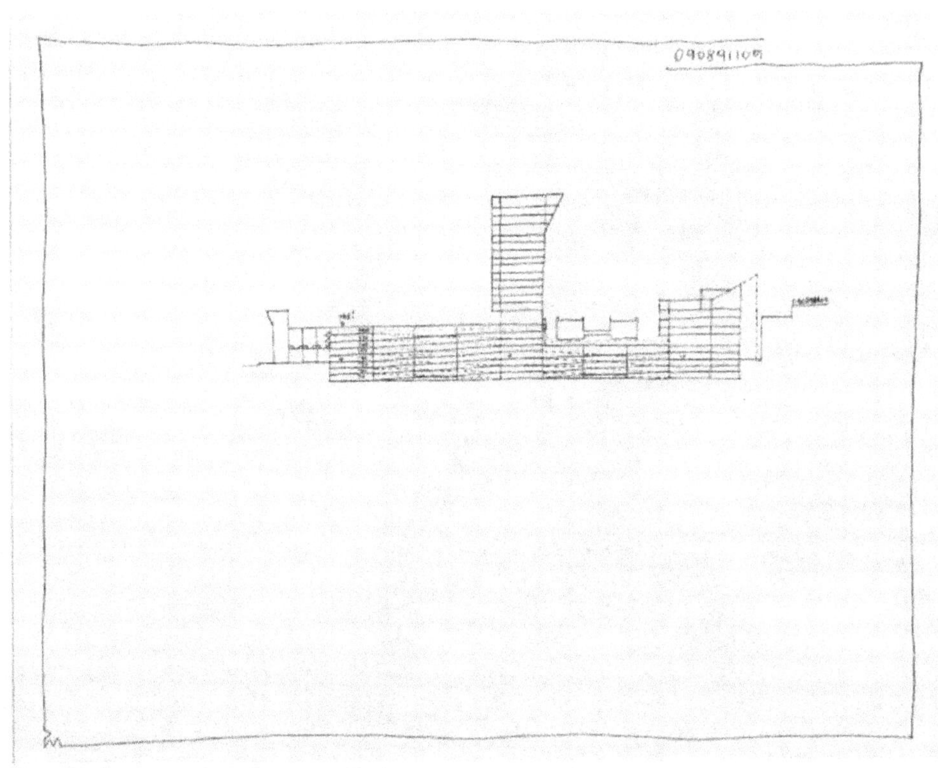

Levels above and underground.

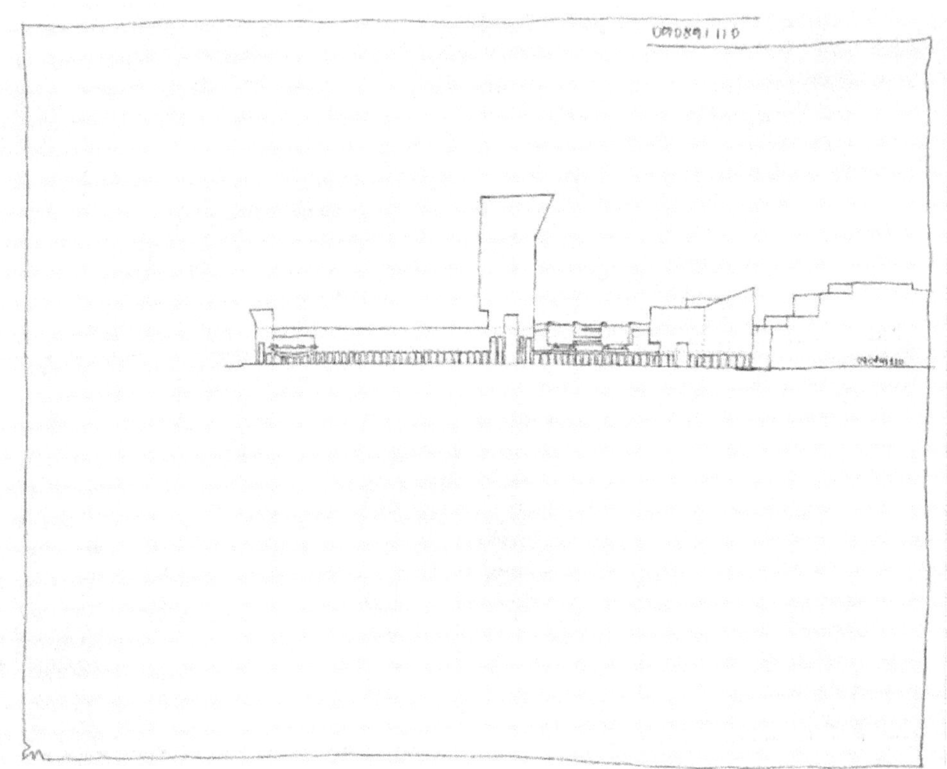

Volume studies from the river.

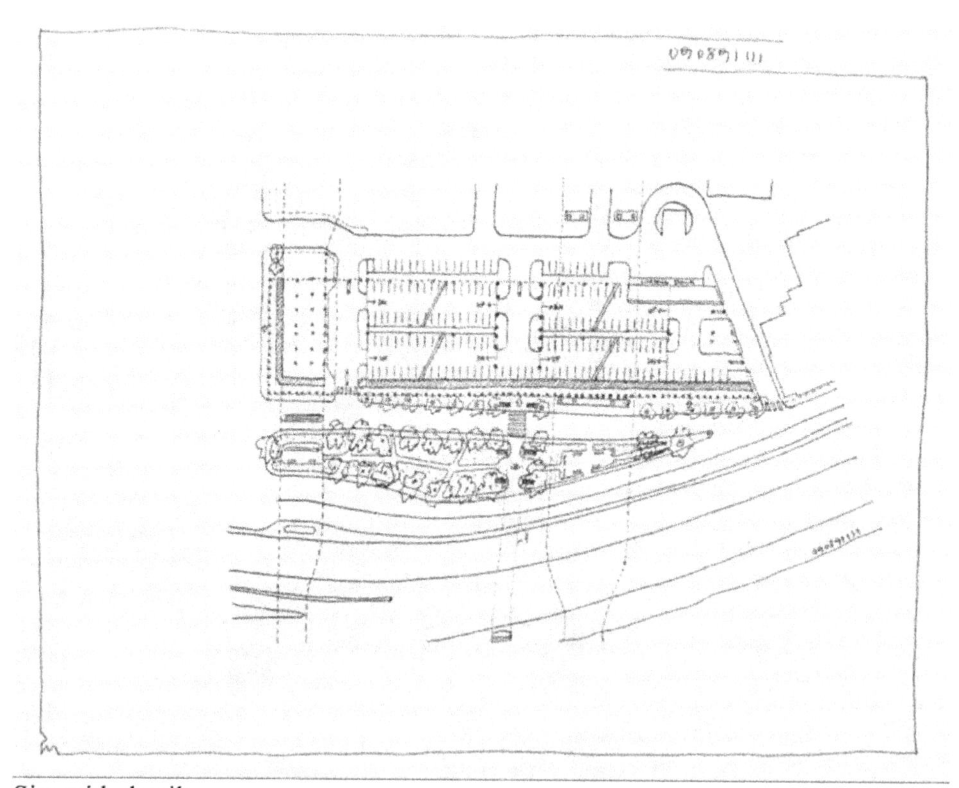

Site with details.

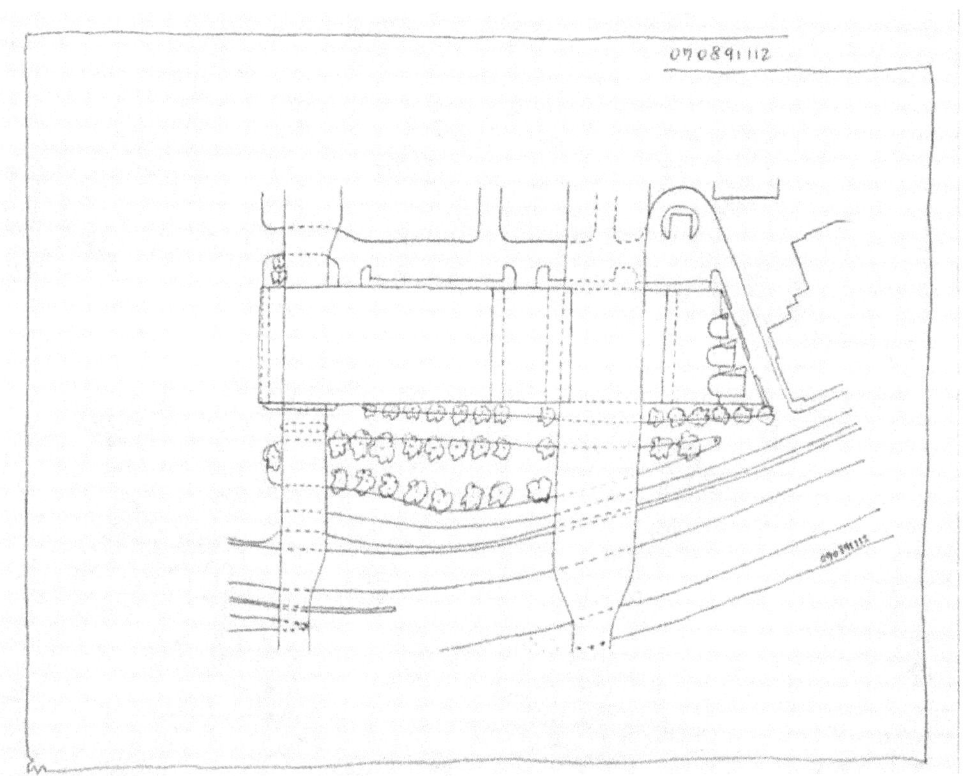

View from above. The dotted lines denote structural overhangs.

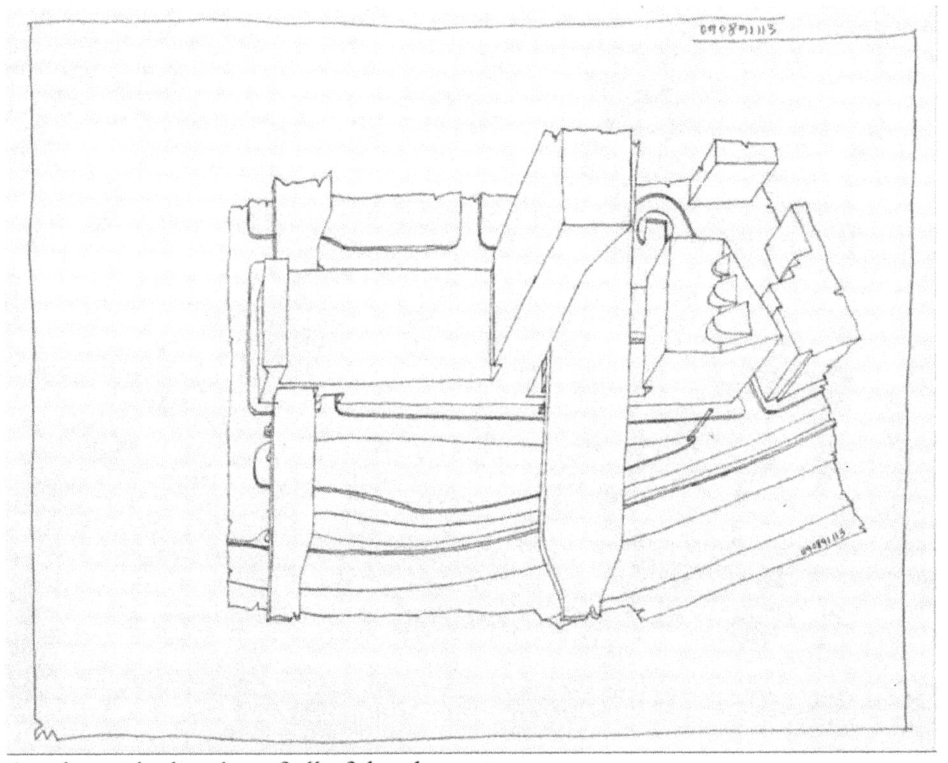

A volumetric drawing of all of the elements.

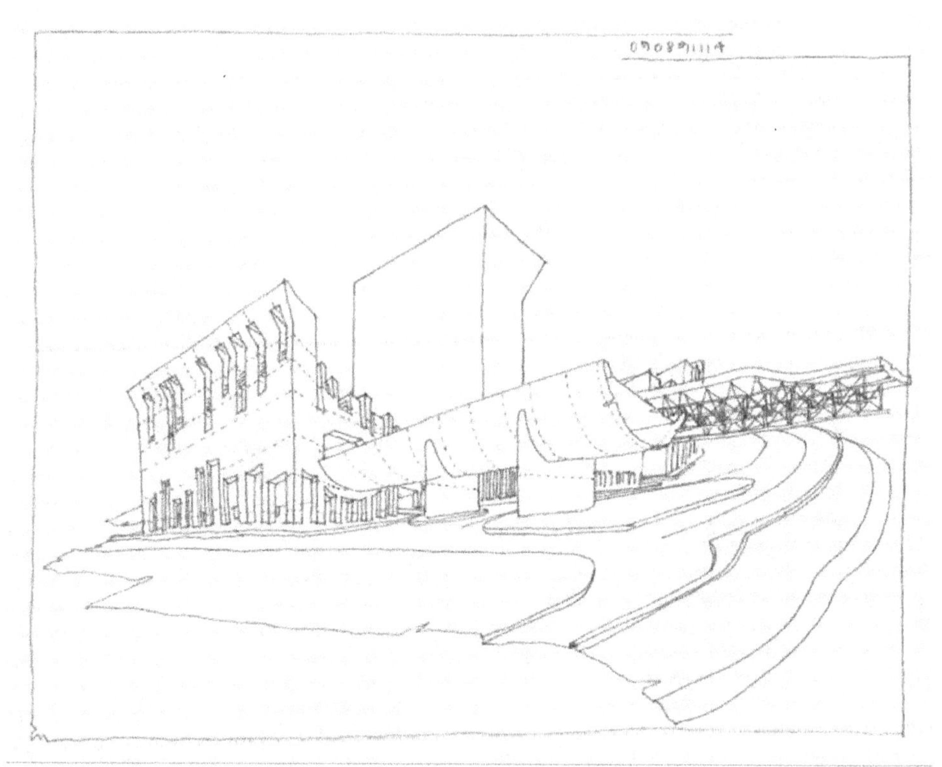

South-West view from the ground.

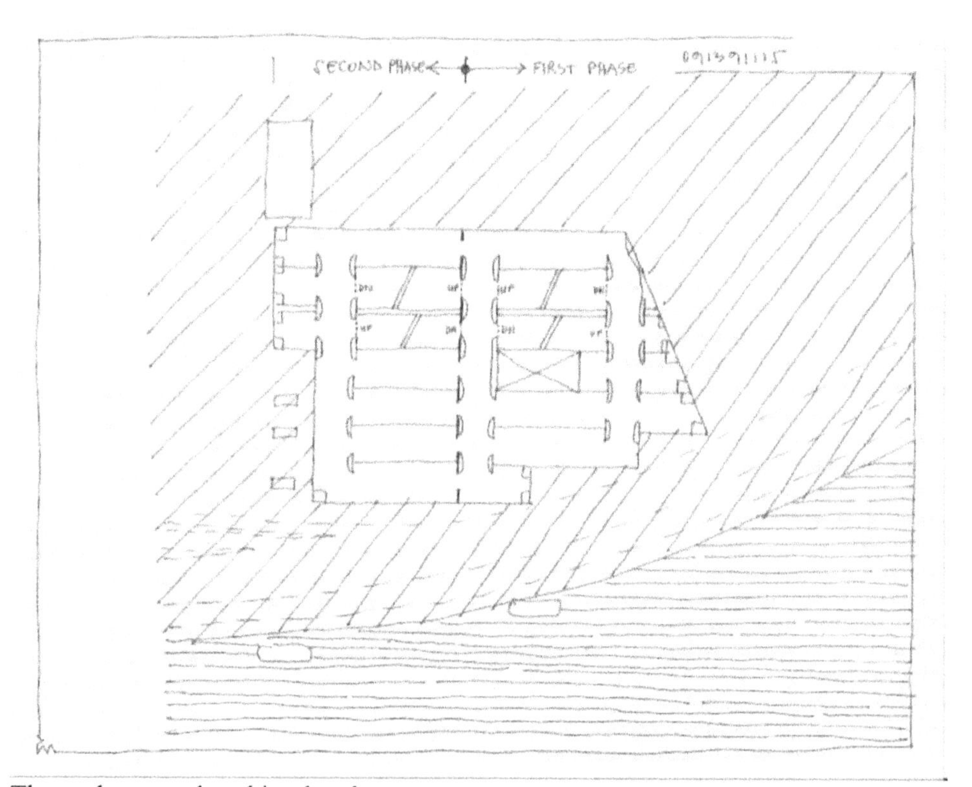

The underground parking levels.

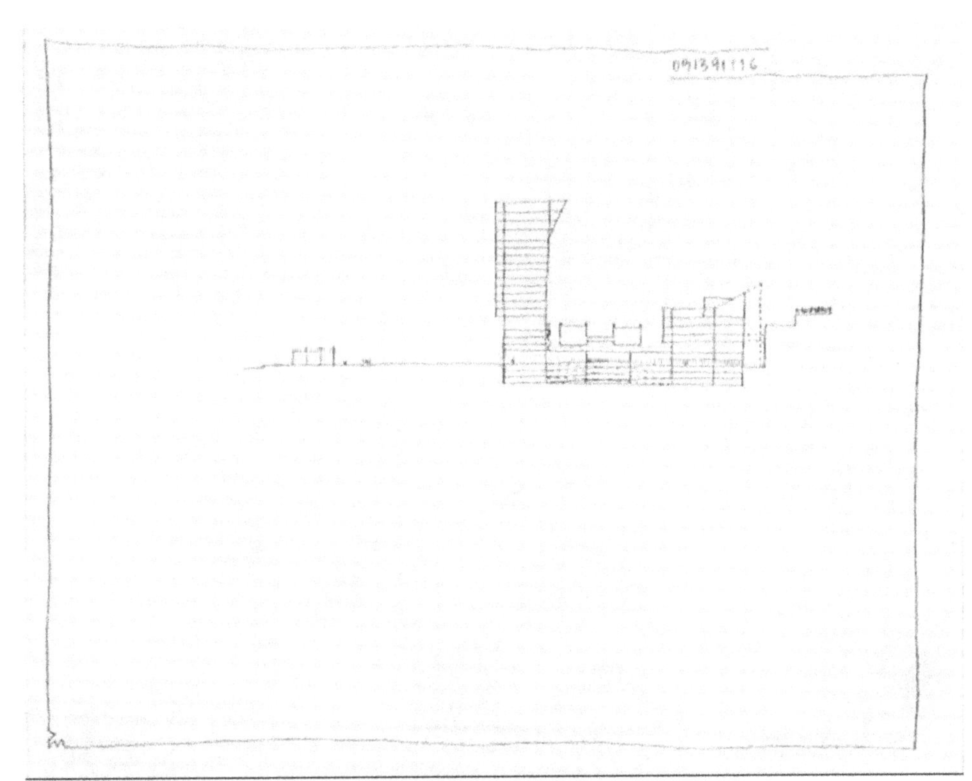

First phase / section.

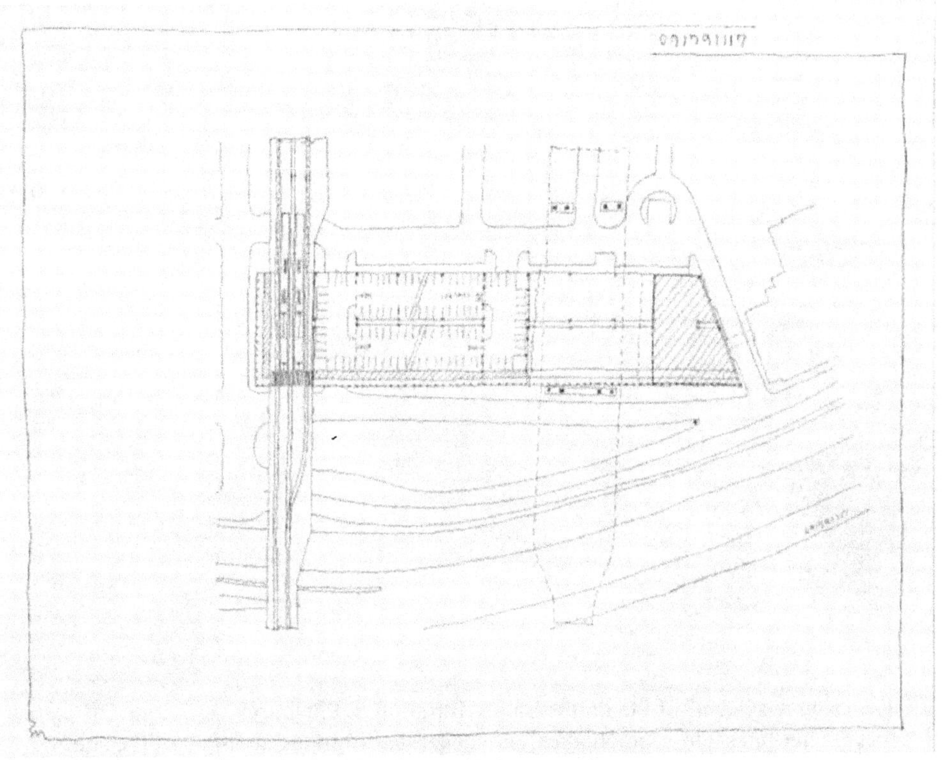

The second floor plan. The hatched area is the courthouse.

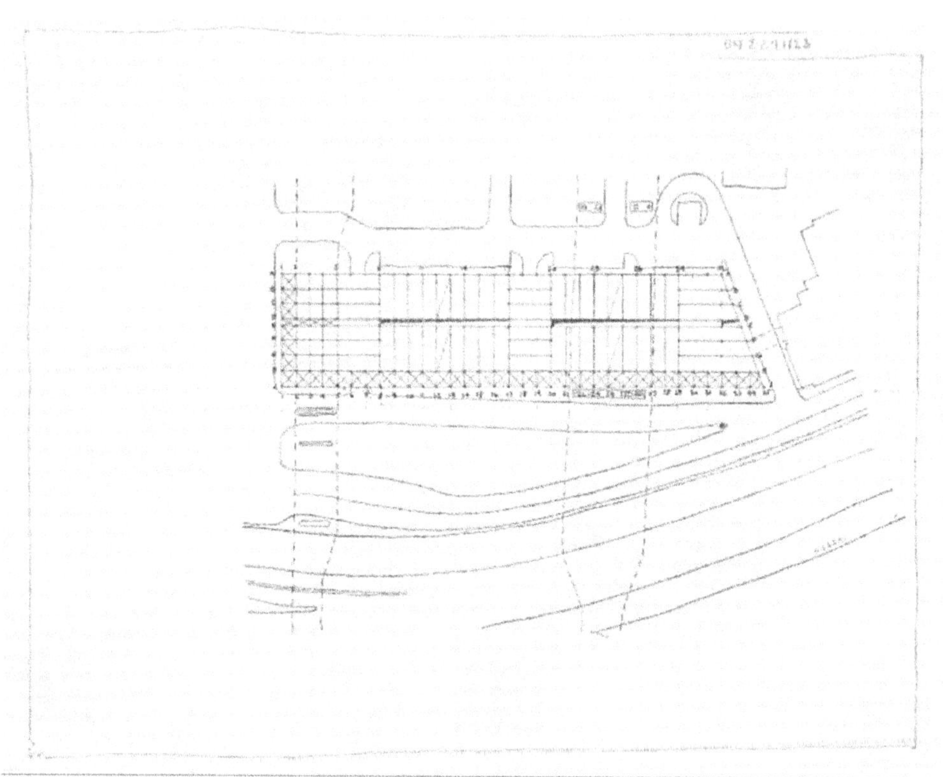

Ground floor plan with the arcades. The structural girders are indicated.

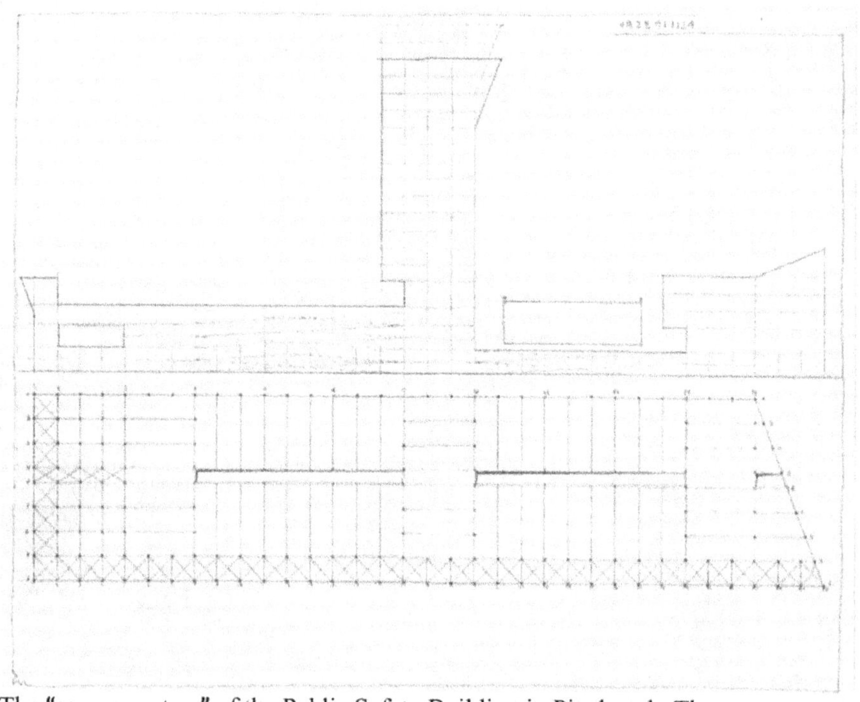

The "source system" of the Public Safety Building in Pittsburgh. The non-rectangular lines, these "anomalies", are generated from the anomaly of the site, and form - due to their identical angles - a 'family of anomalies'.

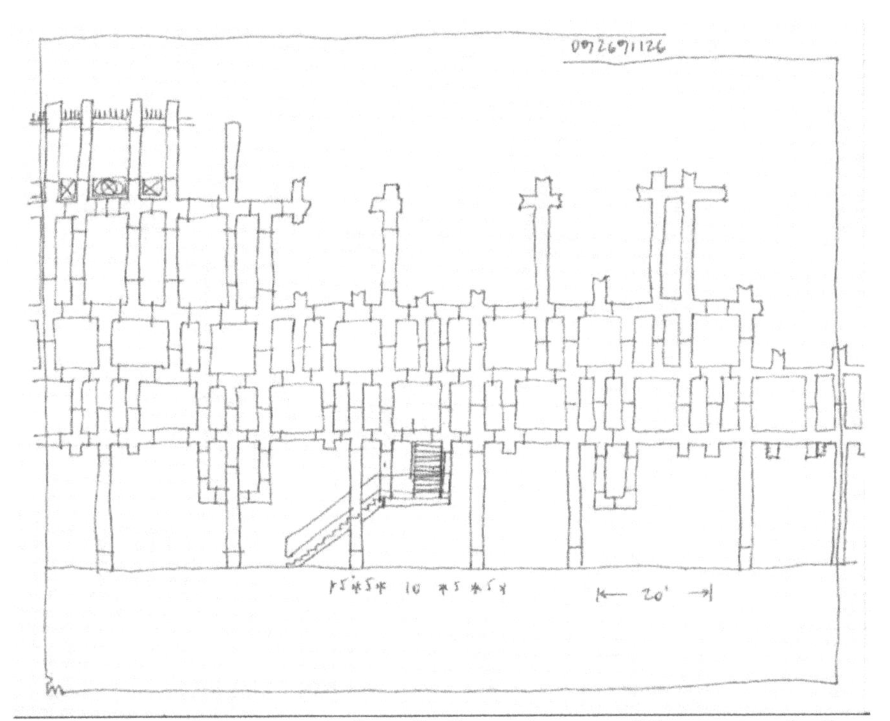

Again the same task: how to transform the linear elements of the structure for the planar envelope of the building.

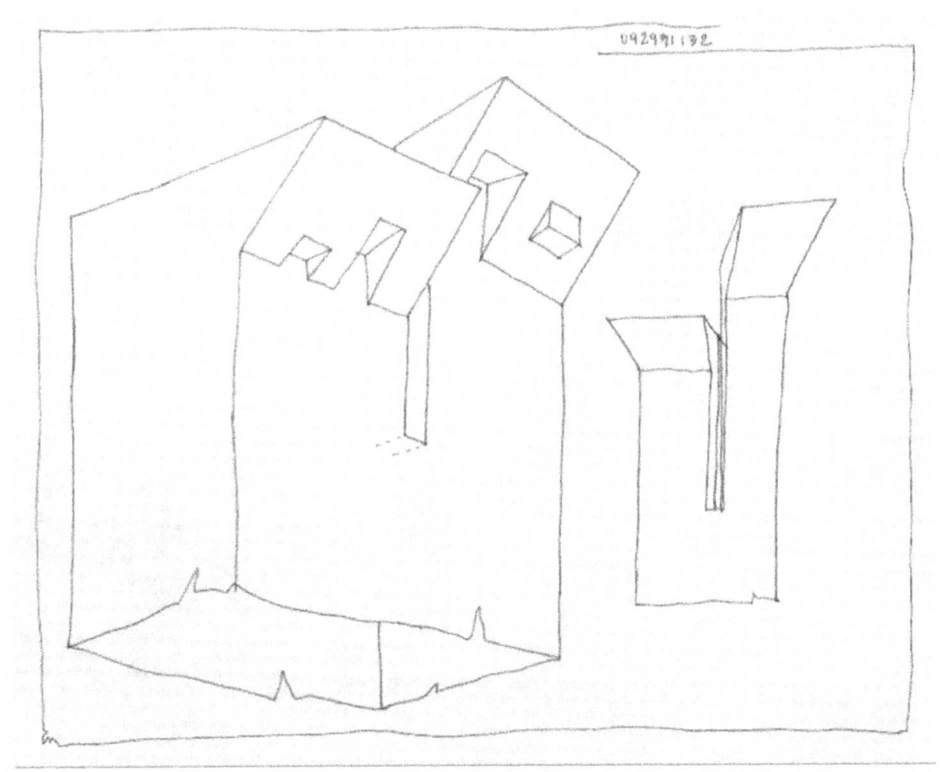

Volumetric variations.

Searching for the system of epidermis.

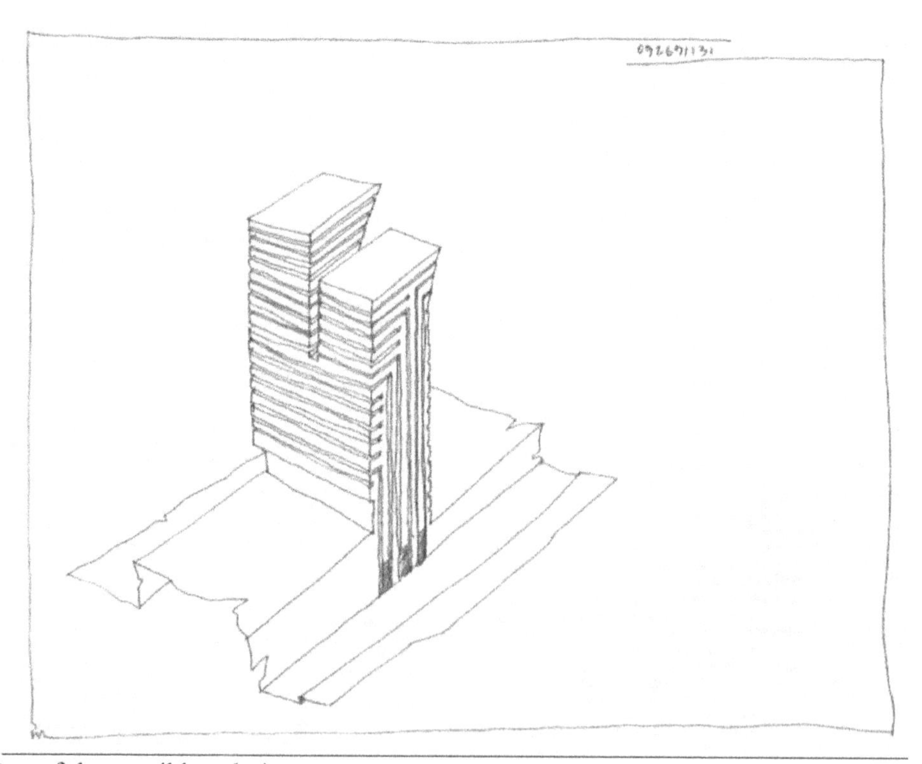

One of the possible solutions.

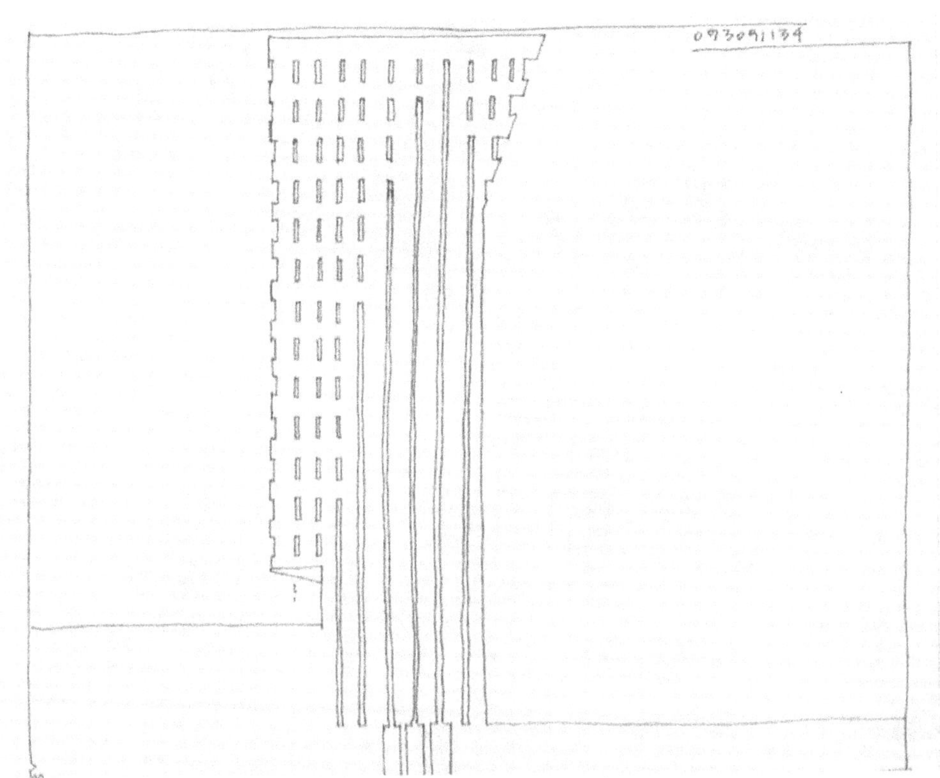

Continuous and punched windows on the side elevation.

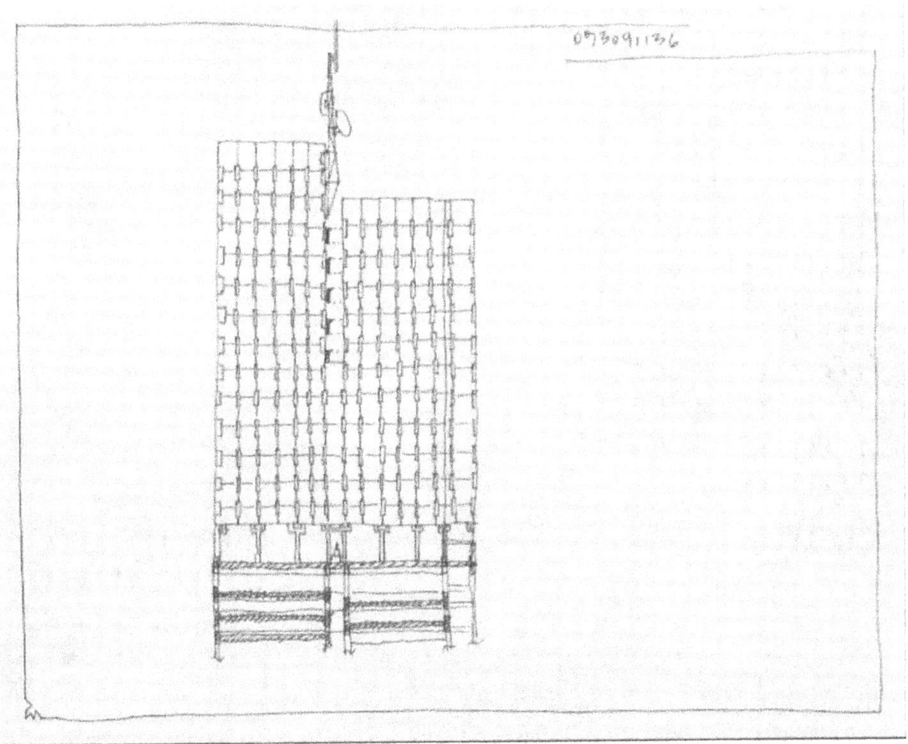

West elevation. Reduced size windows are consistent with minimizing heat-gain.

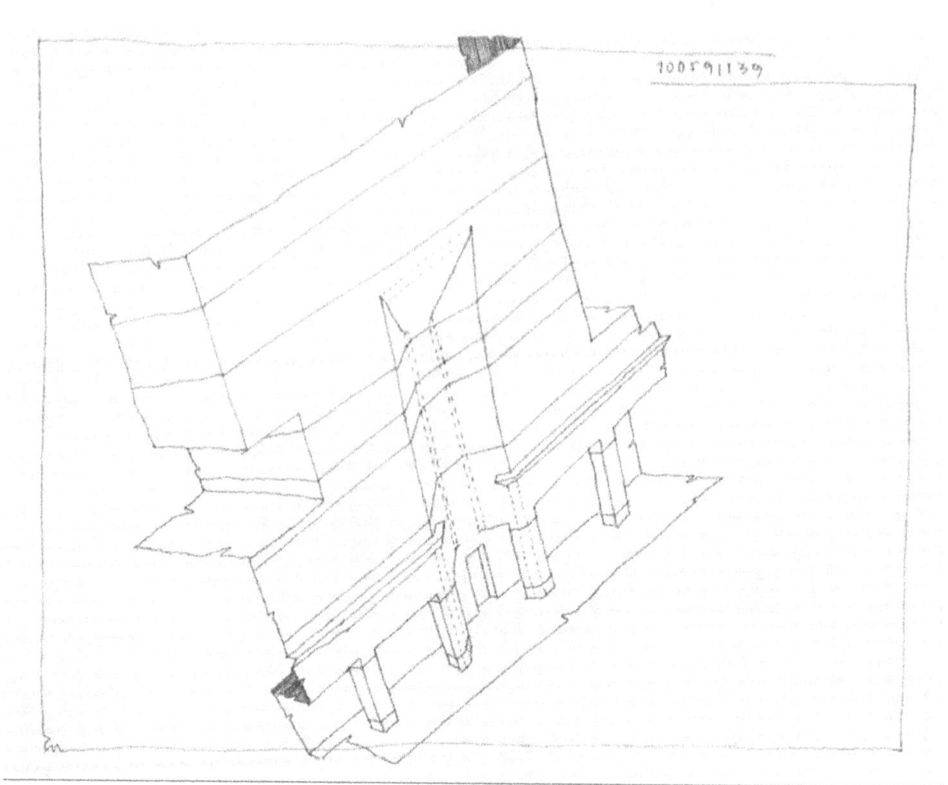

Entrance exploration diagram.

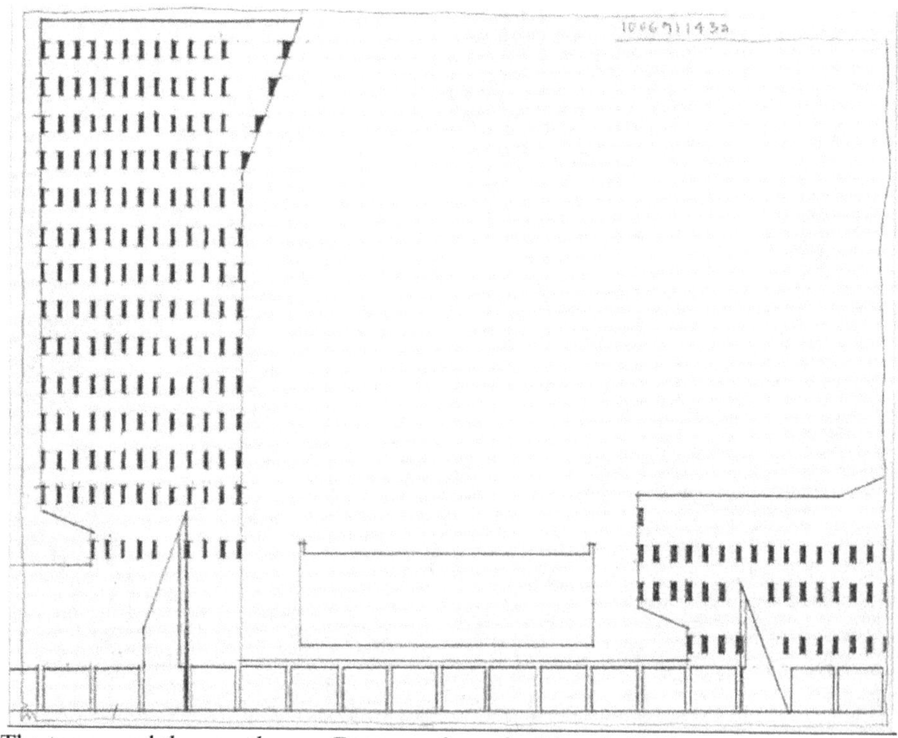

The tower and the courthouse. Between them the Lincoln Bridge goes over the ground floor of the complex.

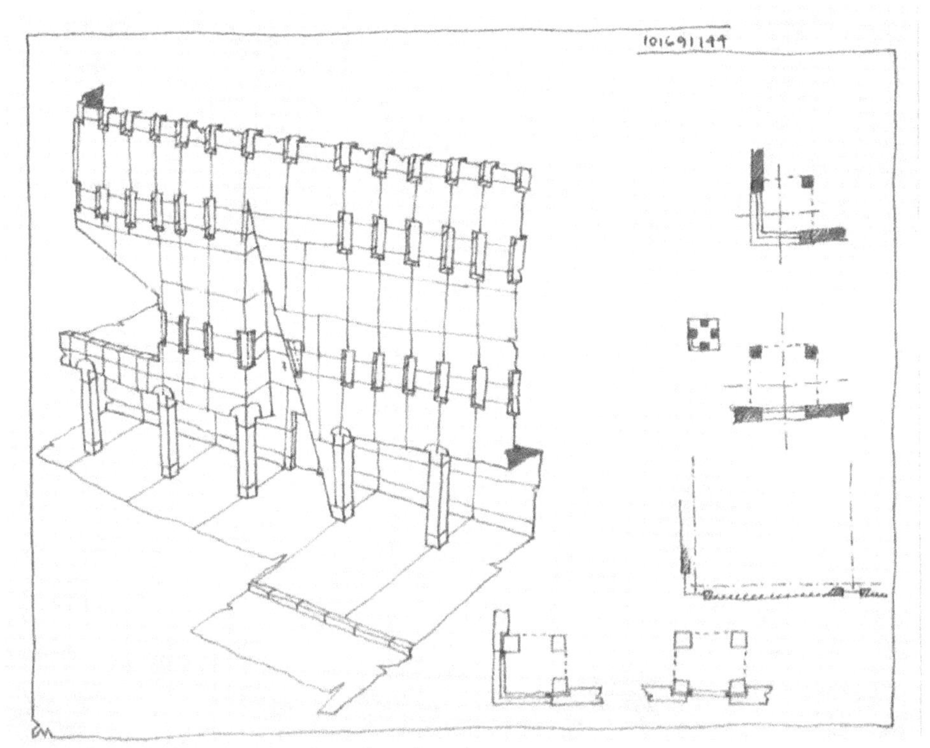

Prefabricated elements, exploration drawings.

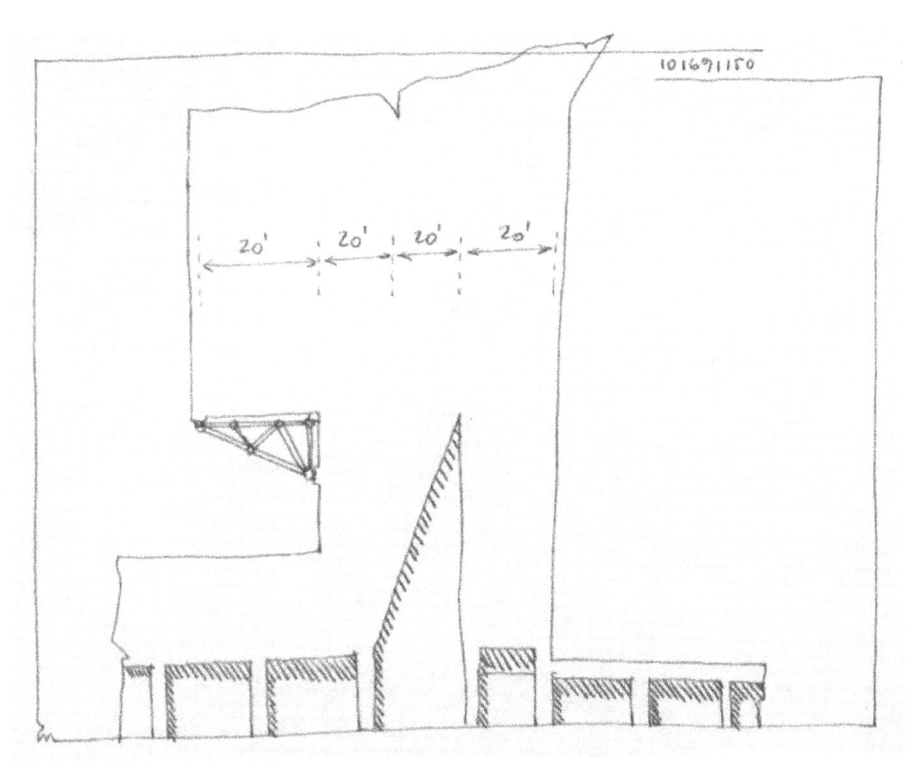

First attempt for a hybrid structure.

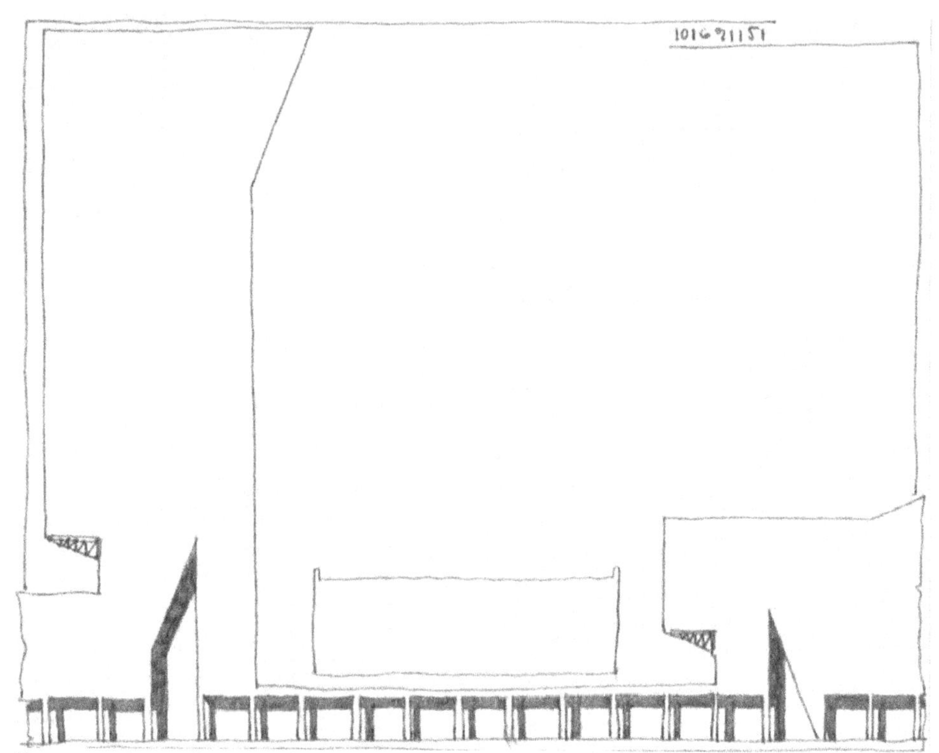

Tower and courthouse. Elevation from the river.

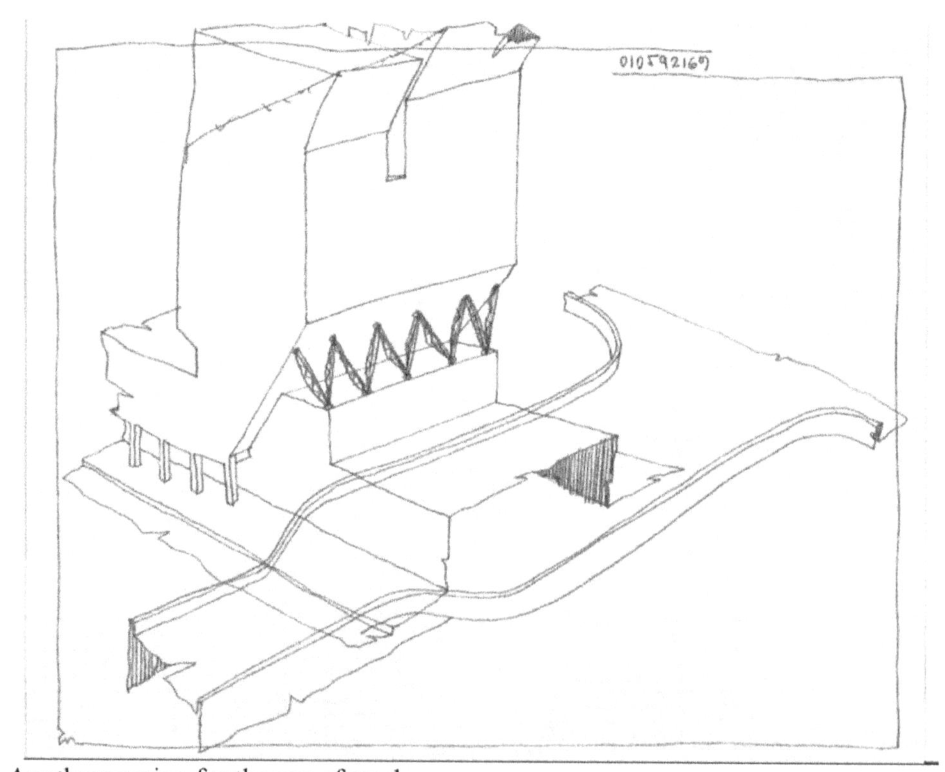

Another version for the use of steel.

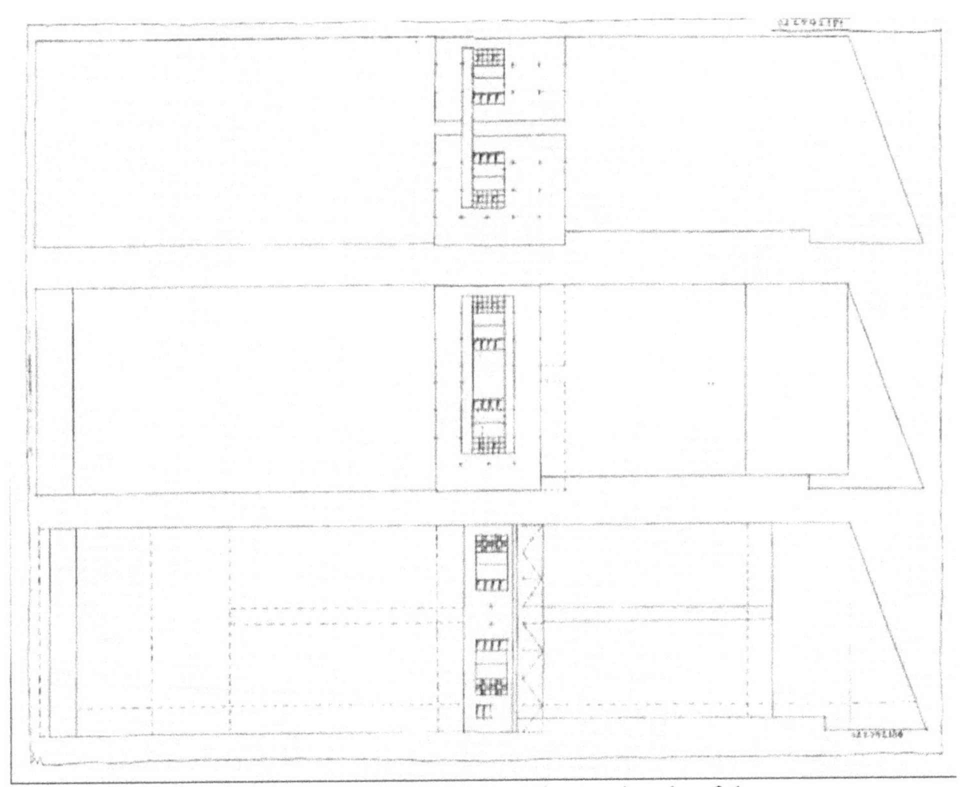

Floor plan systems of the base, the trunk and the top levels of the tower.

This model became the end of this design investigation. The Firm received and accepted a commission for the independent design of the Federal Courthouse, without even a reference for the further development of the site. None of the obvious potentially usable ideas have been observed. Model: Robert Schuster

Chapter 2

LAKE AND FOREST

Pen Zen Diaries #2

Chapter 2

LAKE AND FOREST
BE & K OFFICE BUILDING IN BIRMINGHAM, ALABAMA

As one of my first consulting job in the United State, I was invited by KPS Architects to design a speculative office building to the as yet almost unoccupied area of the city, in the vicinity of a large wooded area and a lake. Since the needs of the occupants of the building could not be predicted, in this case in a way, the forest and the lake became my clients. Designing a building, and its quite large parking area, in an undisturbed natural surrounding will always have a negative consequence, so the first goal was, to minimize that. Several versions of parking arrangements were tested, including to the possible second and third phases.

Eventually, the parking was resolved, so the attention of the design was spent on the massing of the building, and to some solution of the staircases, which would benefit from the view, across the longitudinal axis of the lake. Fortunately, that part of the project has been executed according to my suggestion, but the window system was 'value-engineered' in a terribly unfitting way...

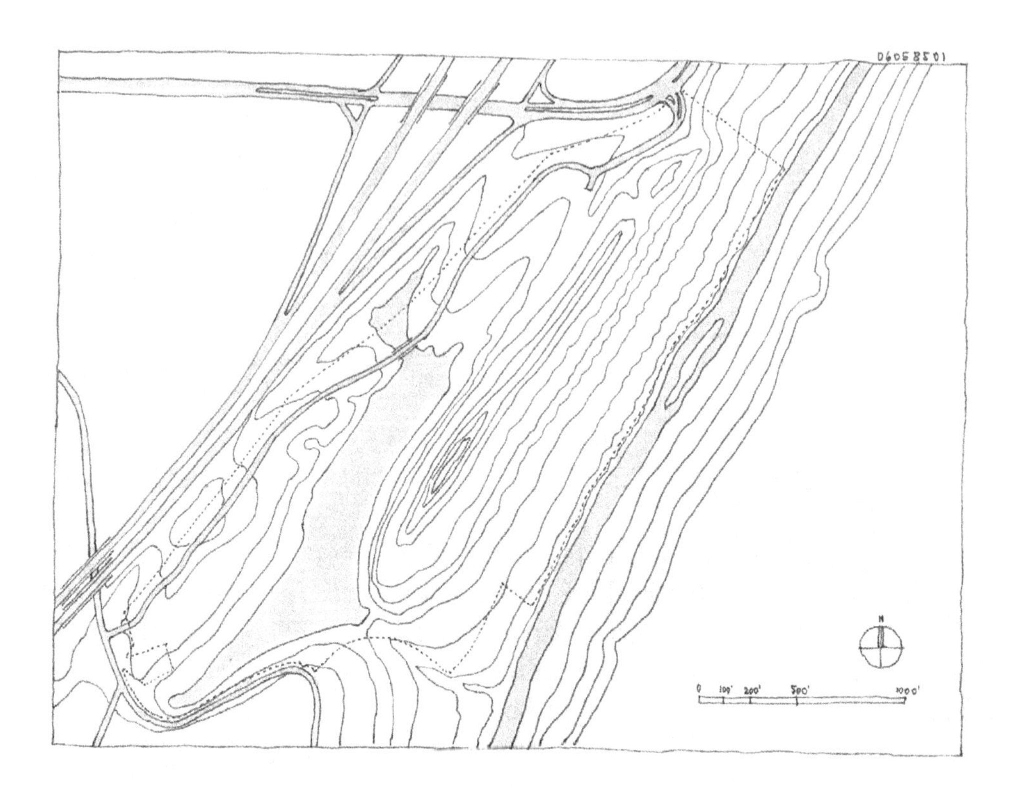
06058501
N
0
100'
200'
500'
1000'

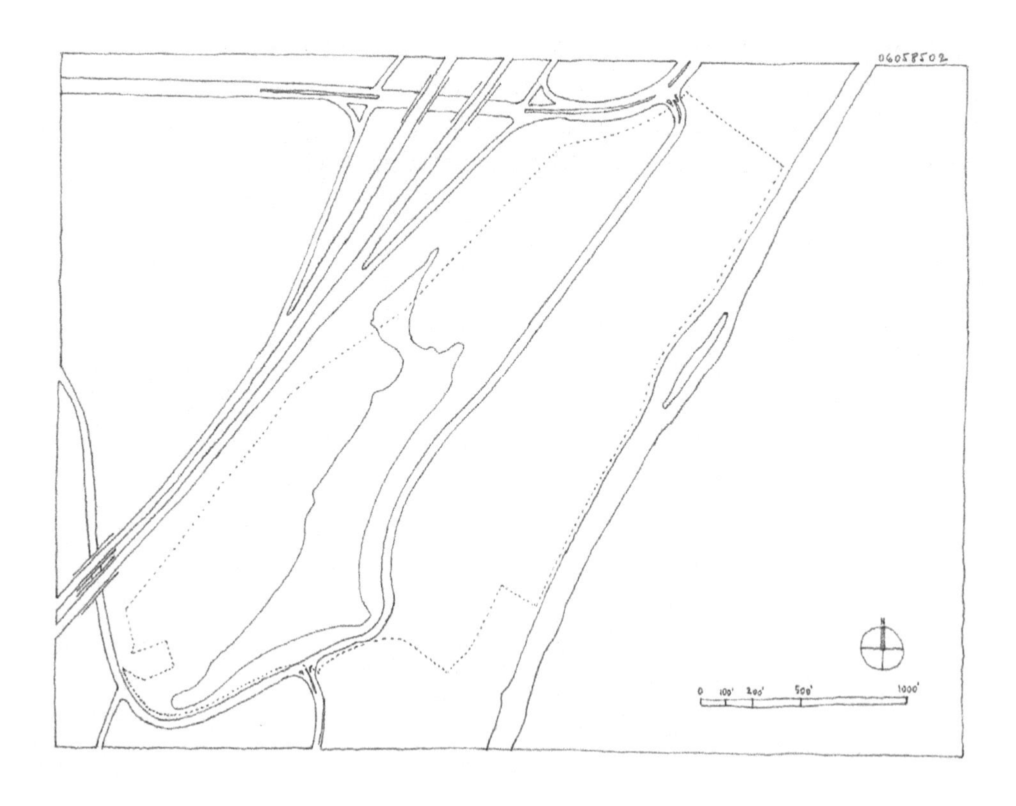
06058502
N
0
100'
200'
500'
1000'

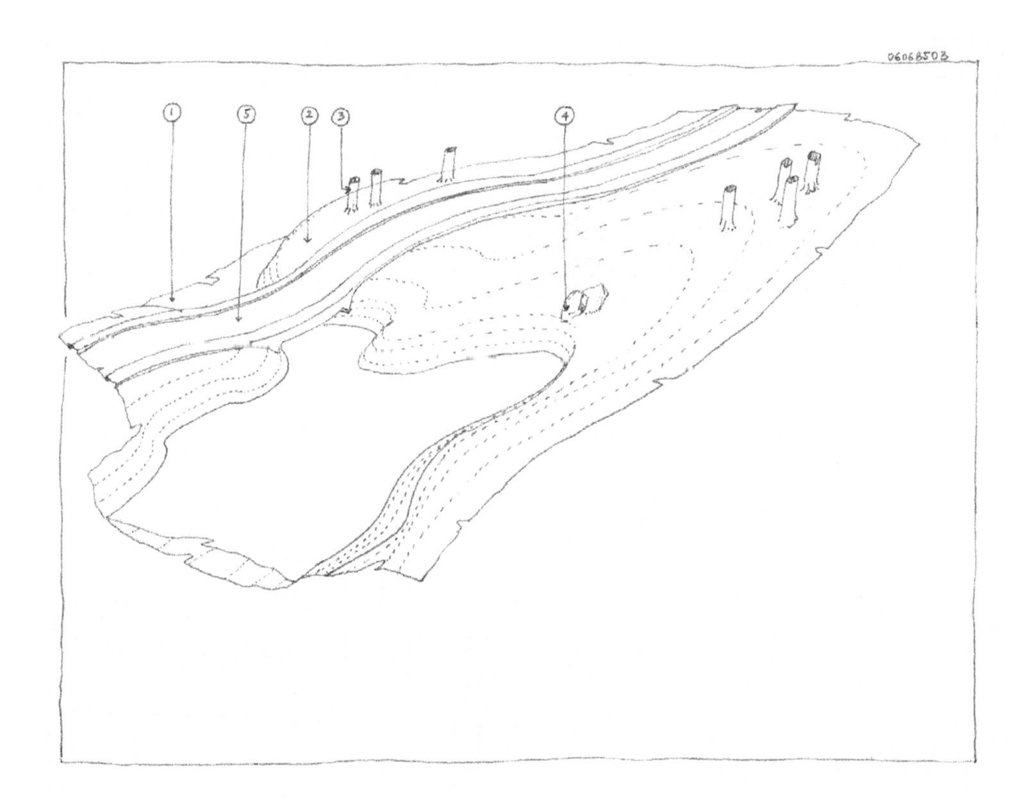
06068503
1
5
2
3
4

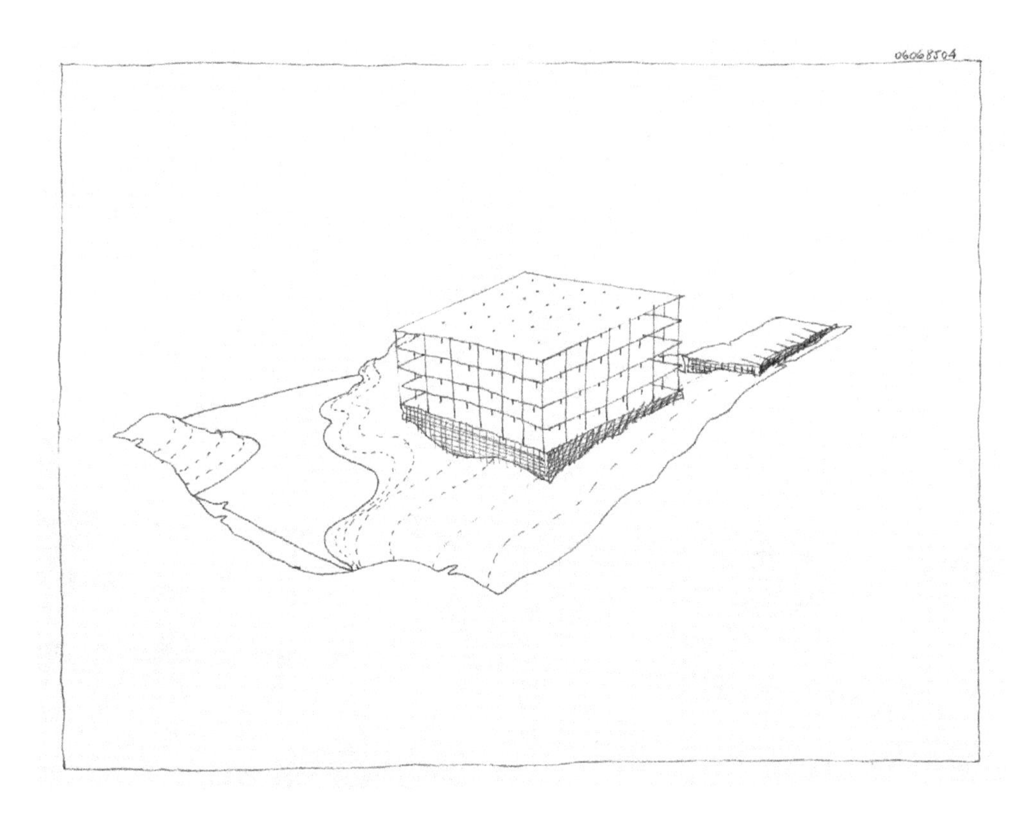
06068504

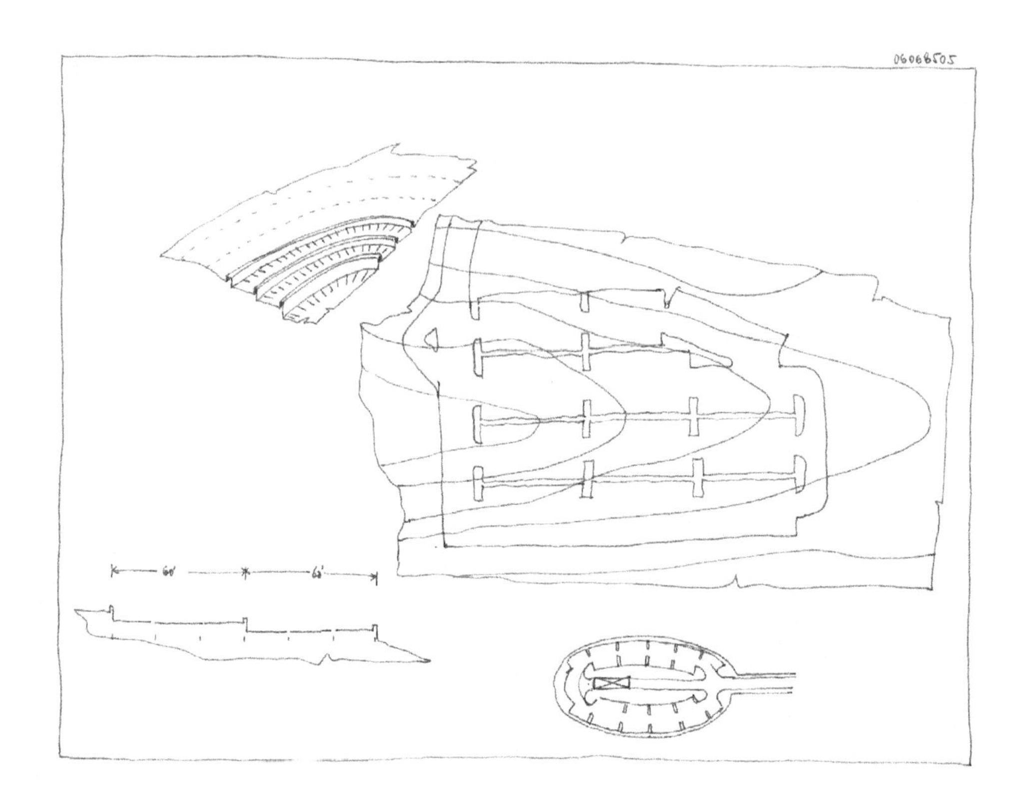
06068505
60'

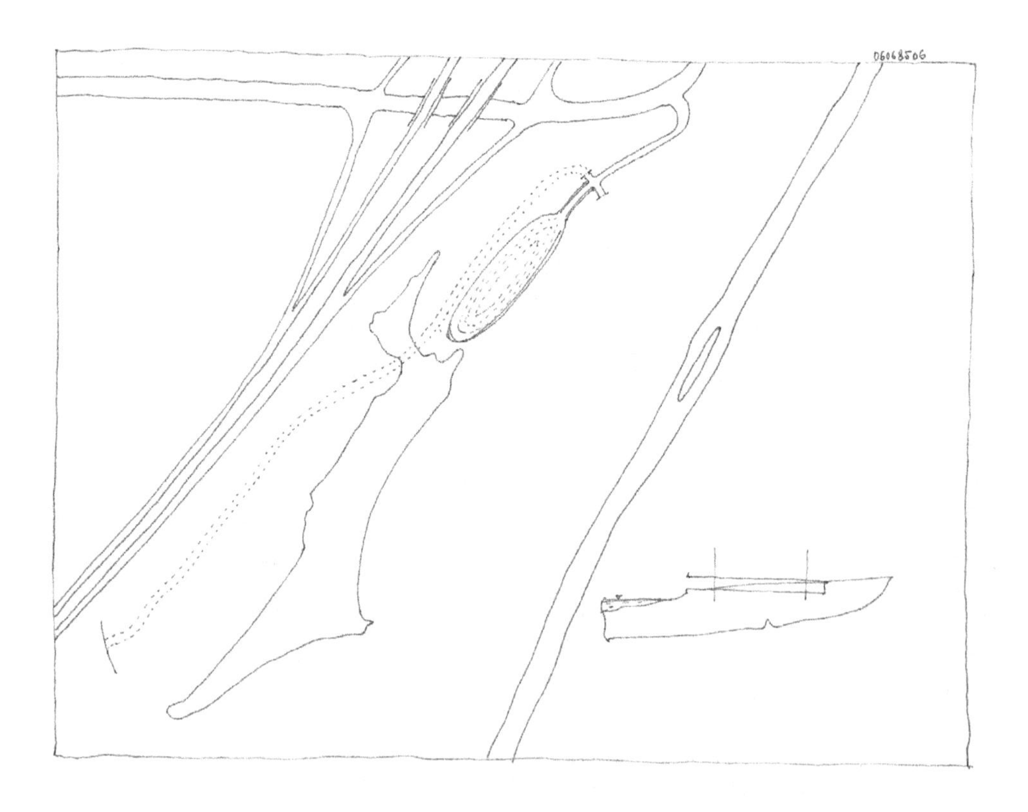
06068506

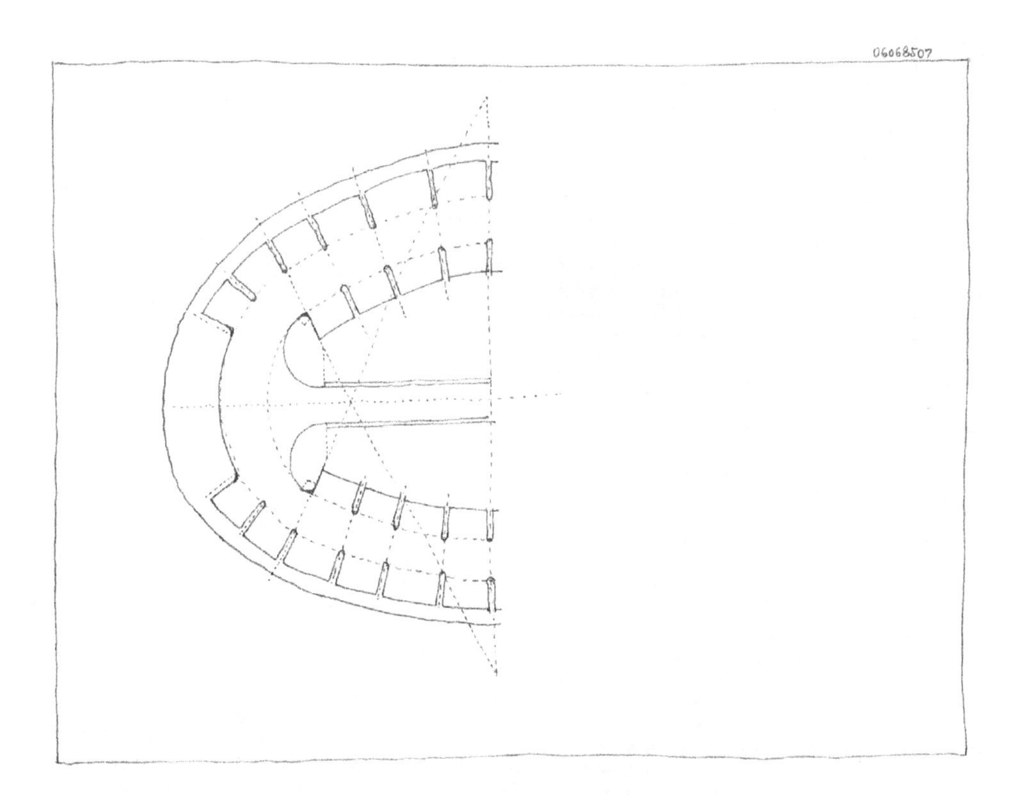
06068507

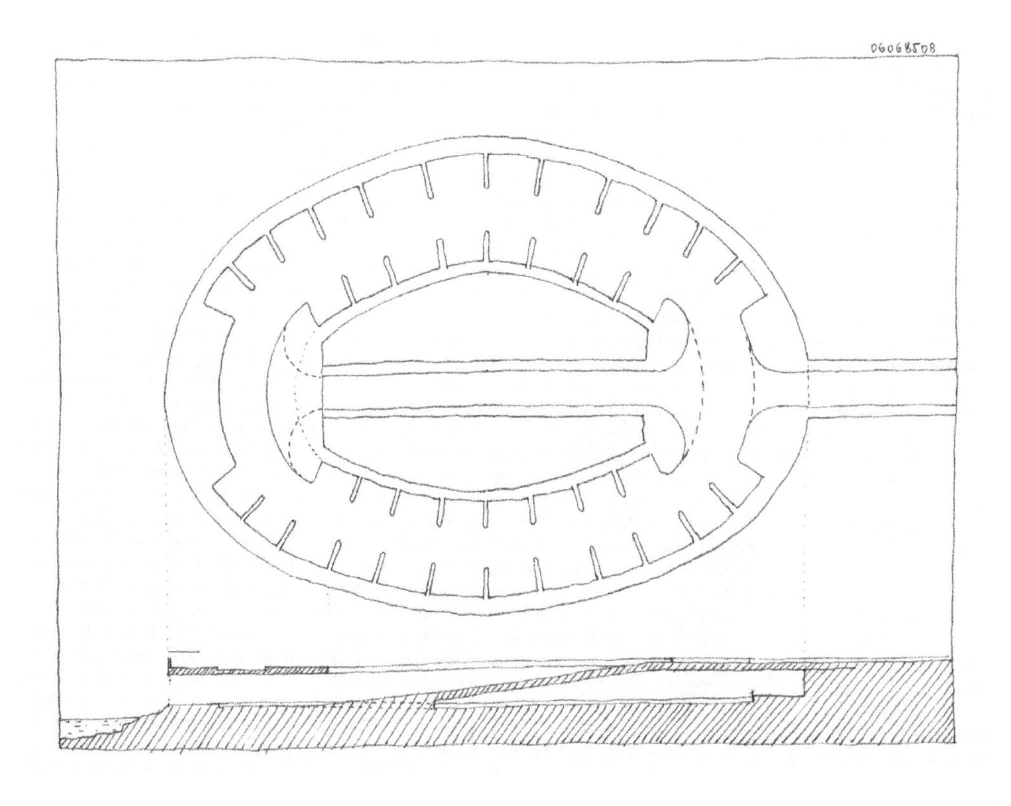
06068508

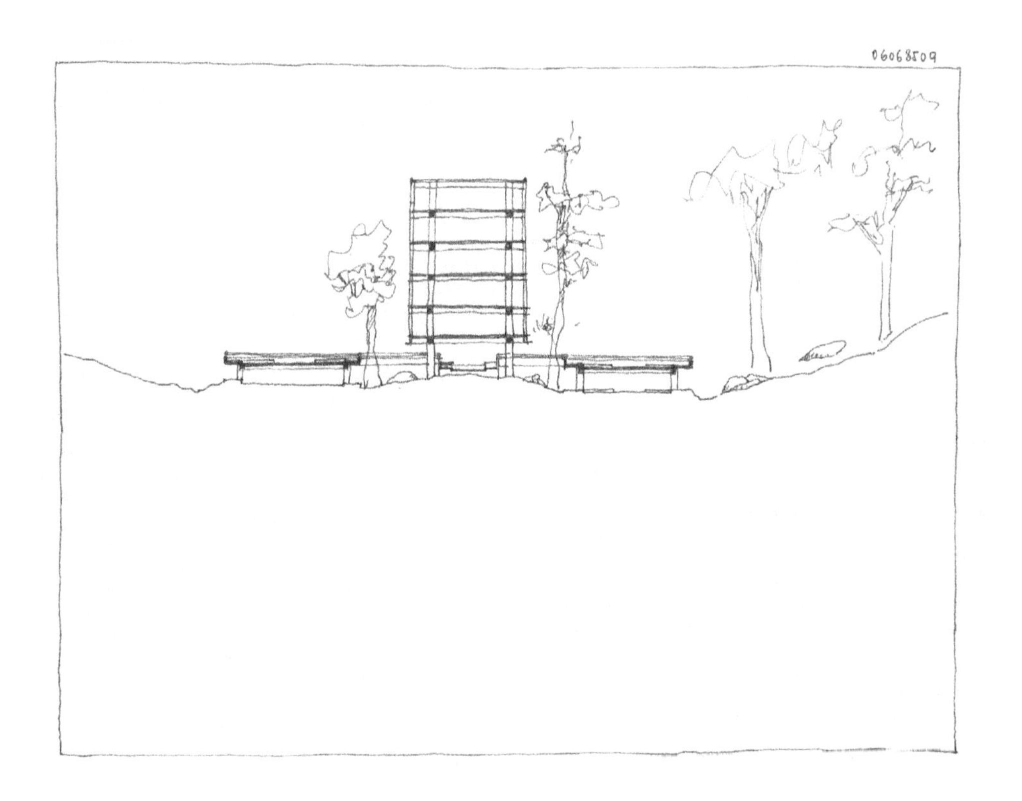
06068509

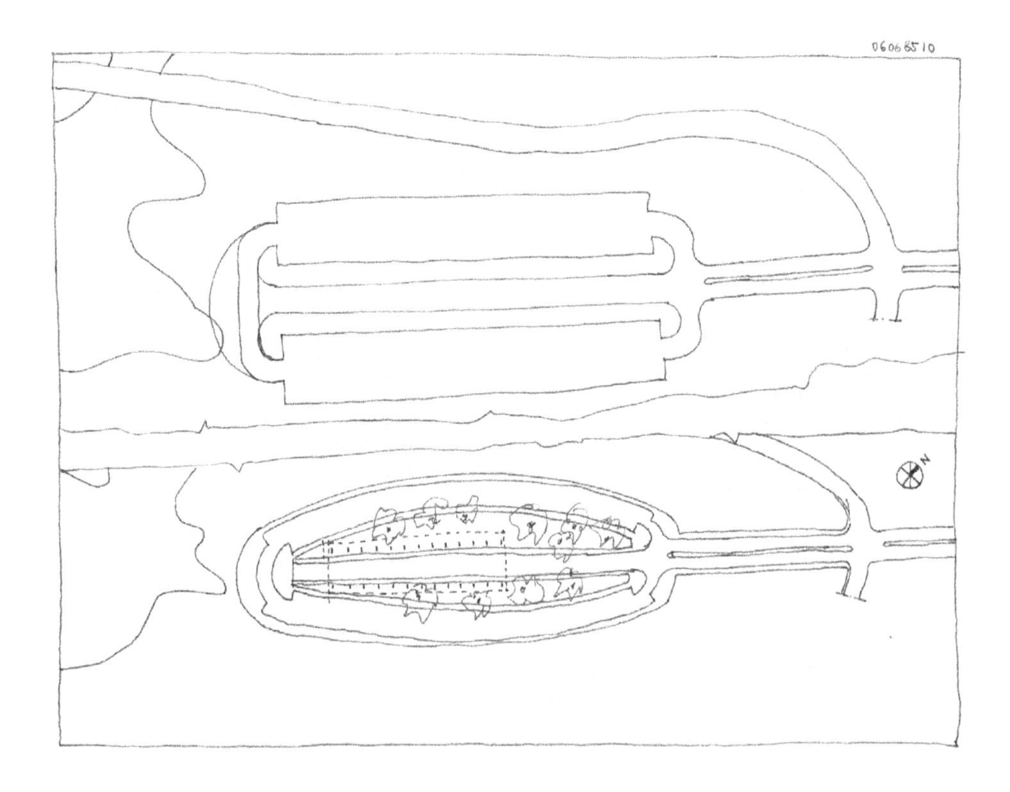
06068510
N

06068511

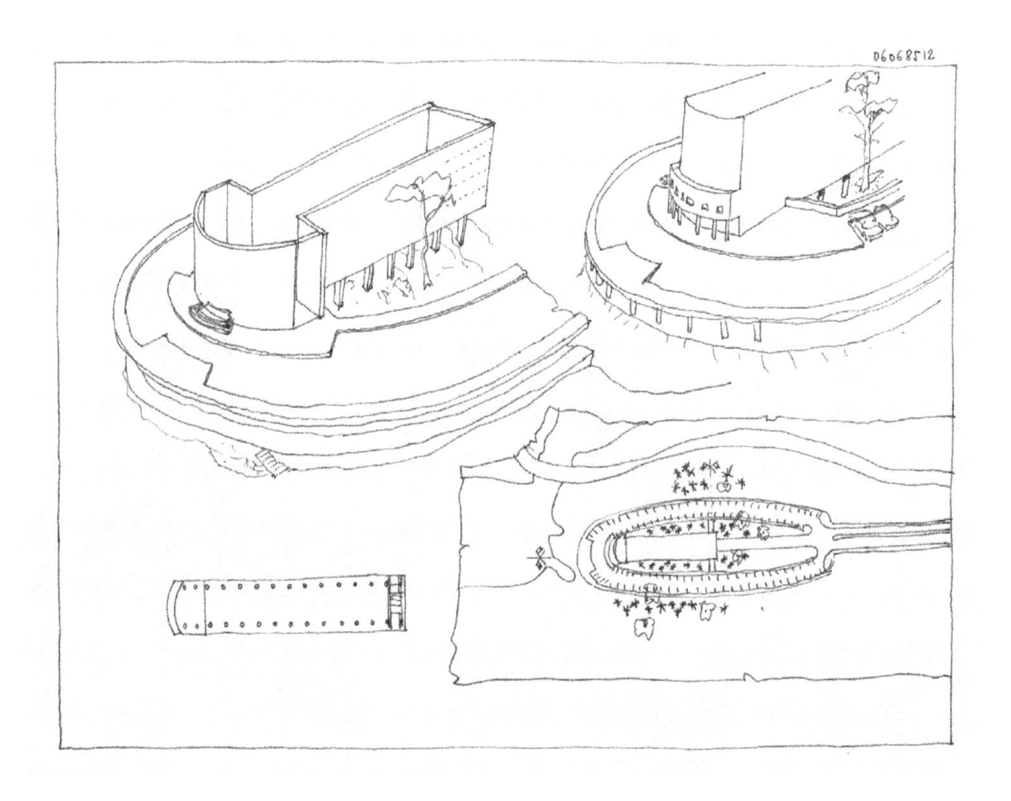
06068512

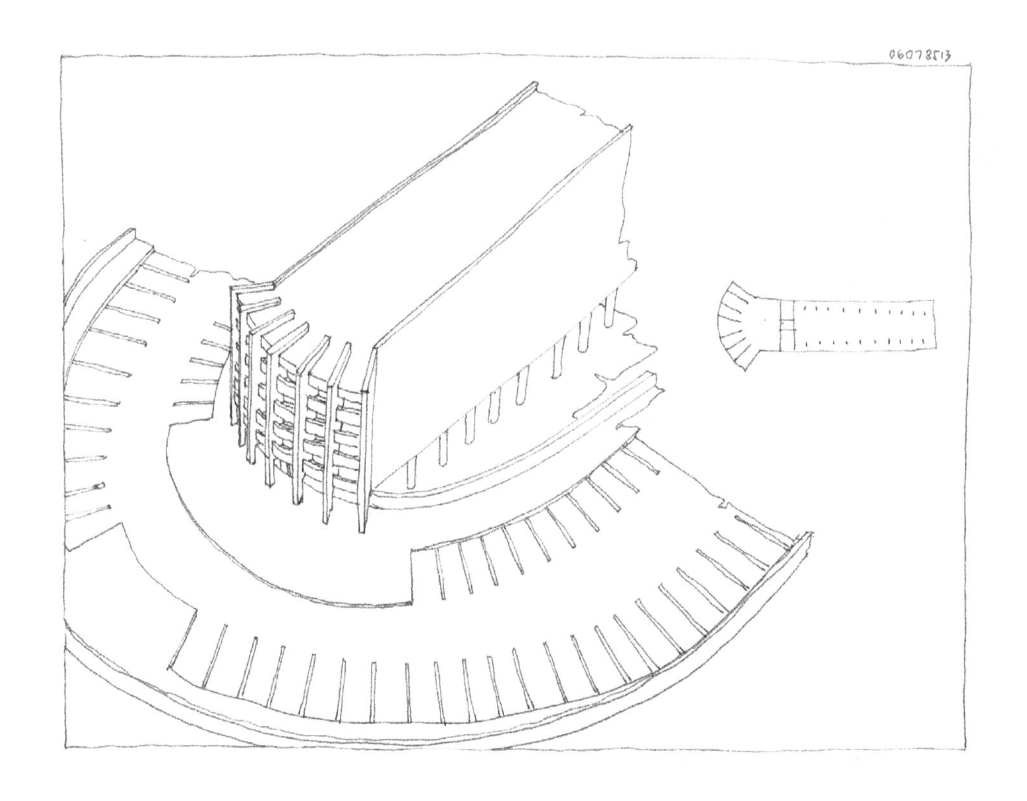
06078513

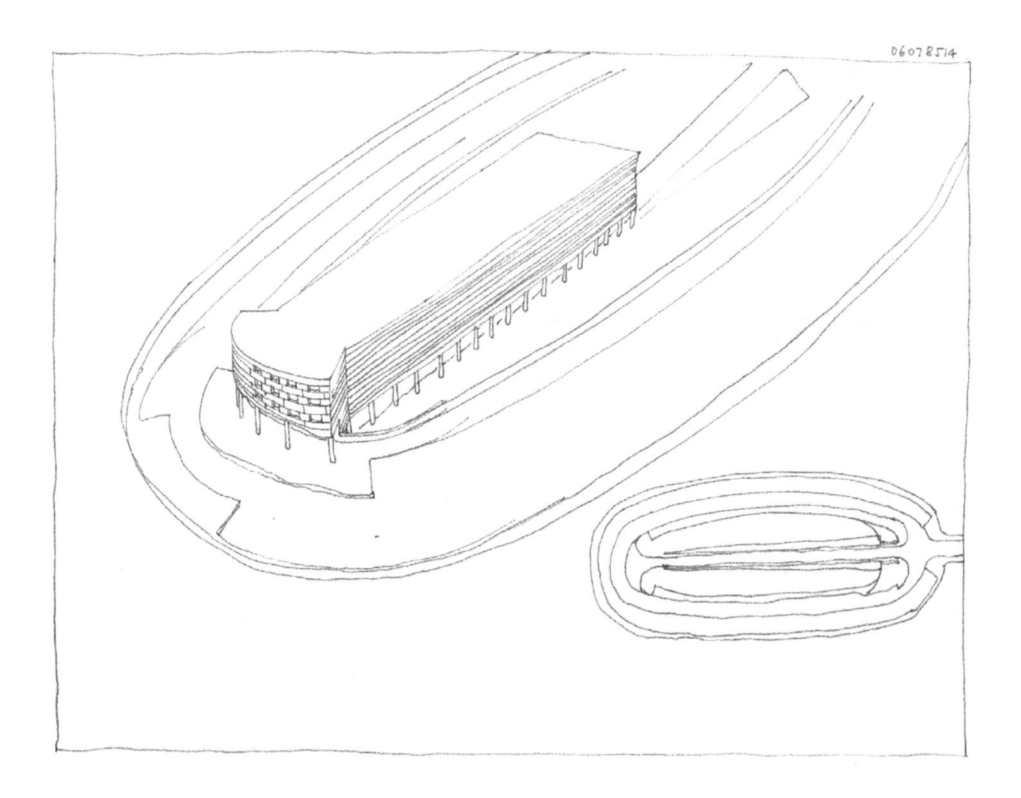
06078514

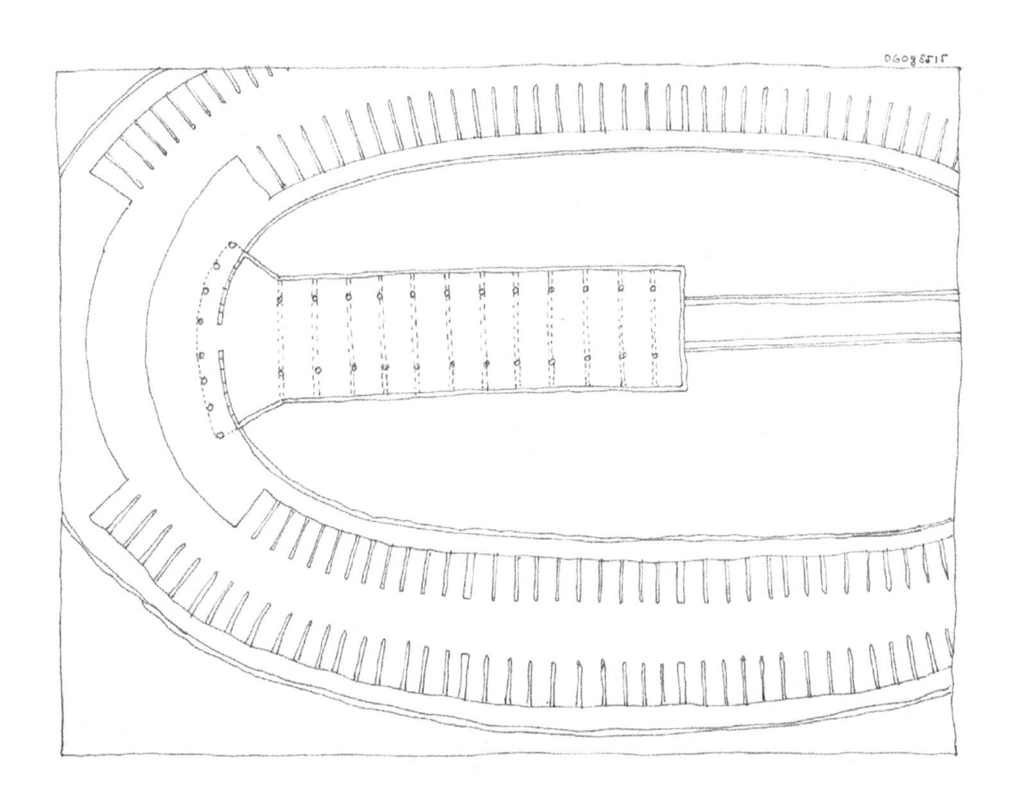
06088515

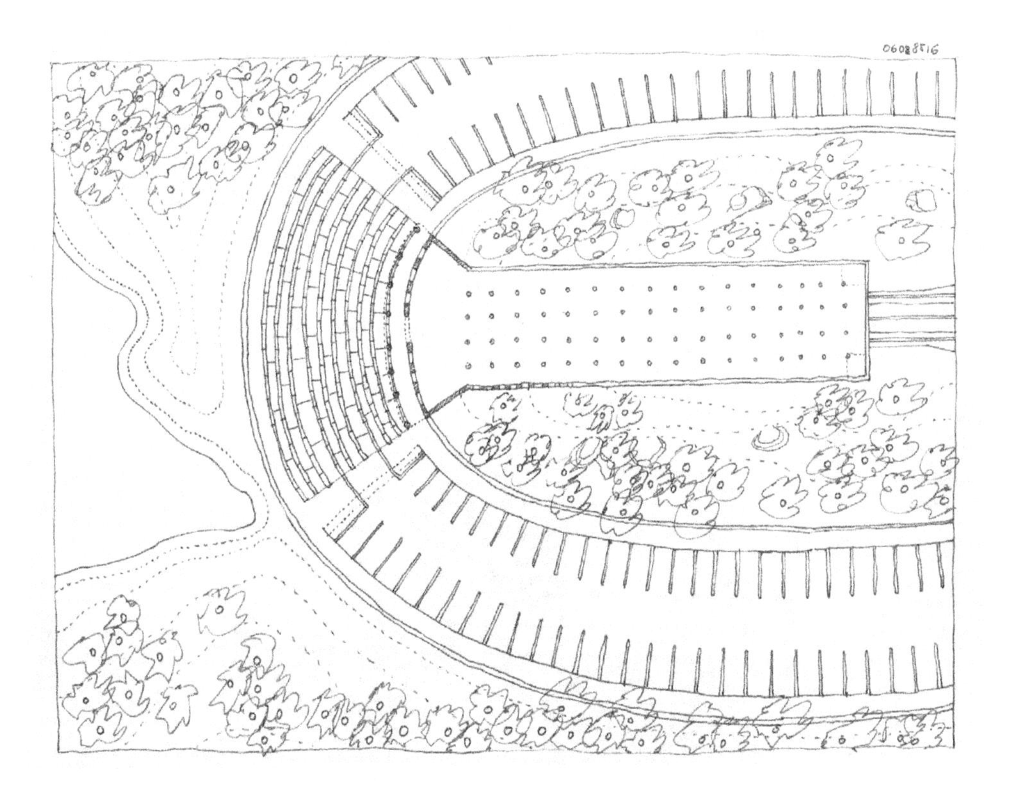
06088516

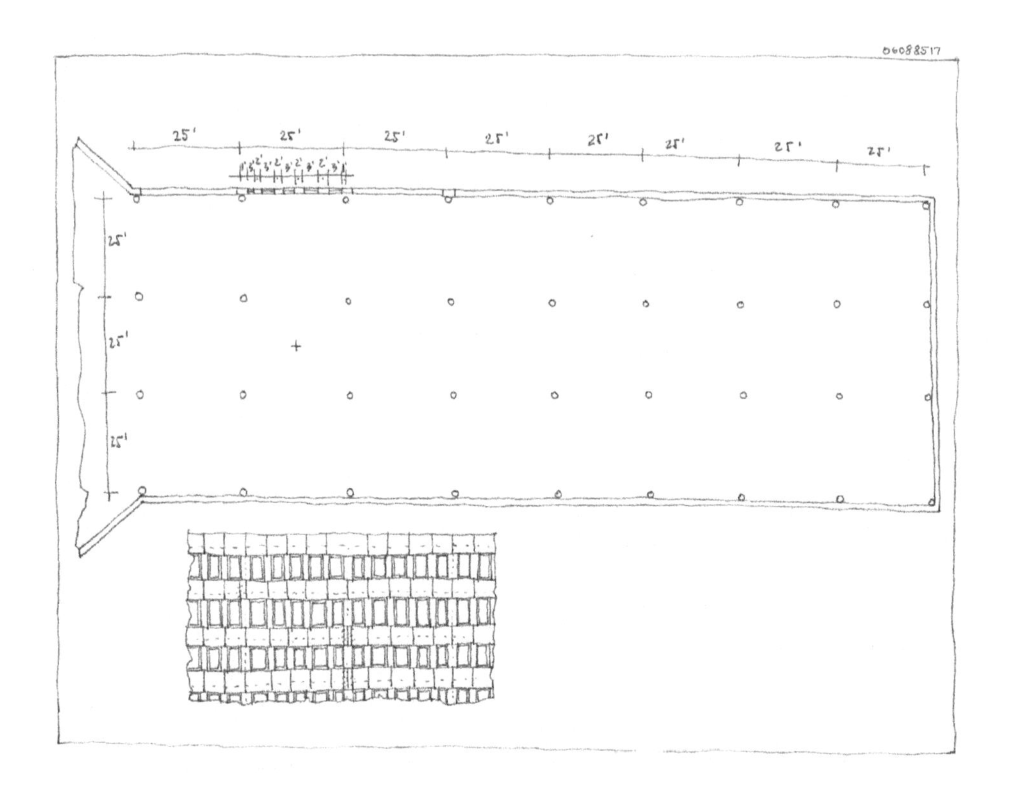
06088517
25'
25'
25'
25'
25'
25'
25'
25'
25'
25'
25'

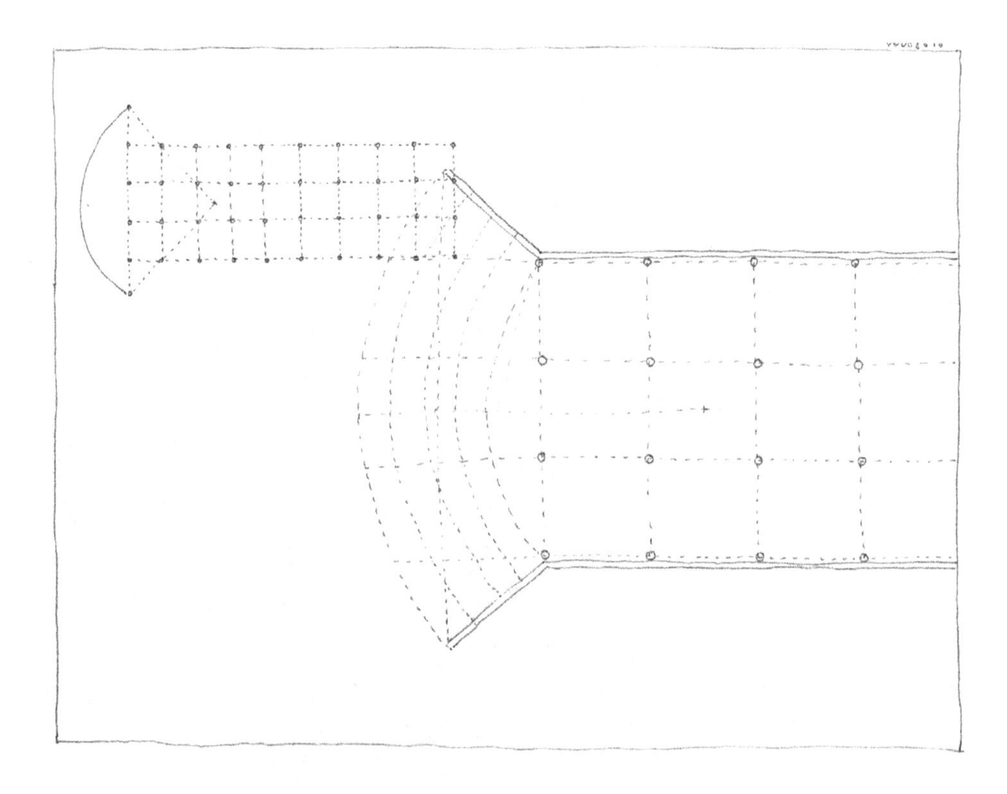

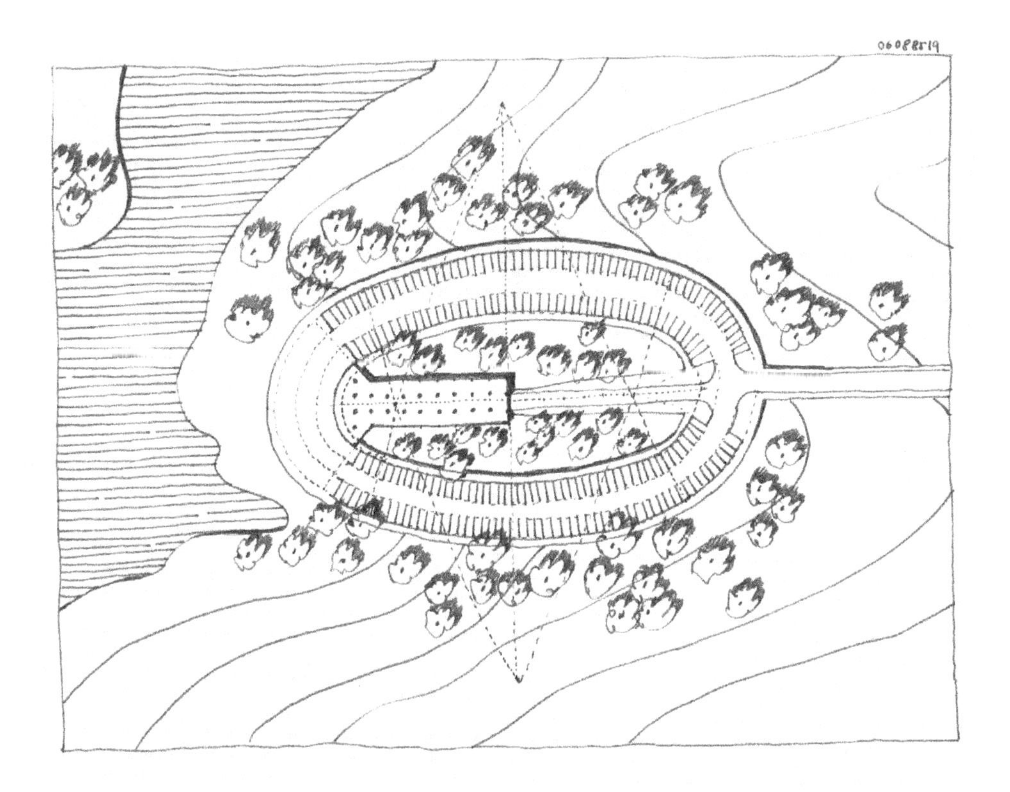
06088519

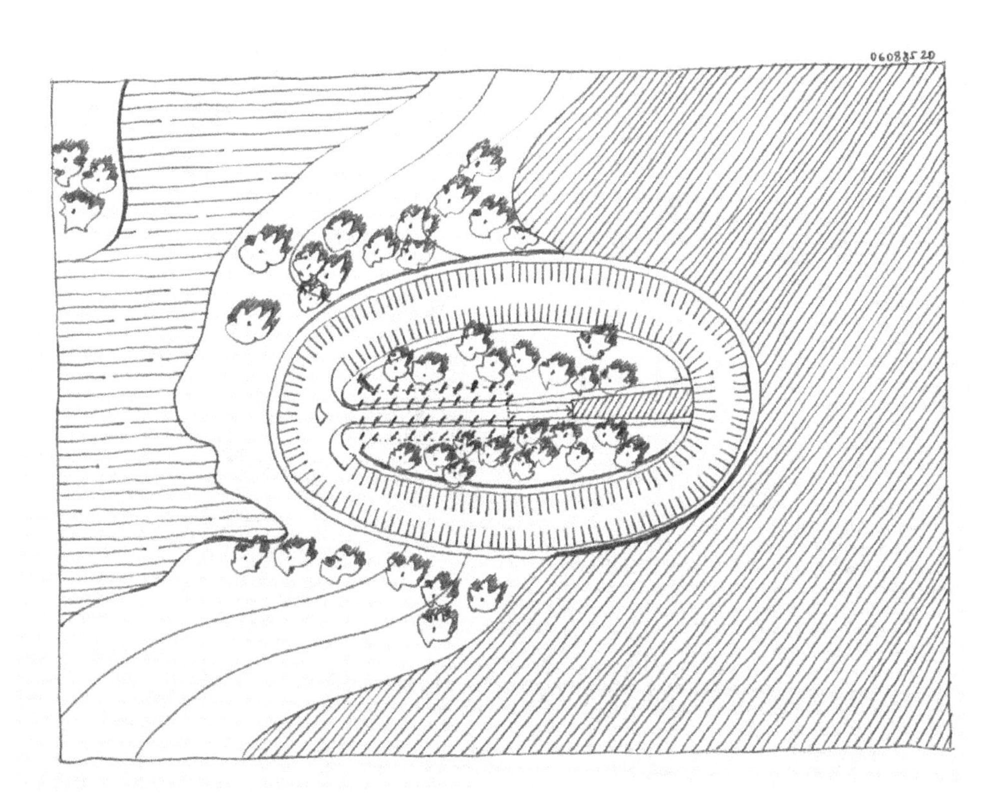
06088520

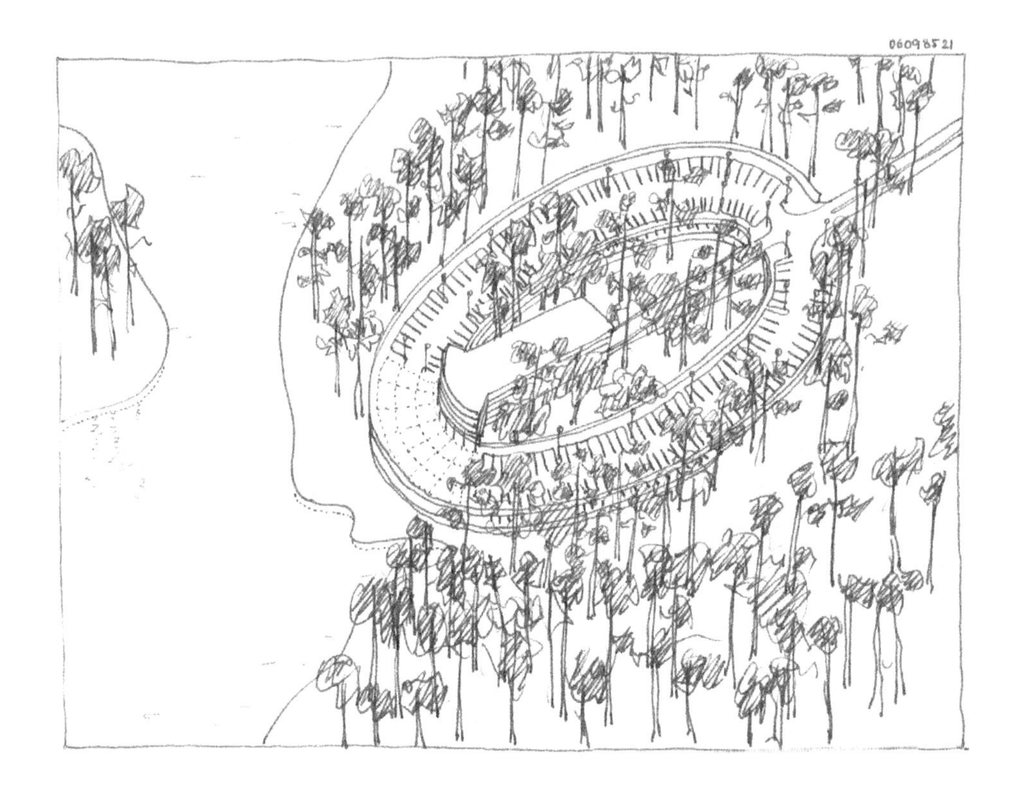
06098521

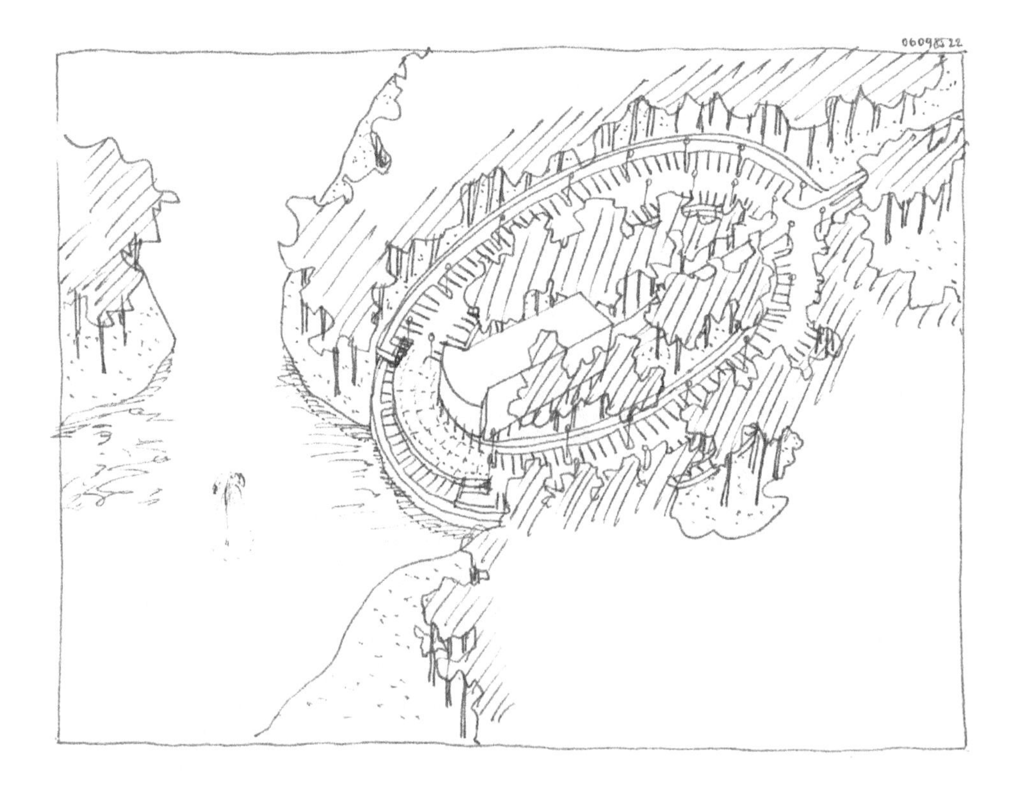
06098522

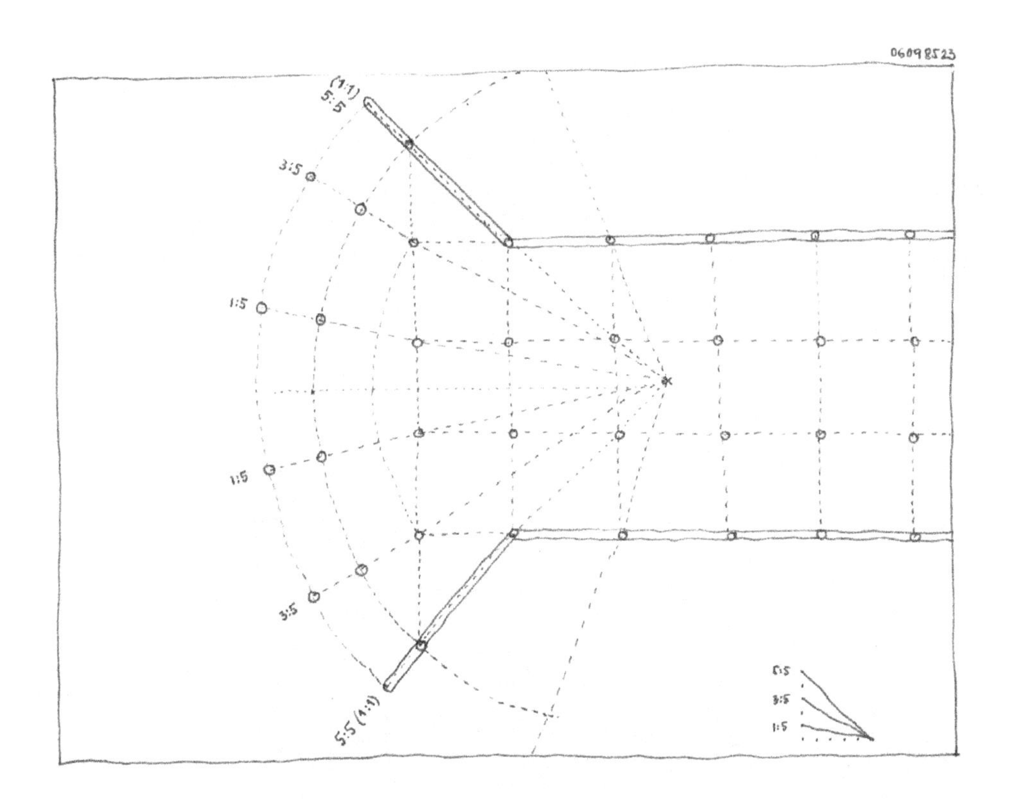
06098523
(1:1)
5:5
3:5
1:5
1:5
3:5
5:5 (1:1)
5:5
3:5
1:5

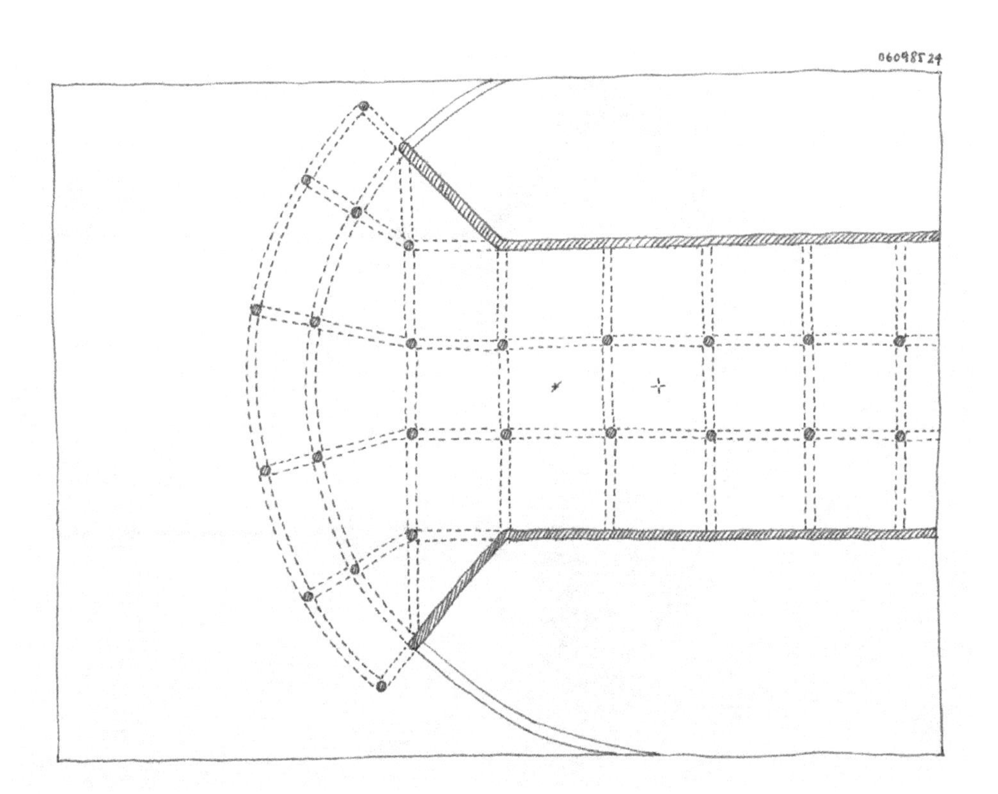
06098524

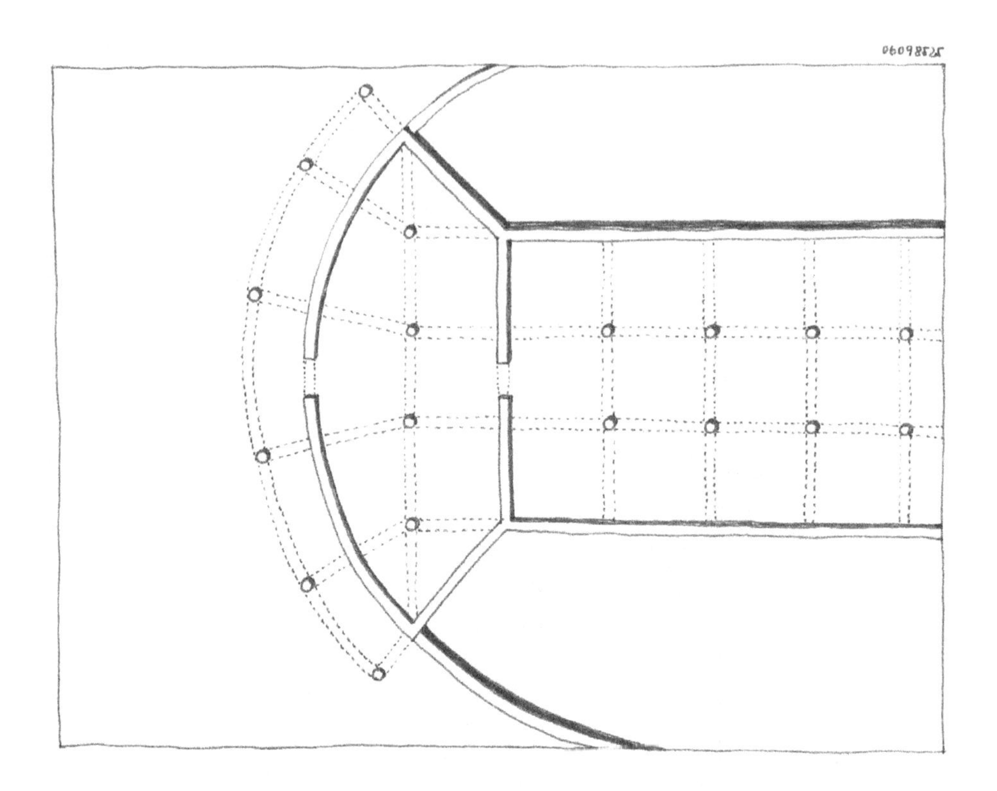

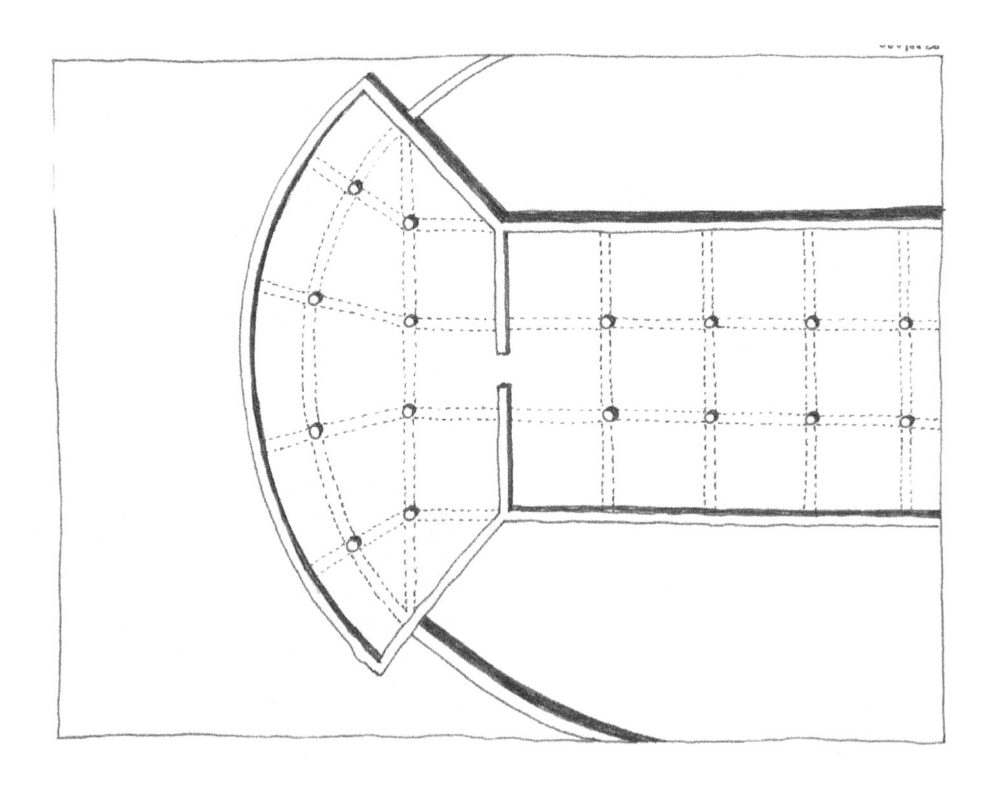

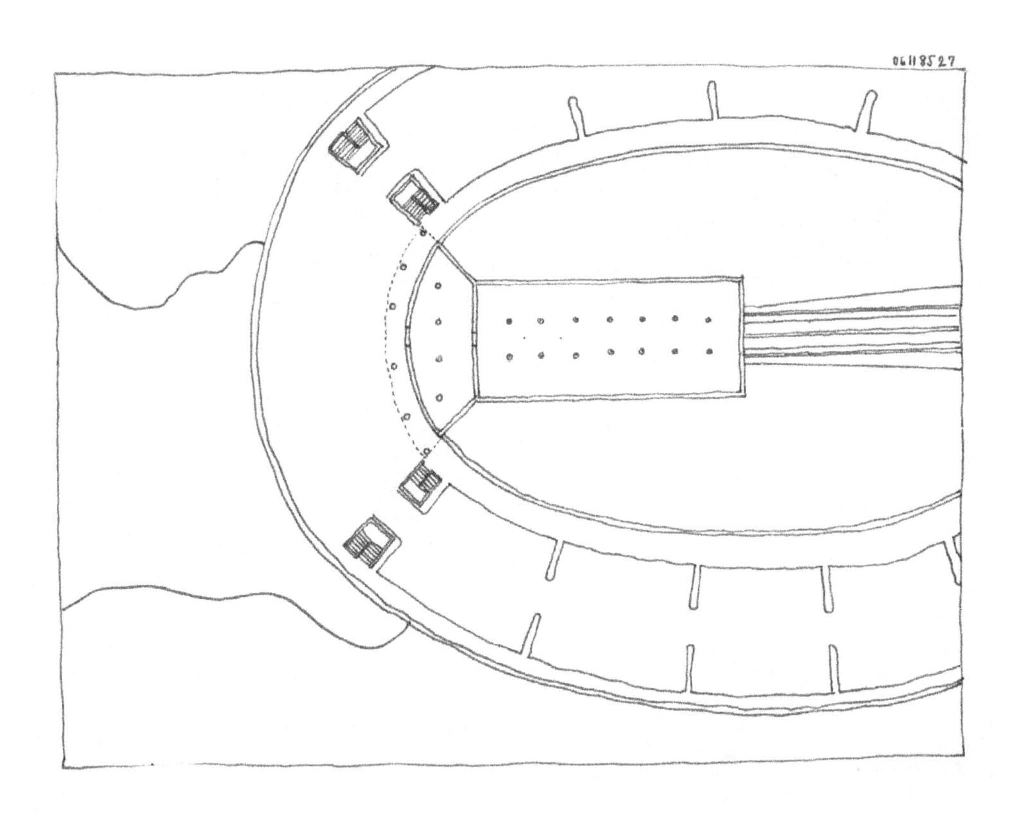
06118527

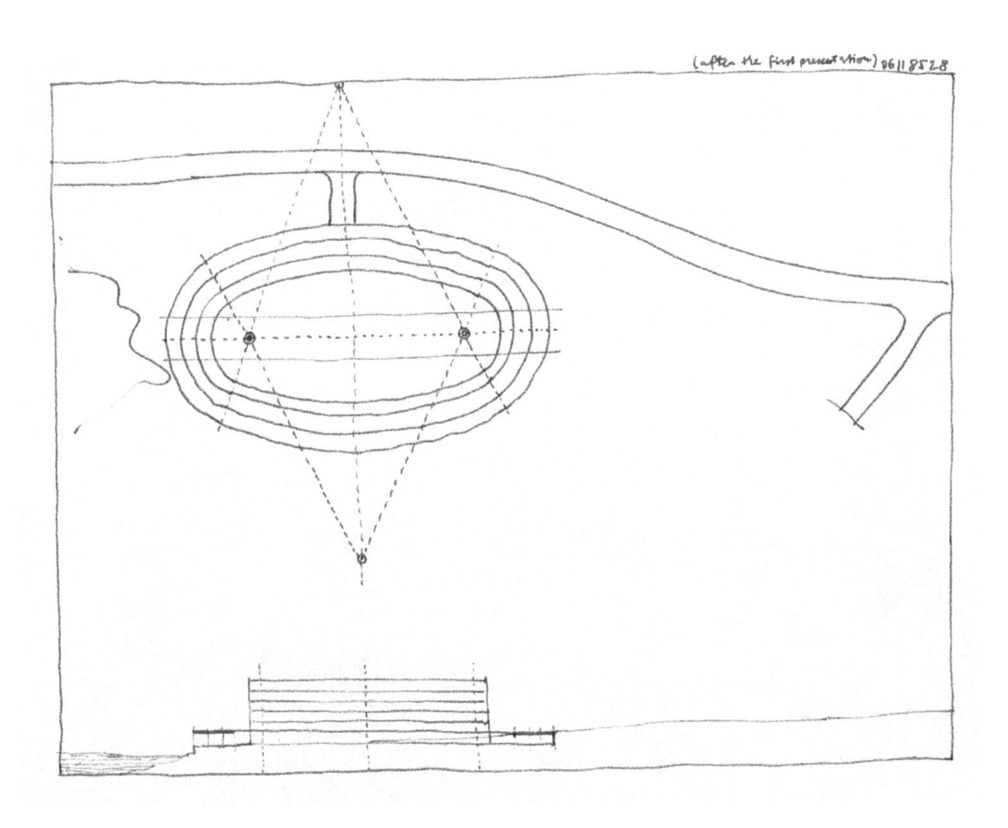
(after the first presentation) 06118528

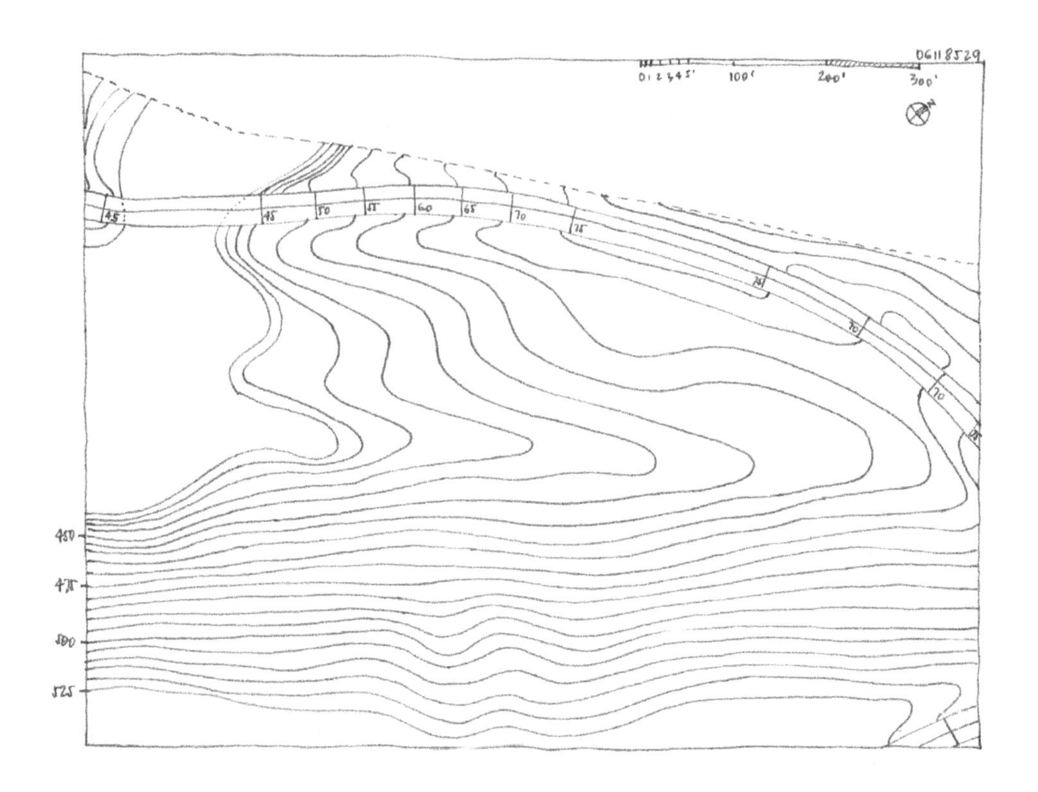

06118529
0 1 2 3 4 5'
100'
200'
300'
45
50
55
60
65
70
75
450
475
500
525

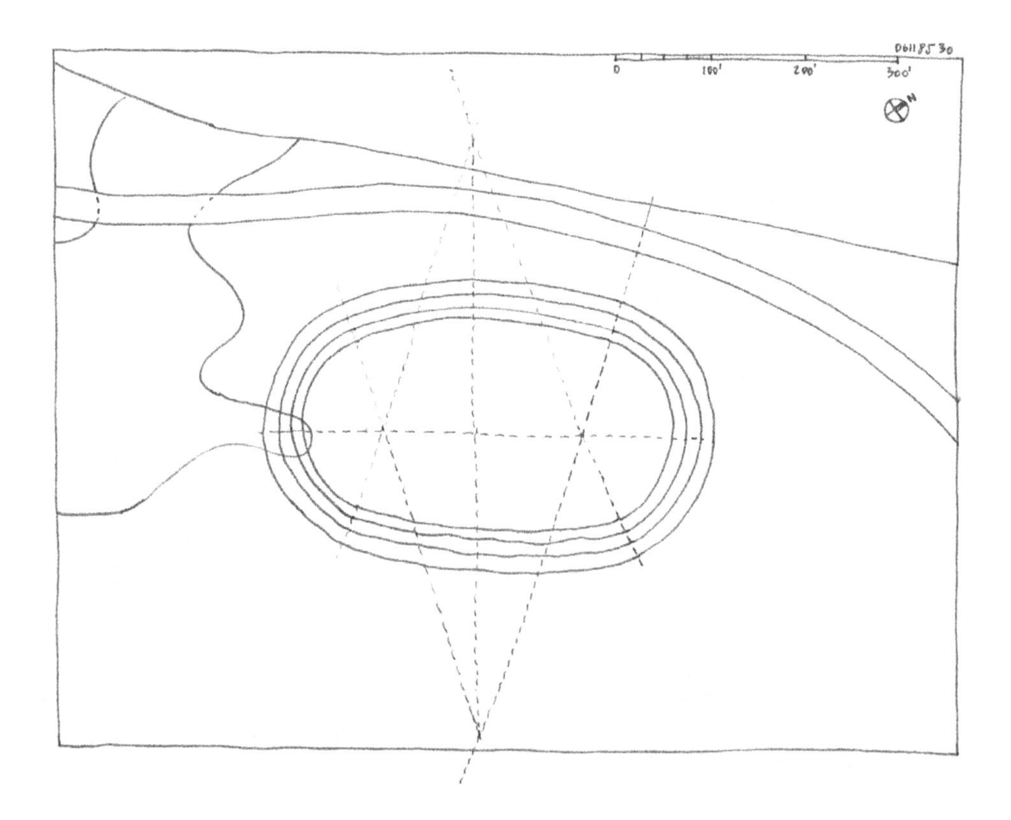

06118530
0
100'
200'
300'

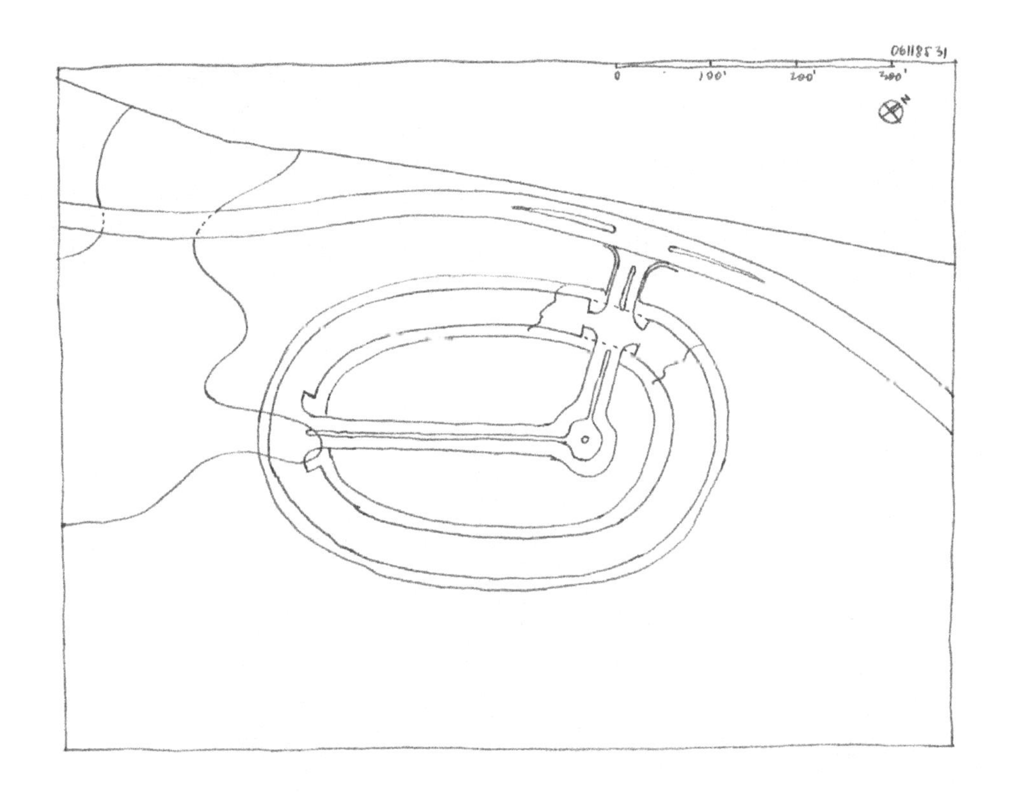
06118531
0
100'
200'
300'
N

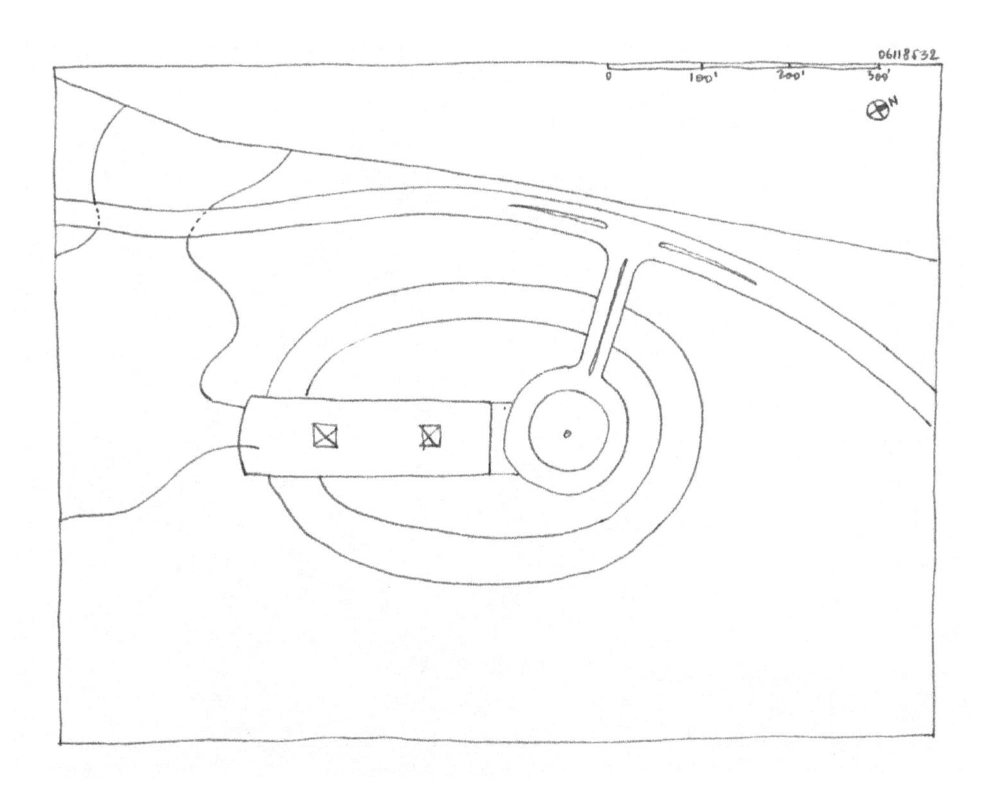
06118532
0
100'
200'
300'
N

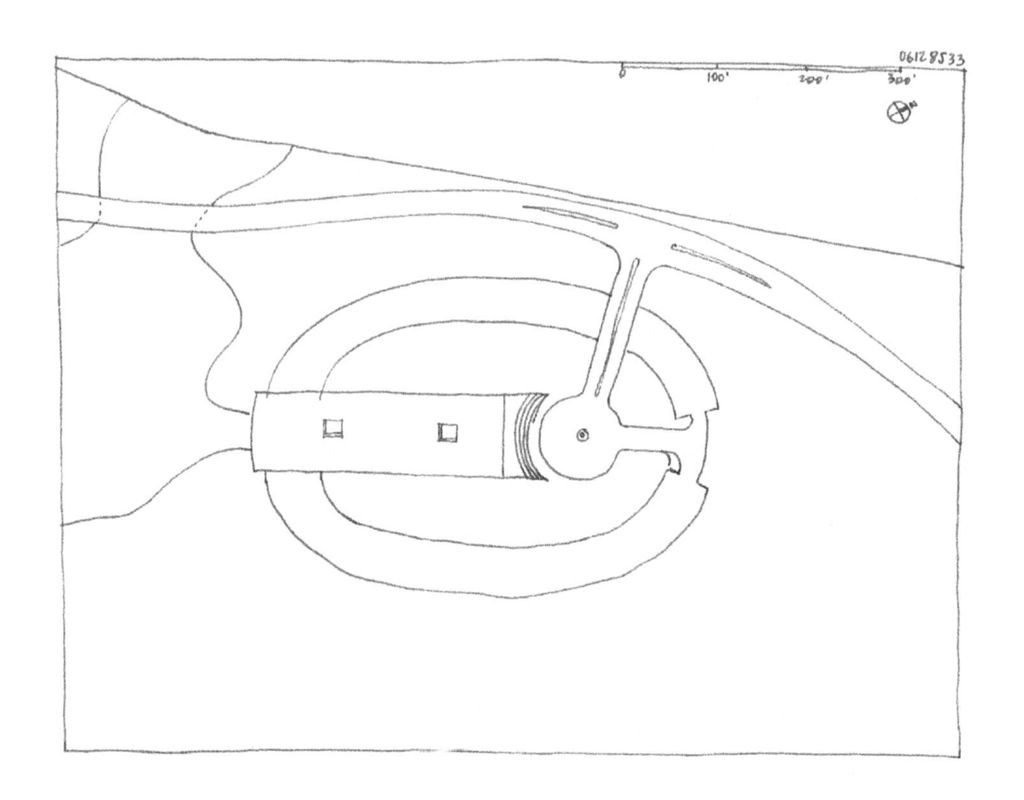
06128533
0
100'
200'
300'

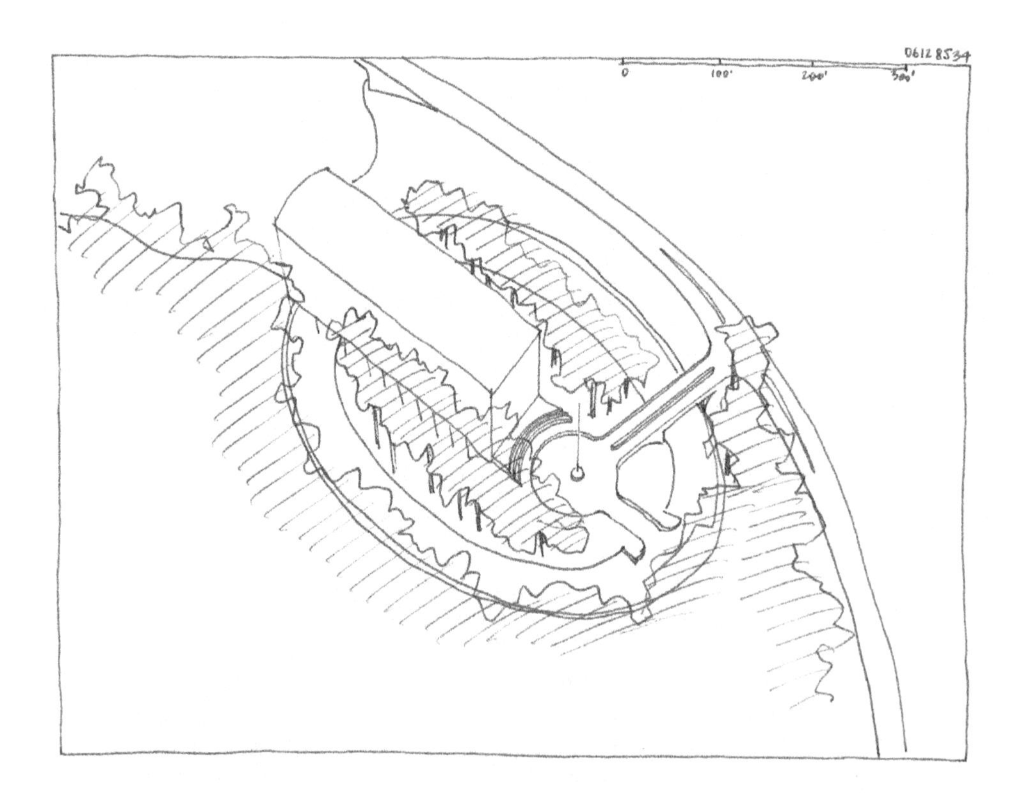
06128534
0
100'
200'
300'

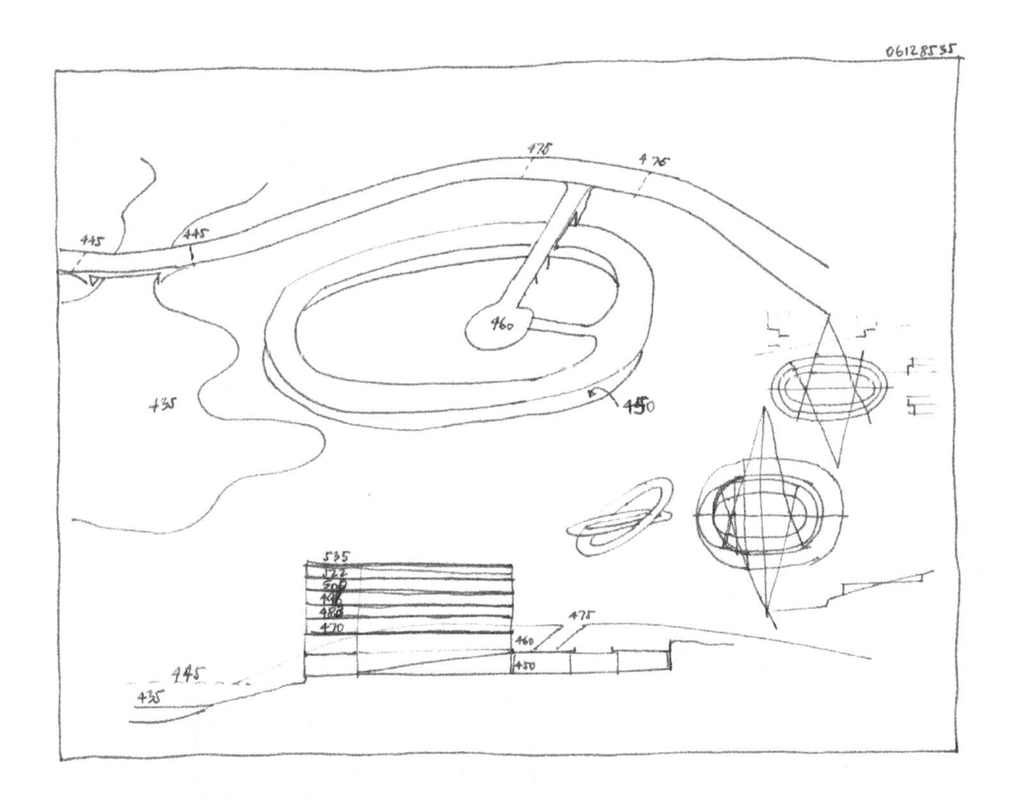
06128535
475
445
445
460
435
450
535
470
475
460
450
445
435

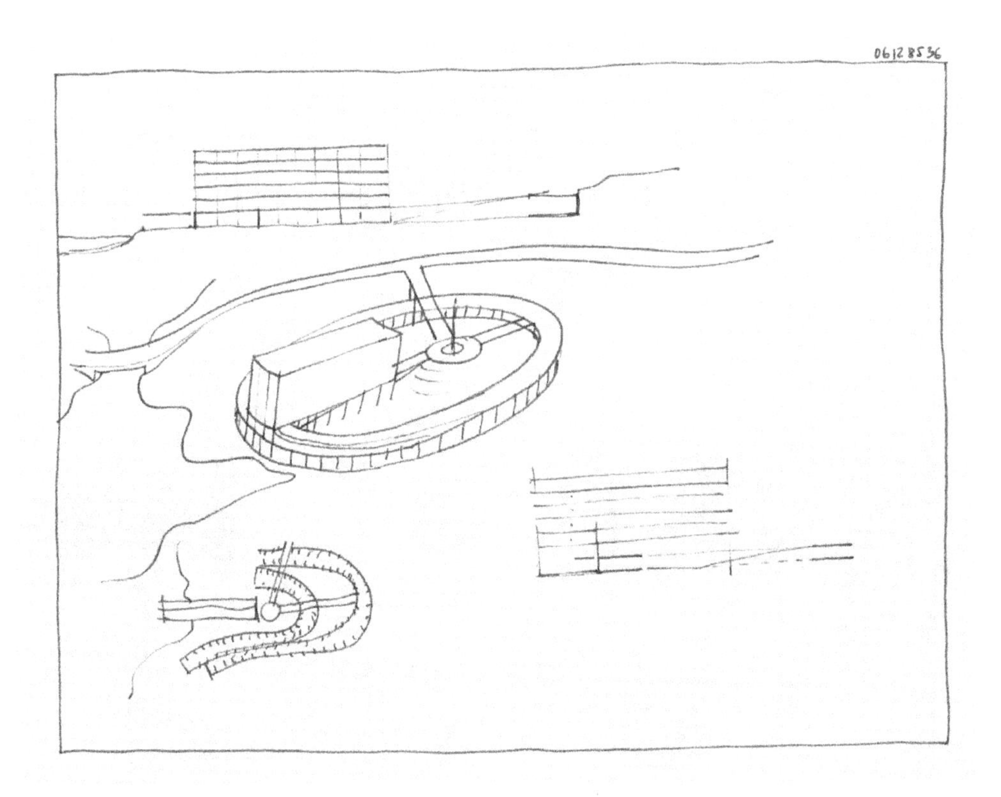
06128536

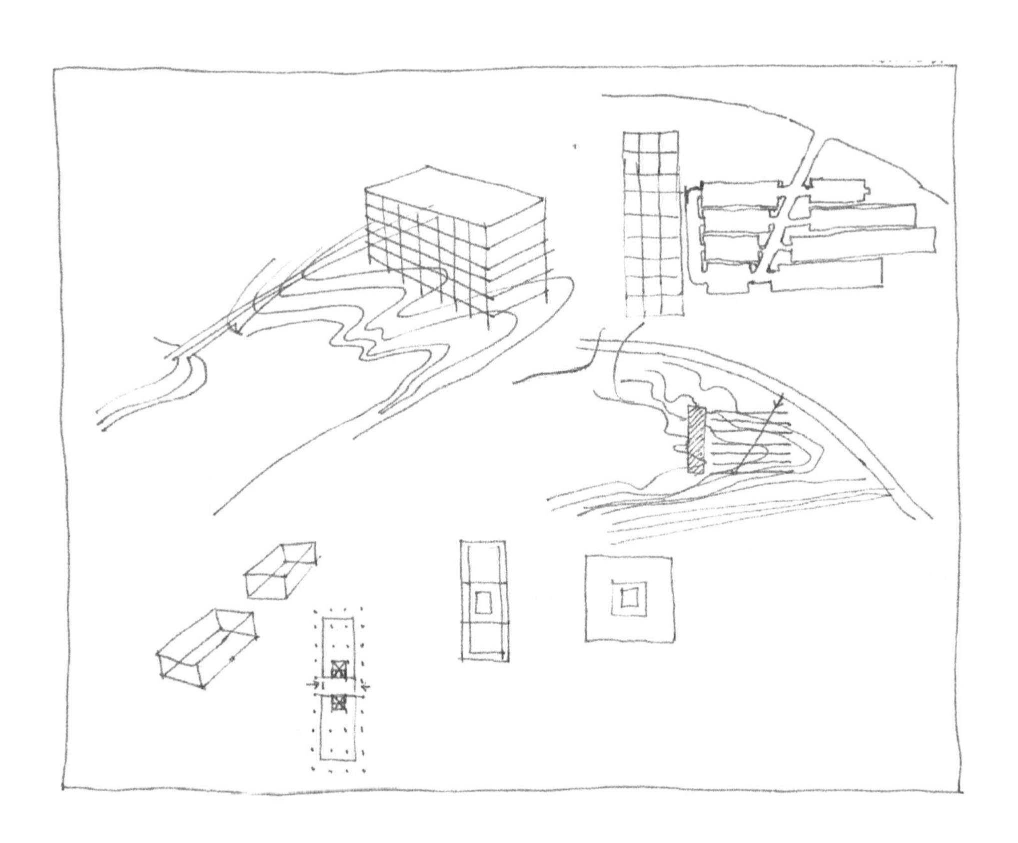

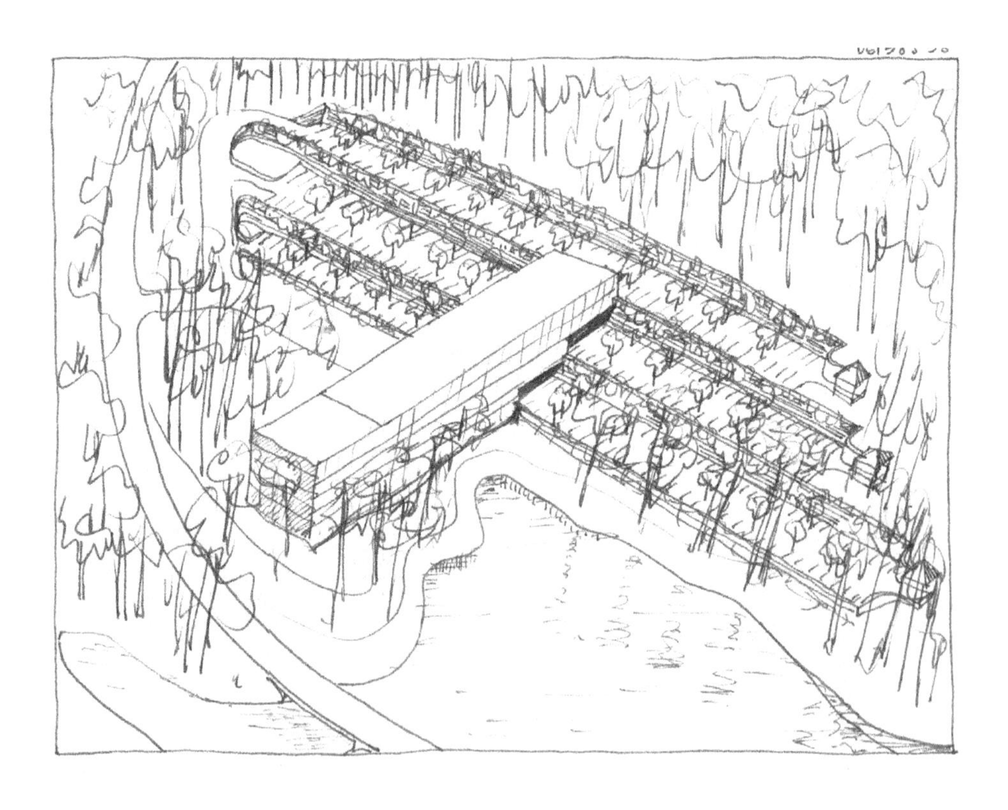

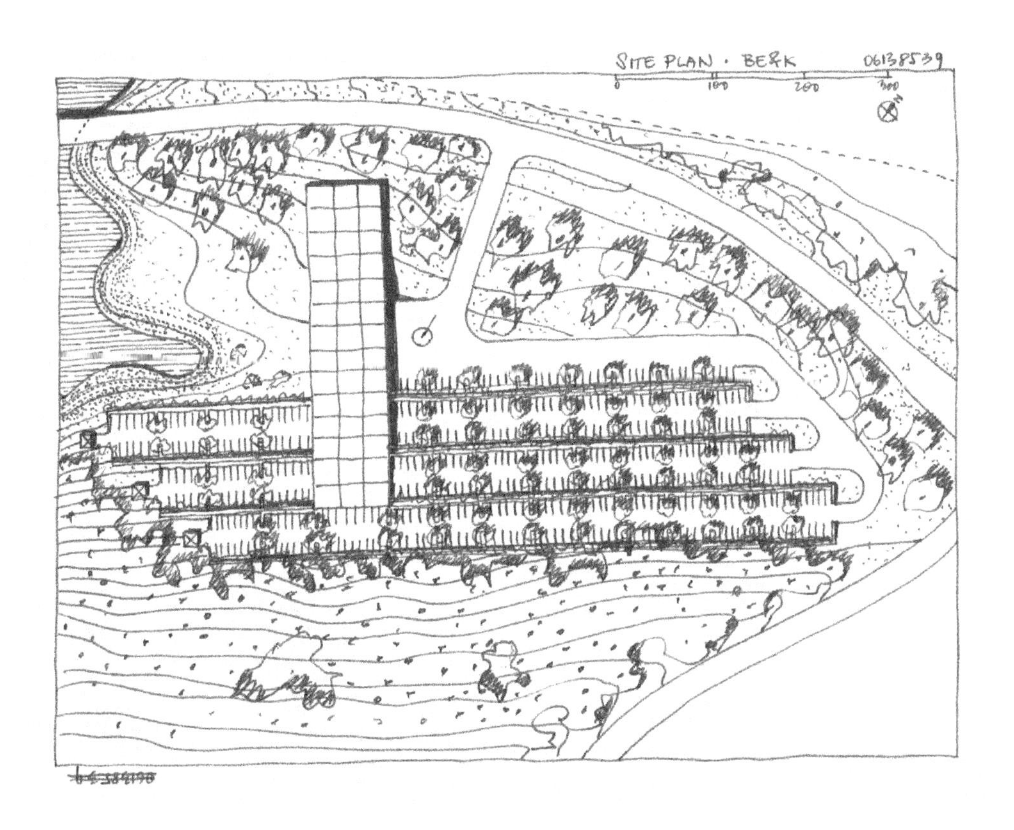
SITE PLAN · BE&K
061385 39
0
100
200
300
N

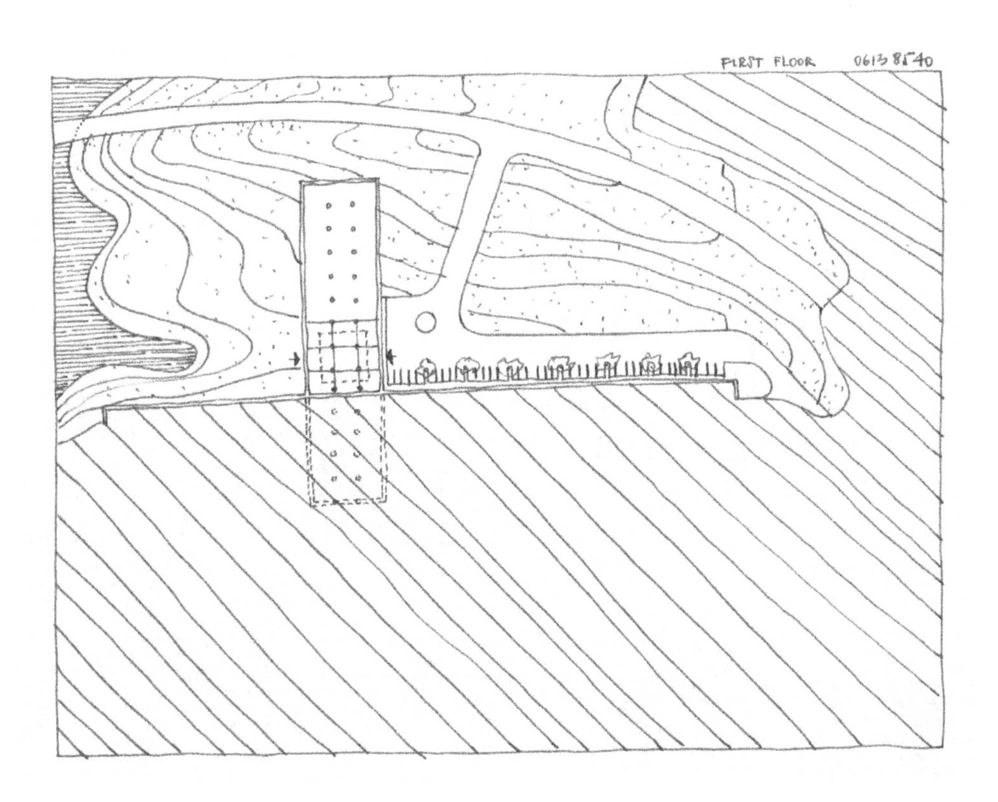
FIRST FLOOR
06138540

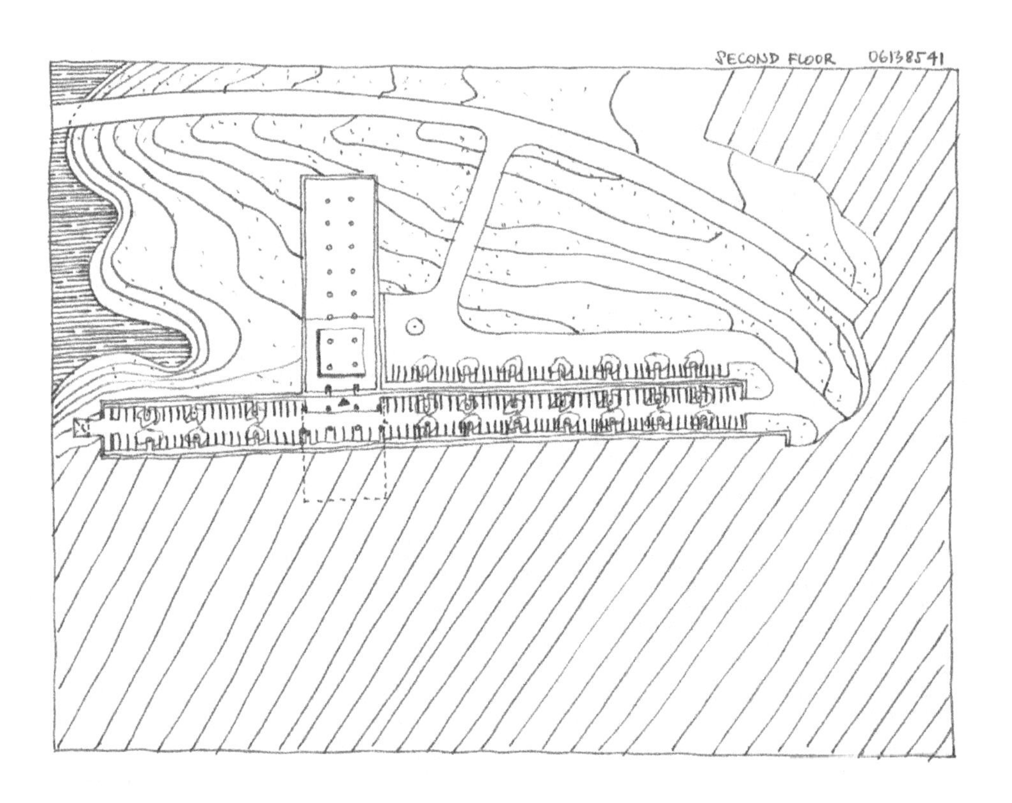
SECOND FLOOR 06138541

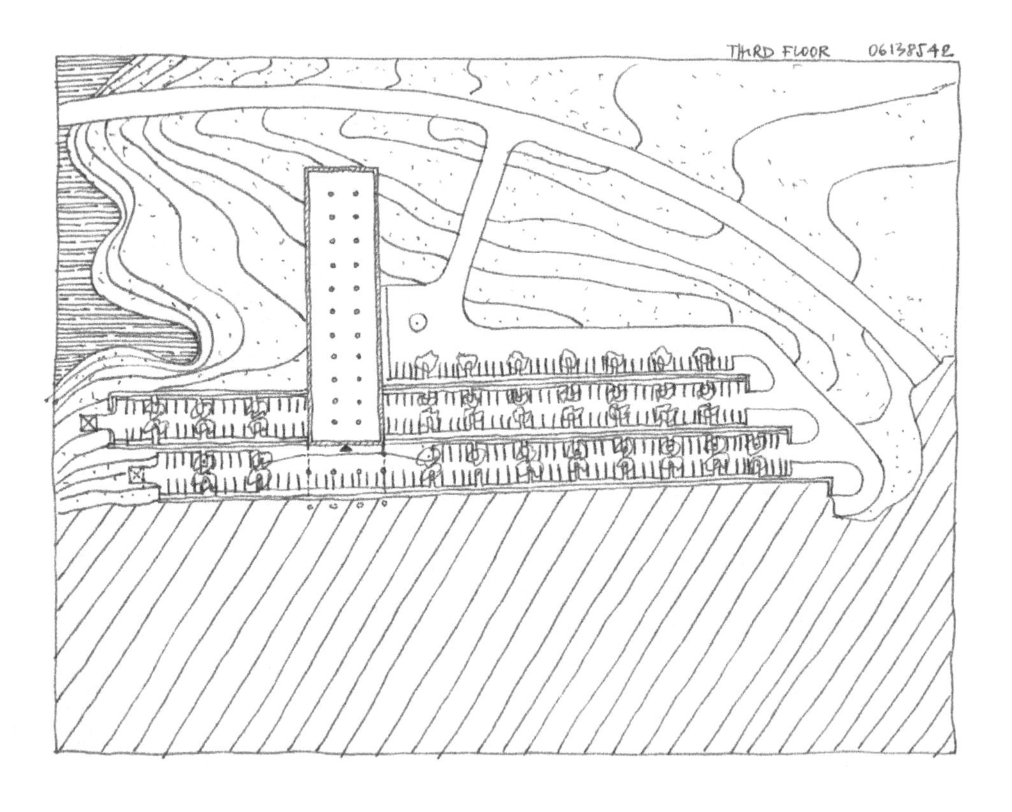
THIRD FLOOR 06138542

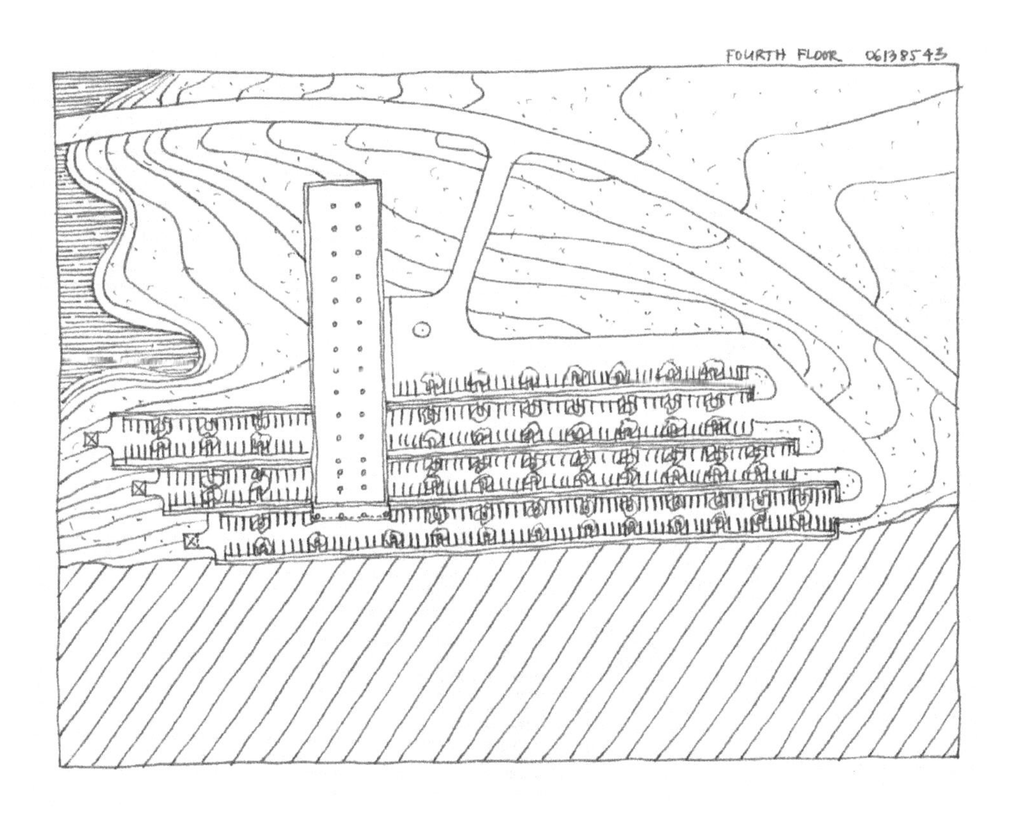
FOURTH FLOOR 06138543

06138544

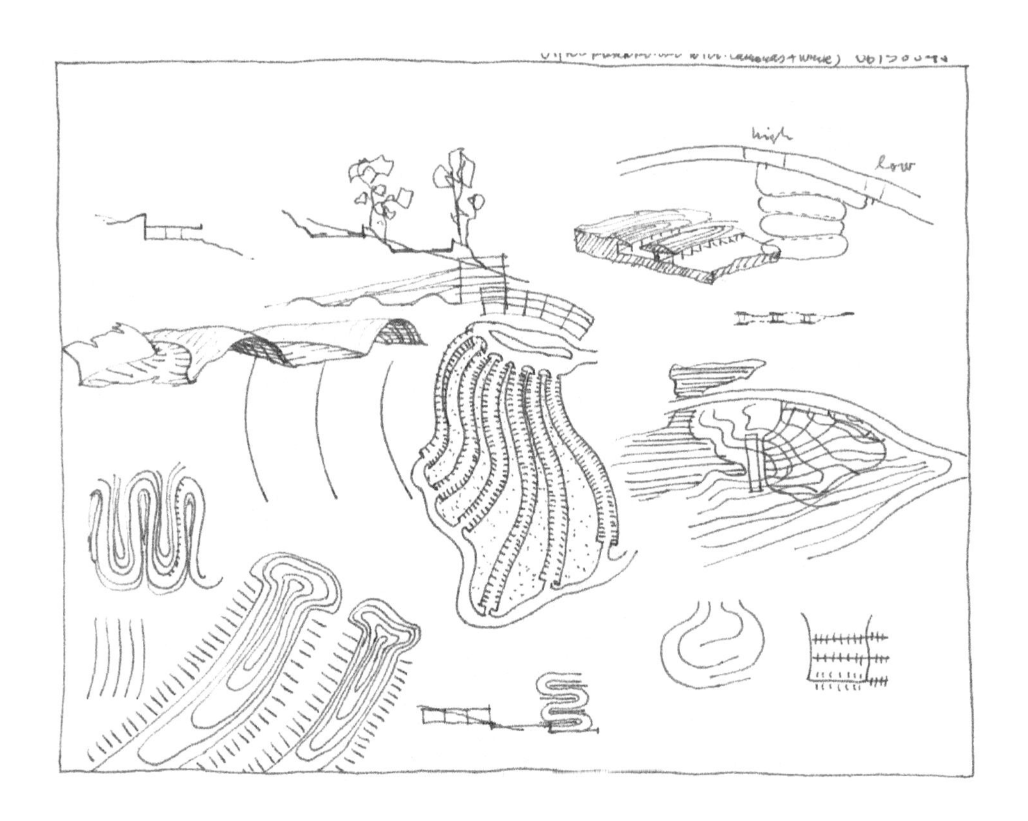
high
low

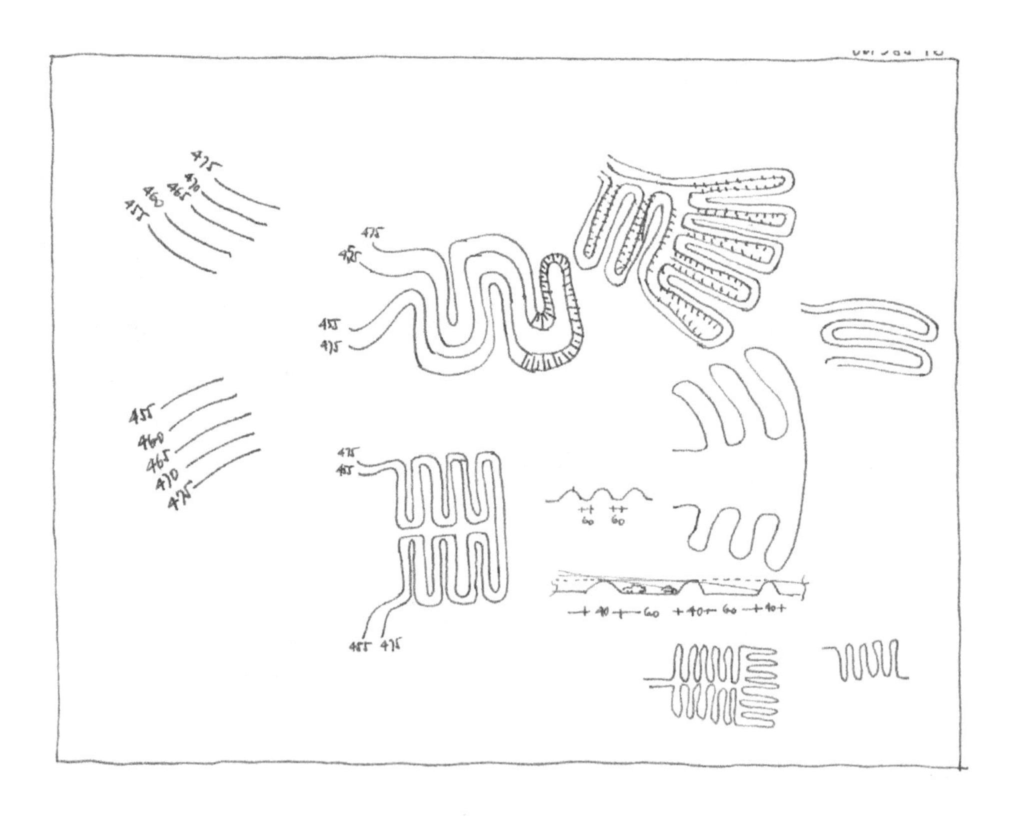
475
470
465
460
455
475
455
455
475
455
460
465
470
475
475
455
455 475
60 60
40 60 40 60 40

RE: 06138546/a

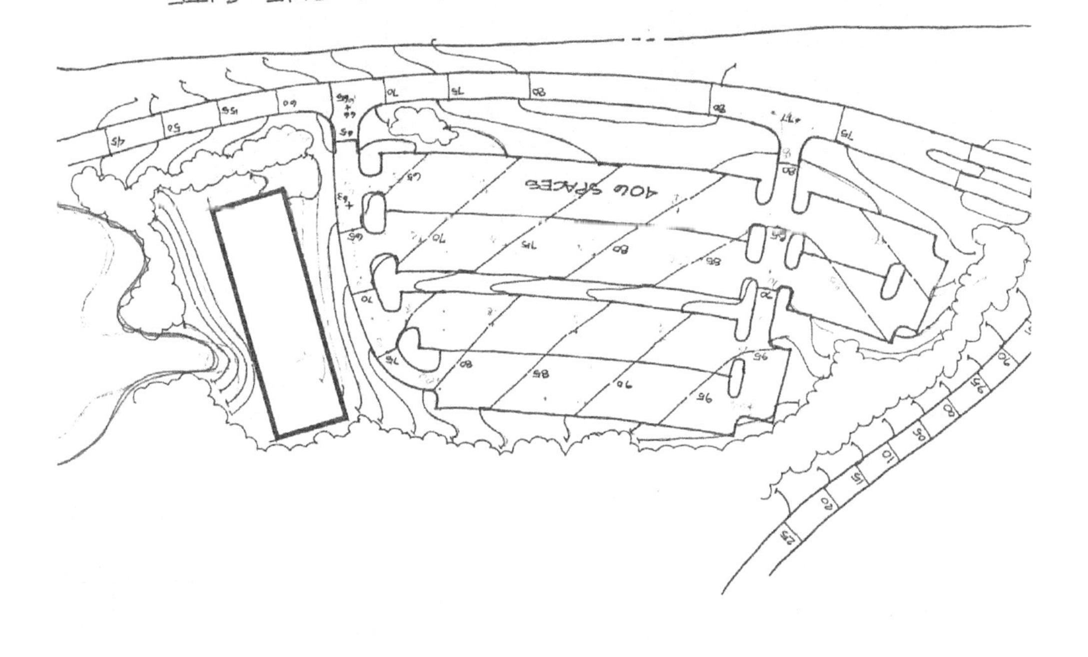

06188547

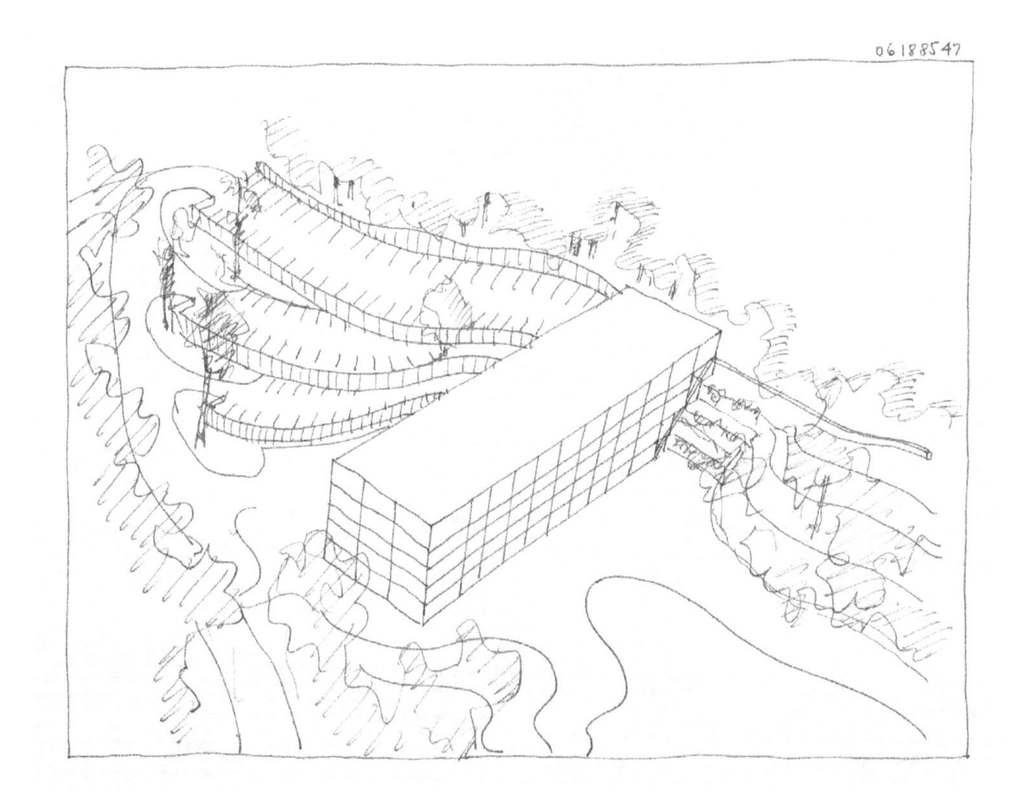

06188548

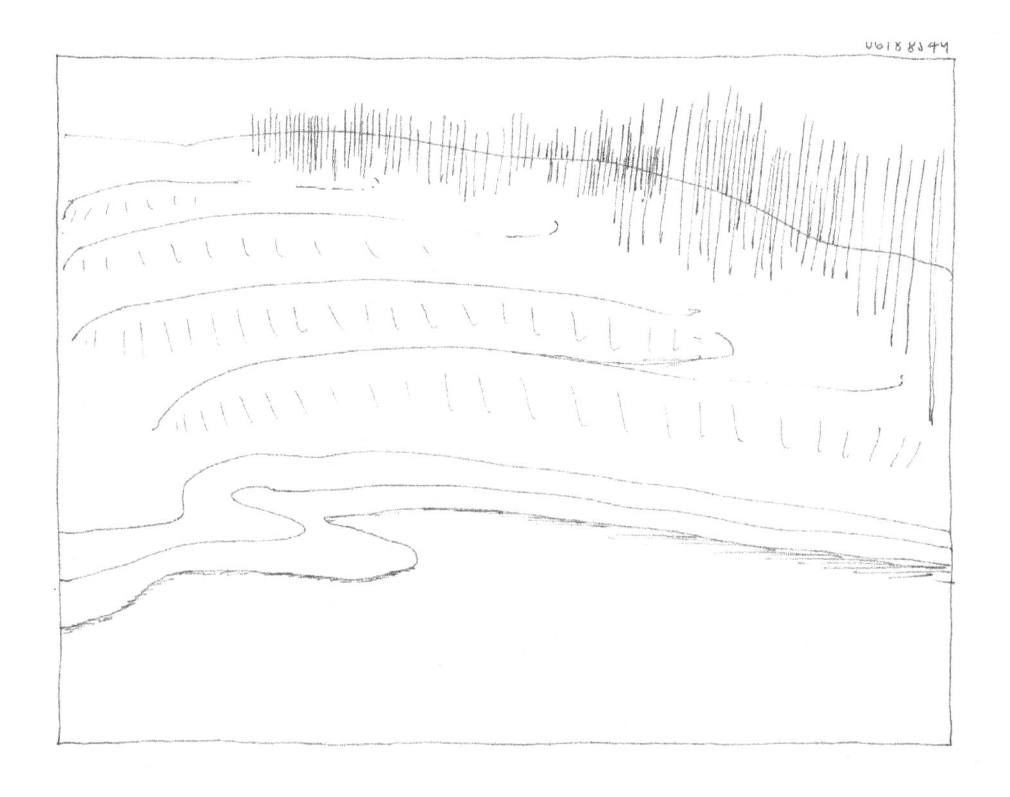
06188544

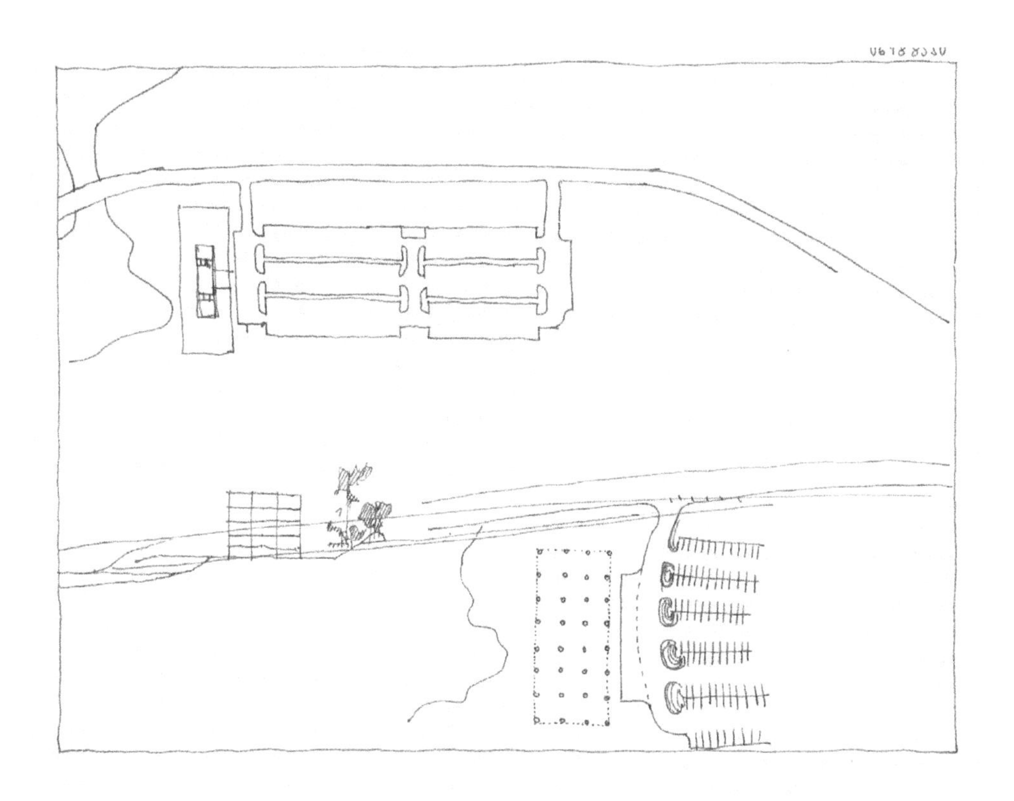

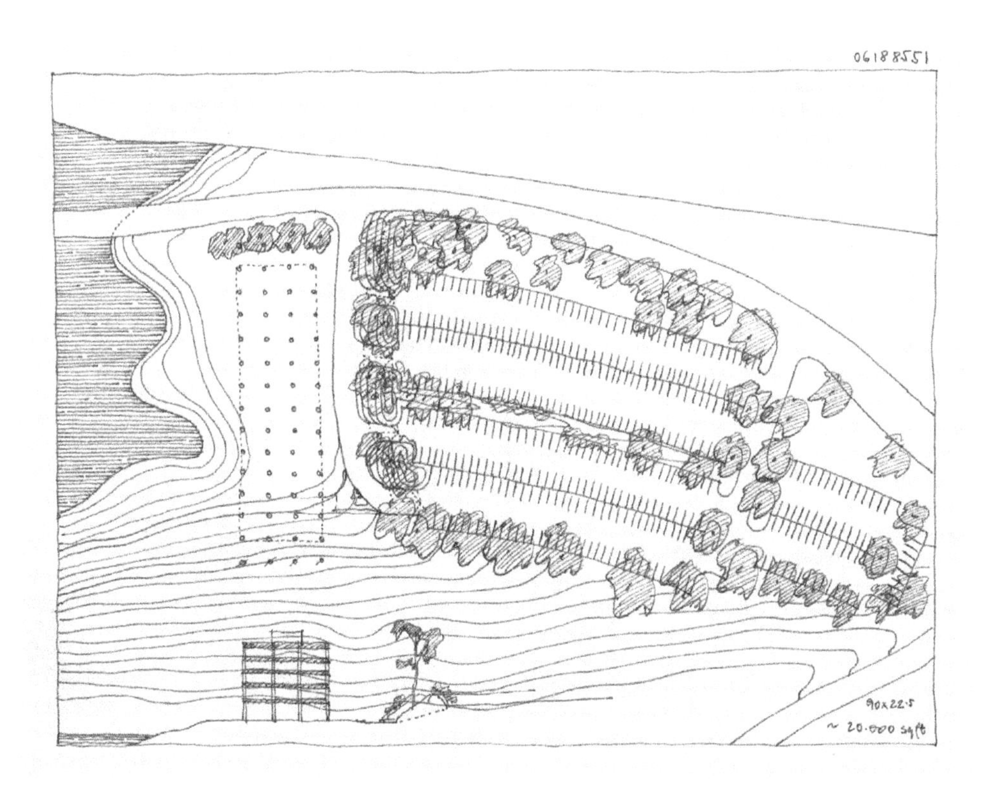
06188551
90x22.5
~ 20.000 sqft

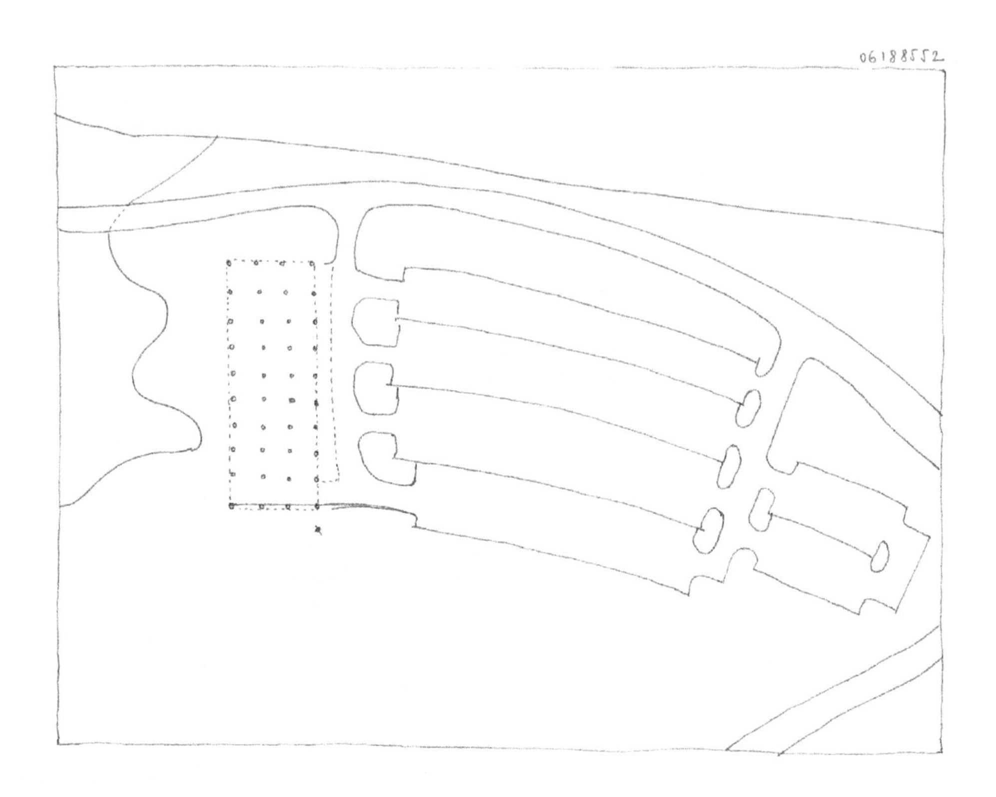
06188552

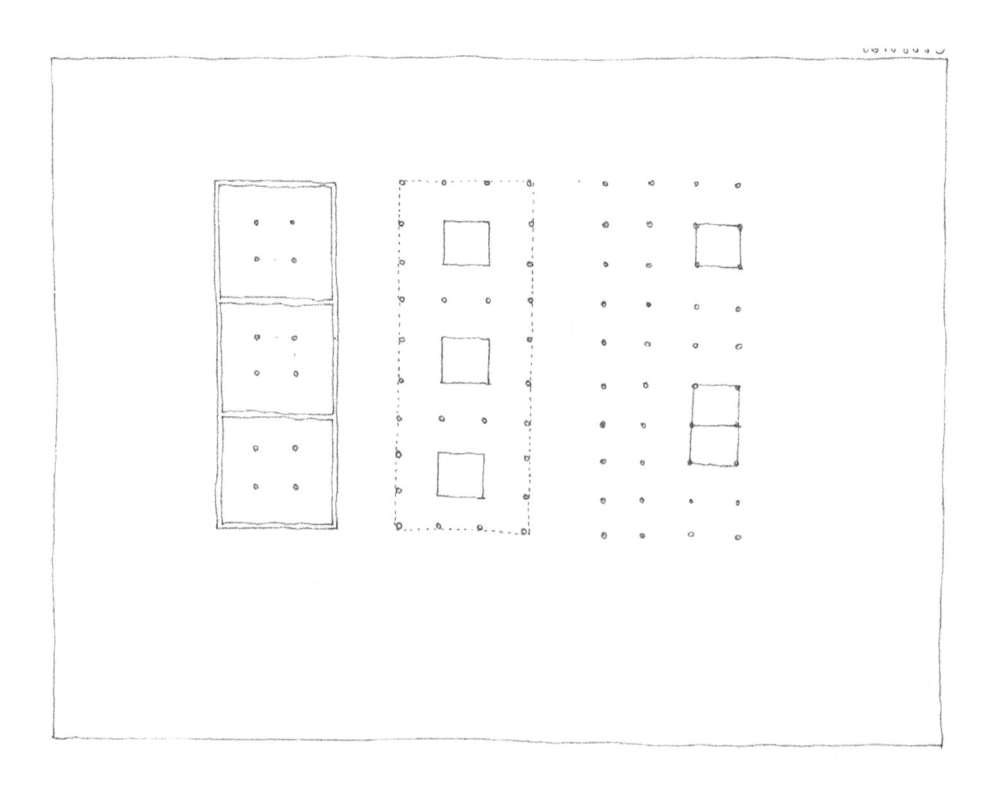

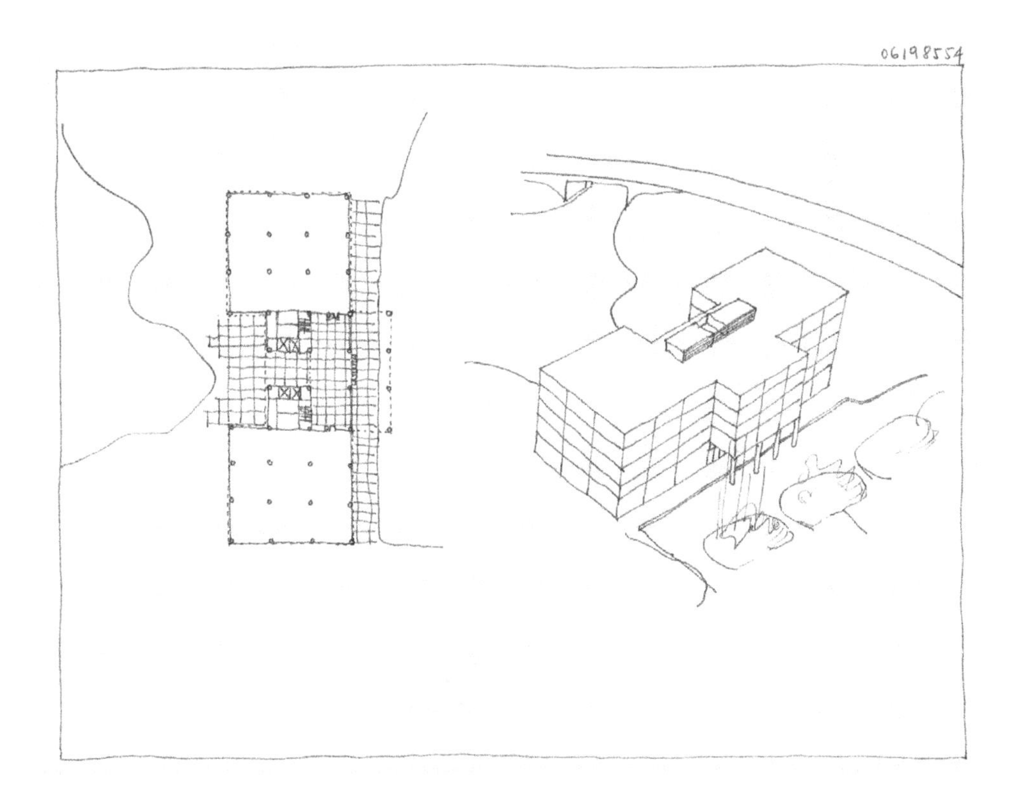
06198554

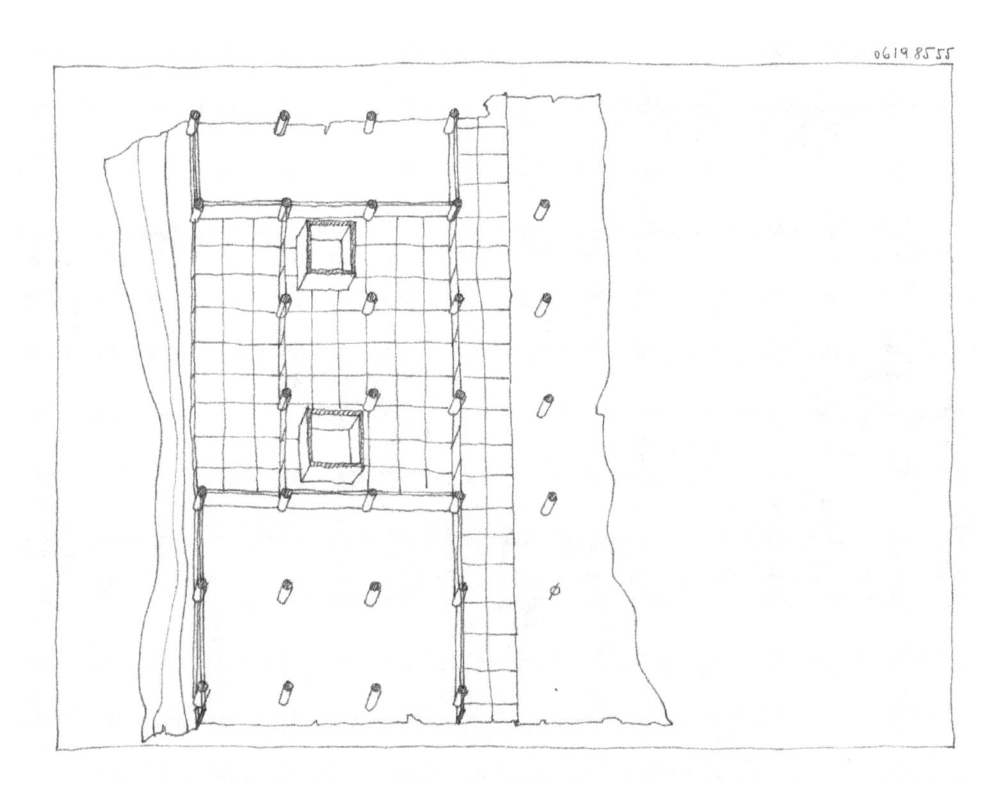
06198555

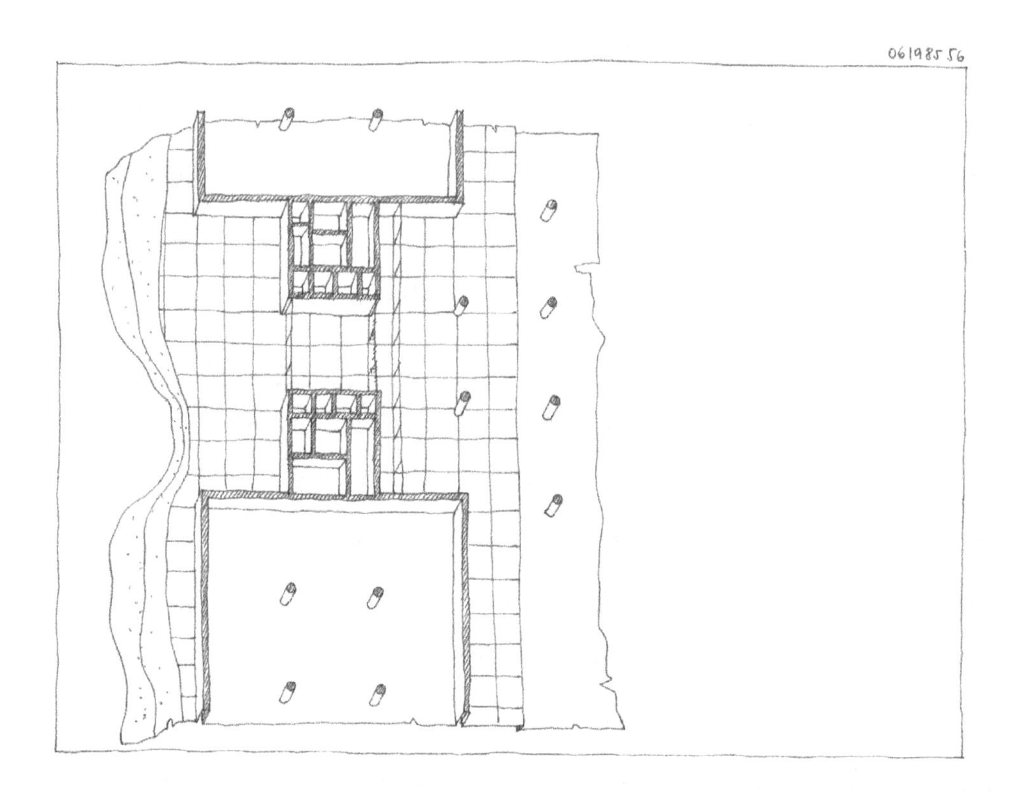

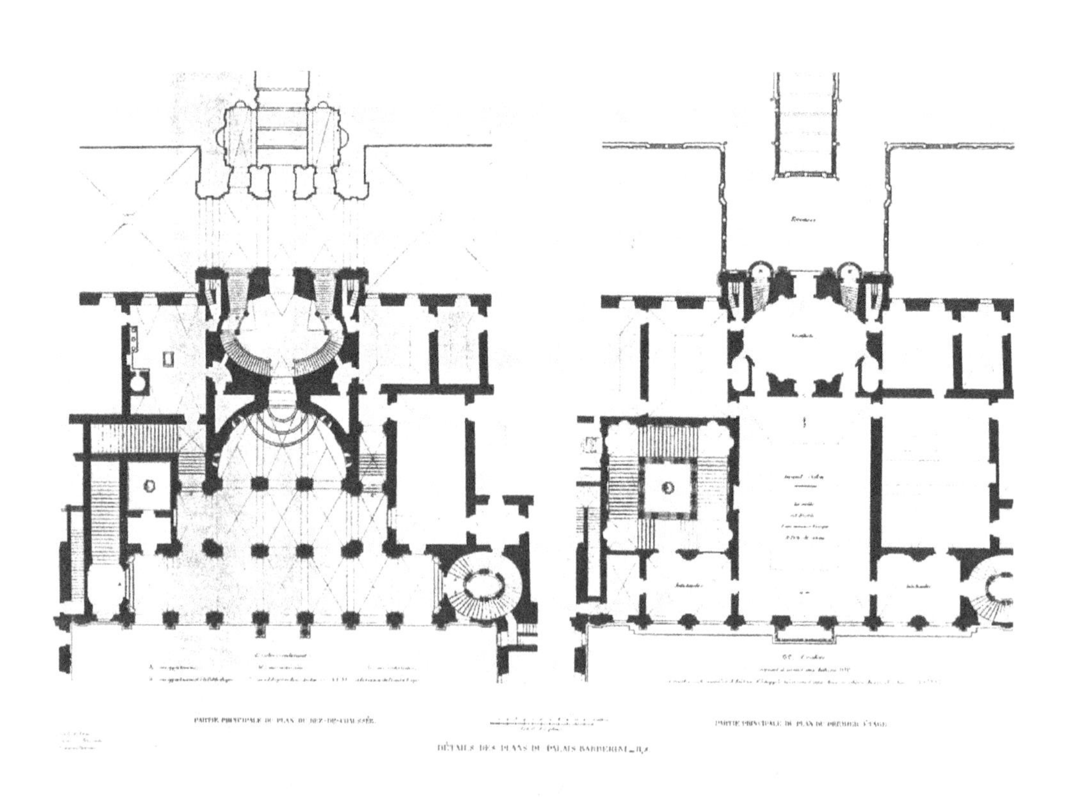
PARTIE PRINCIPALE DU PLAN DU REZ-DE-CHAUSSÉE.
PARTIE PRINCIPALE DU PLAN DU PREMIER ÉTAGE.
DÉTAILS DES PLANS DU PALAIS BARBERINI

Plan du Premier Etage
PALAIS BARBERINI

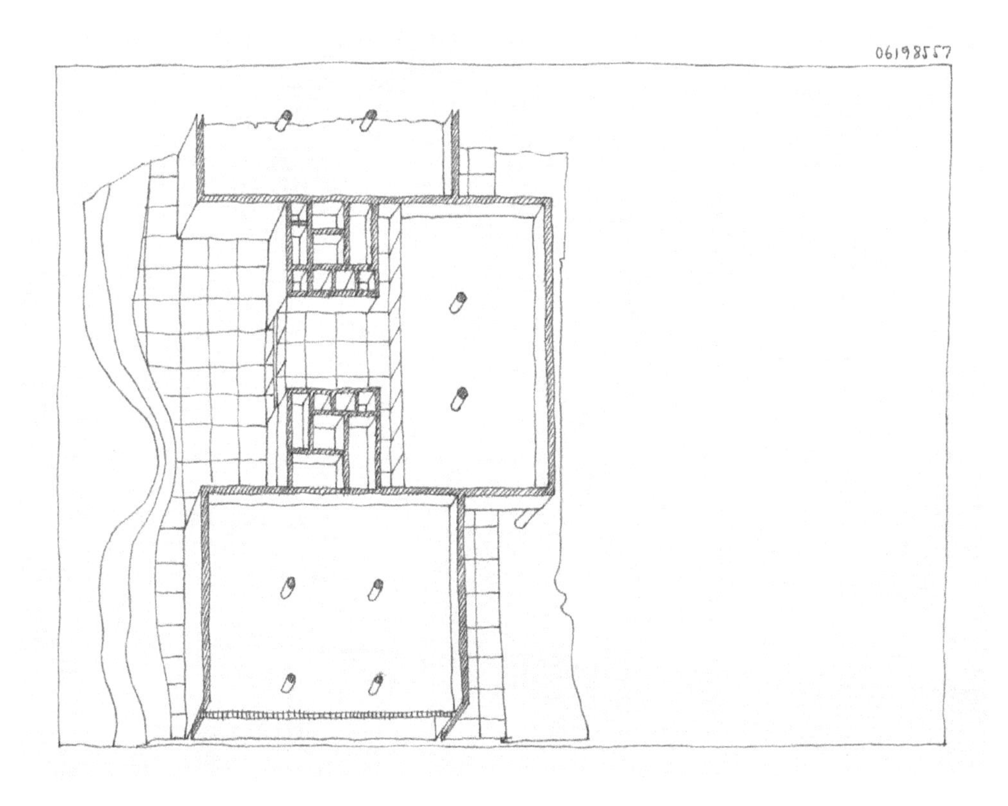
06198557

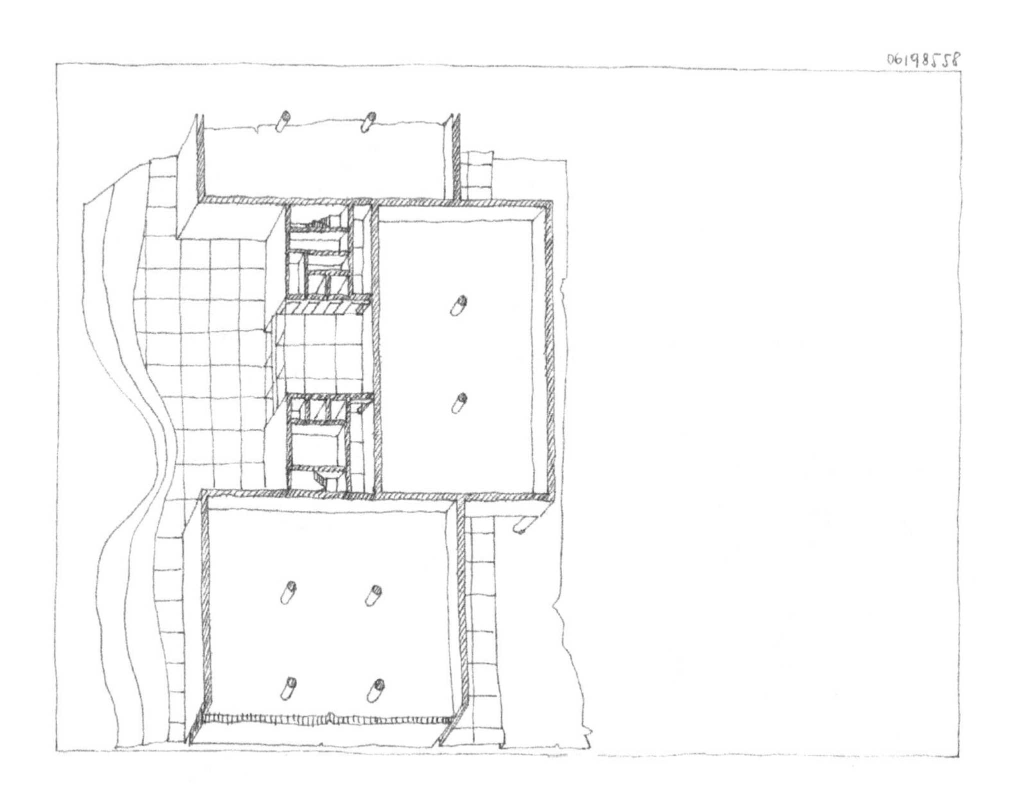
06198558

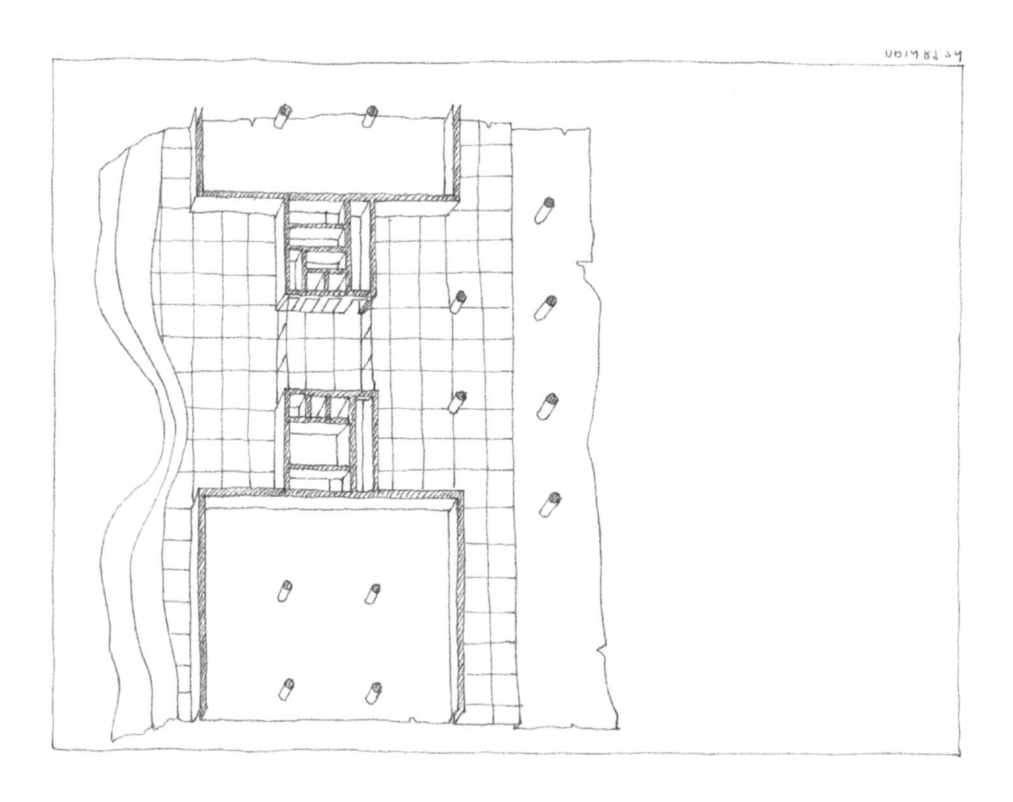

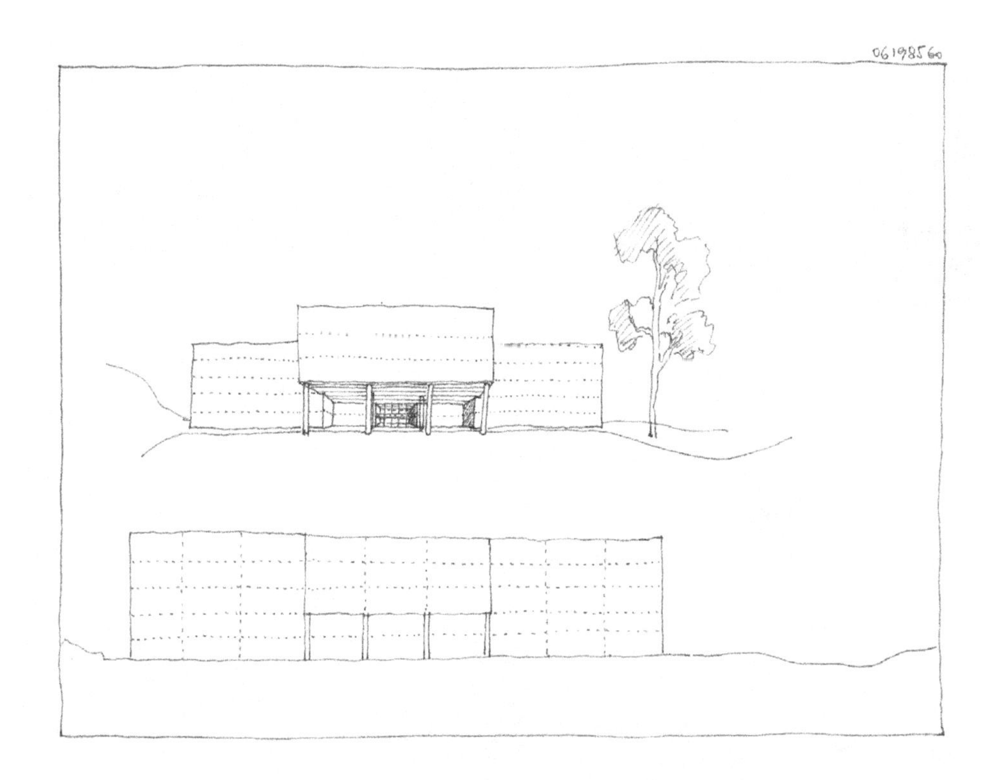
06198560

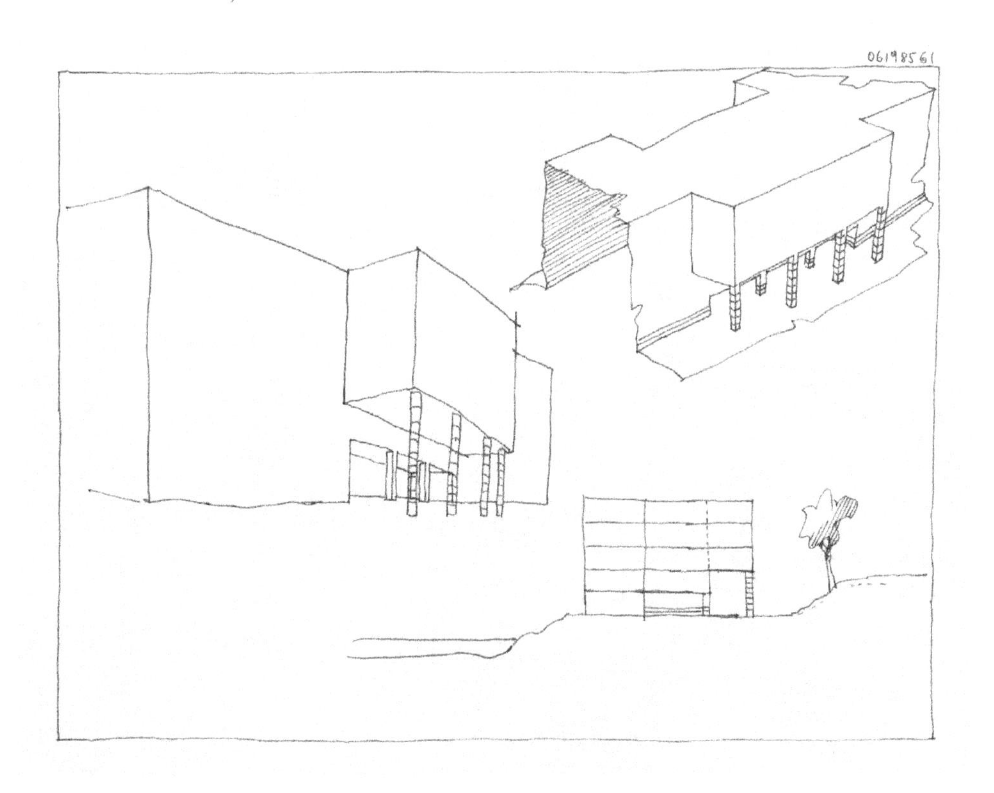
06198561

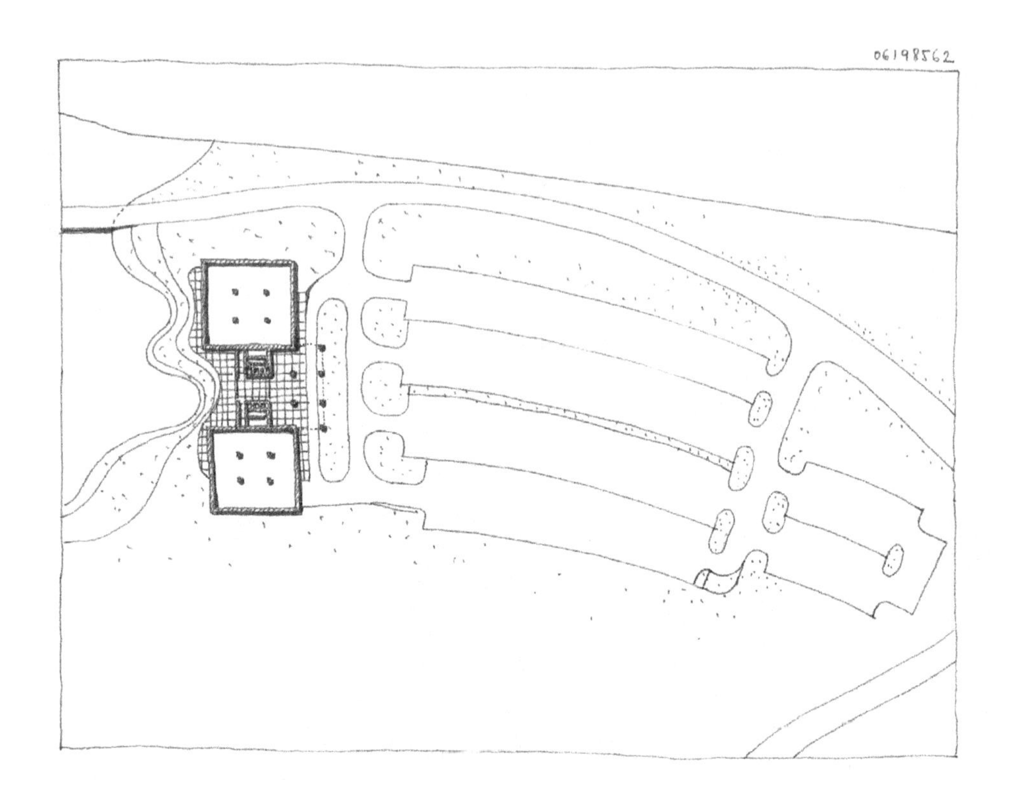
06198562

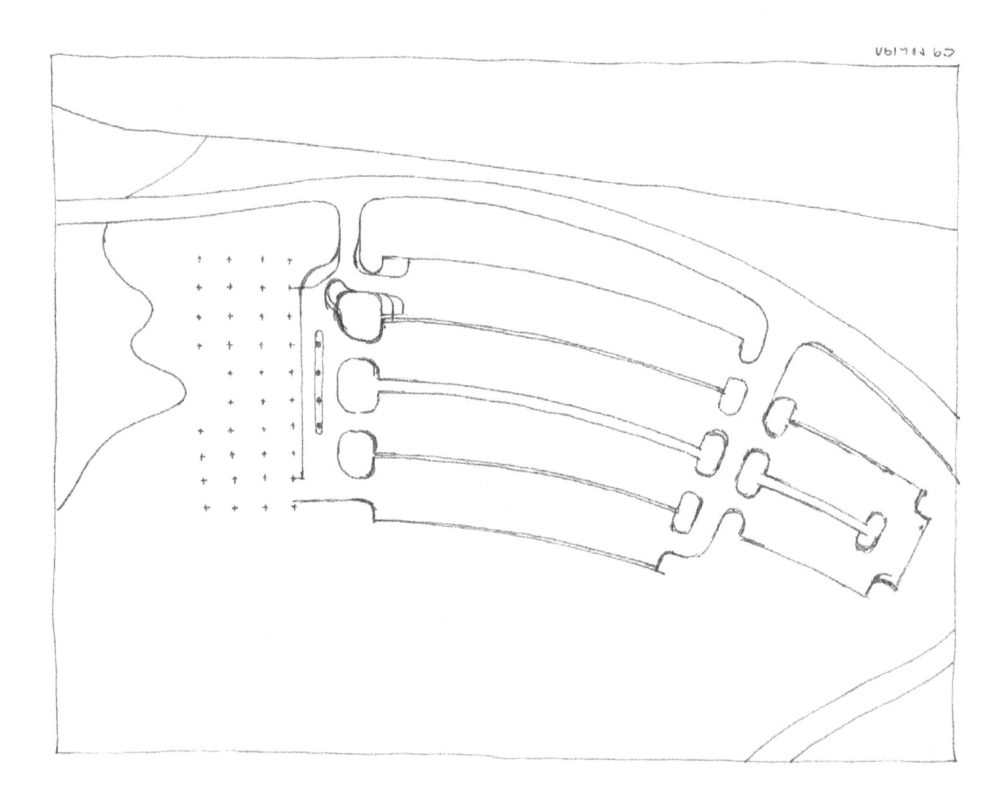

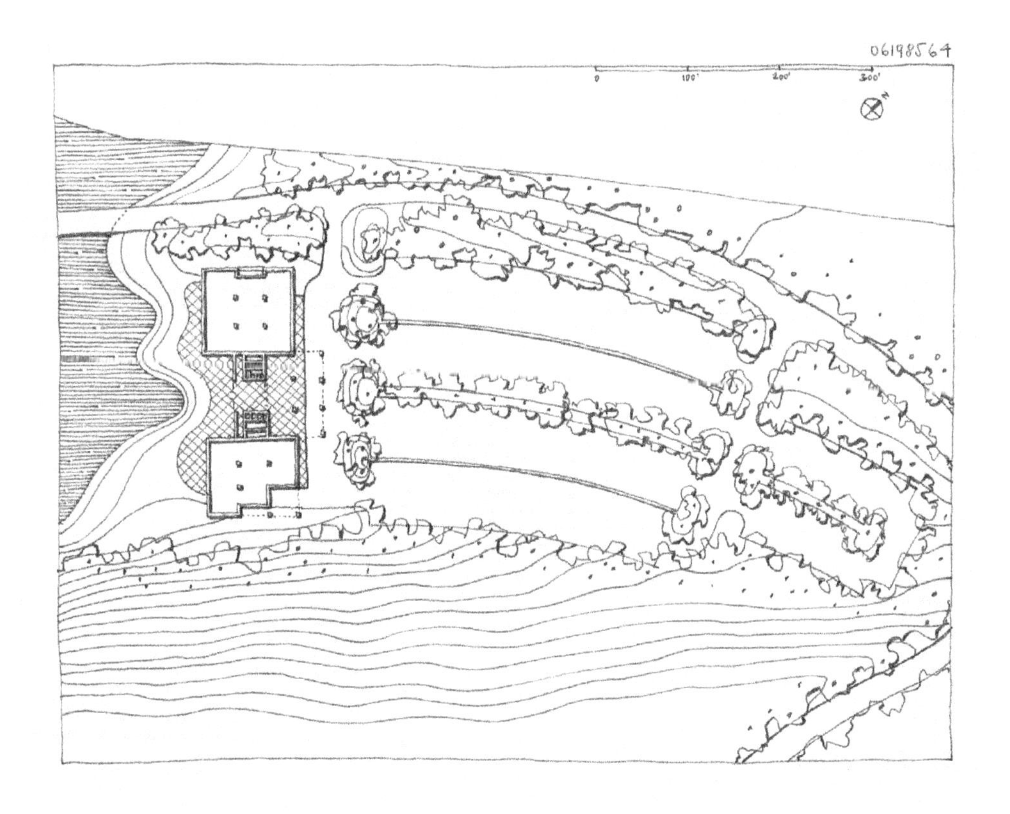
06198564
0
100'
200'
300'
N

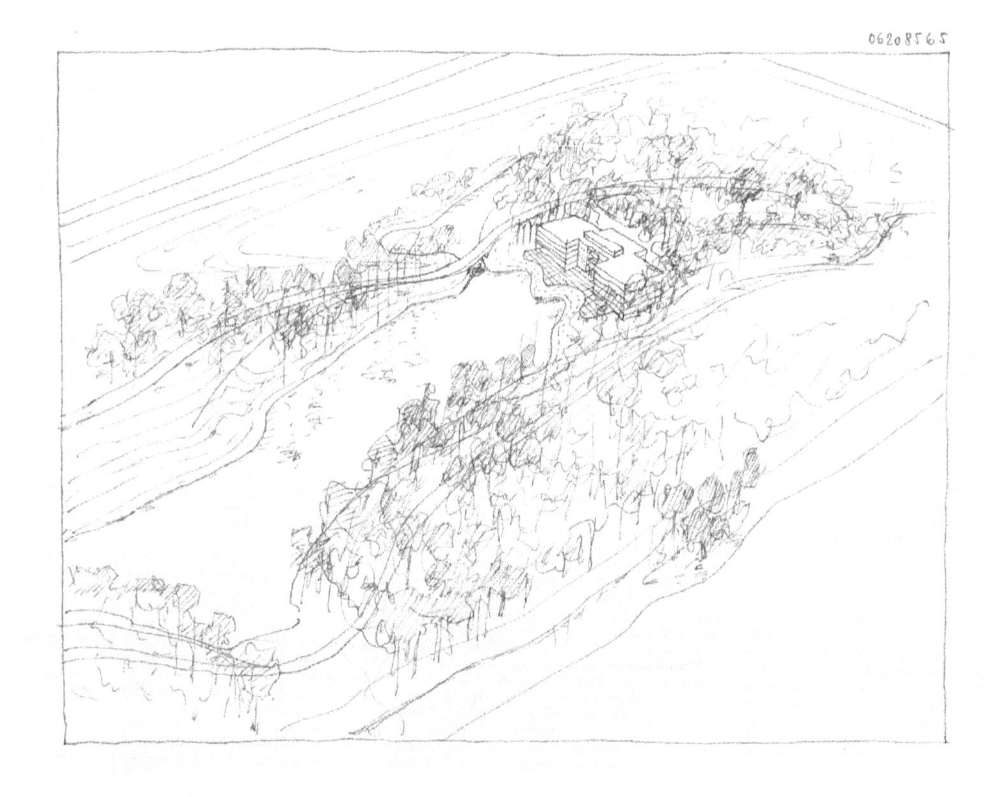
06208565

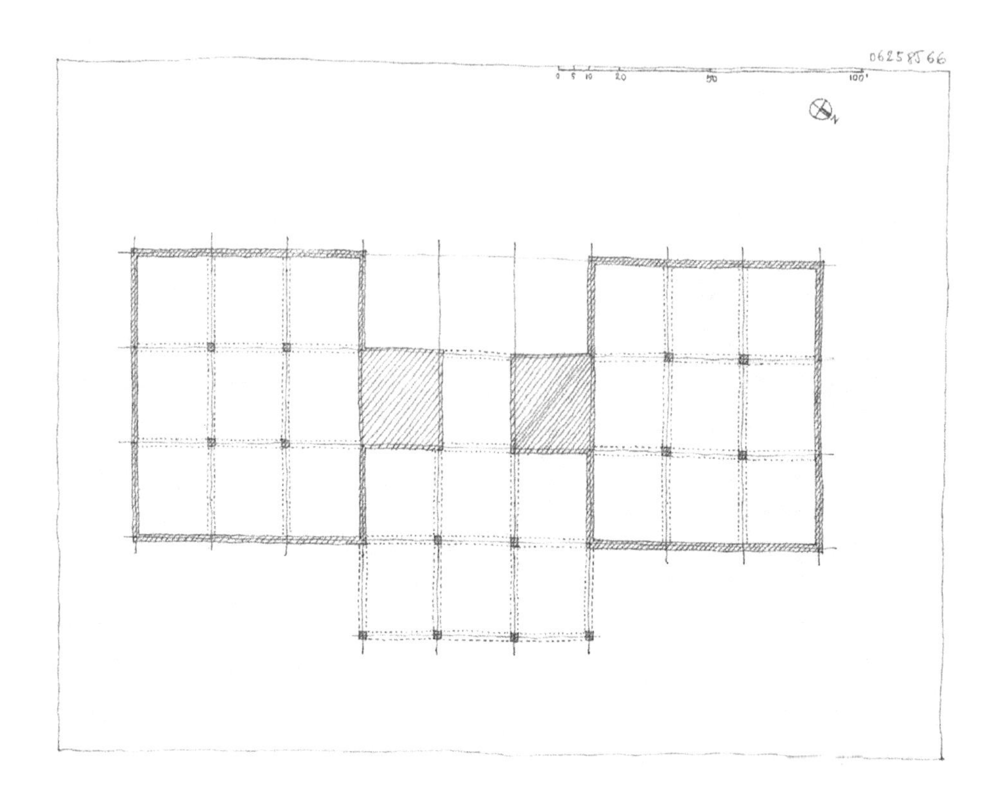
06258566
0 5 10 20 50 100'

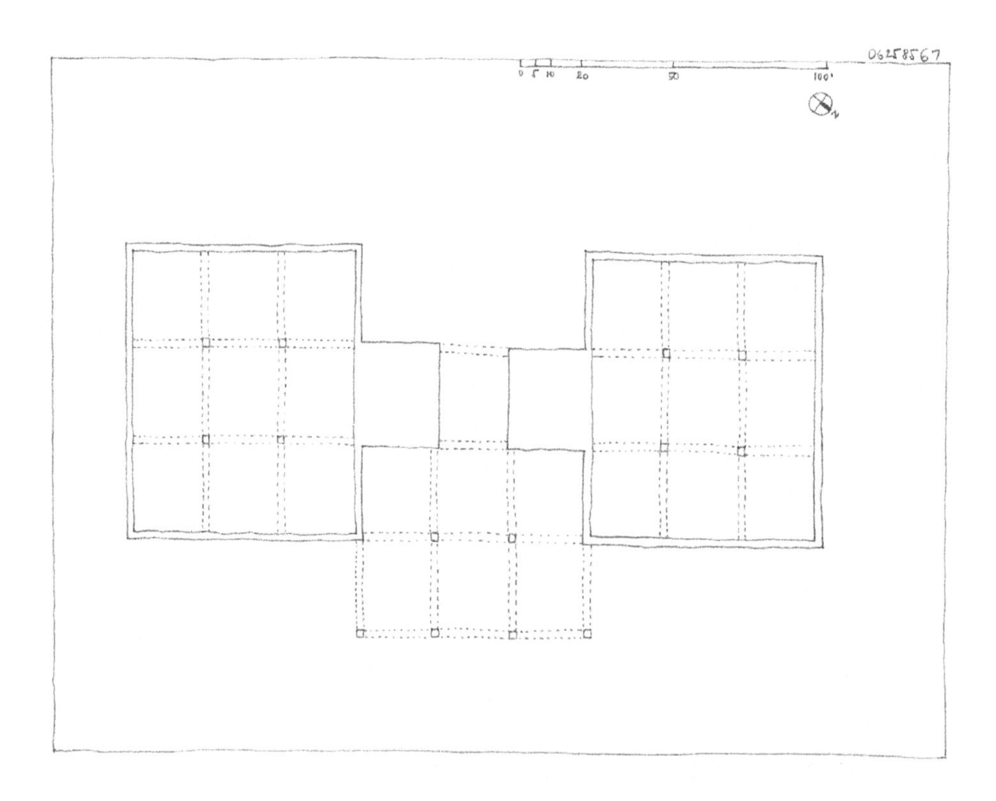
06258567
0 5 10 20 50 100'

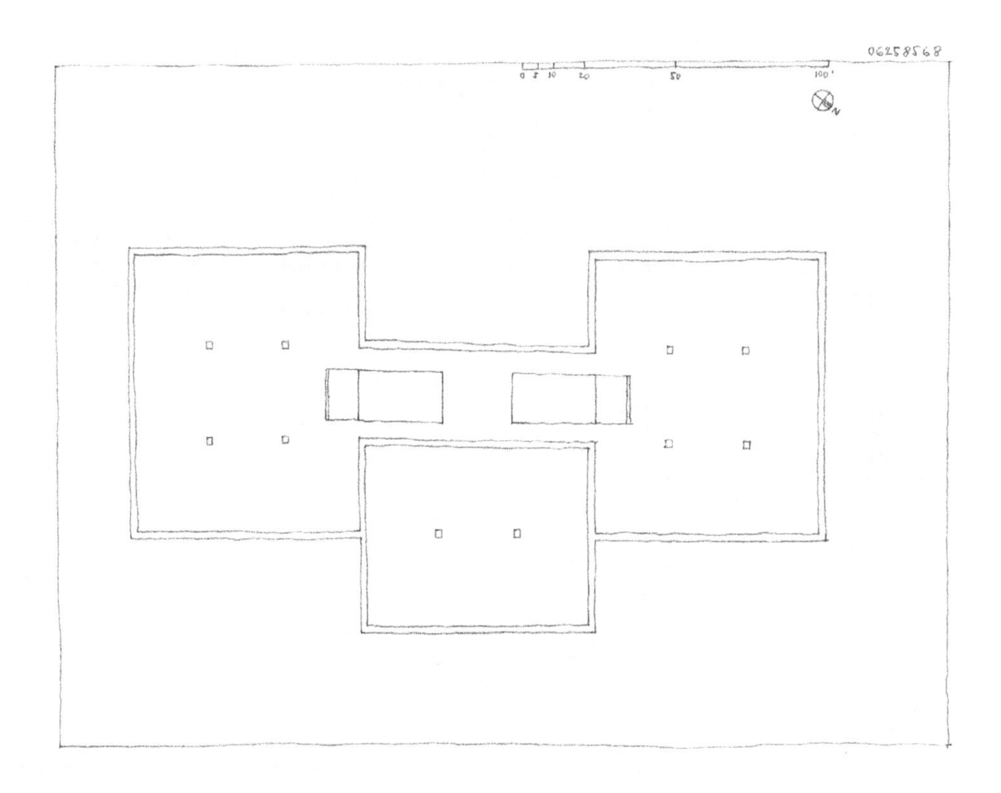
06258568
0 5 10 20 50 100'
N

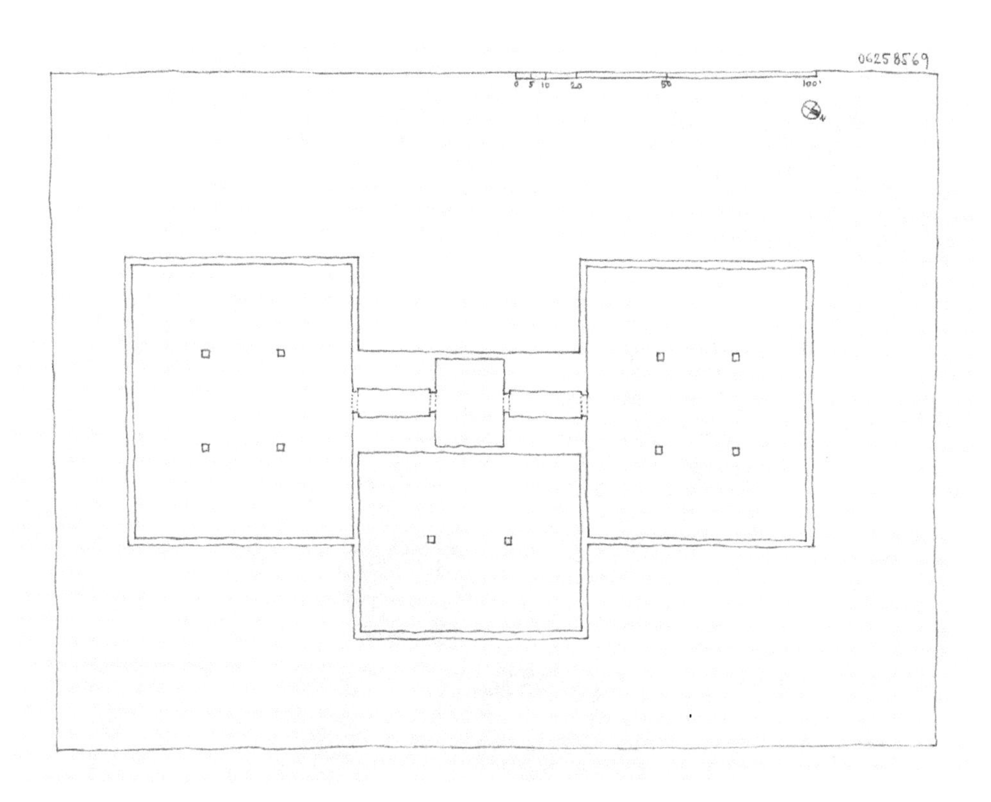
06258569
0 5 10 20 50 100'
N

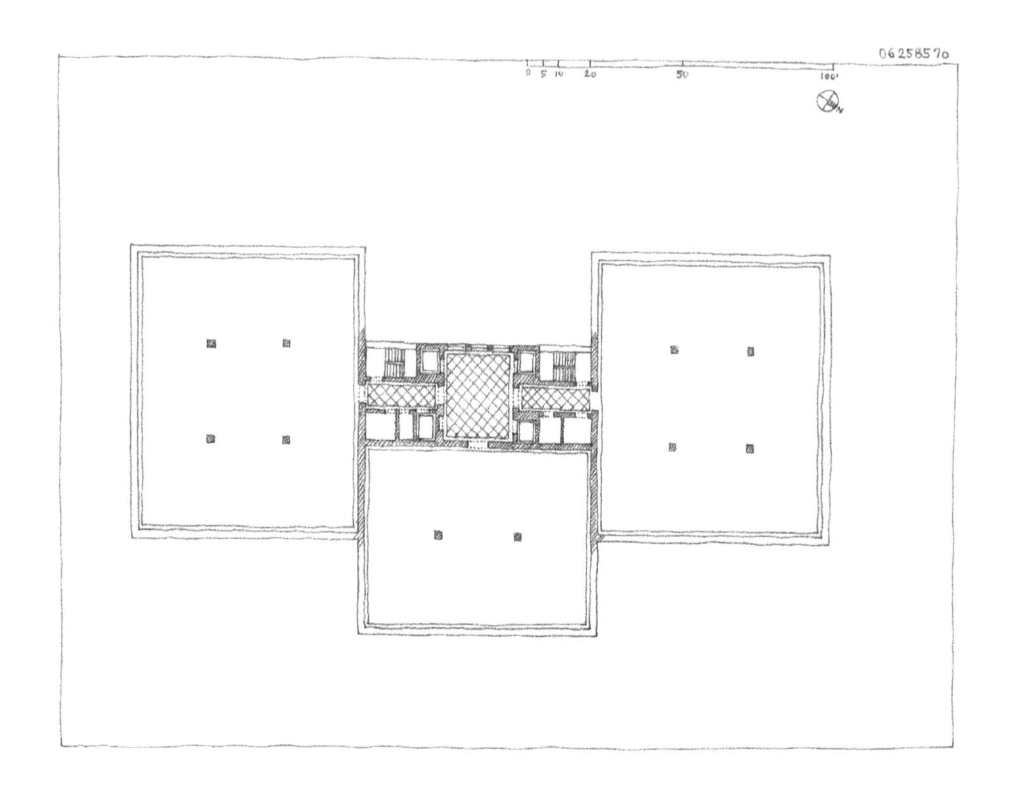
06258570
0
5
10
20
50
100'
N

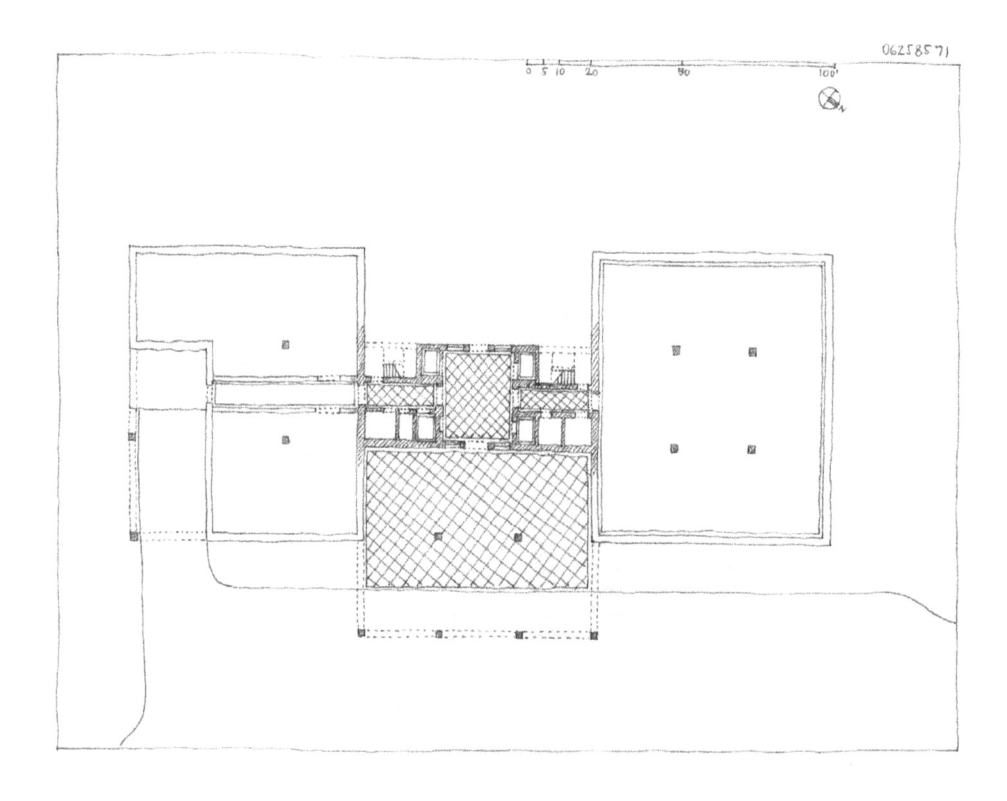
06258571
0
5
10
20
50
100'
N

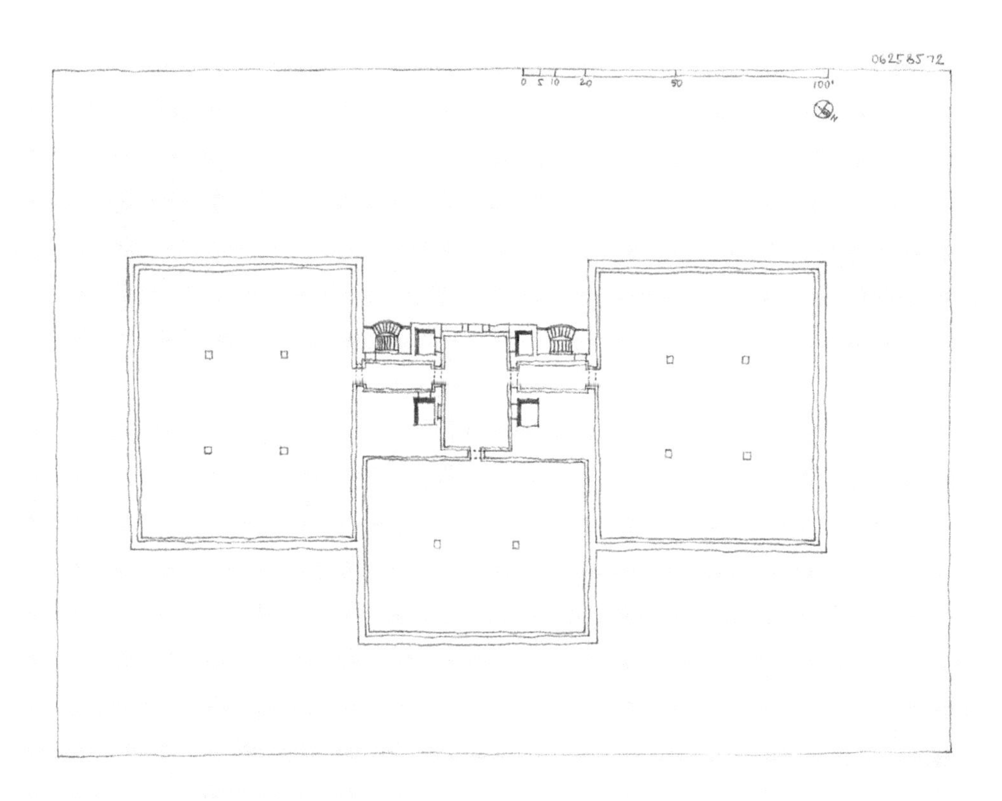
06258572
0 5 10 20 50 100'
N

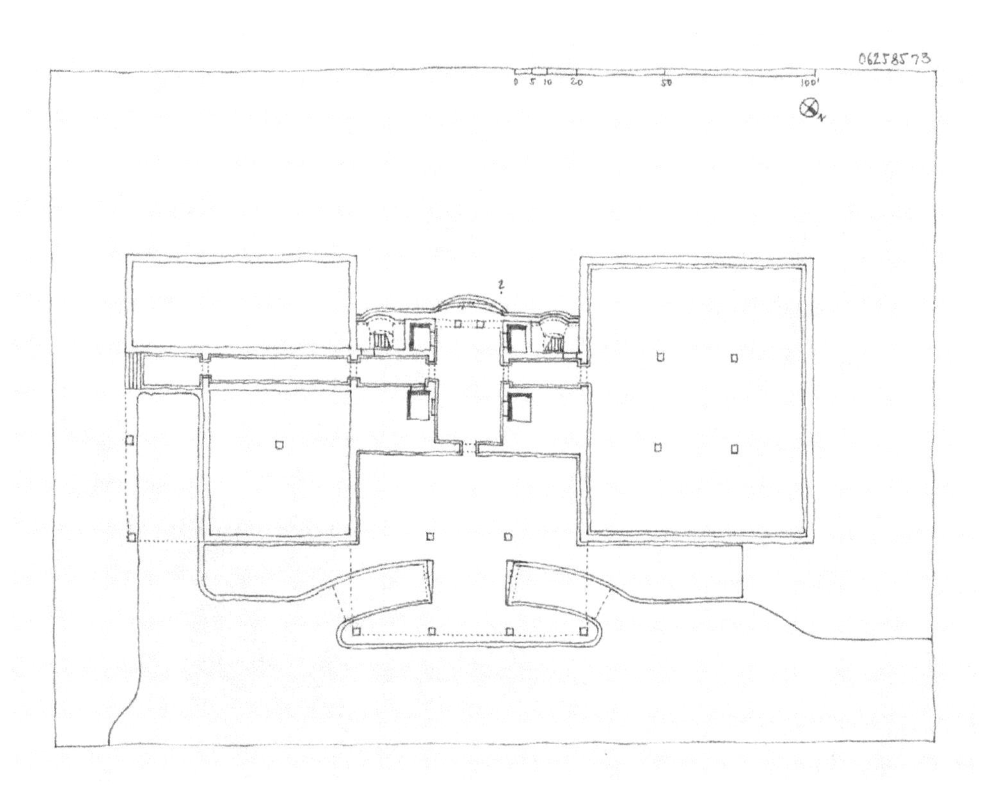
06258573
0 5 10 20 50 100'
N

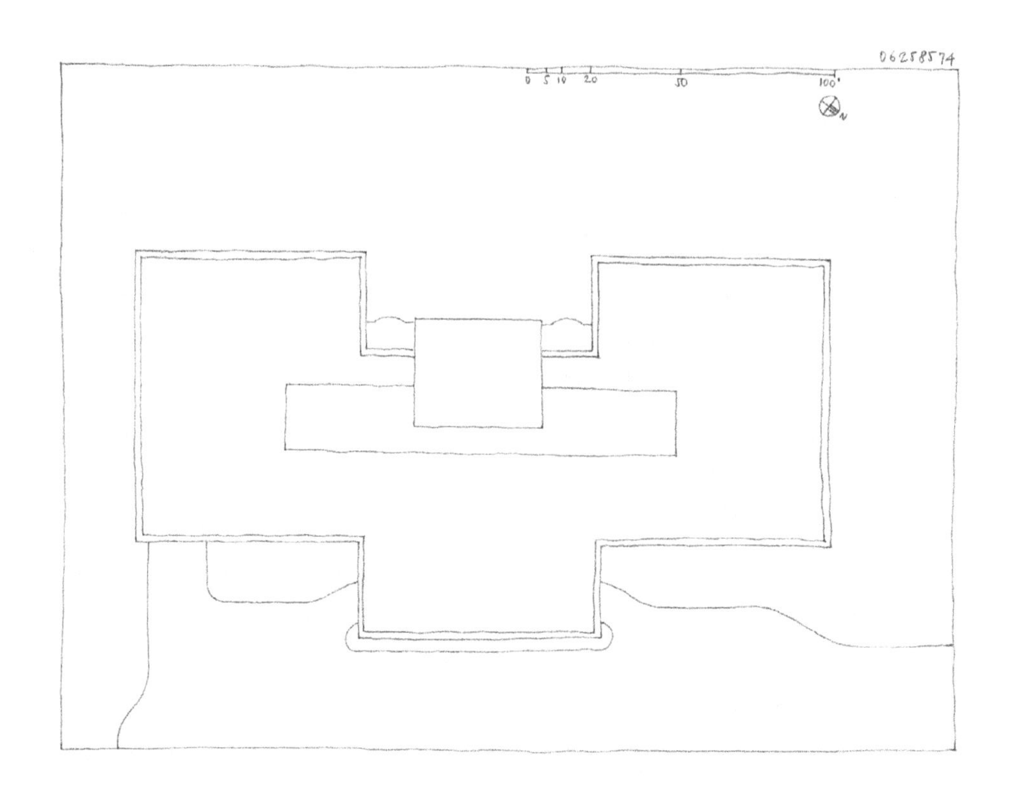
06258574
0 5 10 20 50 100'
N

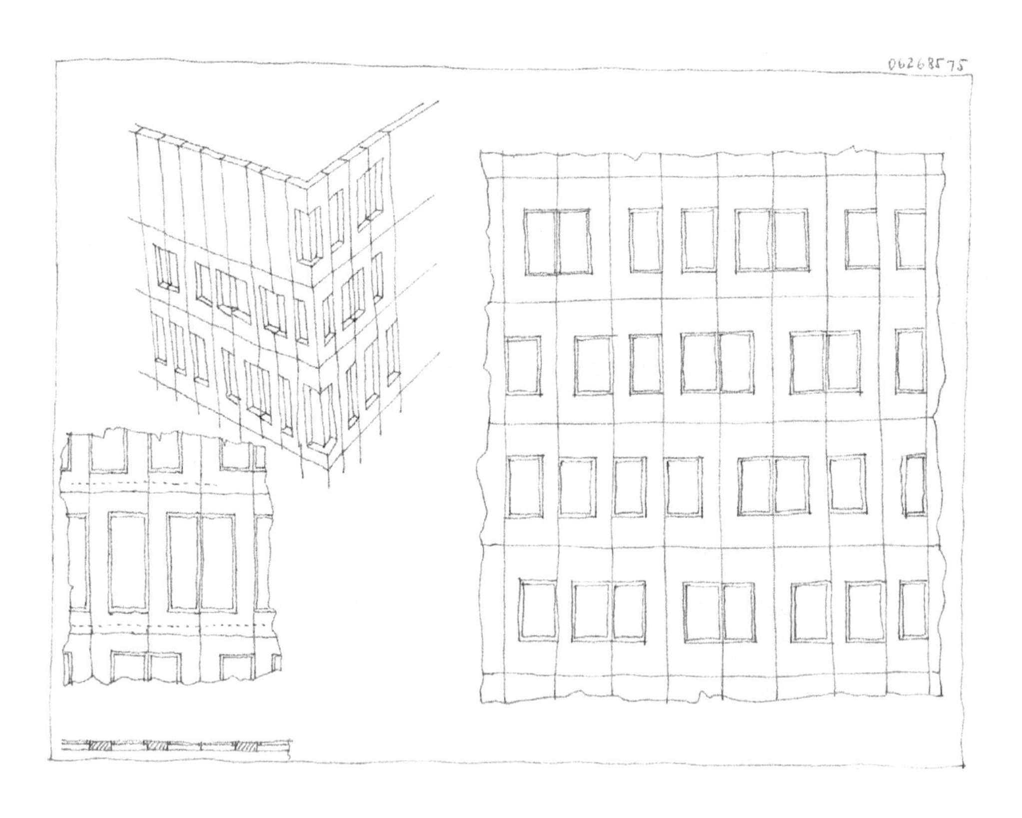
06268575

06268576

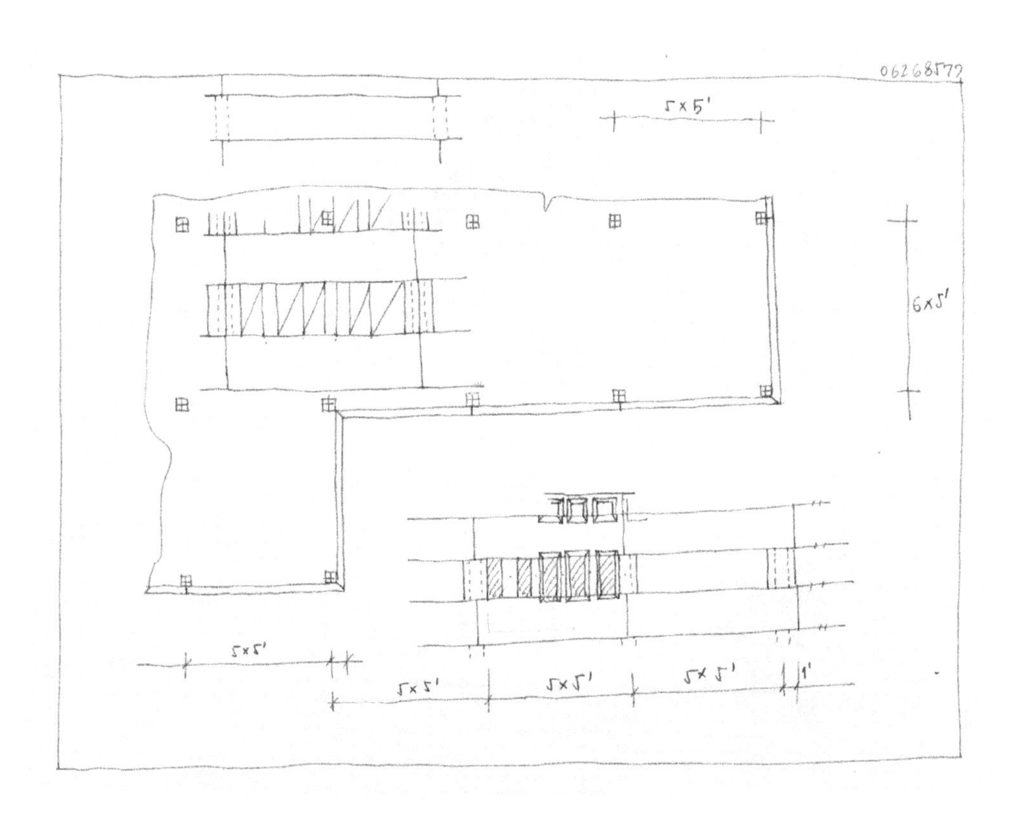
06268577
5 x 5'
6 x 5'
5 x 5'
5 x 5'
5 x 5'
5 x 5'
1'

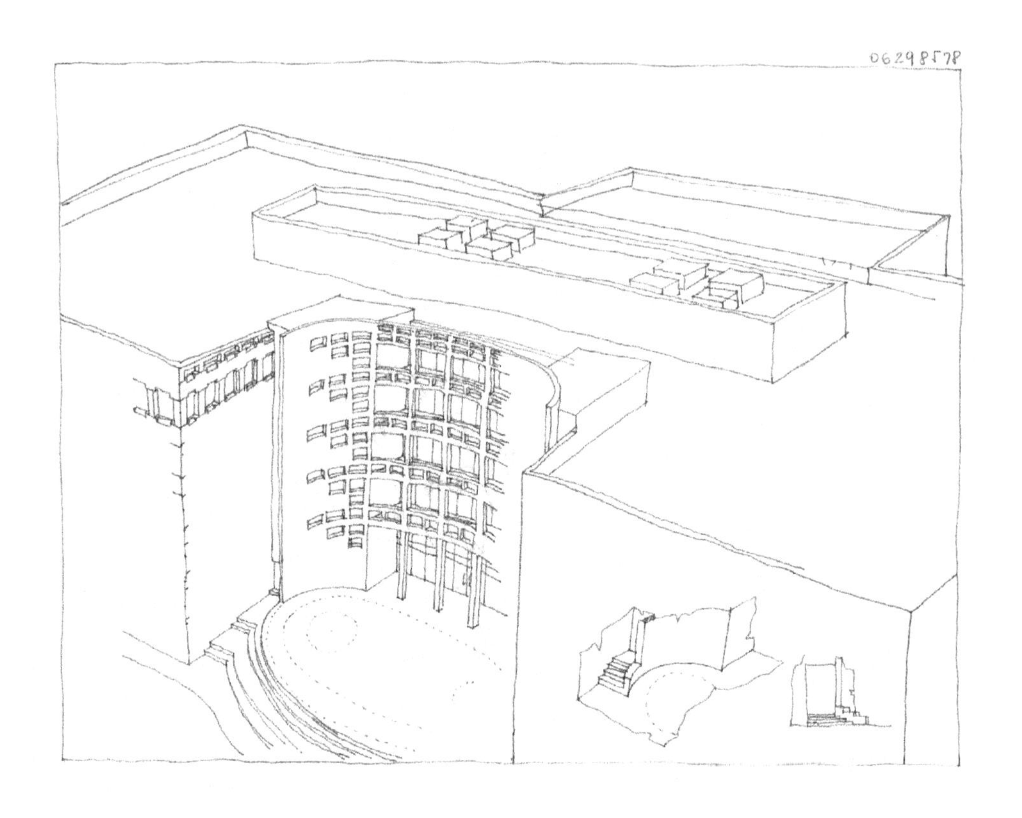
06298578

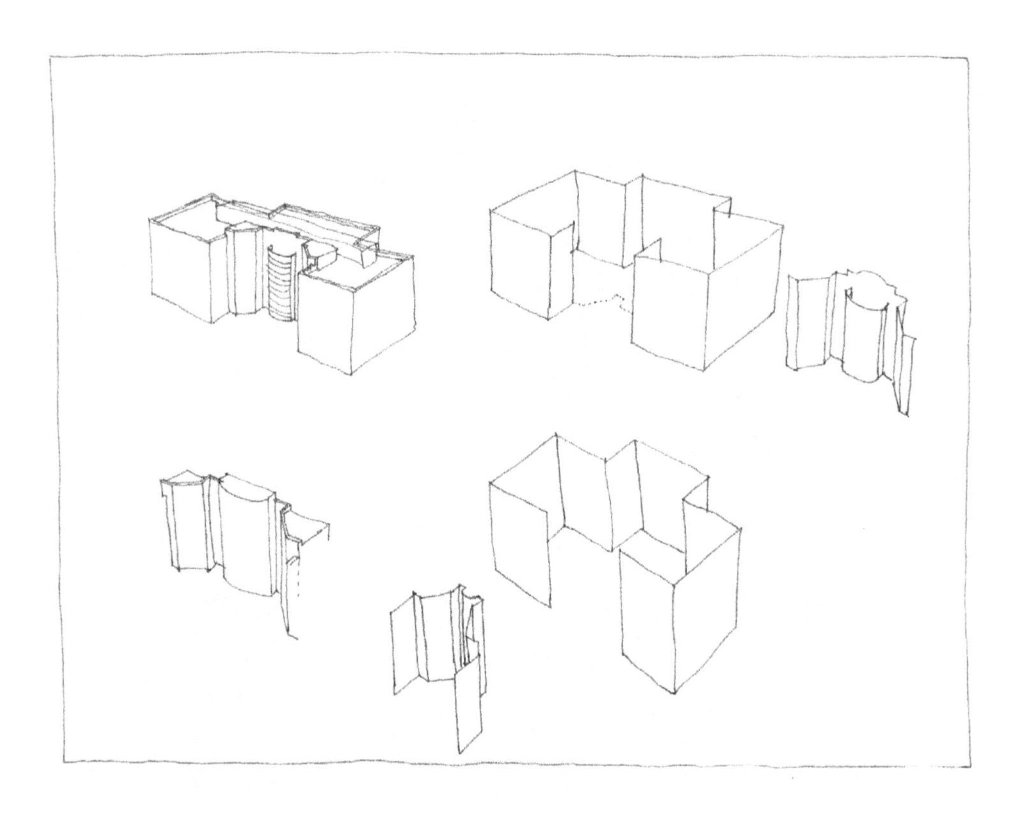

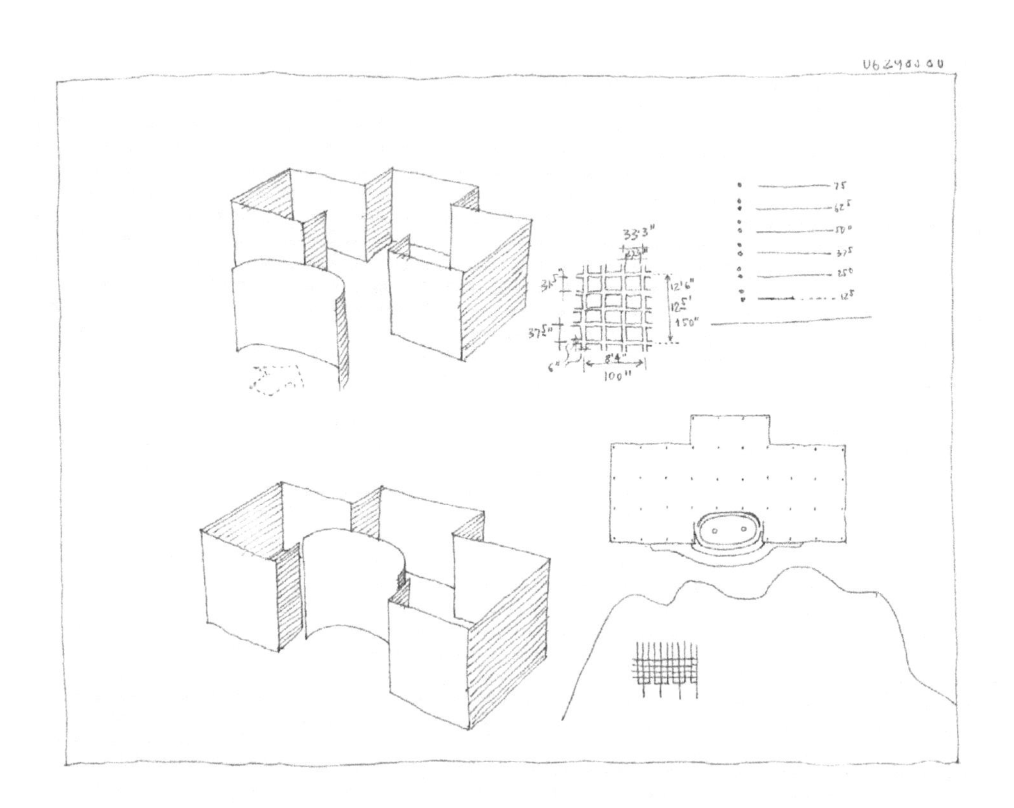

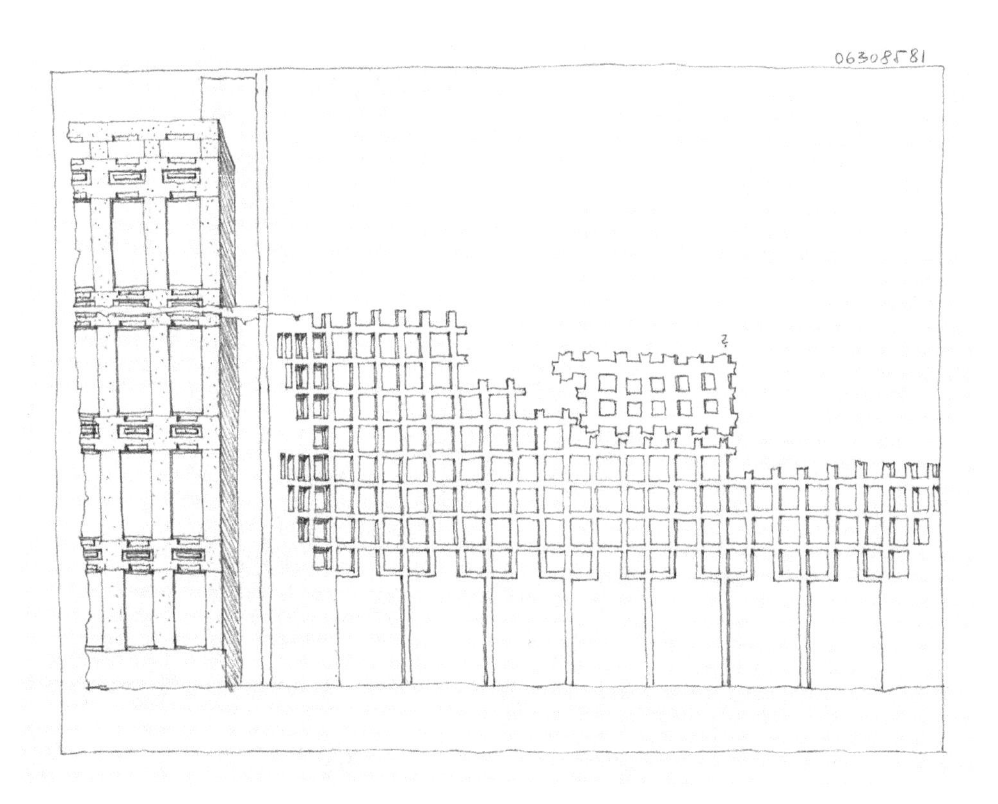

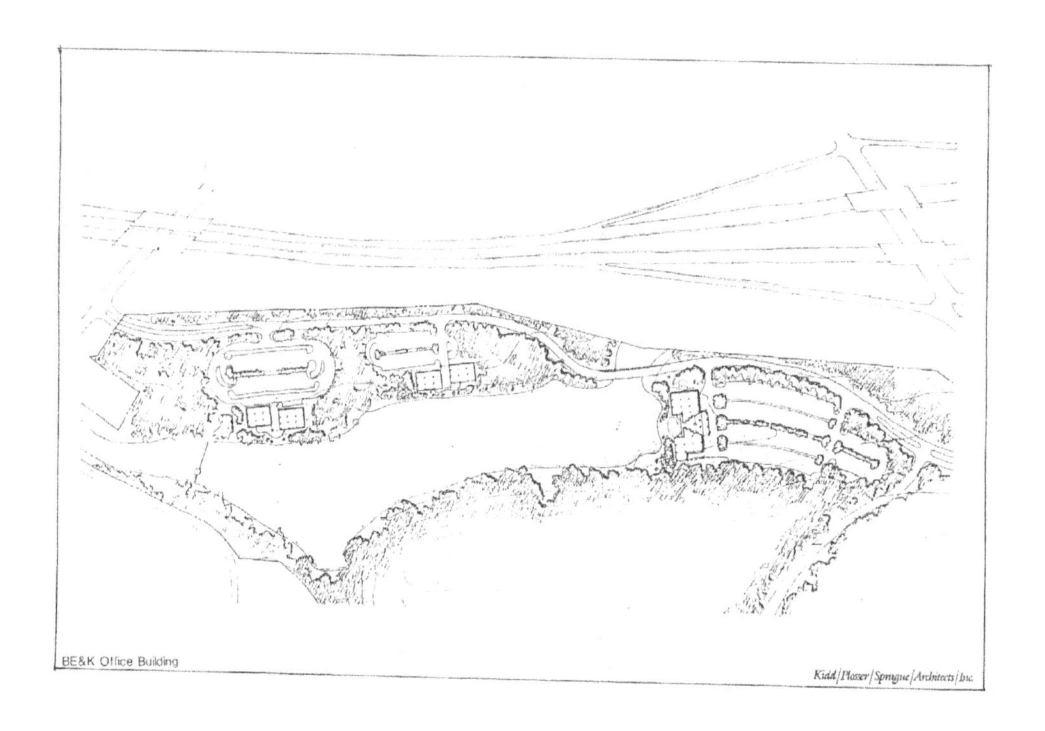
BE&K Office Building
Kidd/Plasser/Sprague/Architects/Inc.

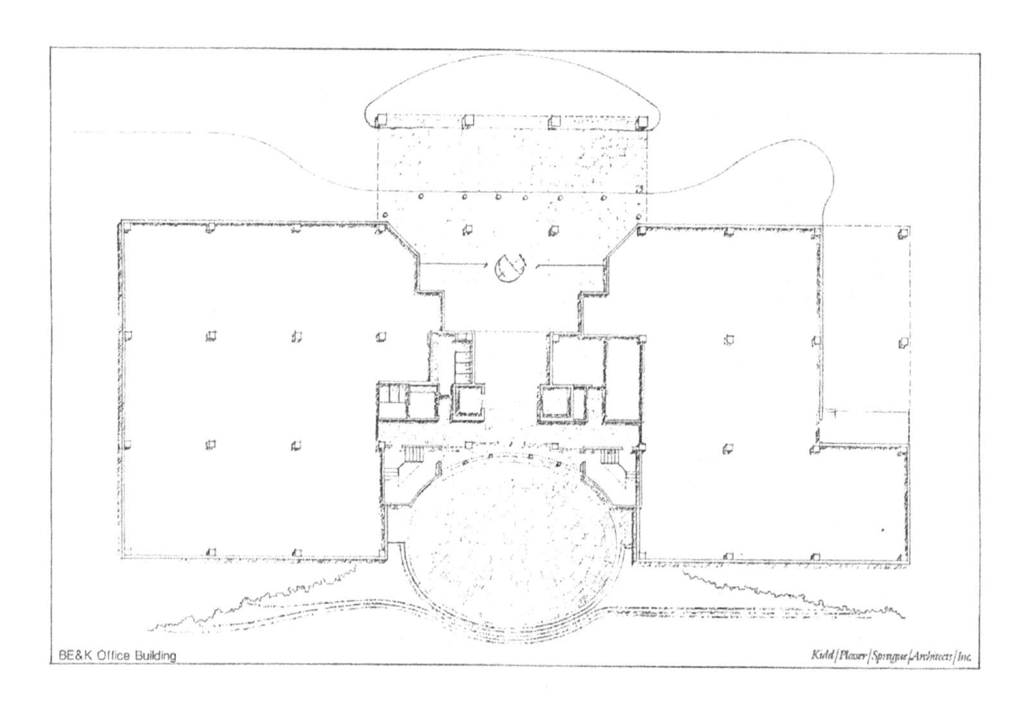
BE&K Office Building
Kidd/Plasser/Sprague/Architects/Inc.

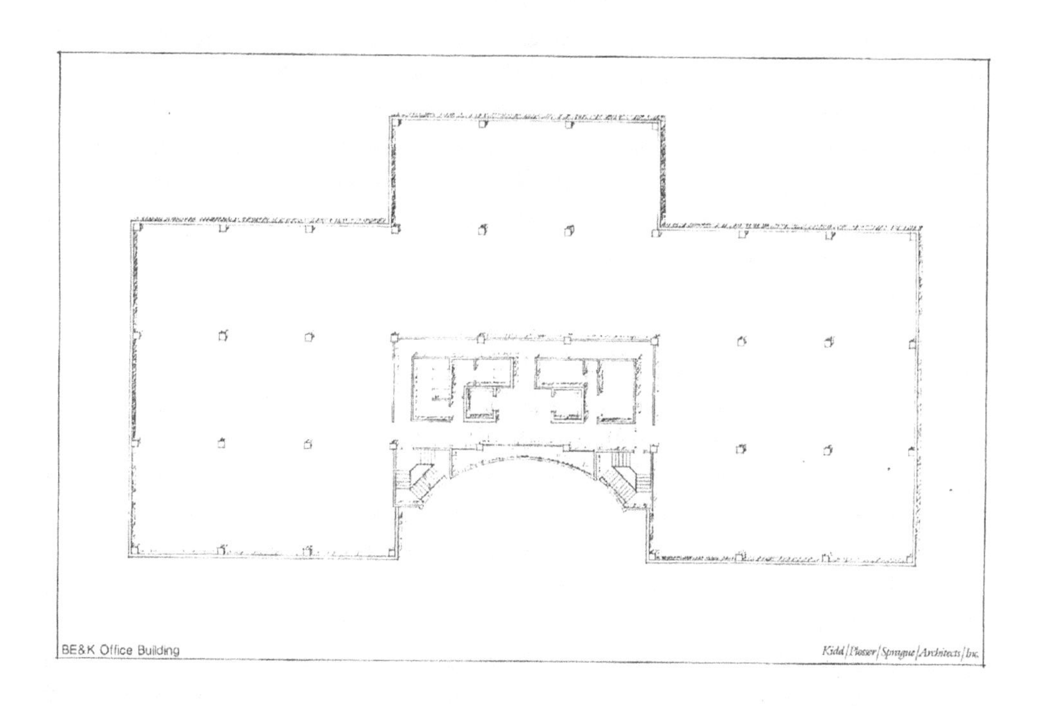
BE&K Office Building
Kidd/Plosser/Sprague/Architects/Inc.

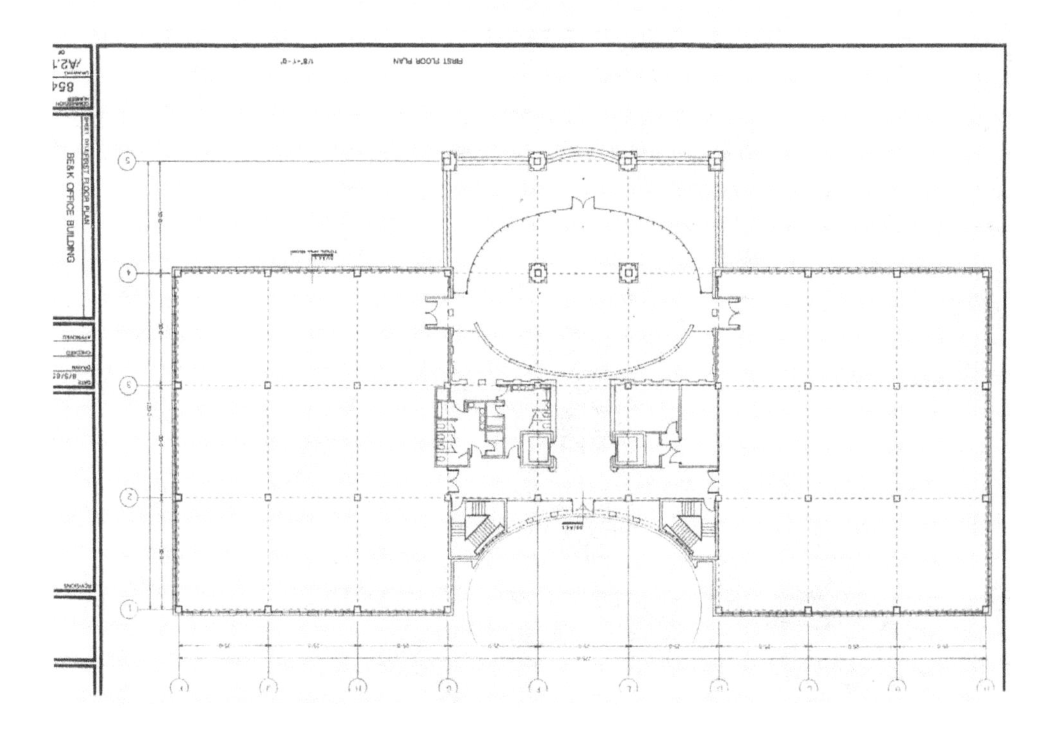
FIRST FLOOR PLAN
BE&K OFFICE BUILDING

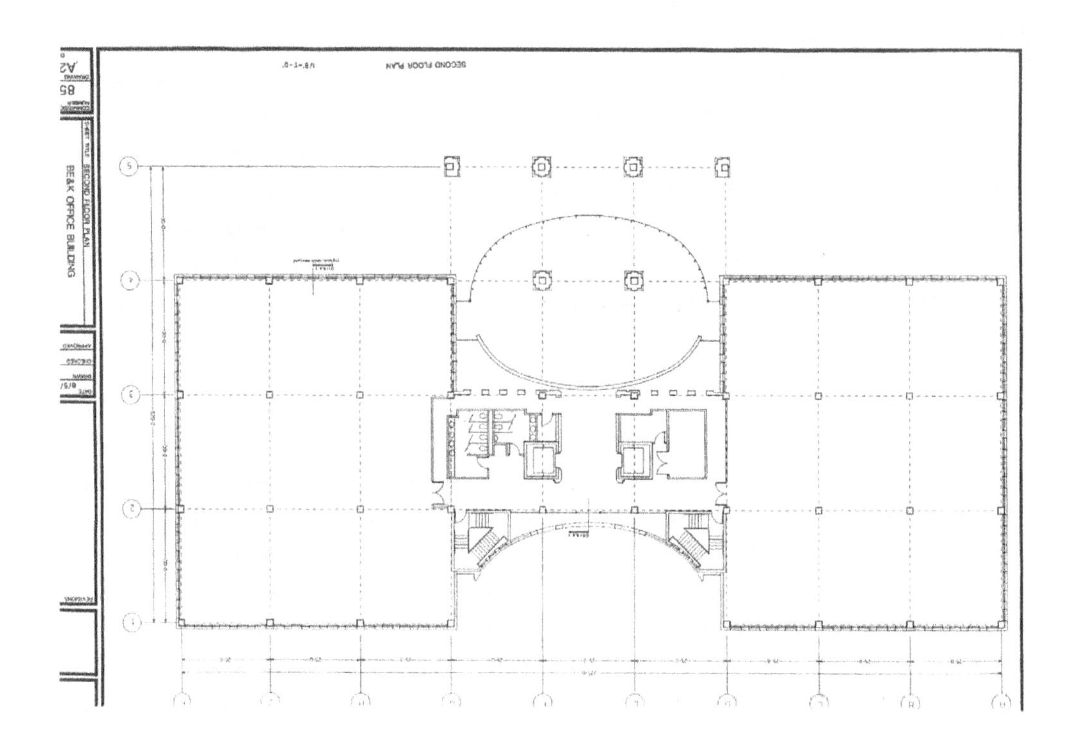
SECOND FLOOR PLAN
BE&K OFFICE BUILDING

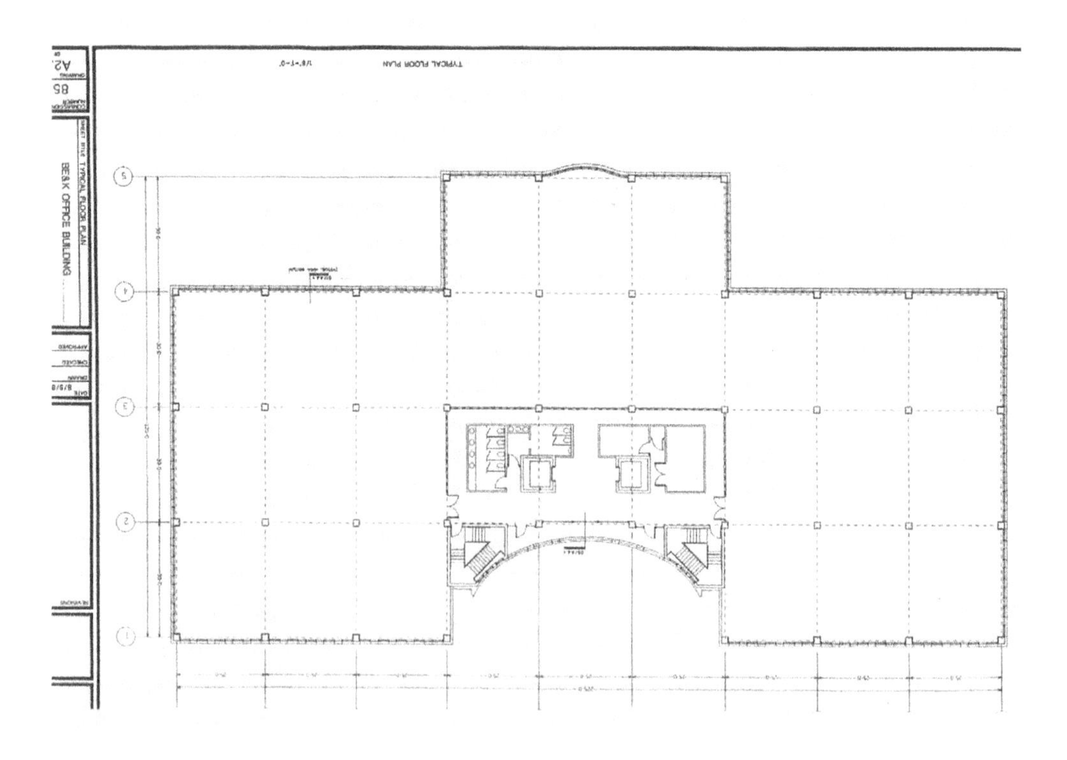
TYPICAL FLOOR PLAN
BE&K OFFICE BUILDING

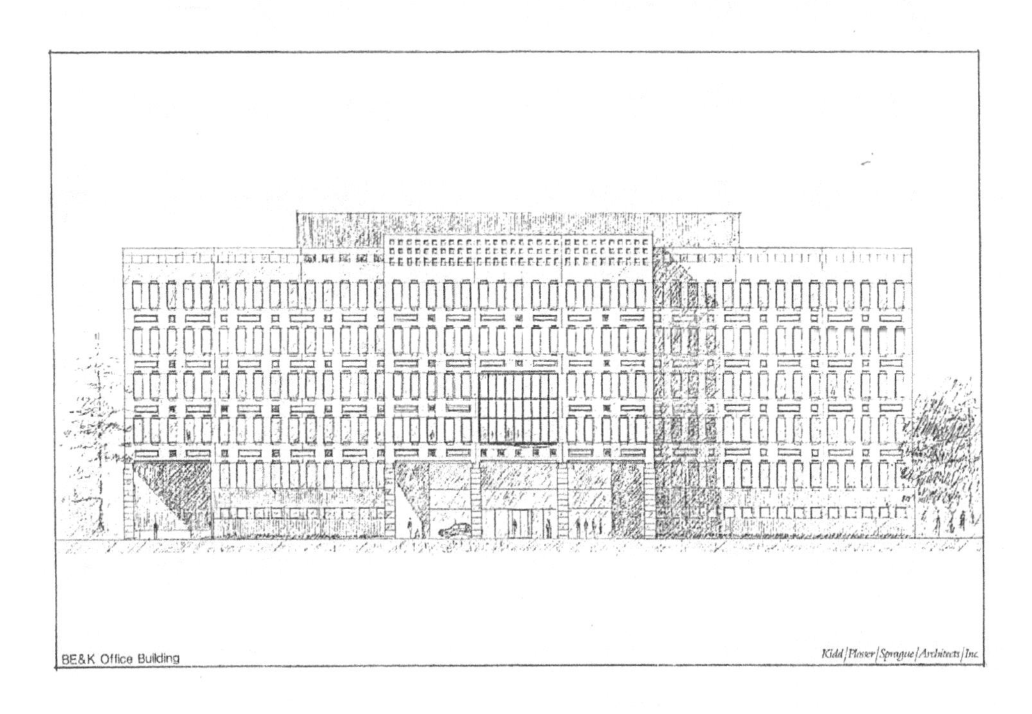
BE&K Office Building
Kidd/Plosser/Sprague/Architects/Inc.

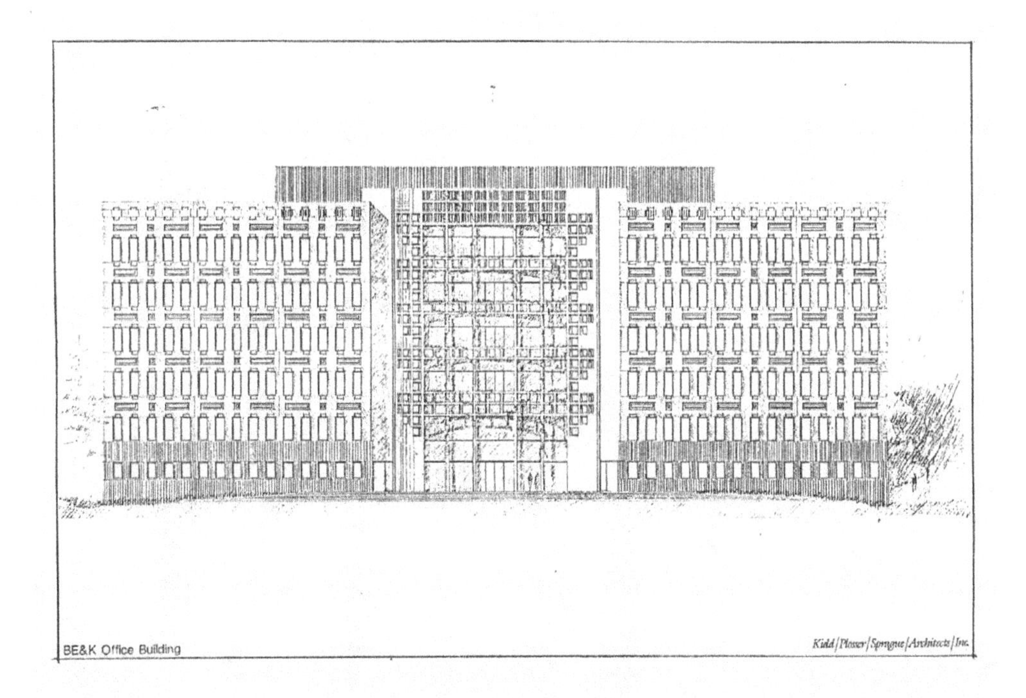
BE&K Office Building
Kidd/Plosser/Sprague/Architects/Inc.

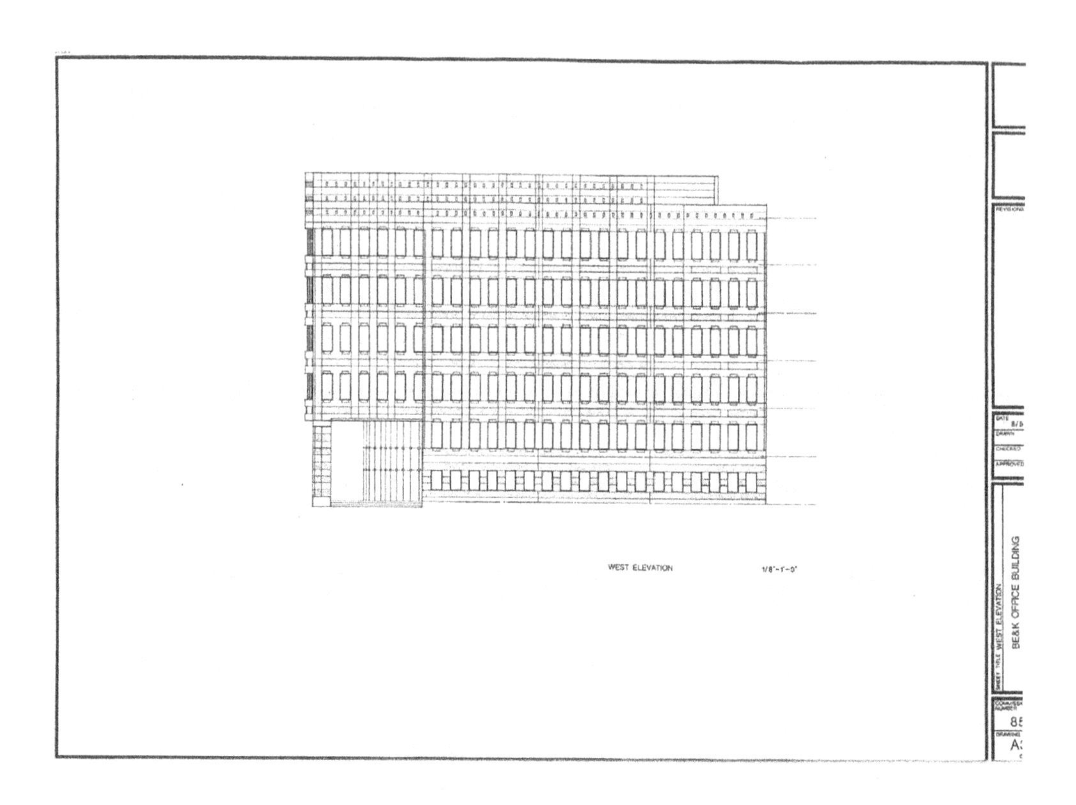
WEST ELEVATION
1/8"-1'-0"
SHEET TITLE WEST ELEVATION
BE&K OFFICE BUILDING

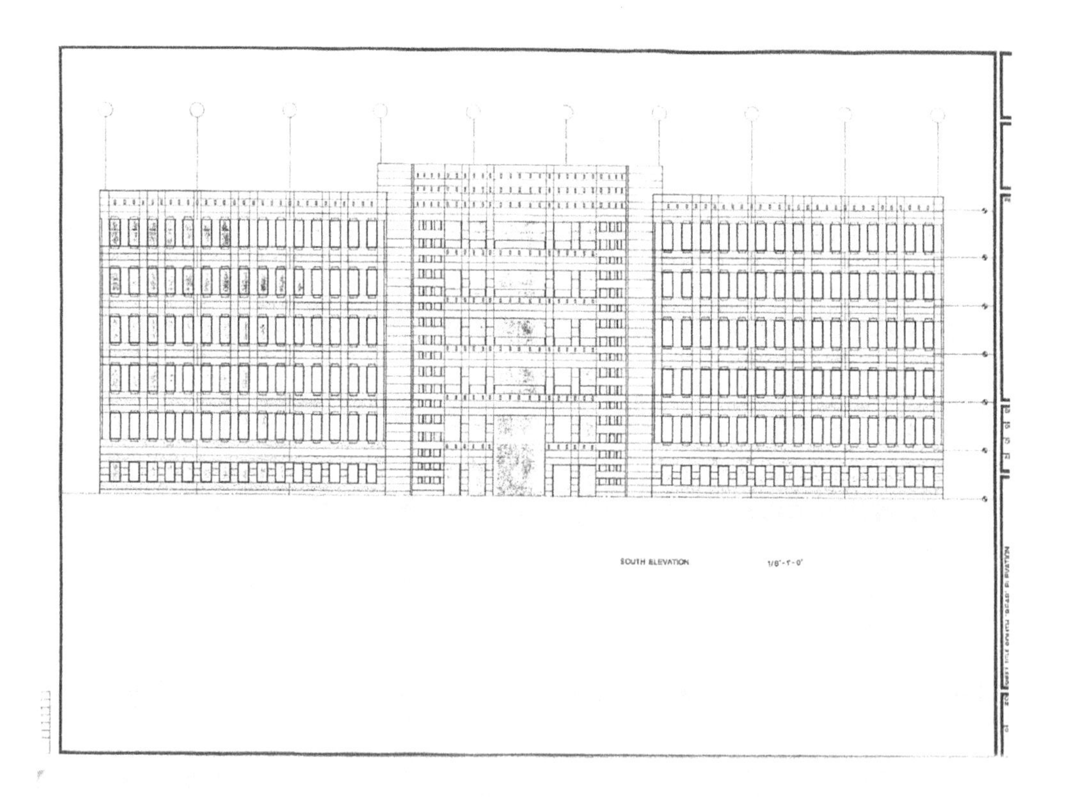
SOUTH ELEVATION
1/8"-1'-0"

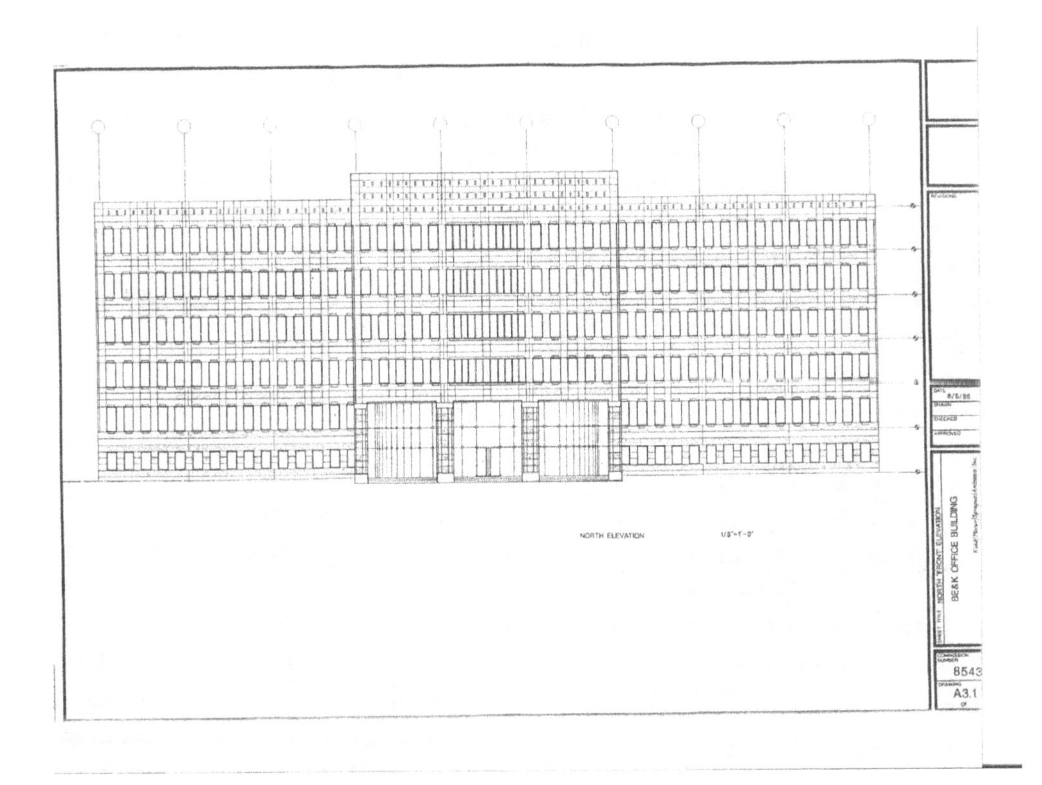
NORTH ELEVATION
BE&K OFFICE BUILDING
8543
A3.1

459
© 2007 Navteq
Google
Pointer 33° 24'35.92"N 86° 45'51.13"W
Streaming 100%
Eye alt 2809 ft

Chapter 3

CONSEQUENTIAL DELIBERATIONS

Pen Zen Diaries #3

Chapter 3

(P.D.Z.3)
Consequential Deliberation / The Peak Club"
Hongkong

This chapter contains the complete design phases of the "The Peak, Hongkong" competition, the subject of which was a design of a "gentleman's club". Since the requirement was to apply aspects of ancient Chinese philosophical treaties (I Ching, Feng Shui), I interpreted myth as context and as a narrative on the belief of a people.

Using my method of surface drawings, the "general space print" referred to the ontological layer, the "particular space print" to the belief layer, and the "space print fragments" to the cosmic layer.

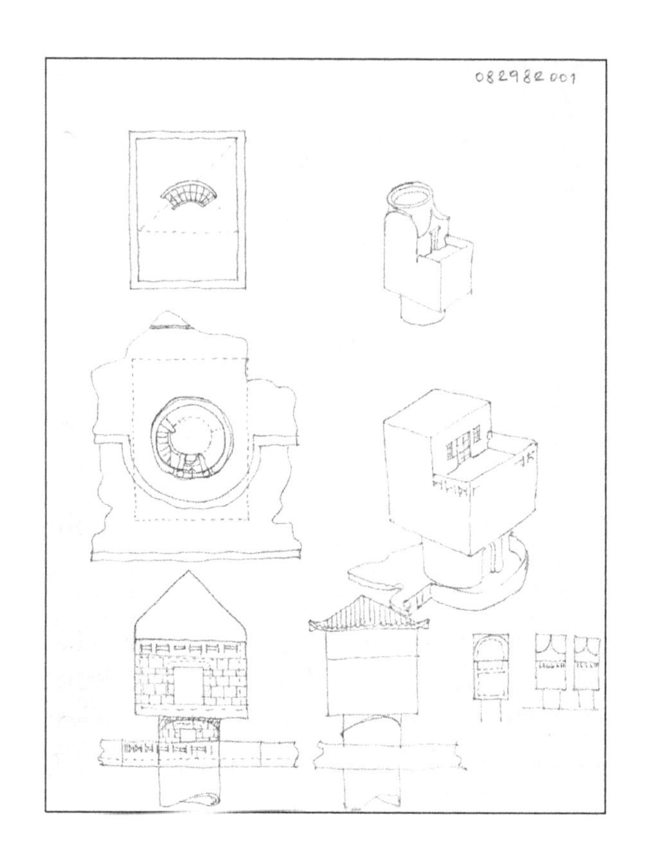
082982001

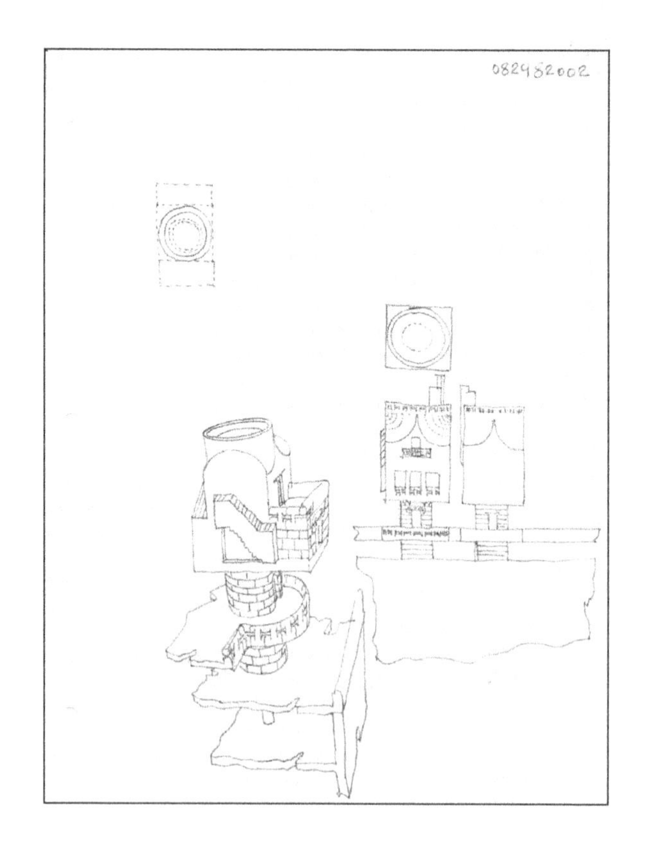
082982002

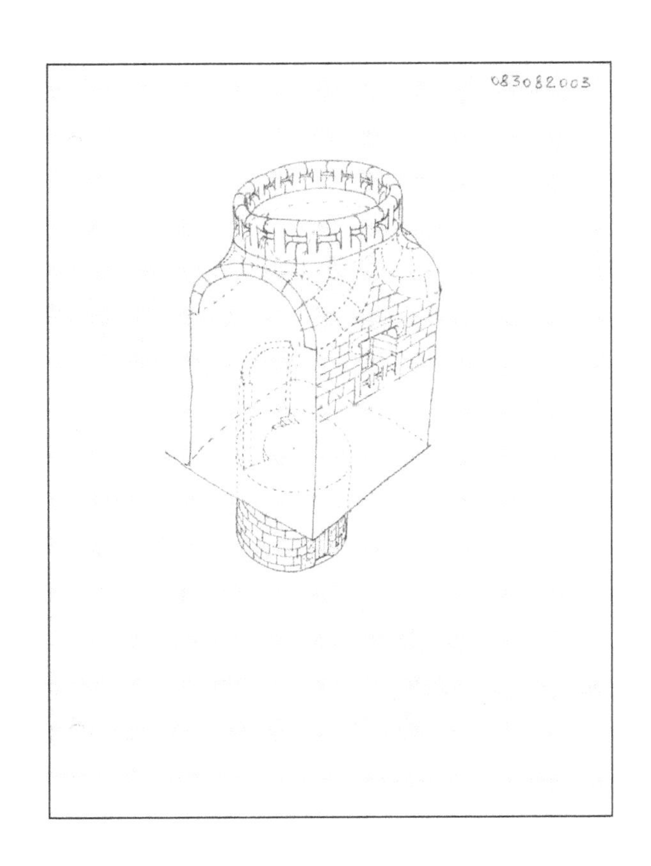
083082003

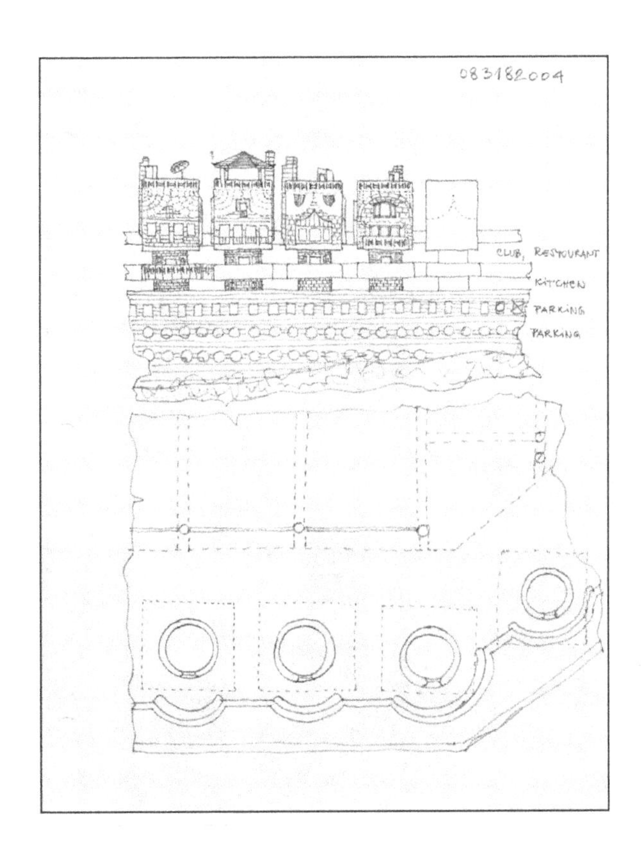
083182004
CLUB, RESTOURANT
KITCHEN
PARKING
PARKING

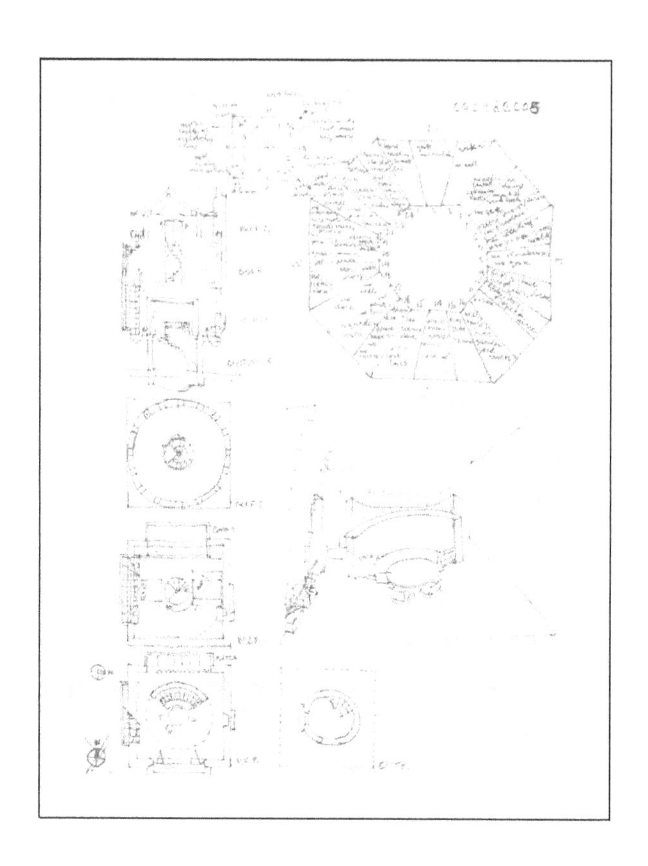

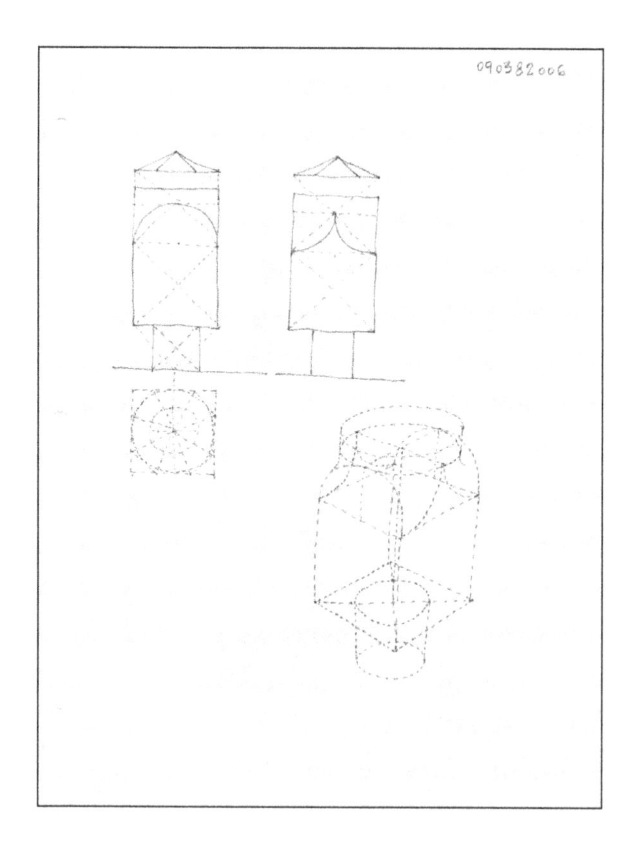
090382006

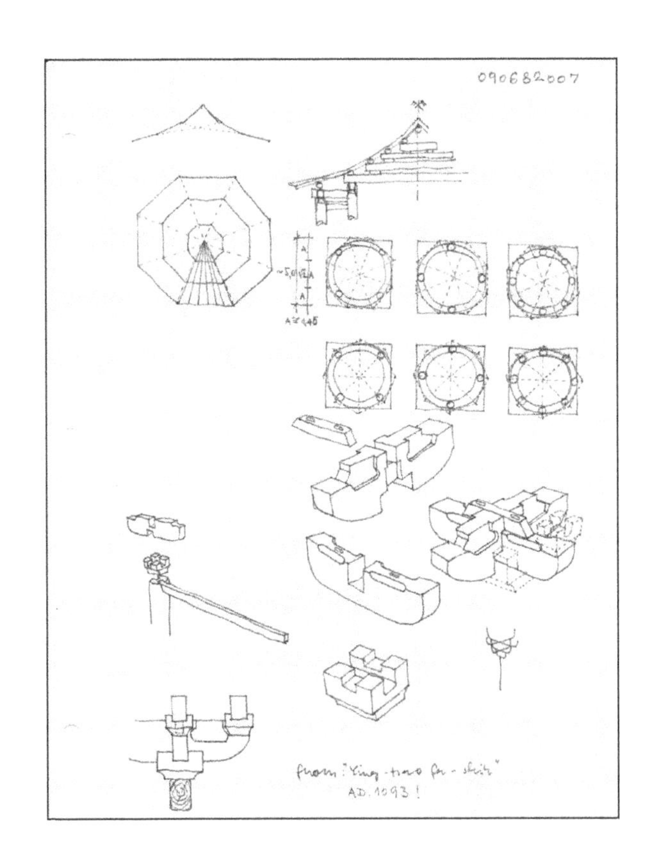
090682007
from: "Ying-tsao fa-shih"
AD. 1093!

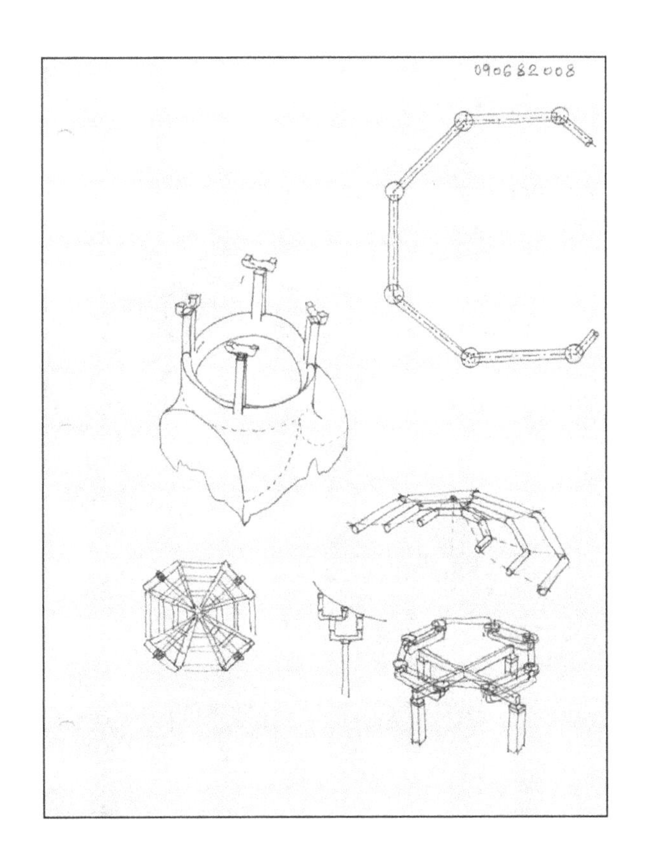
090682008

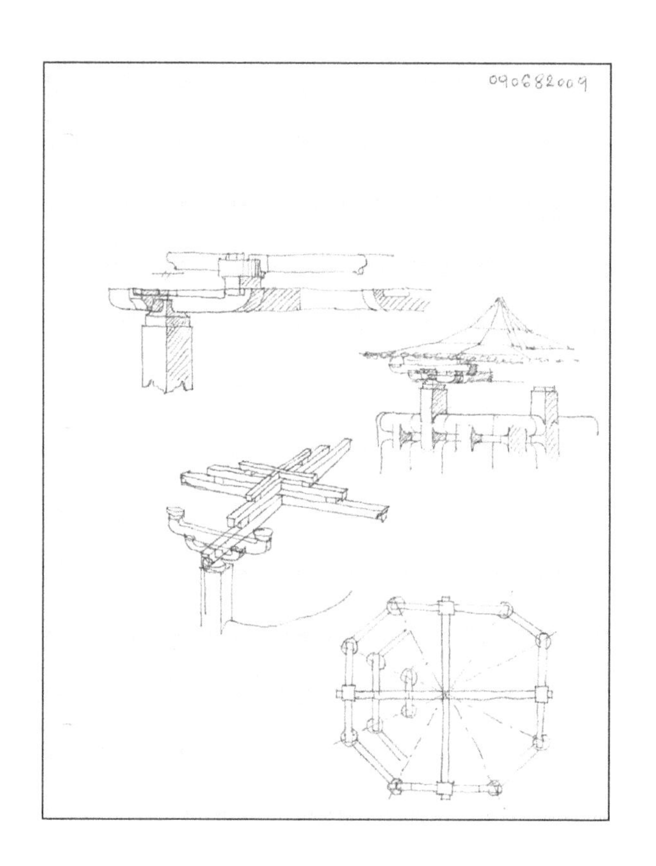
090682009

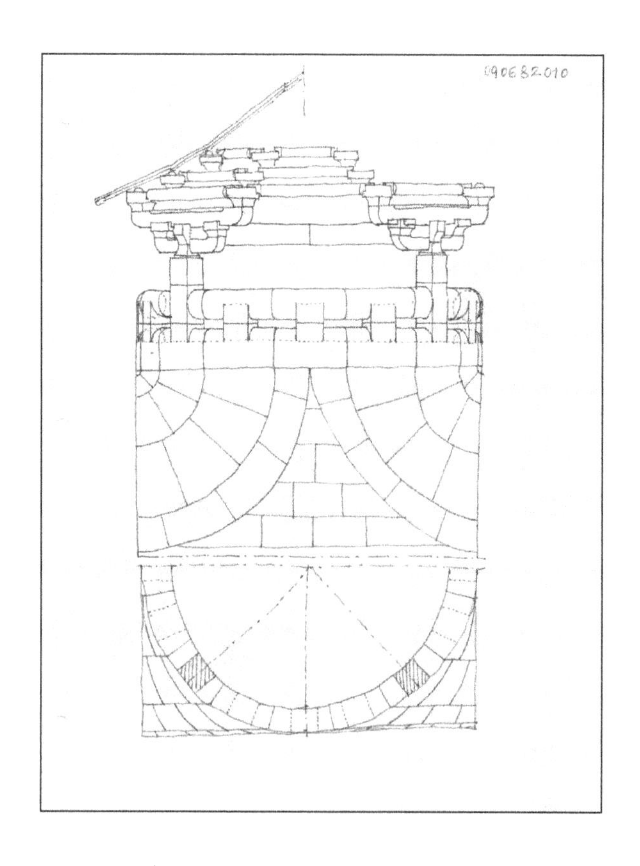
090682010

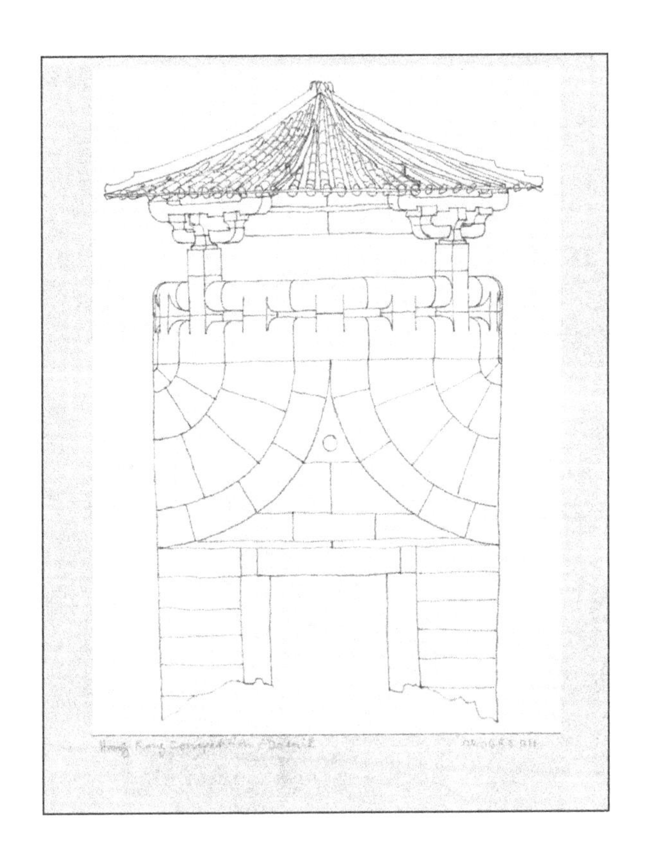
Hong Kong Competition / Detail

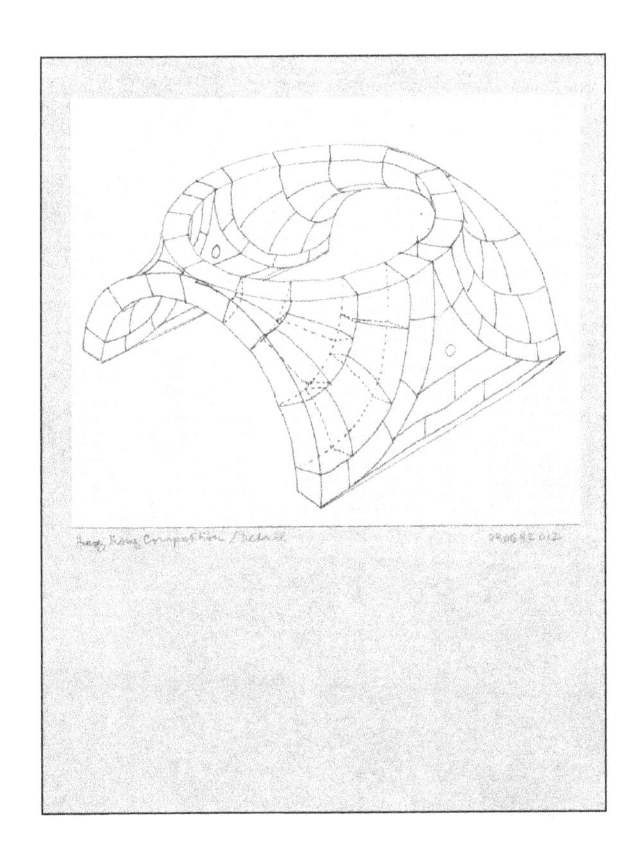
Hong Kong Competition / Detail

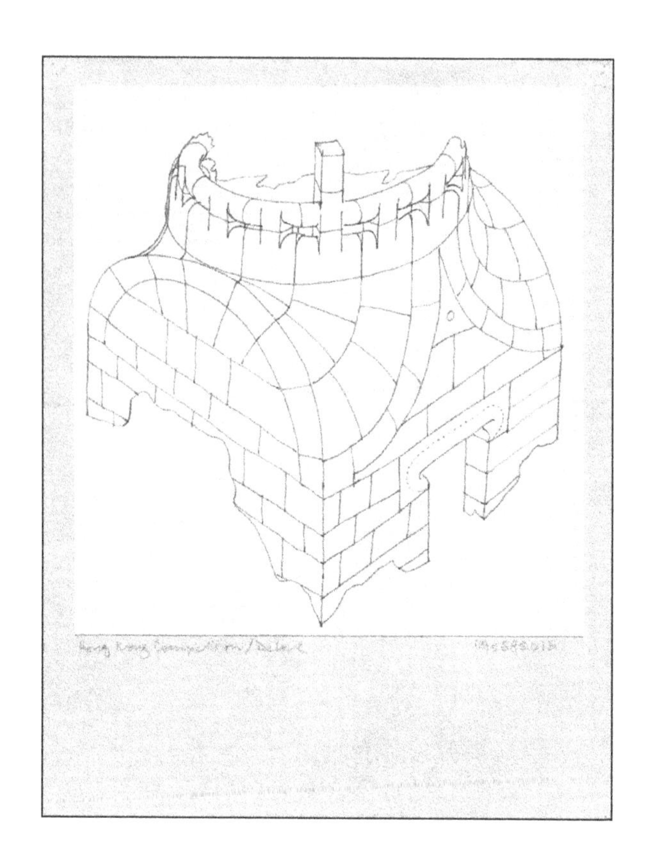

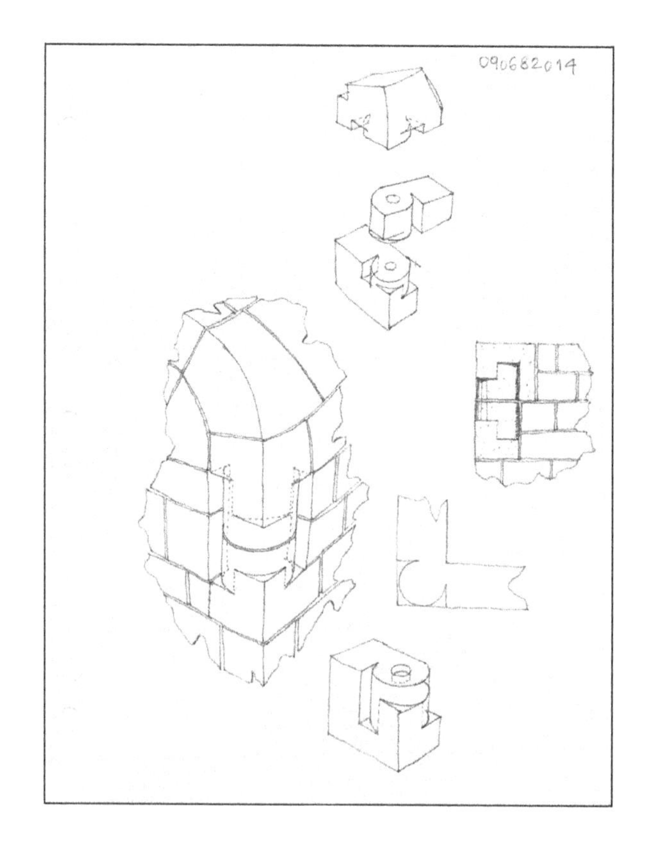
090682014

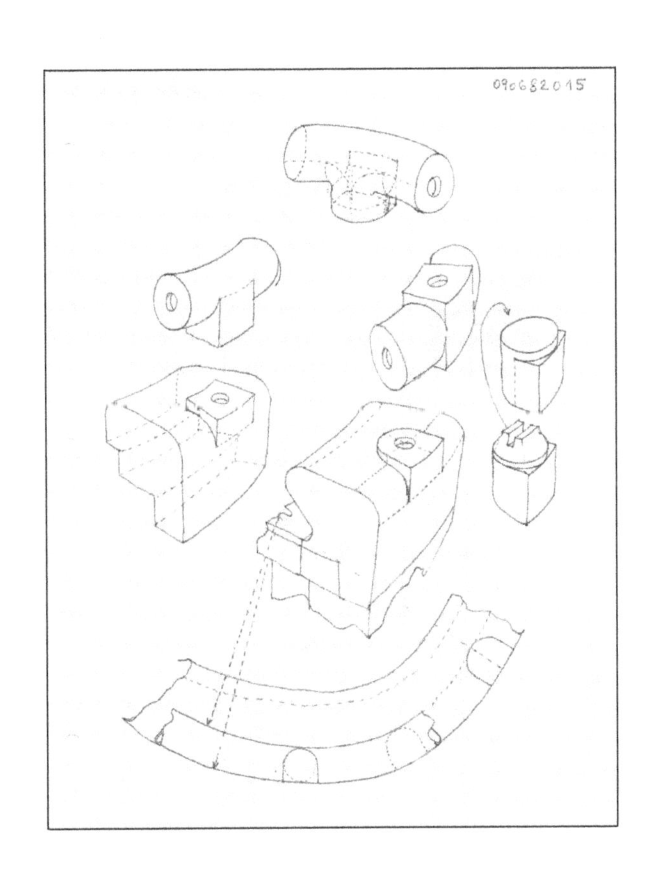
090682015

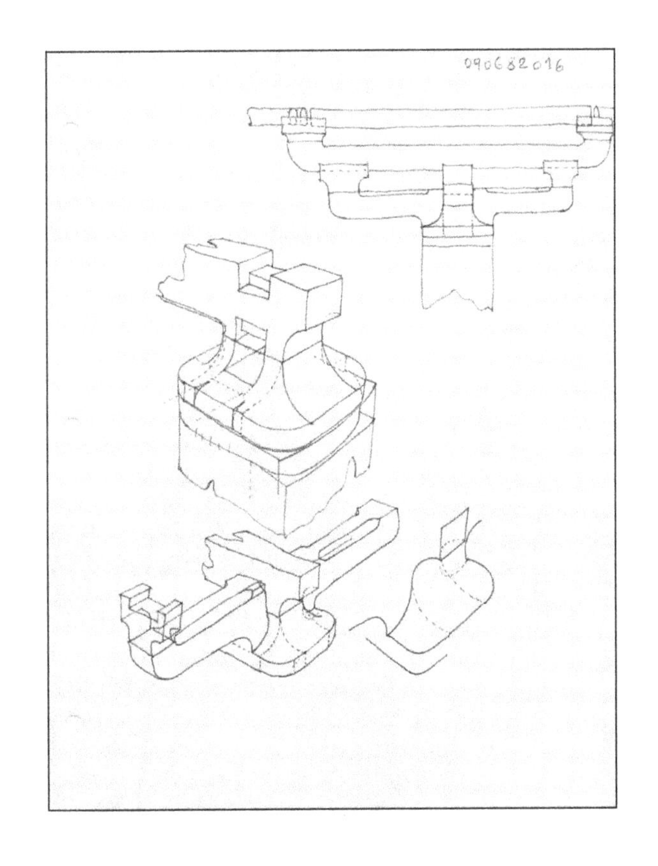
090682016

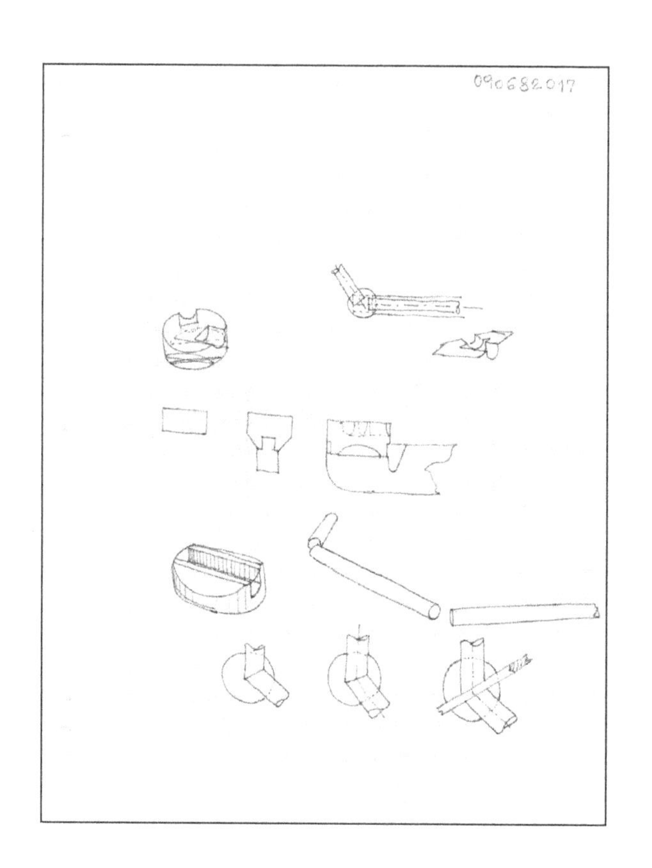
090682017

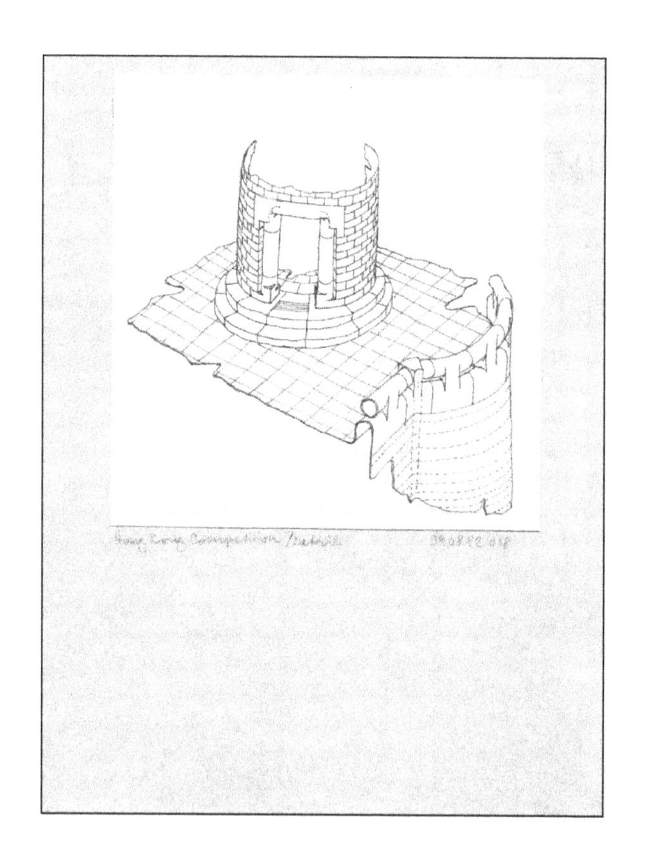
Hong Kong Competition

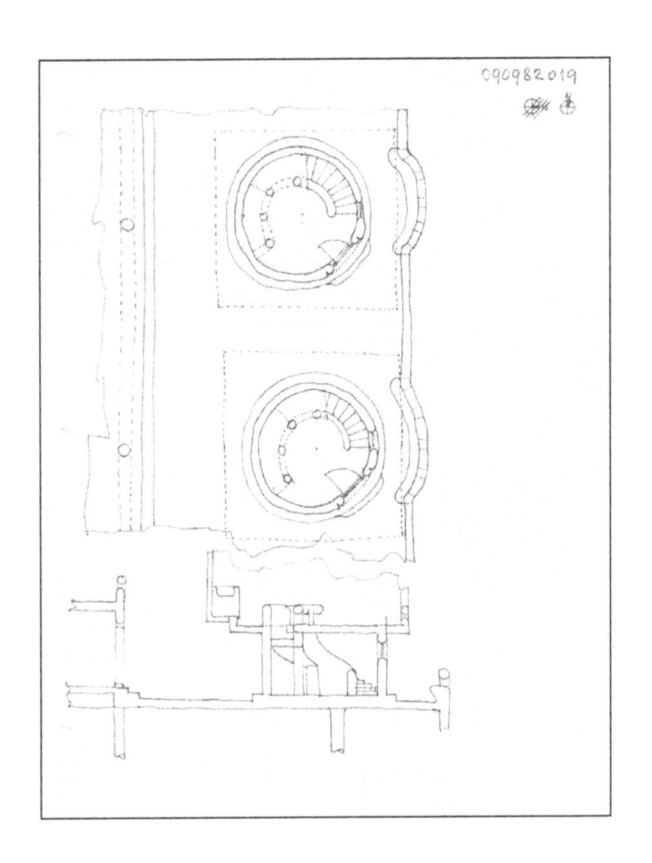
090982019

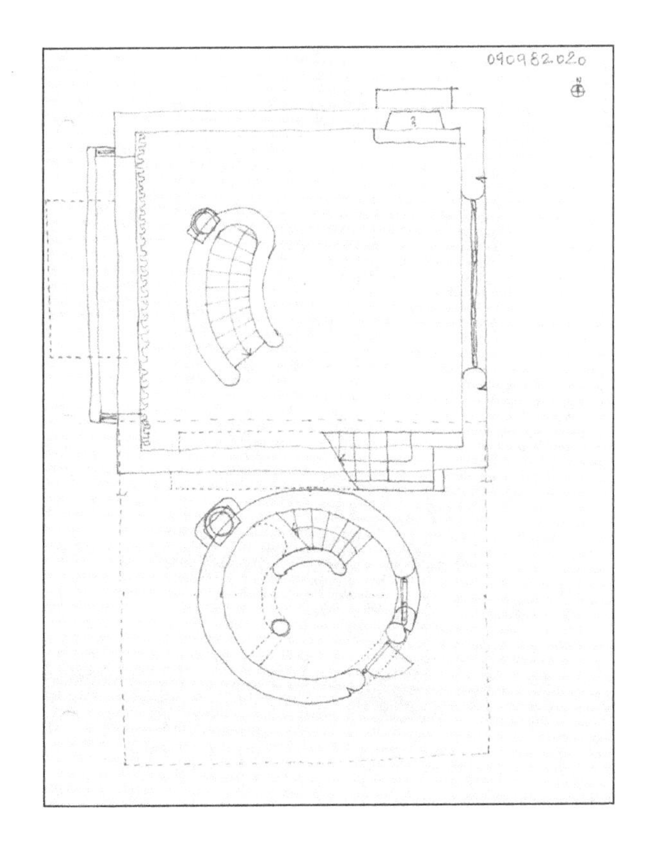
090982020

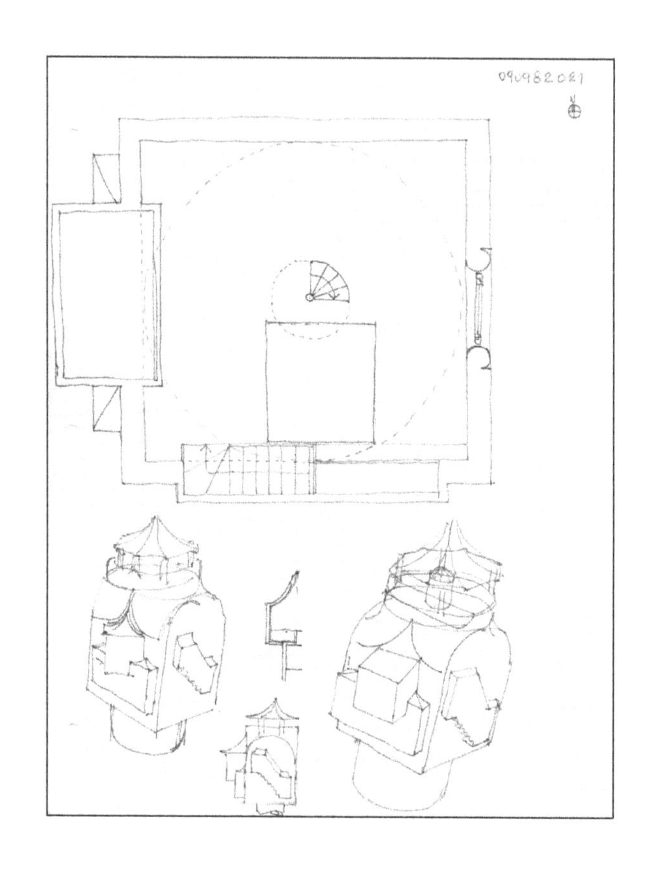
090982.021

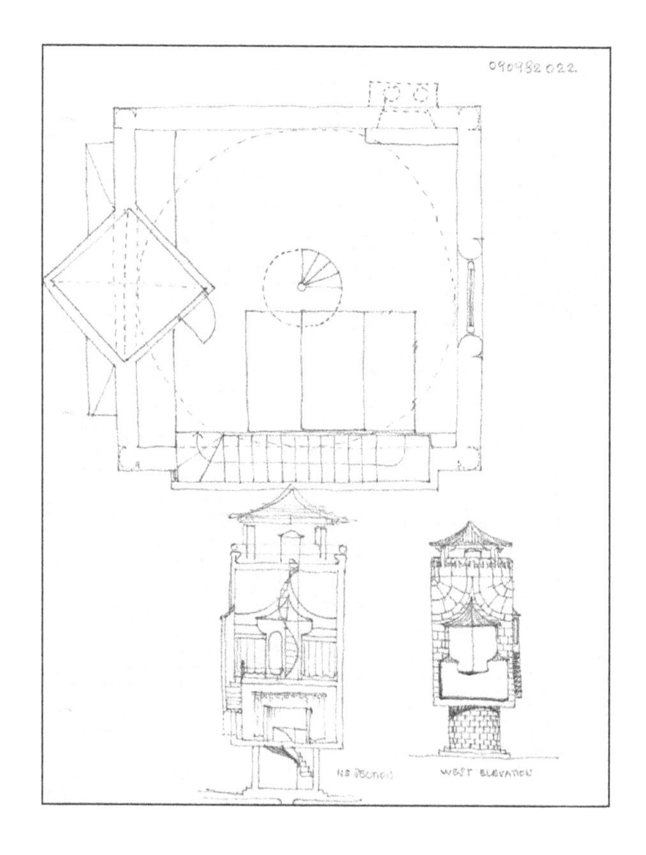
090982.022
NS SECTION
WEST ELEVATION

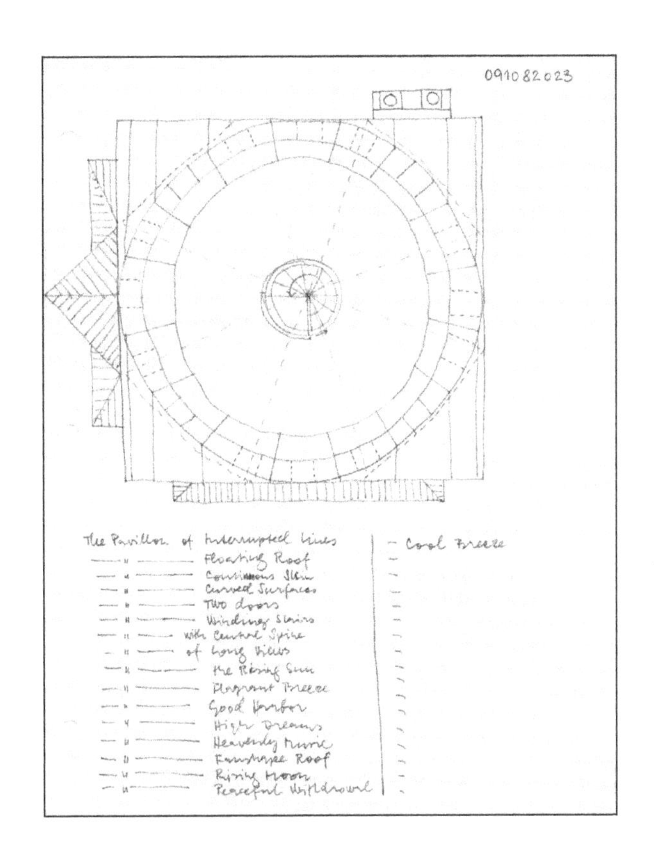
091082023
The Pavillon of Interrupted Lines
Floating Roof
Continuous Skin
Curved Surfaces
Two doors
Winding Stairs
with Central Spine
of Long Views
the Rising Sun
Fragrant Breeze
Good Harbor
High Dreams
Heavenly Music
Fanshape Roof
Rising Moon
Peaceful Withdrawal
Cool Breeze

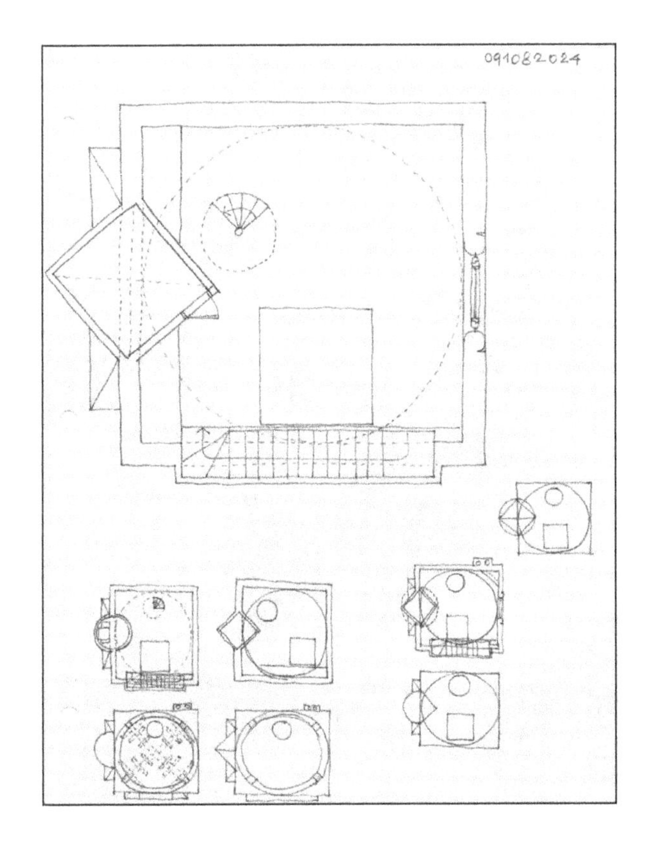
091082024

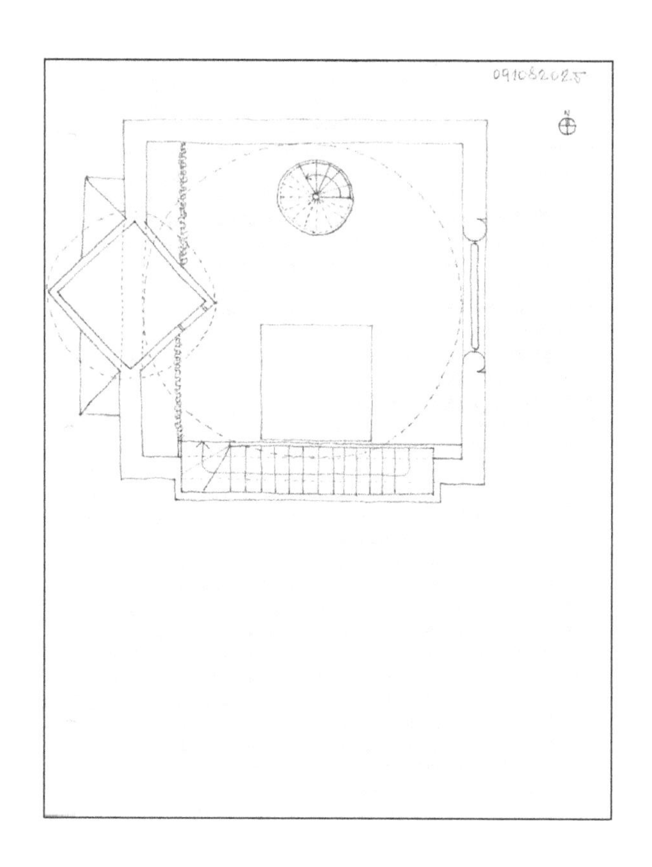
091082025
N

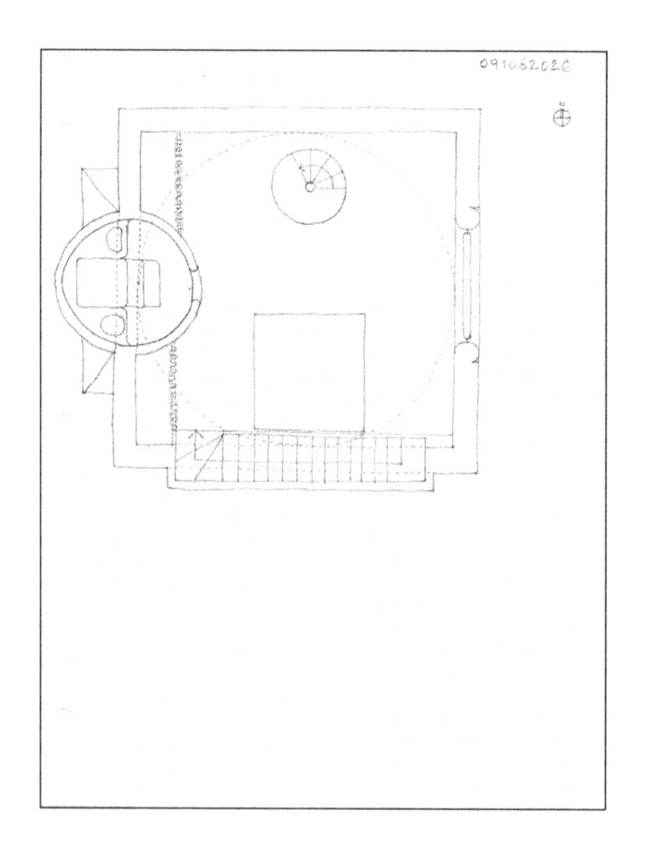
091082026
N

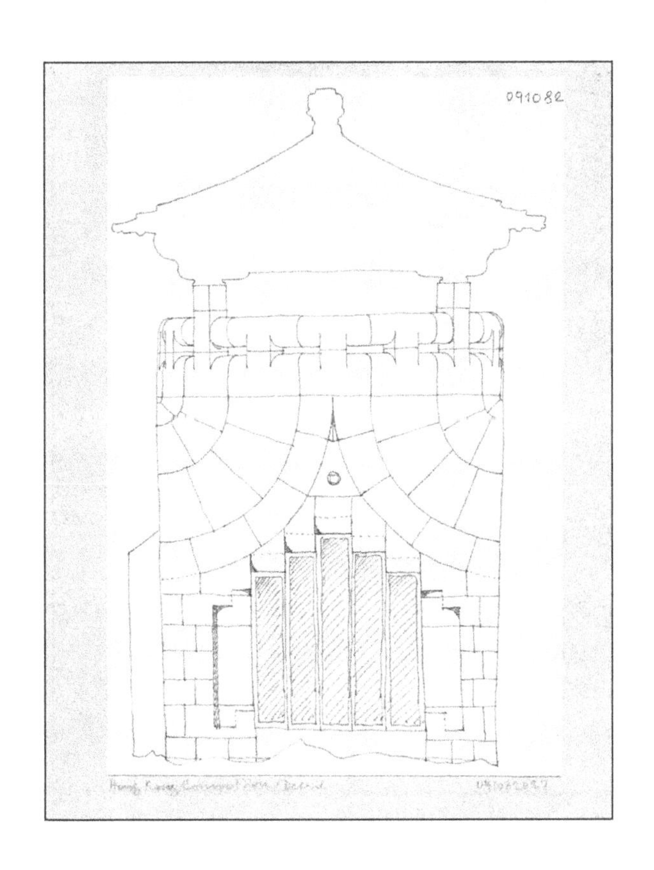
091082

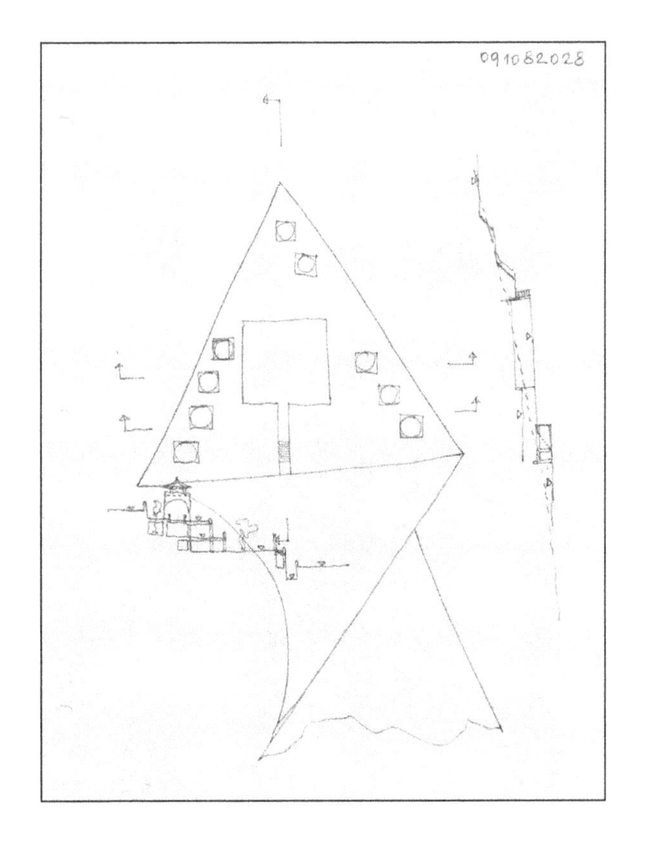
091082028

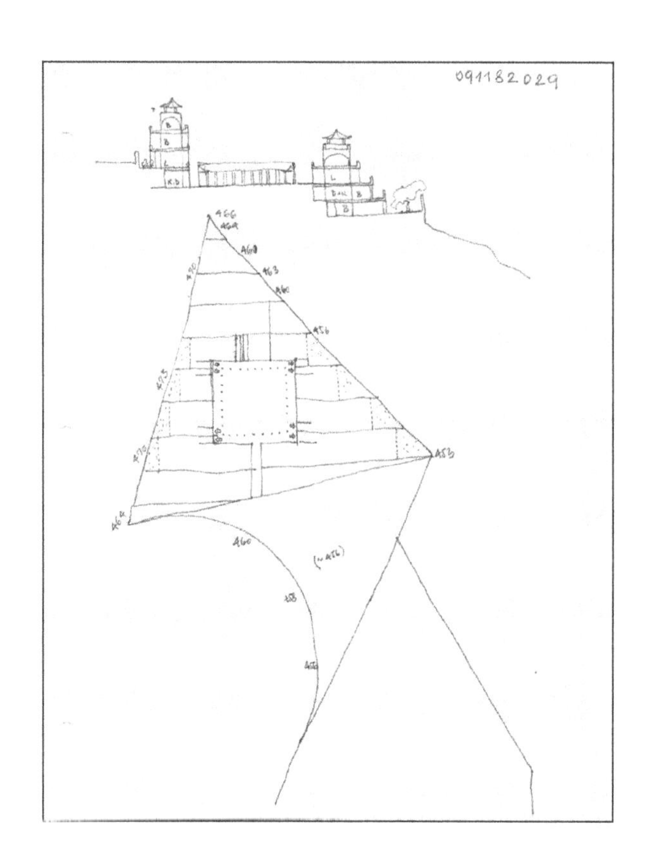
091182029

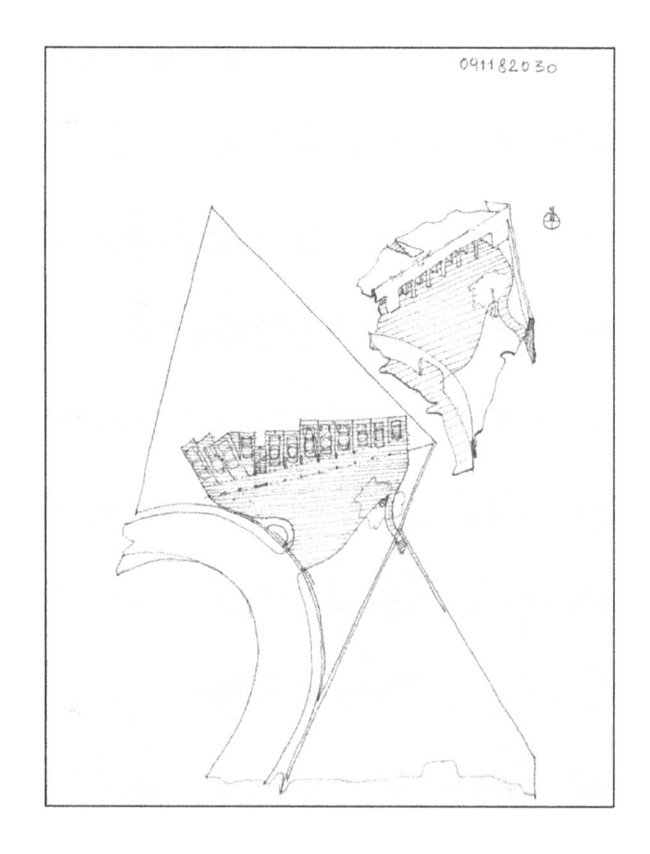
091182030

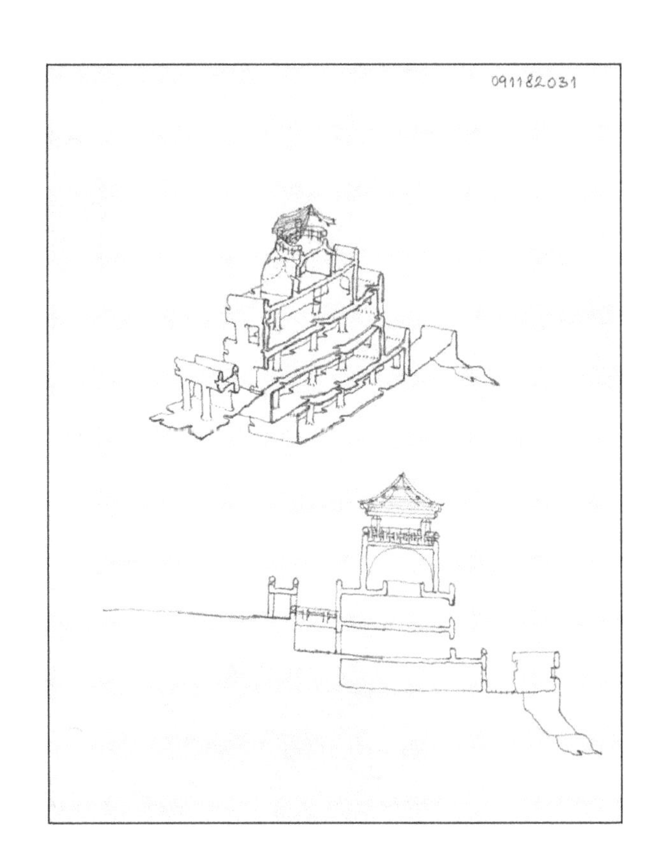
091182031

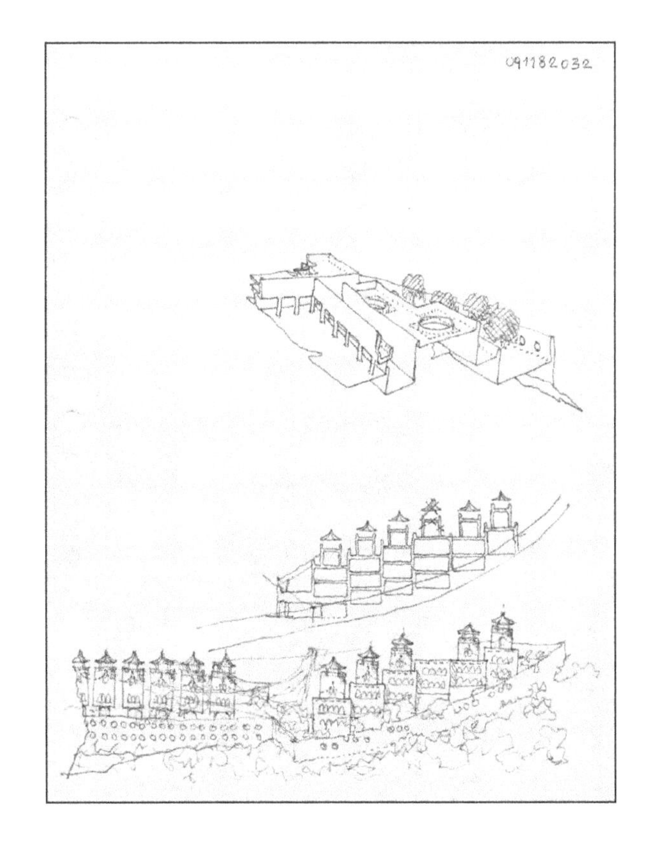
091182032

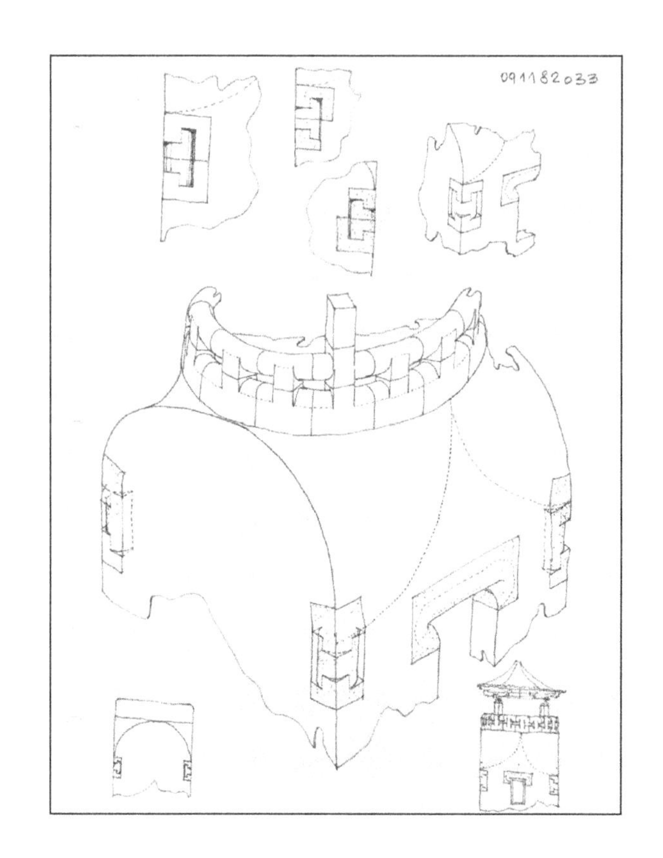
091182033

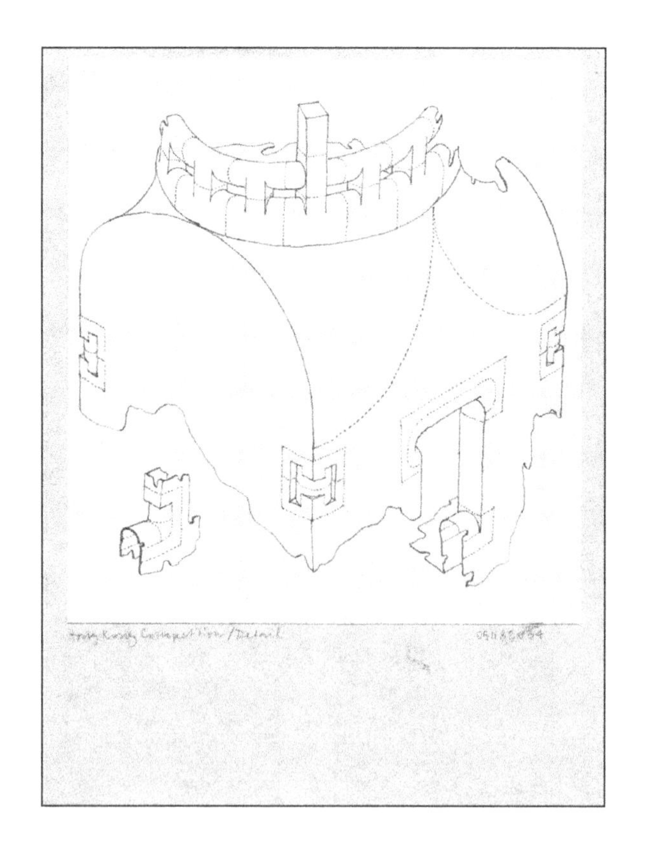
Competition / Detail

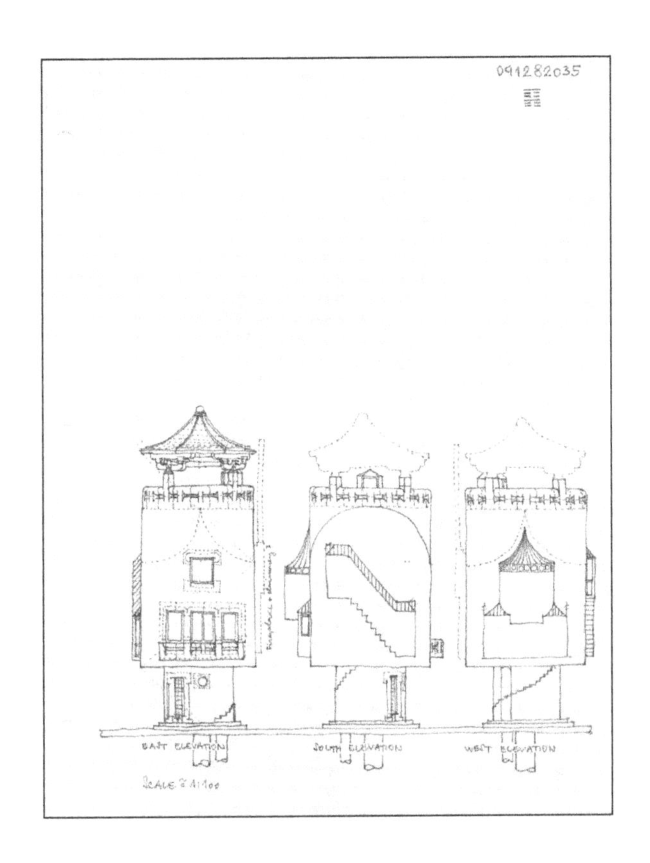
091282035
EAST ELEVATION
SOUTH ELEVATION
WEST ELEVATION

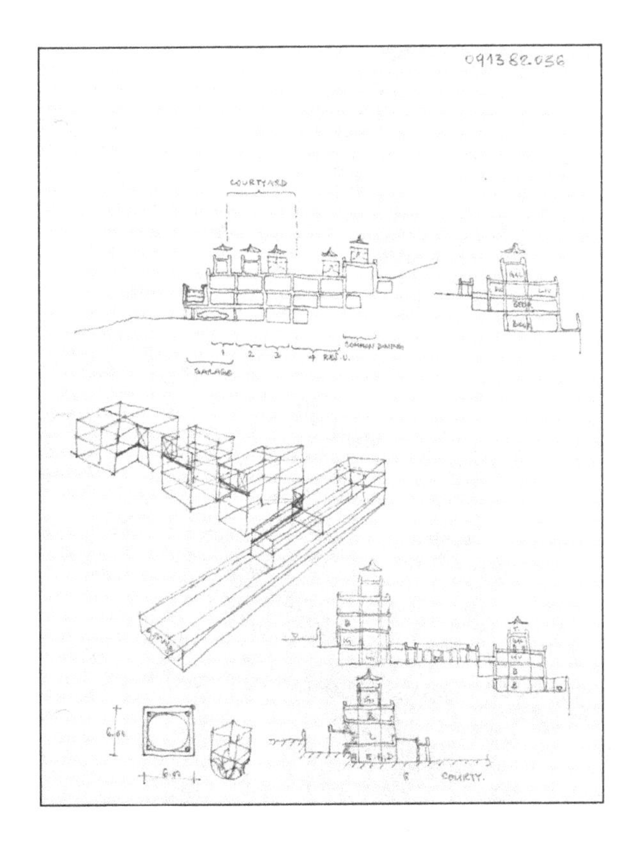
091382.036
COURTYARD
GARAGE
COMMON DINING
COURTY.

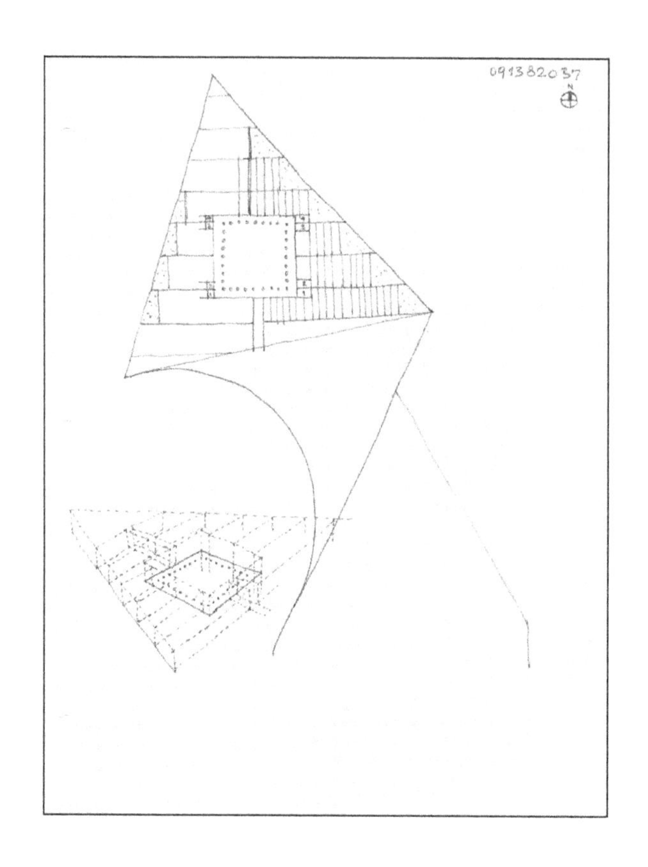
091382037
N

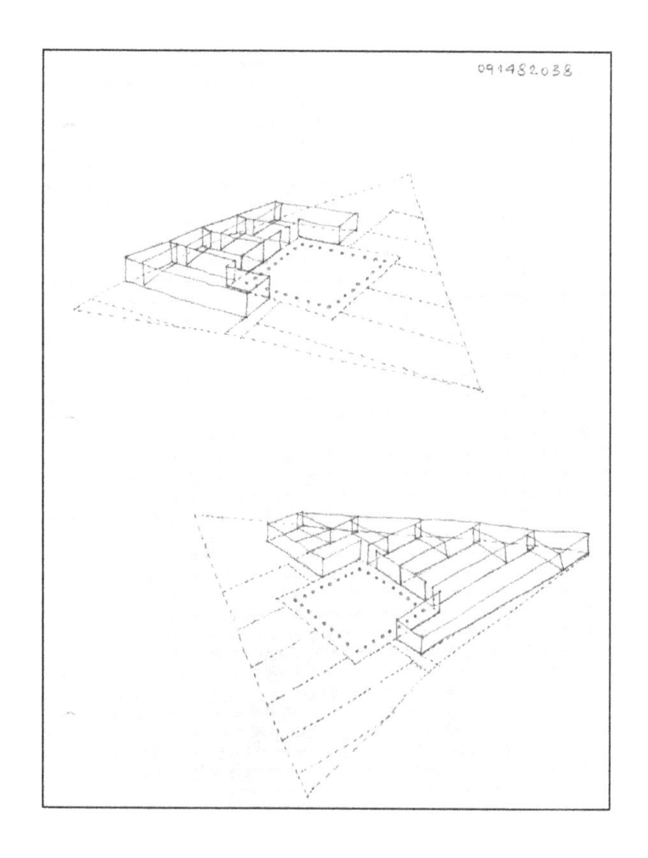
091482038

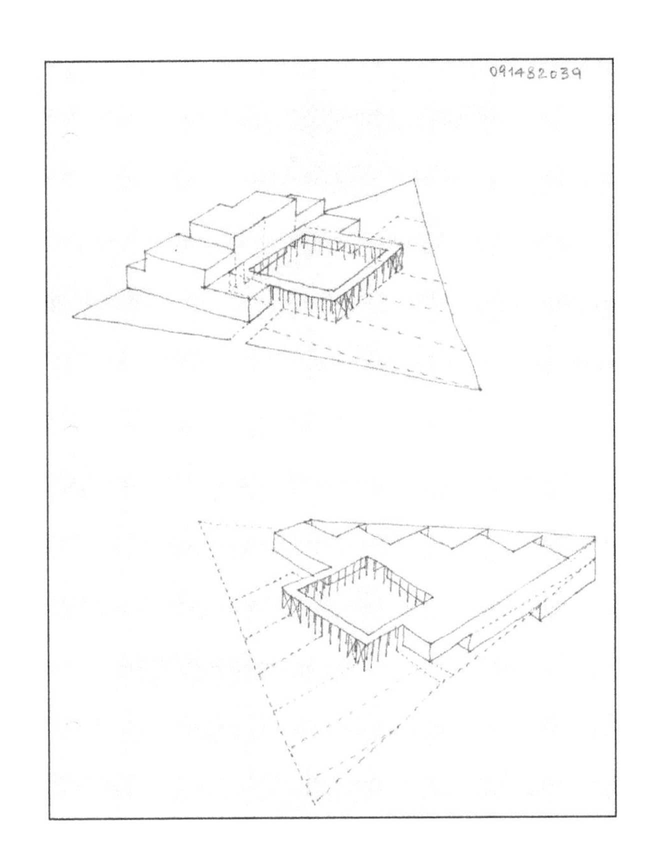
091482039

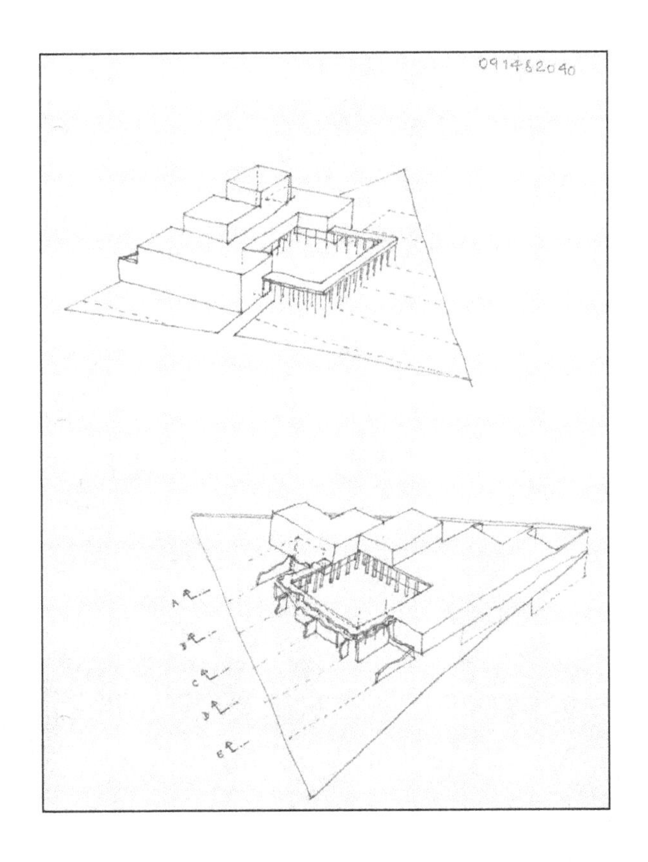
091482040

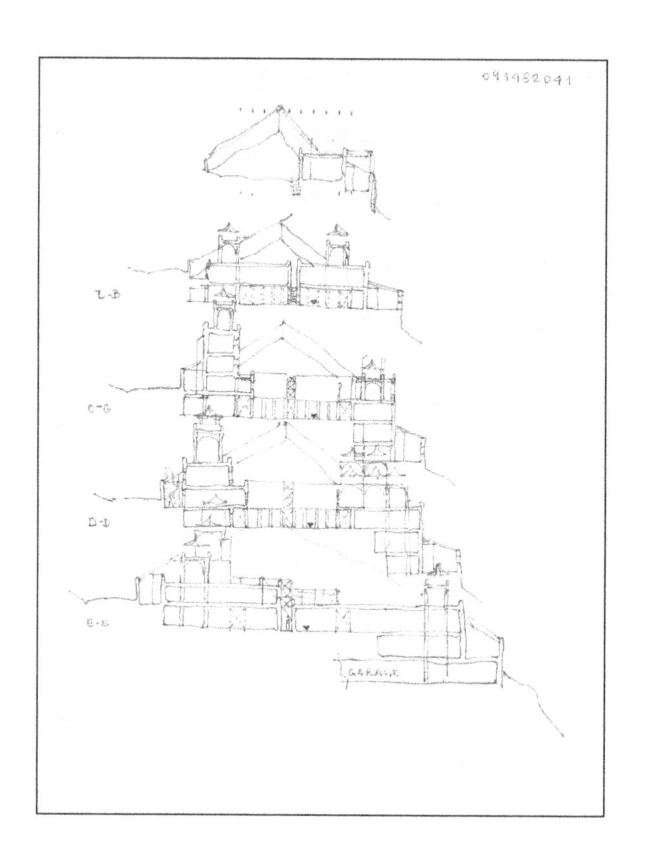
091482041
GARAGE

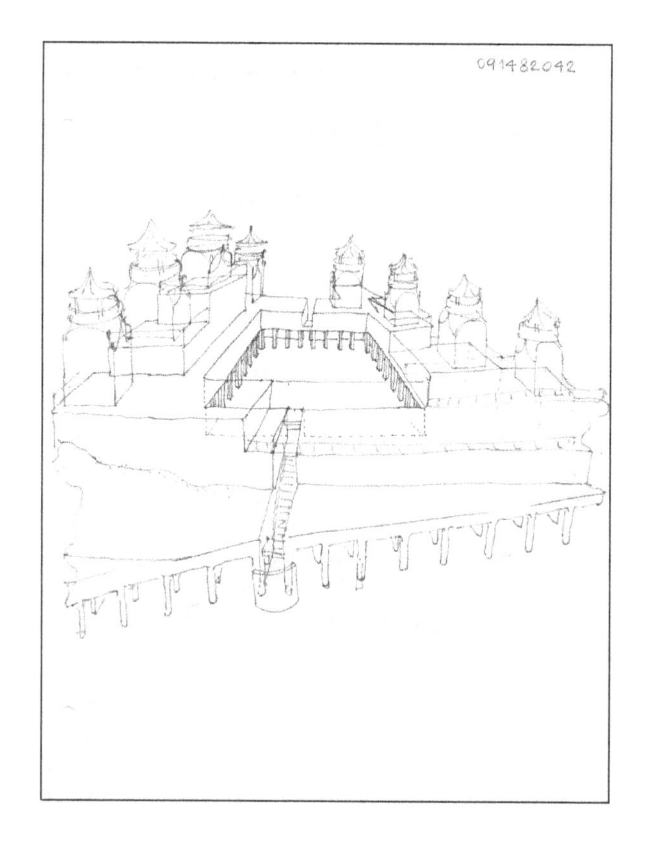
091482042

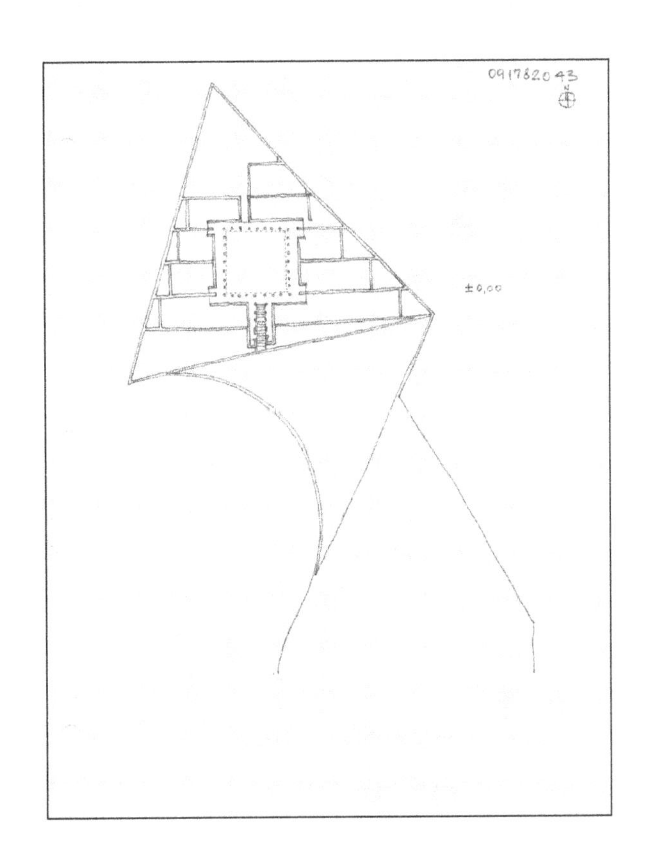
091782043
±0,00

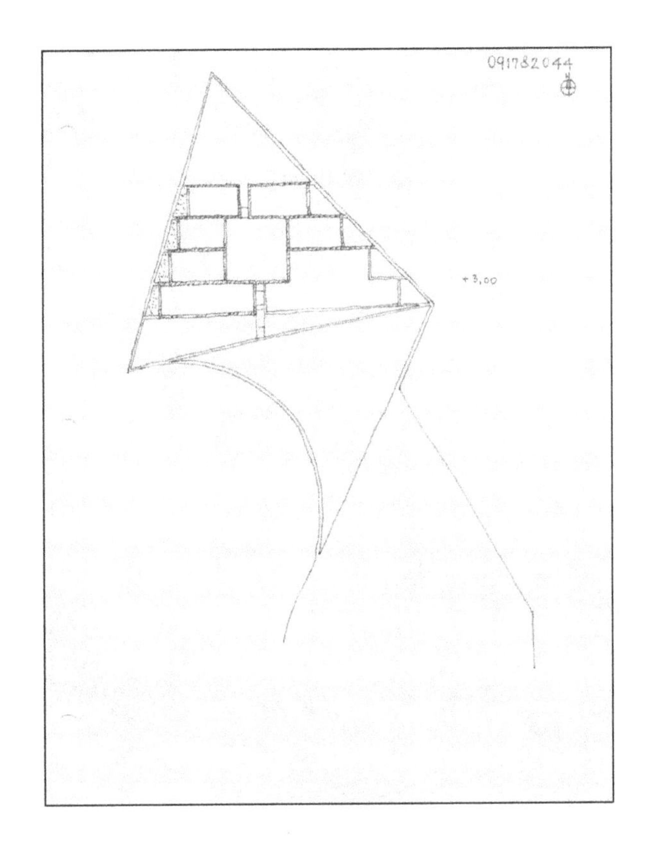
091782044
+3,00

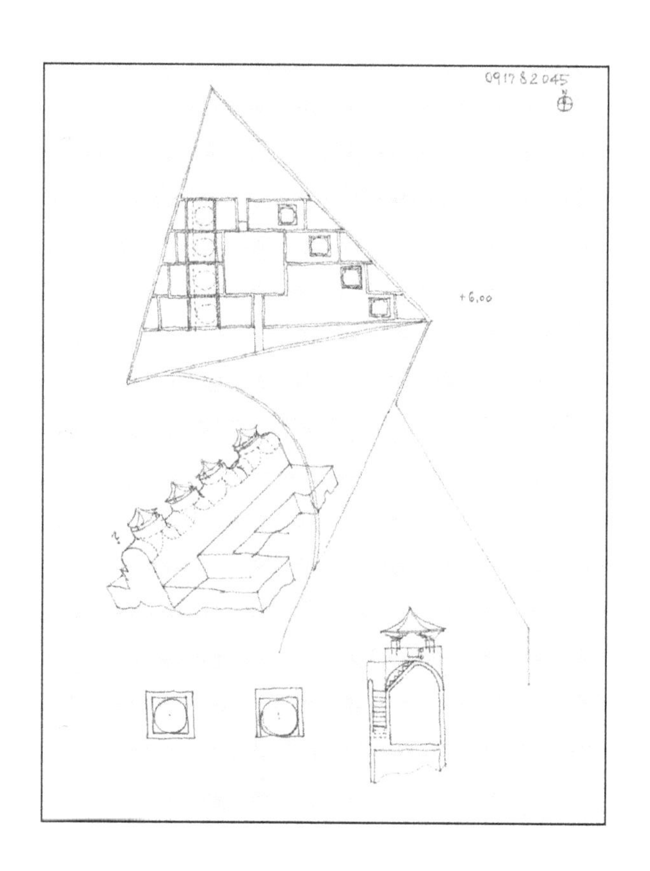

09178 2045
+6,00

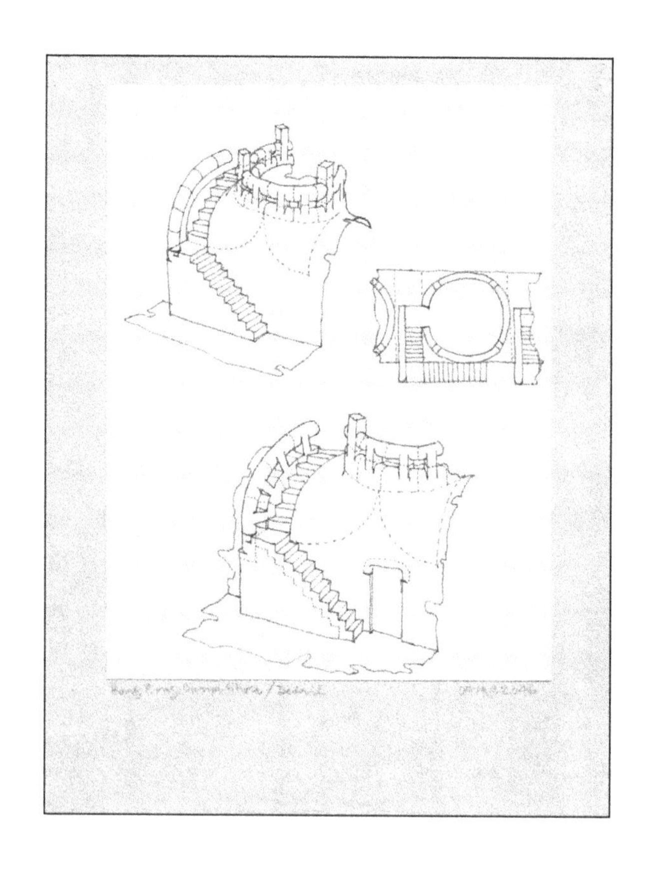

091982047

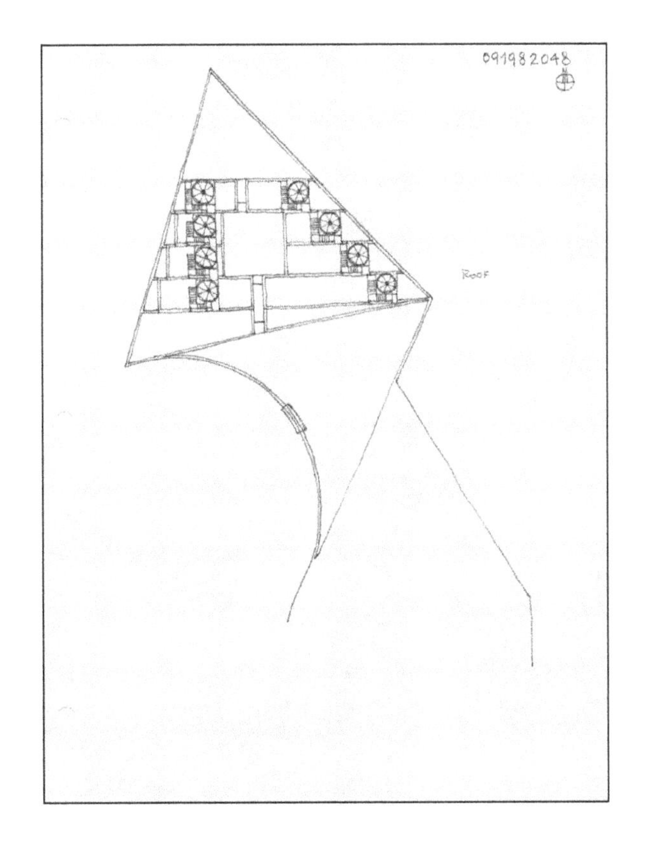
091982048
ROOF

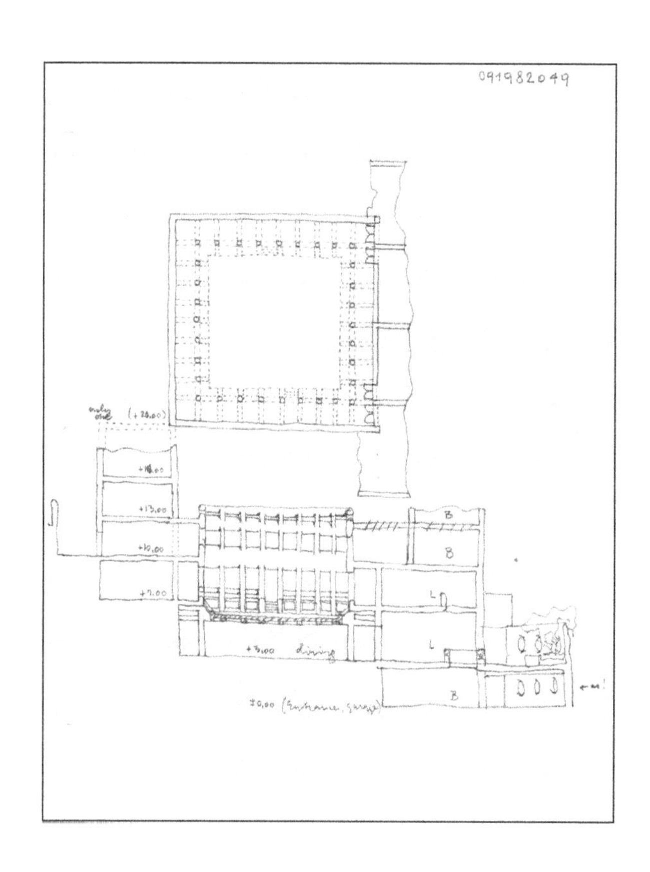
091982049
+13.00
+10.00
+7.00
+3.00 dining
B
L

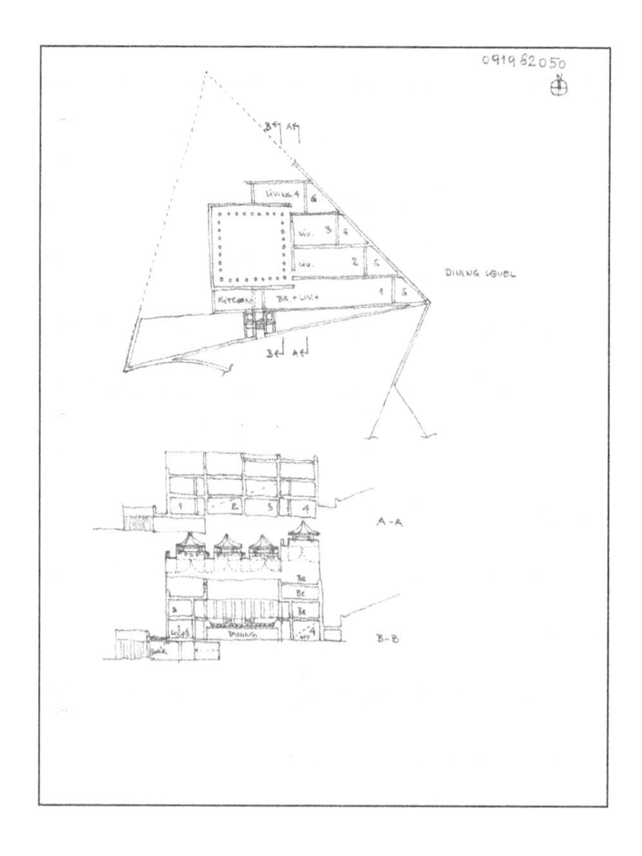
091982050
LIVING 4
DINING LEVEL
KITCHEN
A-A
B-B

091982051

092082052

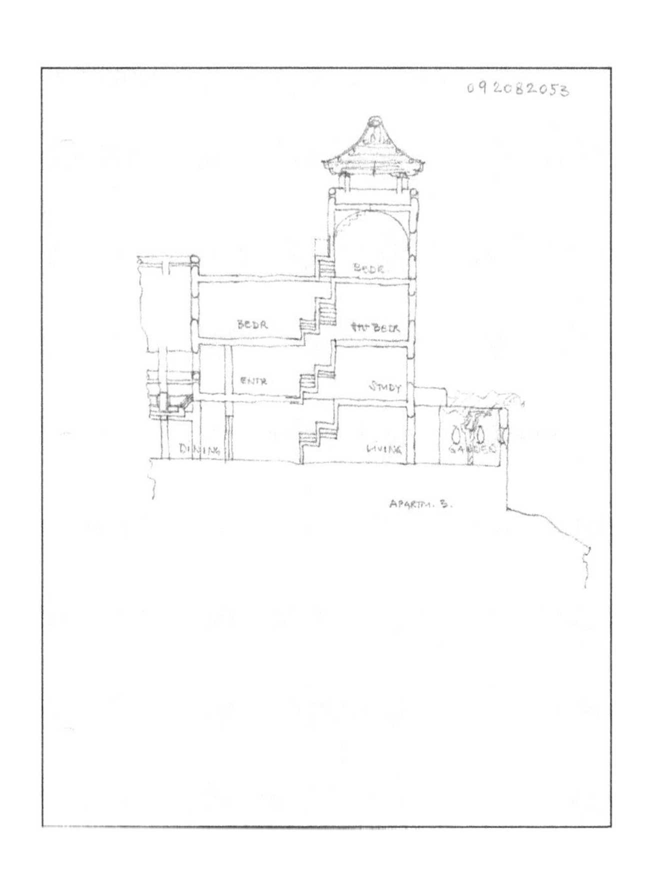
092082053
BEDR
BEDR
BEDR
ENTR
STUDY
DINING
LIVING
GARDEN
APARTM. 3.

092082054
BEDR
ENTR
BEDR
DINING
LIVING
APARTM 2
BEDR.

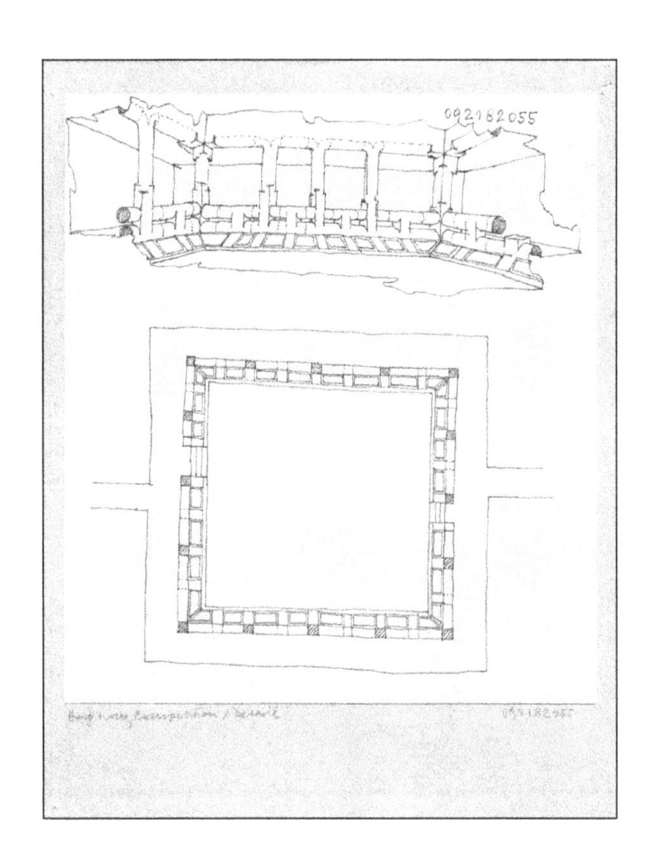
092182055

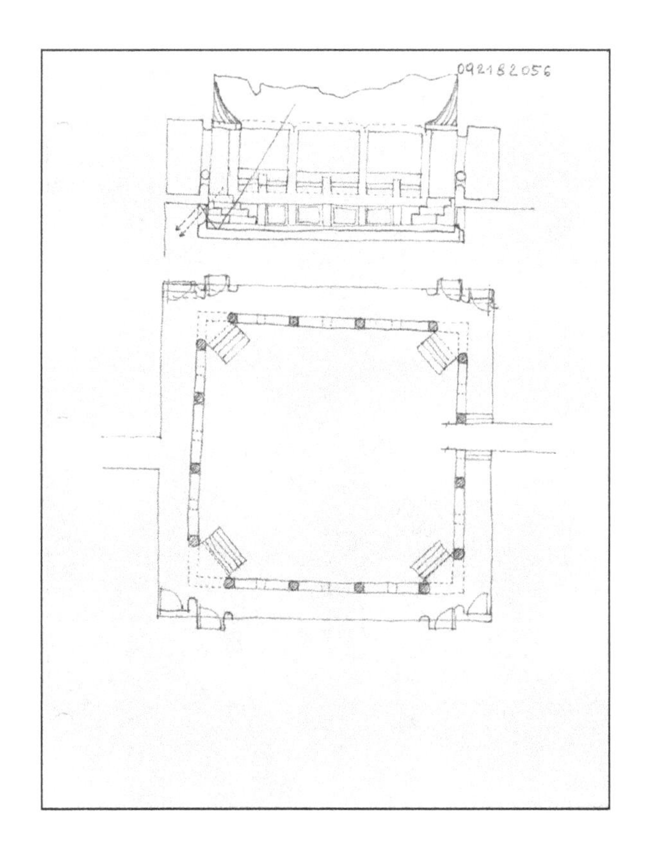
092182056

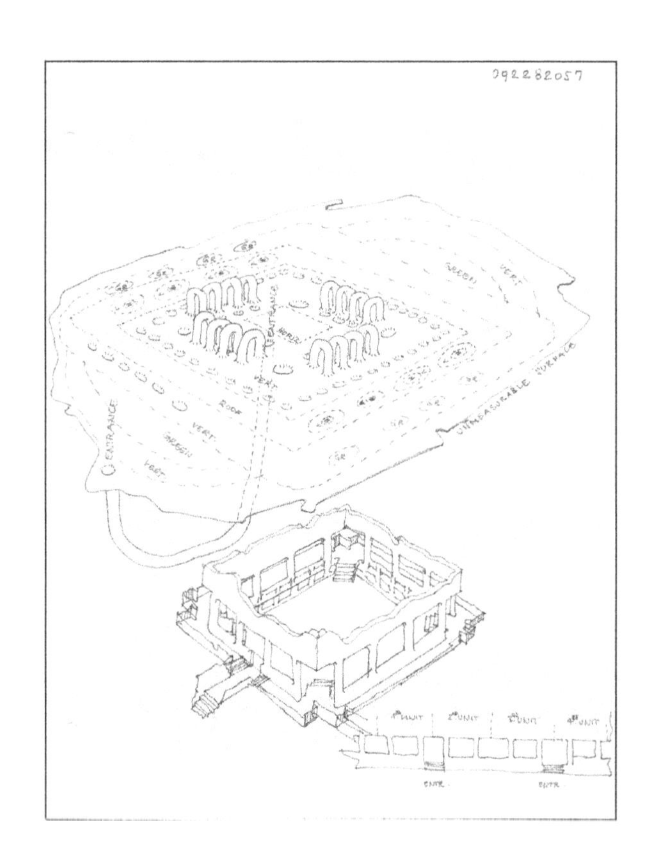
092282057
ENTRANCE
GREEN
VERT.
ROOF
HORIZ.
ENTRANCE
GREEN
VERT.
UNMEASURABLE SURFACE
ENTR.
ENTR.

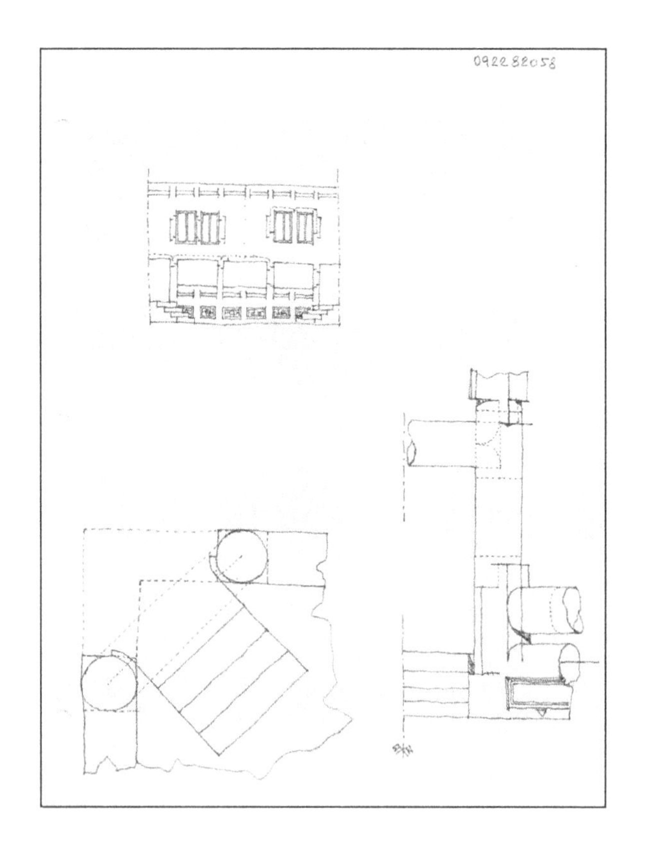
092282058

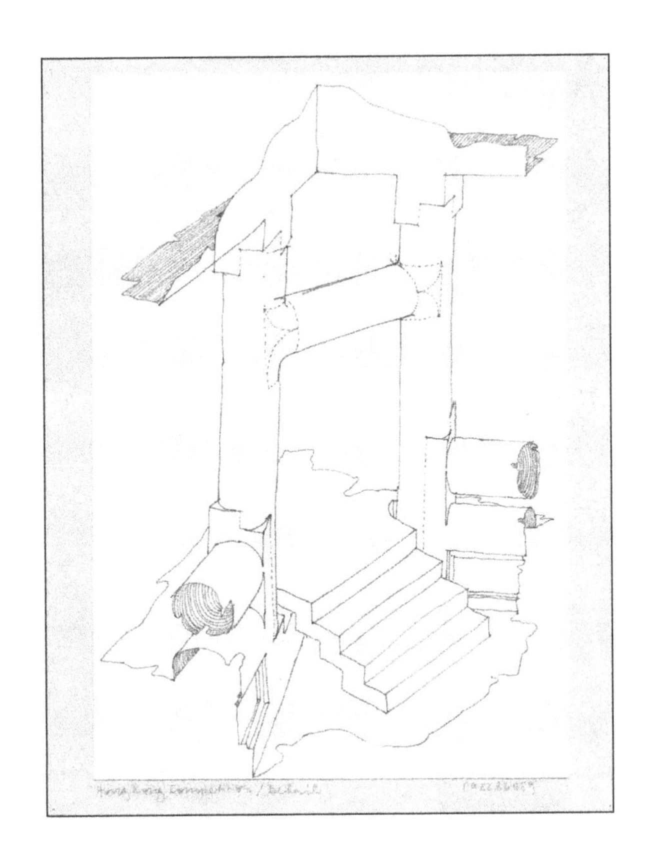
Hong Kong Competition / Detail

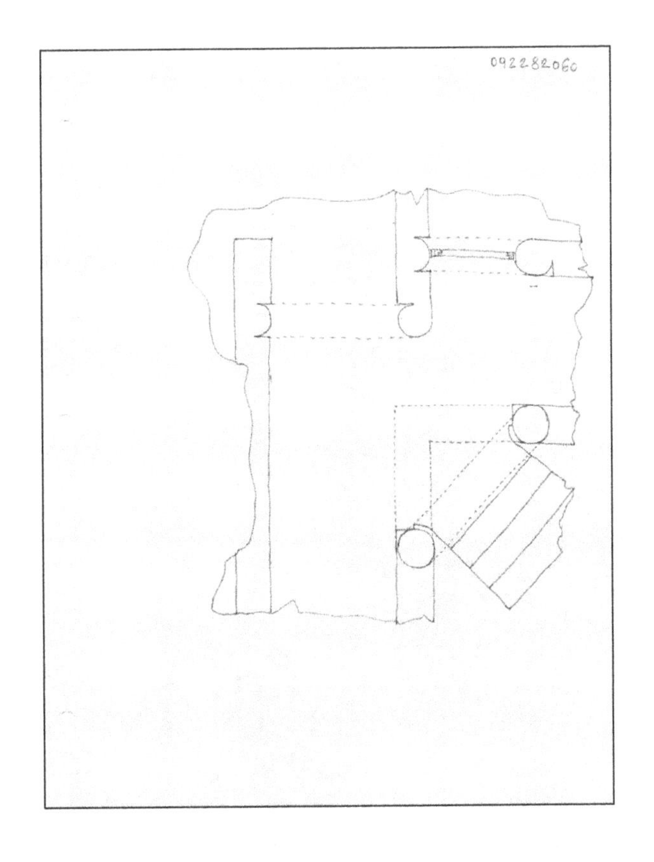
092282060

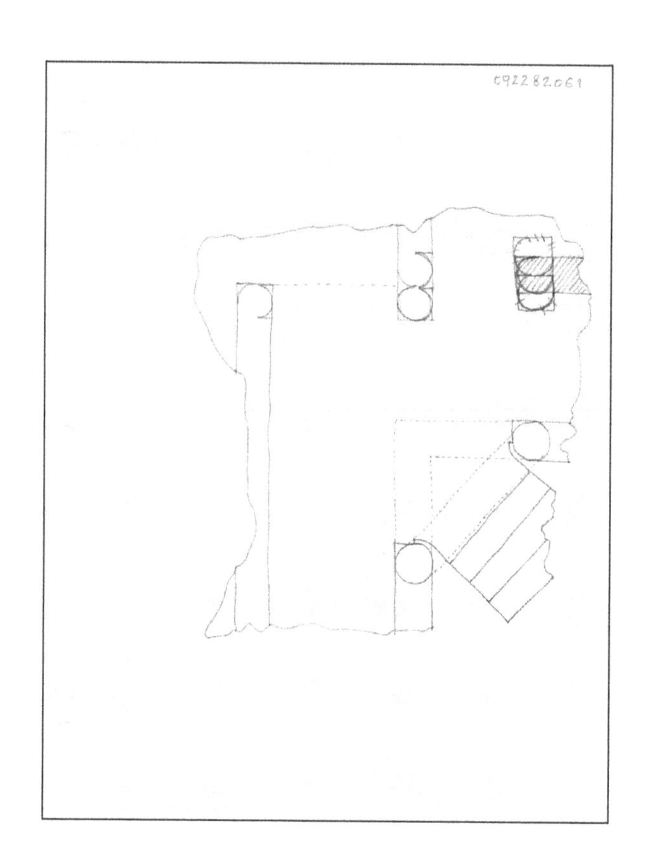
092282061

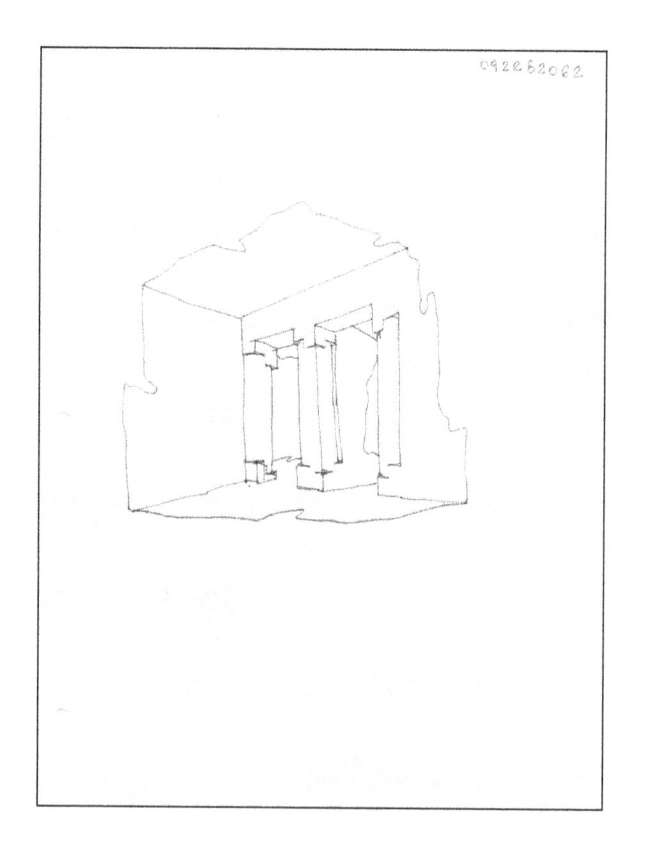
092282062

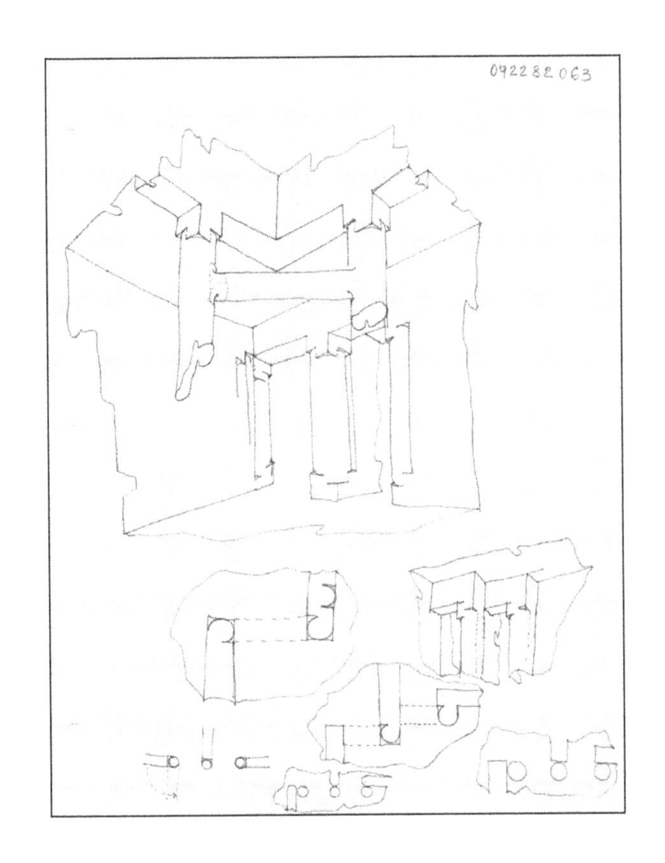

092282.063

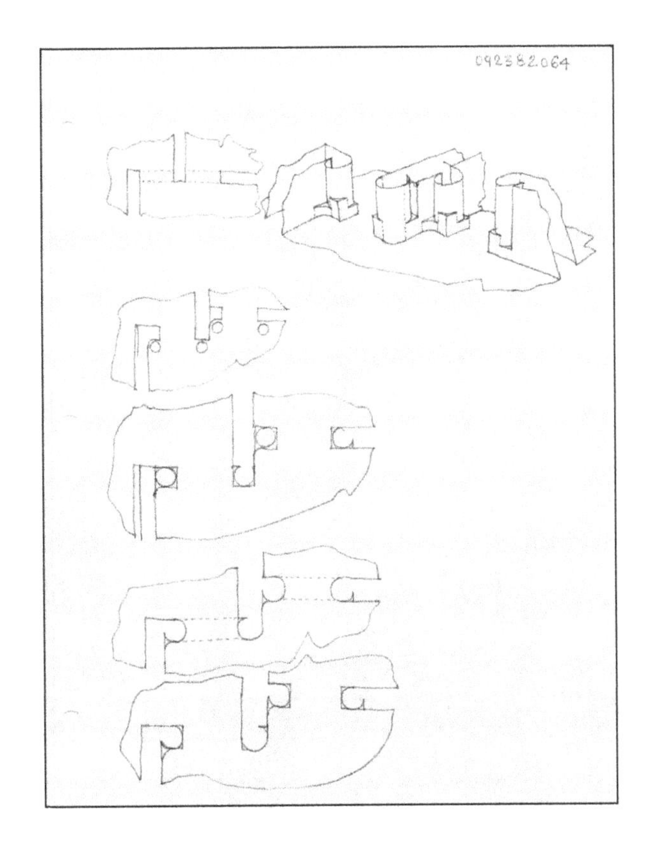

092382.064

092382065

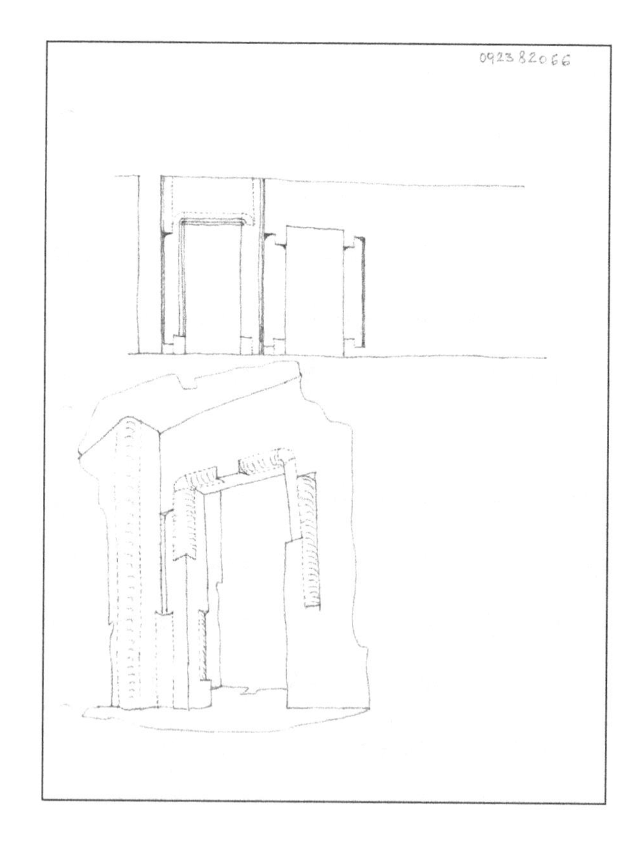
092382066

092382067

092382068

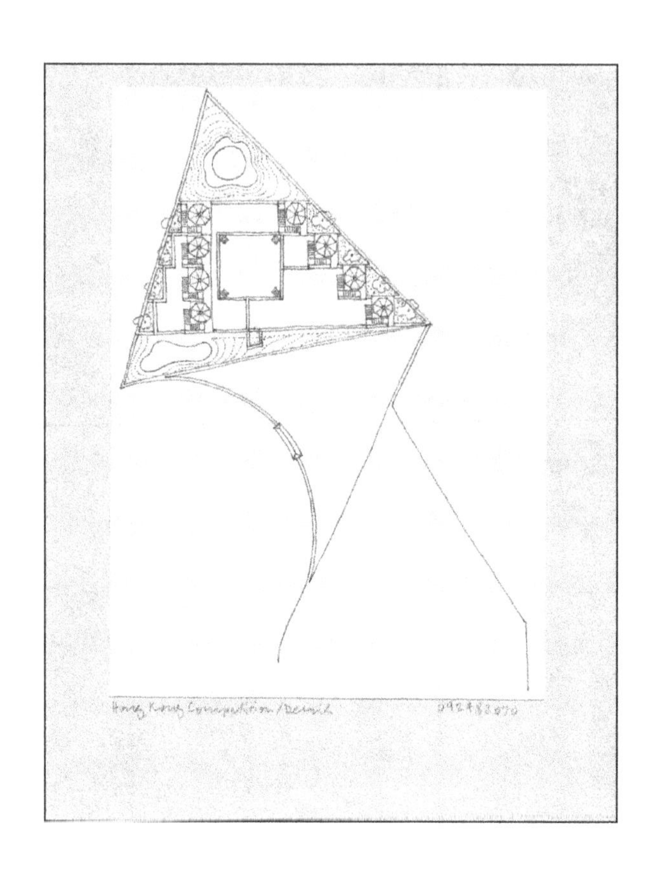
Hong Kong Competition / Detail
092?82070

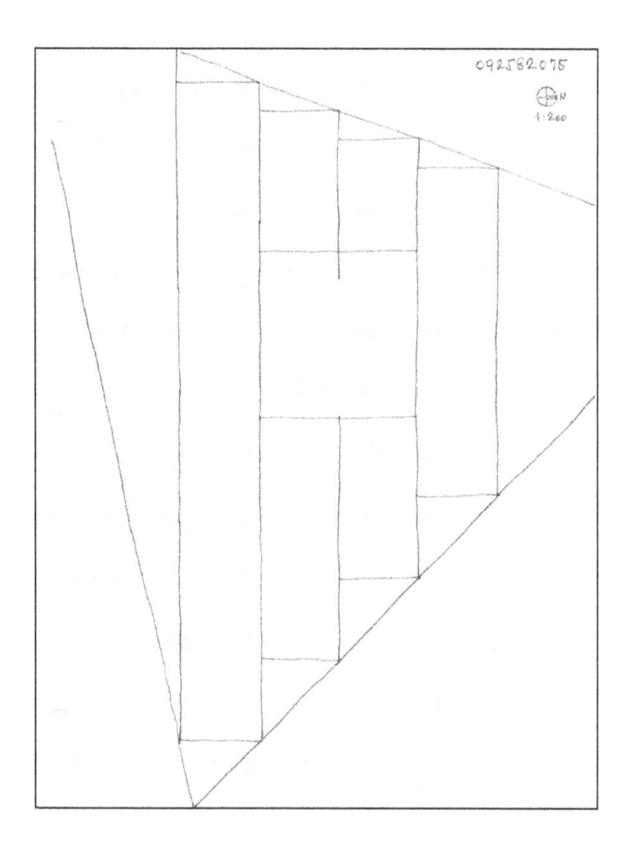
092582075
N
1:200

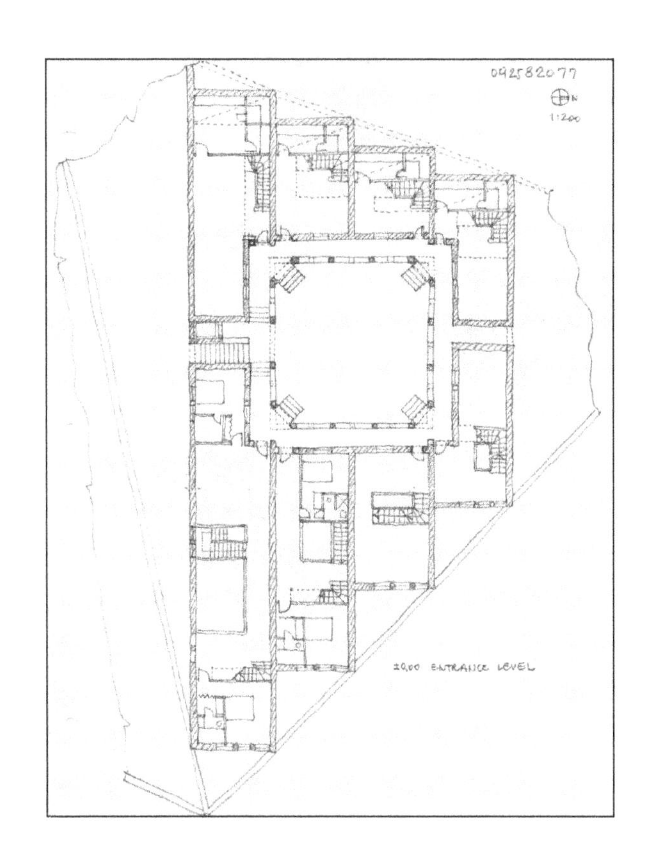
0925820 77
N
1:200
20,00 ENTRANCE LEVEL

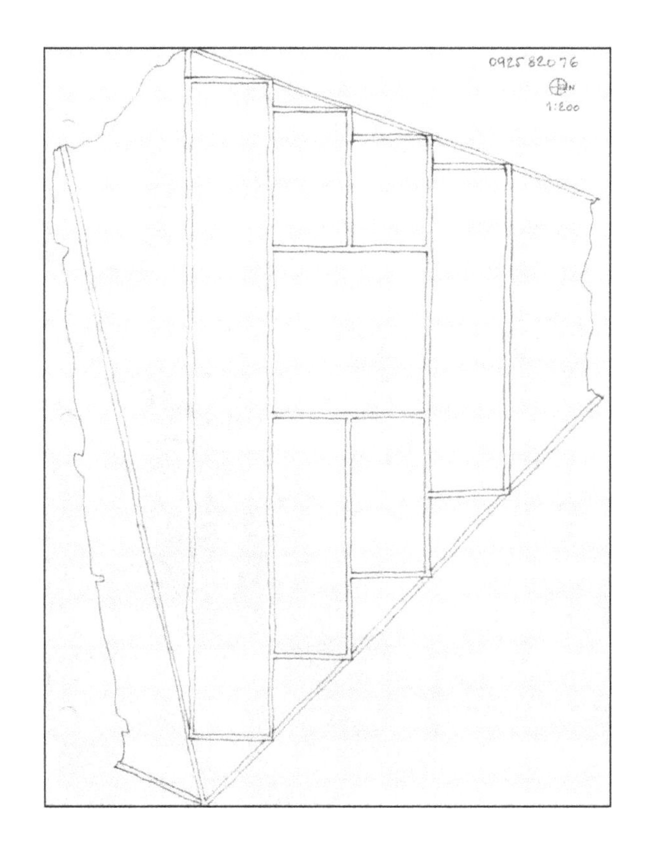
0925820 76
N
1:200

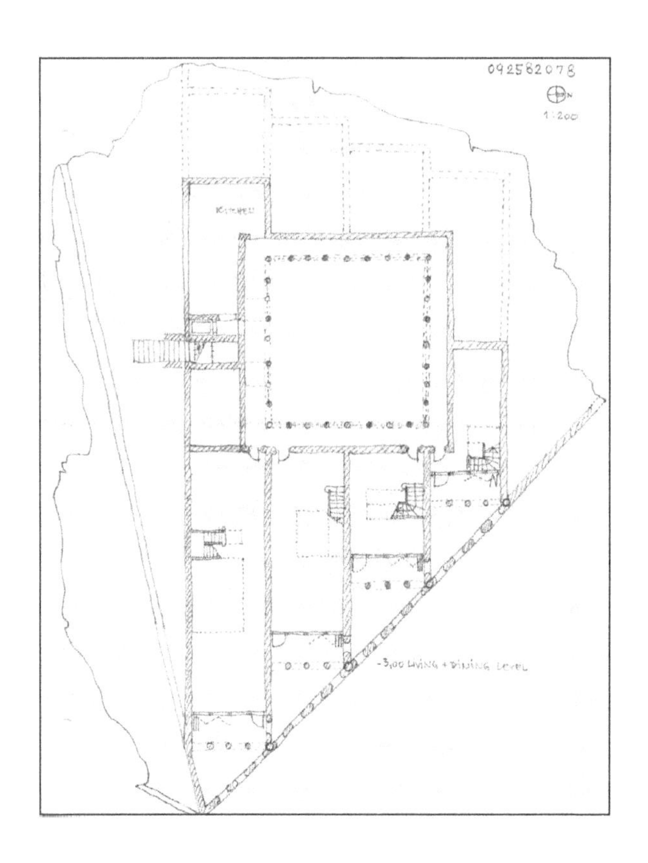
092582078
1:200
KITCHEN
-3,00 LIVING + DINING LEVEL

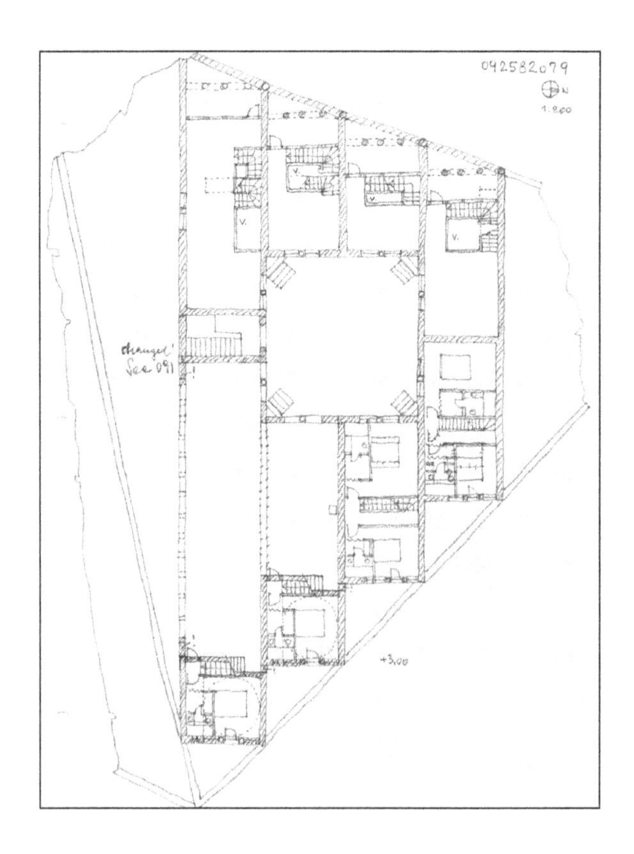
092582079
1:200
changed
See 091
+3,00

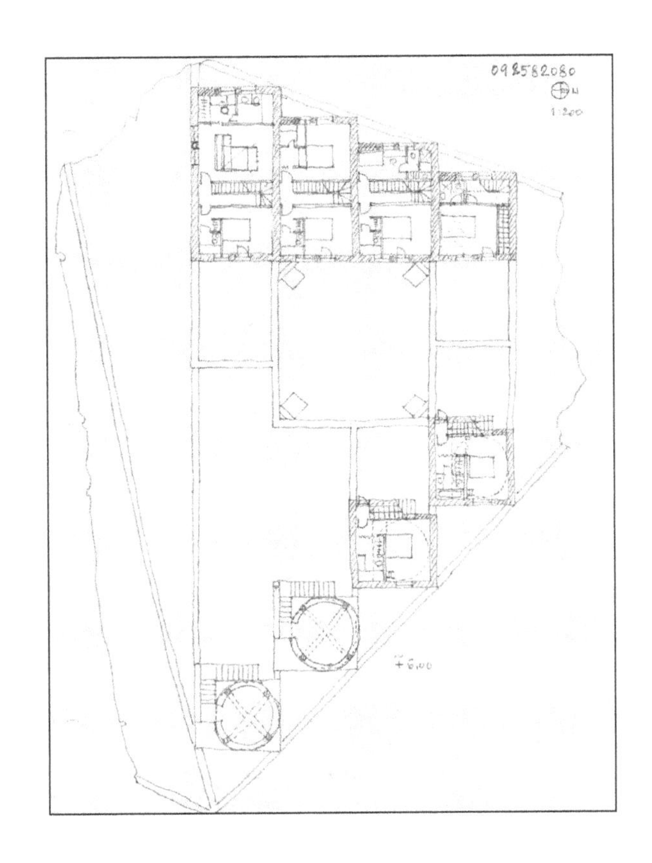

0925820 80
1:200
+6.00

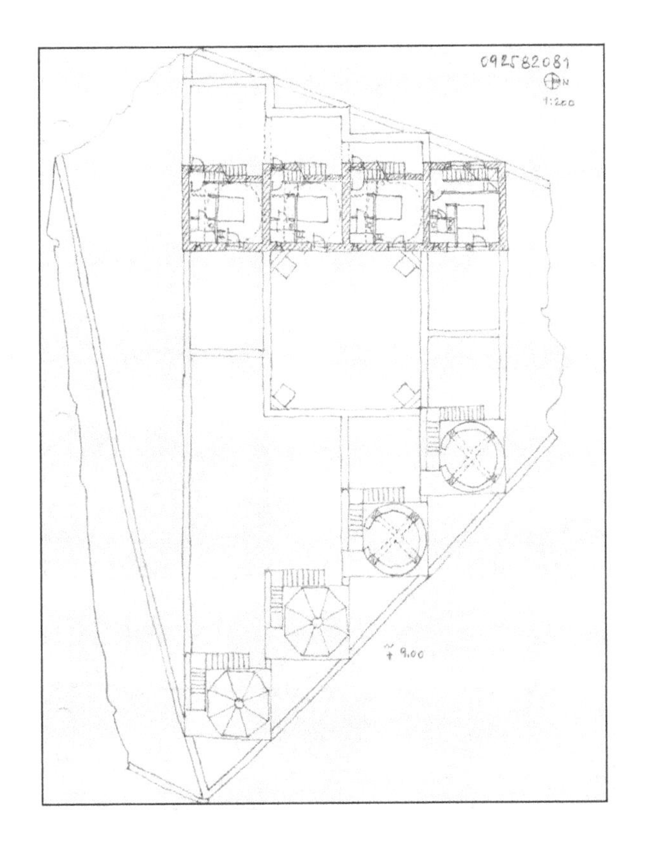

092582081
1:200
+9.00

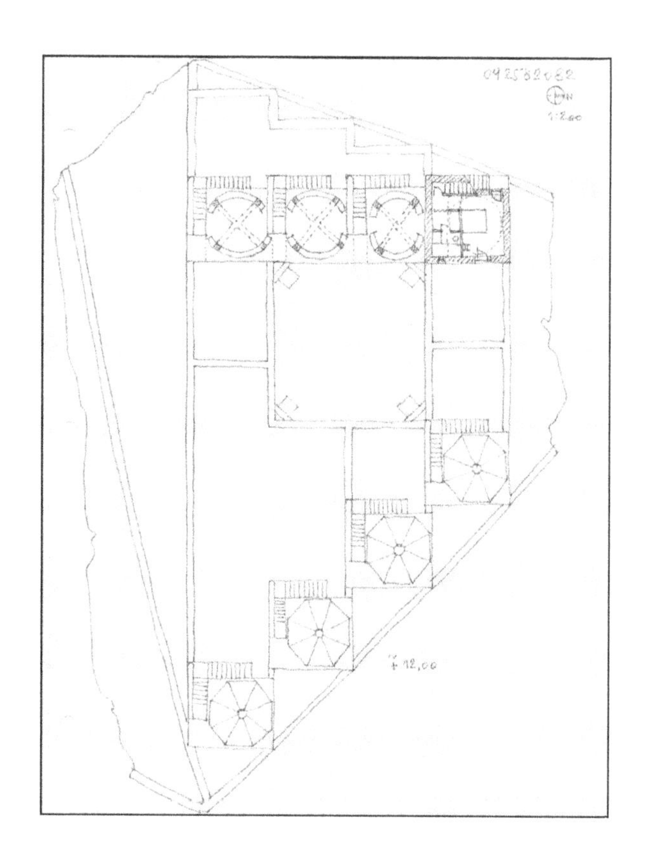

0925B2082
N
1:200
+12,00

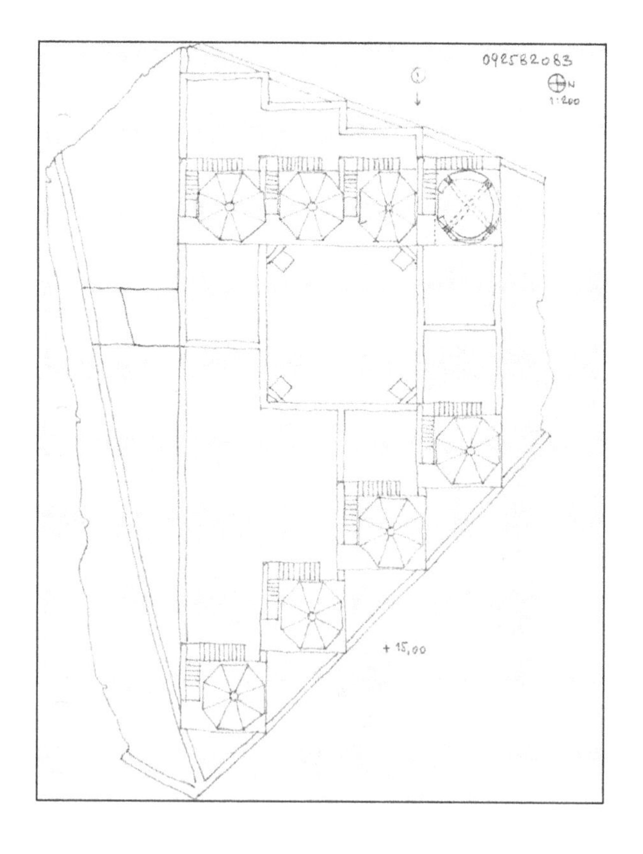

0925B2083
N
1:200
+15,00

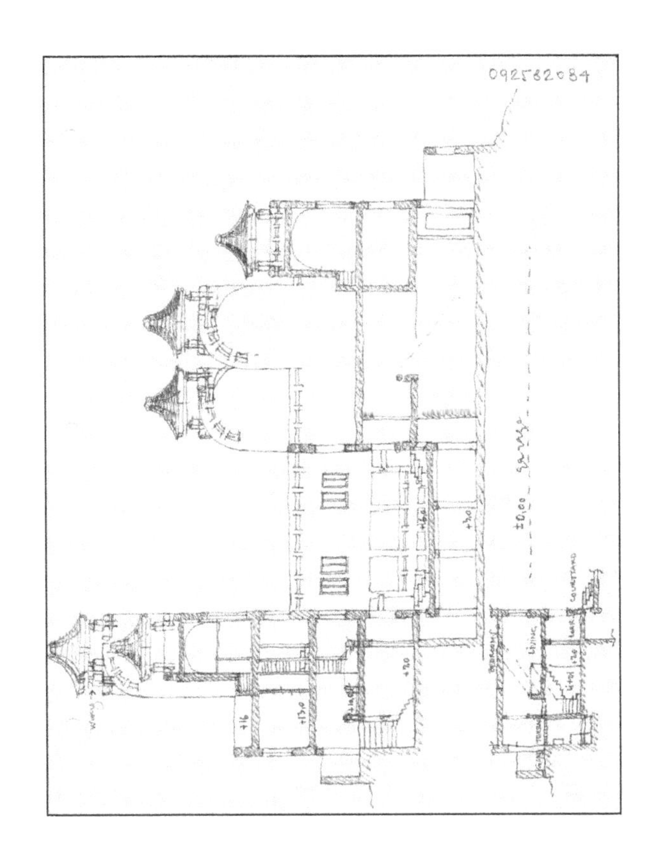
092582084

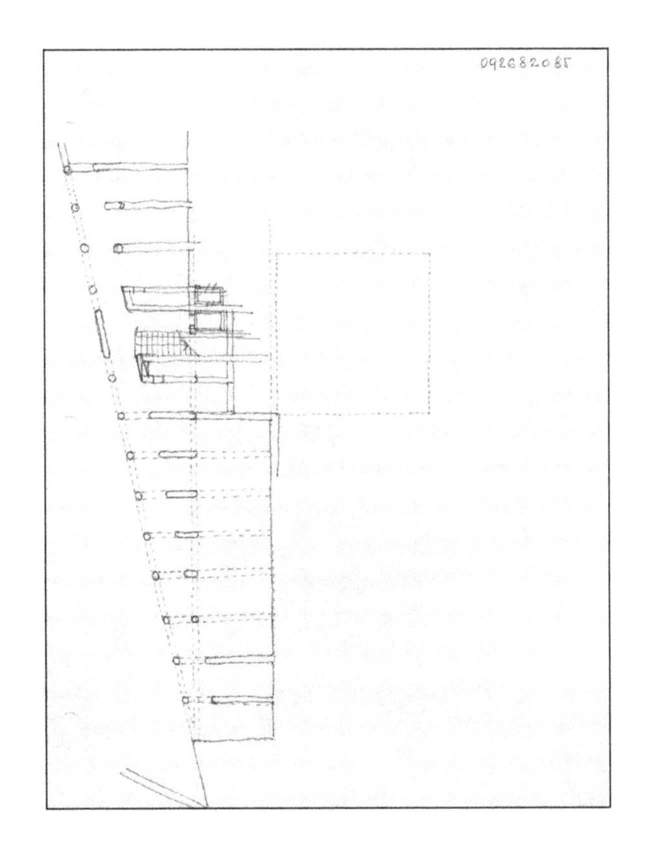
092682085

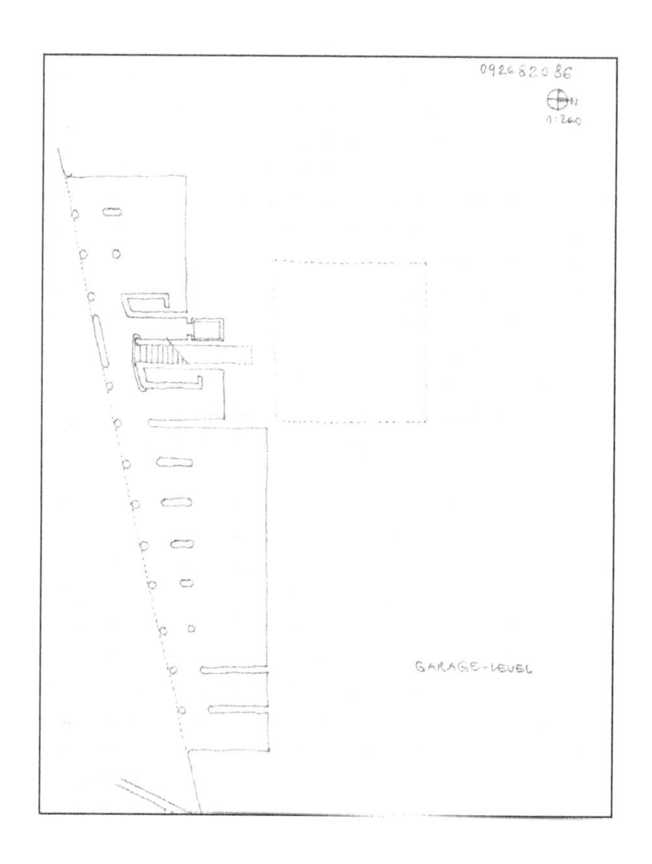
092682086
N
1:200
GARAGE-LEVEL

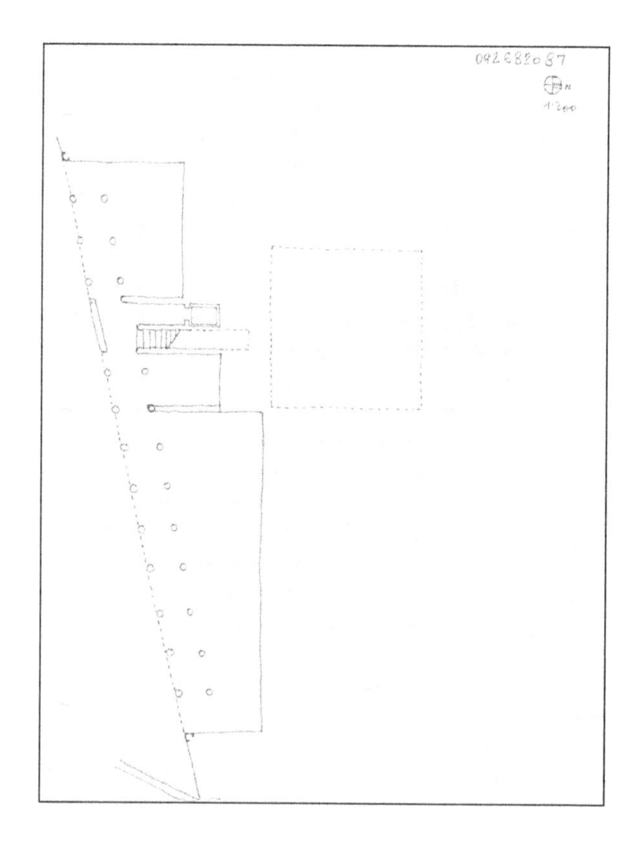
092682087
N

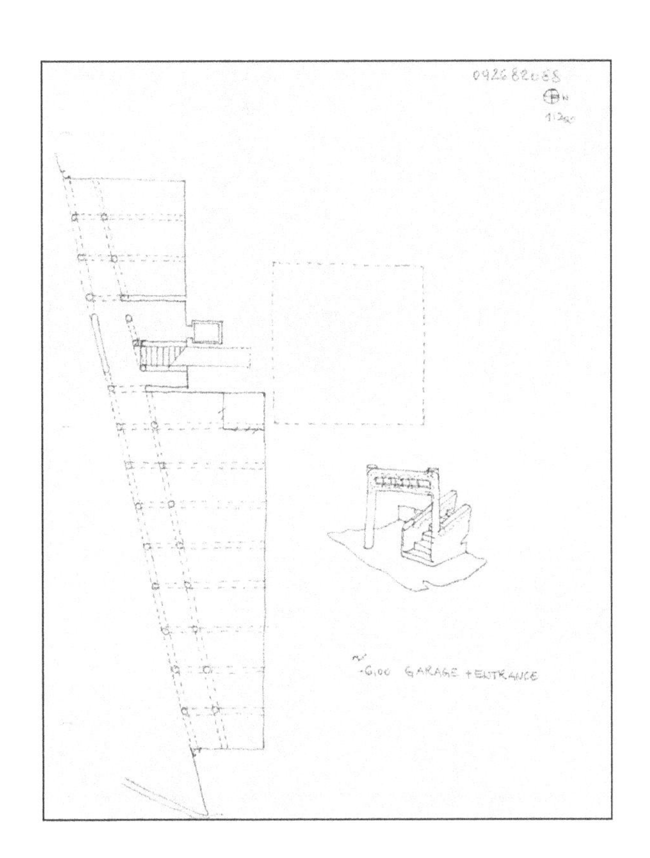
092682088
1:200
-6.00 GARAGE + ENTRANCE

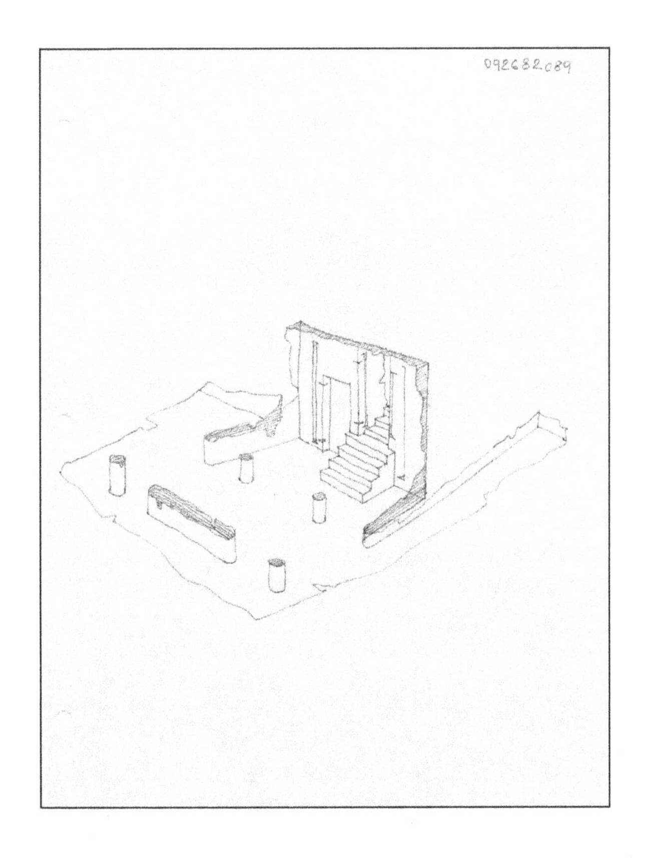
092682089

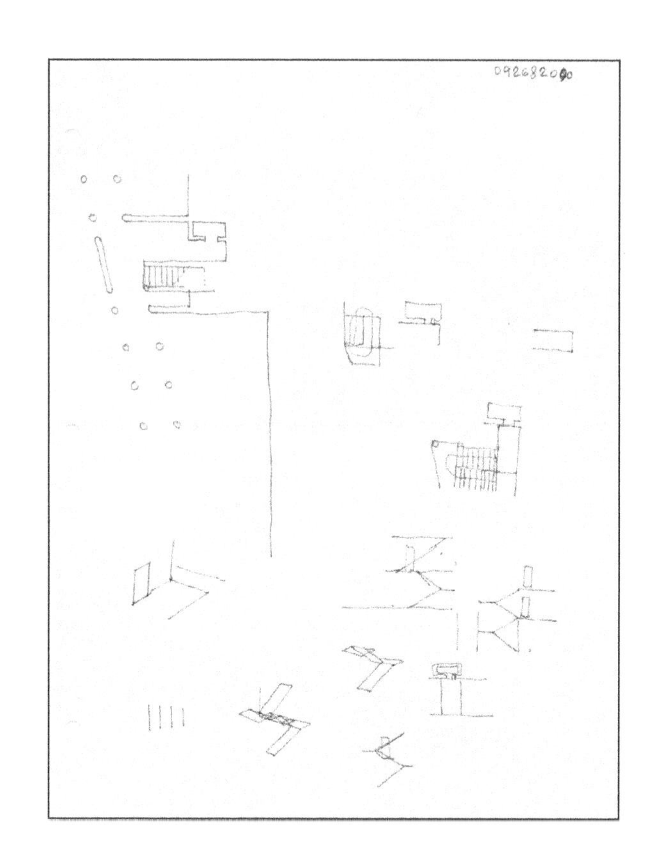

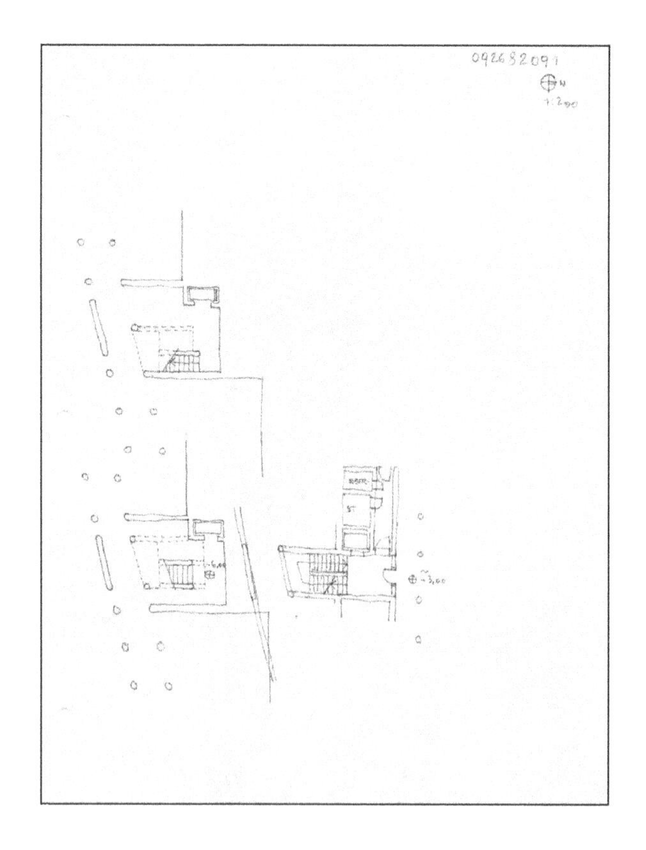

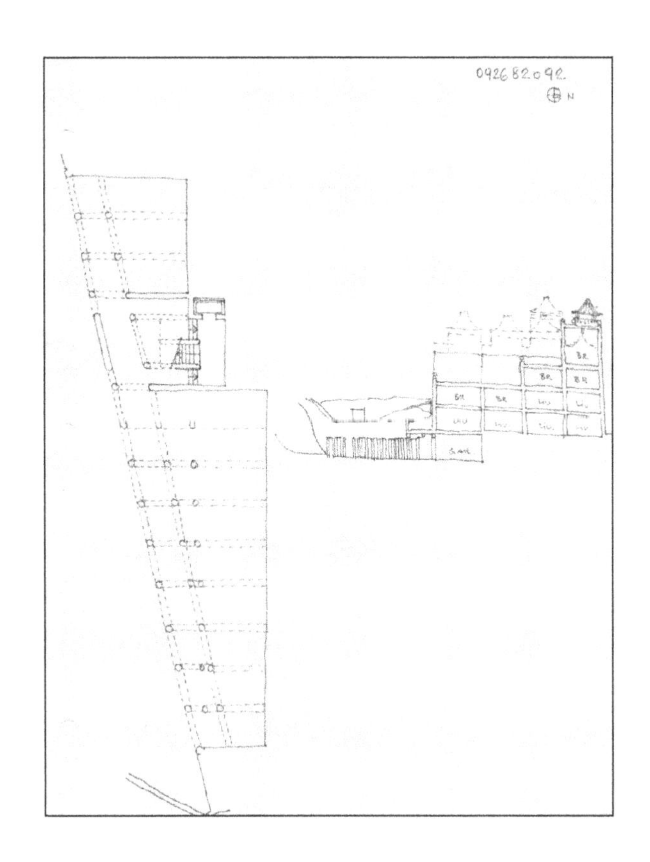
092682092
N
BR
BR
BR
BR
BR
BR
GAR

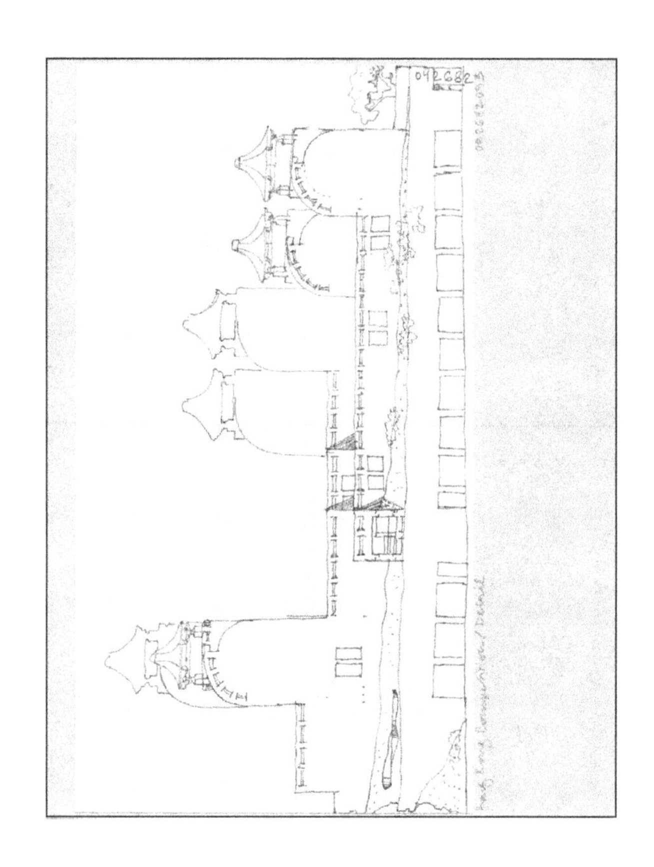

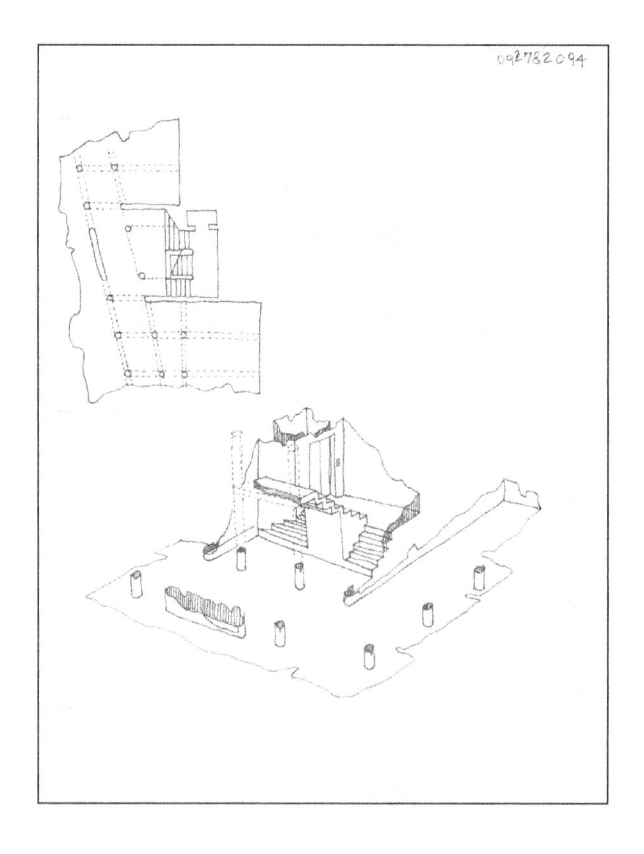

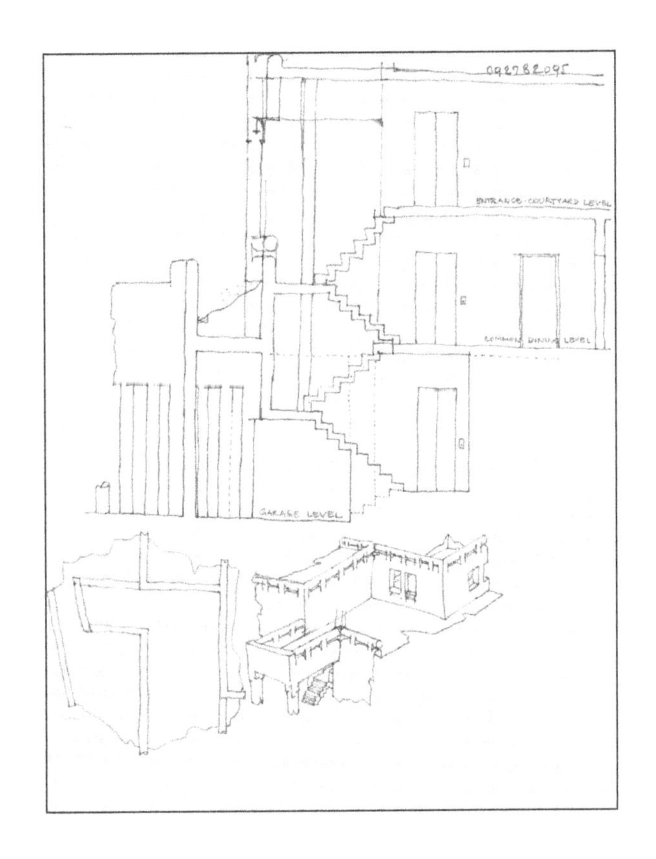
092782095
ENTRANCE-COURTYARD LEVEL
COMMON DINING LEVEL
GARAGE LEVEL

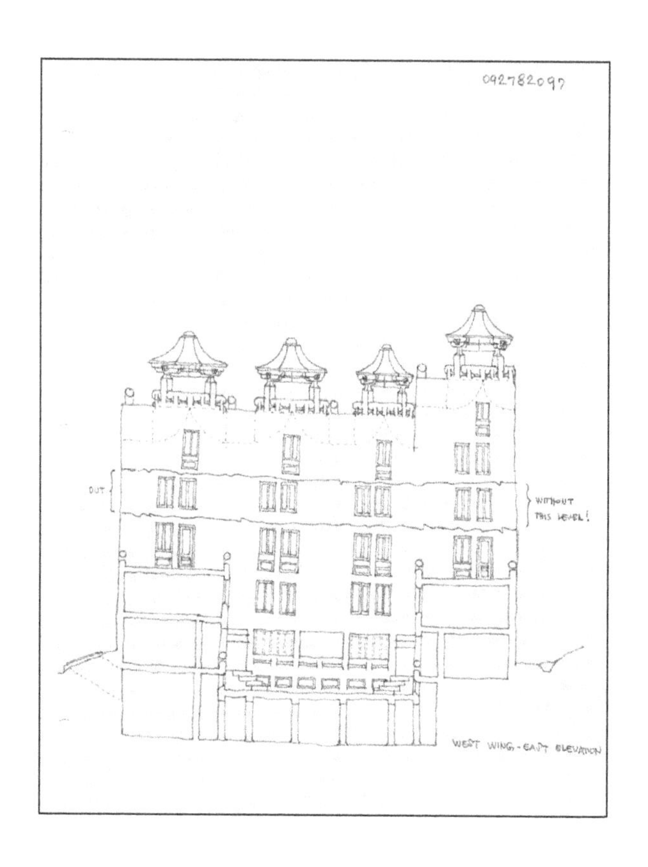
092782097
OUT
WITHOUT
THIS LEVEL!
WEST WING - EAST ELEVATION

092782098

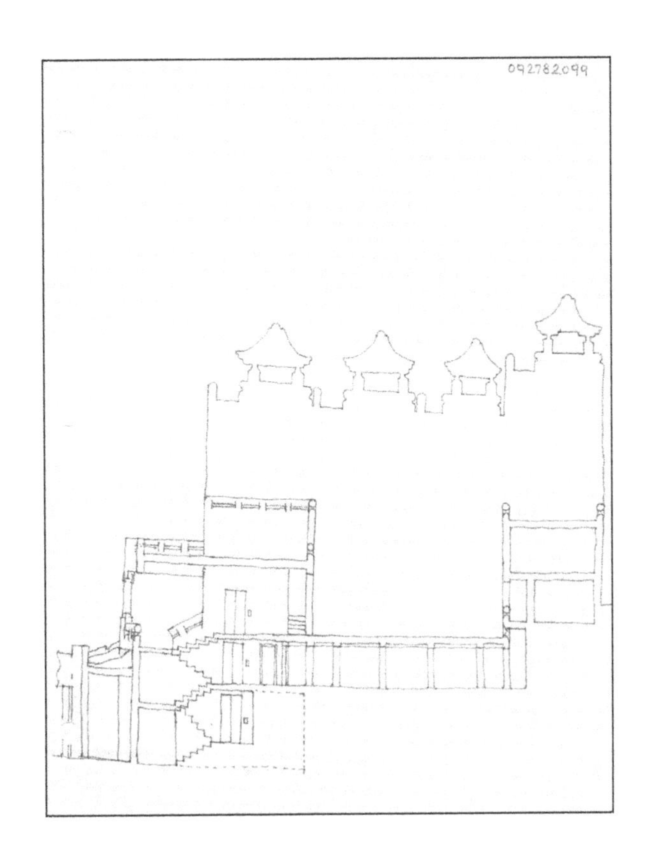
0927820099

092782100

Hong Kong Competition / Detail

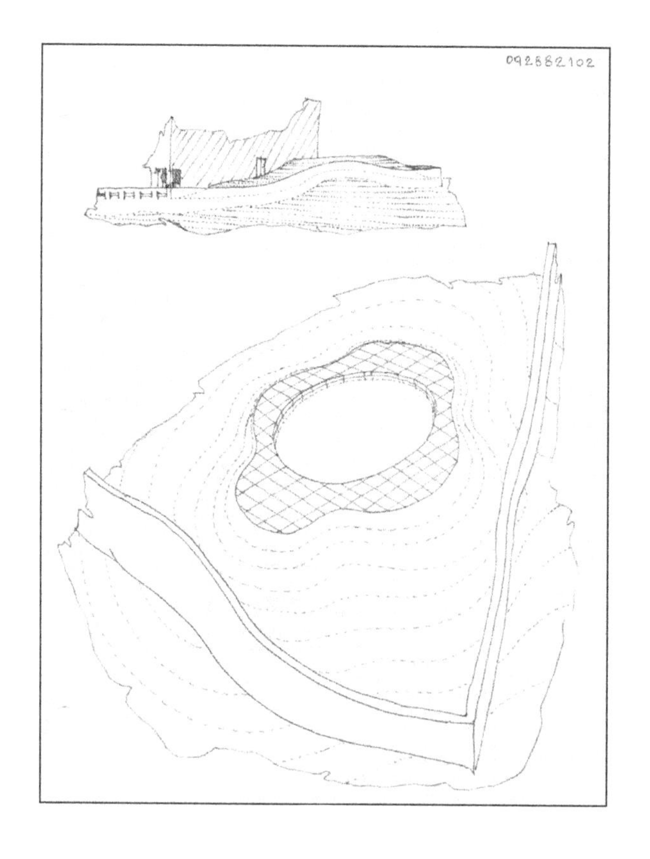
092882102

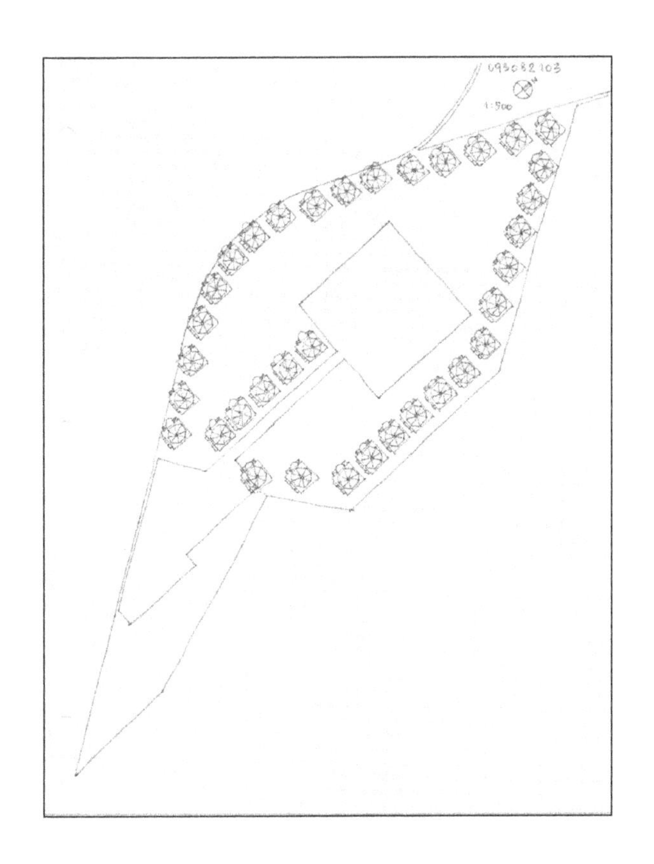
093082103
N
1:500

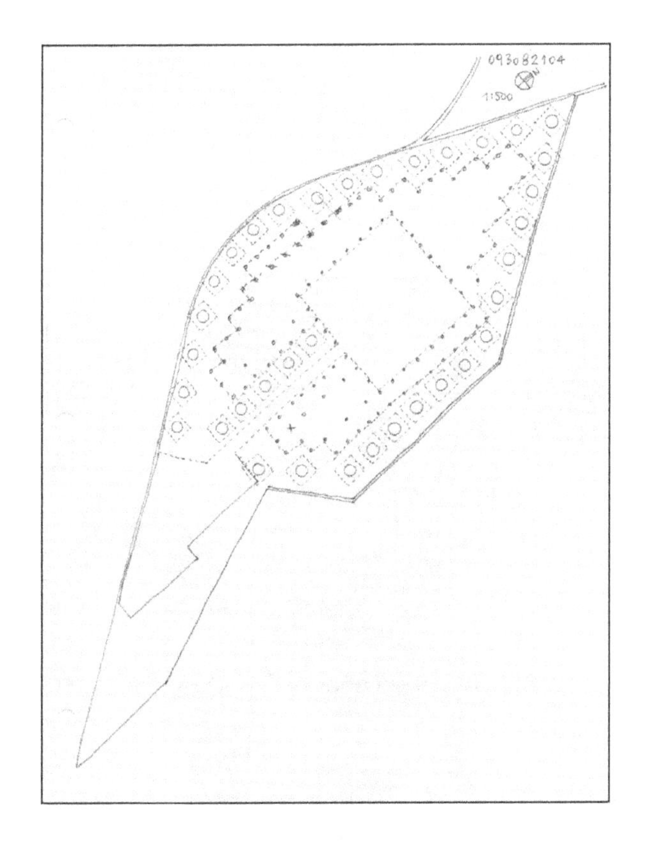
093082104
N
1:500

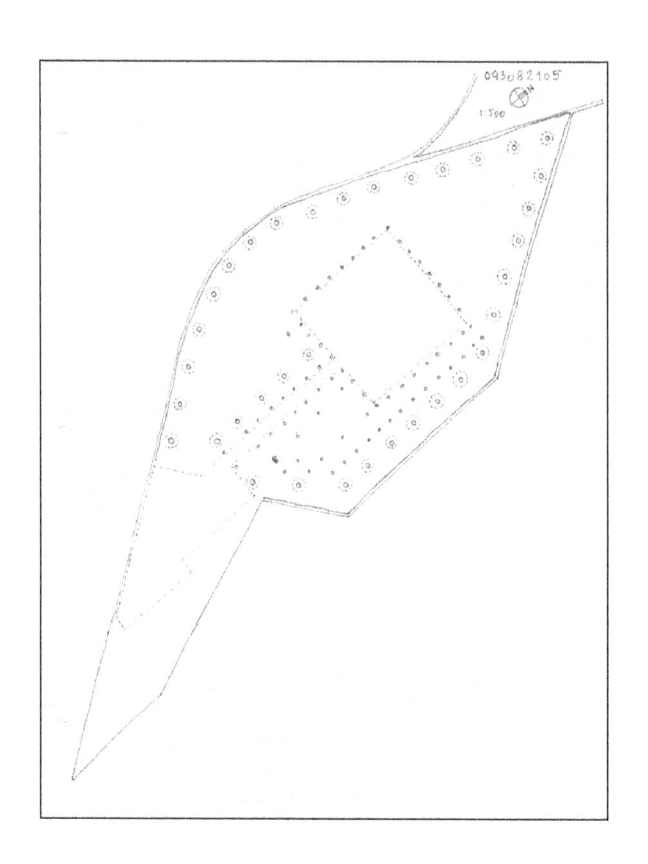

093082105
1:500

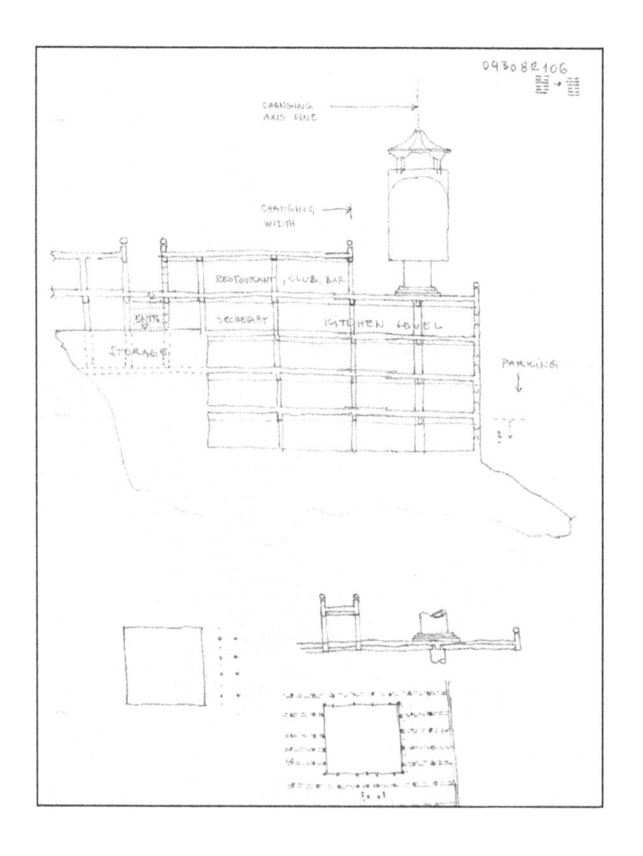

093082106
CHANGING AXIS LINE
CHANGING WIDTH
RESTAURANT, CLUB, BAR
SECRETARY
KITCHEN LEVEL
STORAGE
PARKING

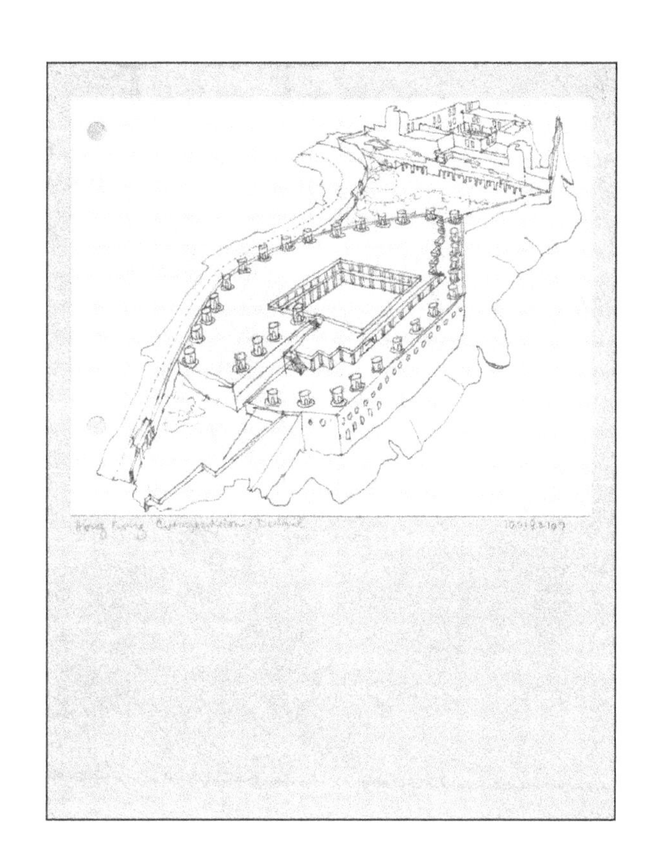
Hong Kong Competition: Detail

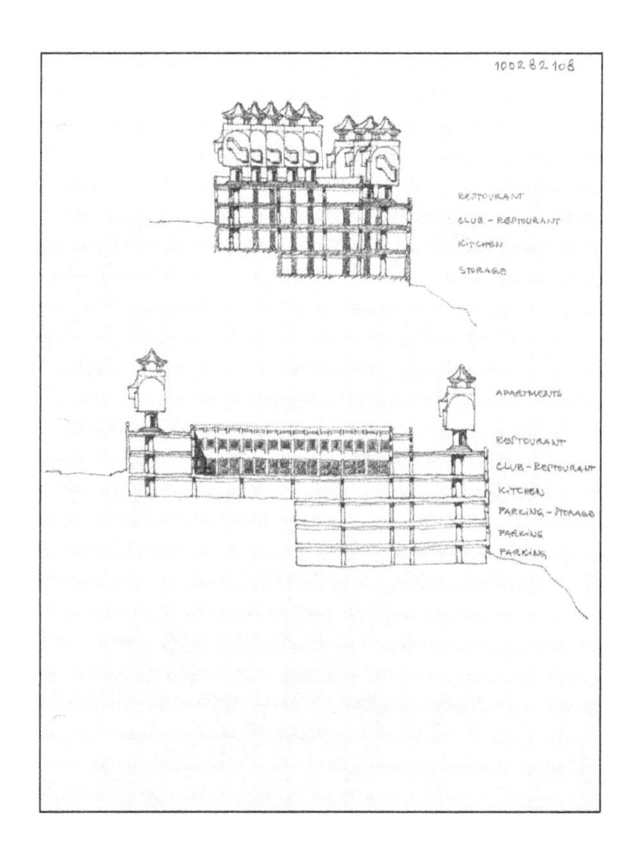
100282108
RESTOURANT
CLUB - RESTOURANT
KITCHEN
STORAGE
APARTMENTS
RESTOURANT
CLUB - RESTOURANT
KITCHEN
PARKING - STORAGE
PARKING
PARKING

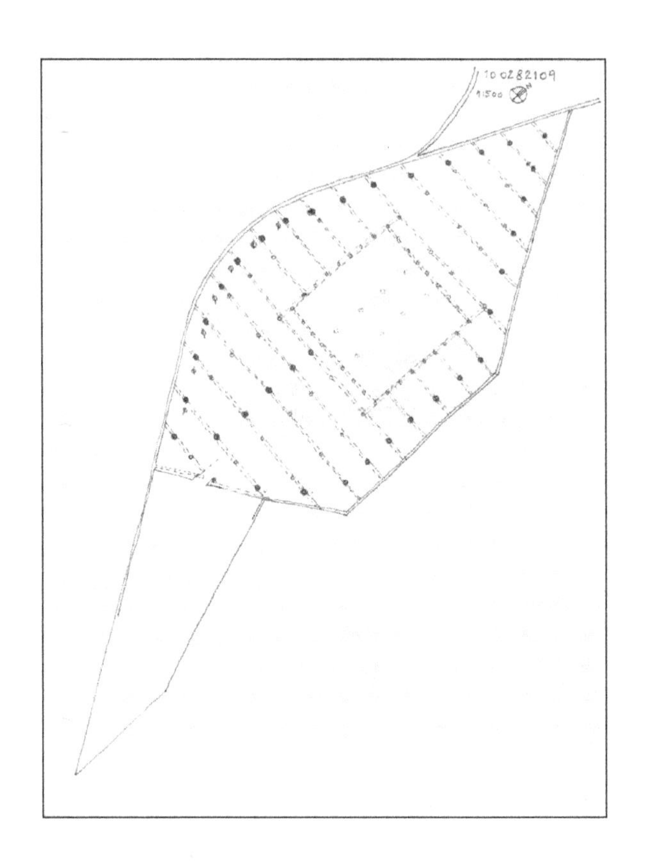
100282109
1:500
N

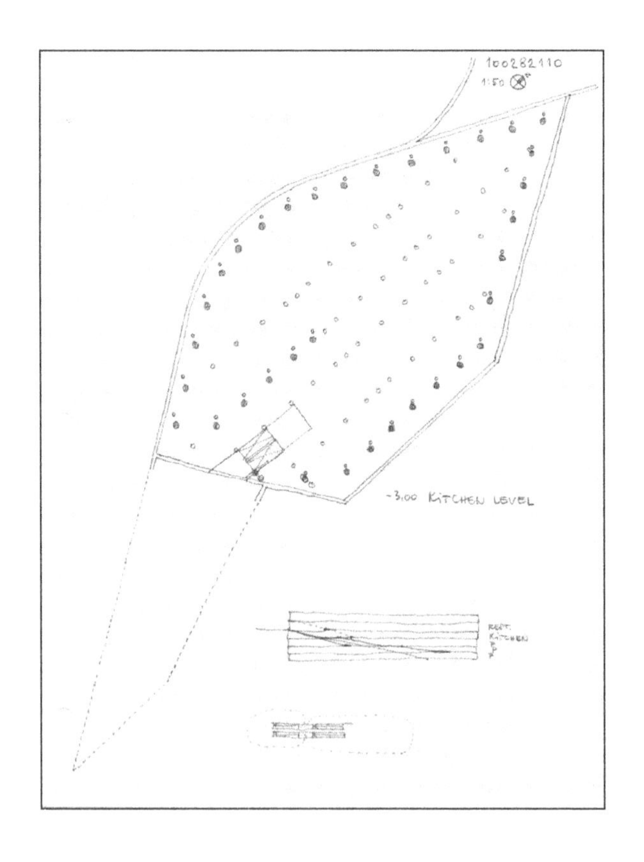
100282110
1:50
-3.00 KITCHEN LEVEL

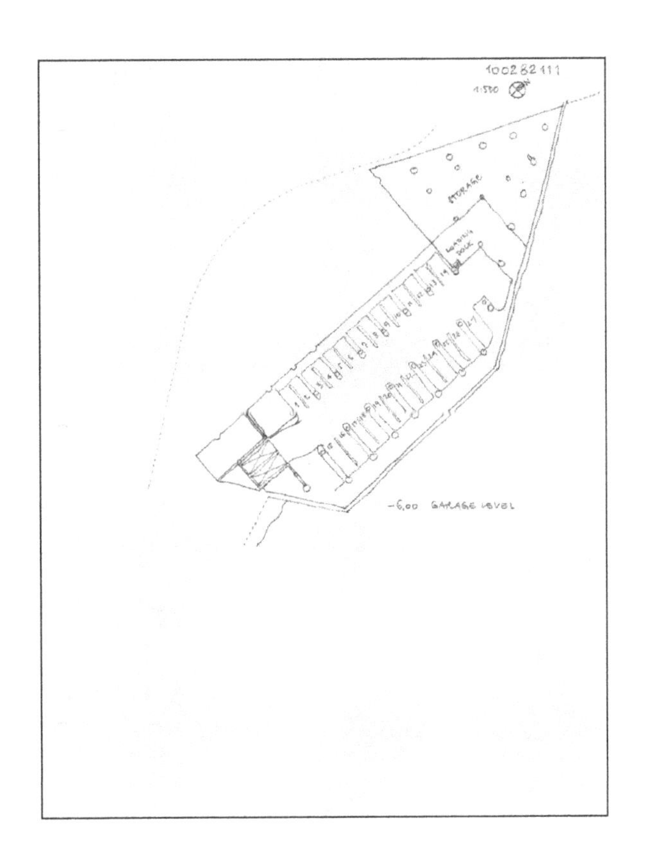
100282111
1:500
STORAGE
-6,00 GARAGE LEVEL

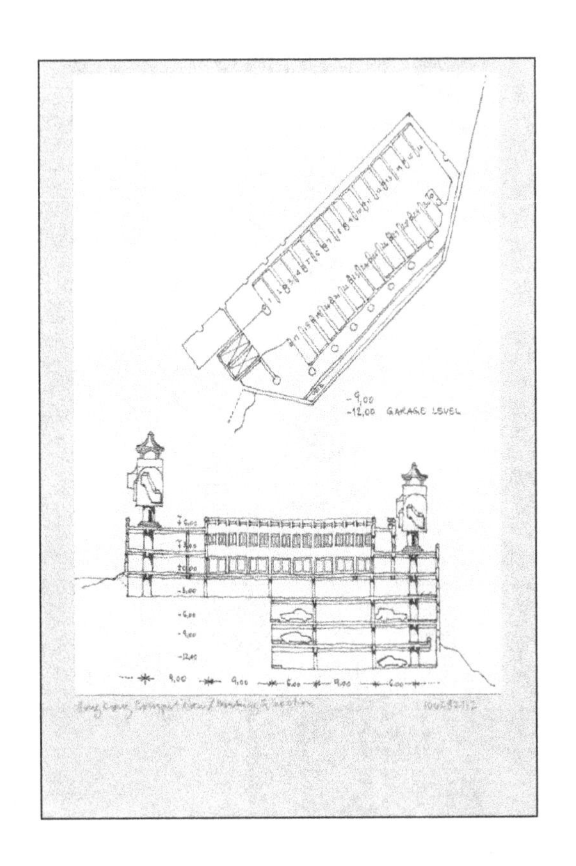
-9,00
-12,00 GARAGE LEVEL

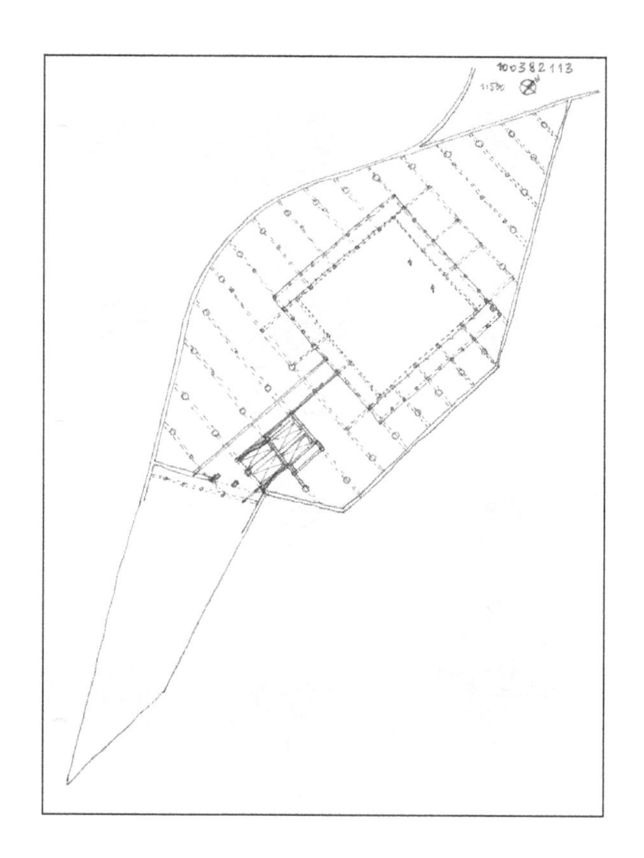

100382113

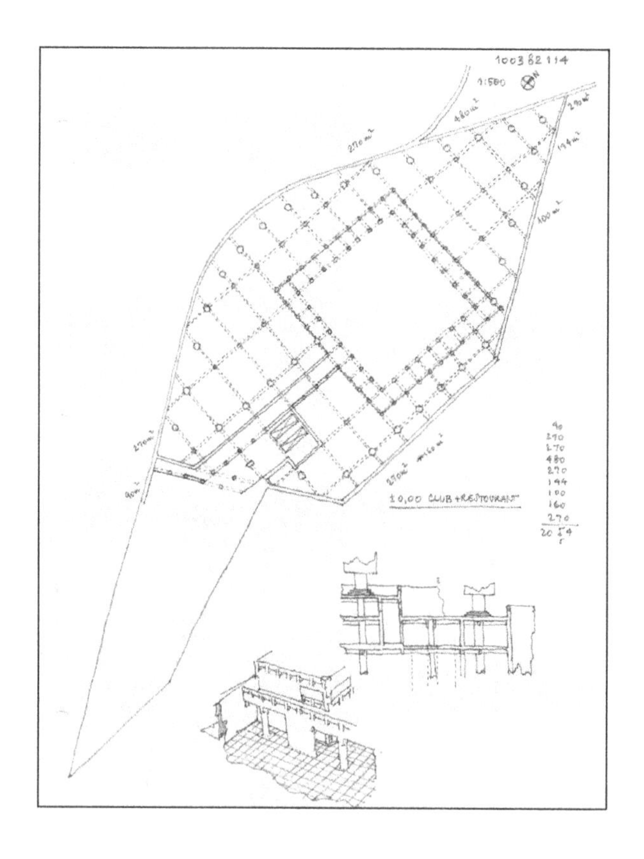

100382114
1:500
480m²
270m²
290m²
144m²
100m²
270m²
90m²
270m²
160m²
10,00 CLUB+RESTOURANT
90
270
270
480
270
144
100
160
270

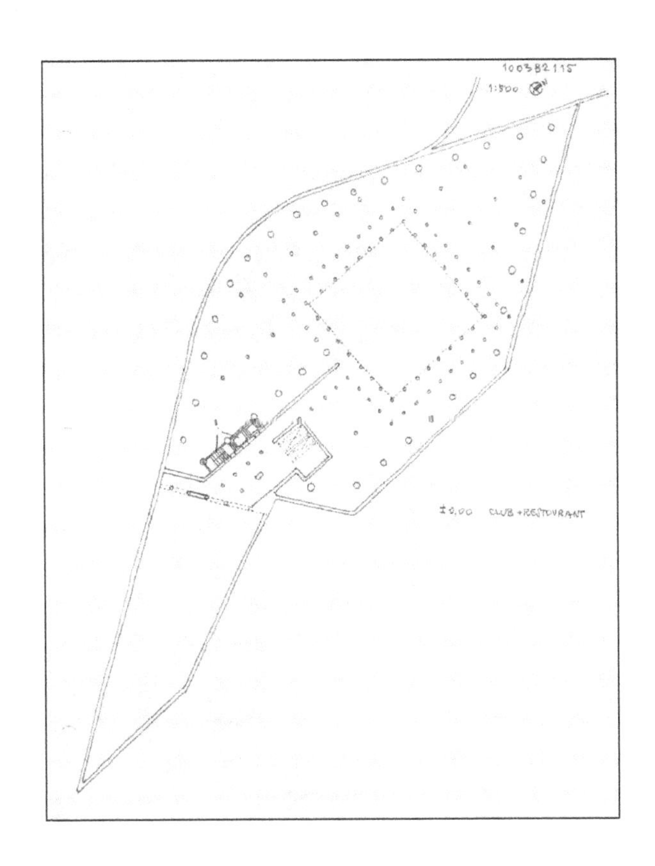
100382115
1:500
±0,00 CLUB + RESTOURANT

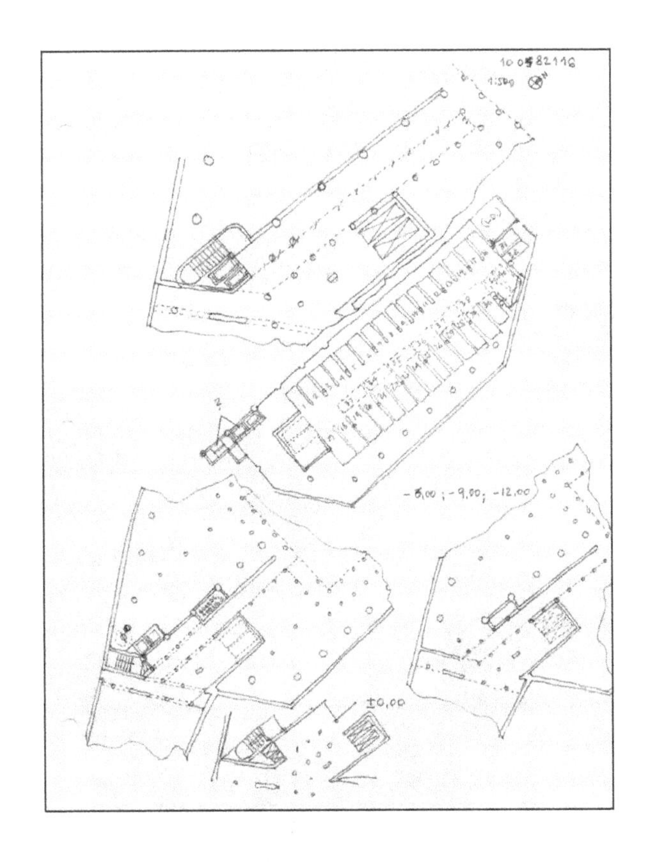
1:500
-6,00 ; -9,00 ; -12,00
±0,00

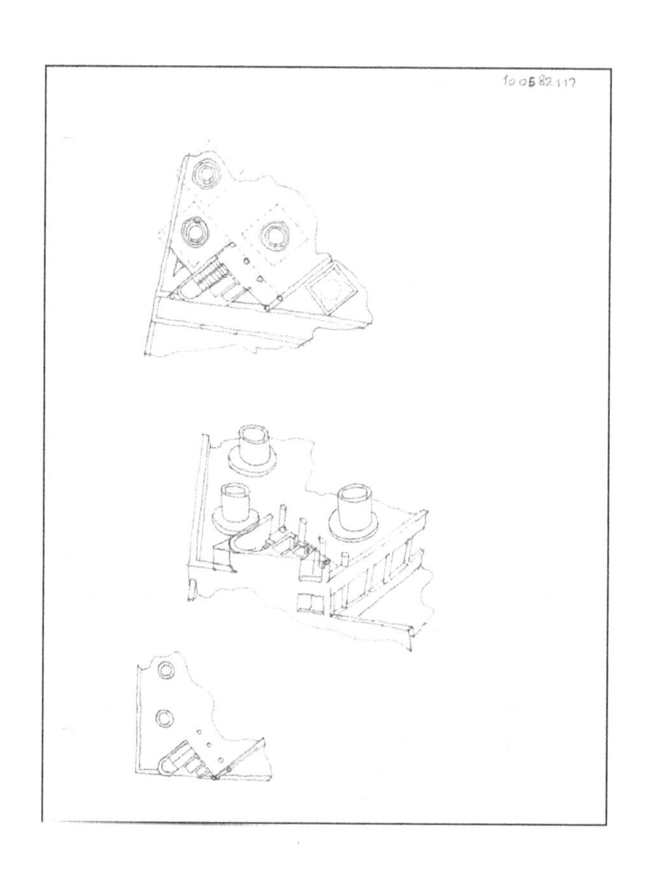
100582117

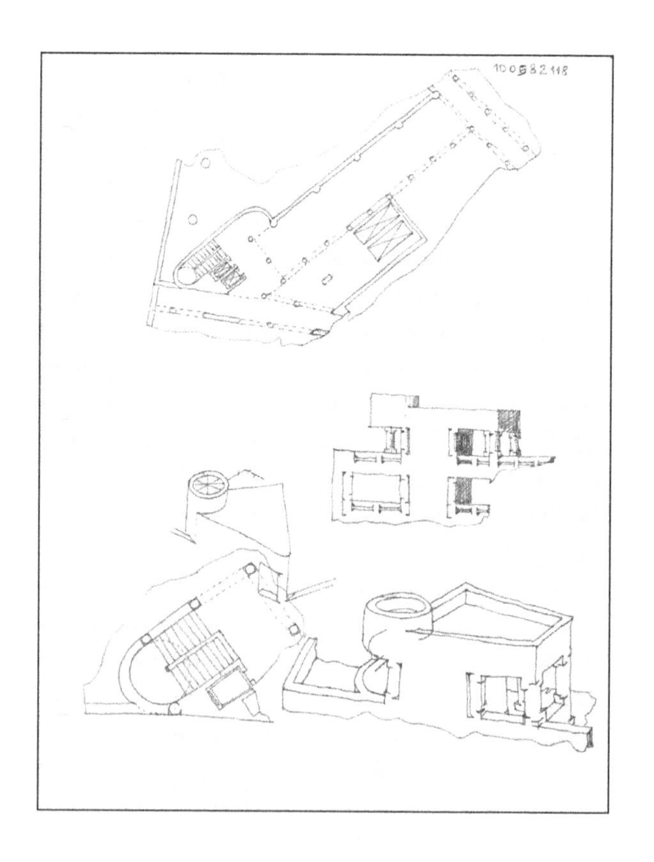
100582118

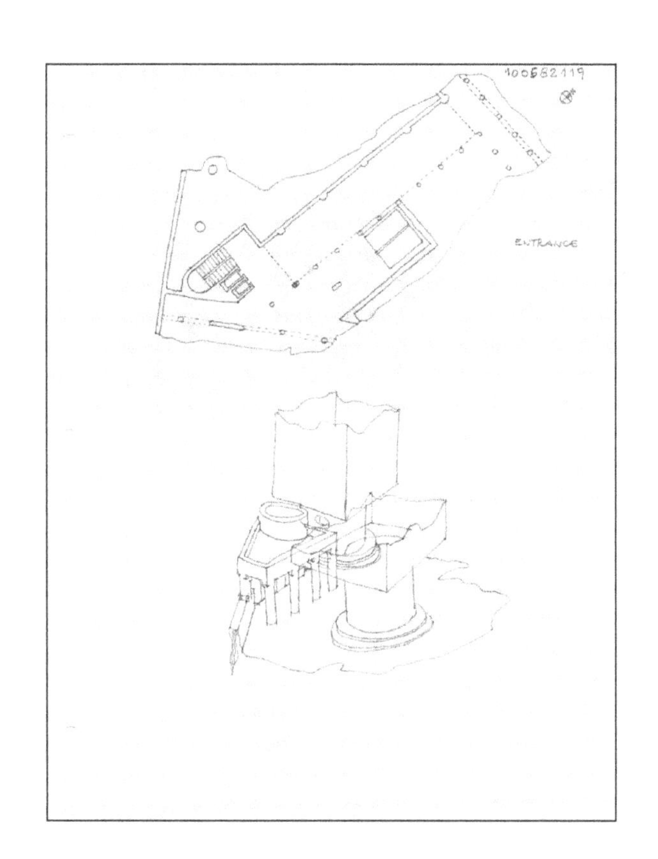
100682119
ENTRANCE

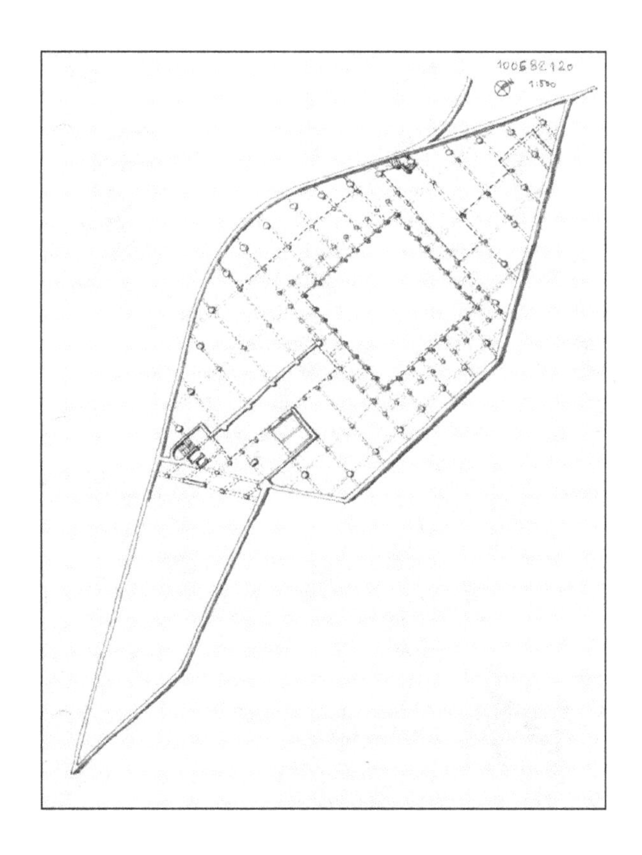
100682120
1:500

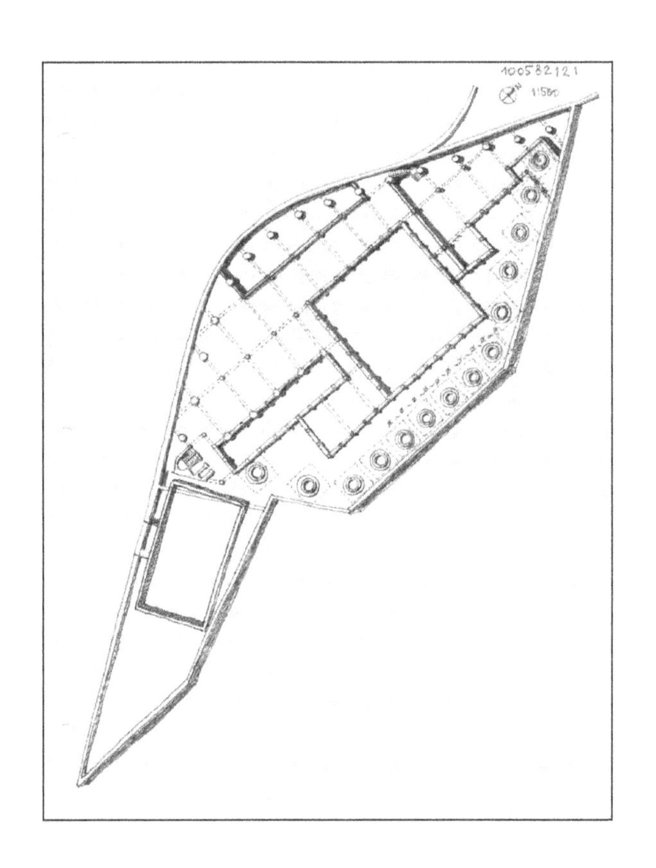
100582121
N
1:500

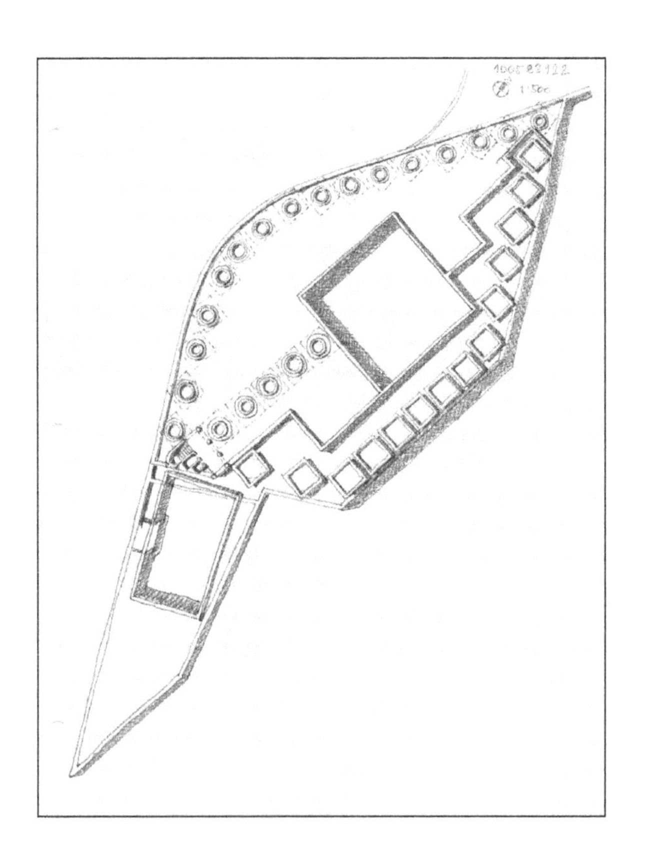
100583122
1:500

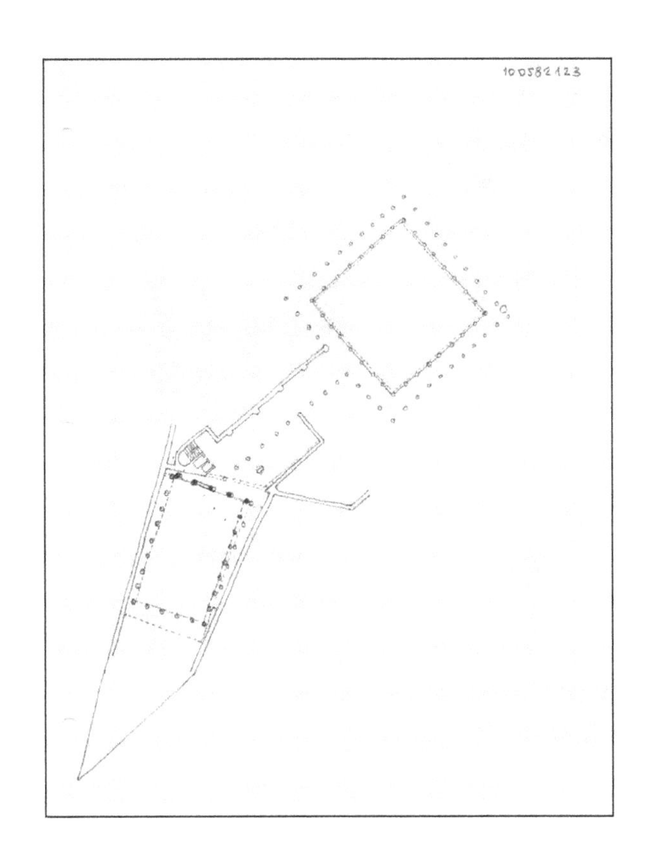
100582123

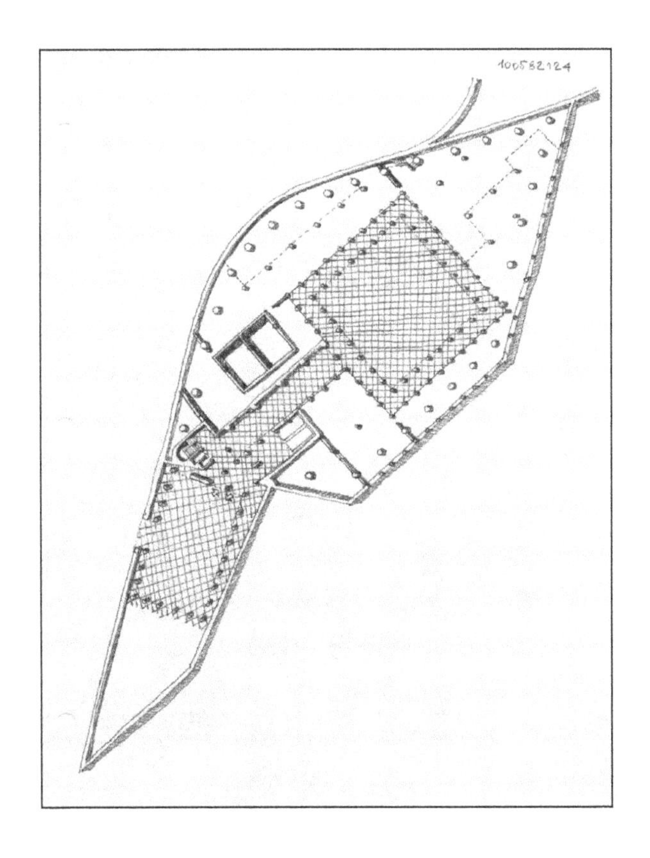
100582124

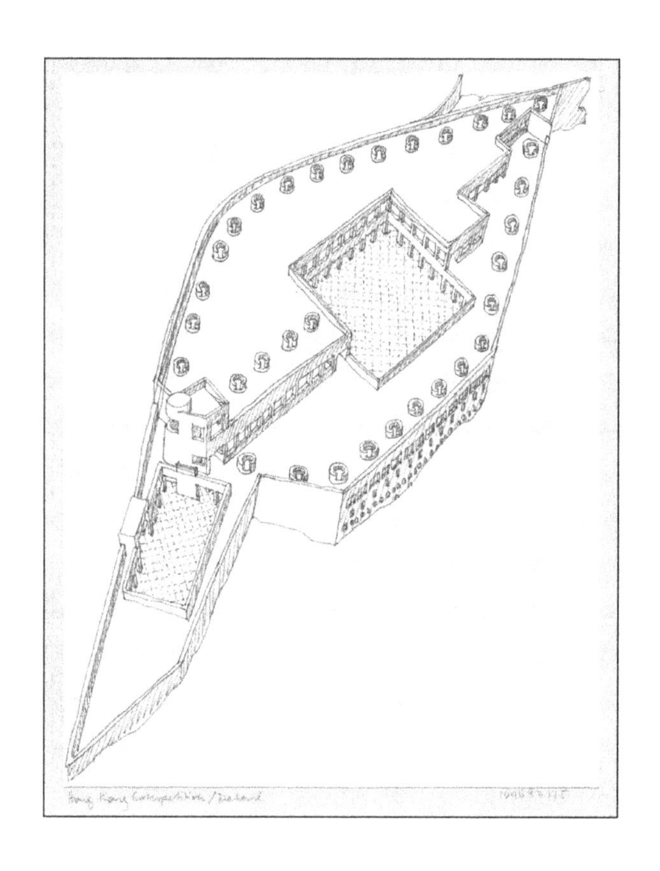

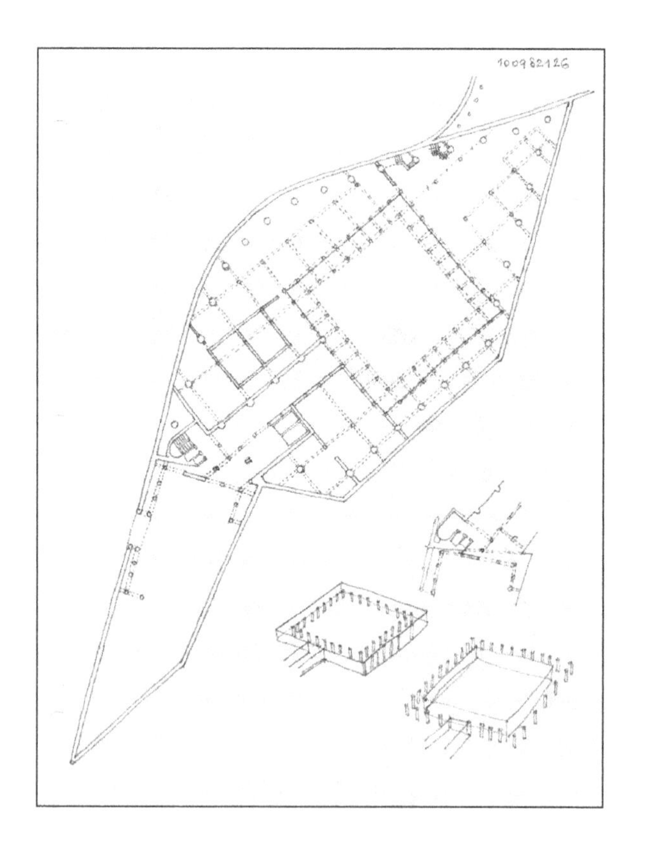

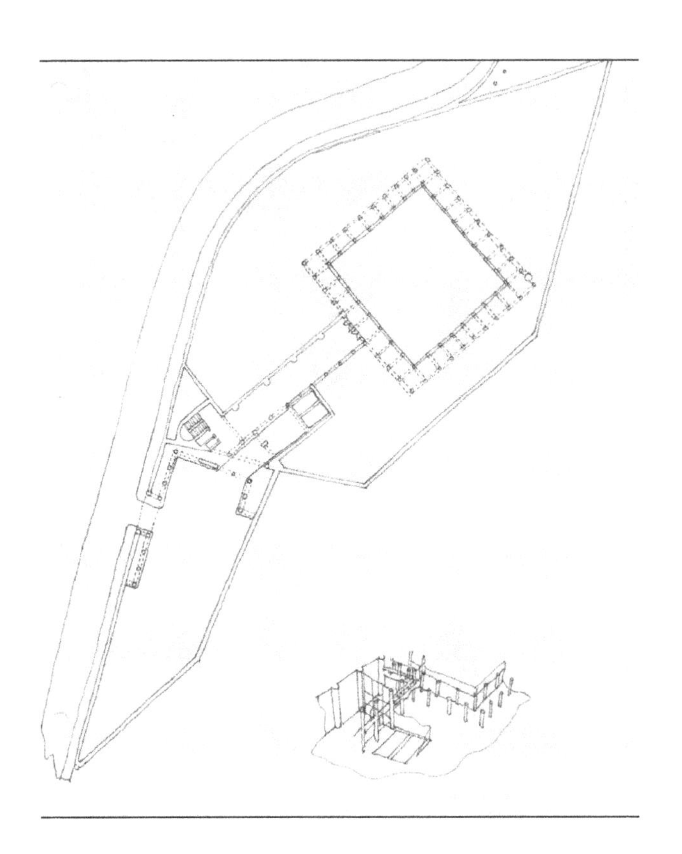

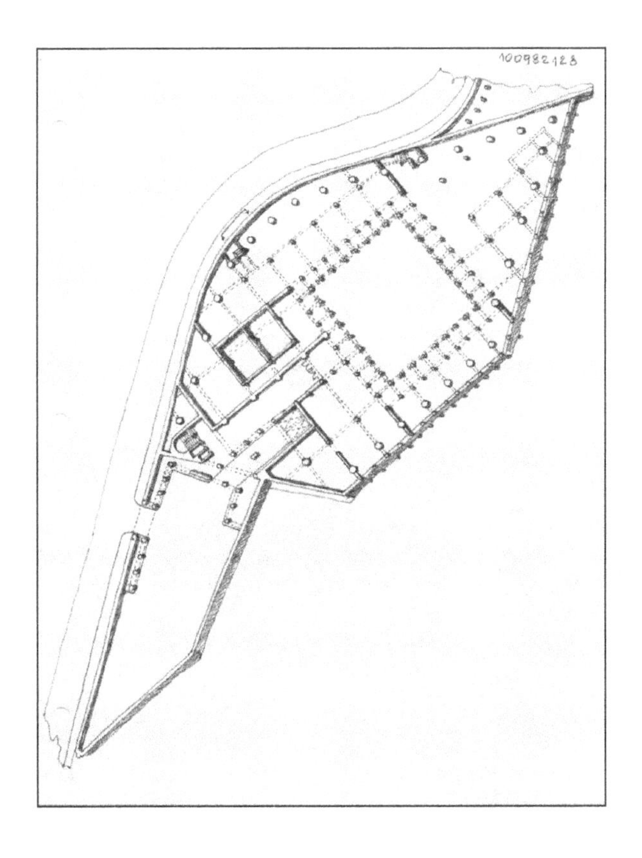
100982128

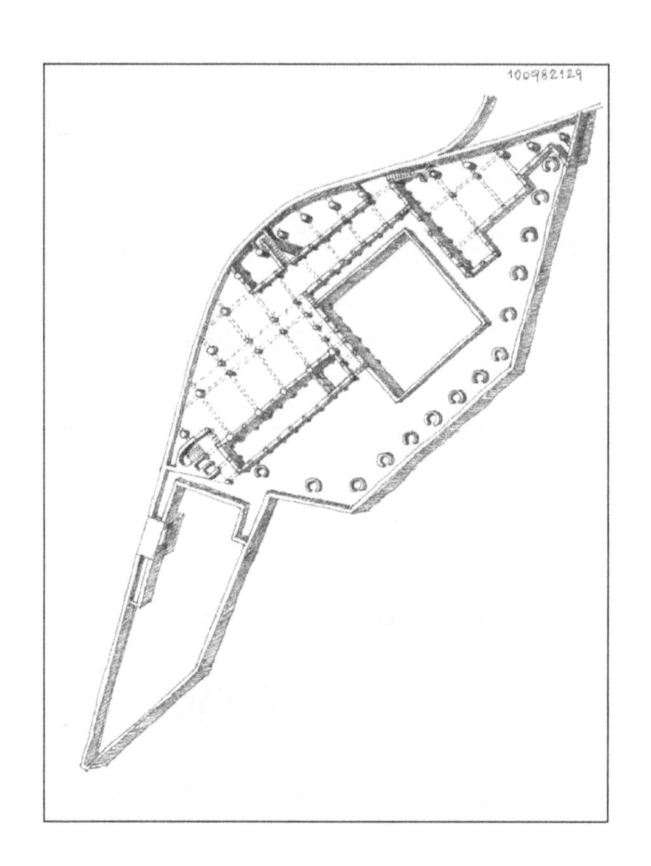
100982129

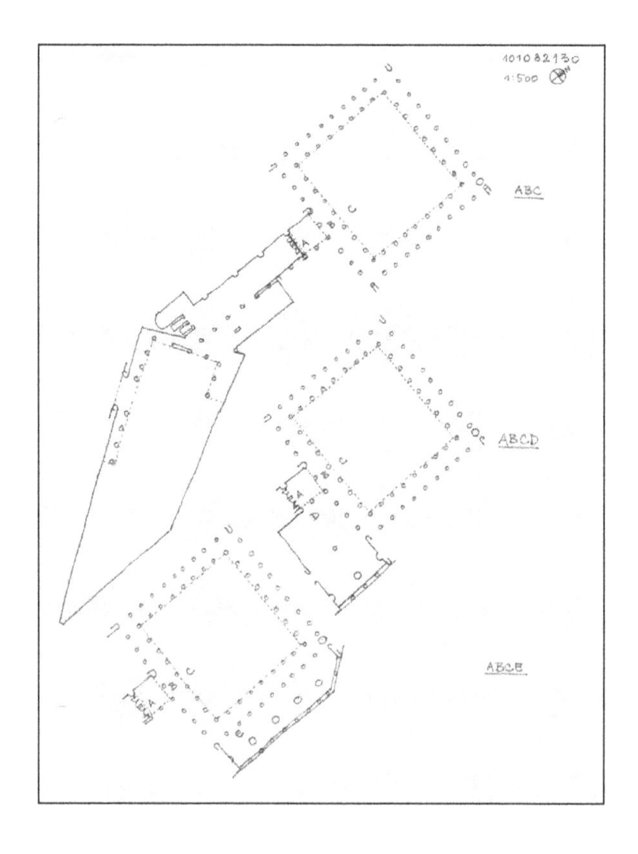
101082130
1:500
ABC
ABCD
ABCE

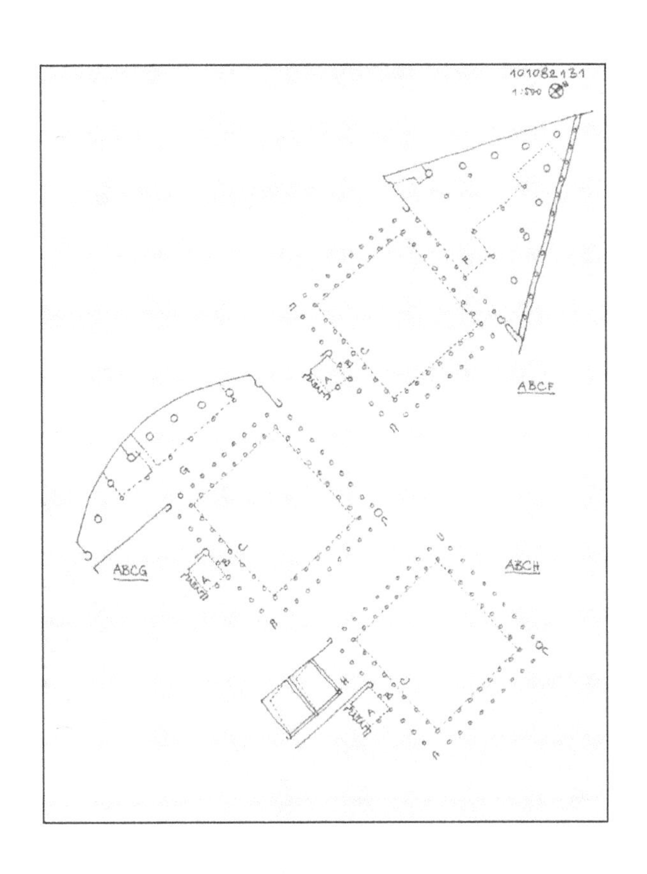

101082131
1:500
ABCF
ABCG
ABCH

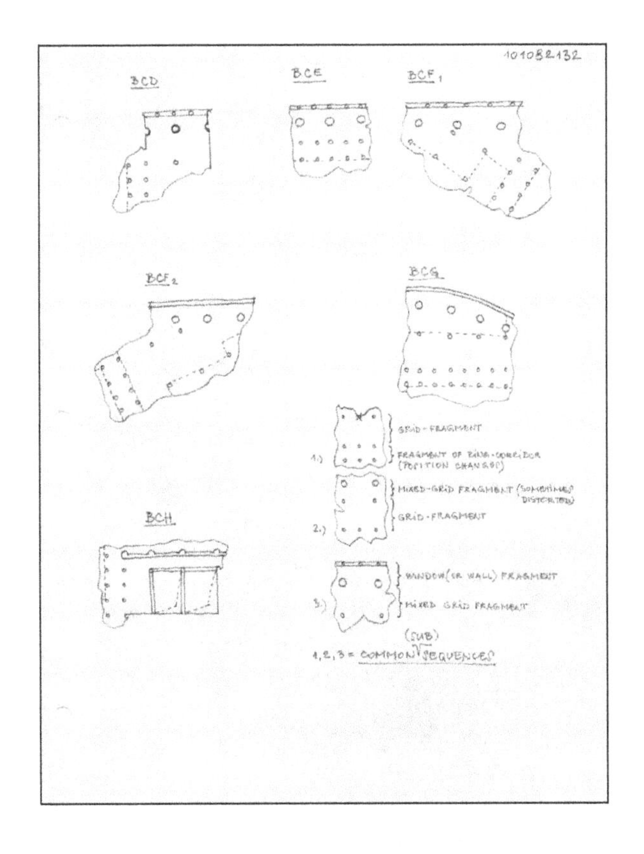

101082132
BCD
BCE
BCF1
BCF2
BCG
BCH
GRID-FRAGMENT
FRAGMENT OF RING-CORRIDOR (POSITION CHANGES)
MIXED-GRID FRAGMENT (SOMETIMES DISTORTED)
GRID-FRAGMENT
WINDOW (OR WALL) FRAGMENT
MIXED GRID FRAGMENT
1.)
2.)
3.)
1, 2, 3 = COMMON (SUB) SEQUENCES

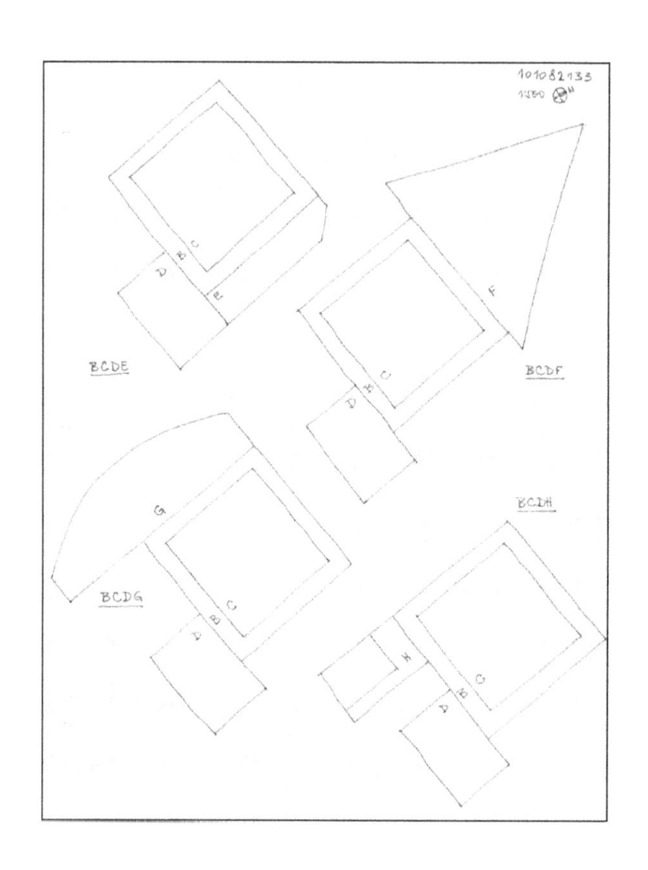
101082133
1:500
BCDE
BCDF
BCDG
BCDH
B
C
D
E
F
G
H

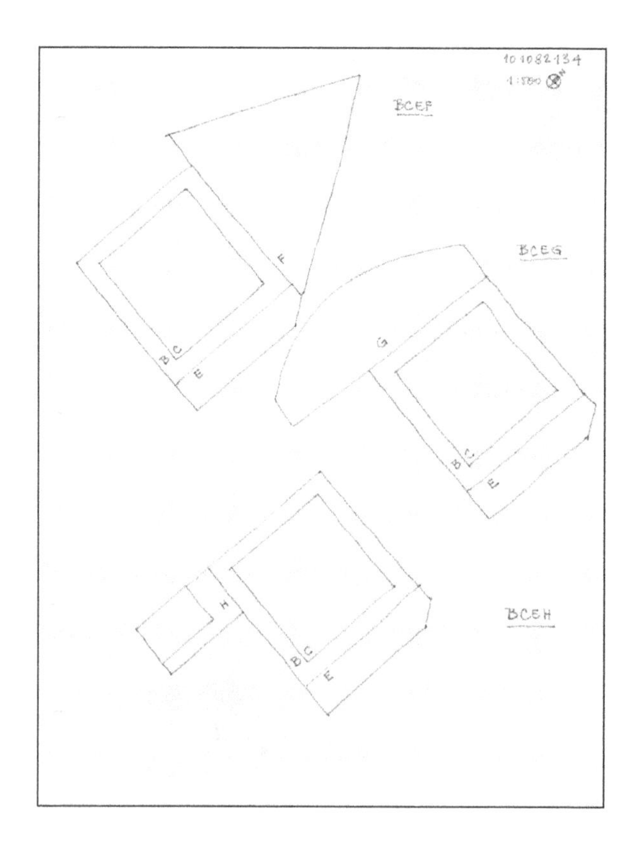
101082134
1:500
BCEF
BCEG
BCEH
B
C
E
F
G
H

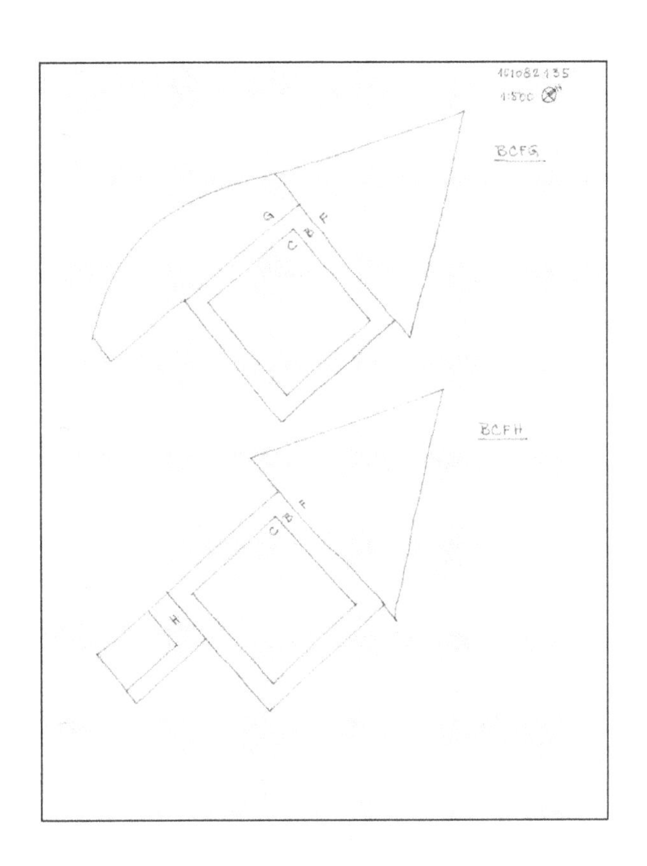
101082135
1:500
BCFG
G
C
B
F
BCFH
C
B
F
H

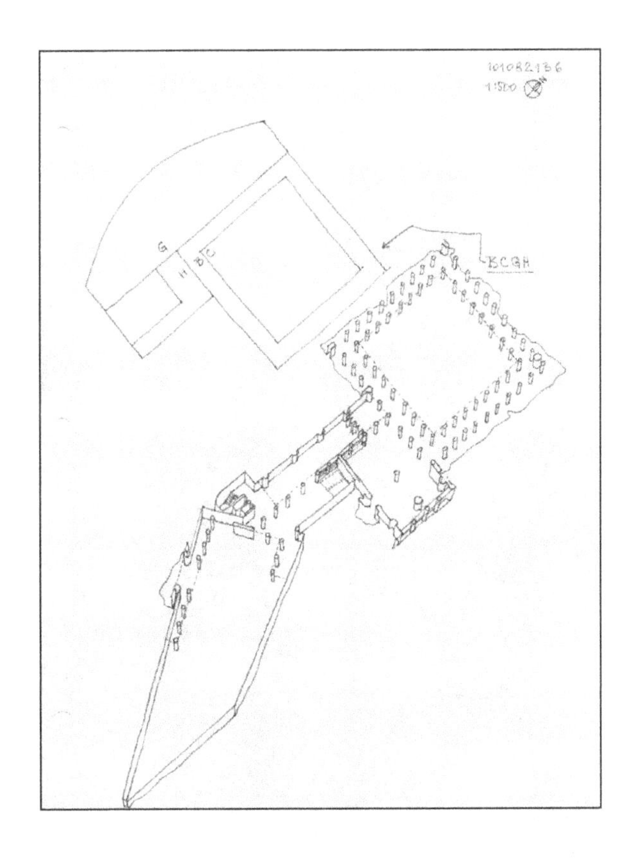
101082136
1:500
BCGH
G
H
B
C

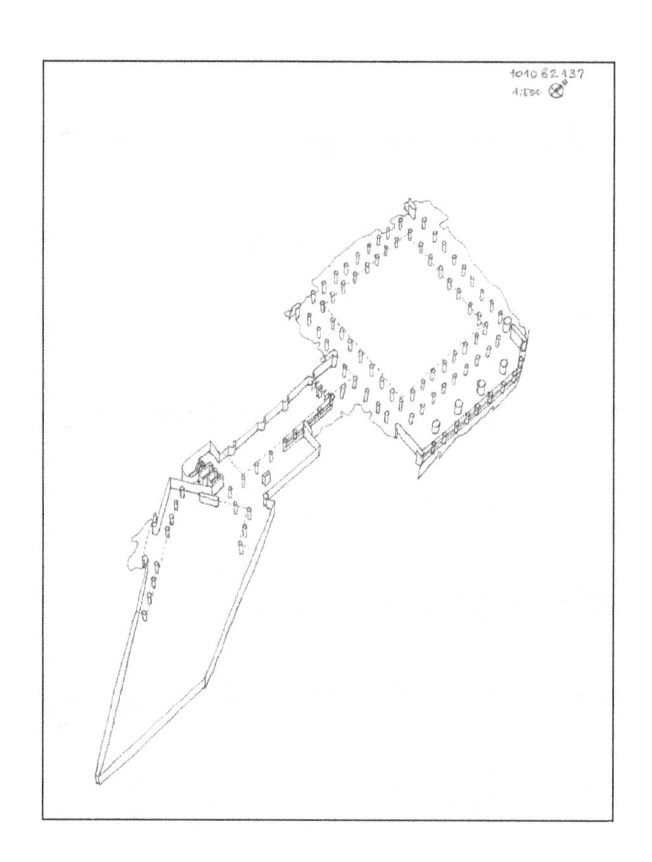
101082137
1:500

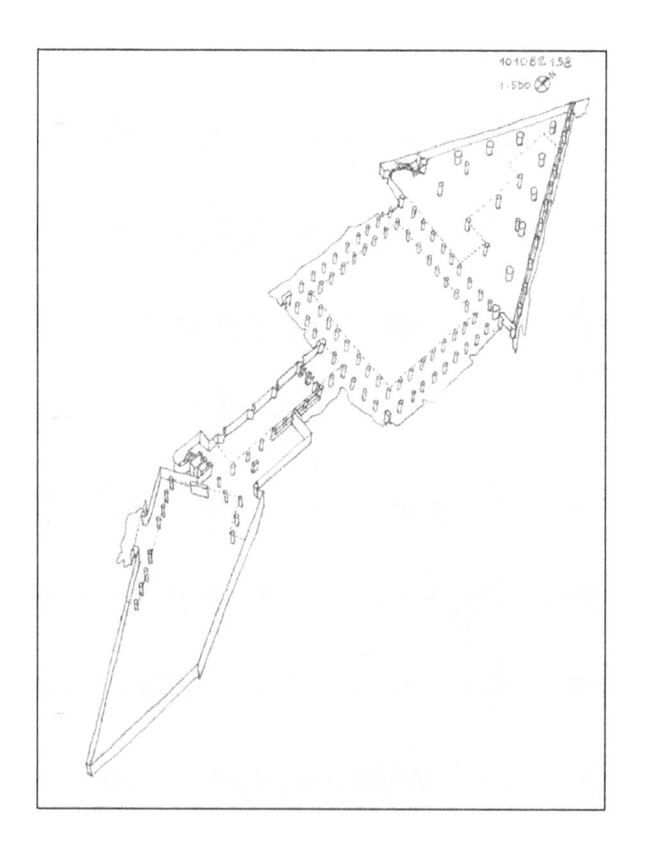
101082158
1:500

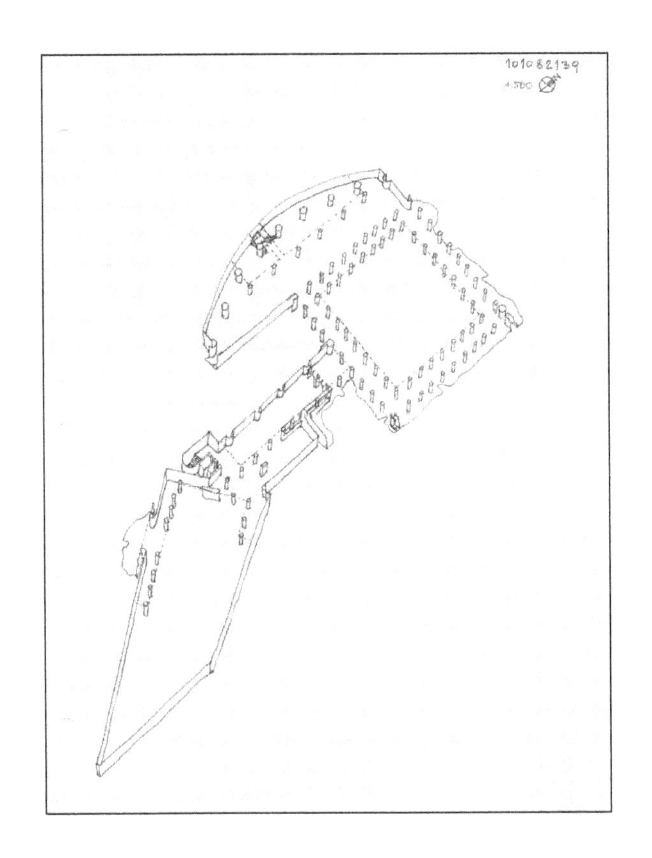
101082139
1:500
N

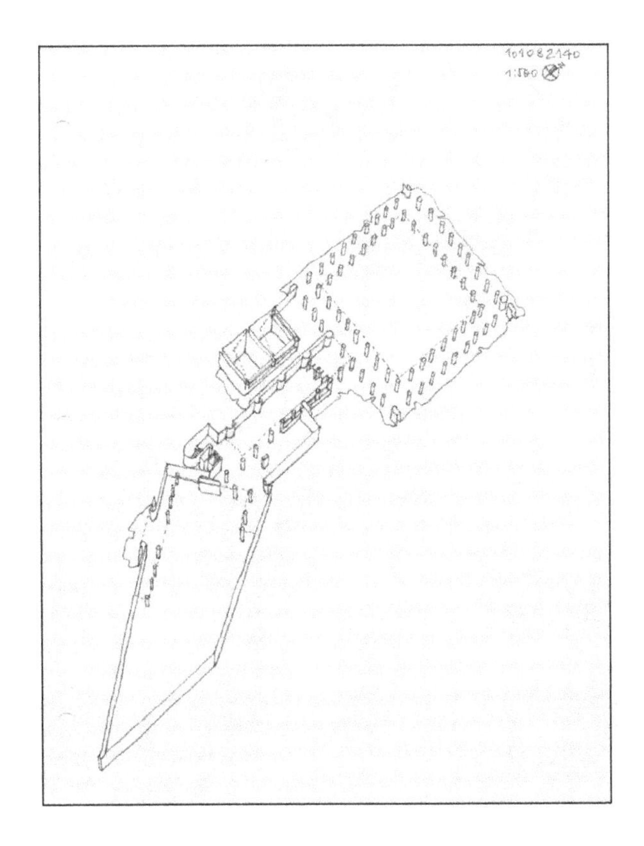
101082140
1:500
N

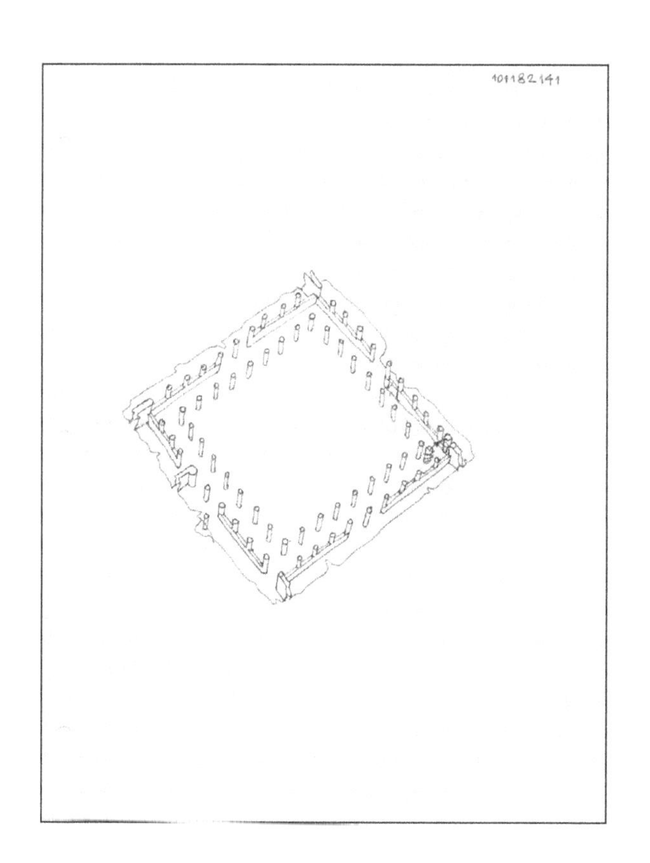

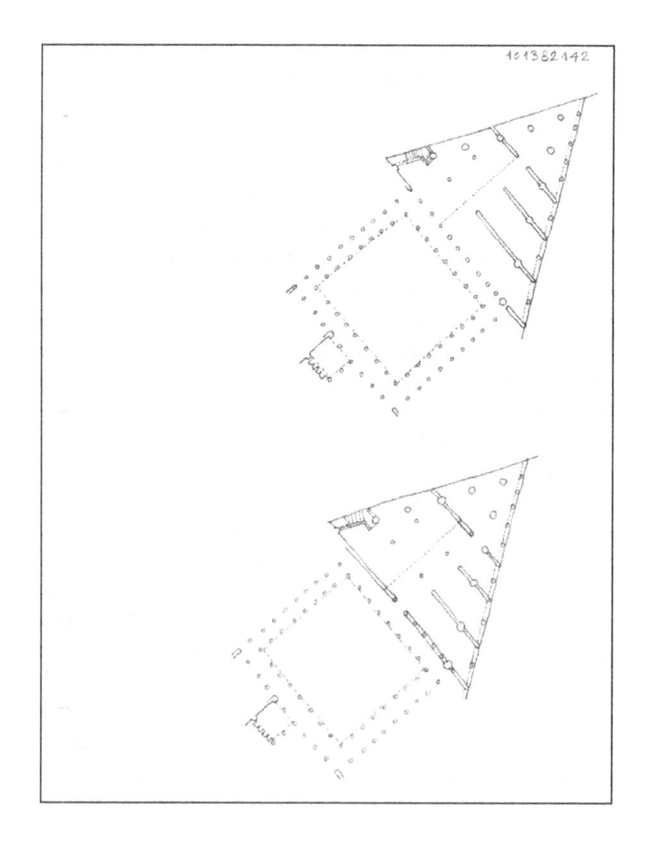

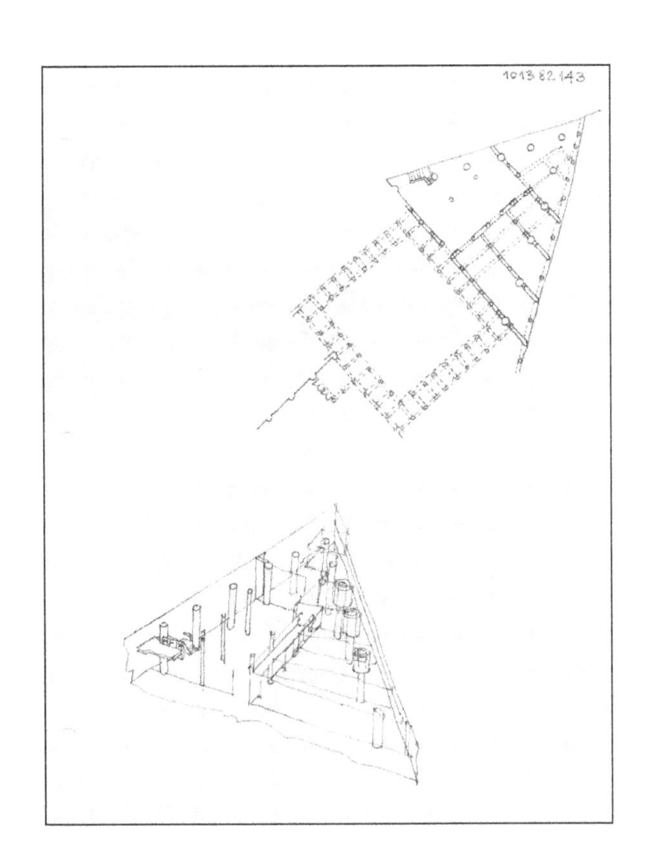
101382143

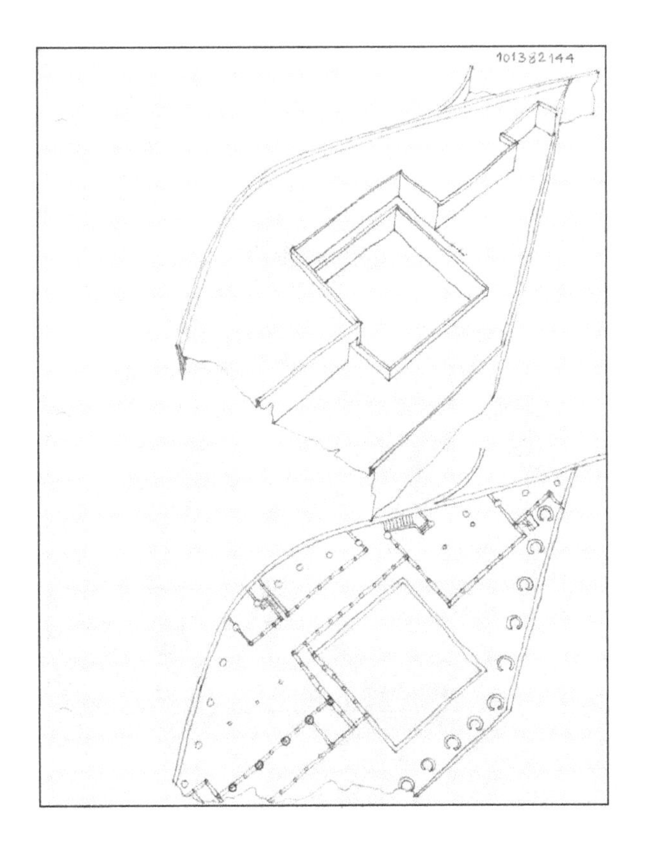
101382144

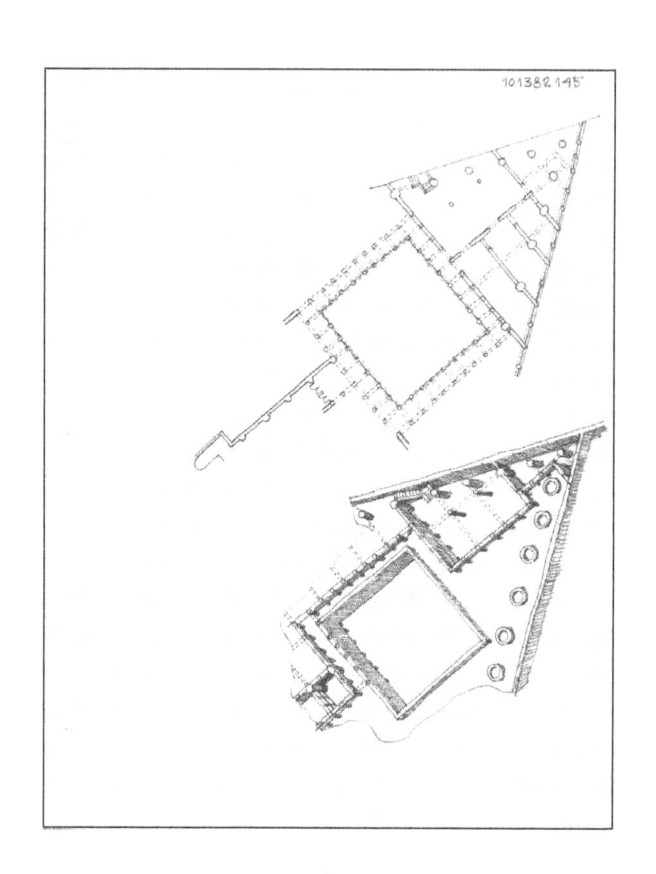
101382145

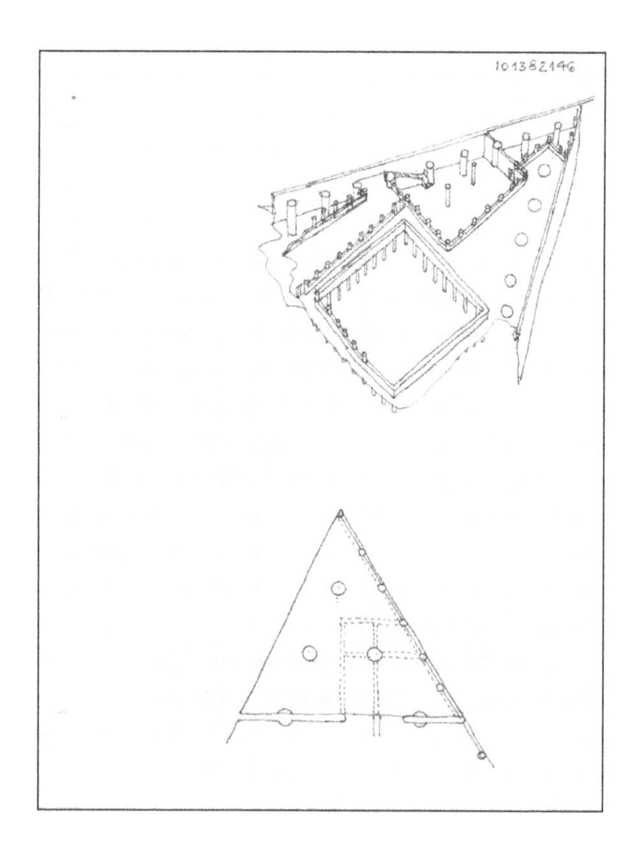
101382146

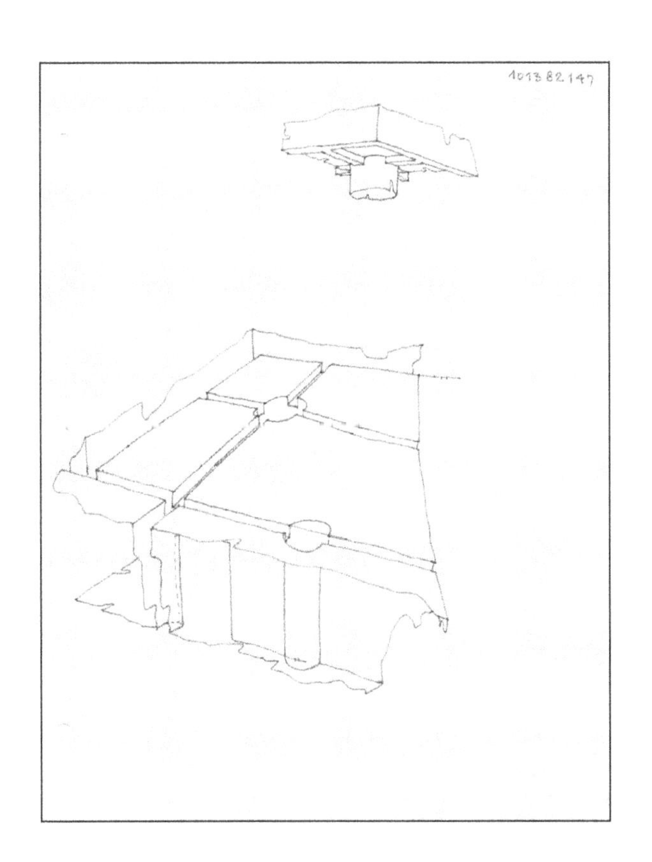
101382147

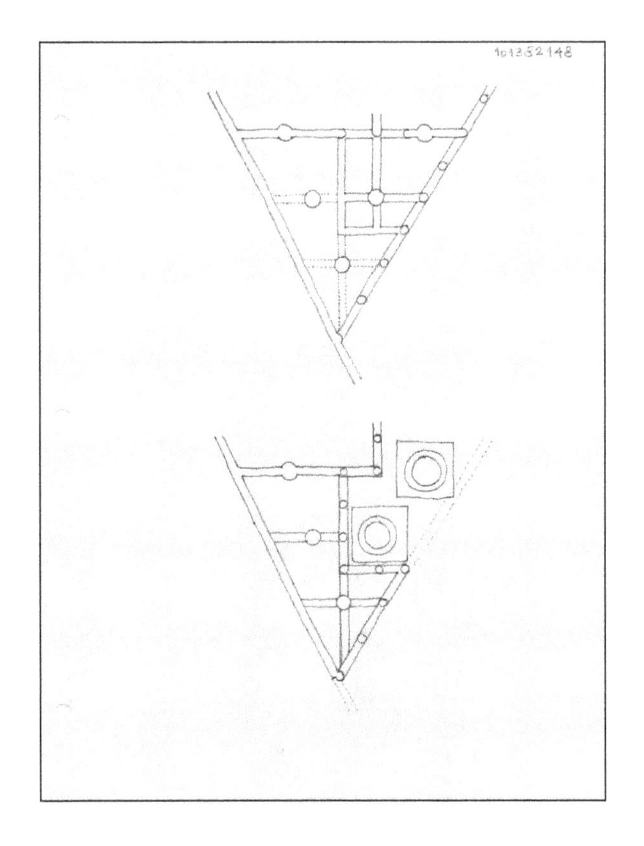
101382148

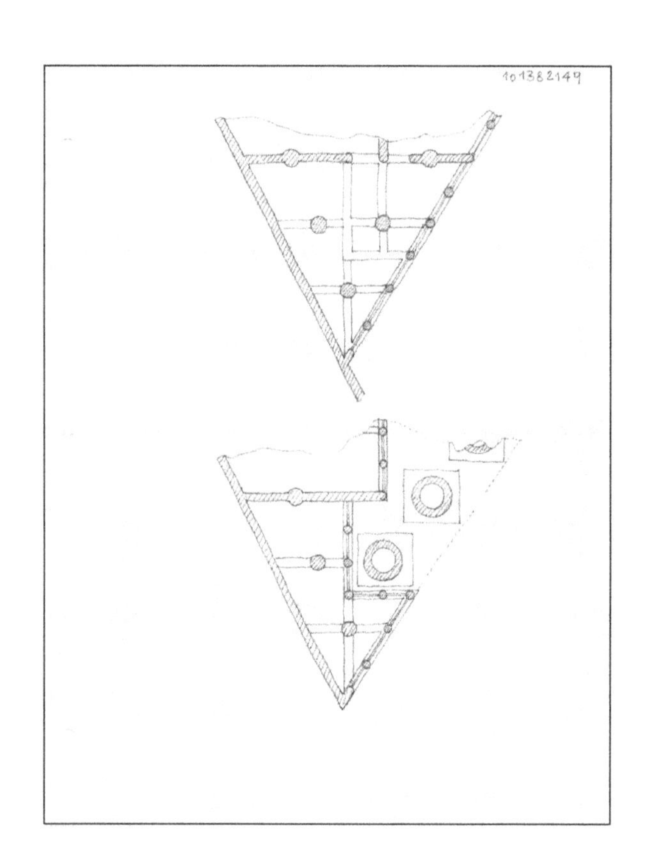
101382149

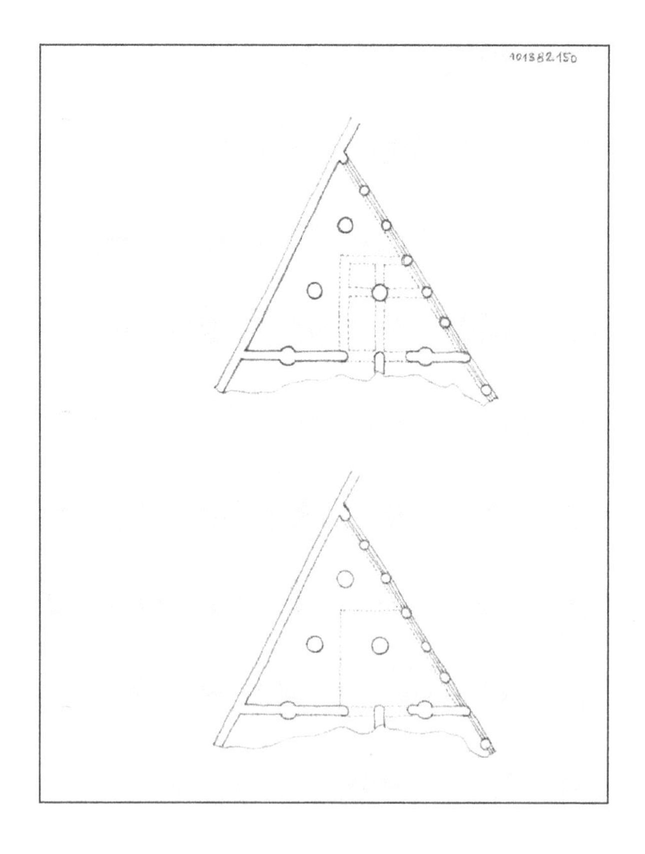
101382150

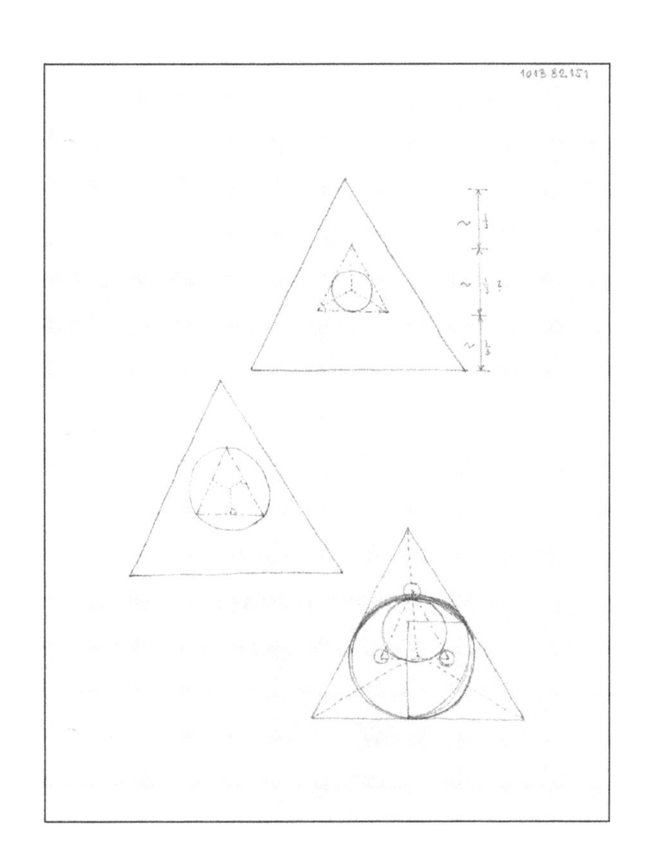
1013.82.151

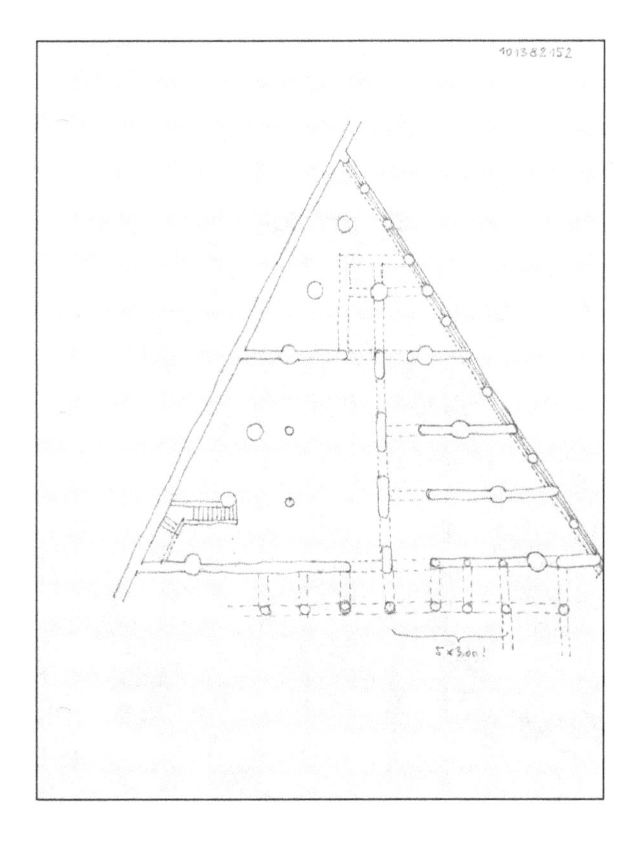
1013.82.152
5 × 3,00 !

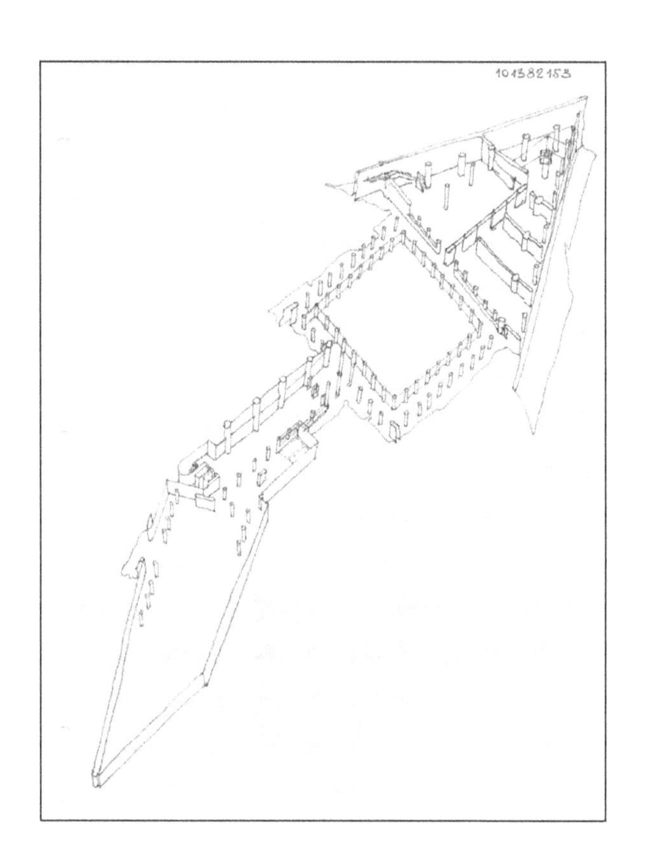
101382153

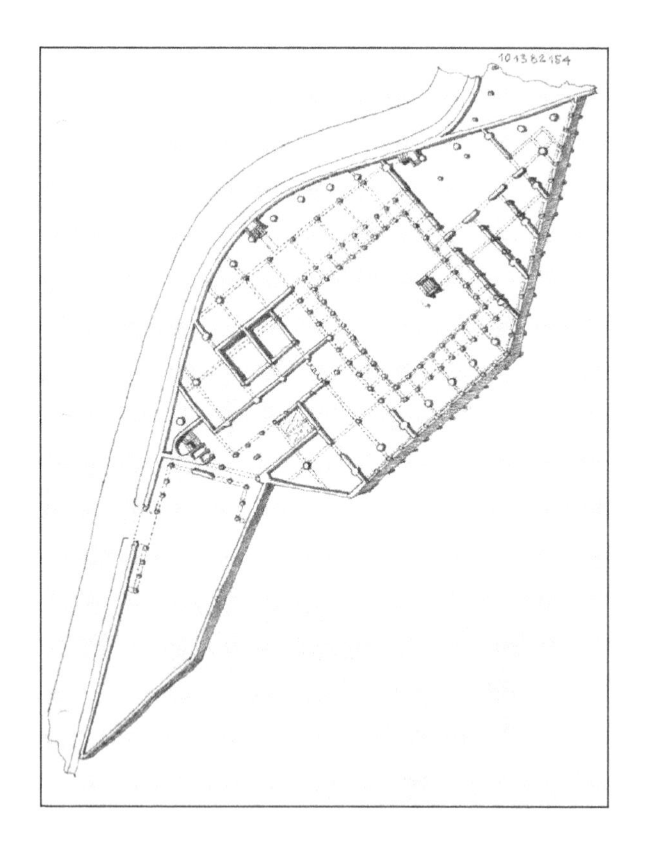
101382154

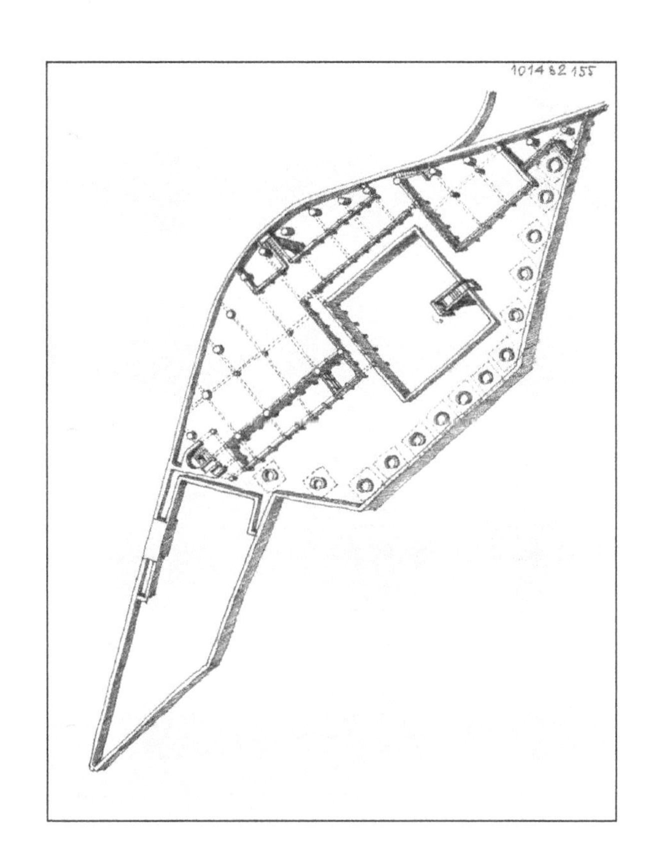
101482155

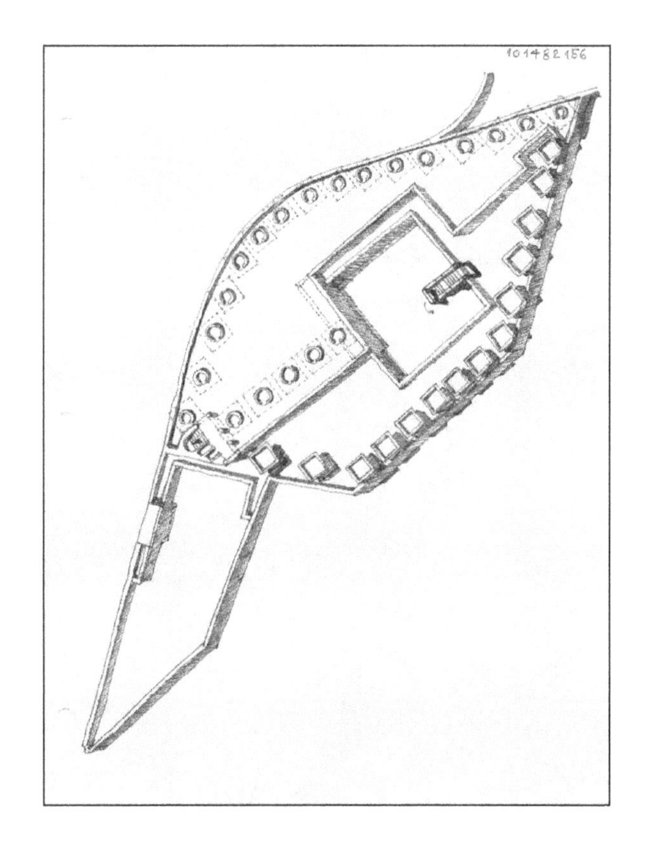
101482156

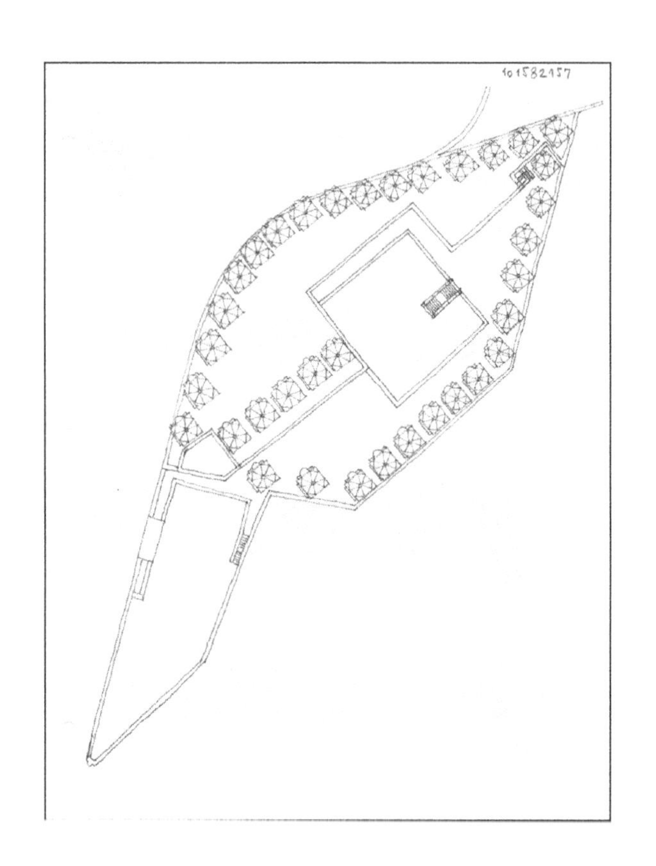
101582157

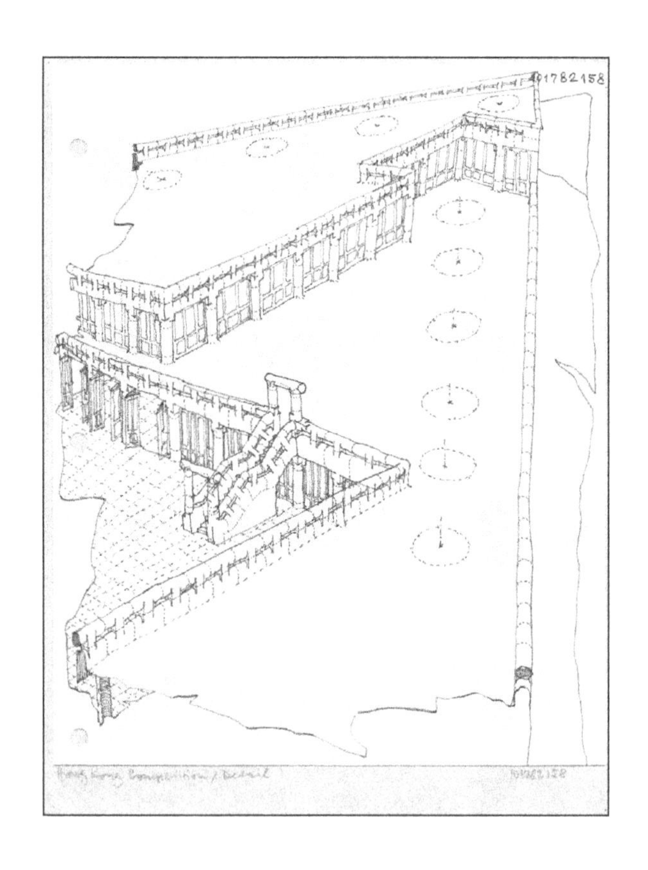
101782158

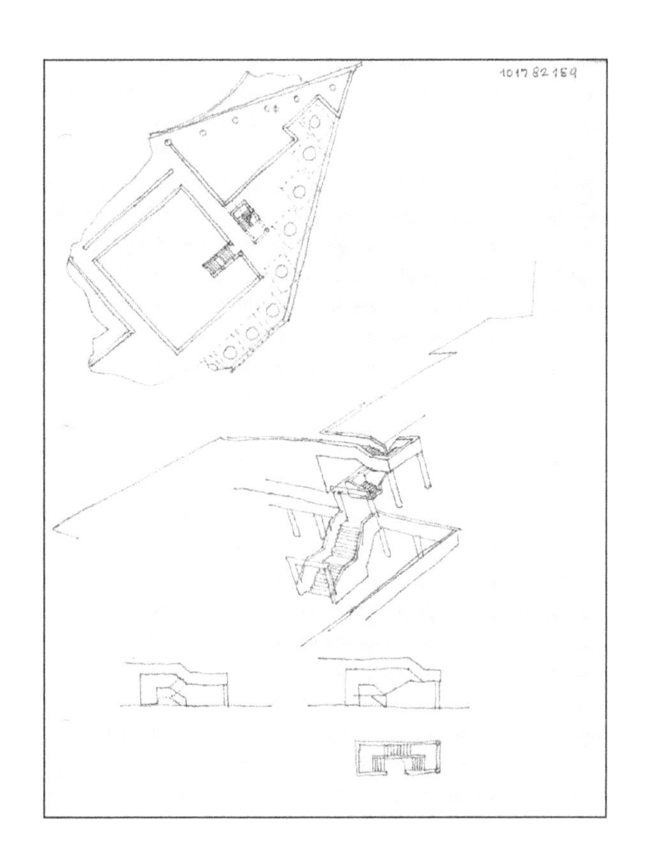
101782159

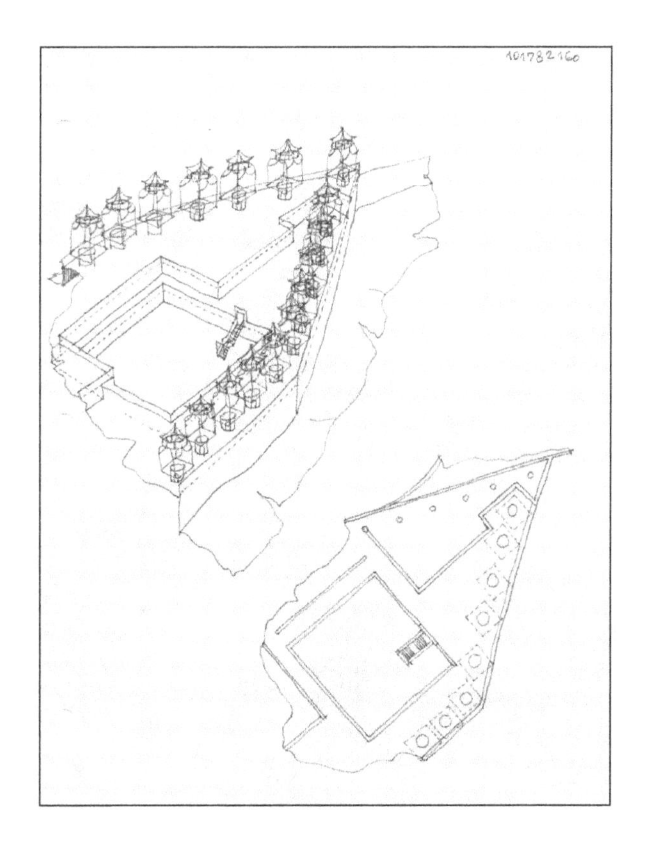
101782160

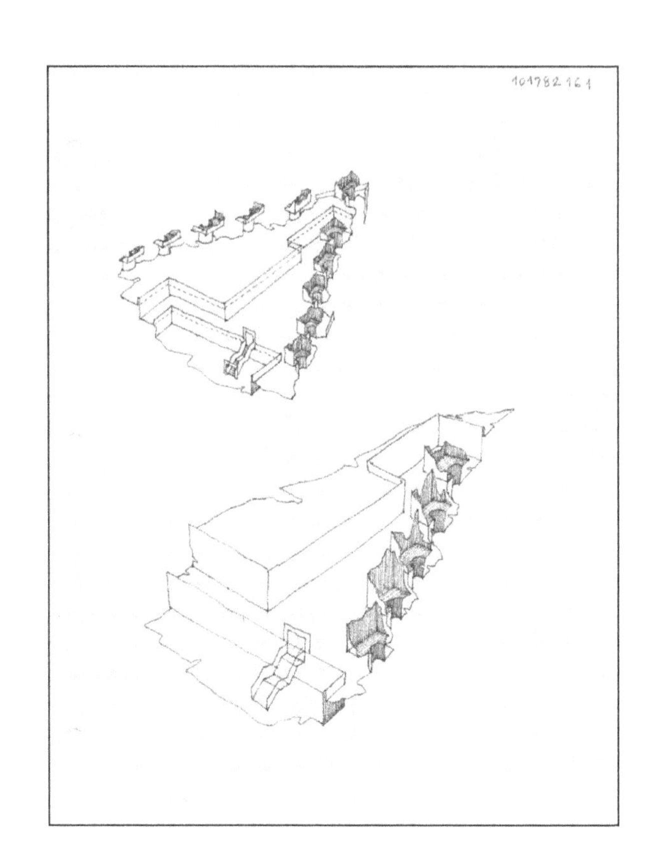
101782161

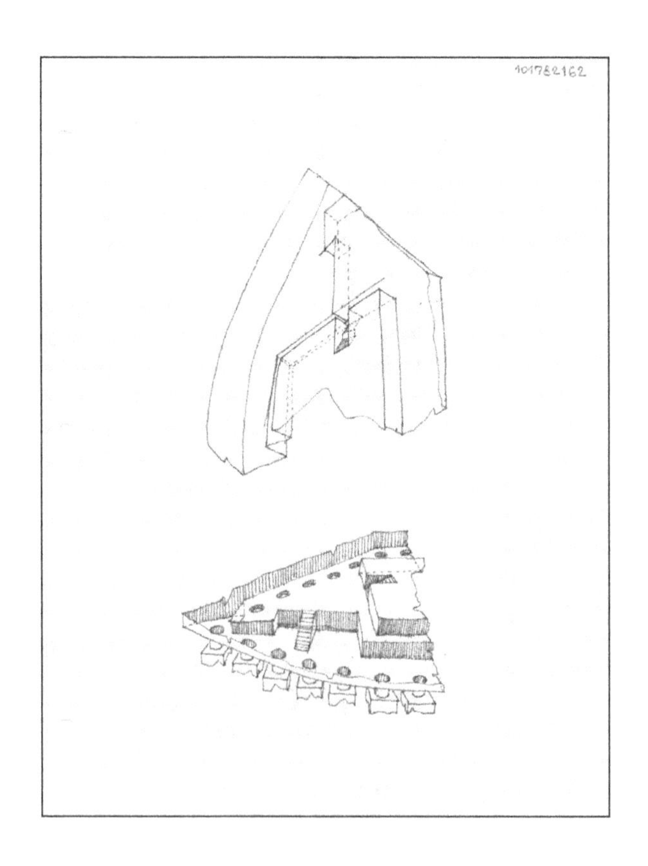
101782162

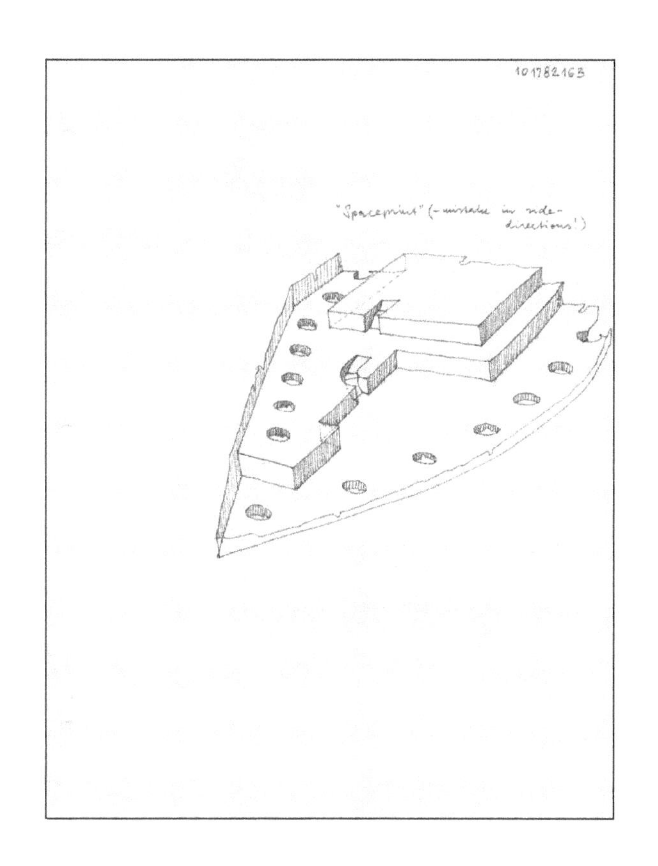
101782163
"Spaceprint" (- mistake in side-
directions!)

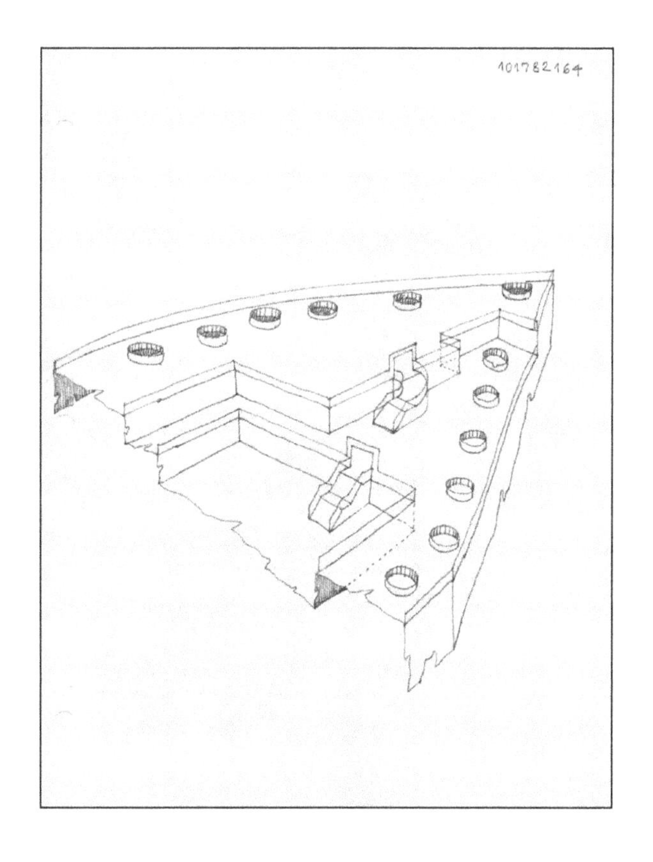
101782164

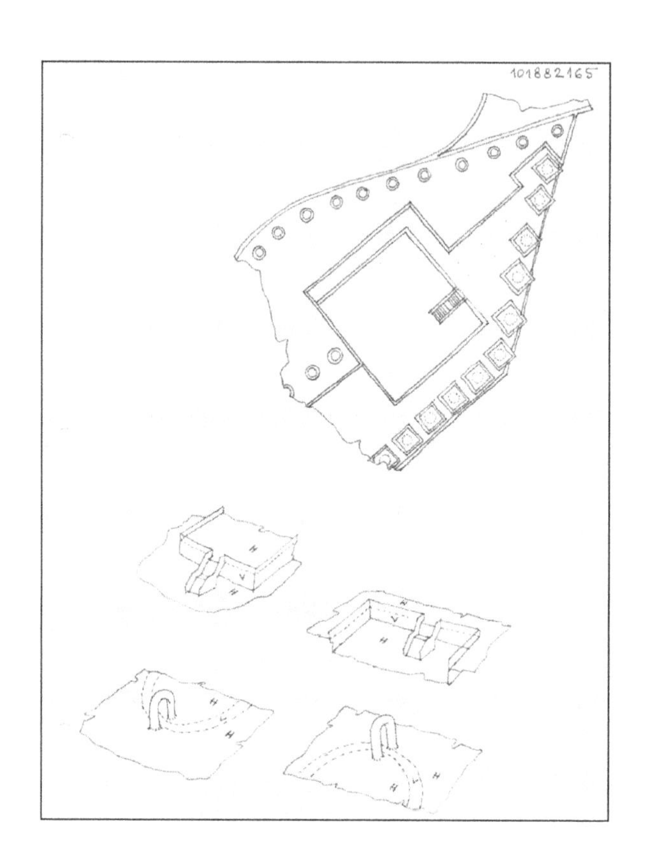
101882165

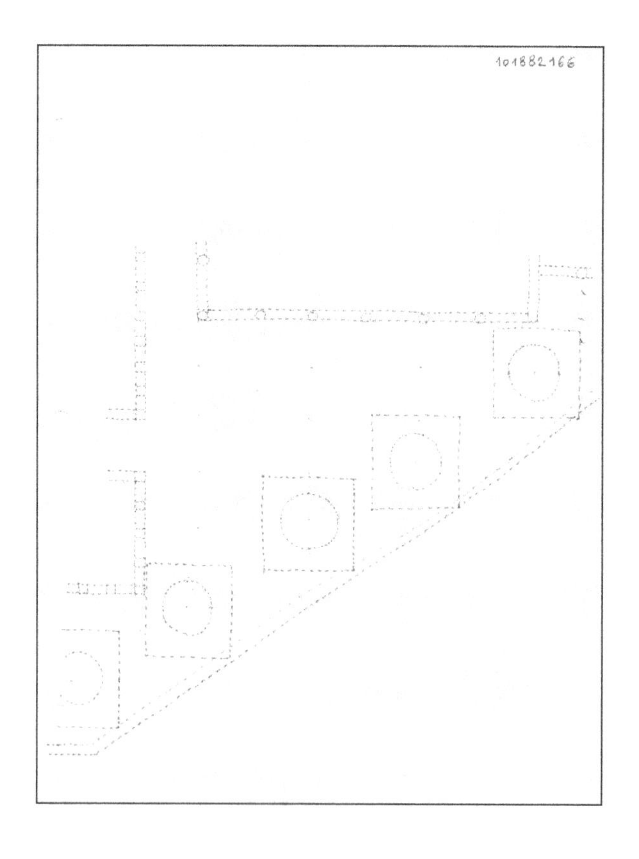
101882166

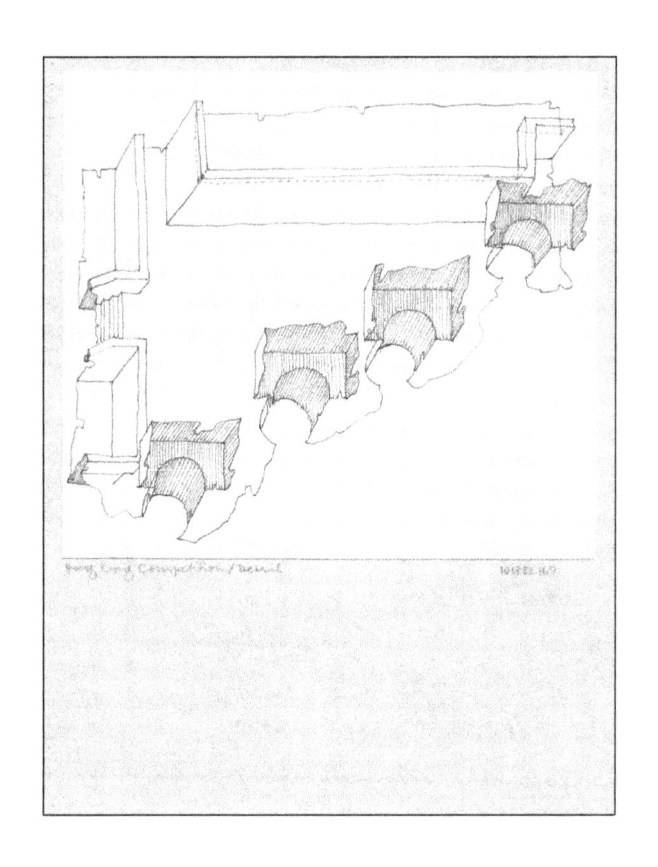
Hong Kong Competition / Detail

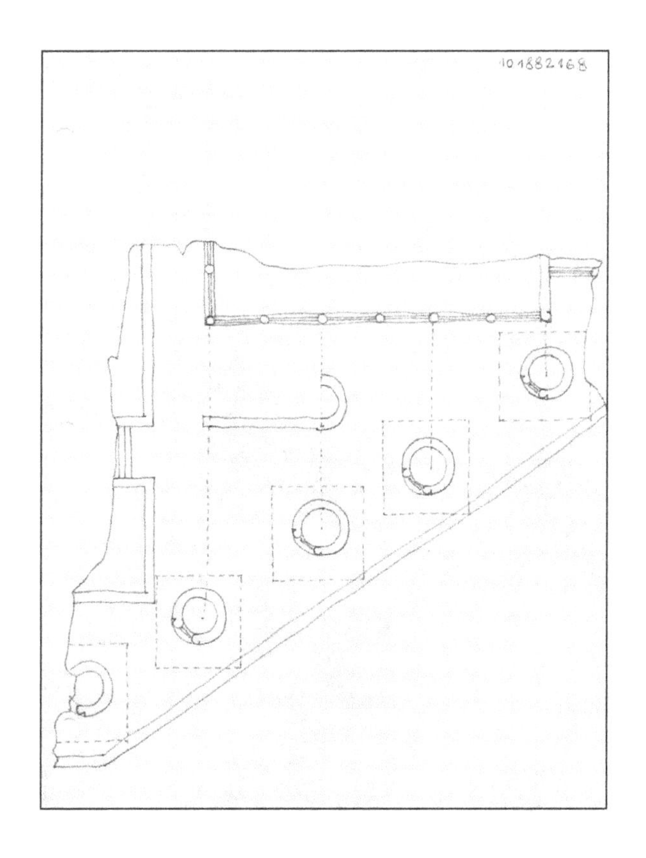
101882168

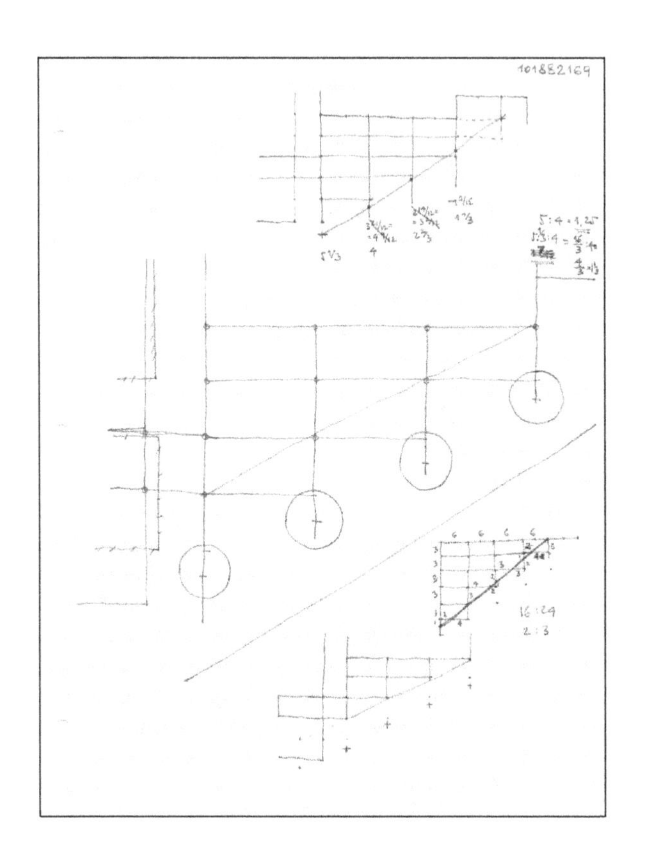
101882169
16:24
2:3

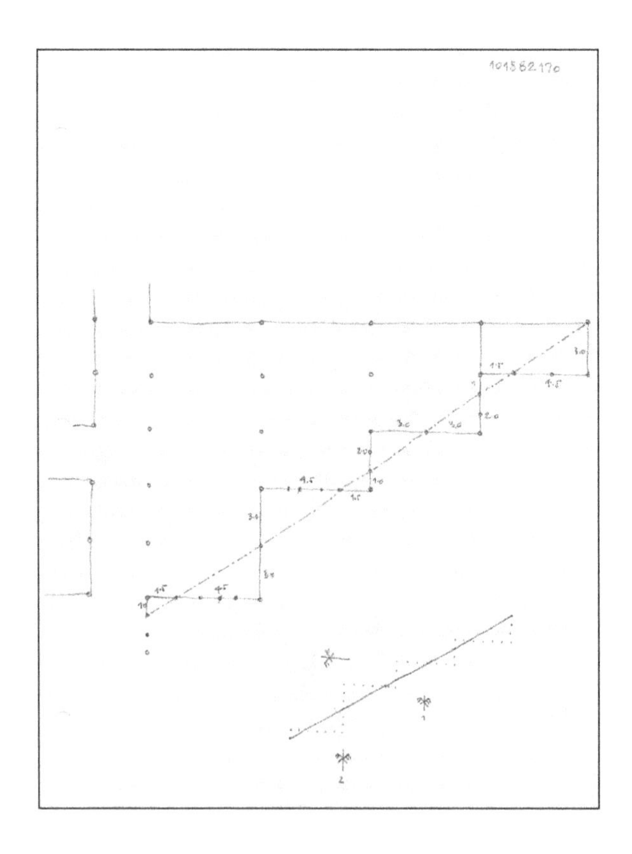
101882170

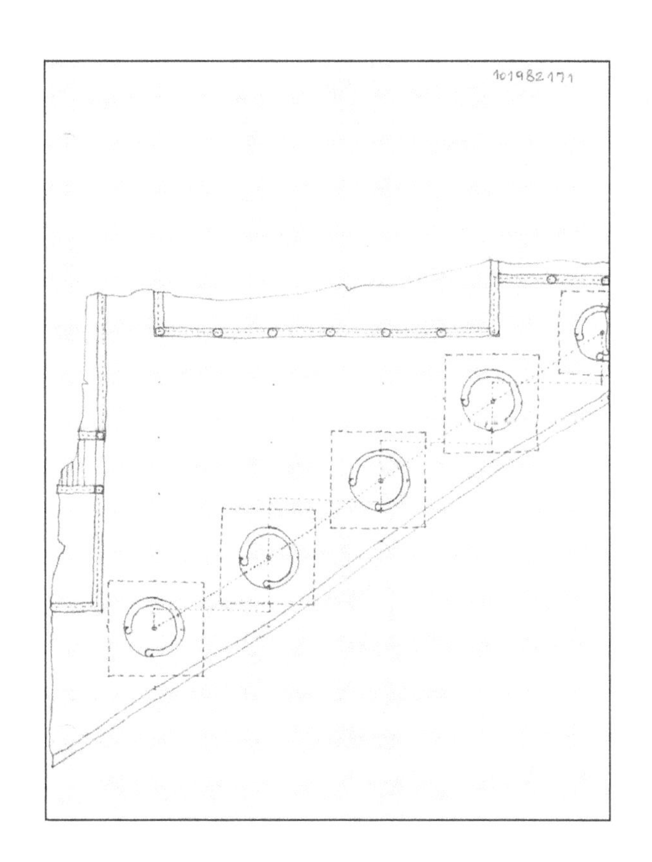
101982171

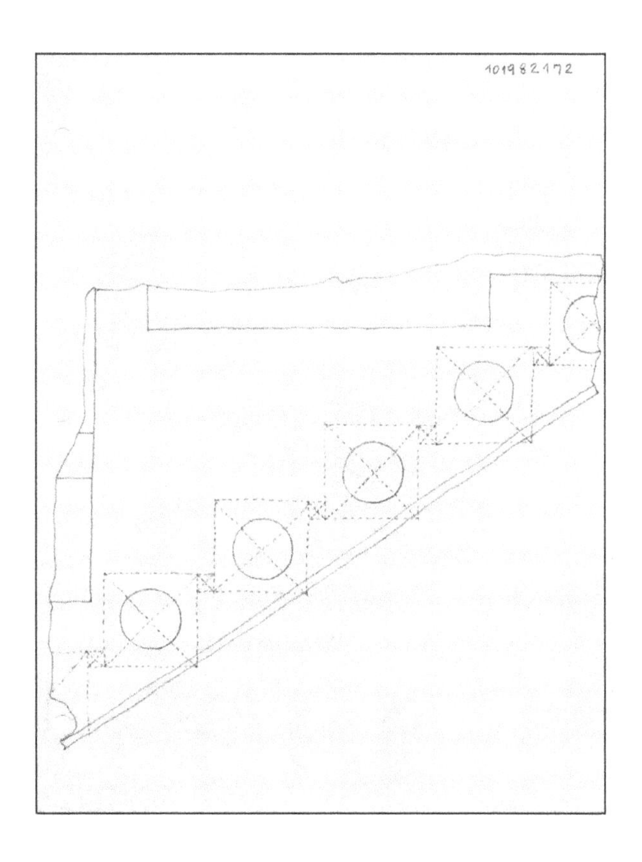
101982172

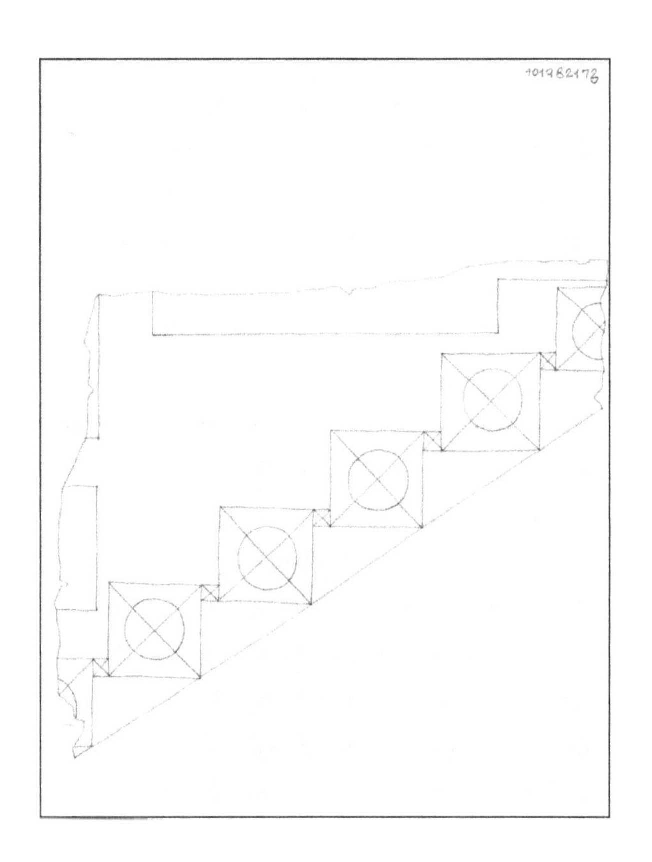

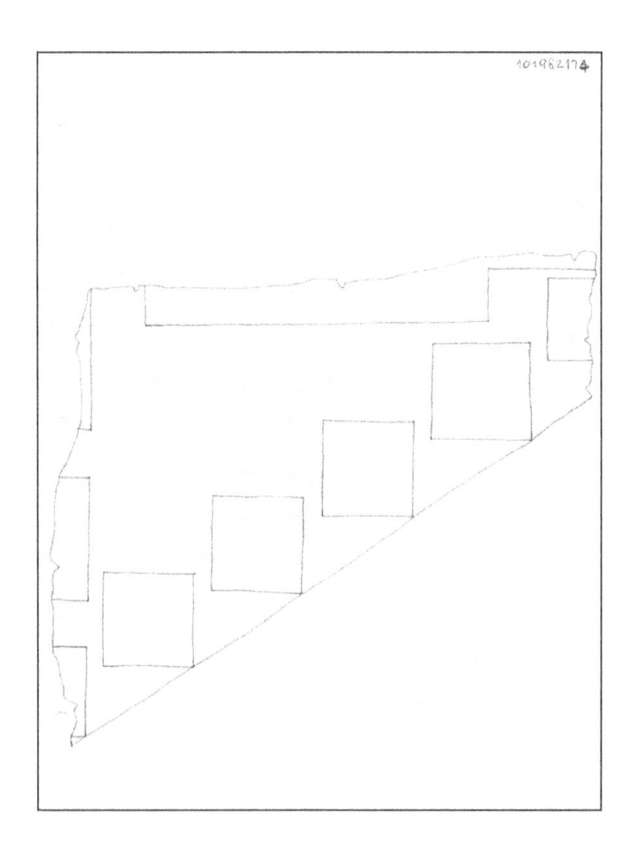

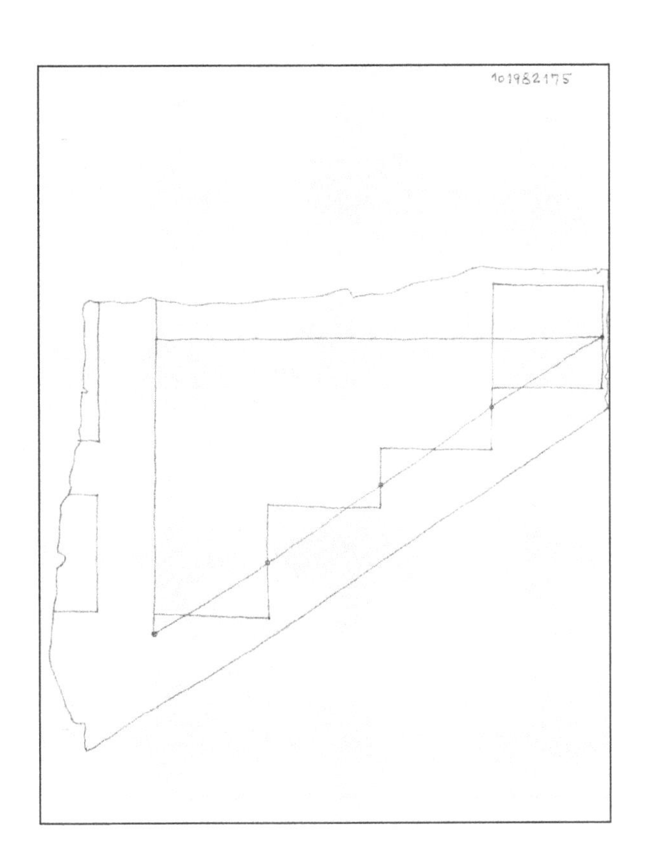
101982175

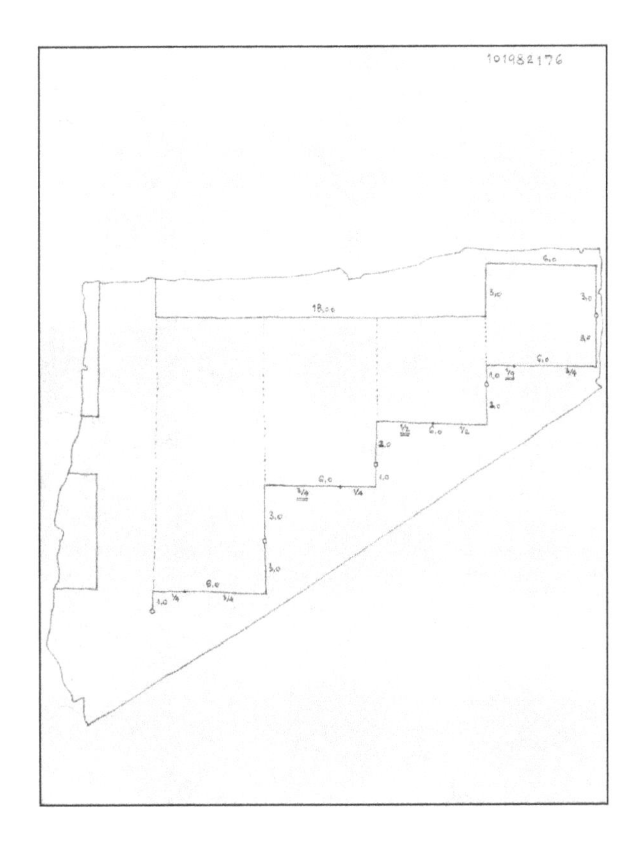
101982176
18,00
6,0
3,0
3,0
6,0
6,0
6,0
6,0
3,0
3,0
2,0
2,0
1,0
1,0

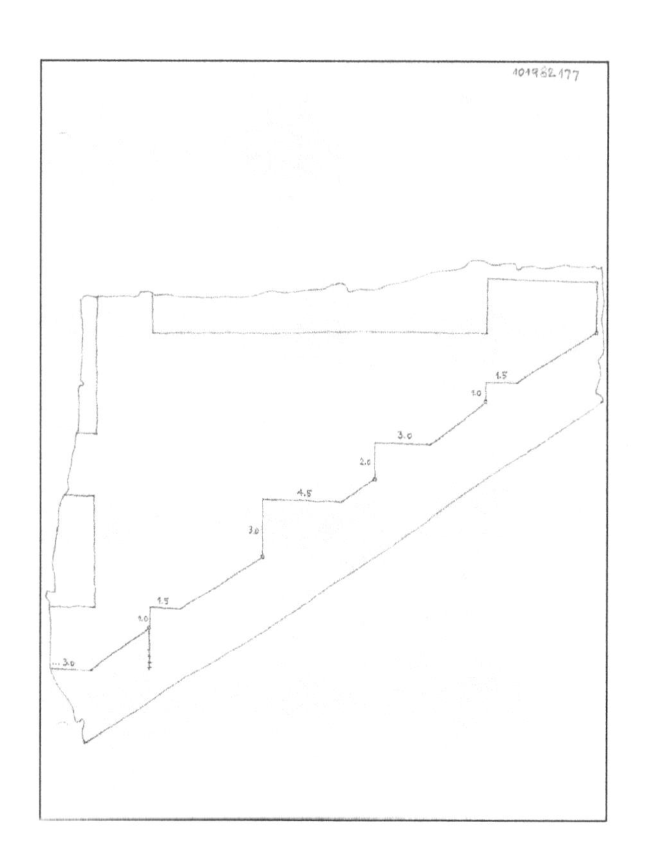
101982.177
1.5
1.0
3.0
2.0
4.5
3.0
1.5
1.0
3.0

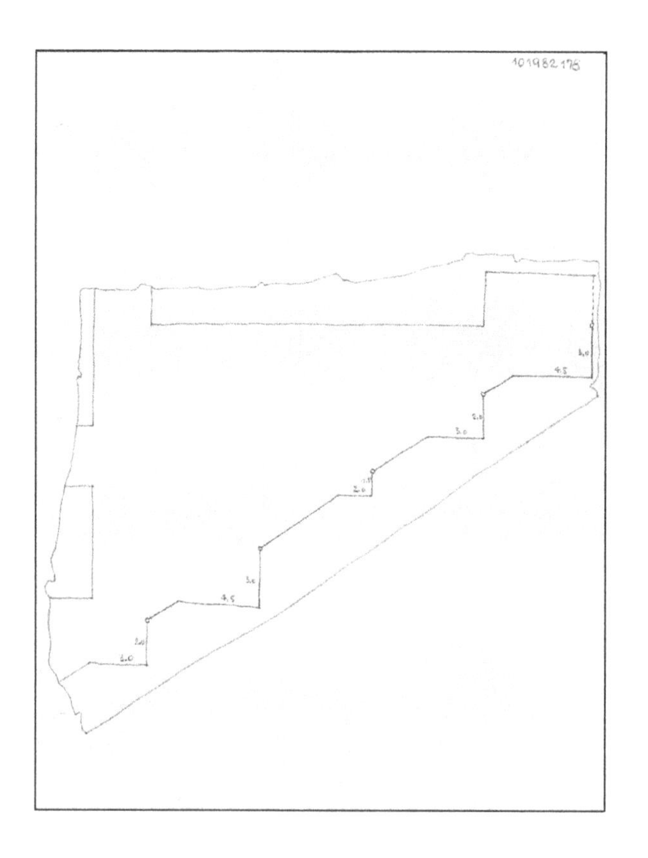
101982.178
4.5
2.0
3.0
4.5
3.0

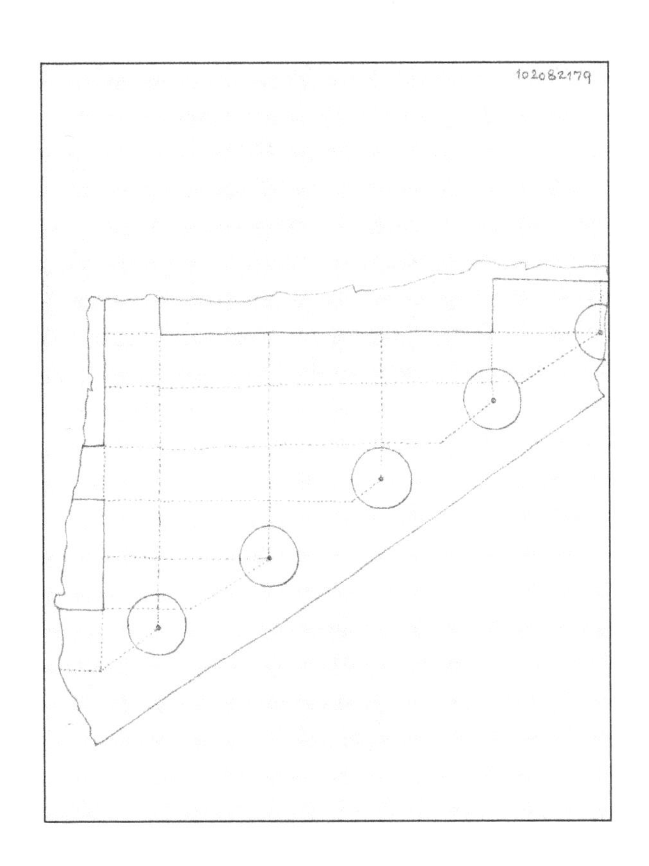
102082179

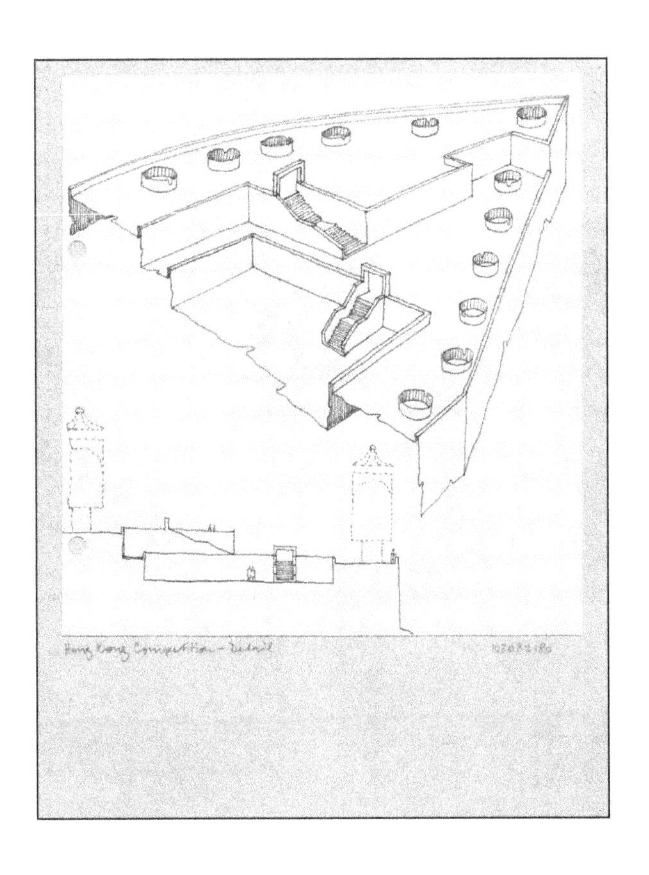
Hong Kong Competition – Detail
102082180

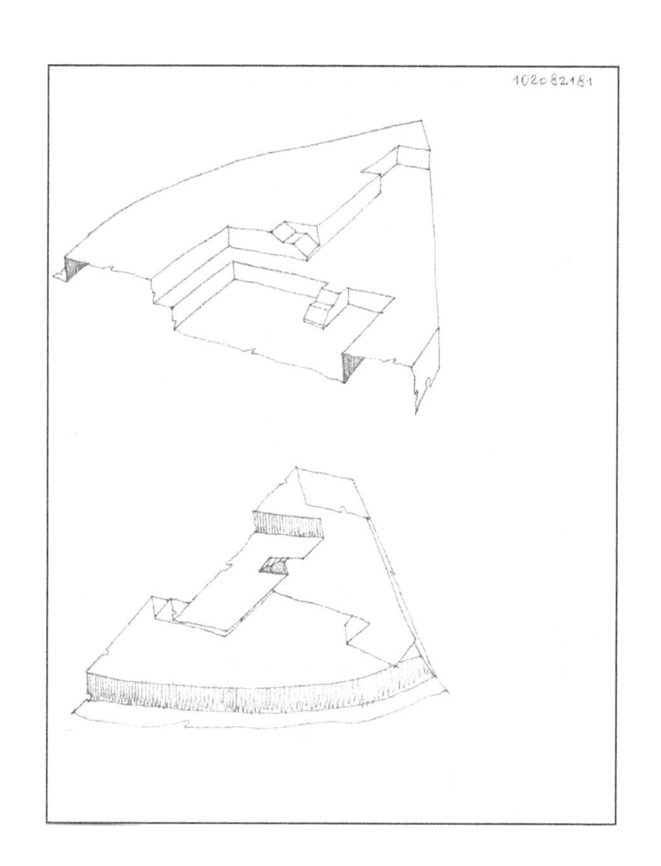
102082181

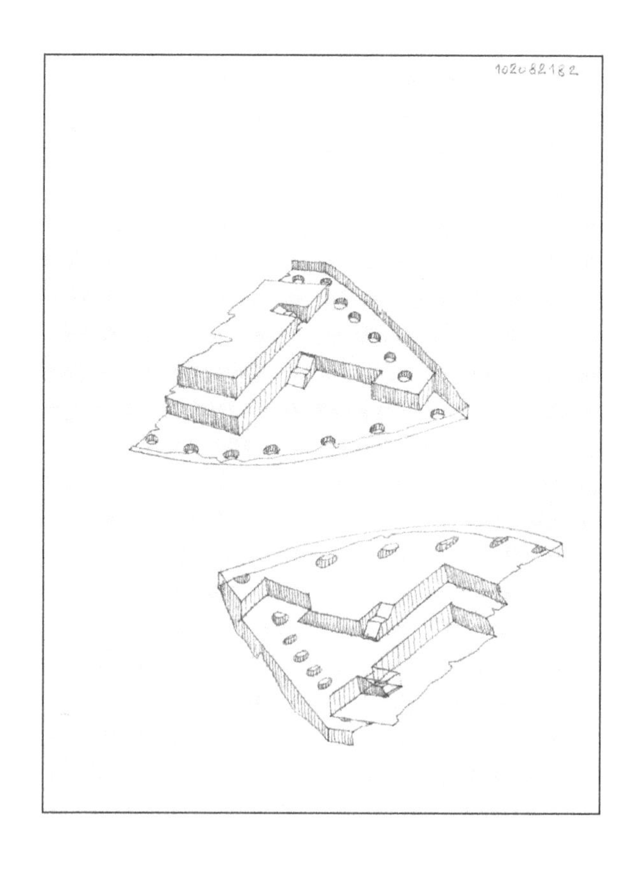
102082182

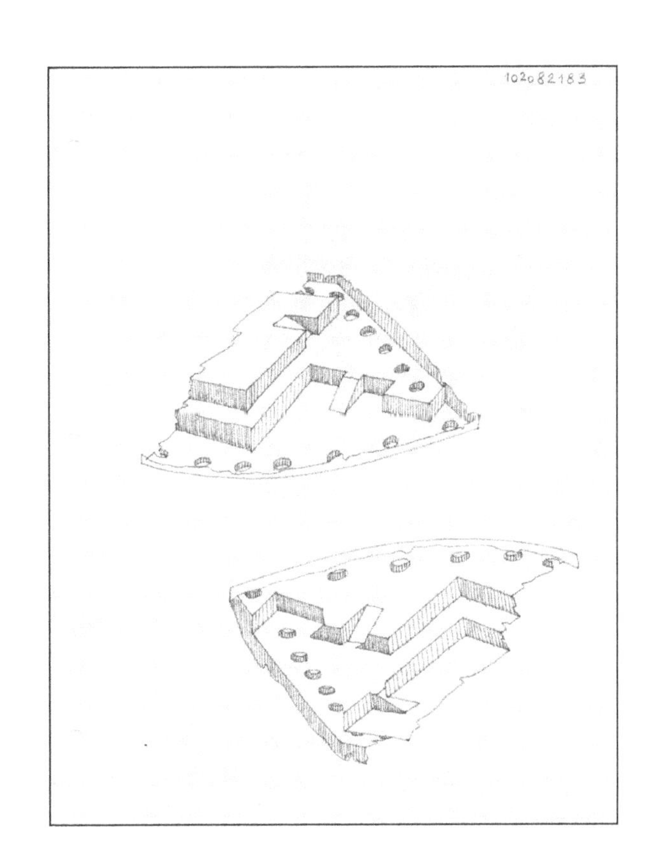
102082183

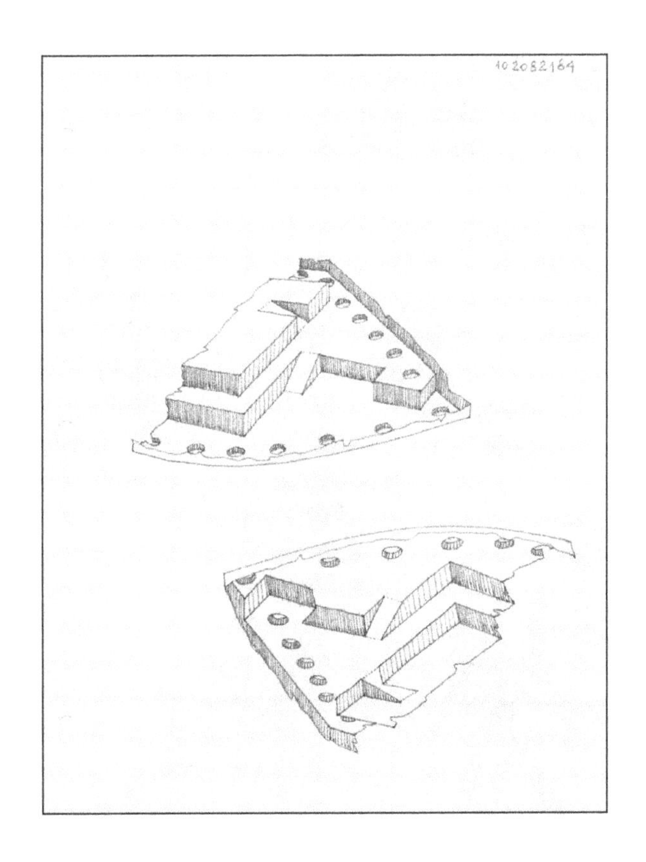
102082184

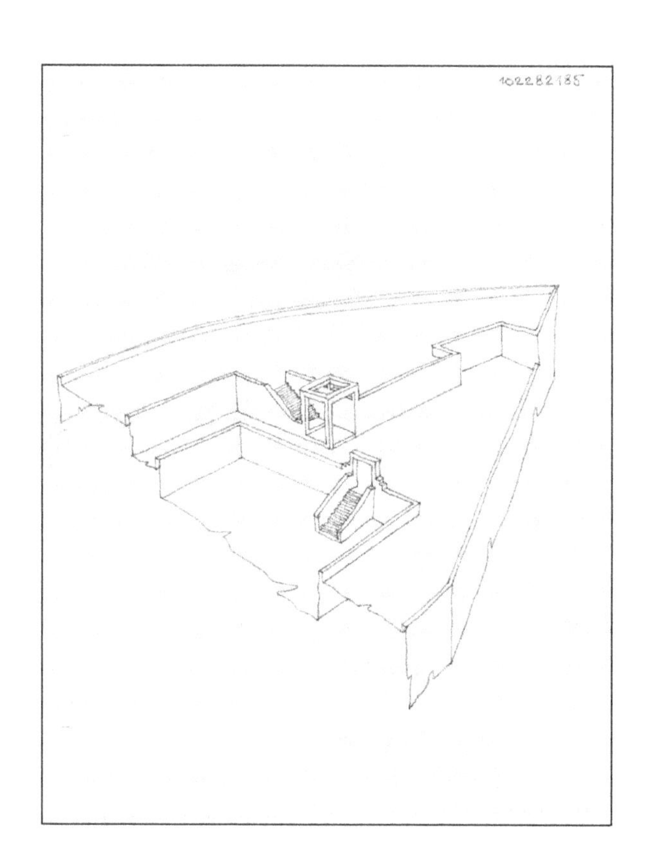
102282185

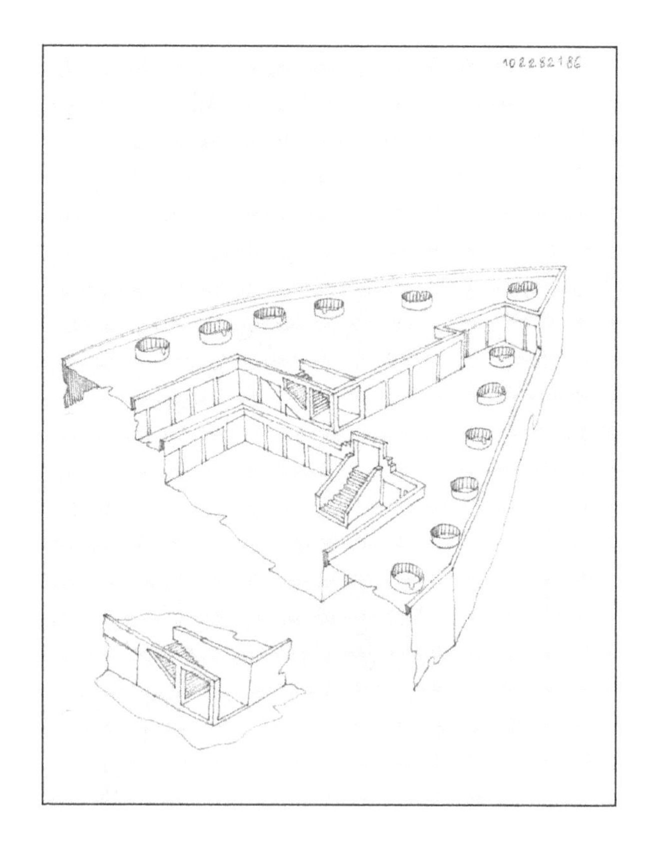
102282186

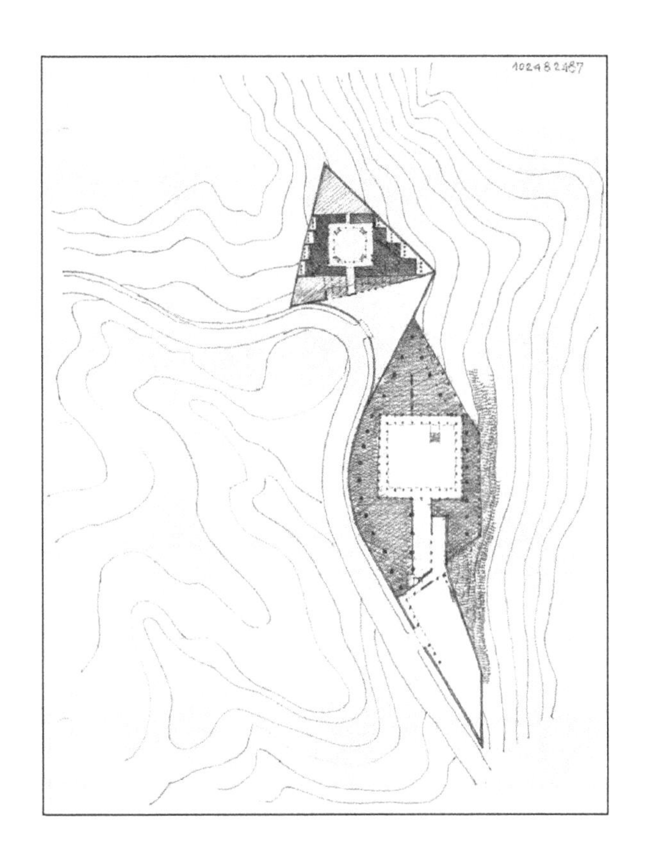
102482187

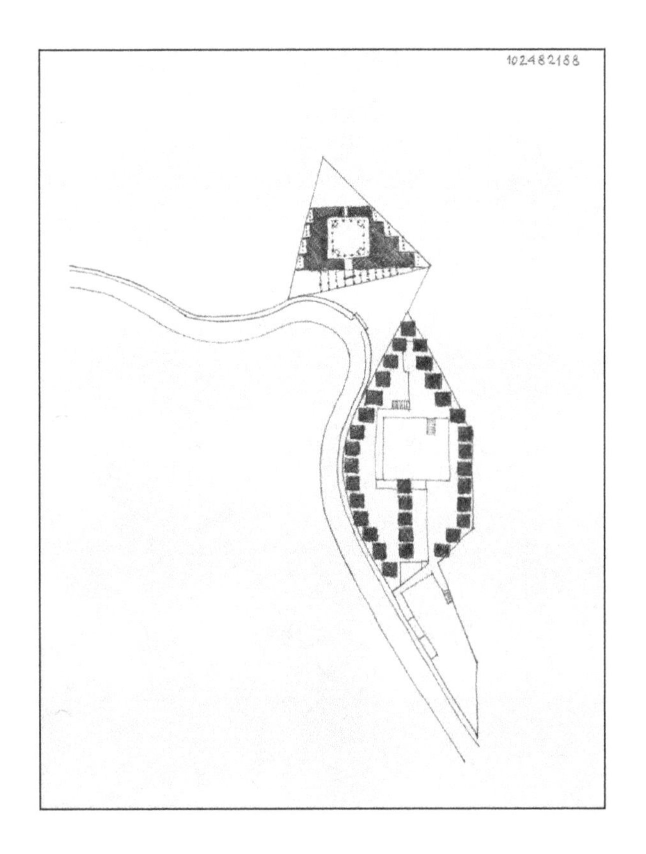
102482188

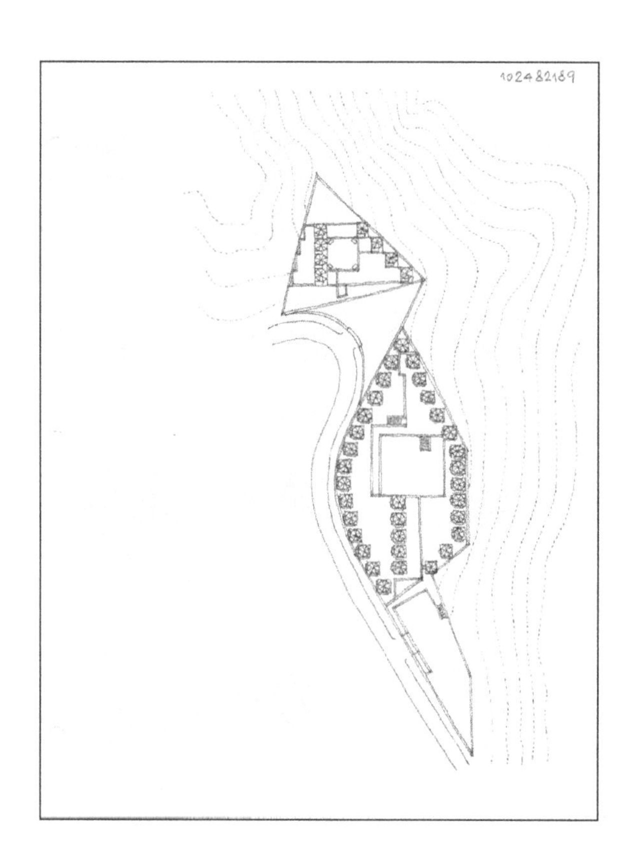
102482189

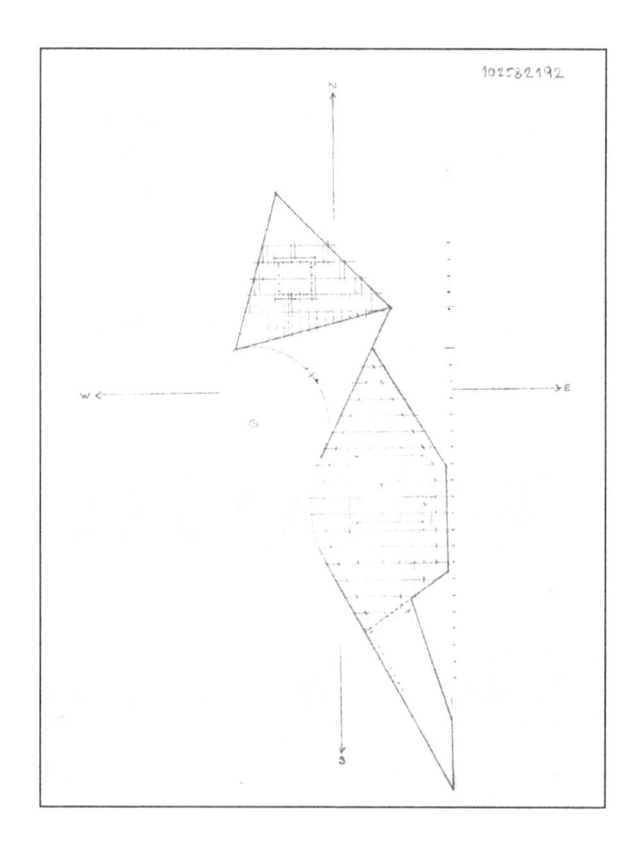
102582192
N
W
E
S

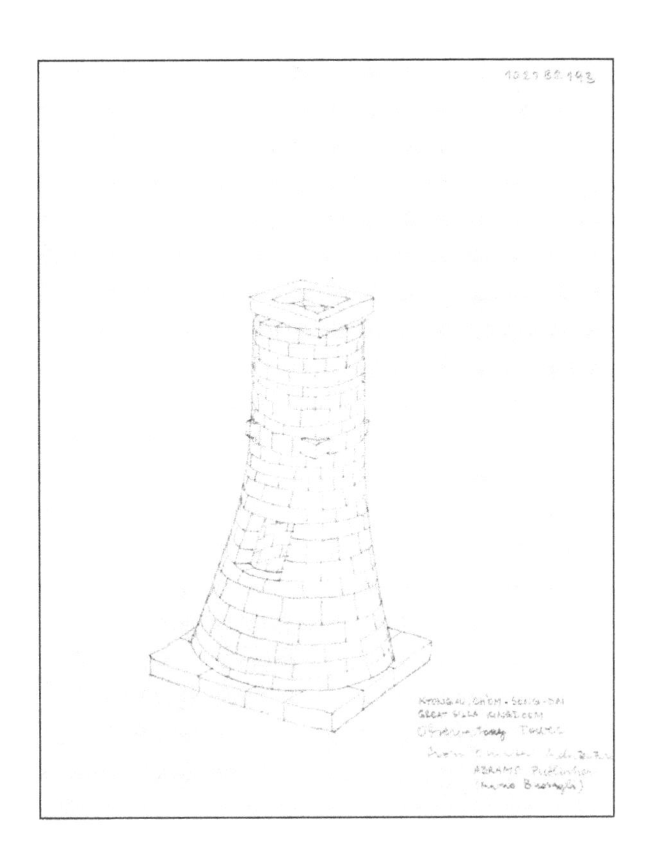

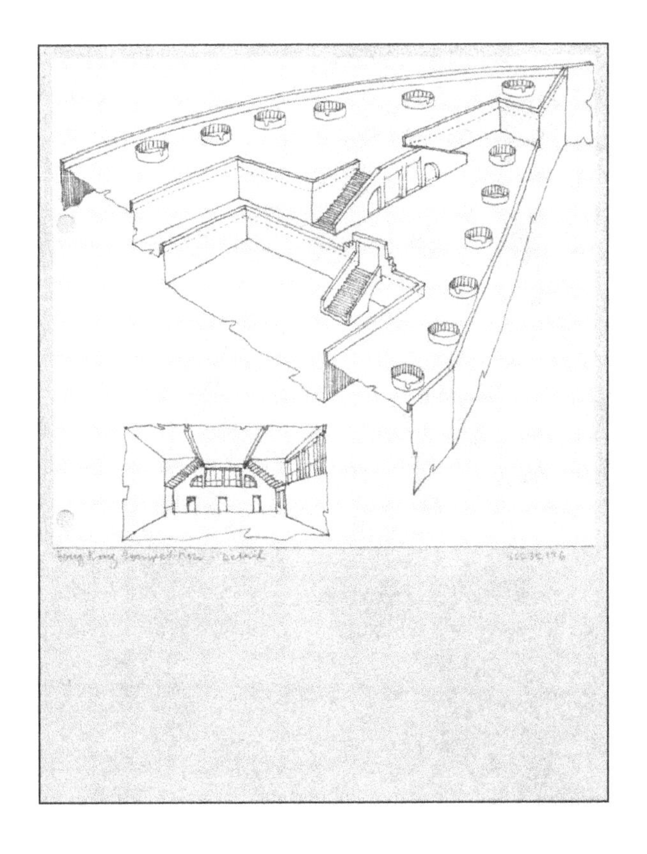

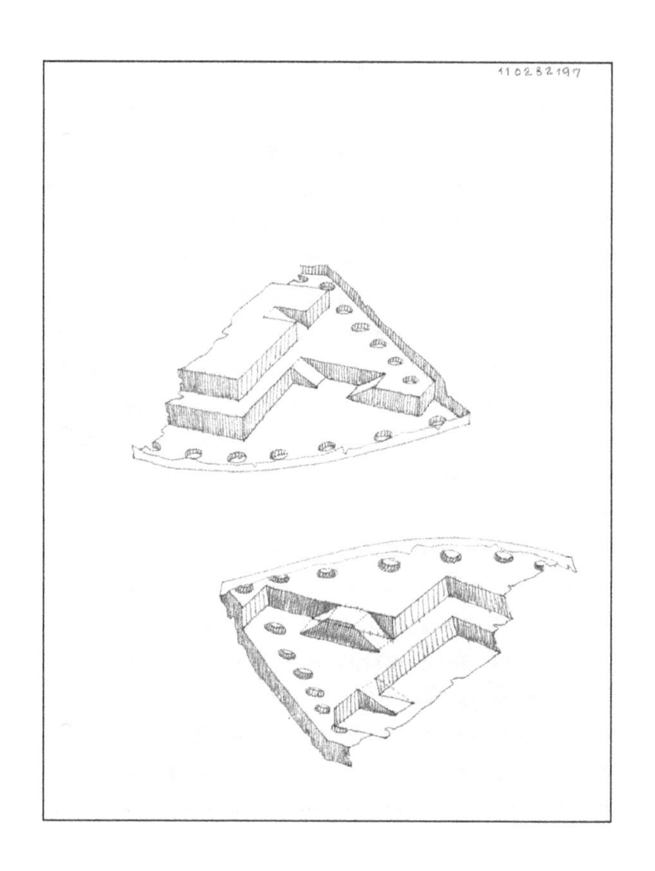

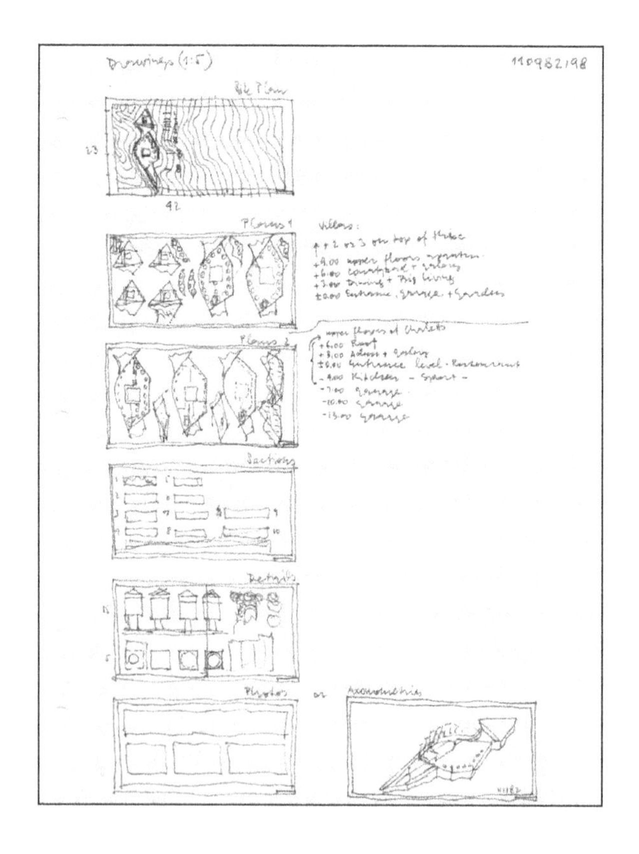
Drawings (1:5)
110982198
Villas:
upper floors of Chalets

110982199
Student, with
modeling skills

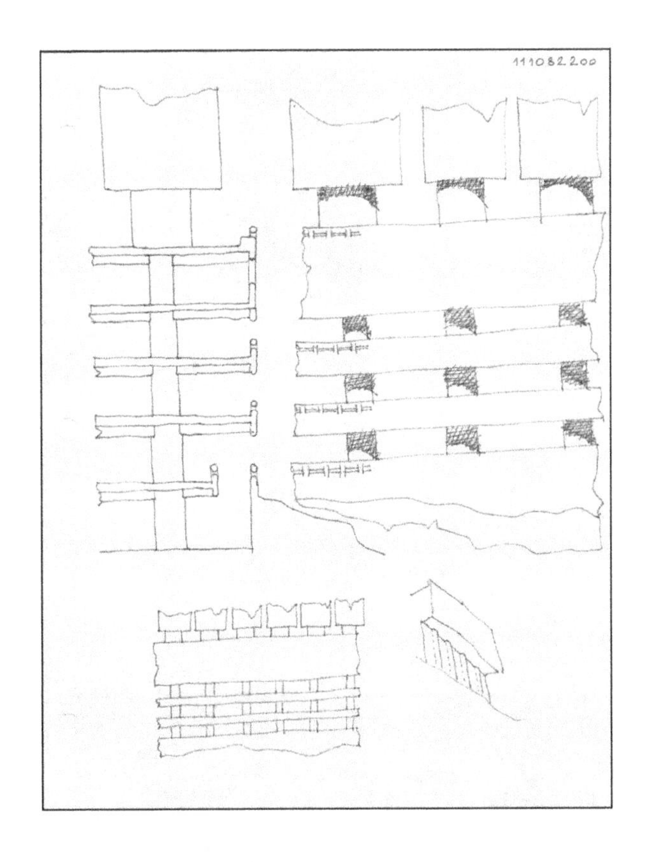
111082200

111282202

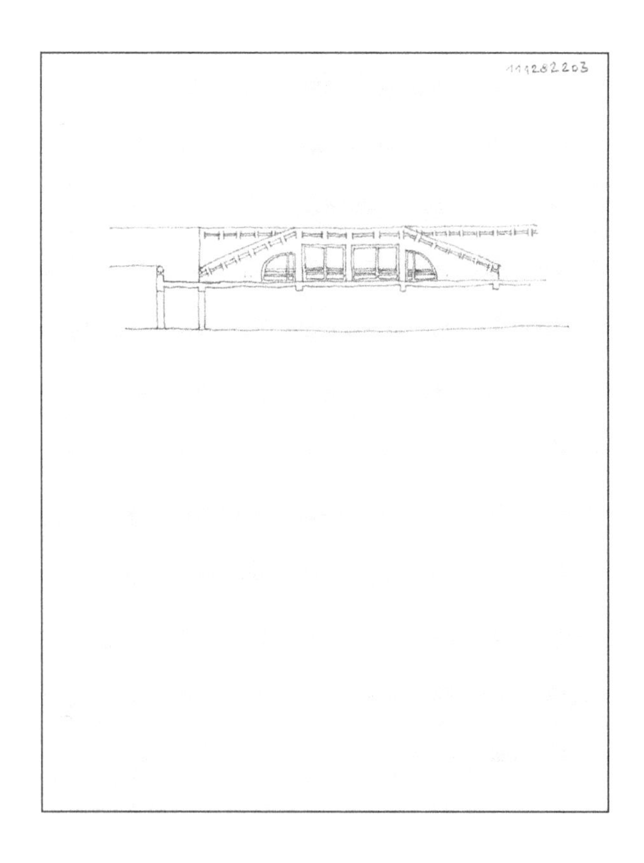
111282203

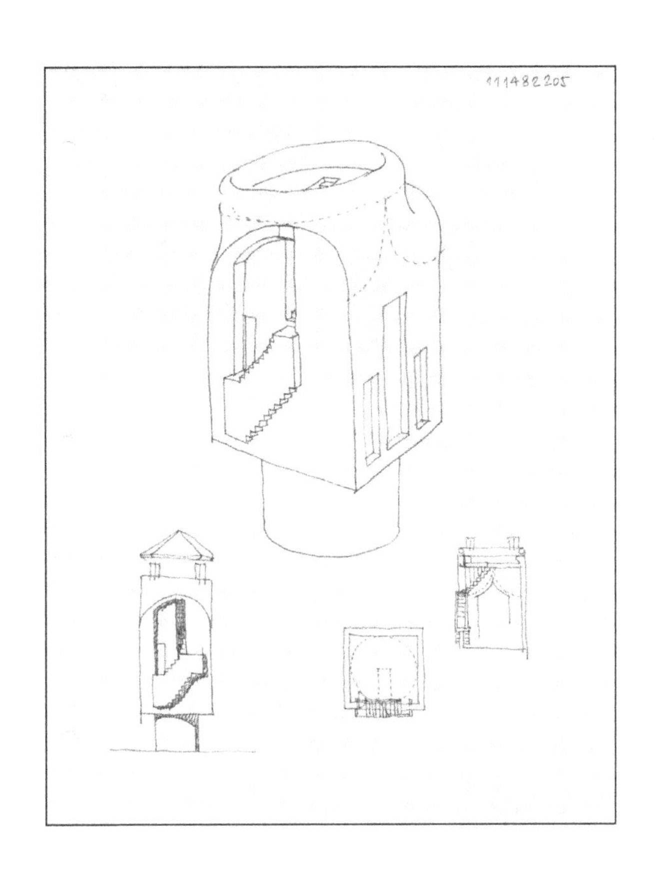
111482205

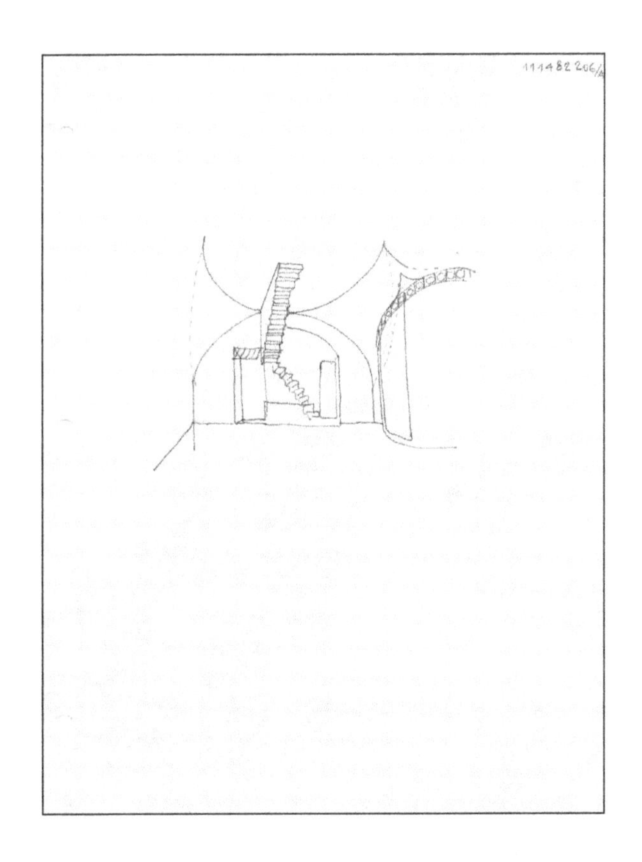
111482206/A

11308220.8.
T'AI-HU STONE
(FROM 'SU YUAN SHIH PU-
BY LIN YU-LIN) – AND ITS
TOPOLOGICALLY EQUIVALENT MODEL
("TEM")

113082/A

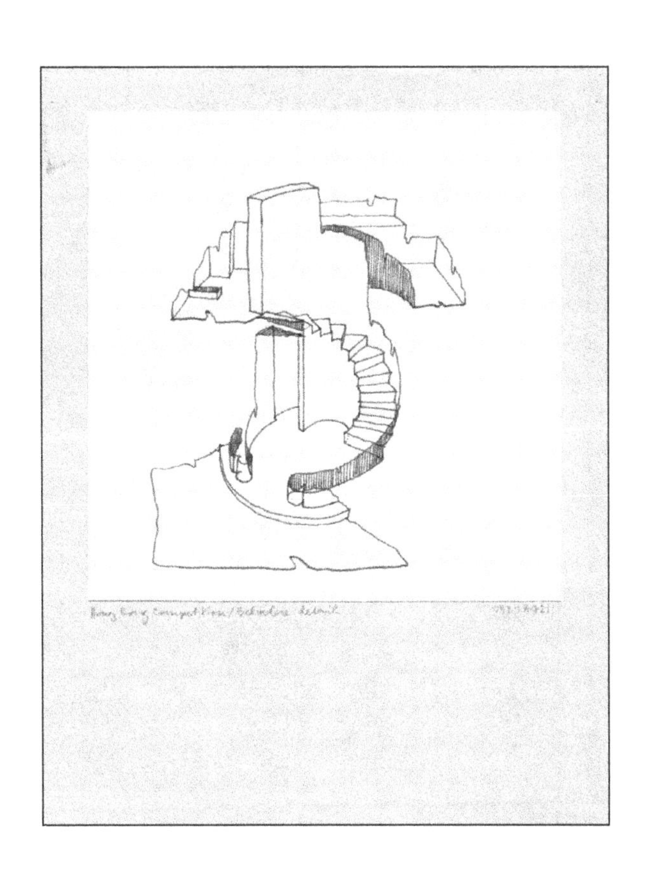
Hong Kong Competition / Belvedere detail

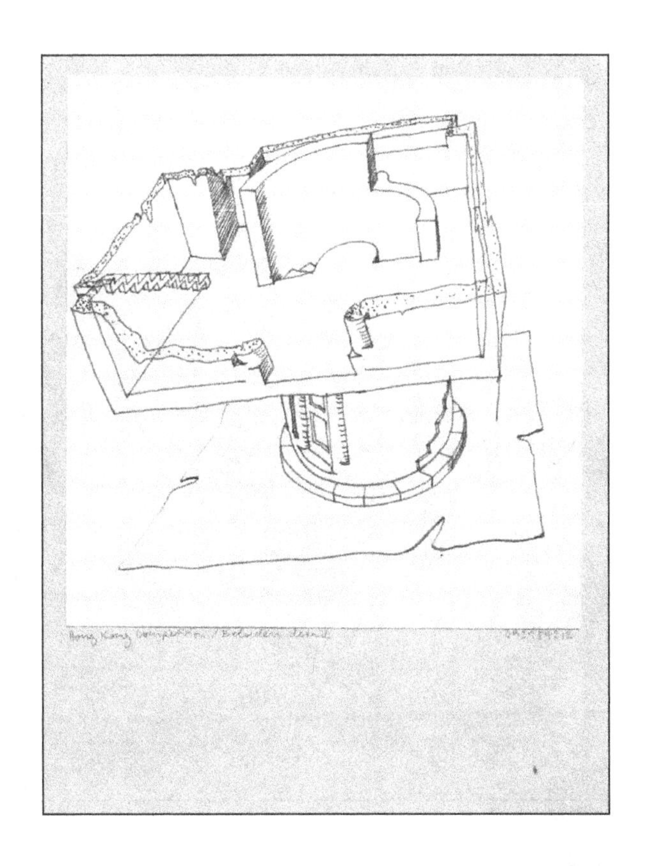
Hong Kong Competition / Belvedere detail

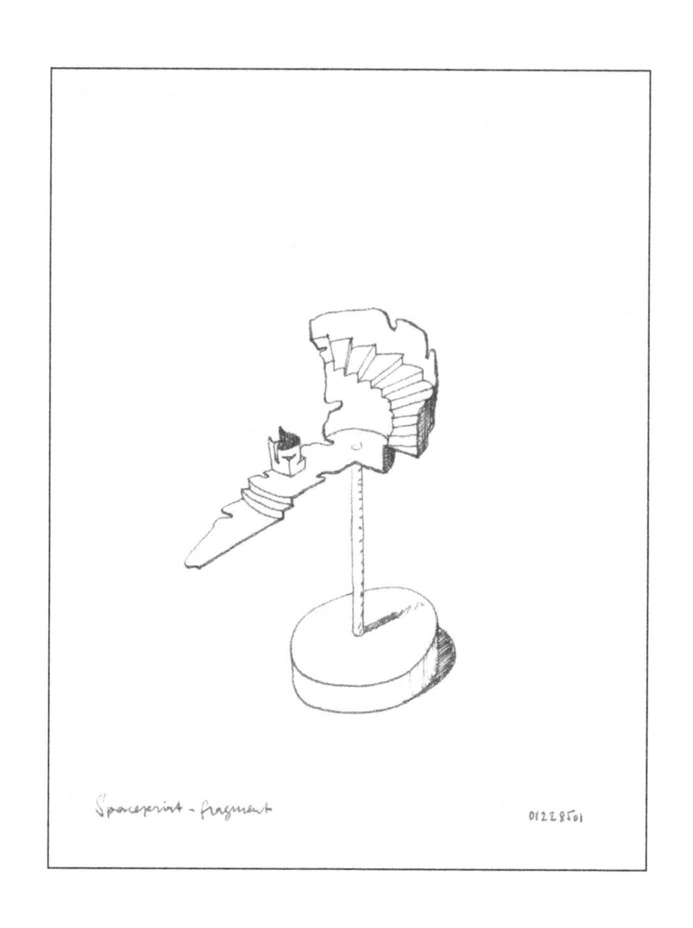
Spaceprint - fragment
01228501

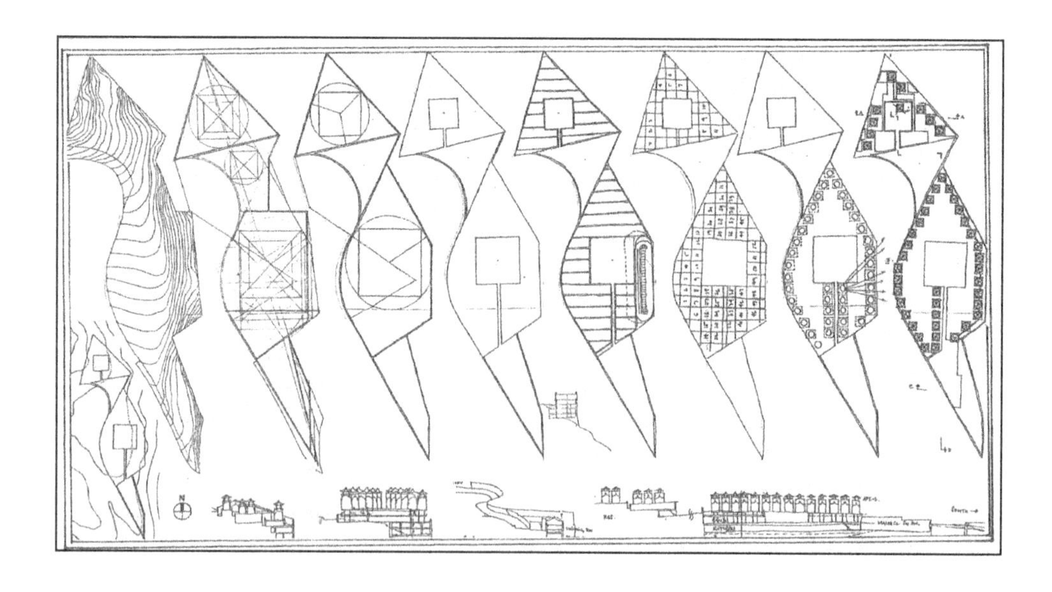

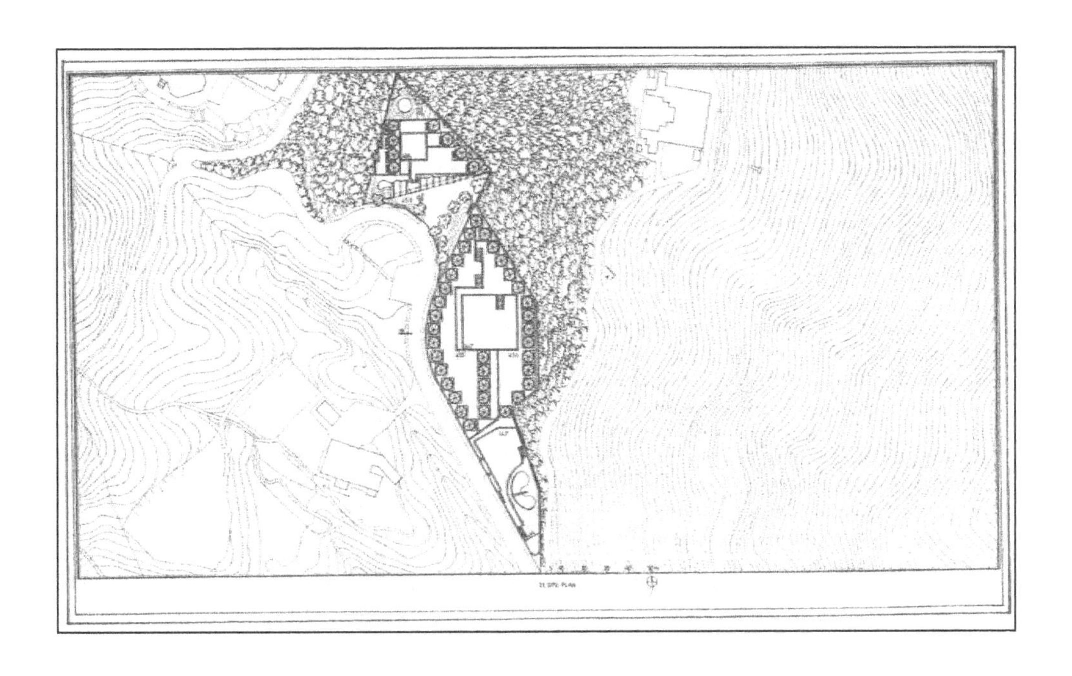

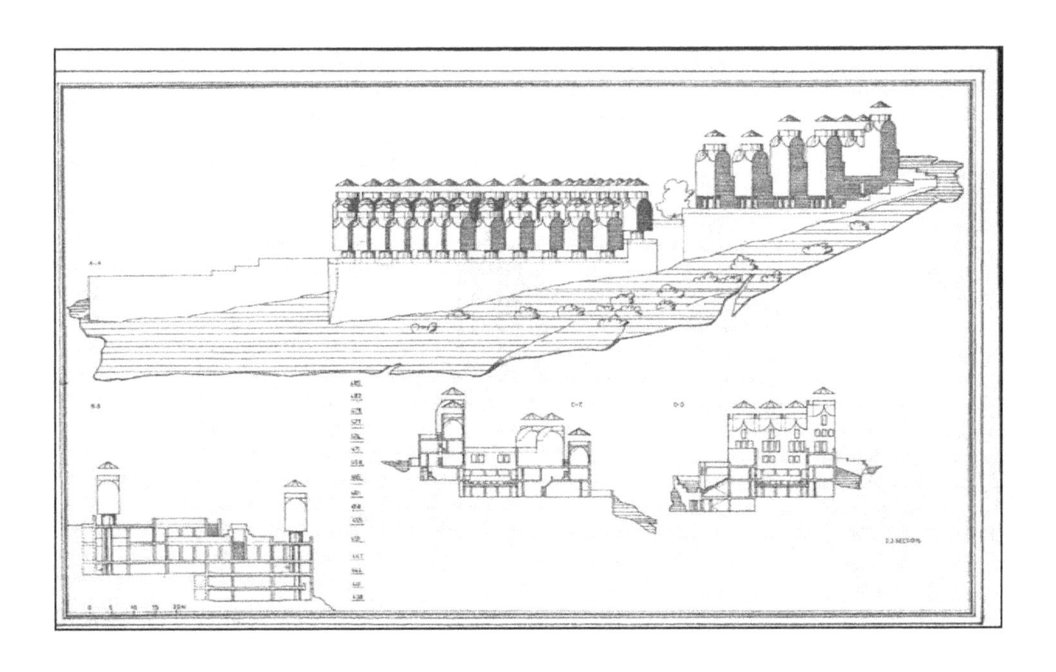

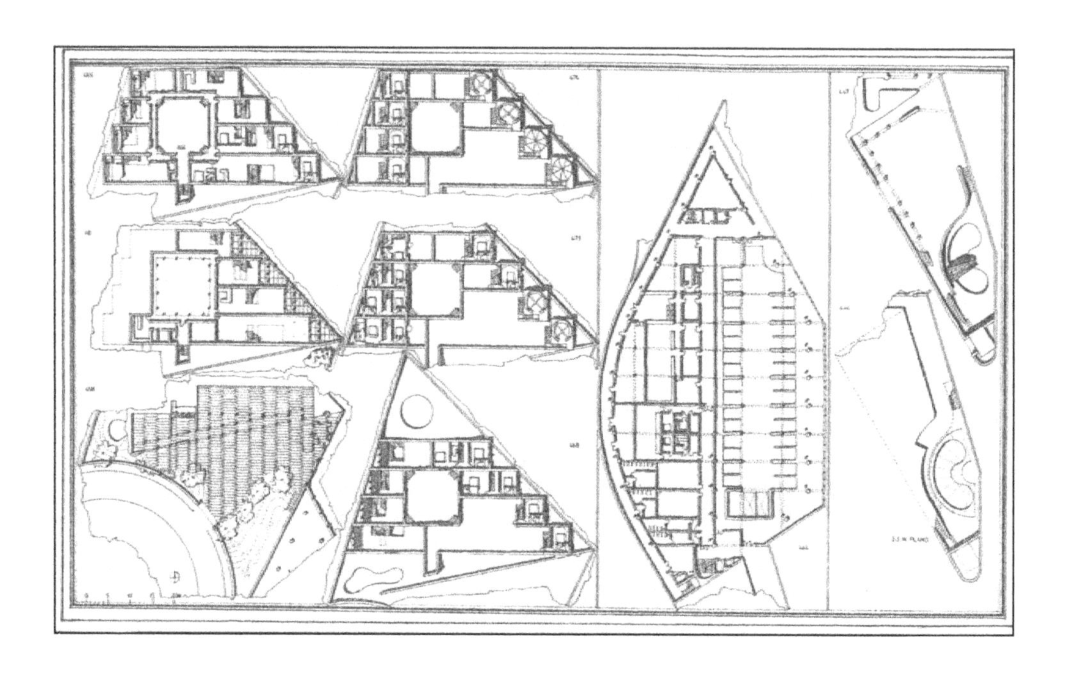

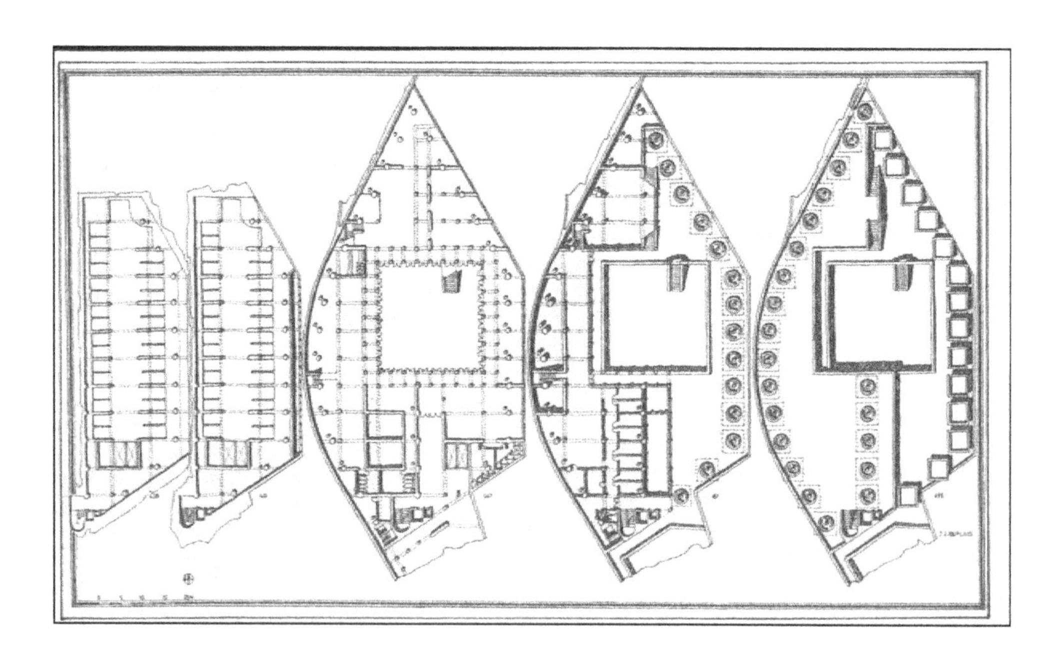

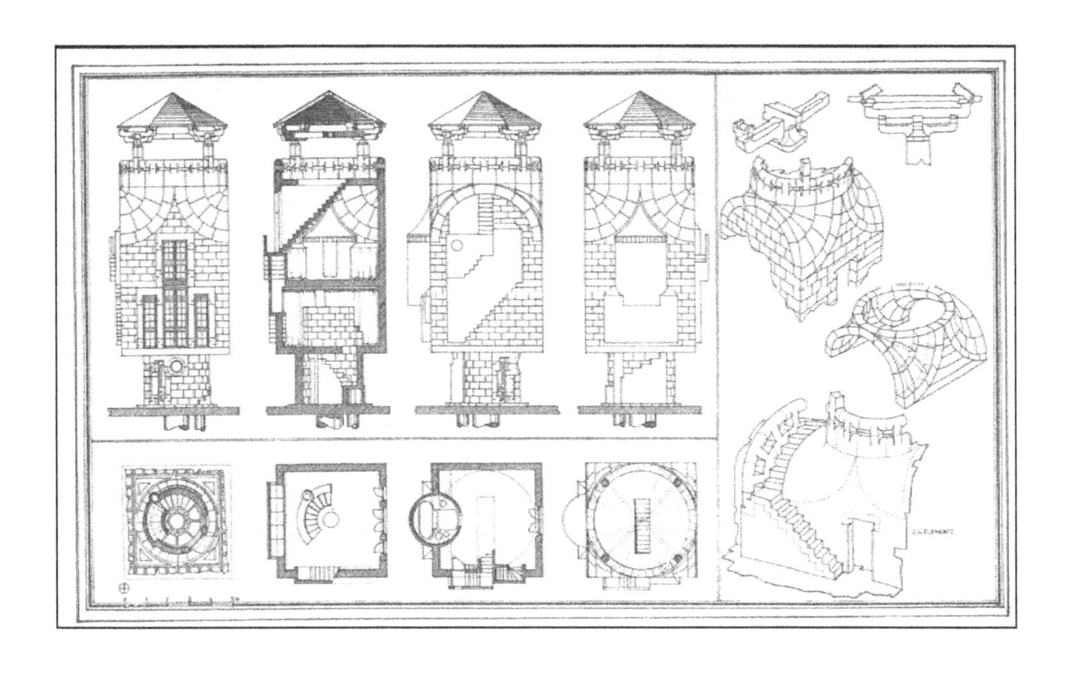

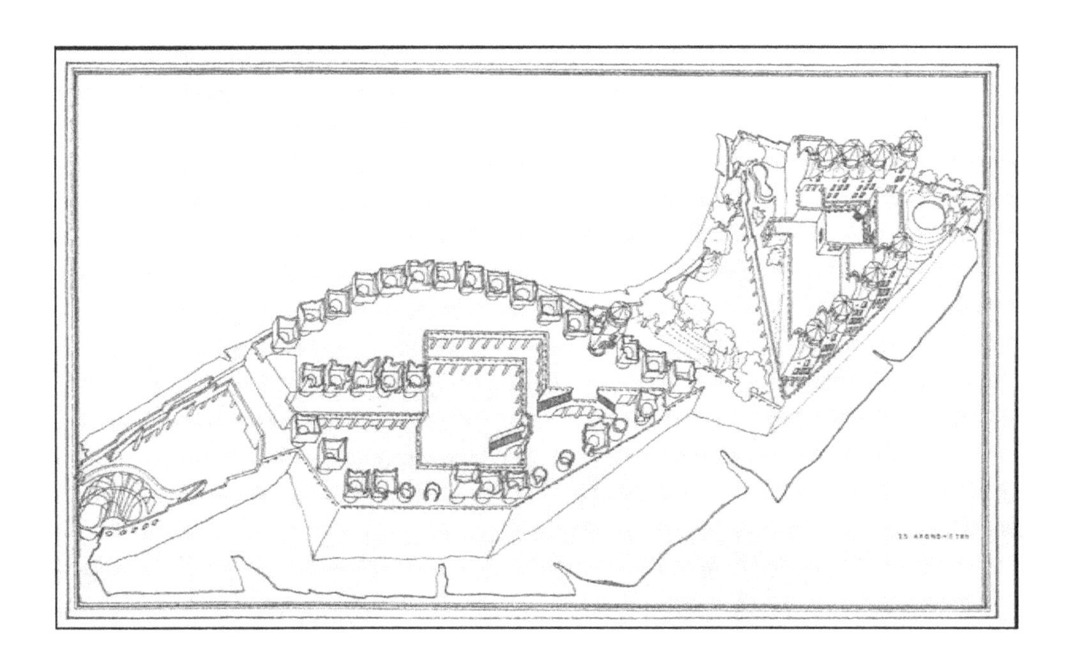

Chapter 4

OPERATION PARIS

Pen Zen Diaries #4

Chapter 4

(P.Z.D.4)
Operation Paris - Opera Bastille

The linear arrangement of the stages of the major auditorium with 2700 seats, the experimental theater with 1600 seats and the fully equipped rehearsal-hall with 100 seats made it possible to serve all of these units with a common back-stage zone. This in turn generated a computer-controlled and operated stage service system, where the middle element of the back stage works as a moving crane-elevator, servicing thus the stages from any of the subterranean storages. The - for economical reasons - oversized requirements, to run six operas simultaneously - demanded a non-traditional solution.

To the contrary, concerning the rites of the arrival, I am very conservative, and view the process equivalently important to that of the performance - I even call it the "stage of the audience". Easier to say, then to preserve the graciousness of the arrival / exit of over four thousand people. For that reason - and to at least partially resolve the notion "...for the people", I've created a sunken plaza, where people converge, coming by car, with one of the three metro-lines, or walking.

All arrive to a stair - which could serve as an amphitheater and also leads to the entrance plaza level.

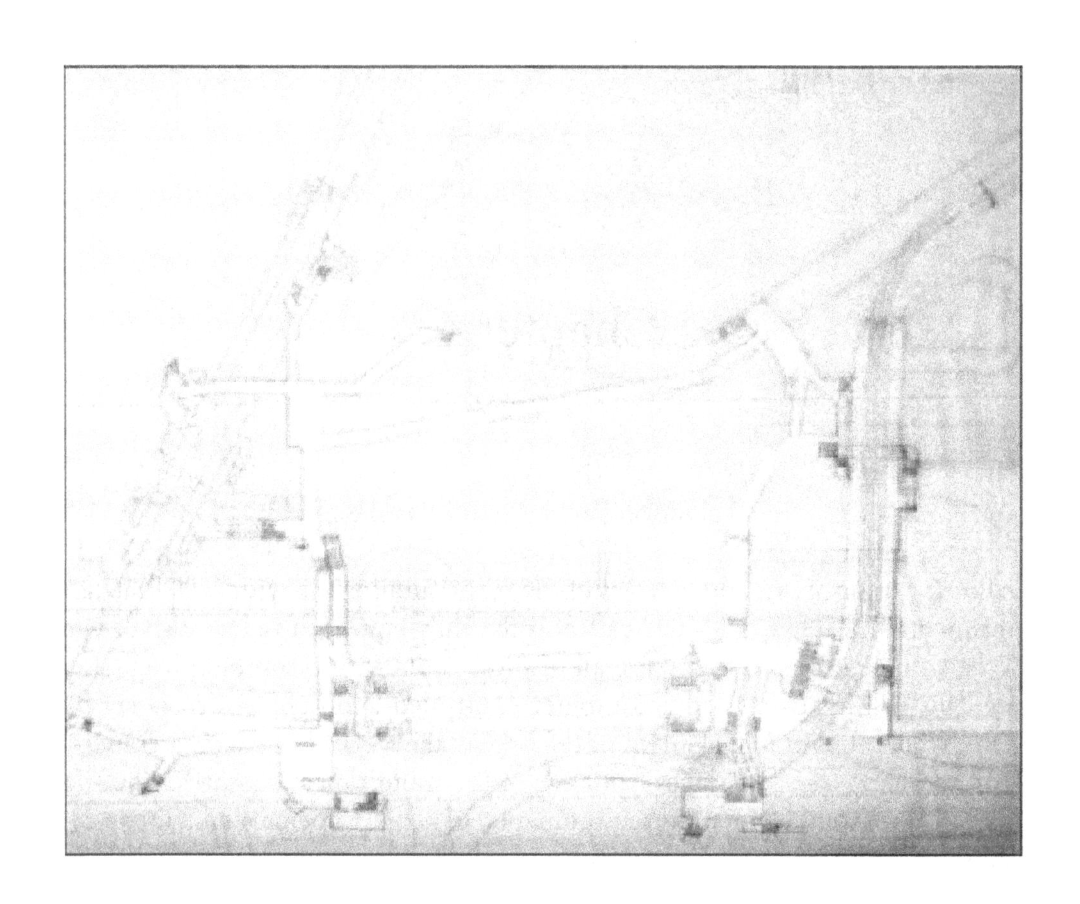

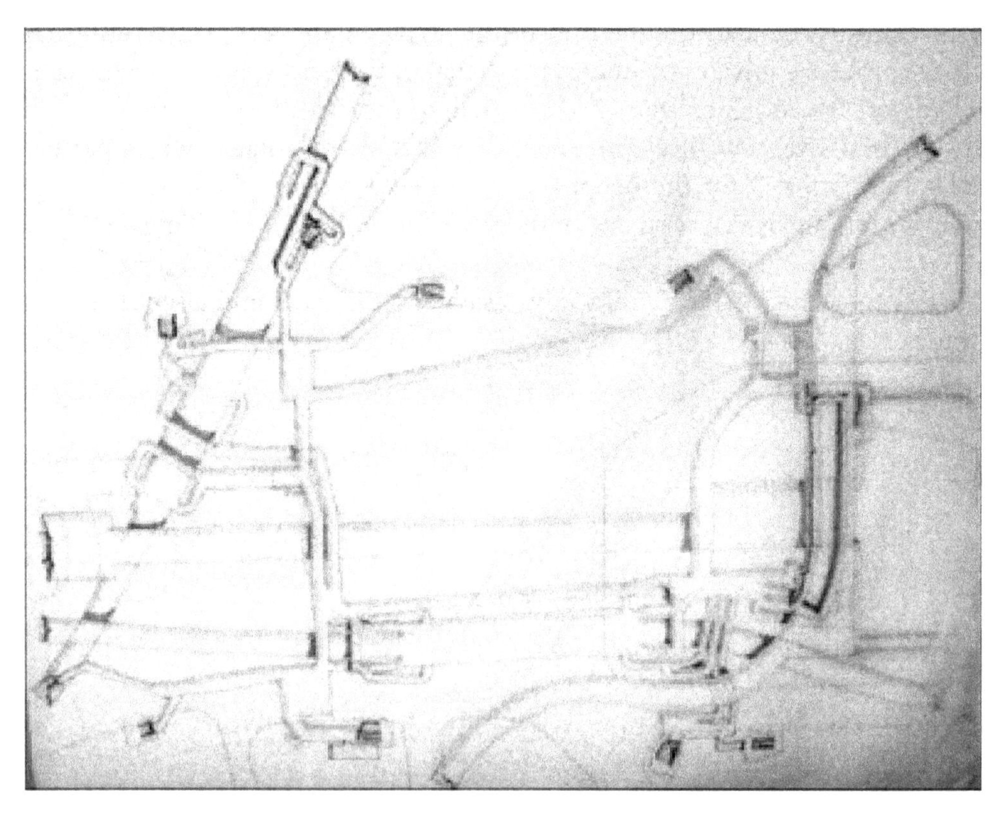

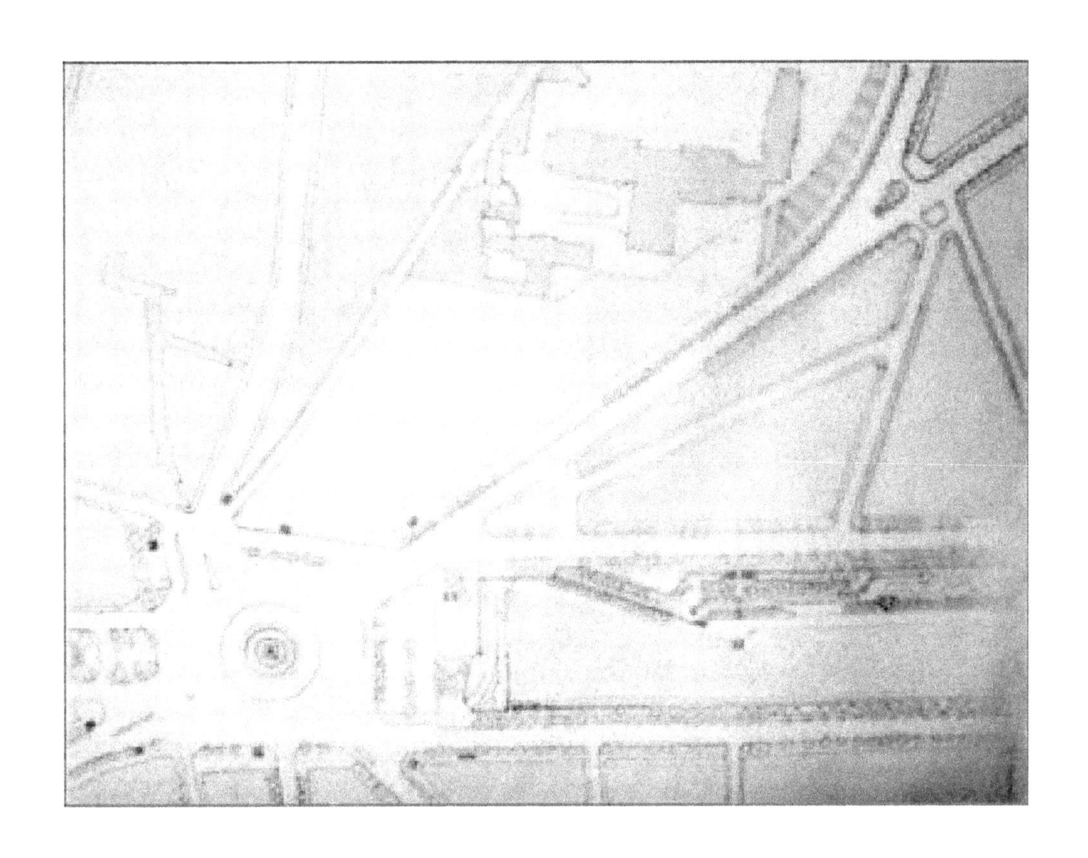

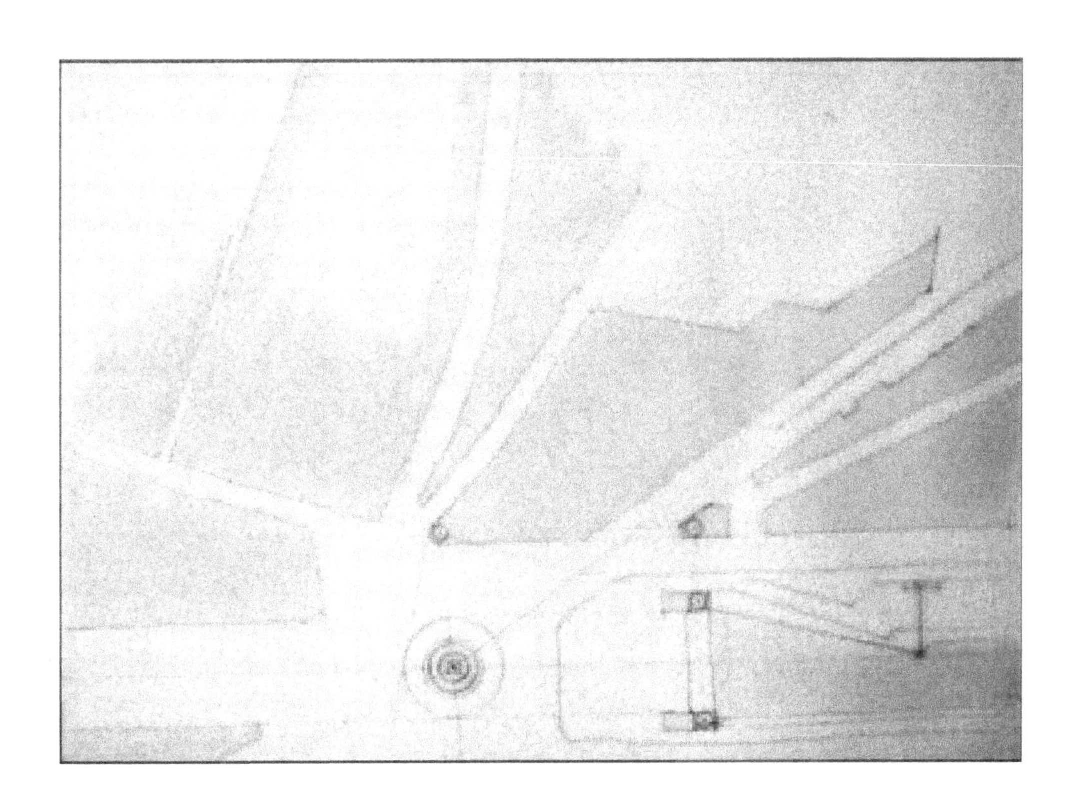

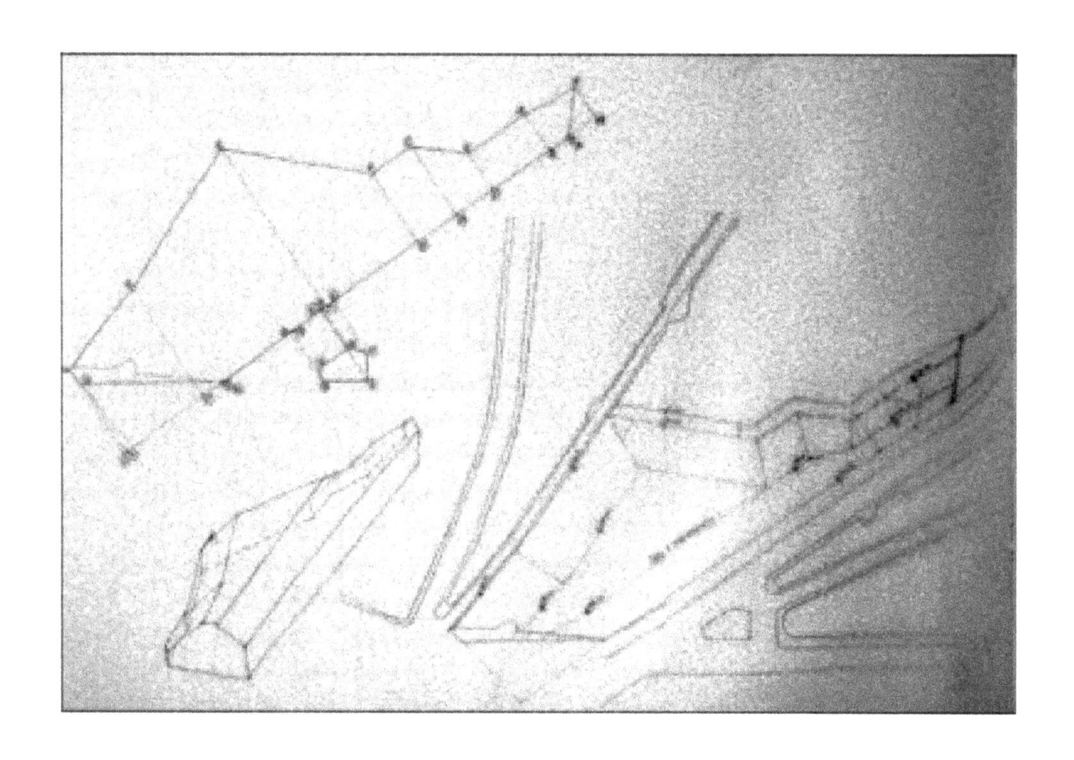

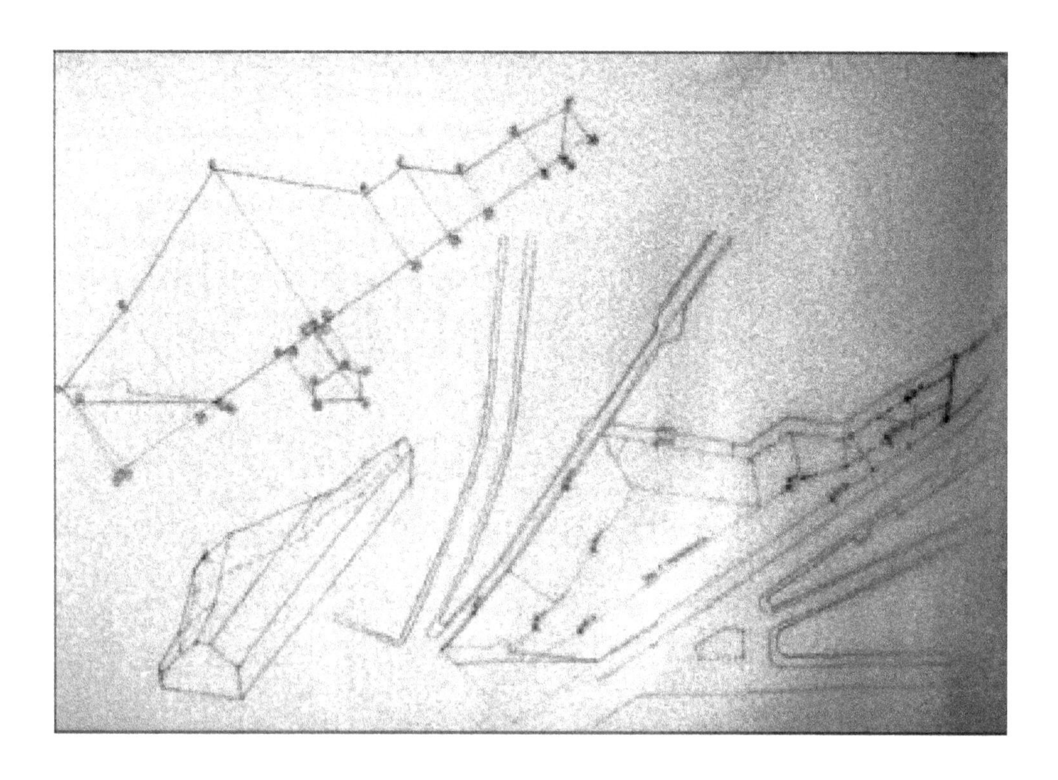

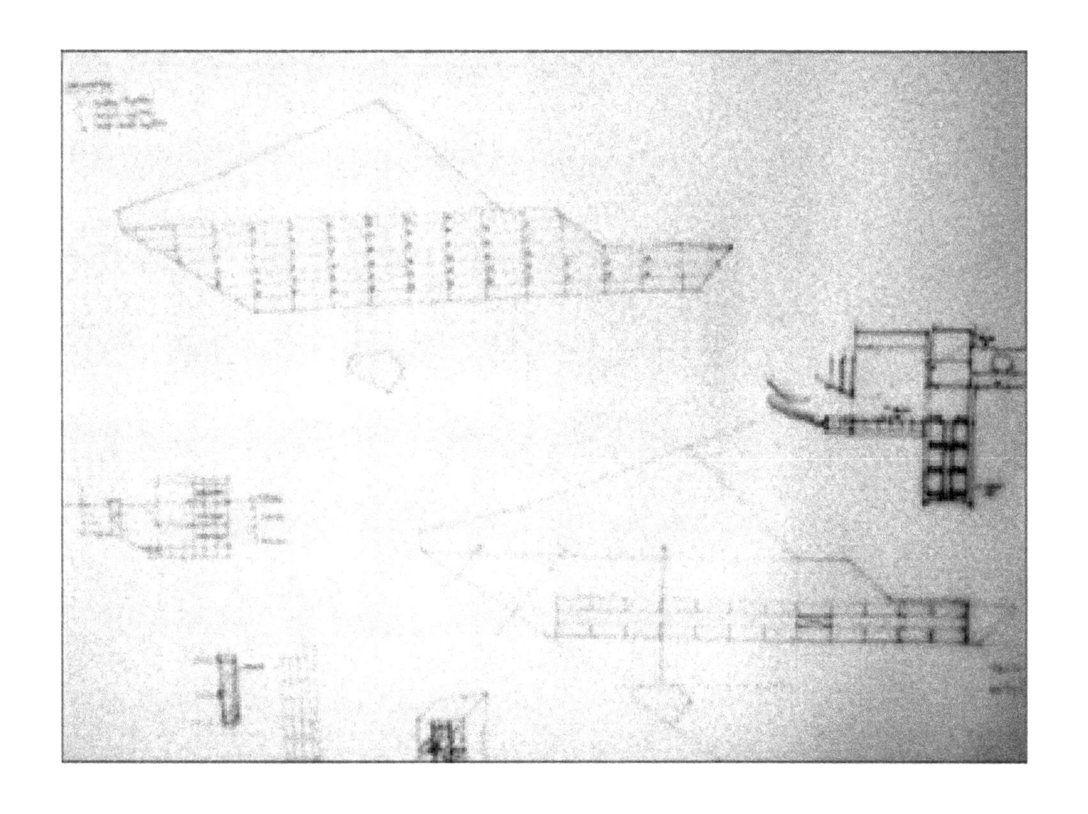

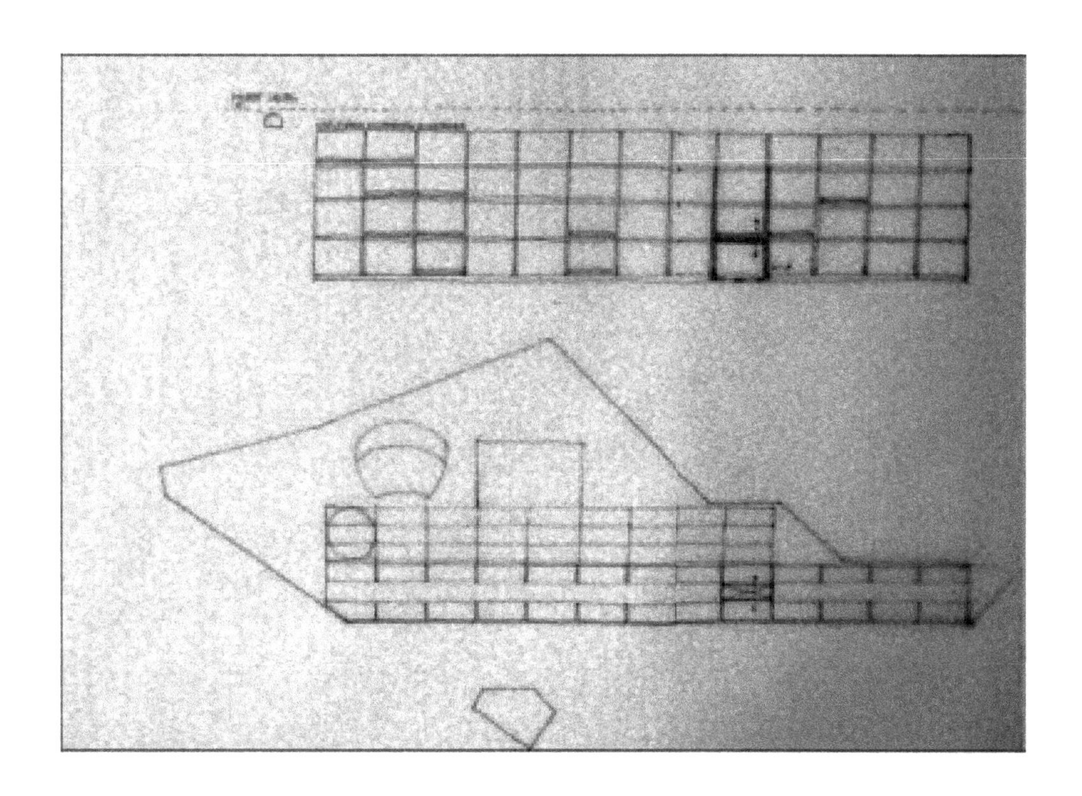

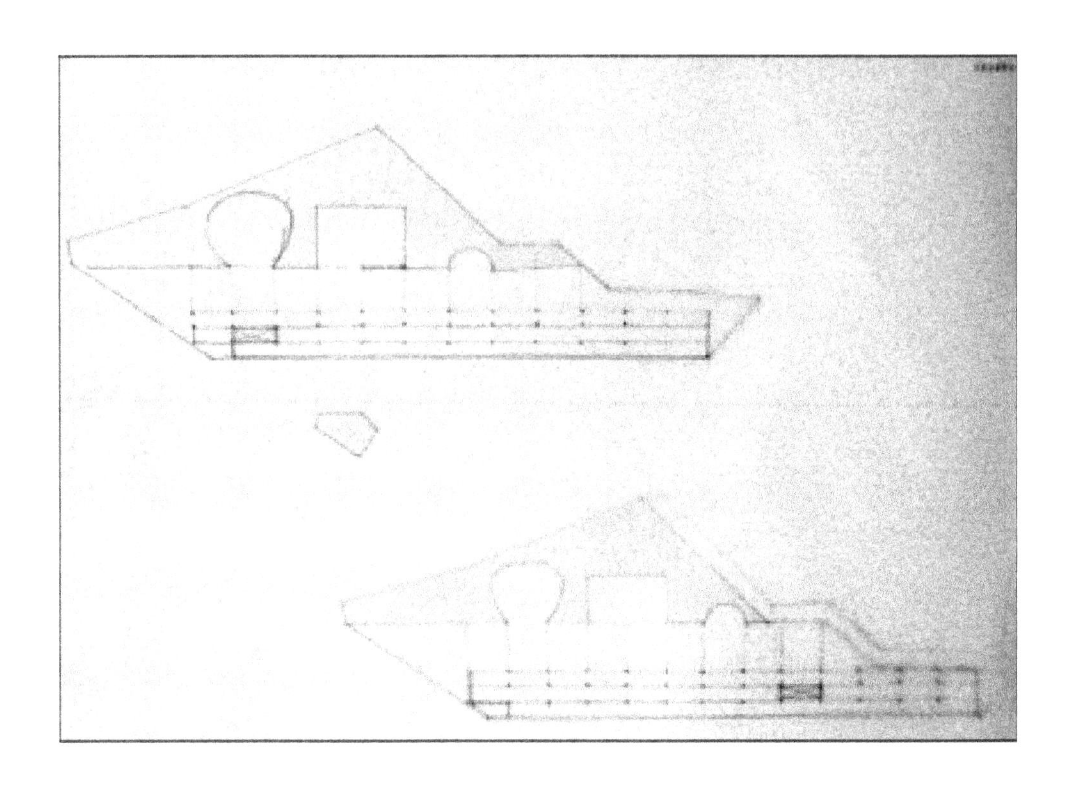

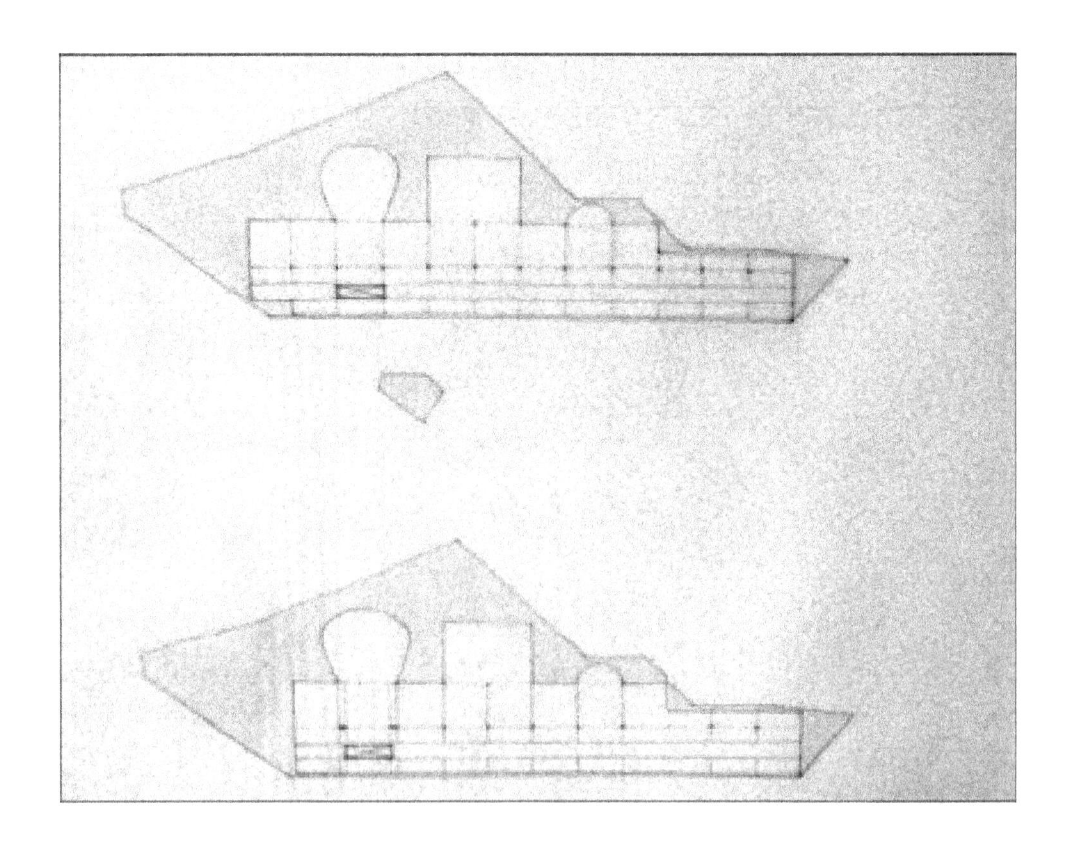

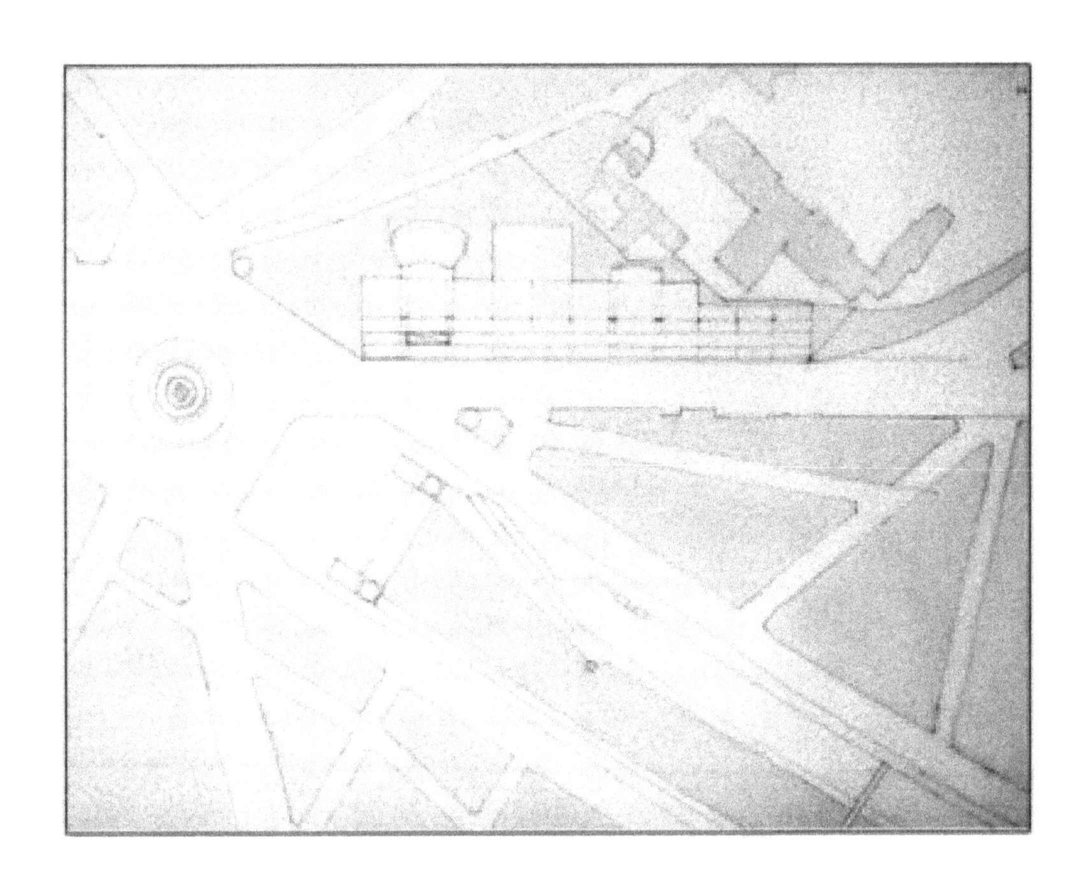

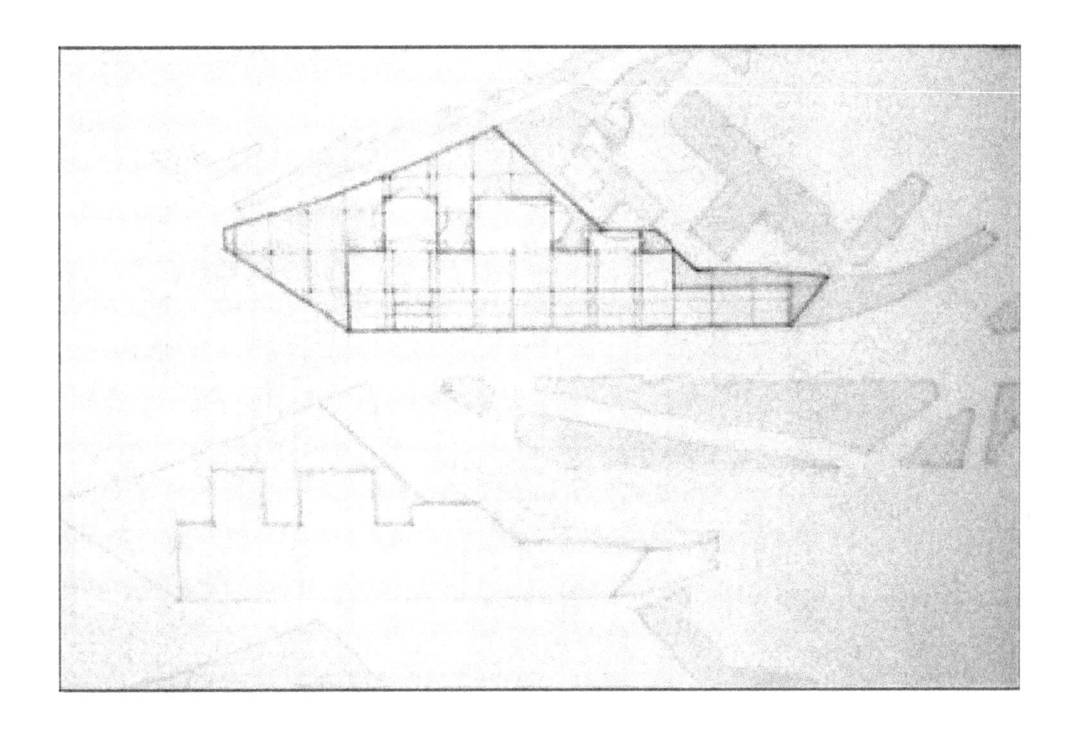

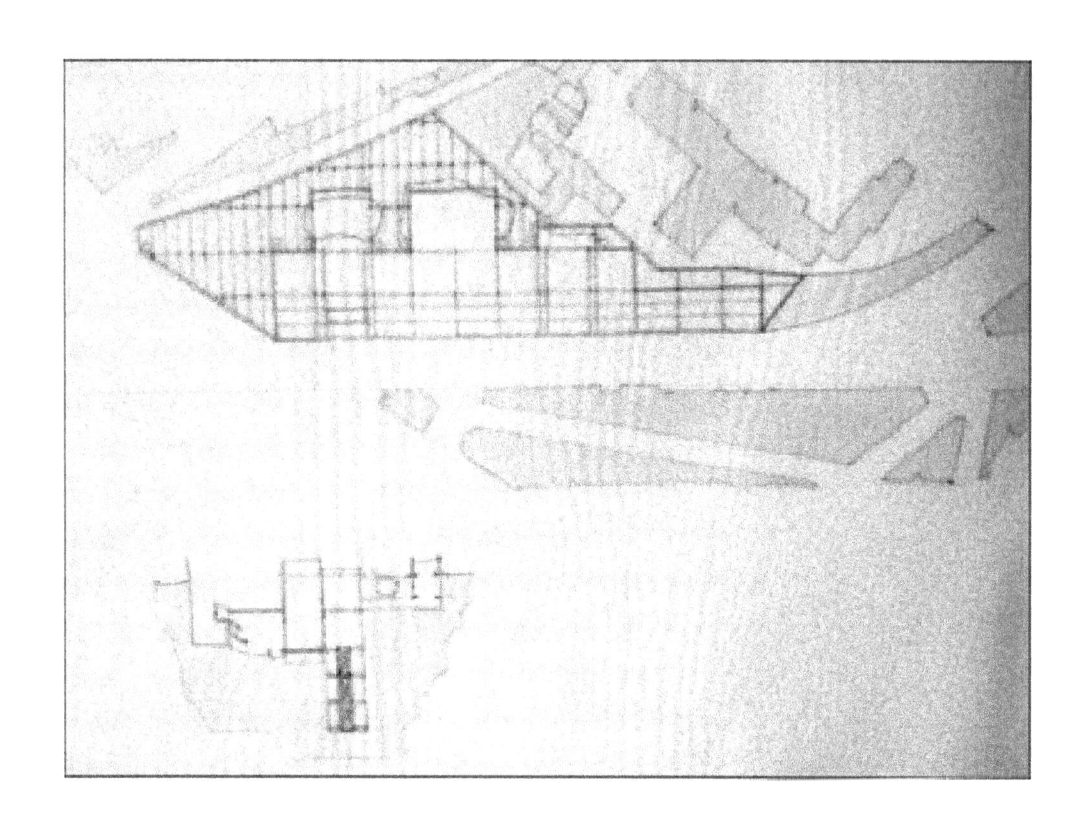

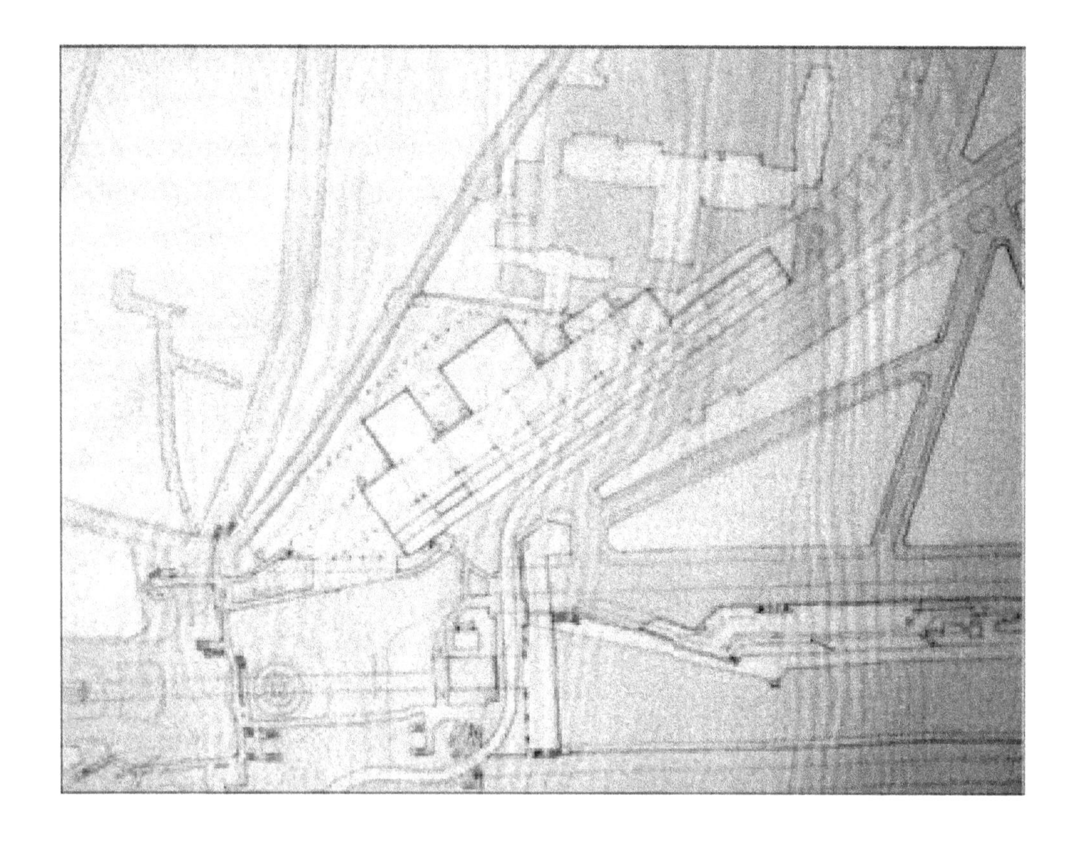

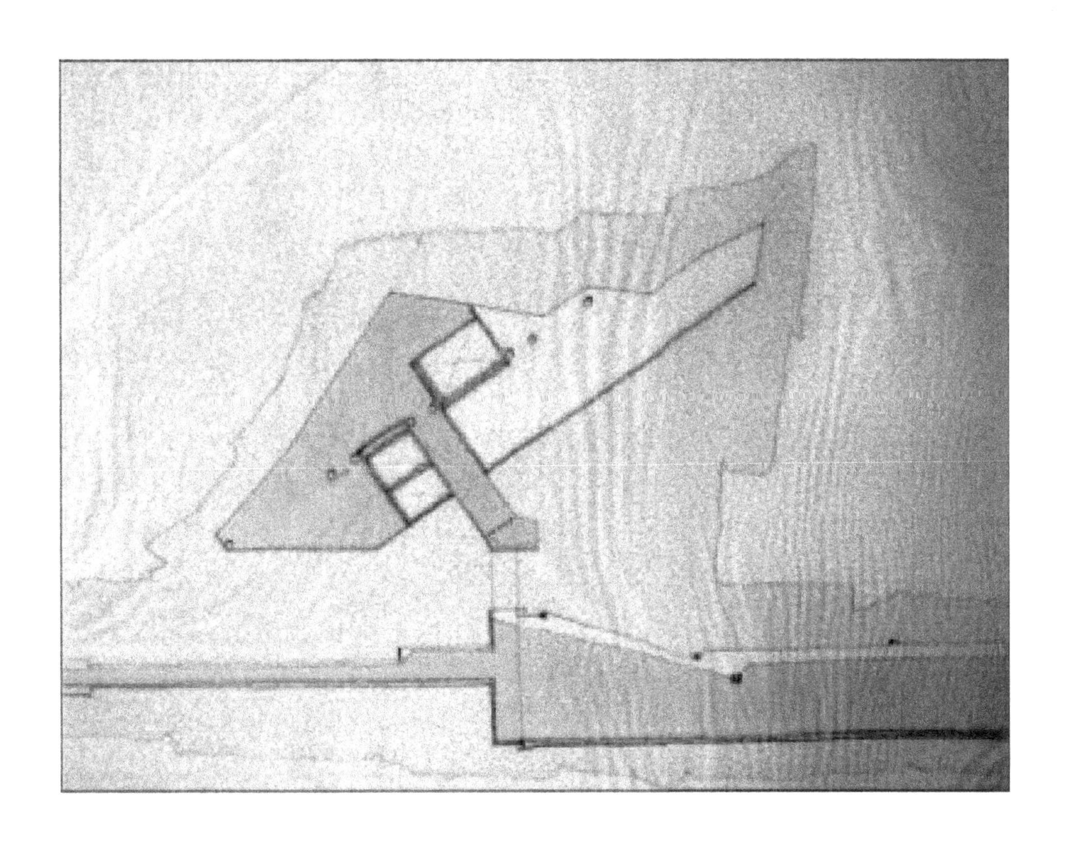

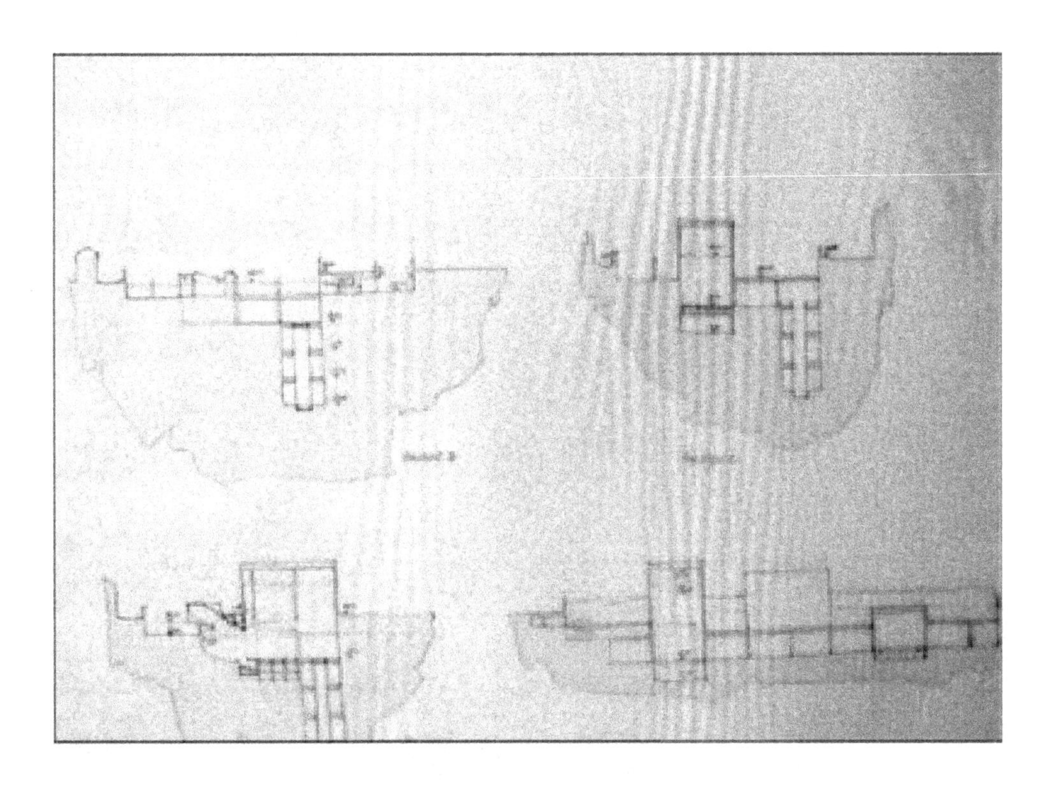

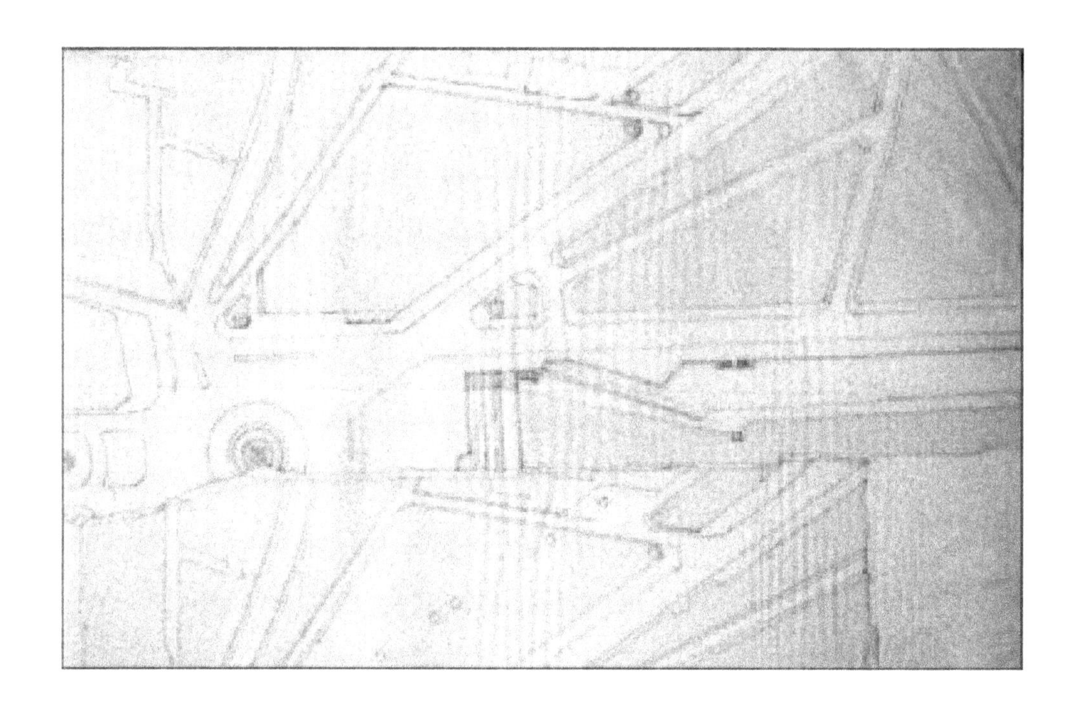

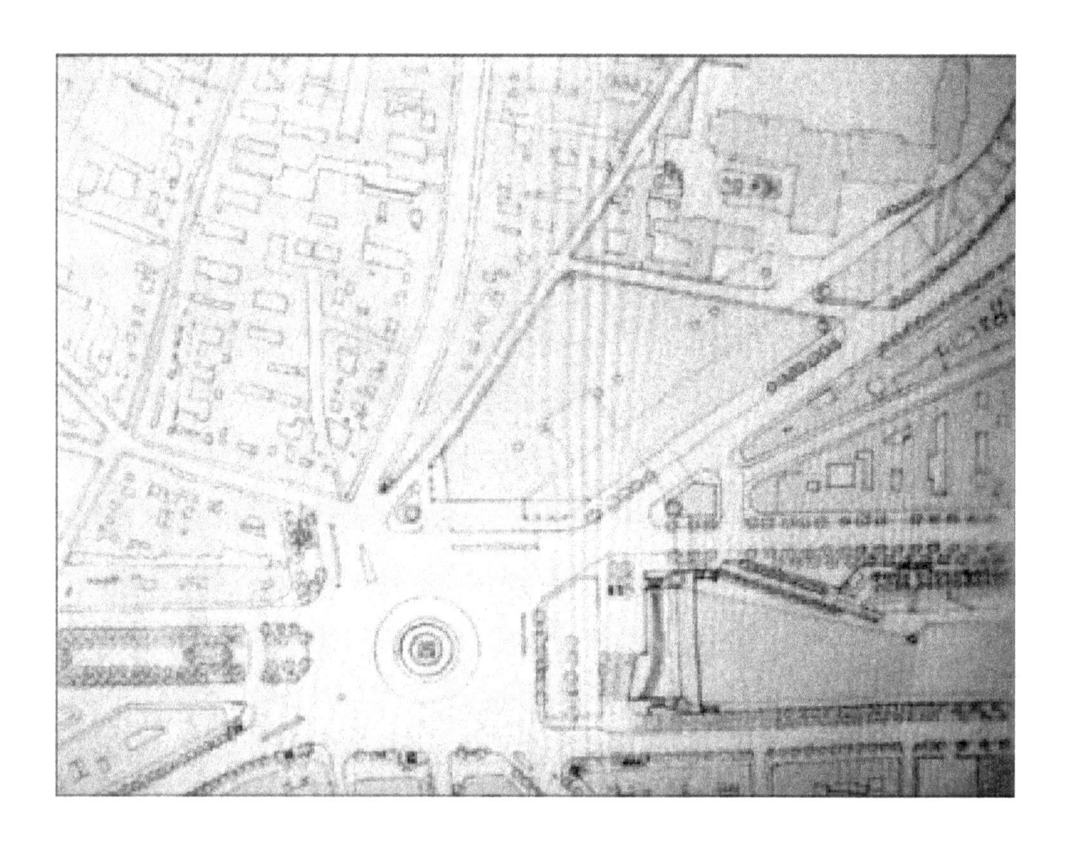

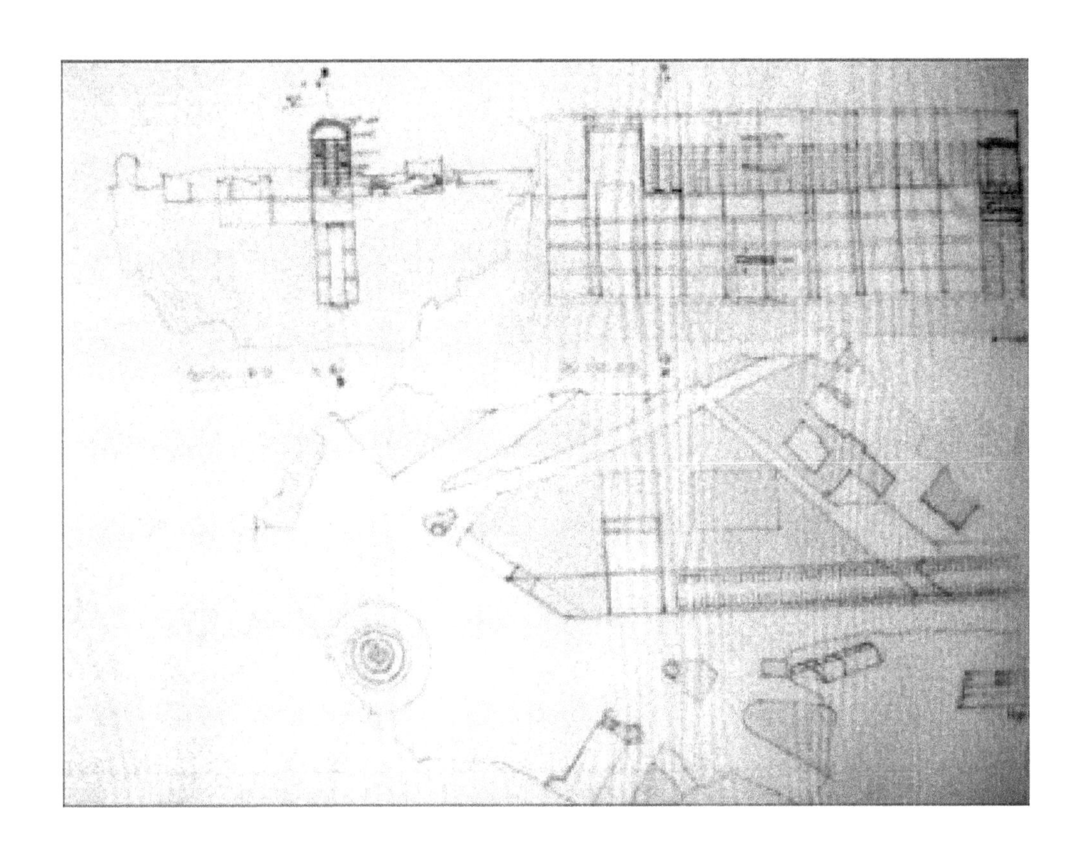

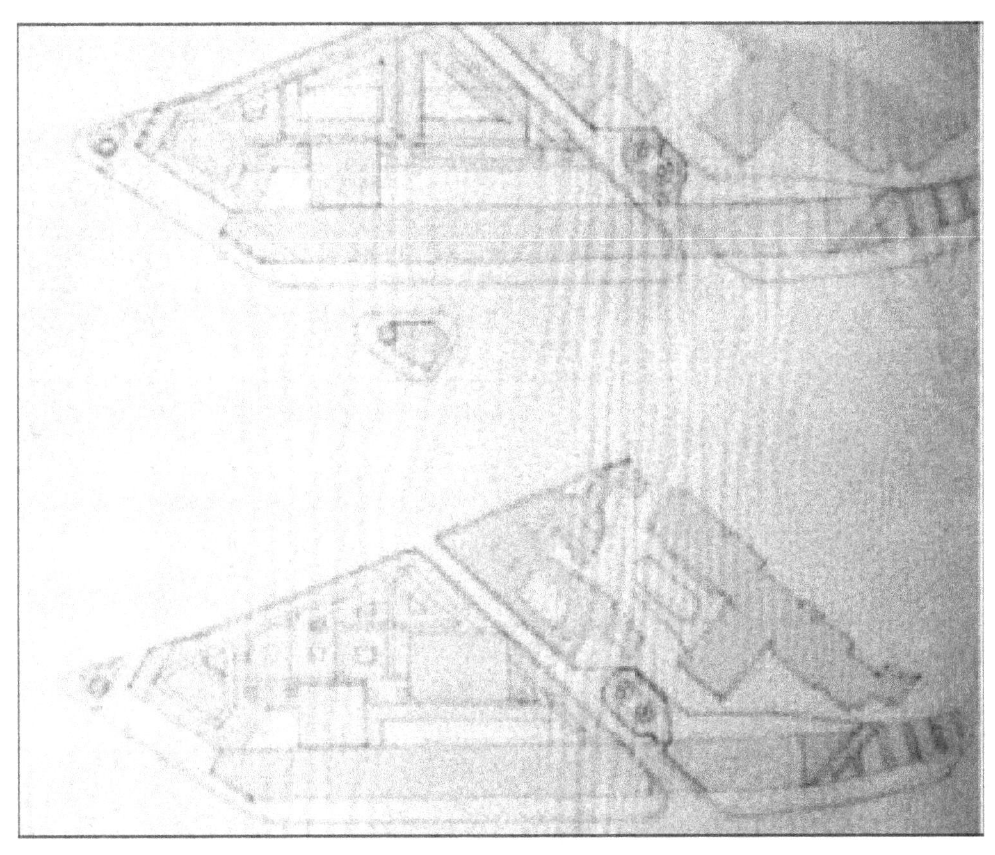

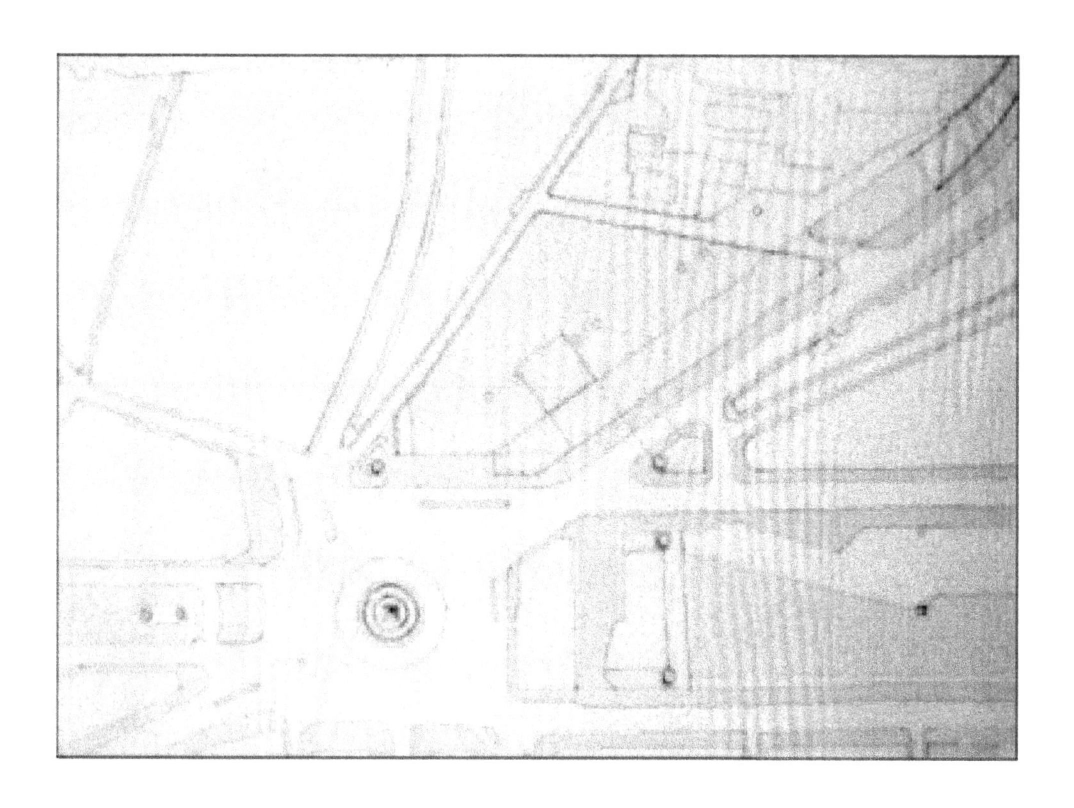

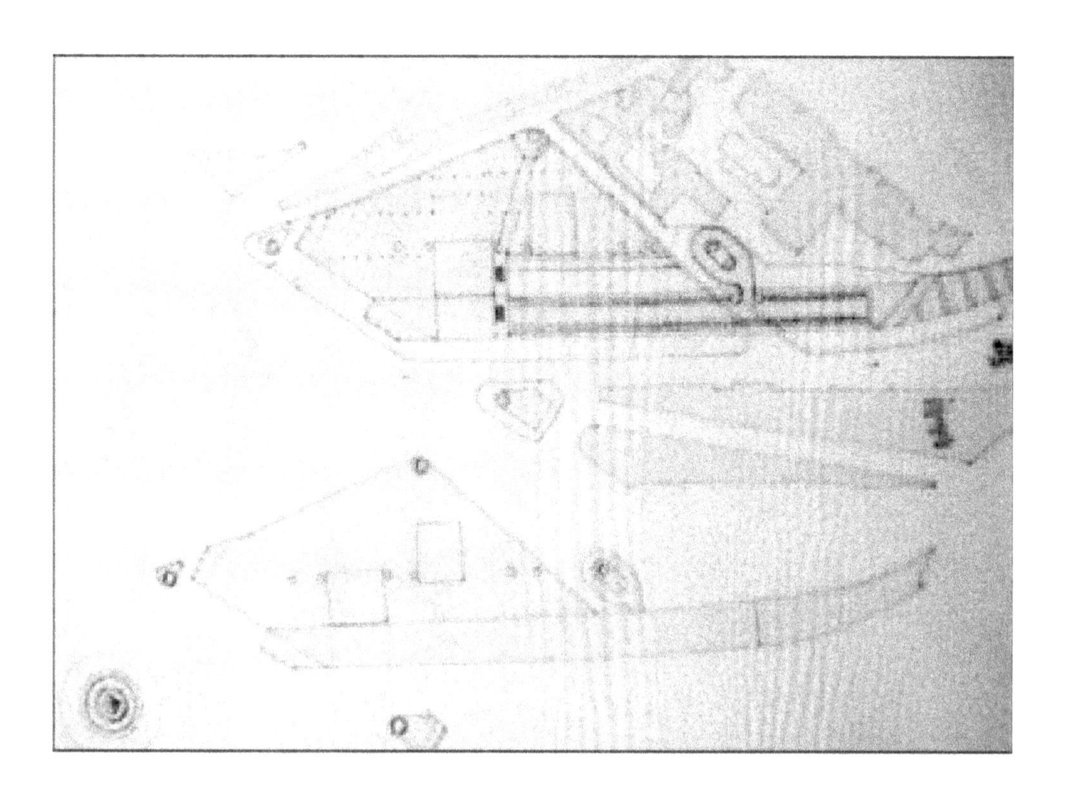

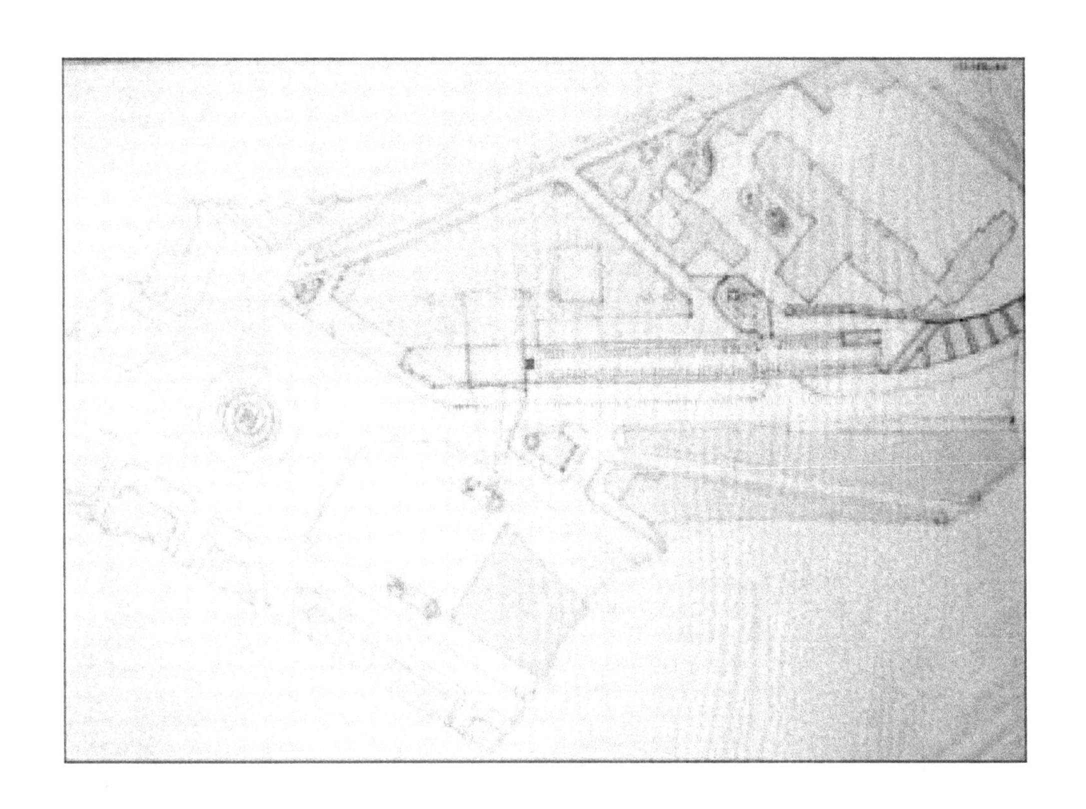

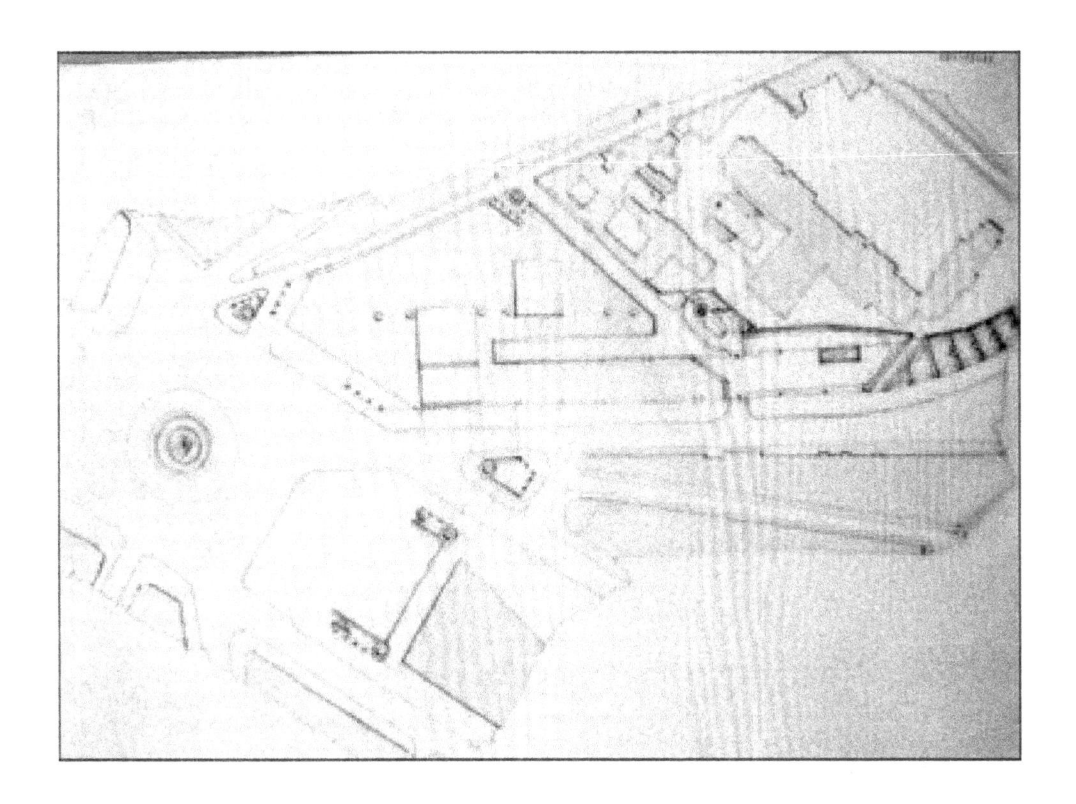

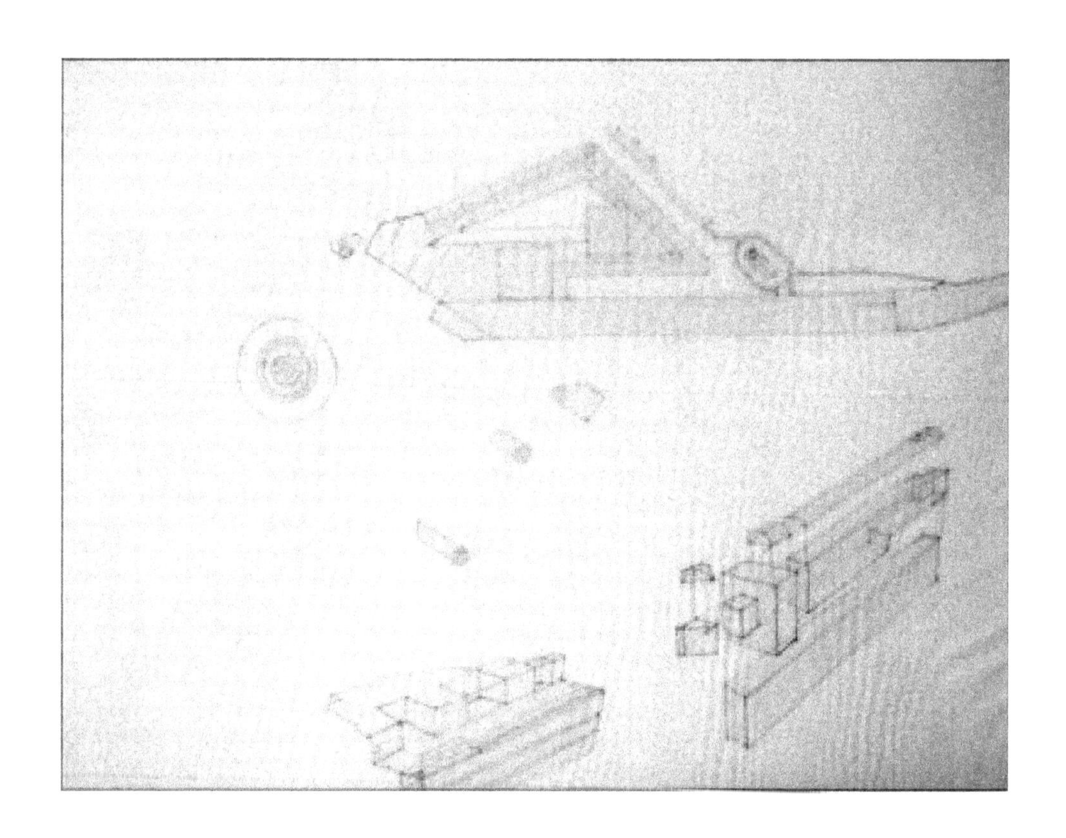

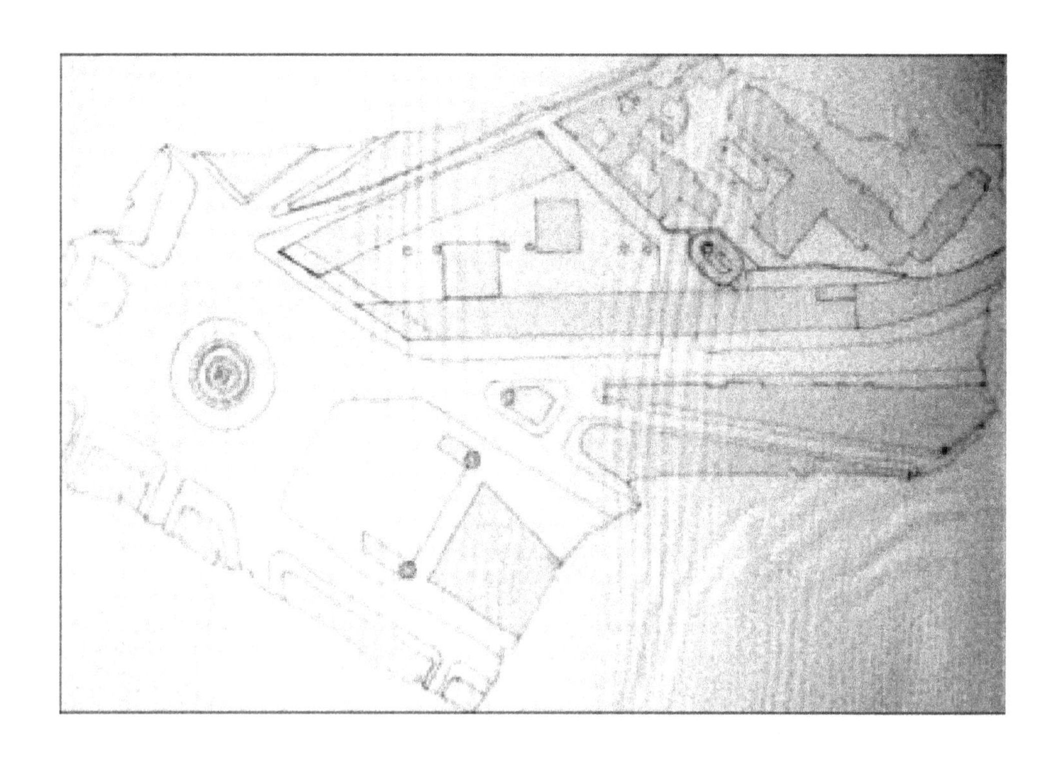

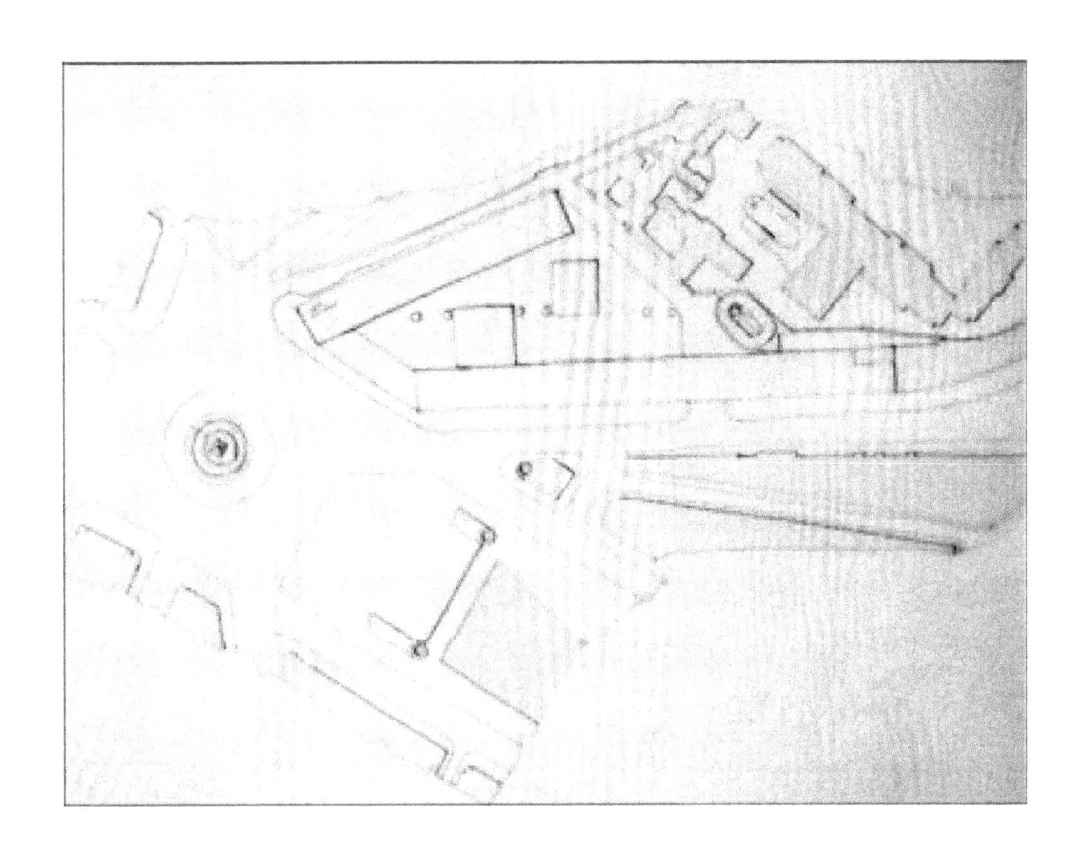

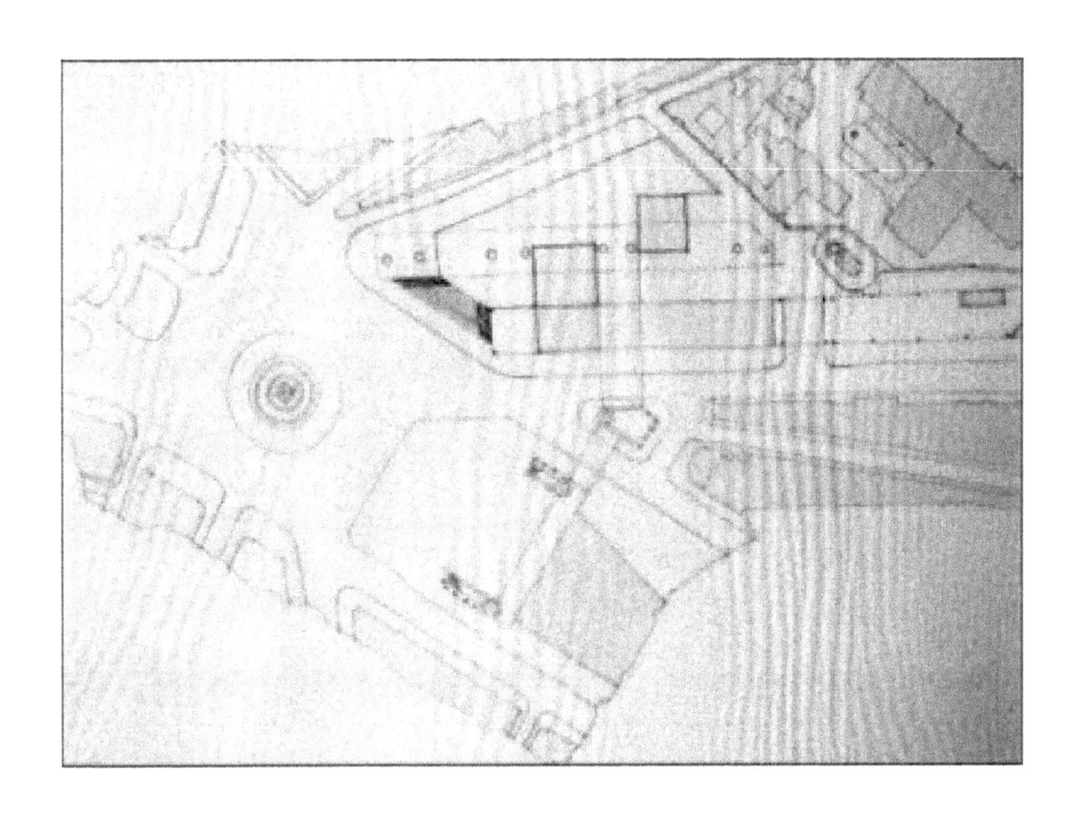

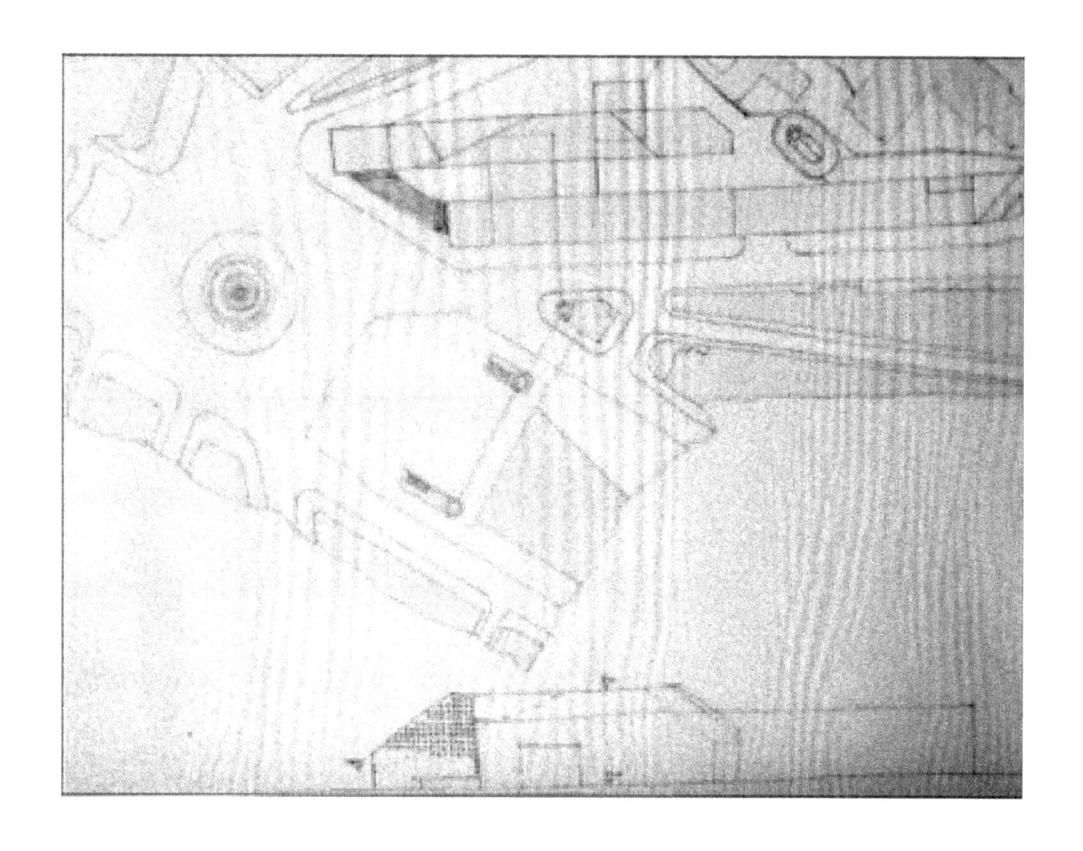

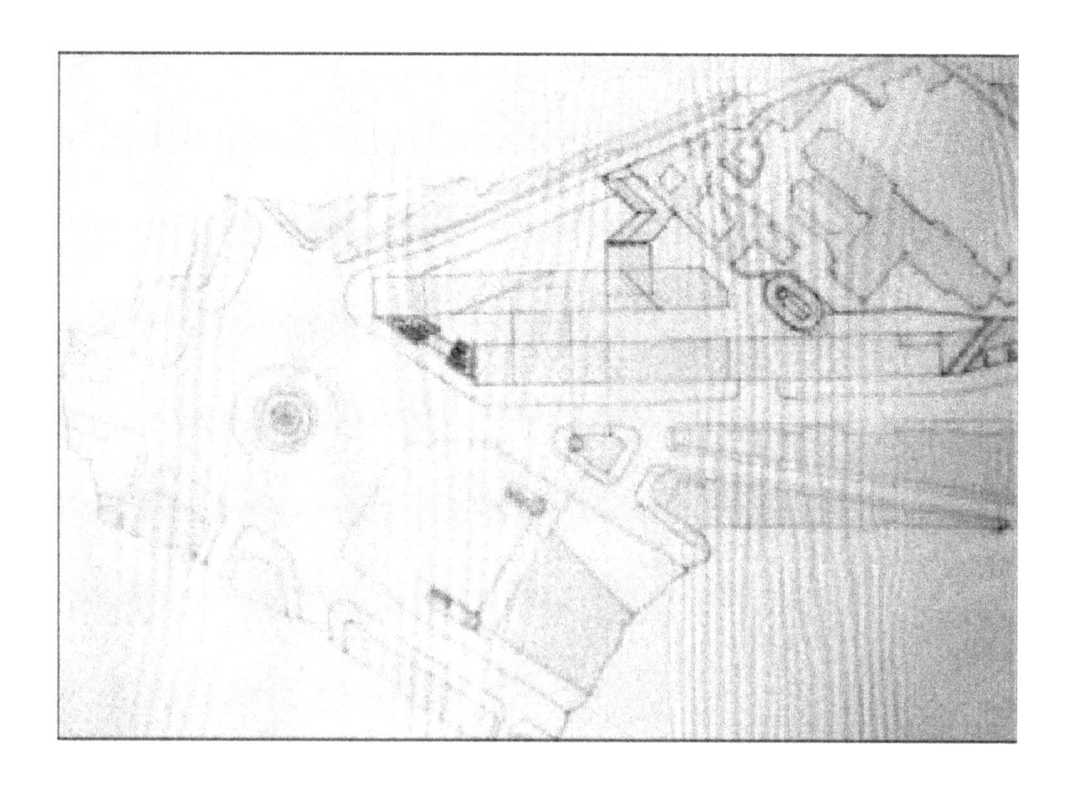

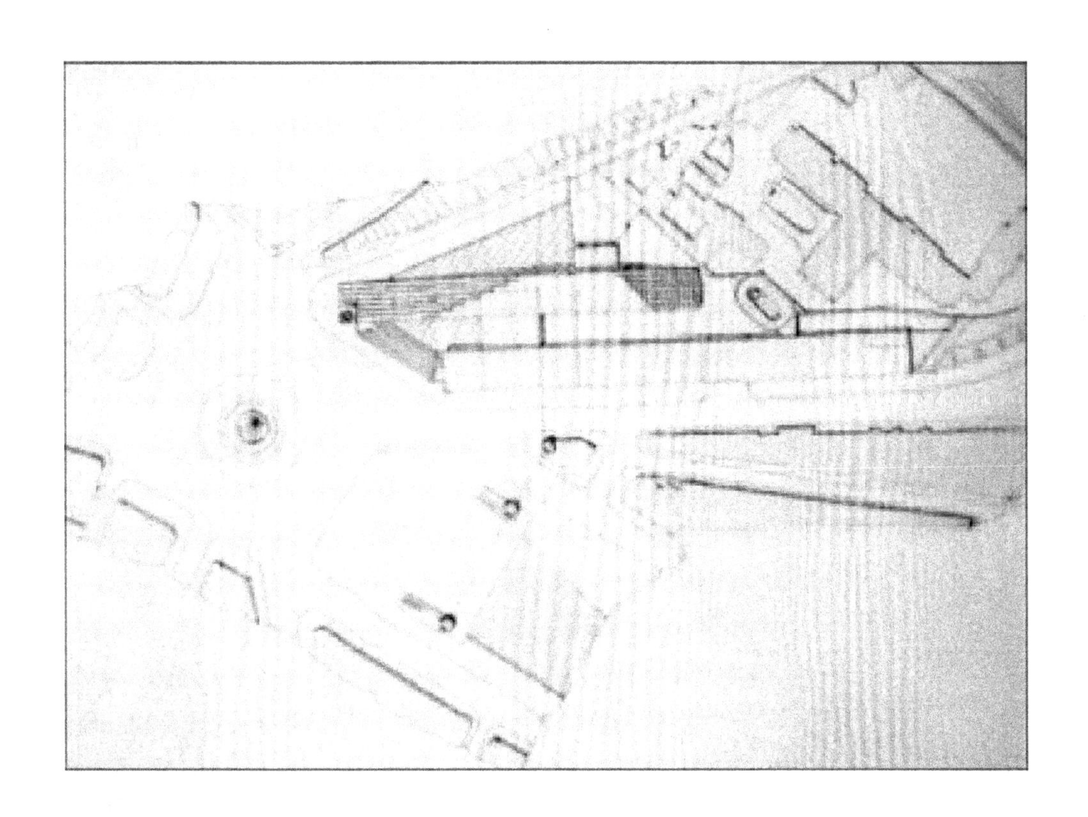

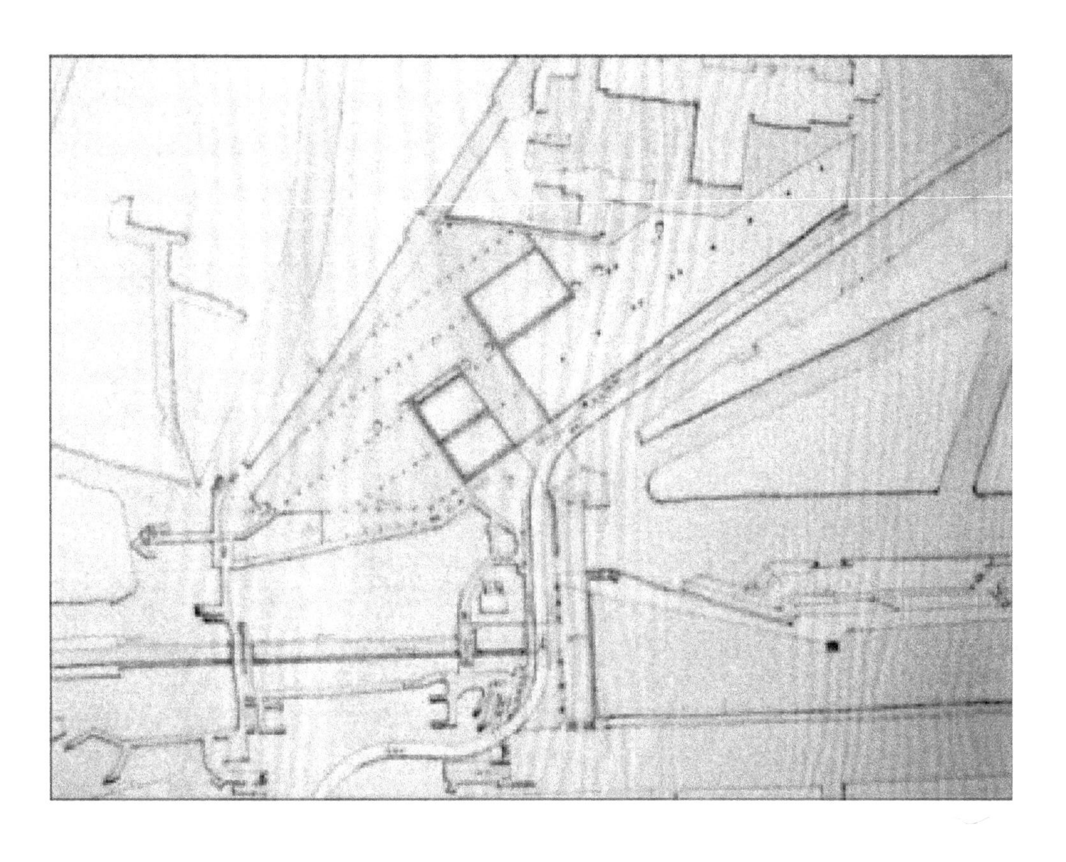

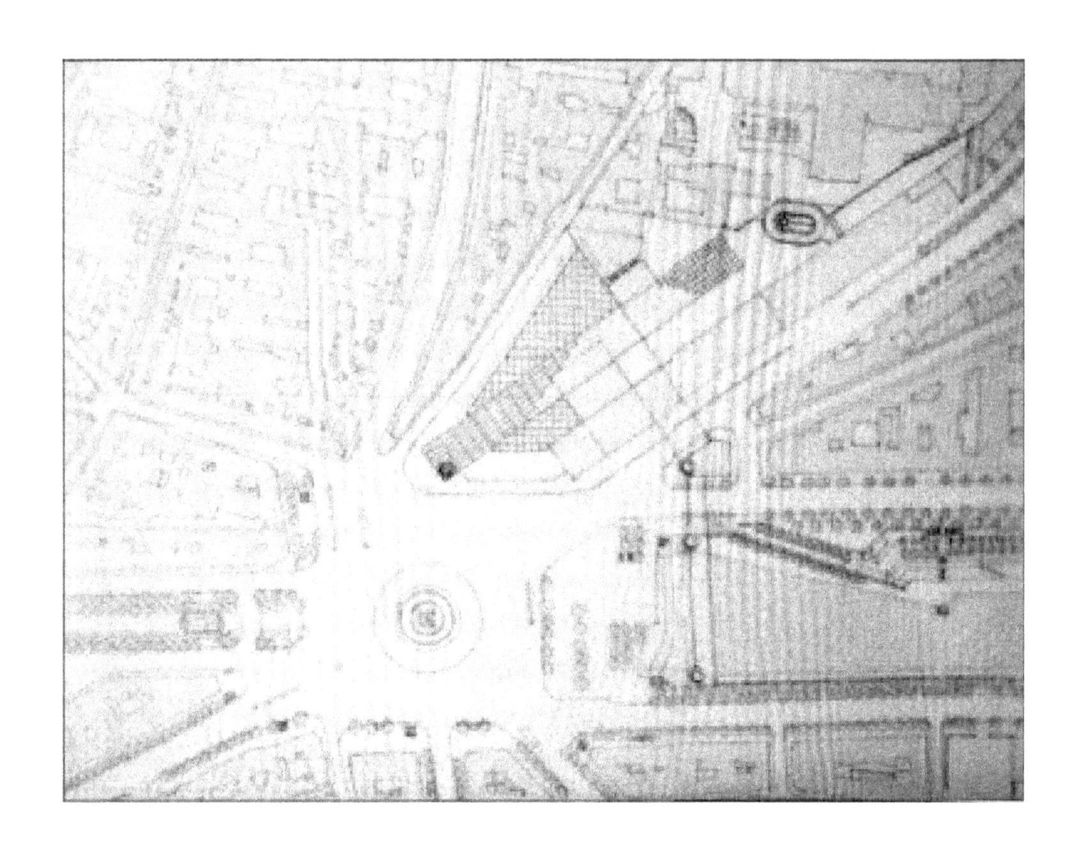

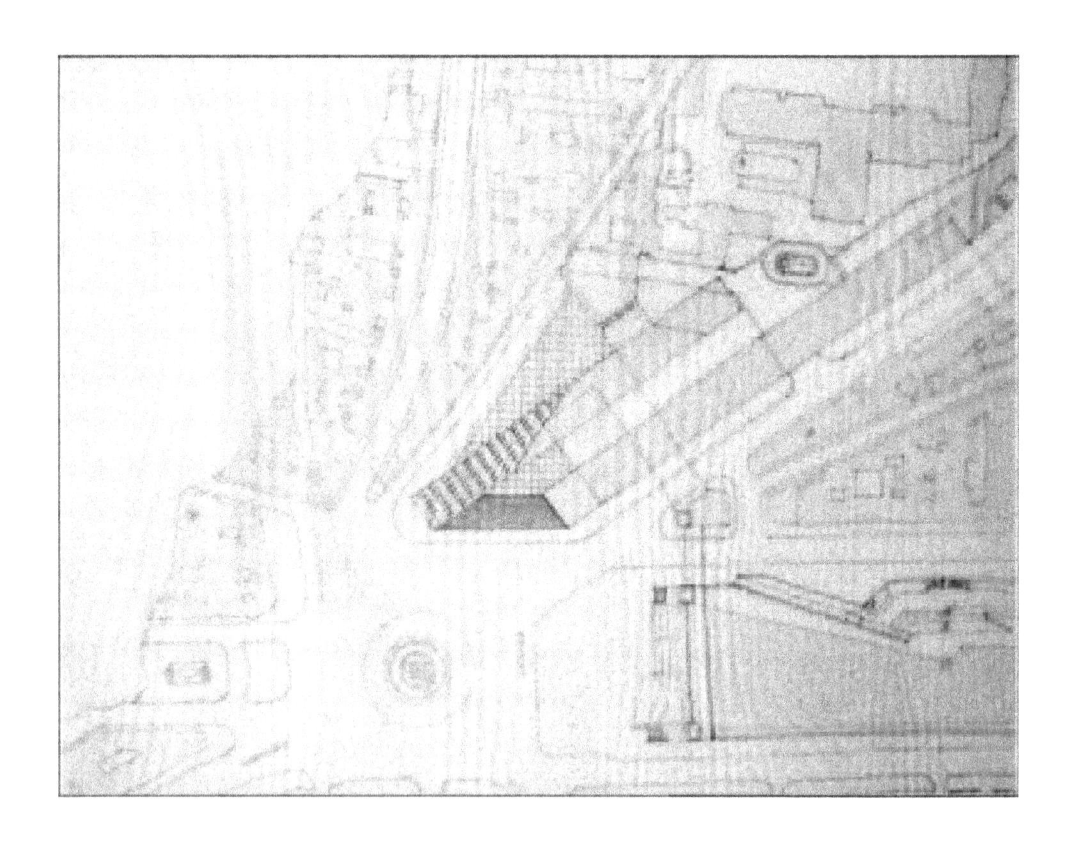

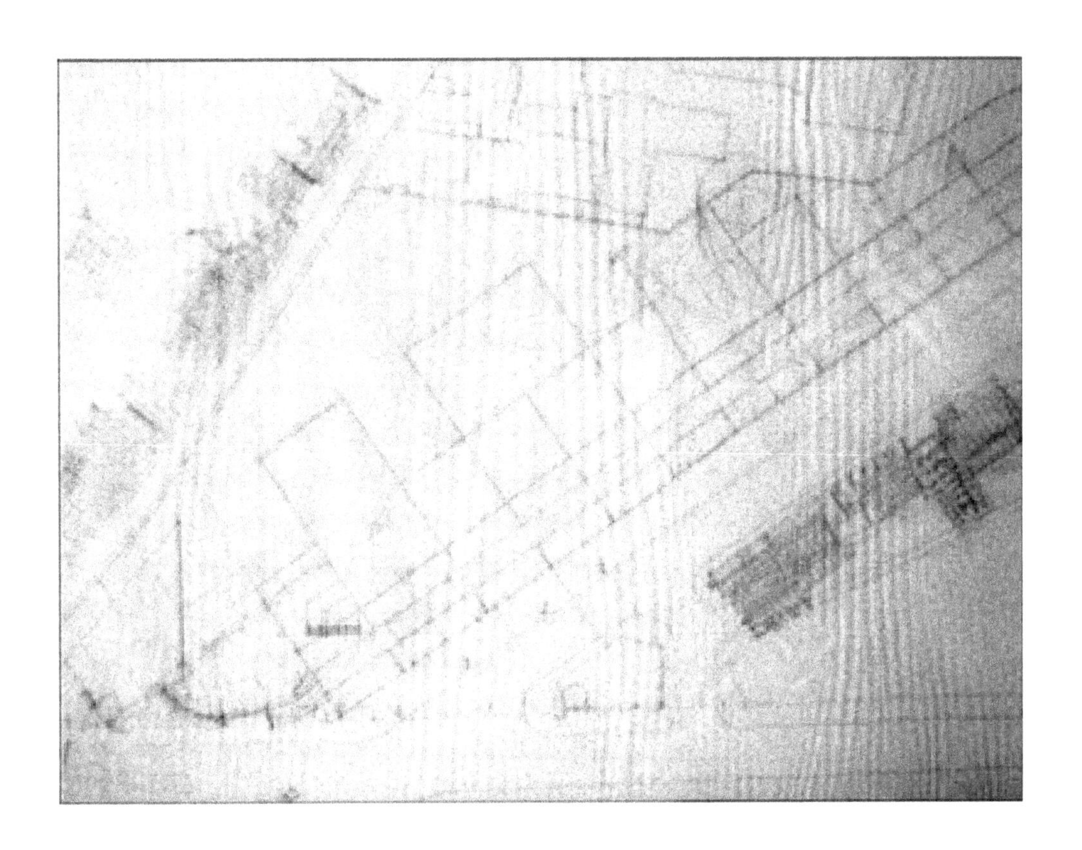

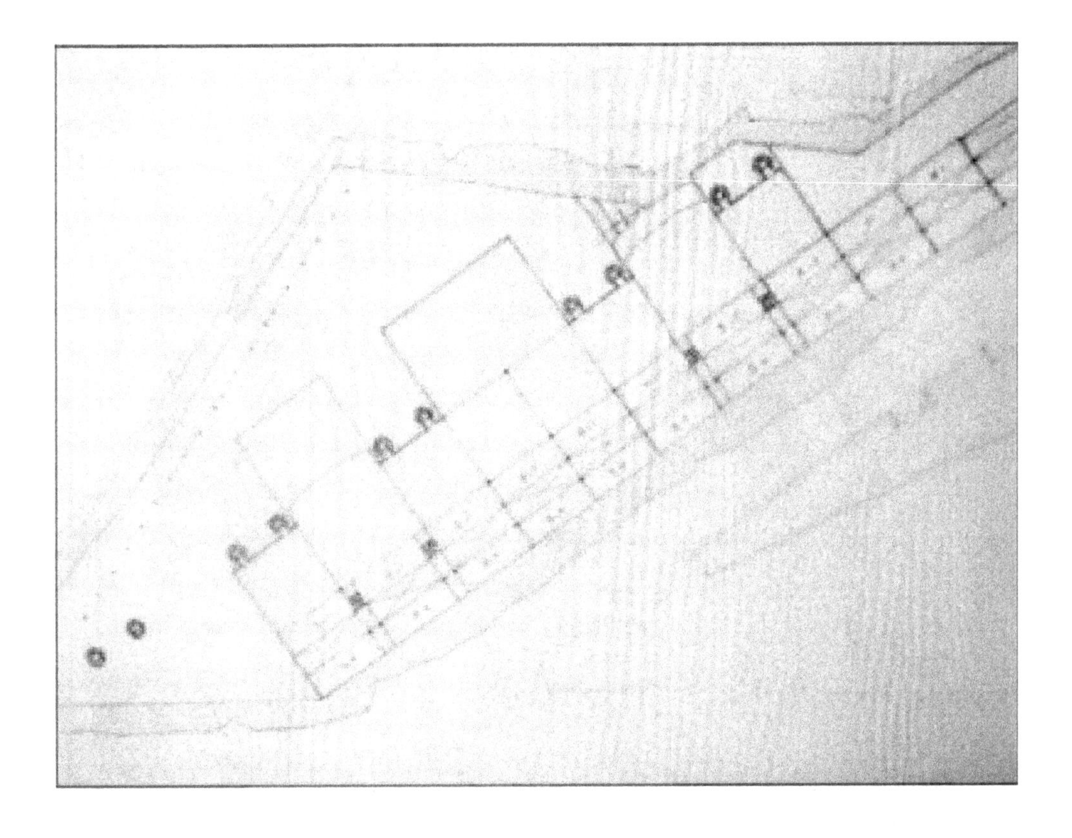

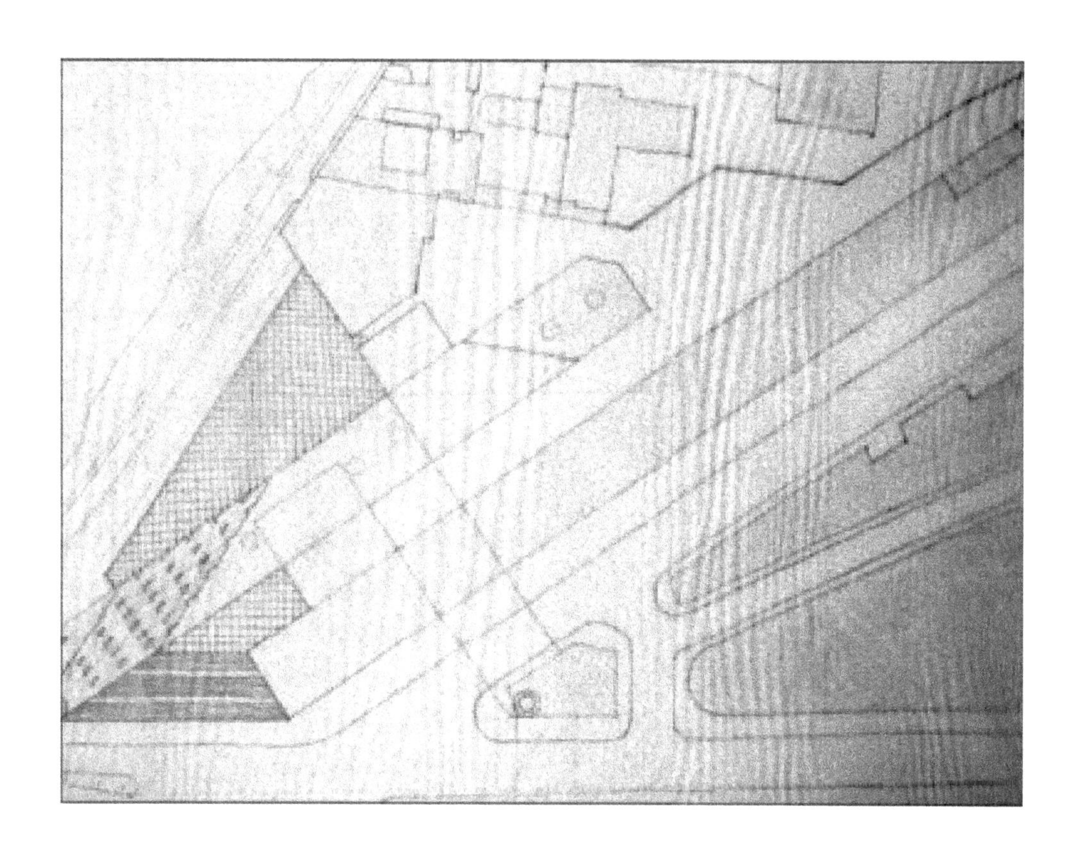

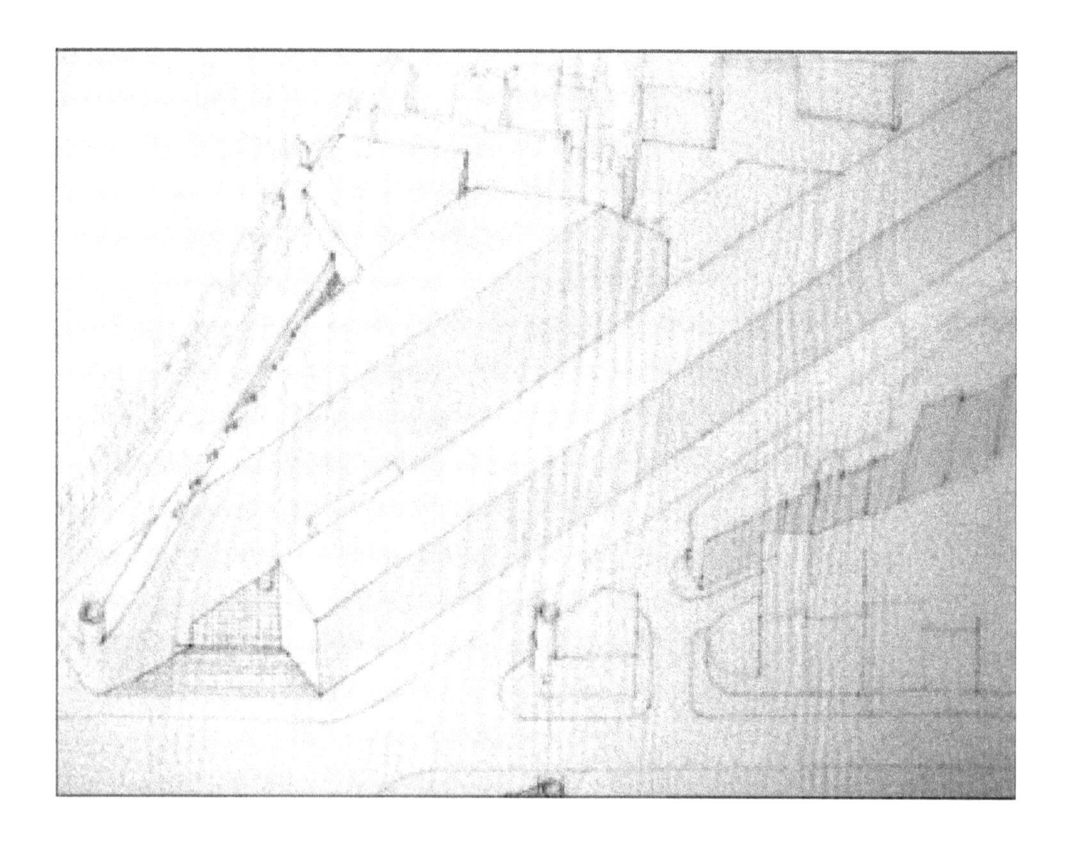

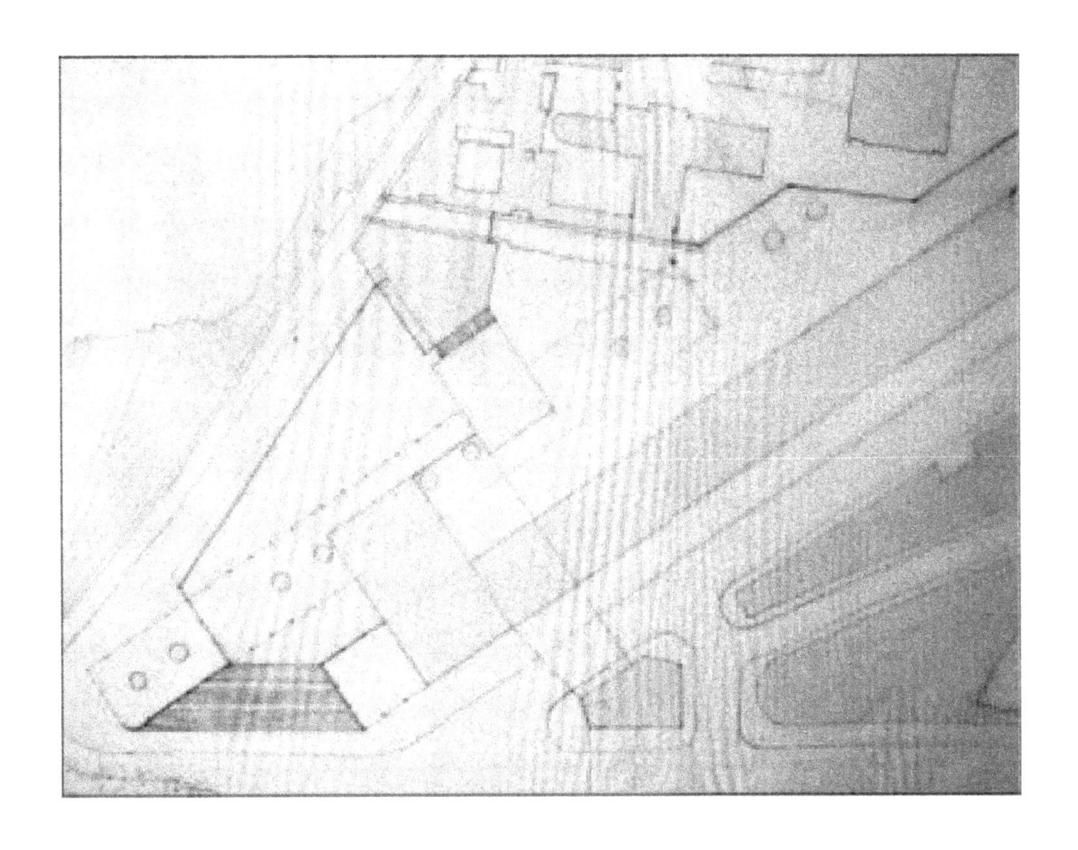

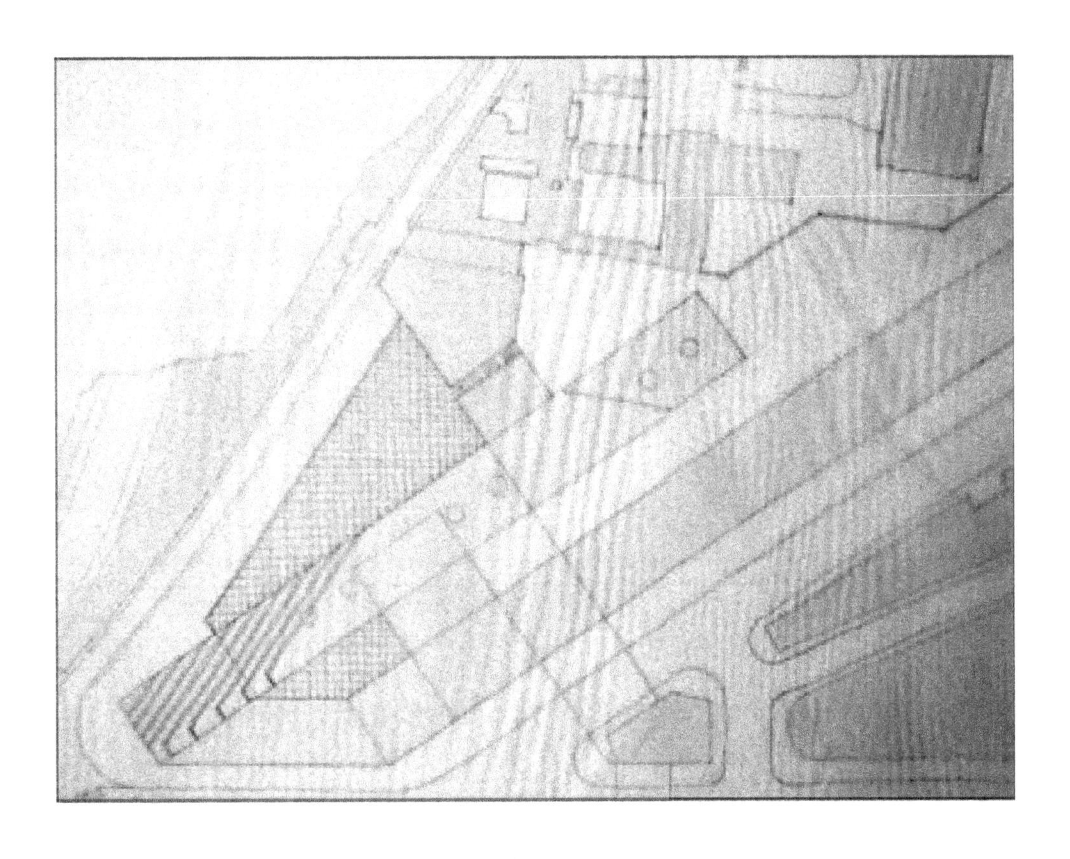

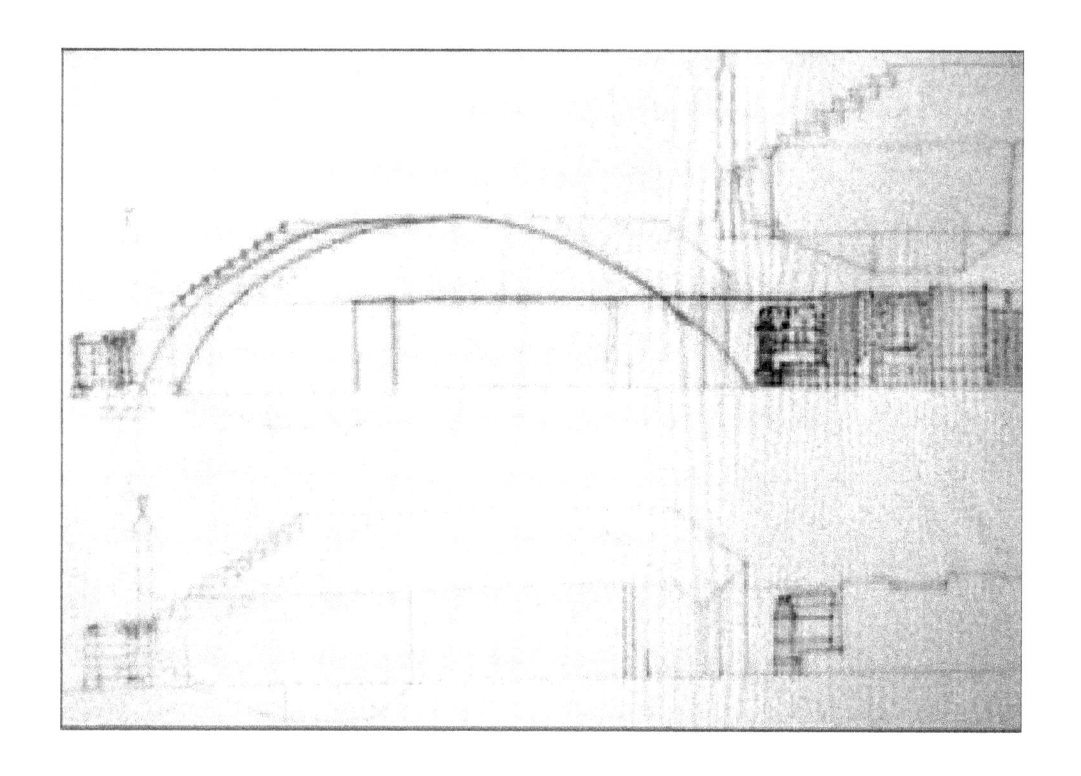

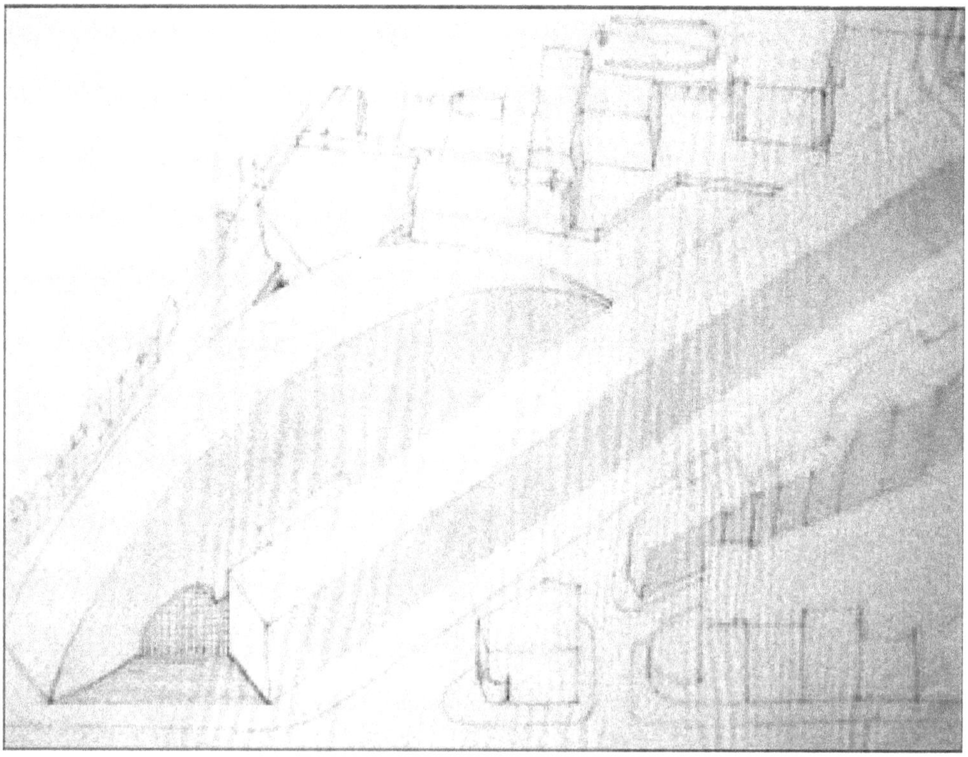

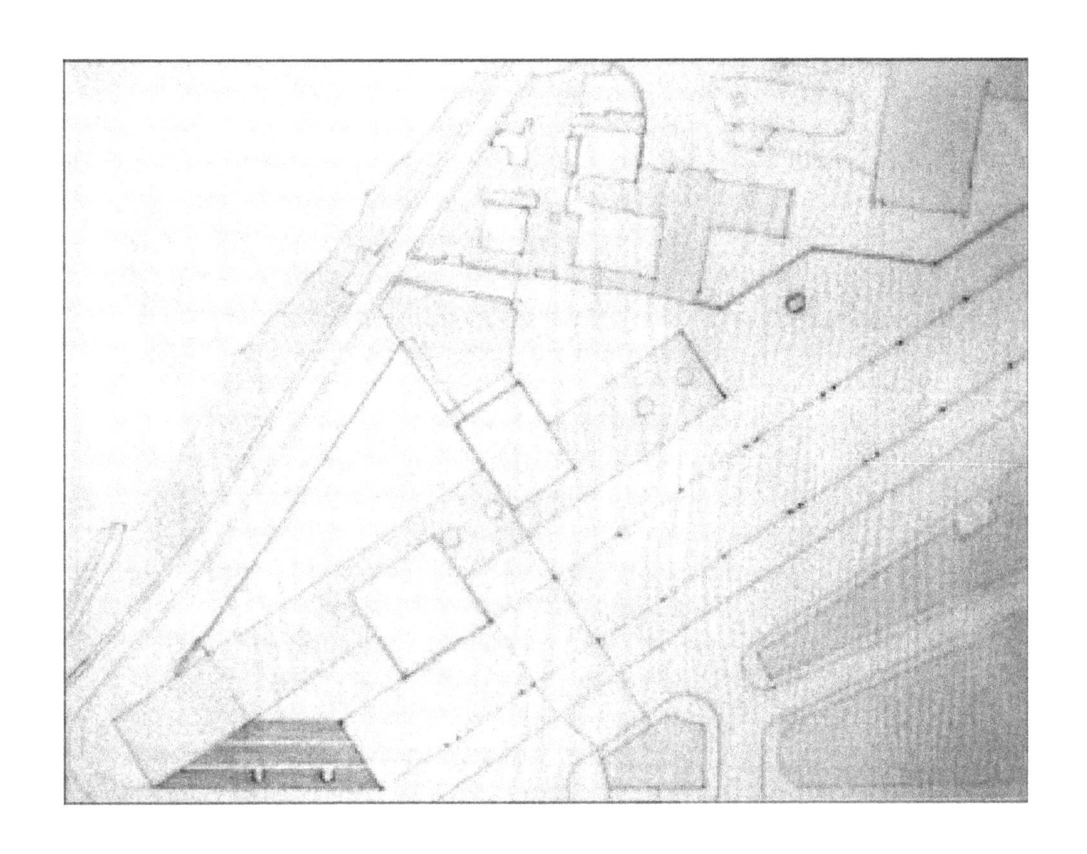

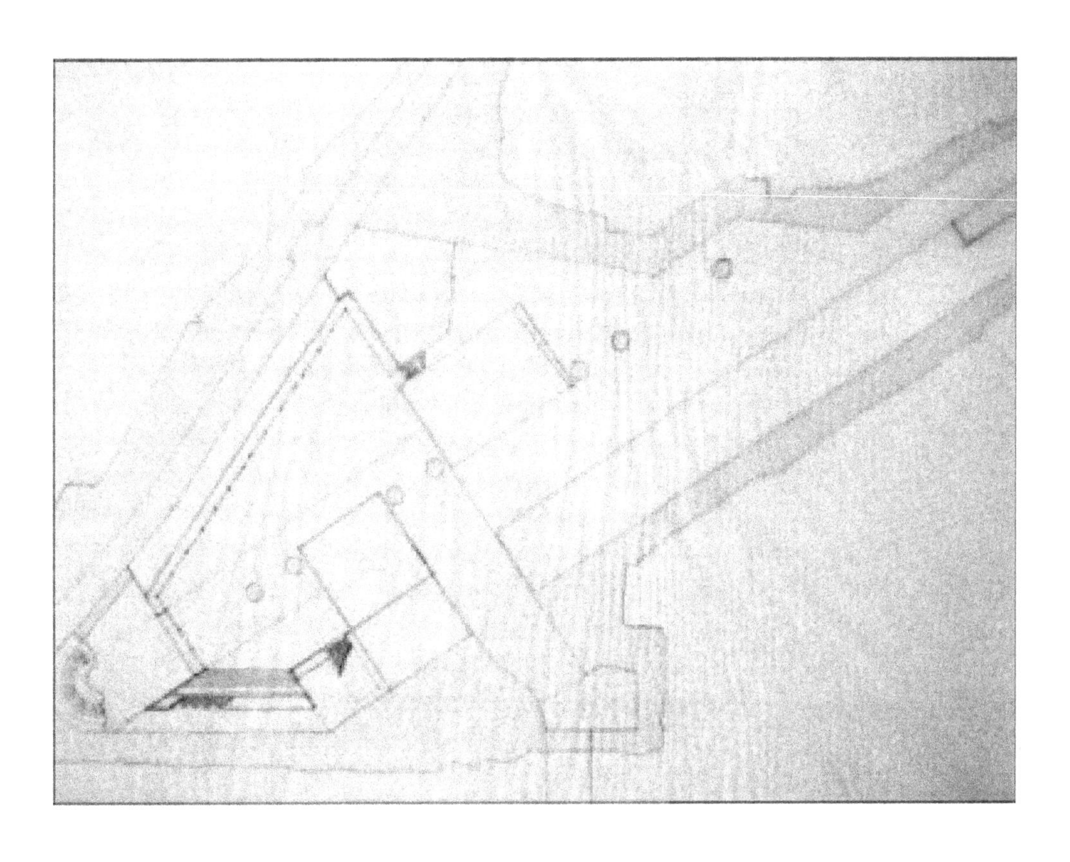

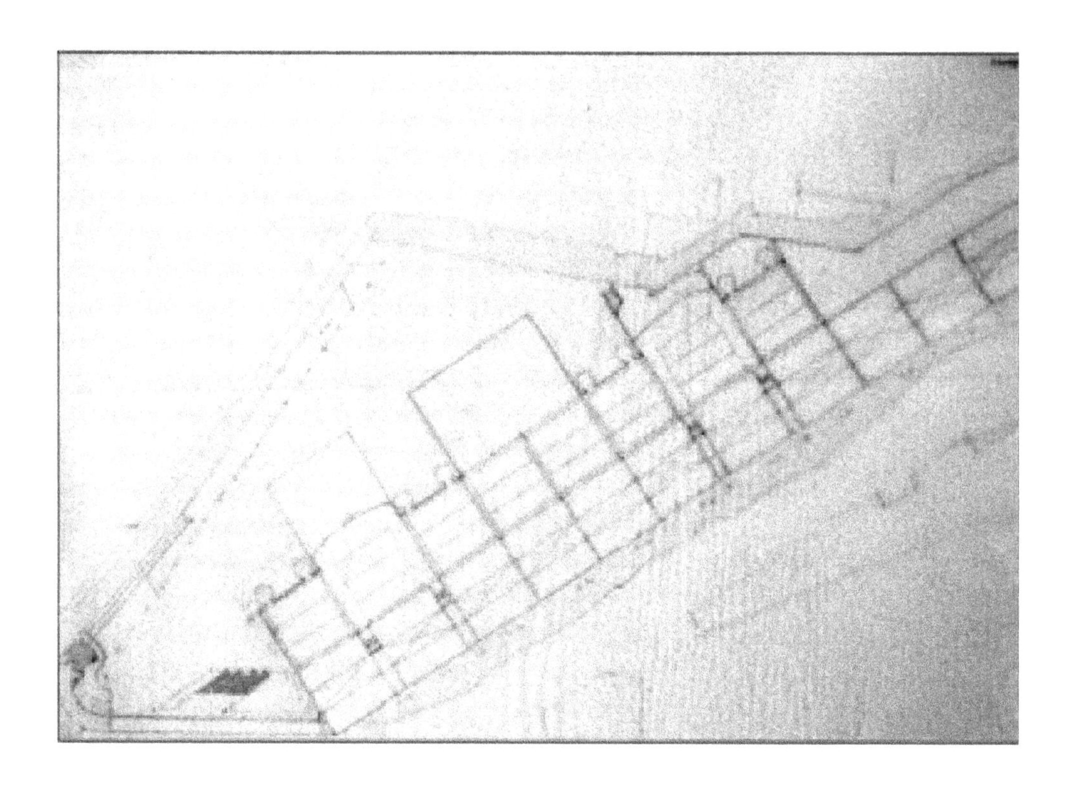

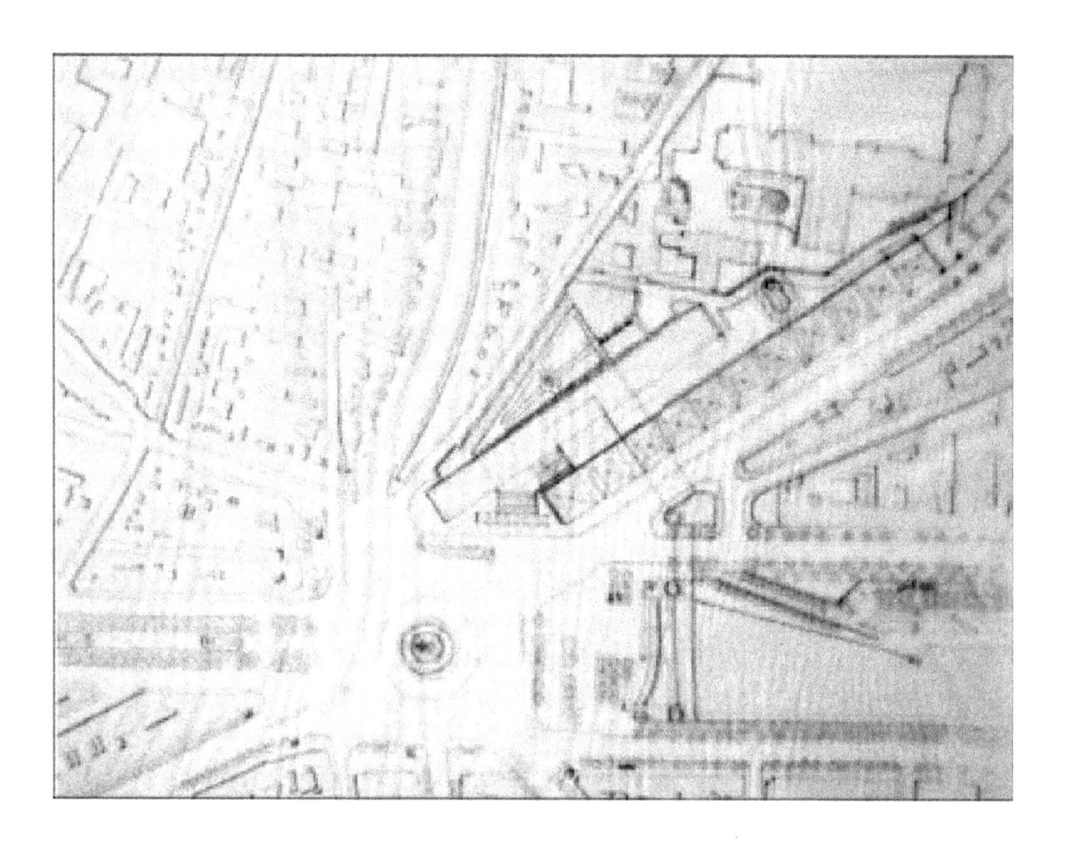

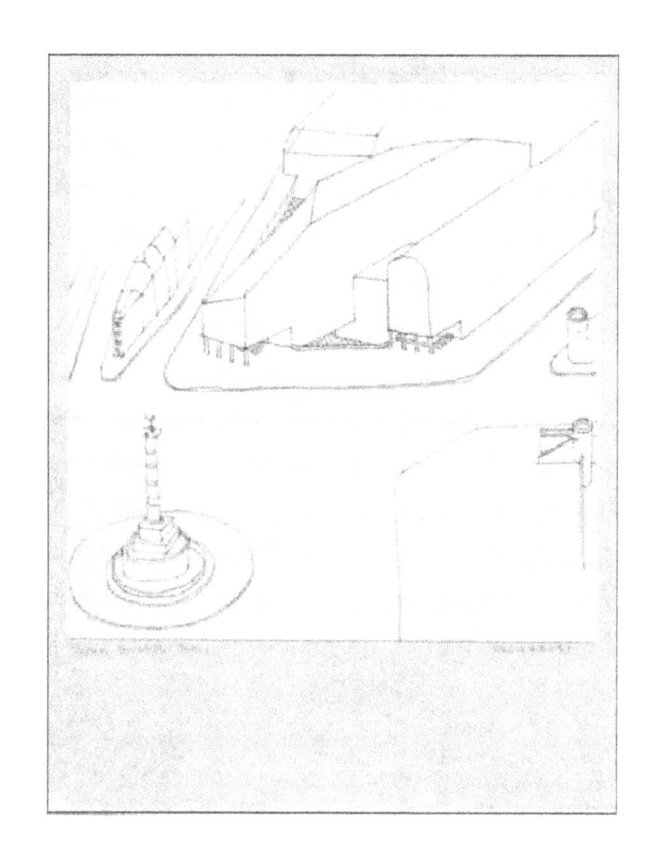

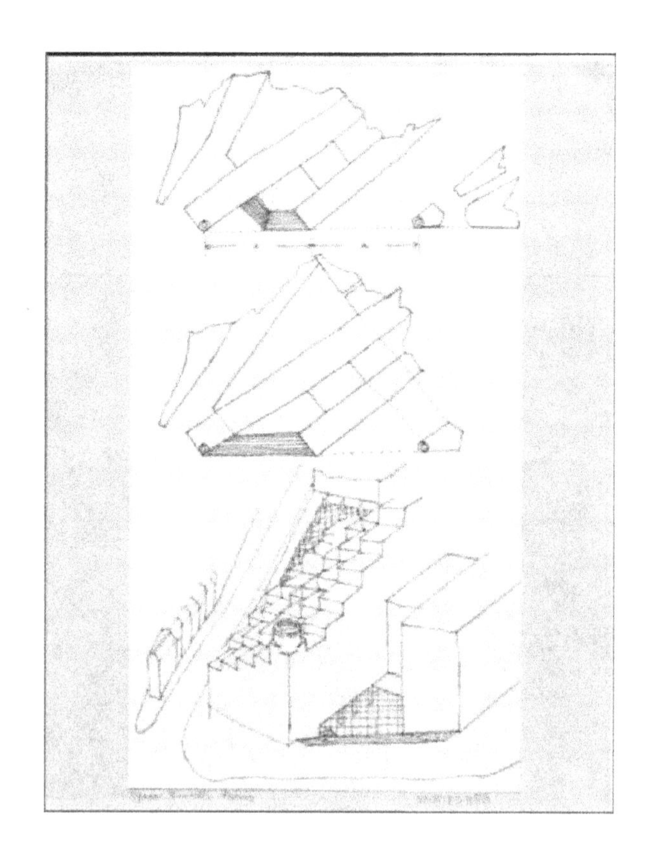

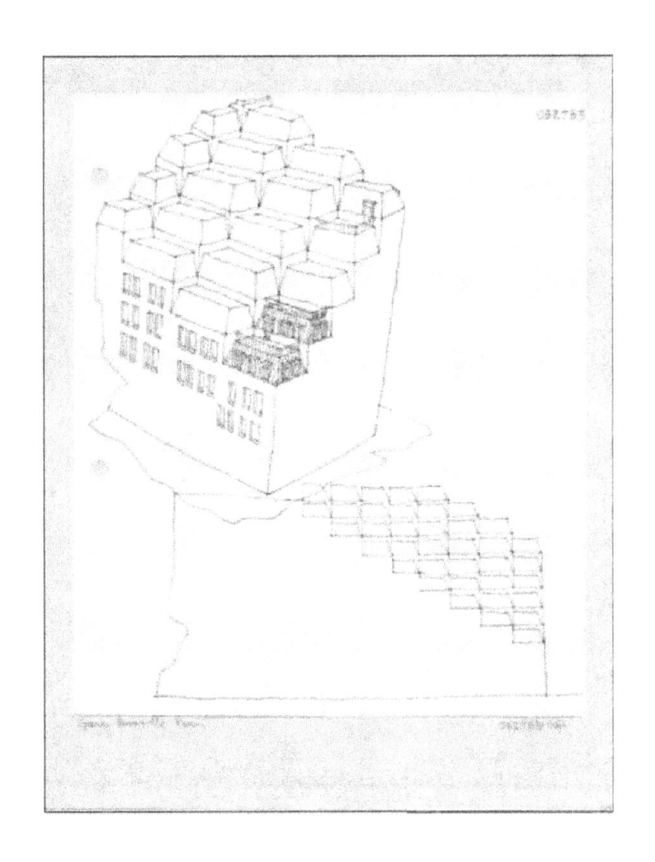

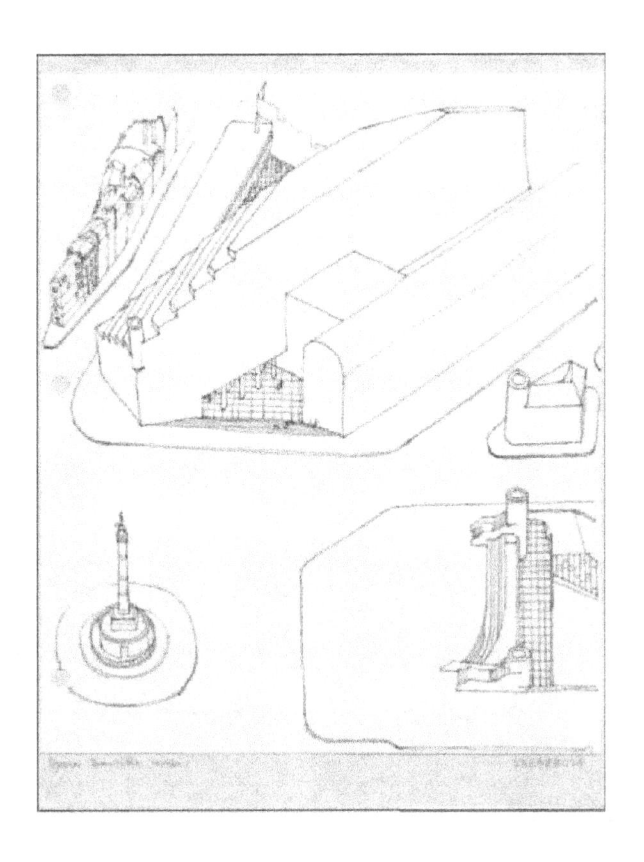

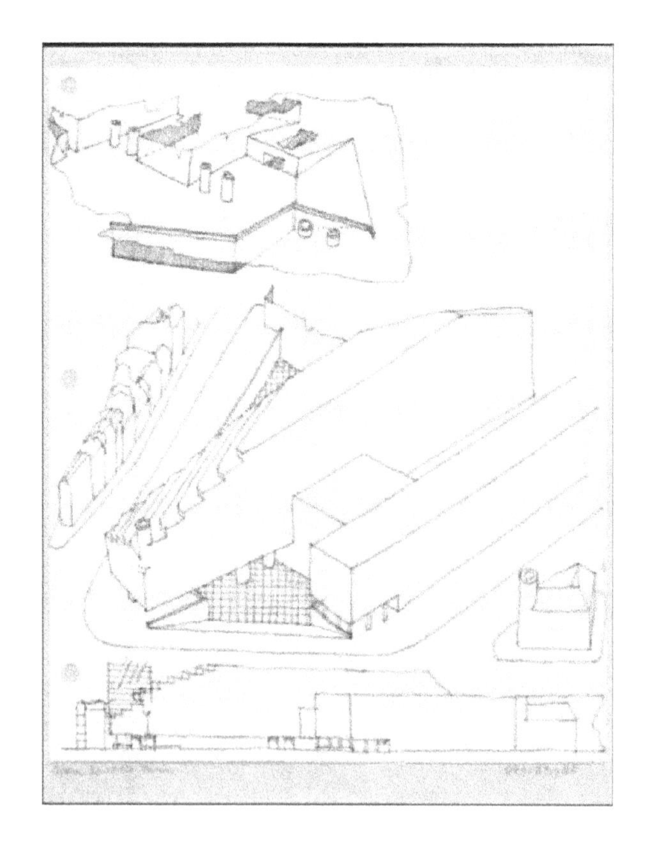

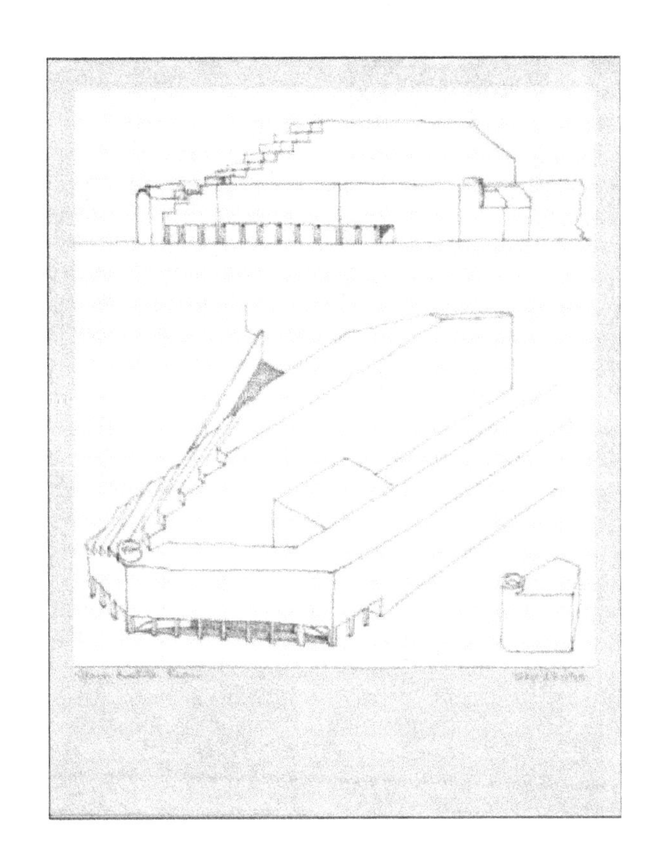

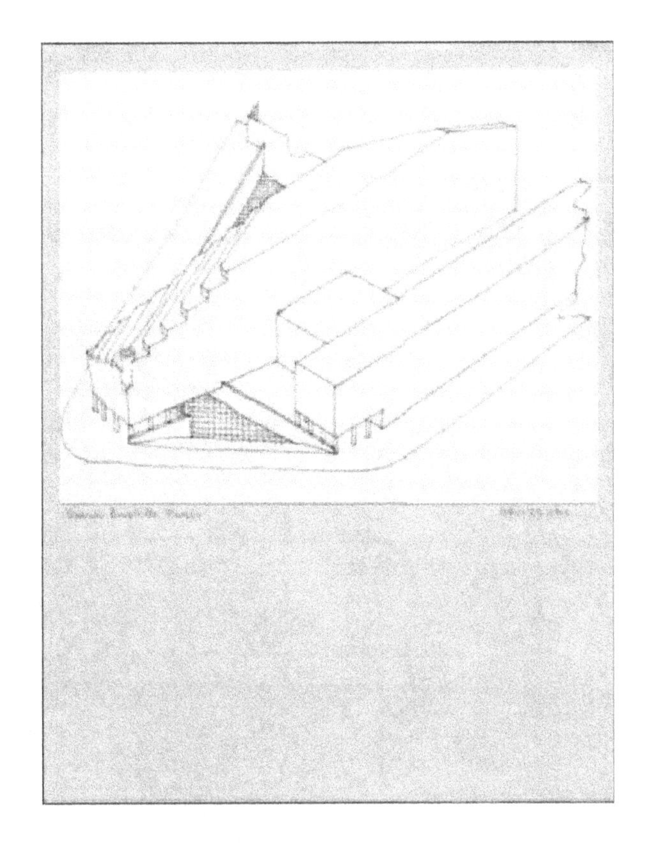

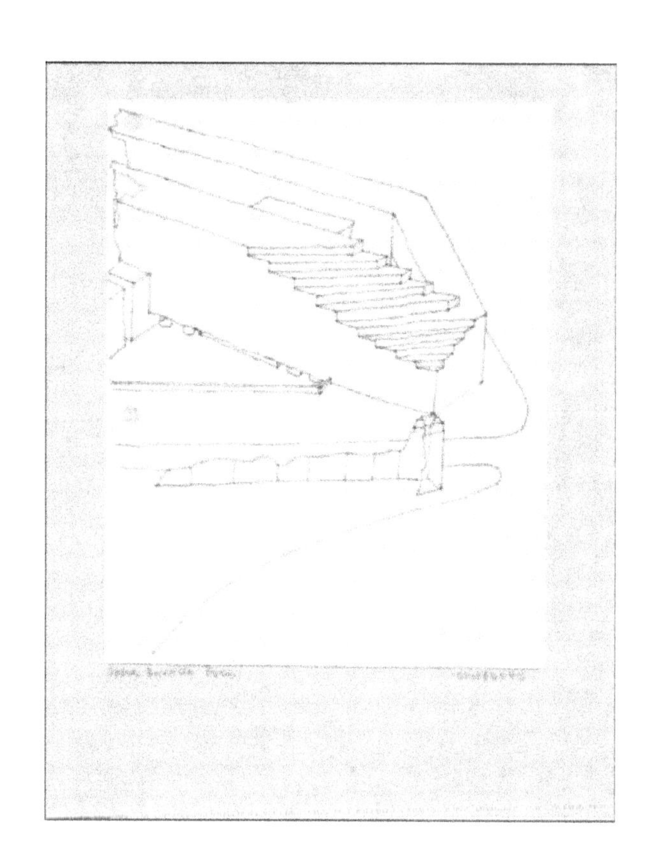

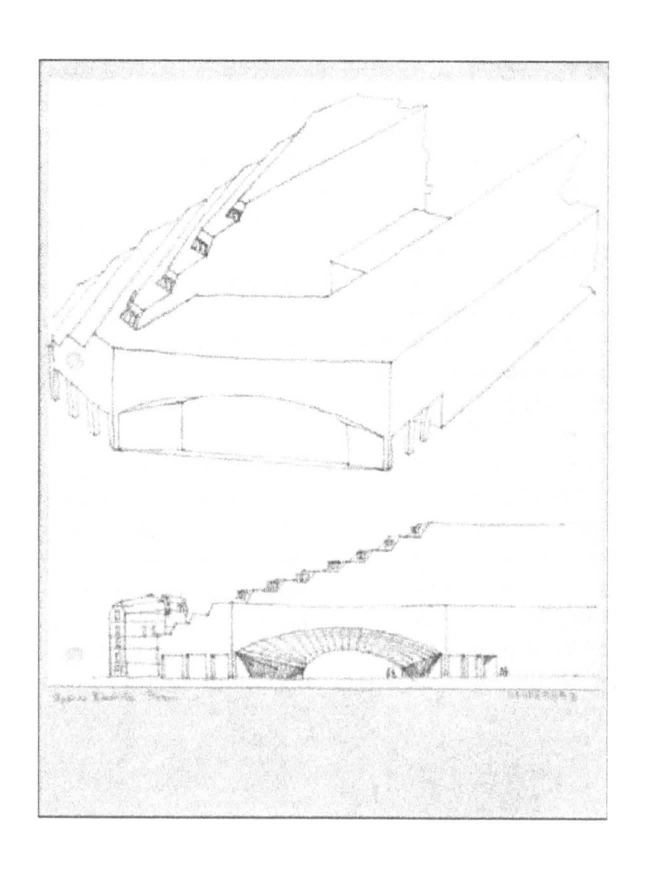

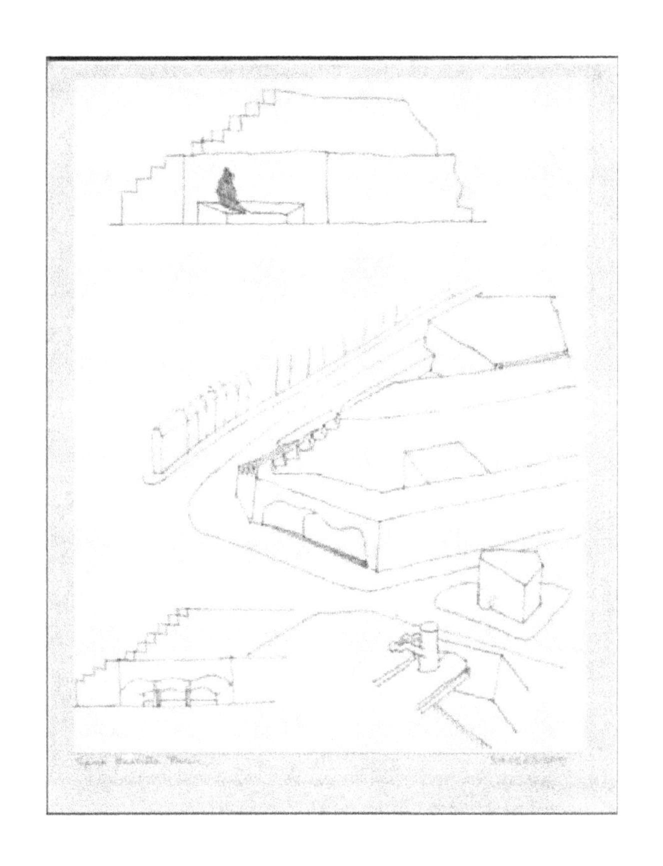

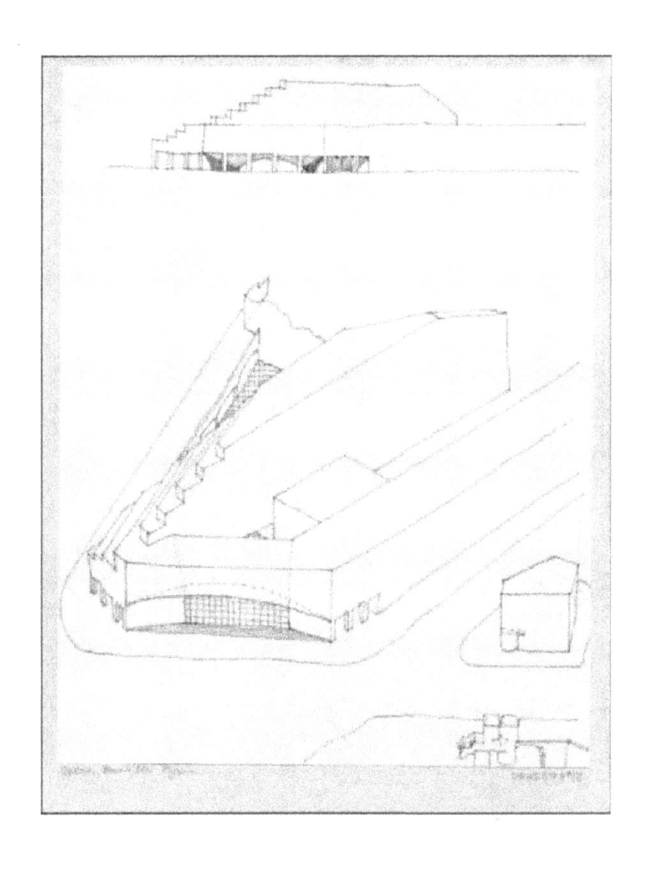

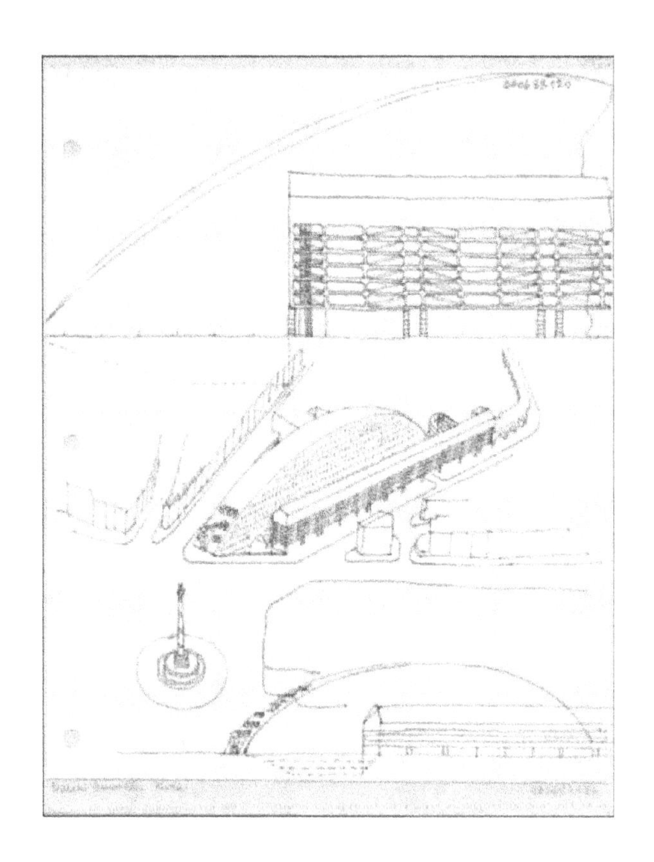

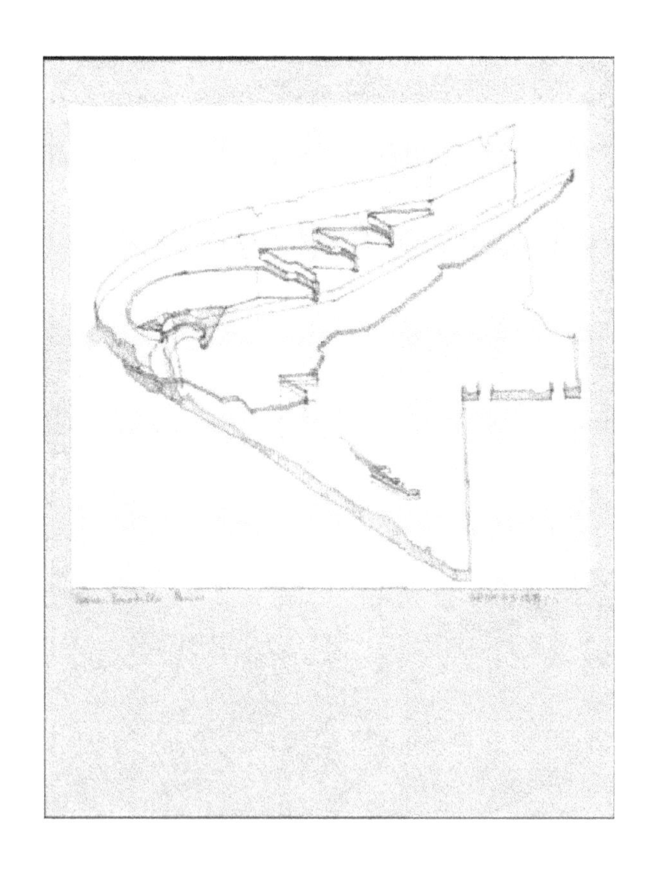

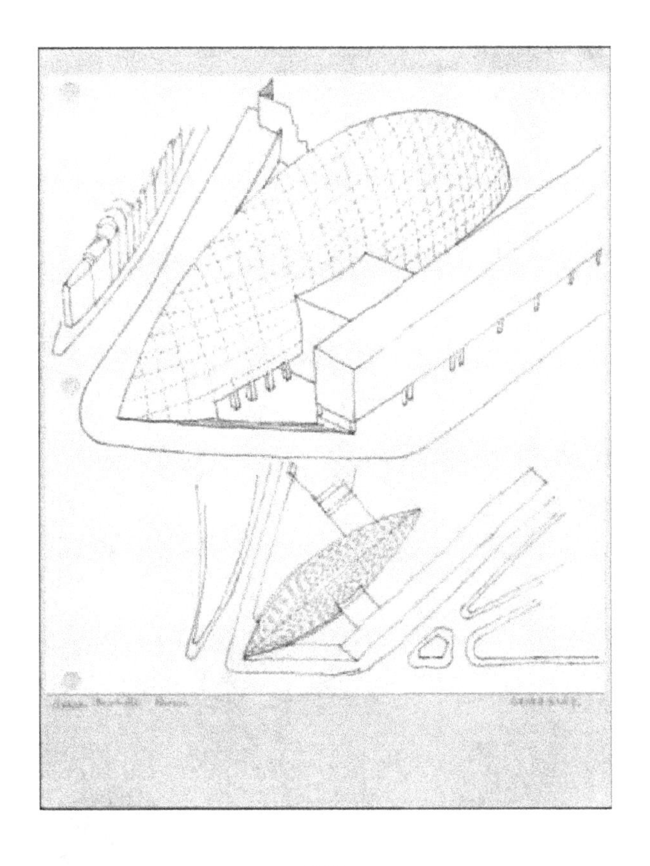

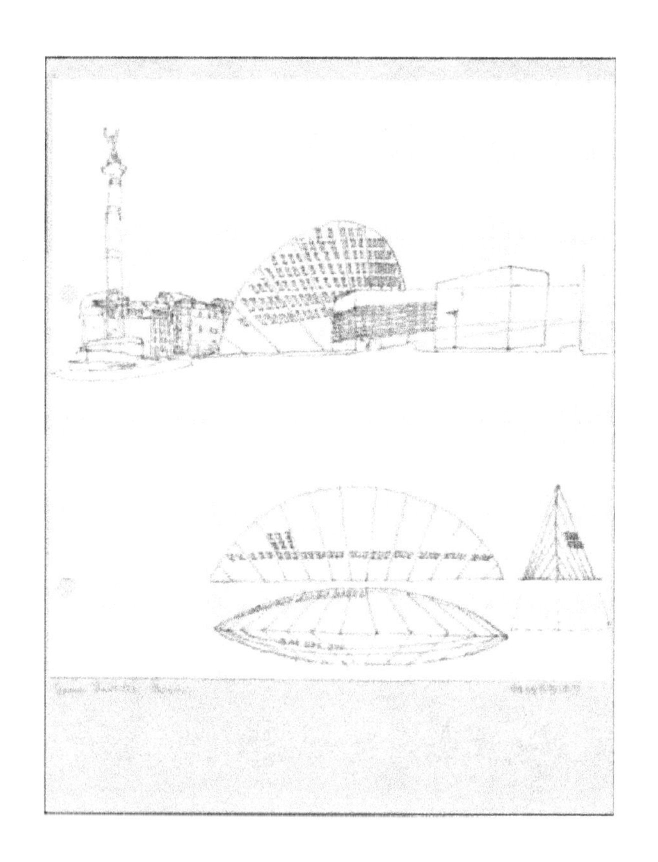

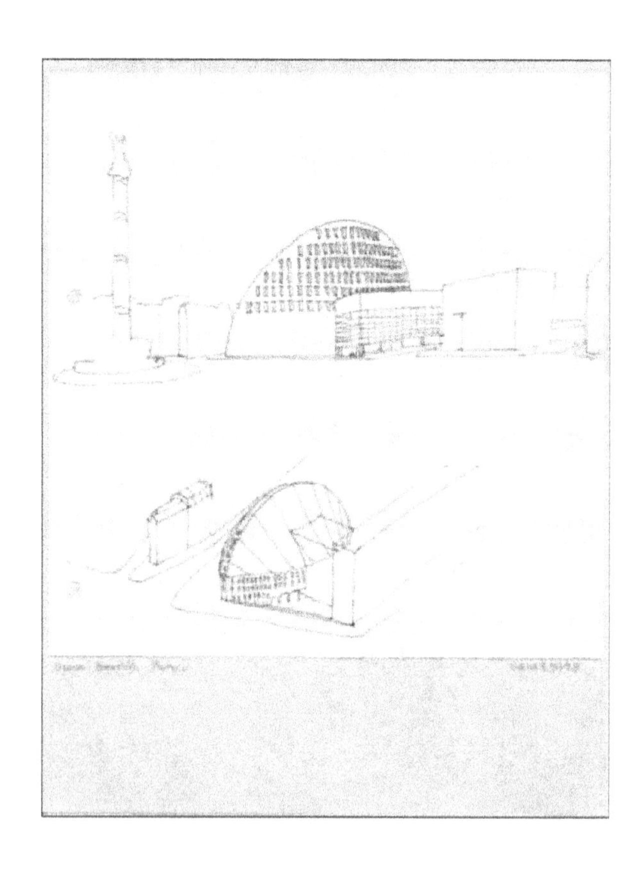

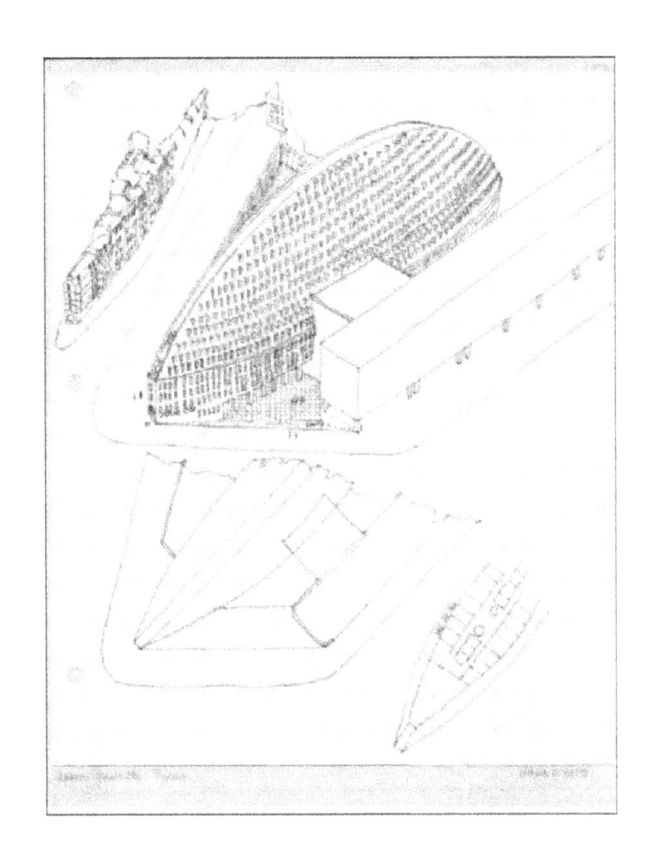

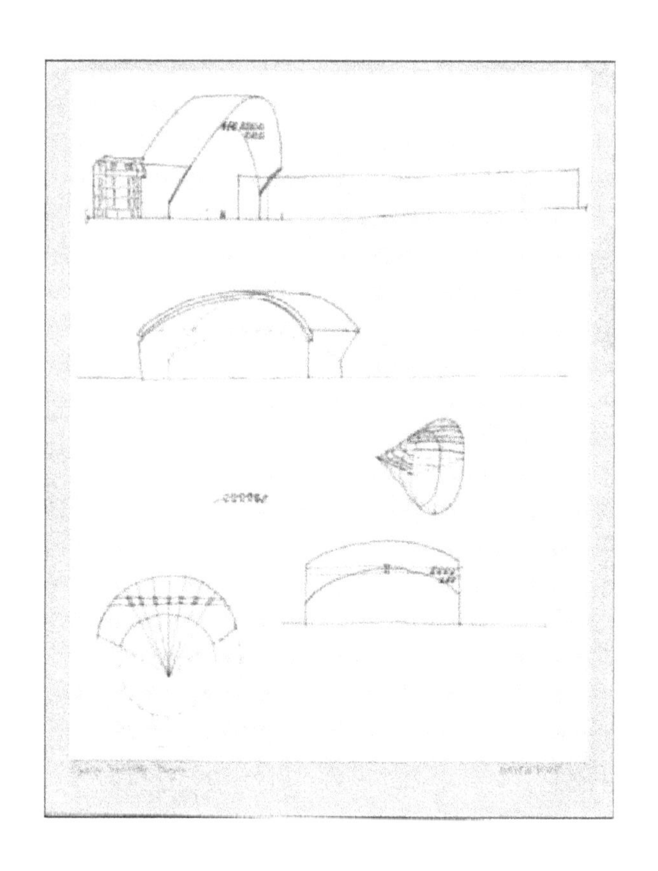

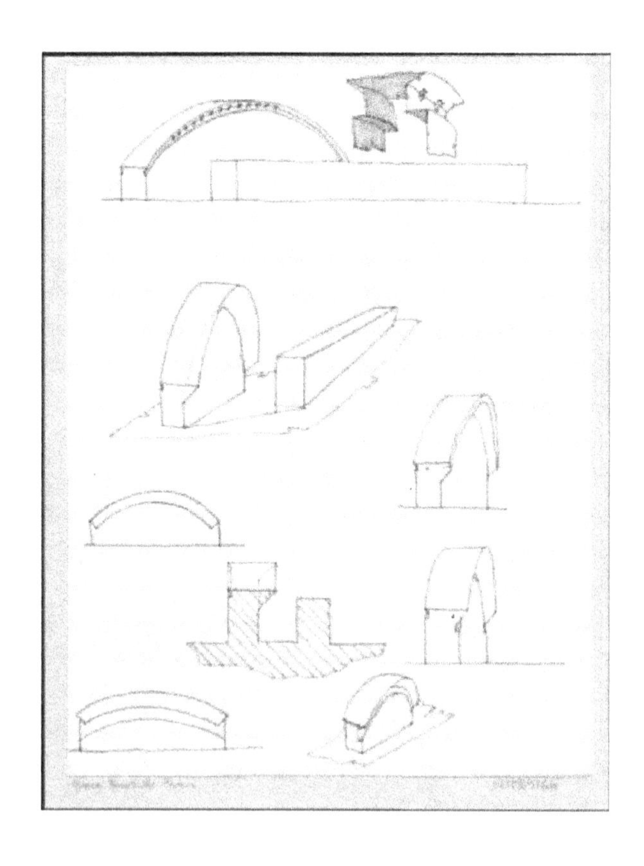

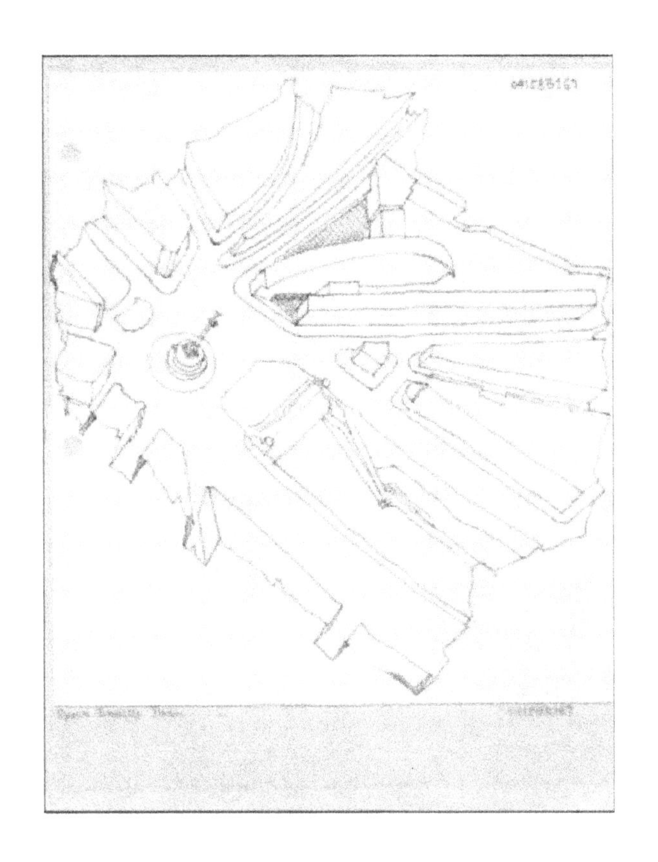

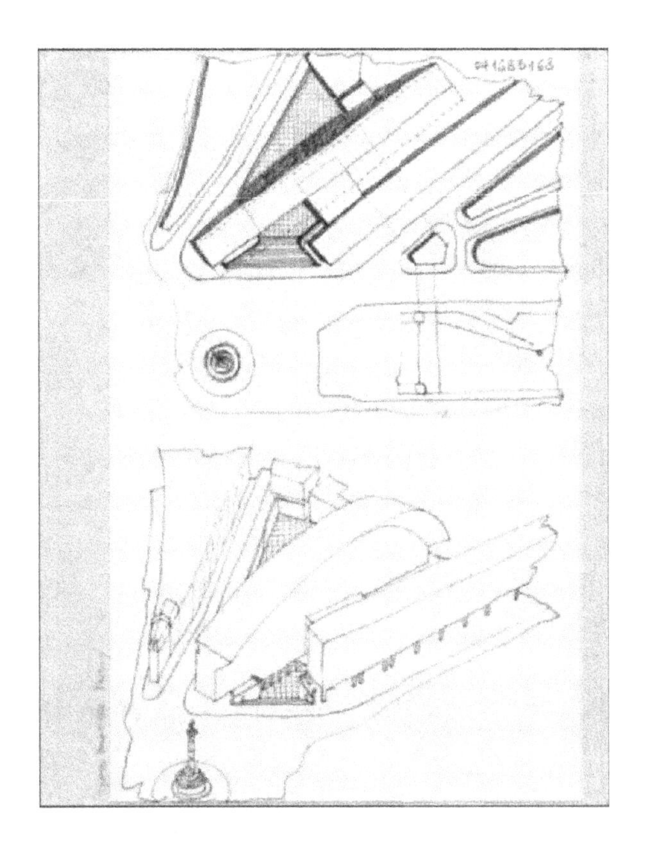

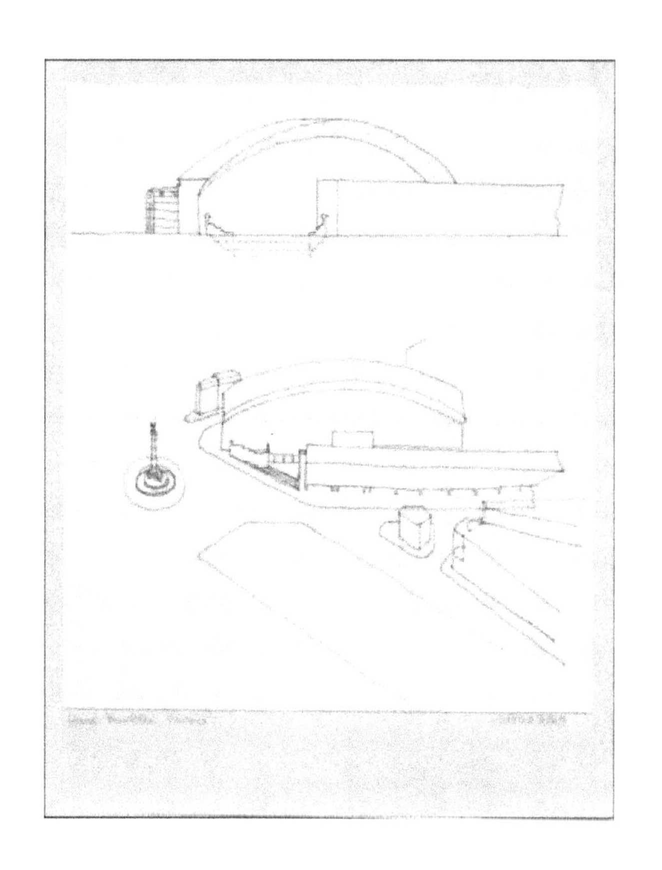

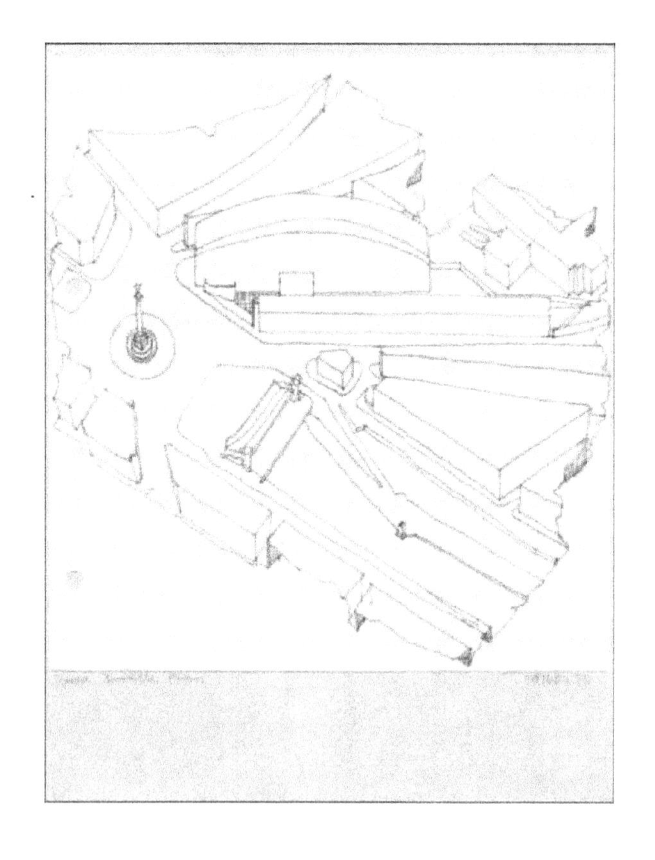

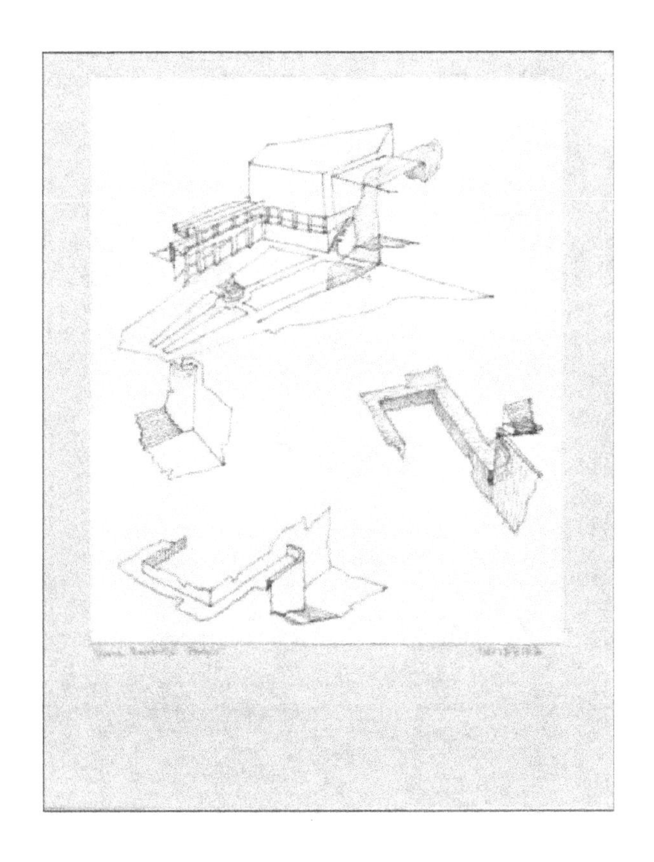

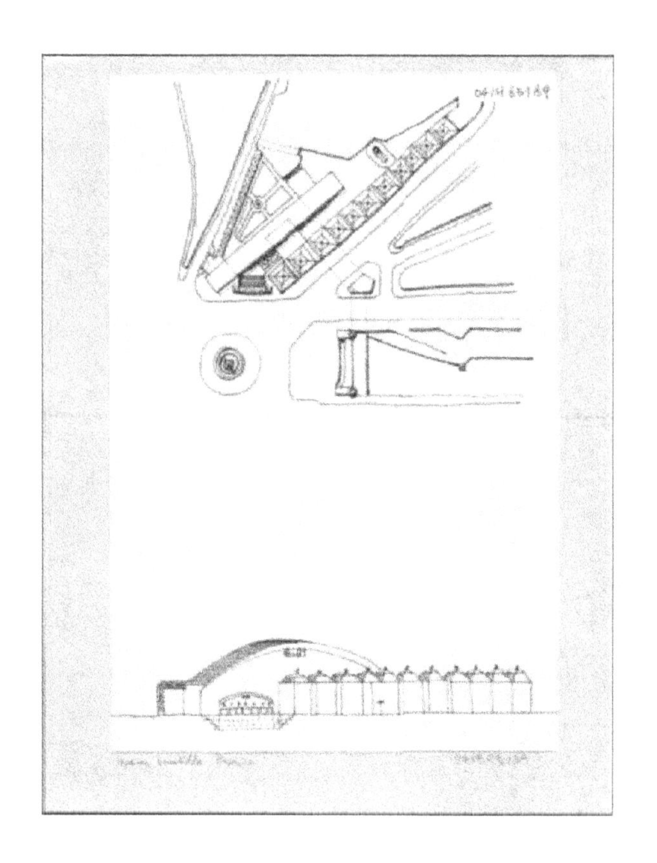

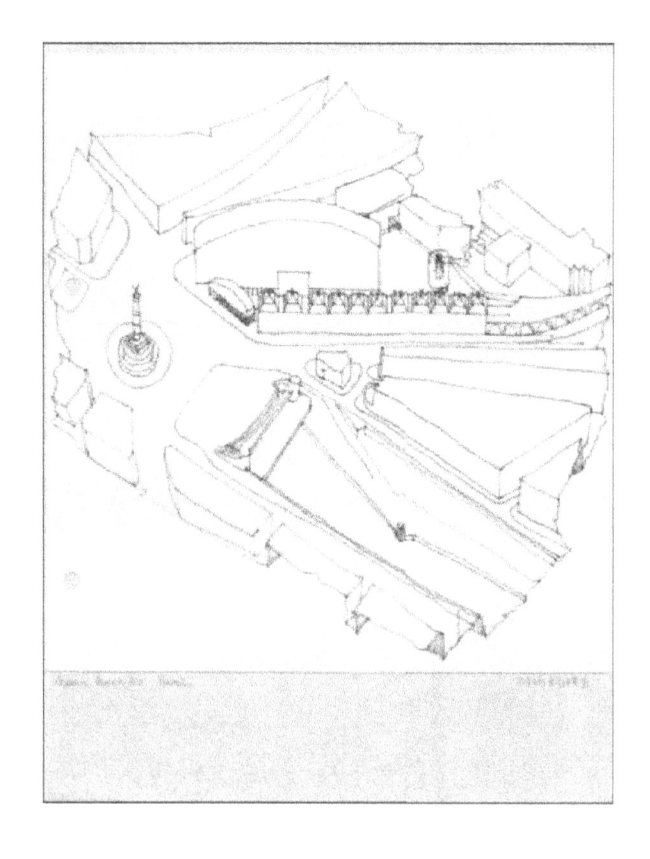

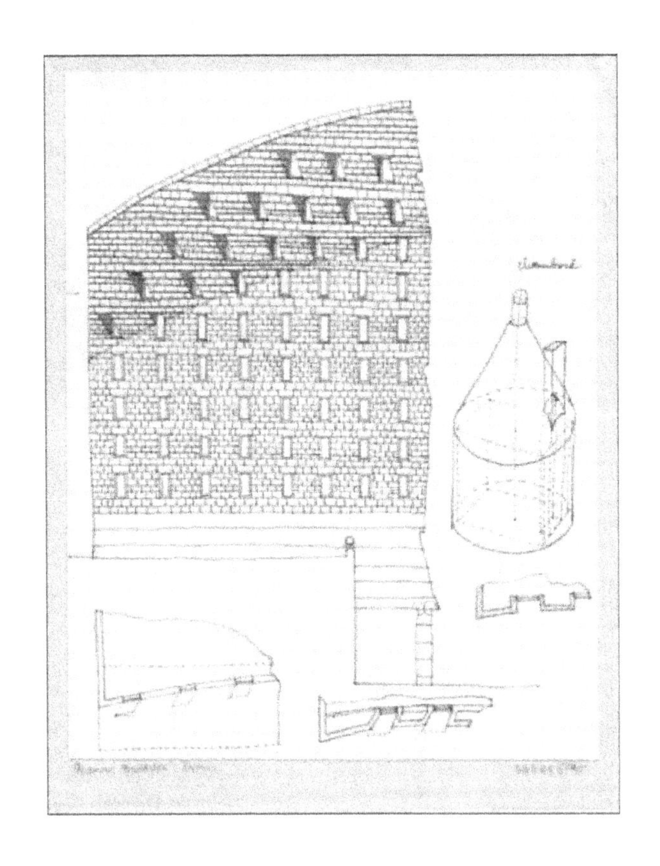

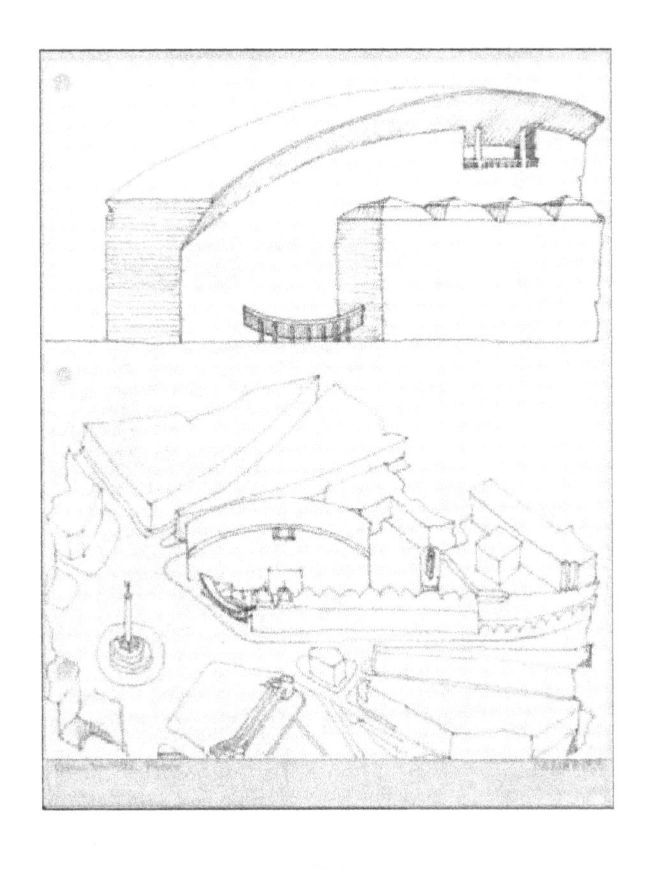

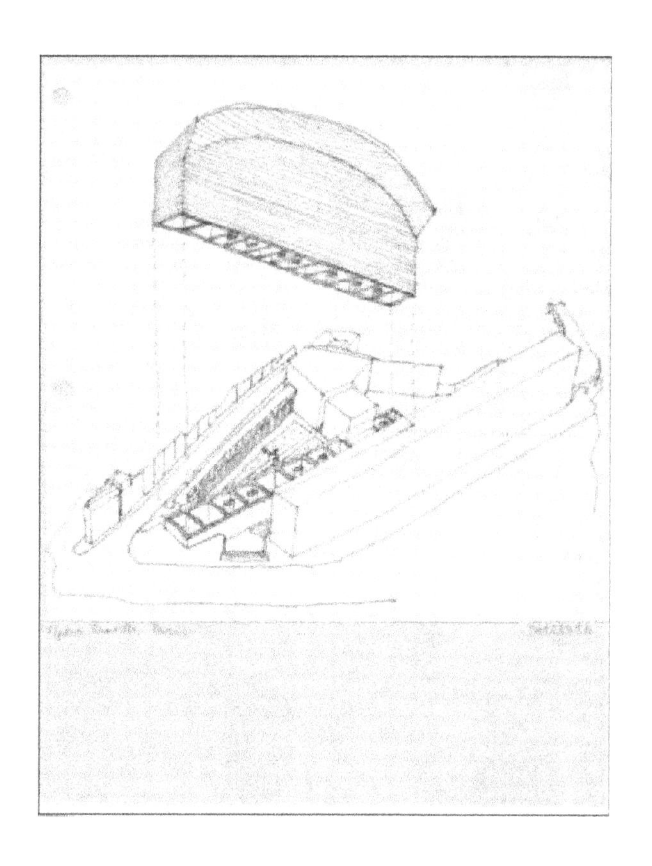

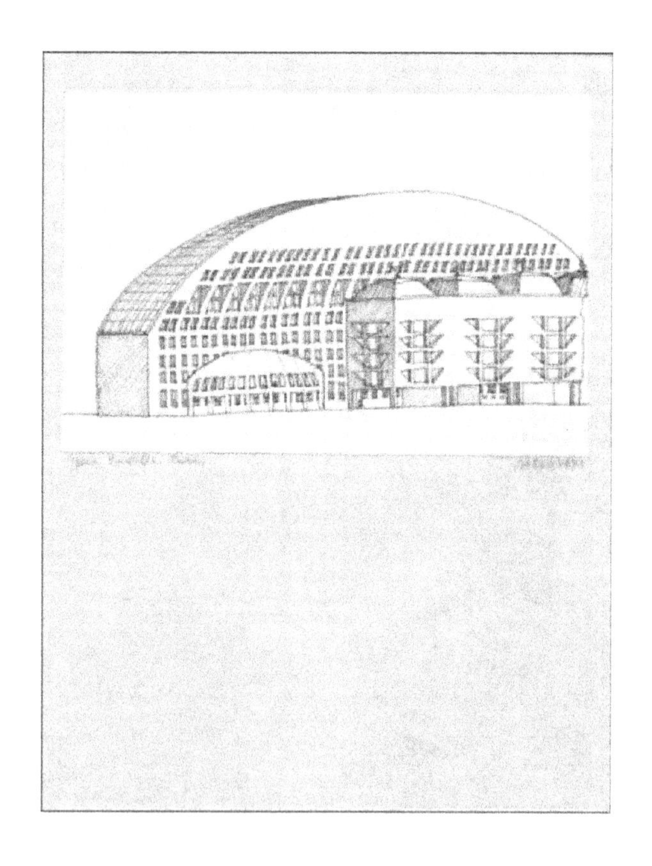

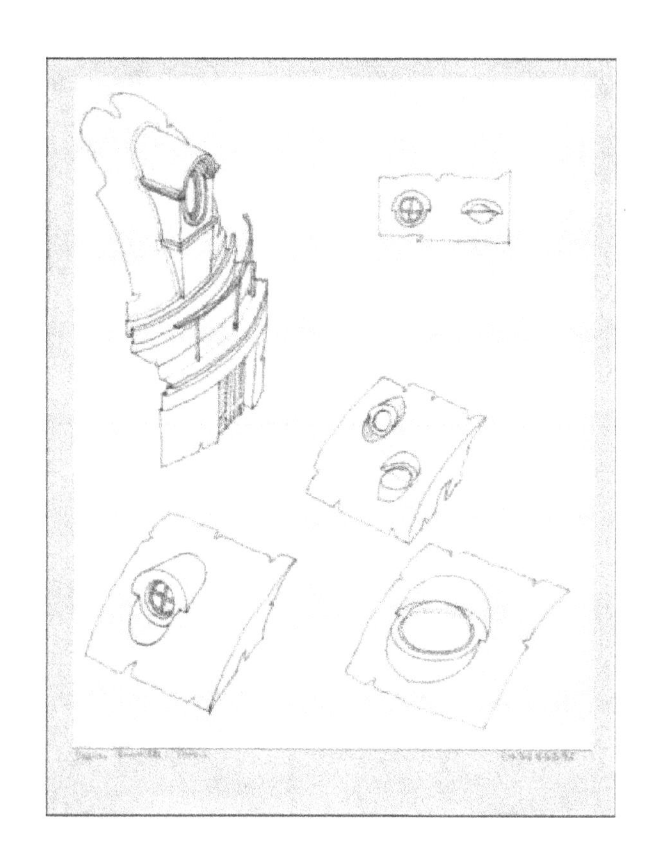

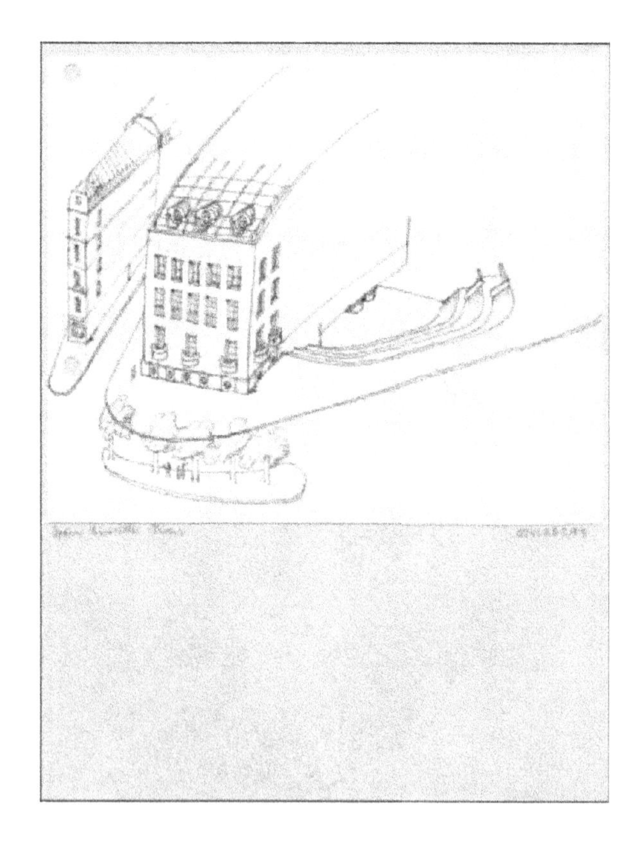

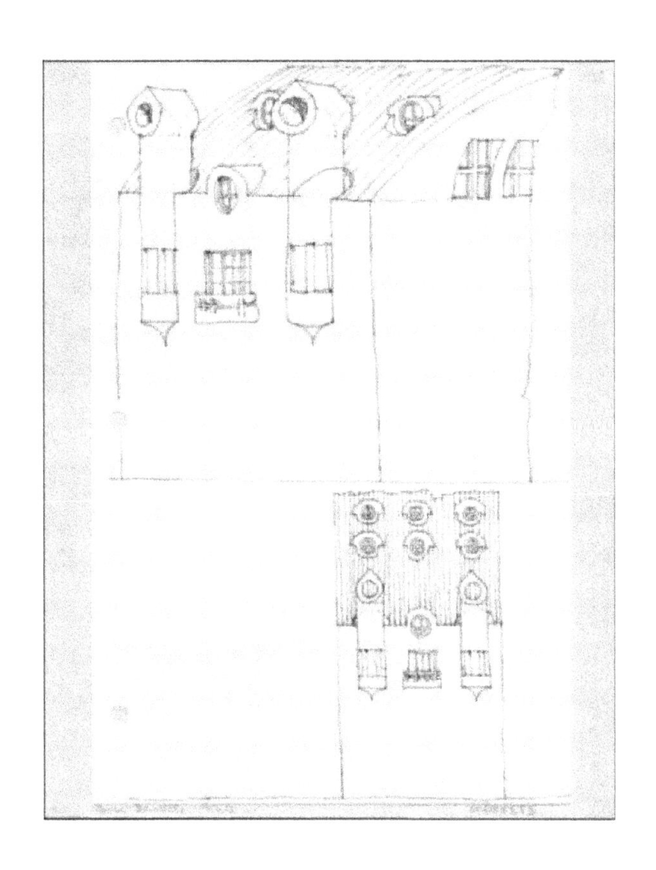

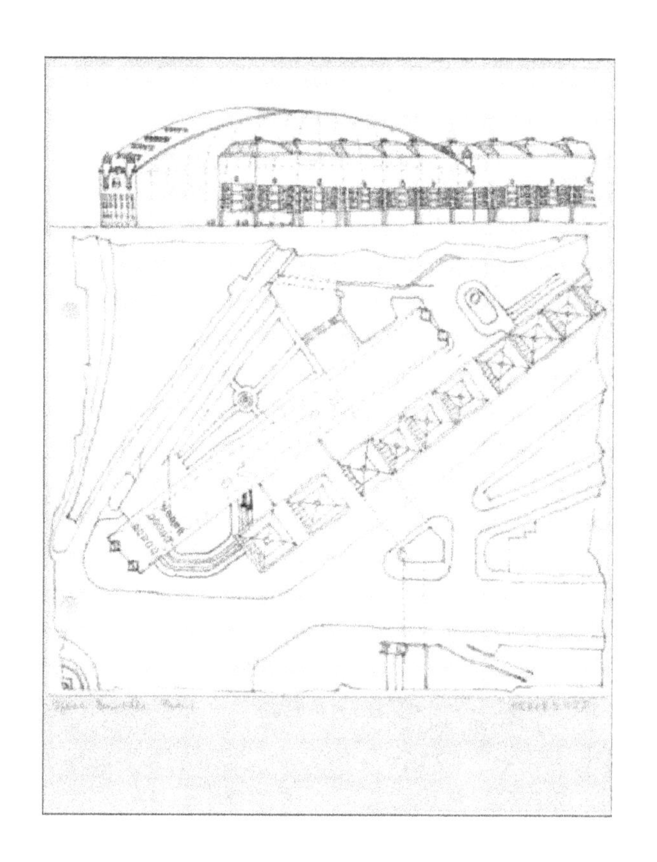

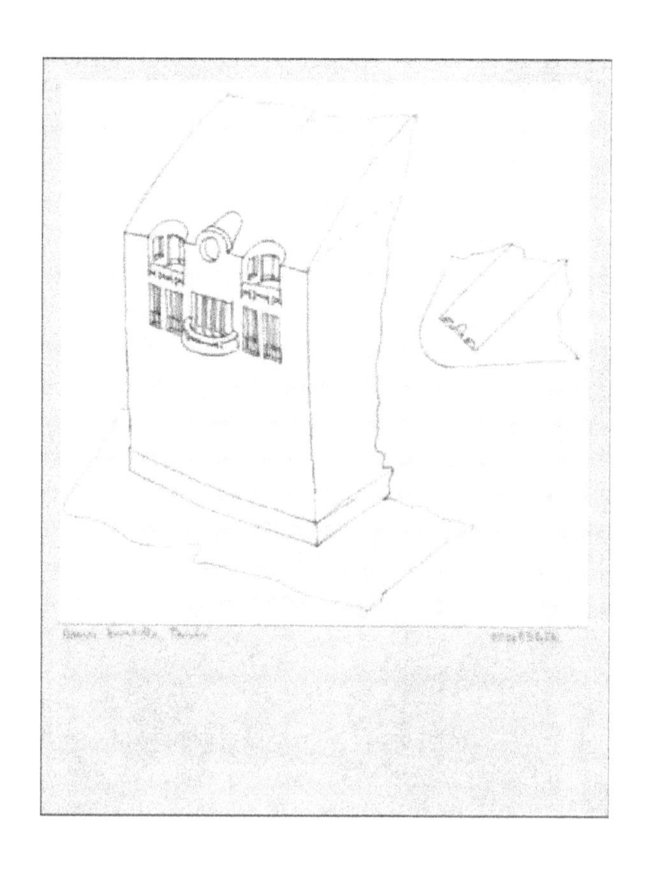

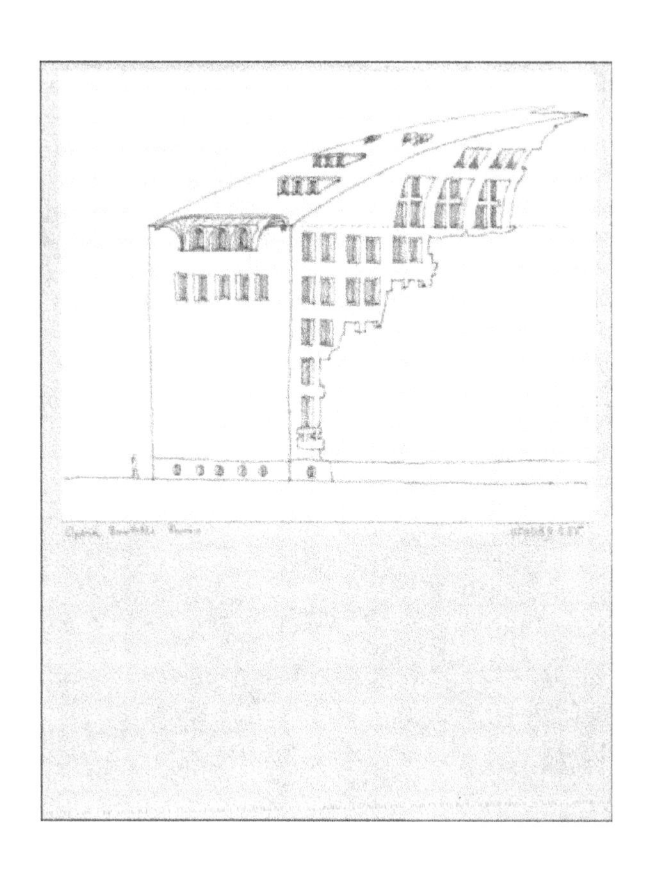

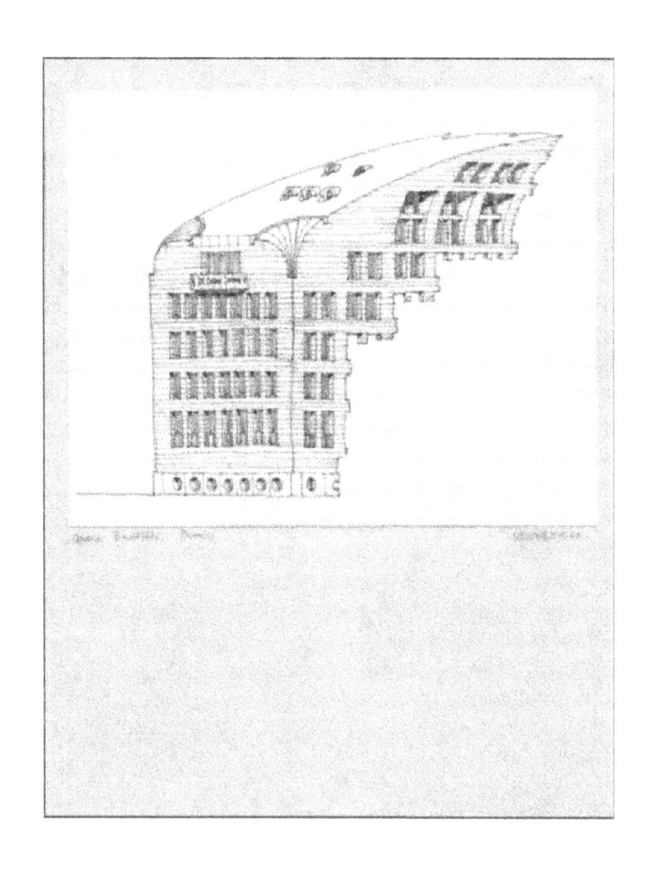

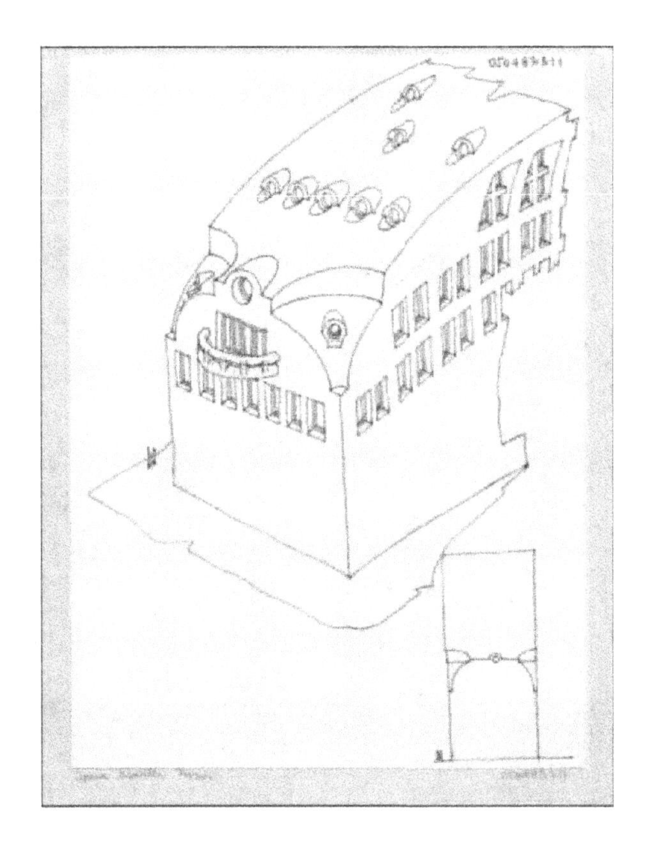

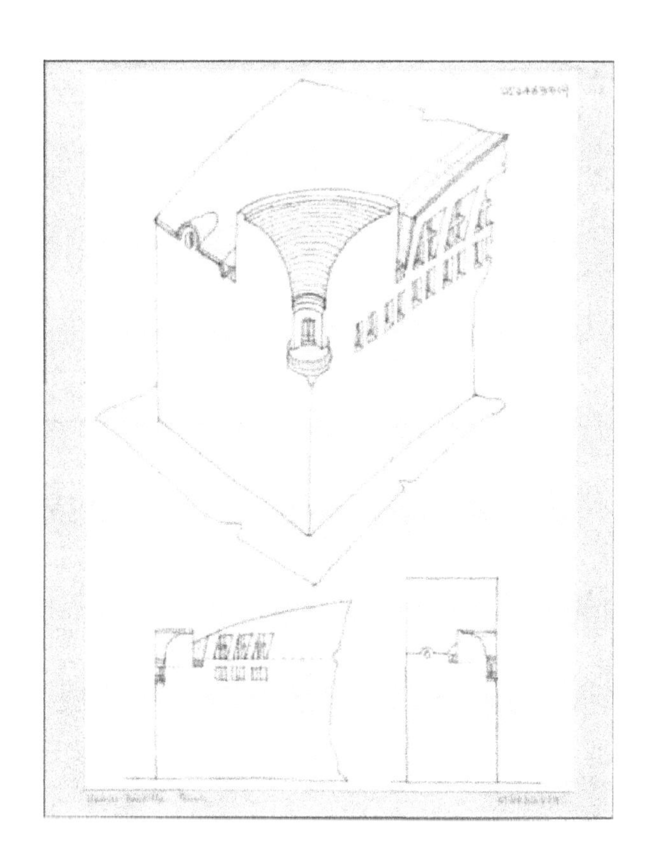

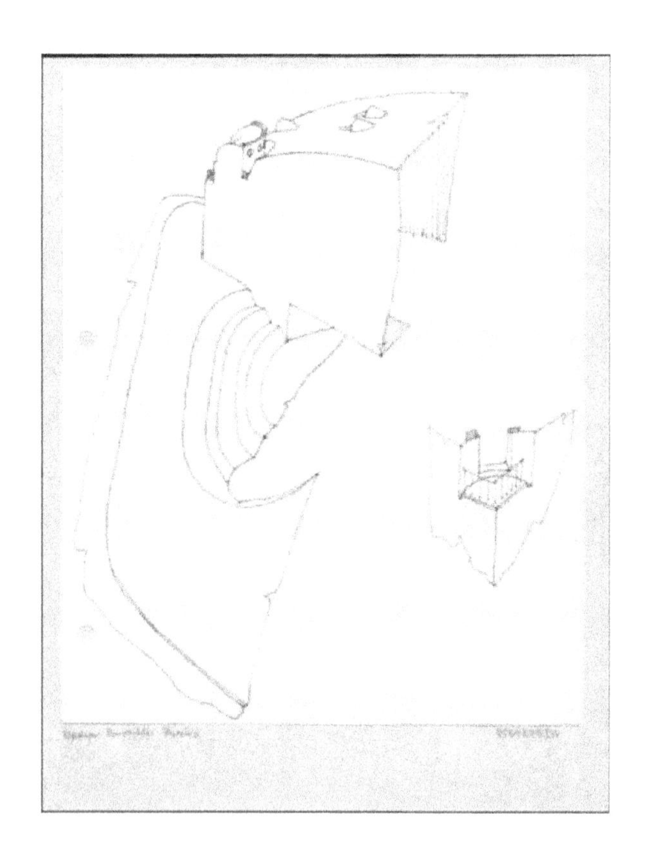

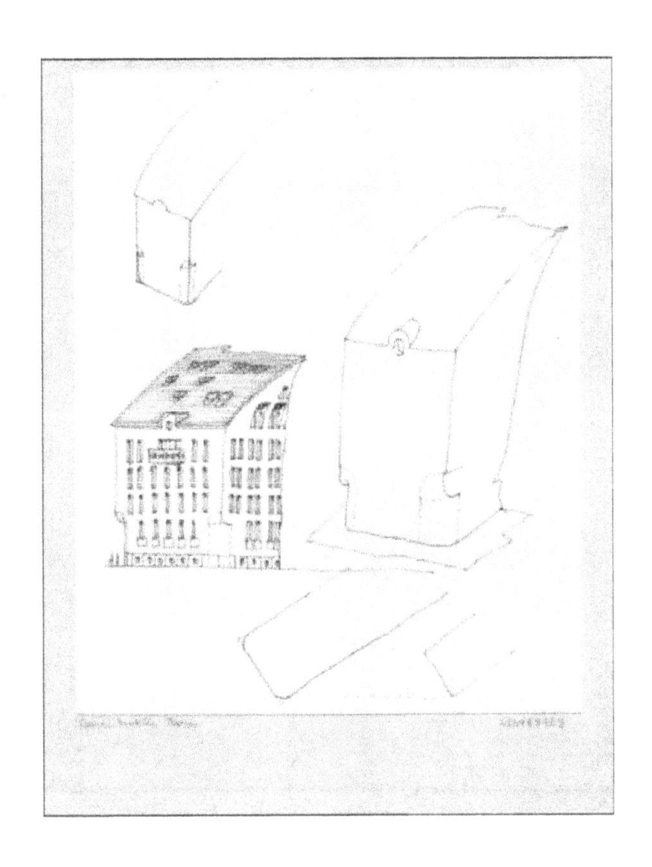

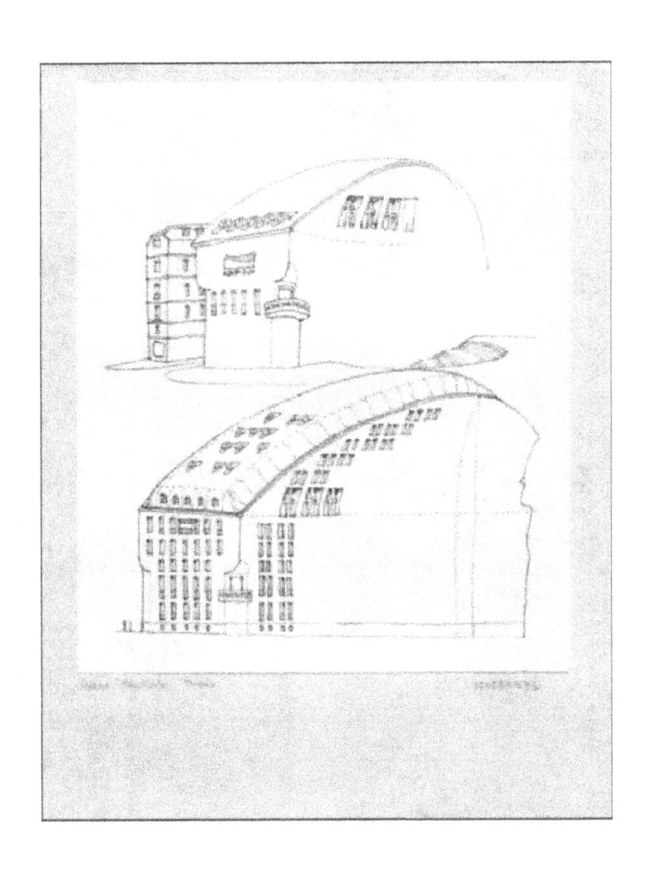

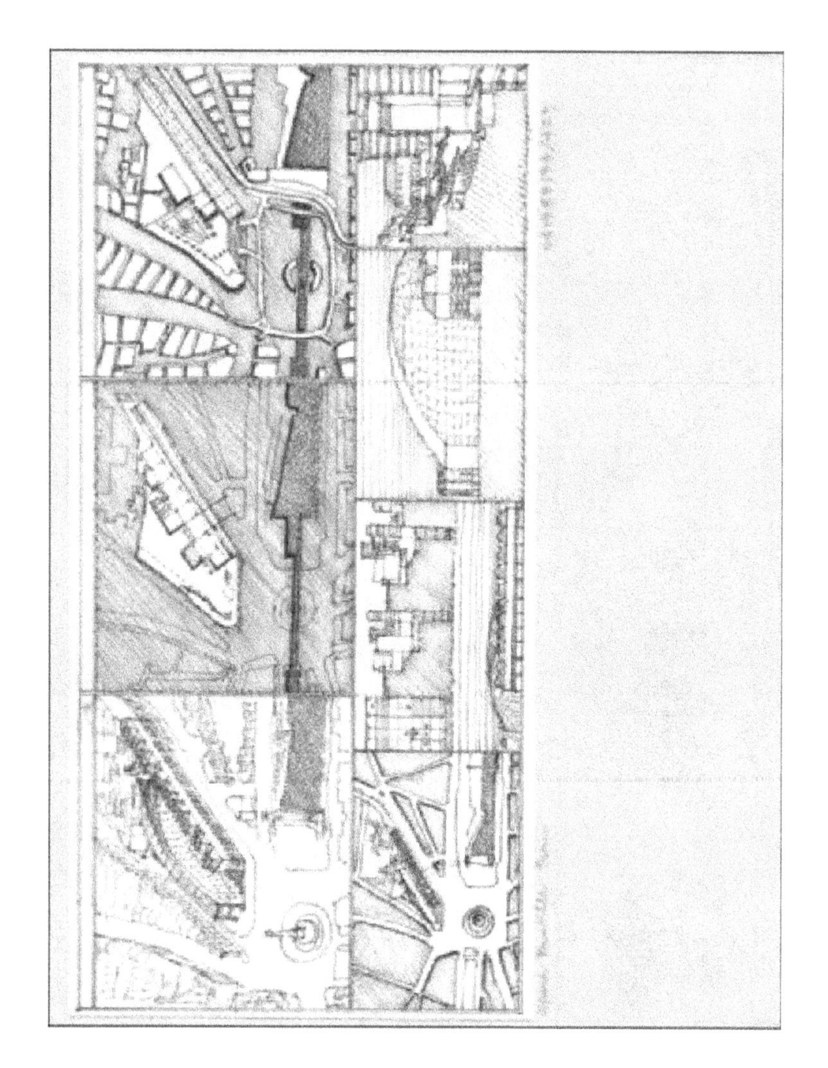

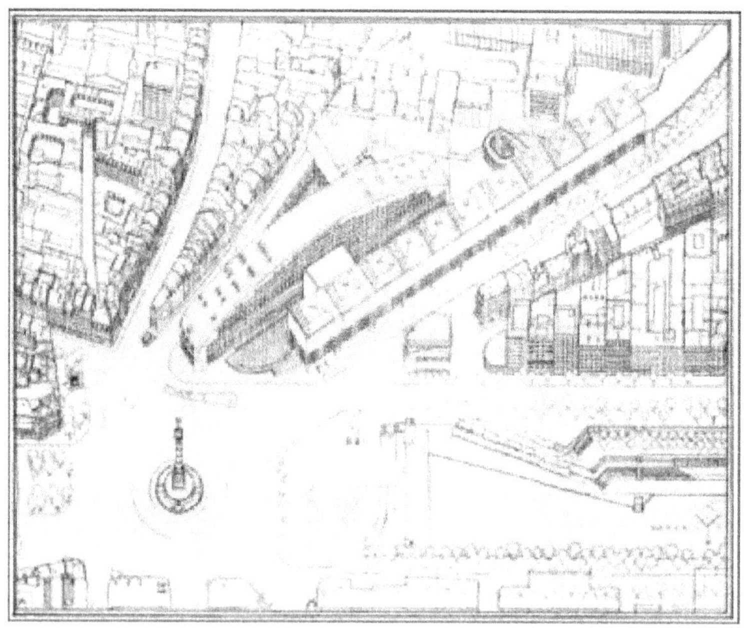

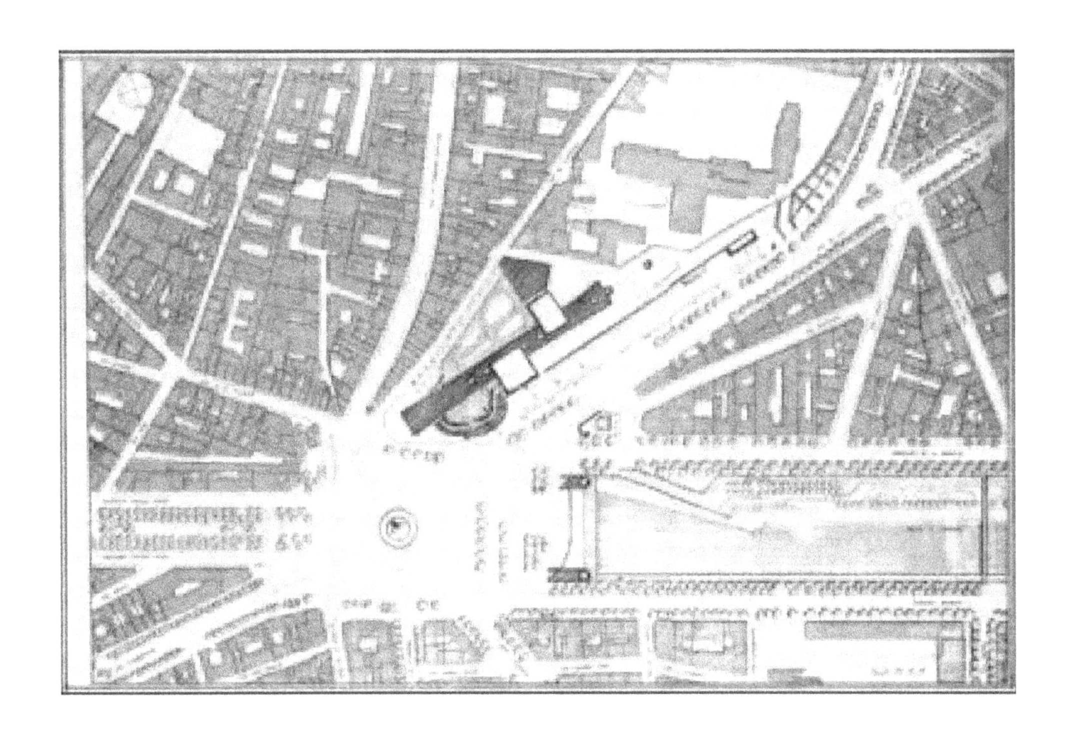

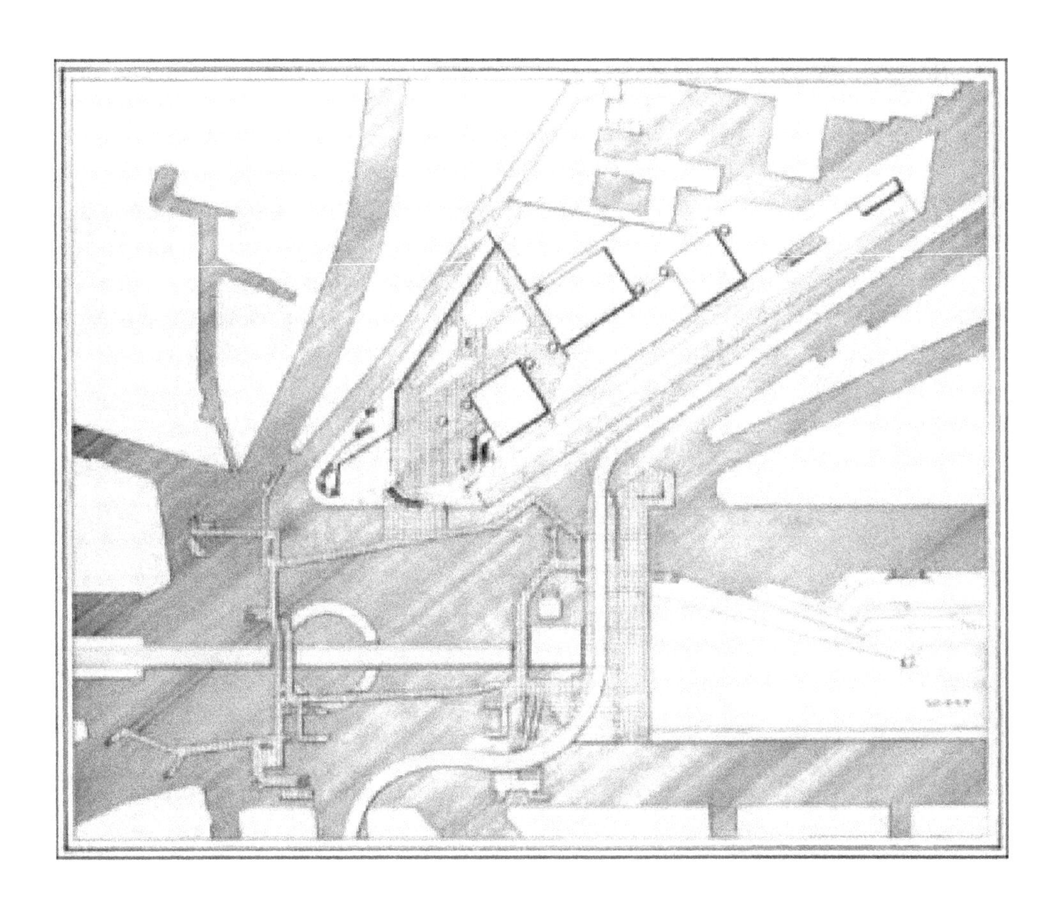

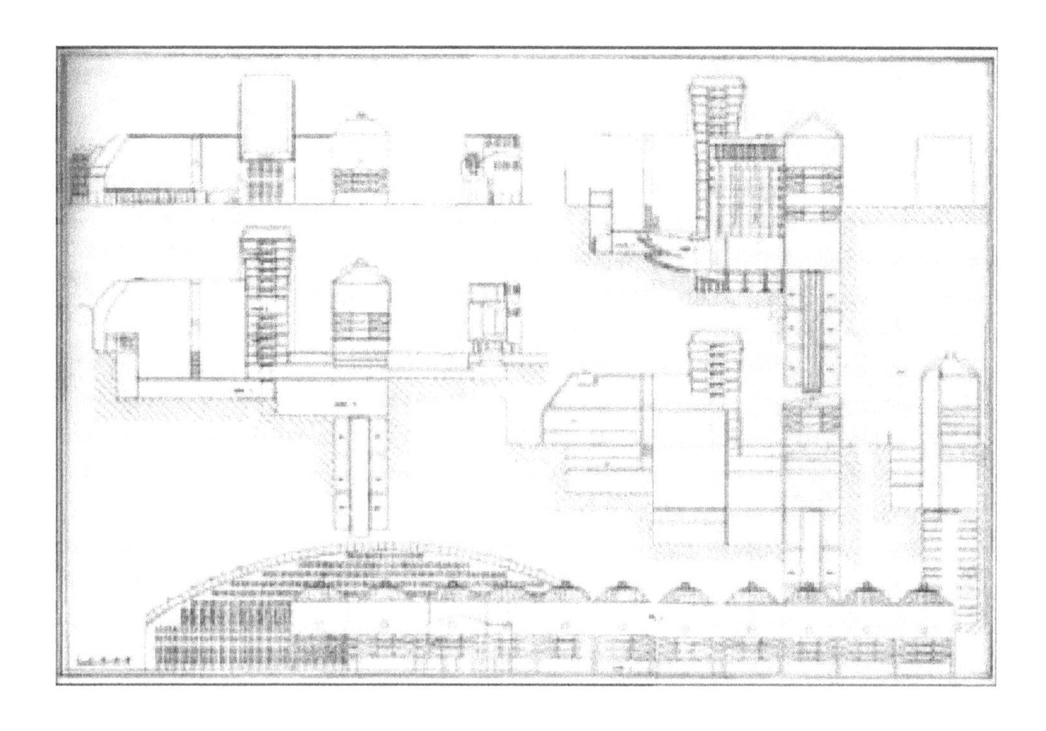

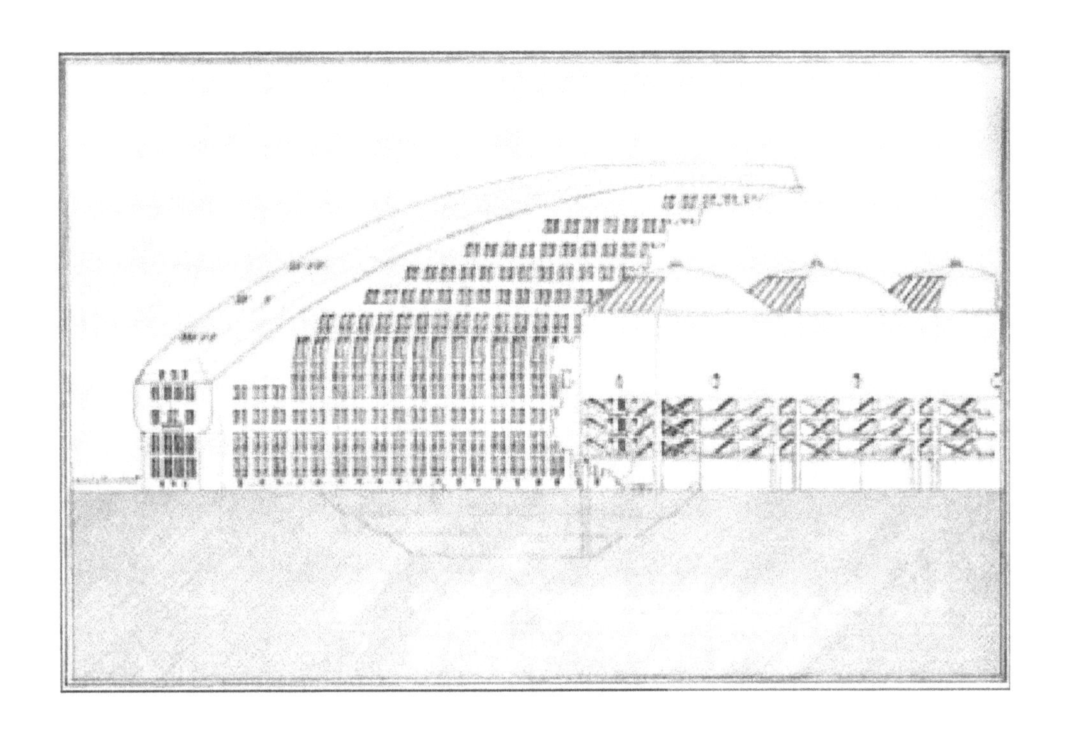

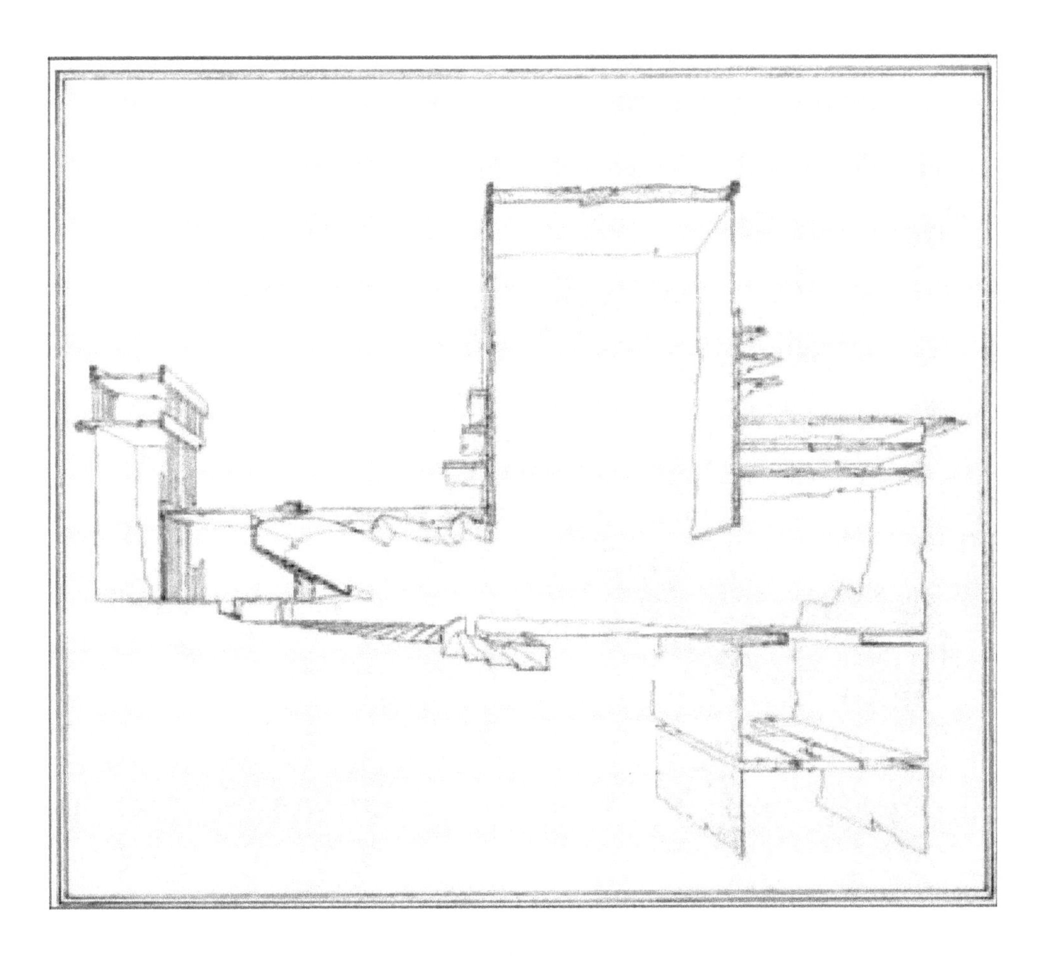

Chapter 5

ANGLES AND ORANGES

Pen Zen Diaries #5

Chapter 5

(P.Z.D.5)
Angles and Oranges - Art School
Orange County, California

In case of a museum building, the question often comes up: should the container just be a reserved depository of art, or should it aspire to express more unabashedly its content. In designing an art school, the dilemna is very similar. Fortunately, in the case of the Art School for the Orange County Community College, for which I served as design consultant to Steven Ehrlich Architects, this prejudice could play very little role. The given site, which contained a theater, designed by Richard Neutra, and where an existing workshop has to be reused, as the exhibition gallery for the school, provided enough restrictions, so this somewhat esoteric aspects did very little in evolving the concept of the design. Like in many other cases, the combined requirements of site, program, structure and in this case the need of natural light were sufficiently complex issues, integrated investigations of these eventually revealed the architectural solution.

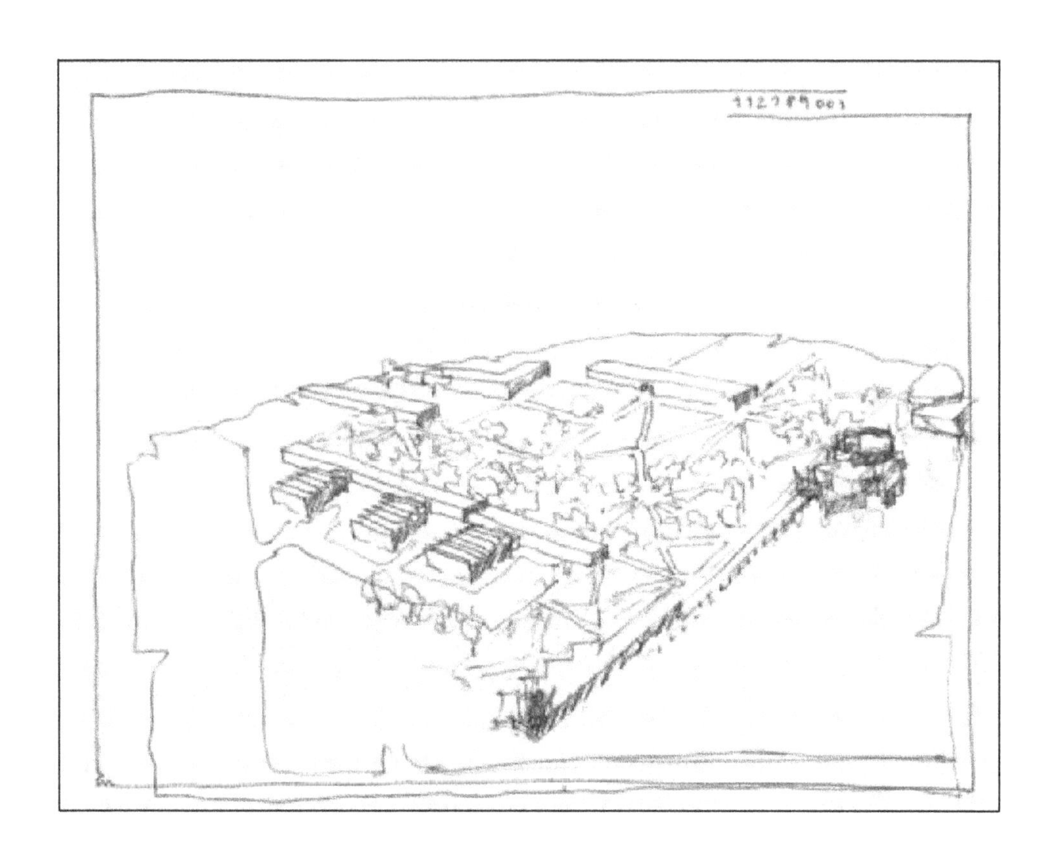
112789001

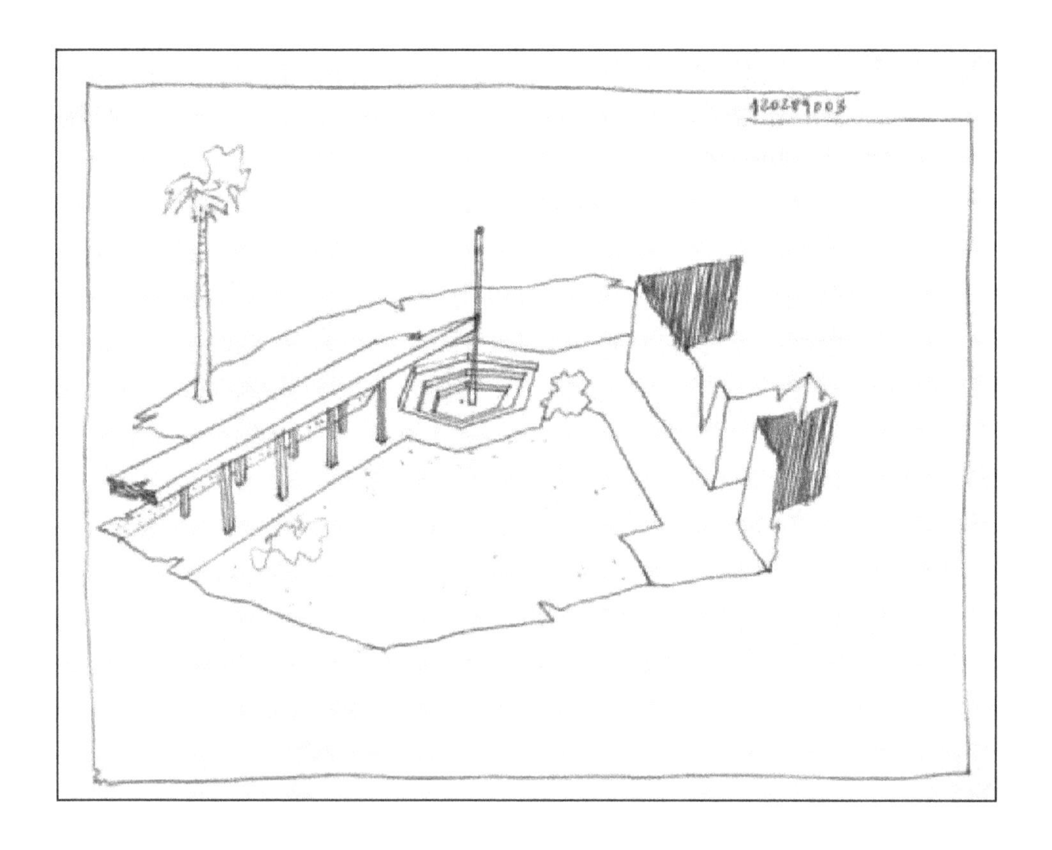
120289003

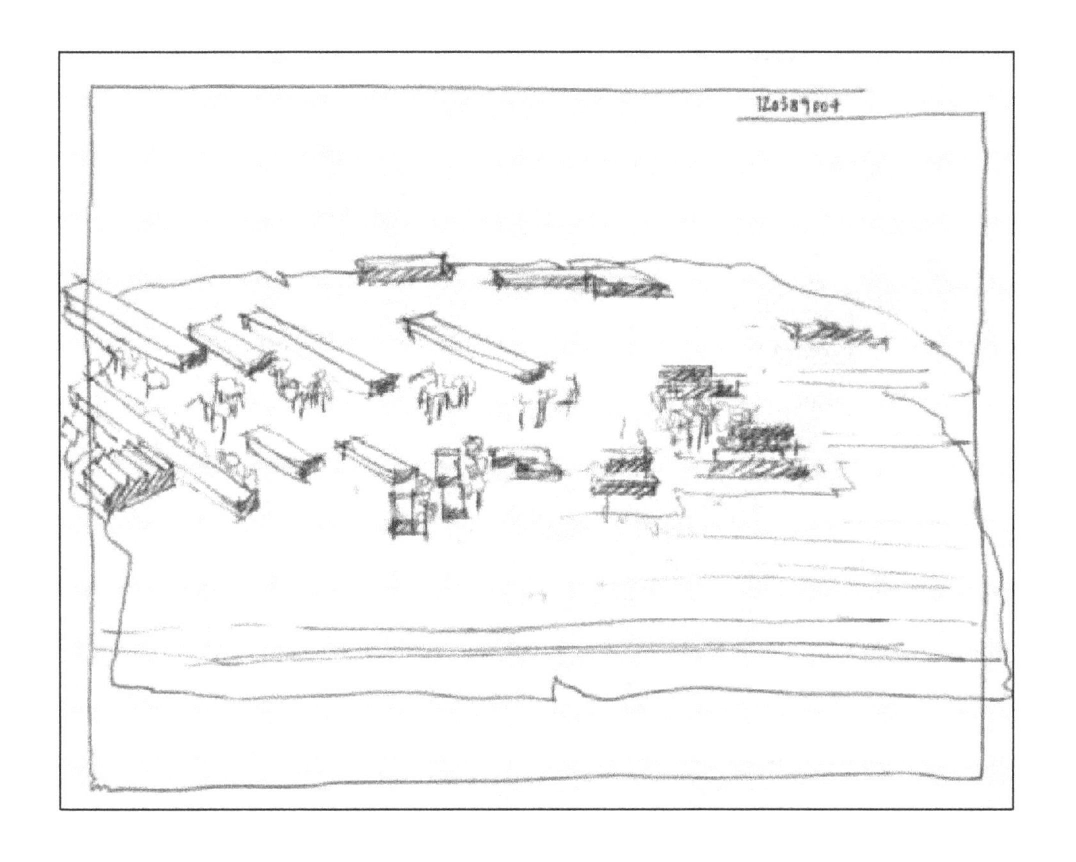
120389004

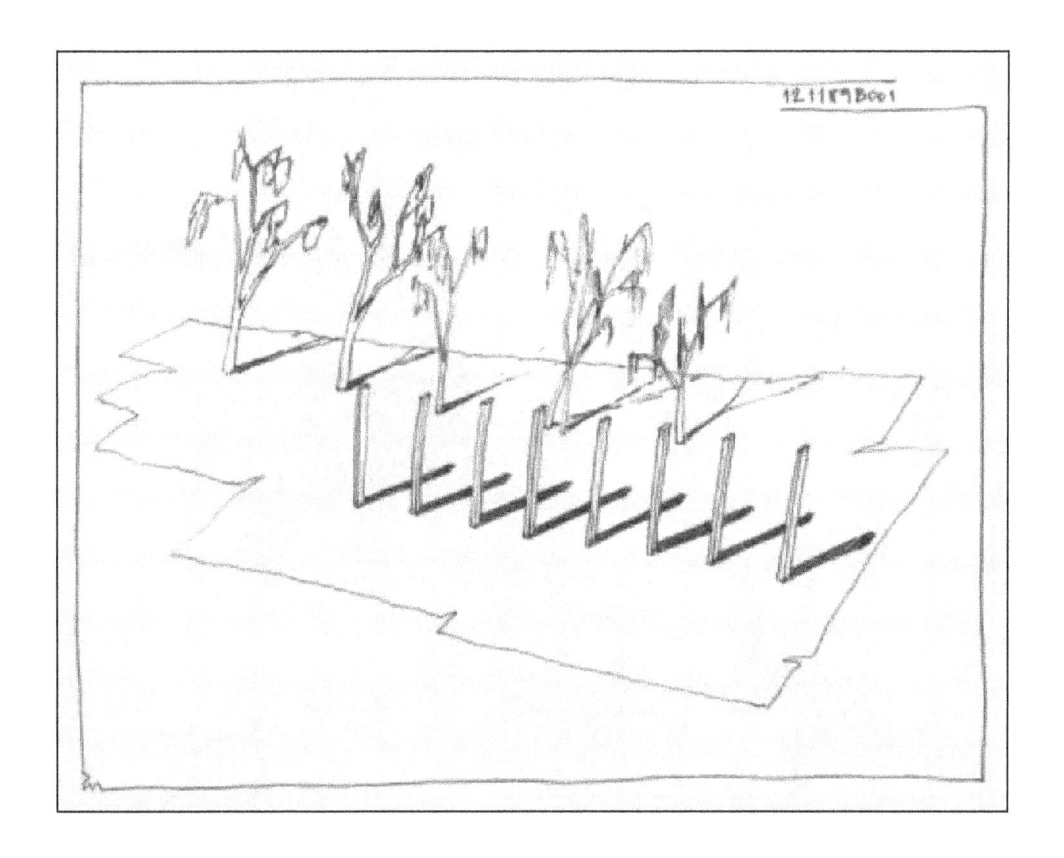
121189B001

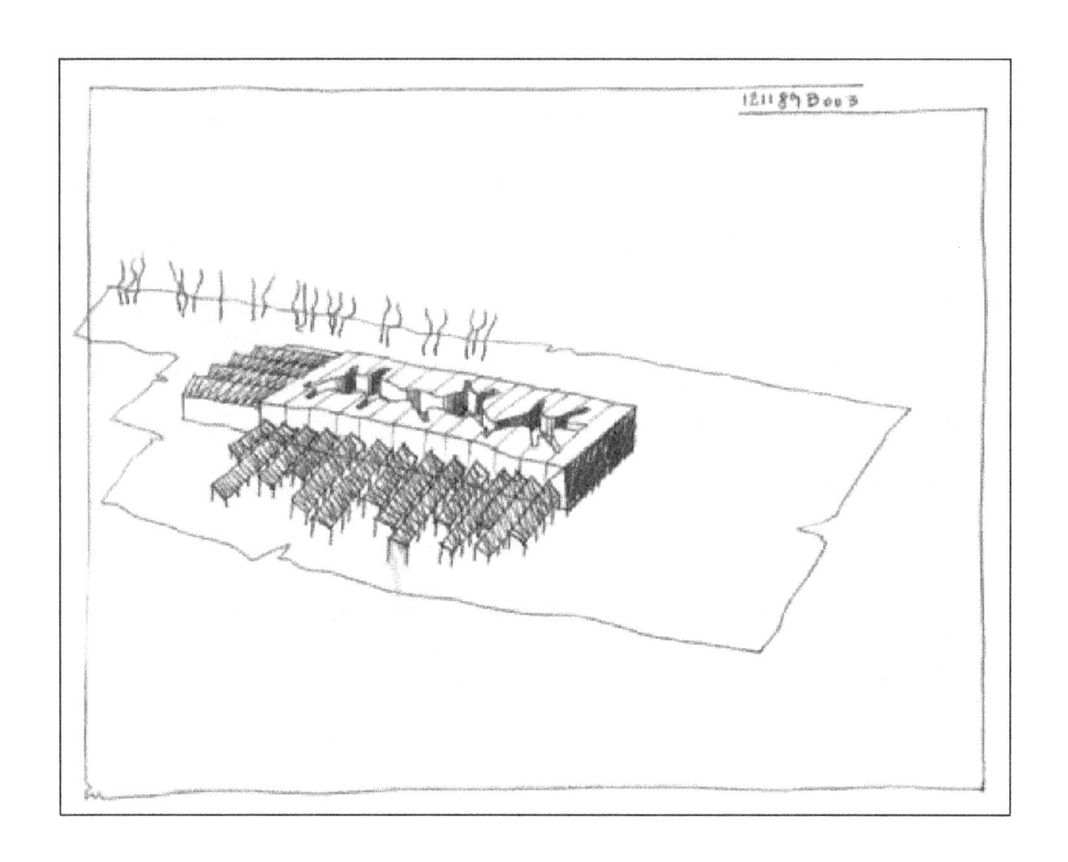
121189B003

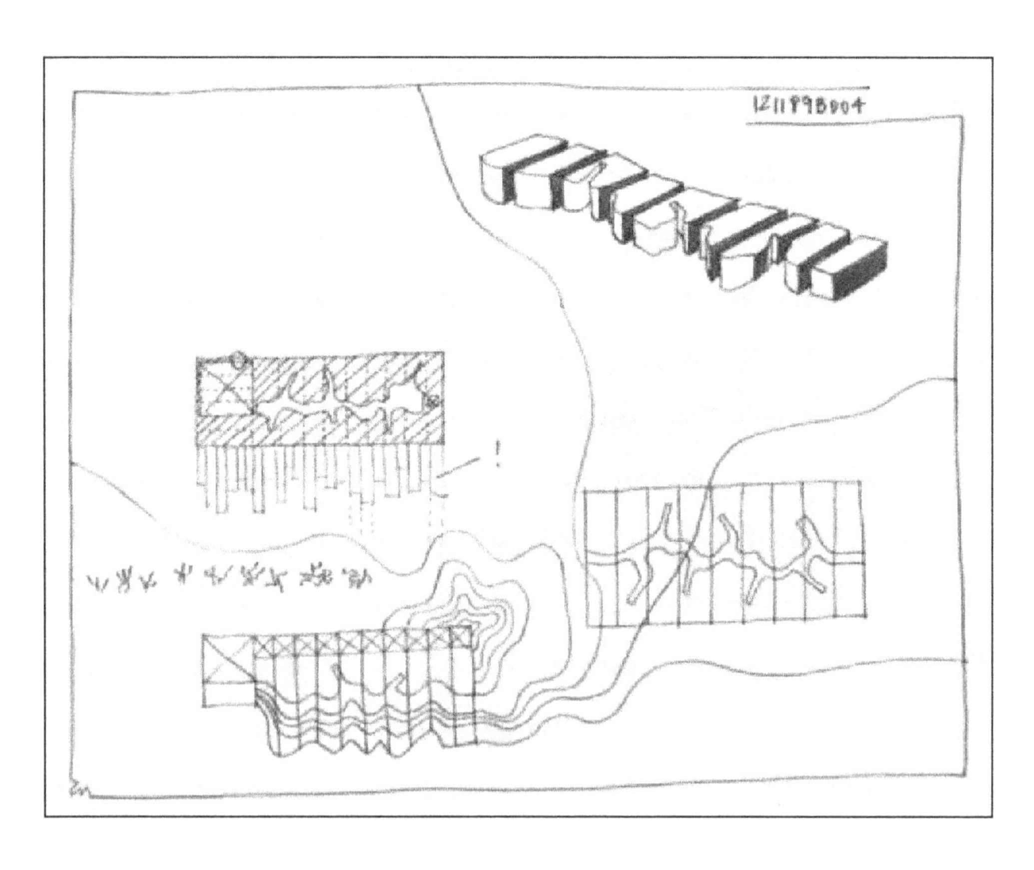
121189B004
!

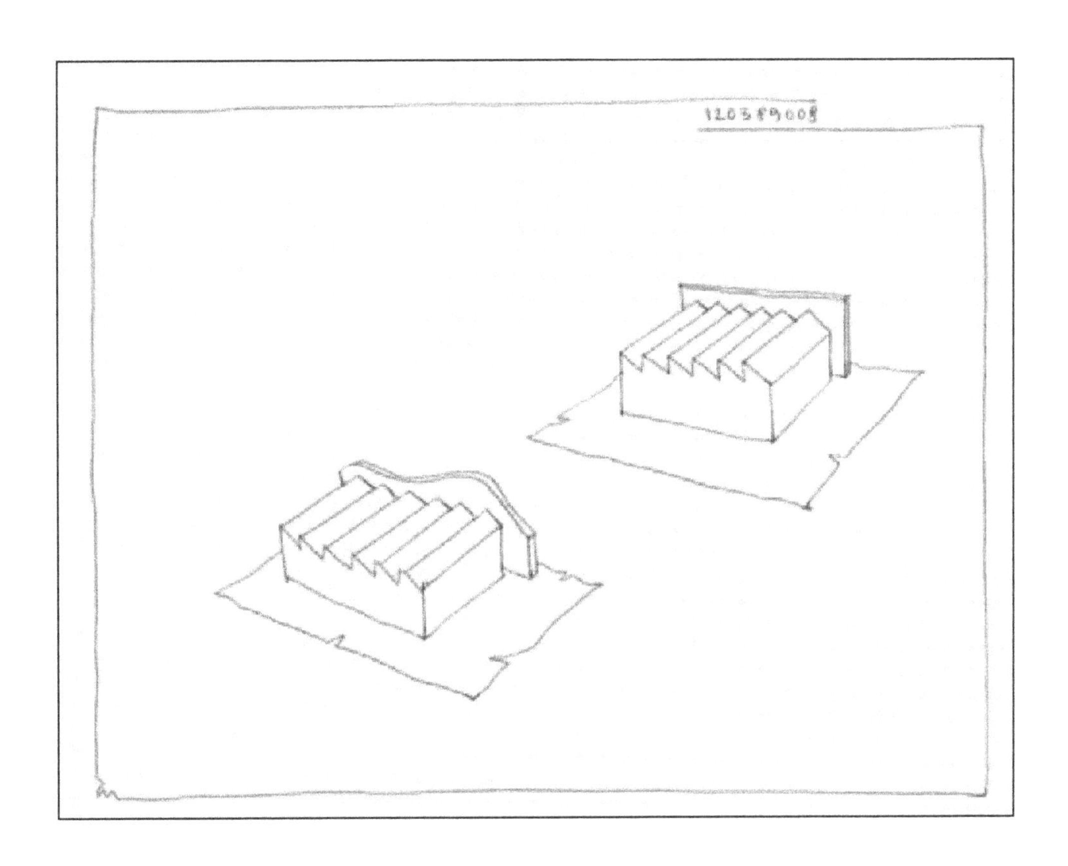

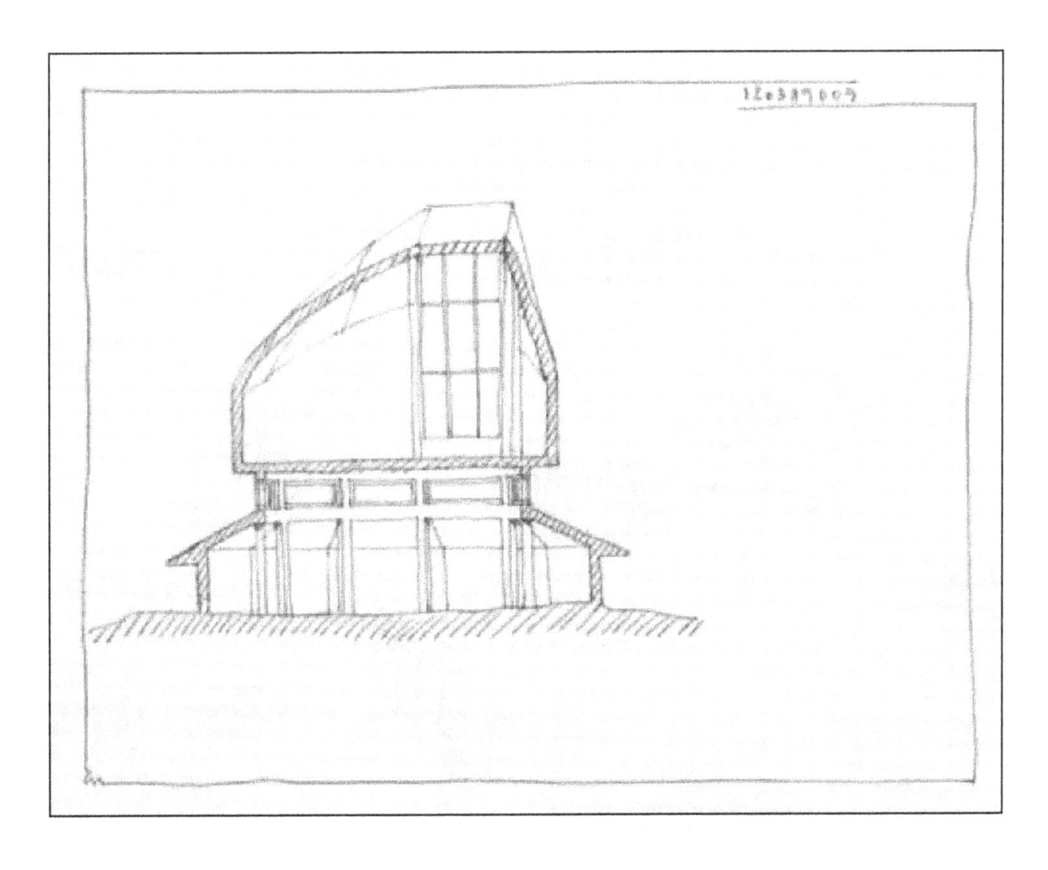

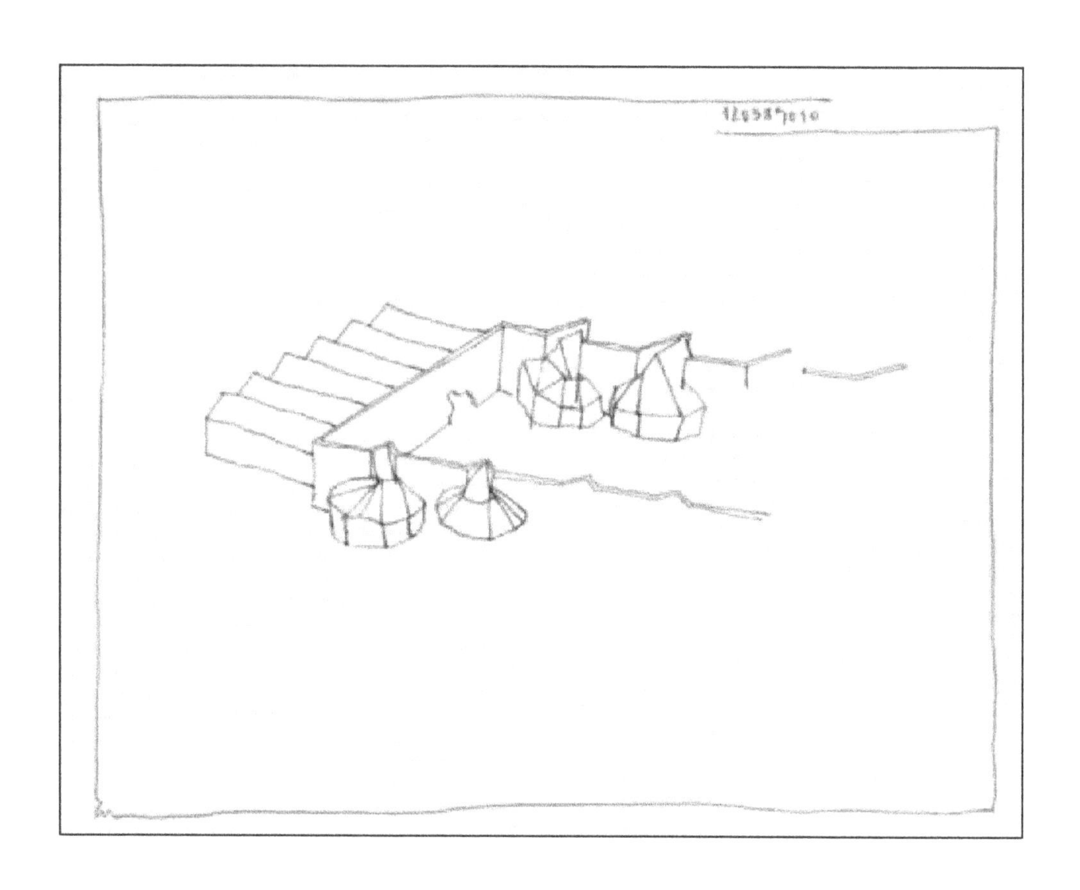

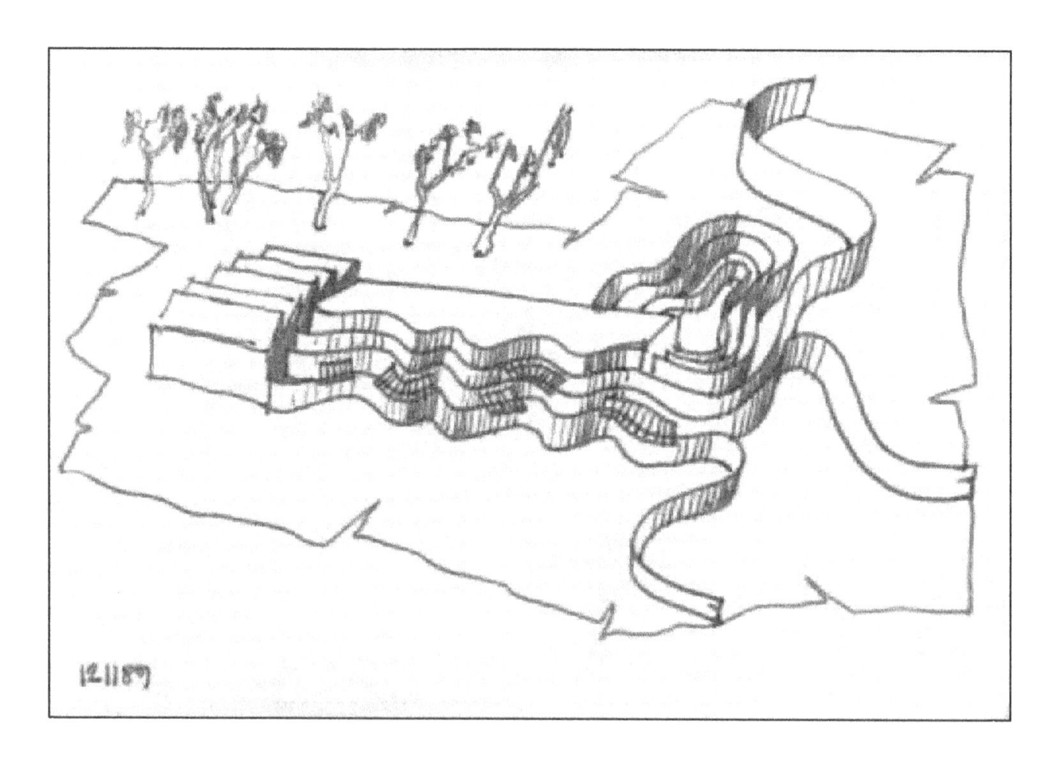
12|11|87

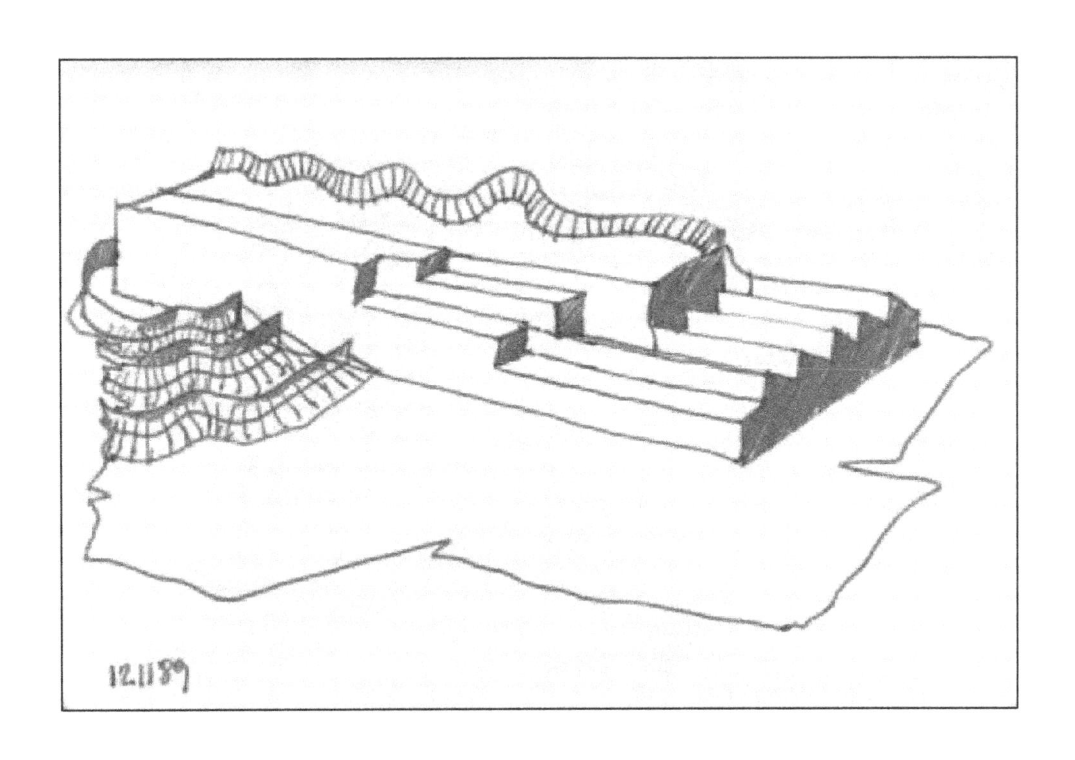

12|1|89

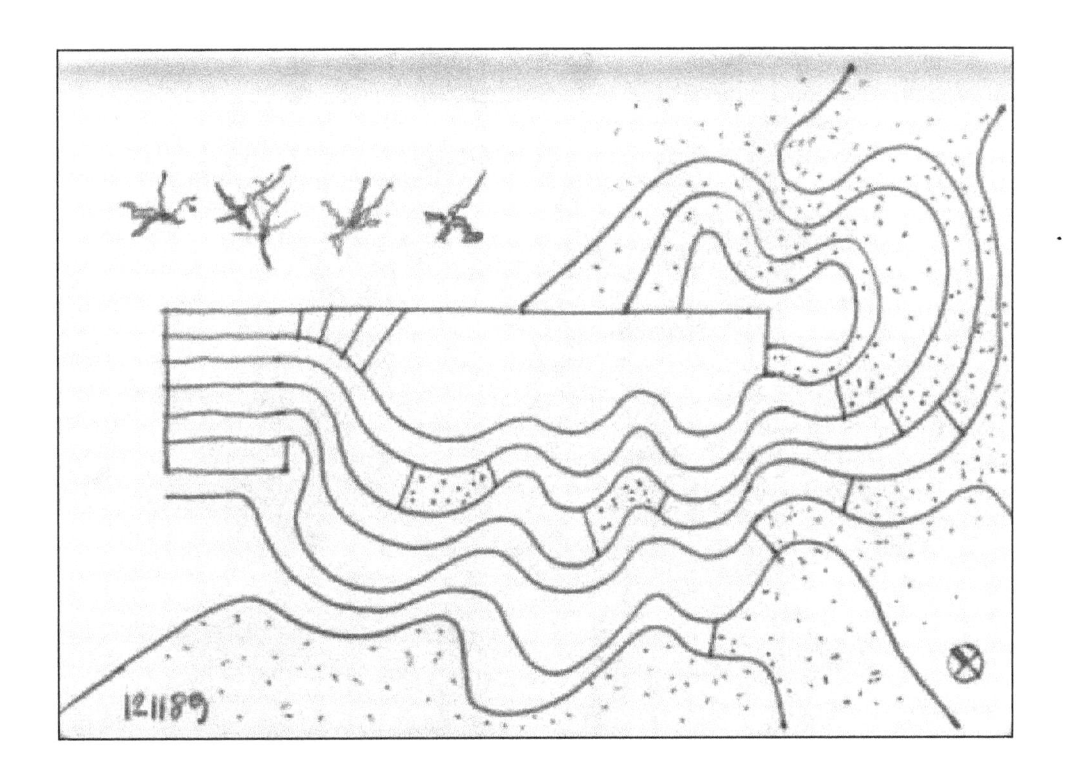

12|1|89

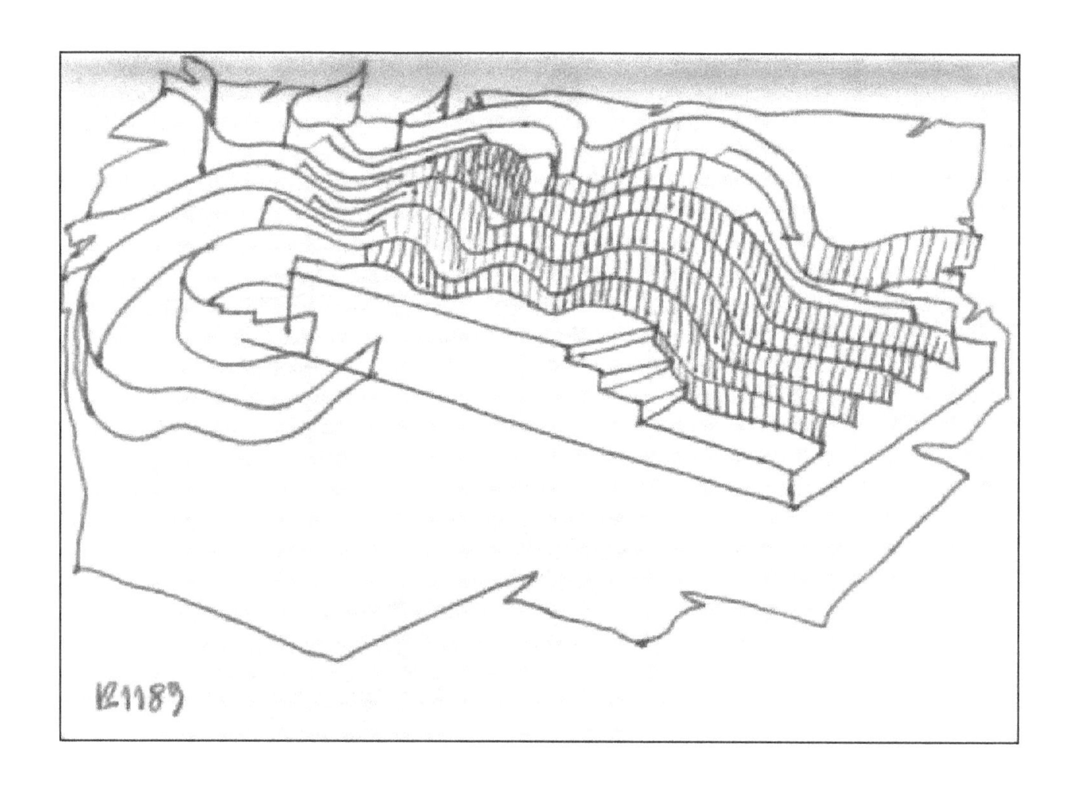

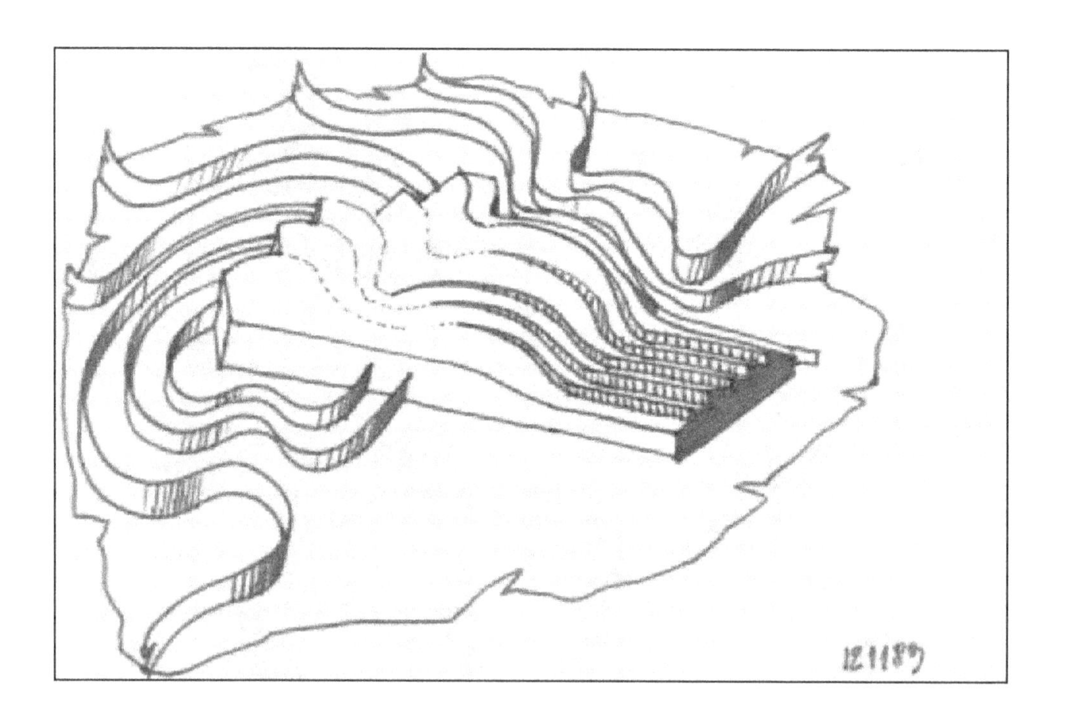

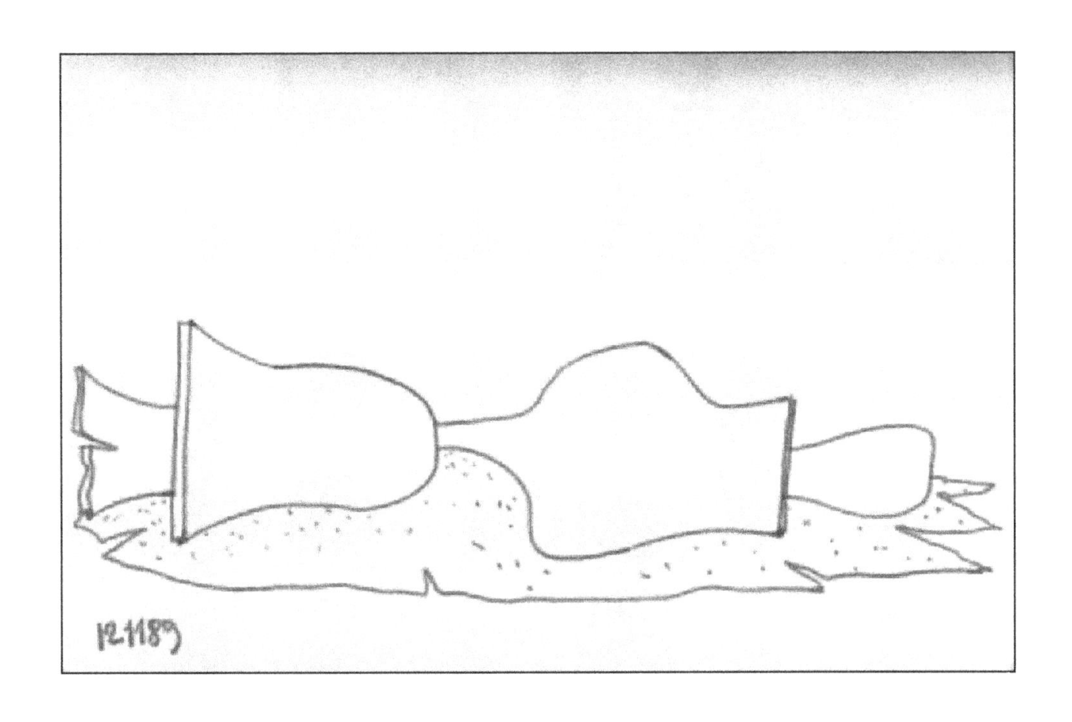
12 11 89

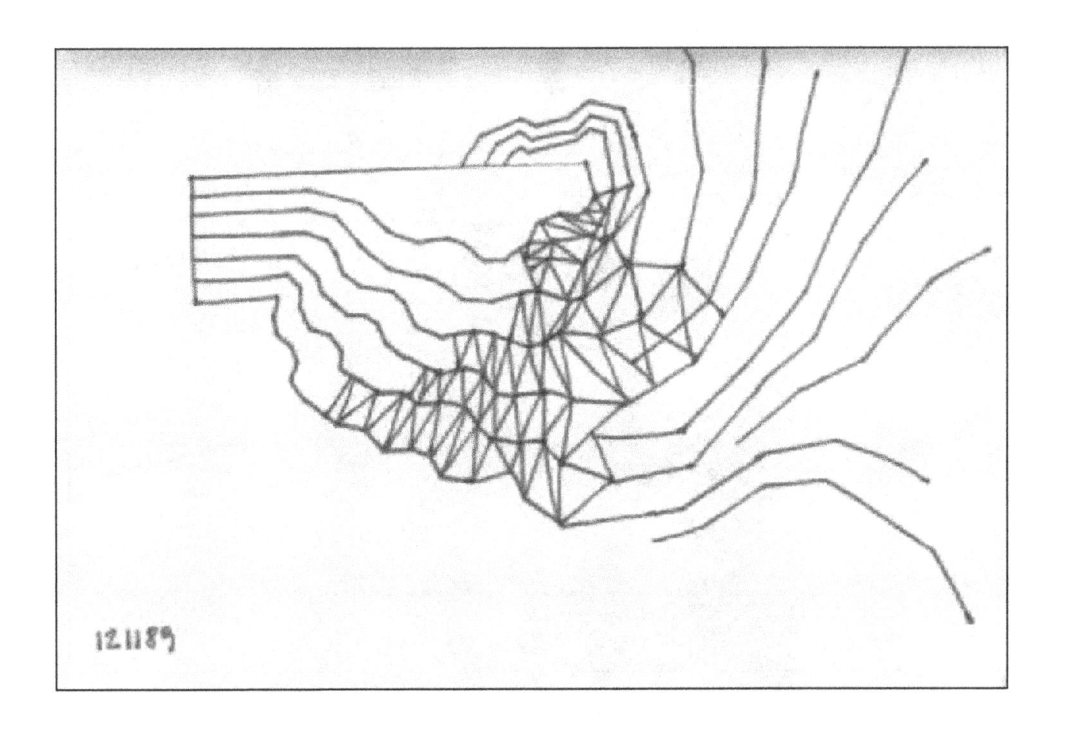
12 11 89

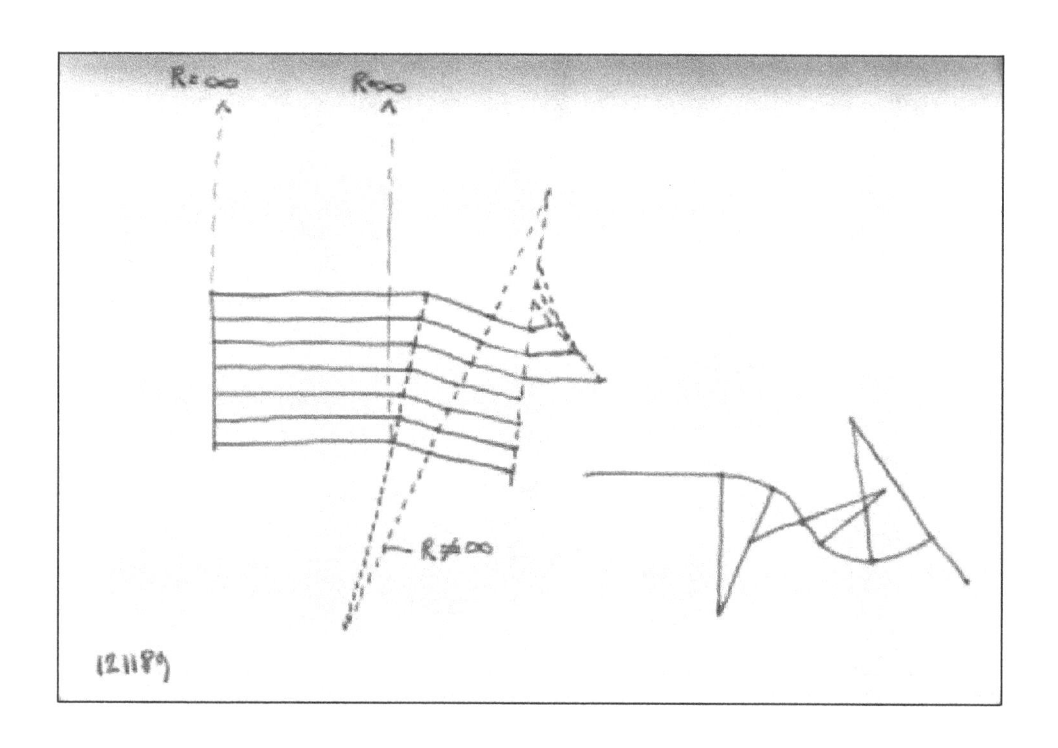
R=∞
R=∞
R≠∞
12/1/89

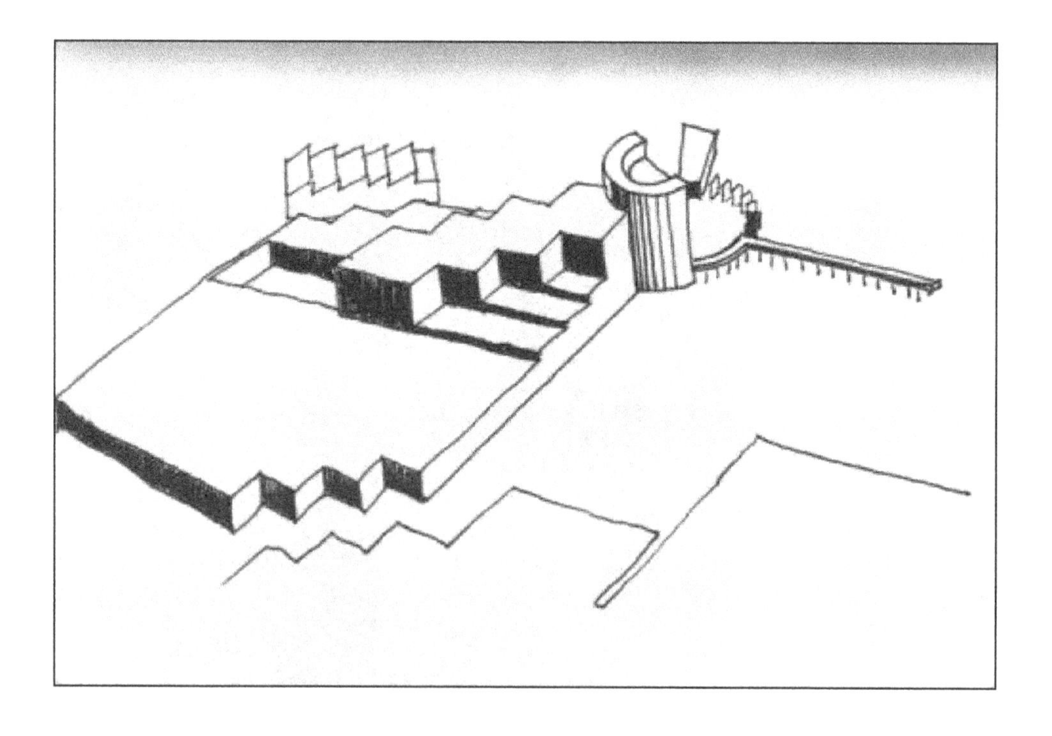

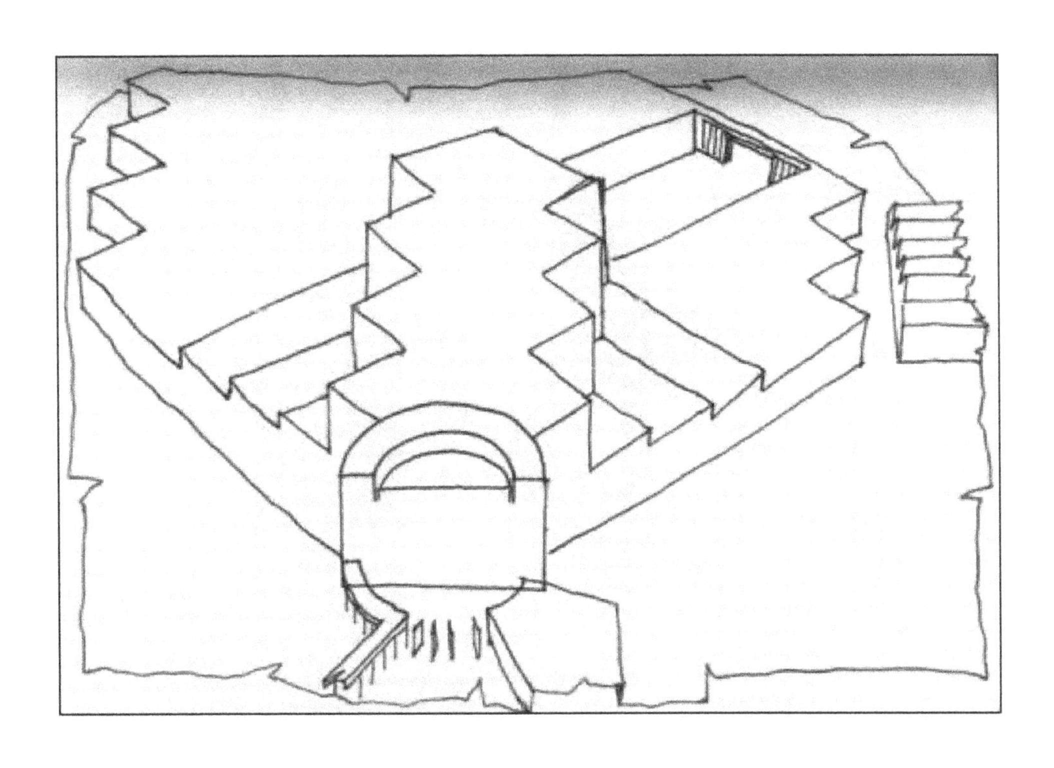

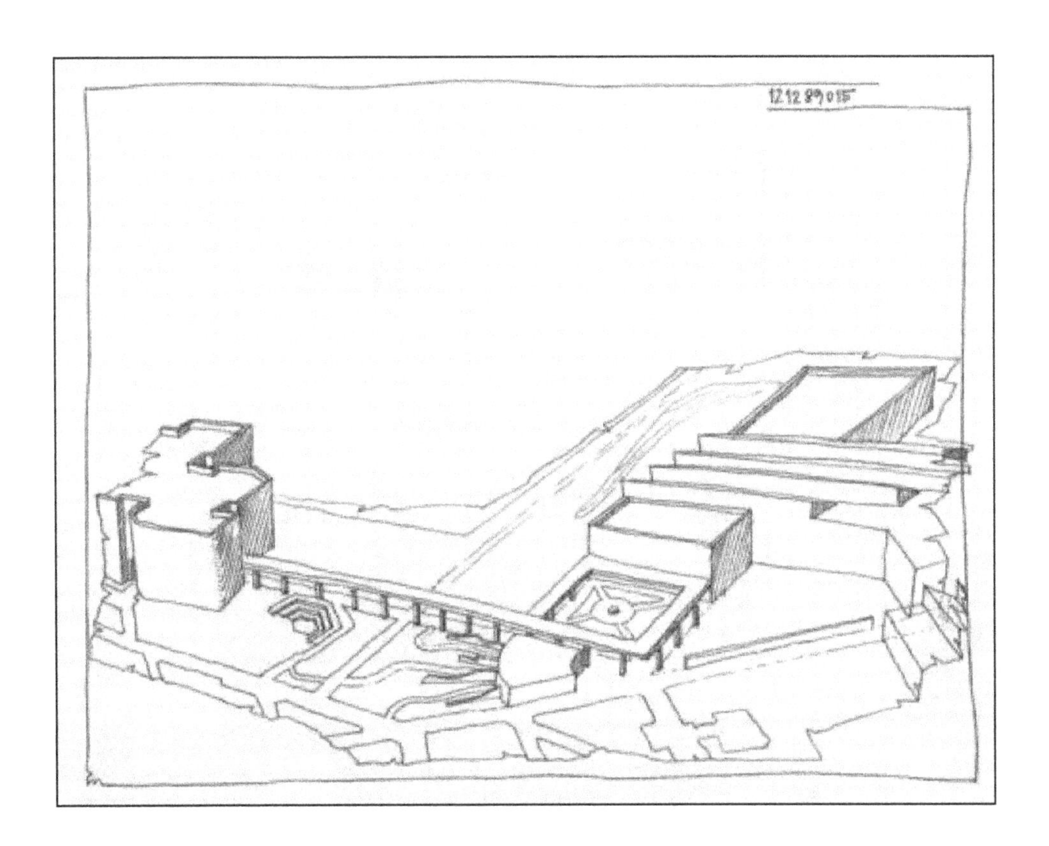

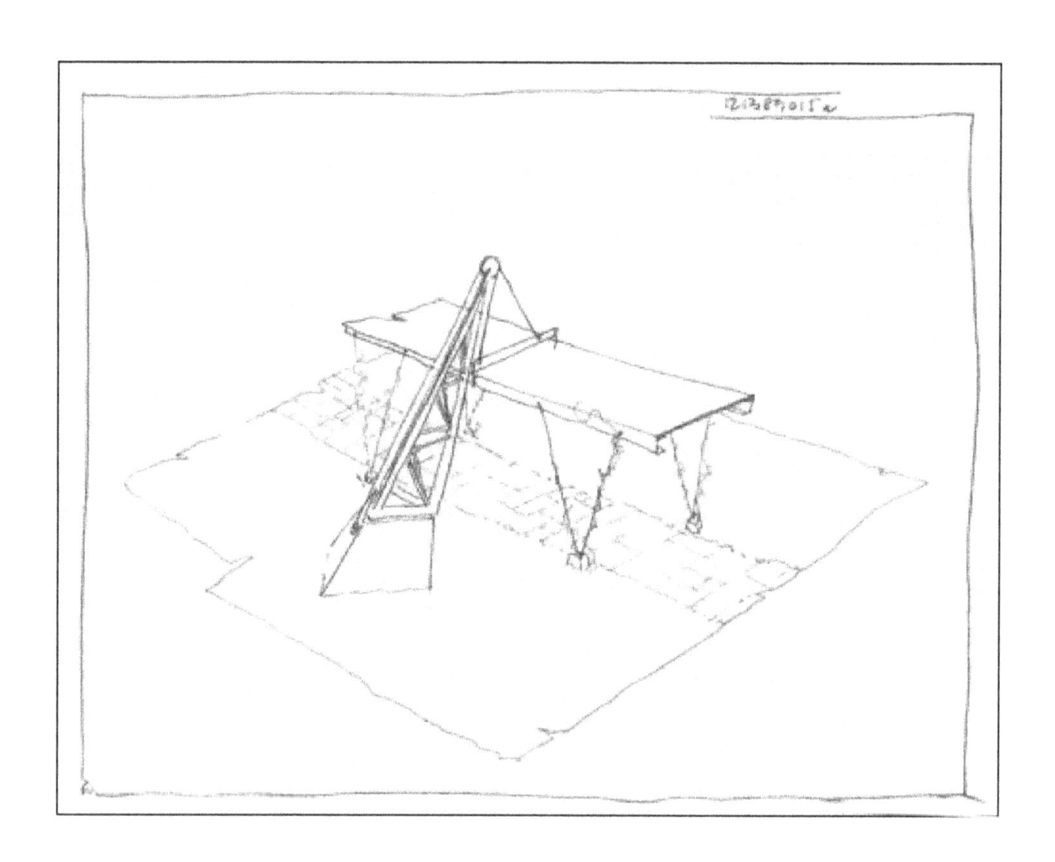

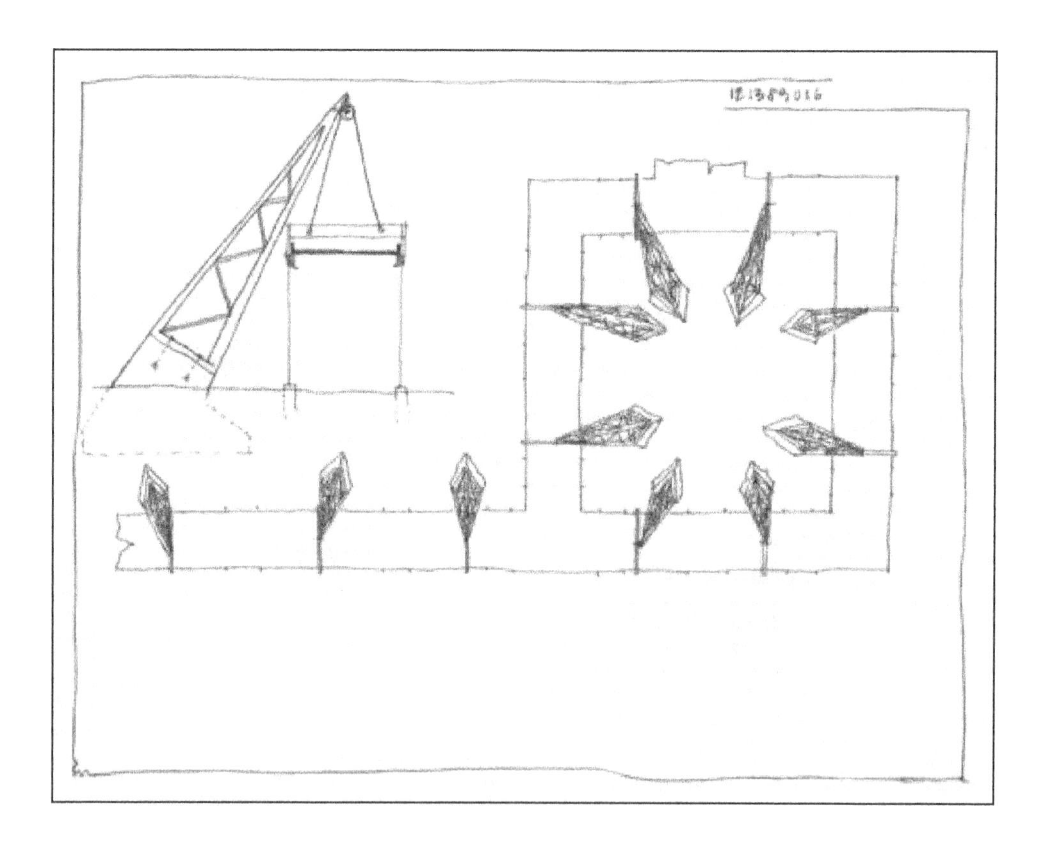

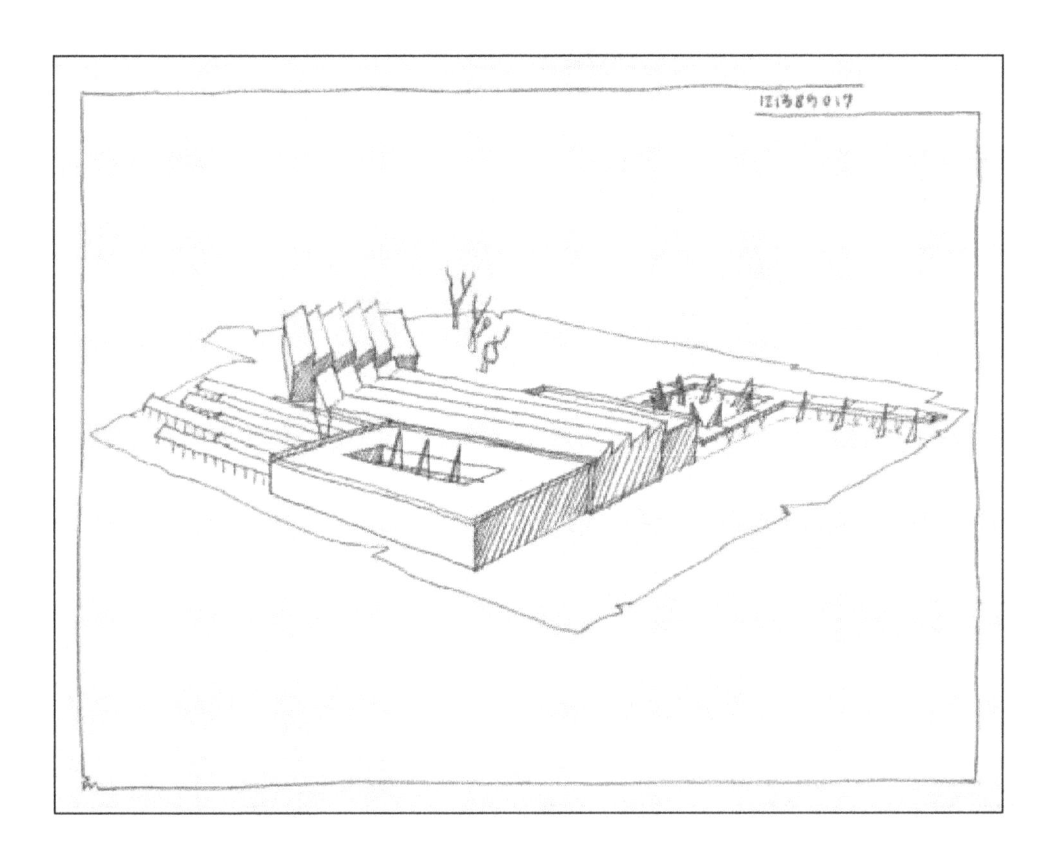

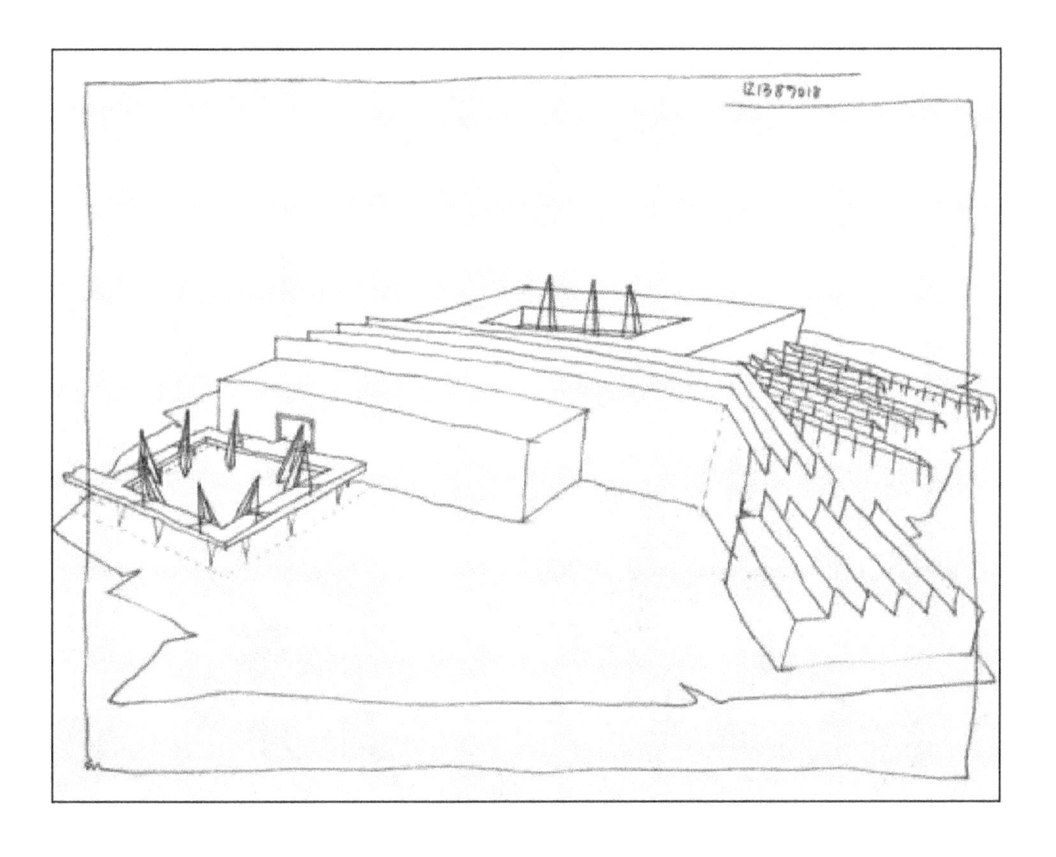

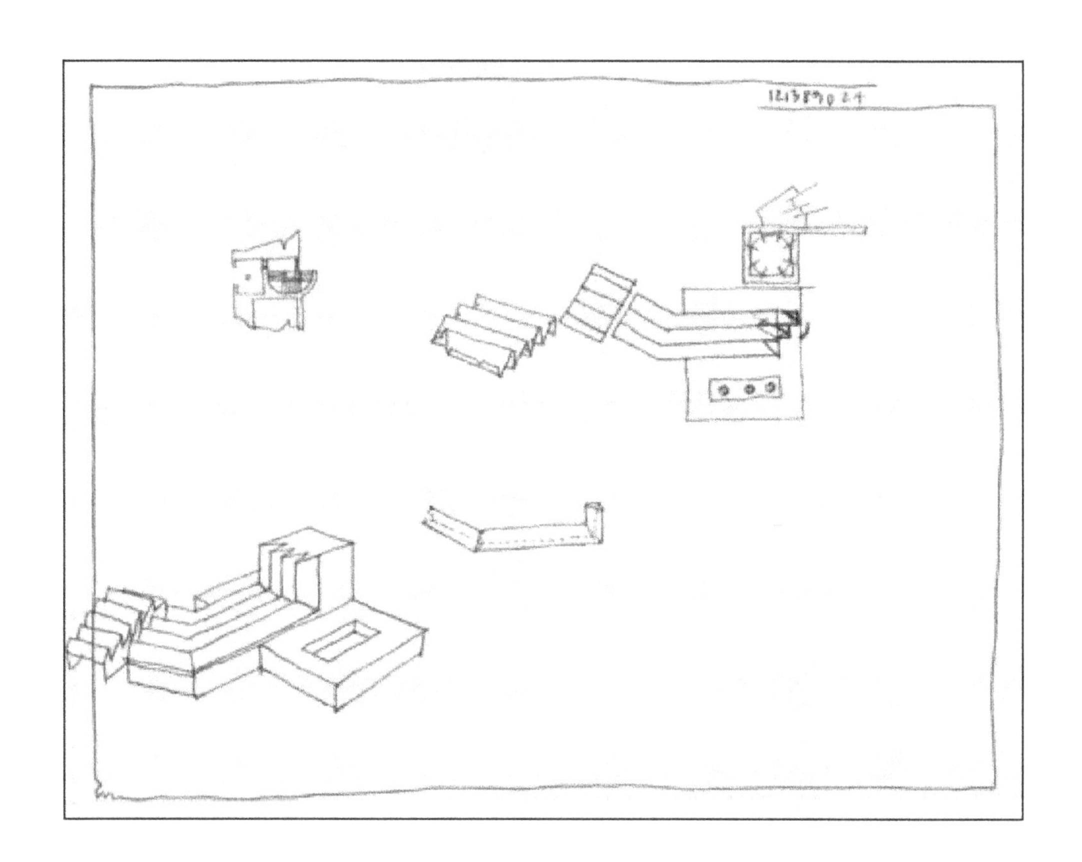

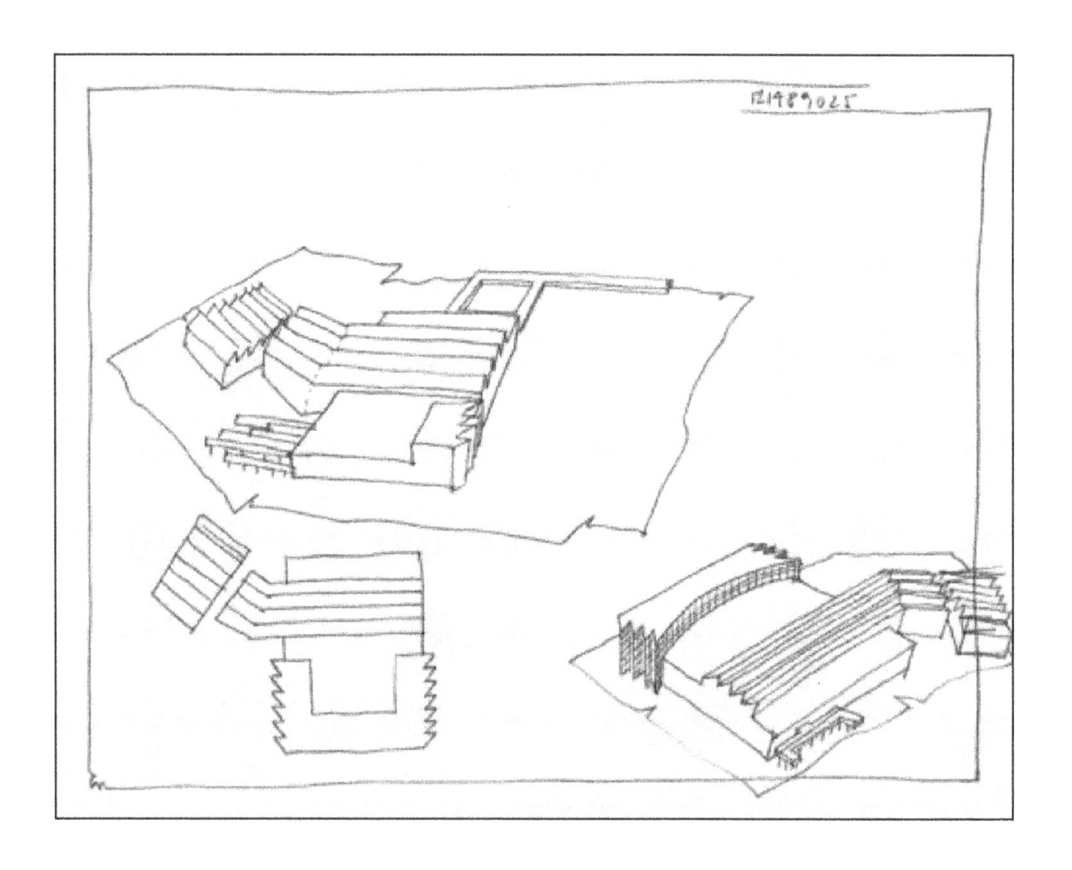

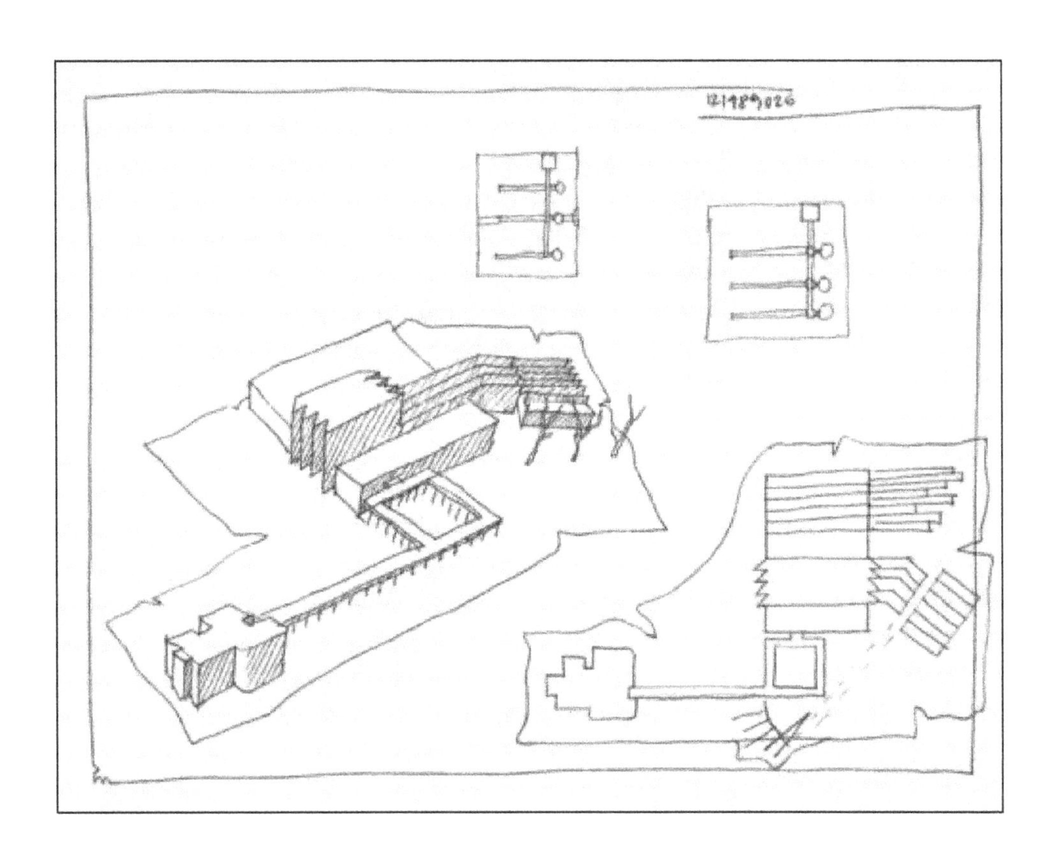
121489026

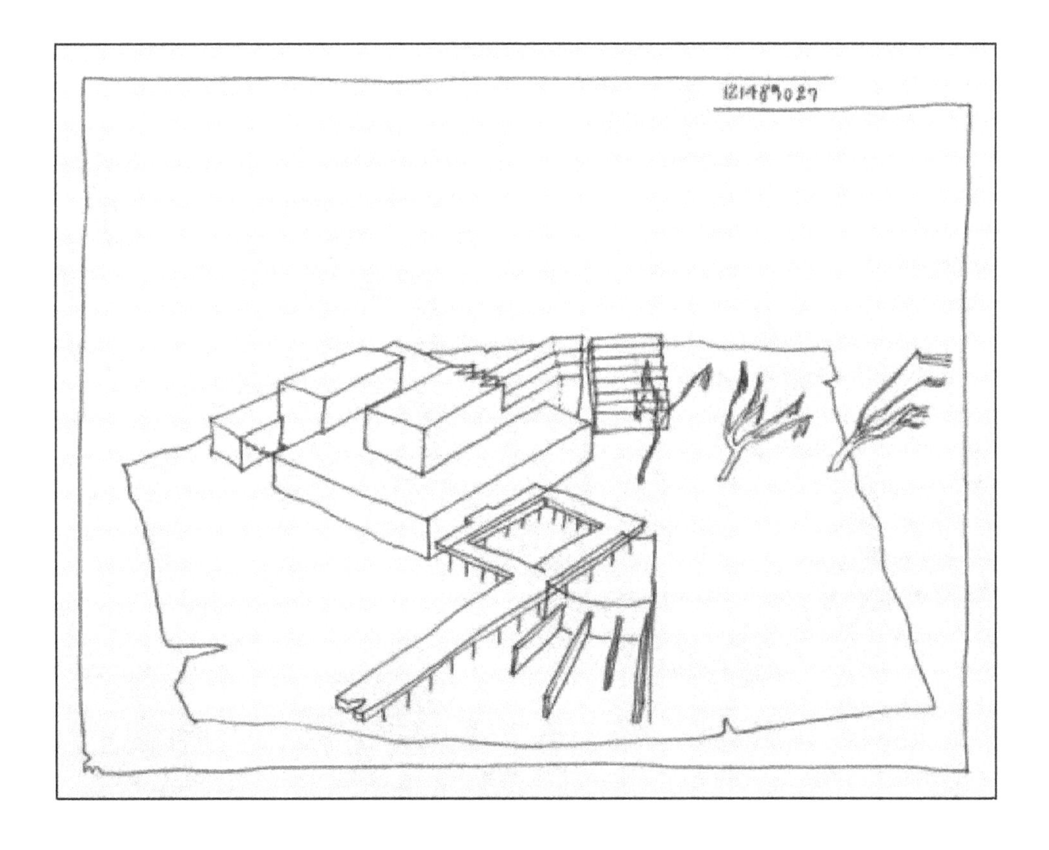
121489027

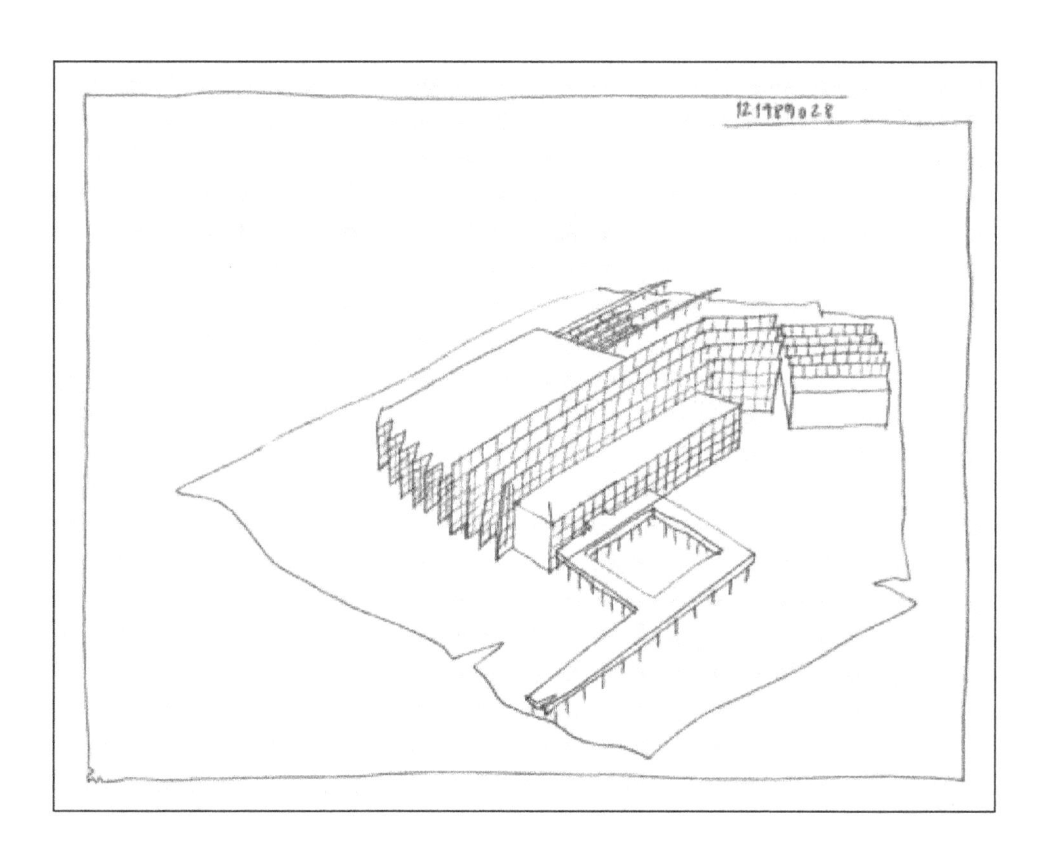
121989028

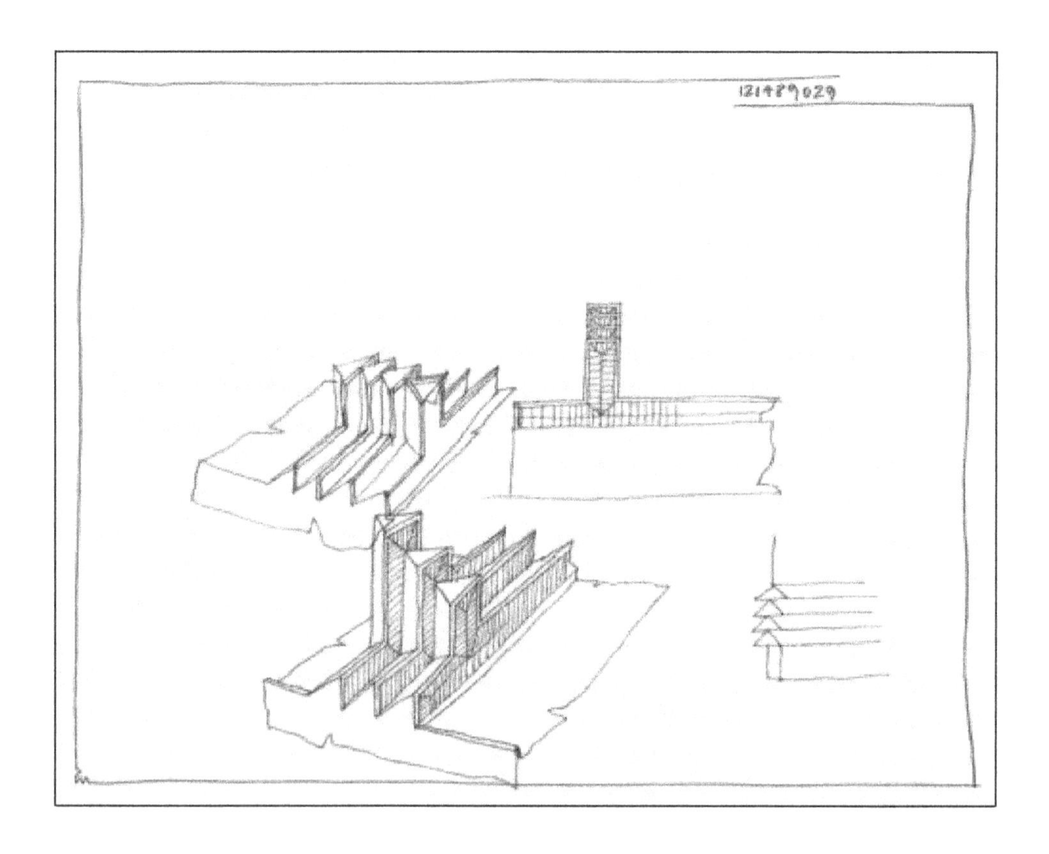
121989029

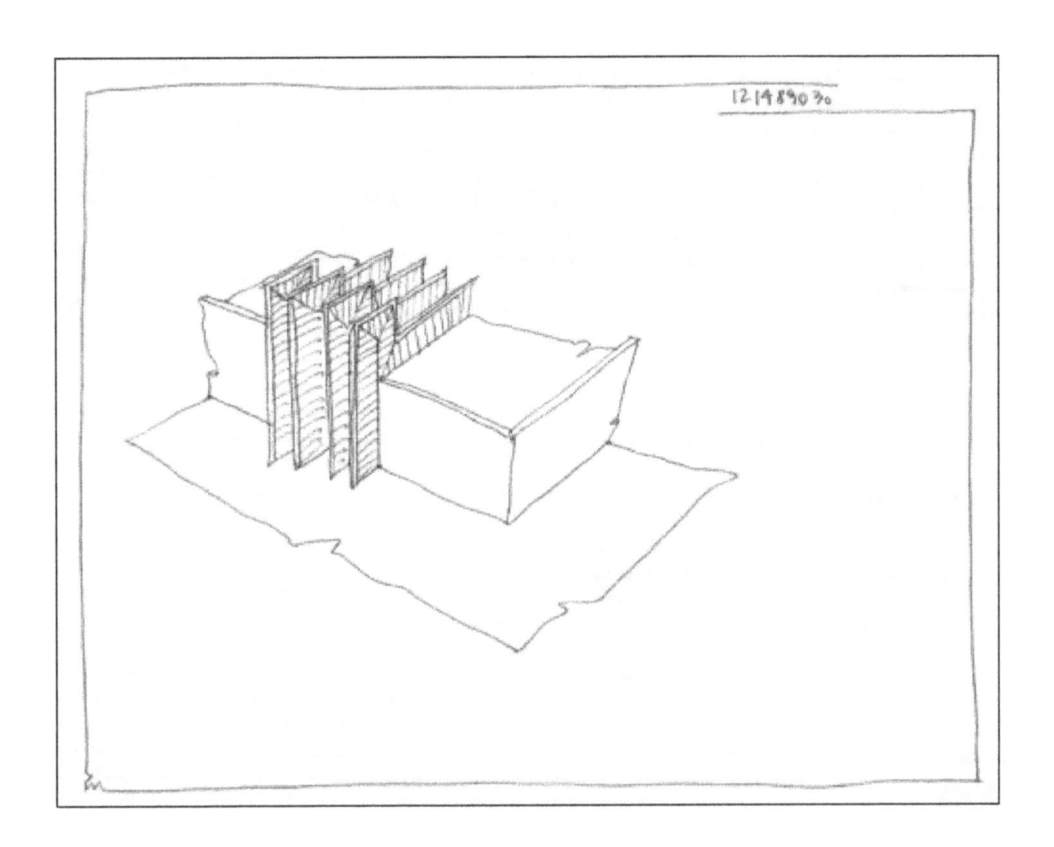
121489030

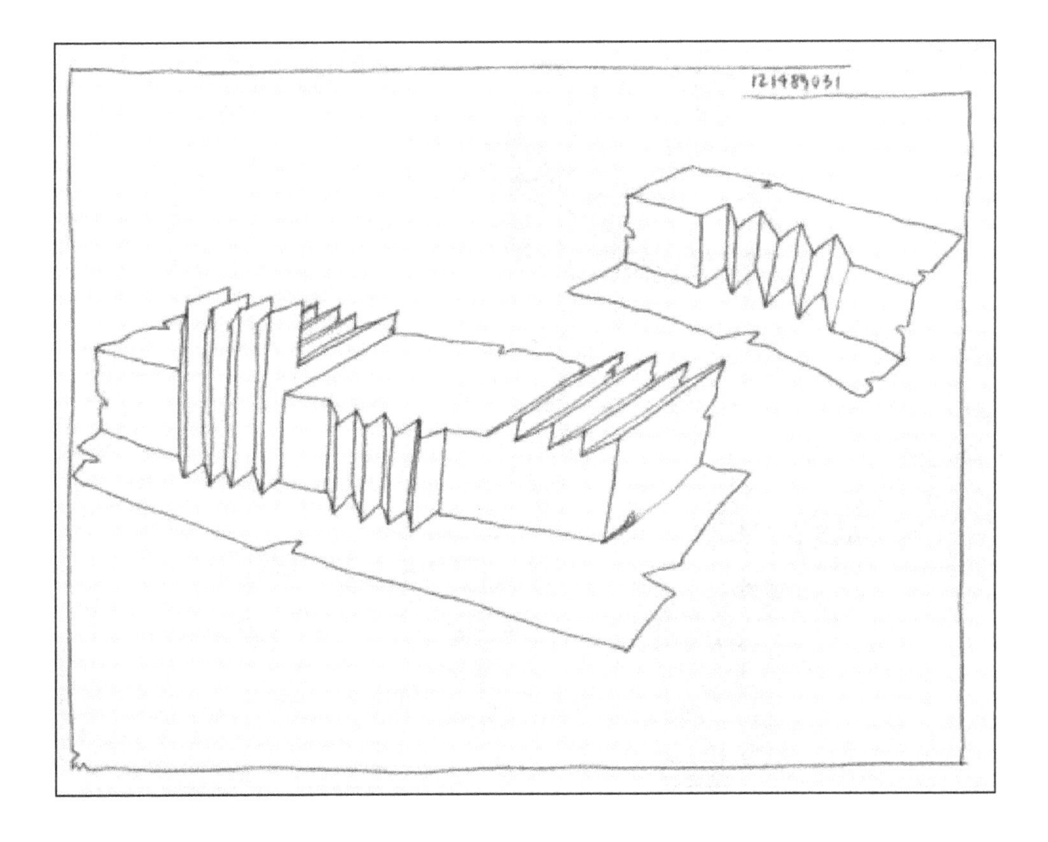
121489031

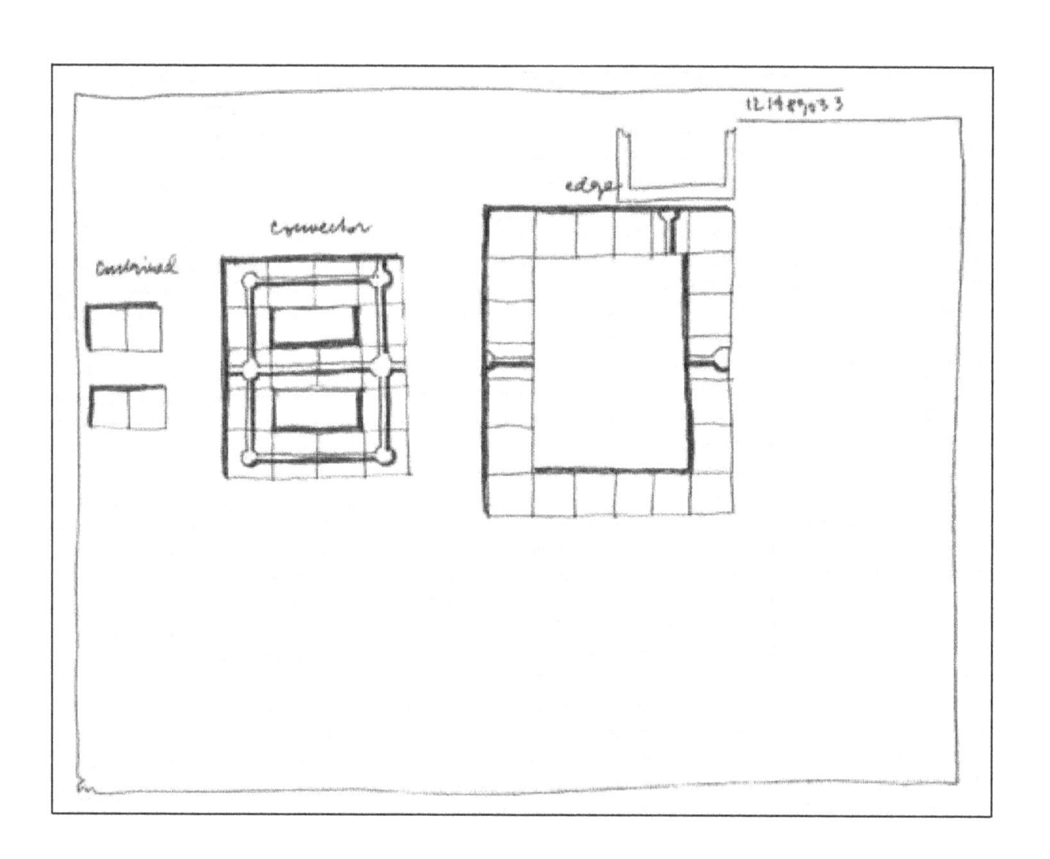
121489033
edge
connector
Combined

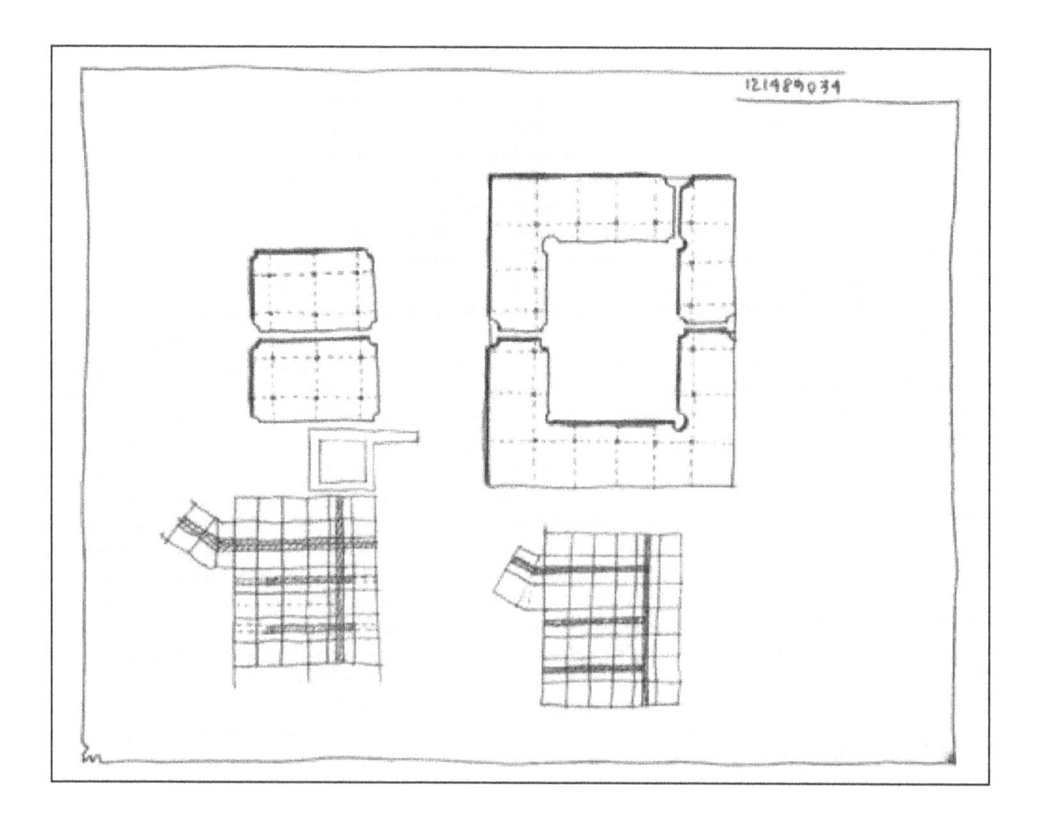
121489034

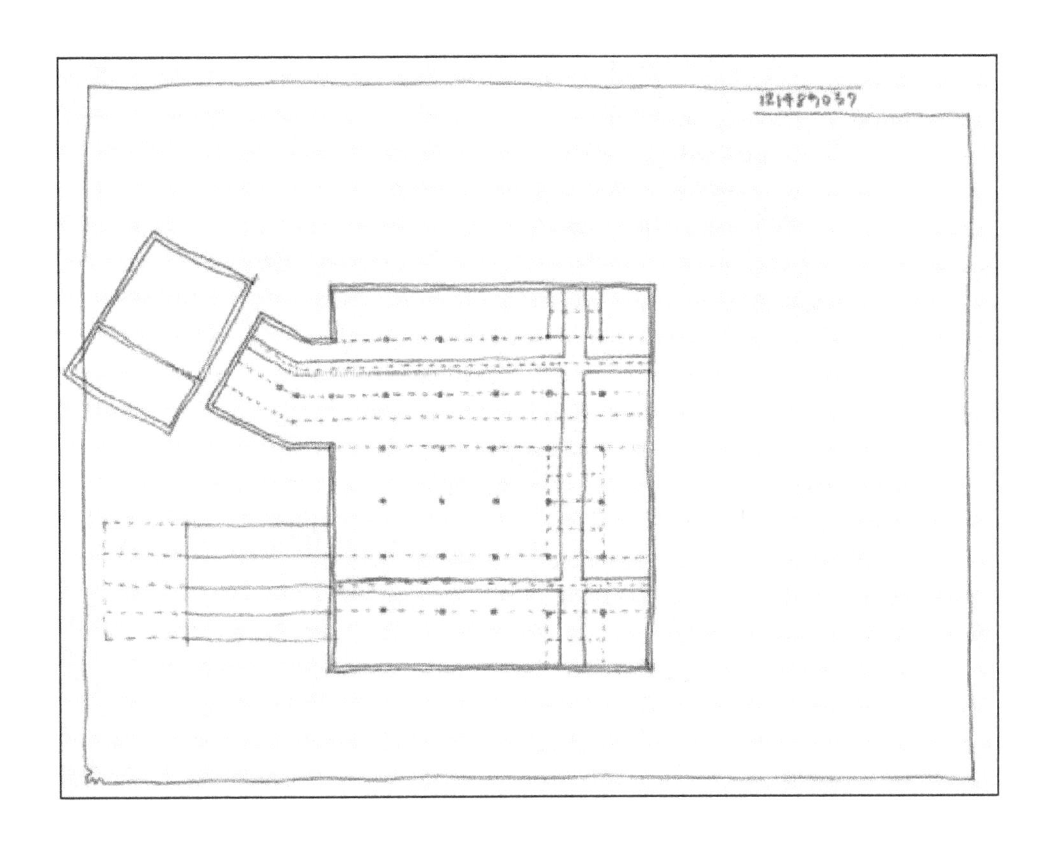
121489037

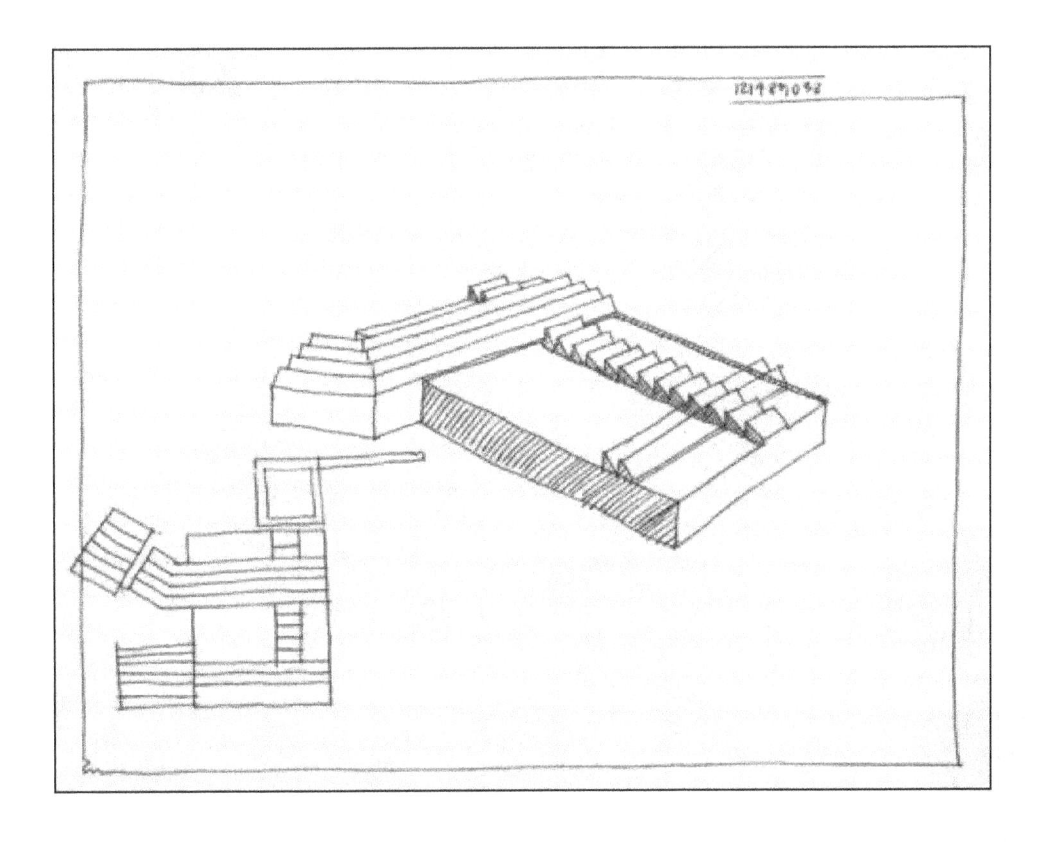
121489038

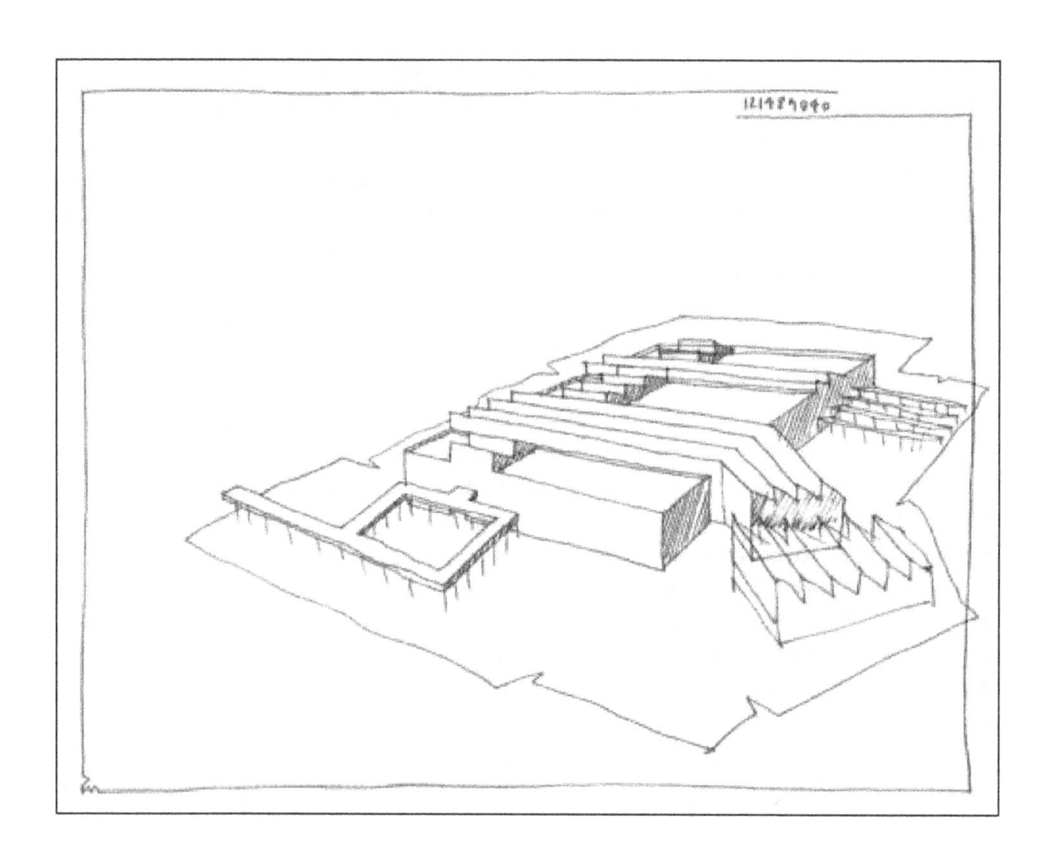

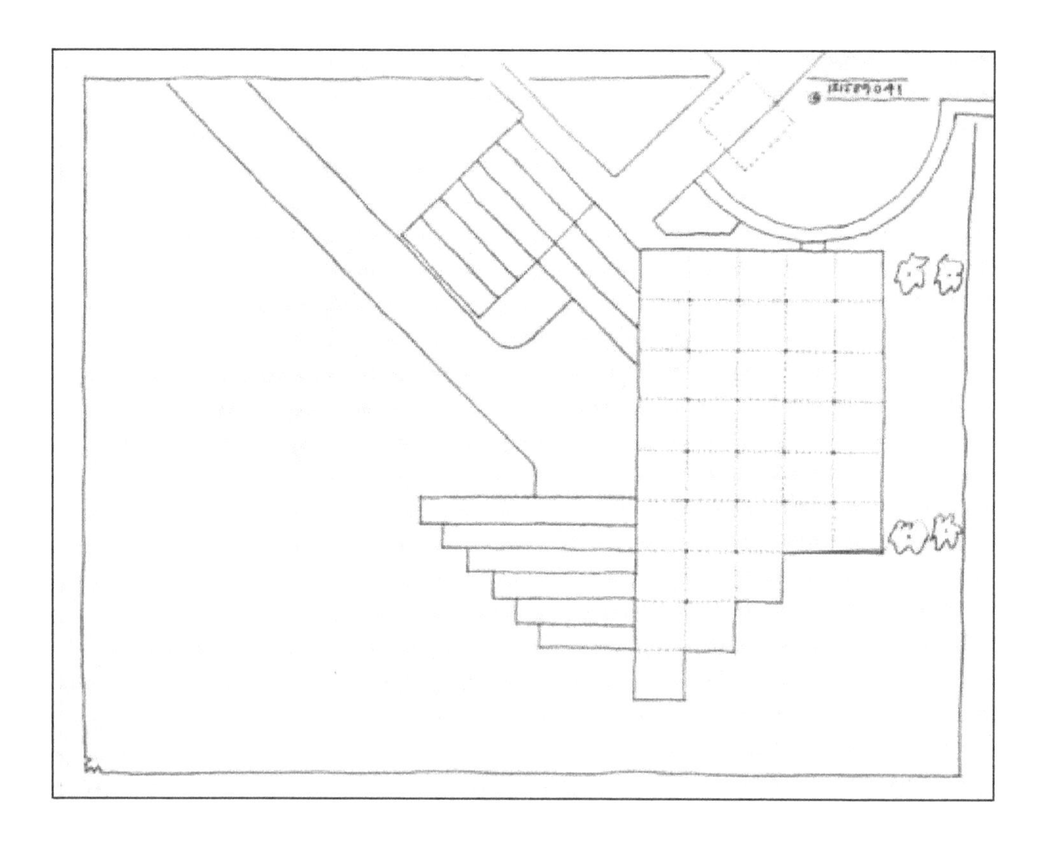

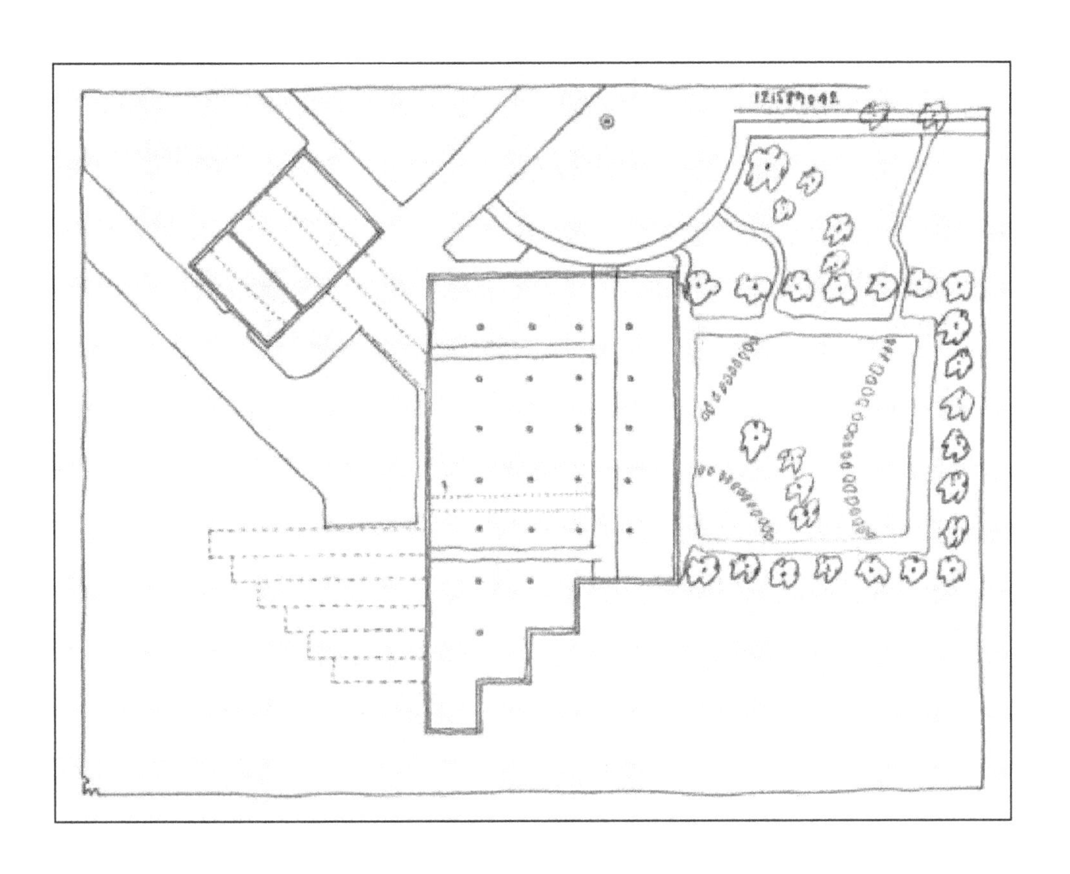
1215879042

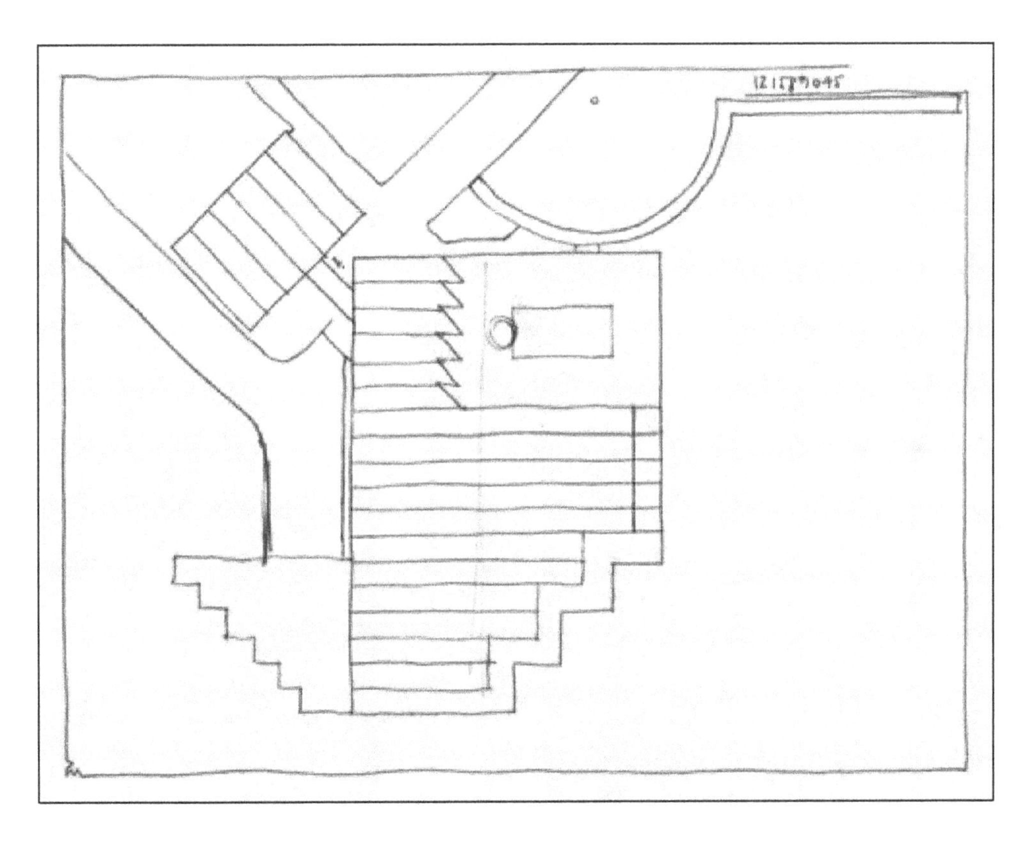
1215879045

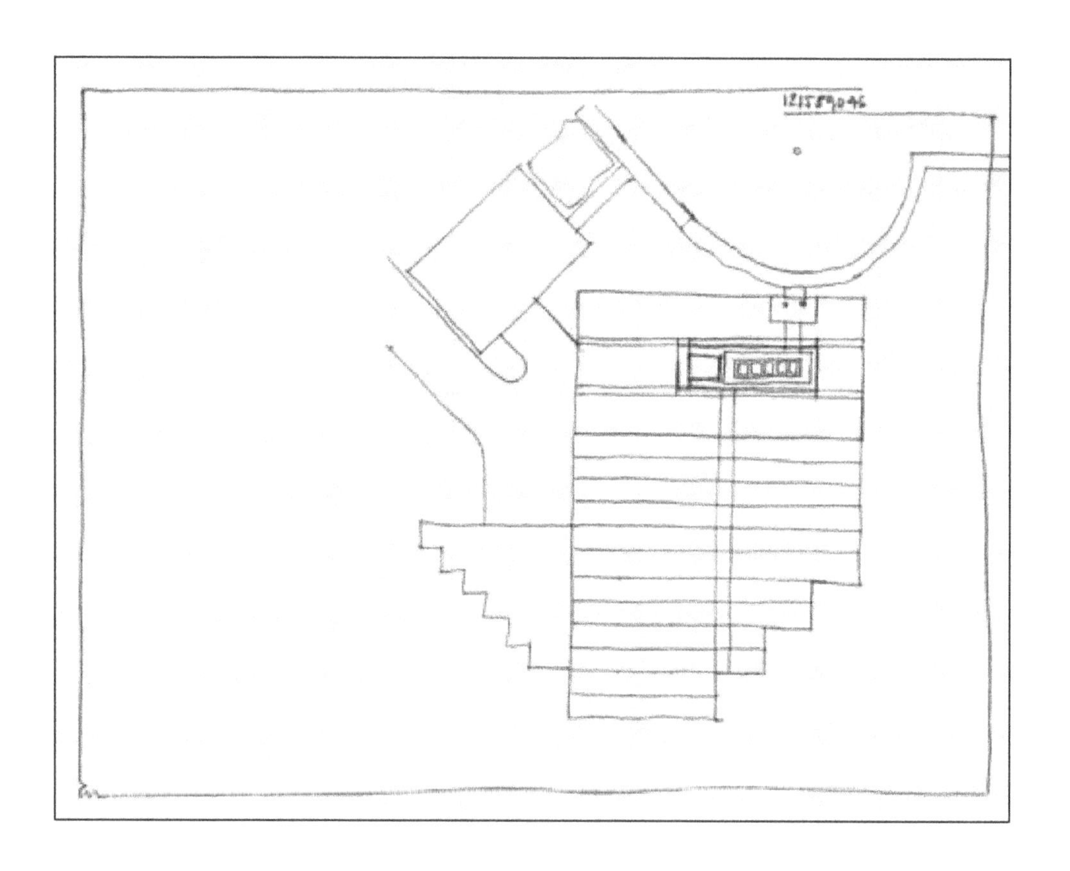

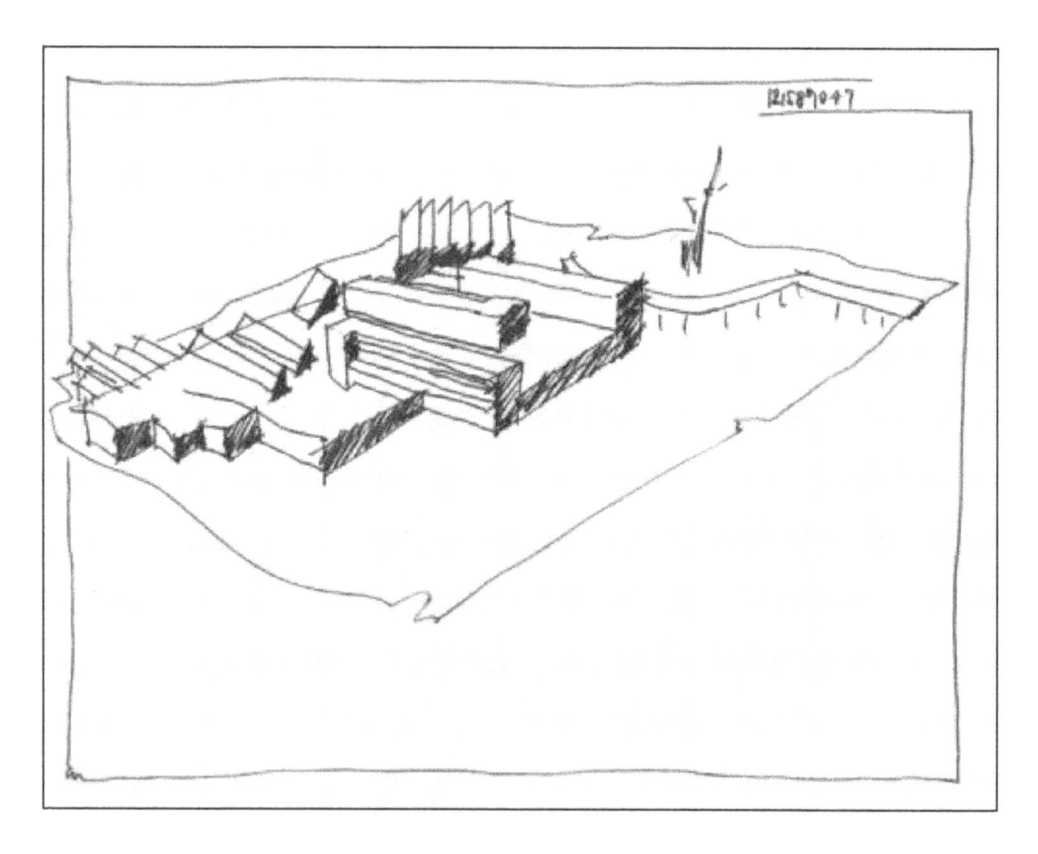

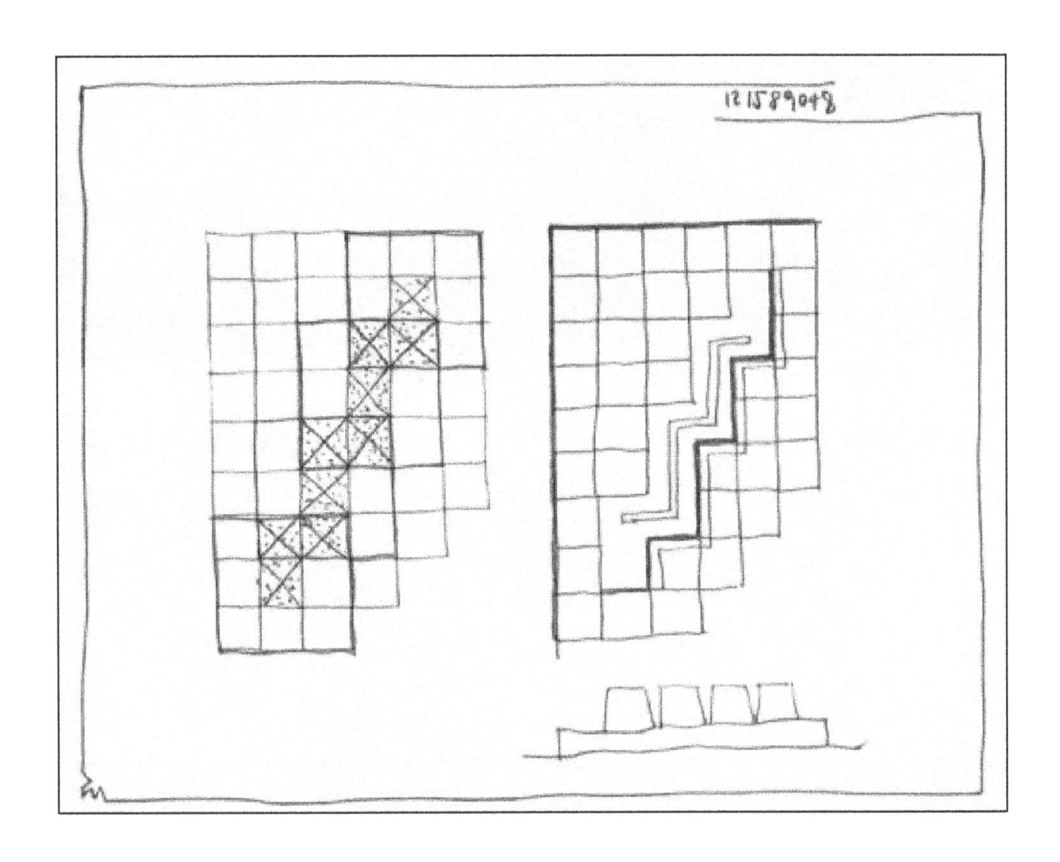
1215890048

1215890049

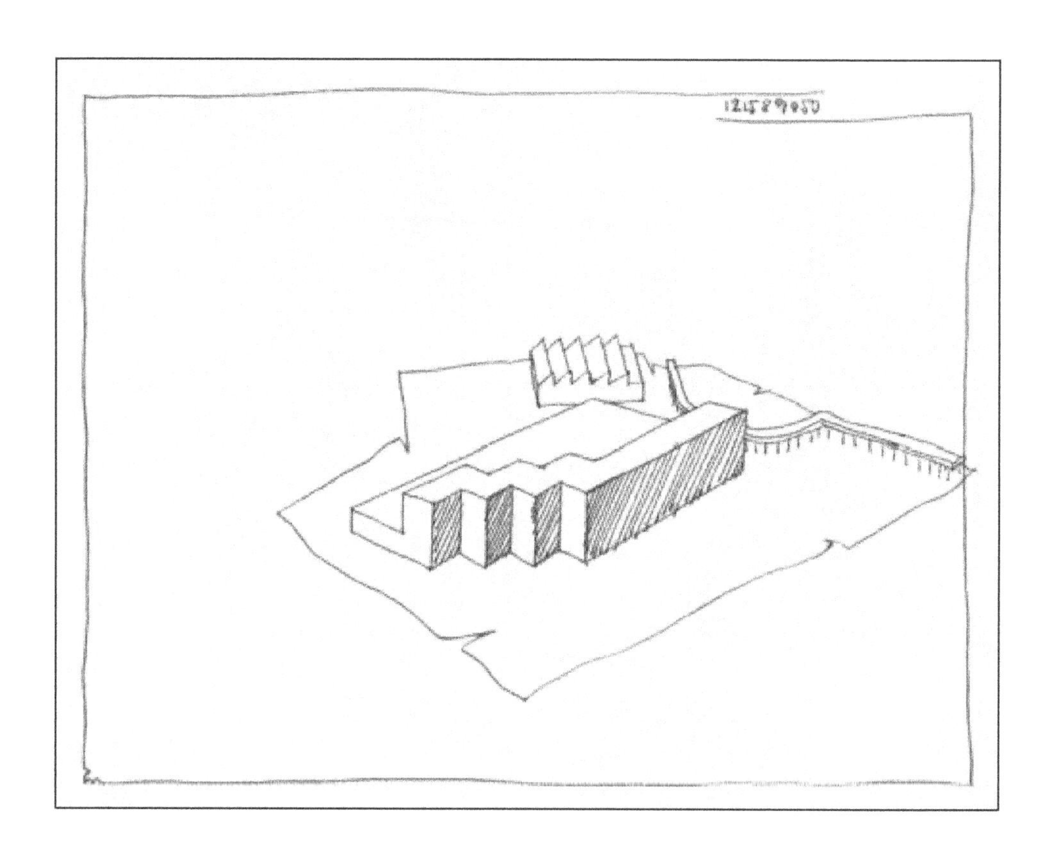
121589050

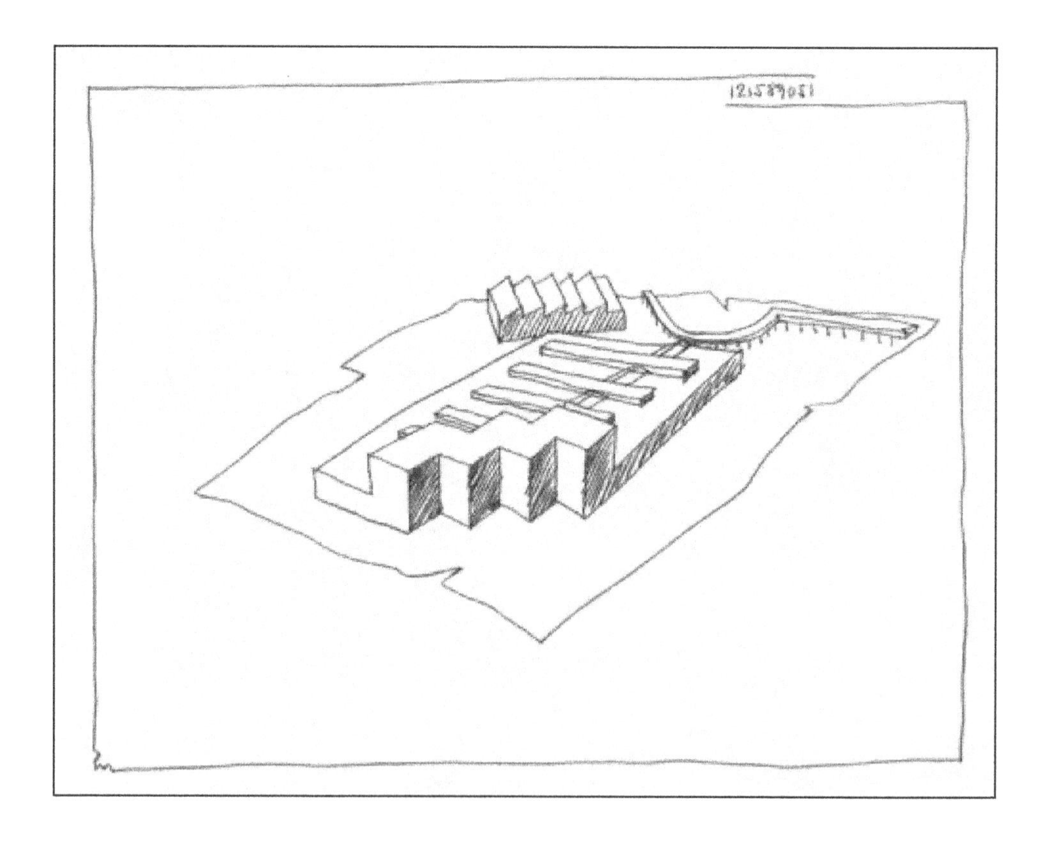
121589051

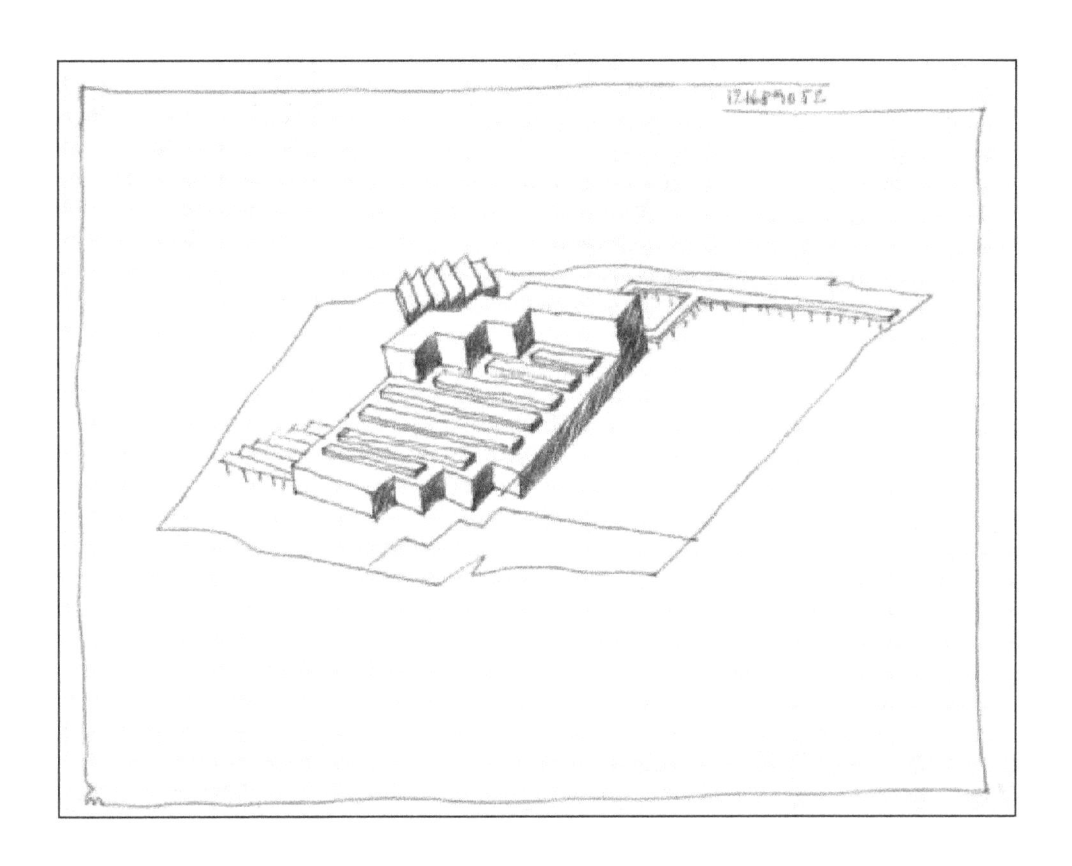
121689052

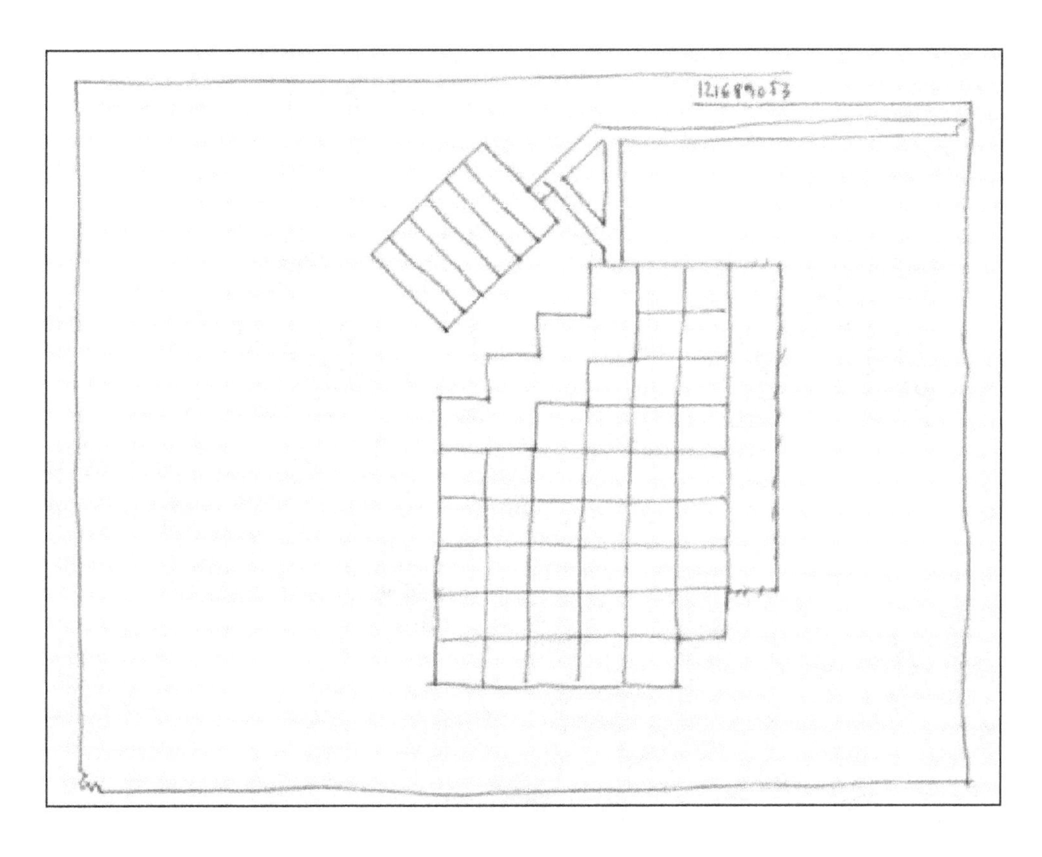
121689053

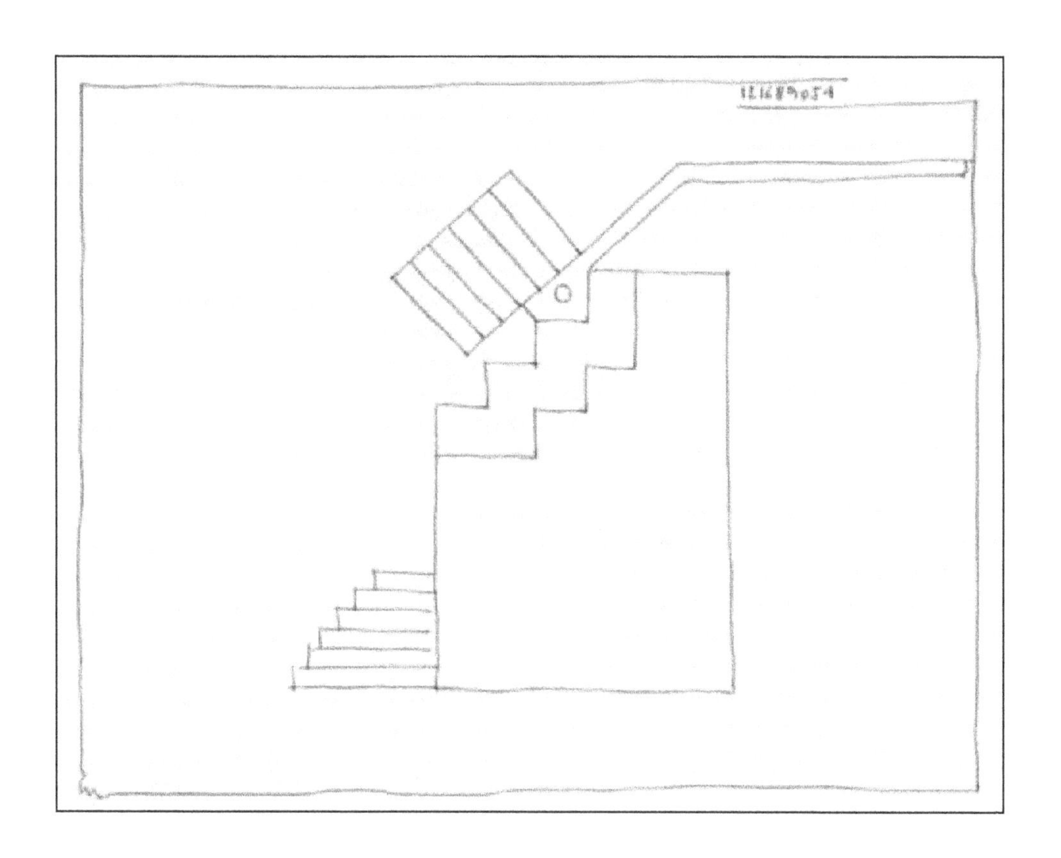

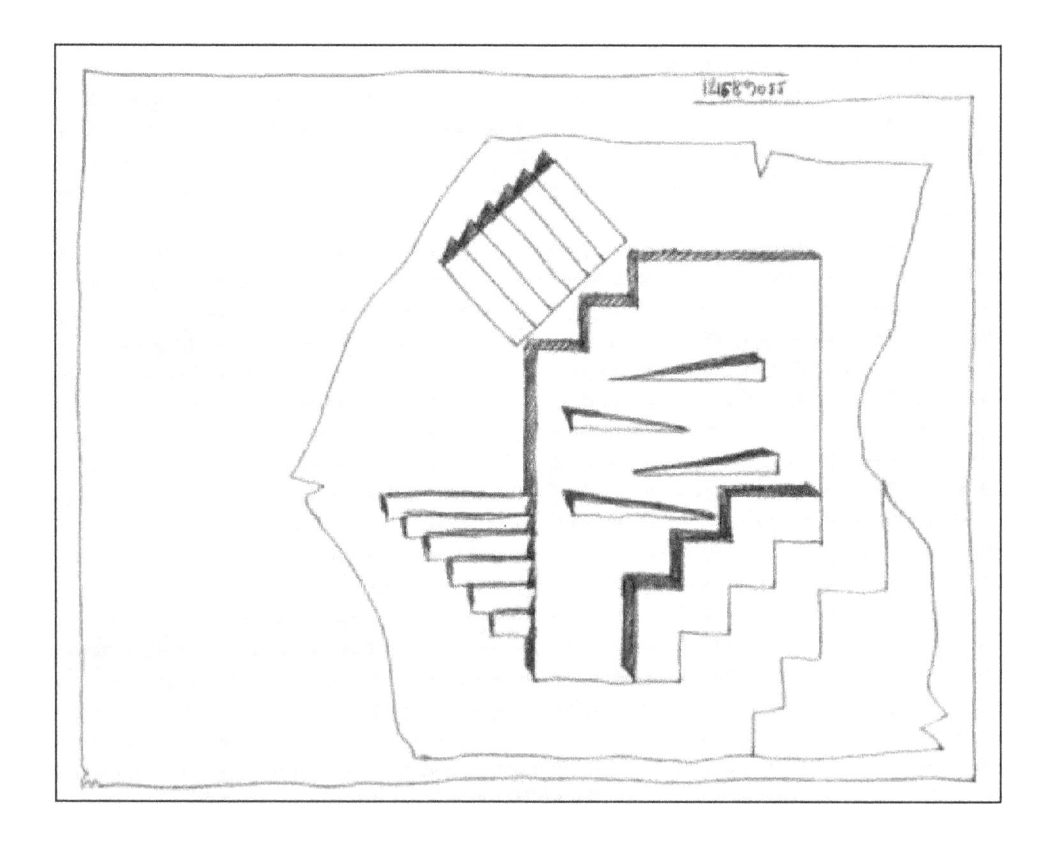

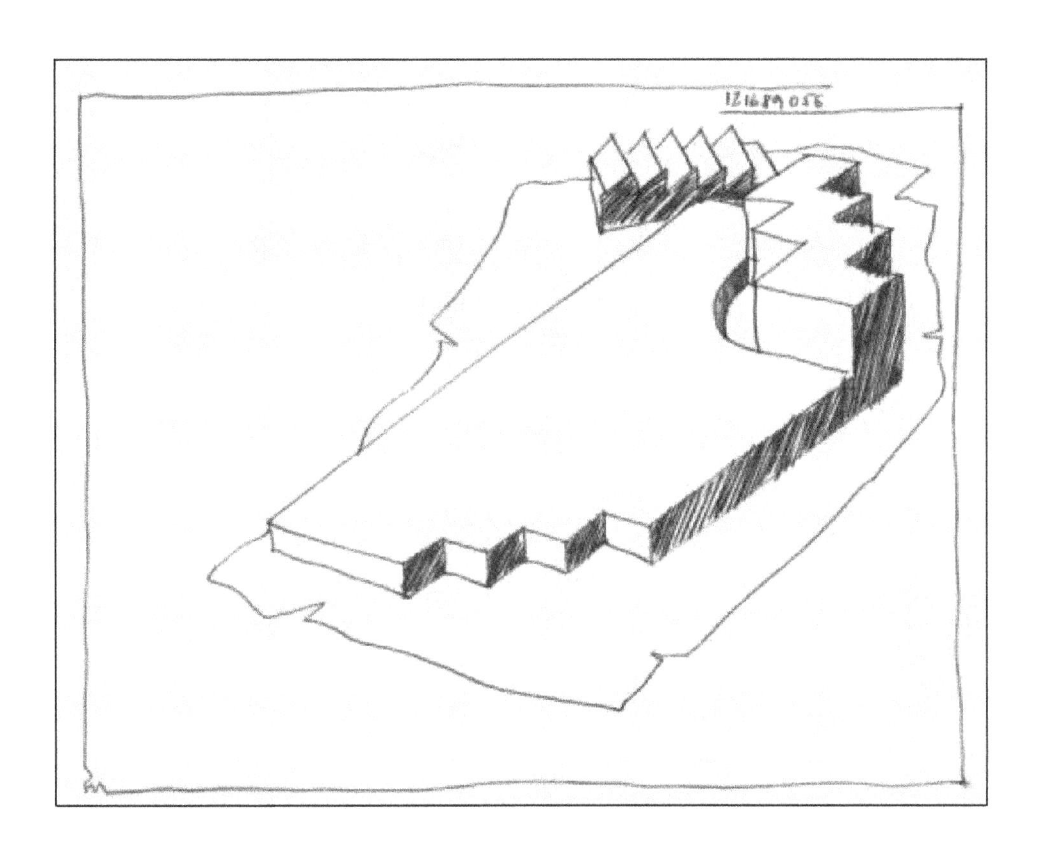
121689056

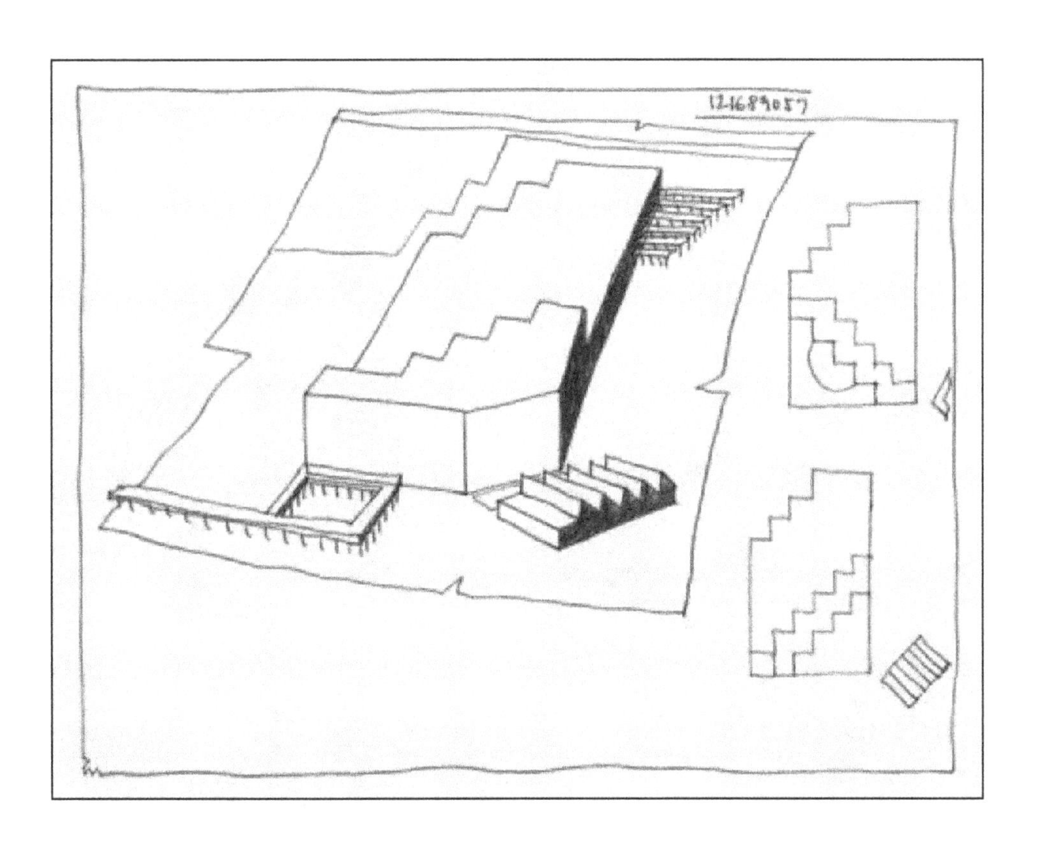
121689057

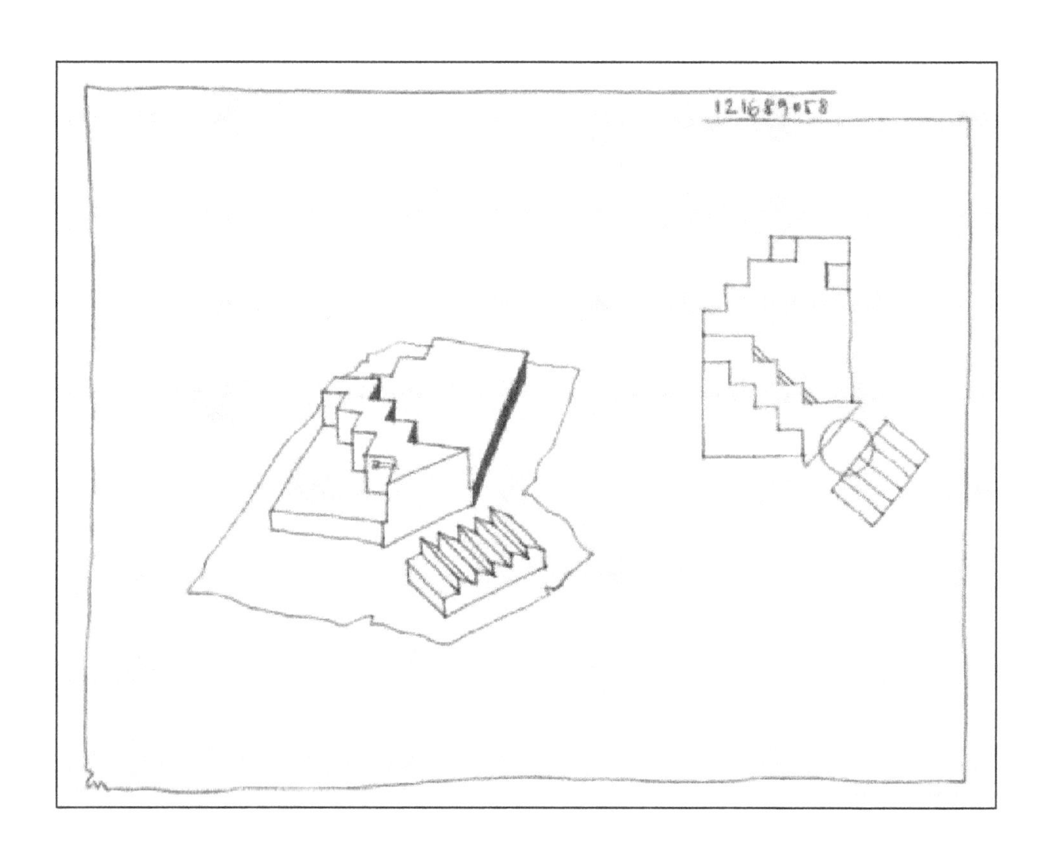
121689058

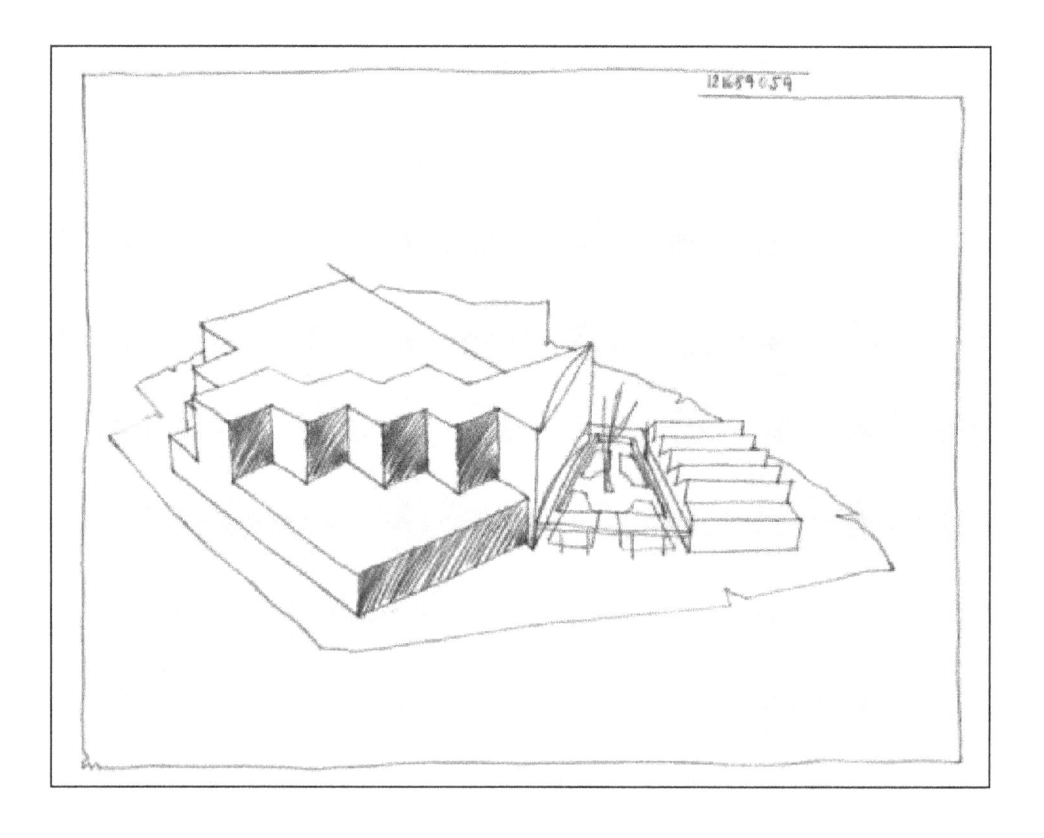
121689059

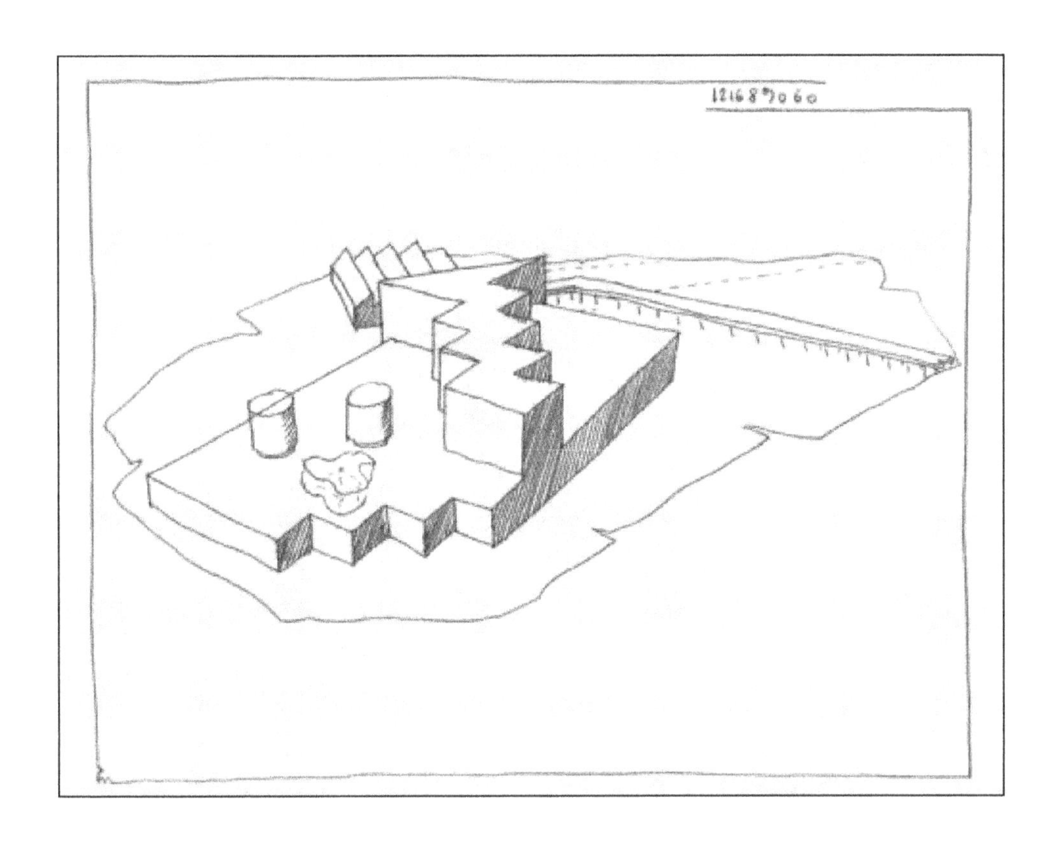

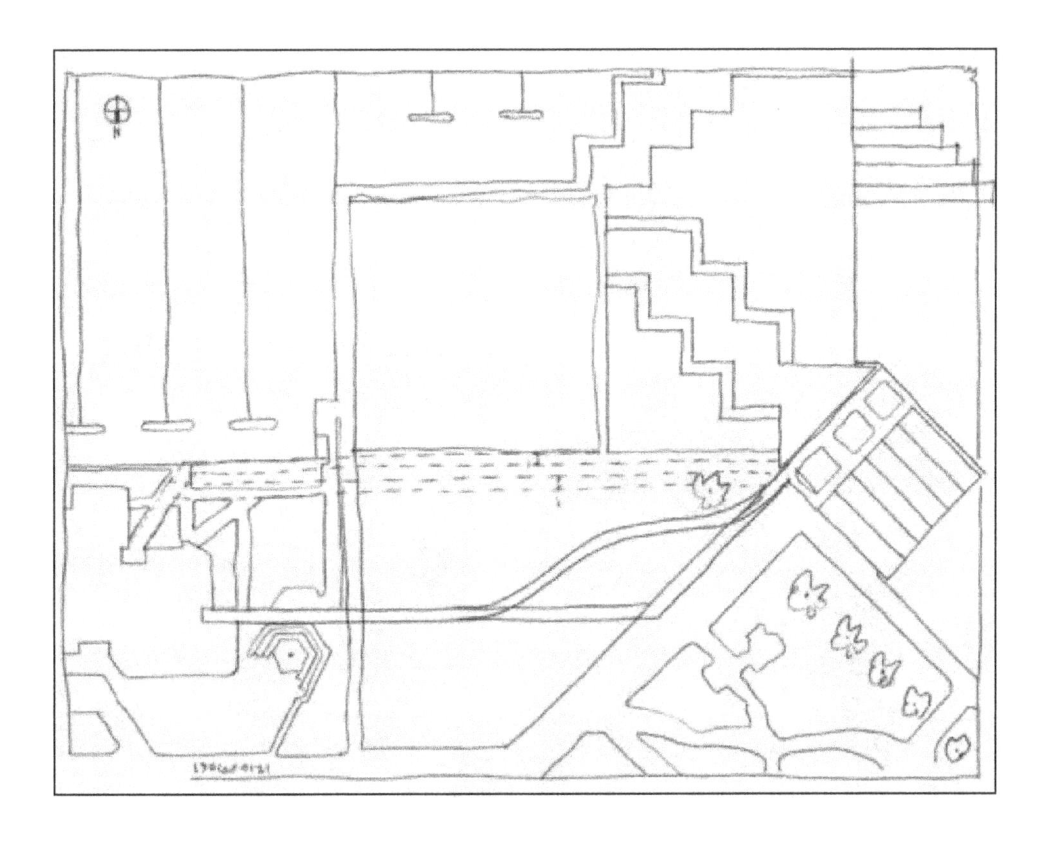

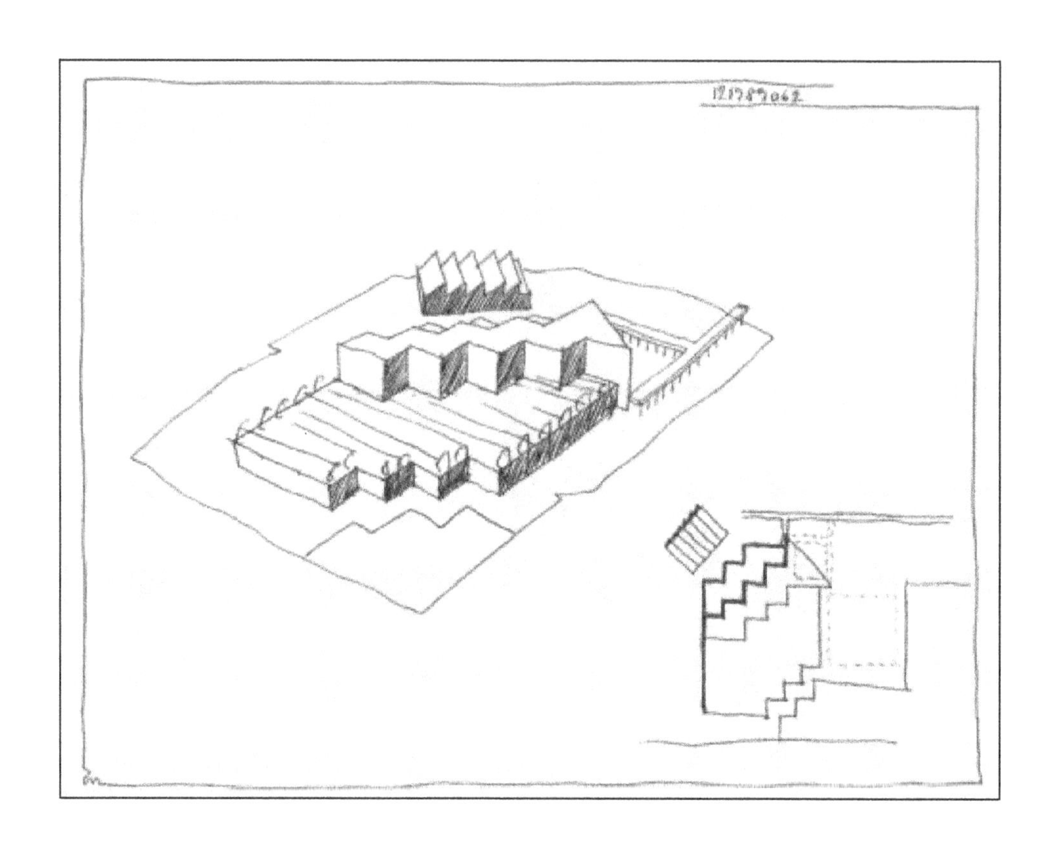

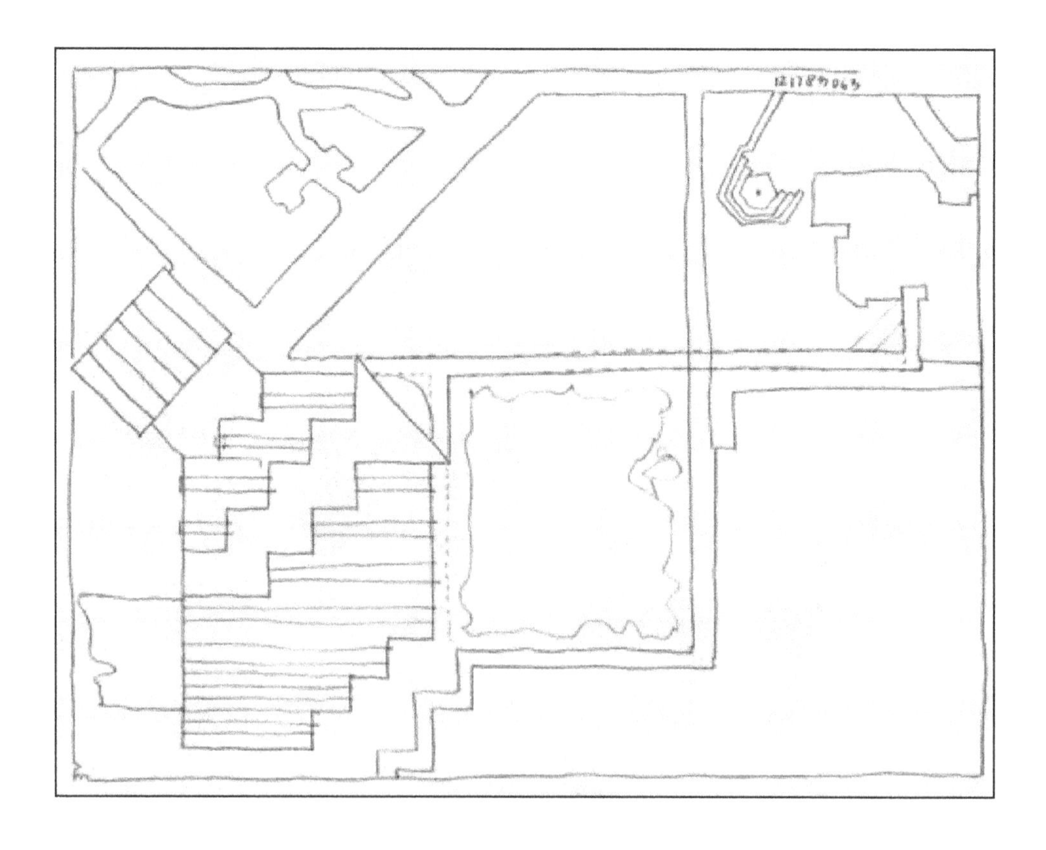

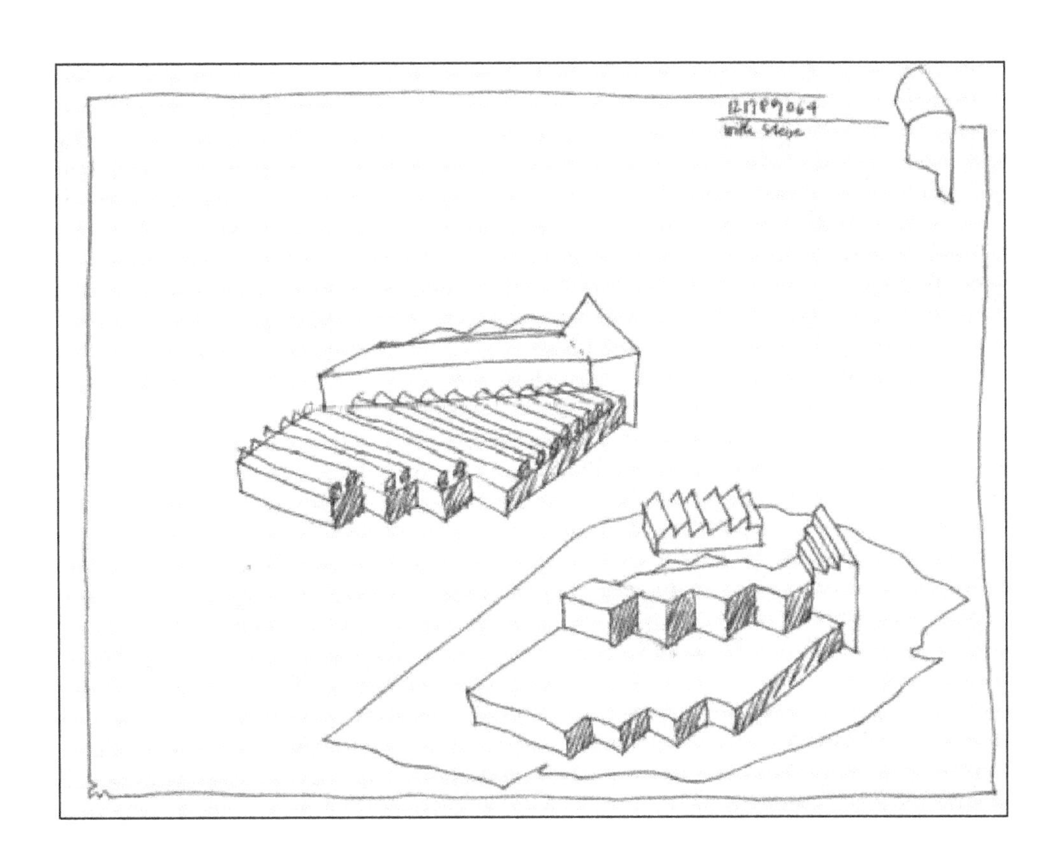
121789064
with Steve

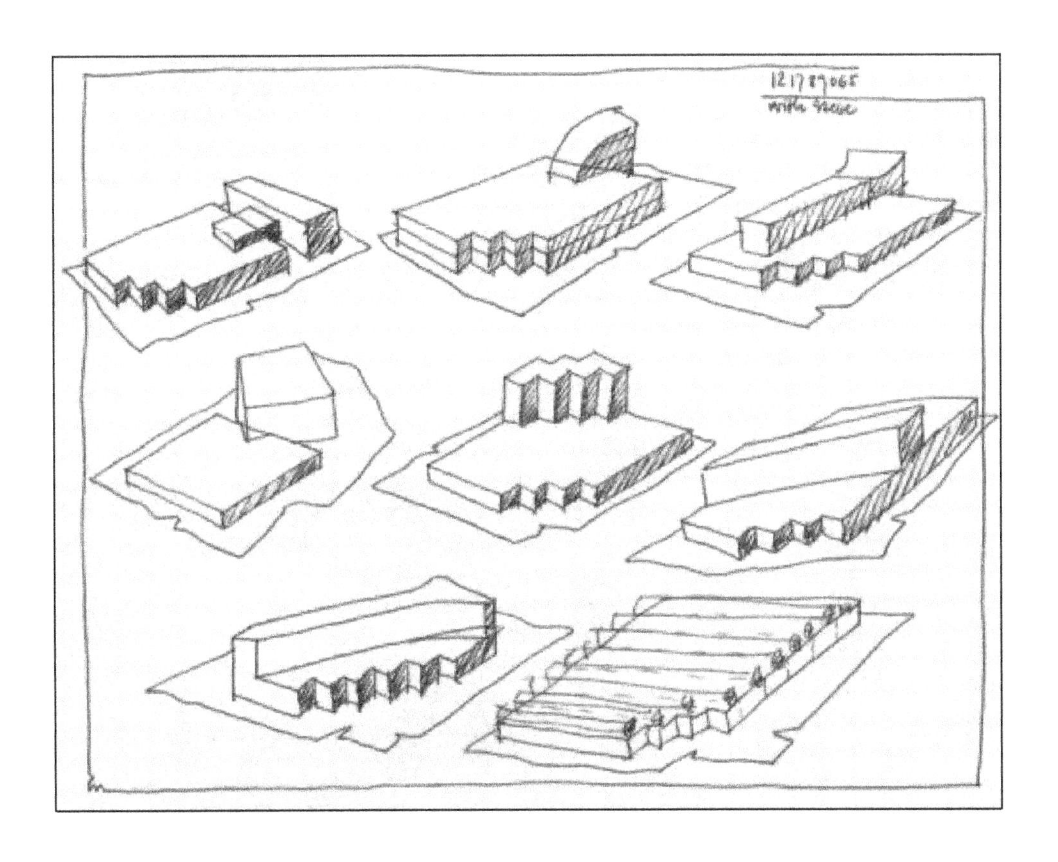
121789065
with Steve

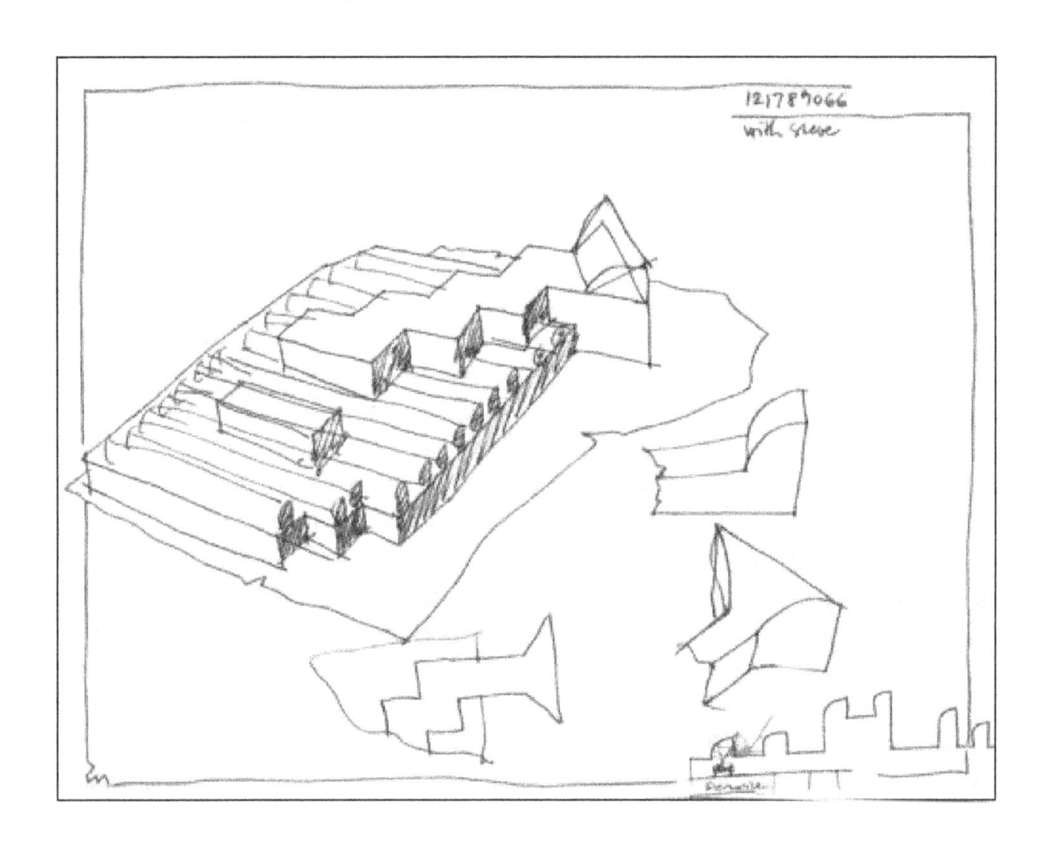
121789066

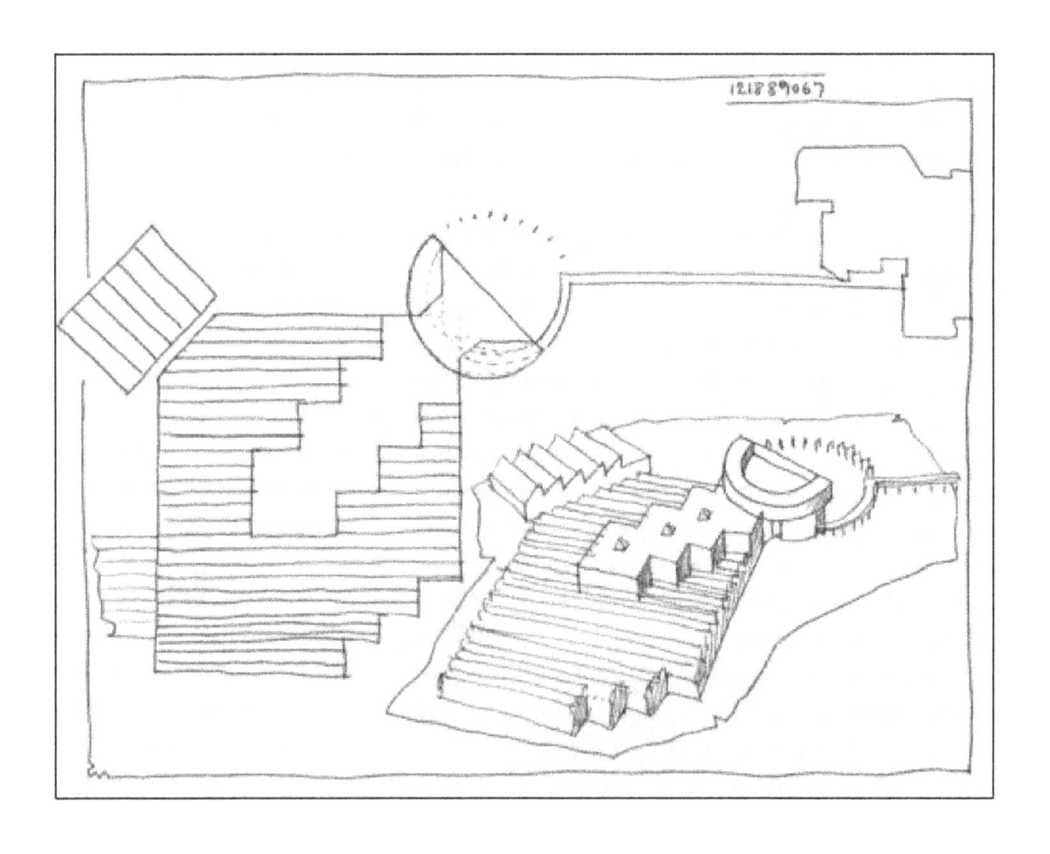
121789067

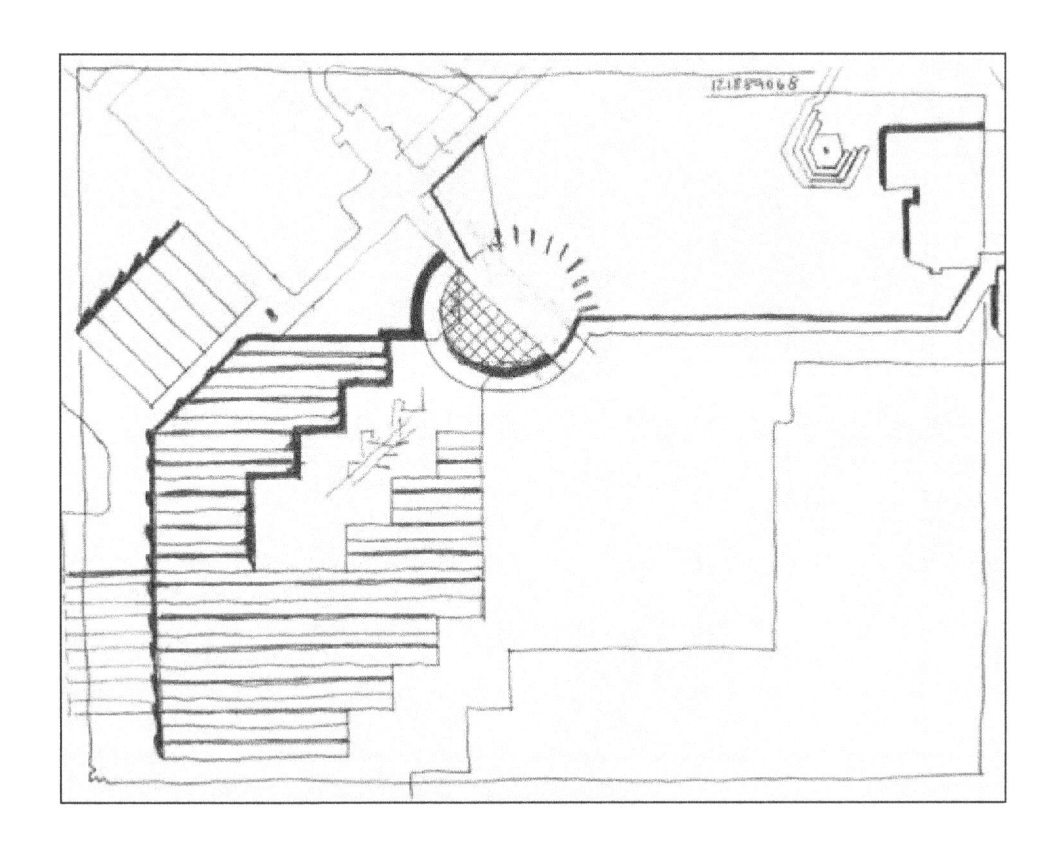
121889068

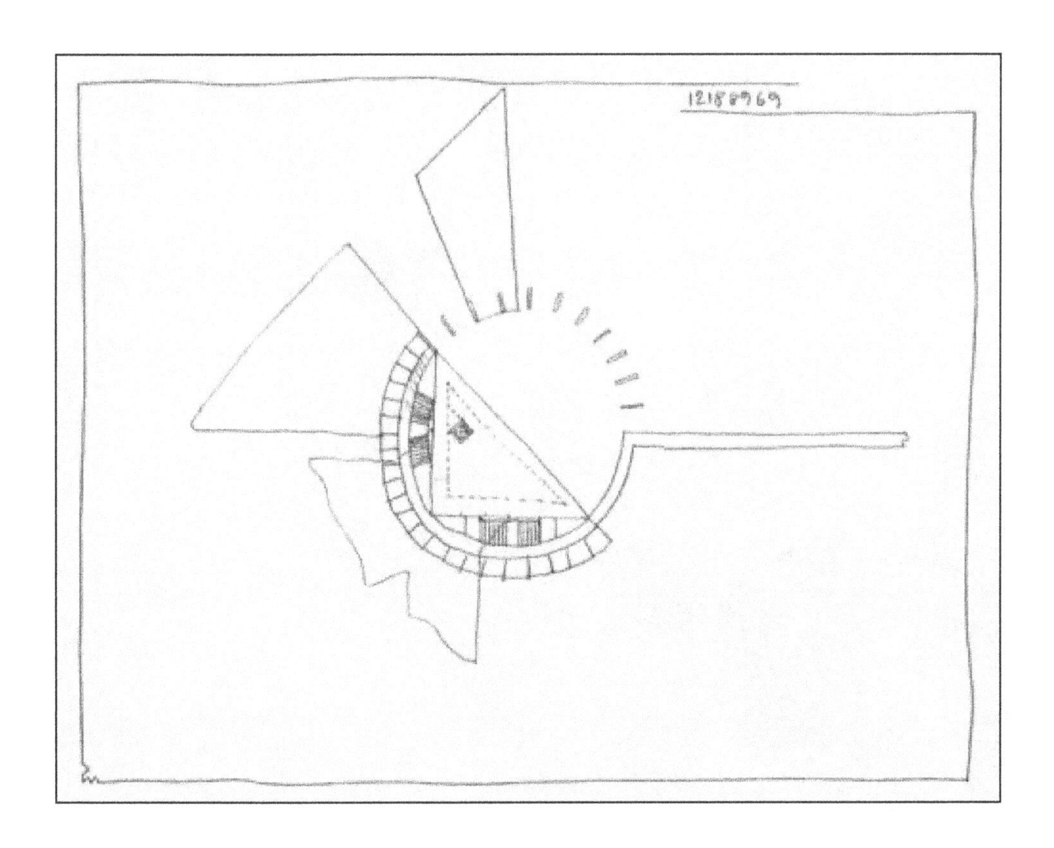
12188969

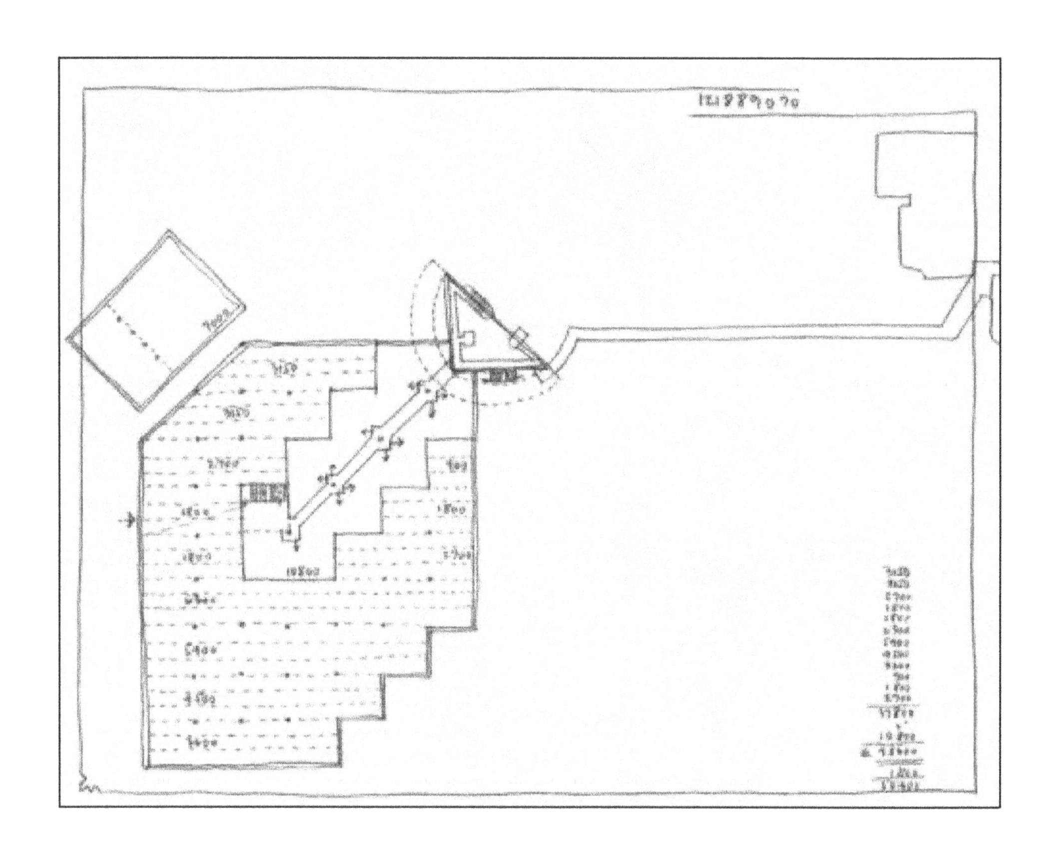

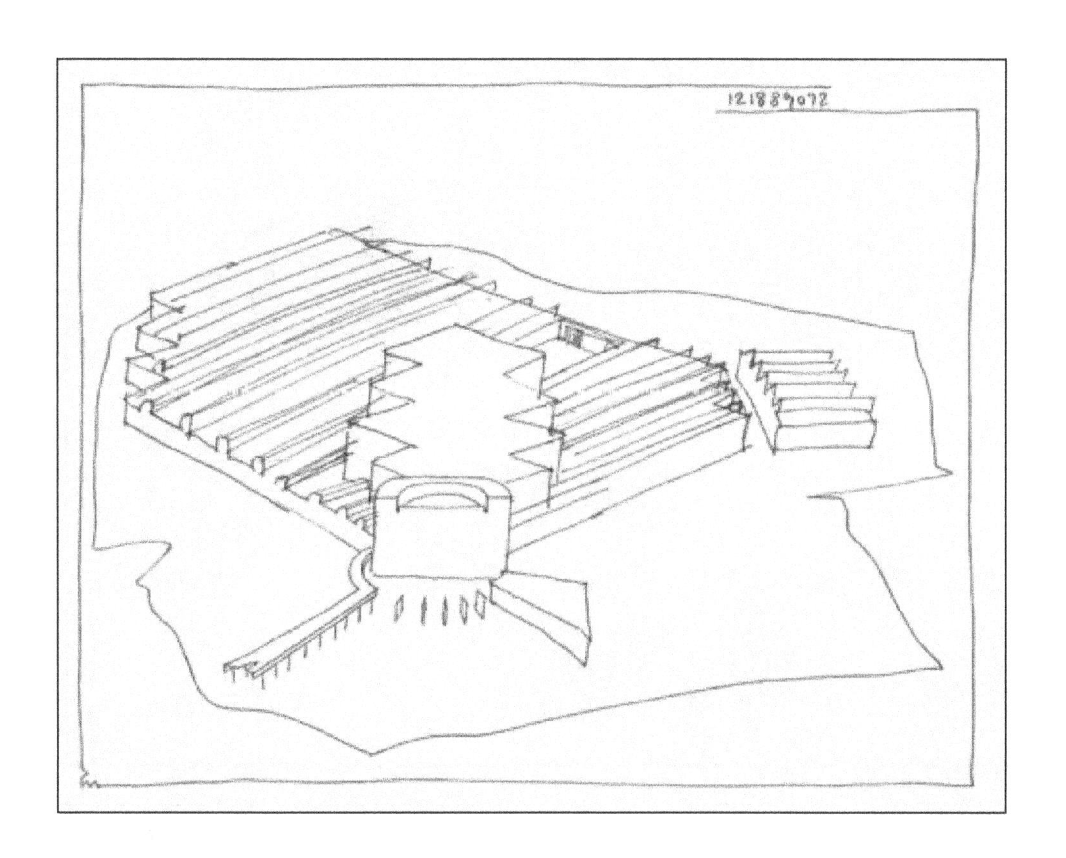
121889072

122089073

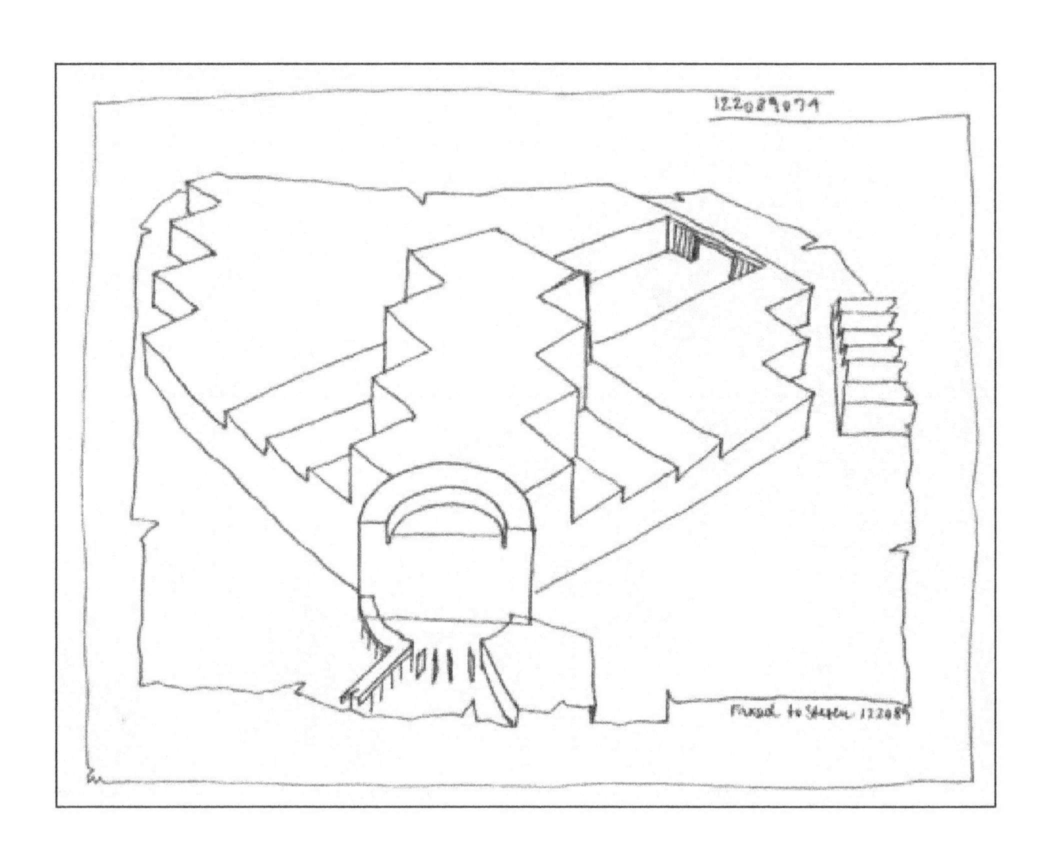
122089074

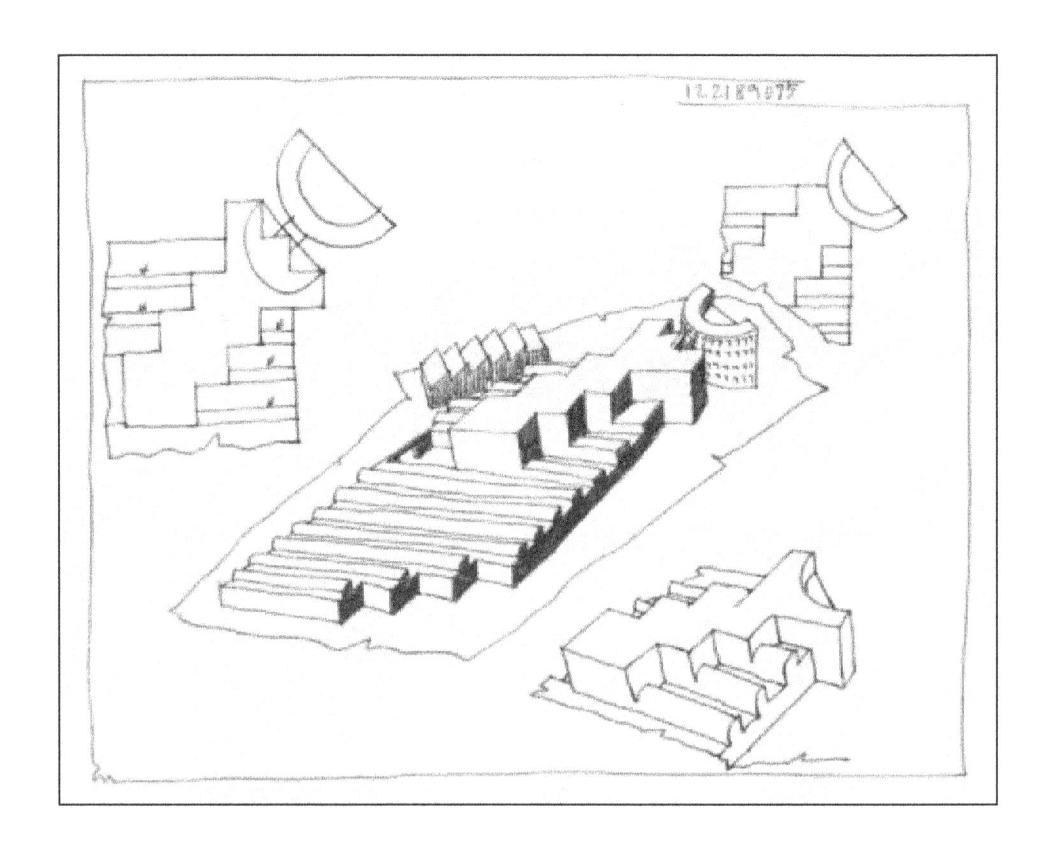
122189075

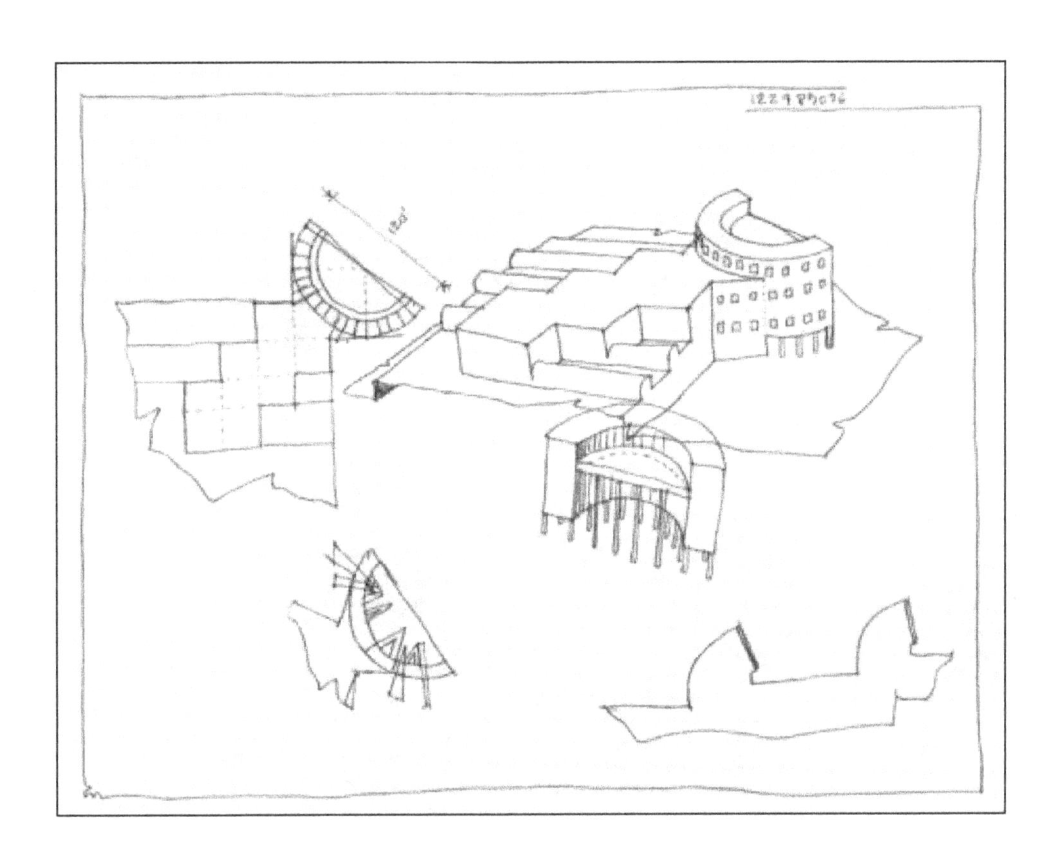

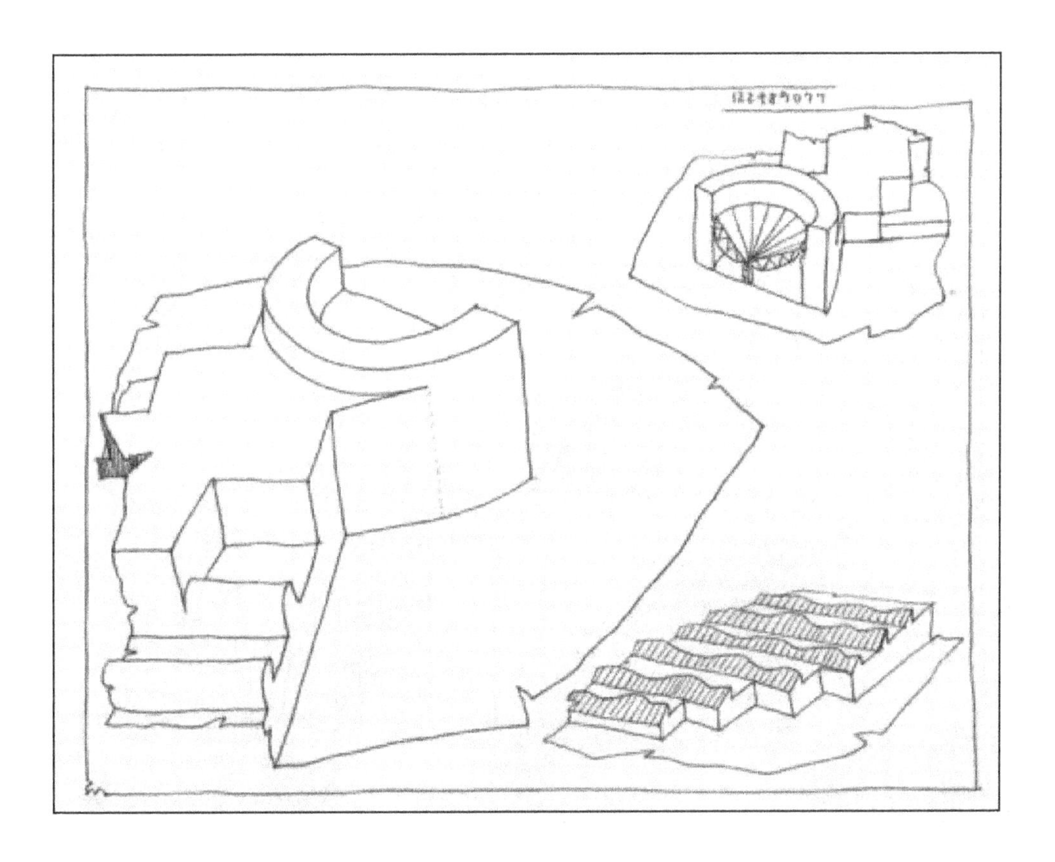

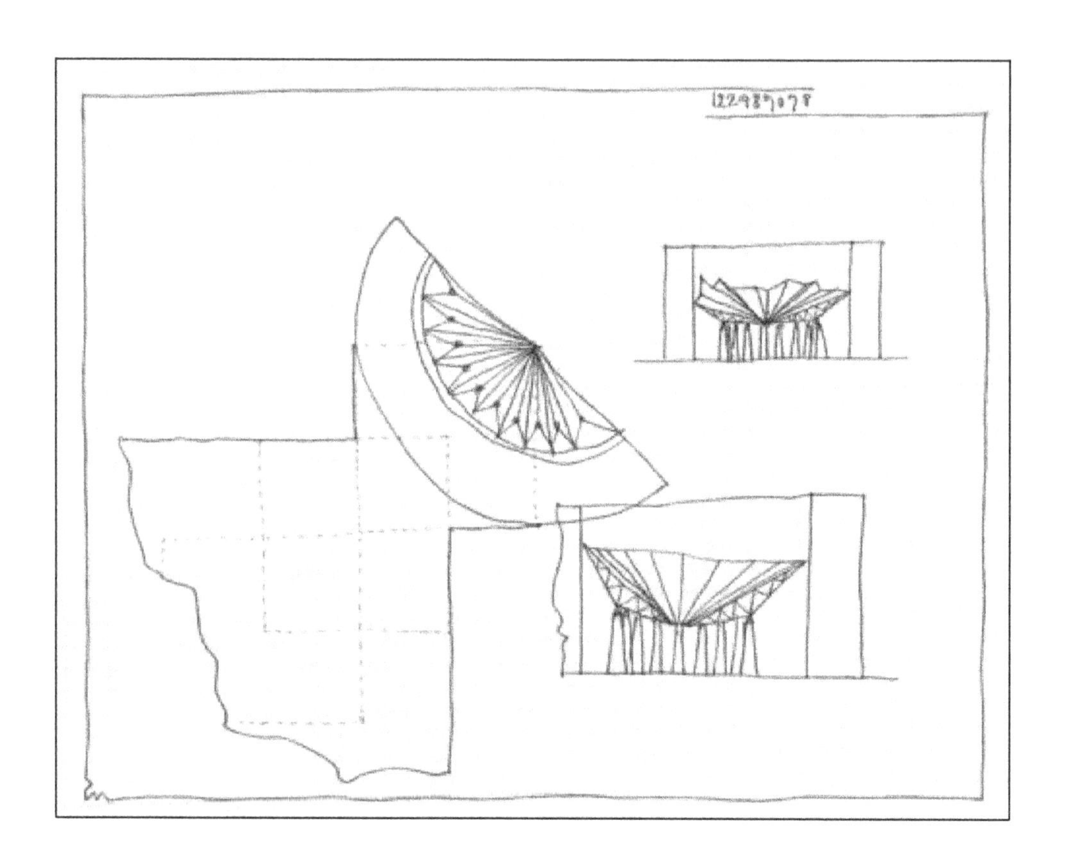

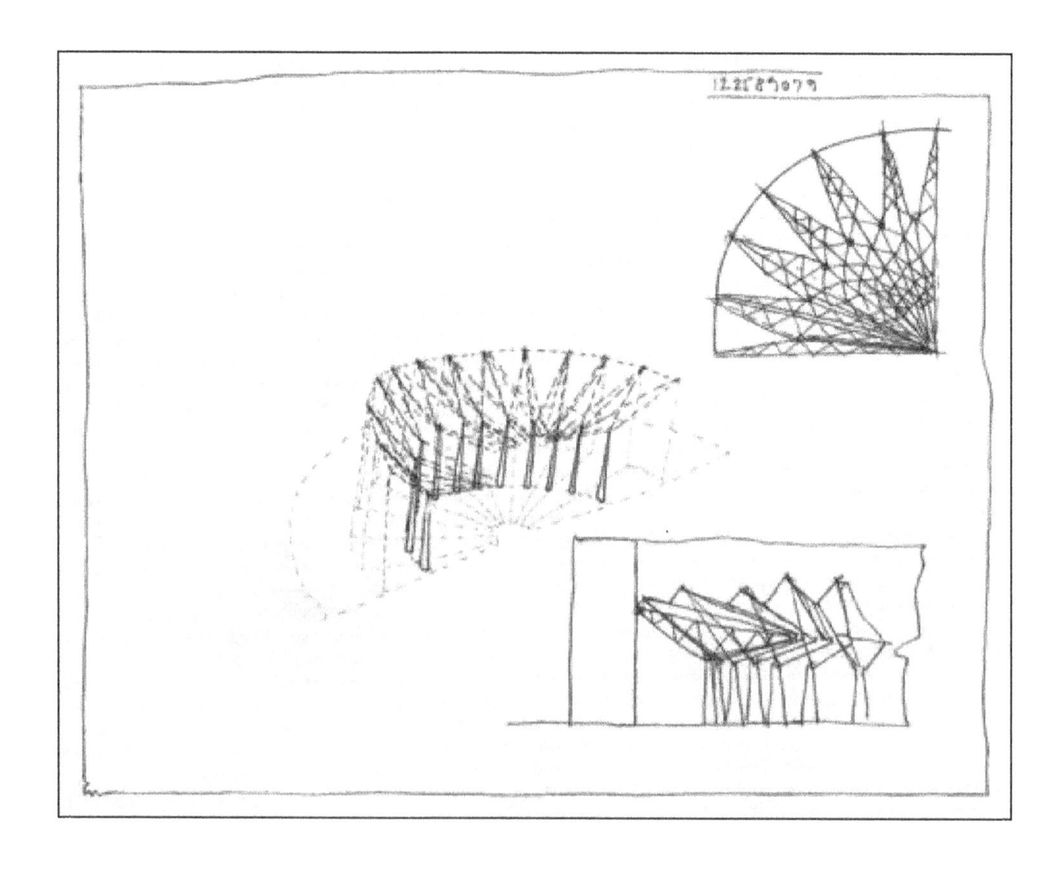

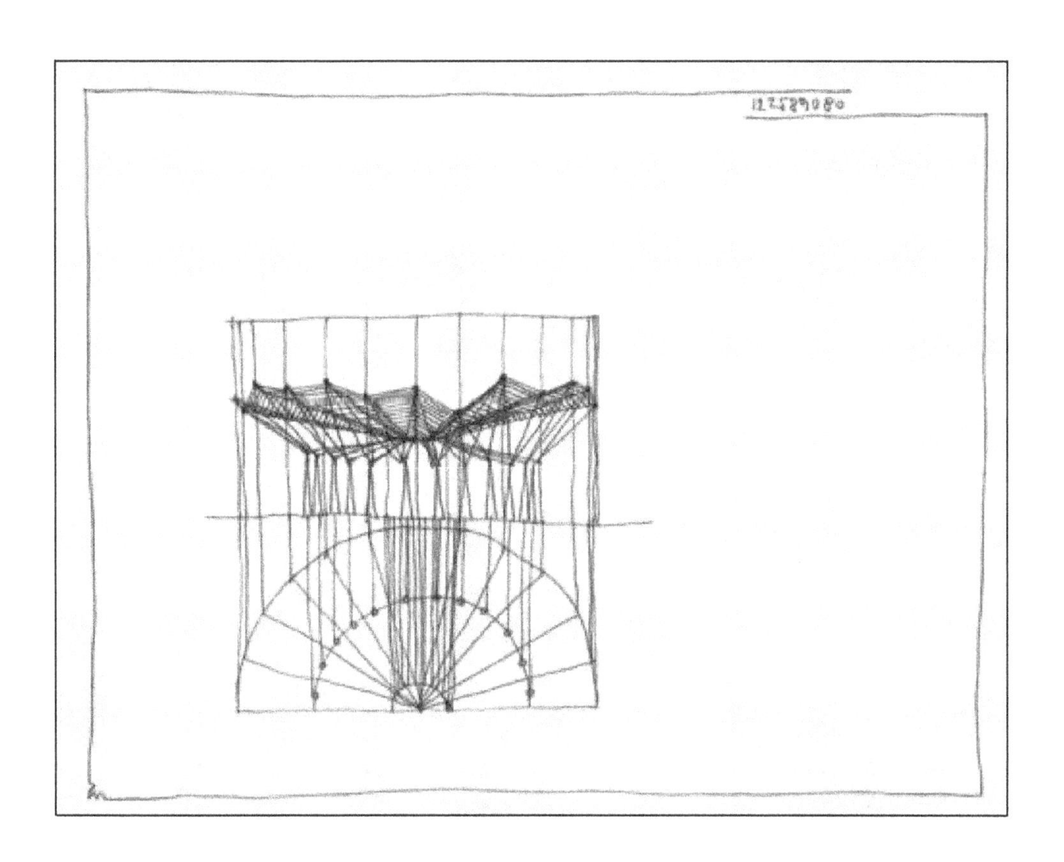
122589080

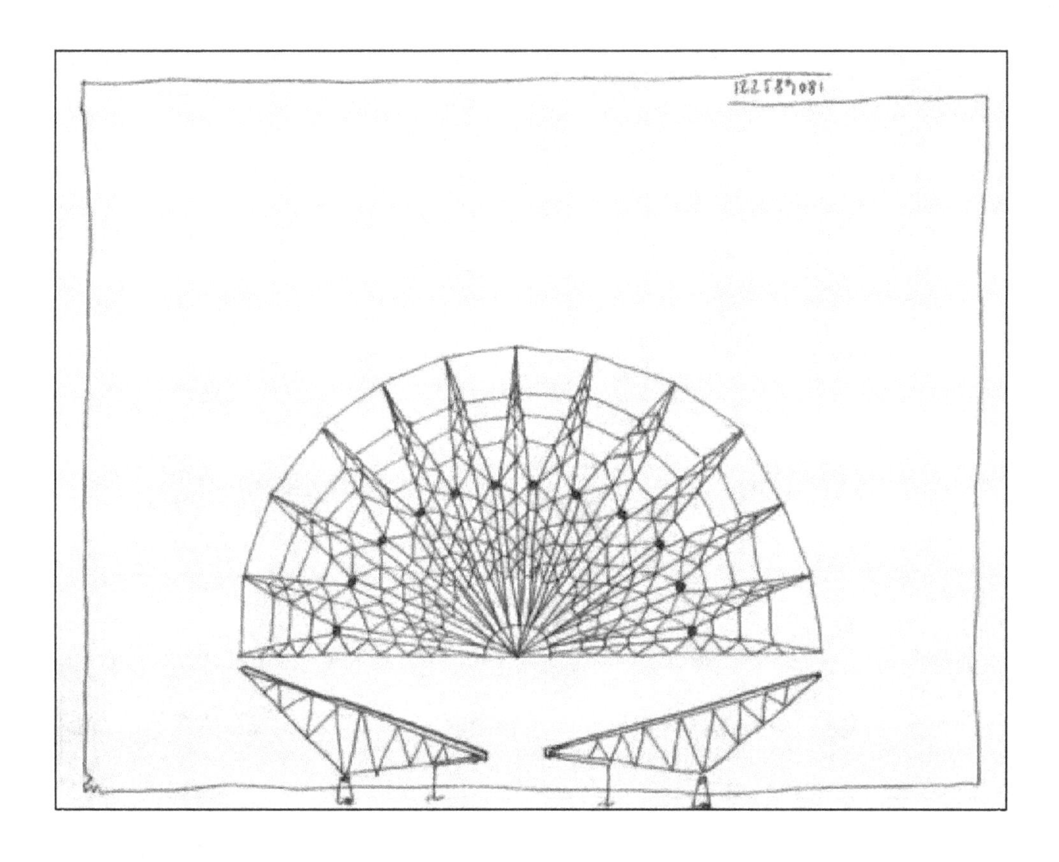
122589081

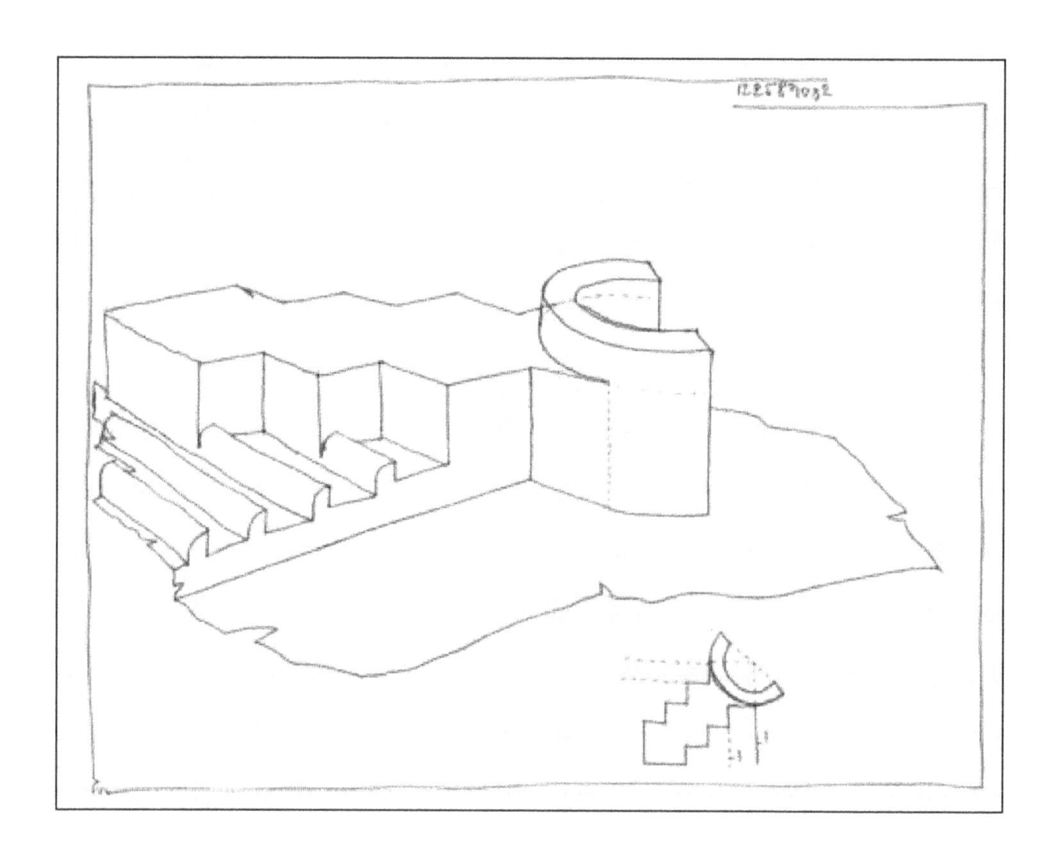

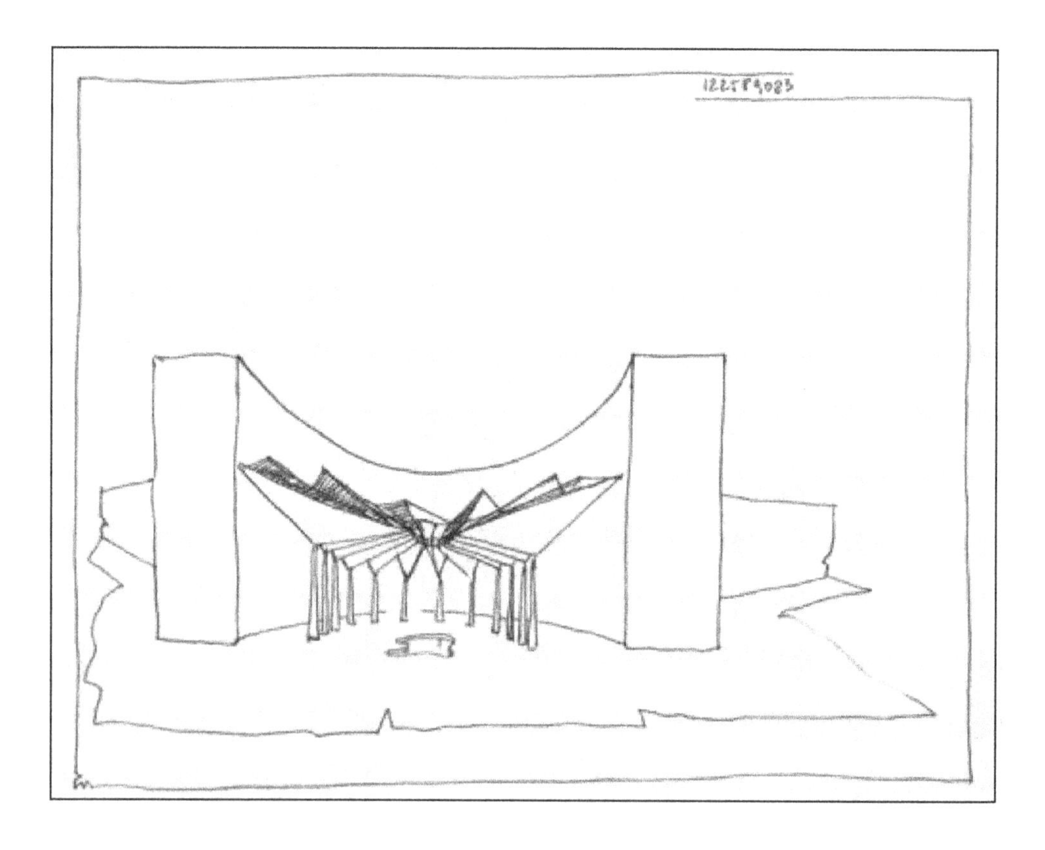

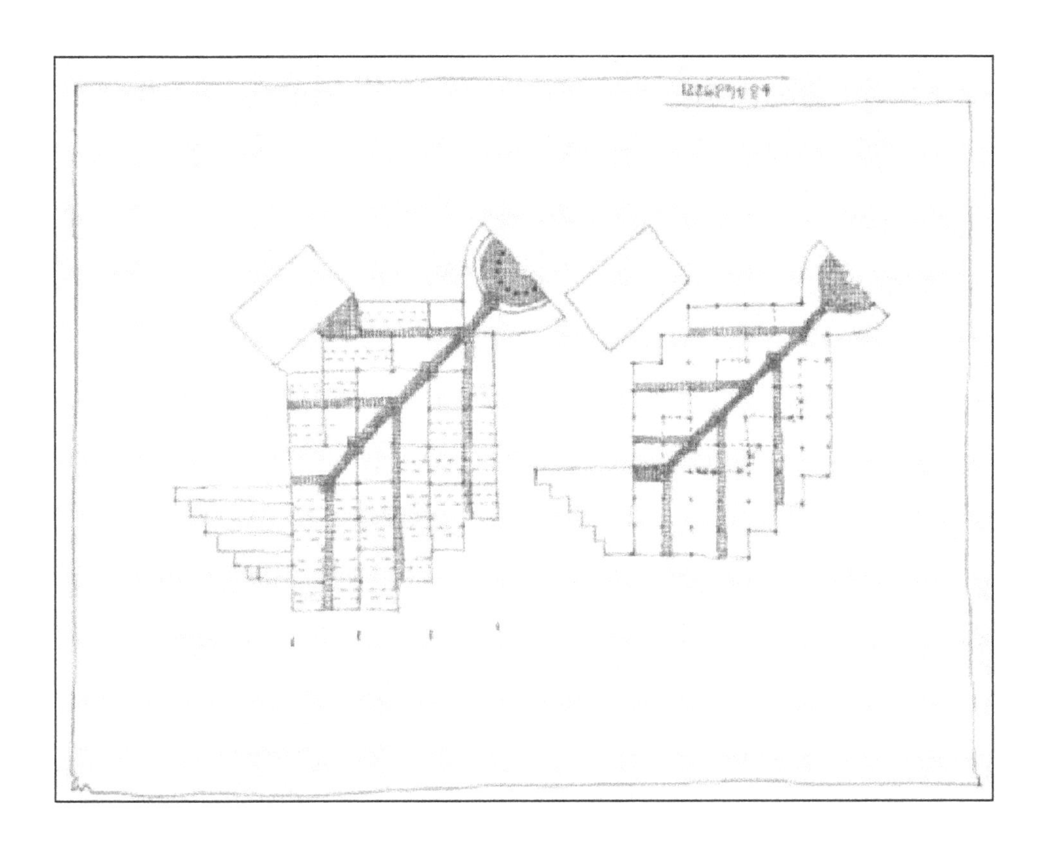

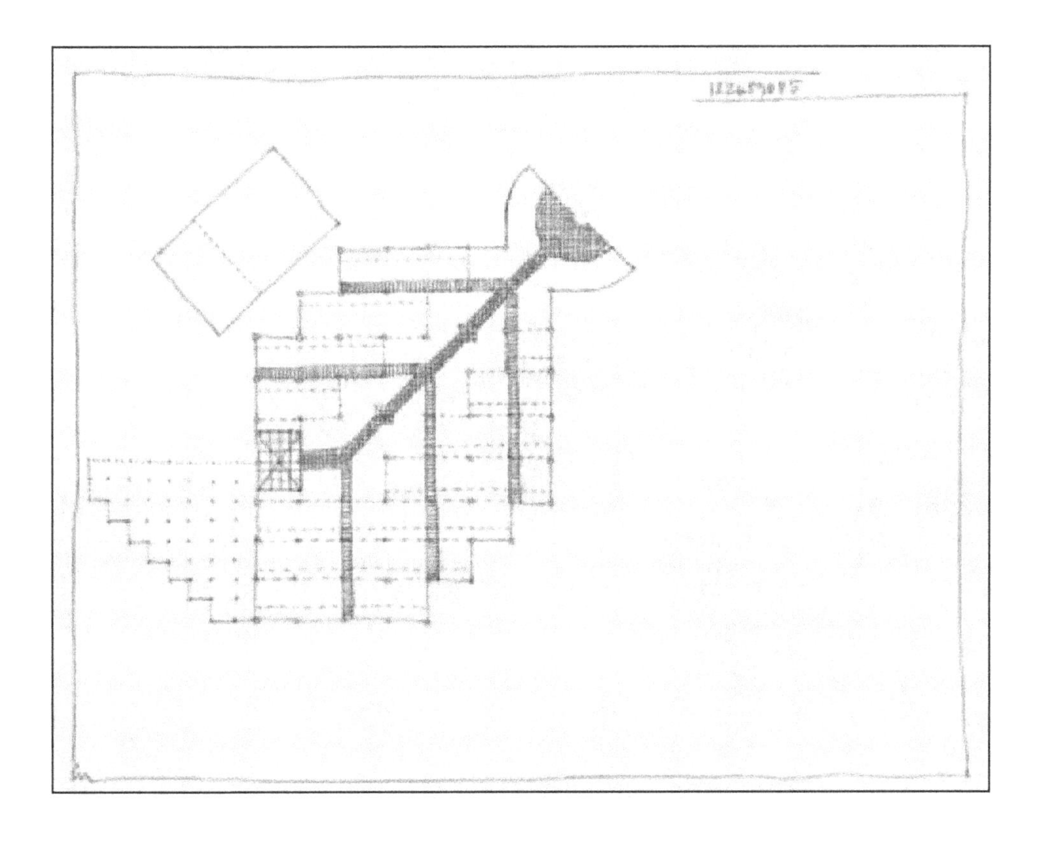

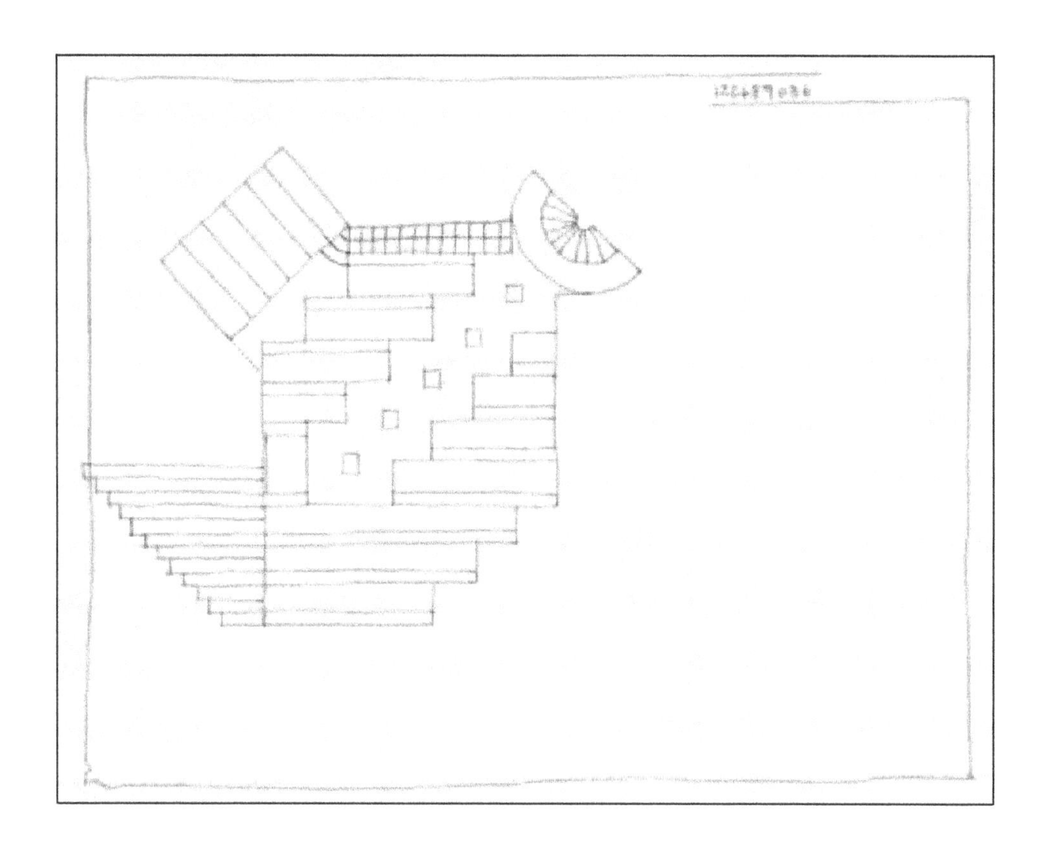

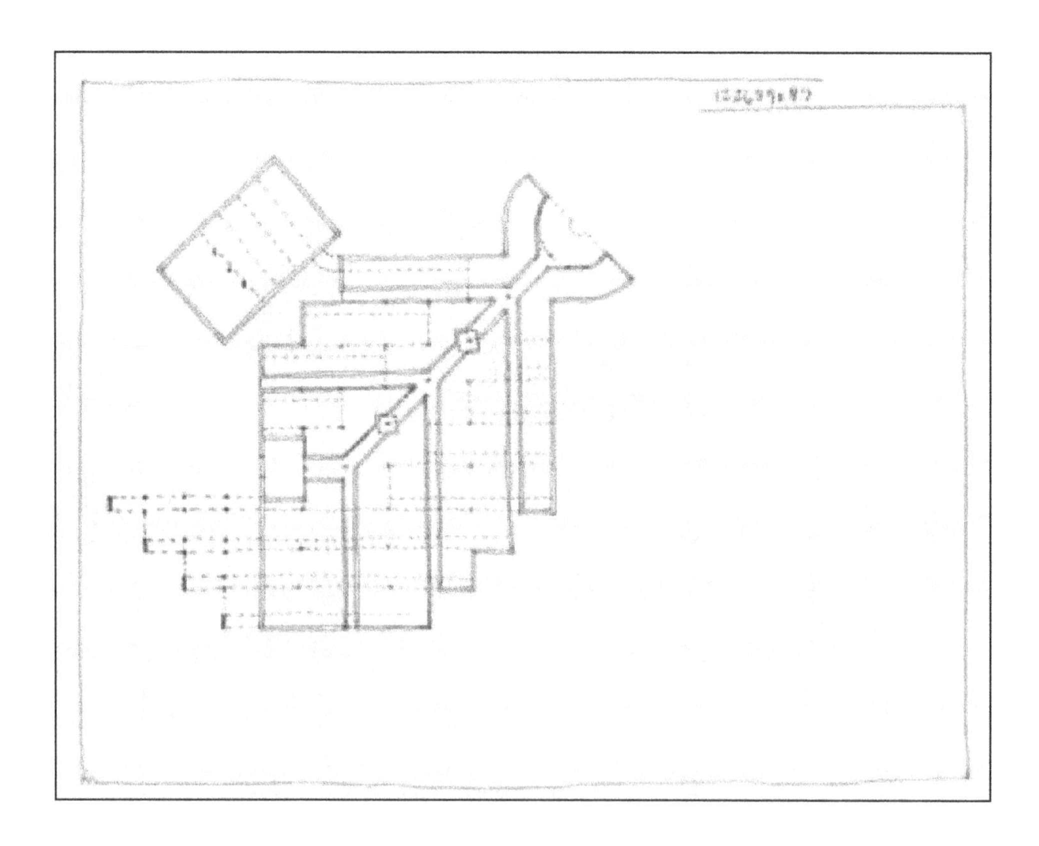

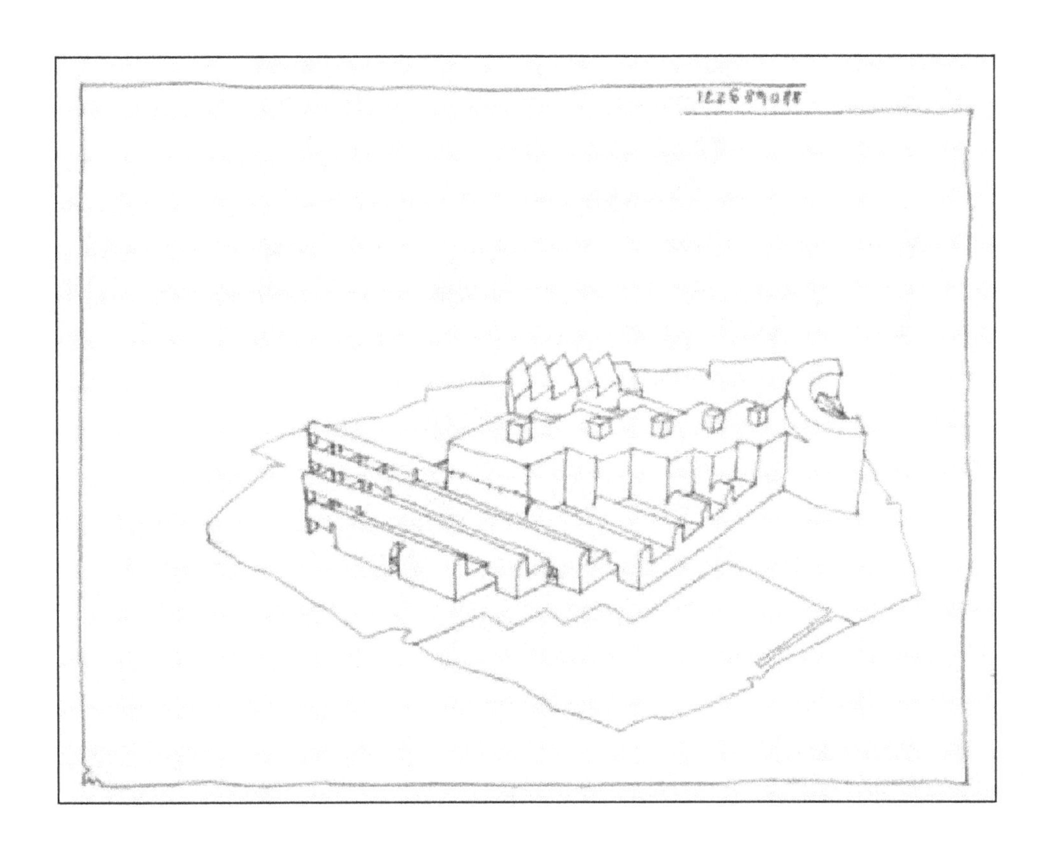

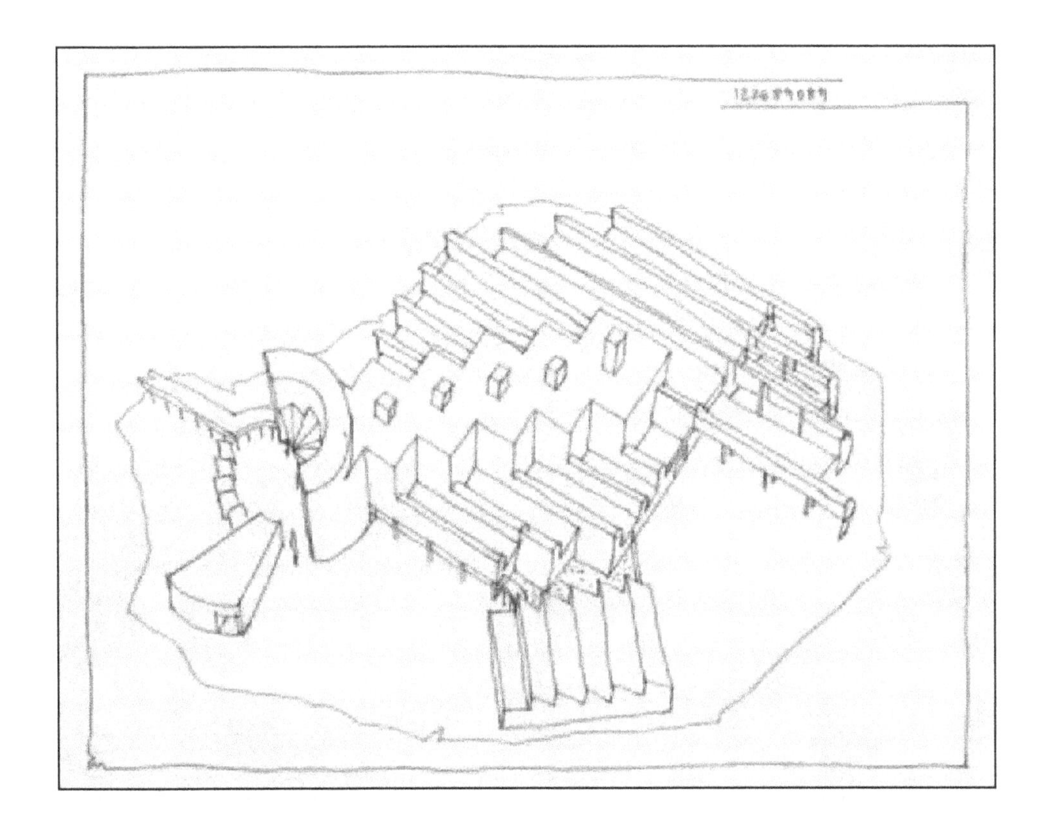

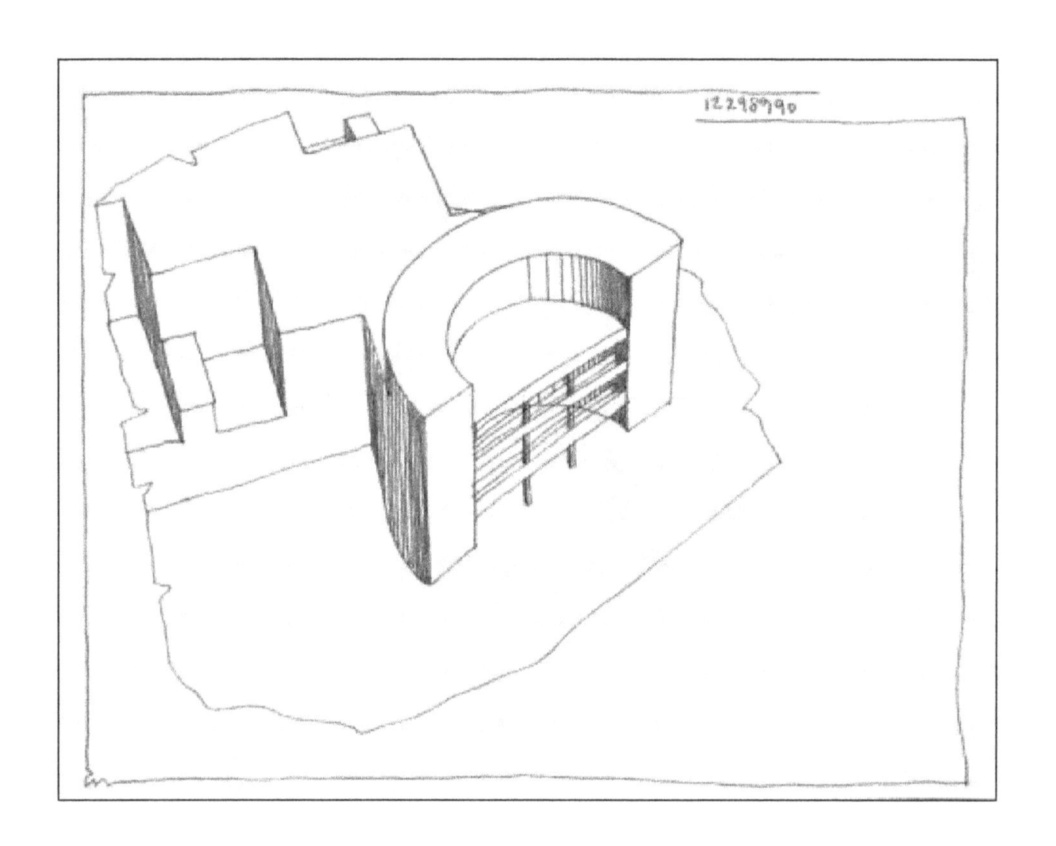
12298990

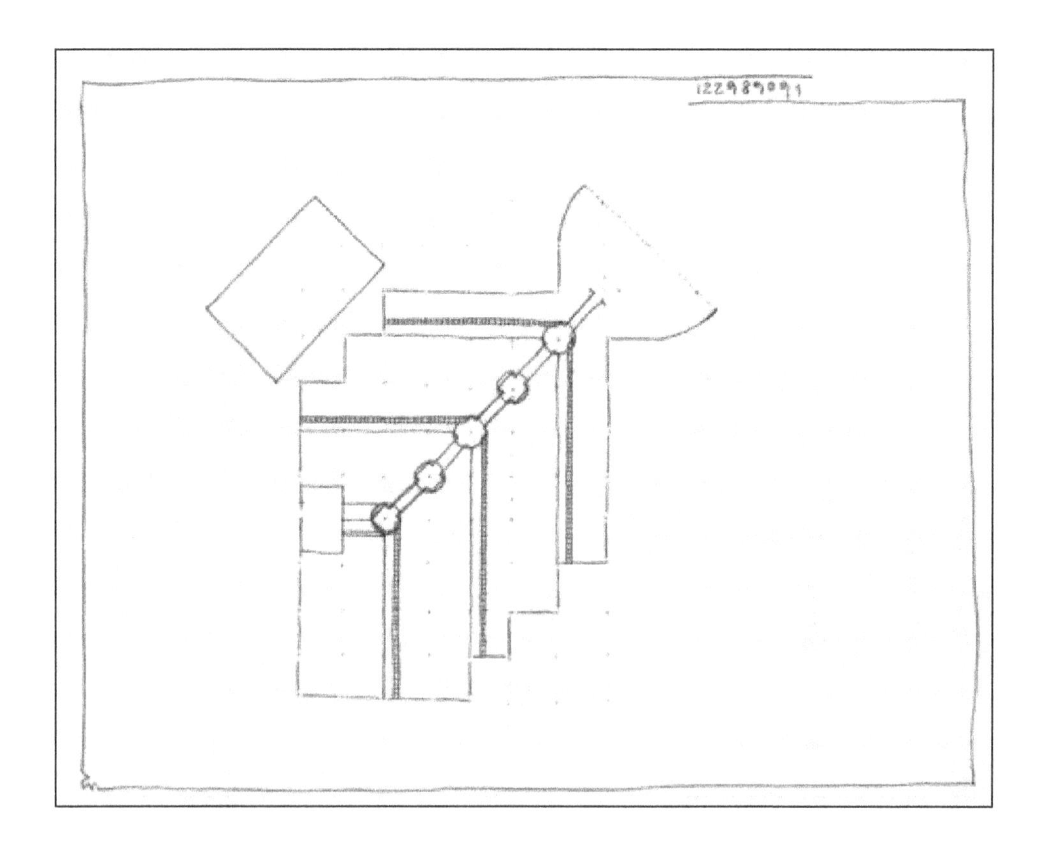
122989091

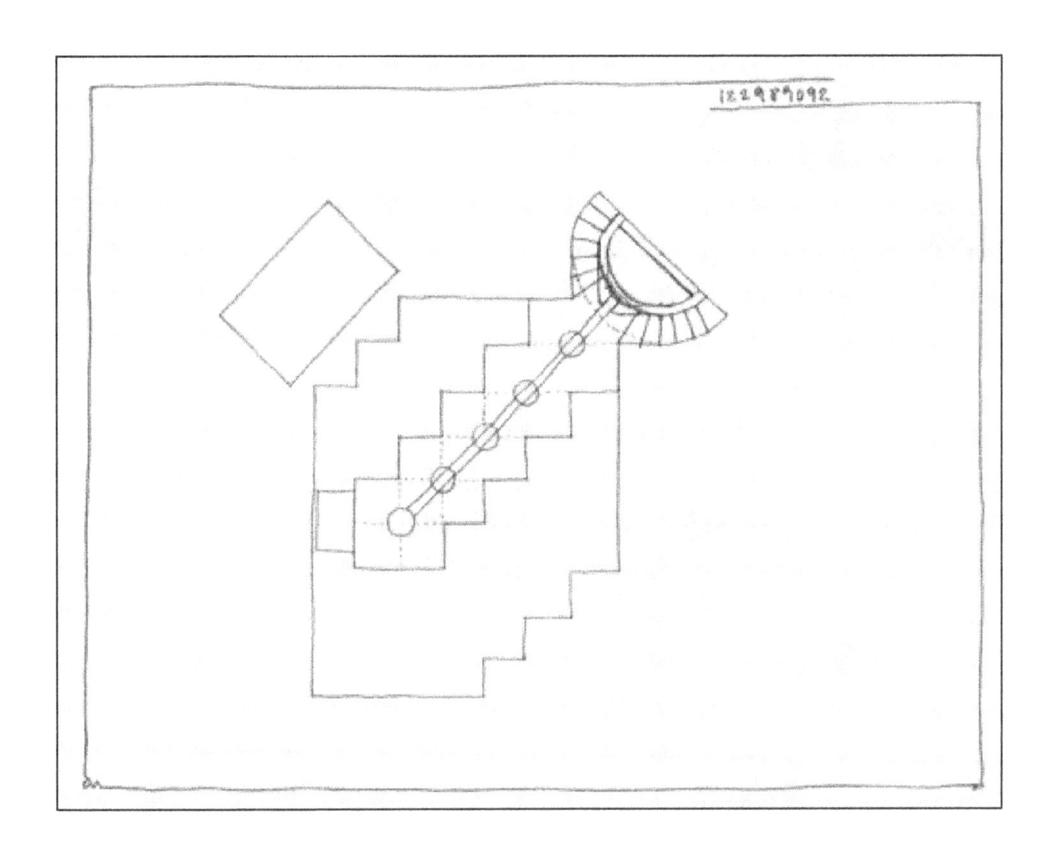
122987092

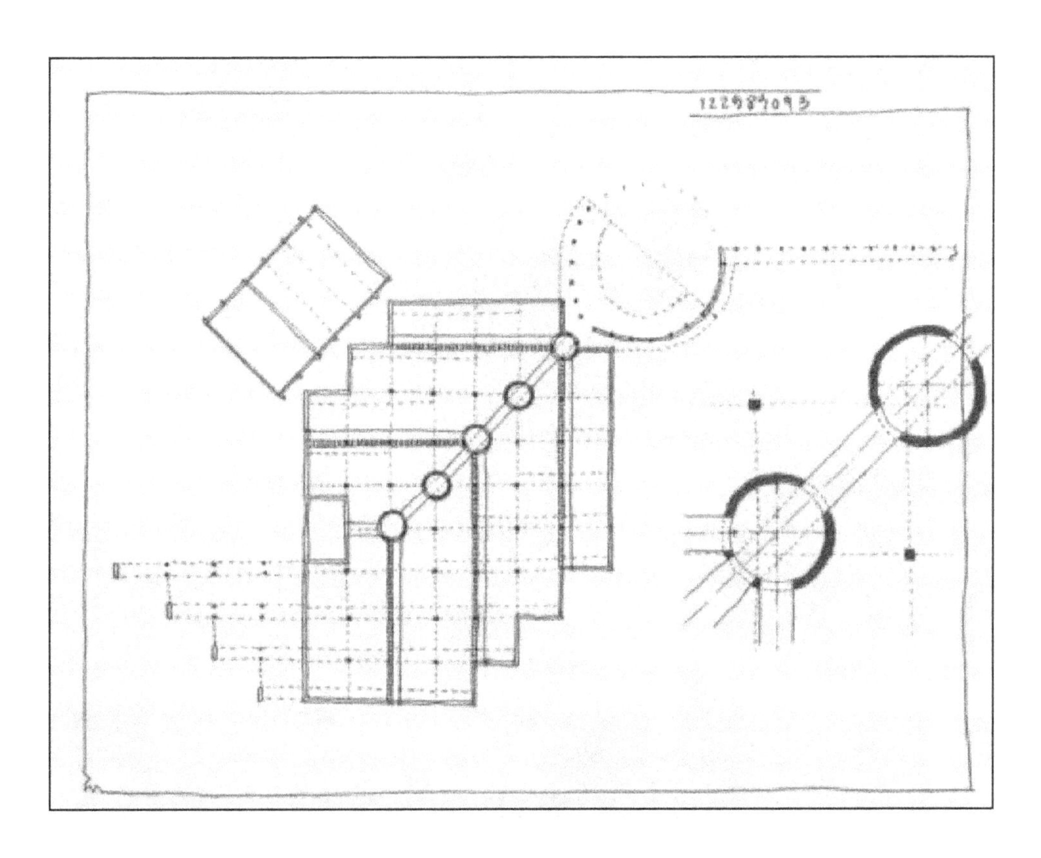
122987093

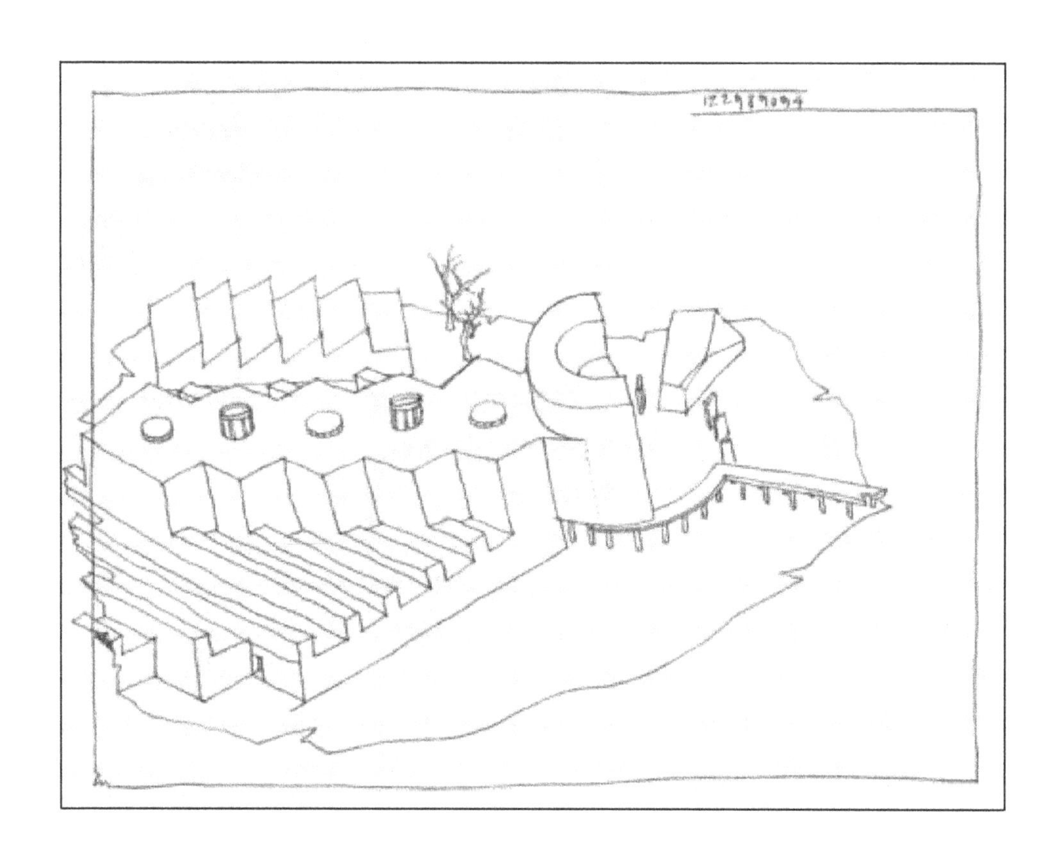
12.29.87094

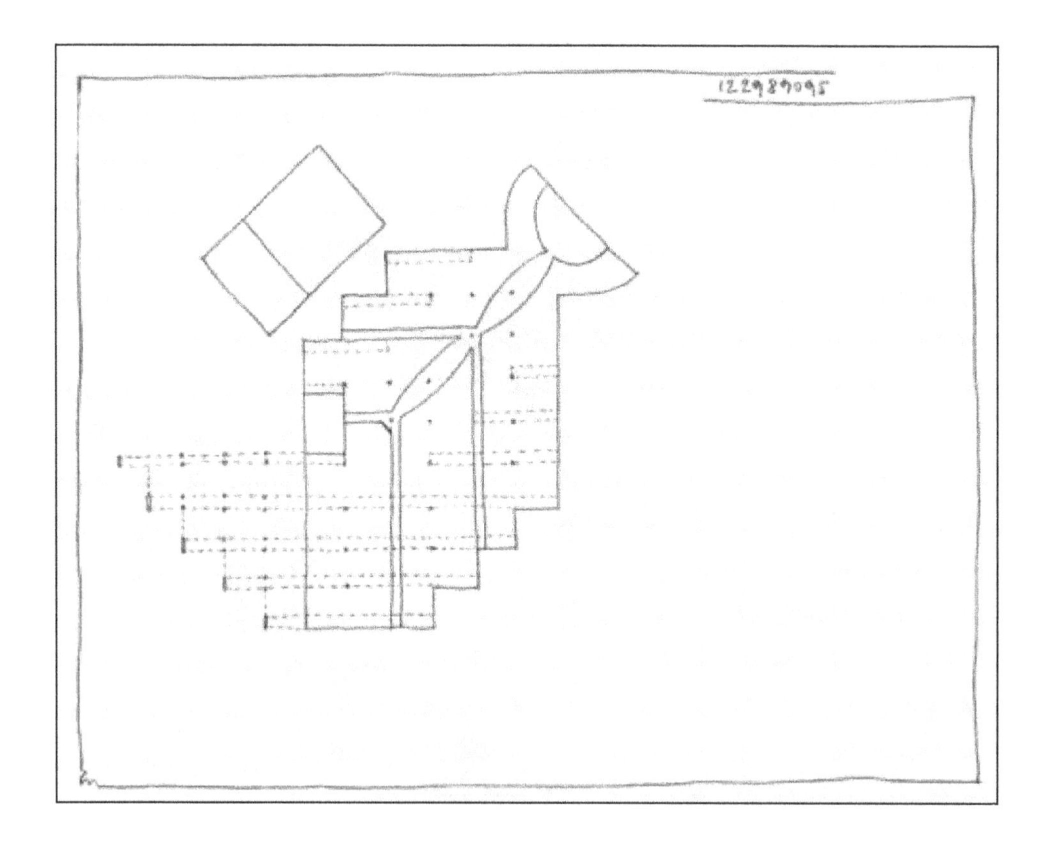
12.29.87095

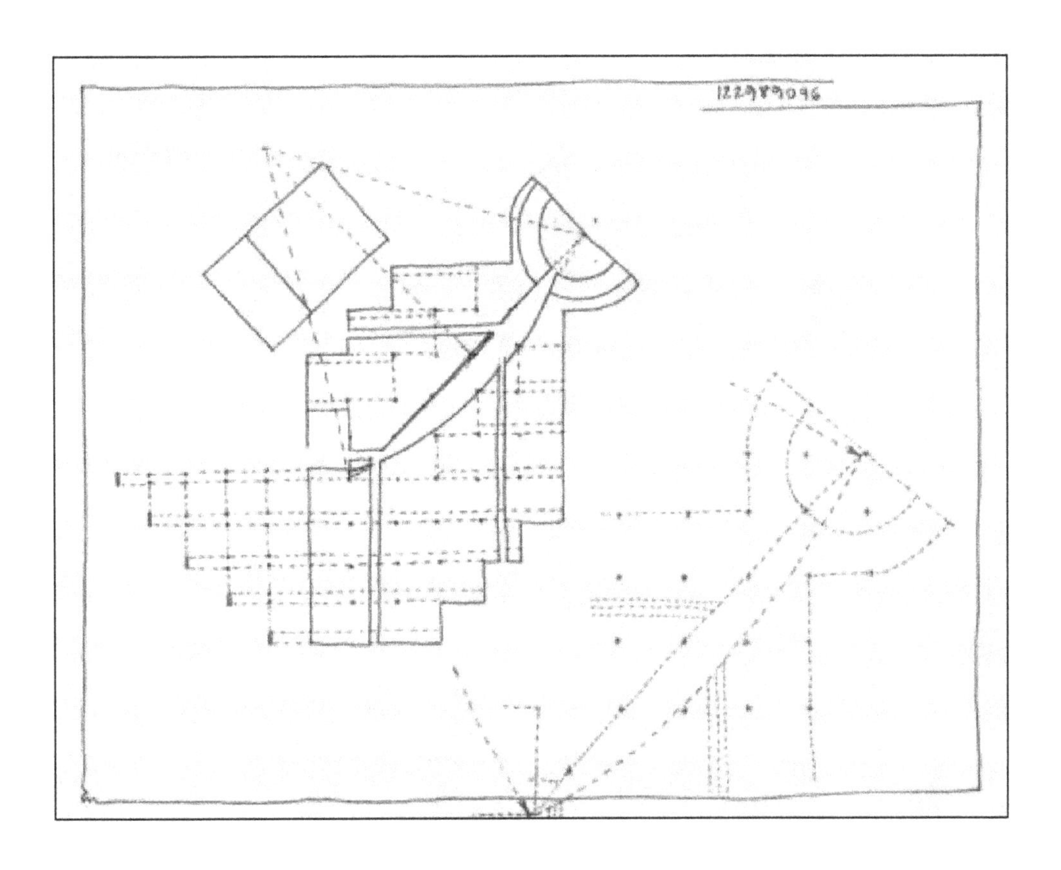
1229899096

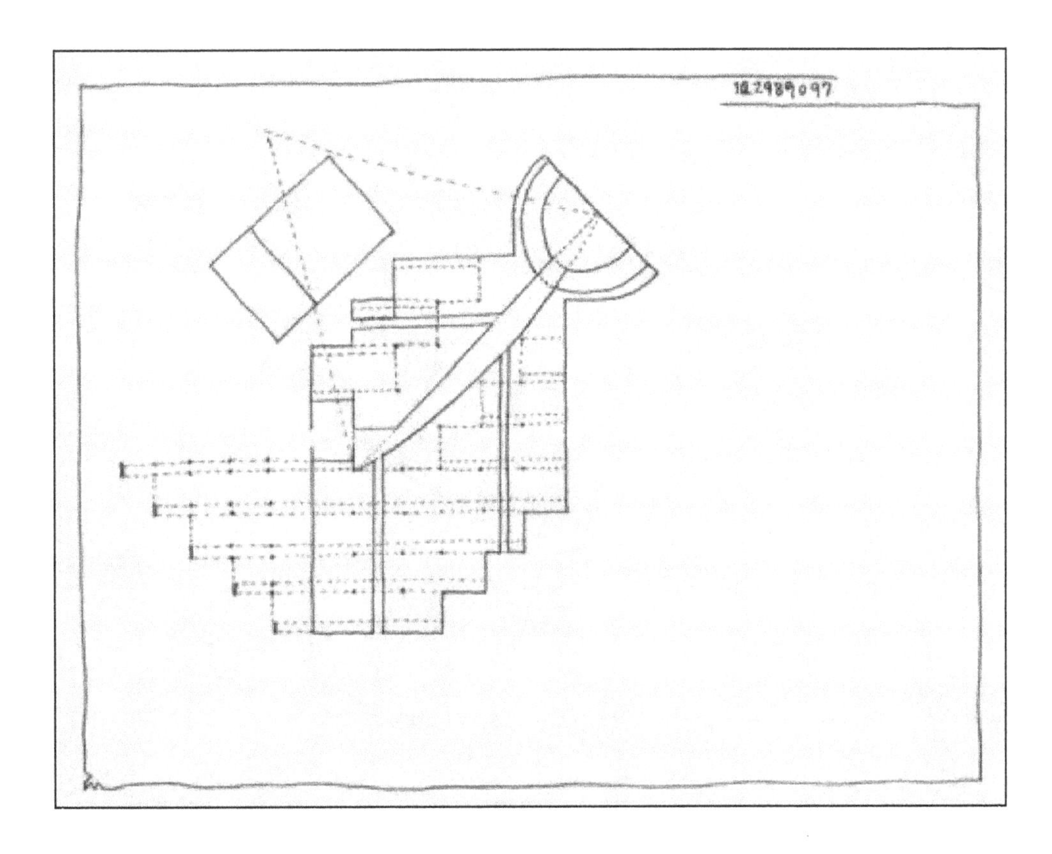
1229899097

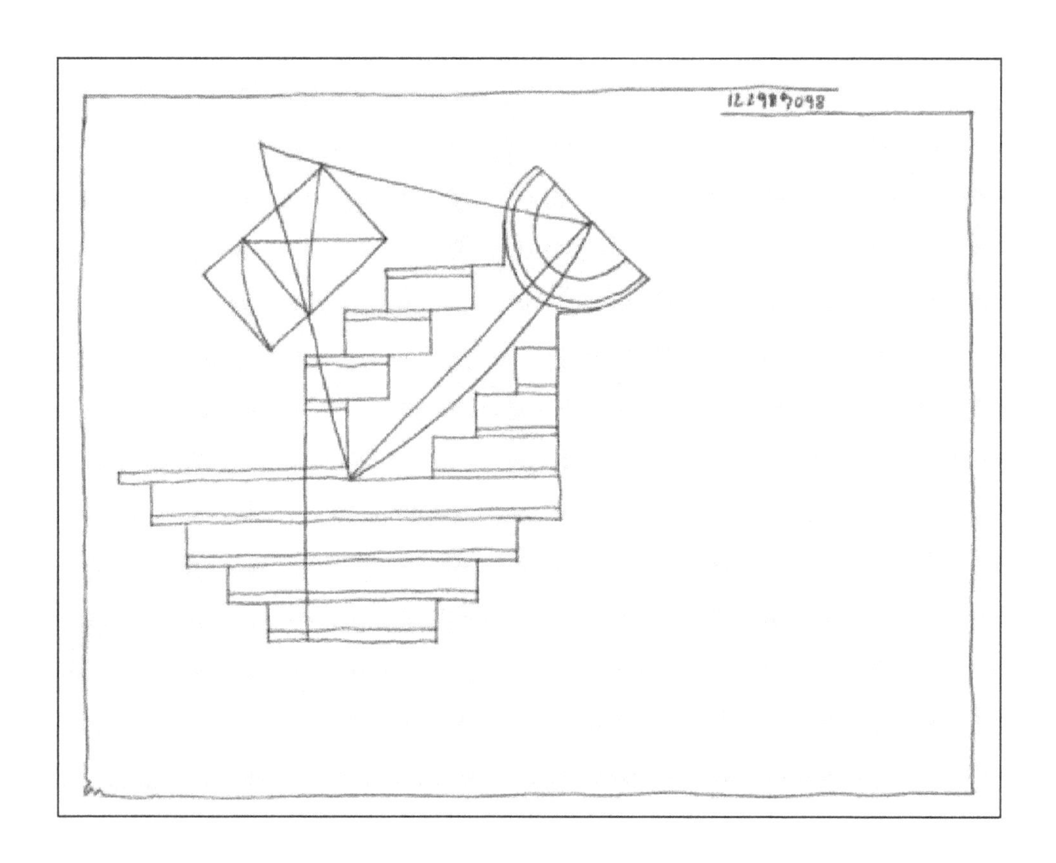
122989098

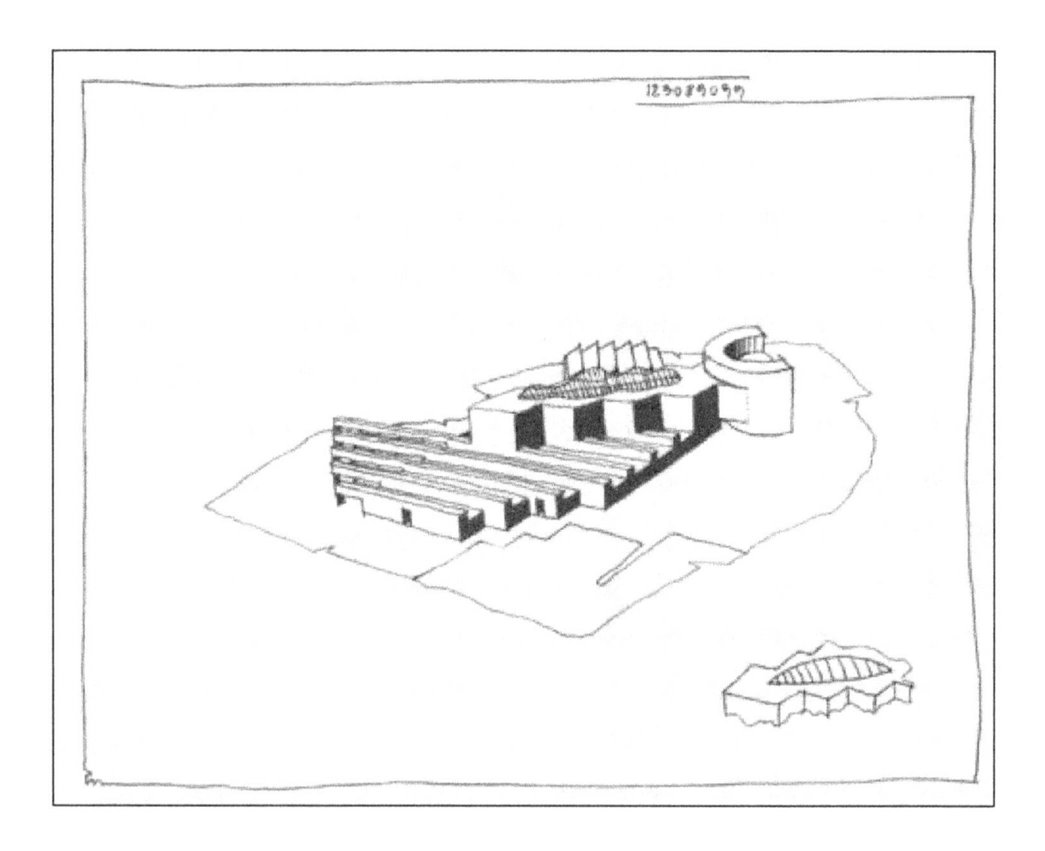
123089099

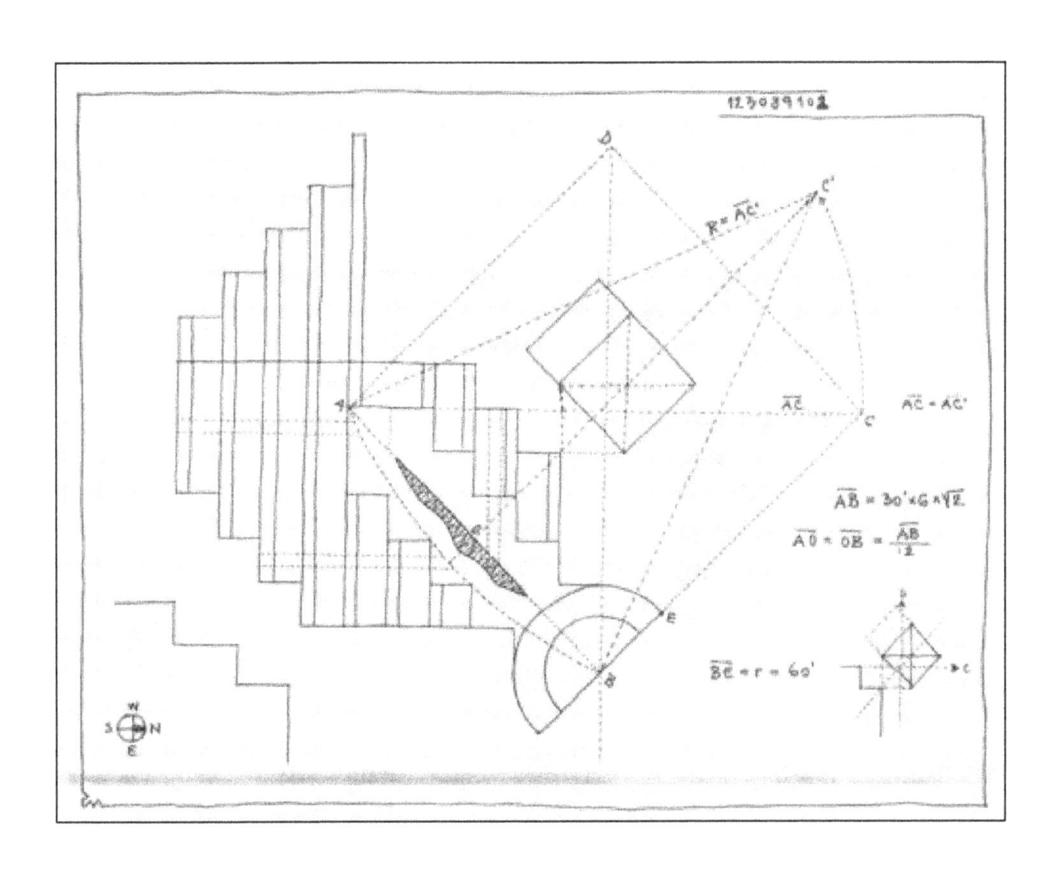

$\overline{AC} = \overline{AC'}$
$\overline{AB} = 30' \times 6 \times \sqrt{2}$
$\overline{BE} = r = 60'$

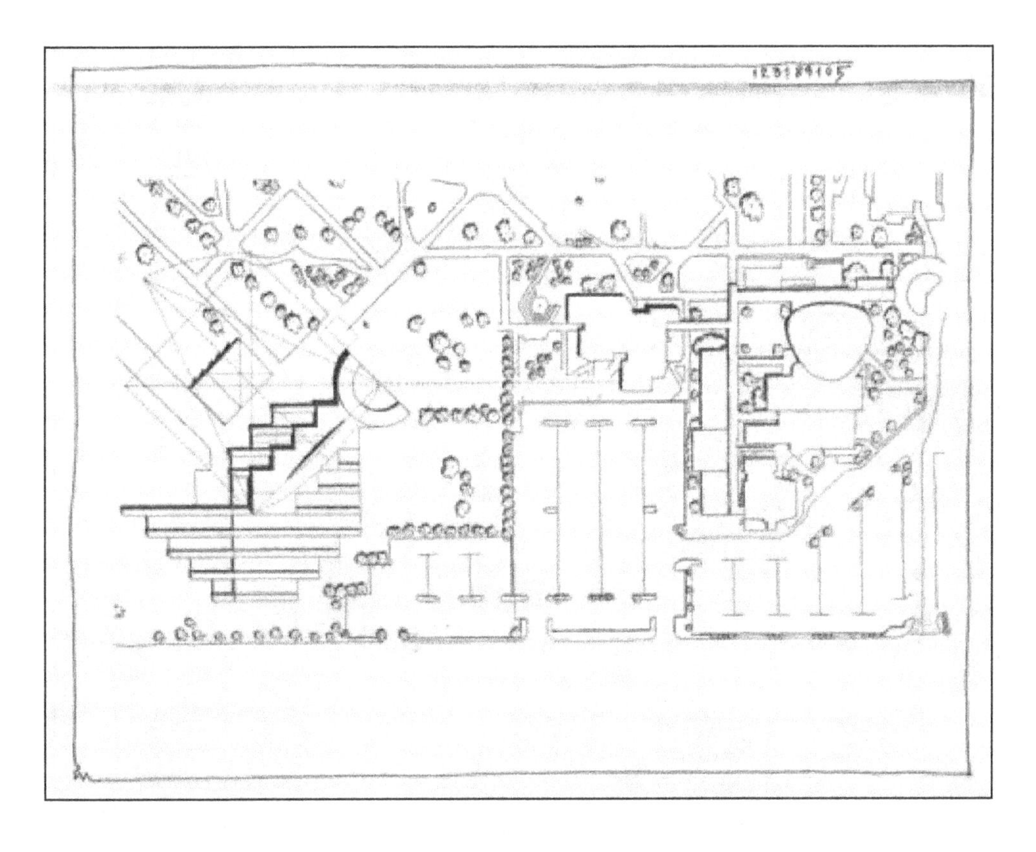

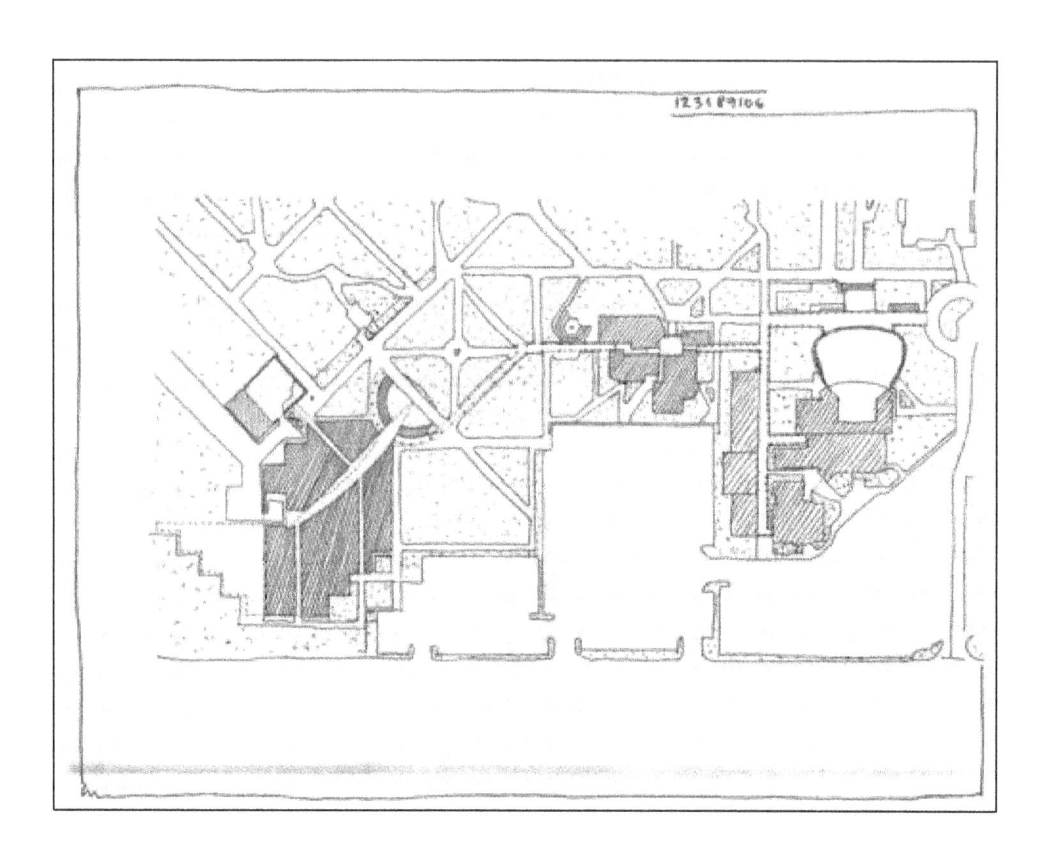
123189106

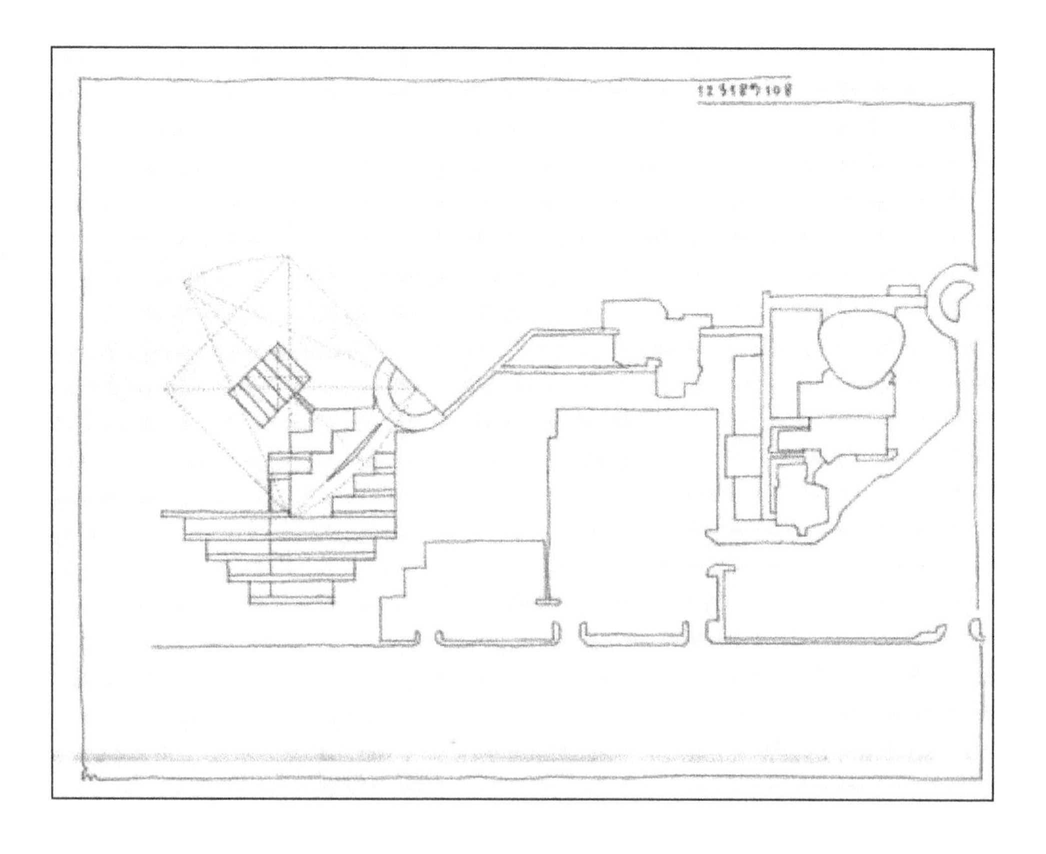
123189108

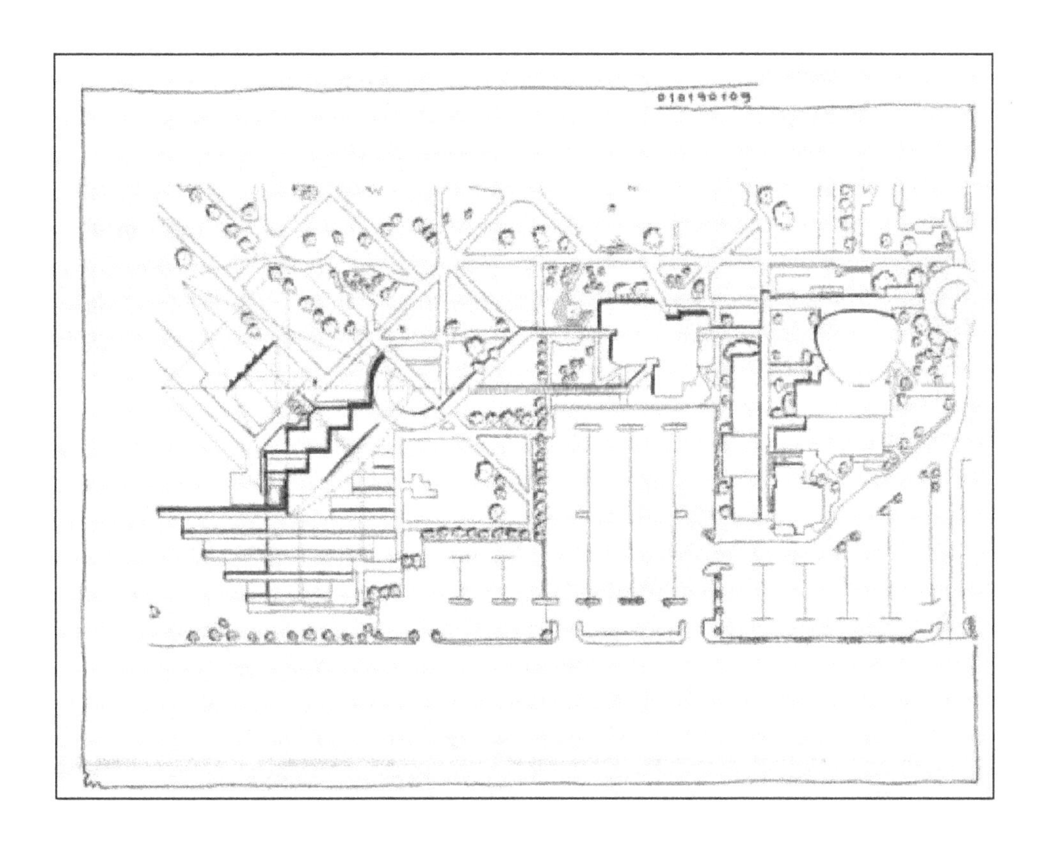
010190109

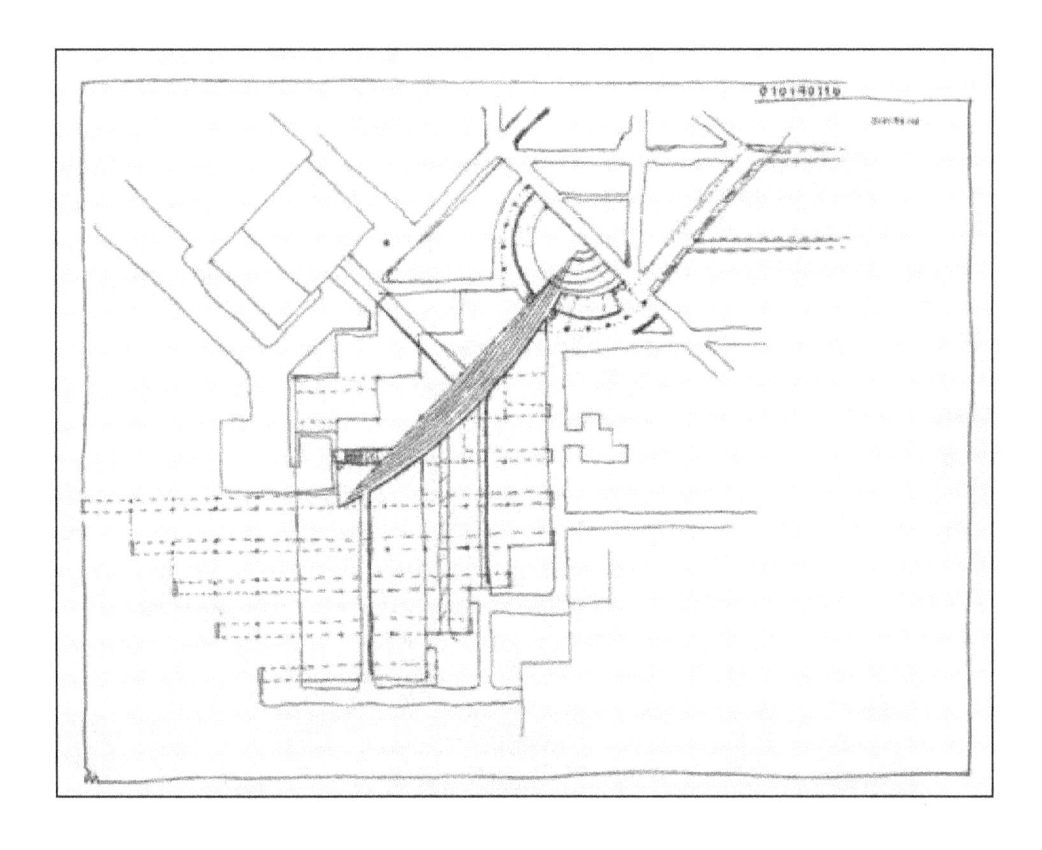

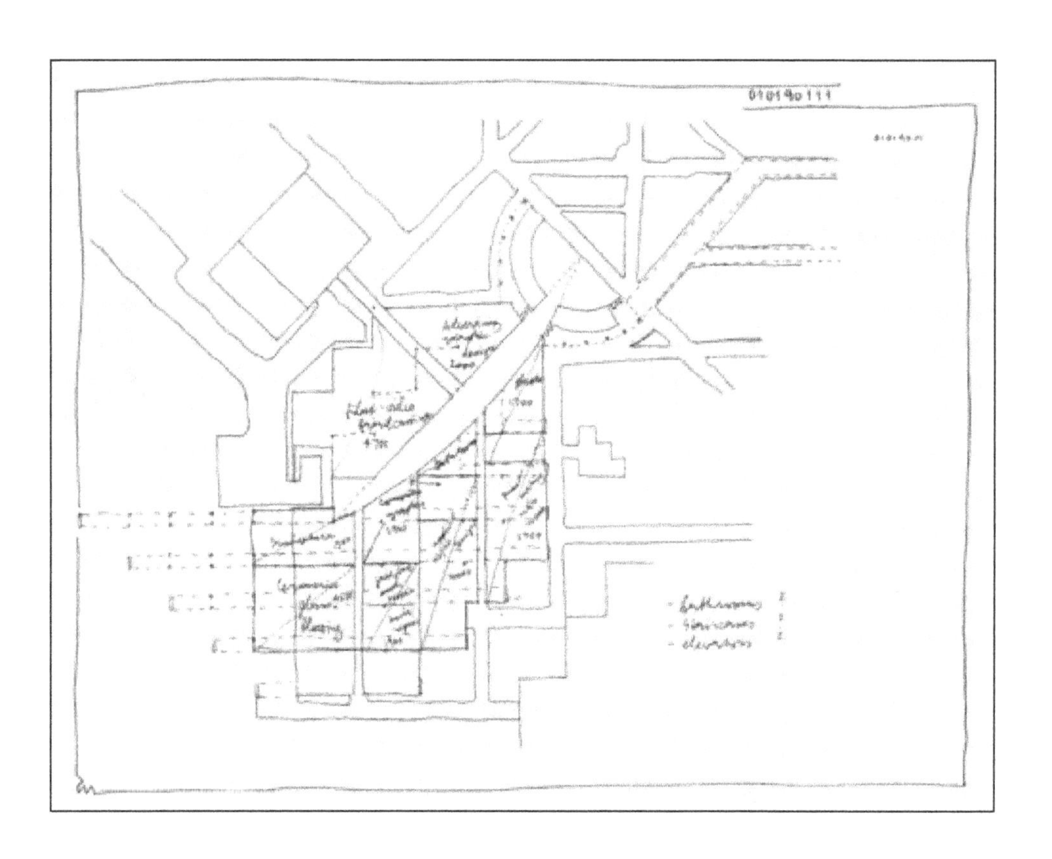
010190111
- bathrooms
- staircases
- elevators

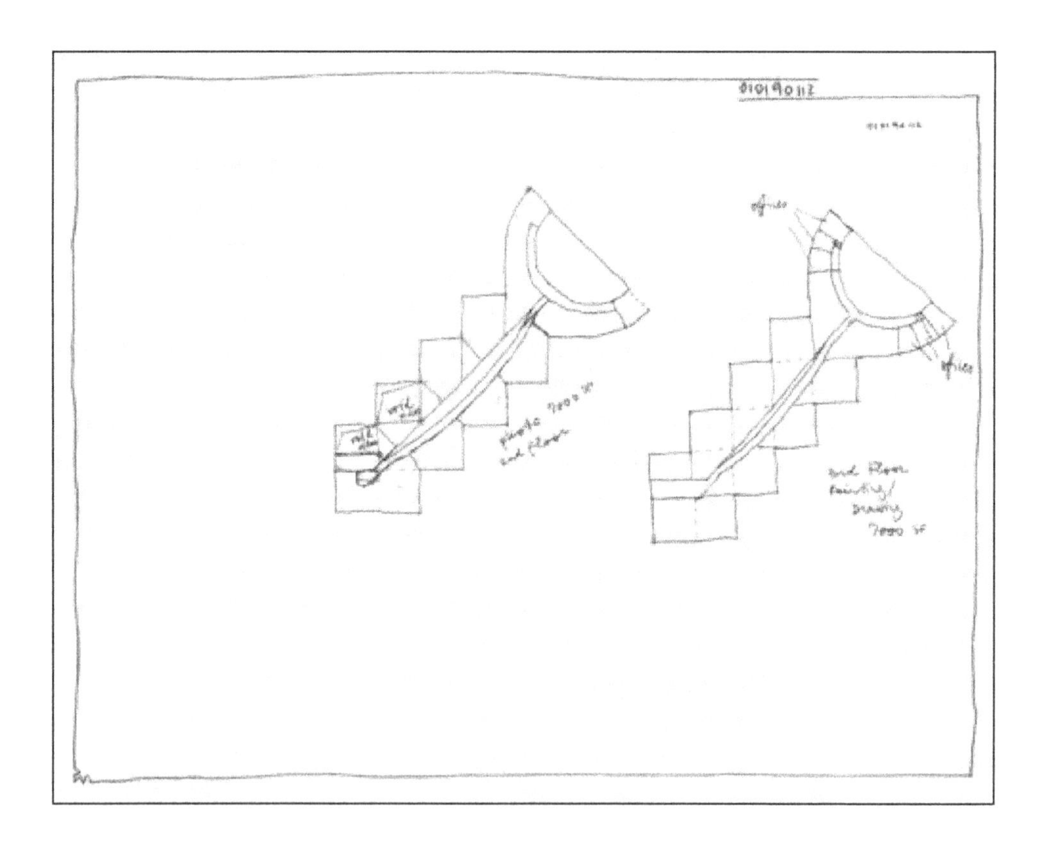
010190112
offices
offices
2nd floor
painting/
drawing
7000 sf

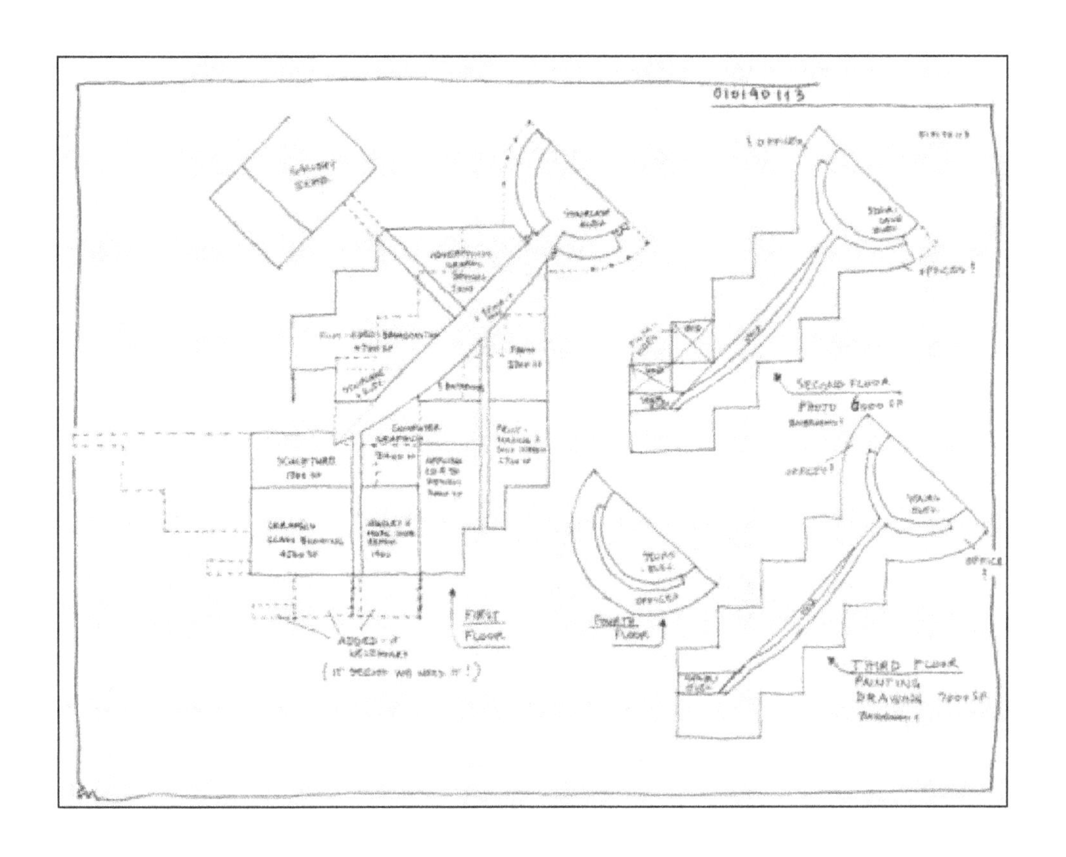
010190113
GALLERY
SCULPTURE
COMPUTER GRAPHICS
FIRST FLOOR
FOURTH FLOOR
SECOND FLOOR
OFFICE
THIRD FLOOR
PAINTING
DRAWING

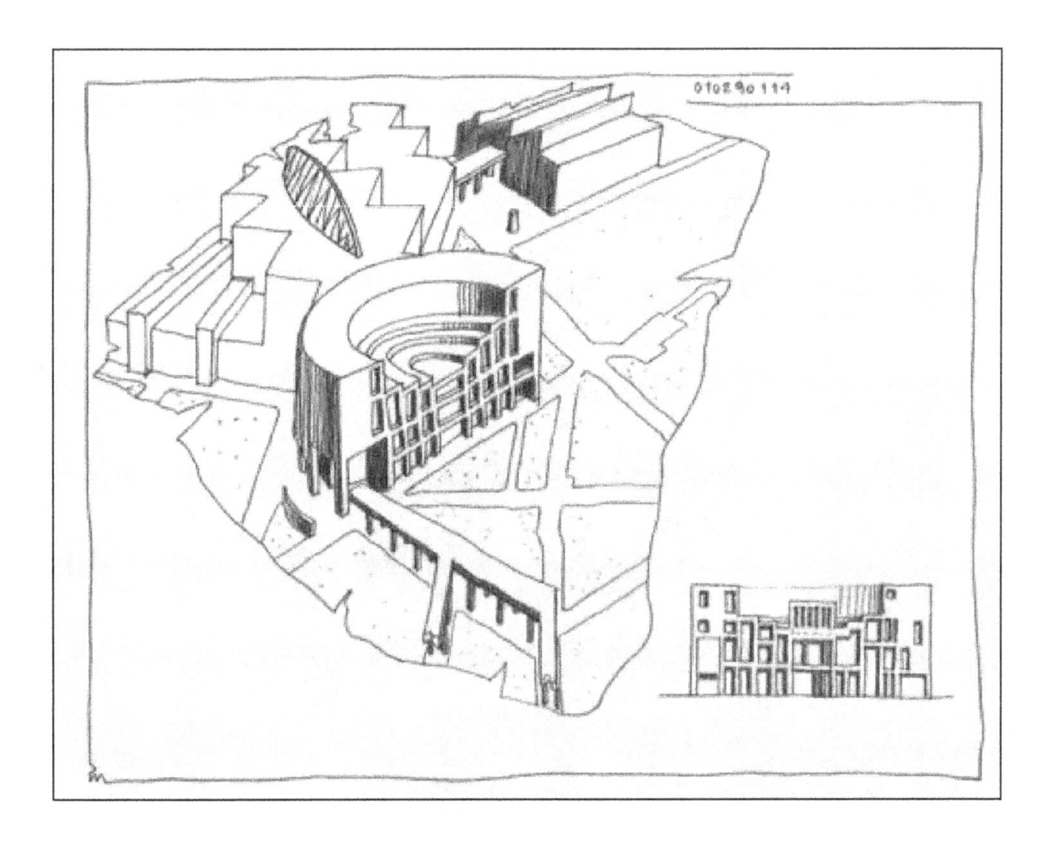
010890114

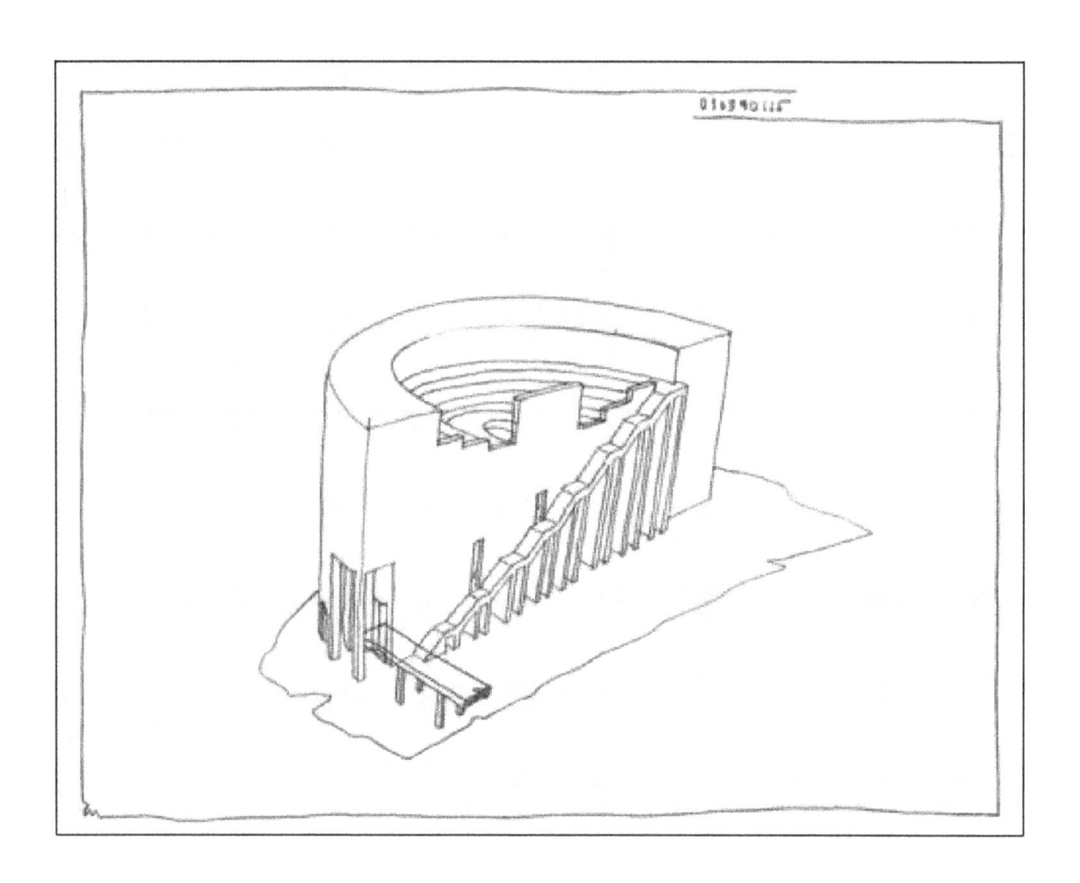

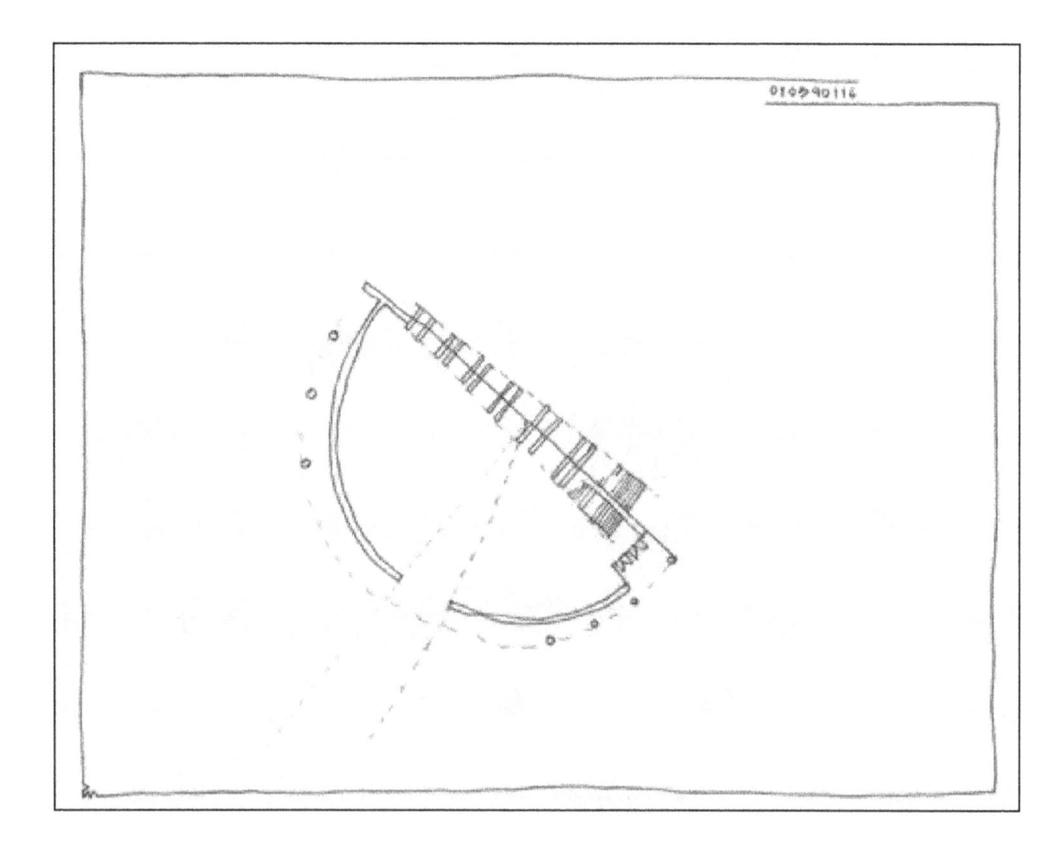

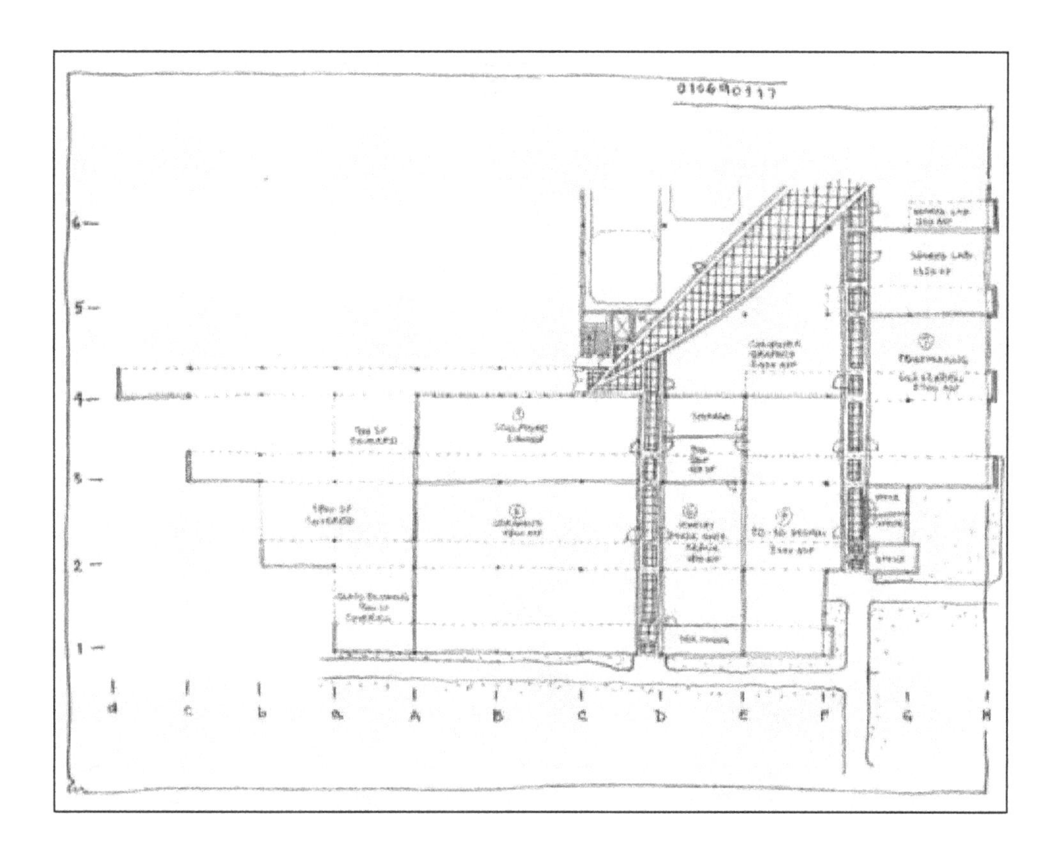

d
c
b
a
A
B
C
D
E
F
G
H

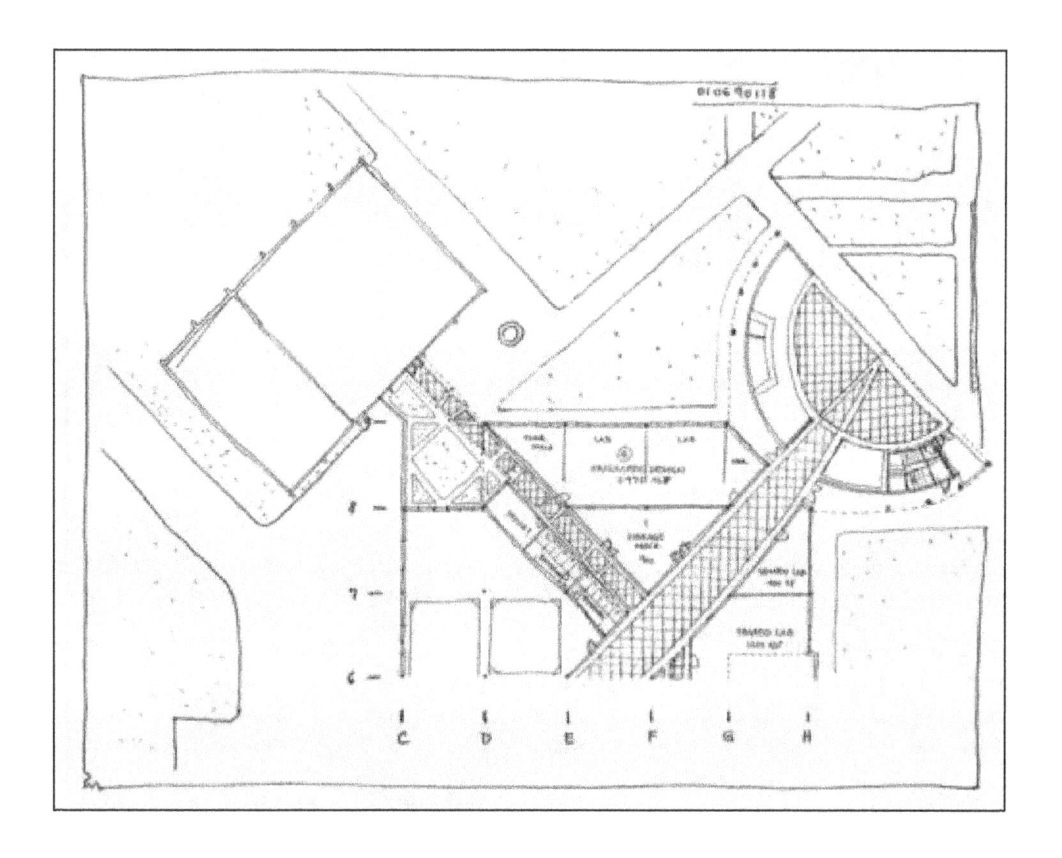

C
D
E
F
G
H

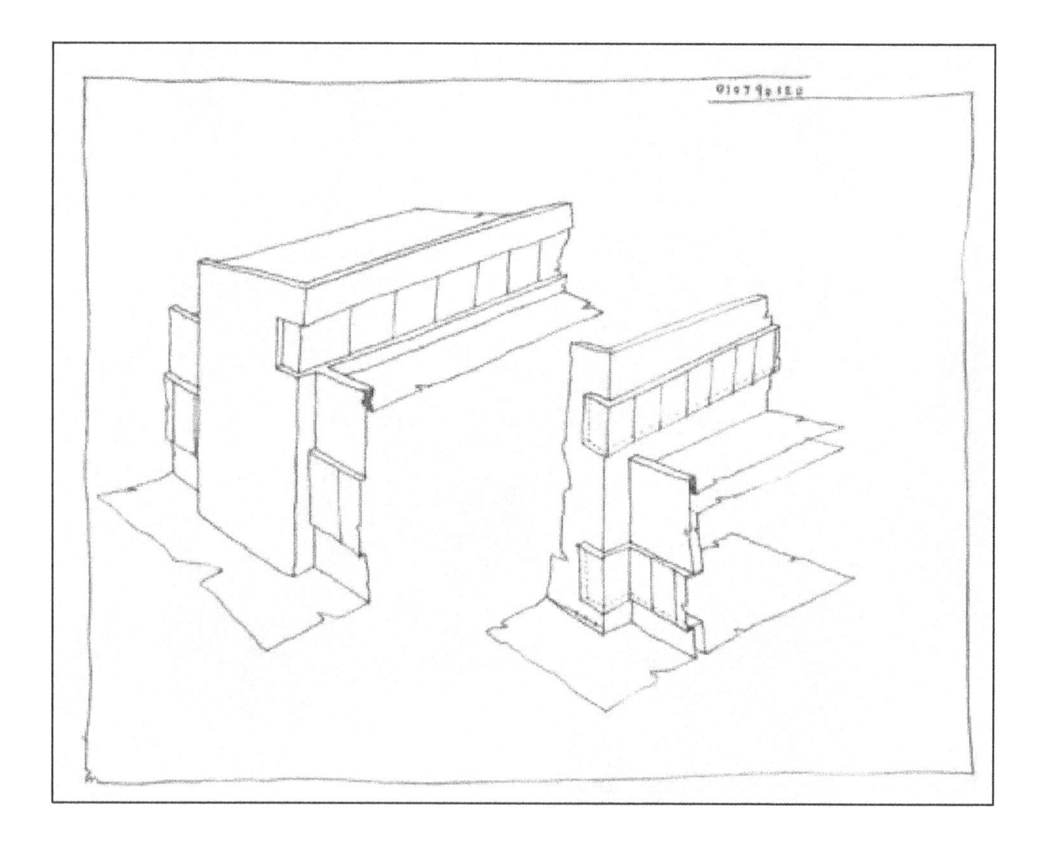

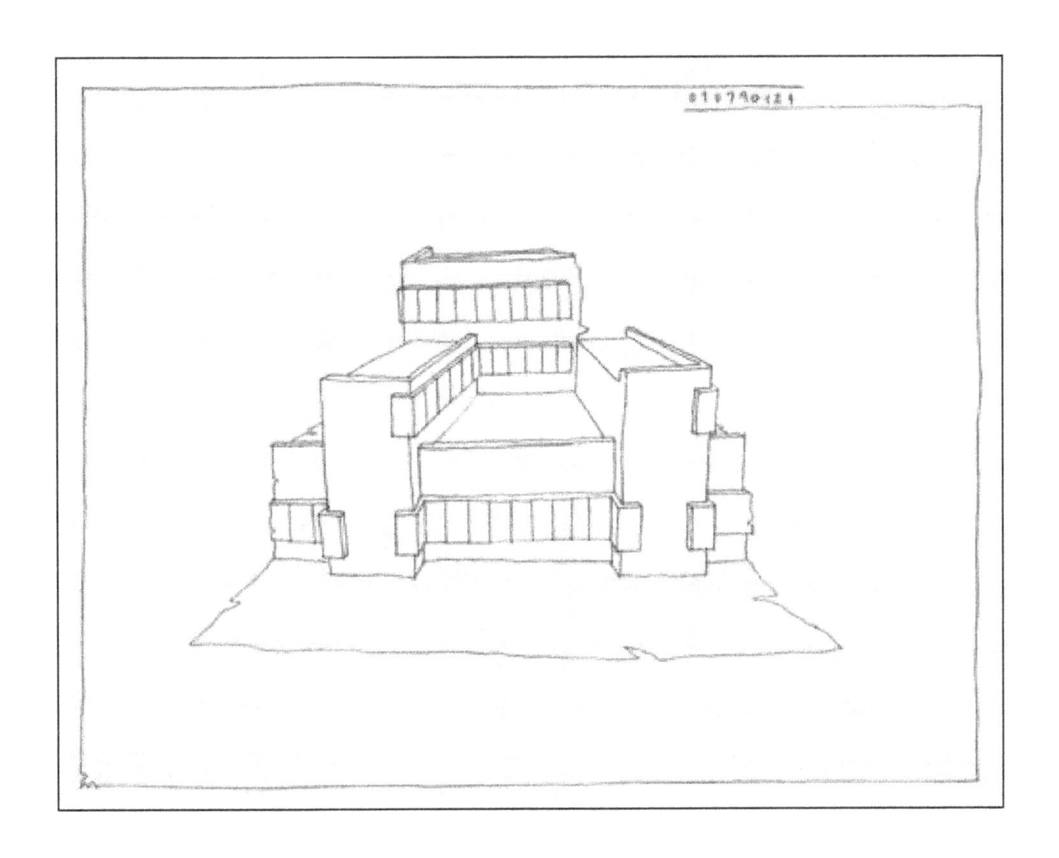
010790121

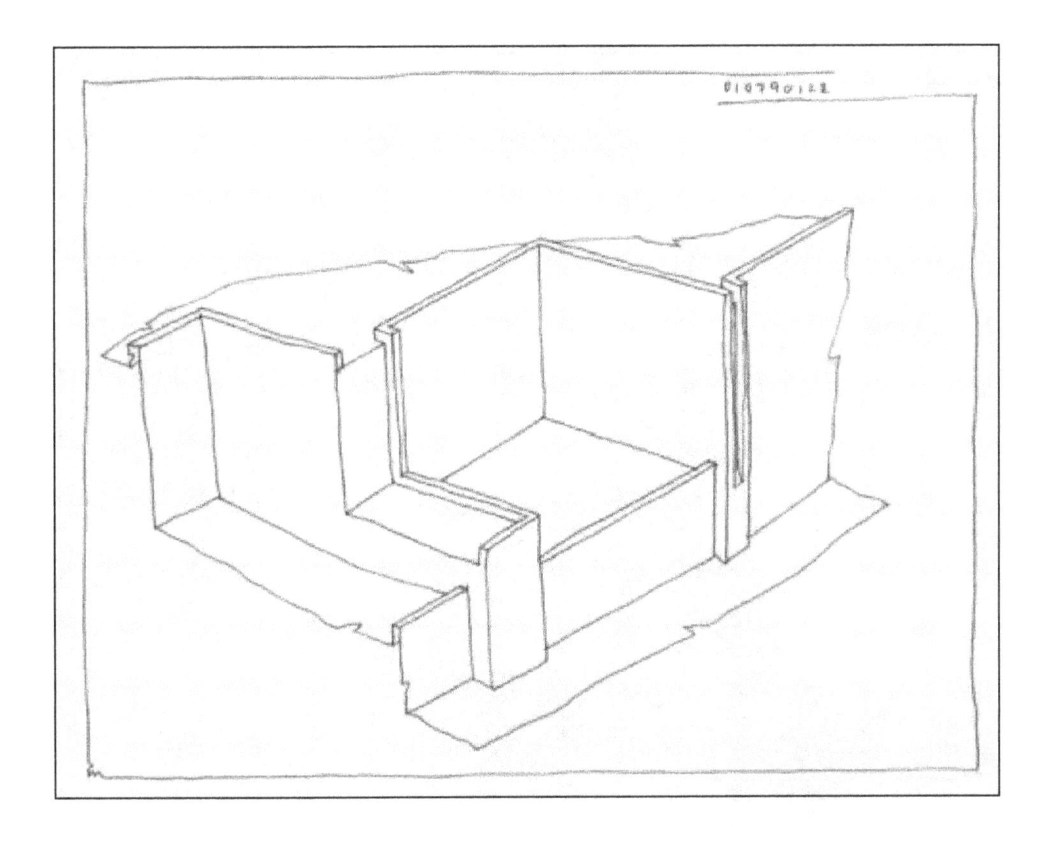
010790122

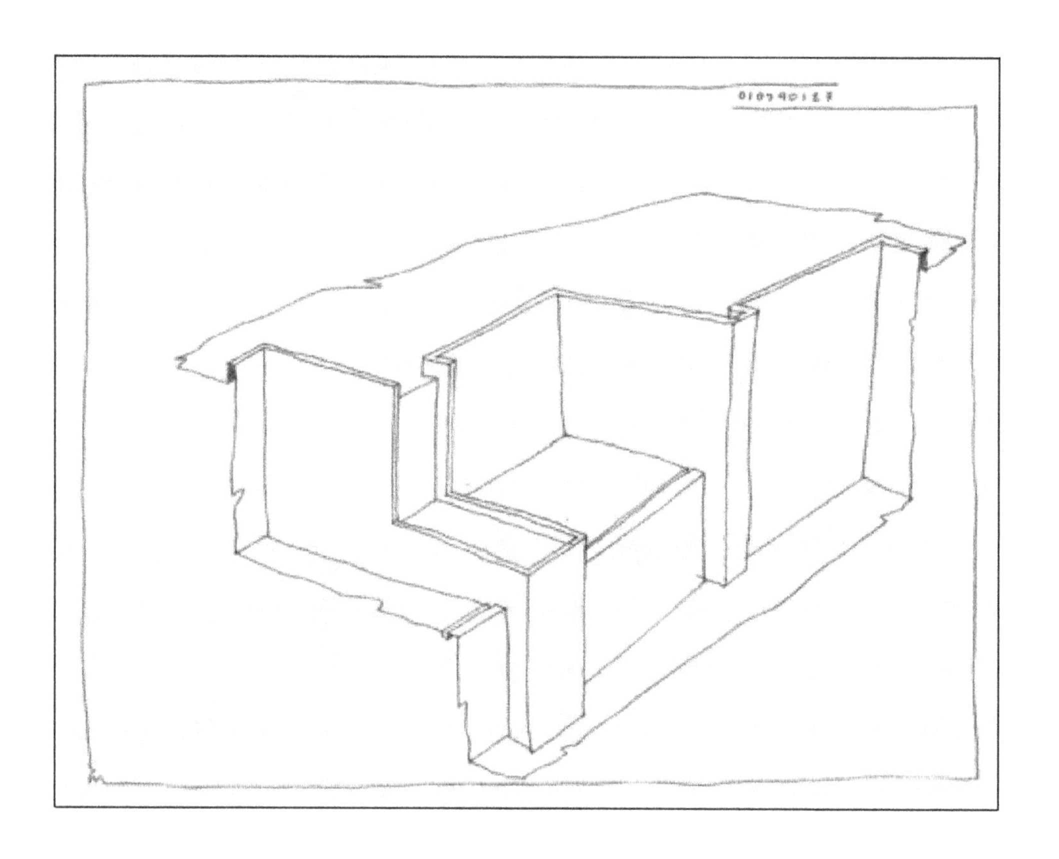

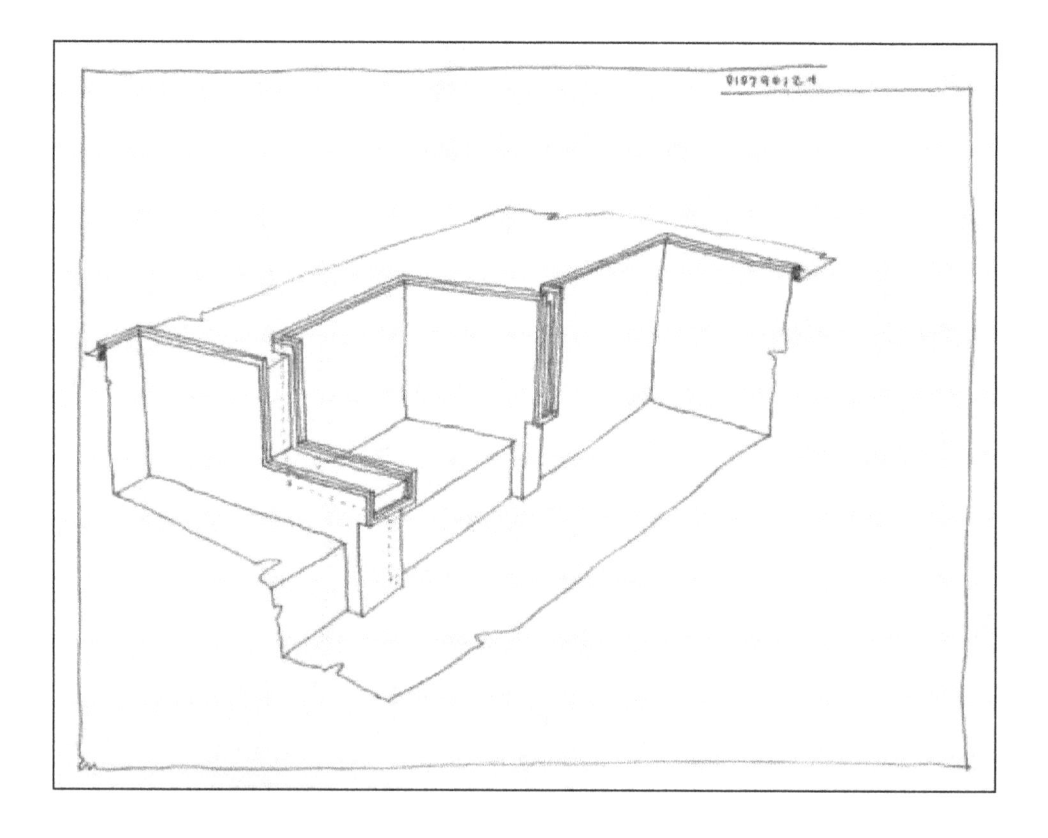

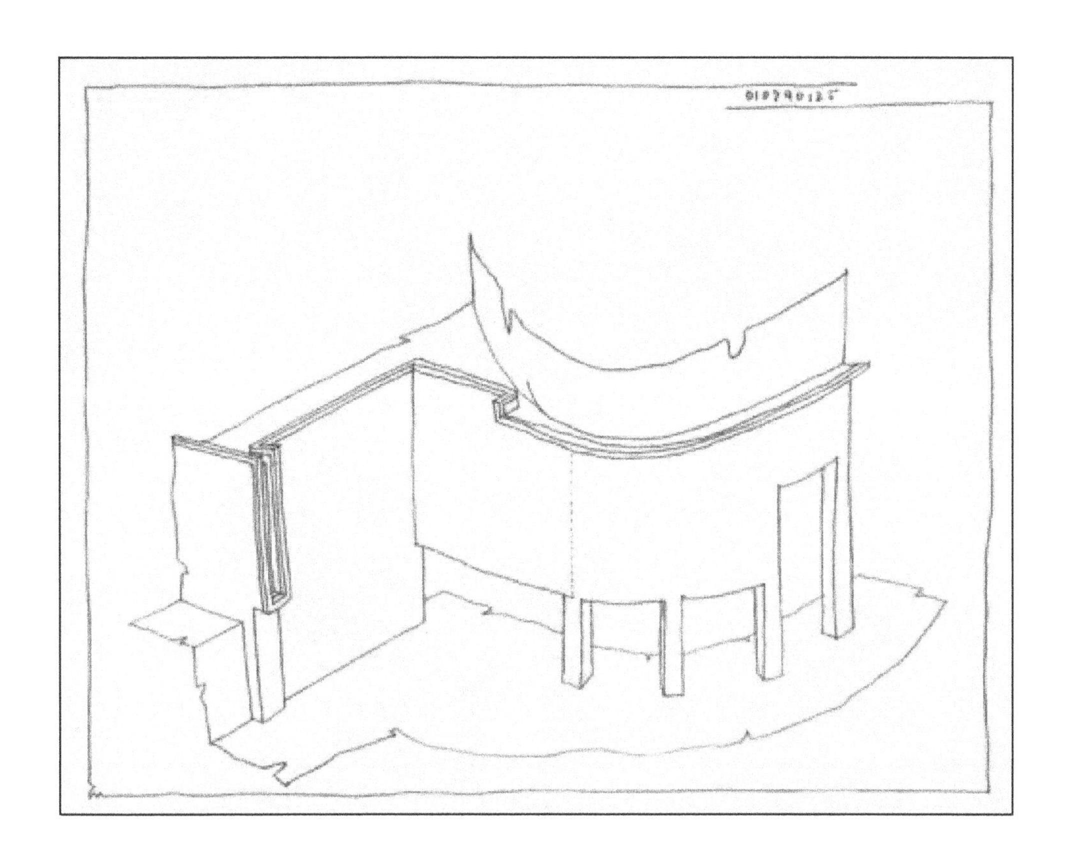

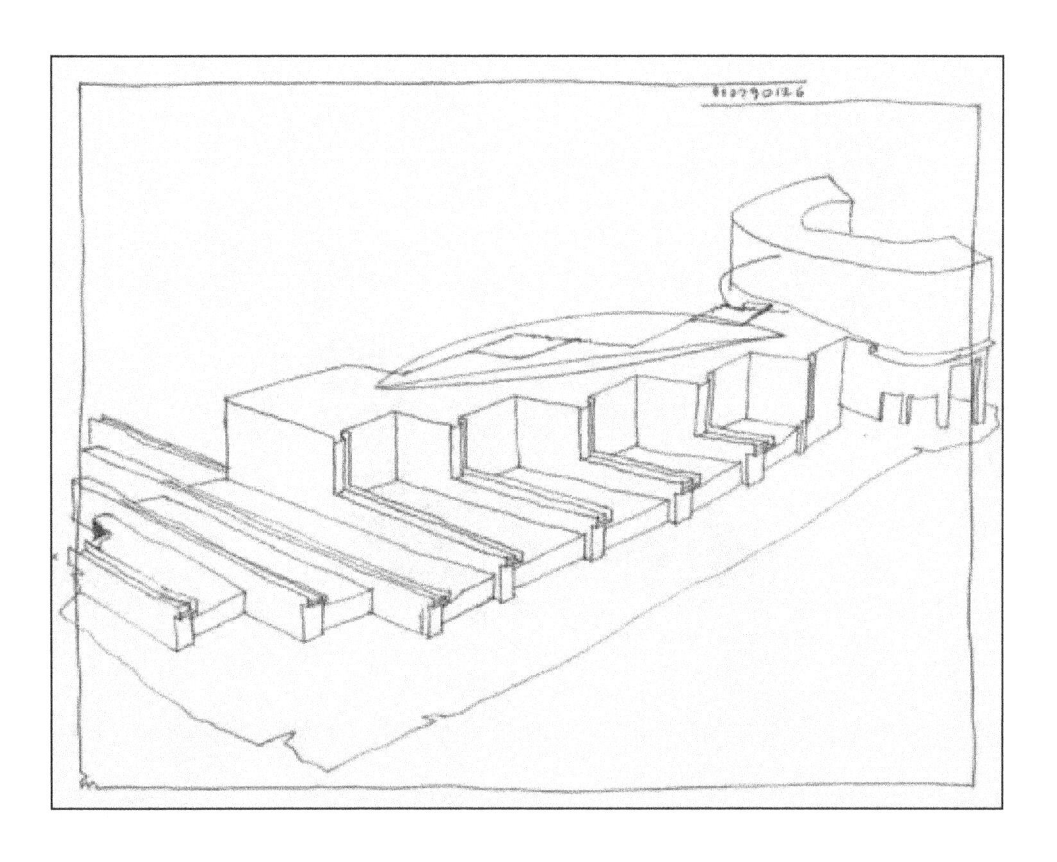

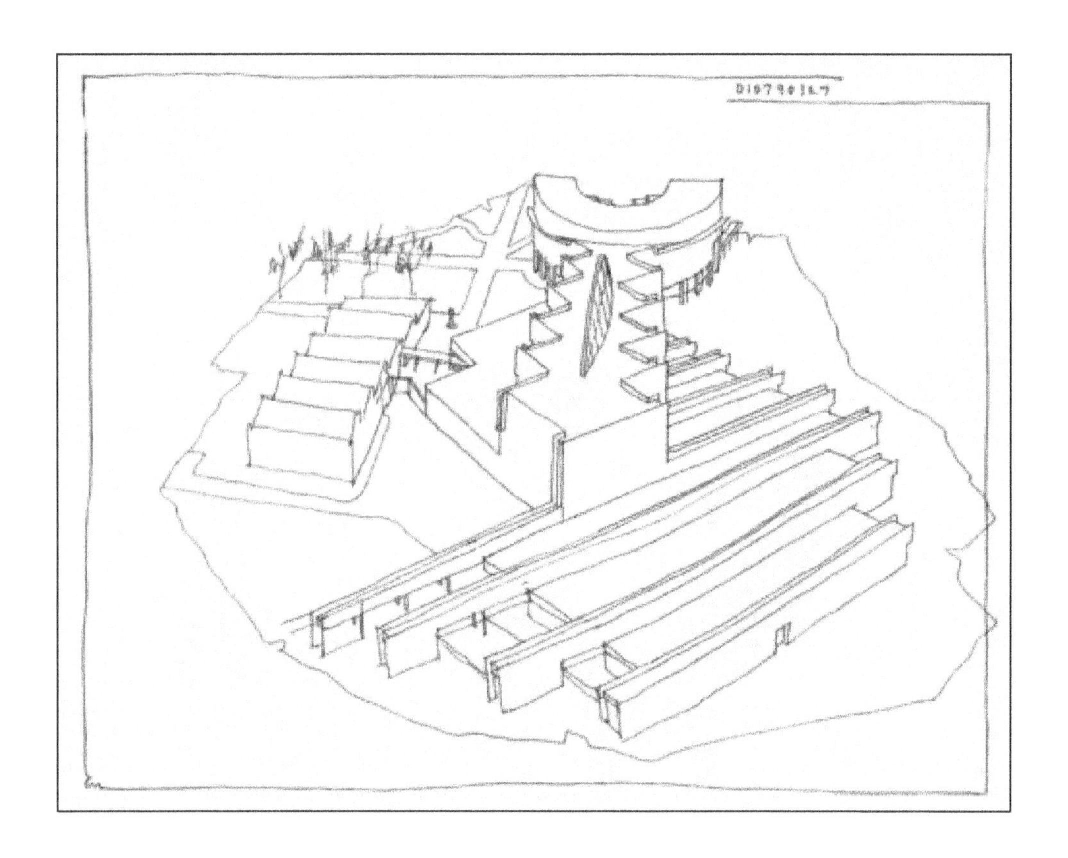

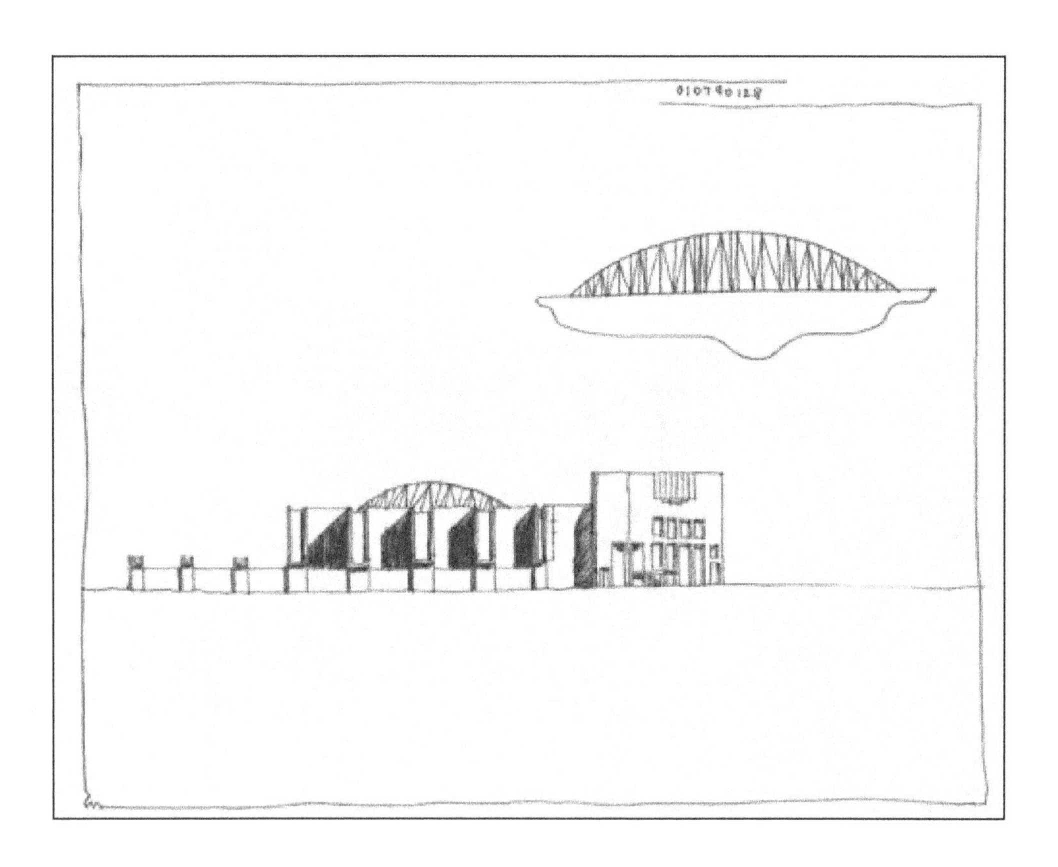

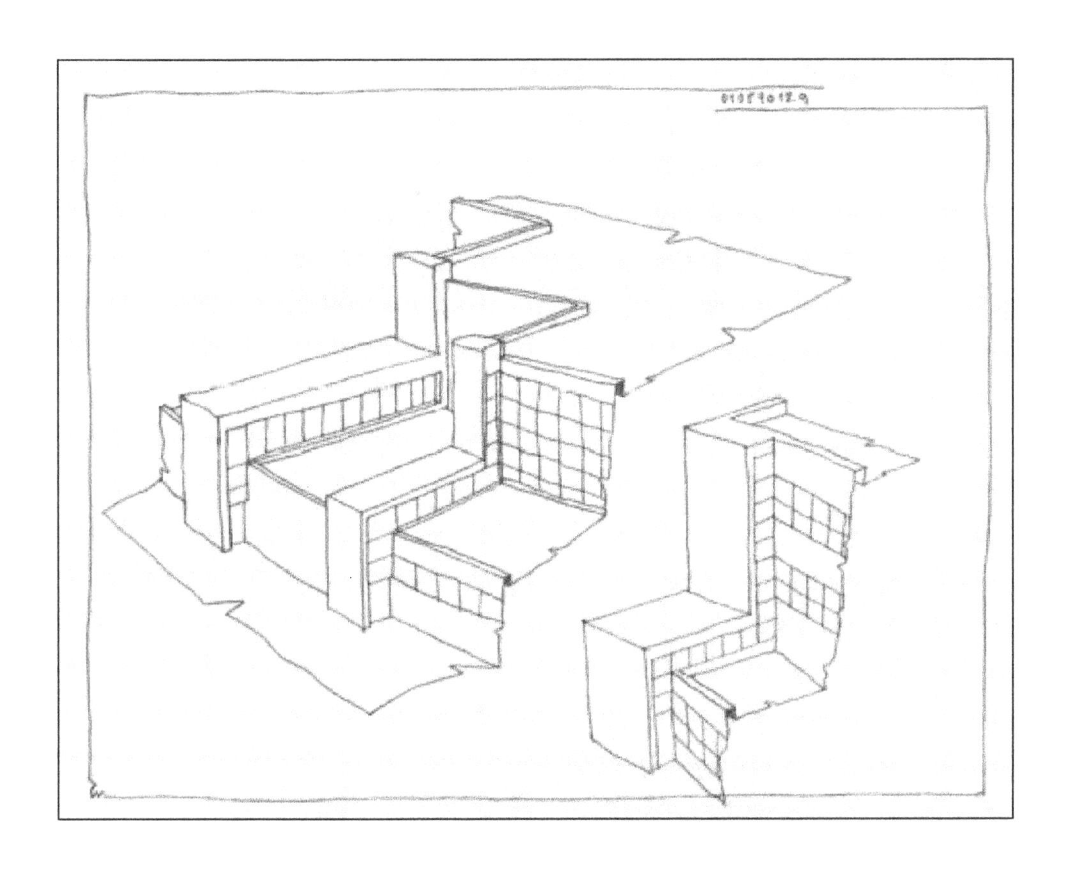

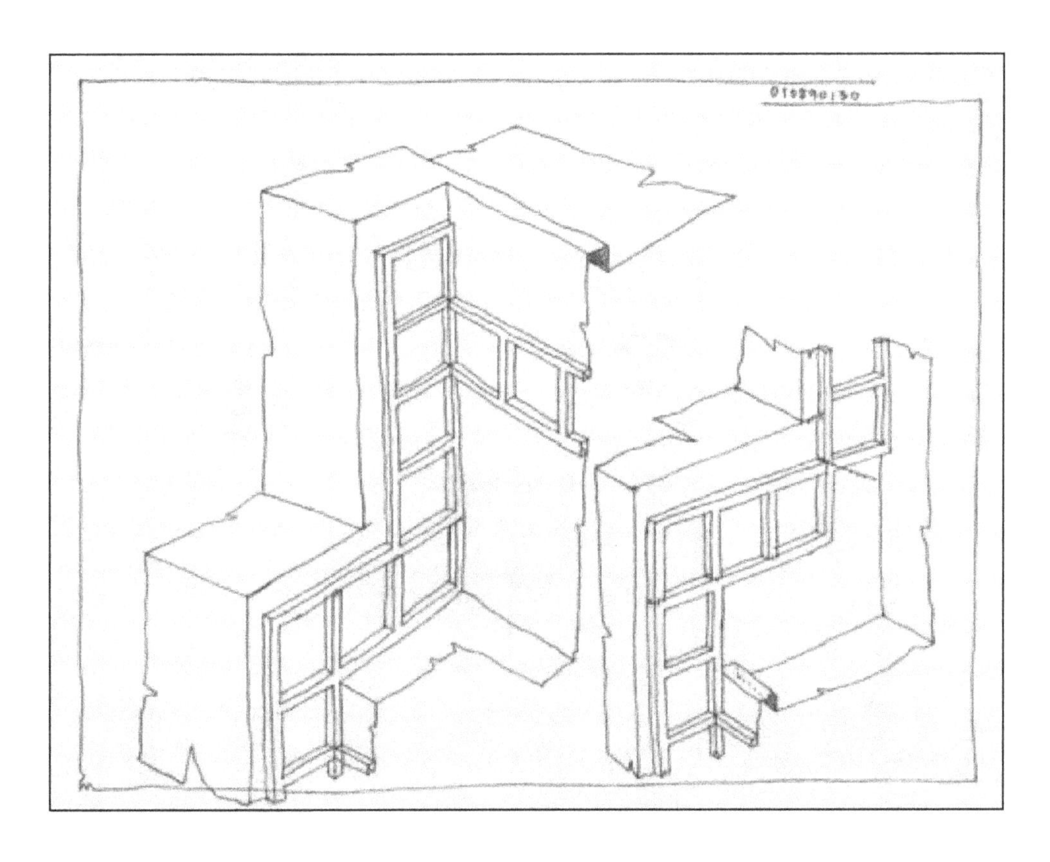

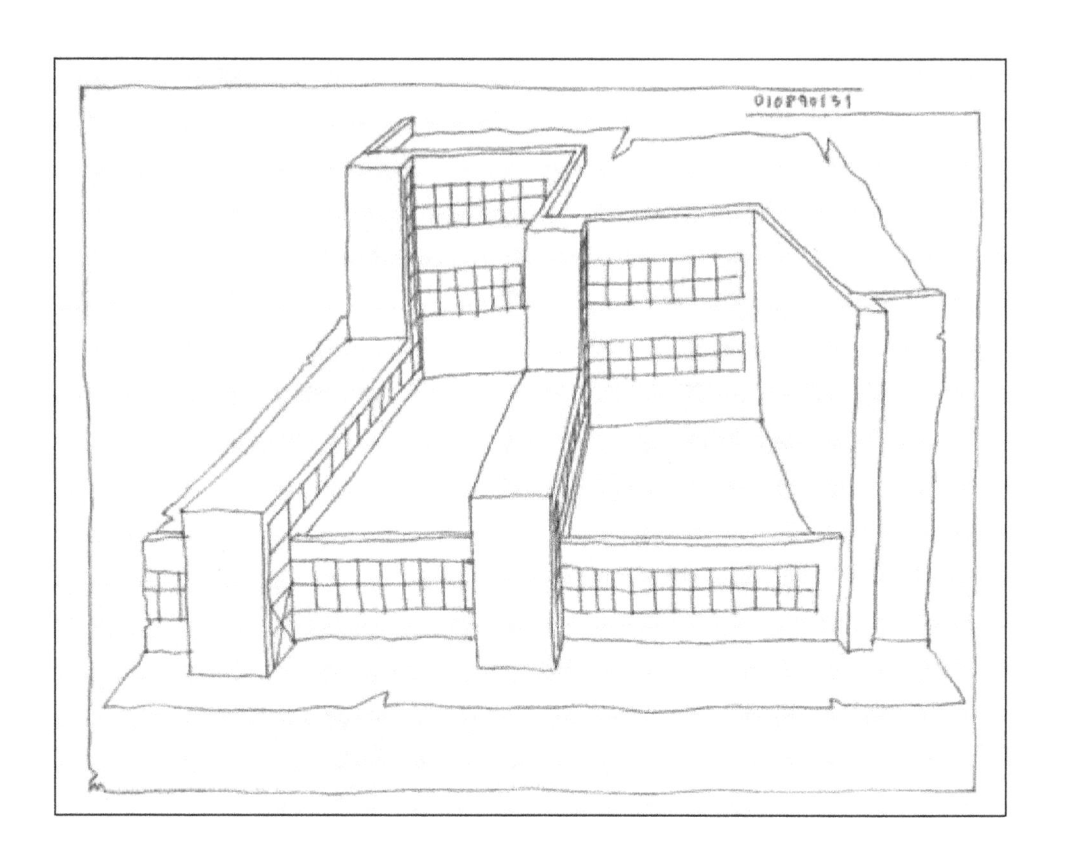
010890131

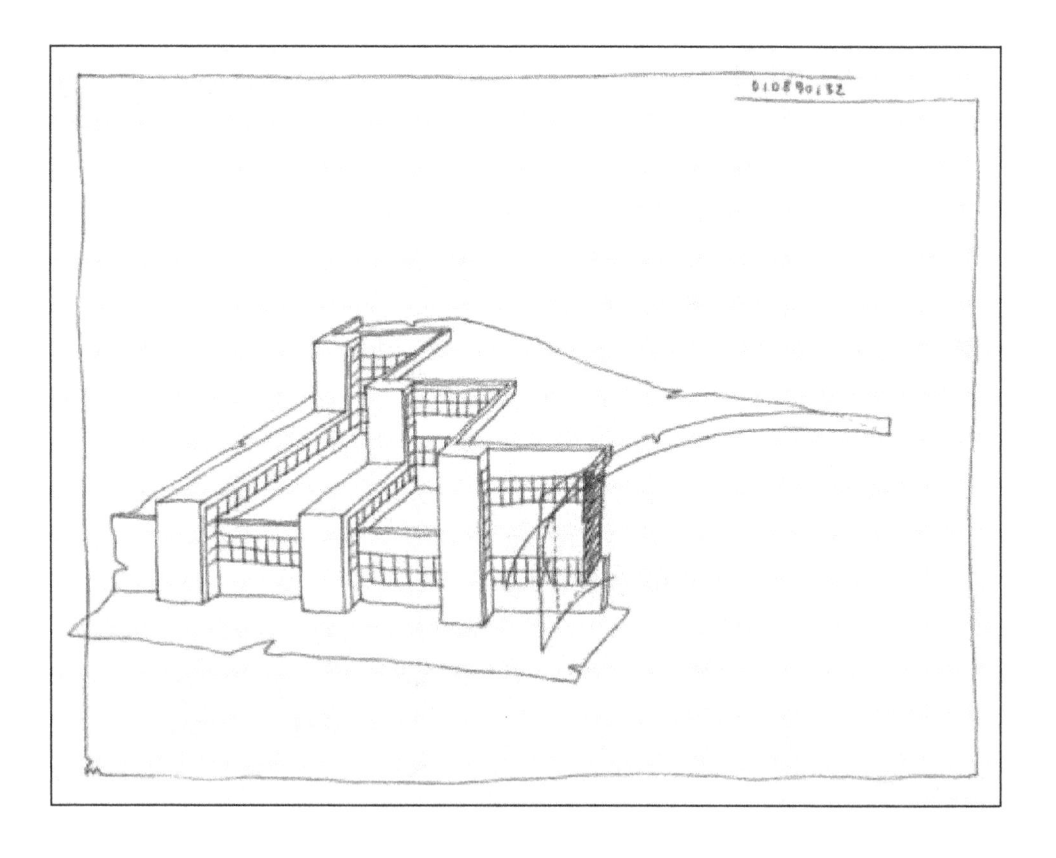
010890132

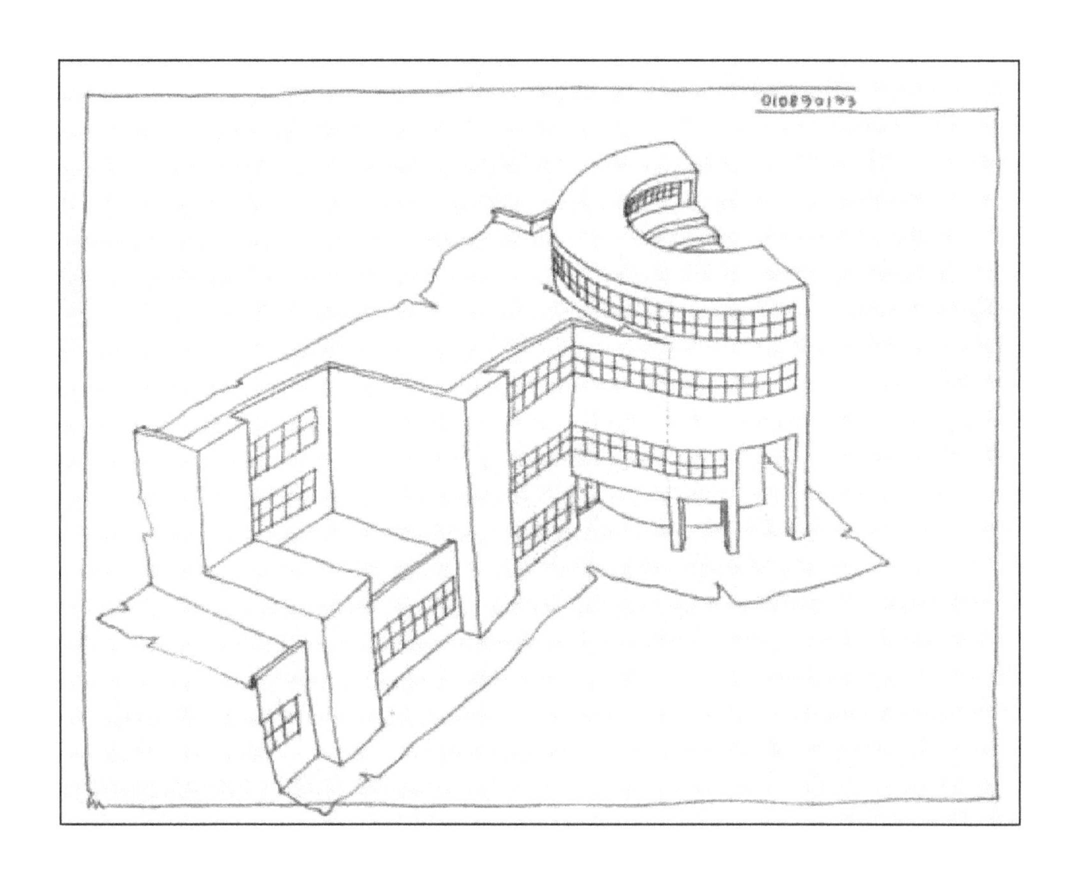

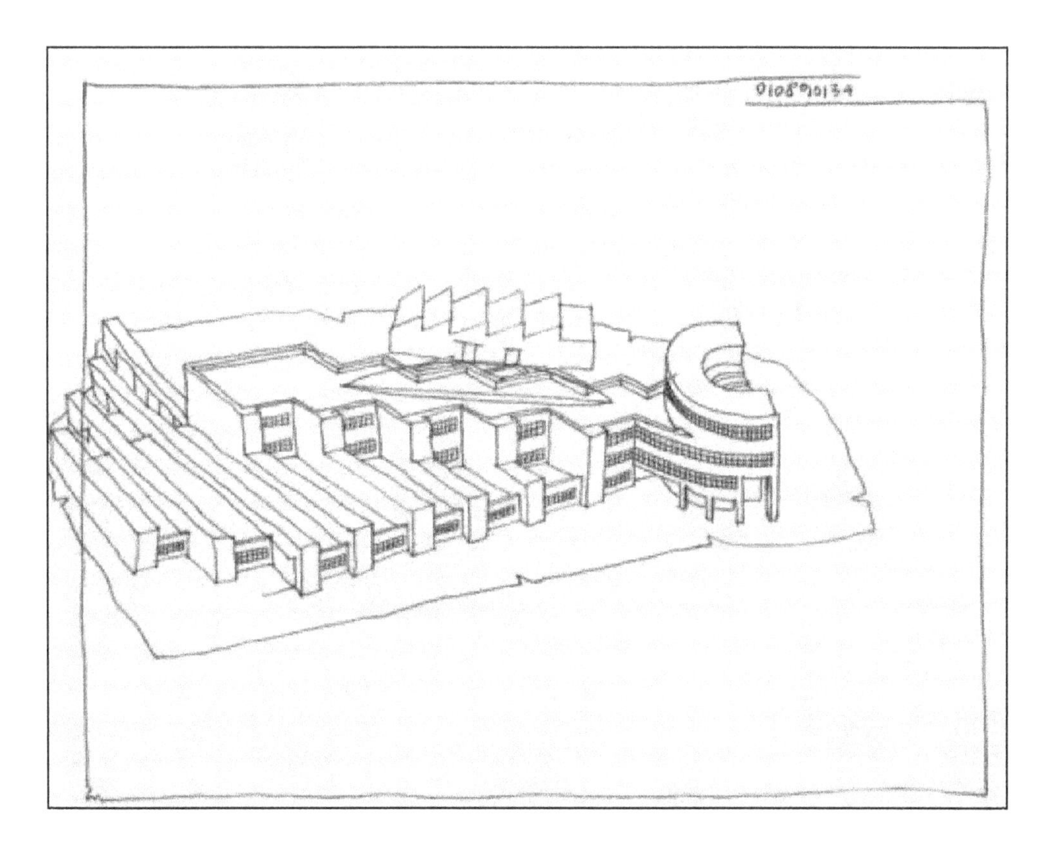

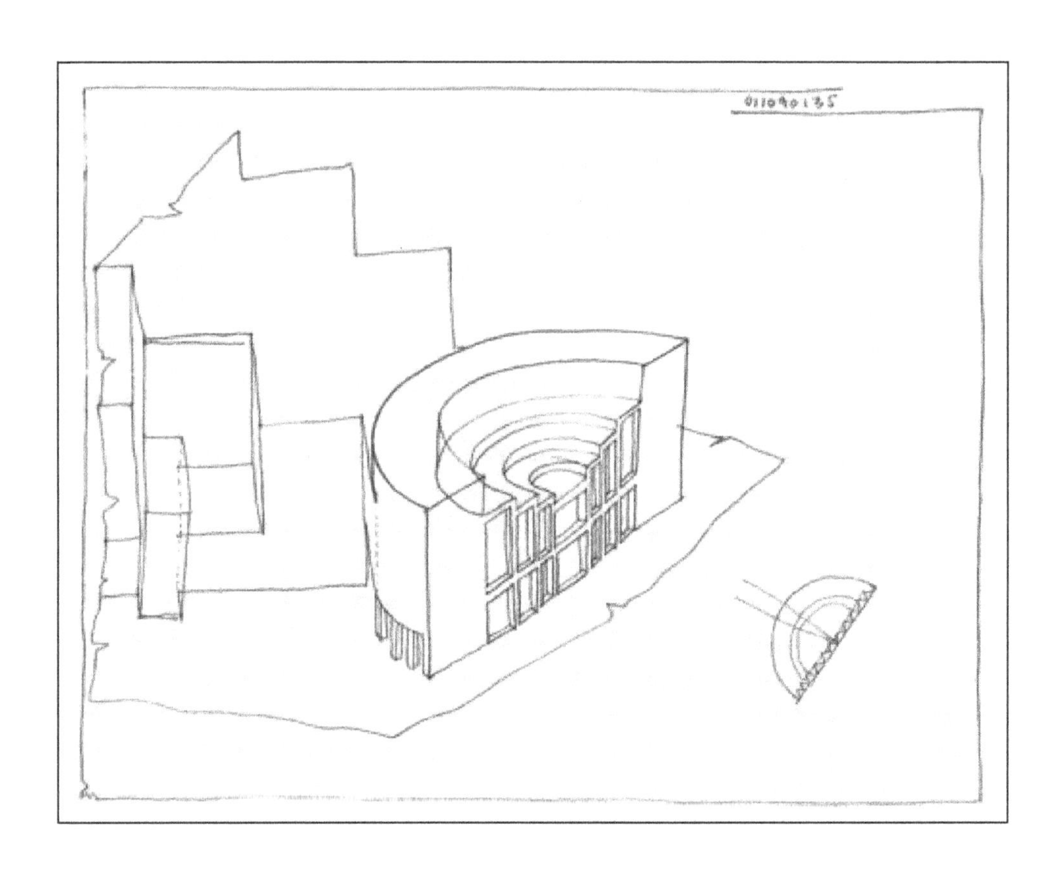
011090135

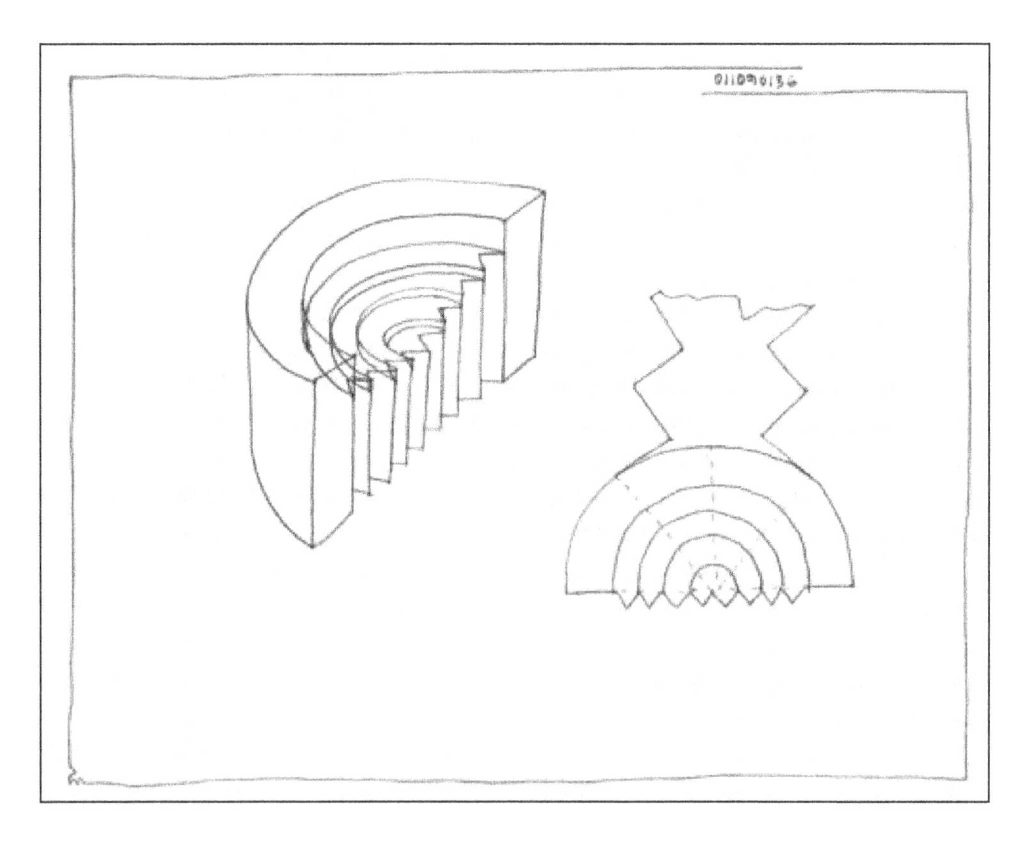
011090136

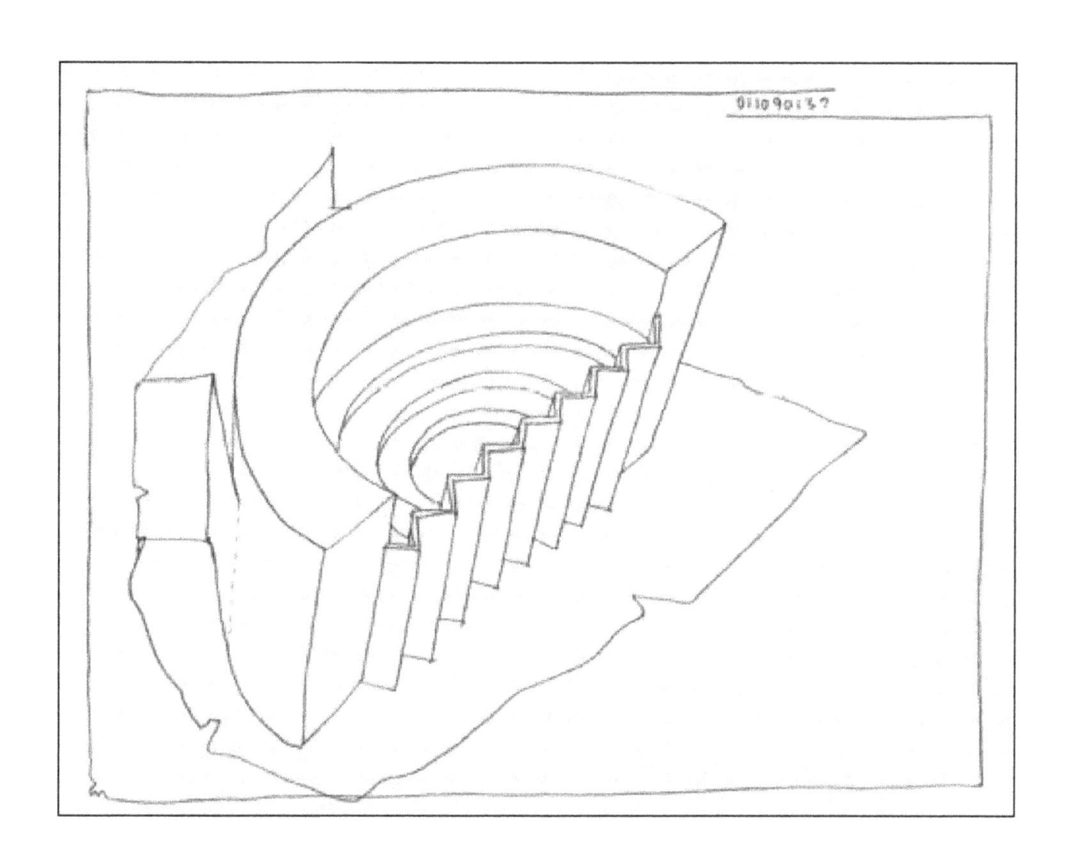
011090137

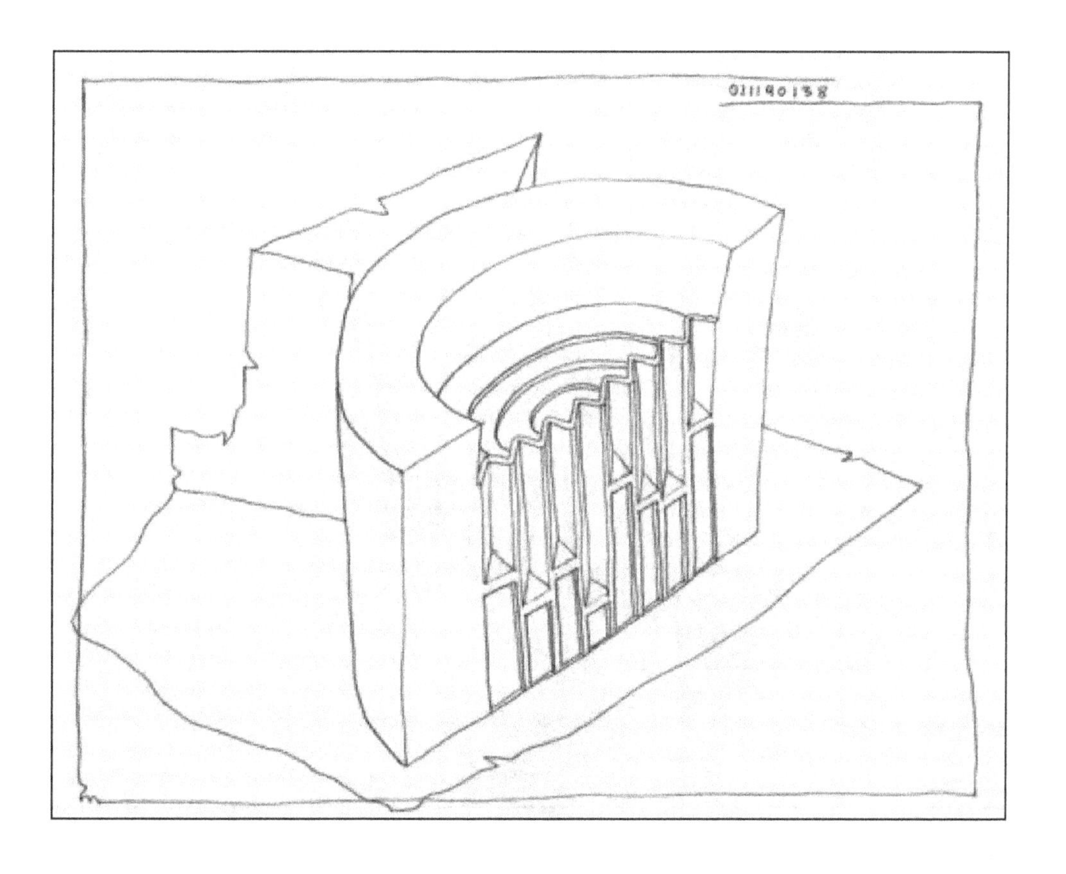
011190138

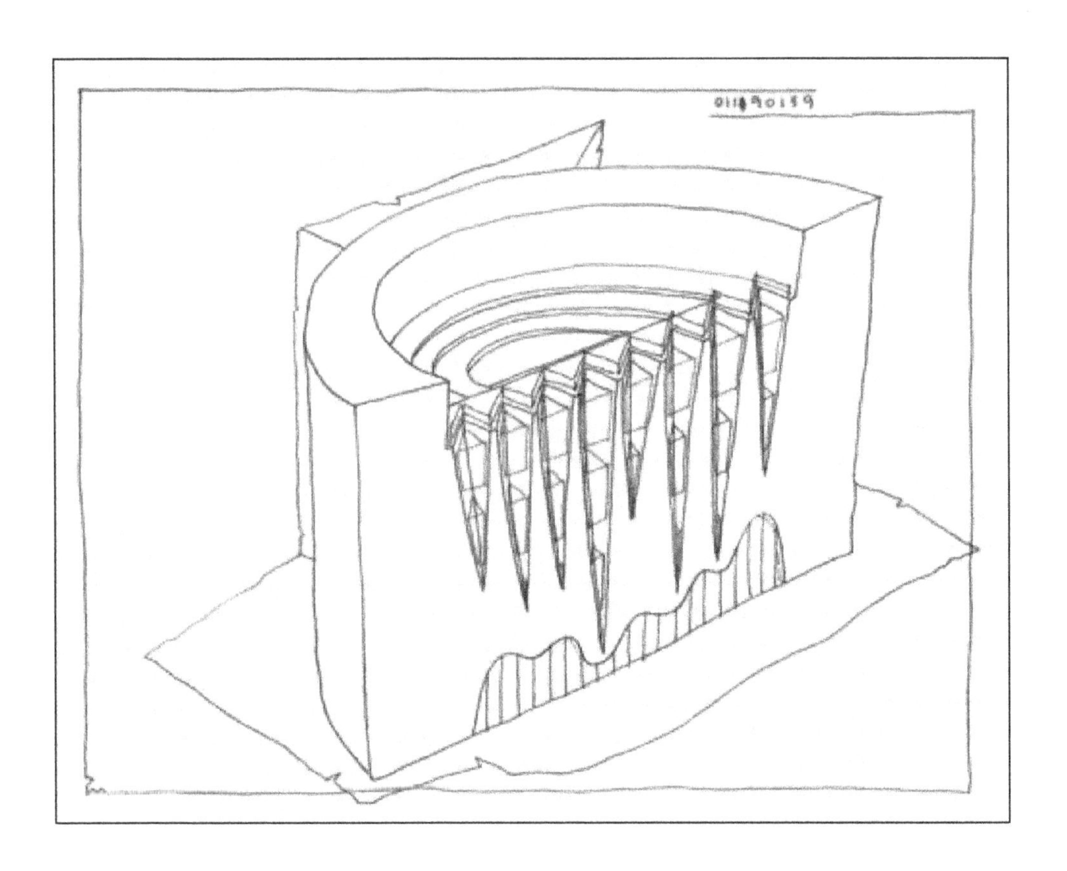

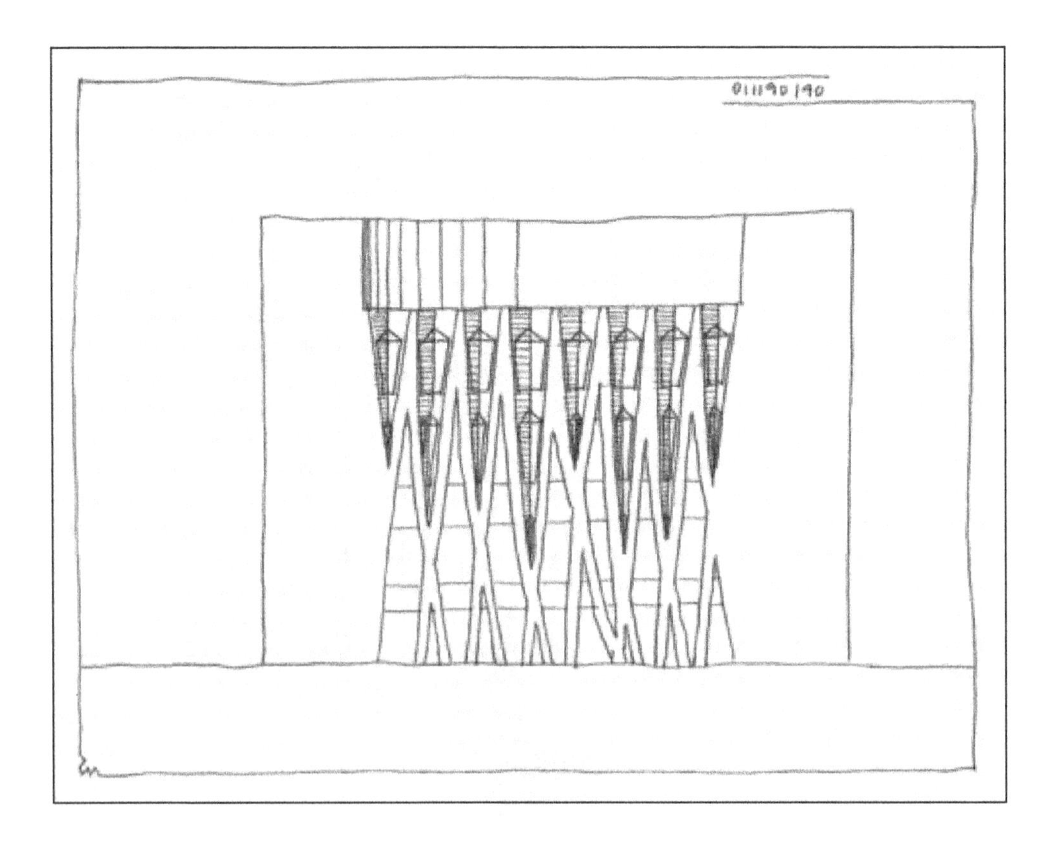
011190190

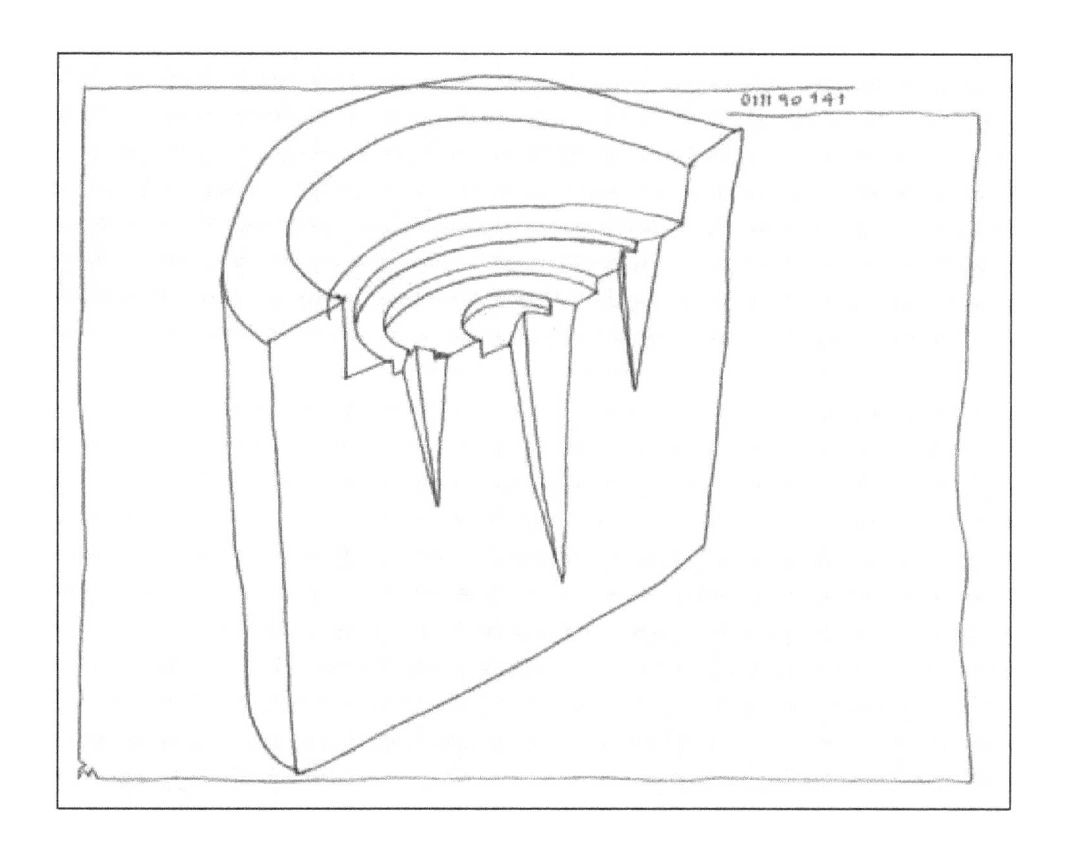
0111 90 141

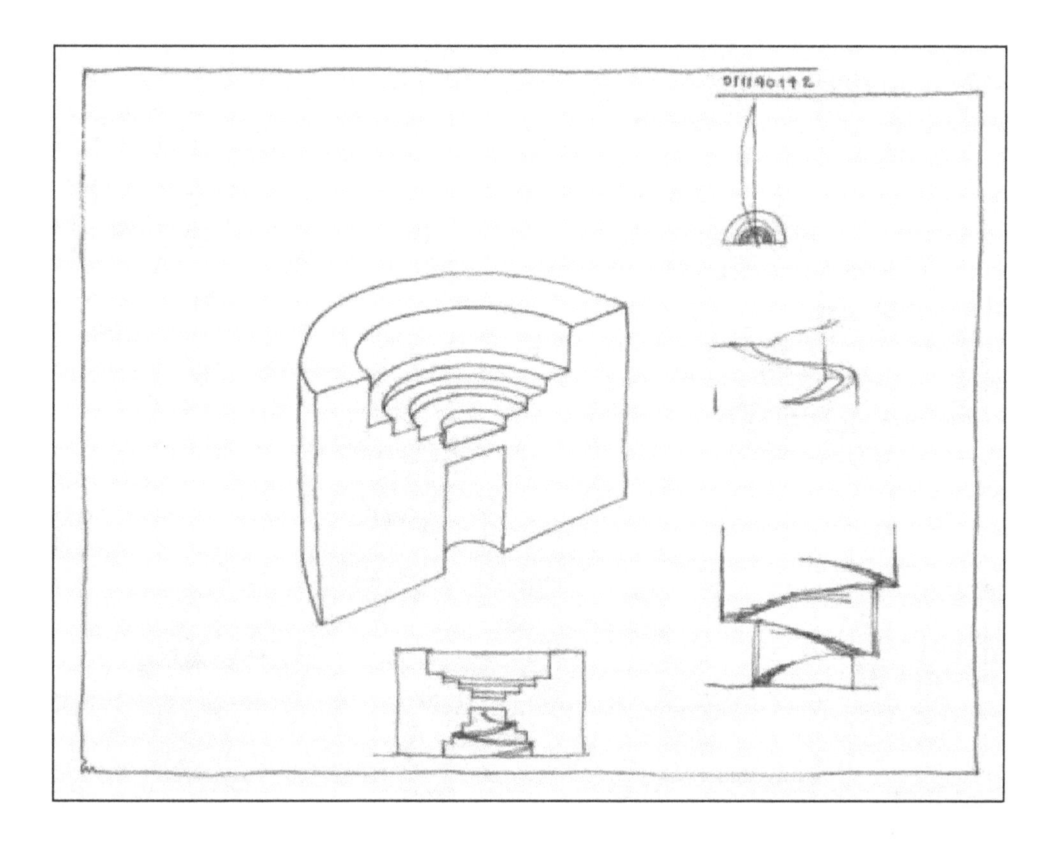
011190142

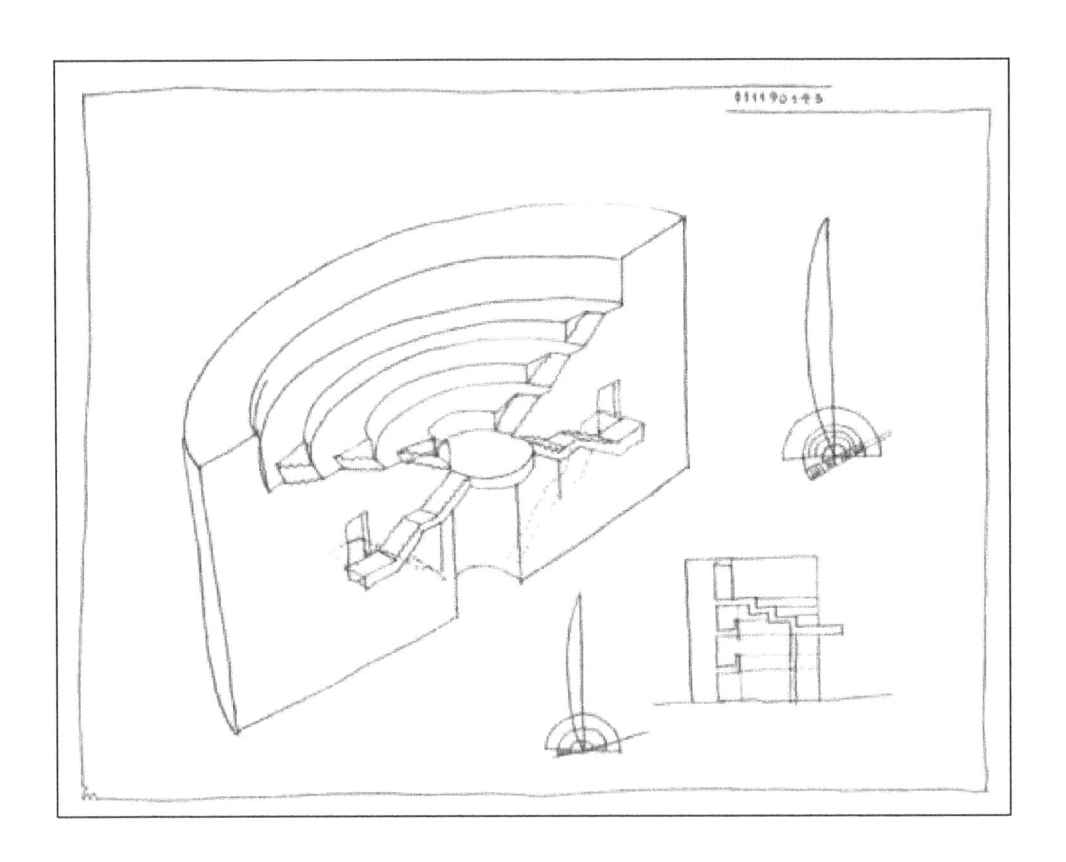

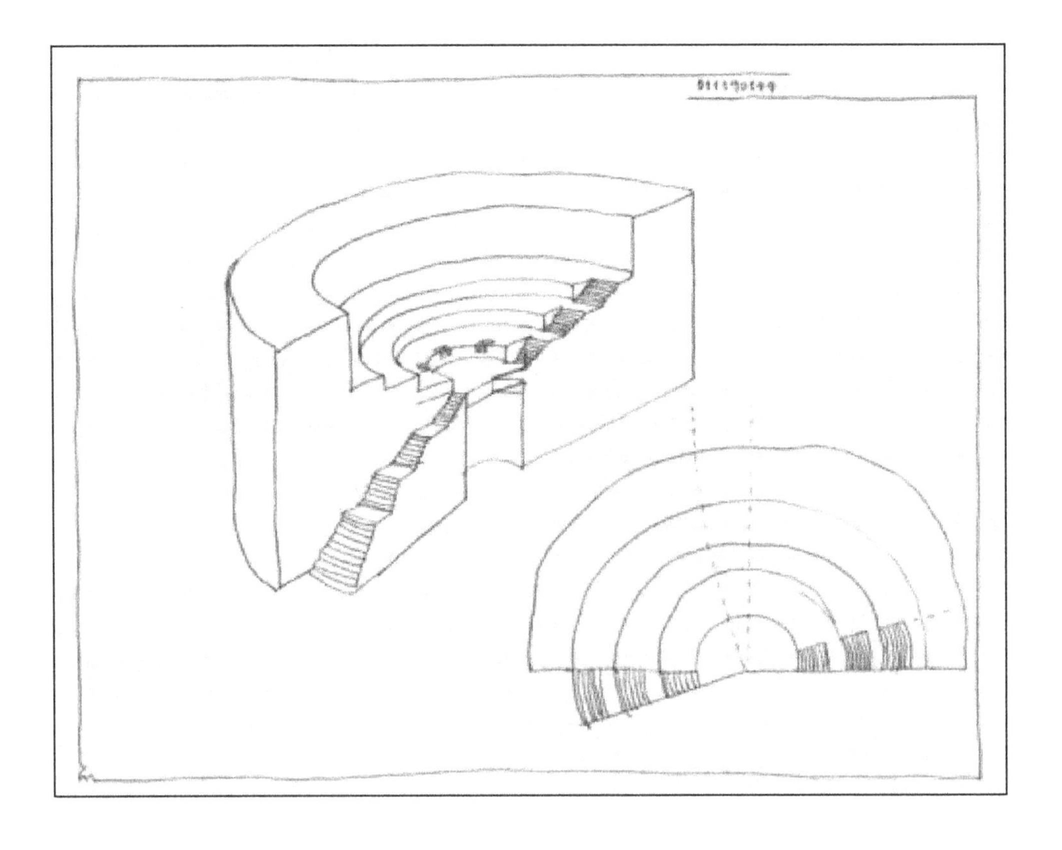

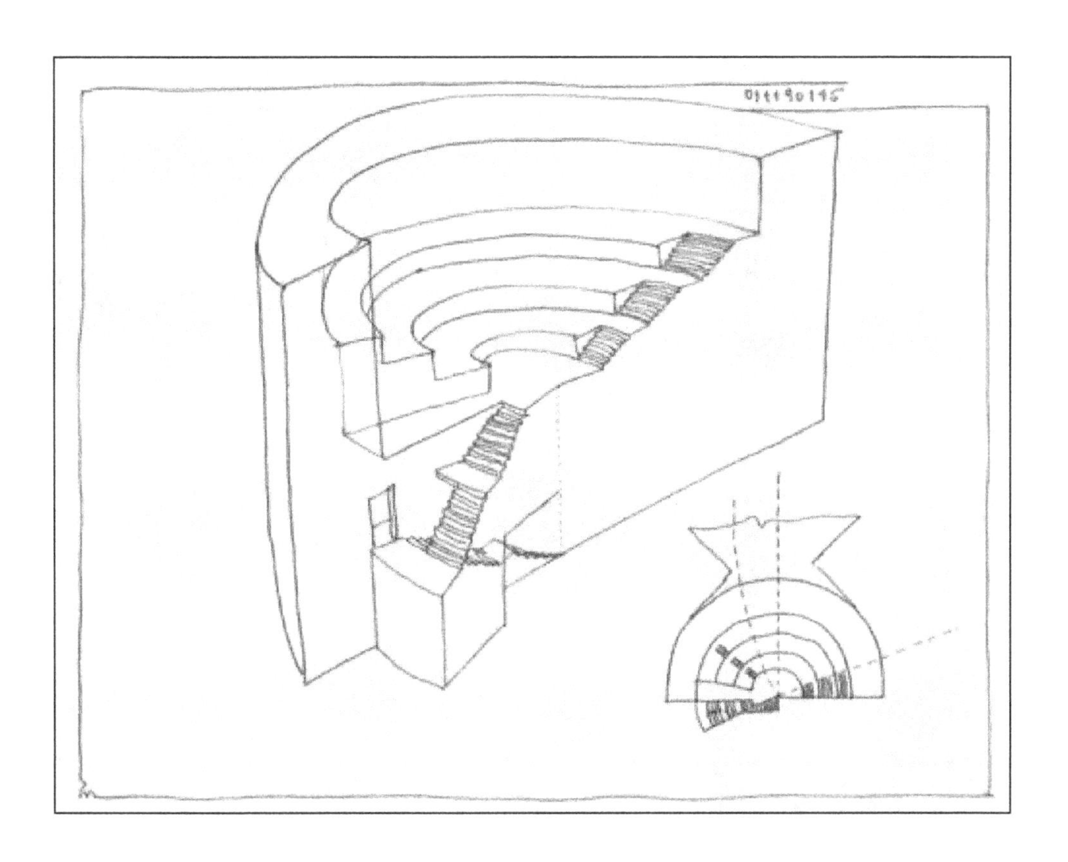
011190145

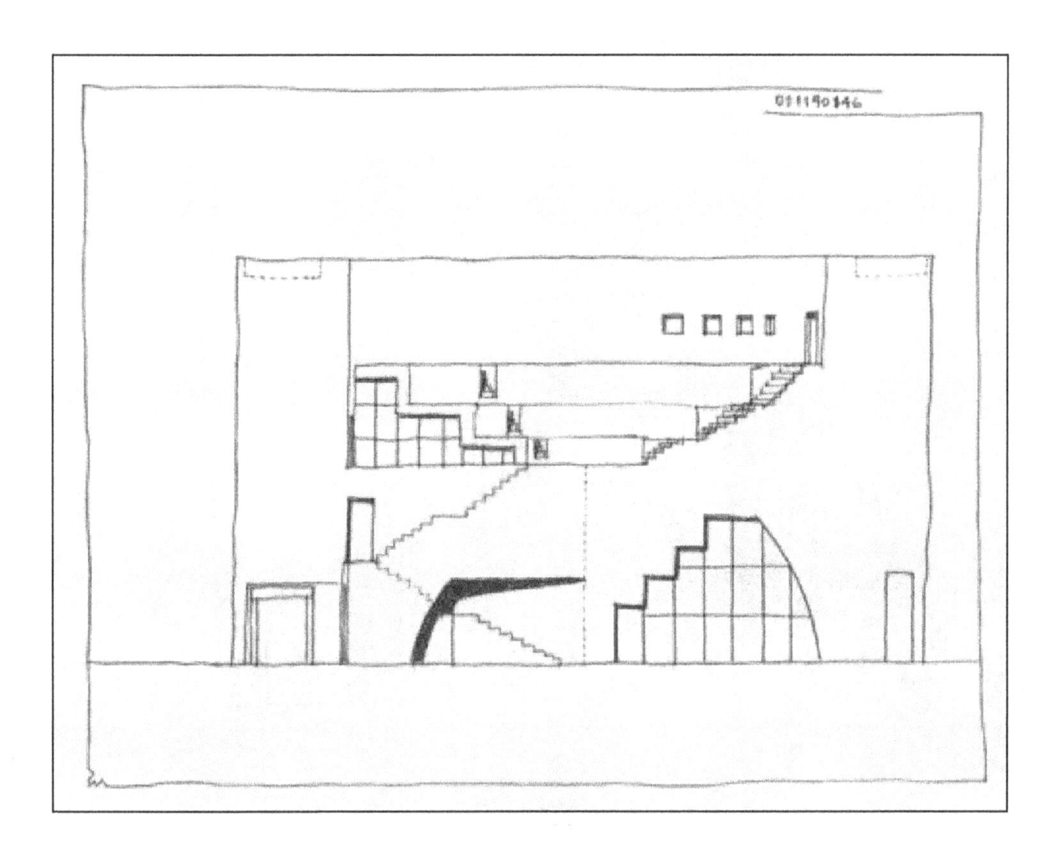
011190146

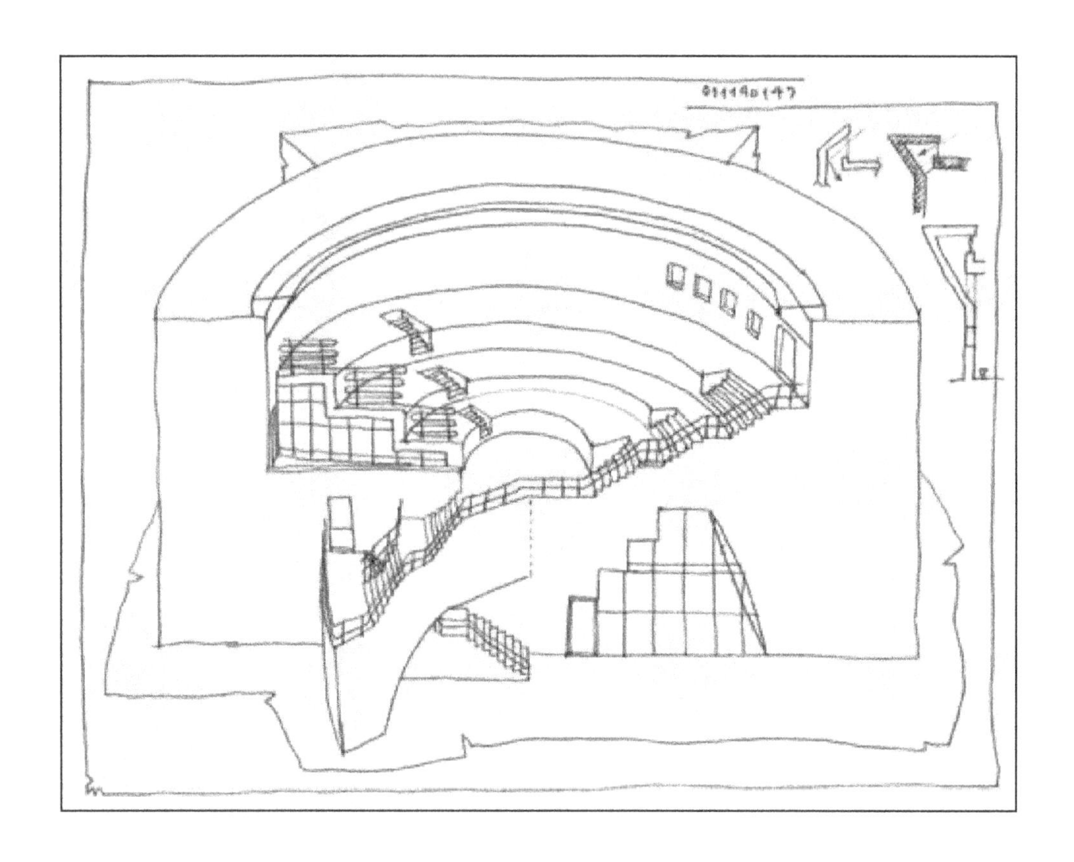

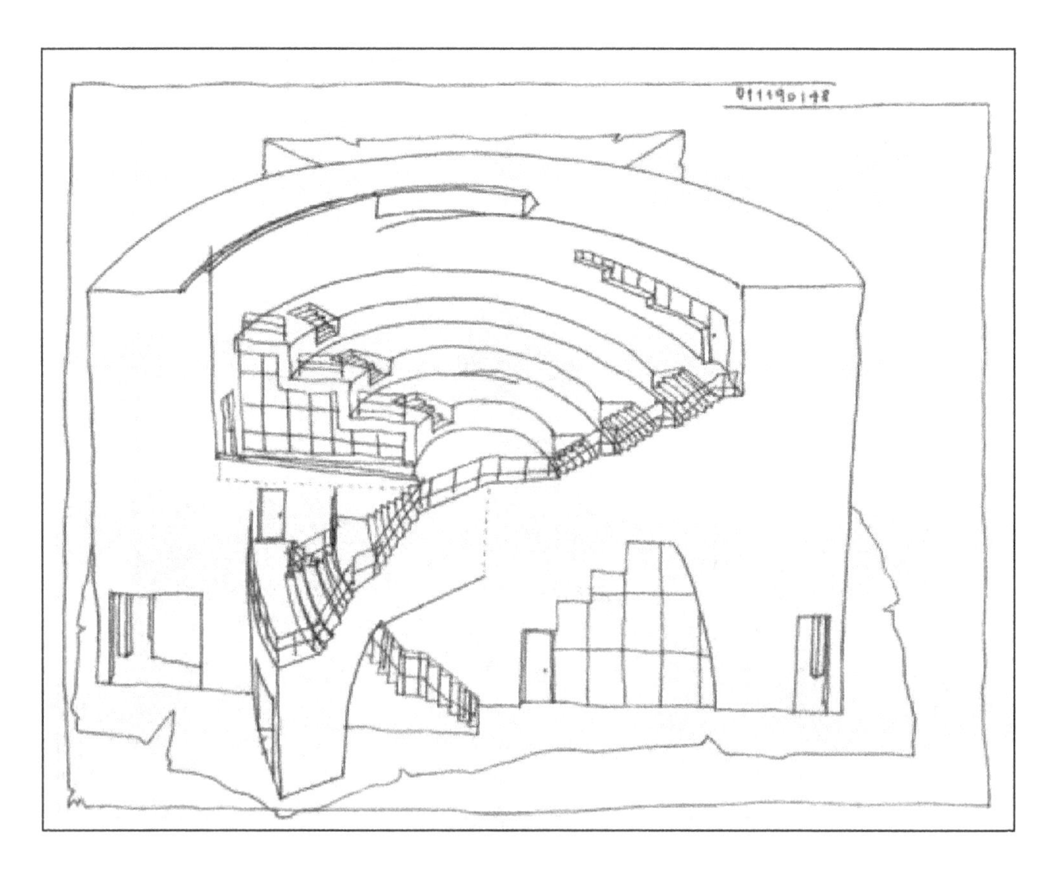

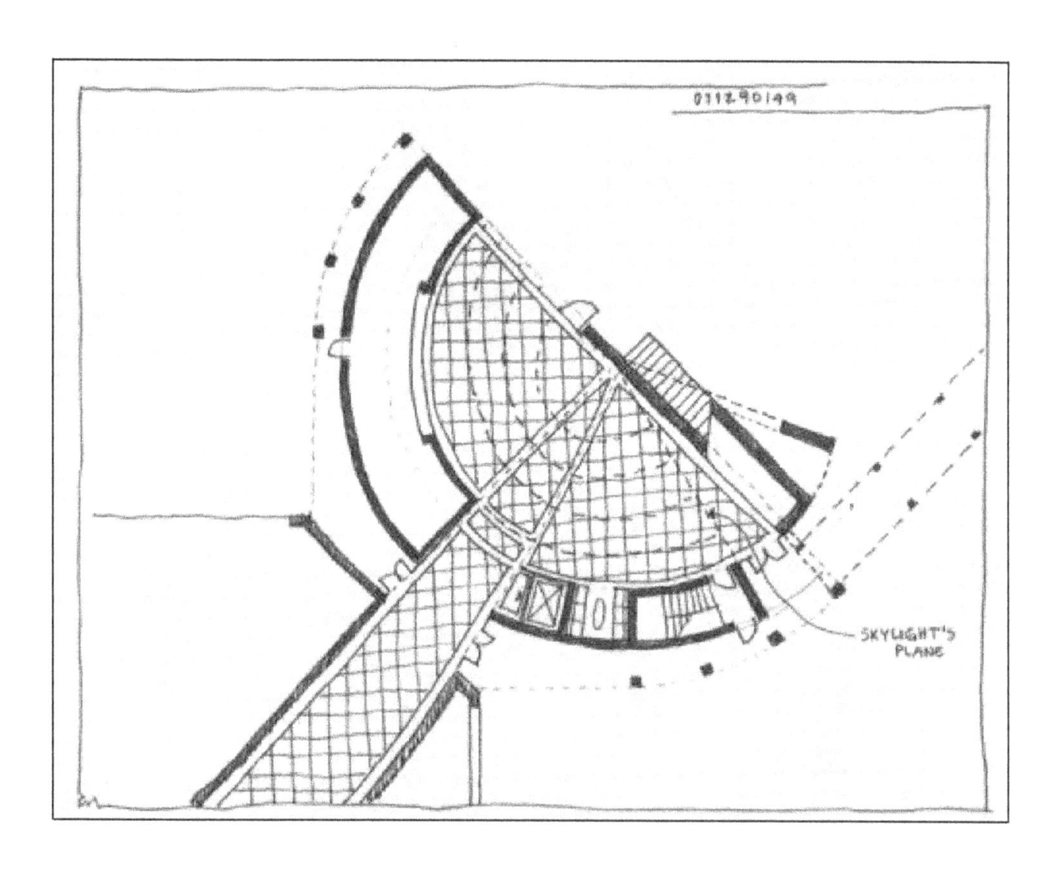
011290149
SKYLIGHT'S
PLANE

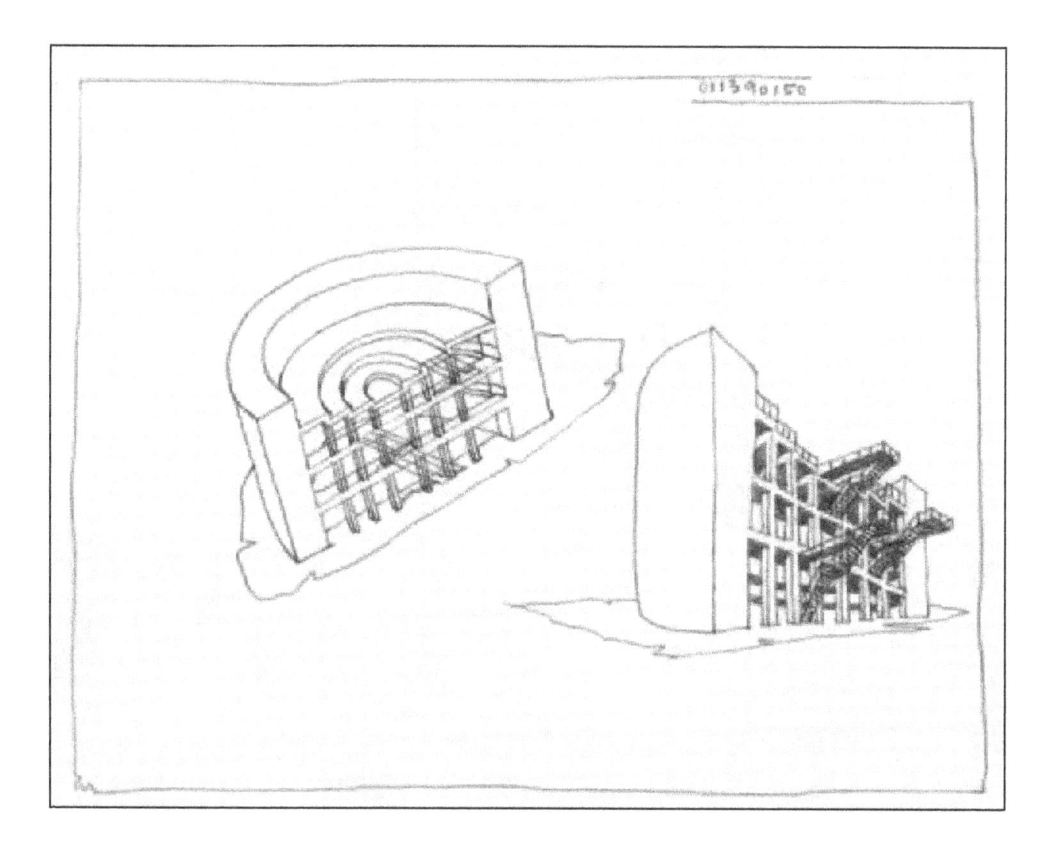
011390150

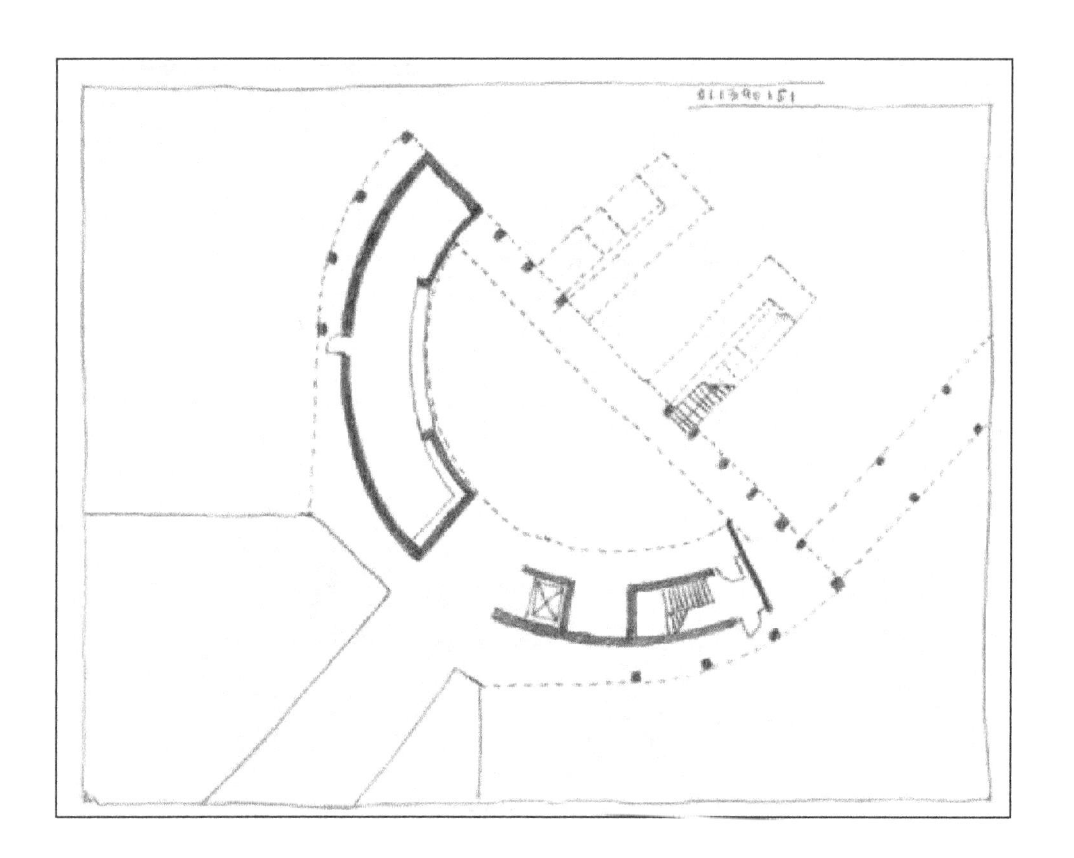
011390151

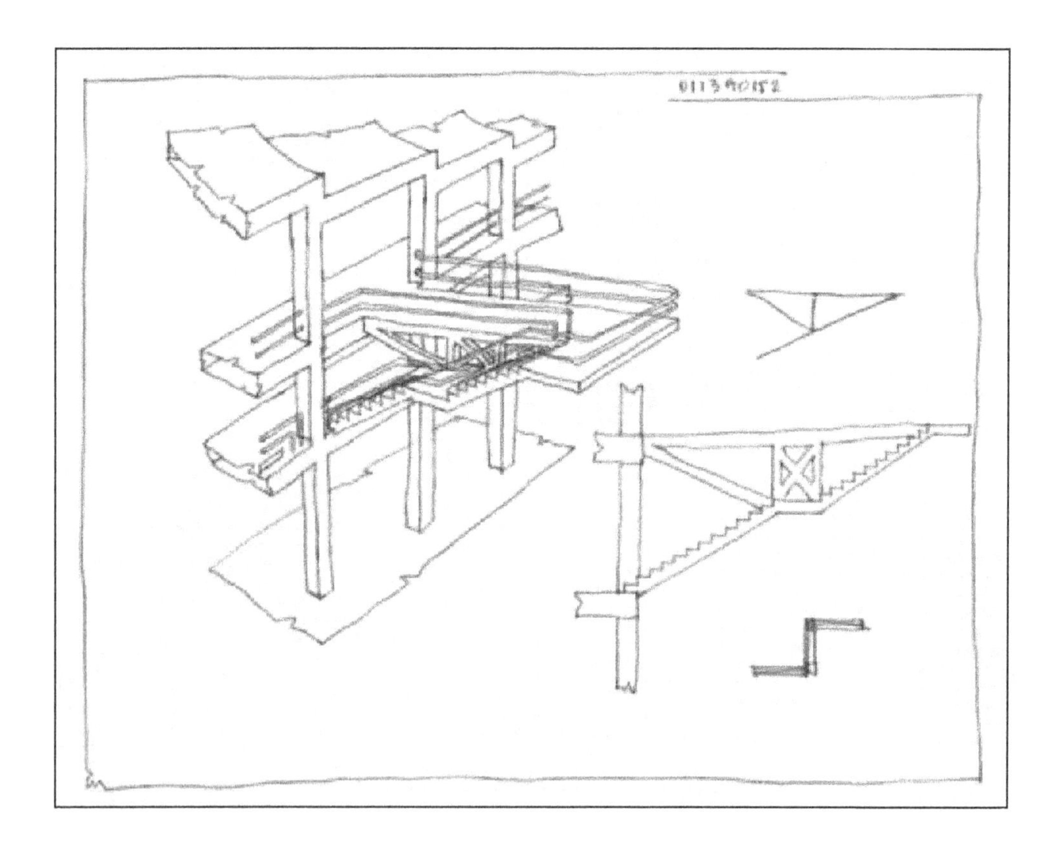
011390152

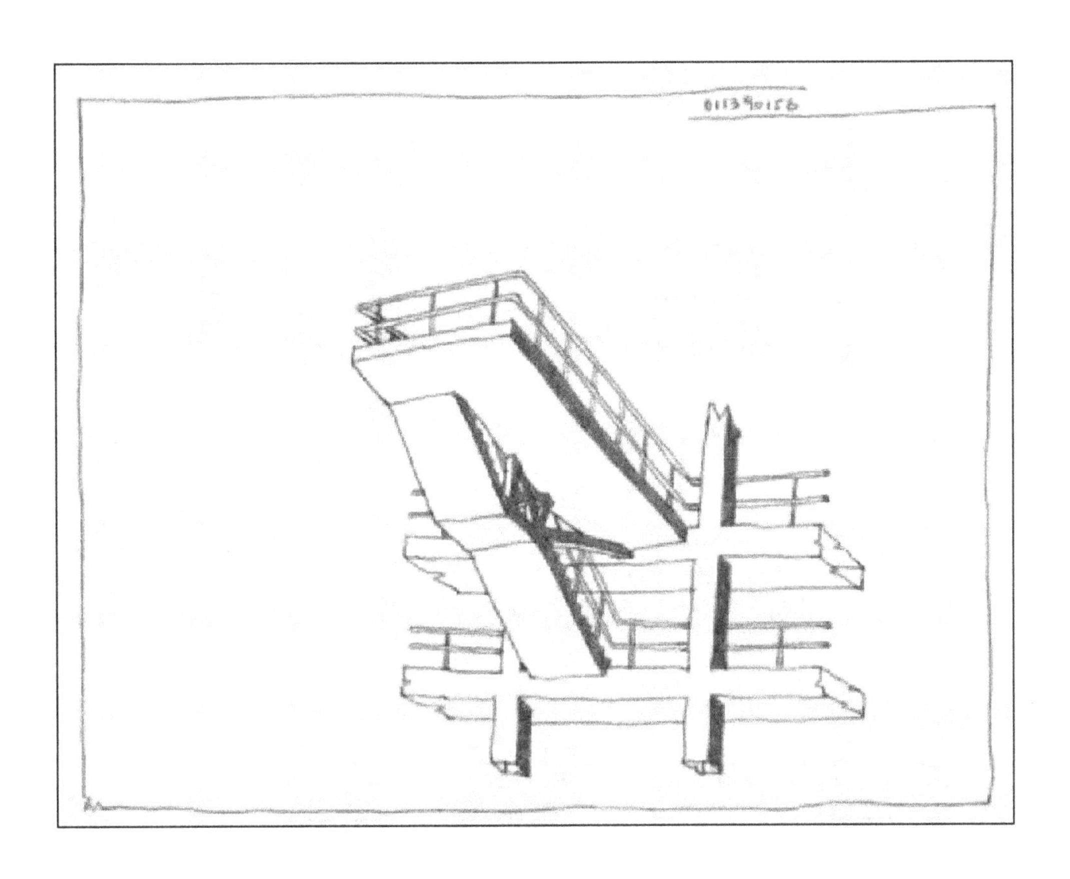
011390156

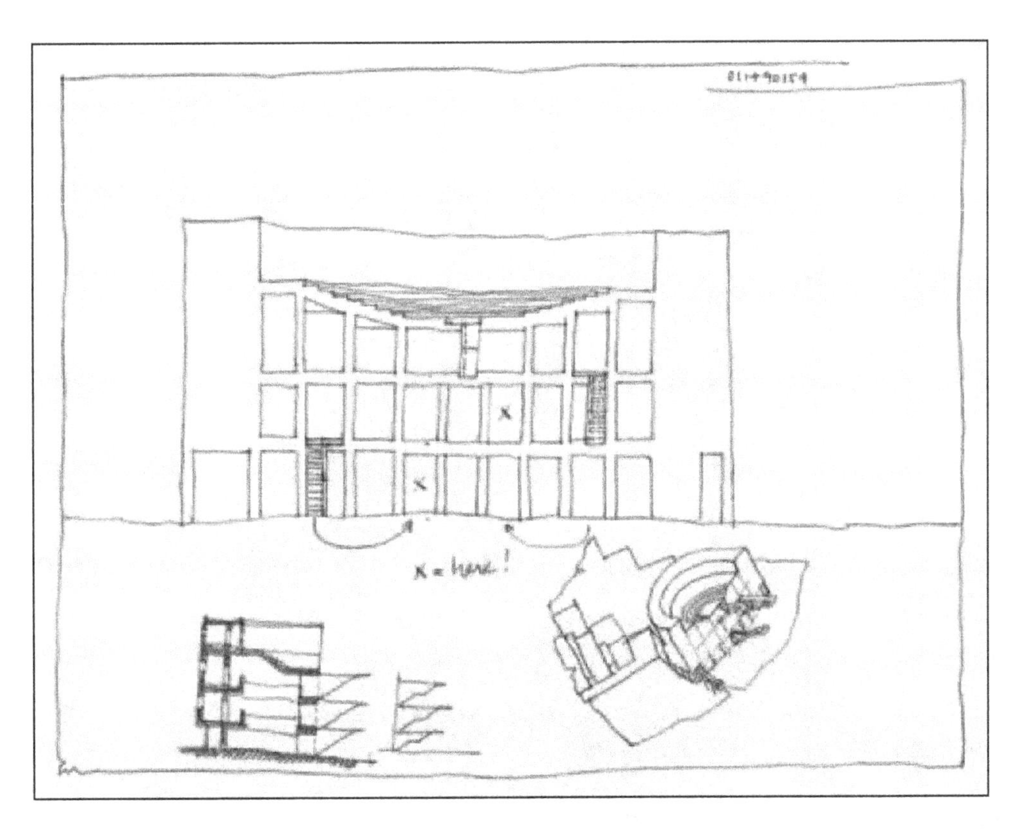
011490154
x = hard!

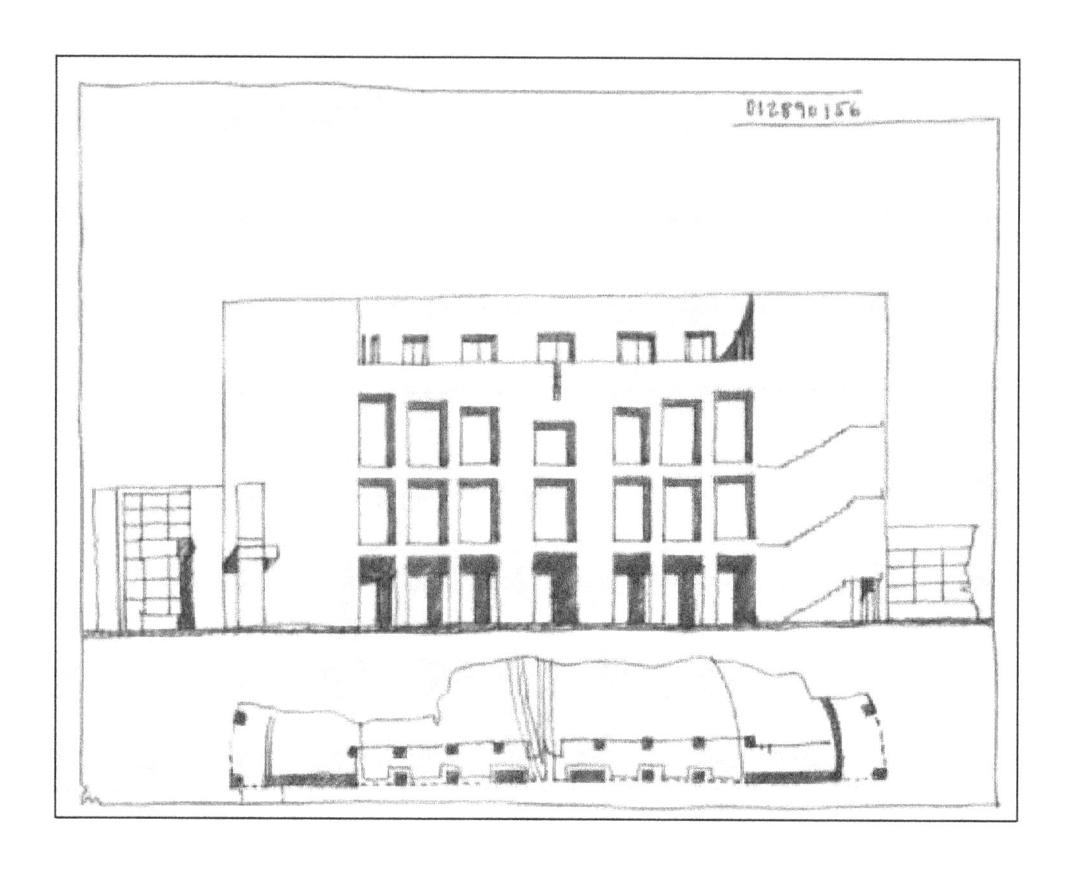
012890156

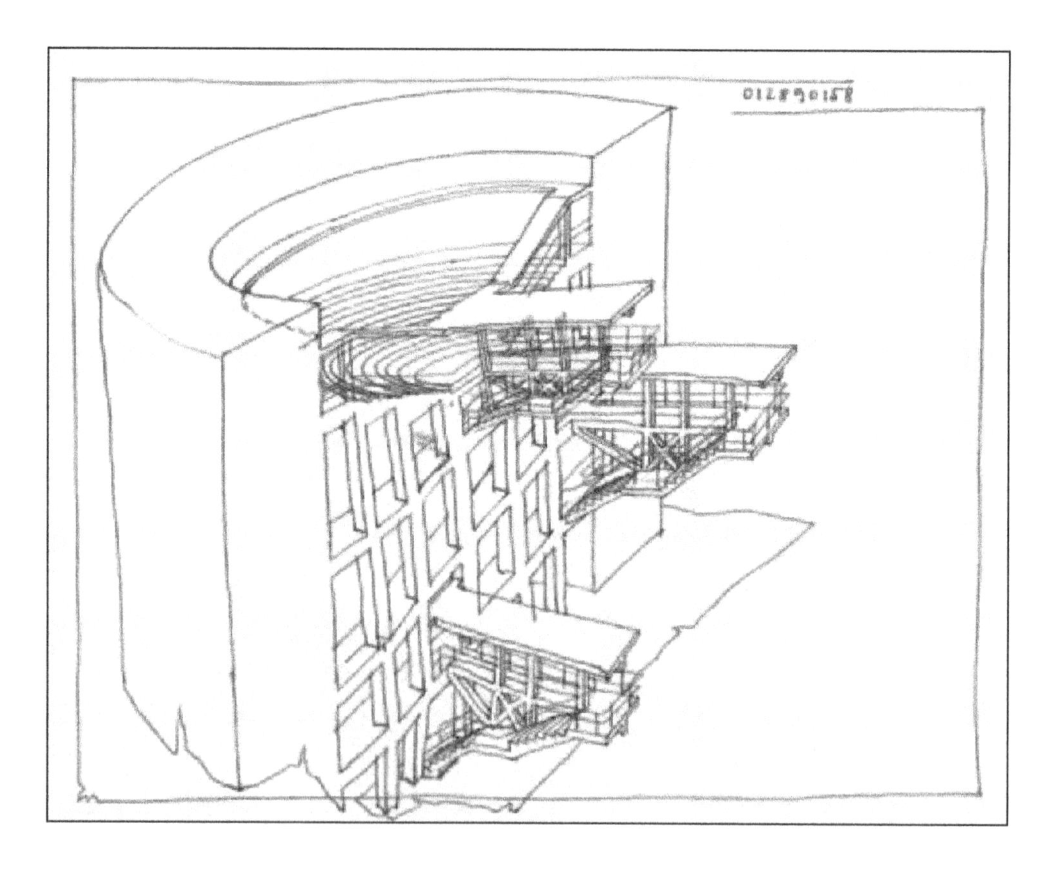
012890158

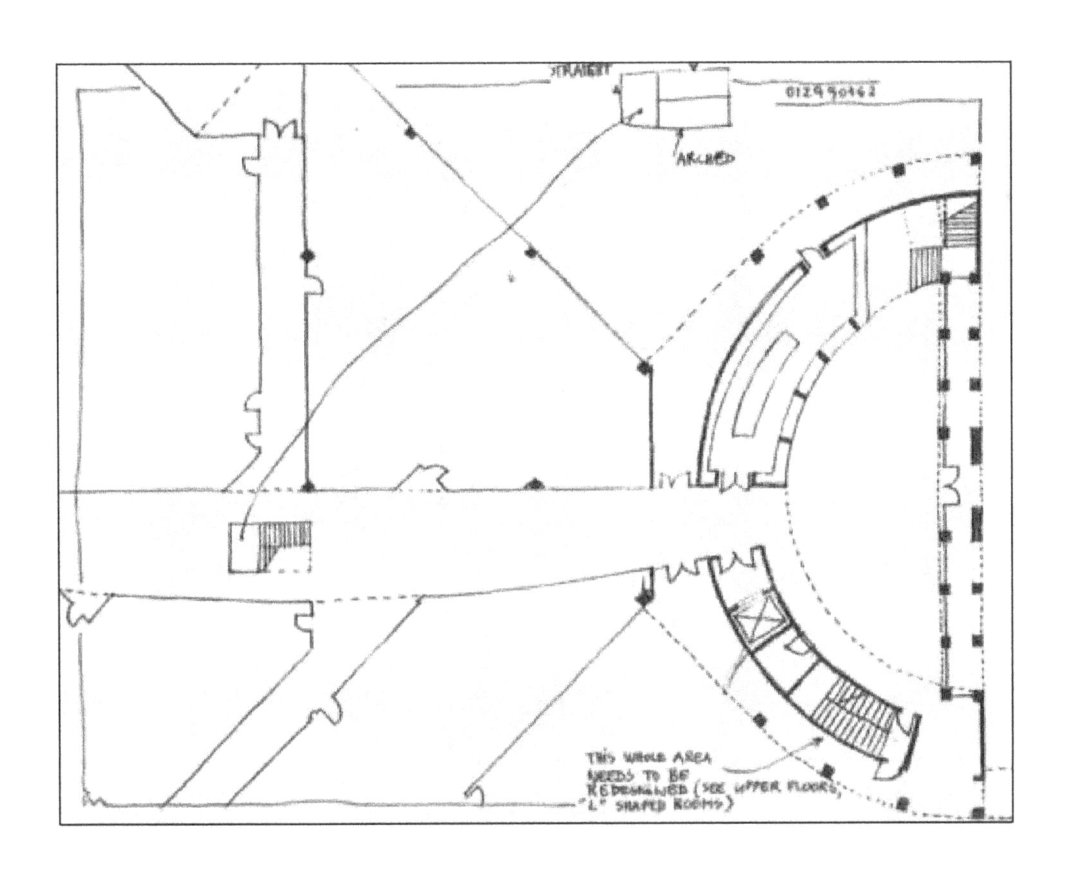
STRAIGHT
ARCHED
012990462
THIS WHOLE AREA NEEDS TO BE REDESIGNED (SEE UPPER FLOORS, "L" SHAPED ROOMS)

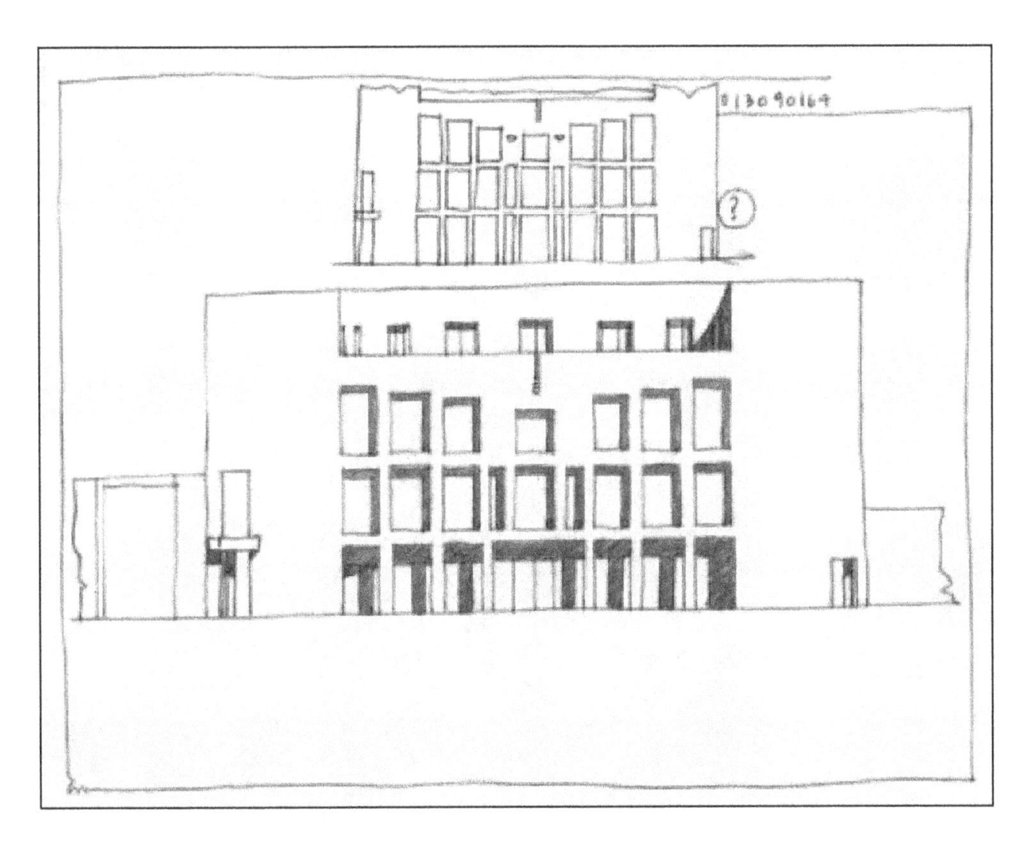
013090164

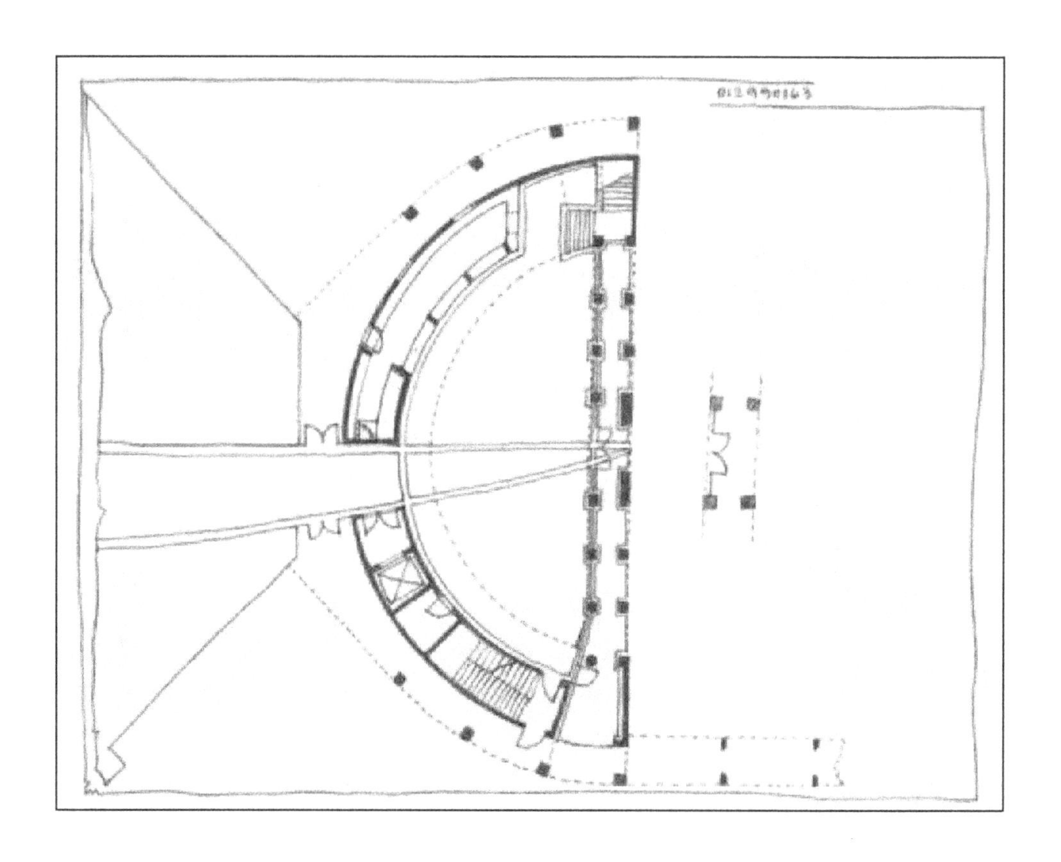

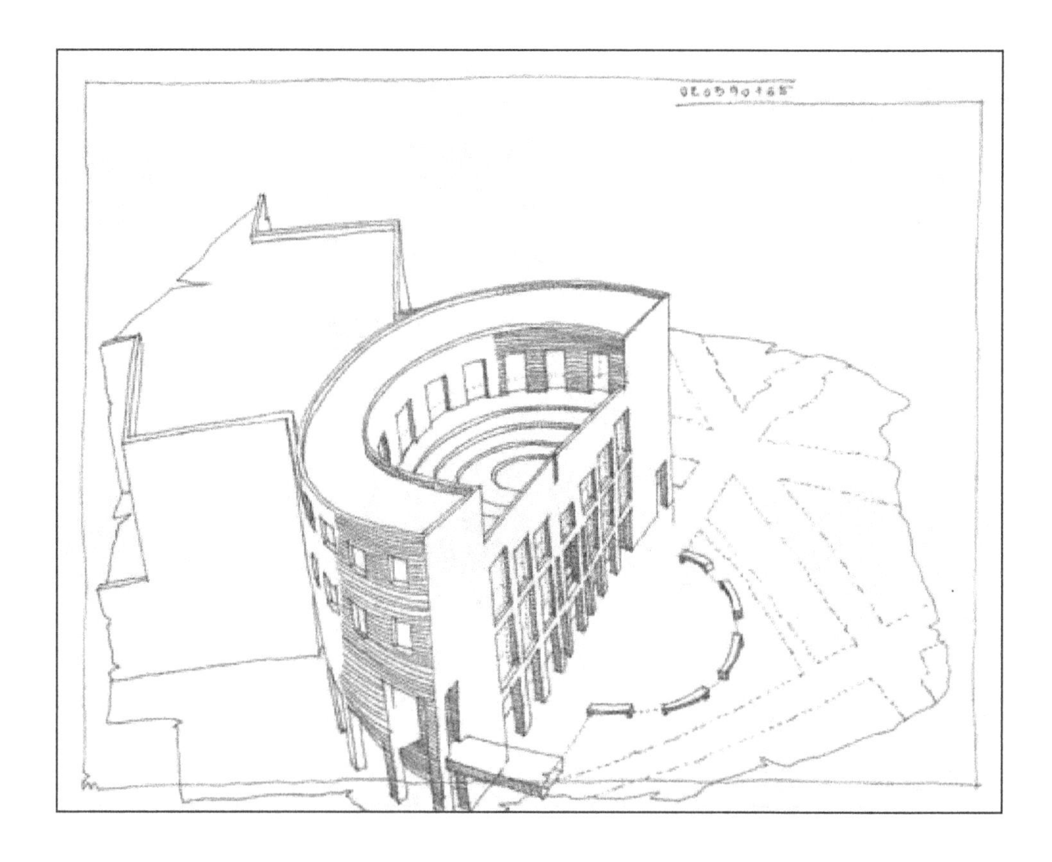

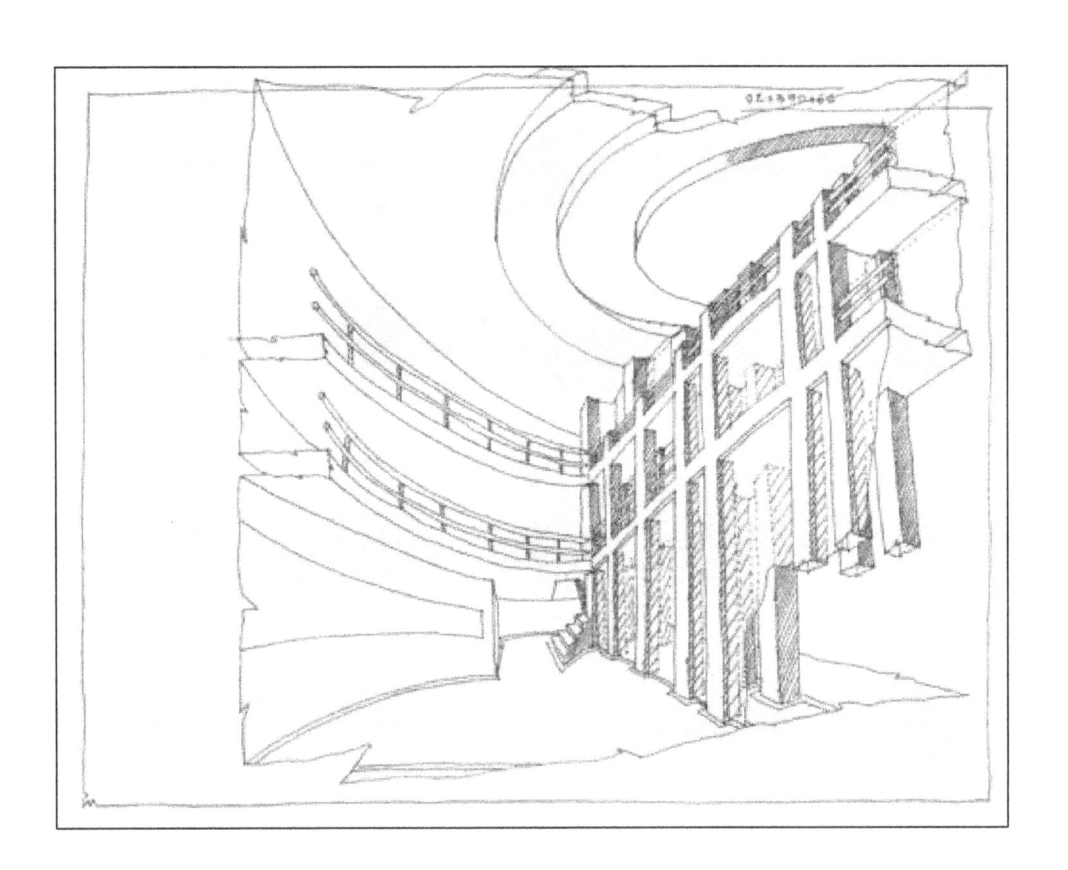

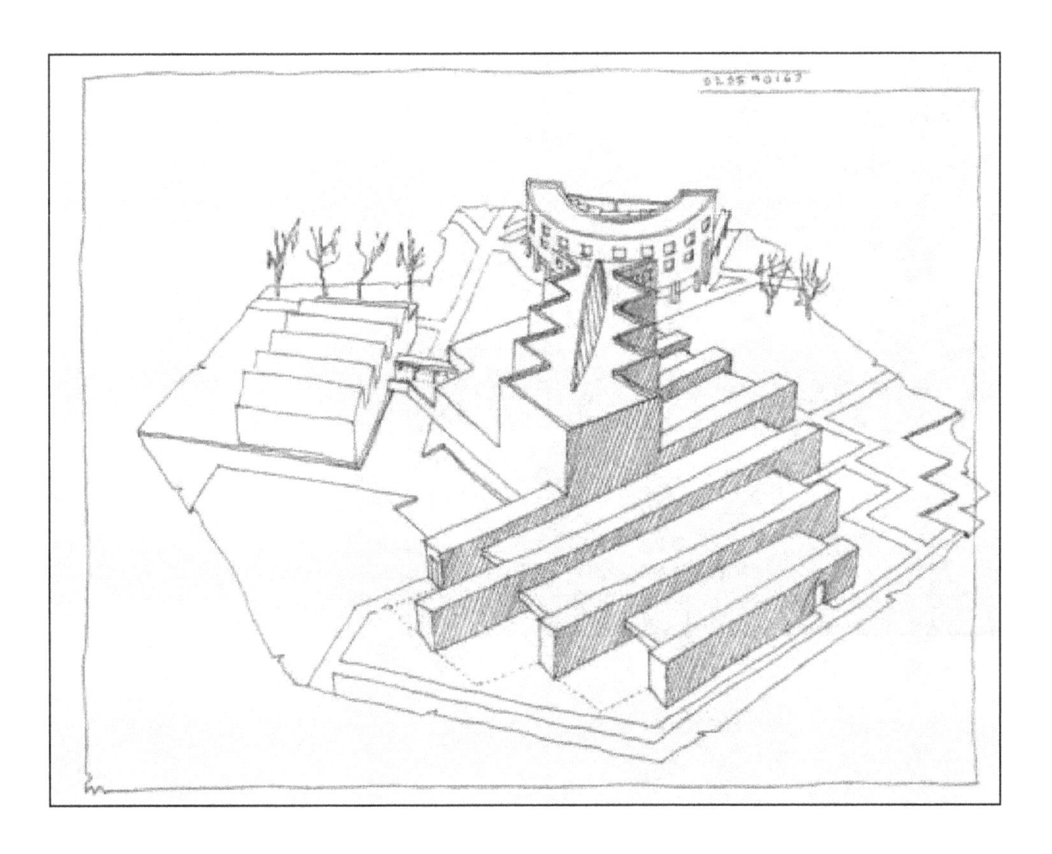

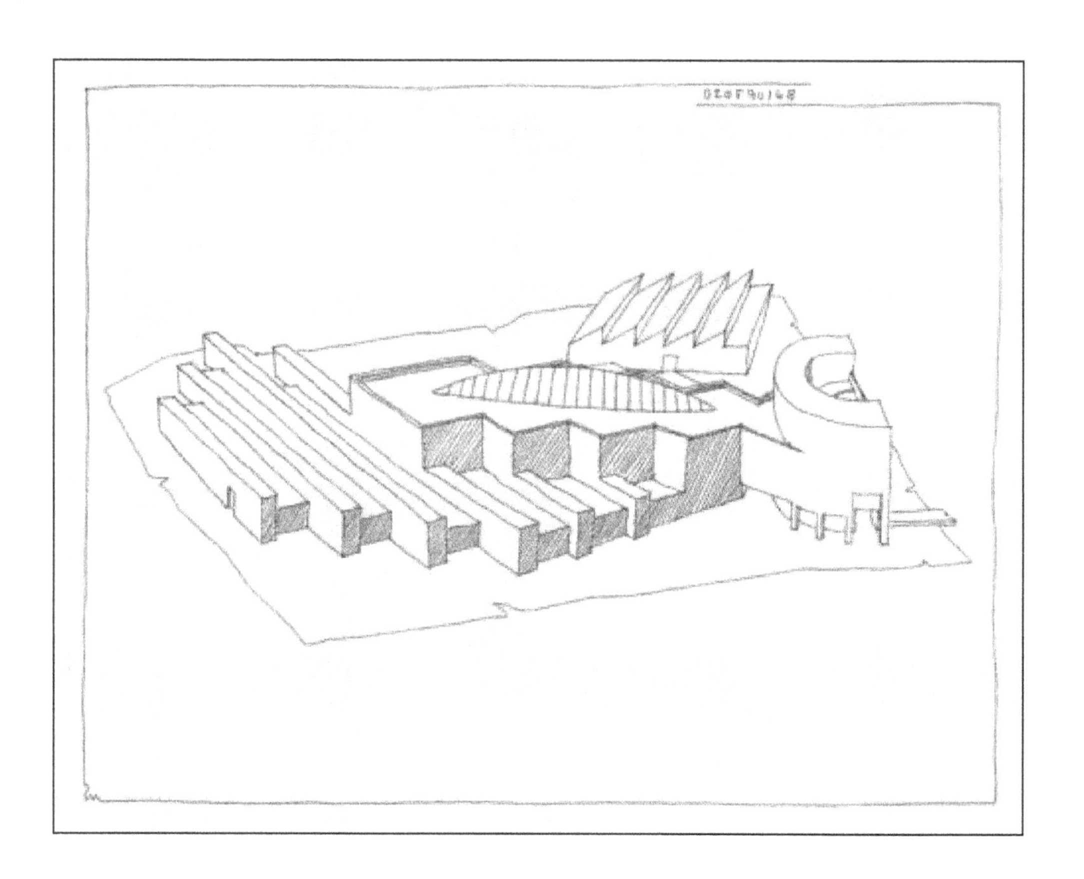

Chapter 6

MULTIPLE HORIZONS

Pen Zen Diaries #6

Chapter 6

(P.Z.D.6)
Multiple Horizons - International Port
Yokohama Japan

This project, the Competition for the International Port of Yokohama, Japan, offered an interesting educational opportunity for authors. A group of 15 students with mixed backgrounds (from second year to masters level) participated in the competition, from idea development to the required submission drawings. The process started in a democratic mode, giving everybody the same option for developing her or his idea for the final project. To demystify the very complex program, everybody was asked to poetically summarize the intentions, which will guide the design of the project. In this phase, in many different ways the result were quite mature products, in varying degrees grasping the symbolic or the rational aspects of the task. Unfortunately, and predictably, the first and later drawn-manifestations of the intents were less successful. Of these, author's attached sketches provide an overview. However, their assistance in inking the final boards is gratefully appreciated.

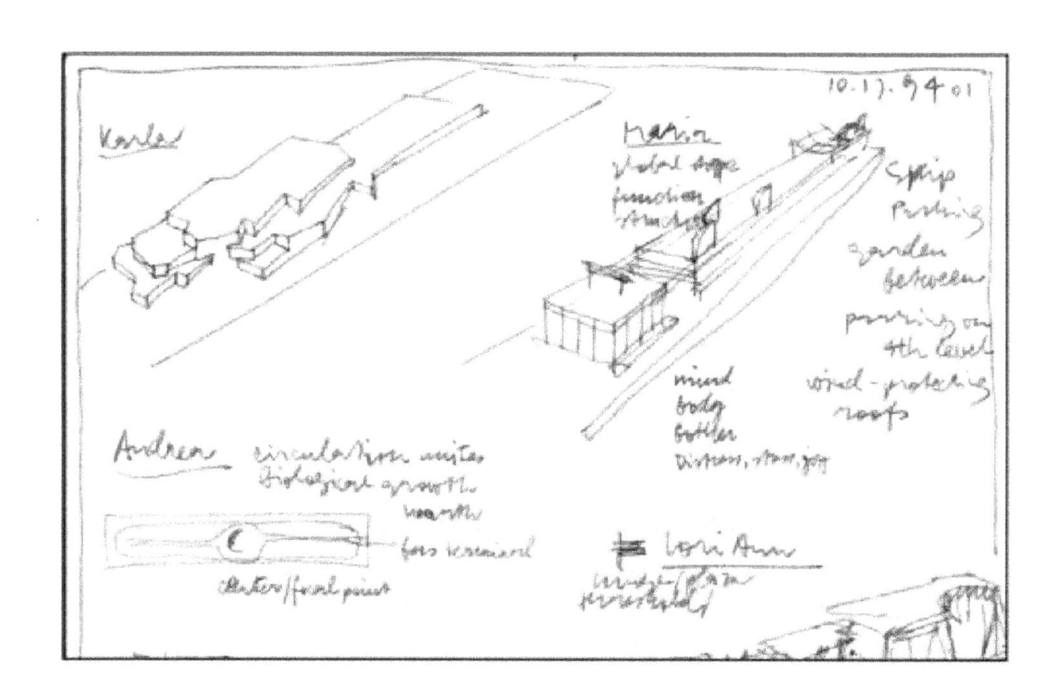

10.17.94 01
Karla
Marion
garden
between
parking on
4th level
wind-protecting
roofs
mind
body
Andrea
circulation unites
biological growth
Lori Ann

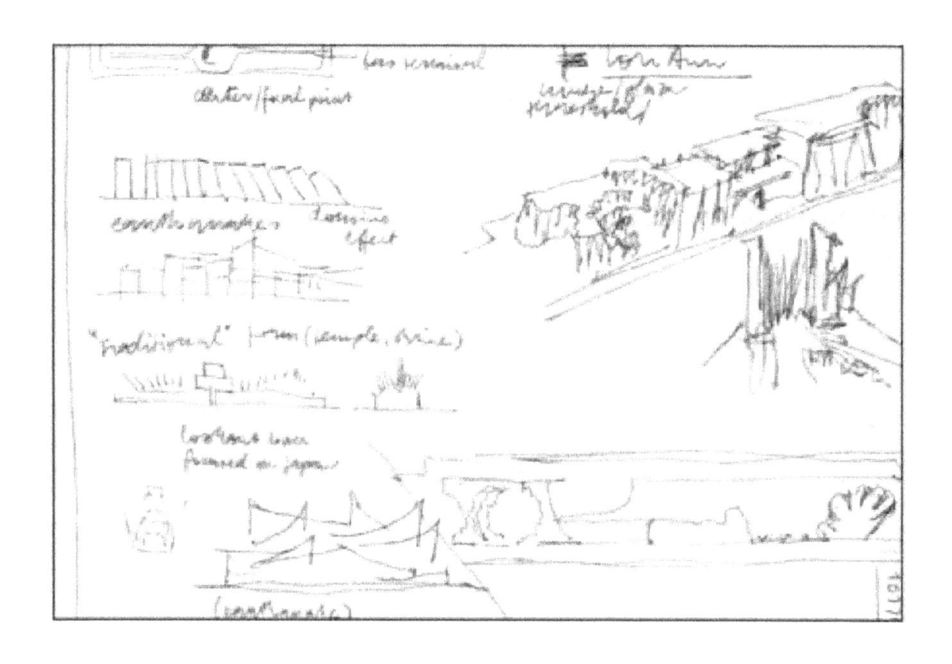

Lori Ann

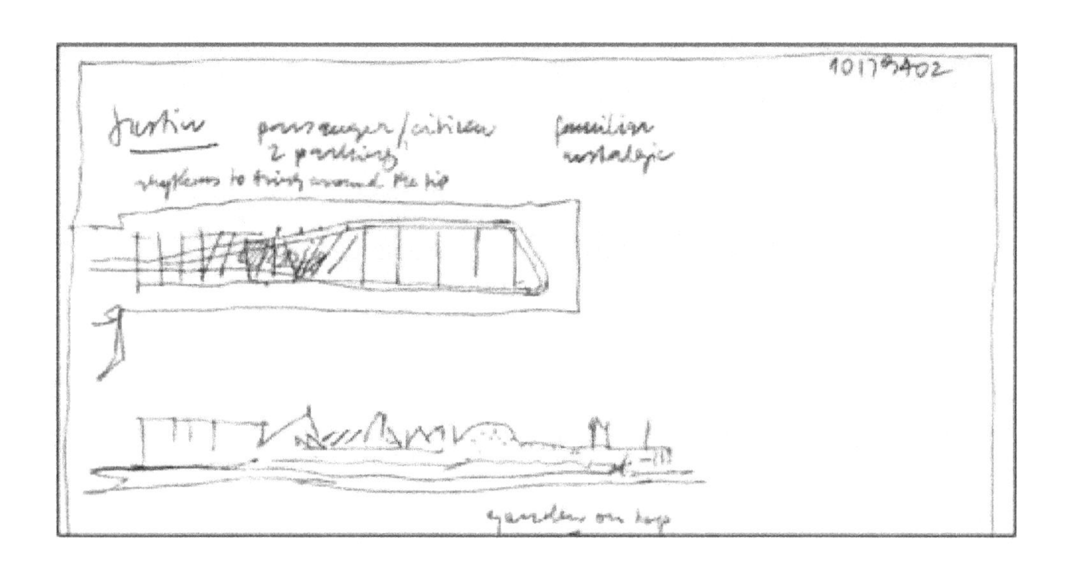

Justin
passenger/citizen
2 parking
familiar
nostalgic
garden on top

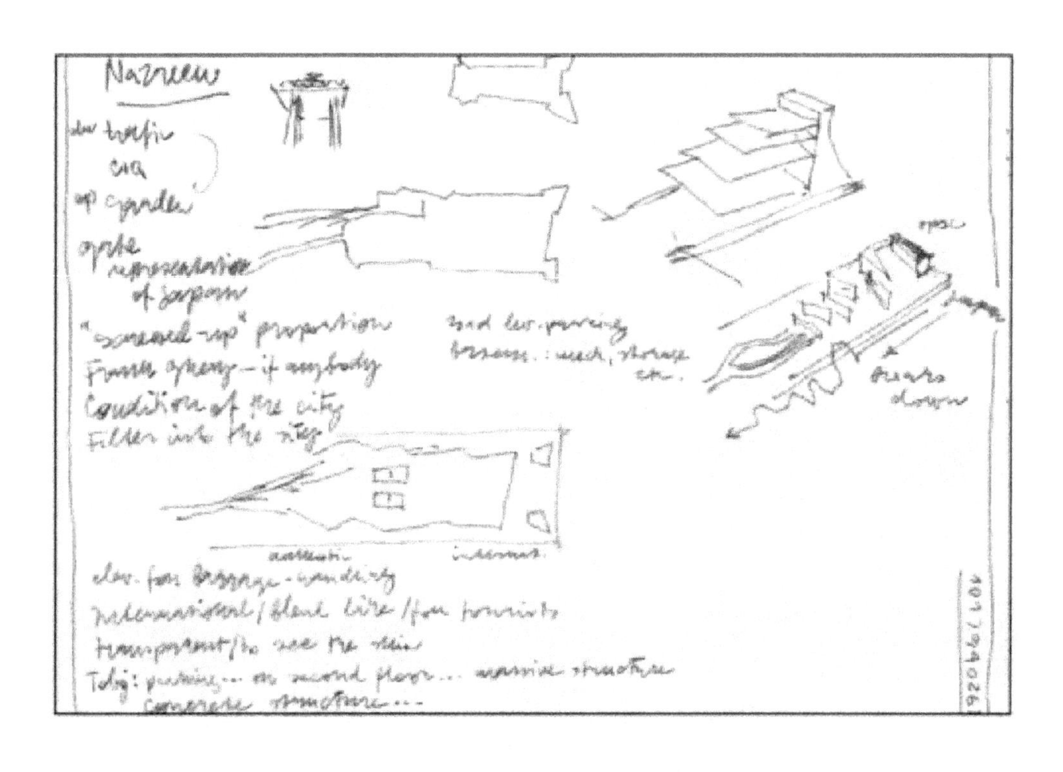

Nazreen
Condition of the city

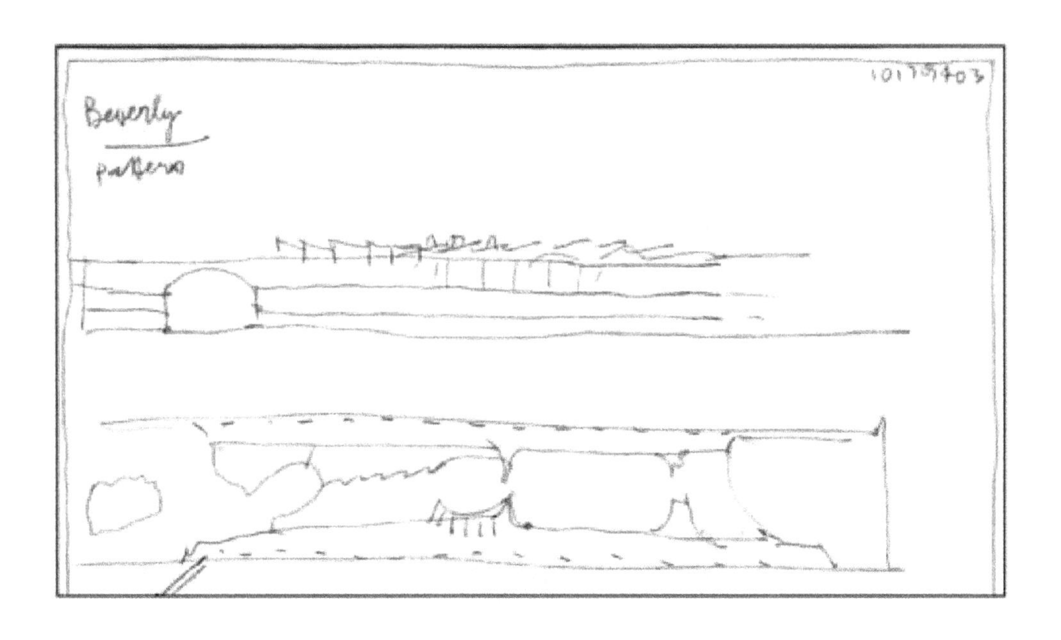
Beverly
pattern
10179703

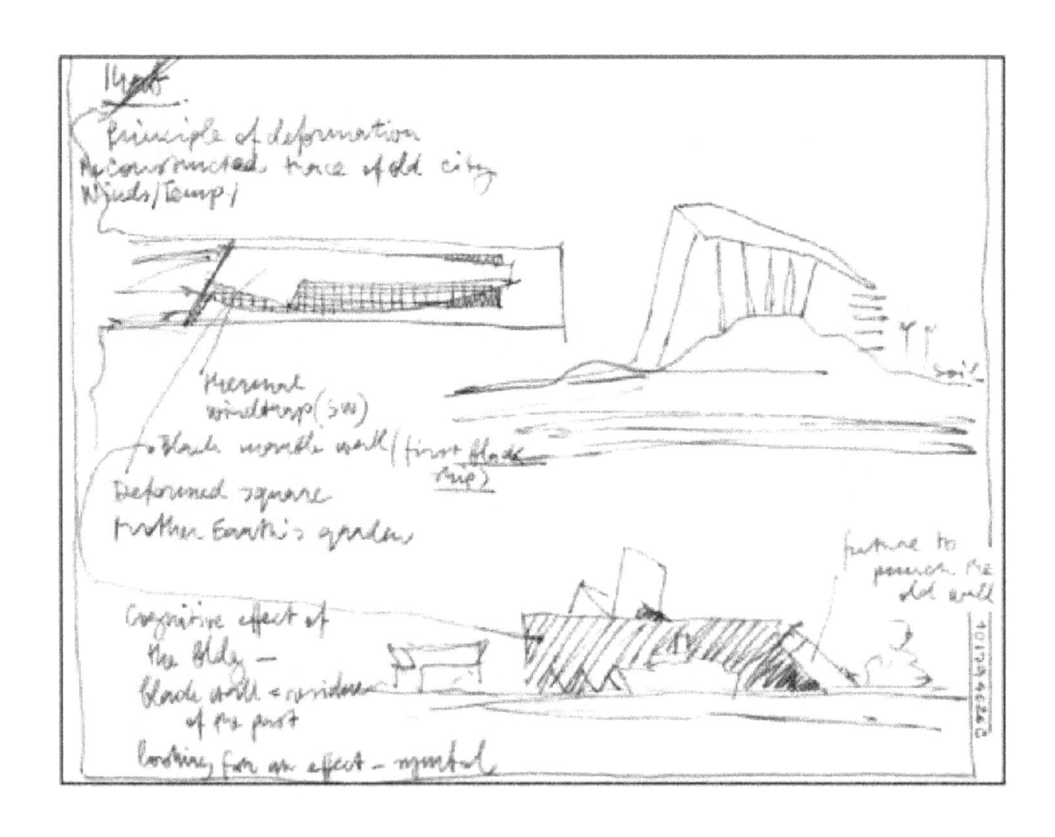
Principle of deformation
Reconstructed trace of old city
Winds/Temp./
seasonal windtrap (SW)
Deformed square
Mother Earth's garden
soil
Cognitive effect of
the Bldg —
black wall = evidence
of the past
looking for an effect – symbol

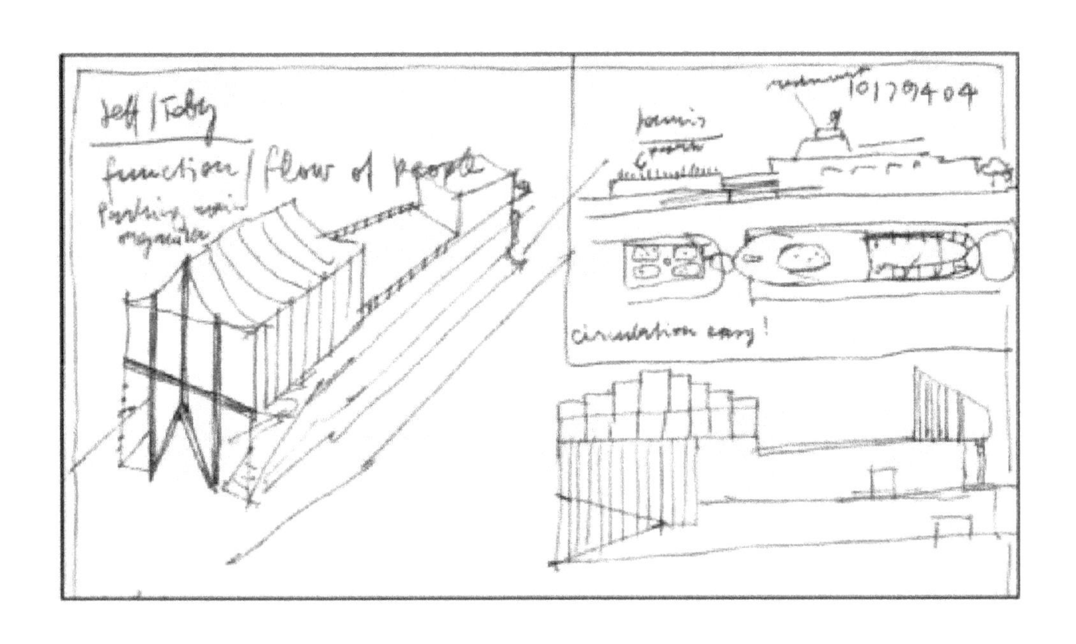
Jeff / Toby
function / flow of people
circulation easy!

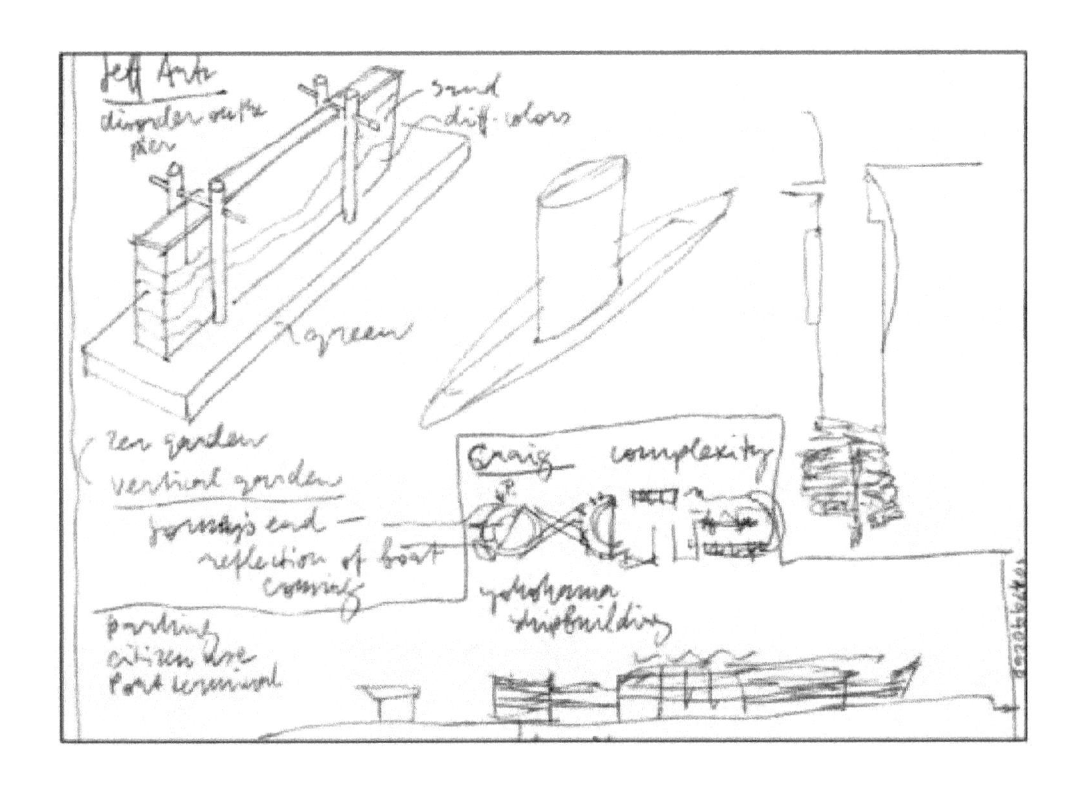
sand
diff. colors
zen garden
vertical garden
reflection of boat
coming
Craig
complexity
yokohama
shipbuilding
parking
citizen use
Port terminal

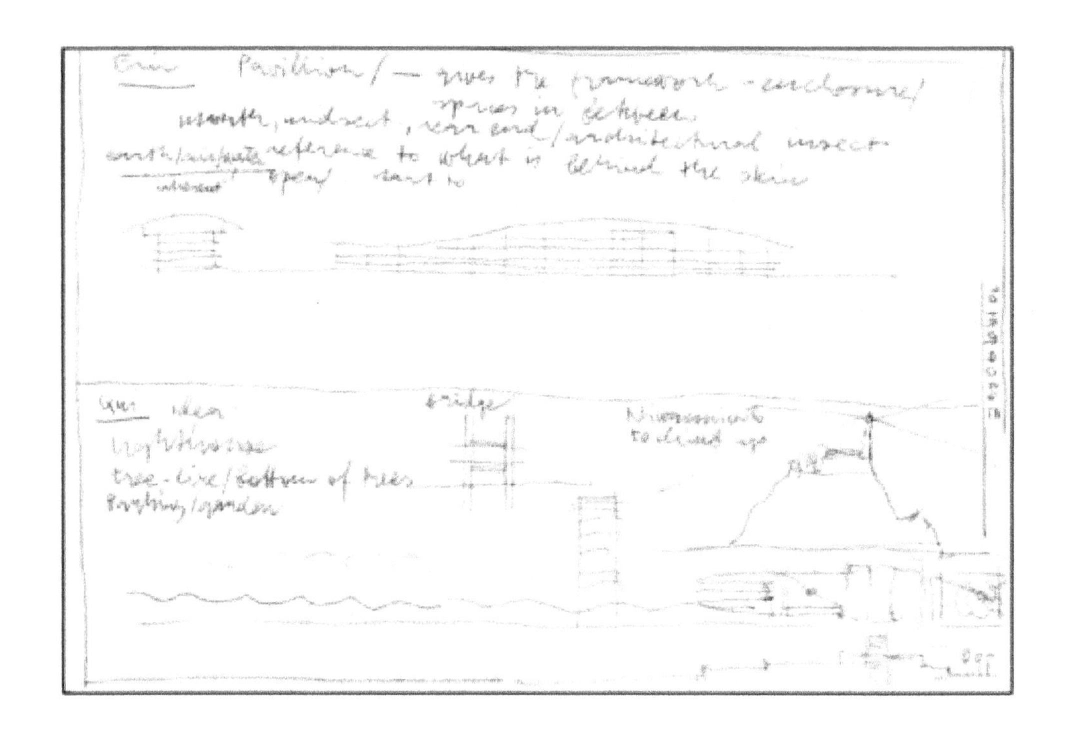
Pavilion / — gives the framework - enclosure /
spaces in between
bridge
lighthouse
tree-line / bottom of trees
Parking / garden

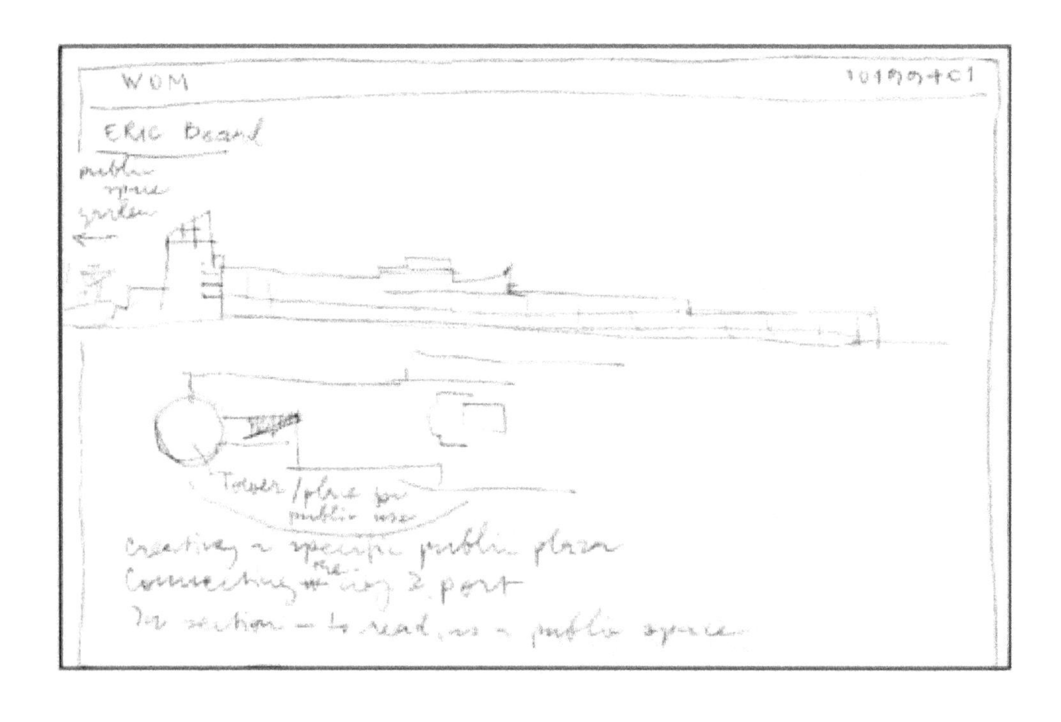
WOM
ERIC Beard
public
space
garden
Tower / place for
public use
Creating a specific public plaza
The section — to read as a public space

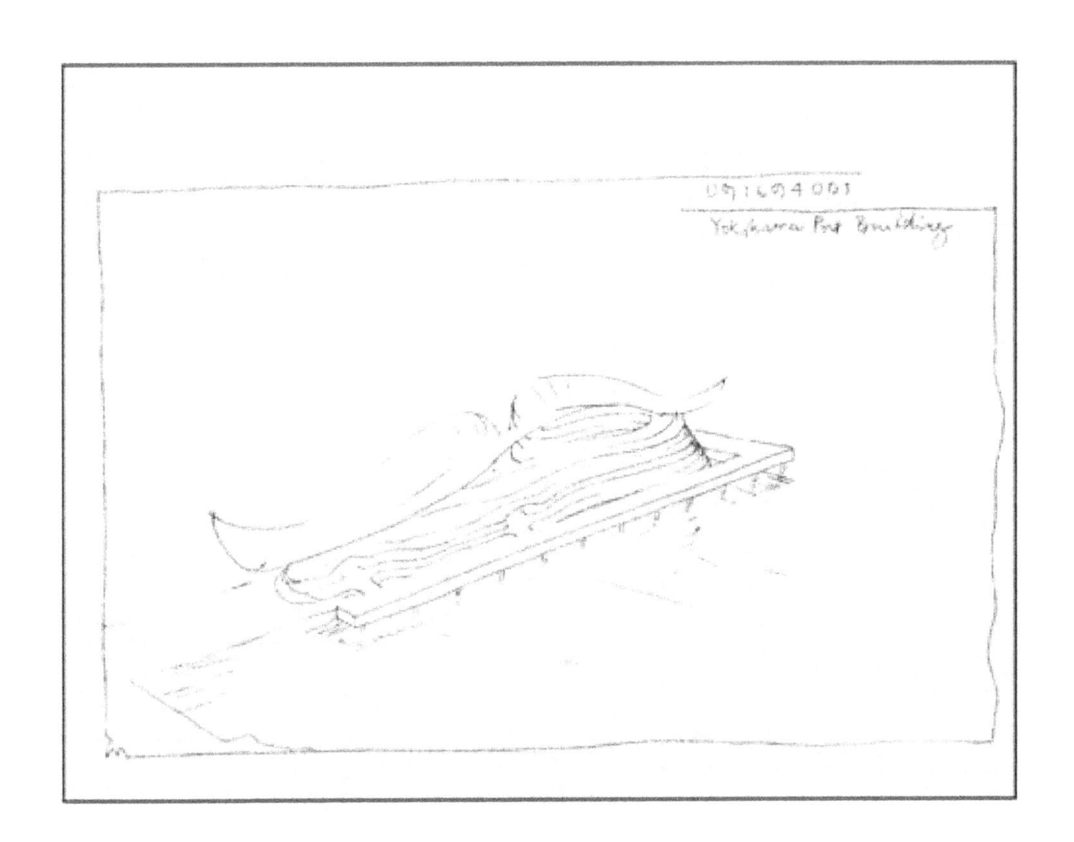
091694001
Yokohama Port Building

091694002

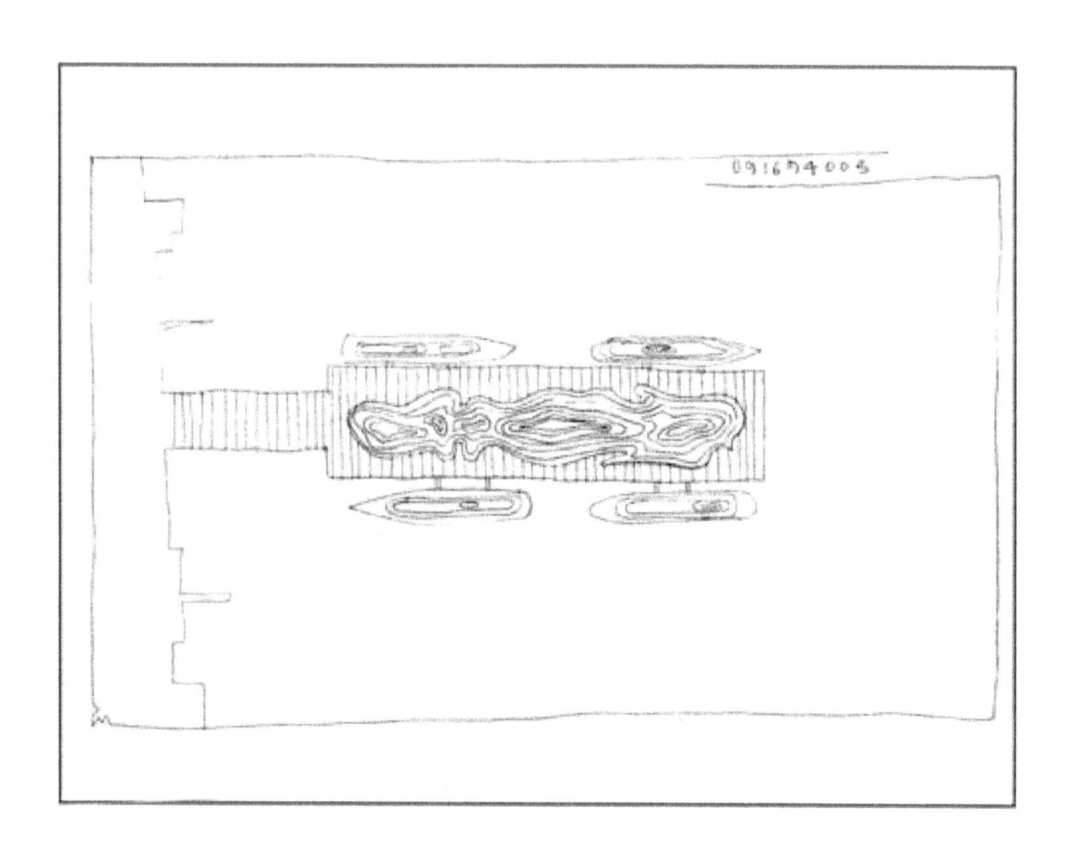
091634005

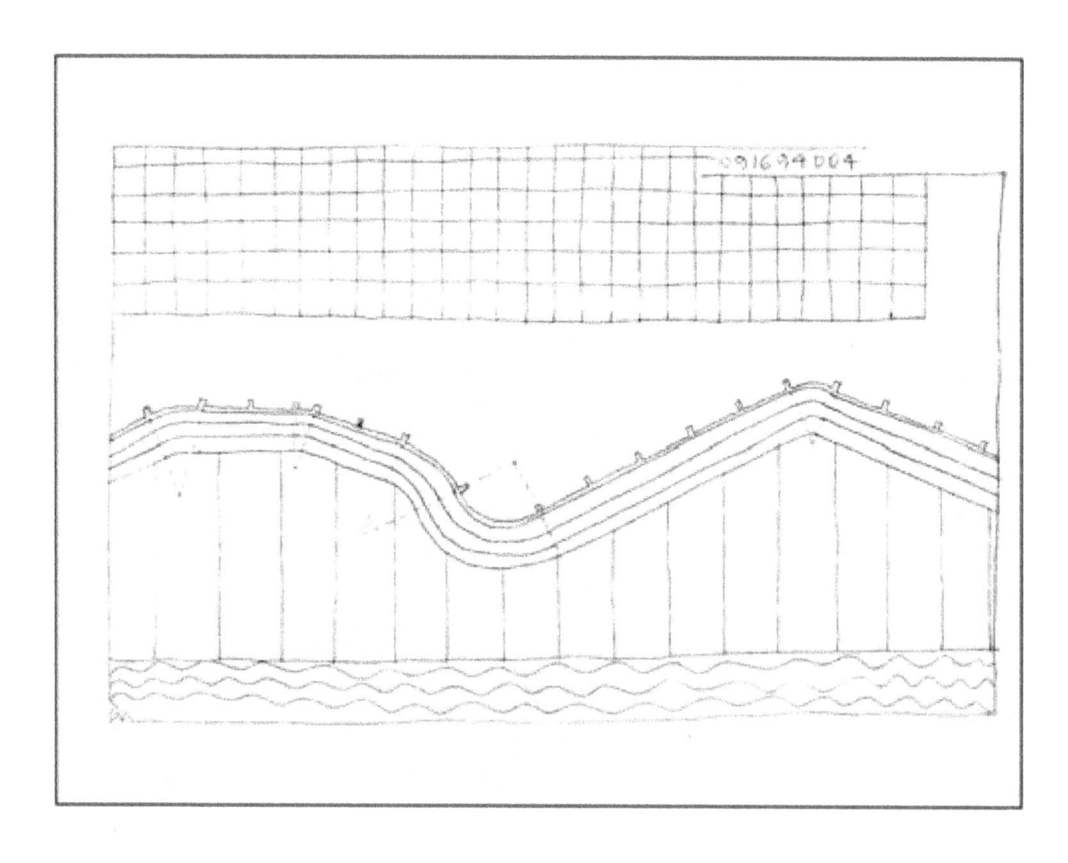
091634004

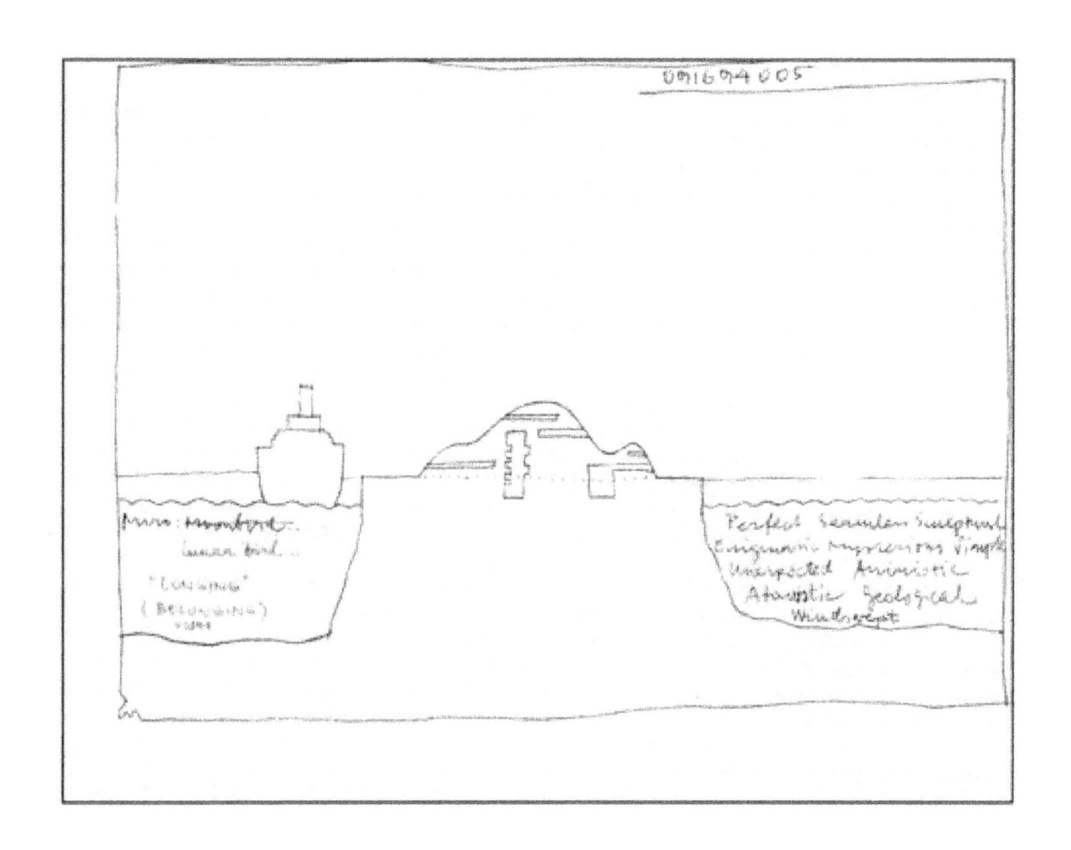
091694005
Unexpected Animistic
Atavistic Geological
Windswept

092294006

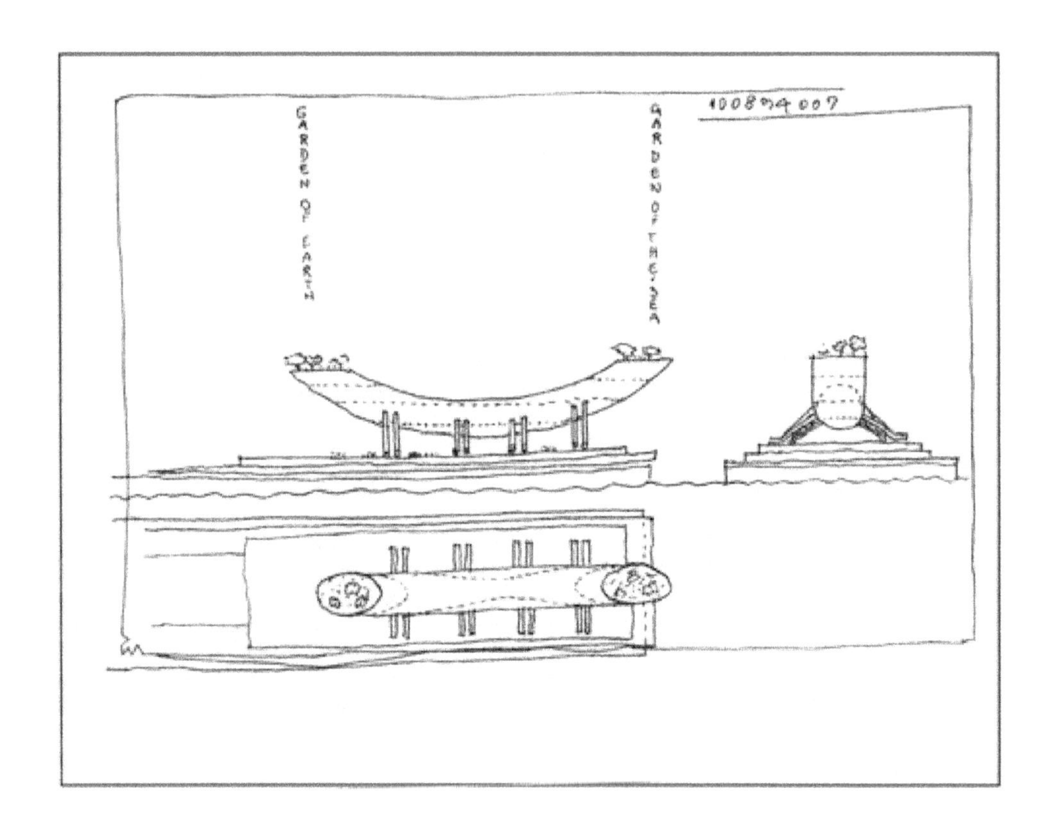
GARDEN OF EARTH
GARDEN OF THE SEA

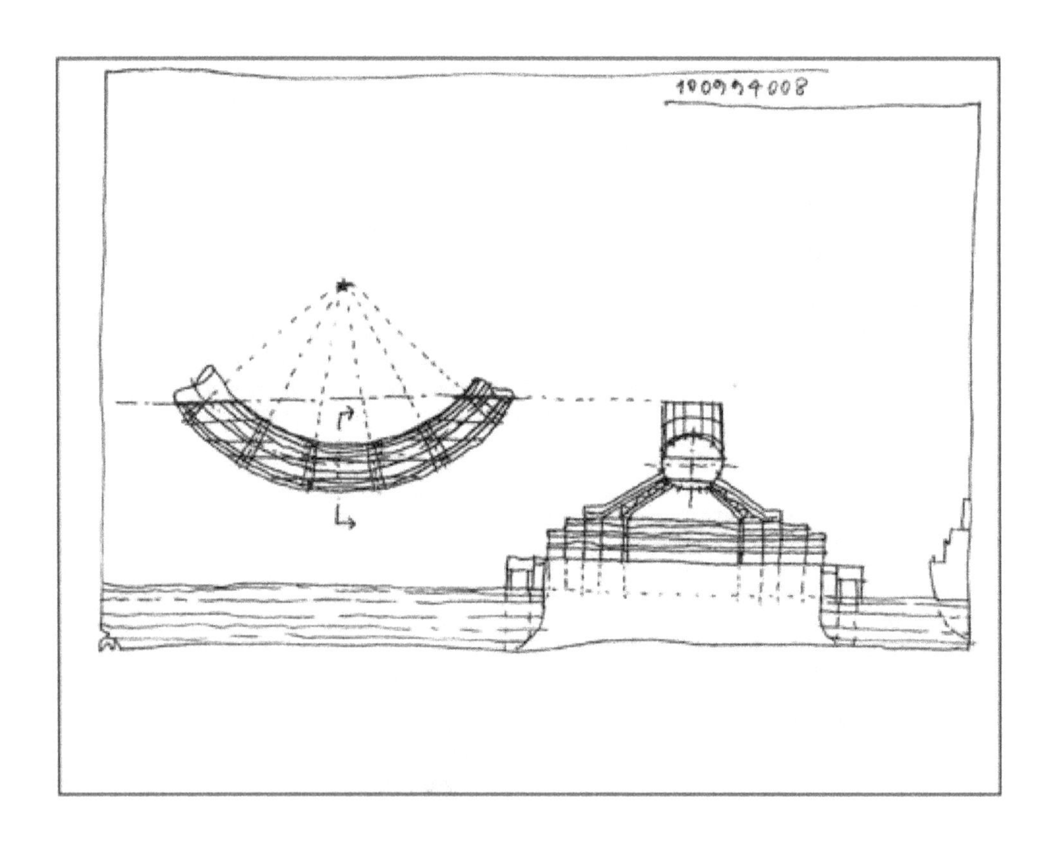

100974009

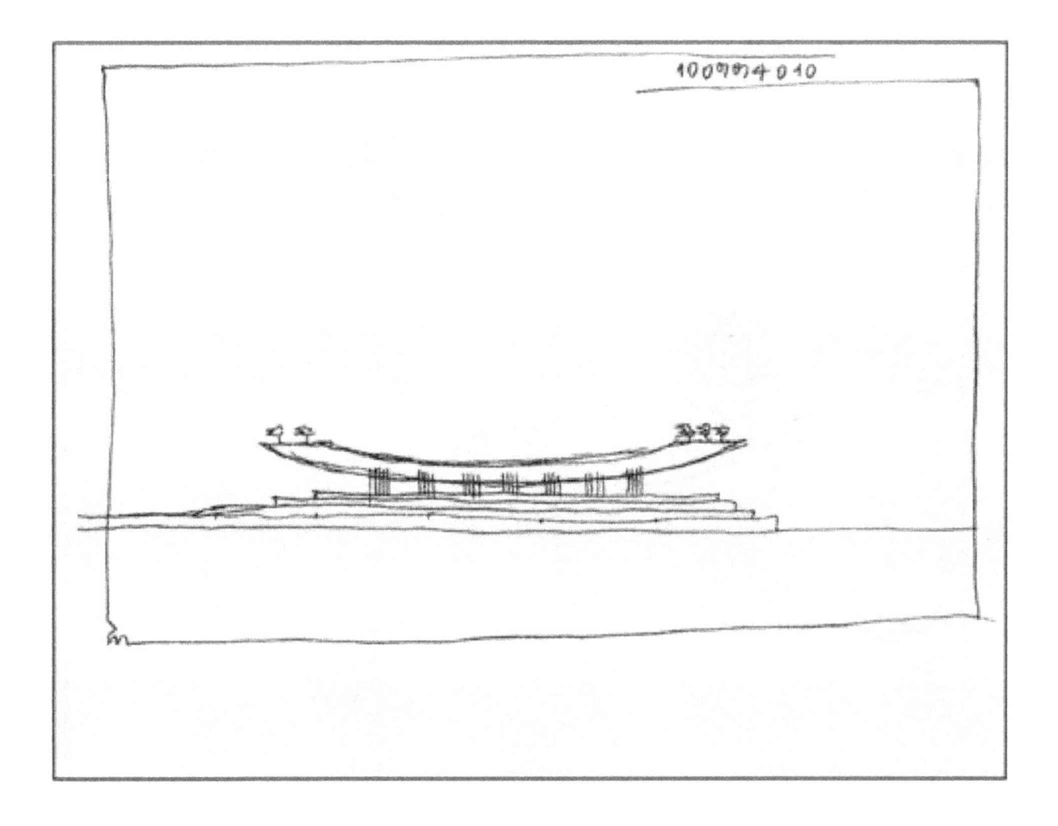
100974010

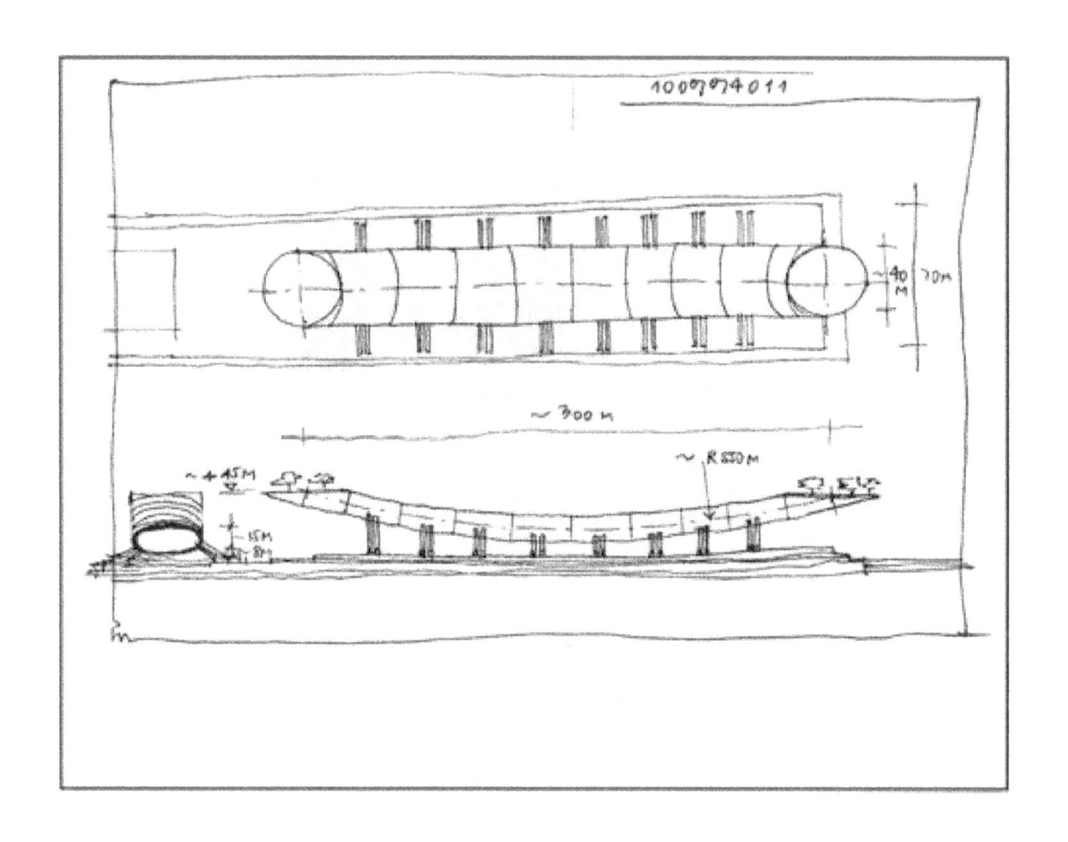
~300 m
~+45M
15M
8M
~40 M
70m

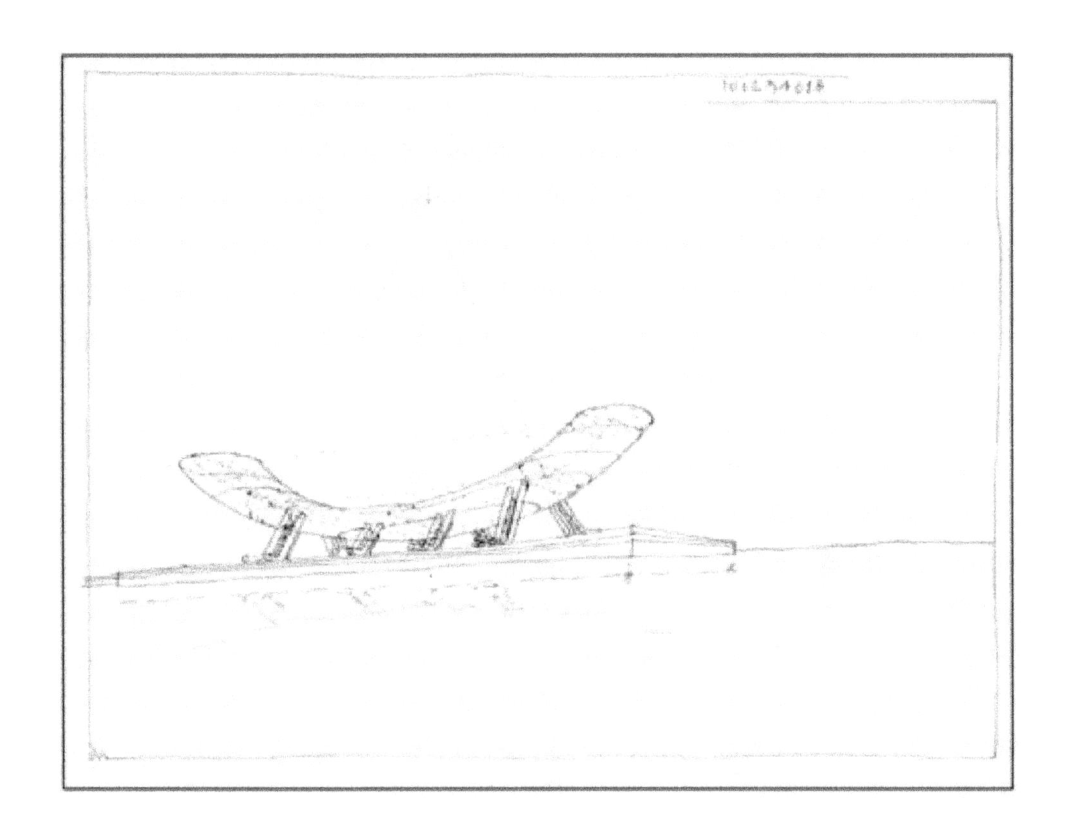

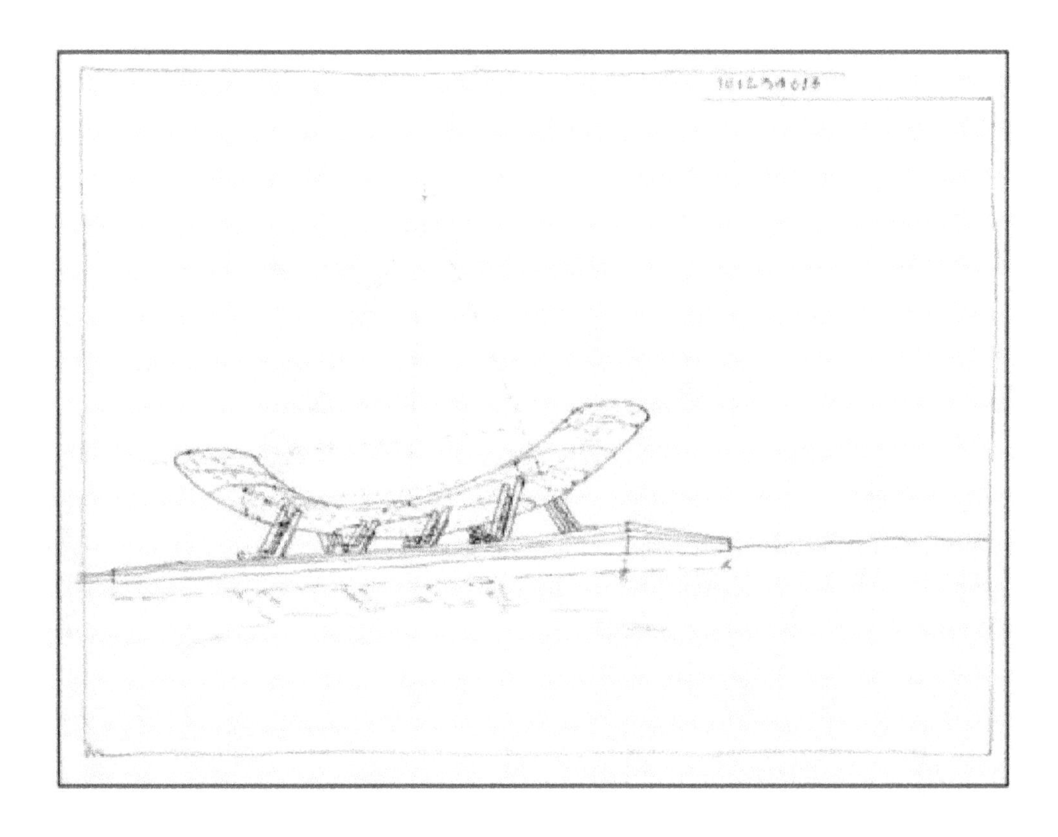

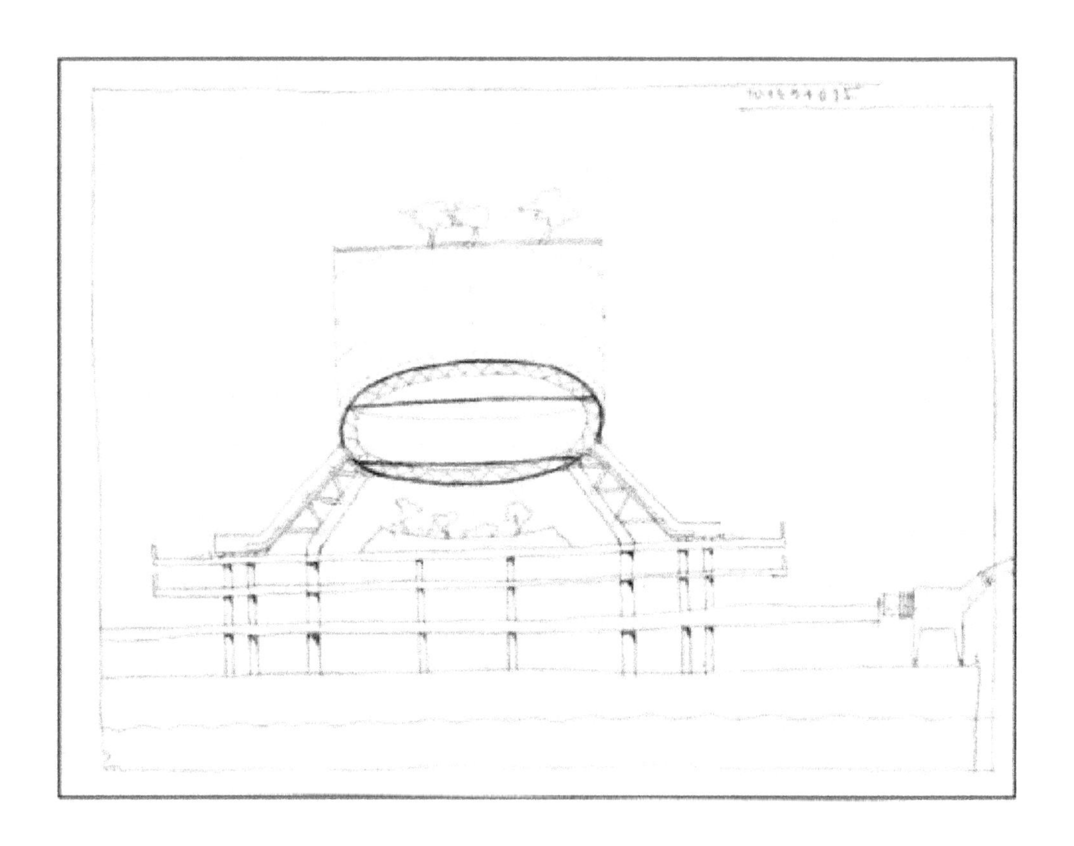

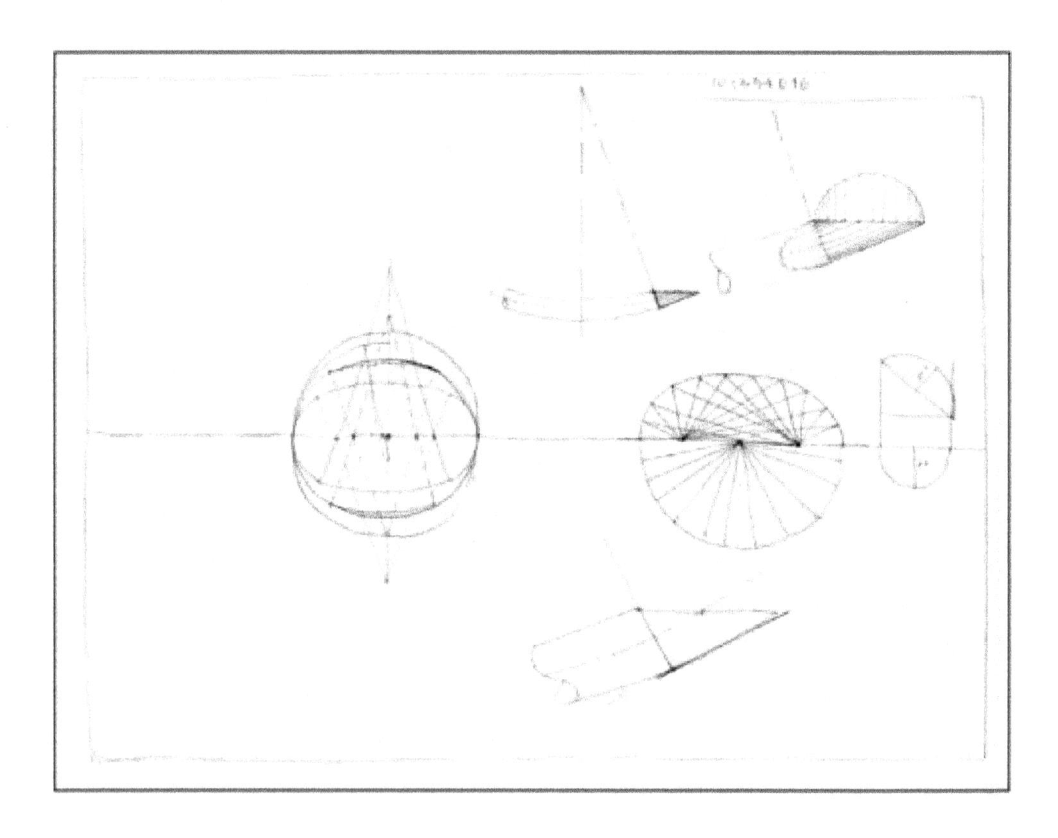

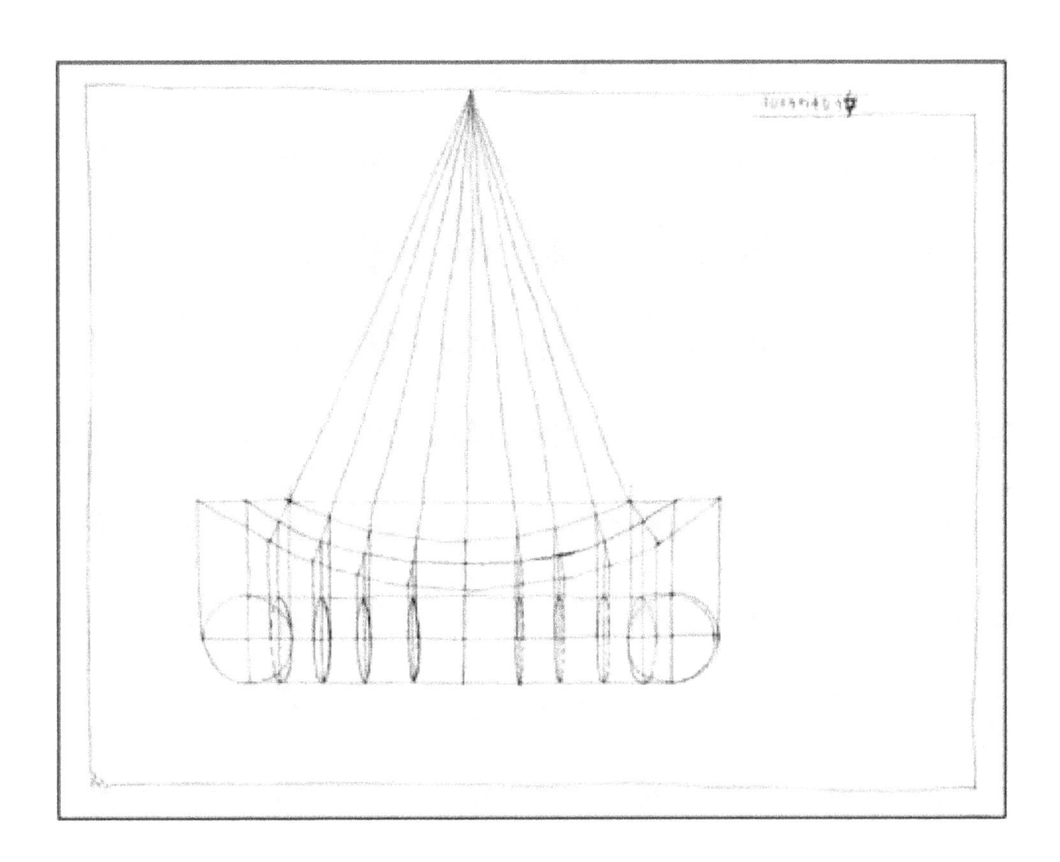

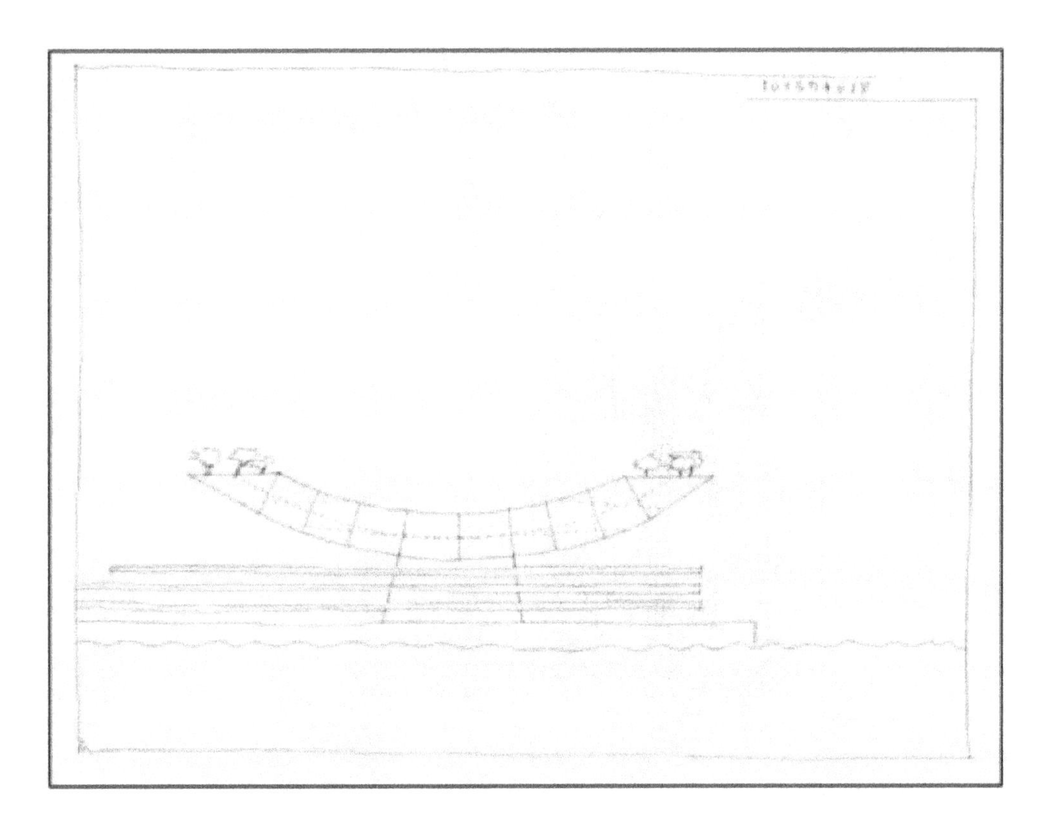

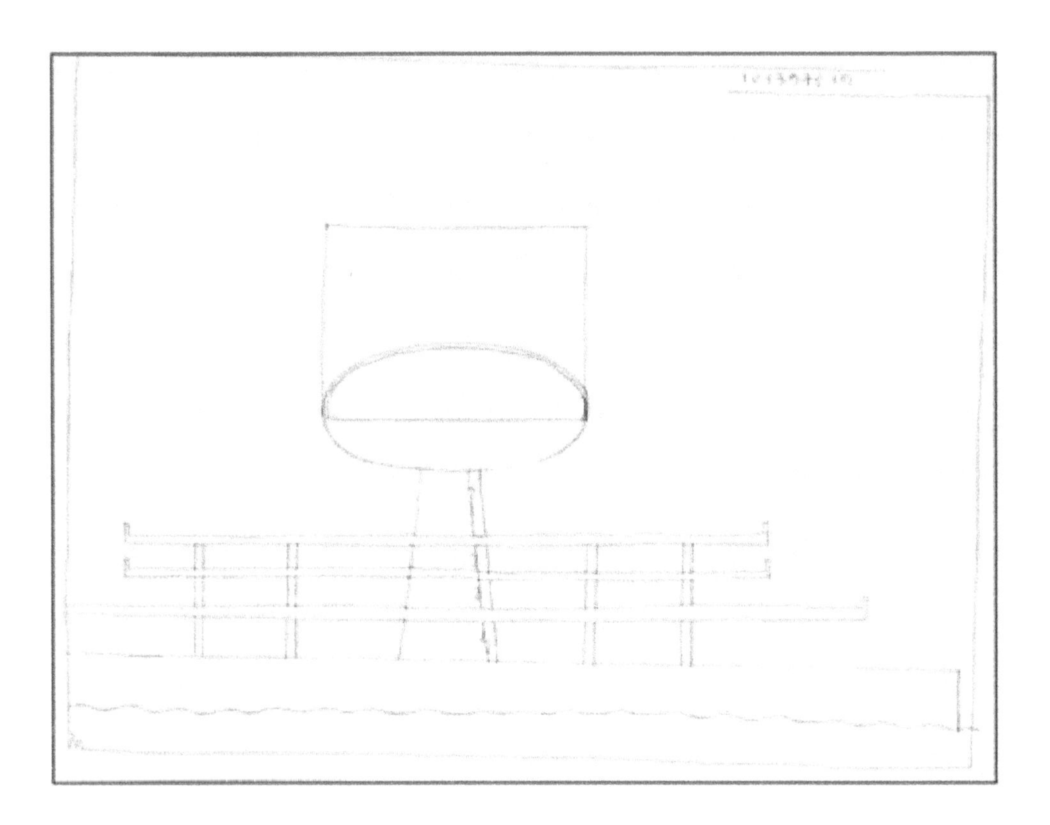

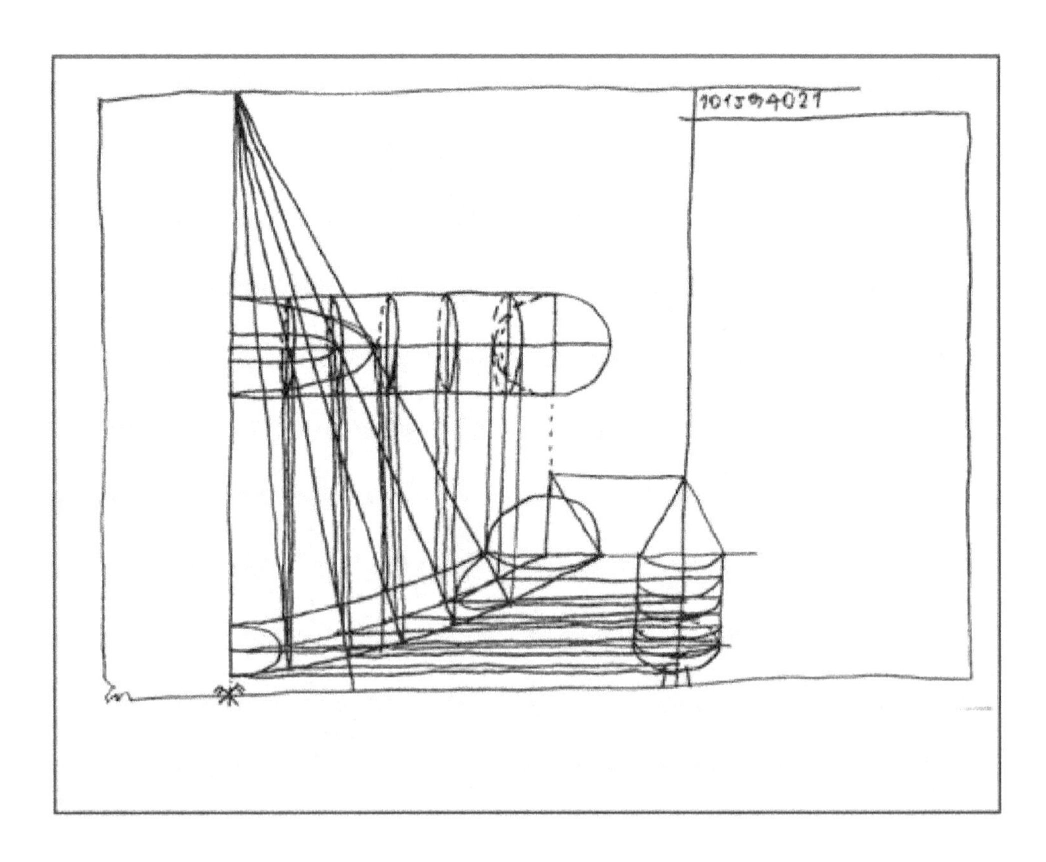
1015の4027

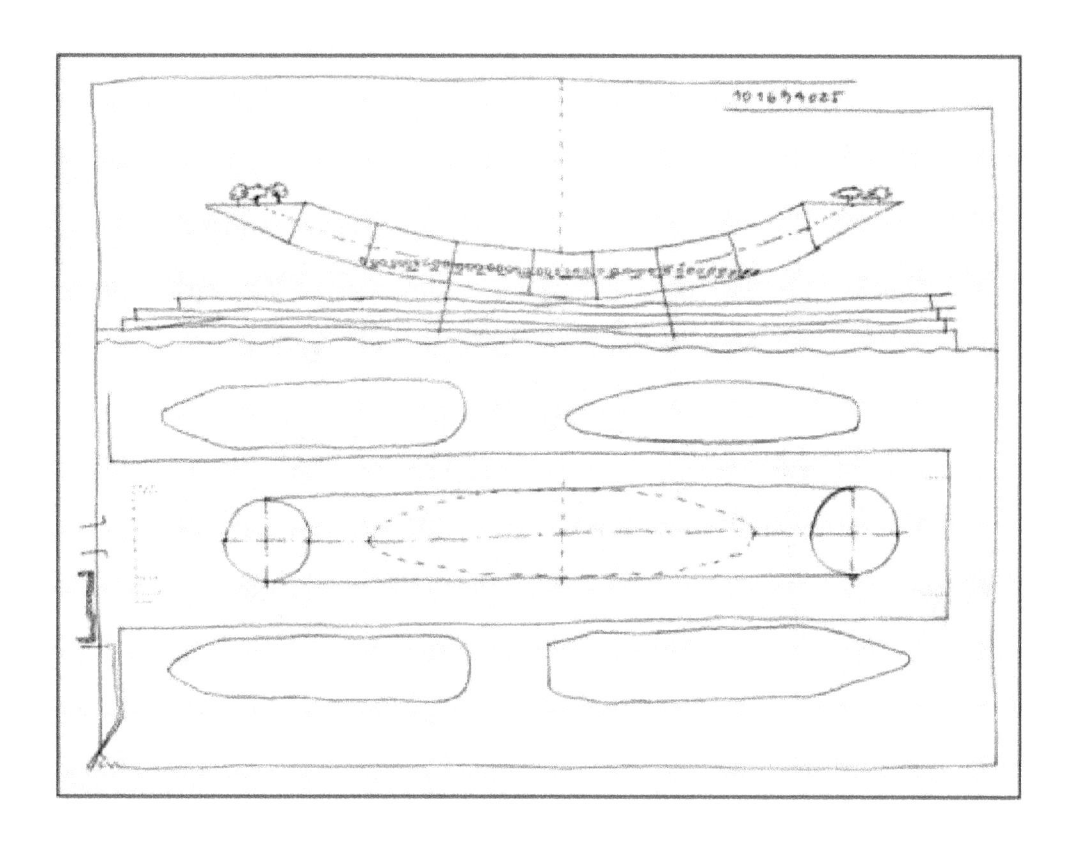

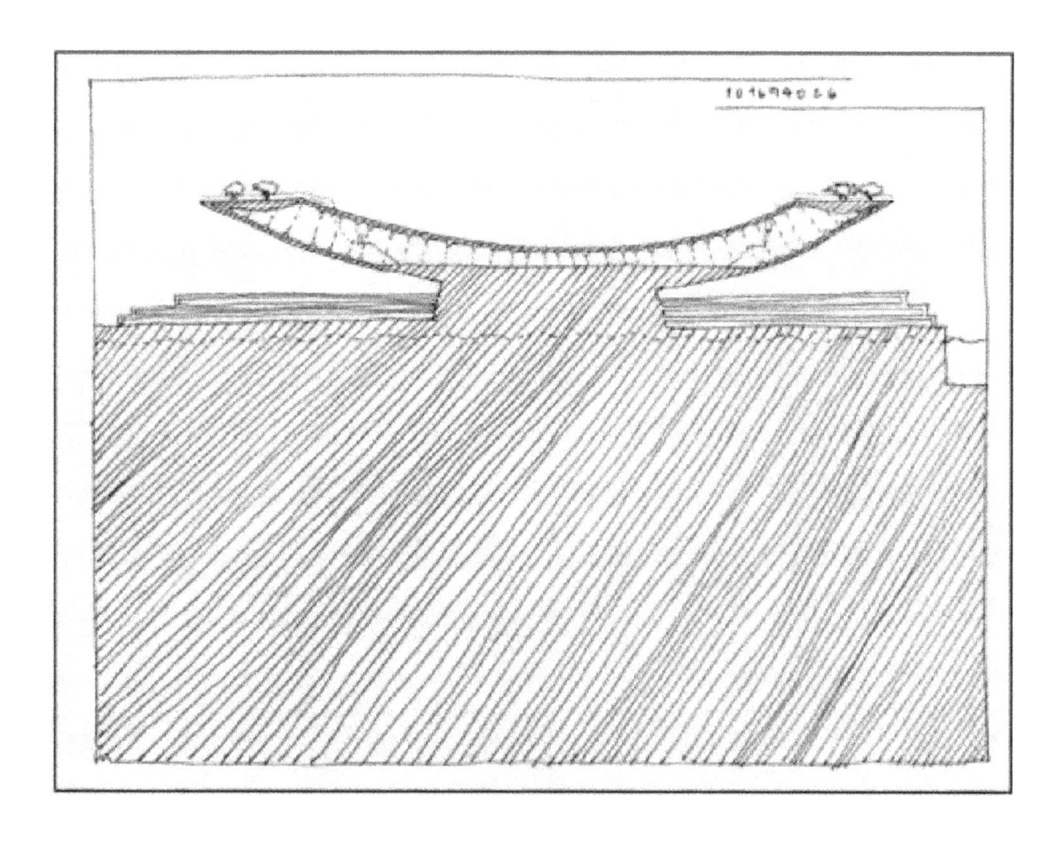

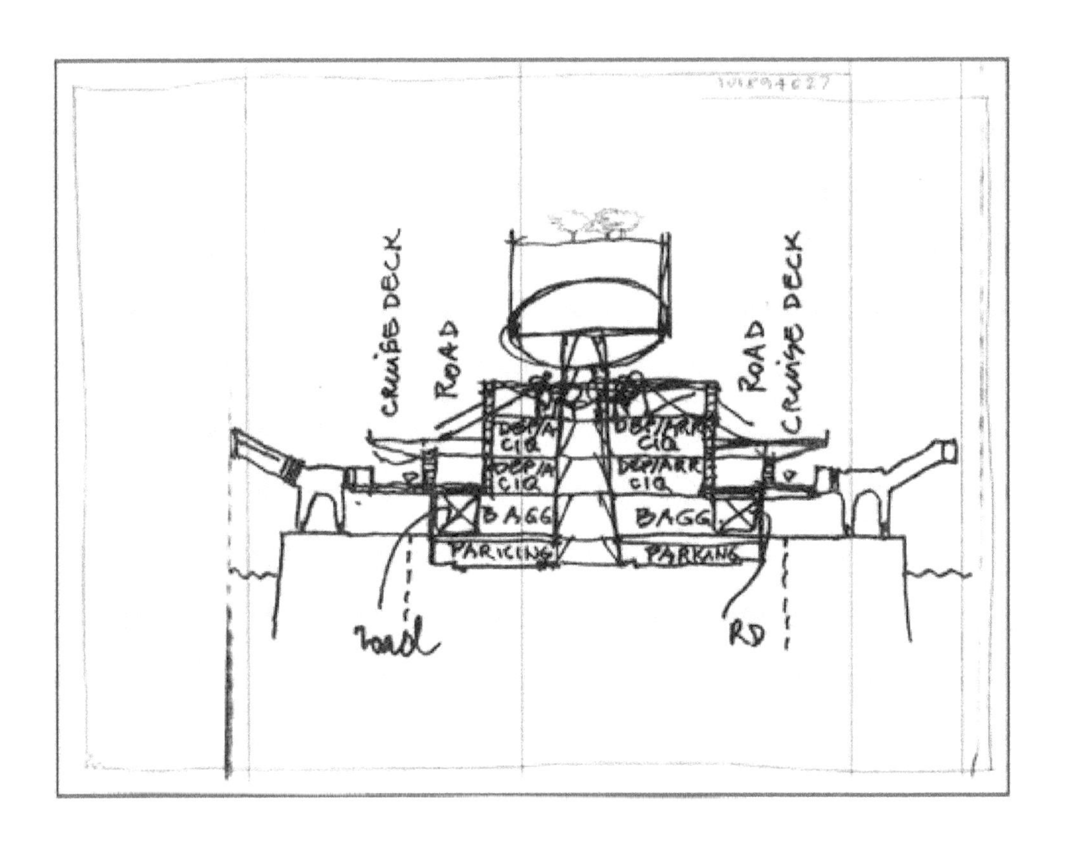
CRUISE DECK
ROAD
ROAD
CRUISE DECK
CIQ
DEP/ARR
CIQ
BAGG
BAGG
PARKING
PARKING
road
RD

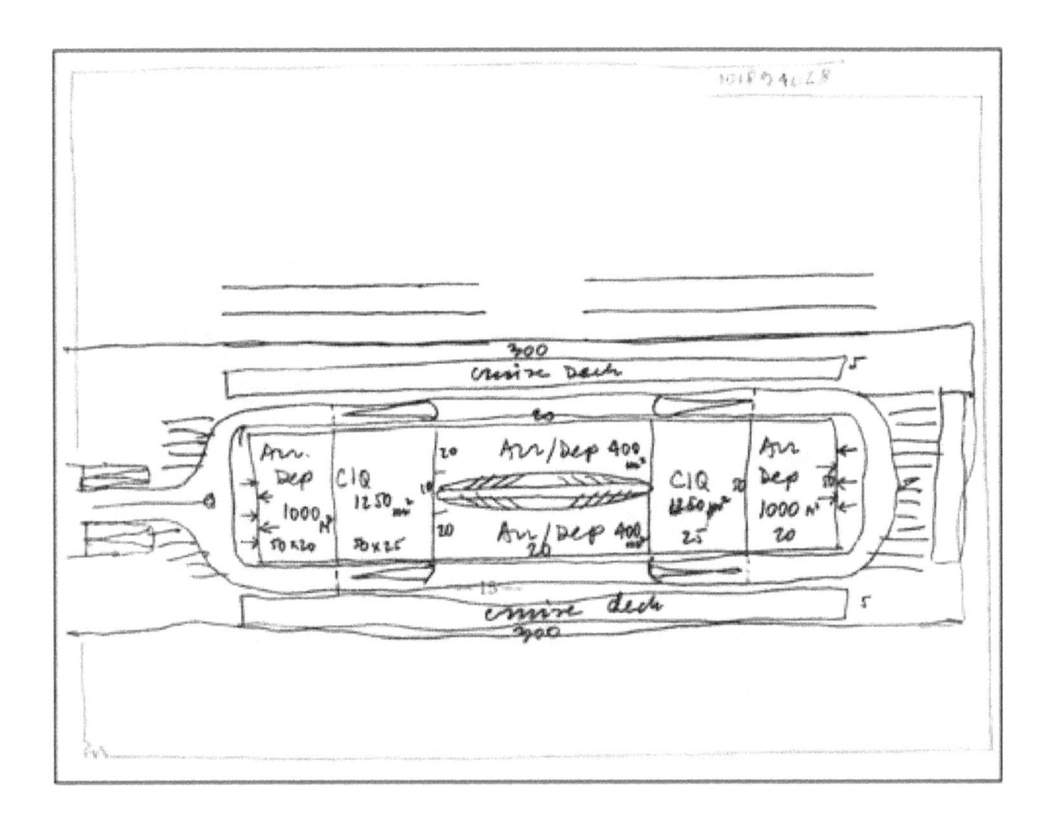
300
cruise deck
5
Arr/Dep 400
Arr.
Dep
1000
CIQ
CIQ
Arr
Dep
1000
Arr/Dep 400
cruise deck
5
300

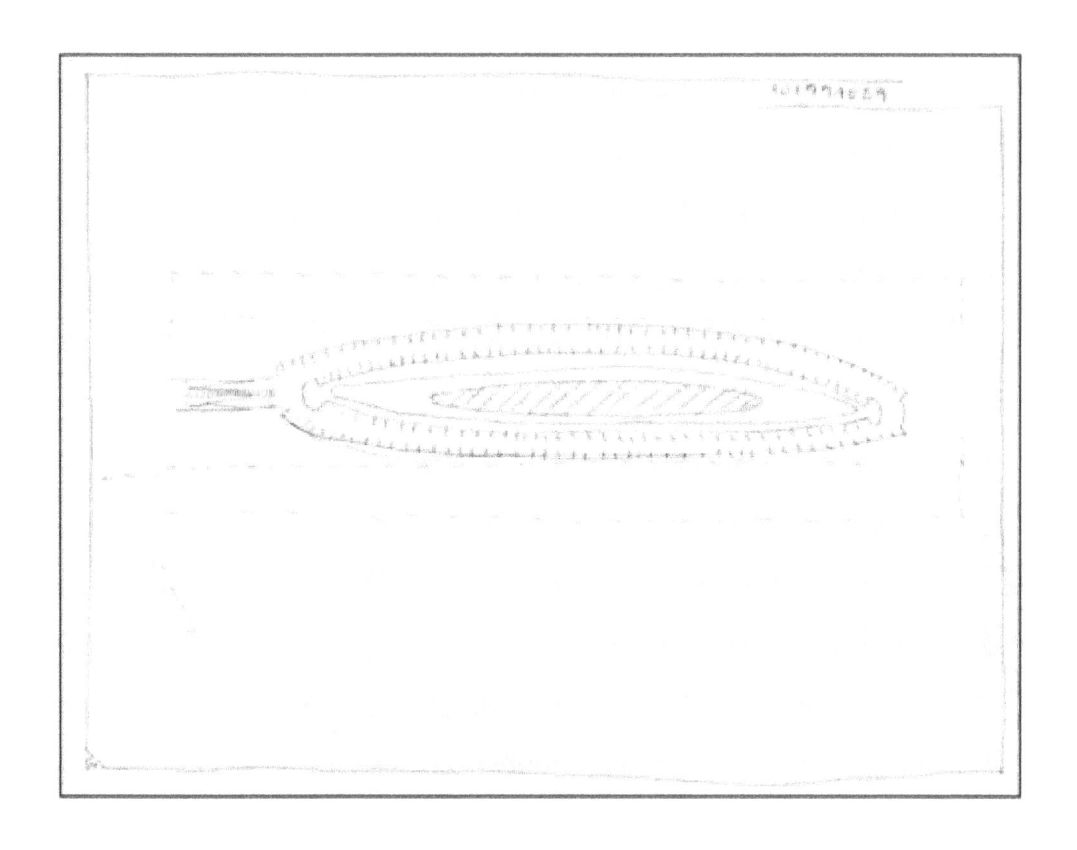

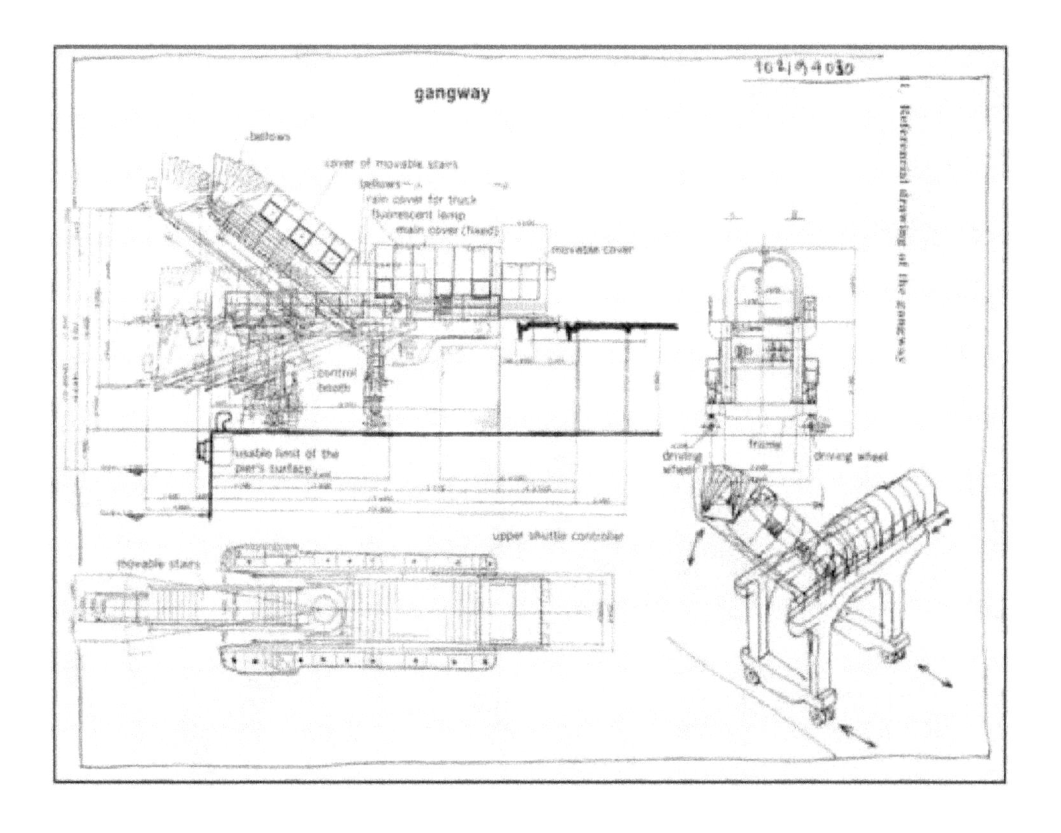
gangway
bellows
cover of movable stairs
bellows
rain cover for truck
fluorescent lamp
main cover (fixed)
movable cover
control booth
usable limit of the pier's surface
upper shuttle controller
movable stairs
frame
driving wheel
driving wheel
Referential drawing of the gangway

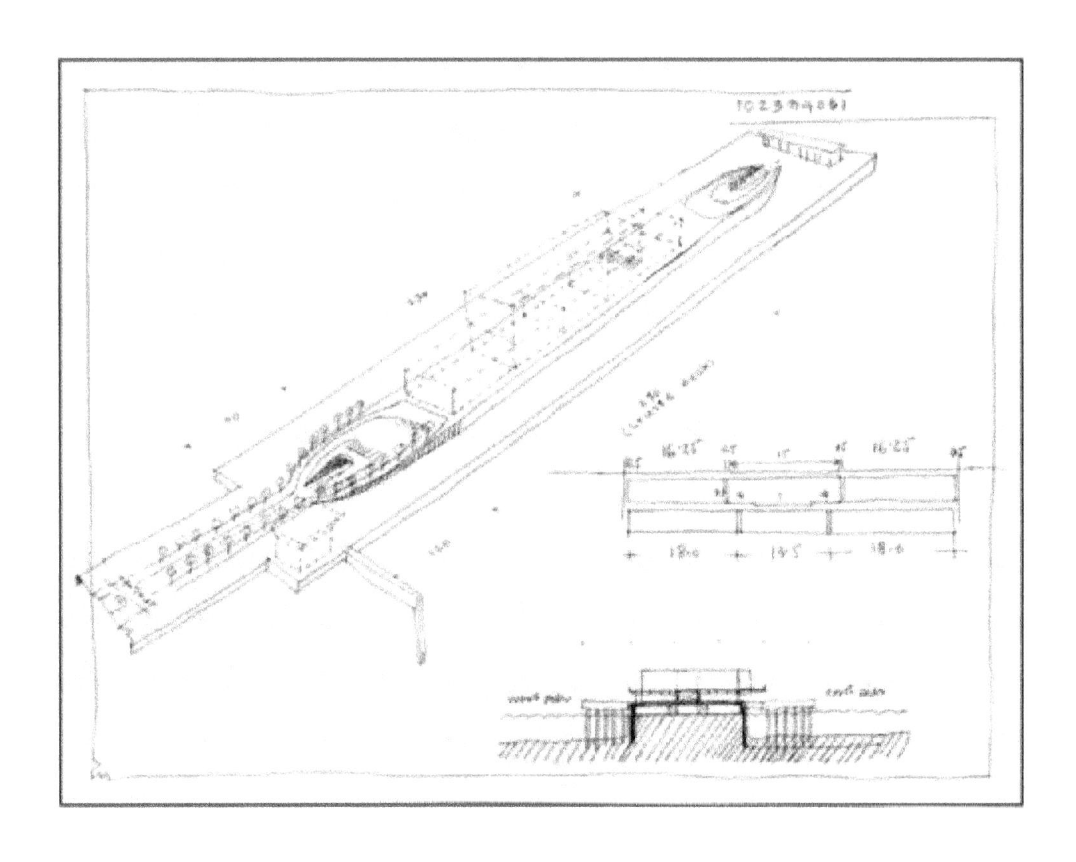

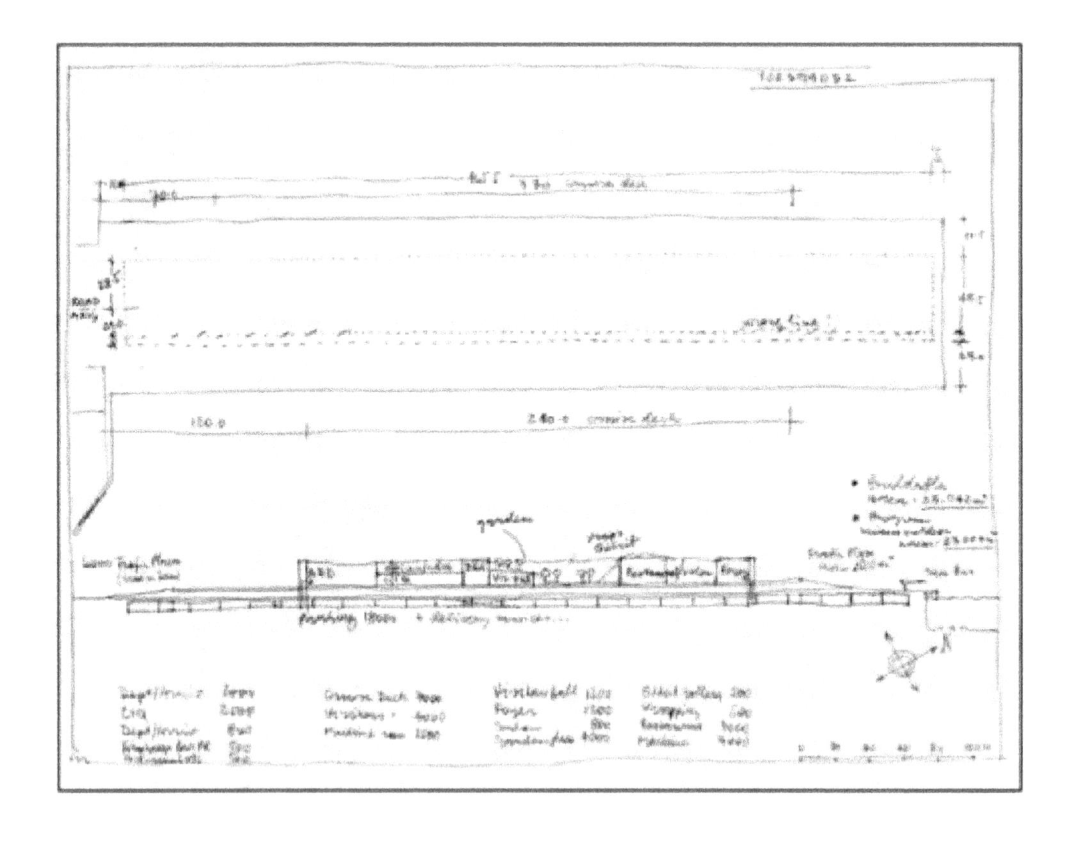

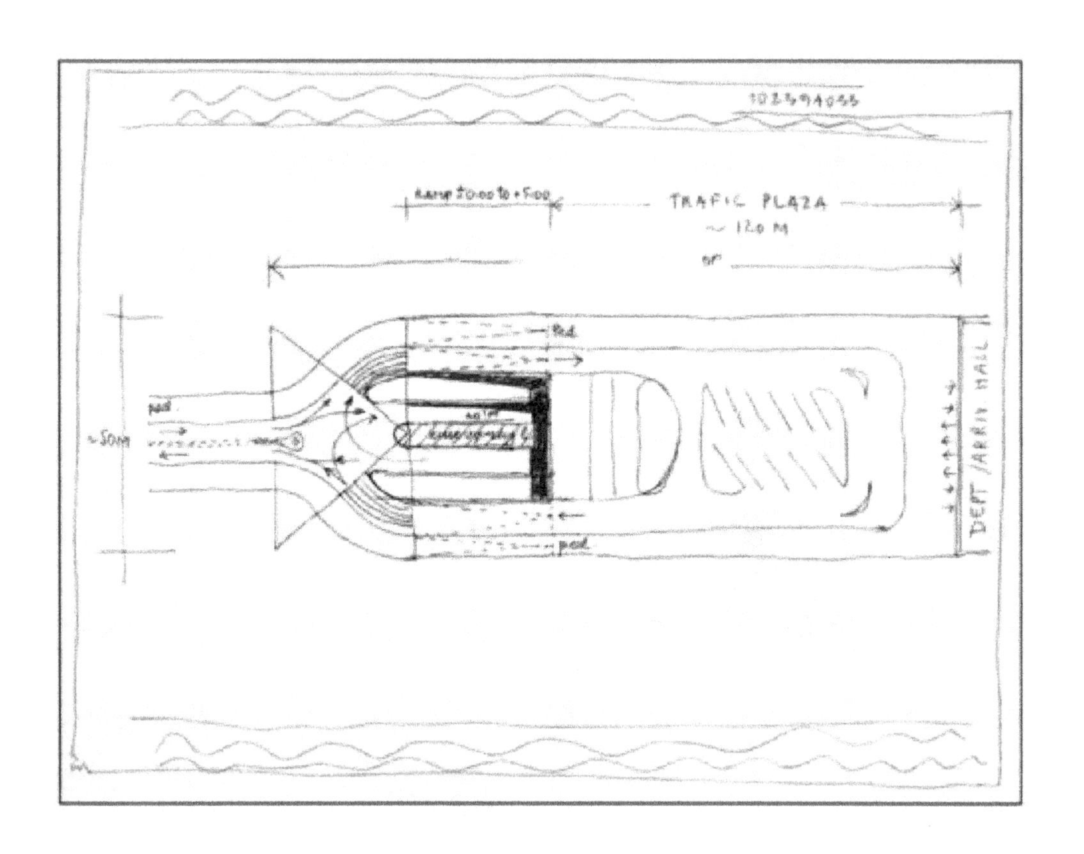
TRAFIC PLAZA
~ 120 M
ped
DEPT / ARRIV HALL

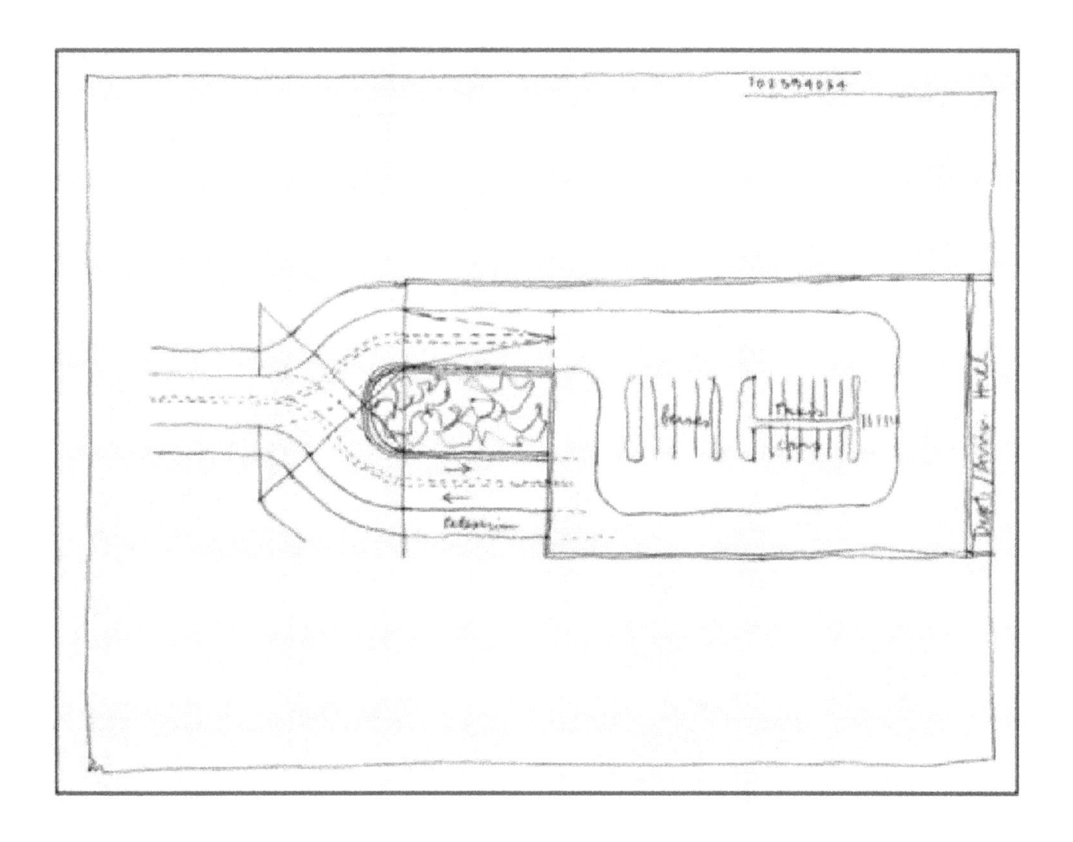
Dept / Arriv Hall

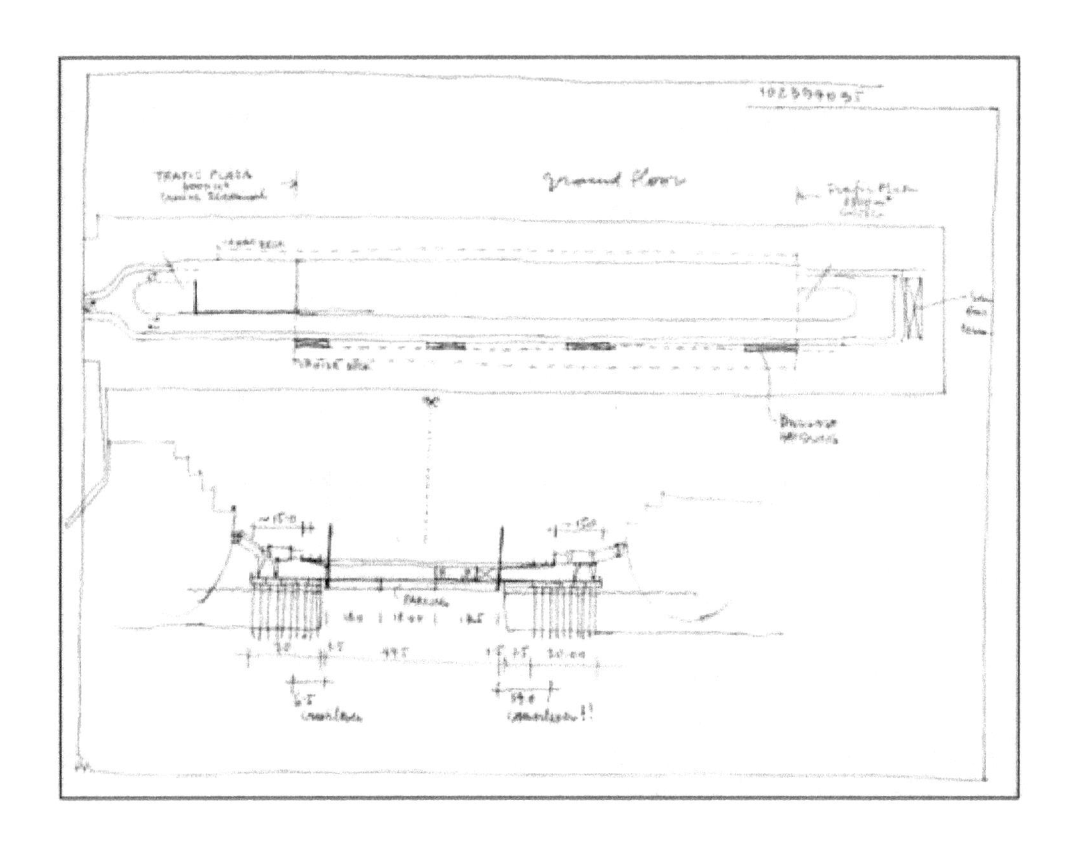
Ground Floor

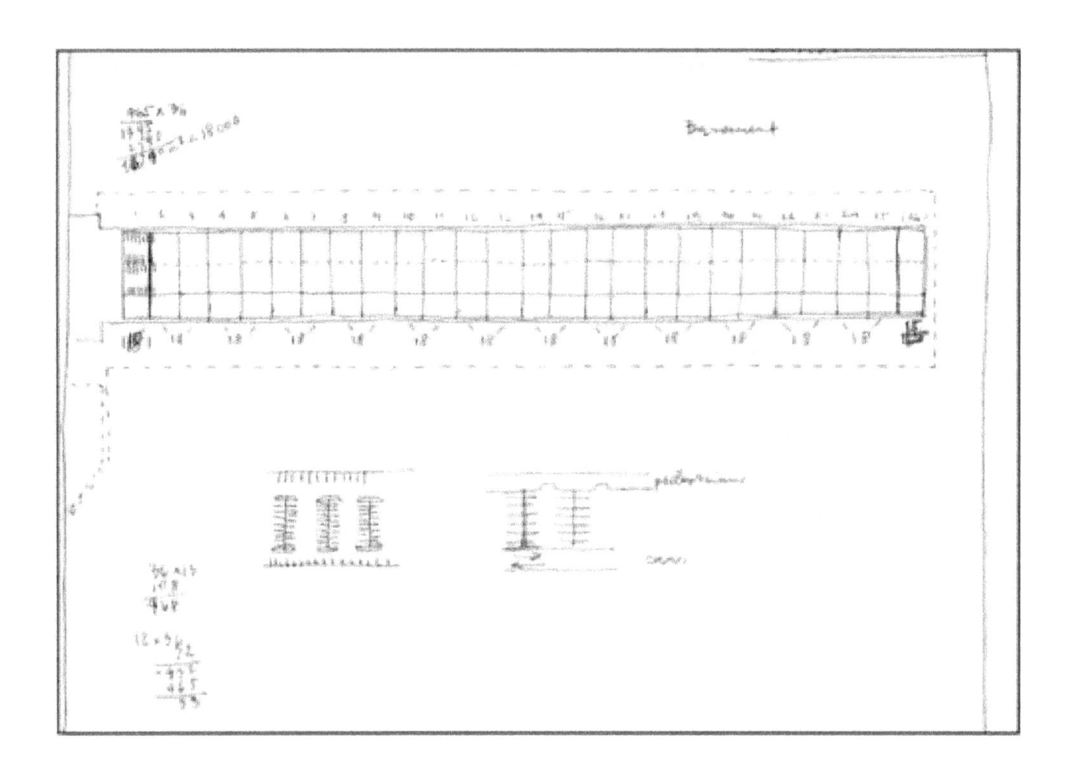
Basement

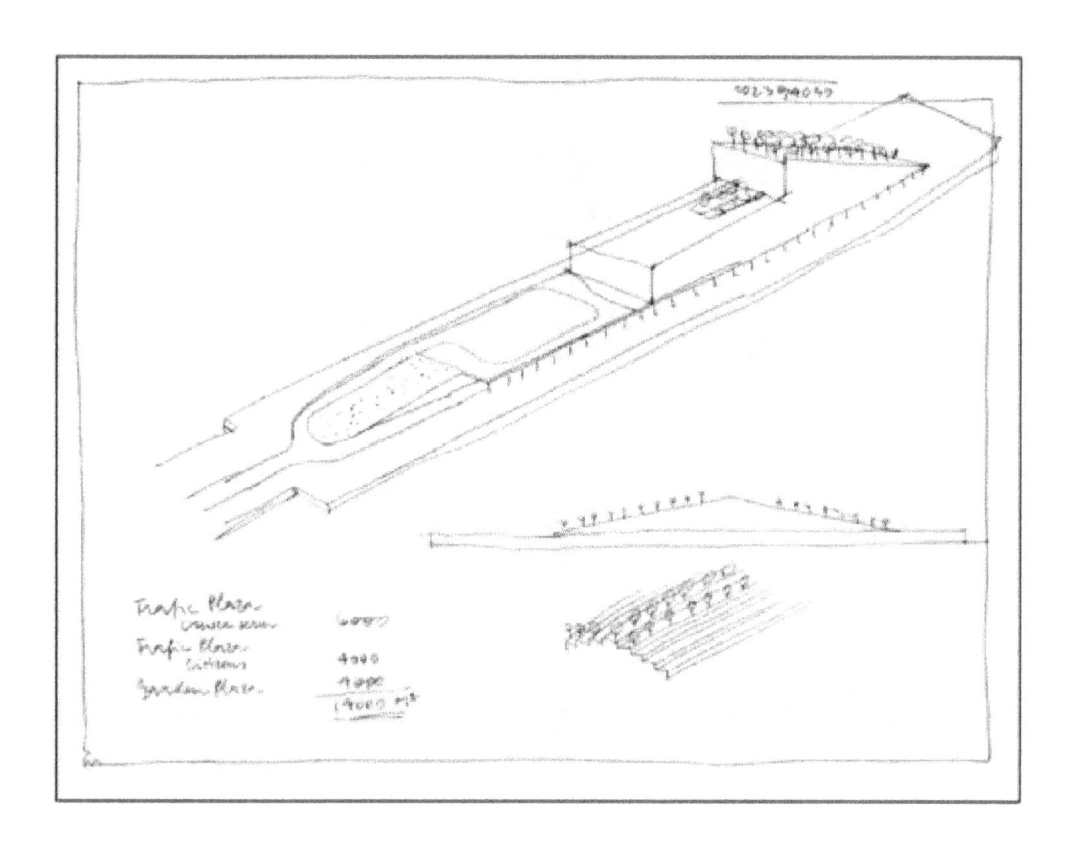
Trafic Plaza
Trafic Plaza

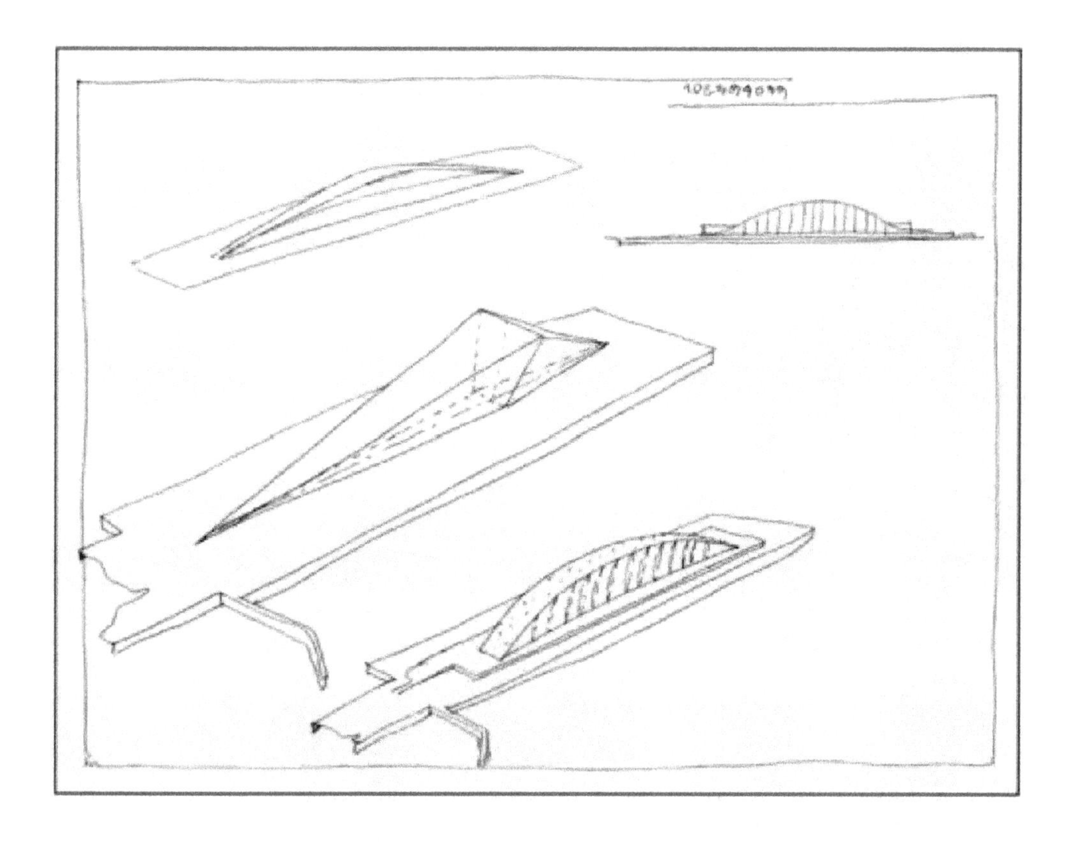

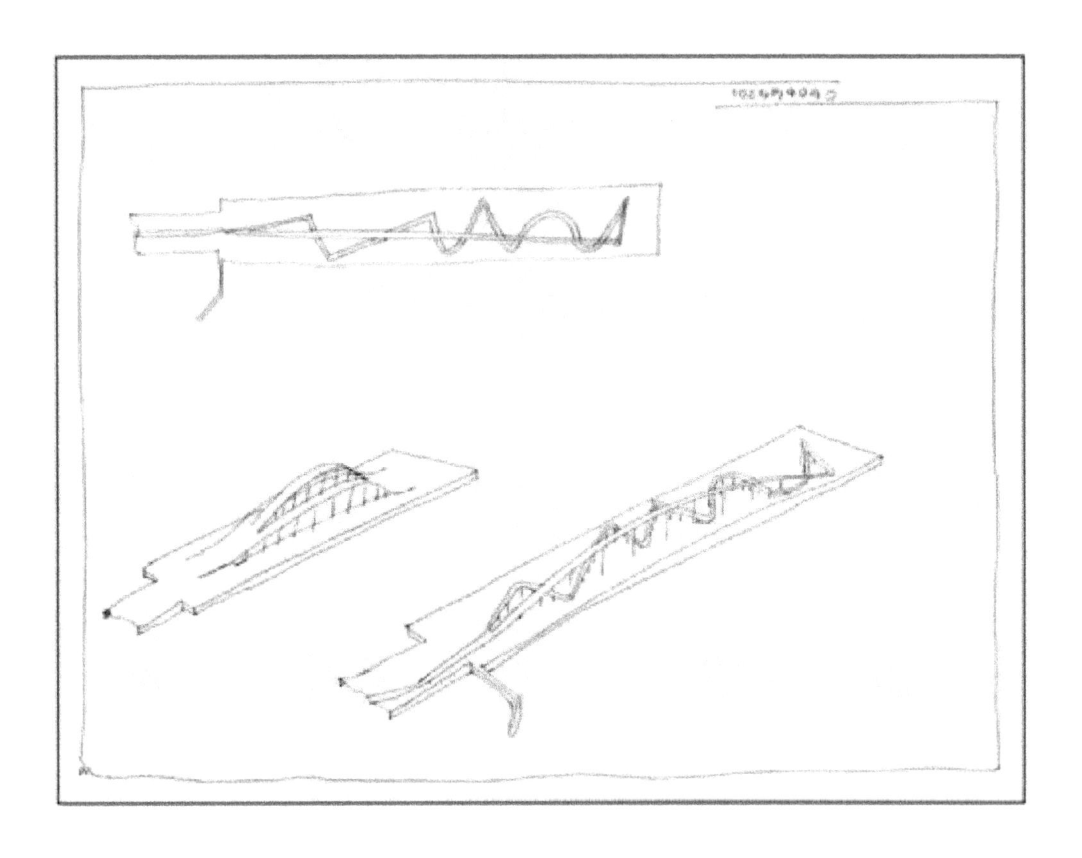

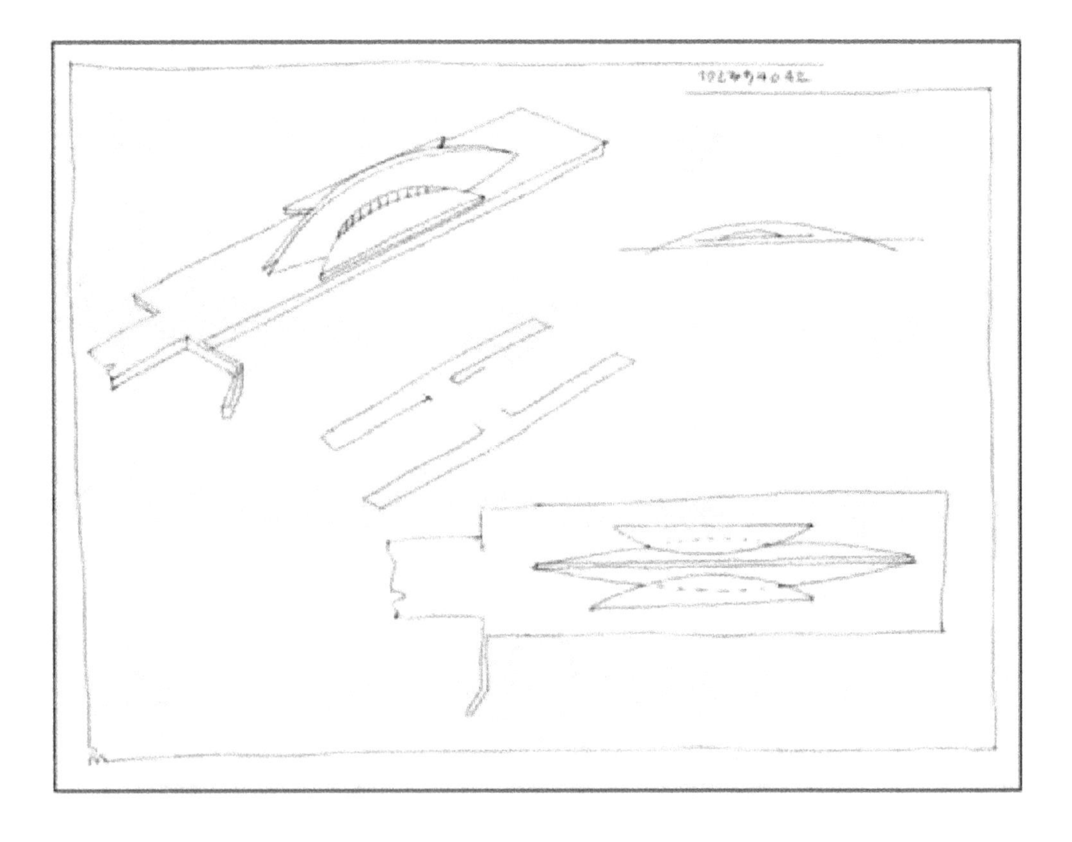

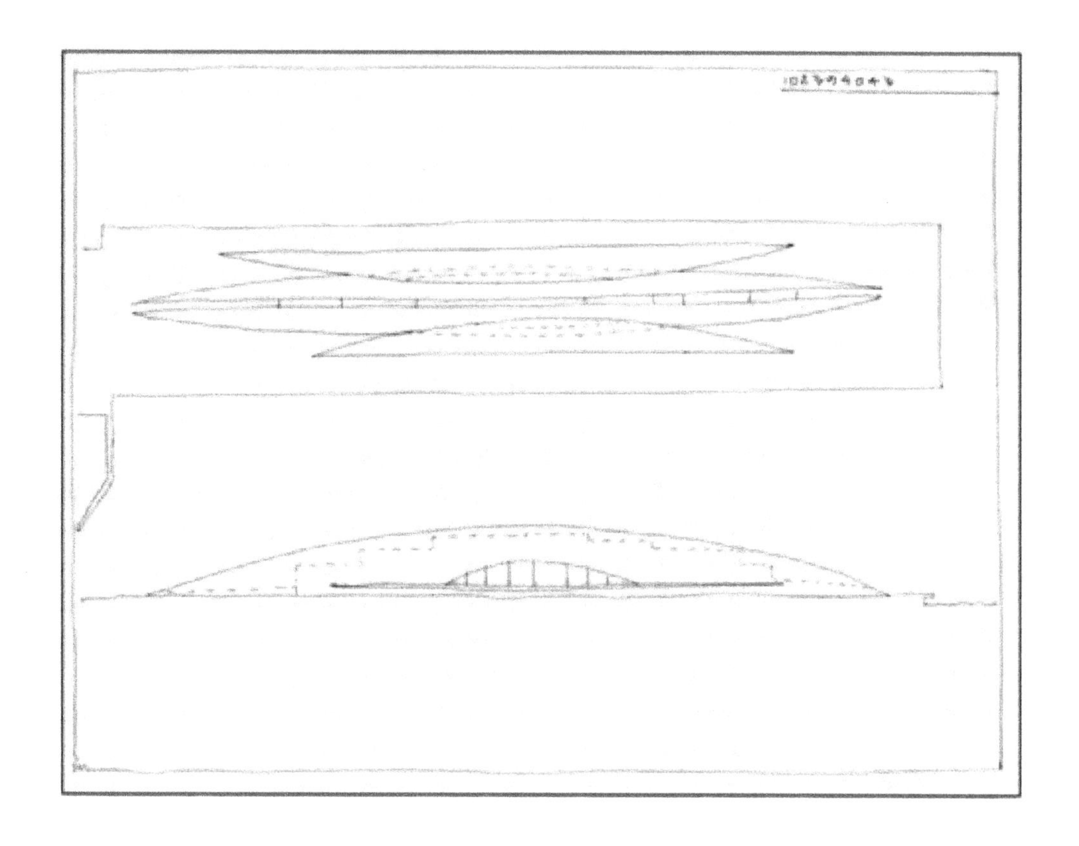

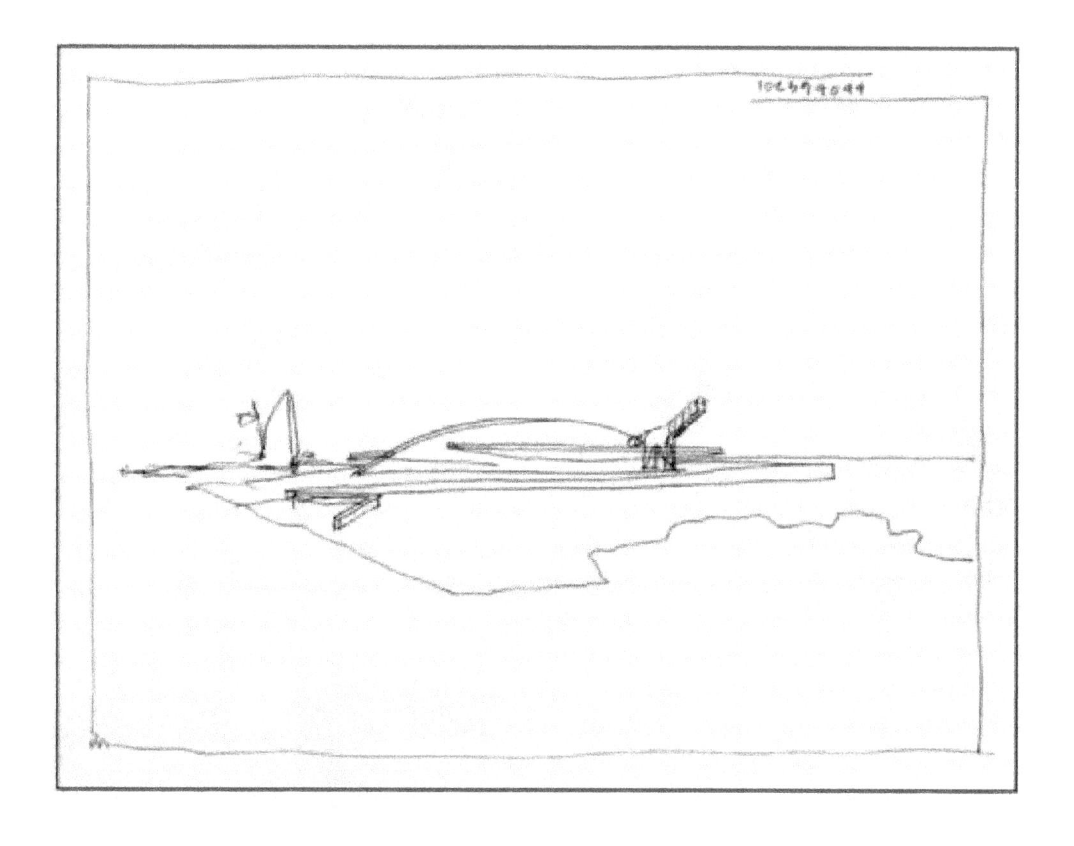

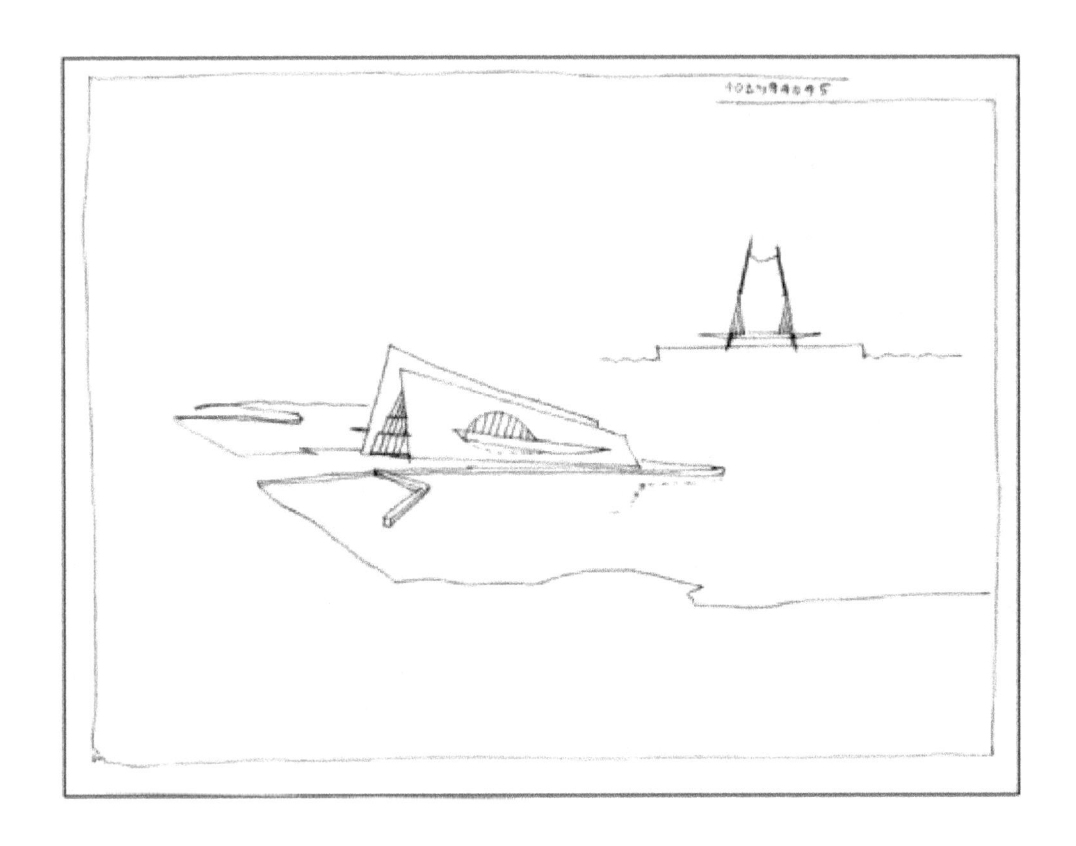

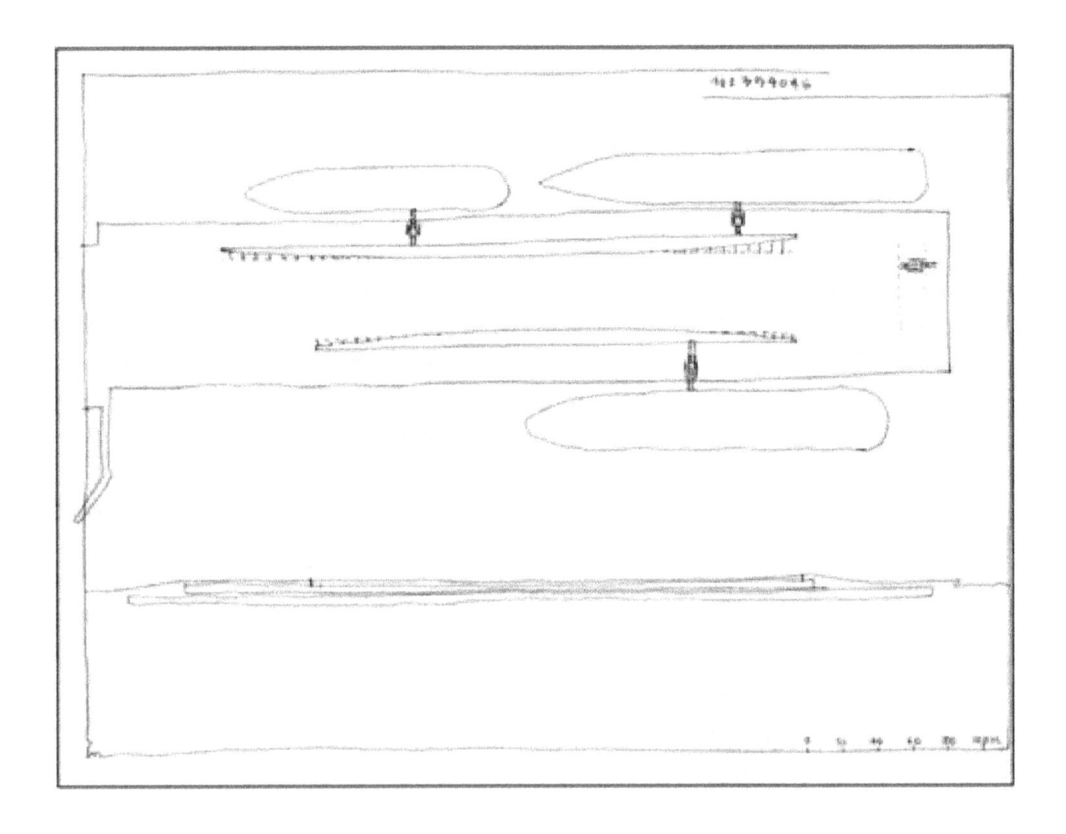

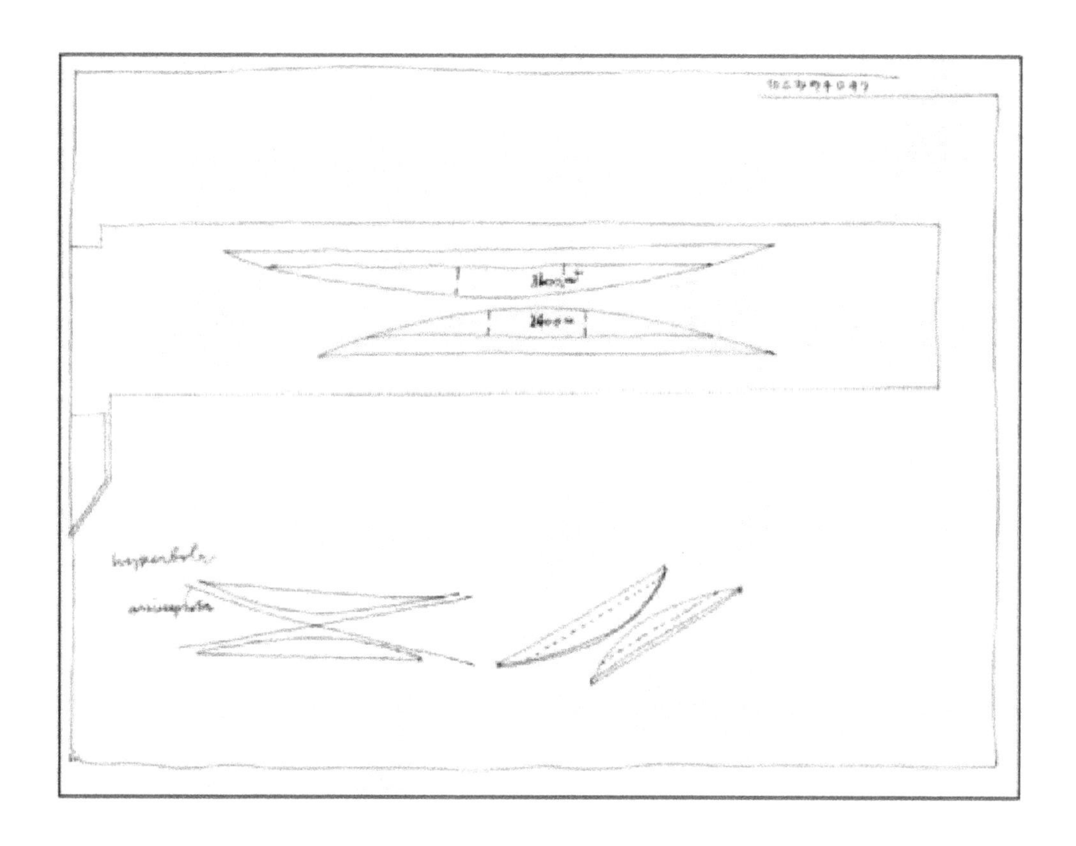

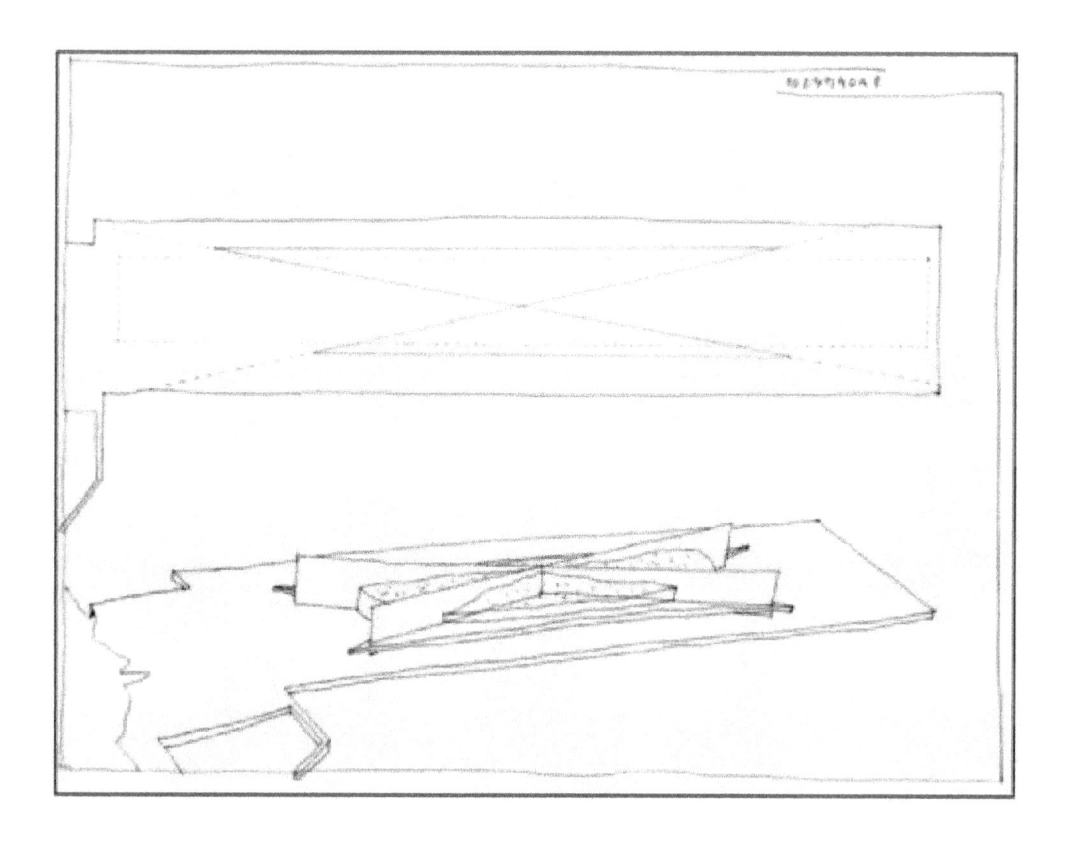

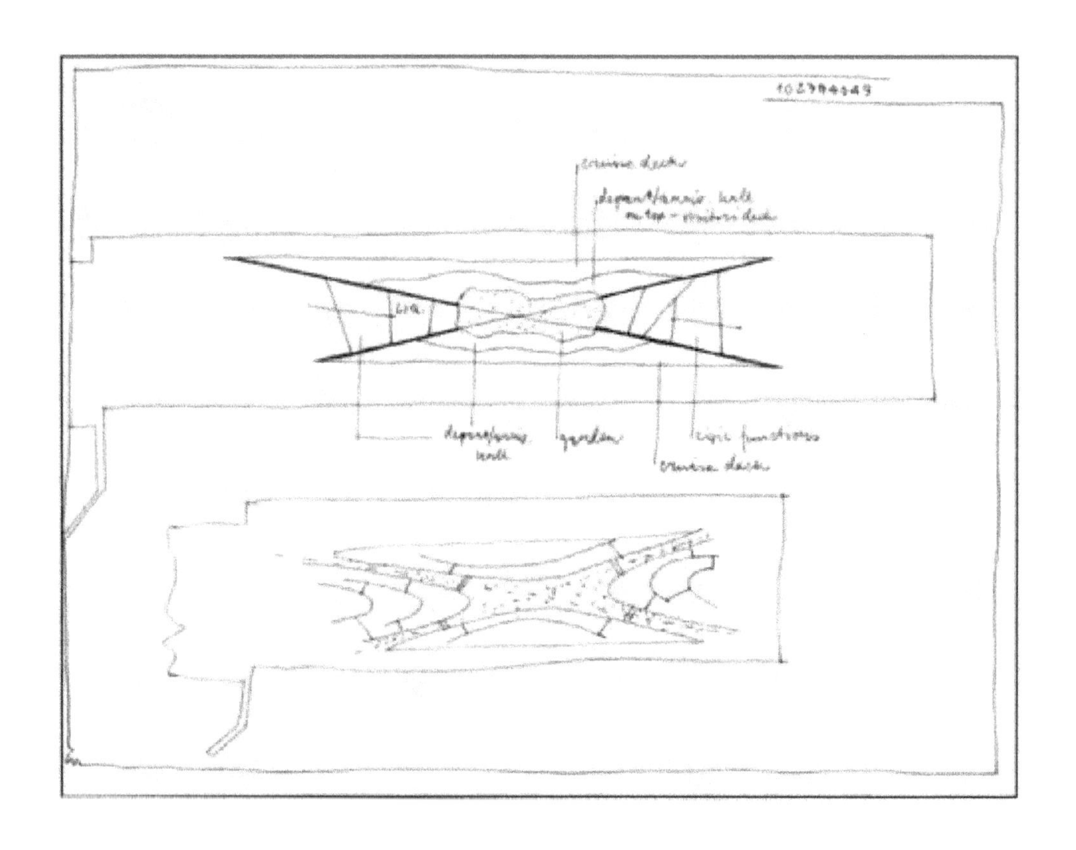
garden

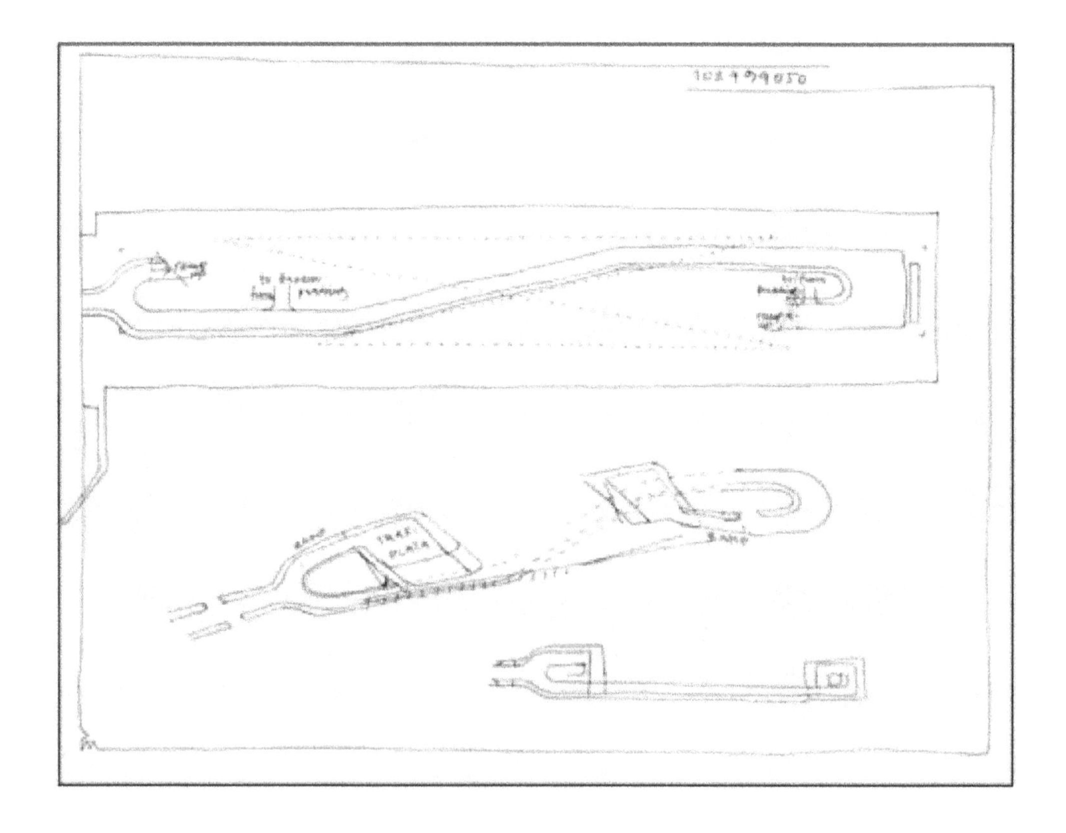

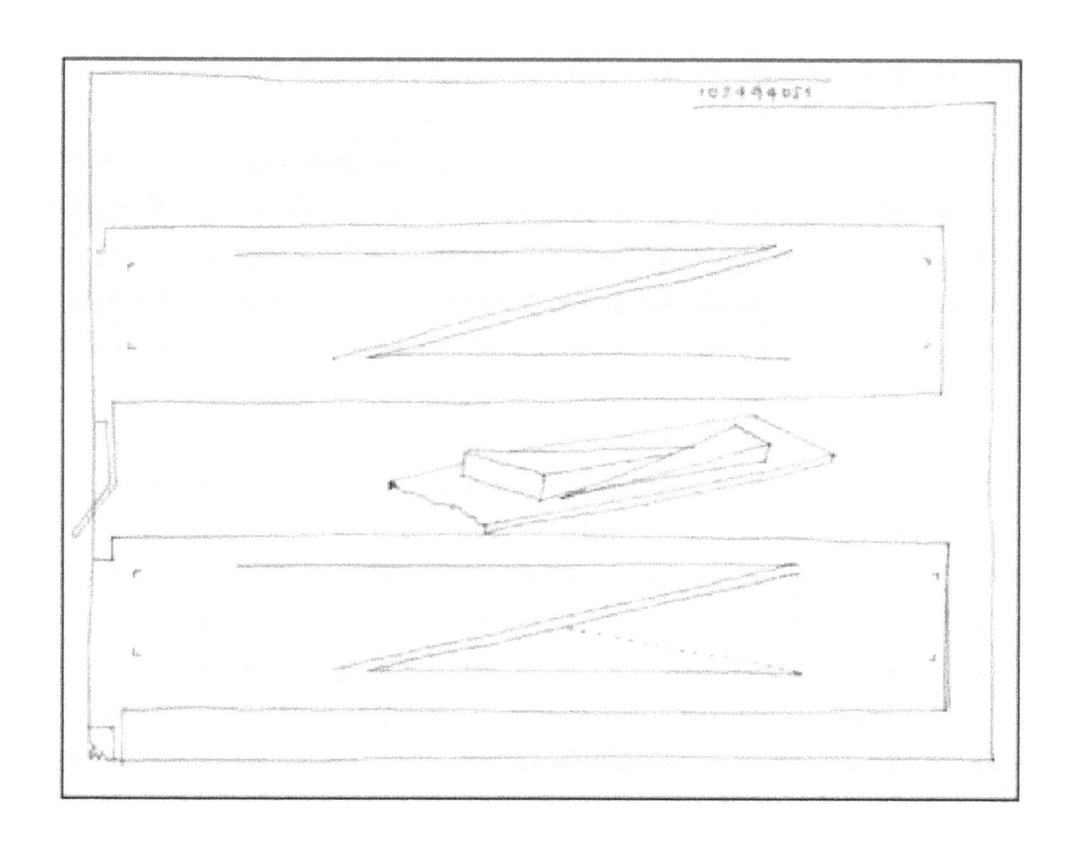

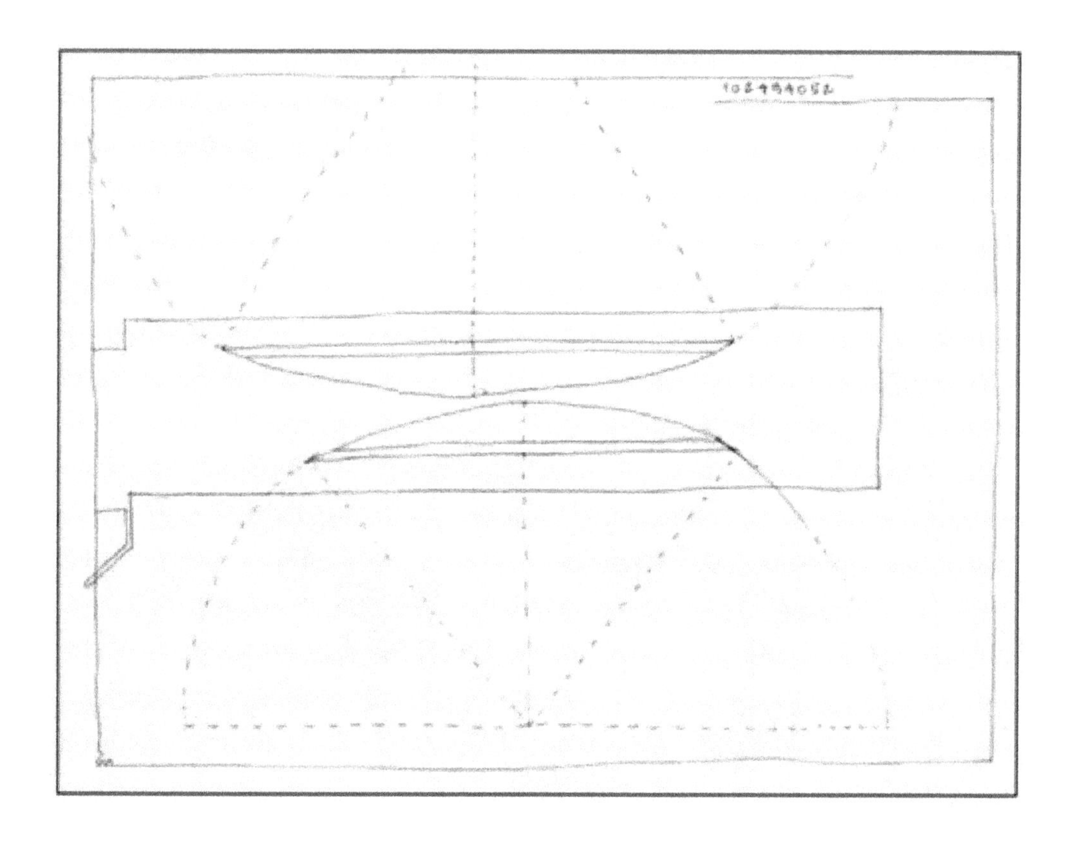

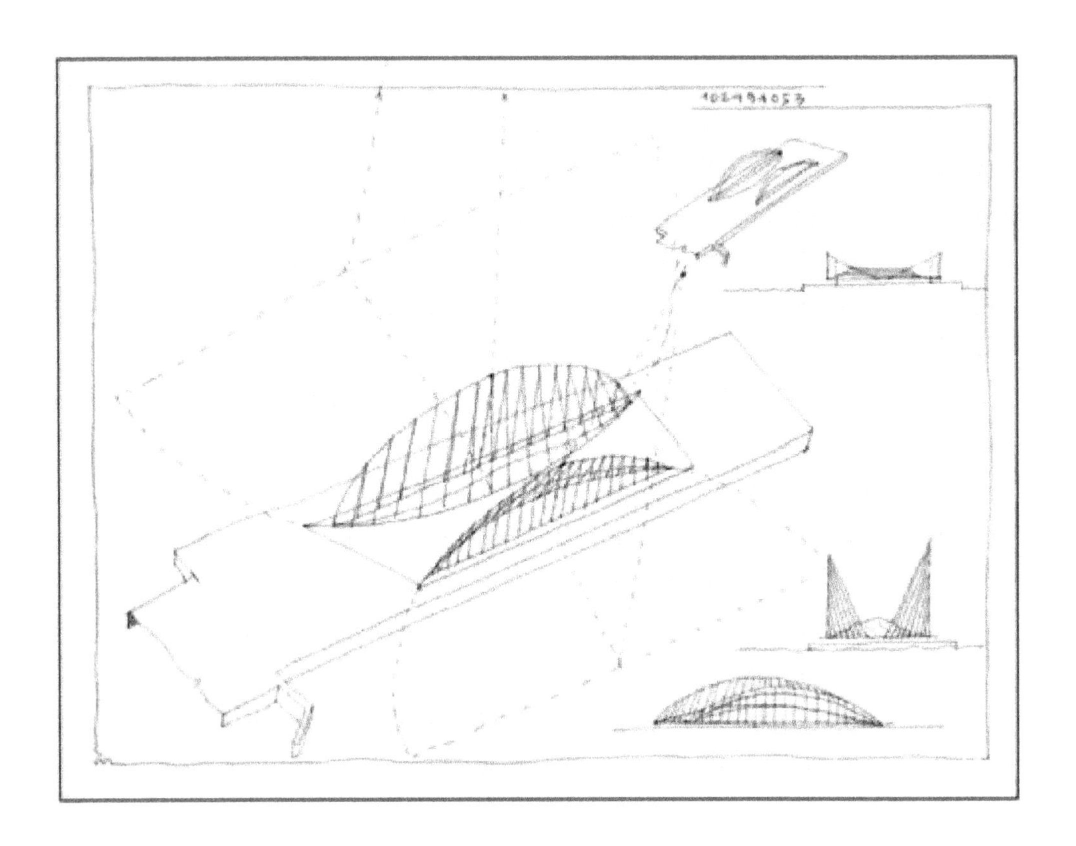

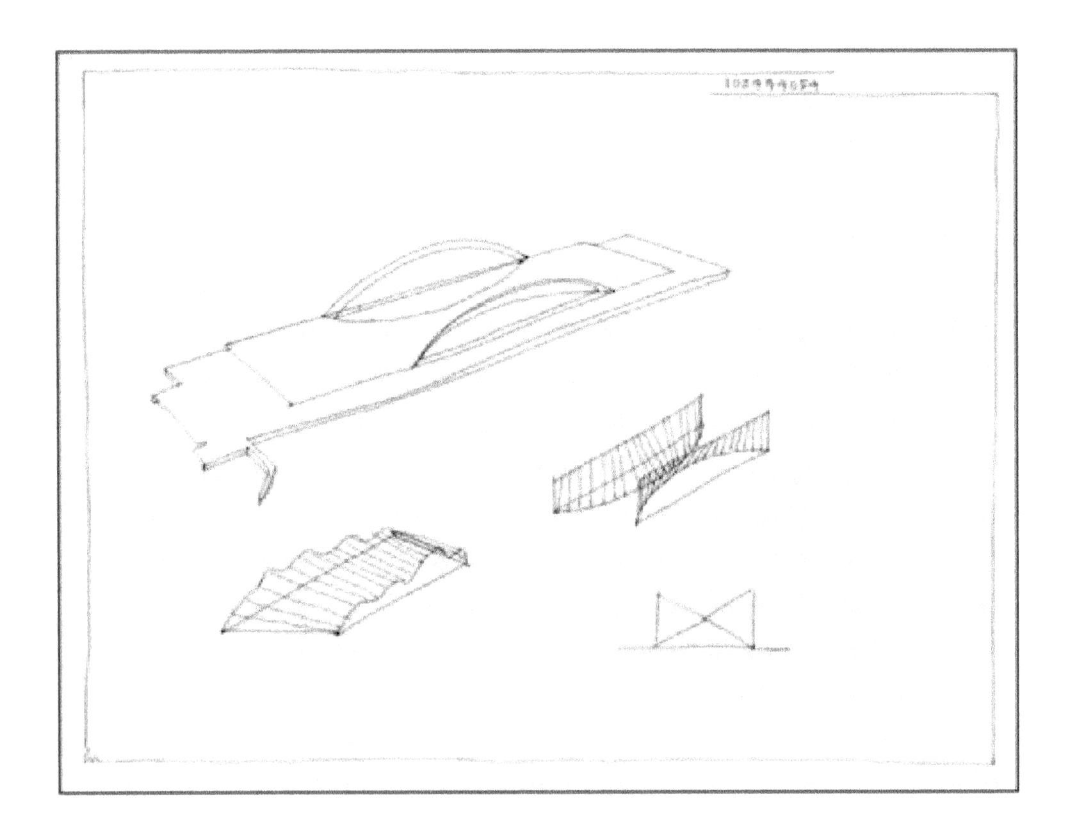

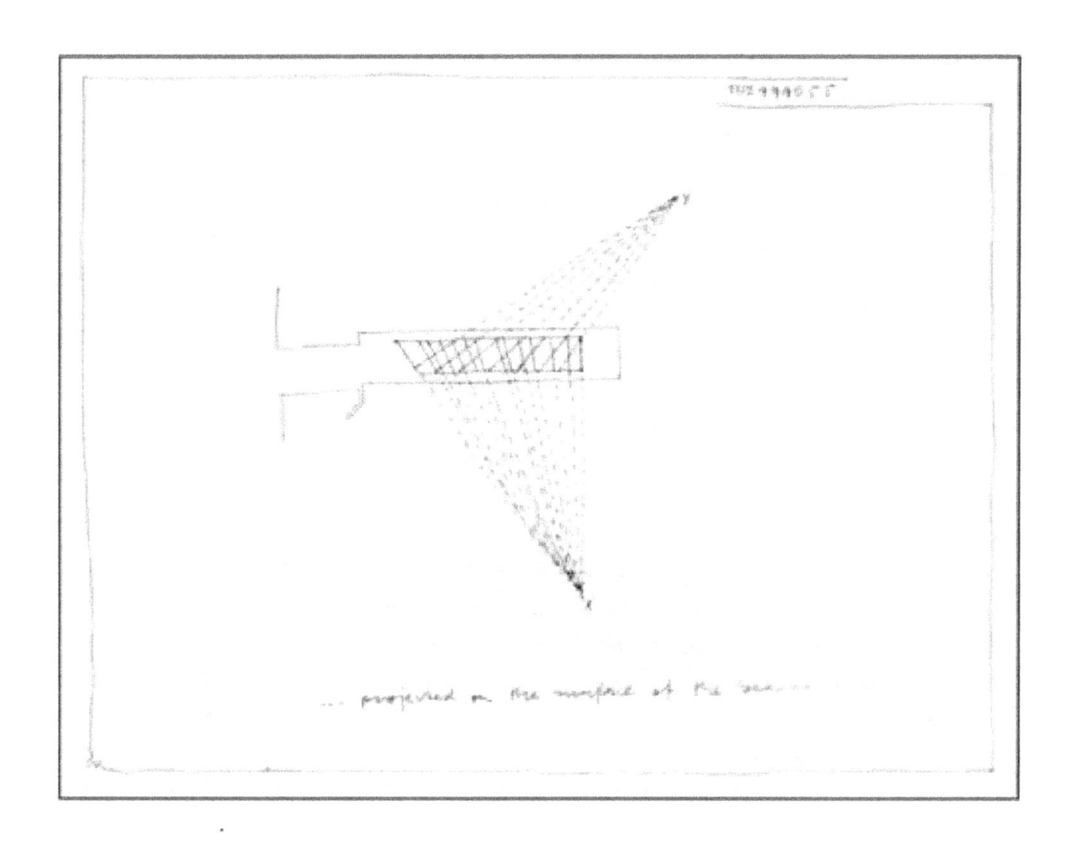
... projected on the surface of the sea...

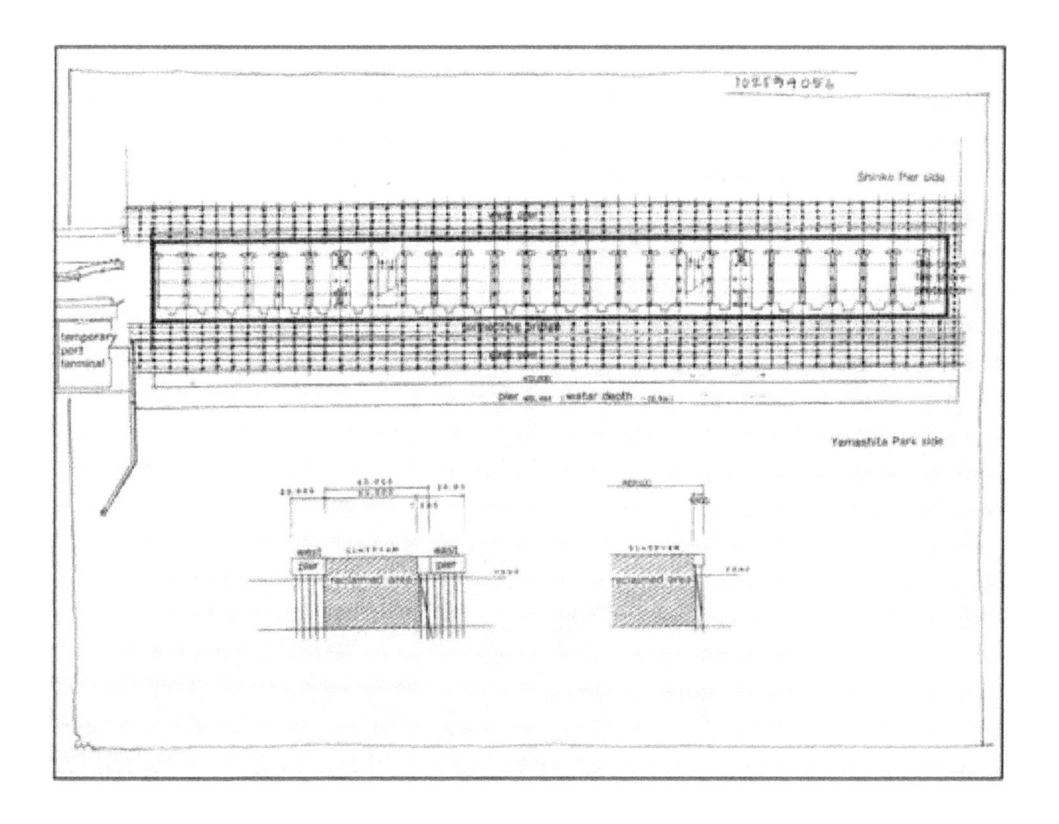
Shinko Pier side
temporary port terminal
pier
water depth
Yamashita Park side
pier
reclaimed area
reclaimed area

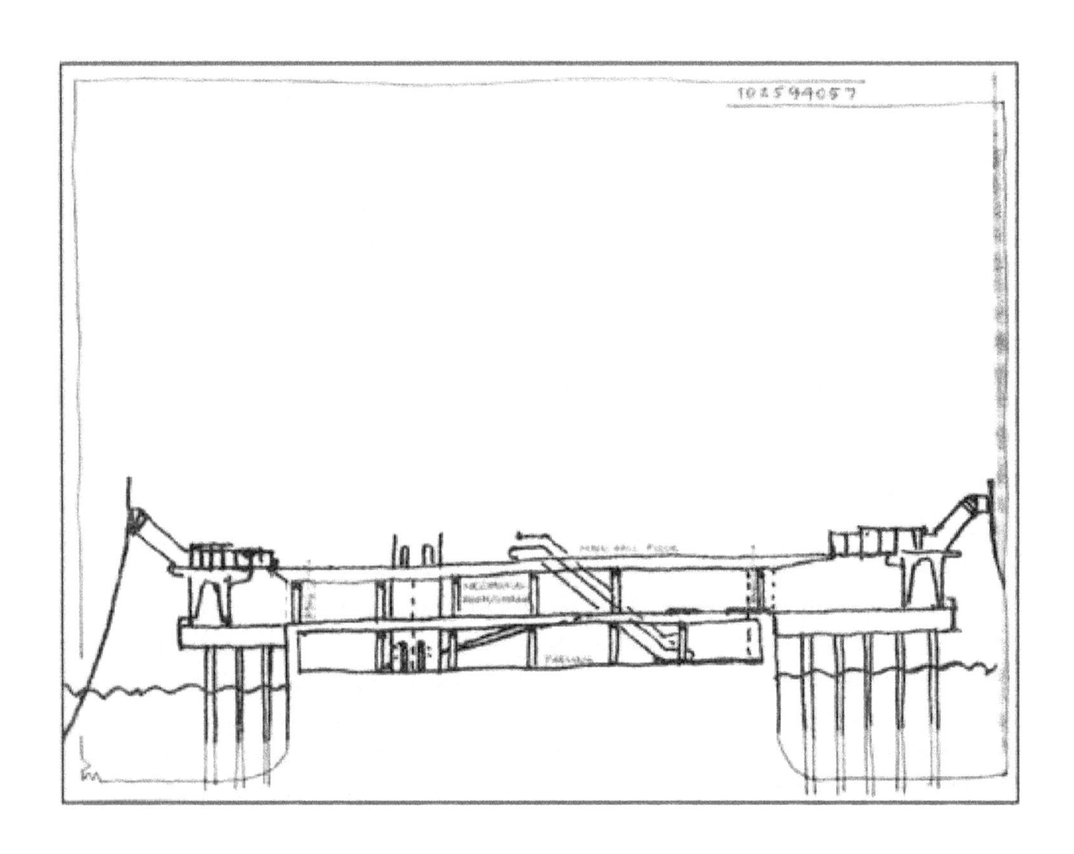

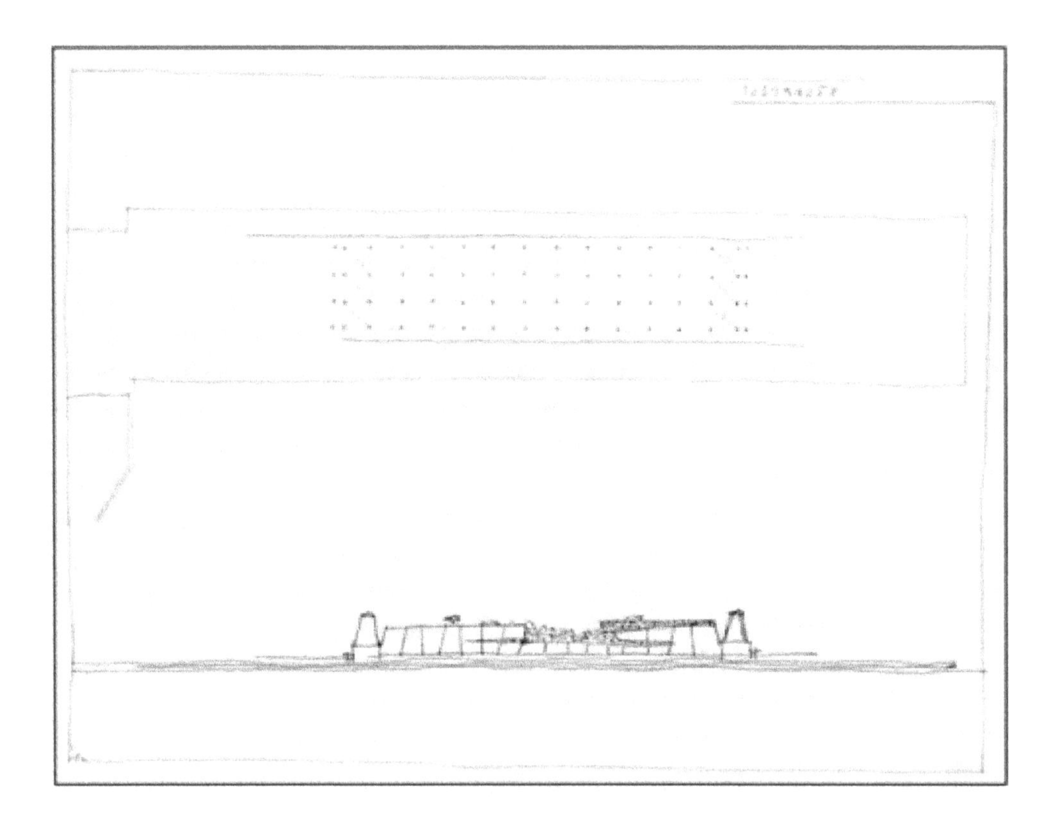

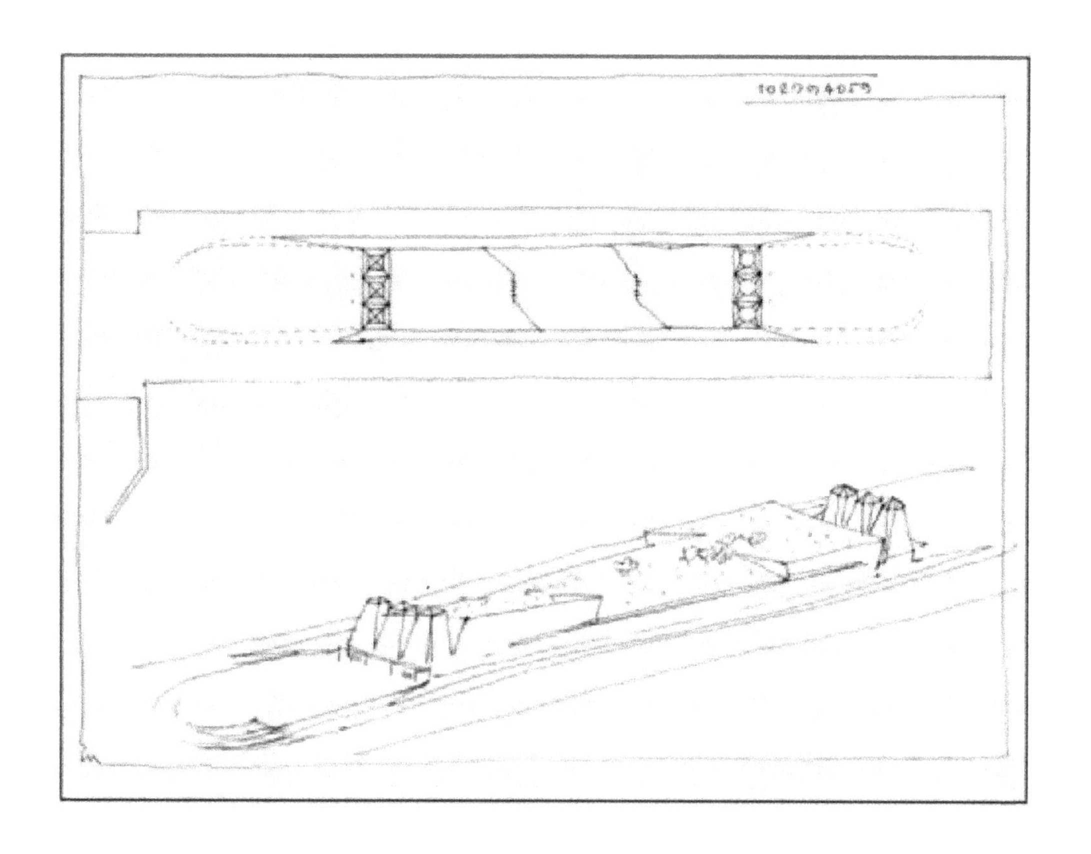

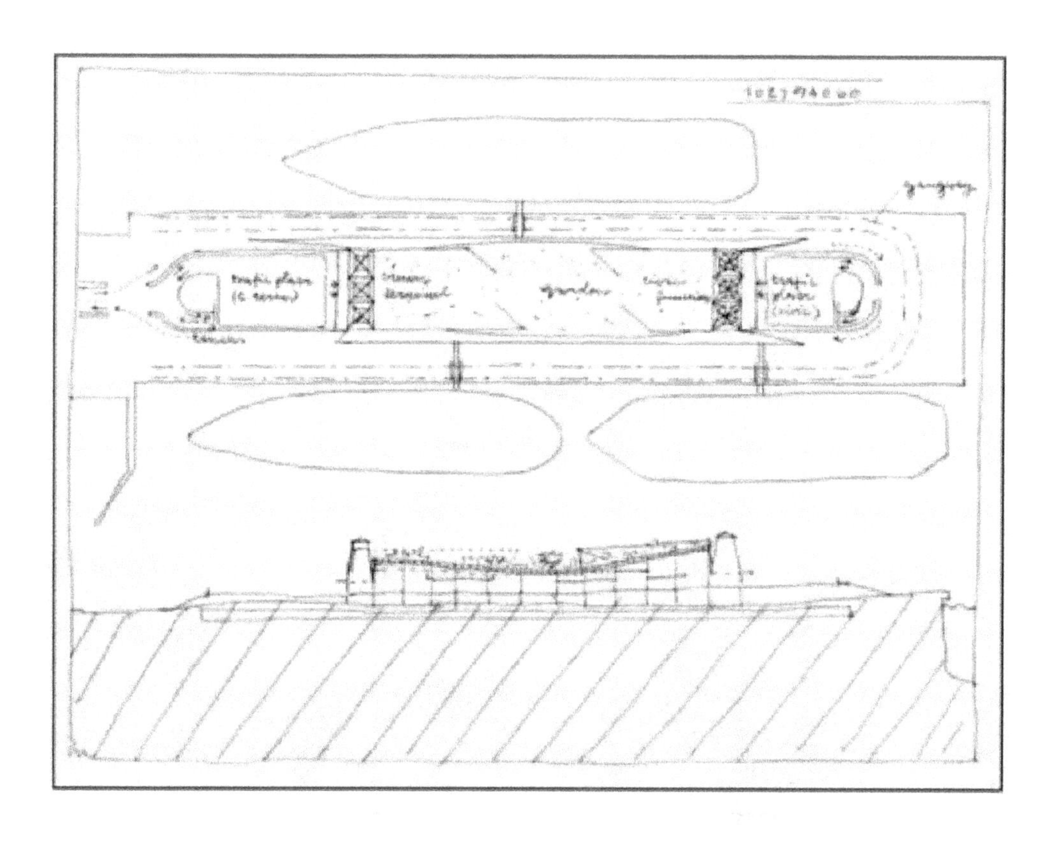

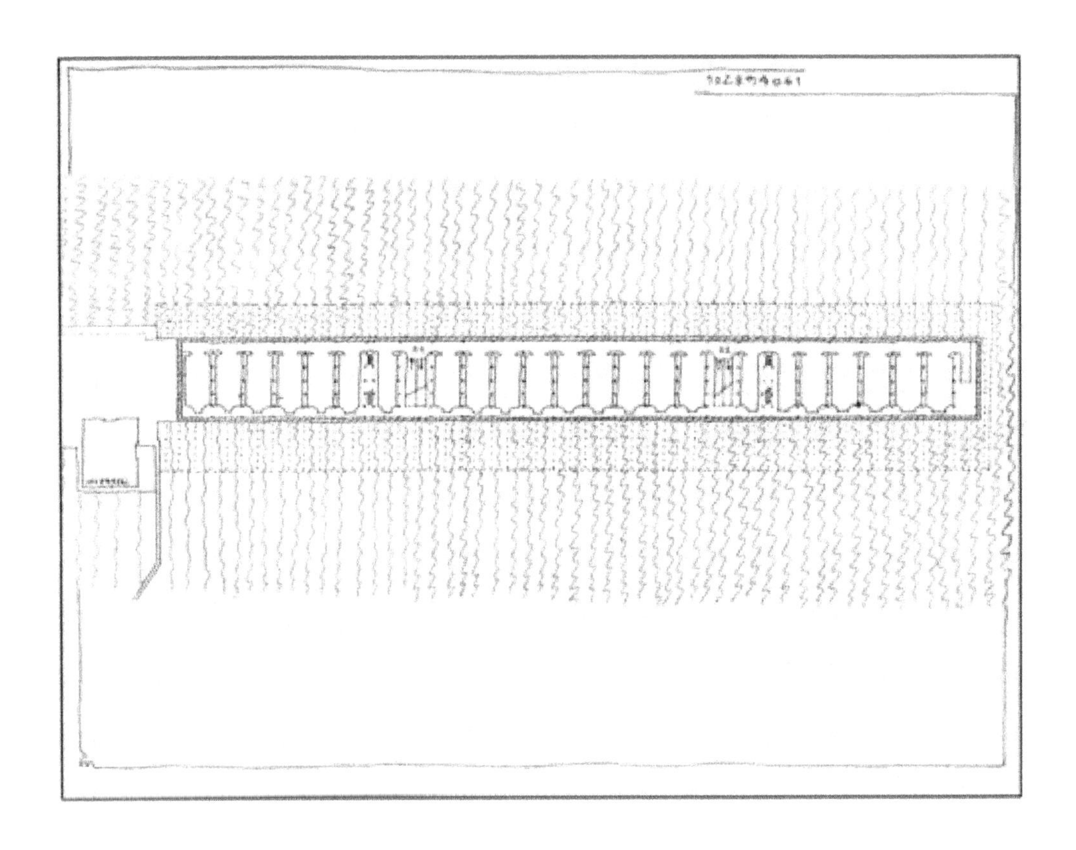

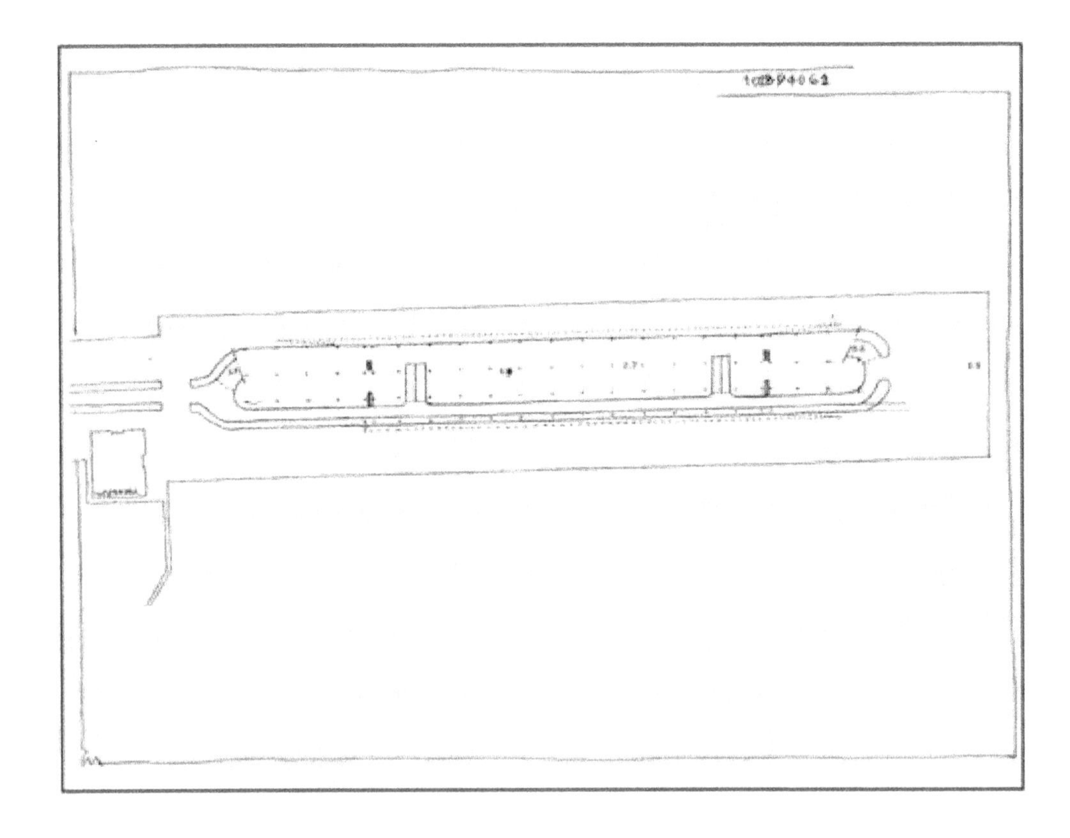

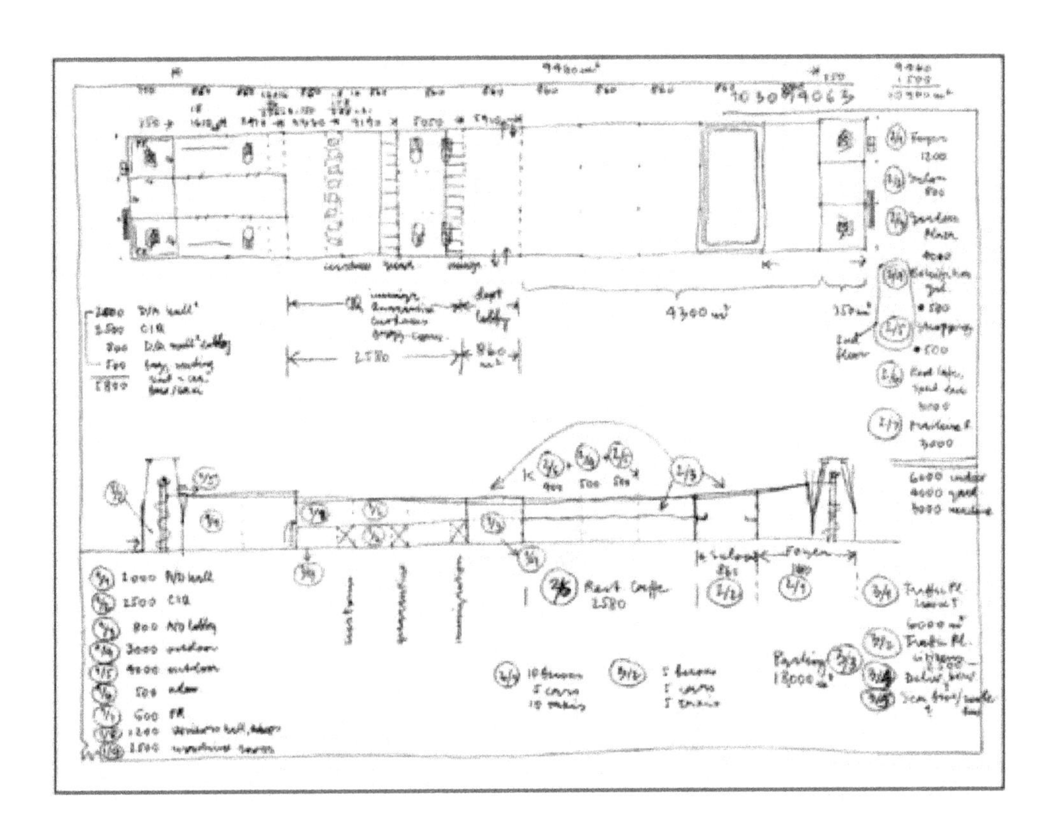

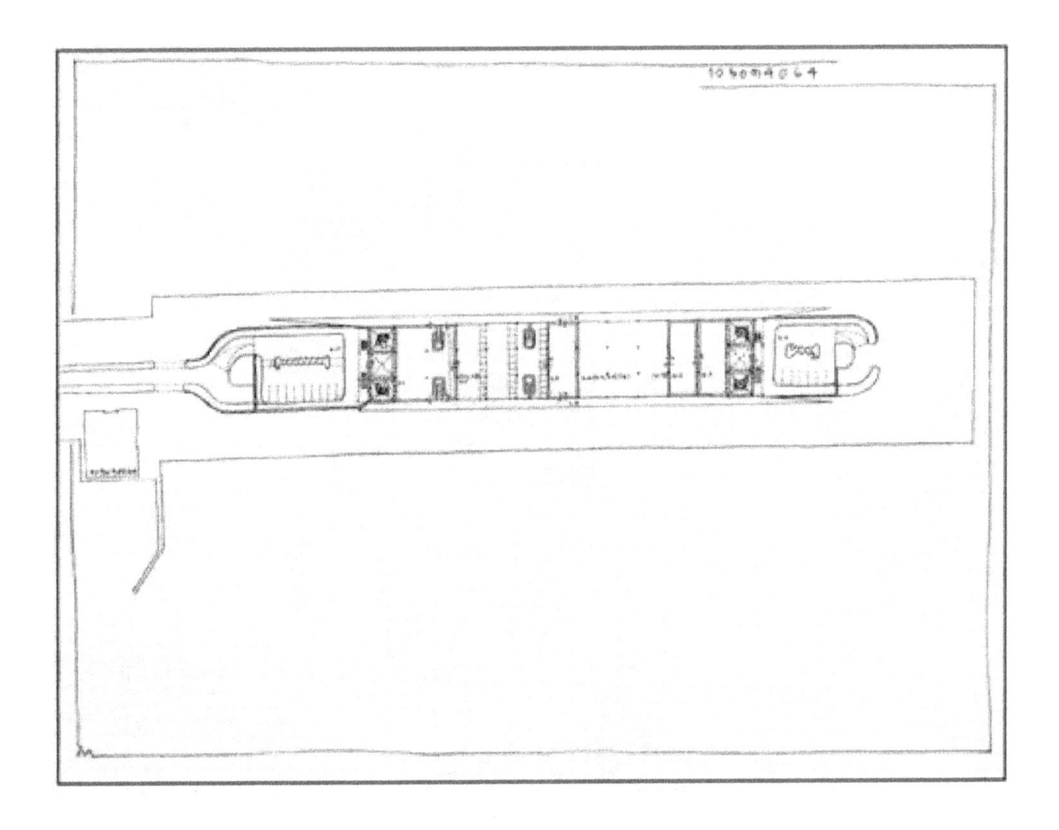

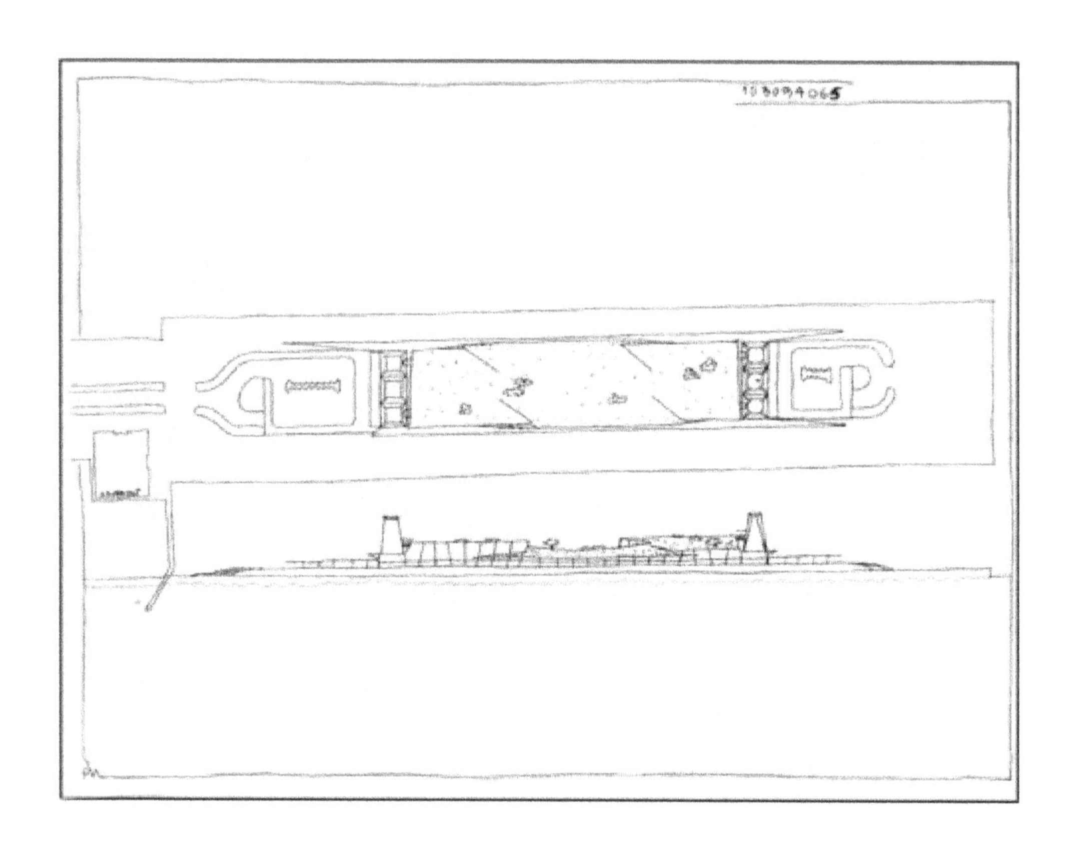

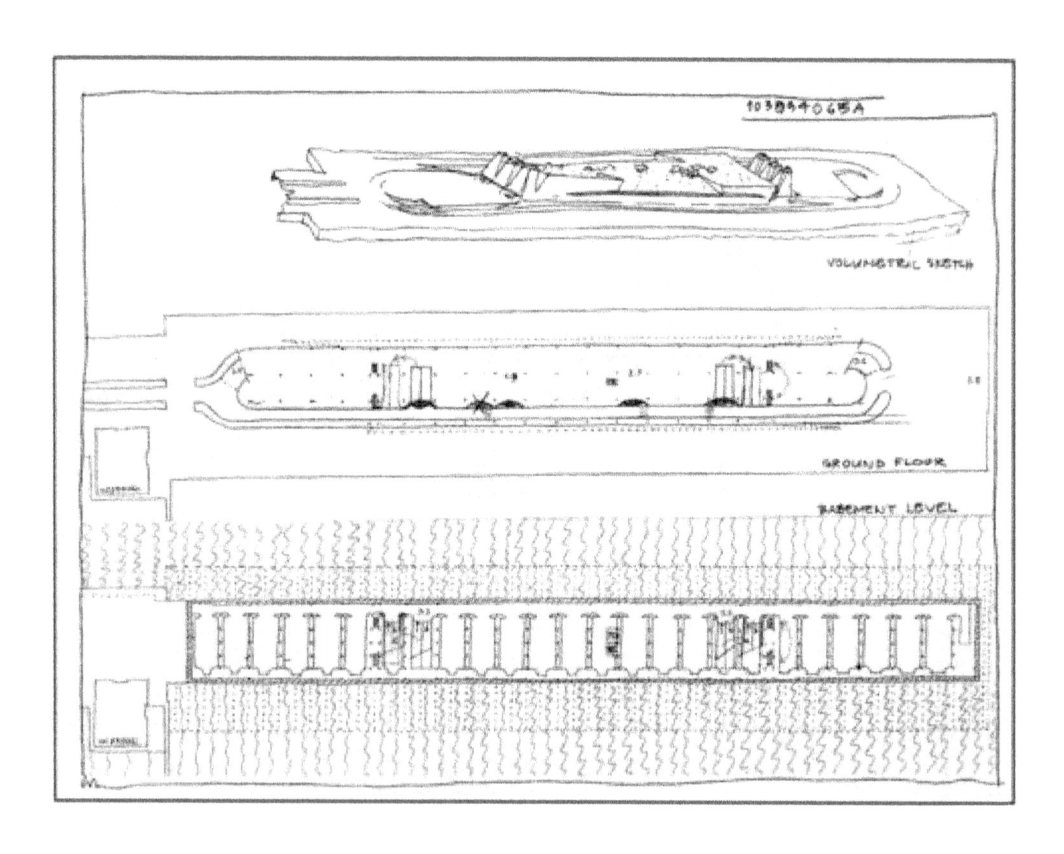
VOLUMETRIC SKETCH
GROUND FLOOR
BASEMENT LEVEL

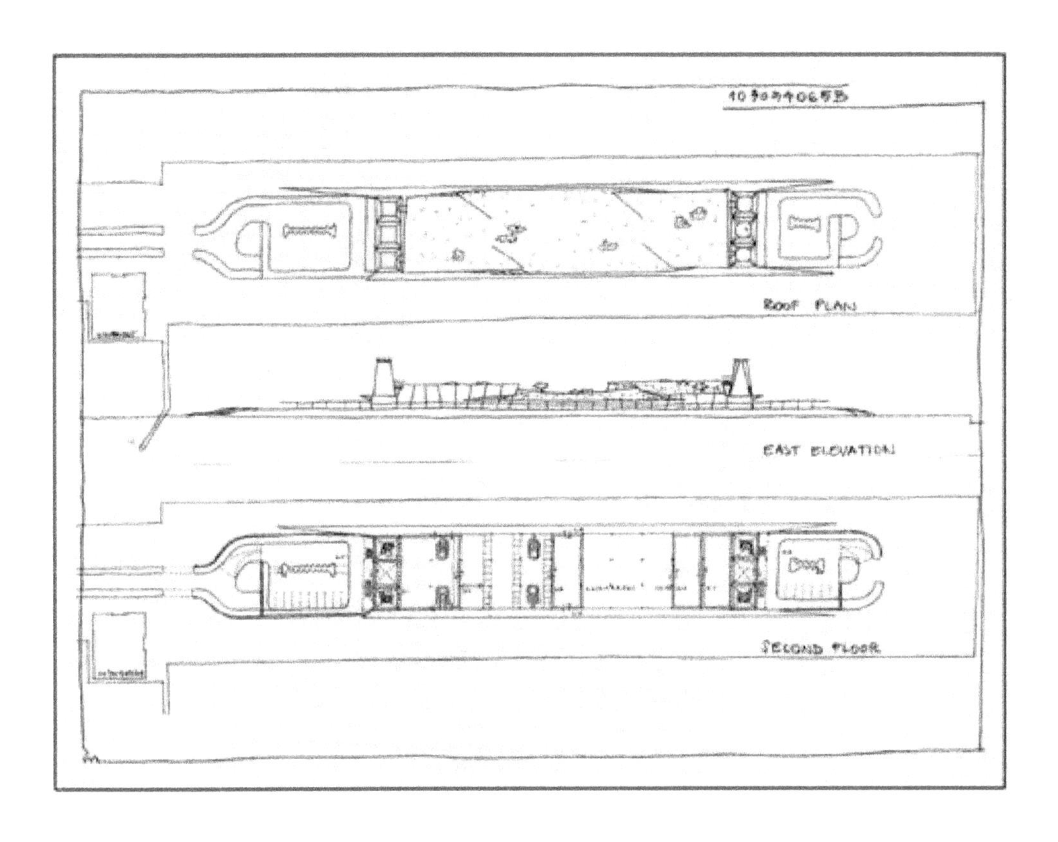
ROOF PLAN
EAST ELEVATION
SECOND FLOOR

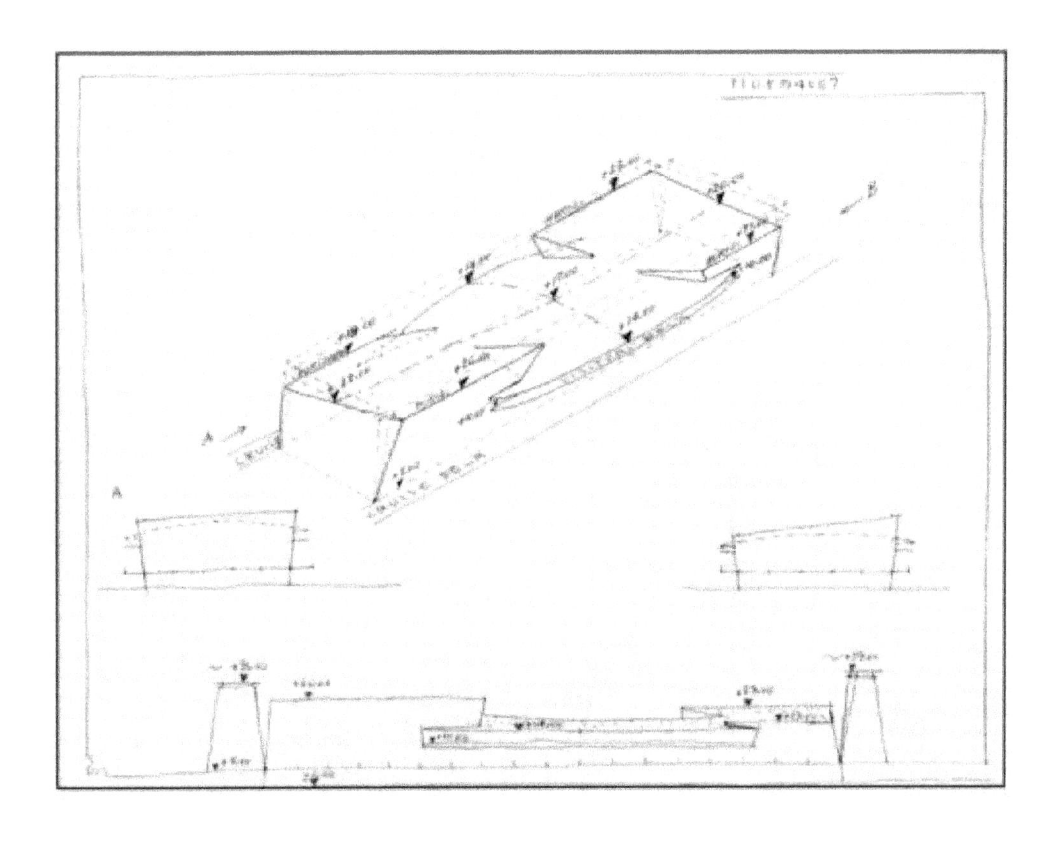

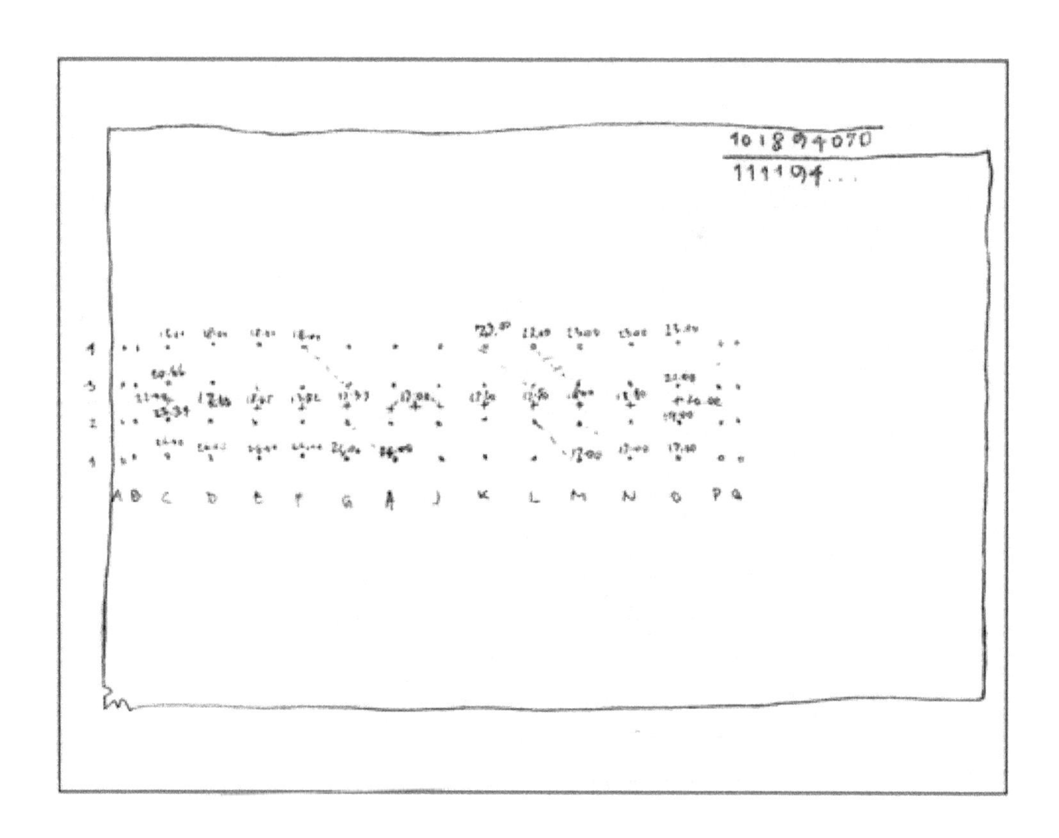

101894070
111194...
4
3
2
1
A B C D E F G H J K L M N O P Q

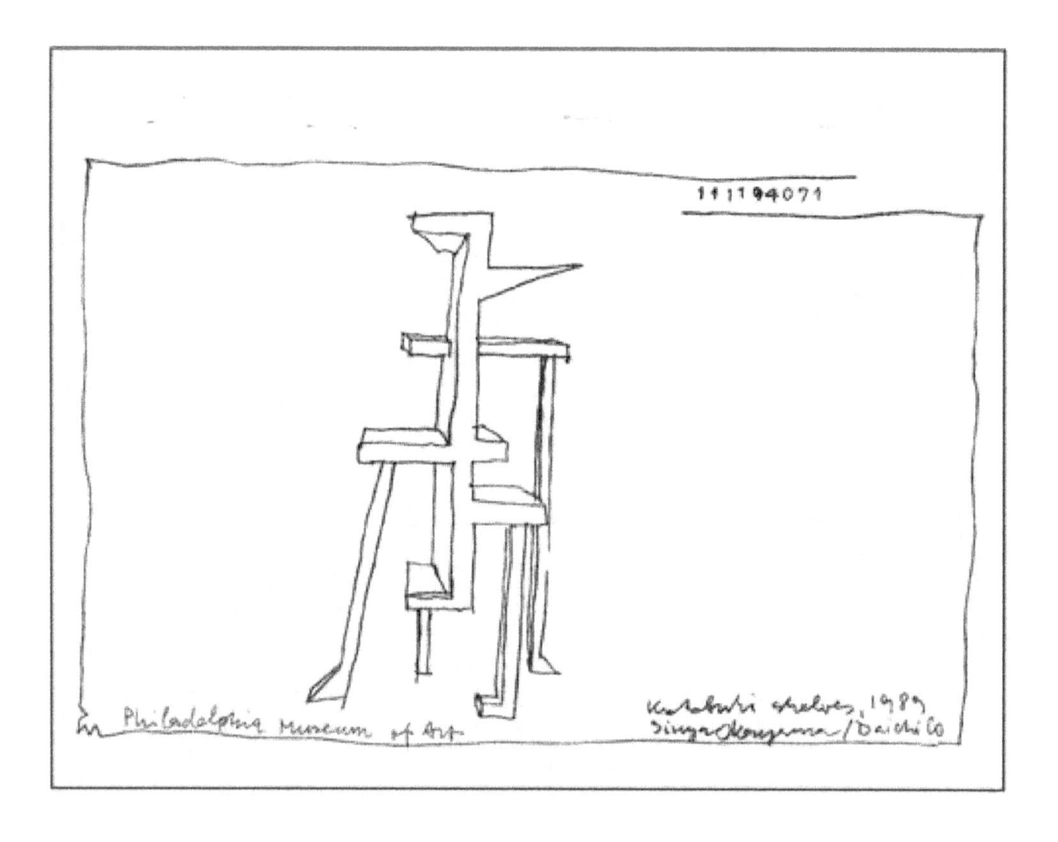

111194071
Philadelphia Museum of Art
shelves, 1989

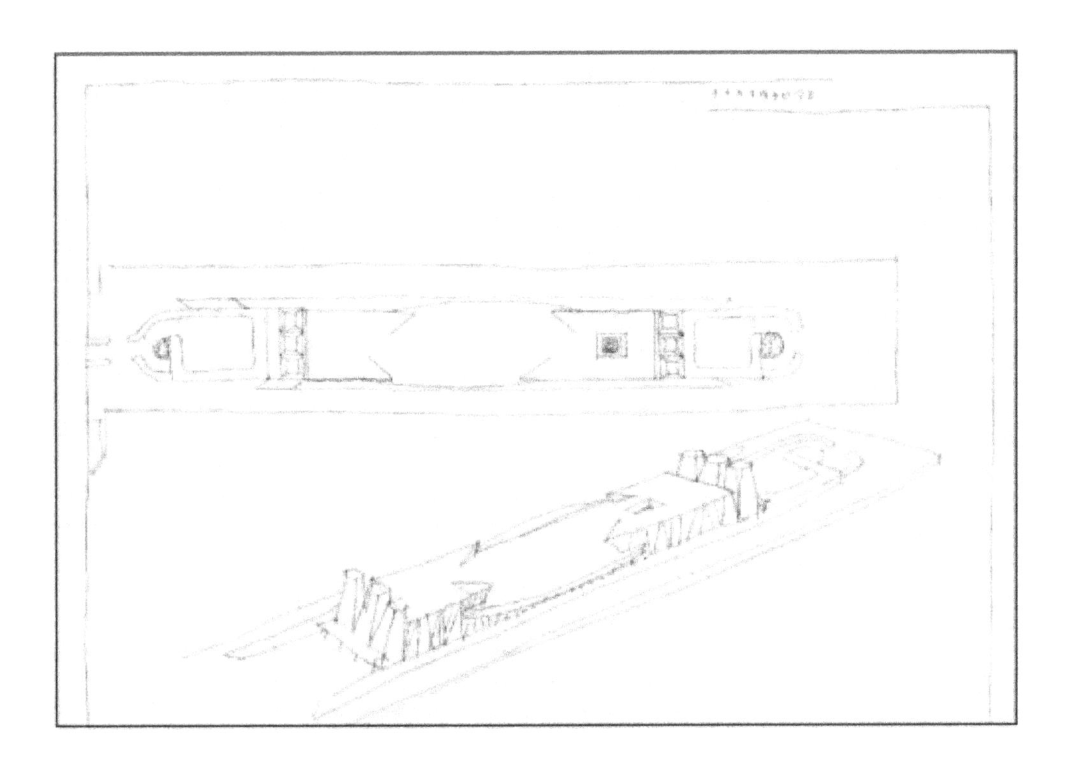

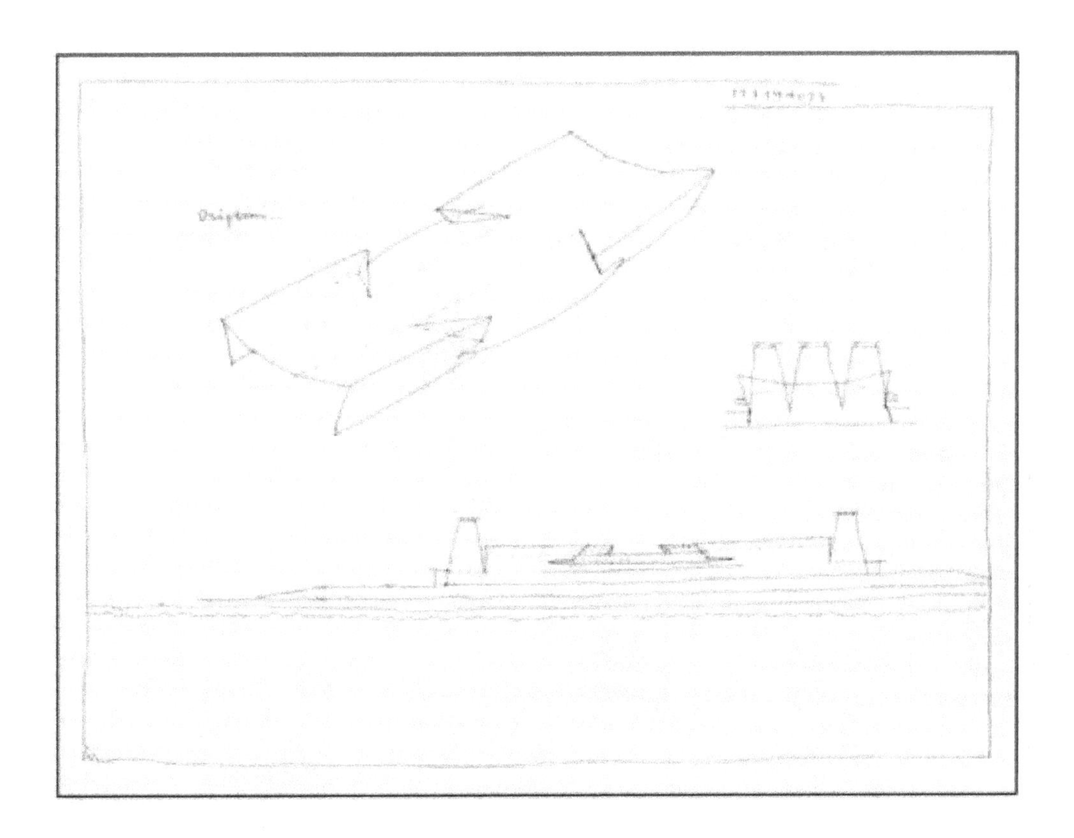

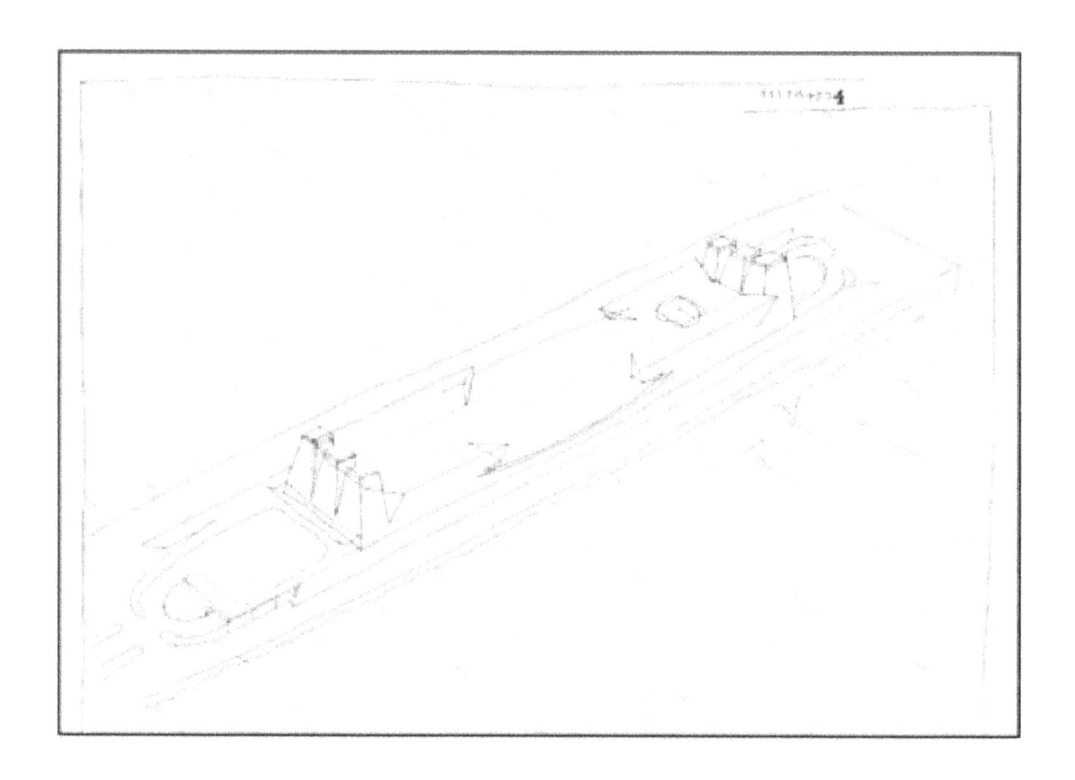

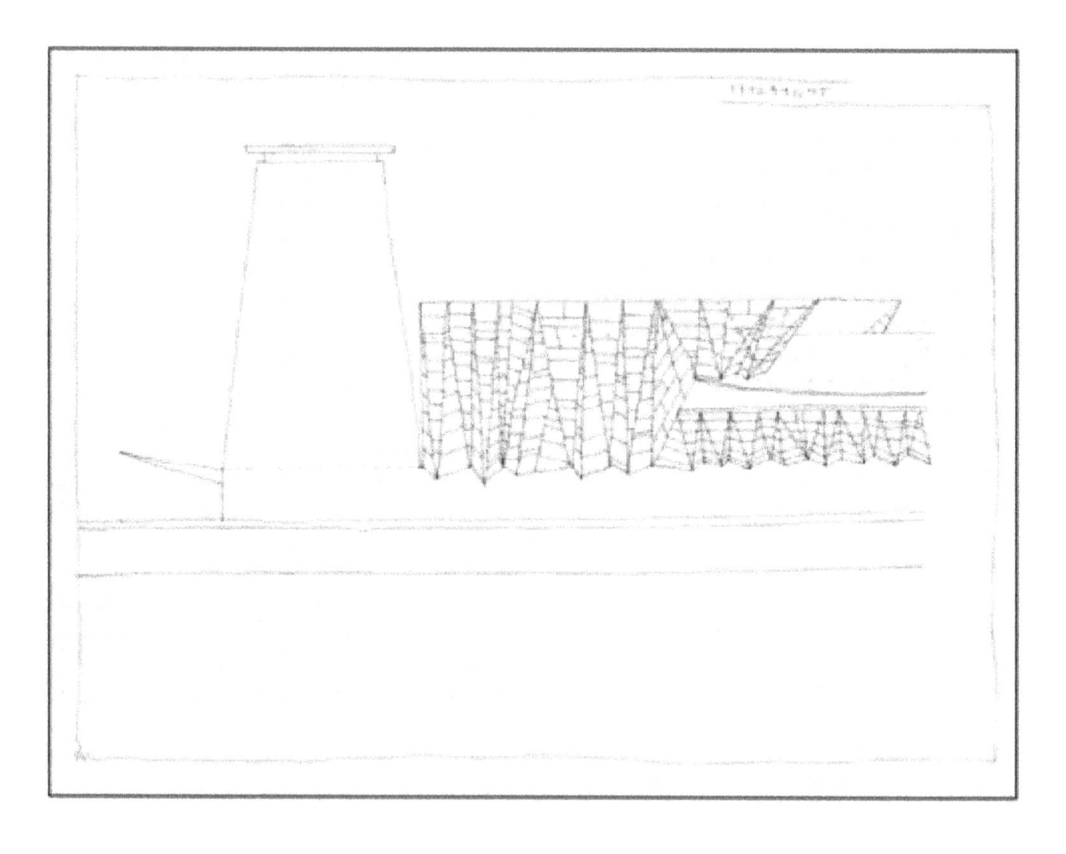

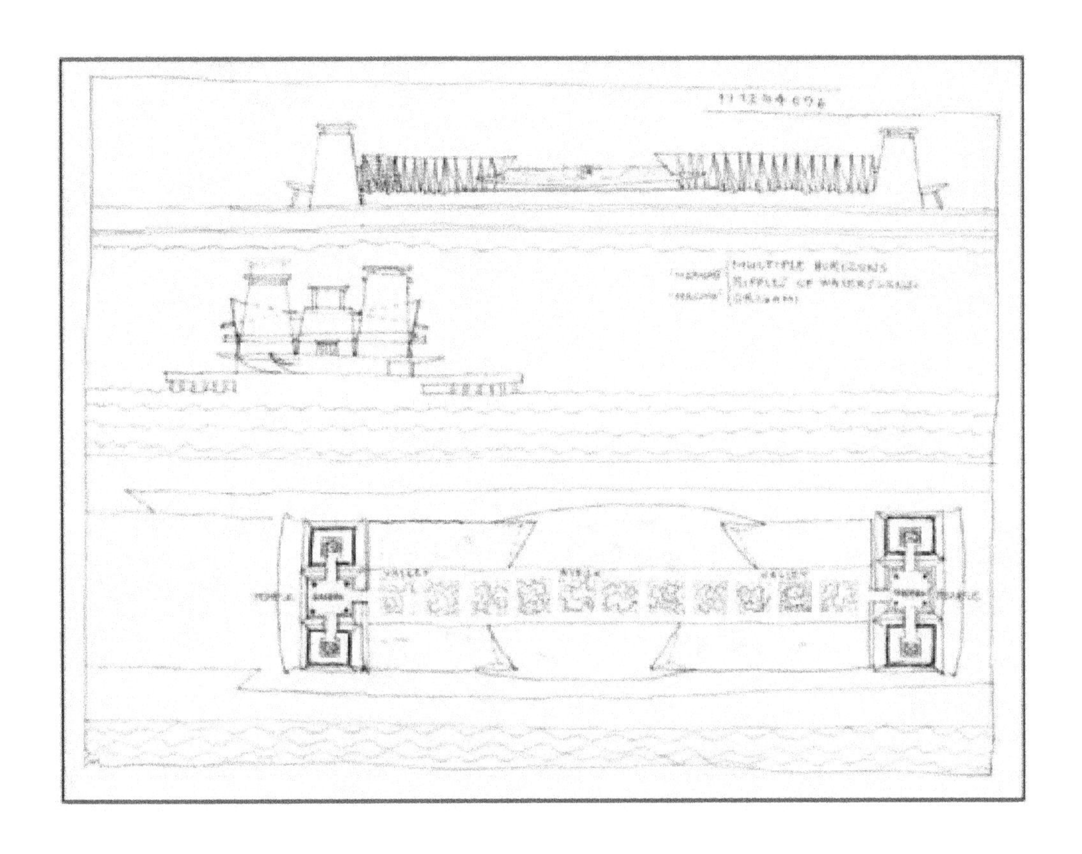
MULTIPLE HORIZONS

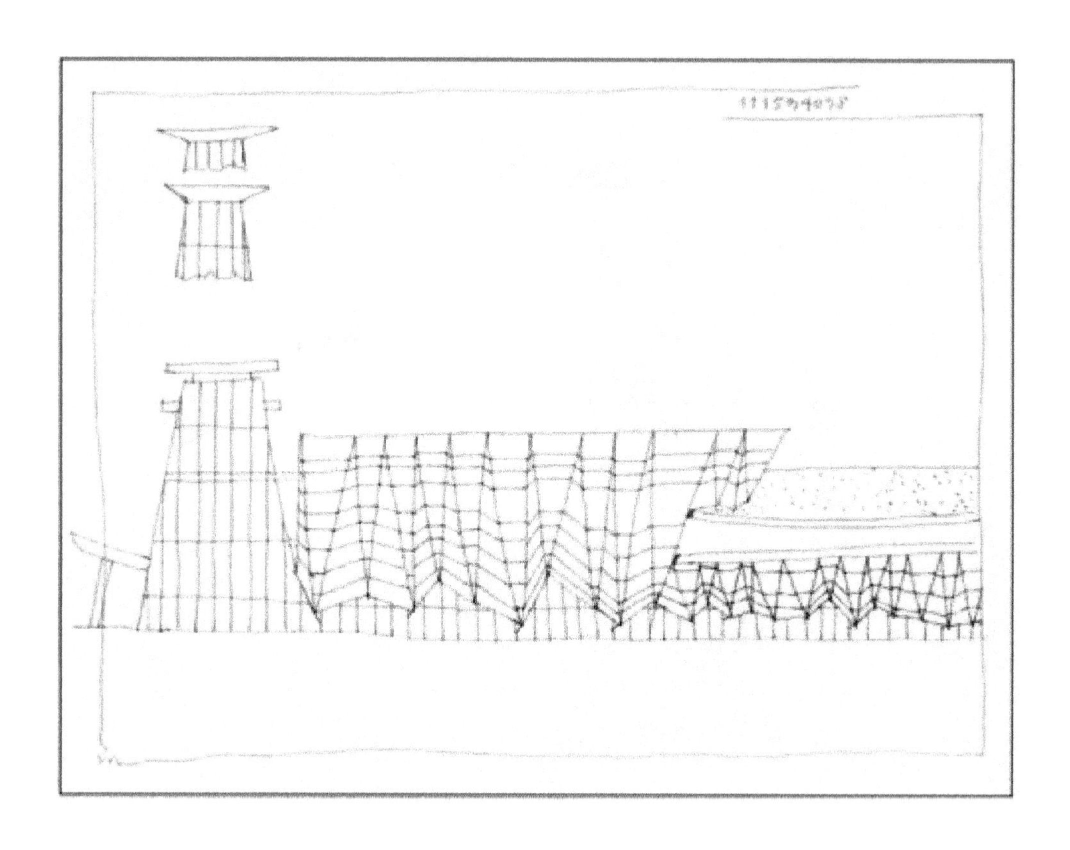

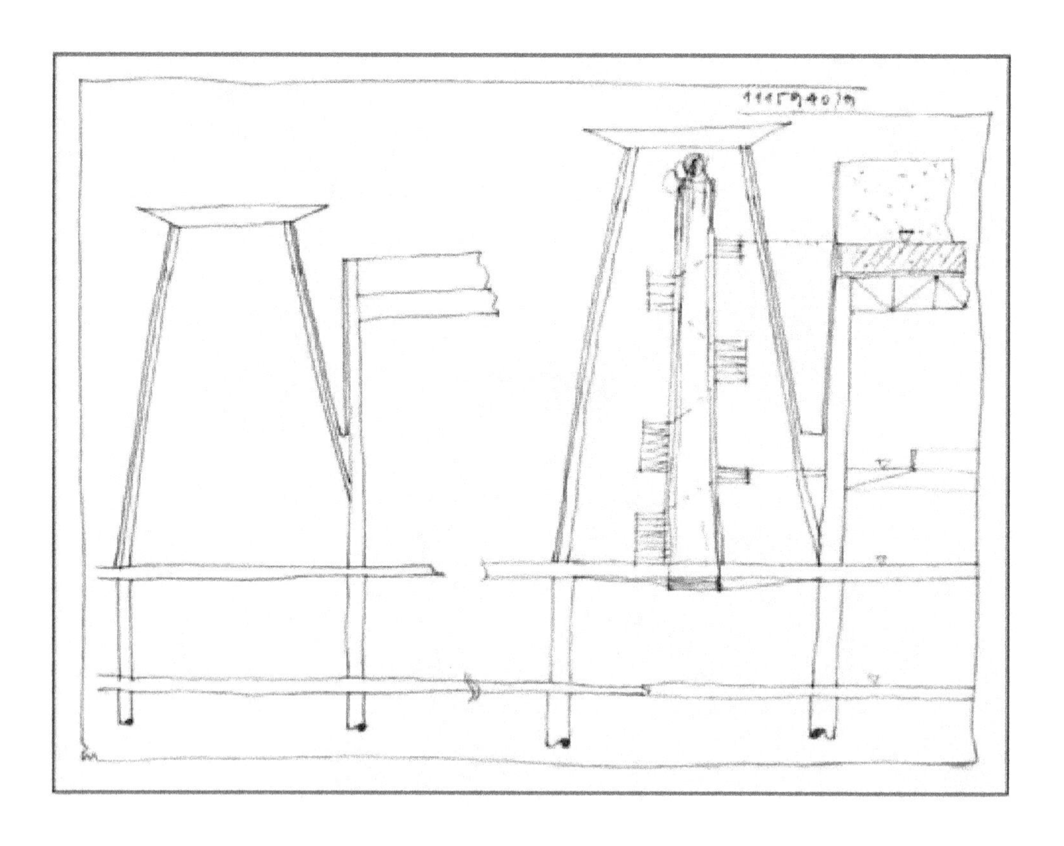

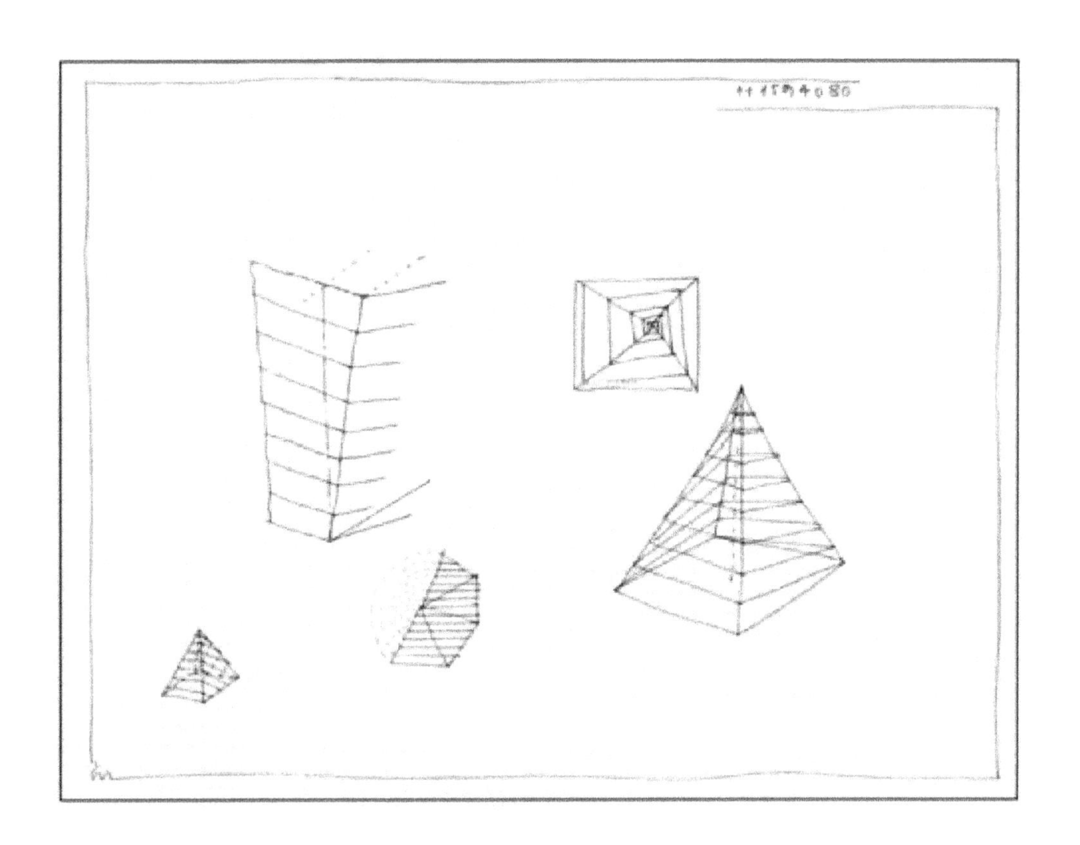

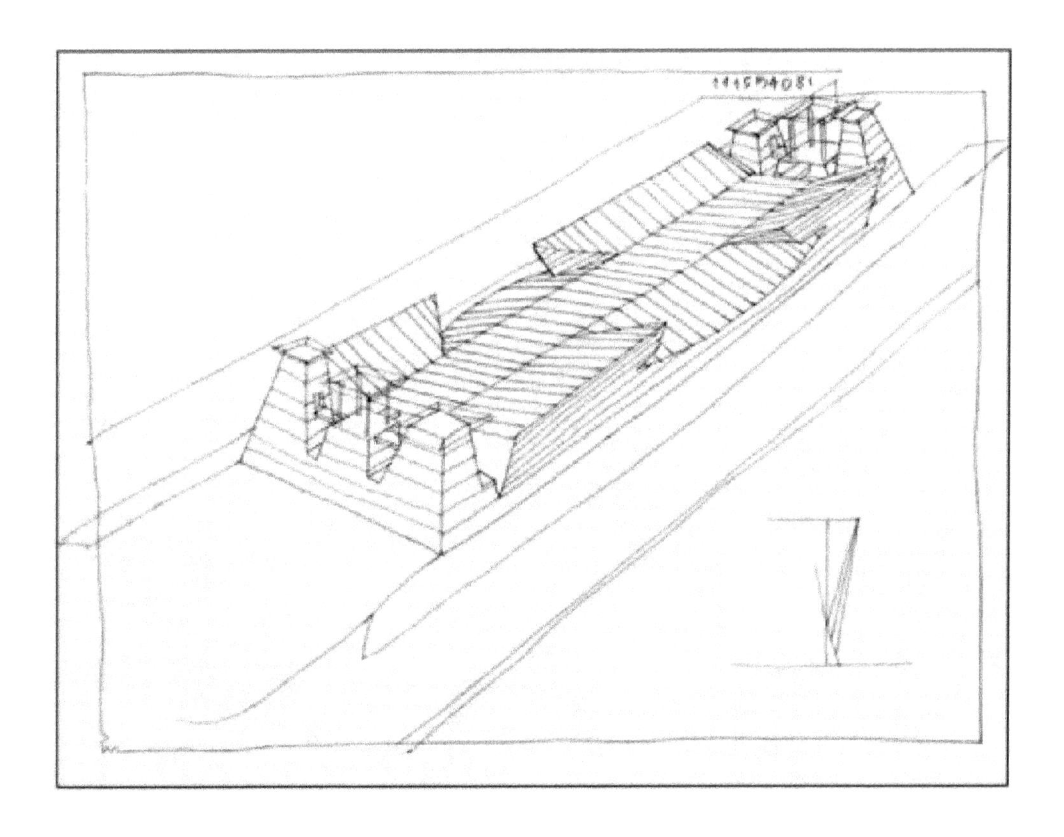

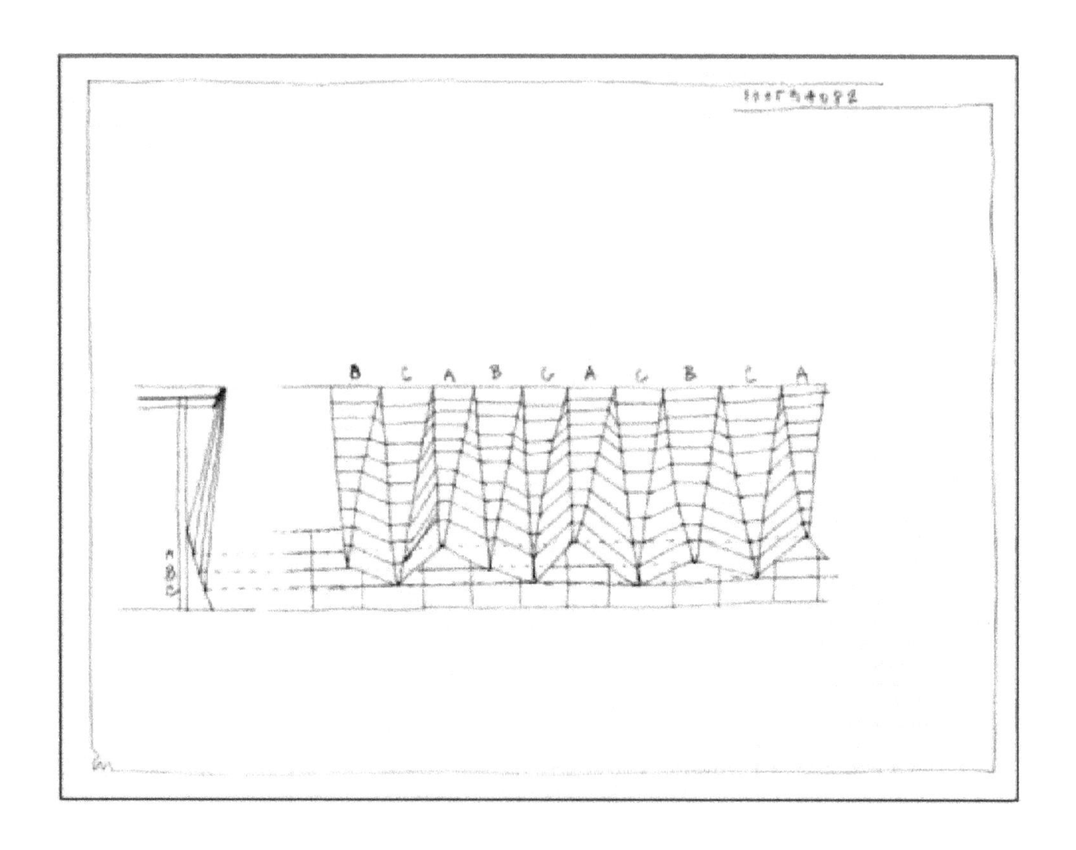
B C A B C A C B C A
A B C

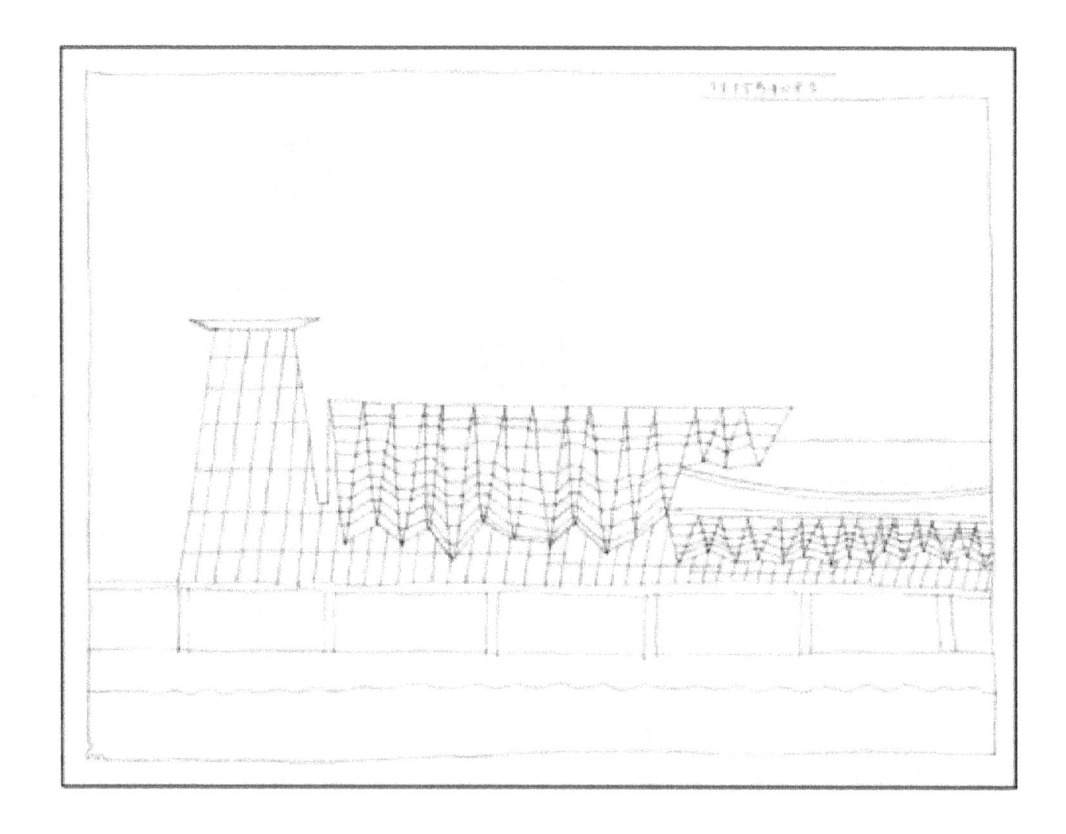

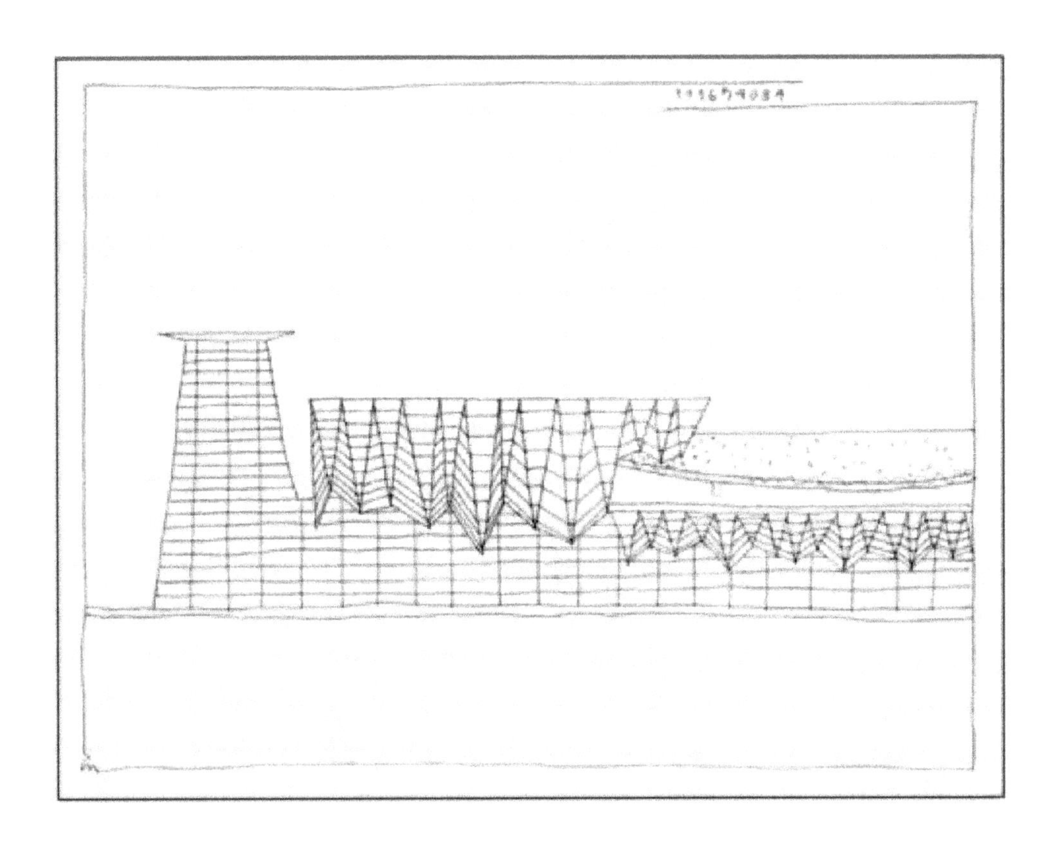

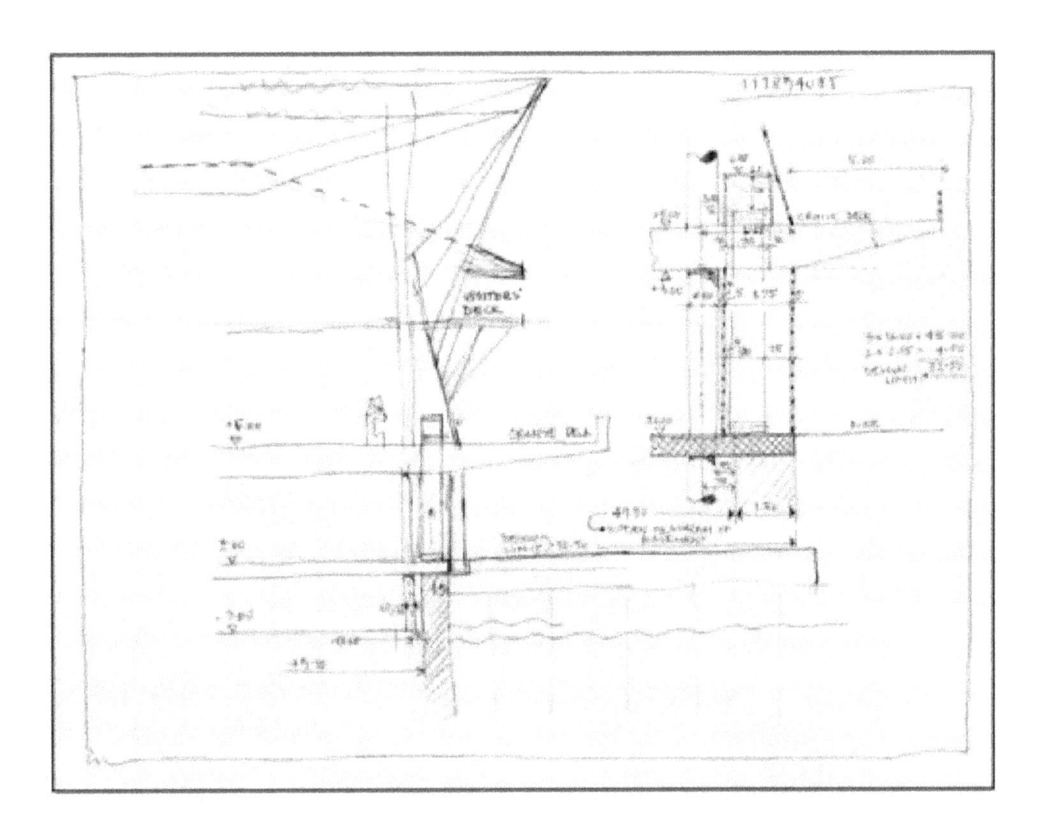
VISITORS'
DECK

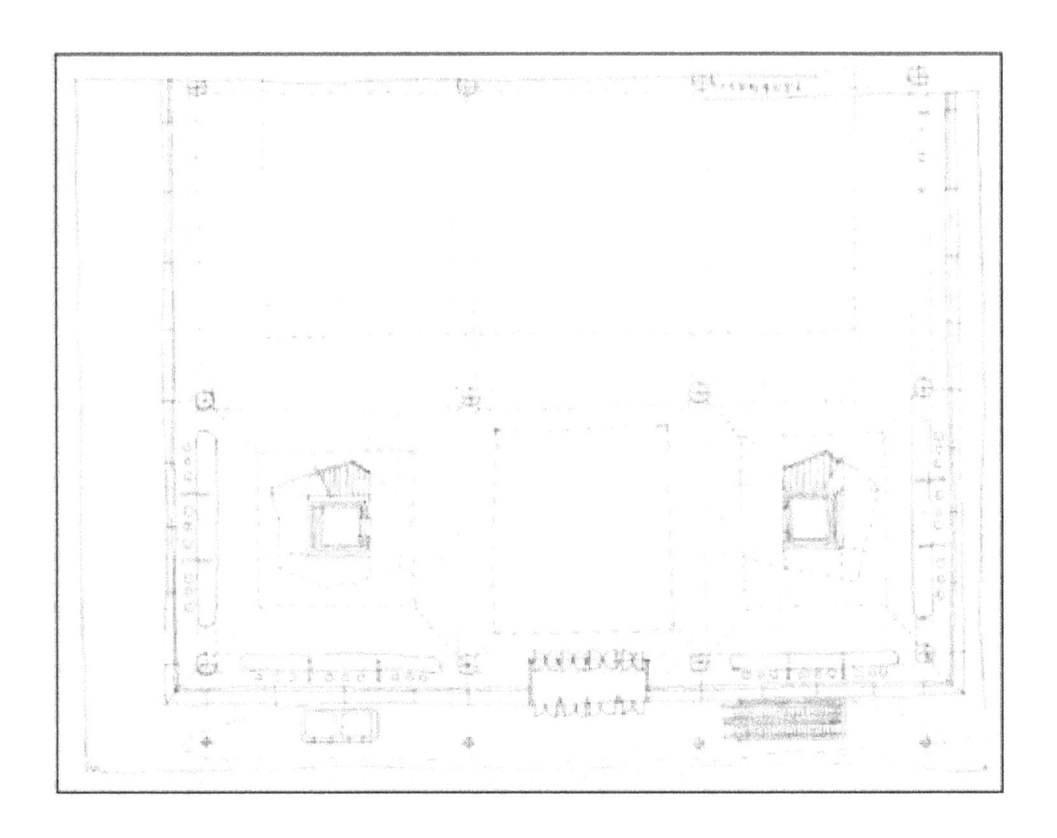

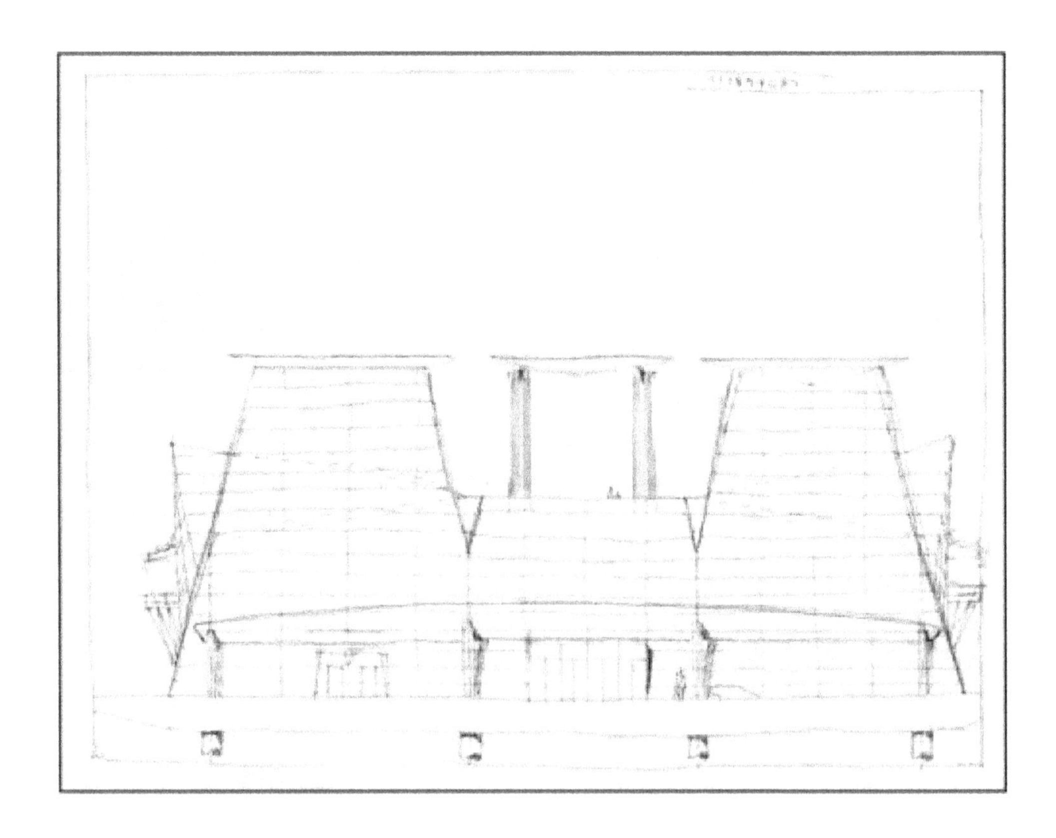

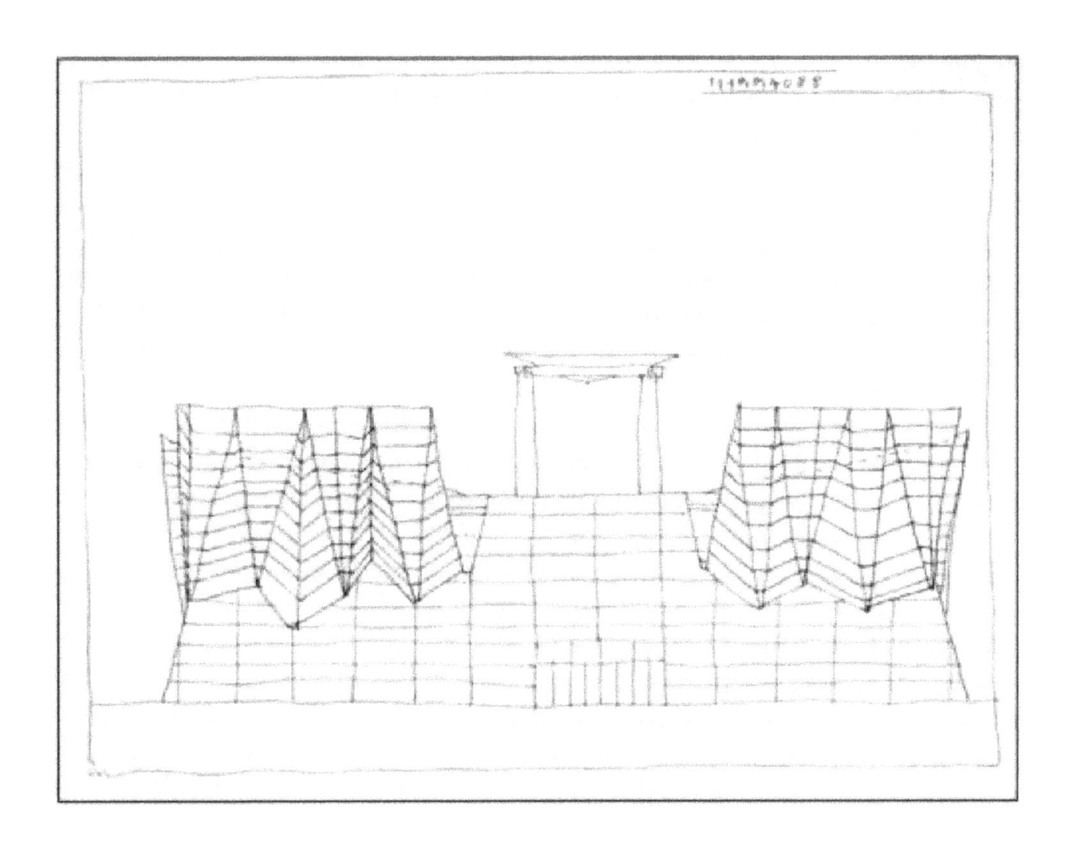

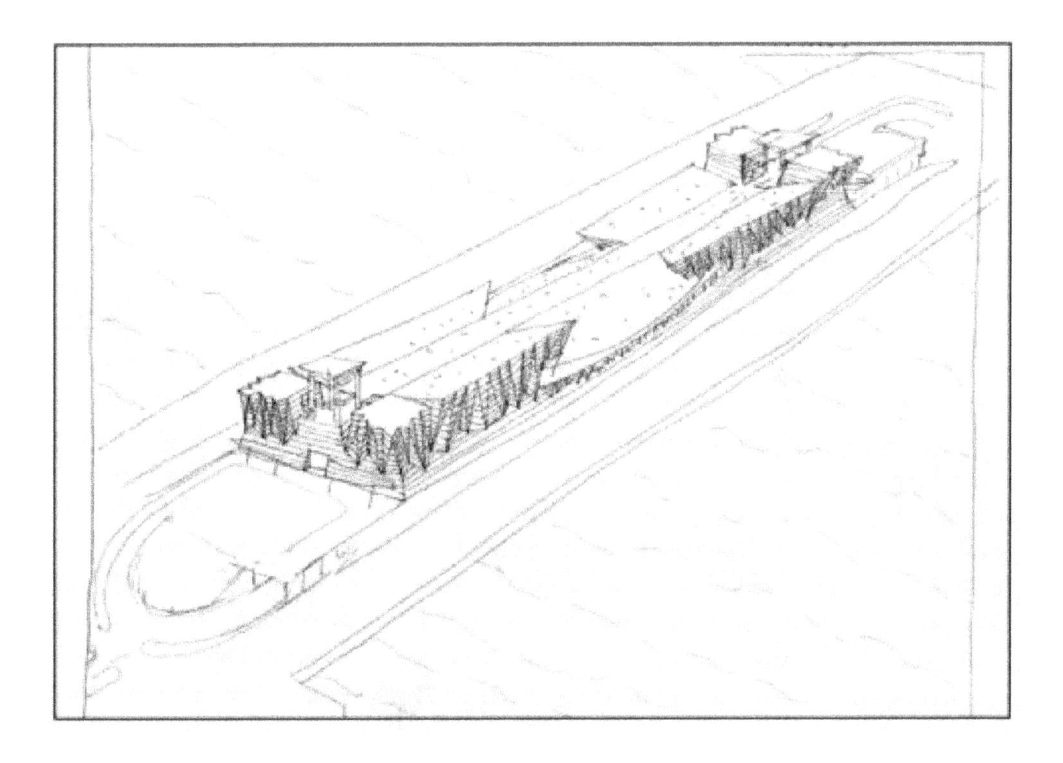

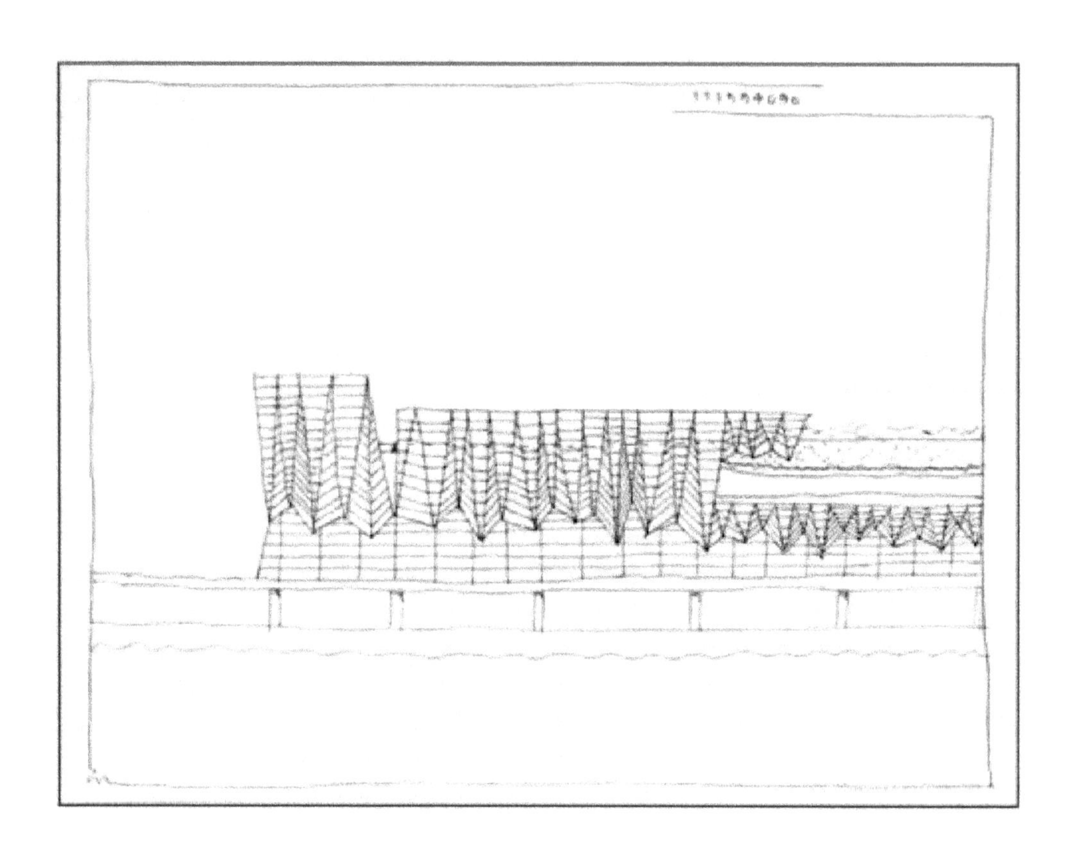

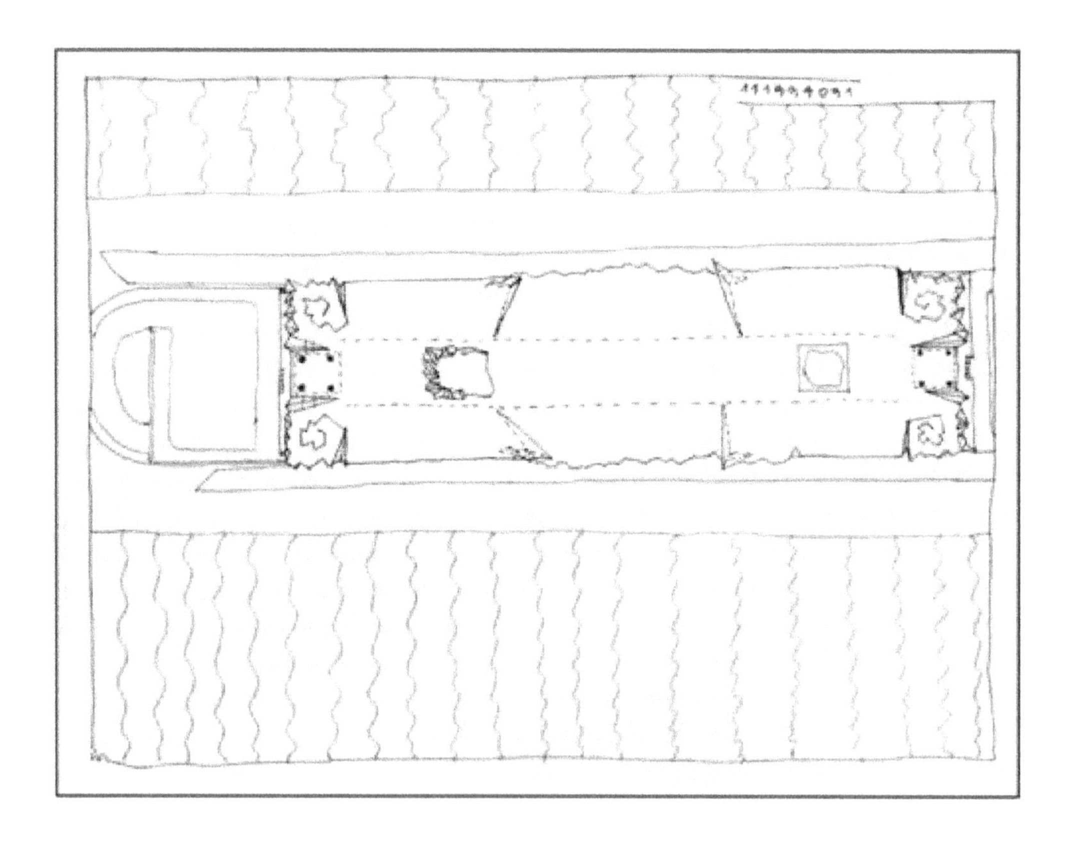

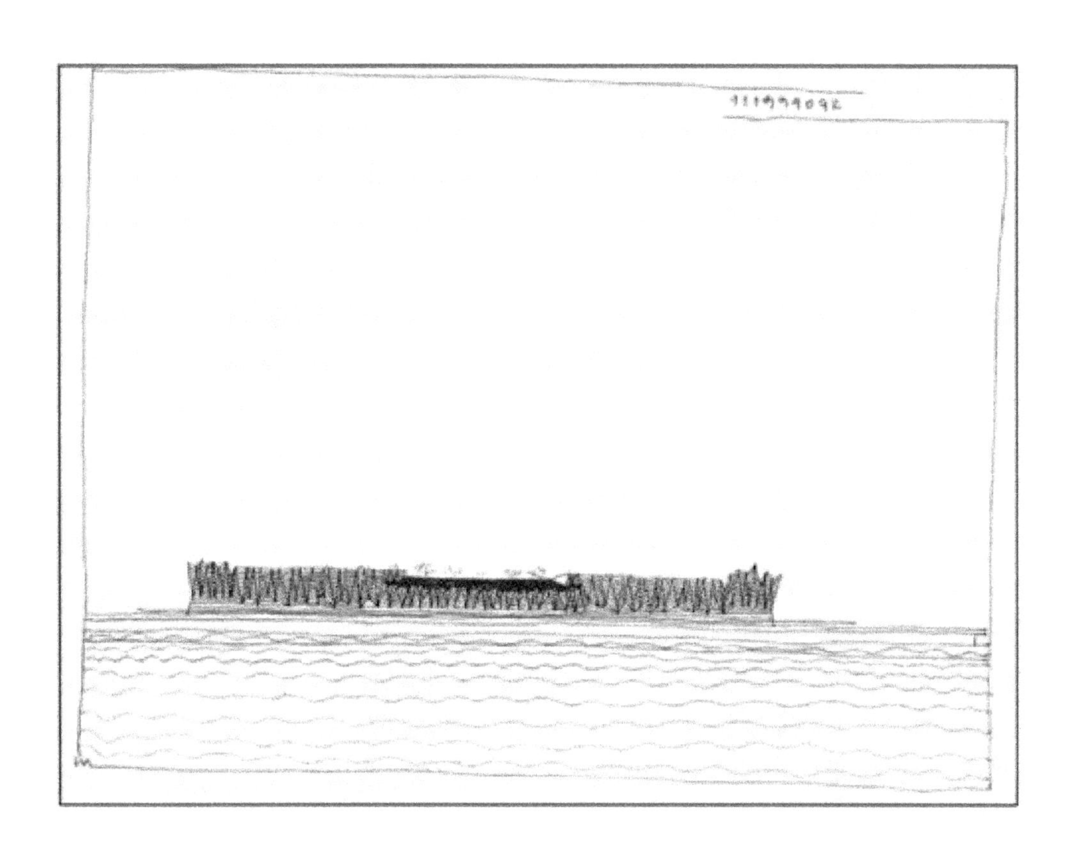

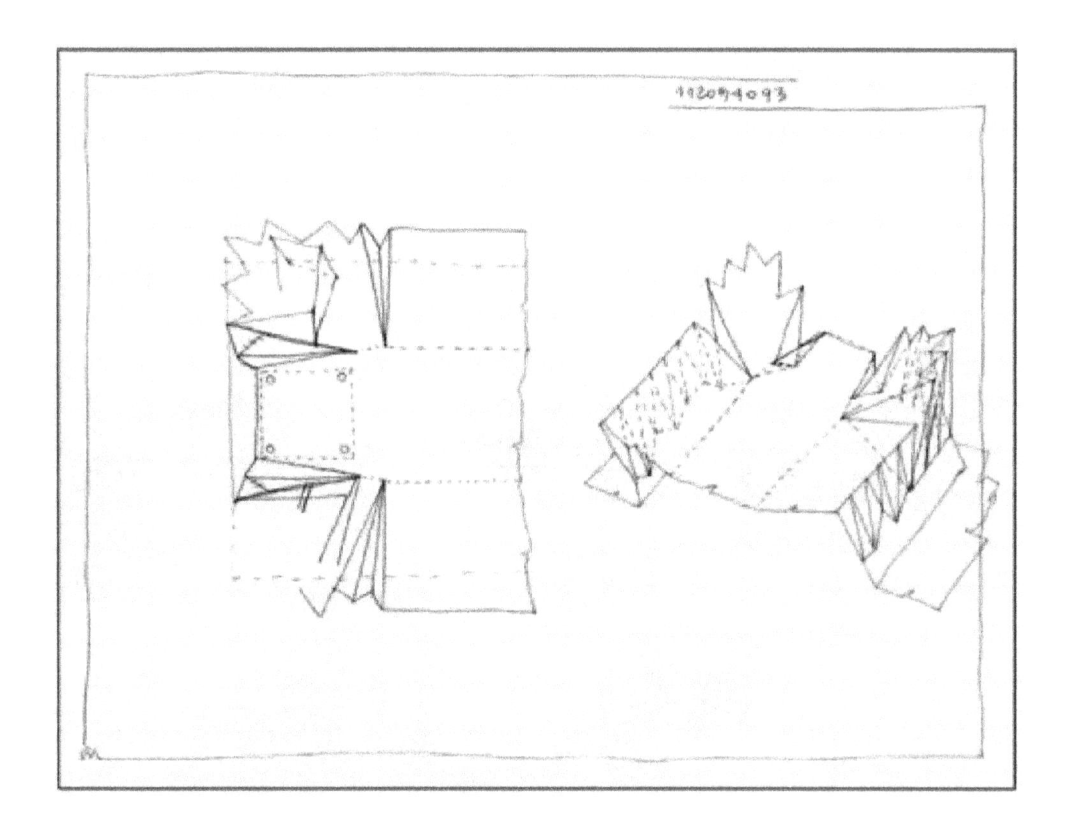

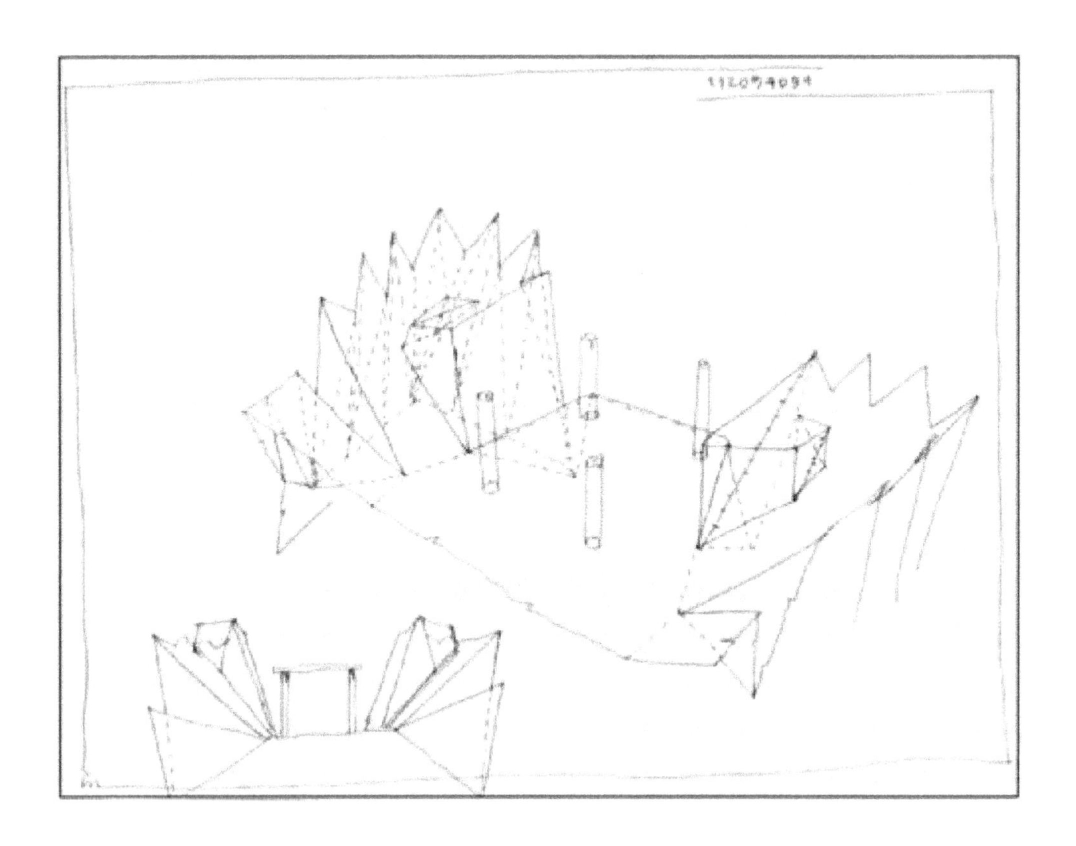

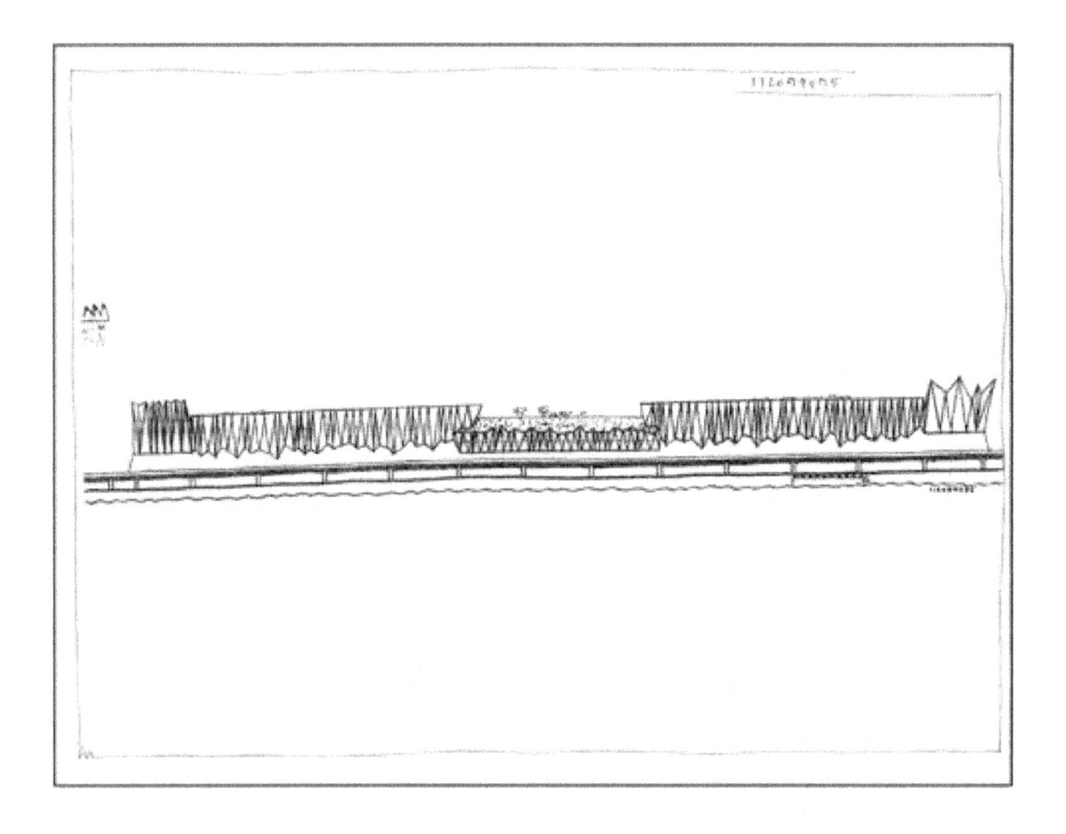

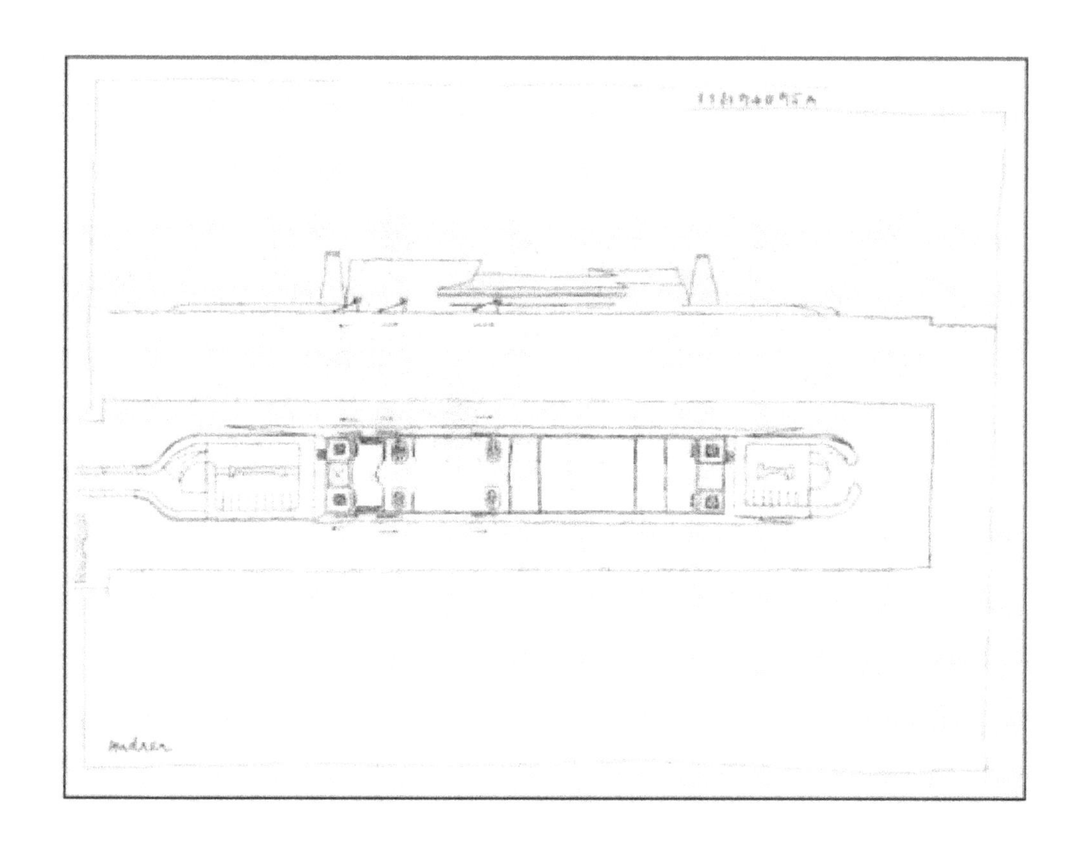

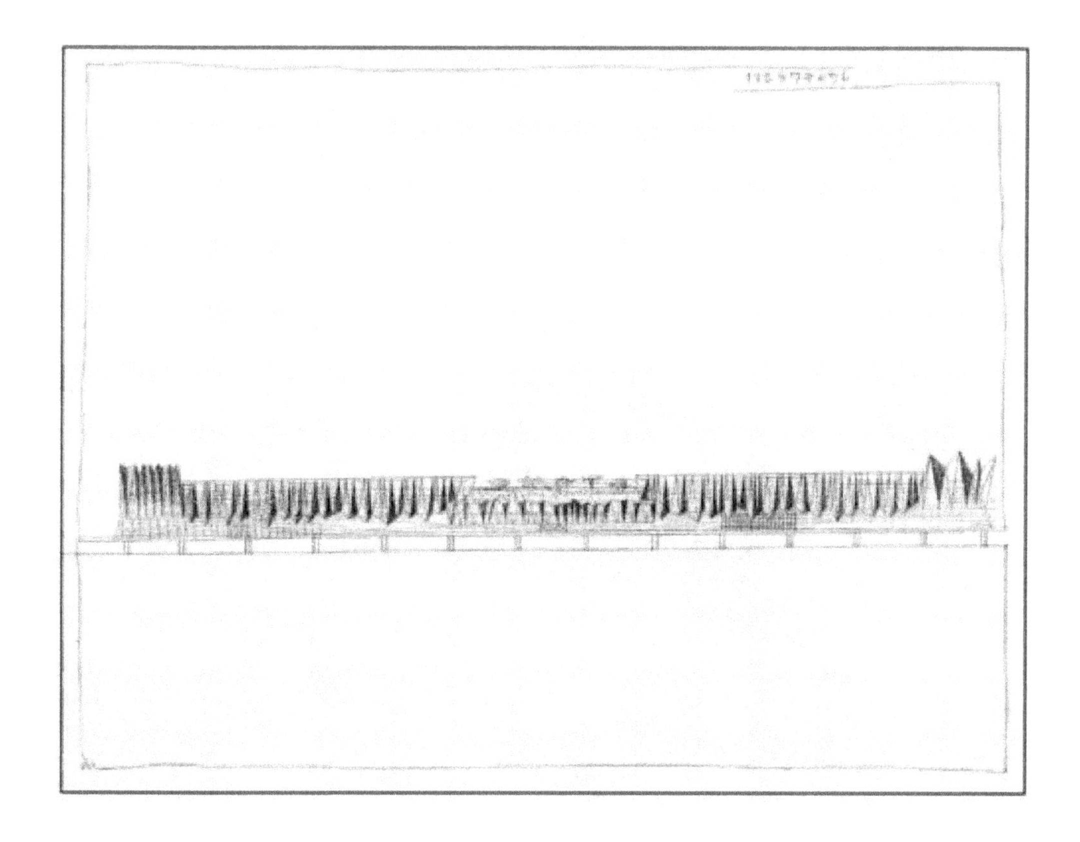

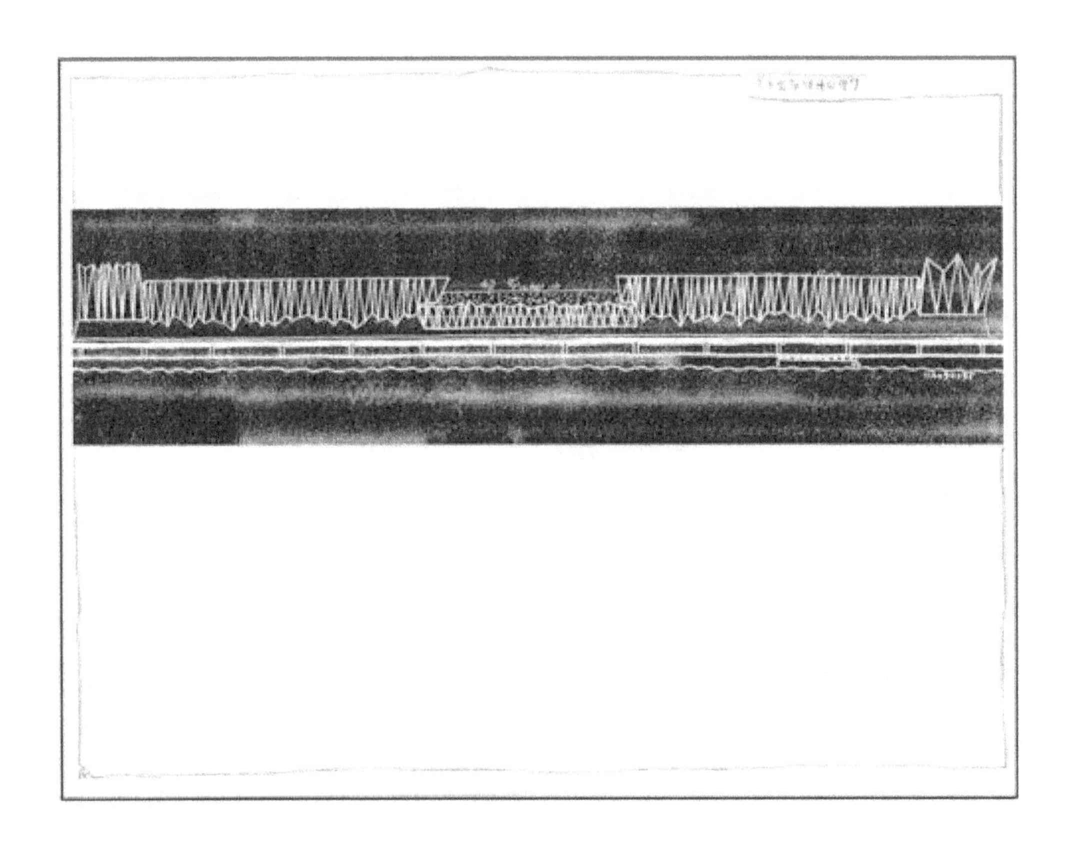

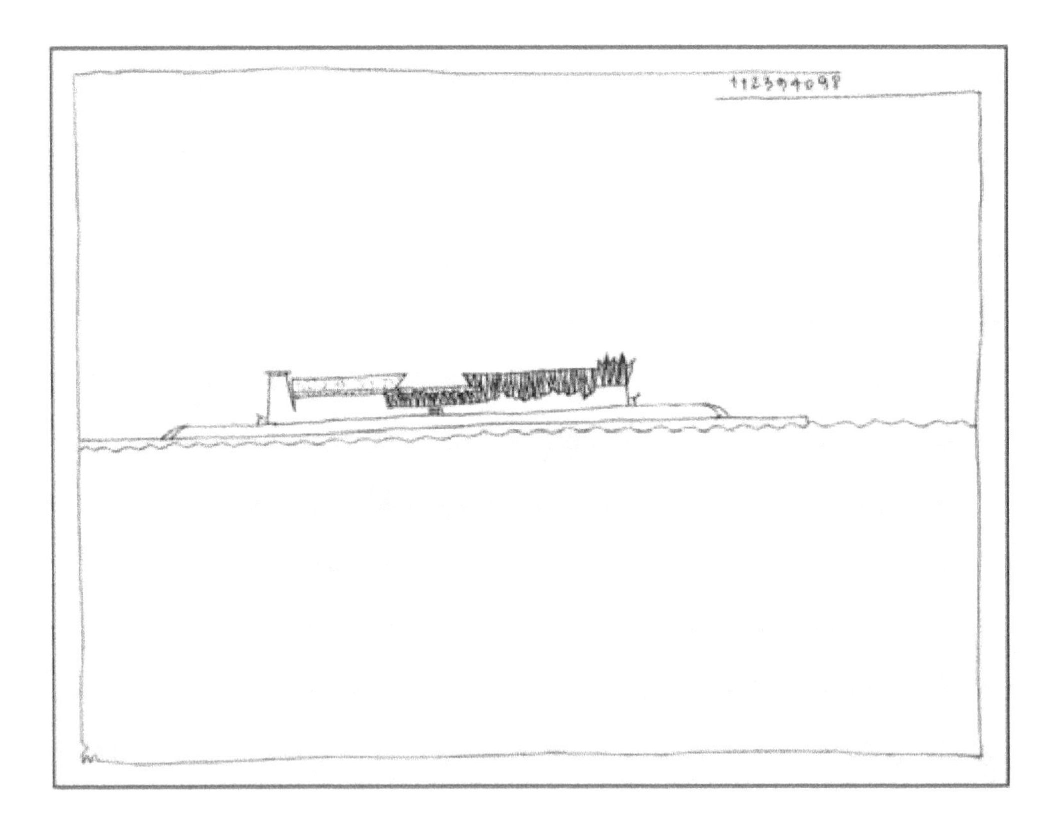

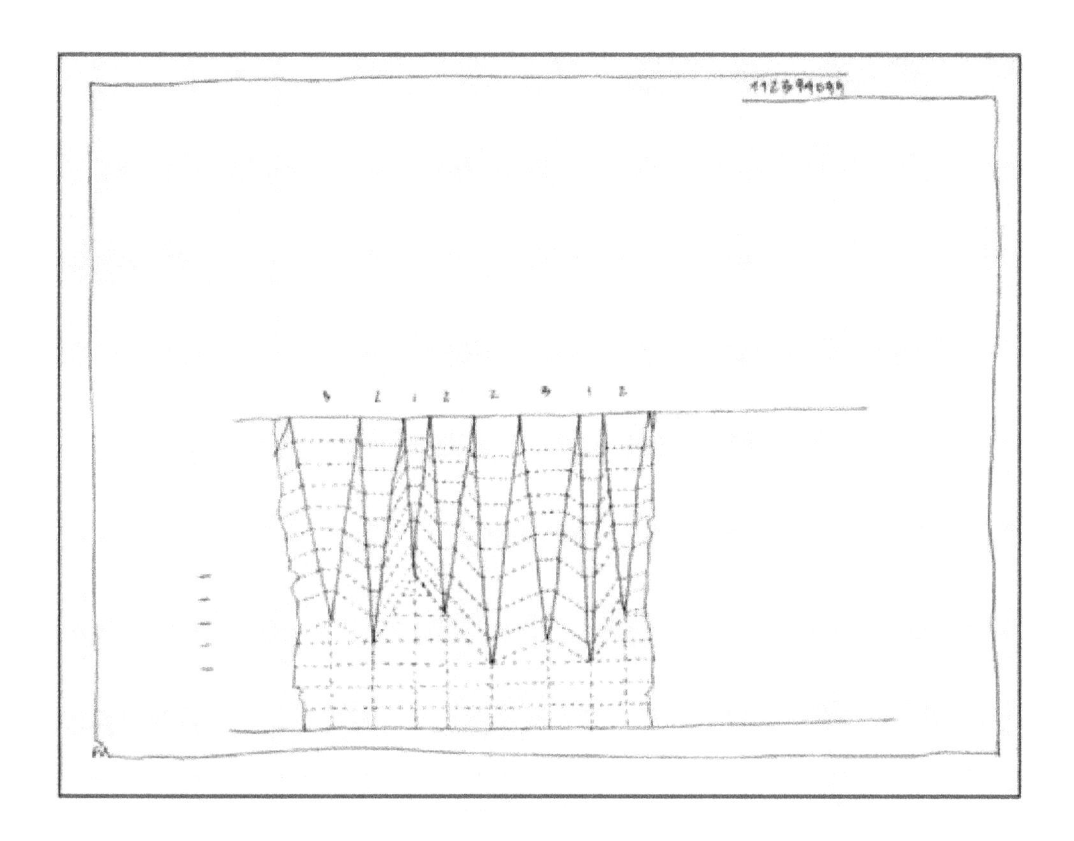

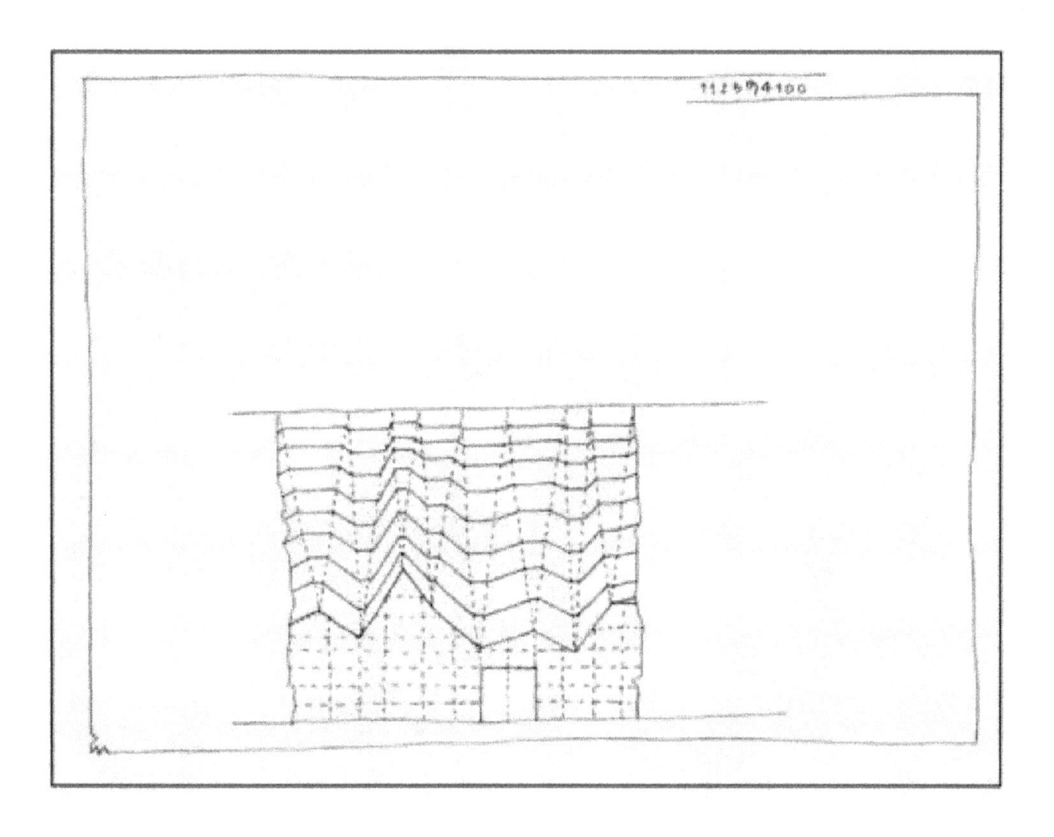

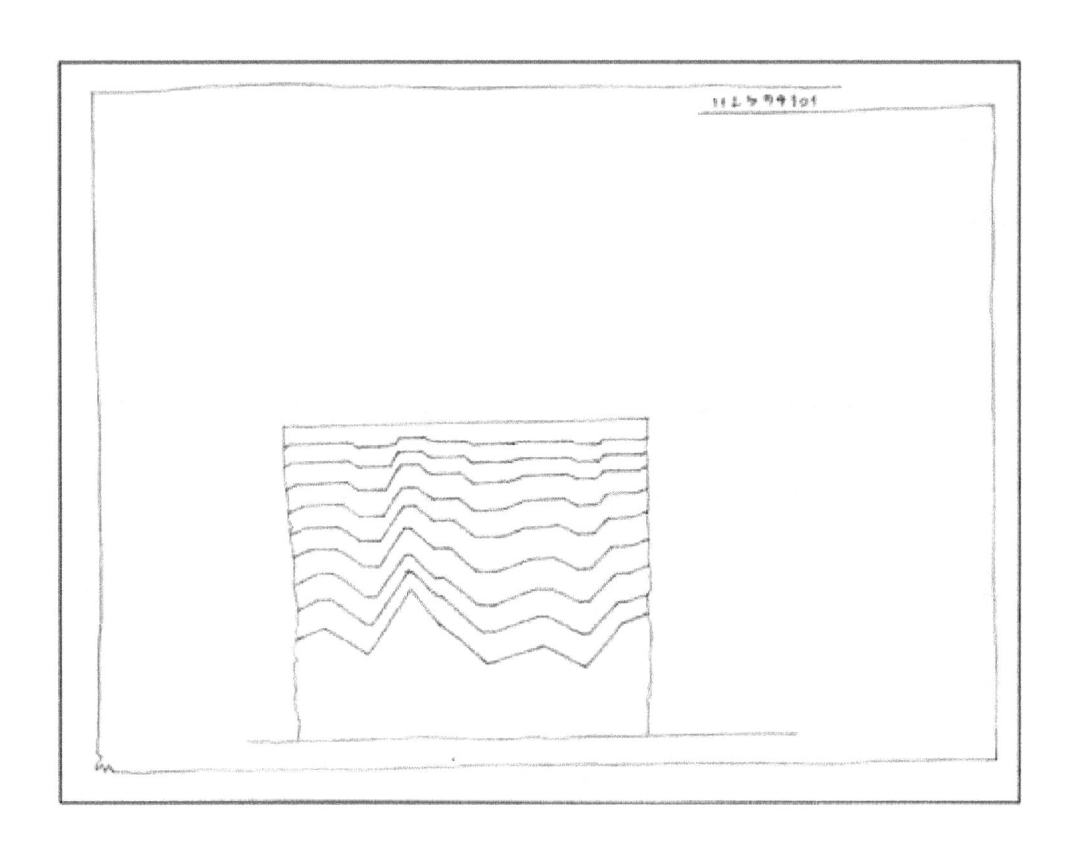

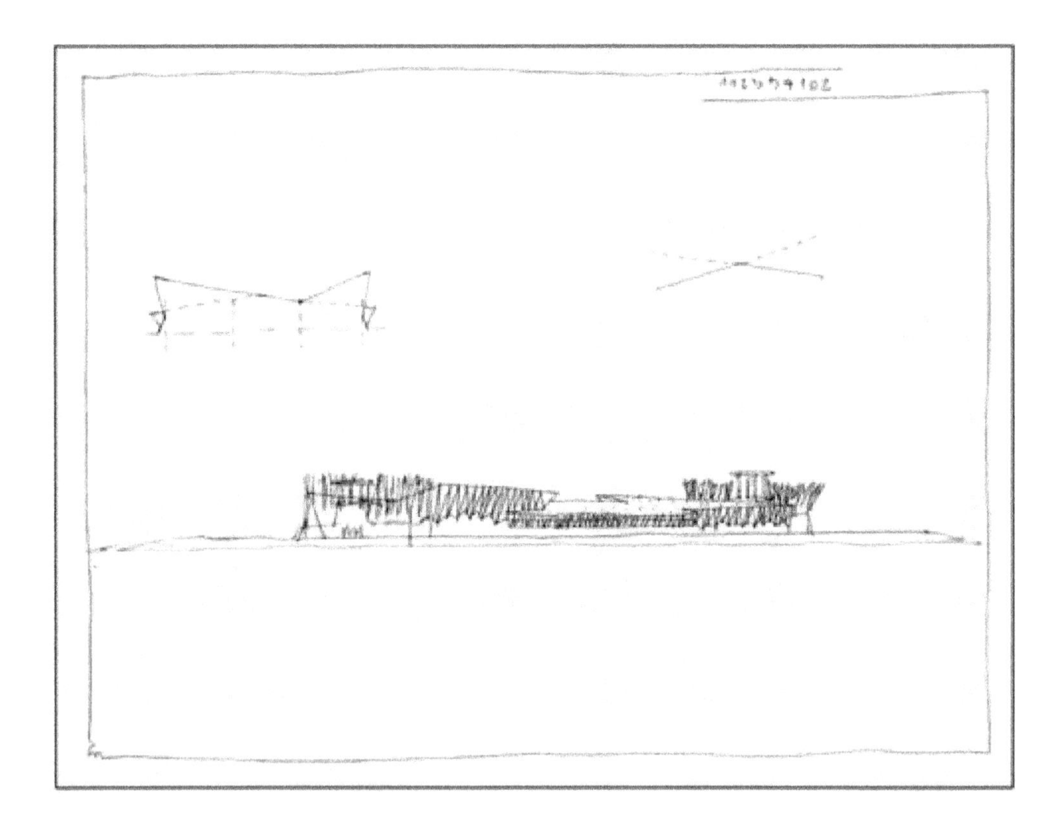

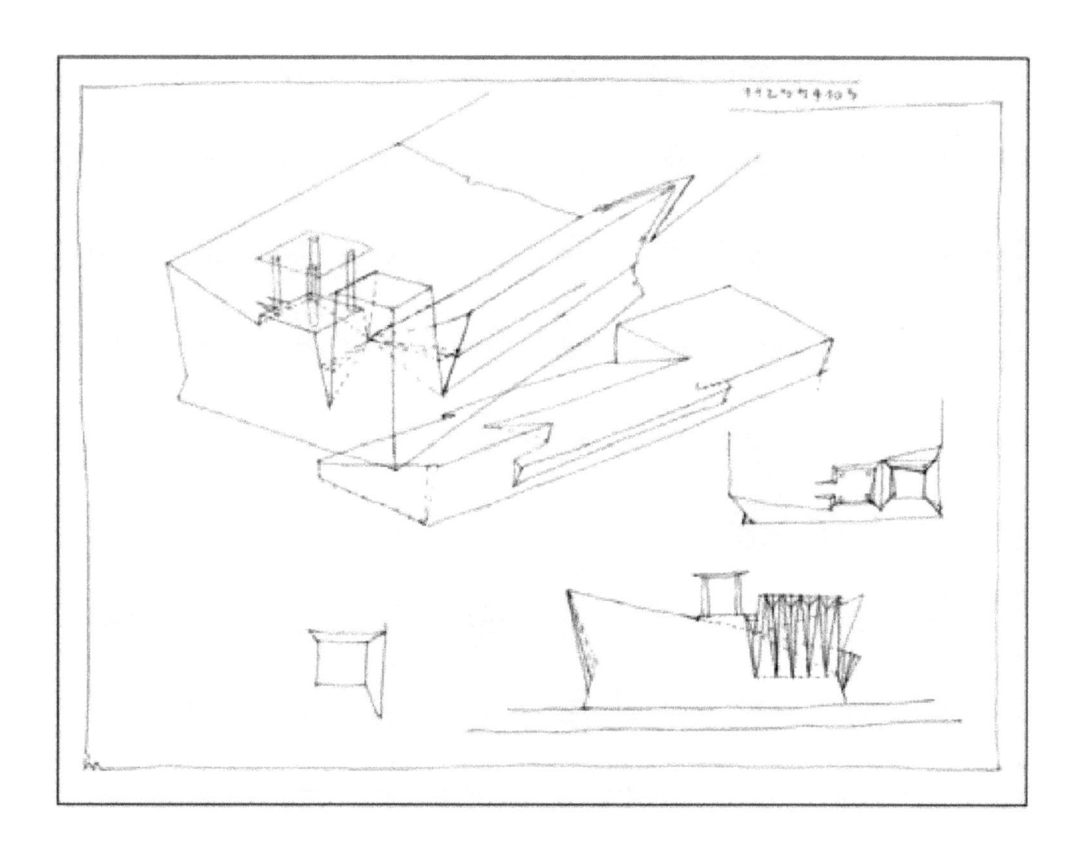

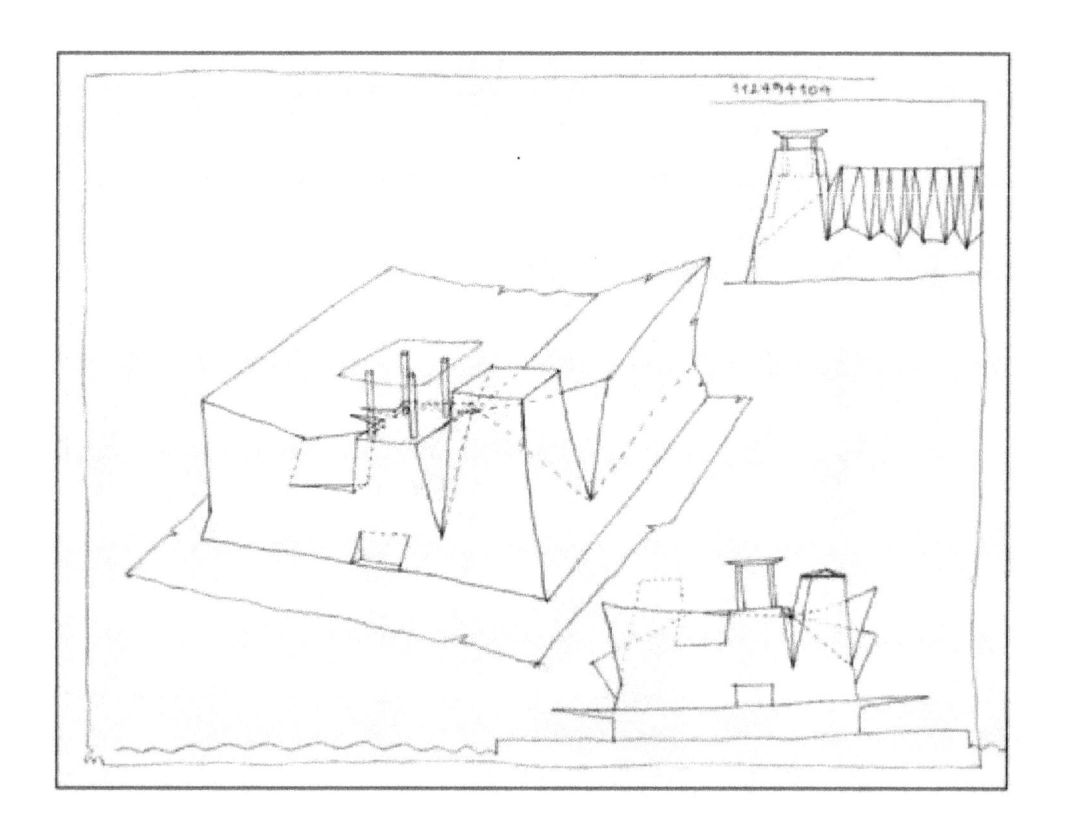

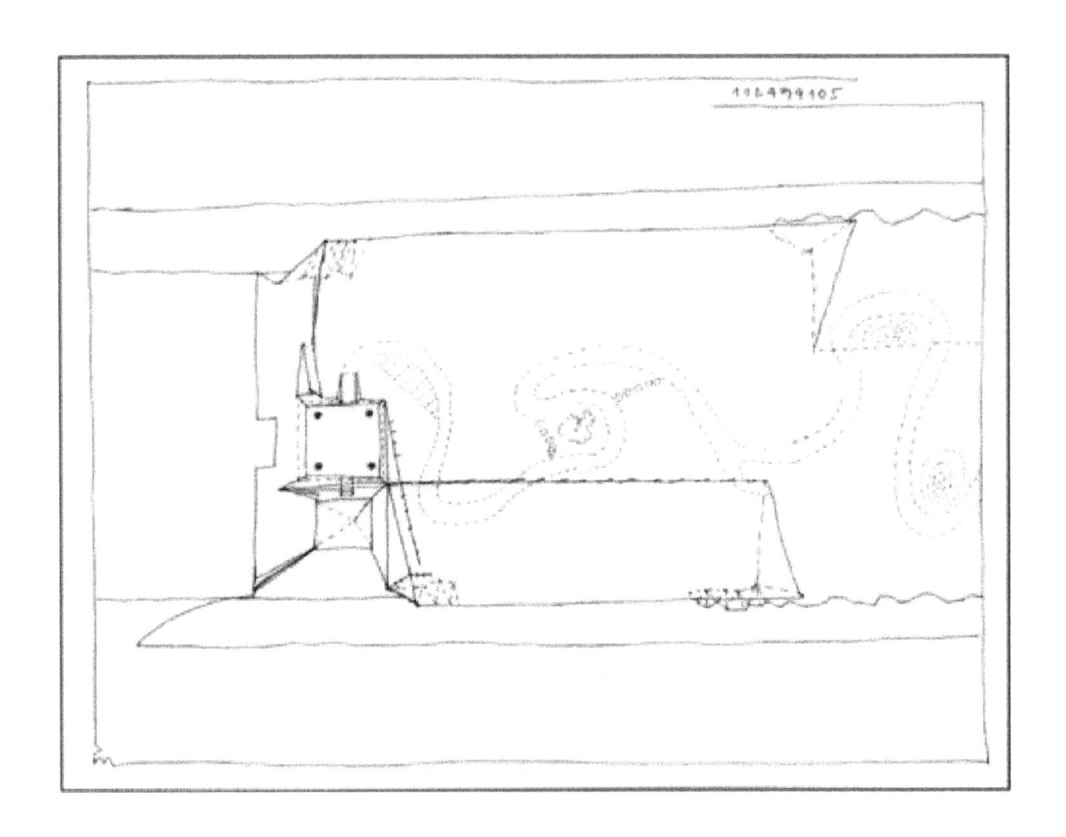

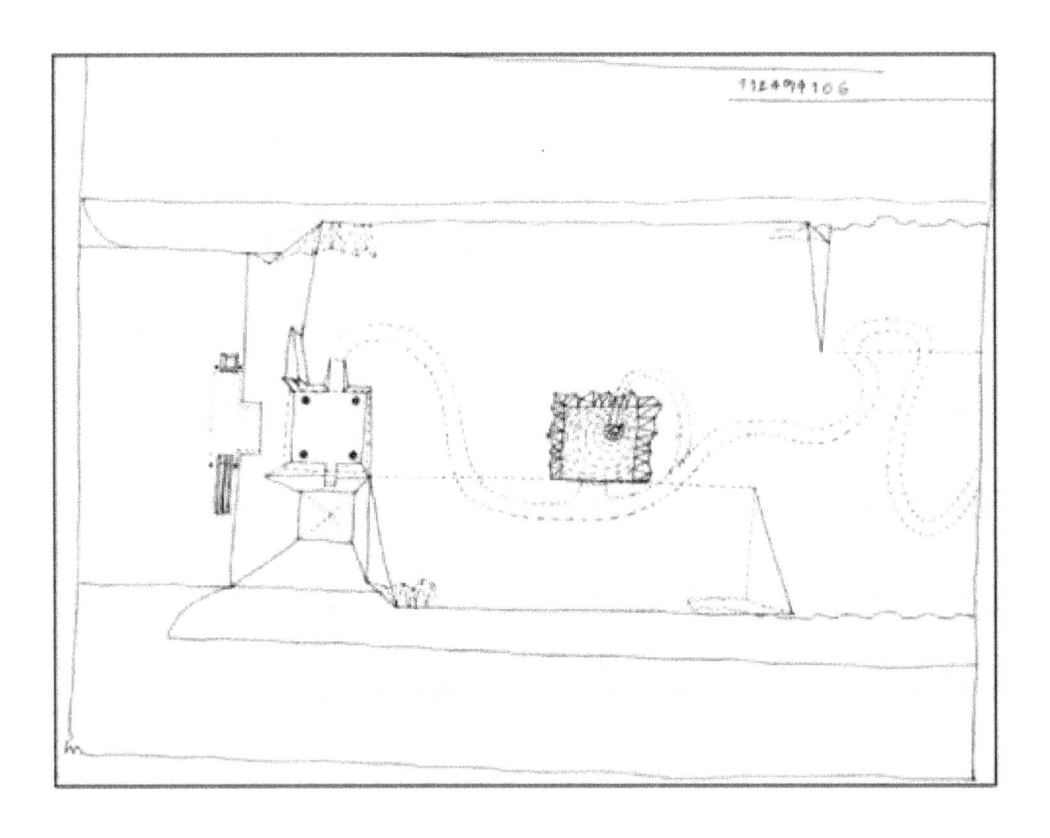

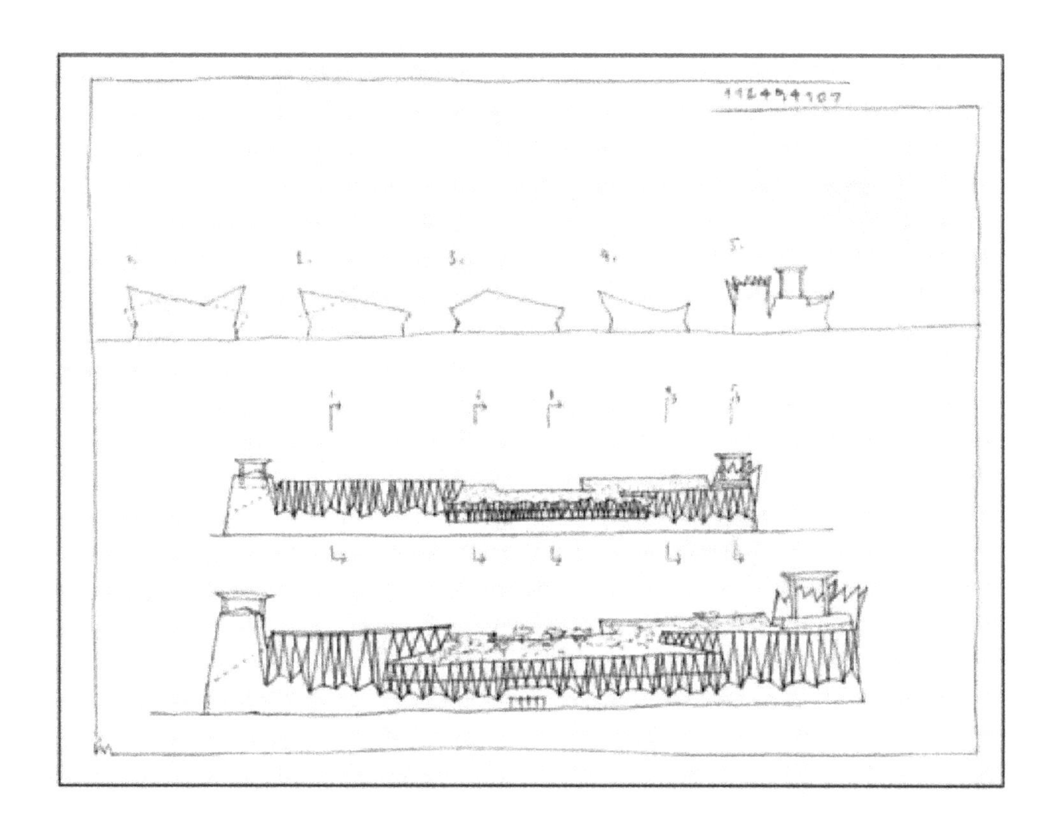

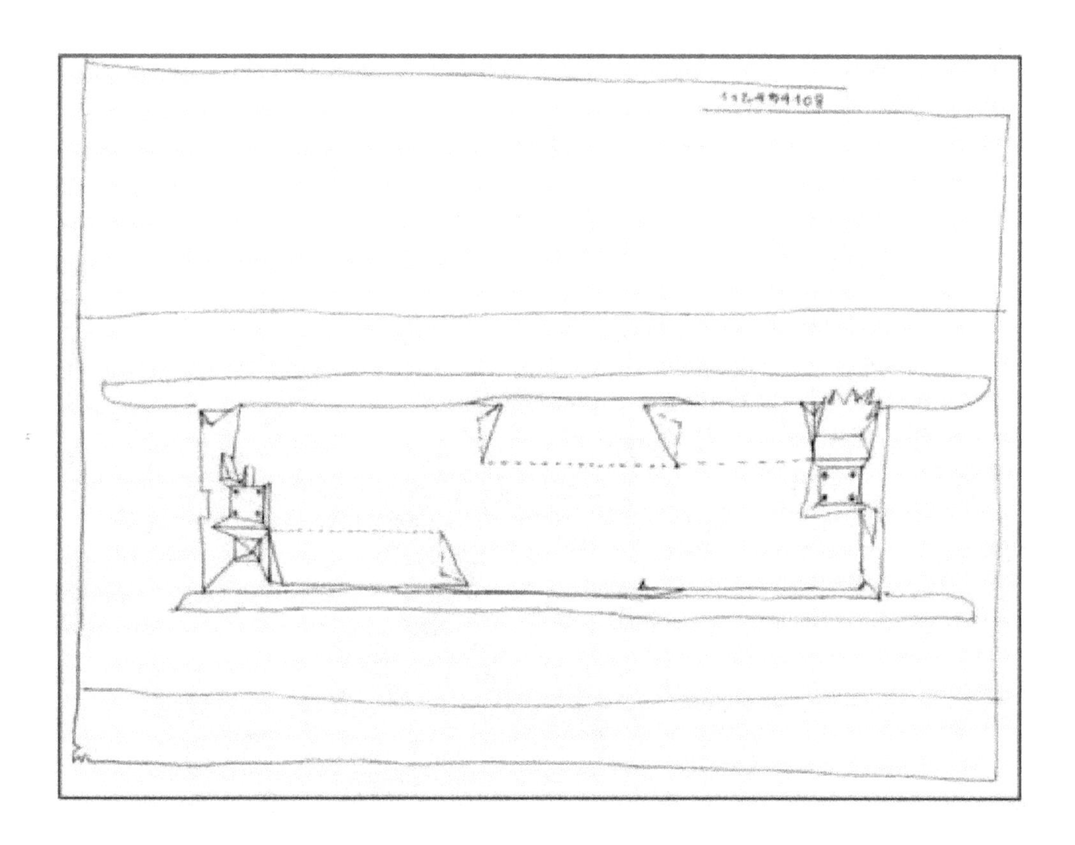

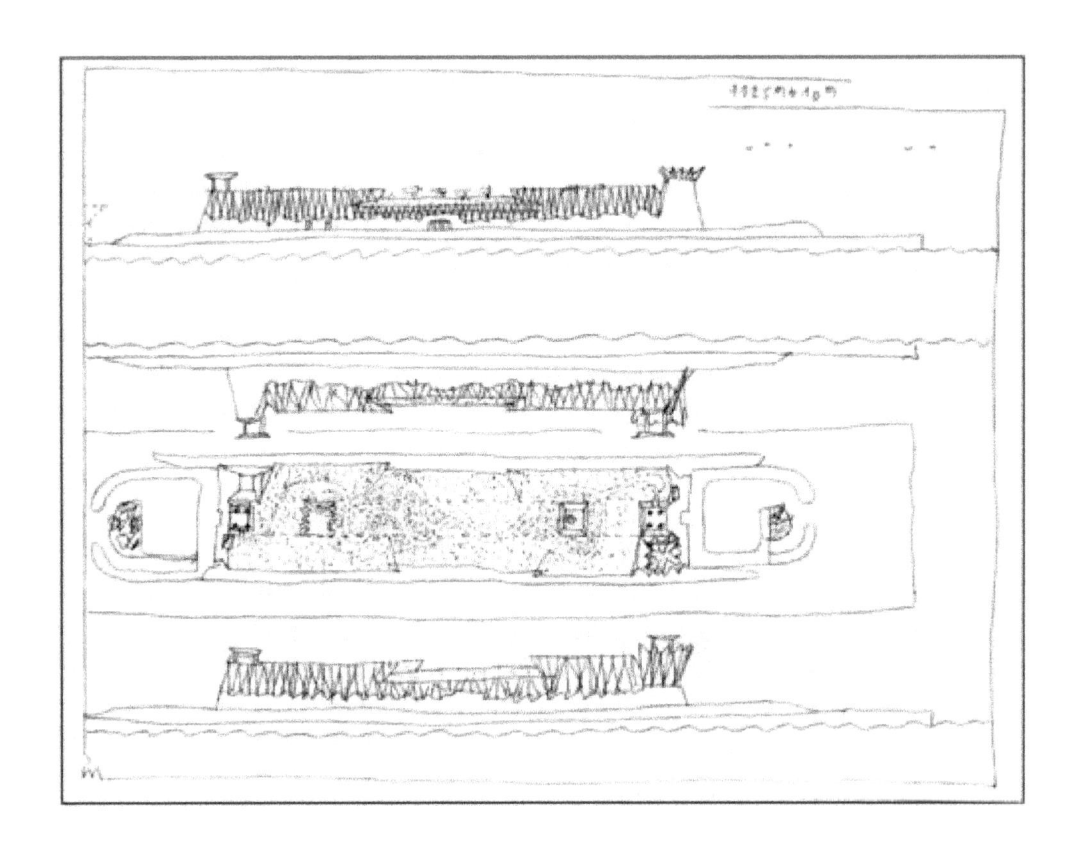

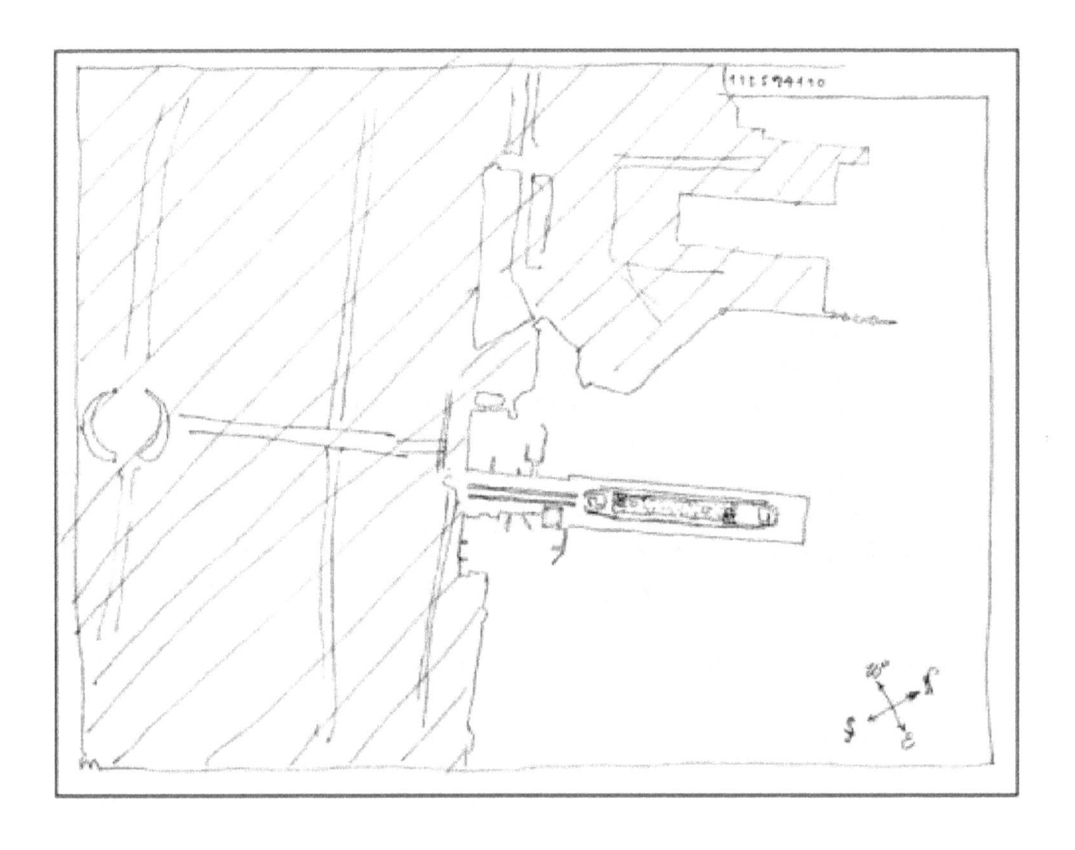

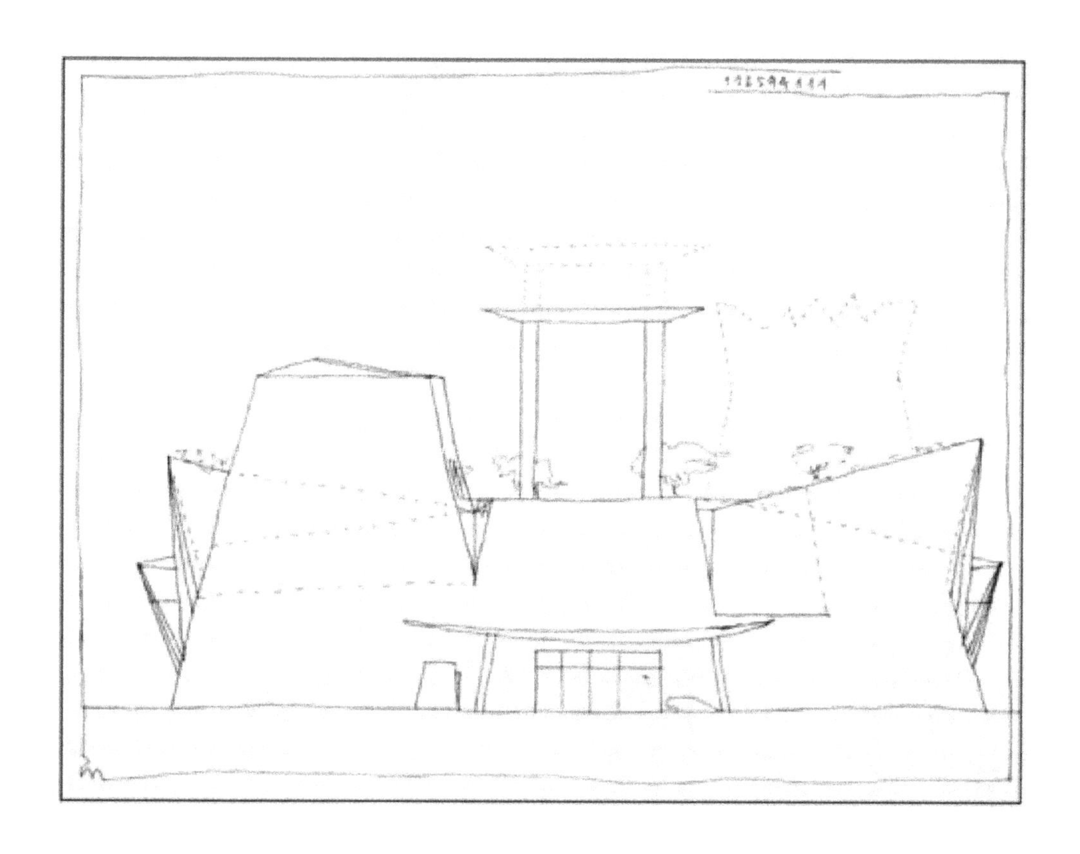

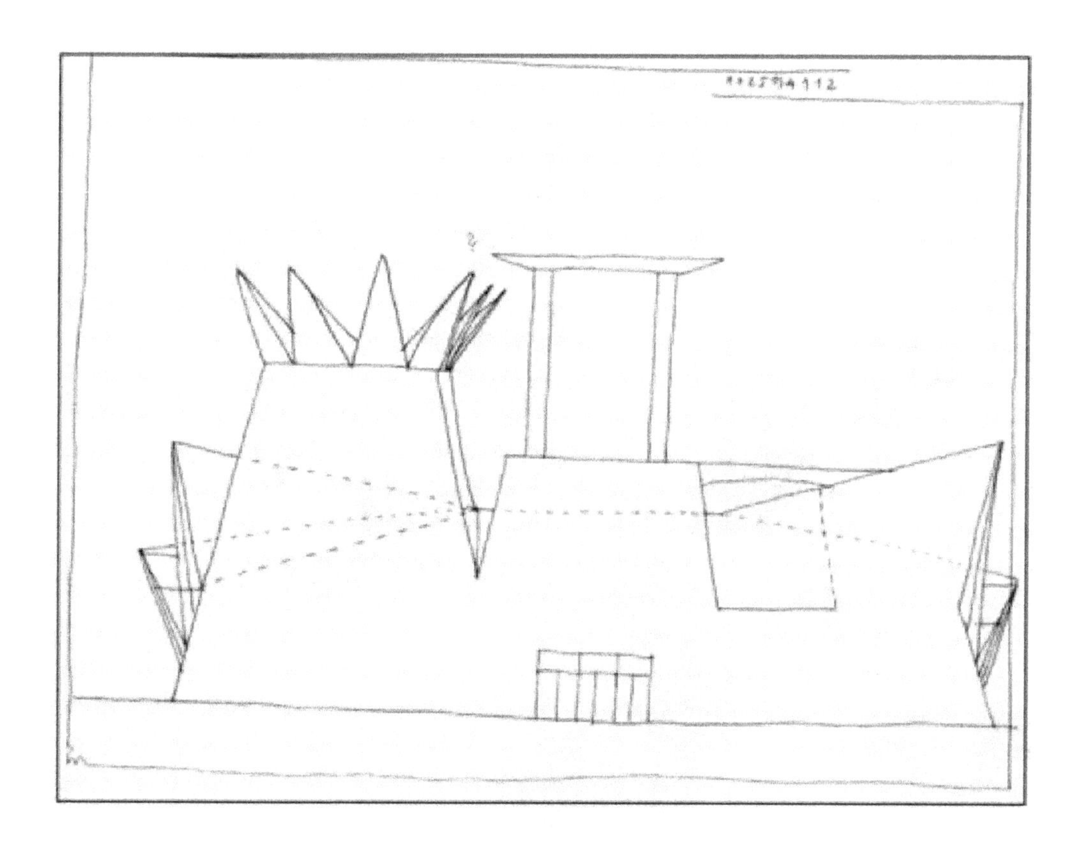

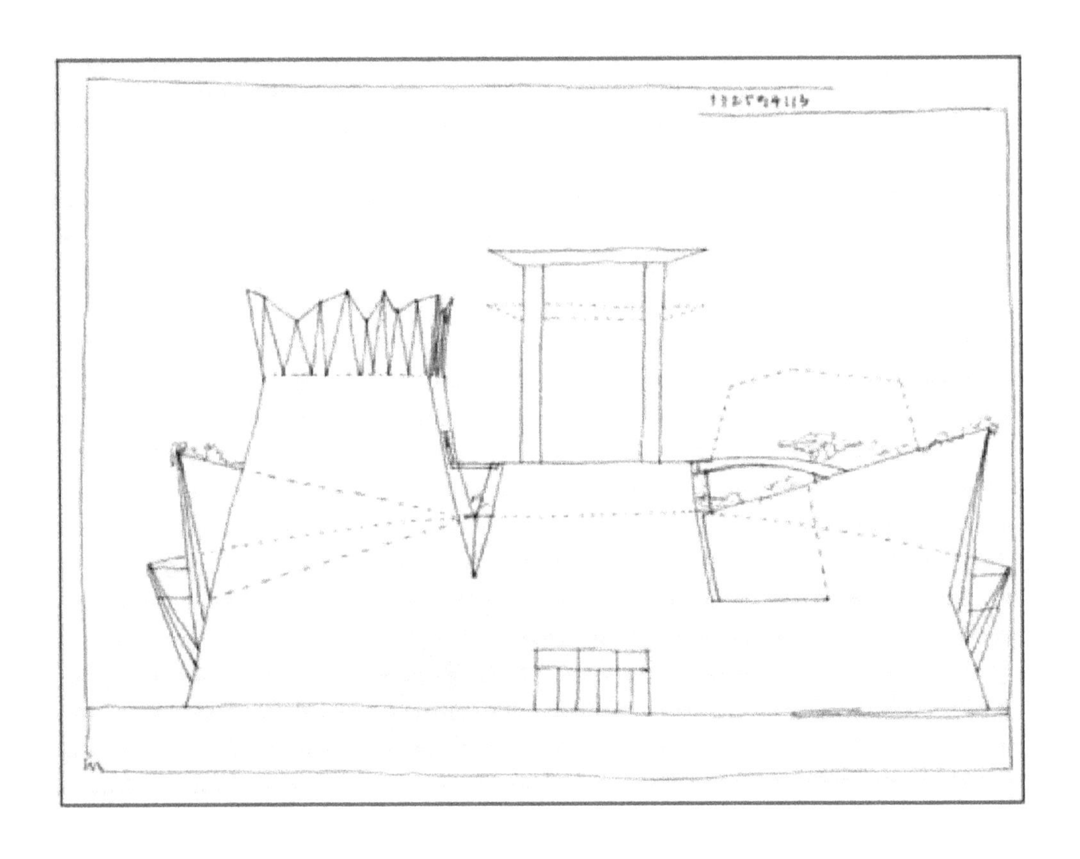

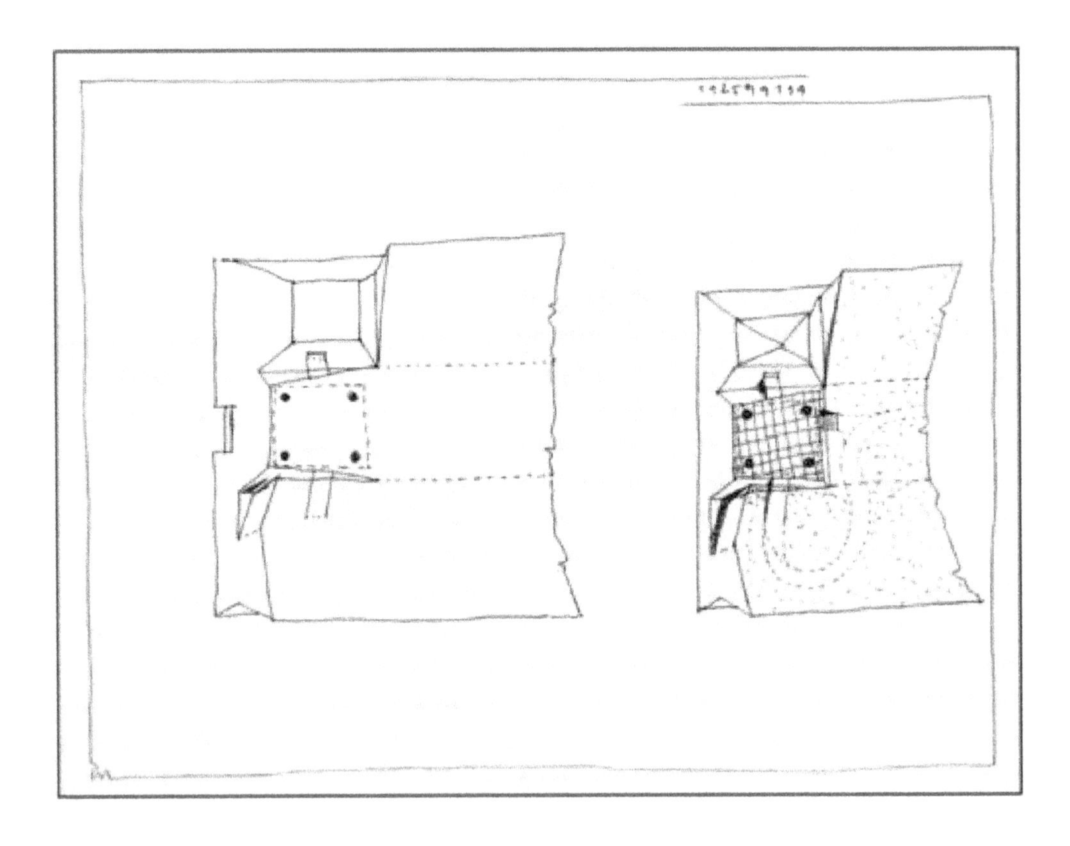

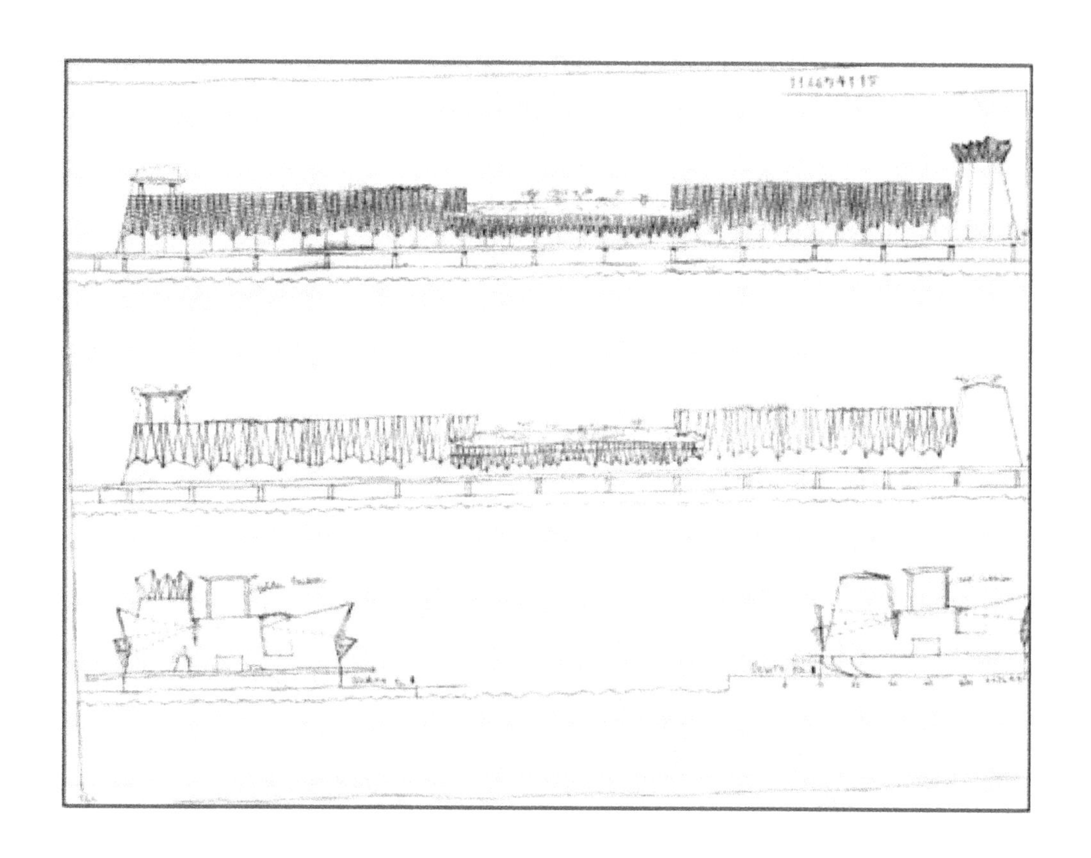

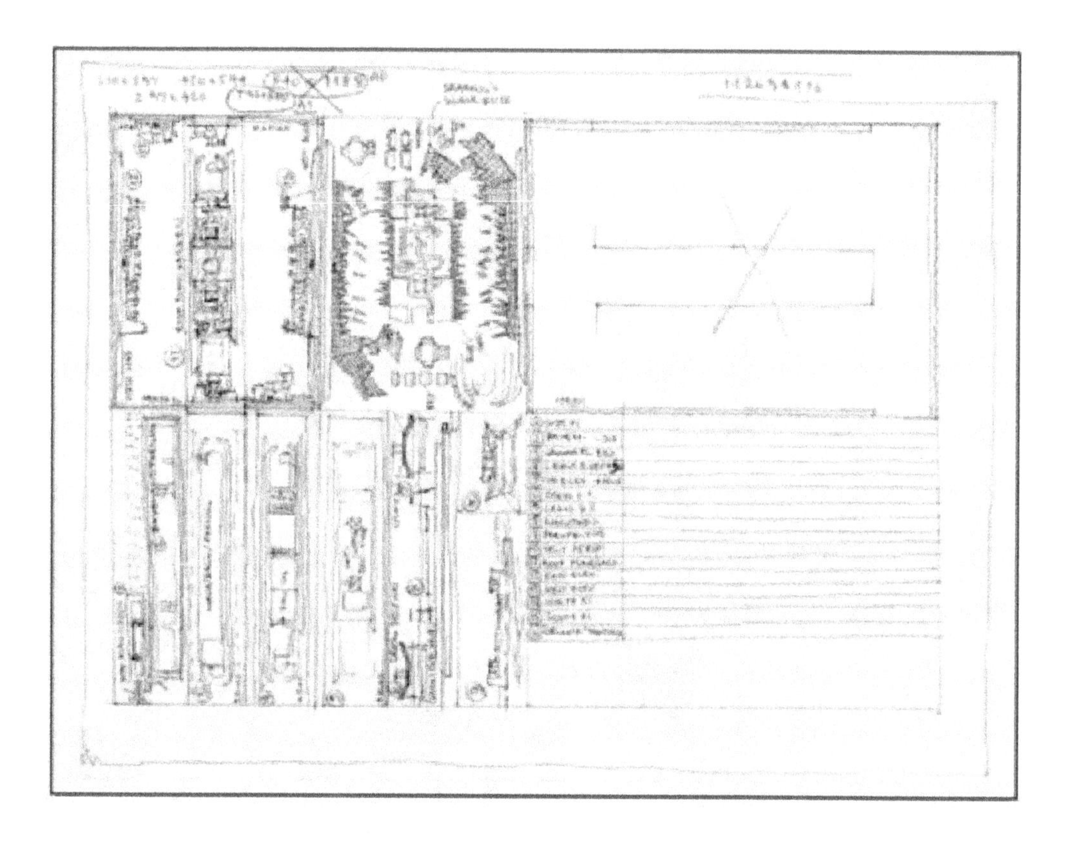

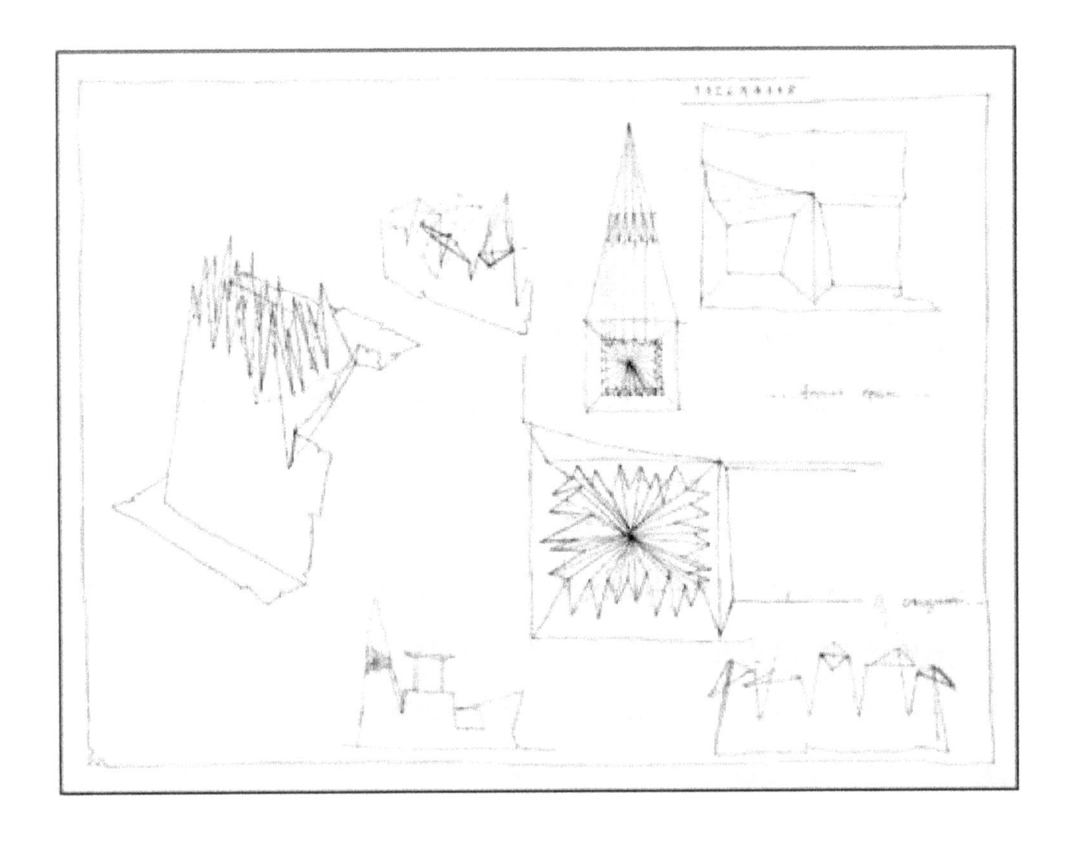

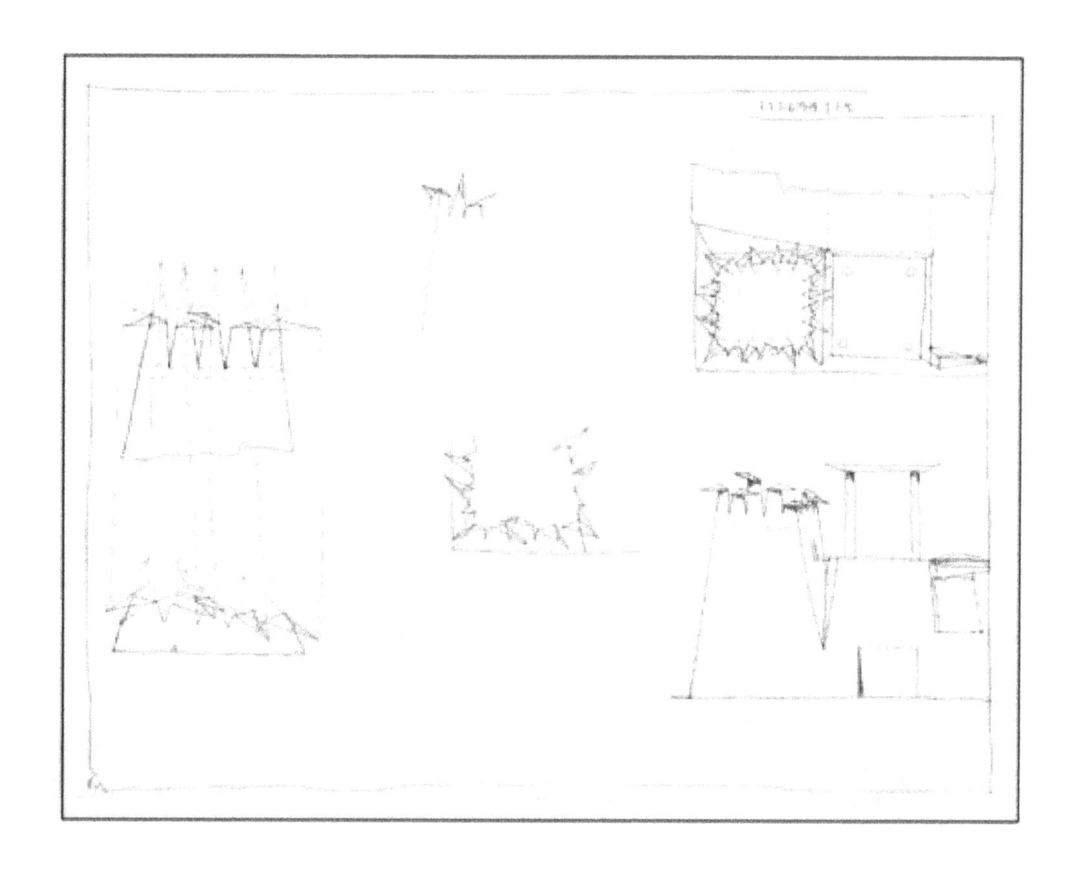

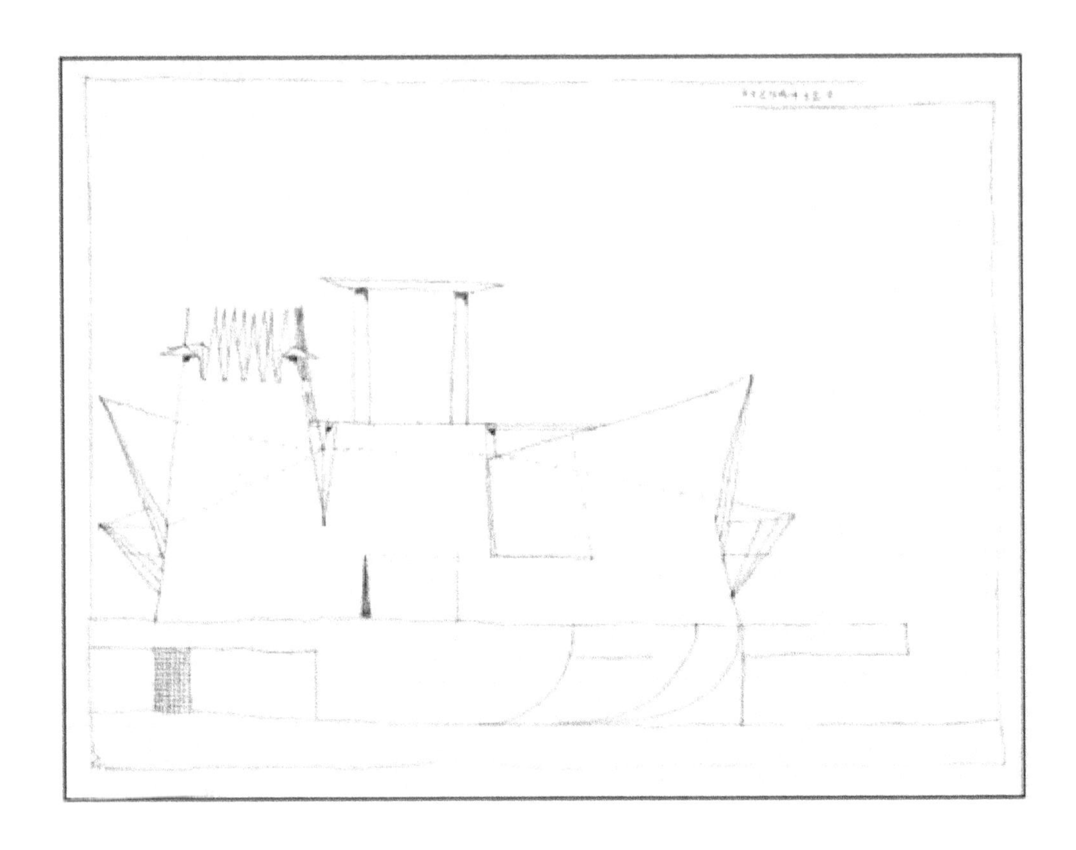

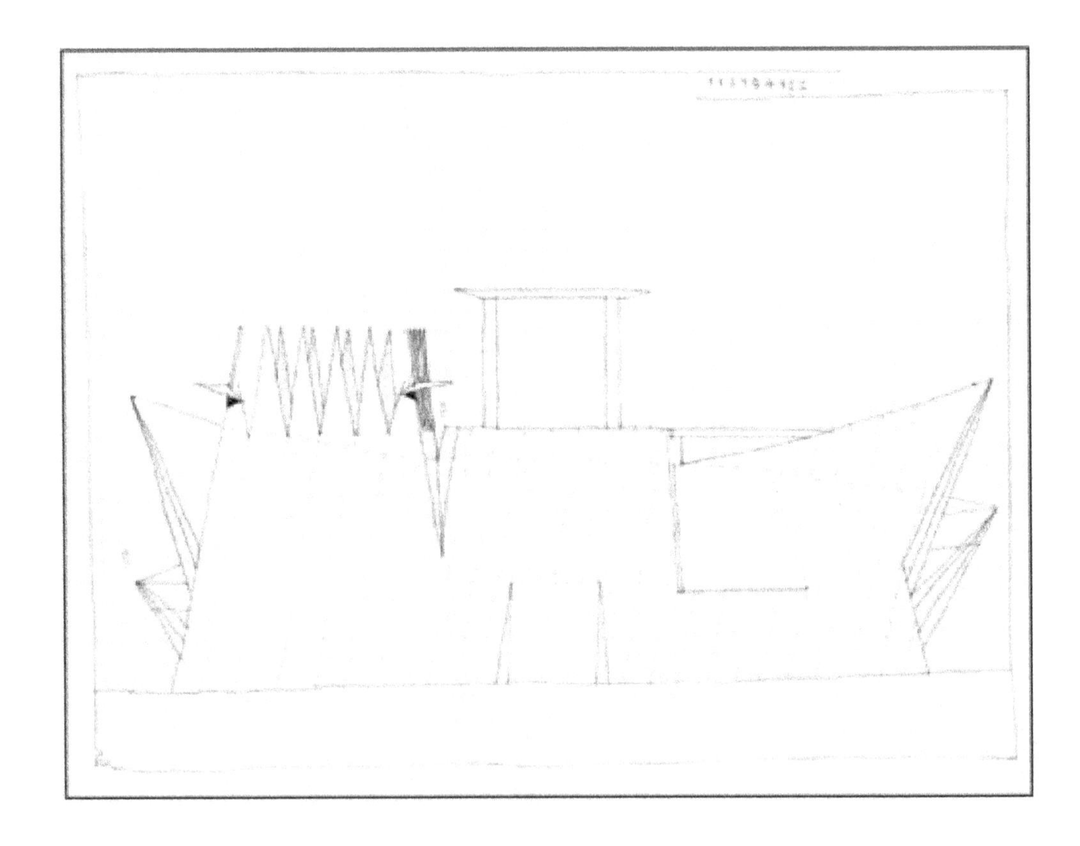

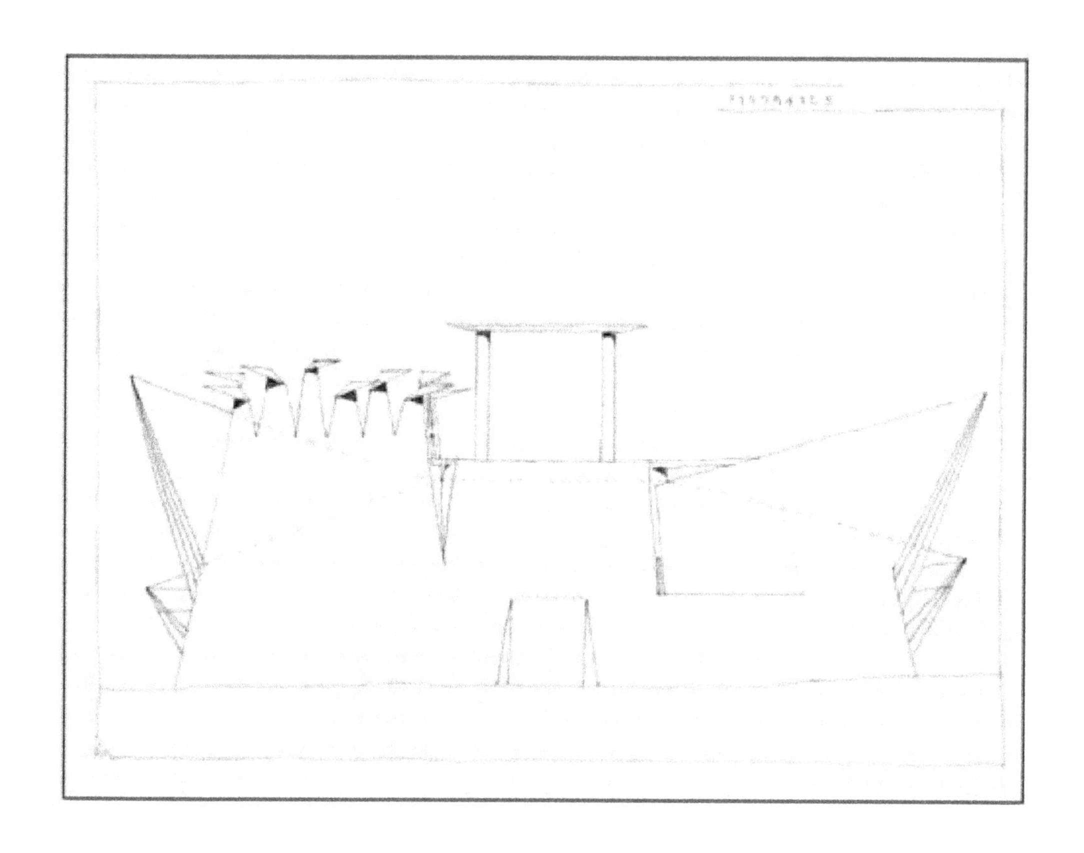

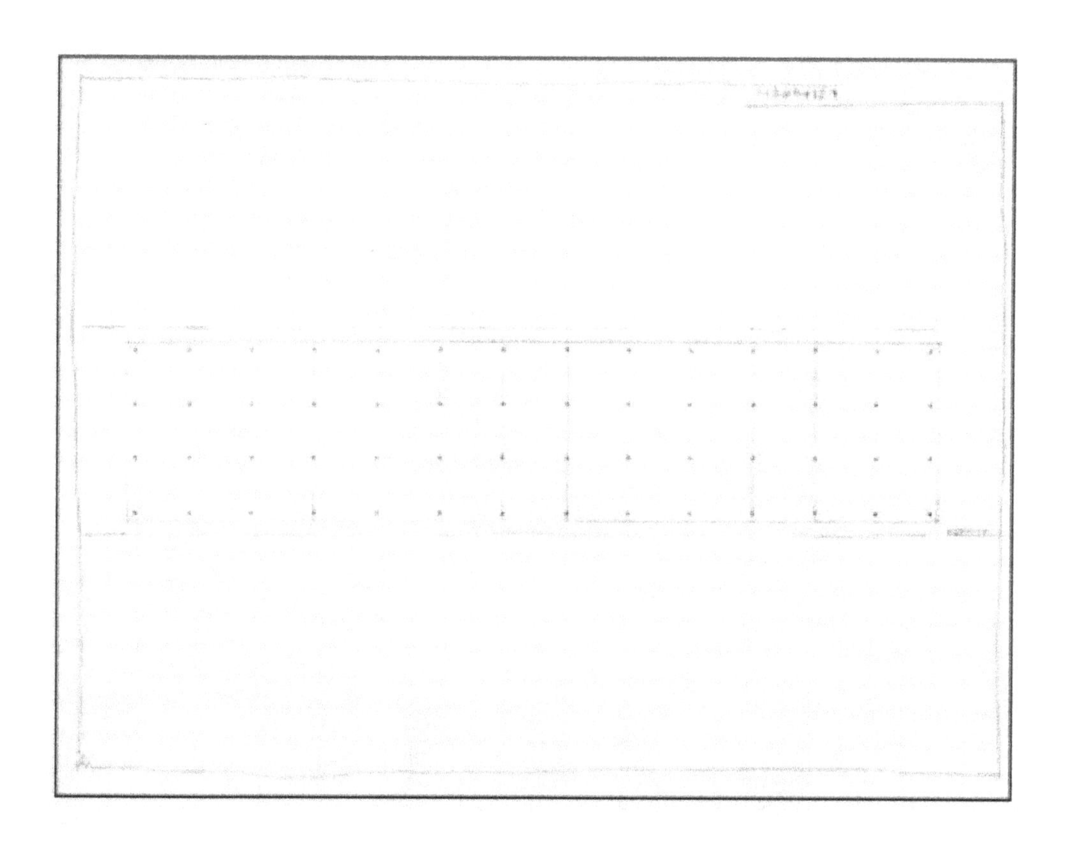

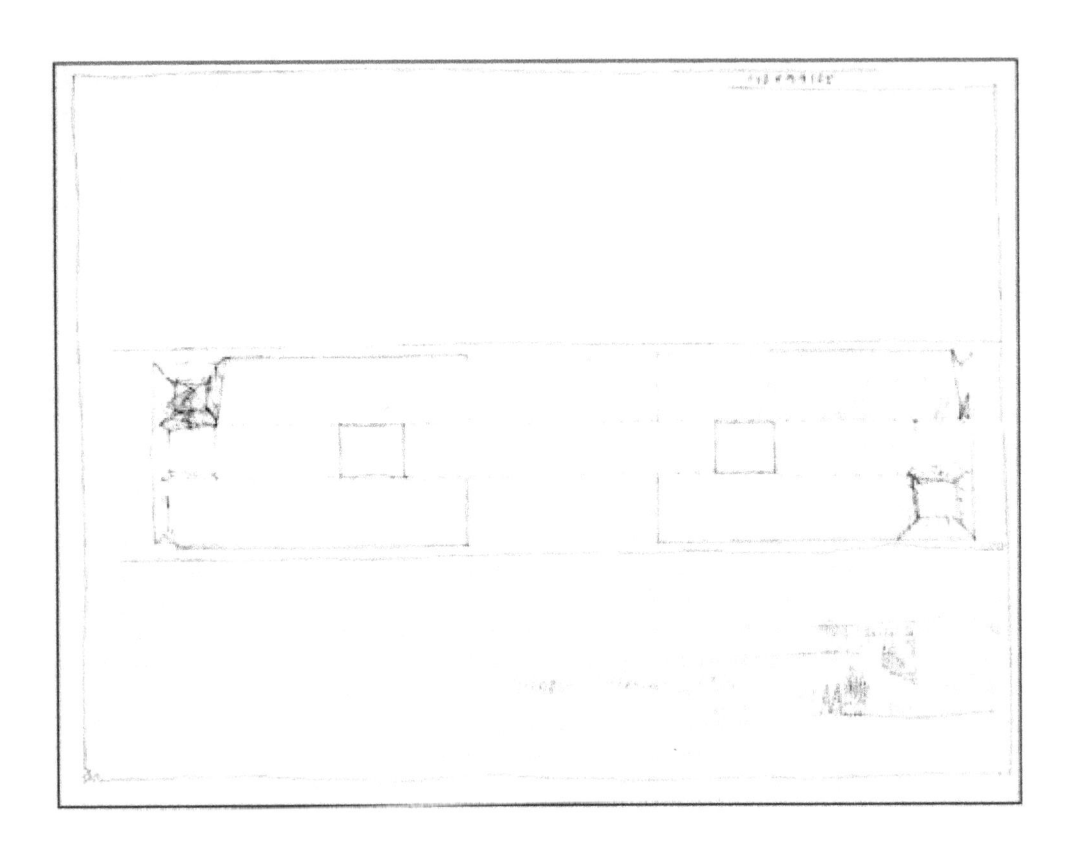

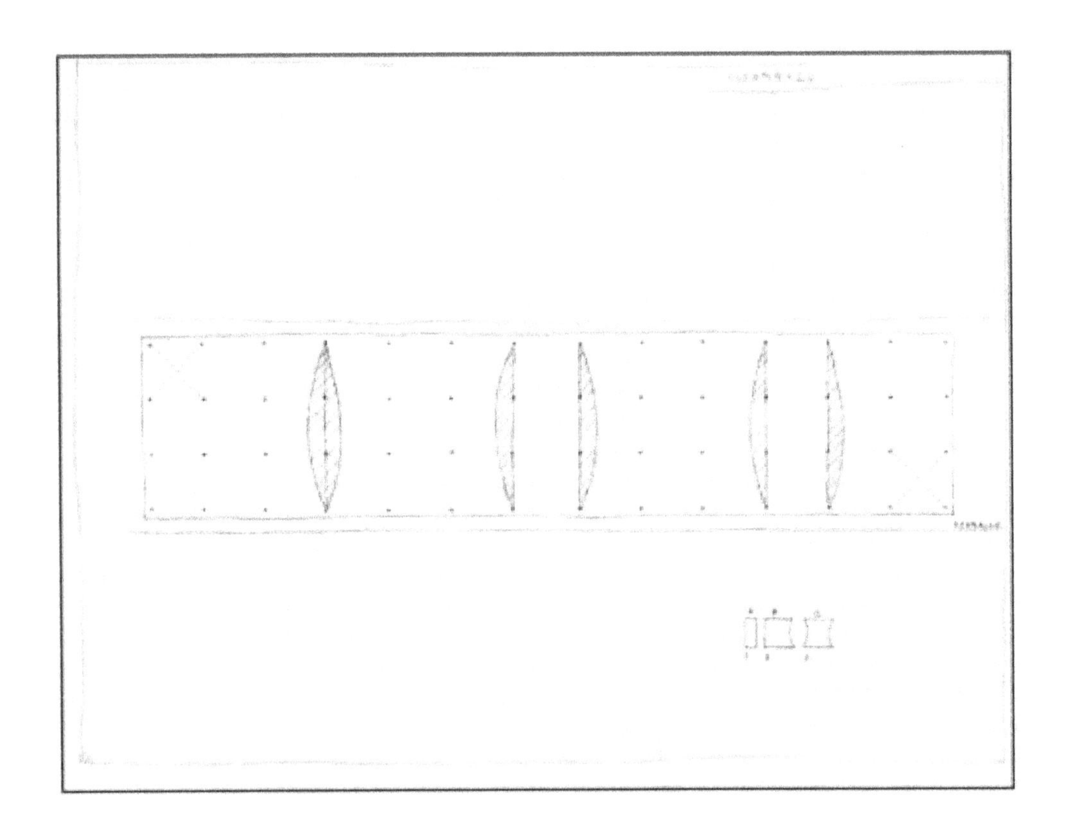

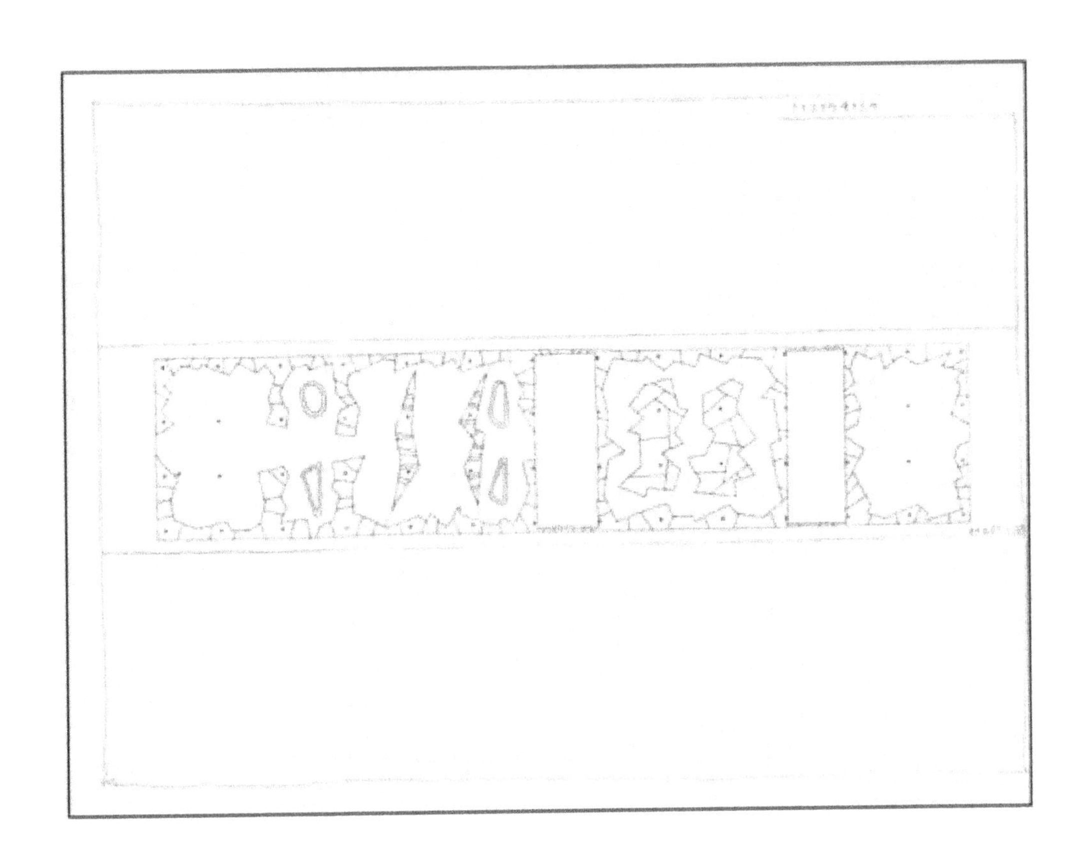

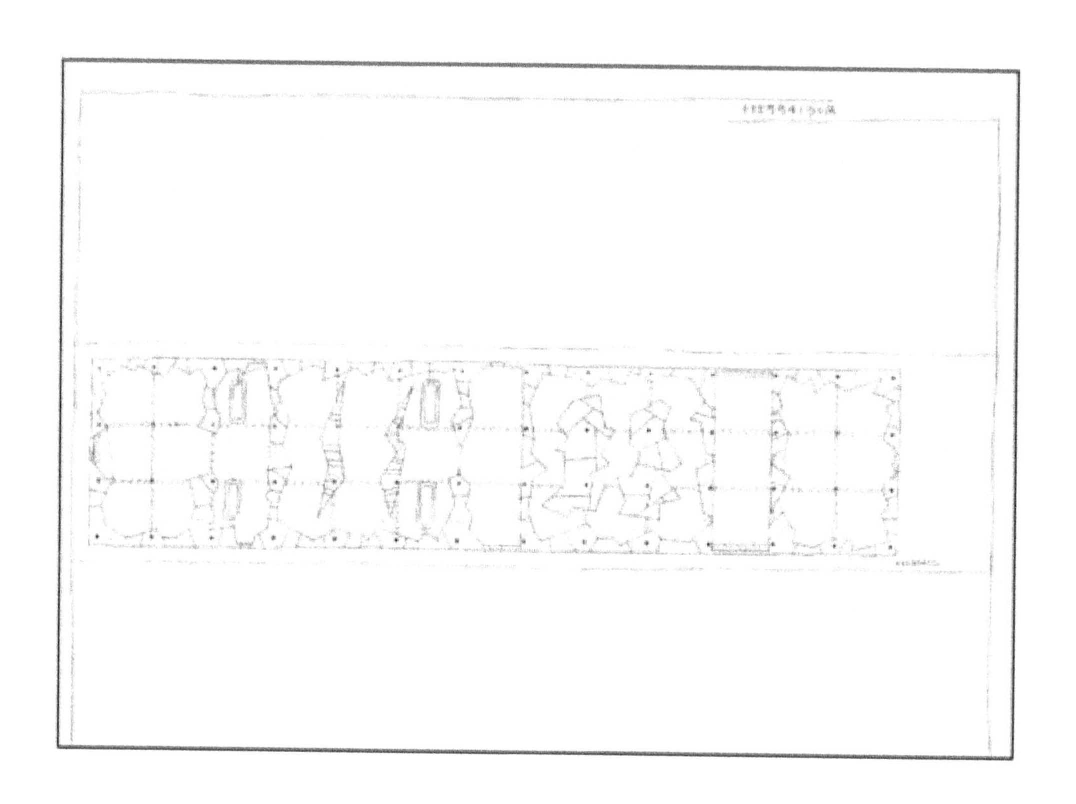

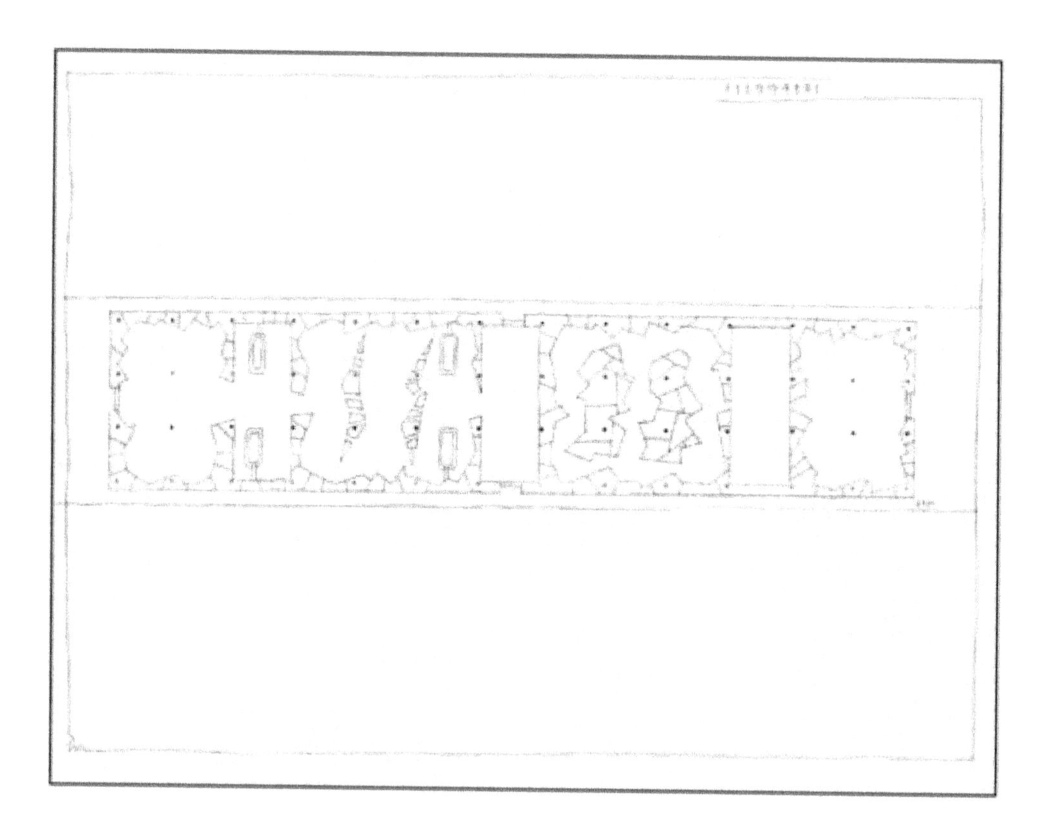

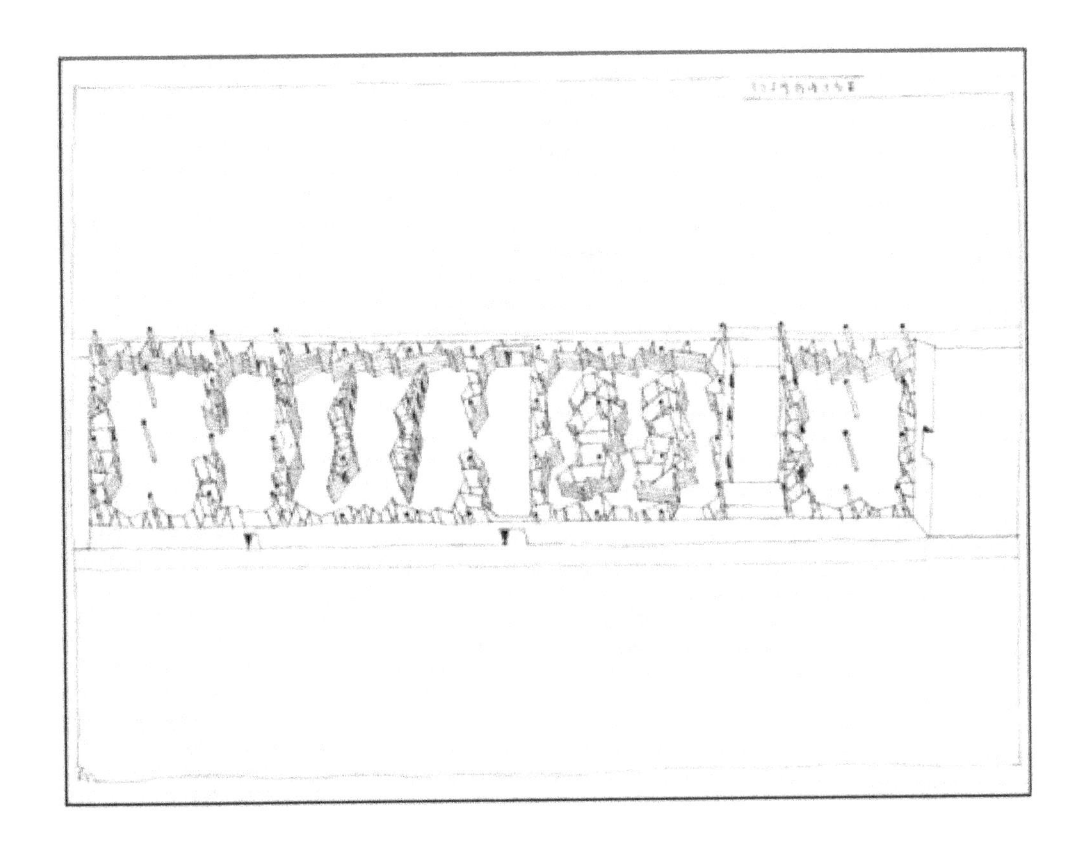

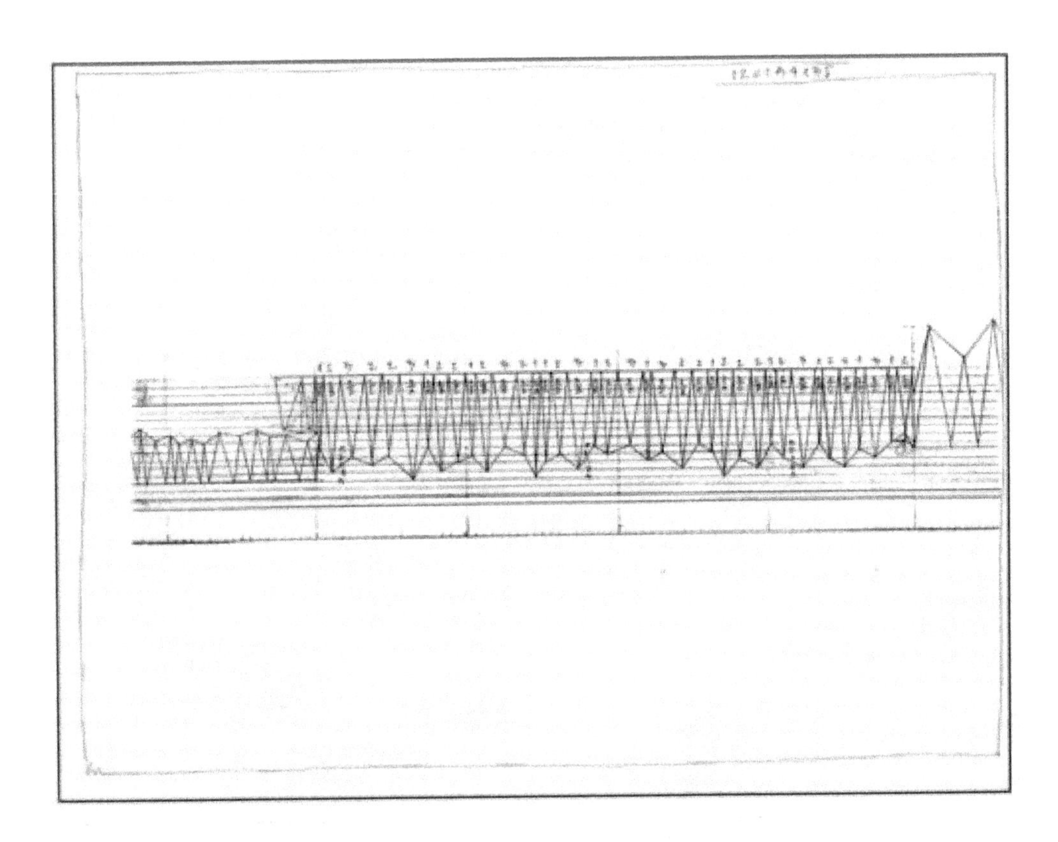

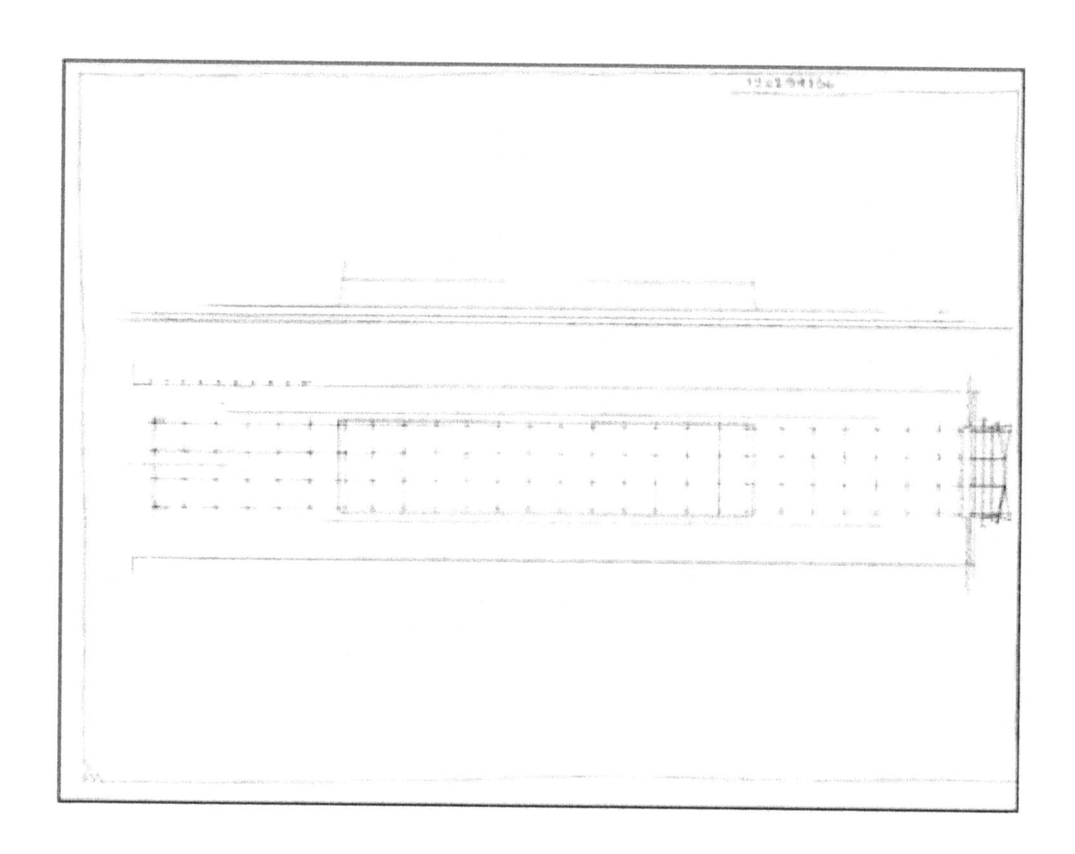

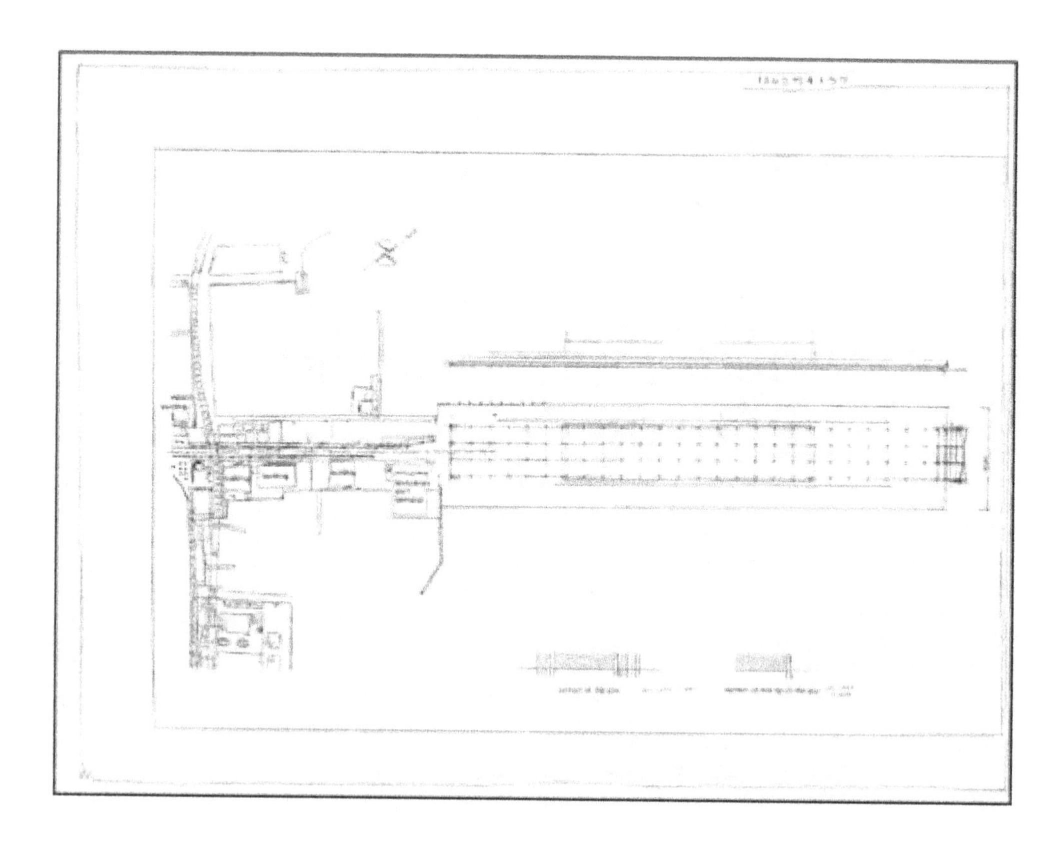

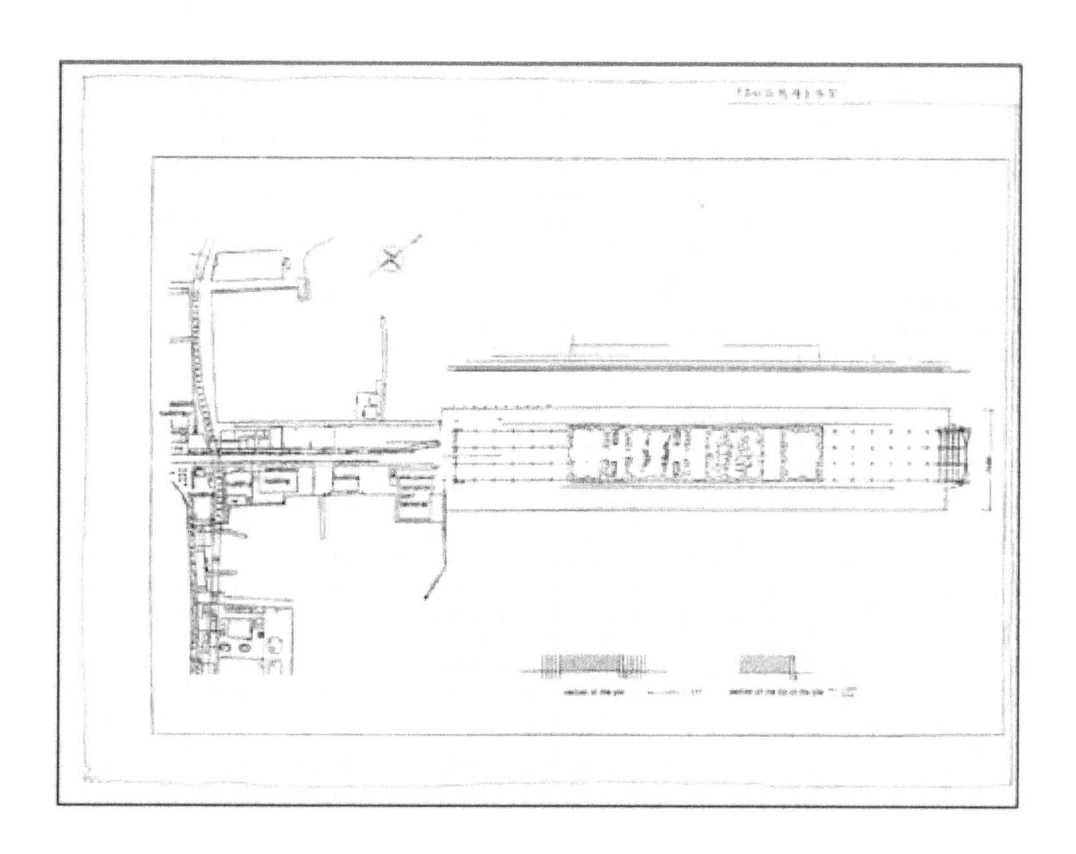

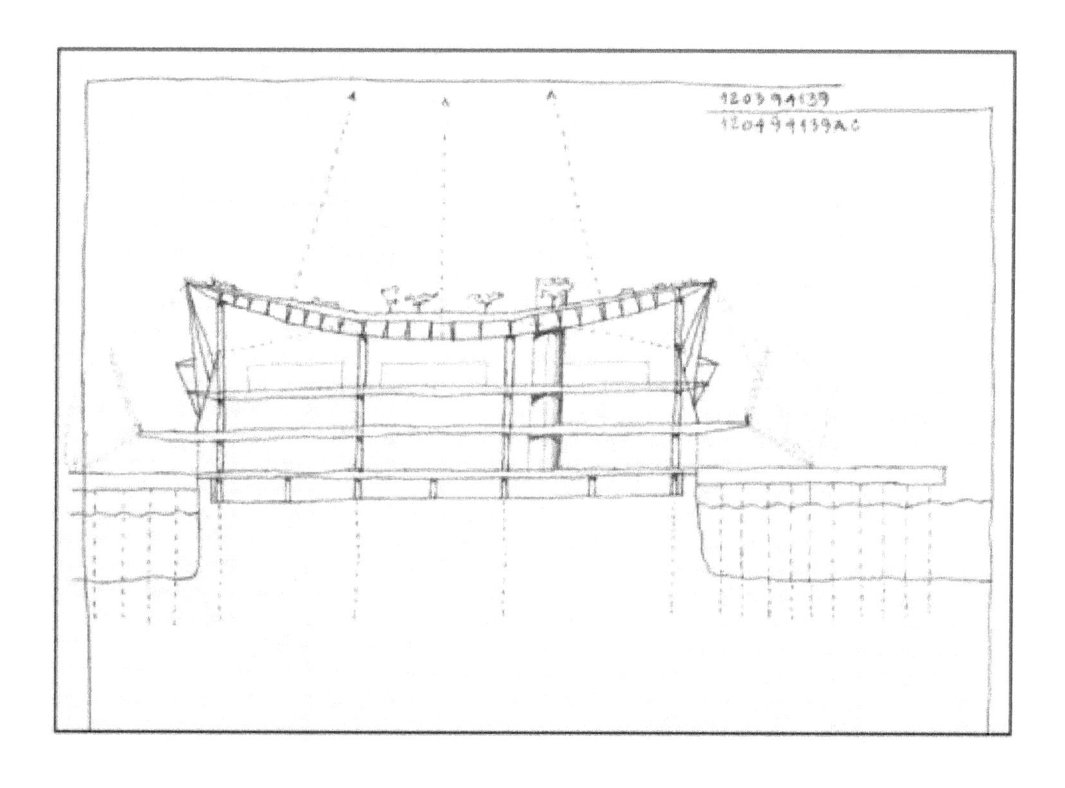
1203 94139
1204 94139 AC

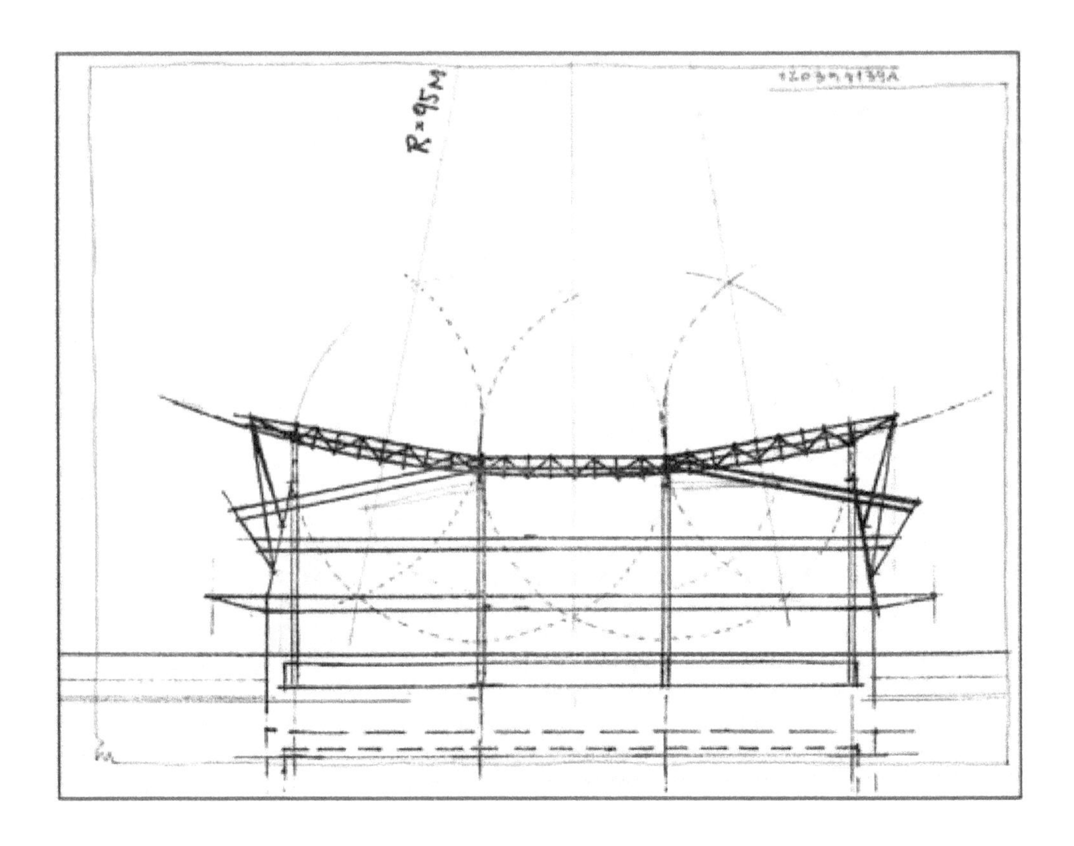
R=95M

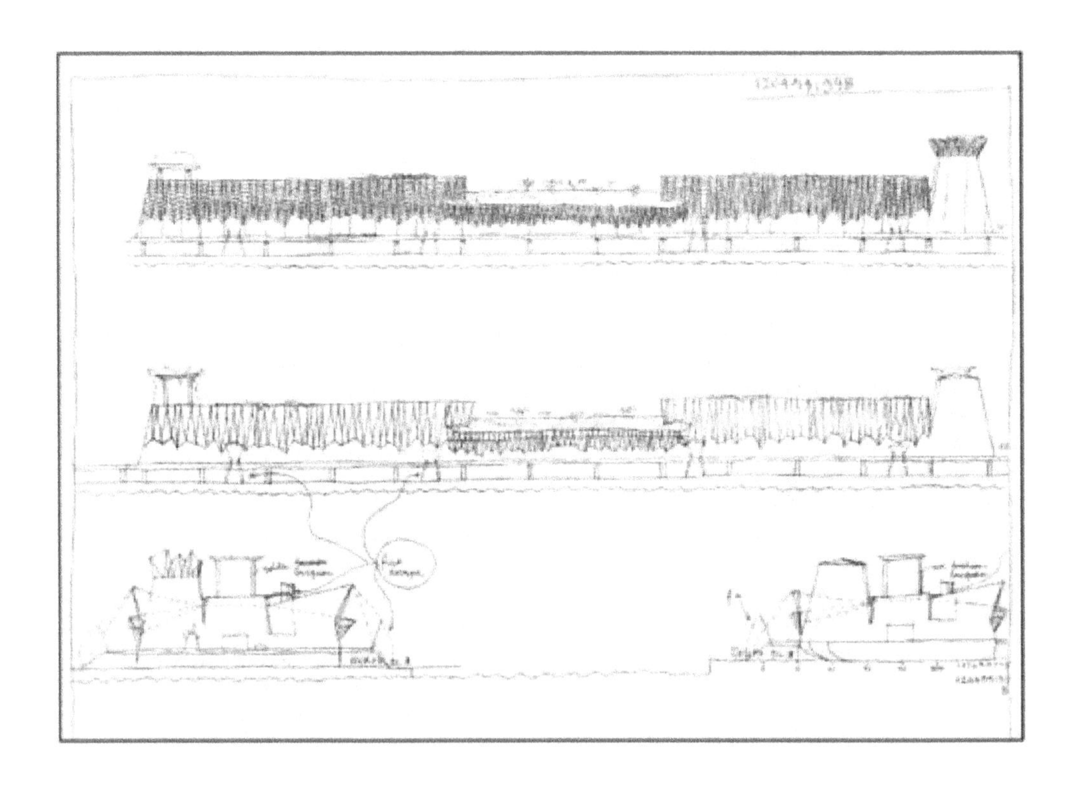

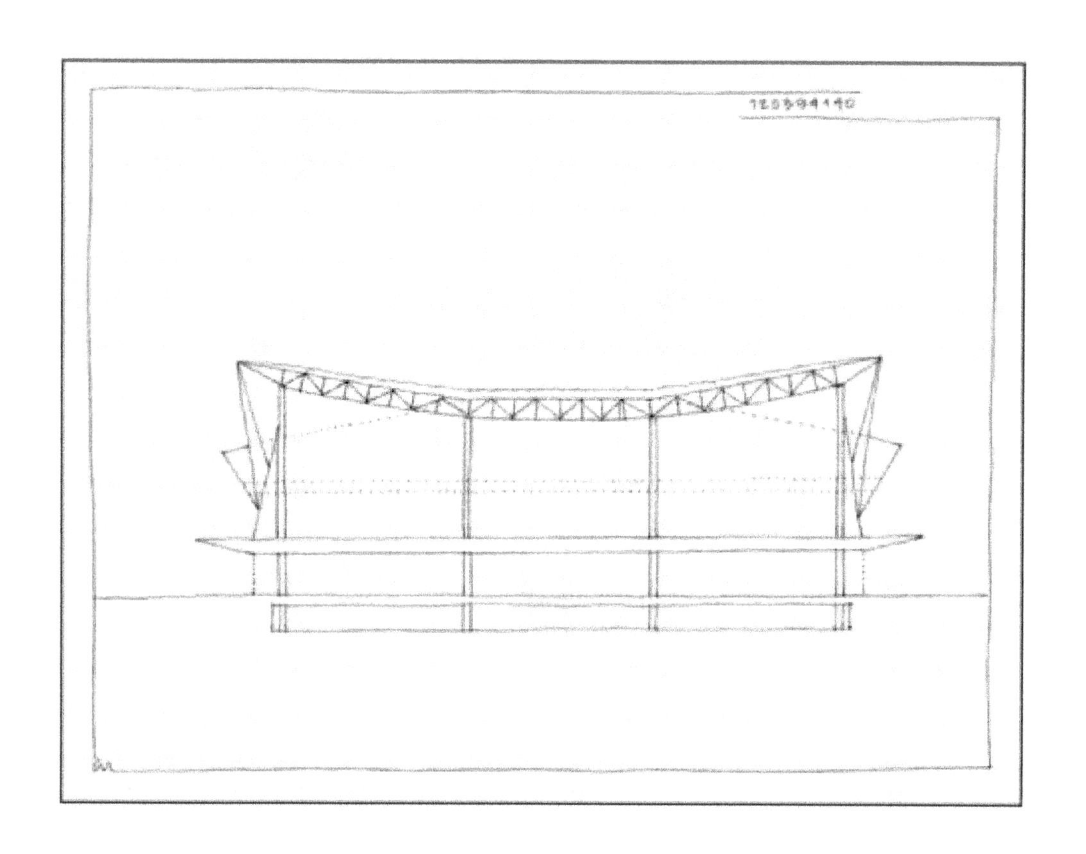

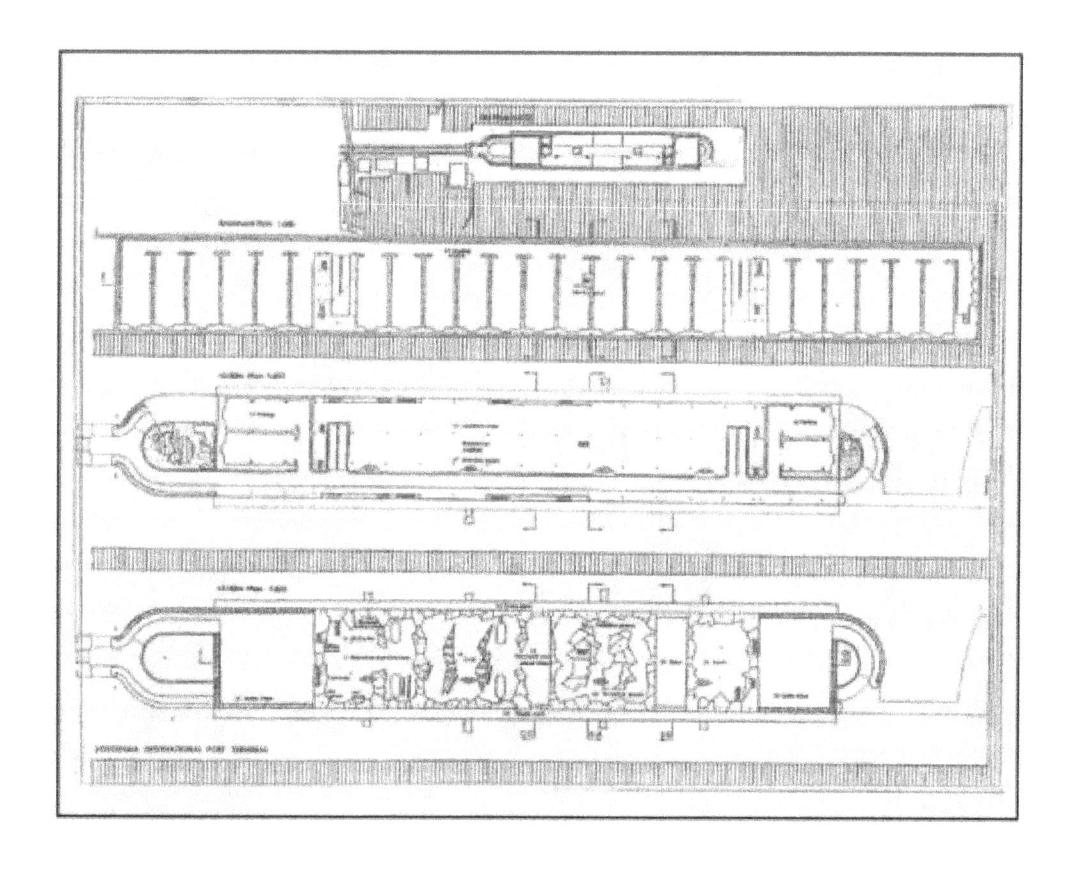

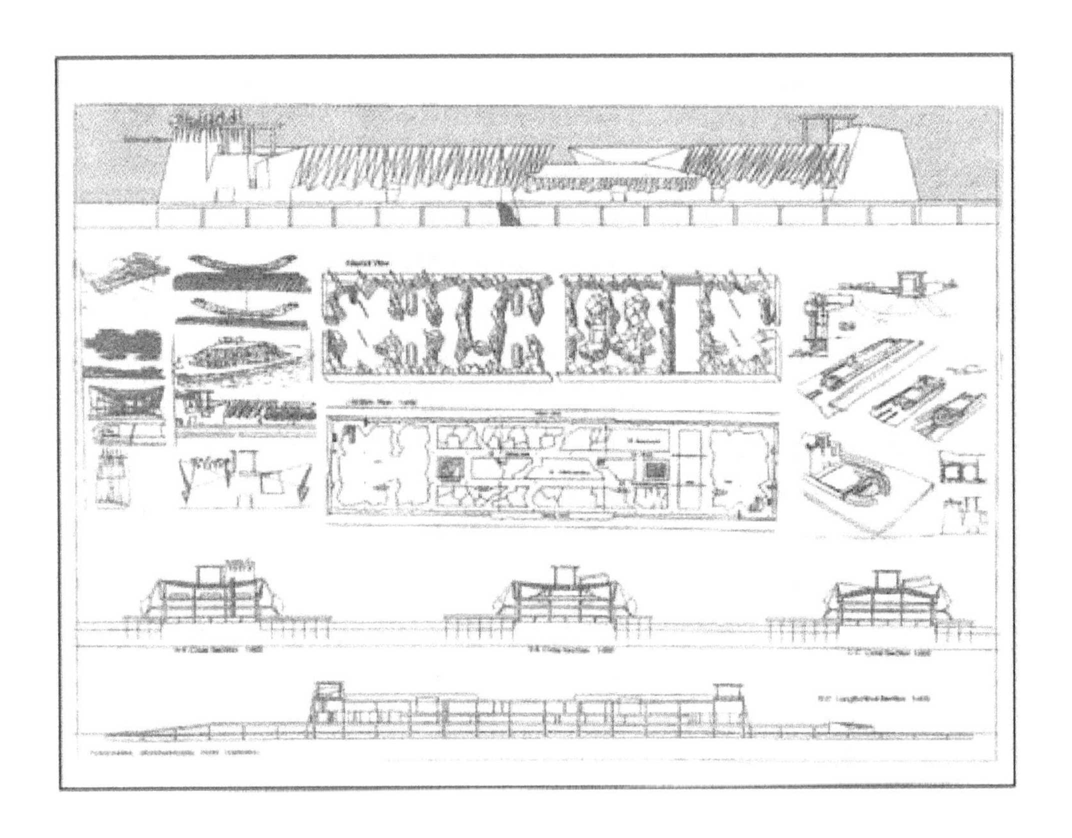

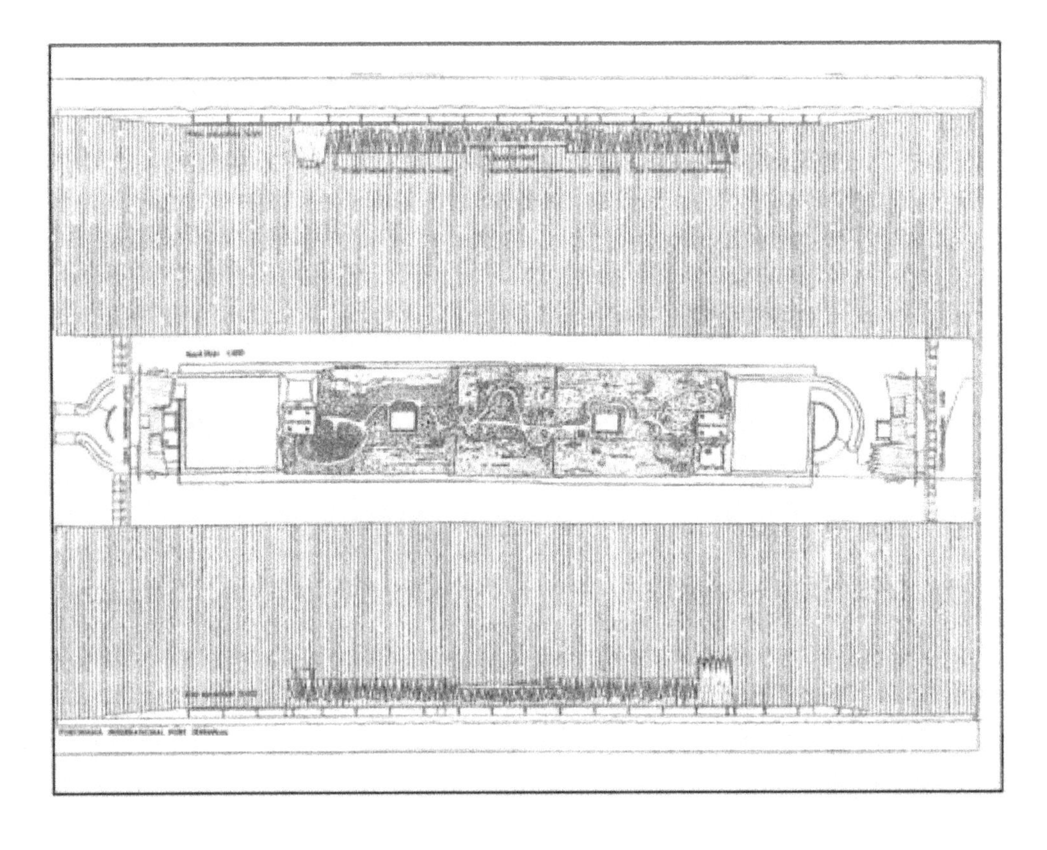

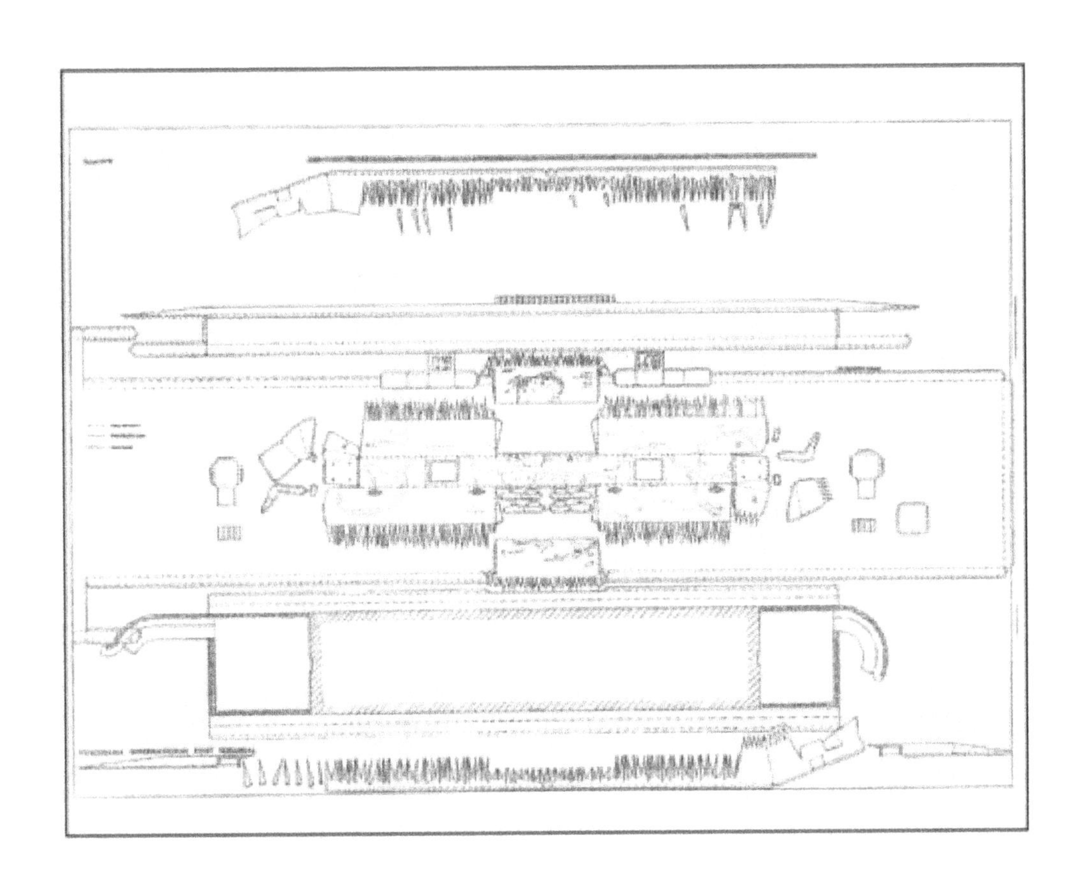

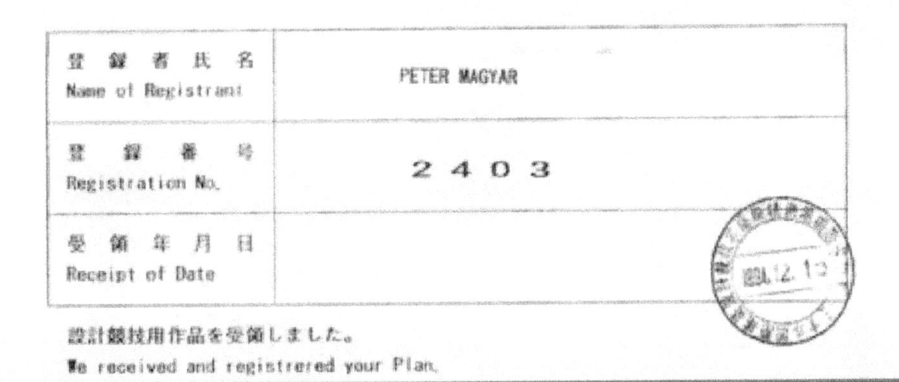

横浜港国際客船ターミナル国際建築設計競技
YOKOHAMA INTERNATIONAL PORT TERMINAL DESIGN COMPETITION

作品受領書
Receipt

登録者氏名 Name of Registrant	PETER MAGYAR
登録番号 Registration No.	2403
受領年月日 Receipt of Date	

設計競技用作品を受領しました。
We received and registrered your Plan.

Chapter 7

HESITANT DECISIONS

Pen Zen Diaries #7

Chapter 7

(P.Z.D.7)
Hesitans Decisions - "Spike Hall" Sports and Cultural Center
Budapest, Hungary

This collection of sketches differ from the previous ones, because they led to the - at least - partial construction of the large urban ensemble of the Budapest Sports and Cultural Center. It was a result of another competition, when the winners were invited to the design of the complex. We -with Dr. Antal Lazar and the A&D Studio - won the first prize, and eventually the commission. Interesting distant cooperation resumed, between Pennsylvania and later Florida, and the office in Budapest, Hungary. More than eight hundred drawings were faxed back and forth, from which just a bit over a hundred are depicted here, my ink drawings, if not otherwise noted. The creative talent of my partner and friend, Toni, and his colleagues, tested and amended the sketches, and eventually executed the construction documents. We had a very fruitful and constructive collaboration, making from the tentative and sometimes crazy drawn ideas a physical reality. It didn't help that the change of government and following delays resulted in a decade-long postponement and several changes in the completion of the project. At the time of the writing of these lines, the construction resumed and the long stagnant "thorn hall", as it is called by the press, finally opened its gates to the expectant public.

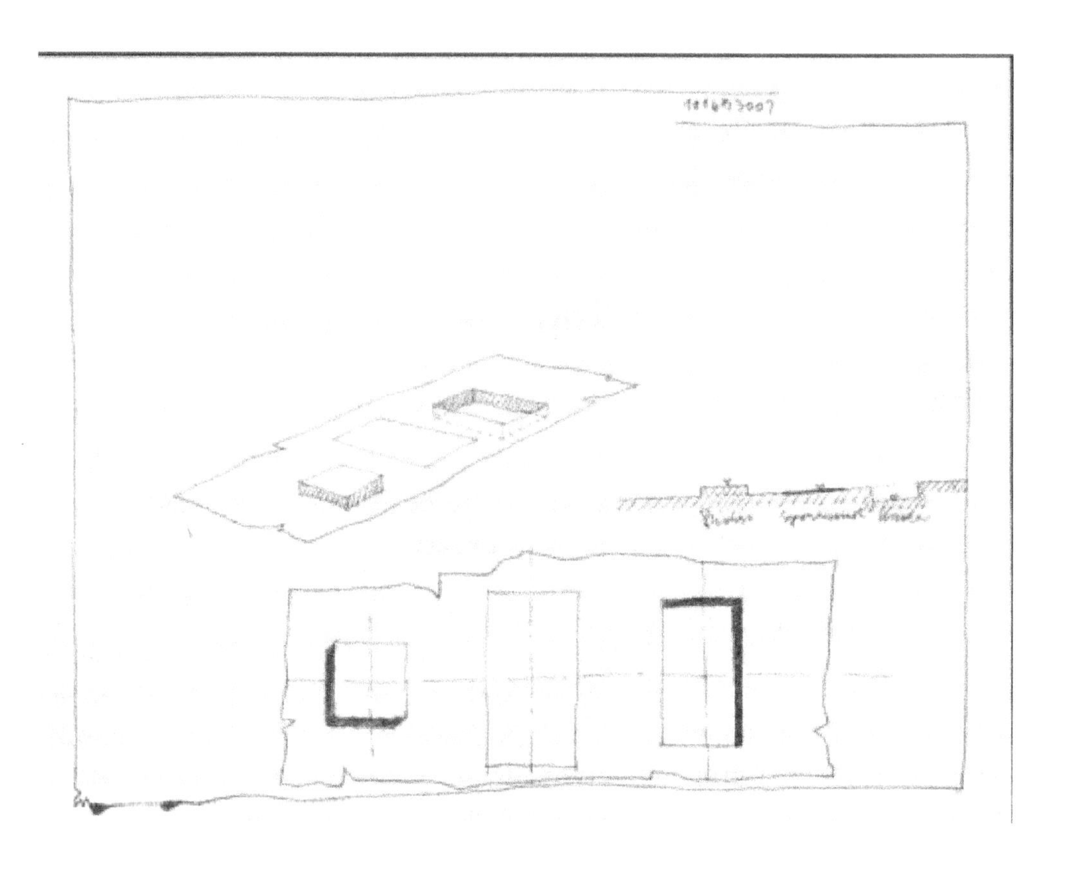

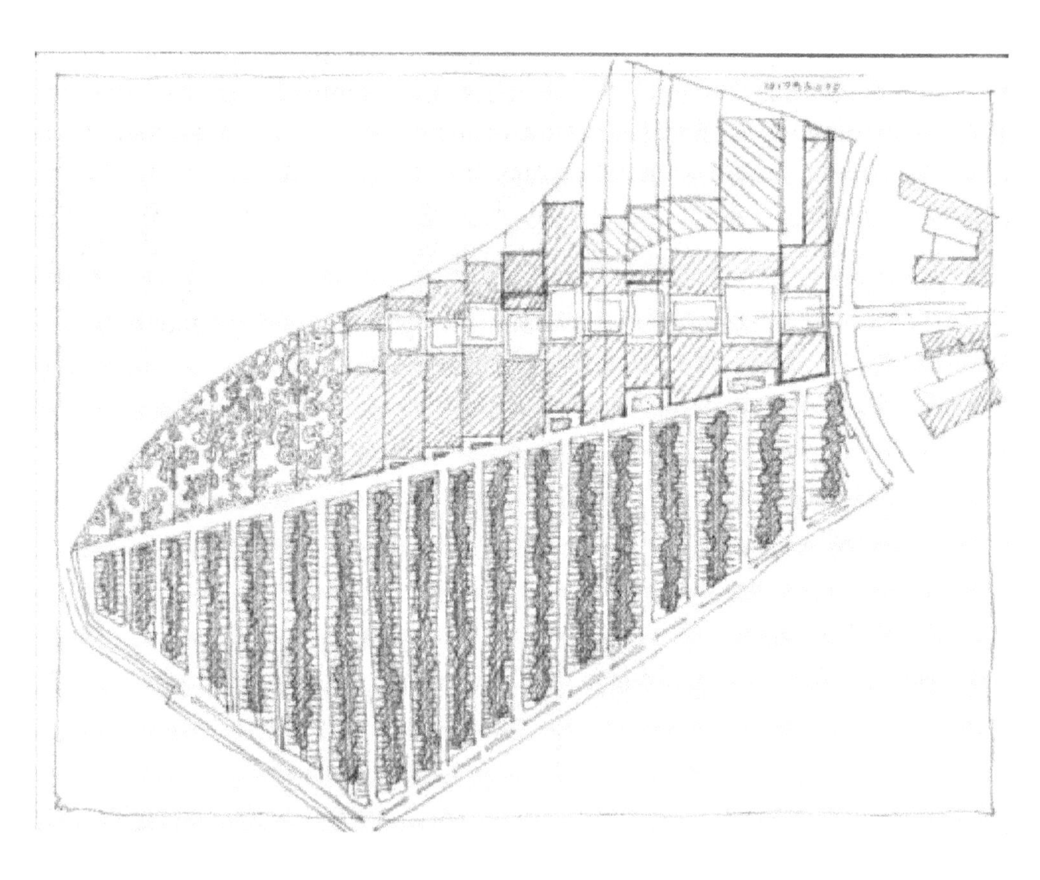

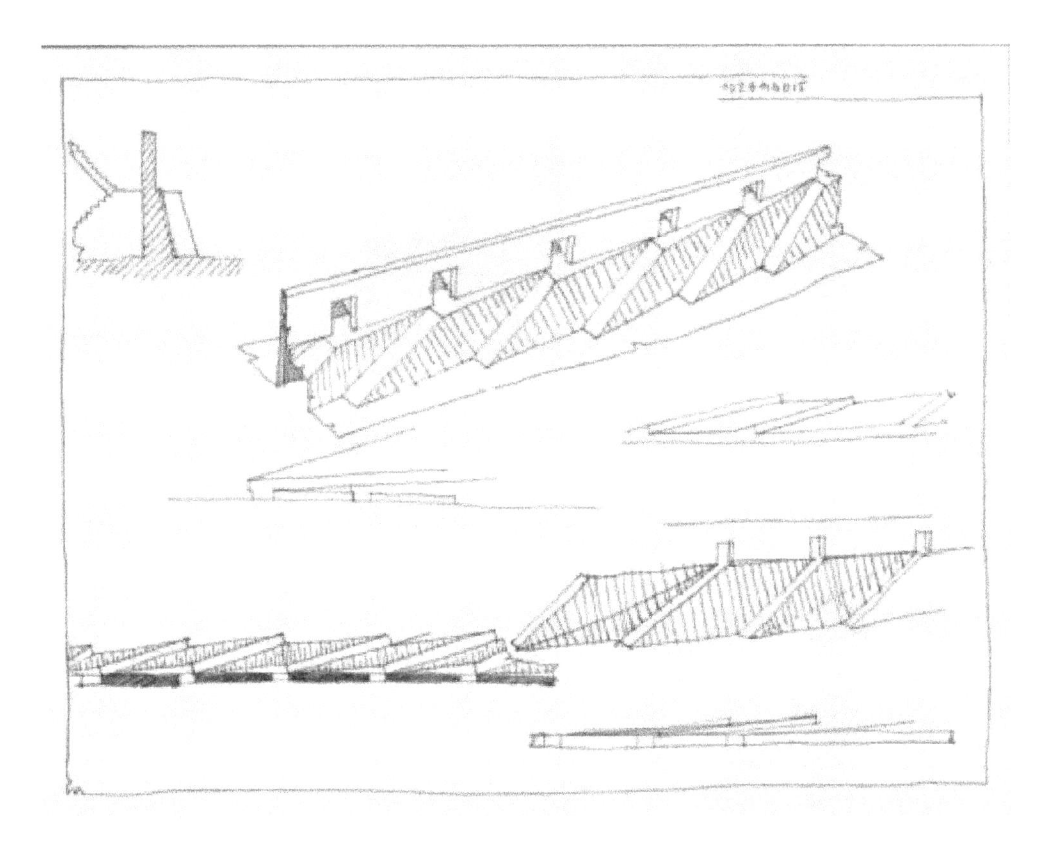

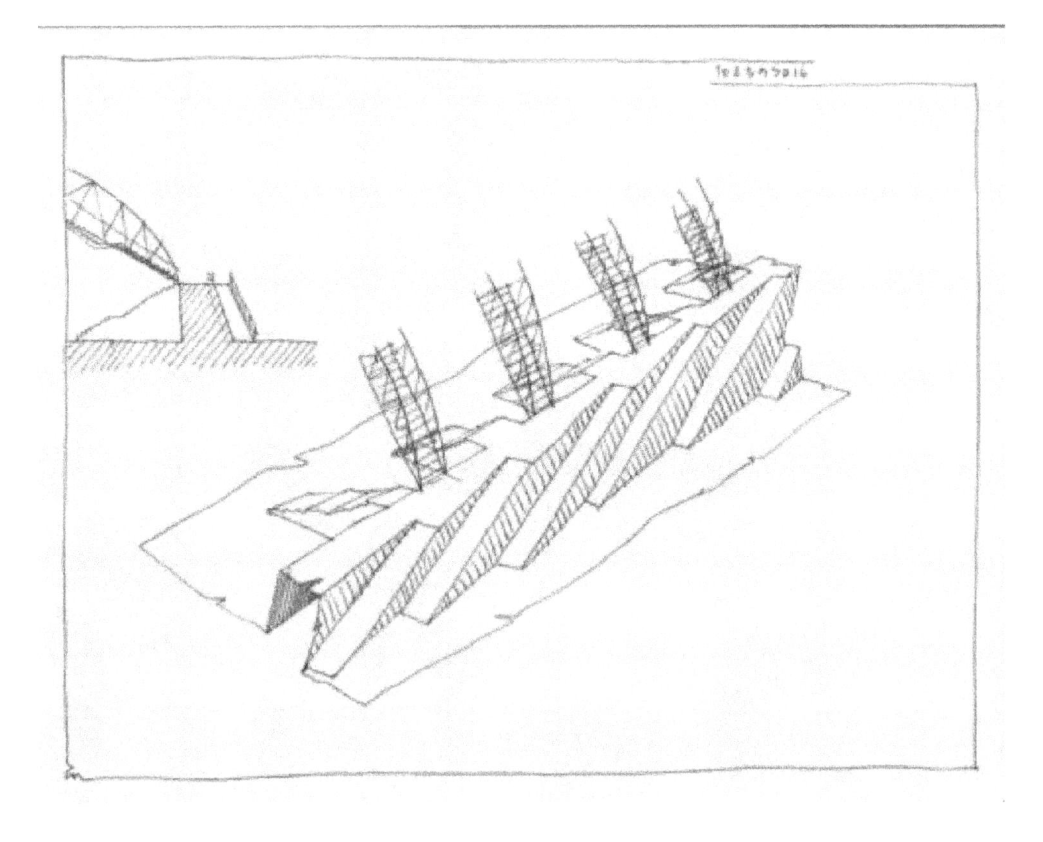

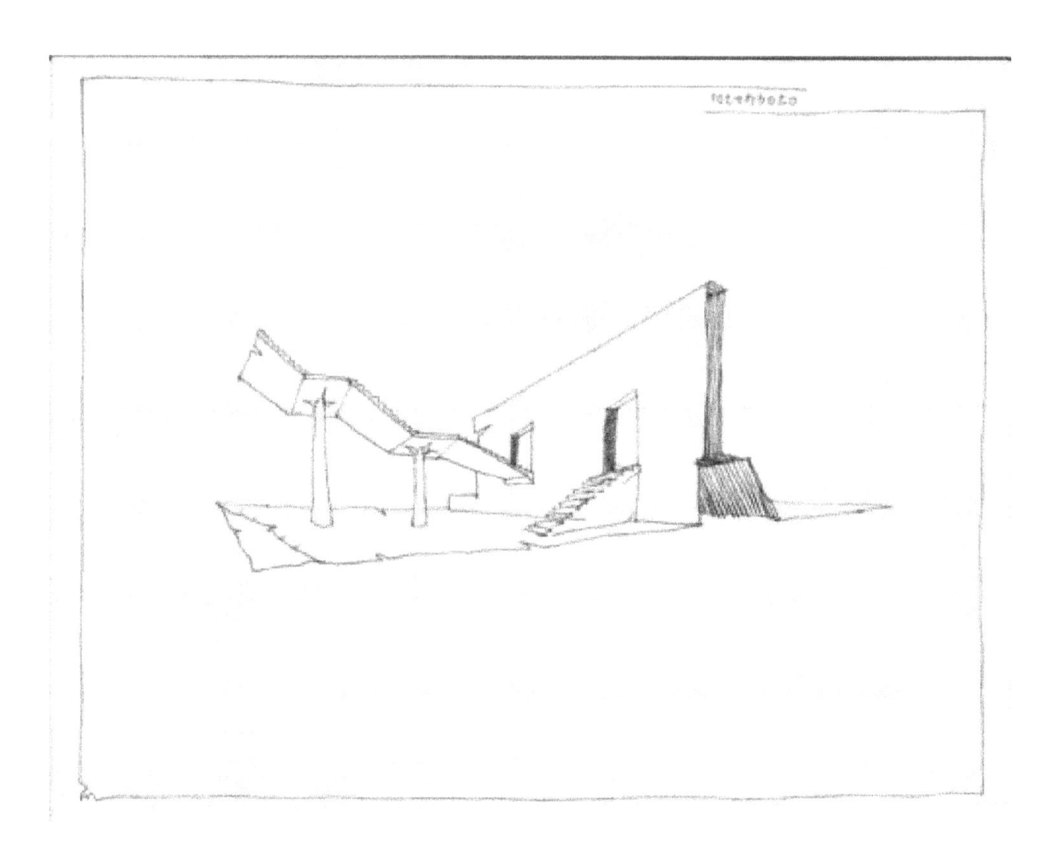

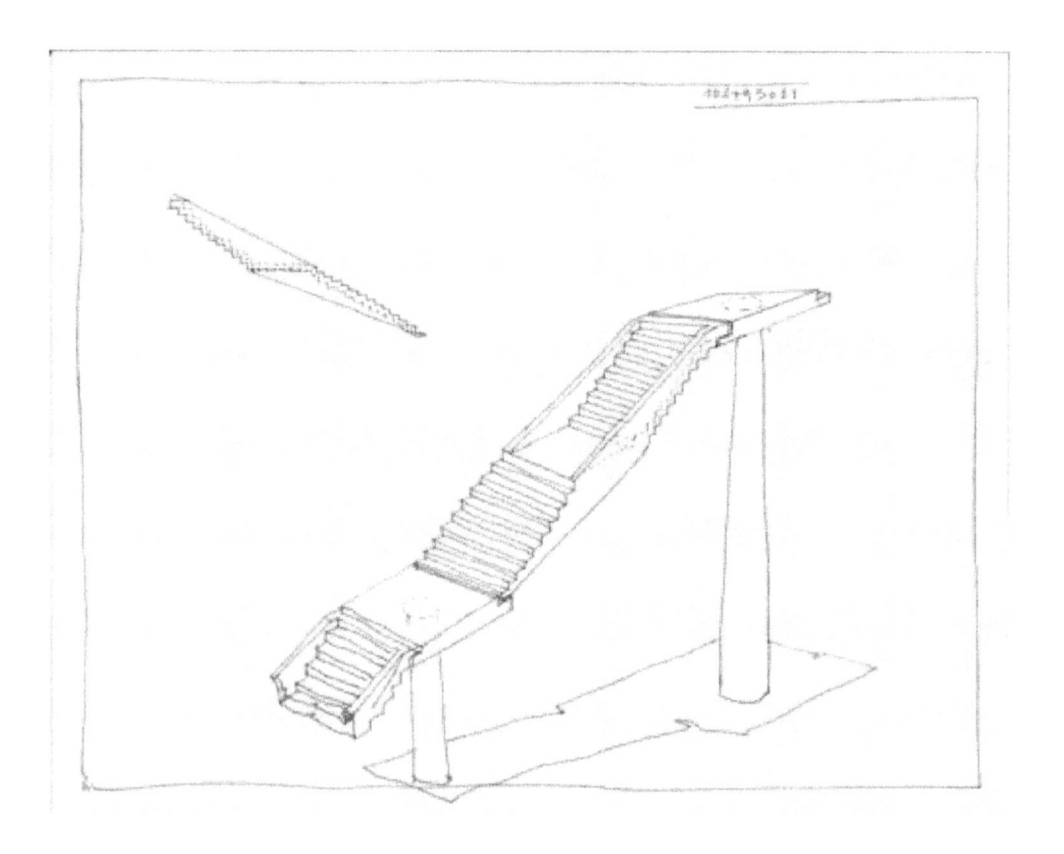

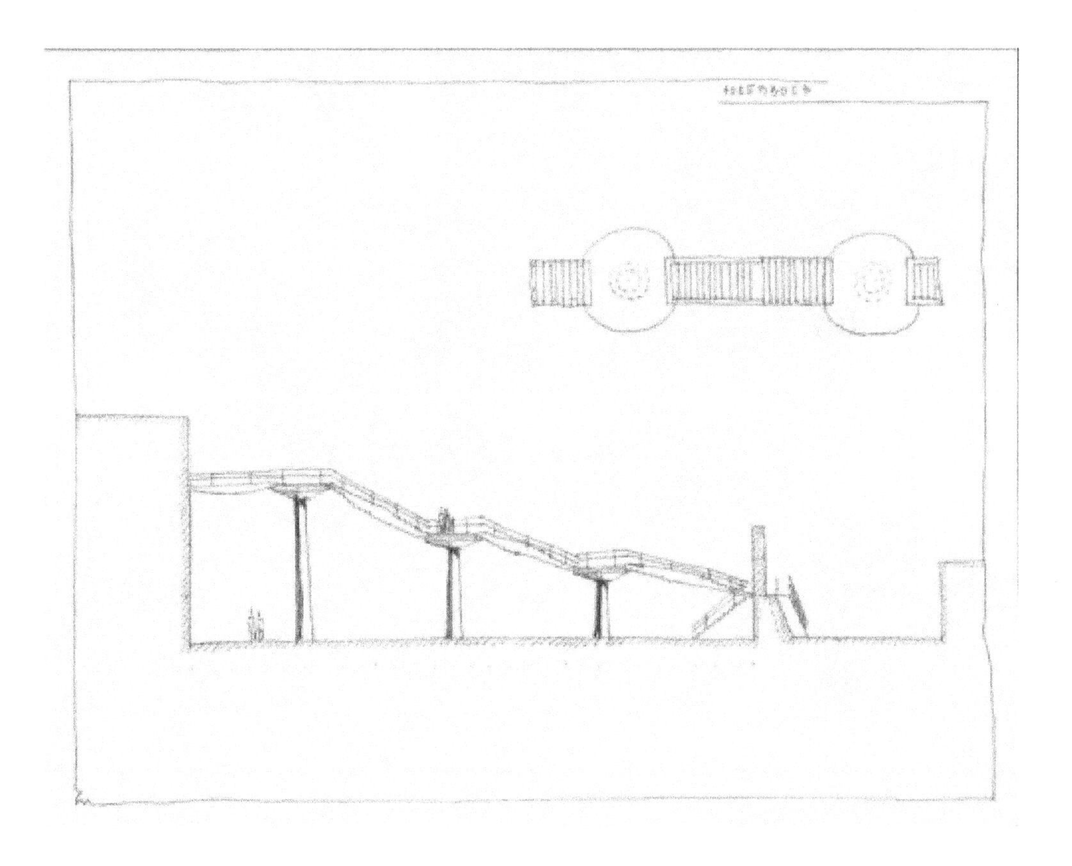

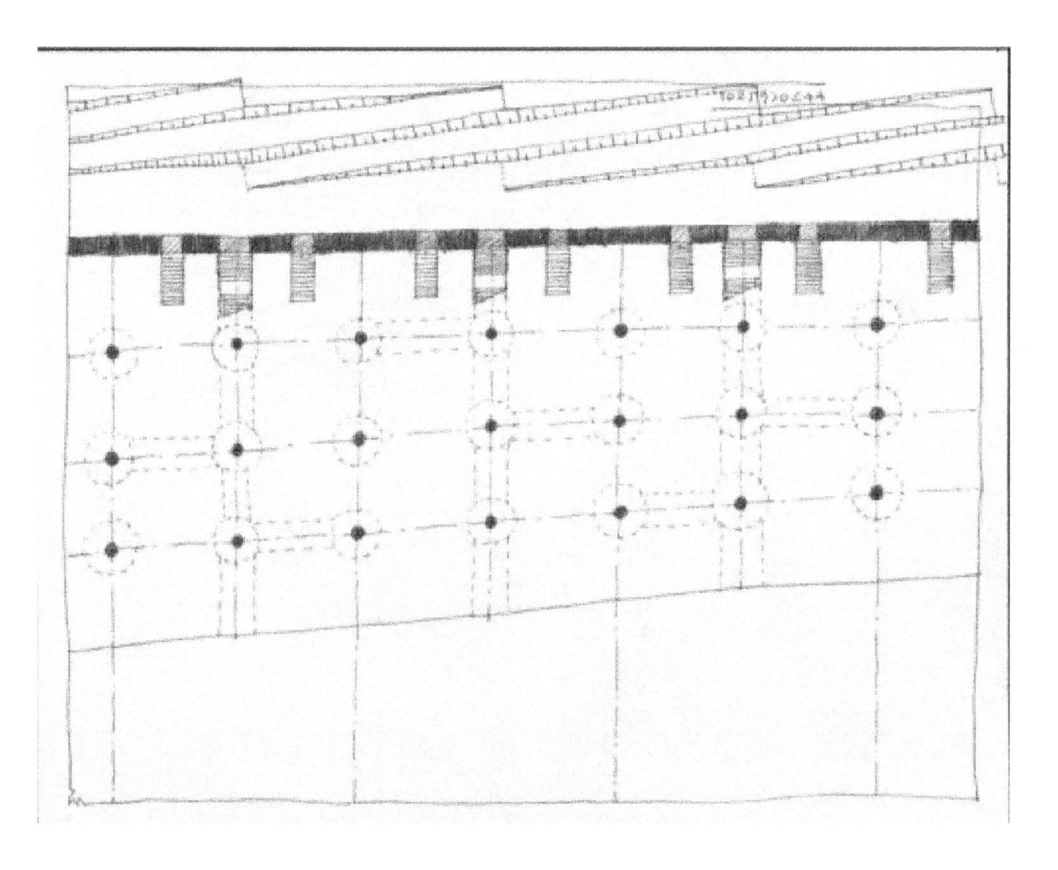

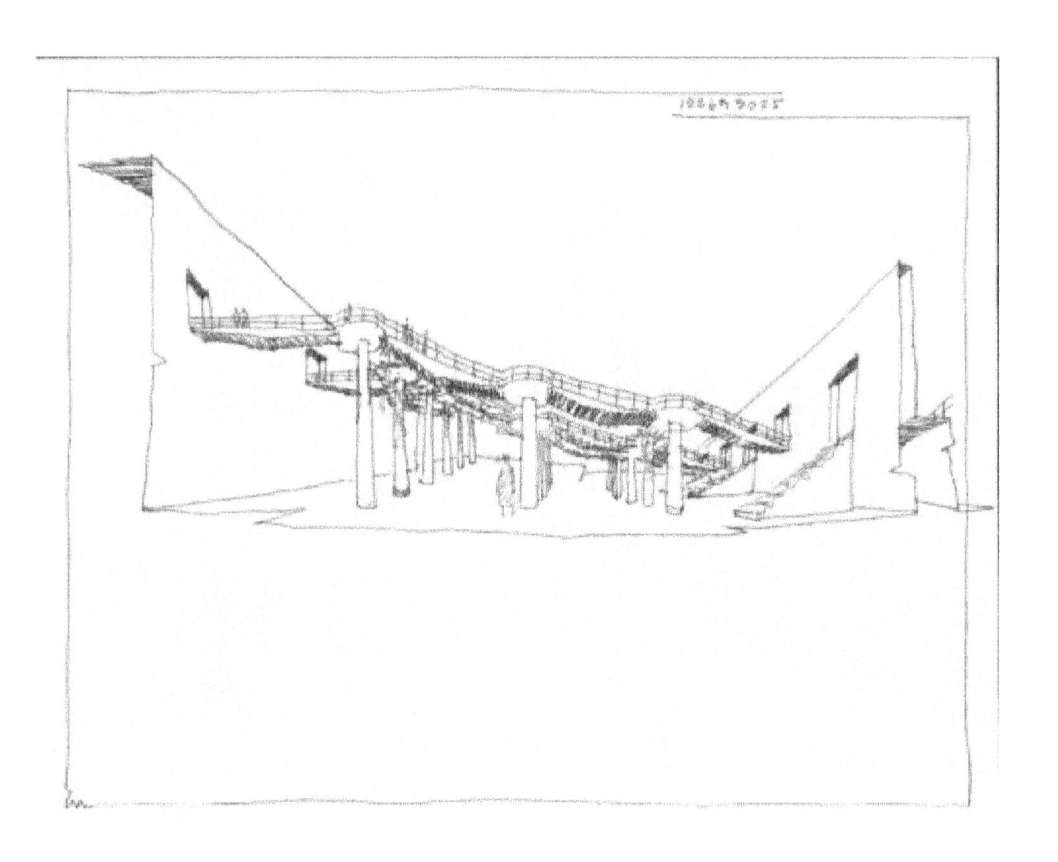

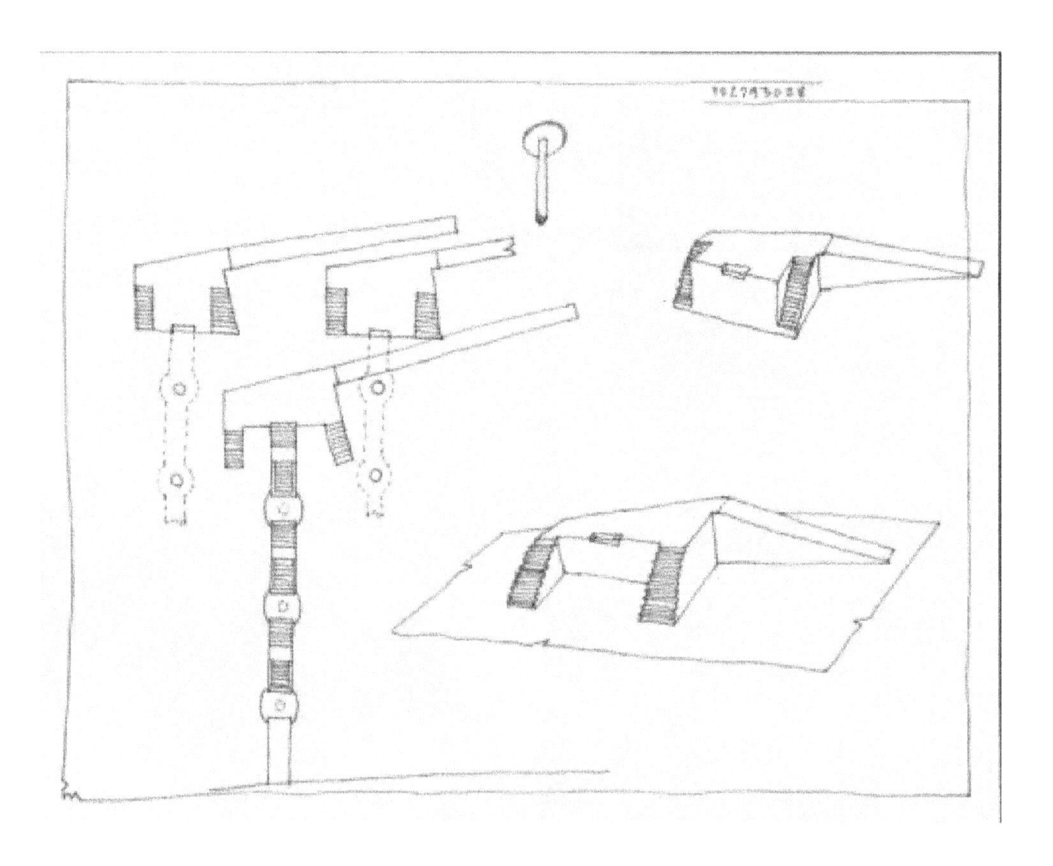

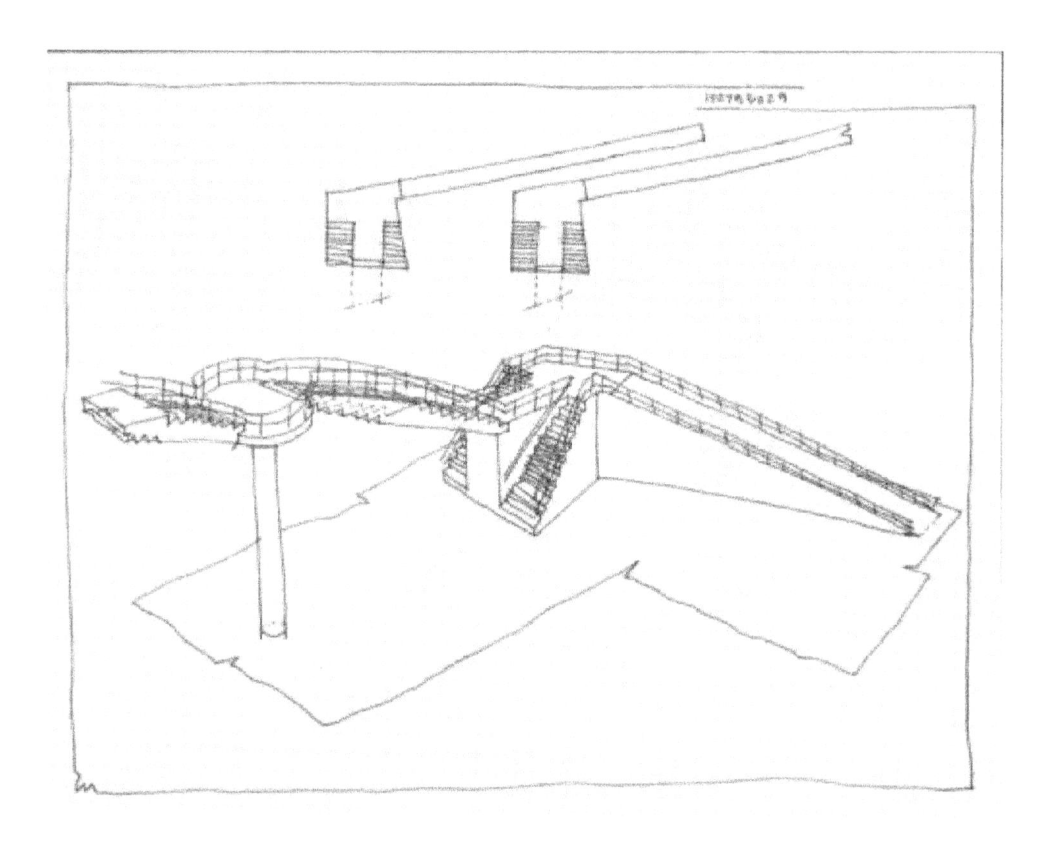

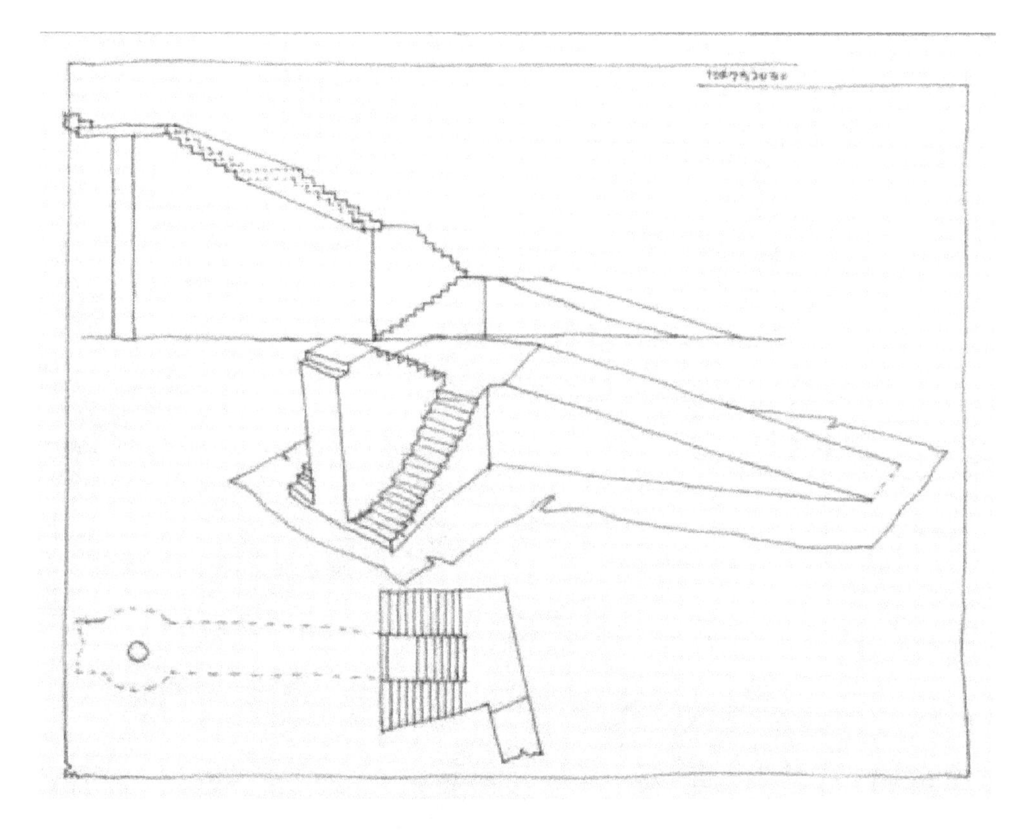

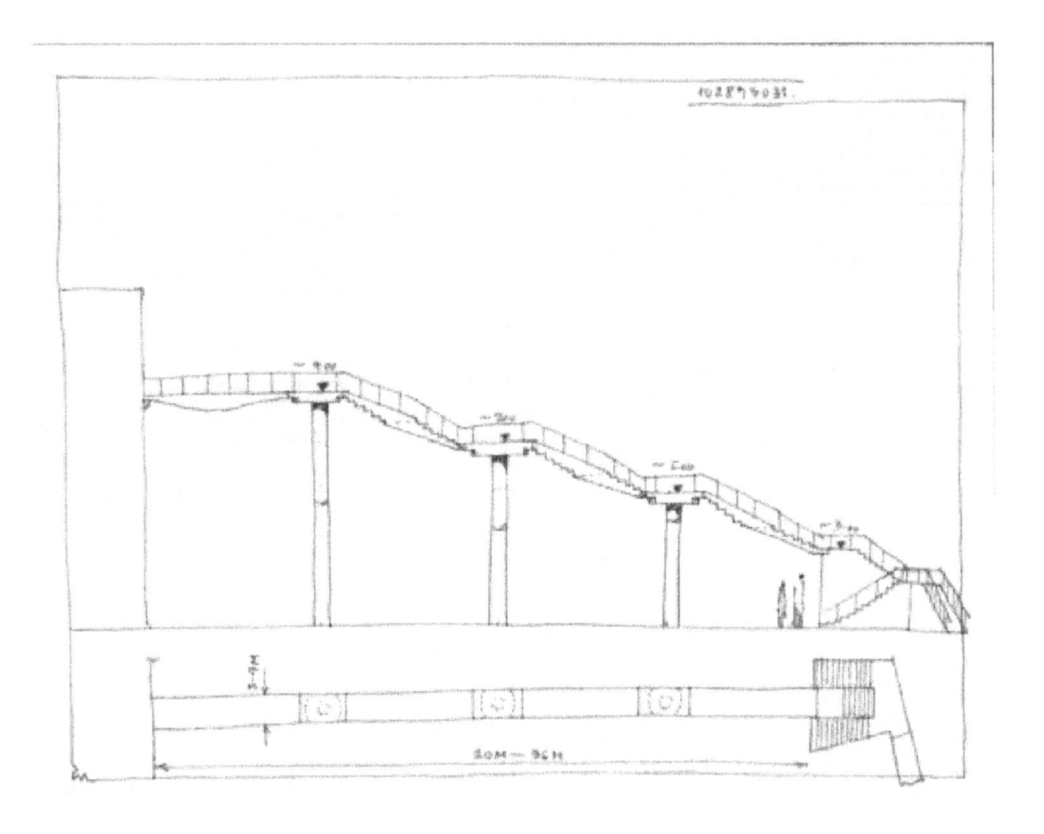

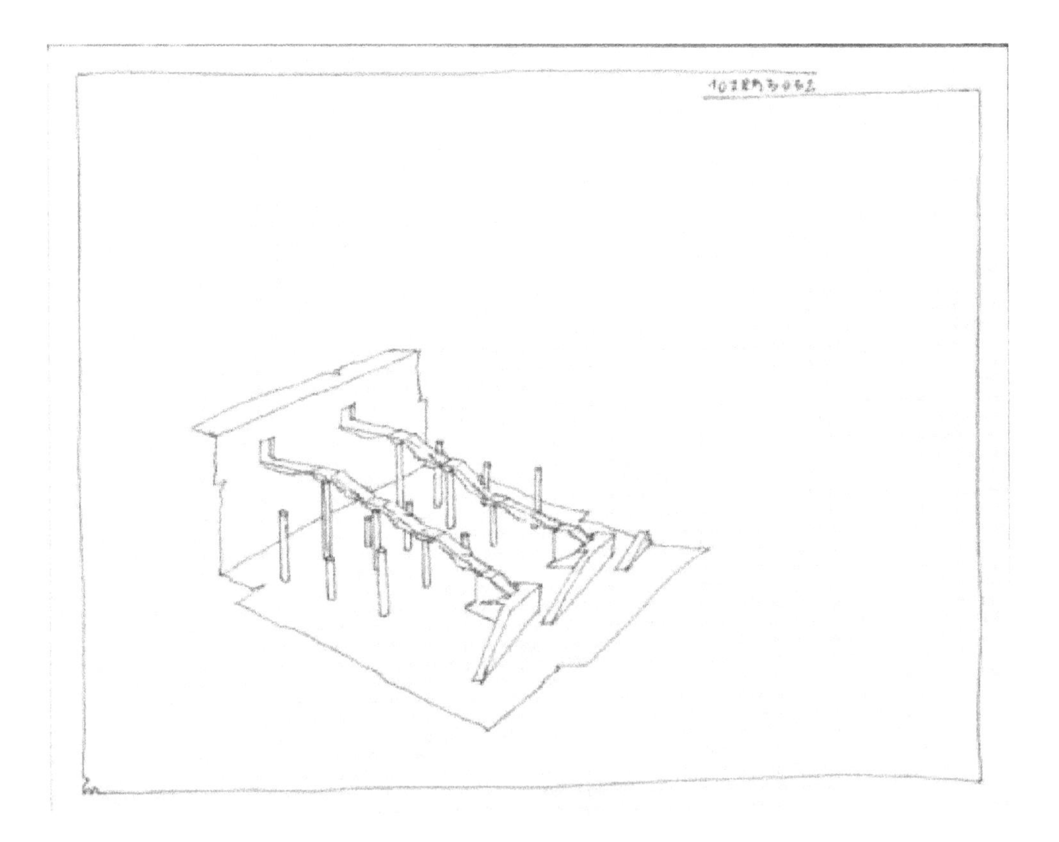

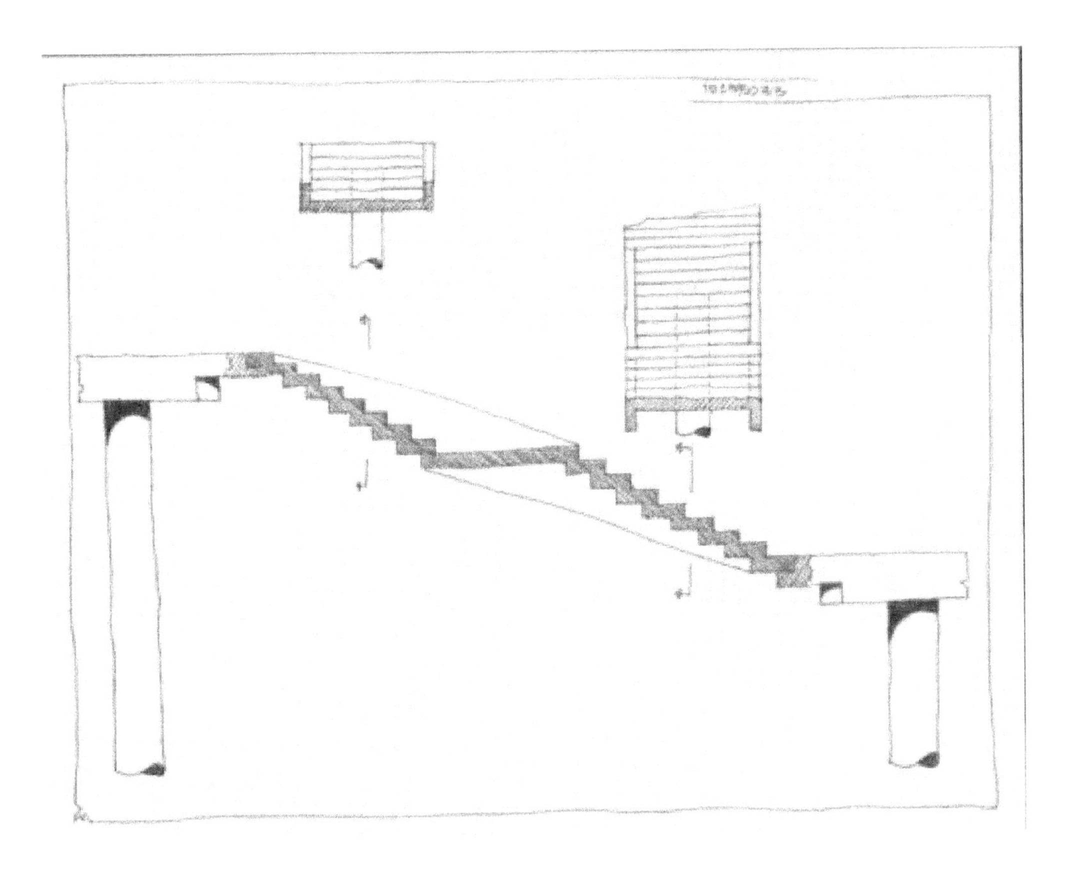

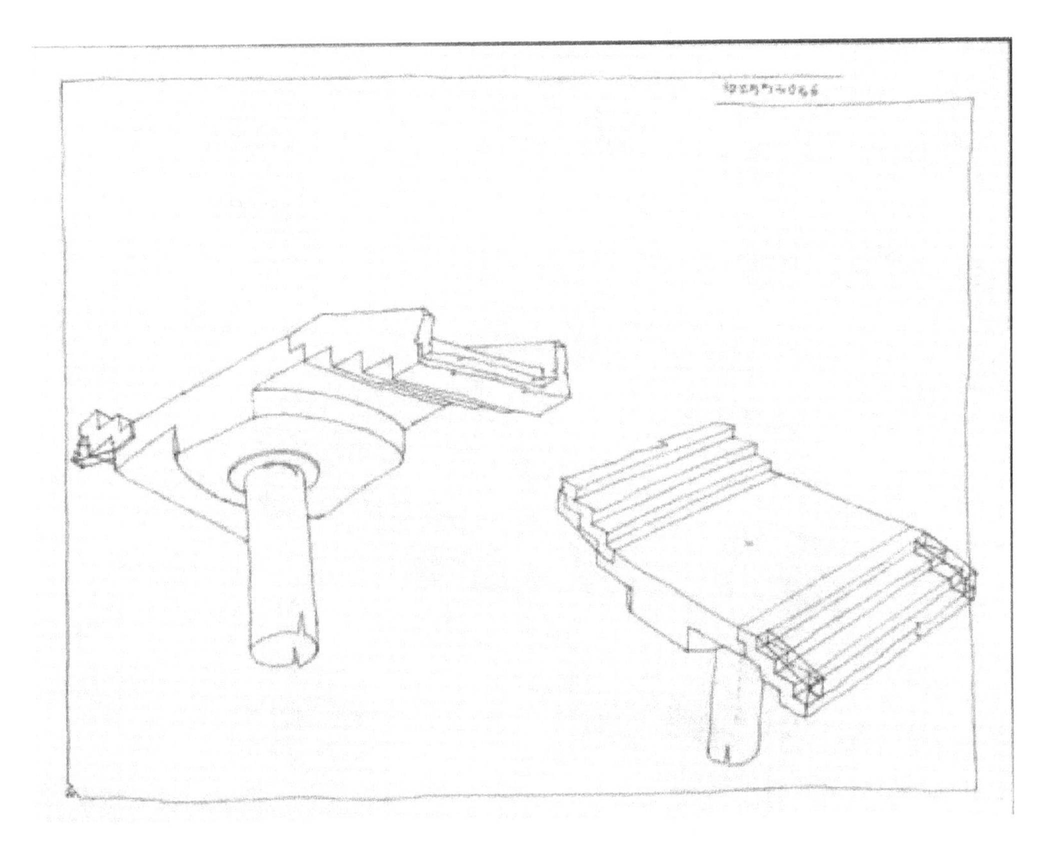

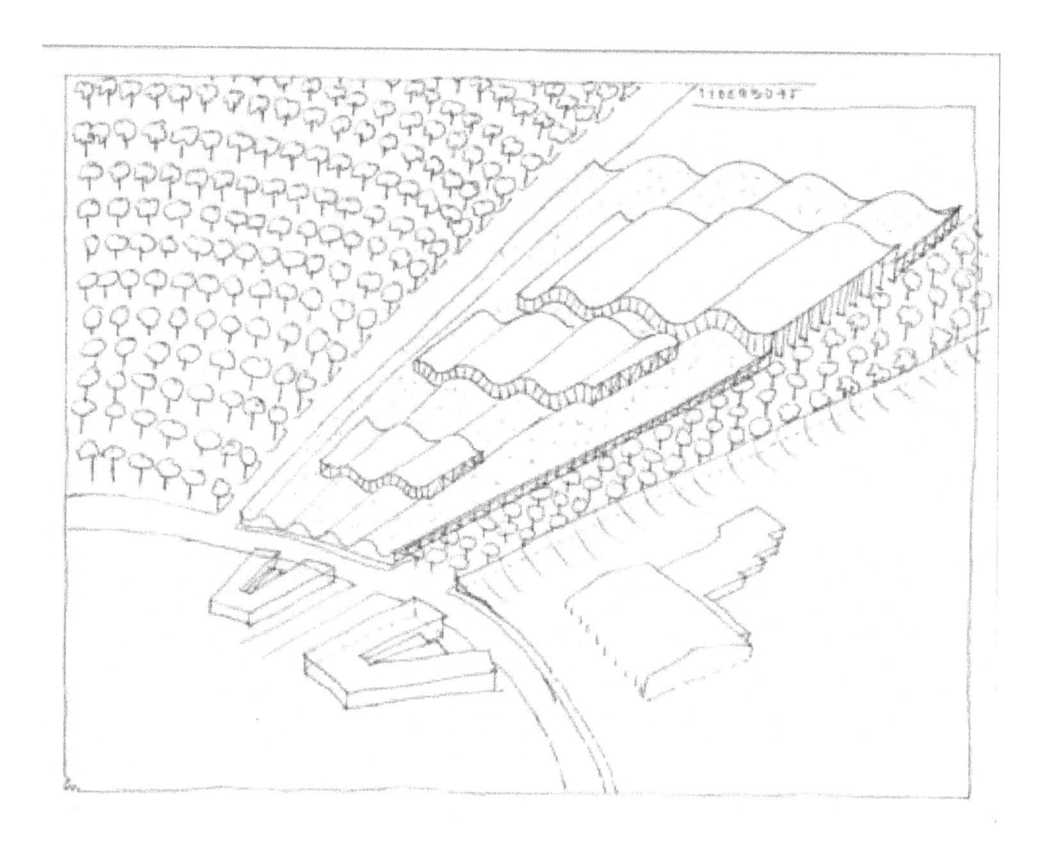

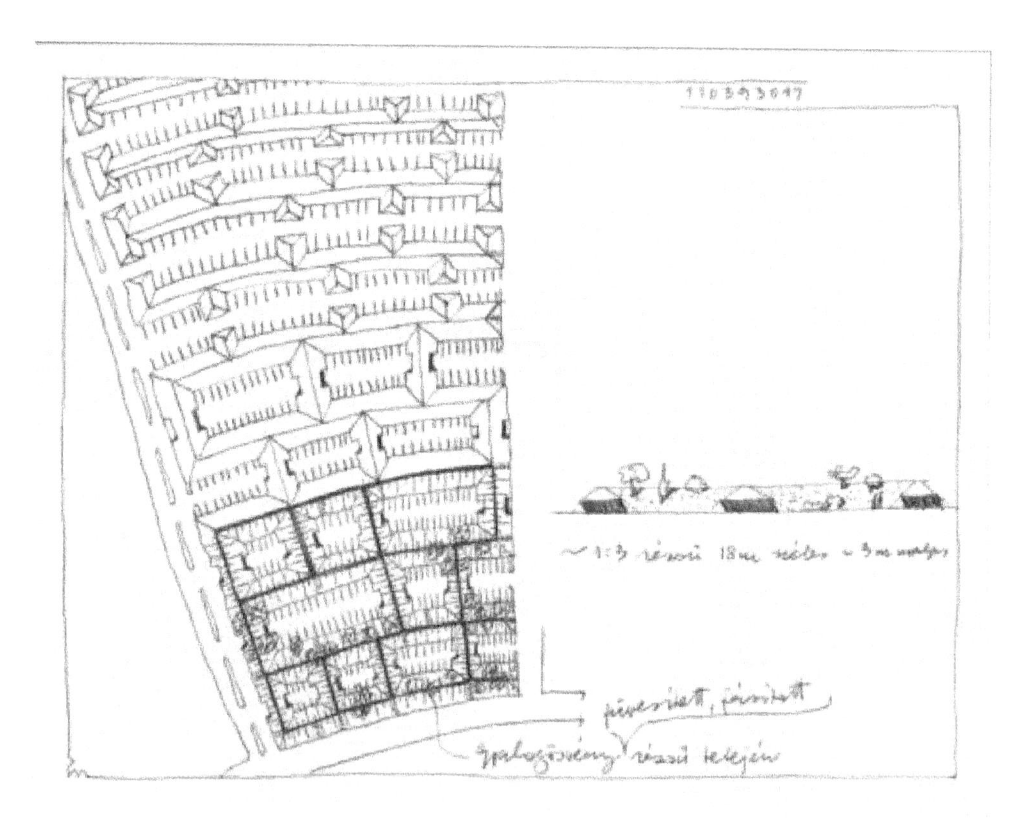

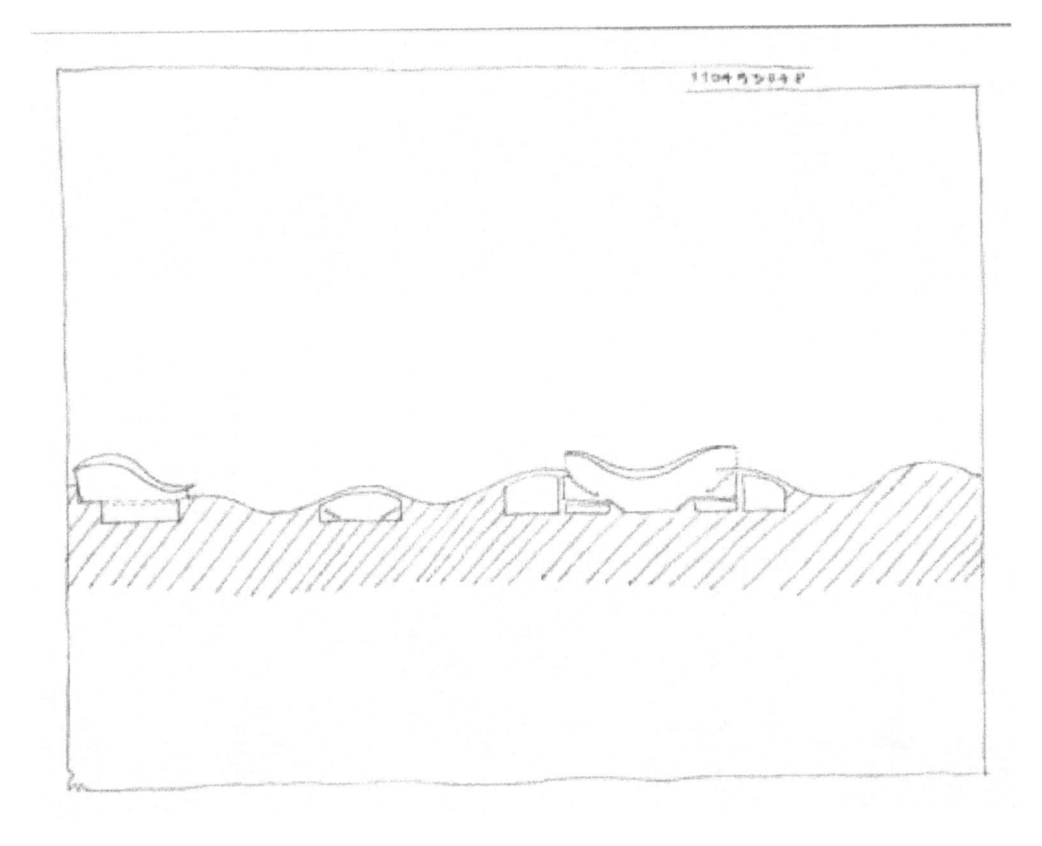

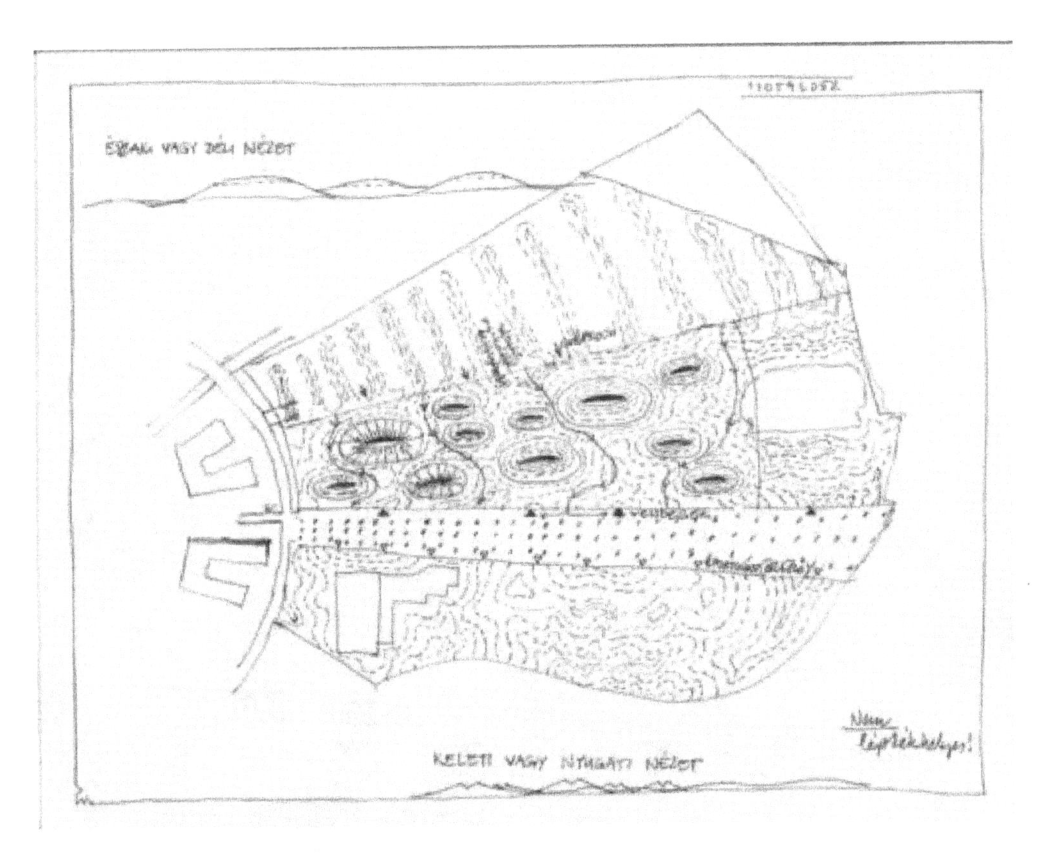
ÉSZAKI VAGY DÉLI NÉZET
KELETI VAGY NYUGATI NÉZET
Nem léptékhelyes!

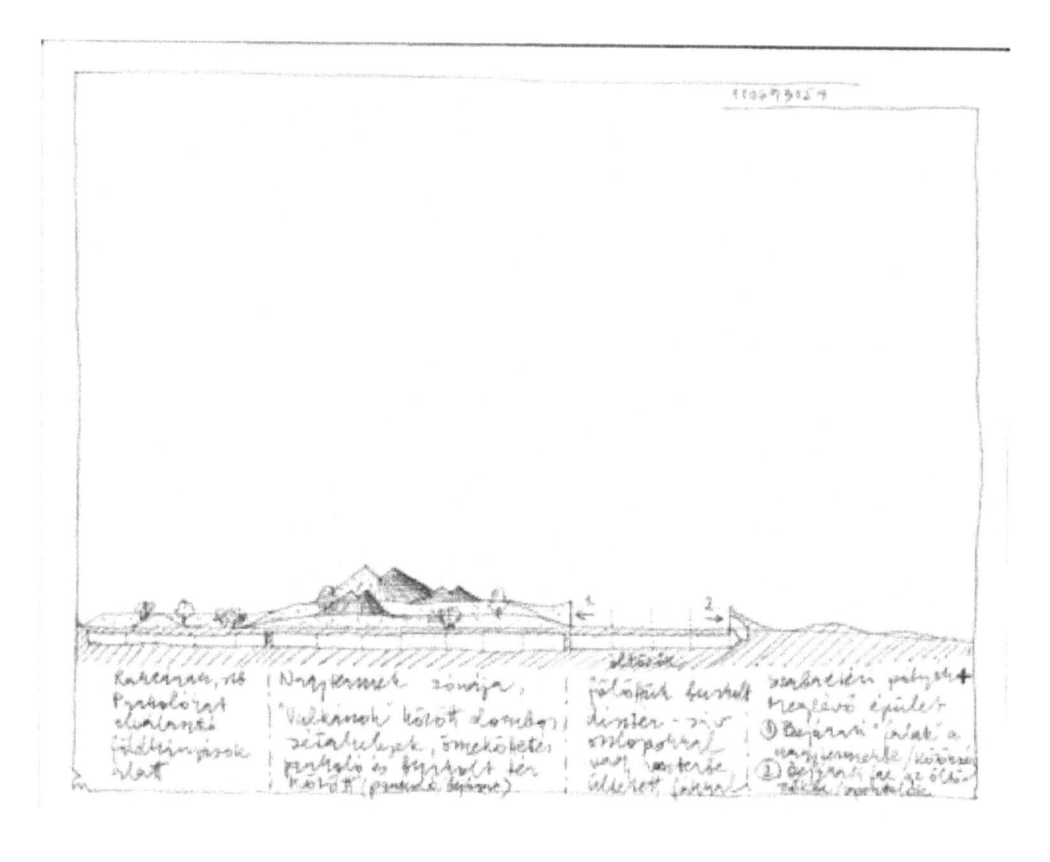

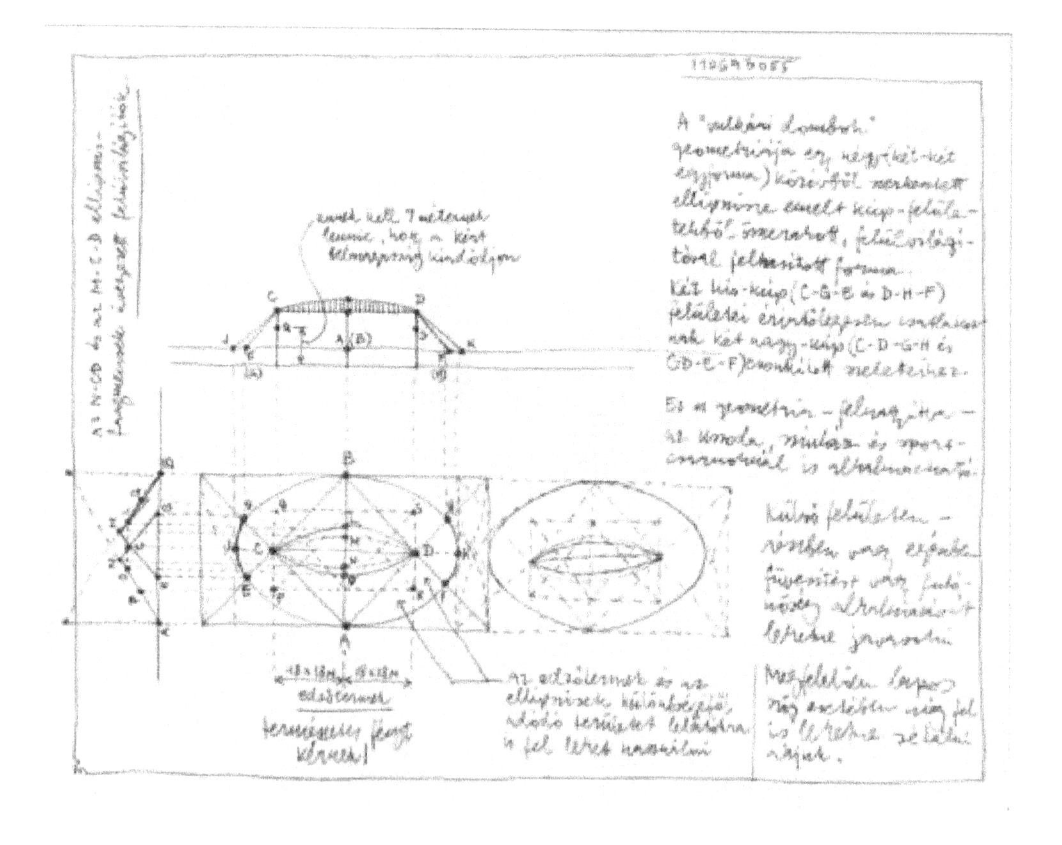

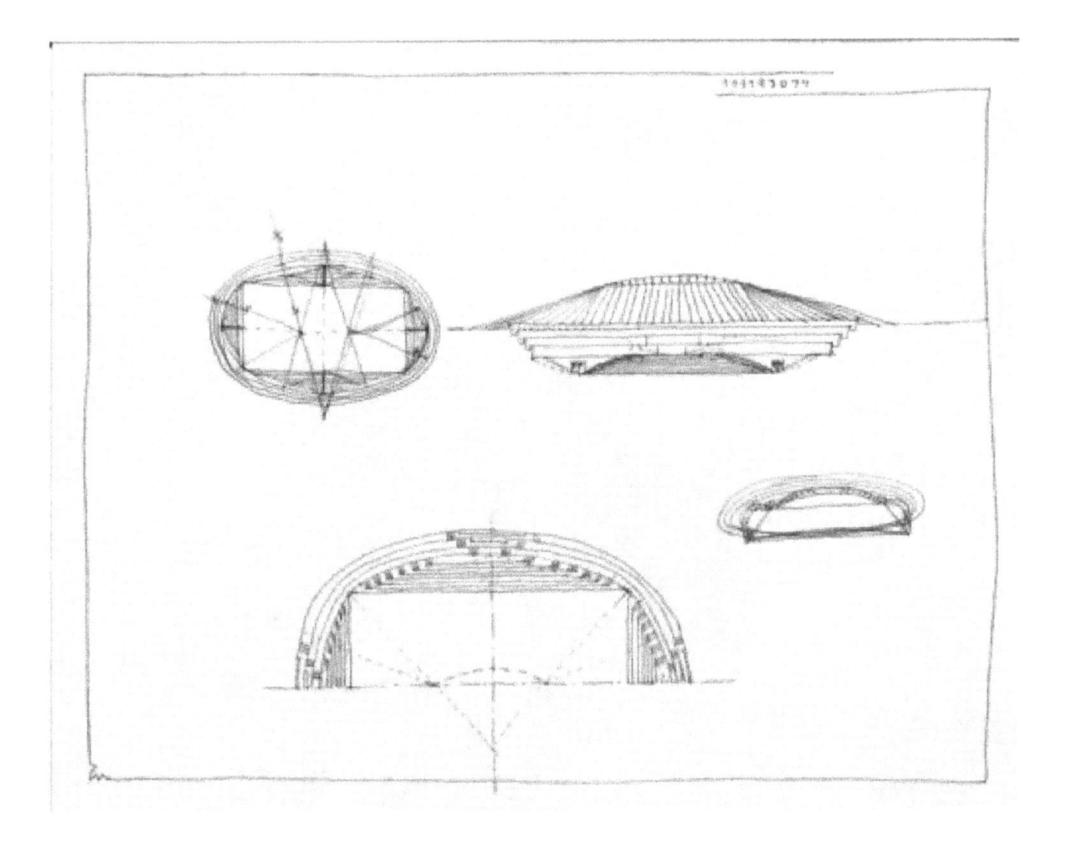

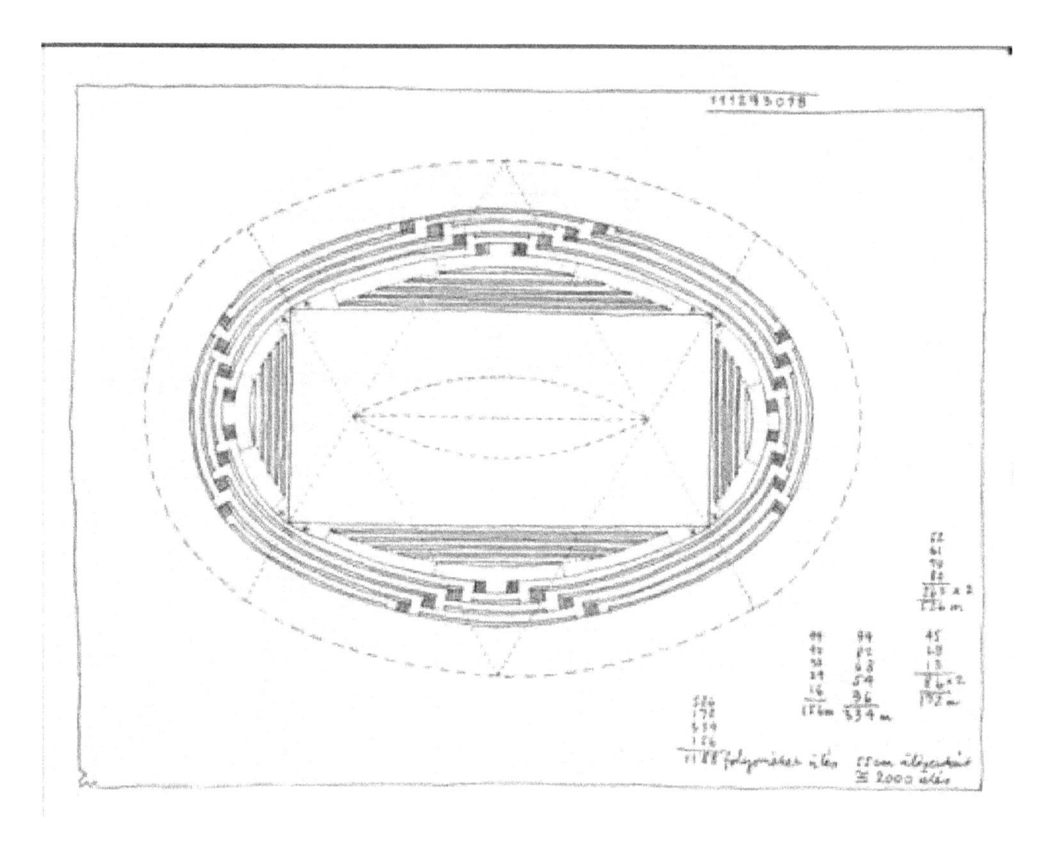

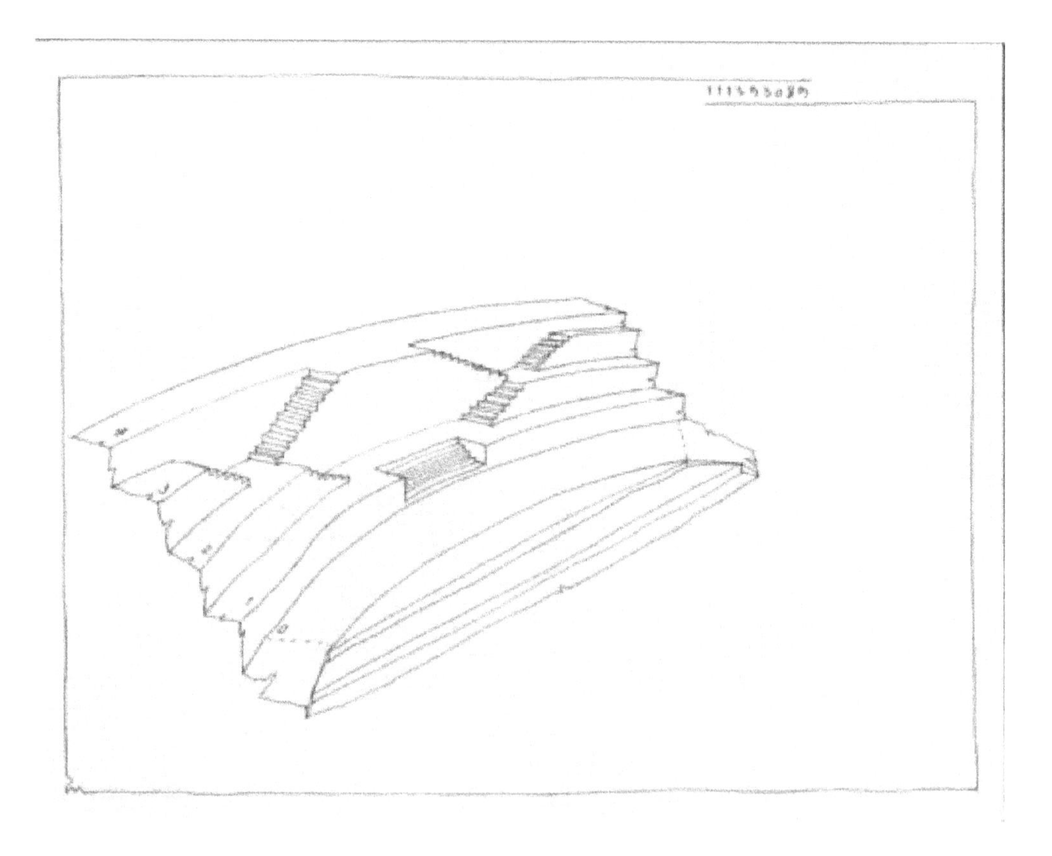

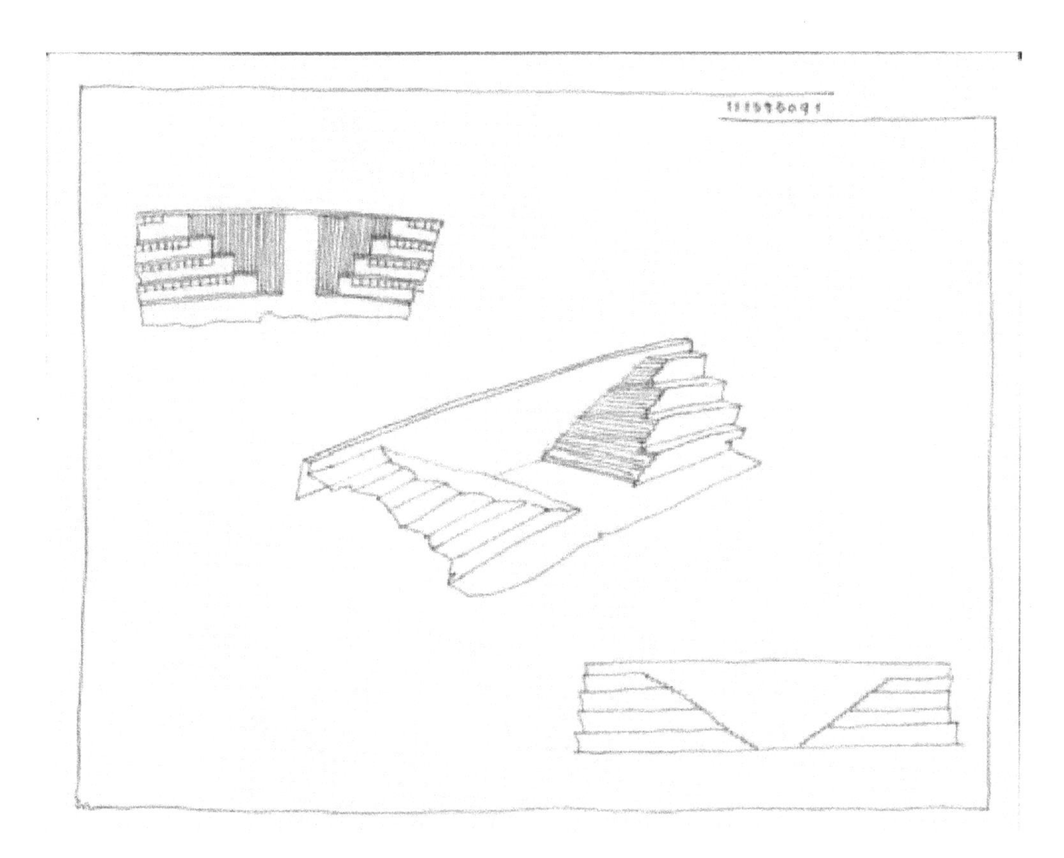

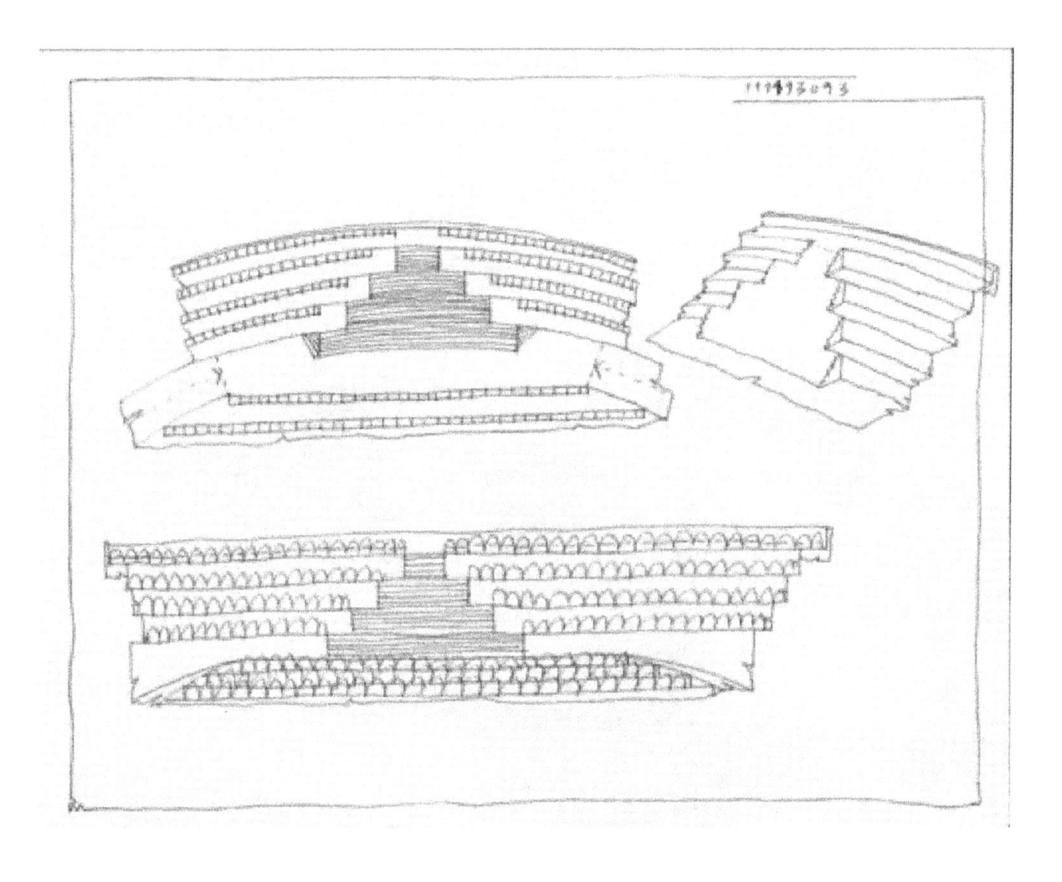

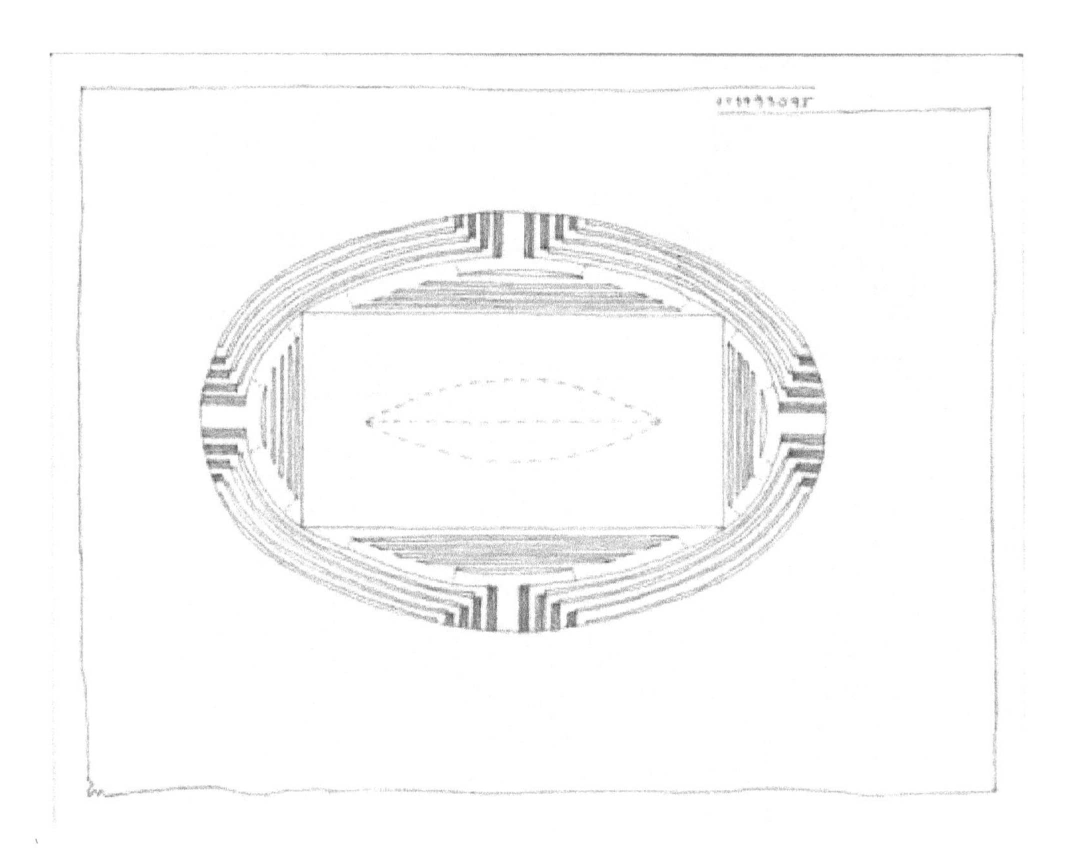

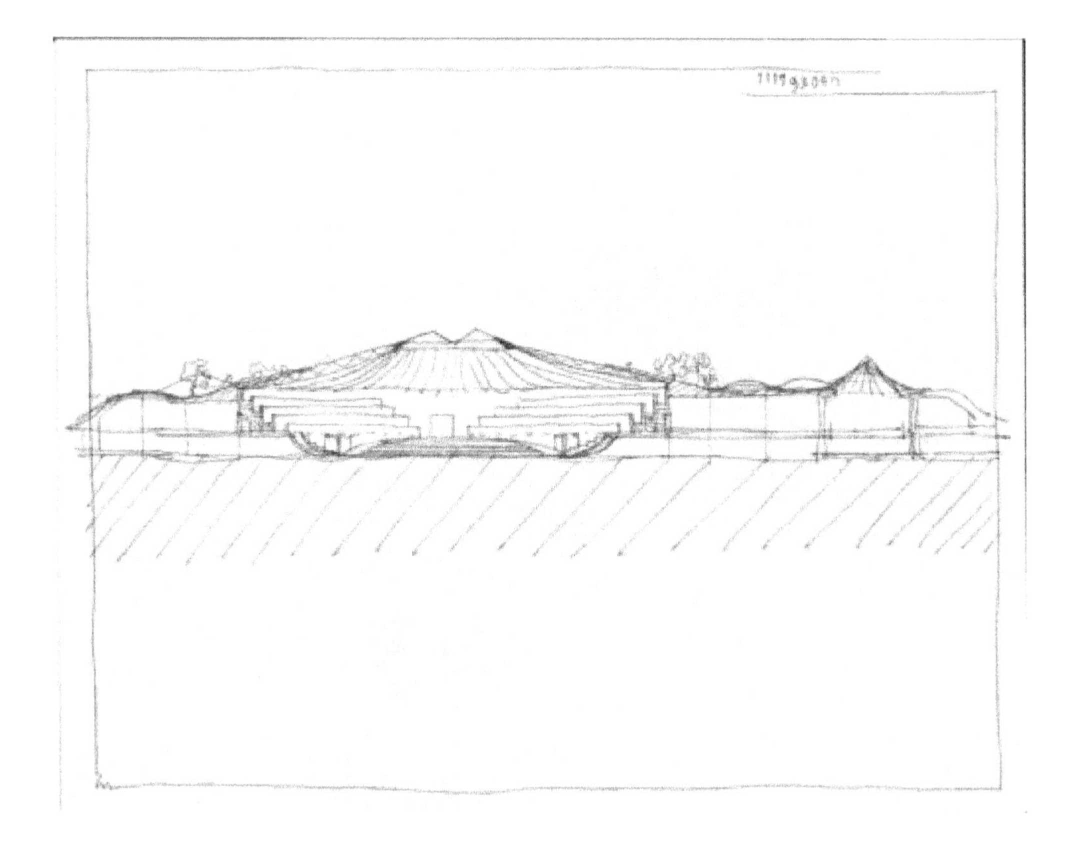

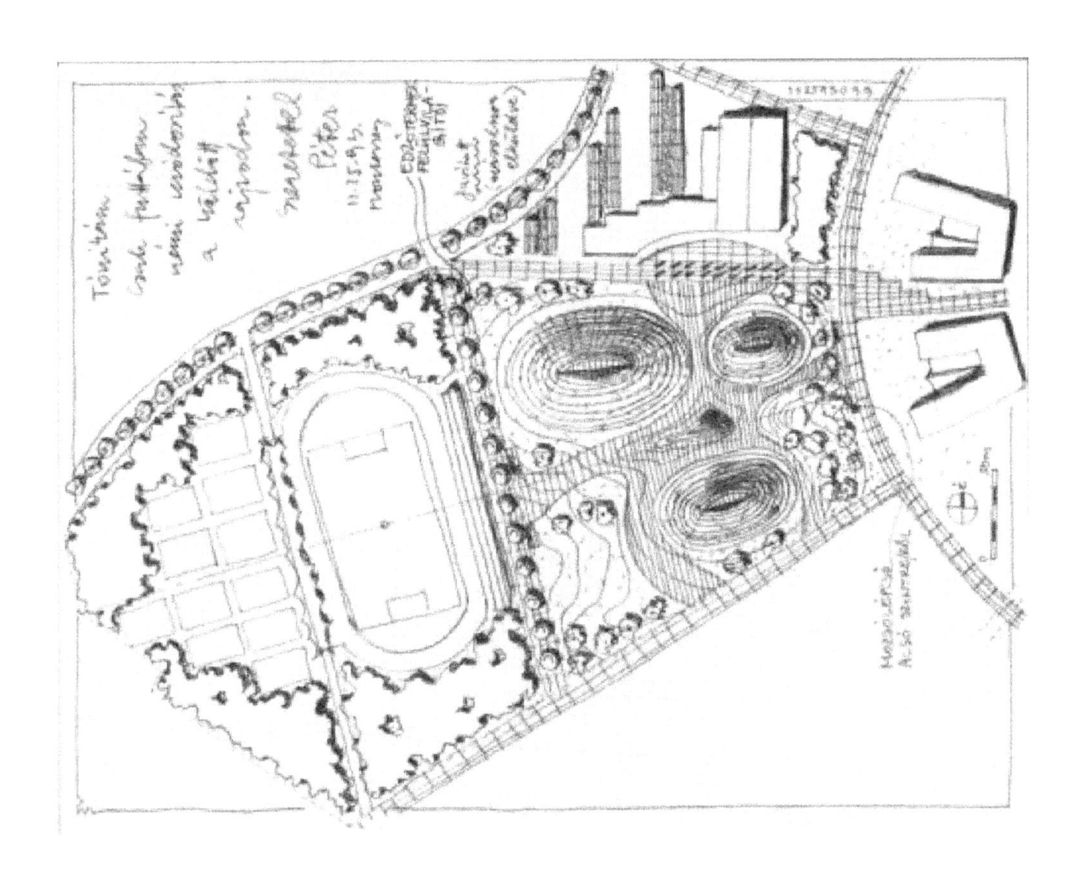

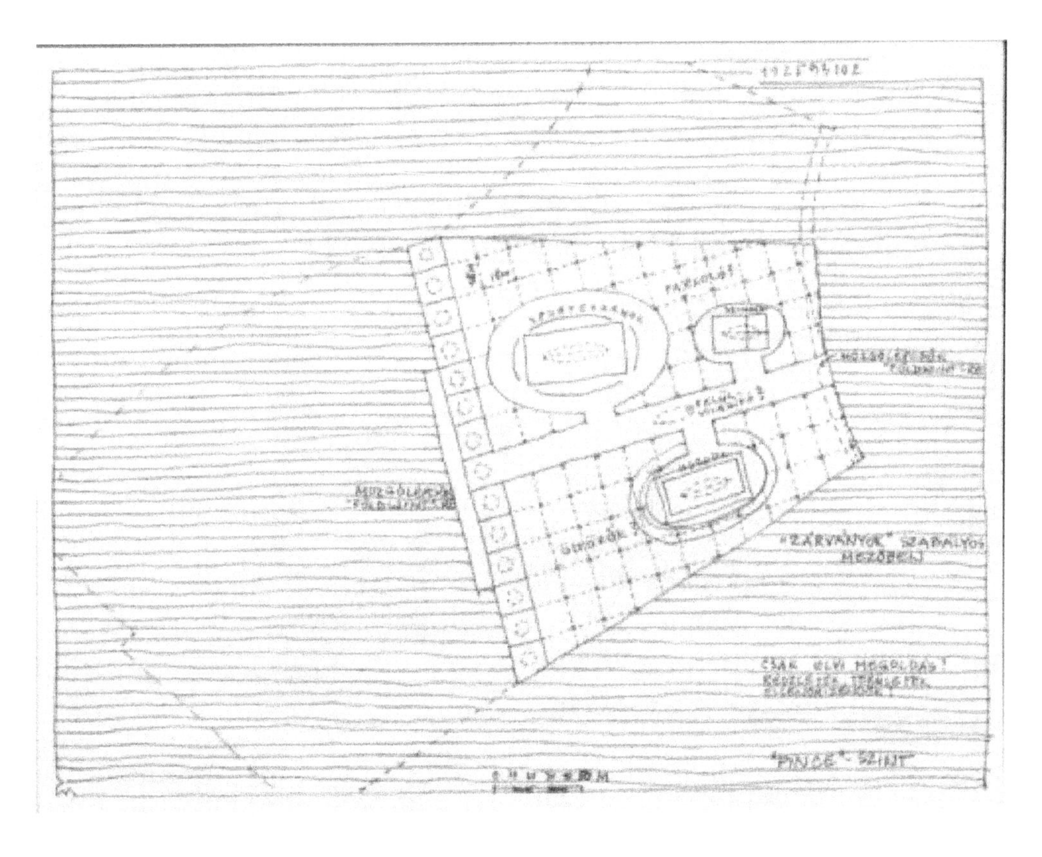

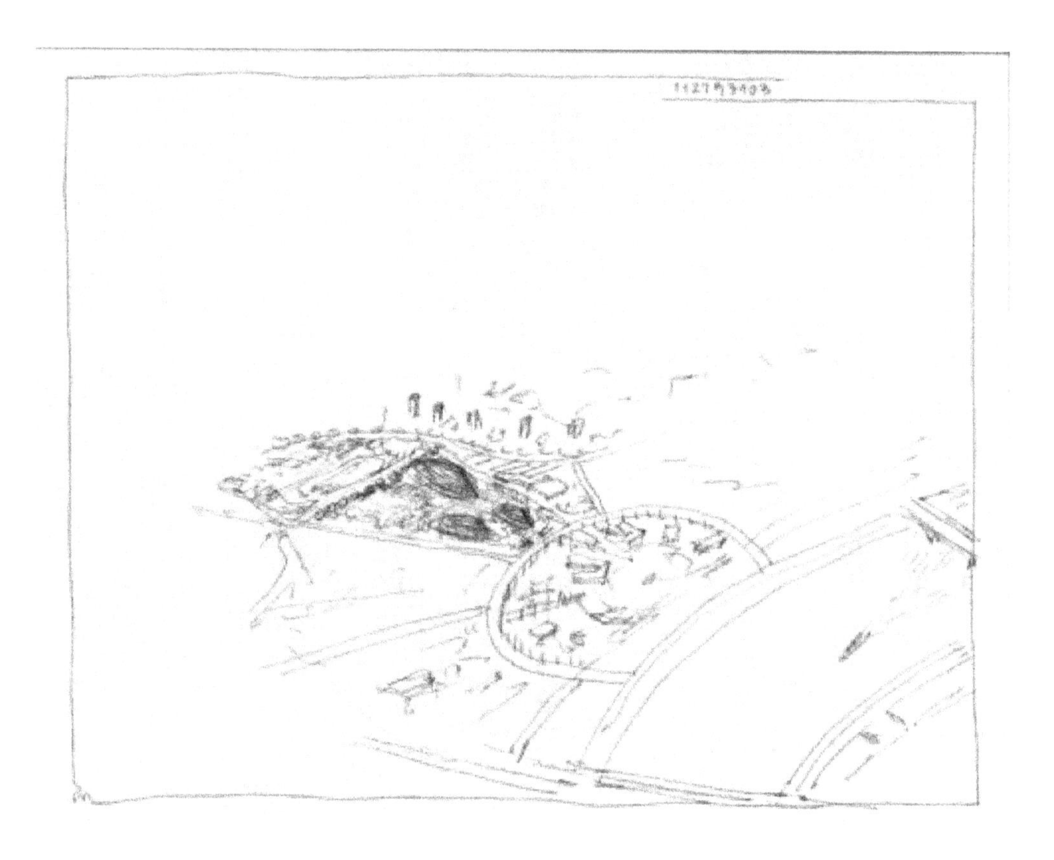

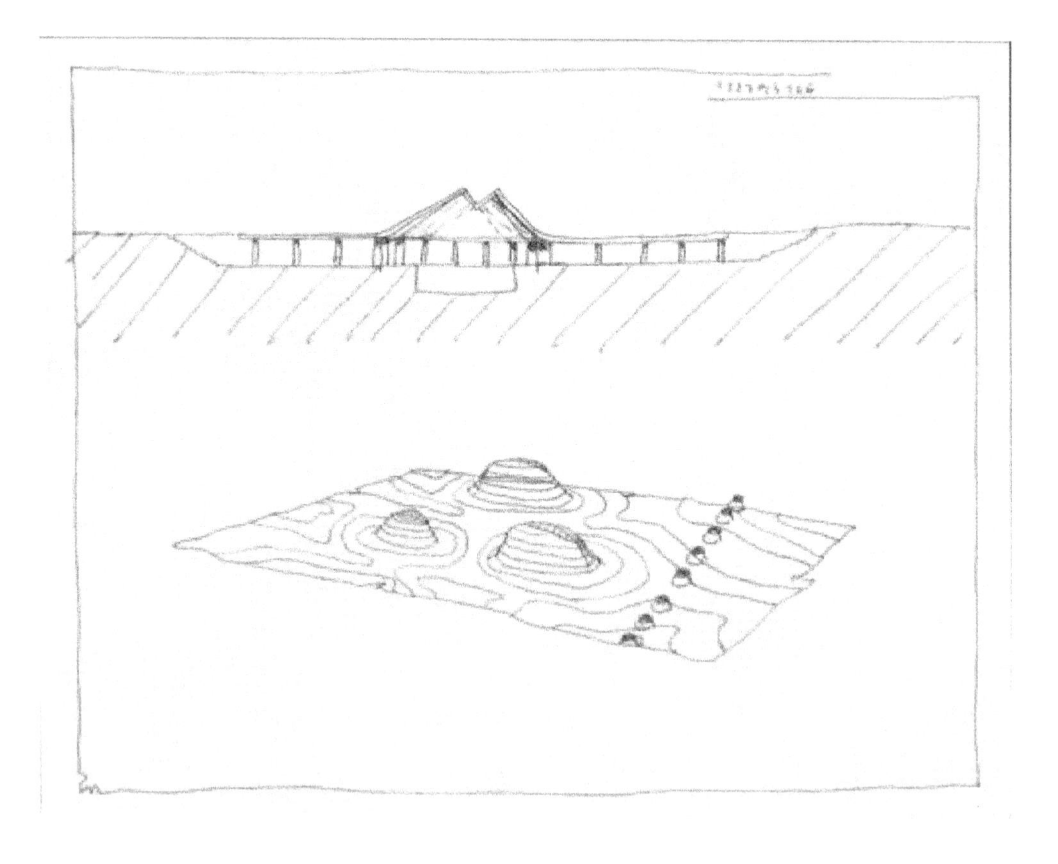

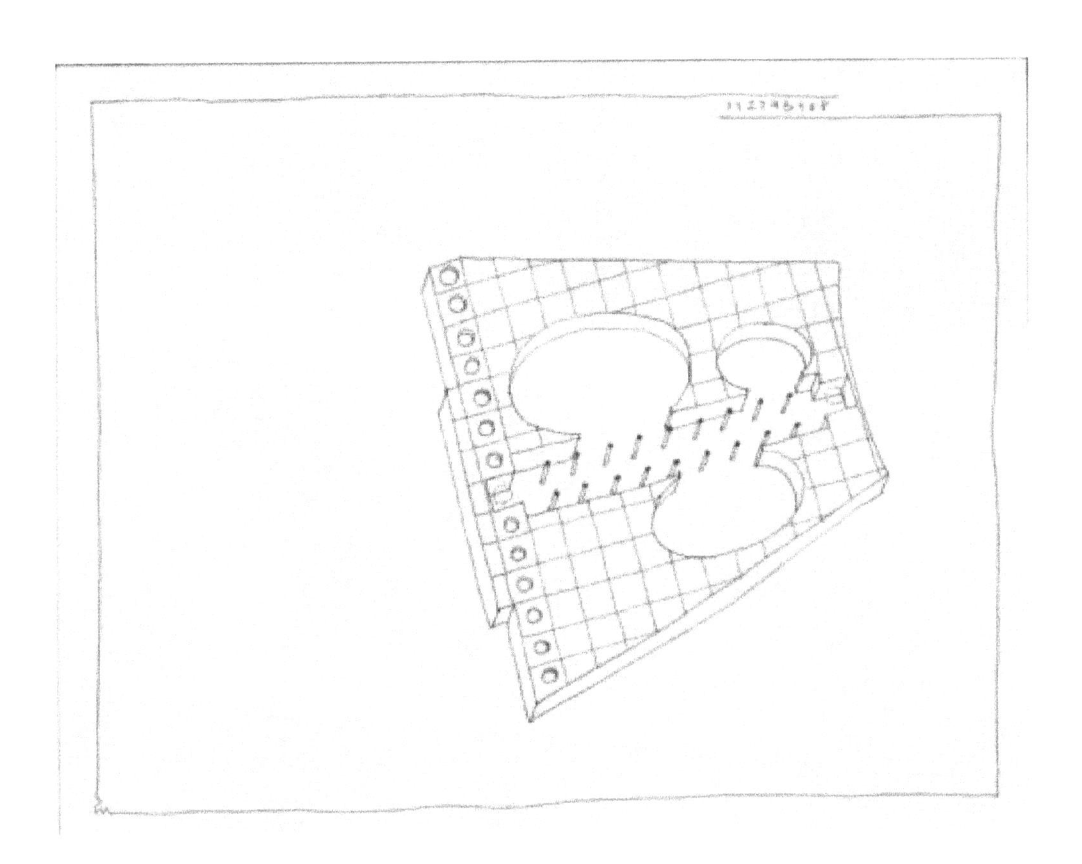

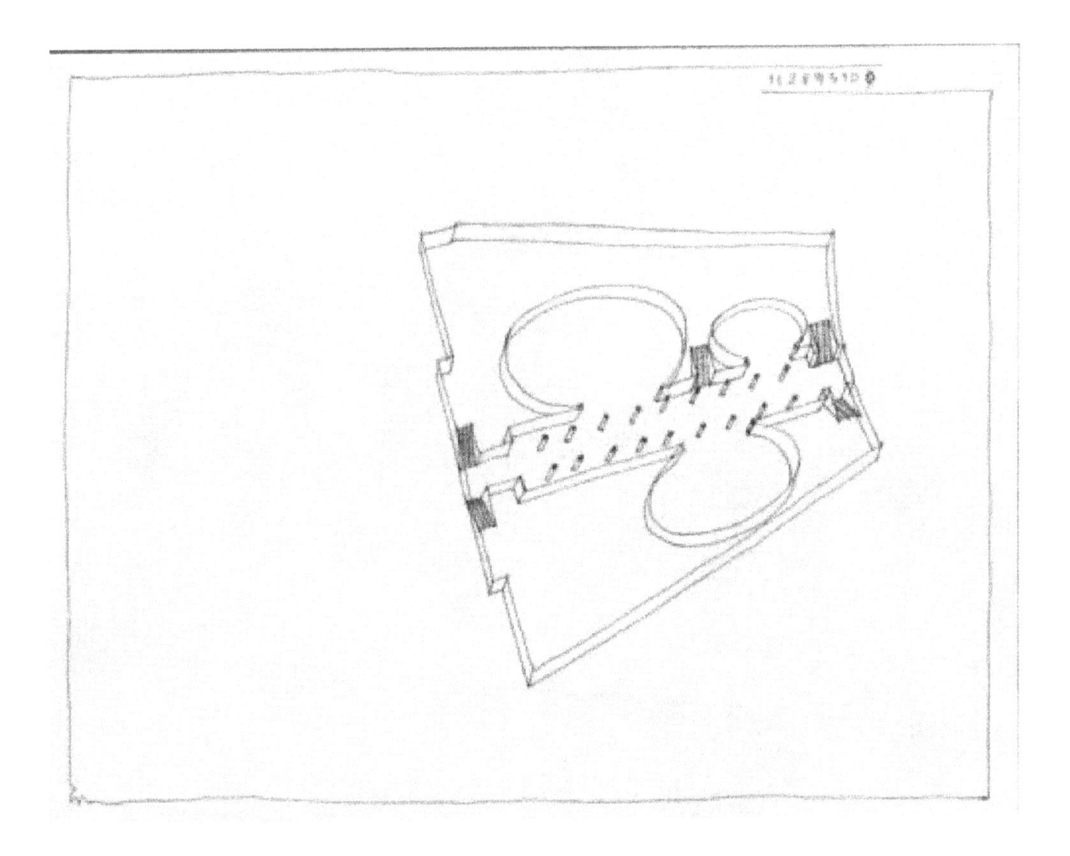

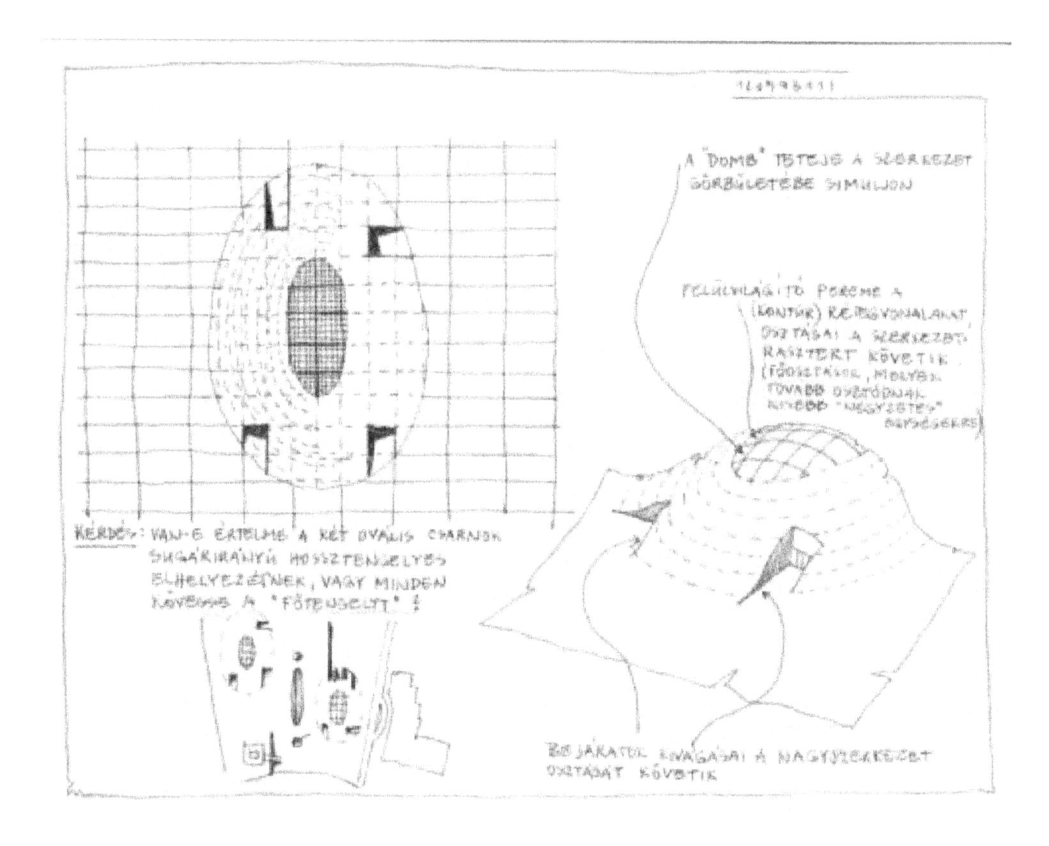
A „DOMB" TETEJE A SZERKEZET GÖRBÜLETÉBE SIMULJON
KÉRDÉS: VAN-E ÉRTELME A KÉT OVÁLIS CSARNOK
ELHELYEZÉSÉNEK, VAGY MINDEN
KÖVETIK

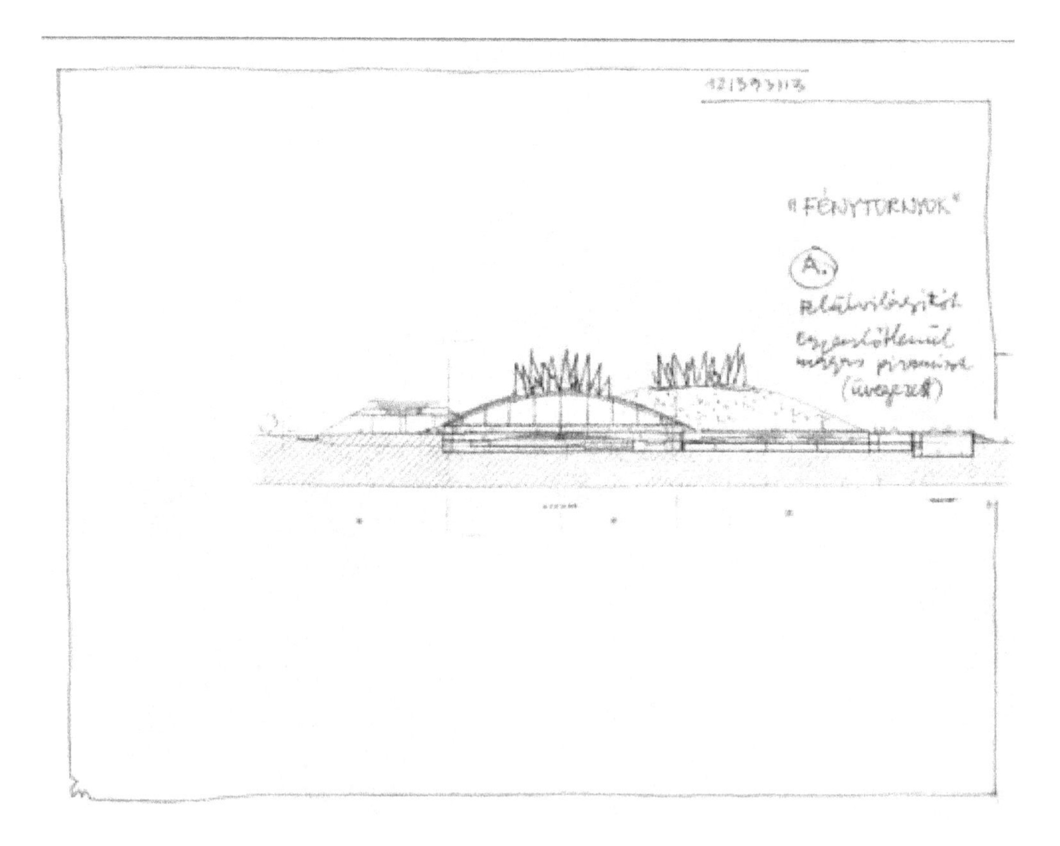
„FÉNYTORNYOK"
A.

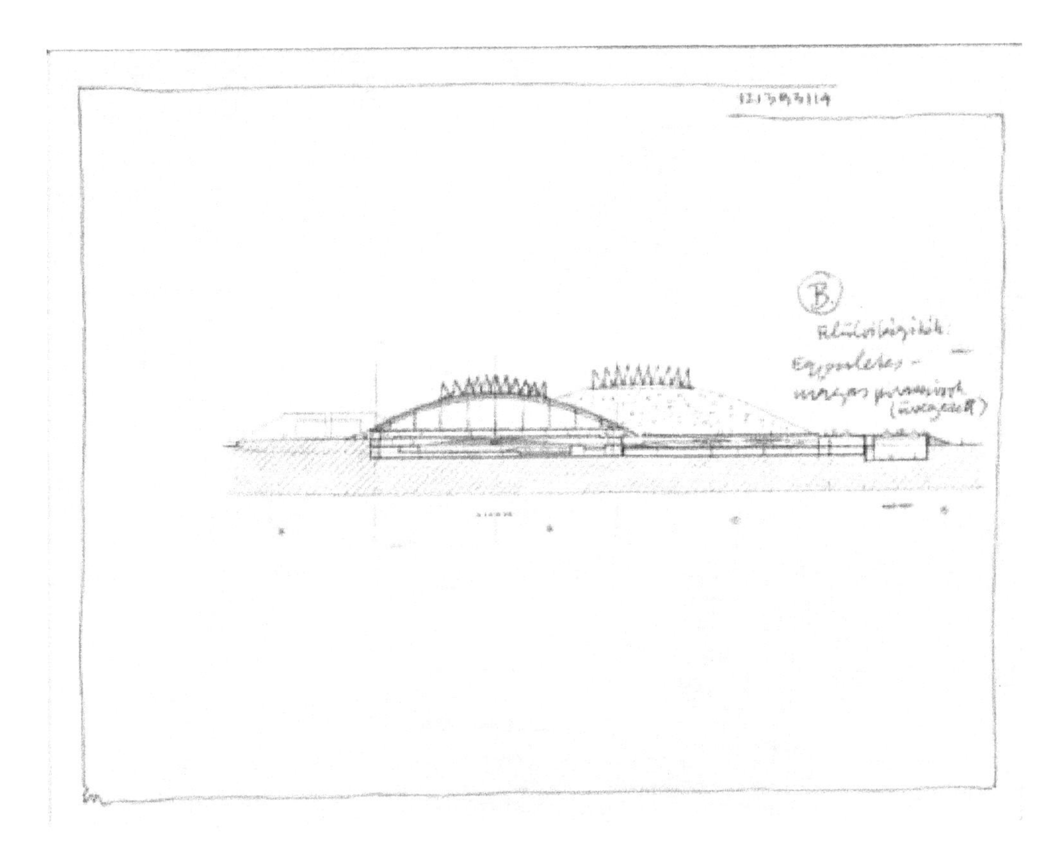
B

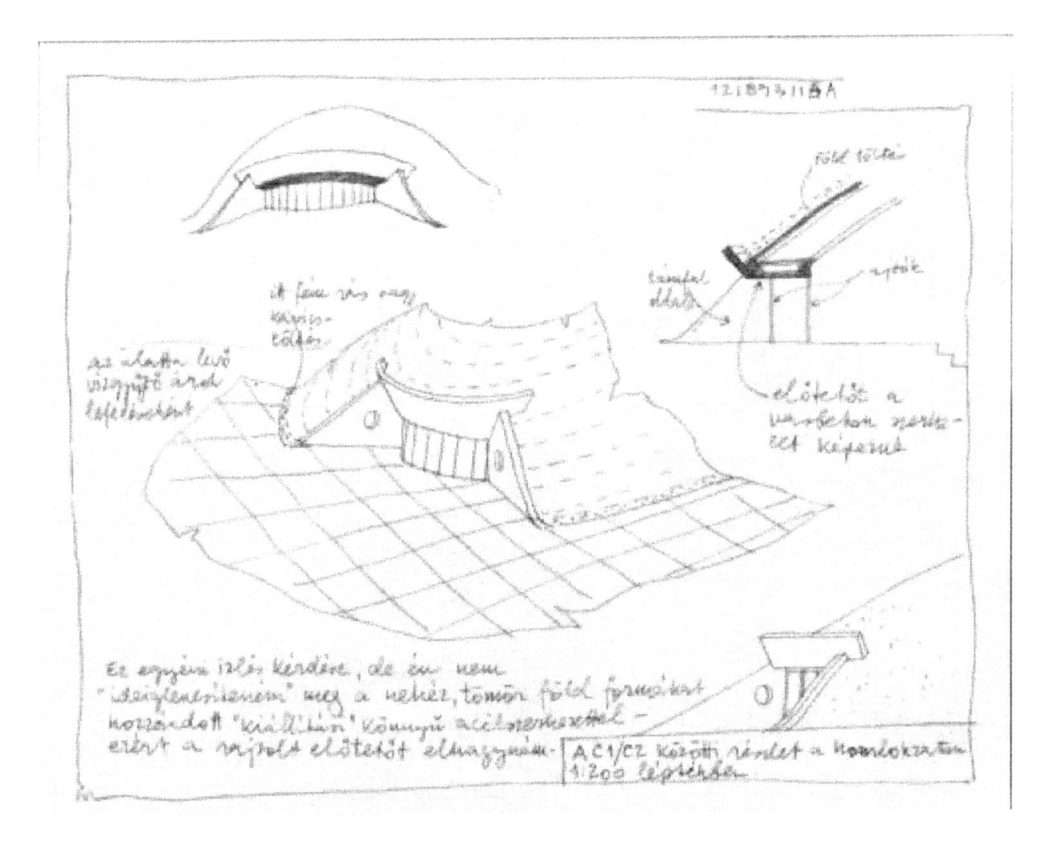
AC1/C2 közötti részlet a homlokzaton
1:200 léptékben

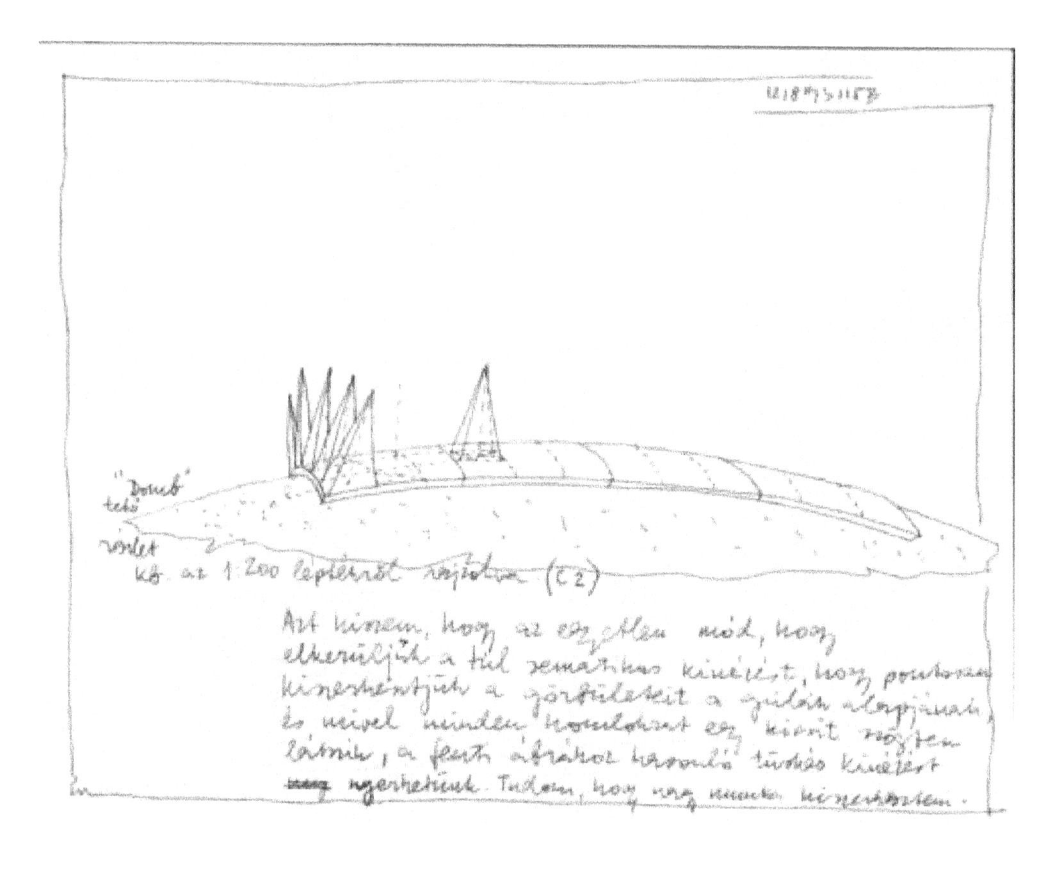
"Domb"
tető
(C2)

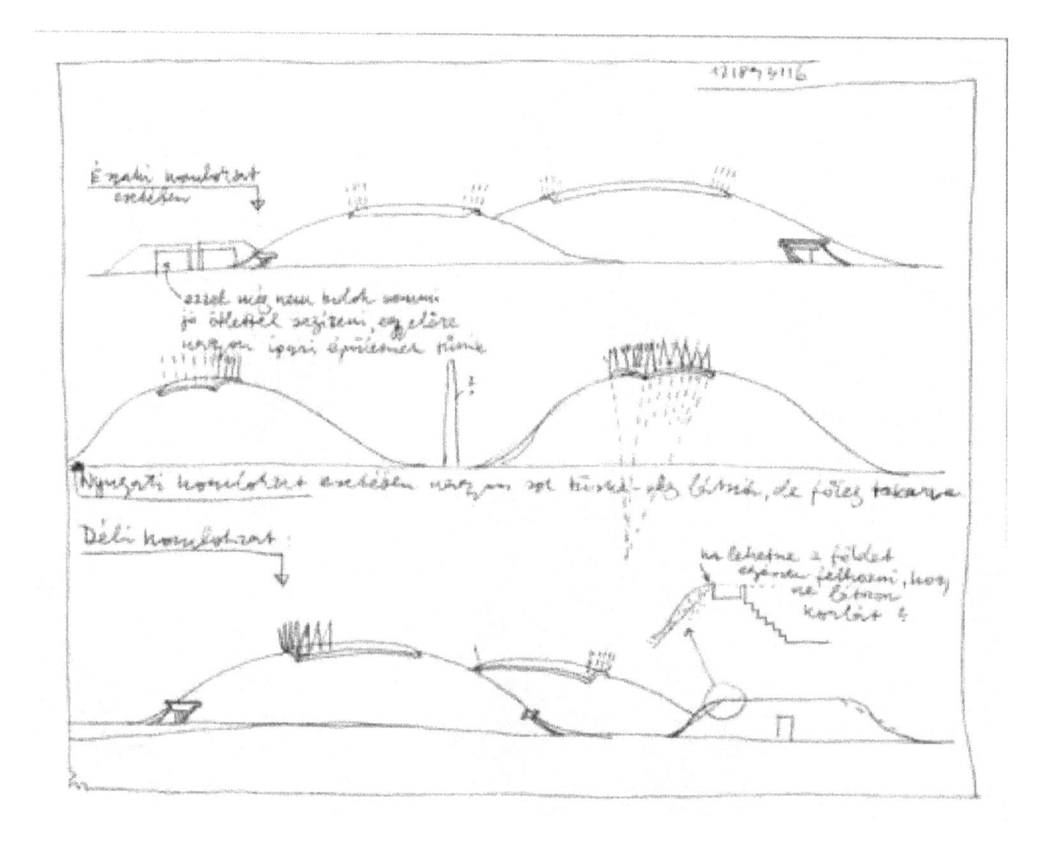
Északi homlokzat
Déli homlokzat

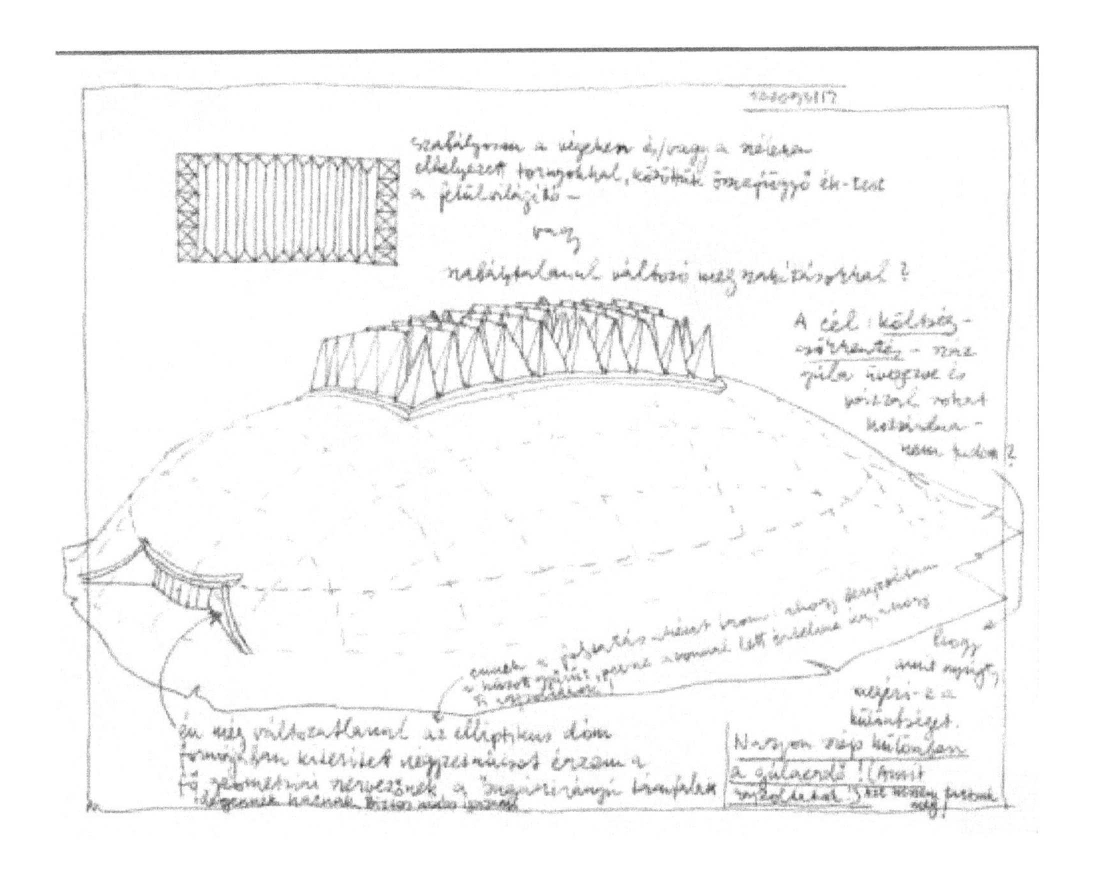
vagy
A cél: költség-
Nagyon szép különben
a gúlaerdő!

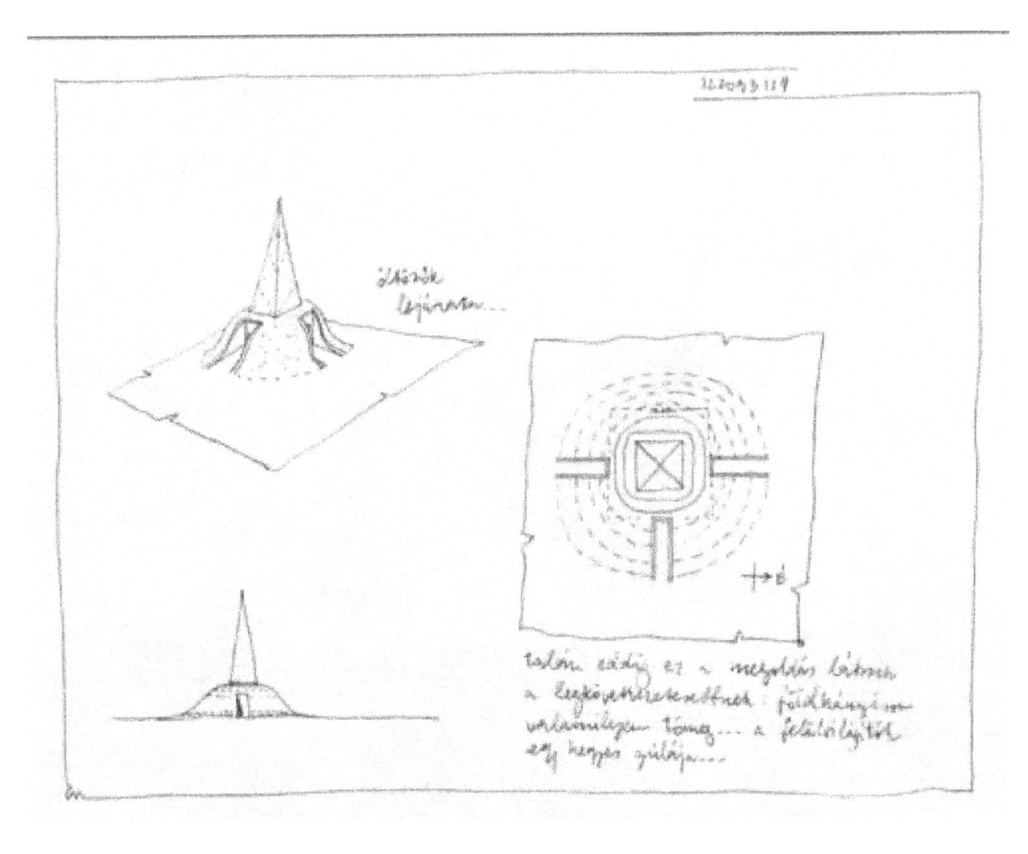

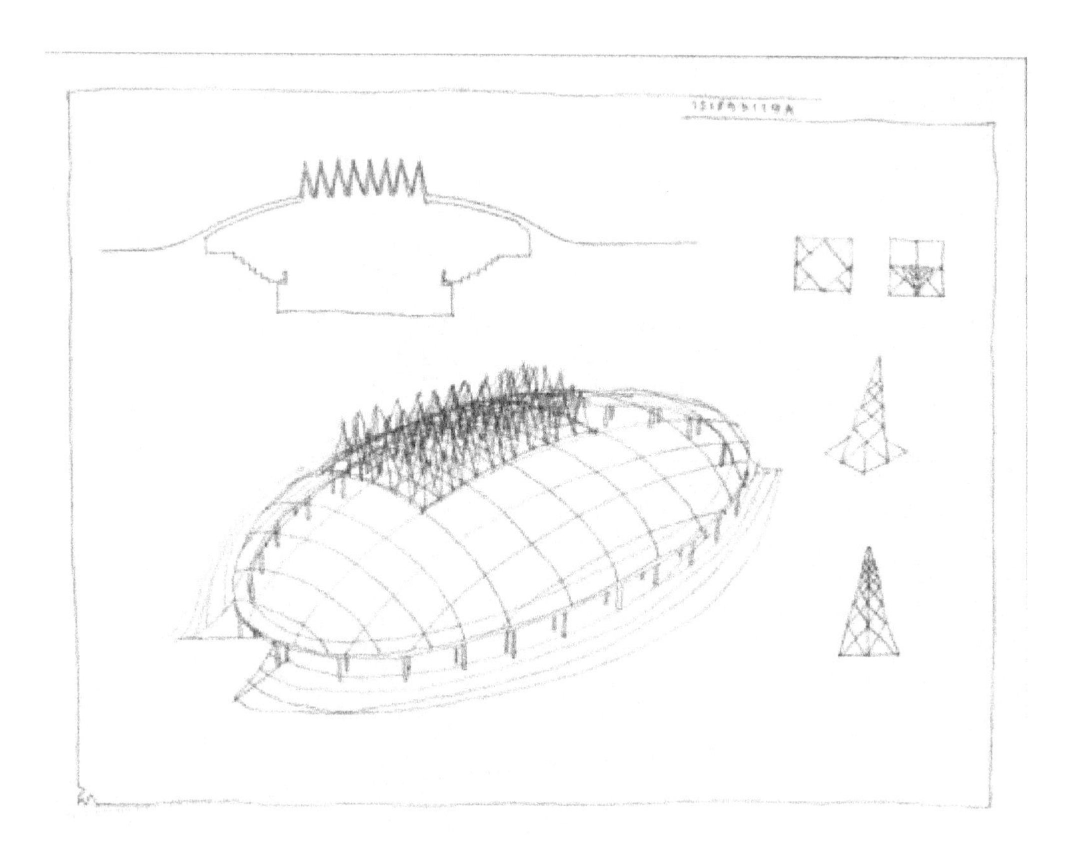

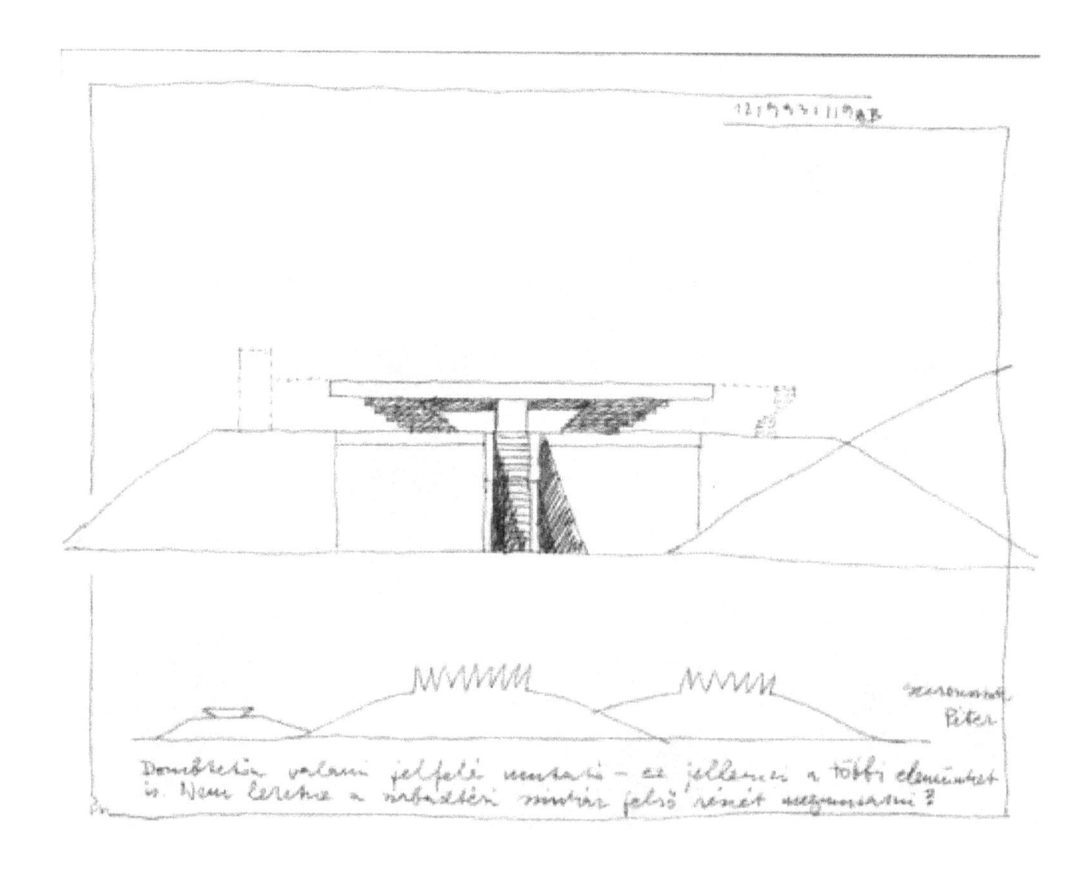
Dombtetőn valami felfelé mutató – ez jellemzi a többi elemünket
is. Nem lehetne a szabadtéri színház felső részét
Péter

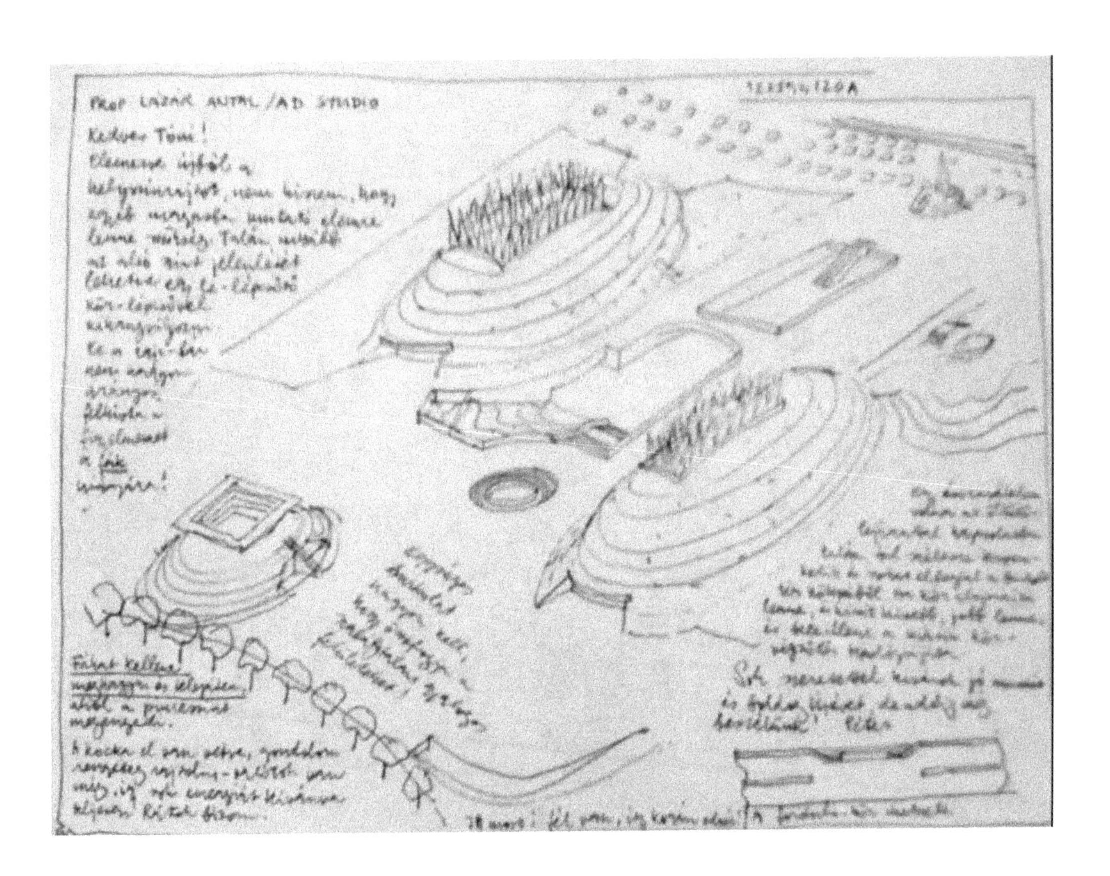
PROF LÁZÁR ANTAL / AD STUDIO
Kedves Tóni!

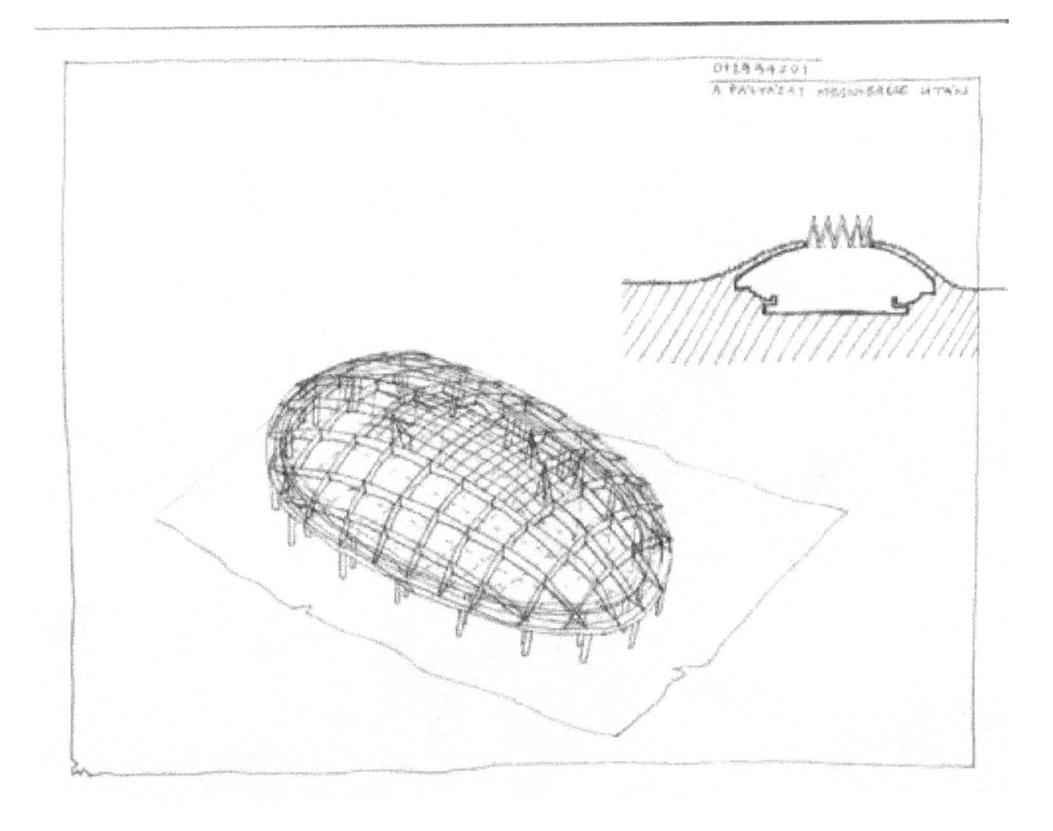
A PÁLYÁZAT MEGNYERÉSE UTÁN

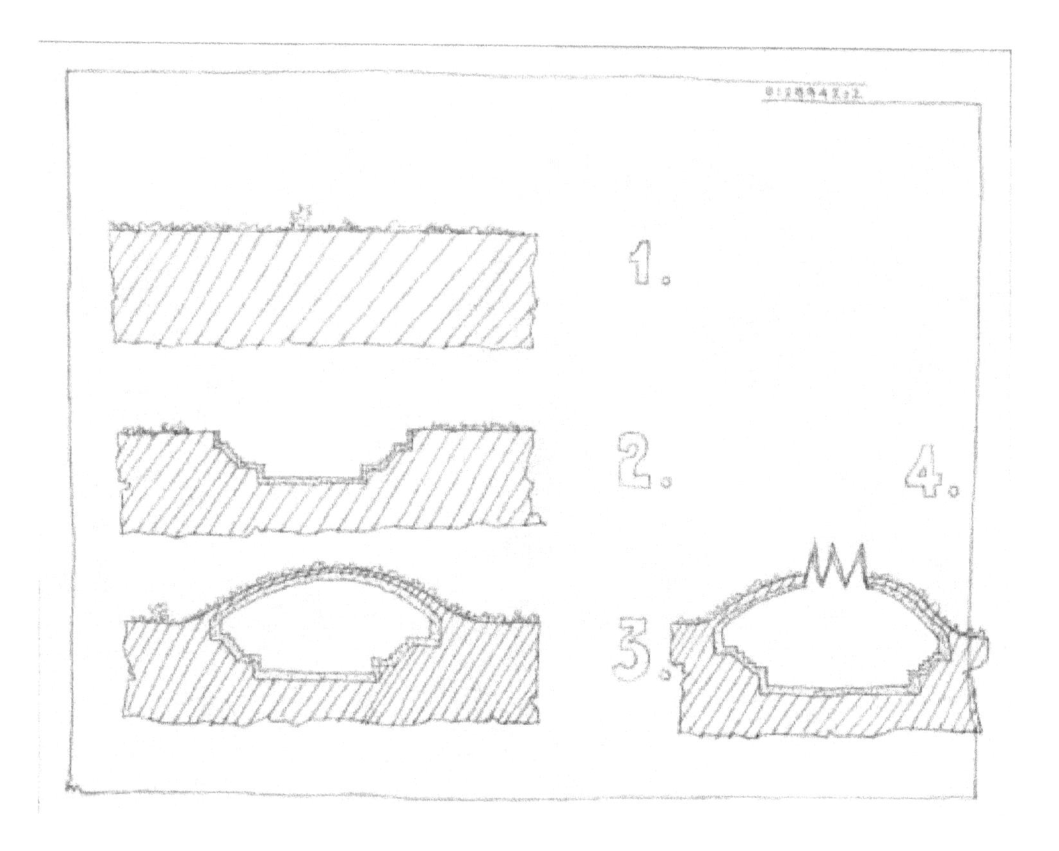

1.
2.
4.
3.

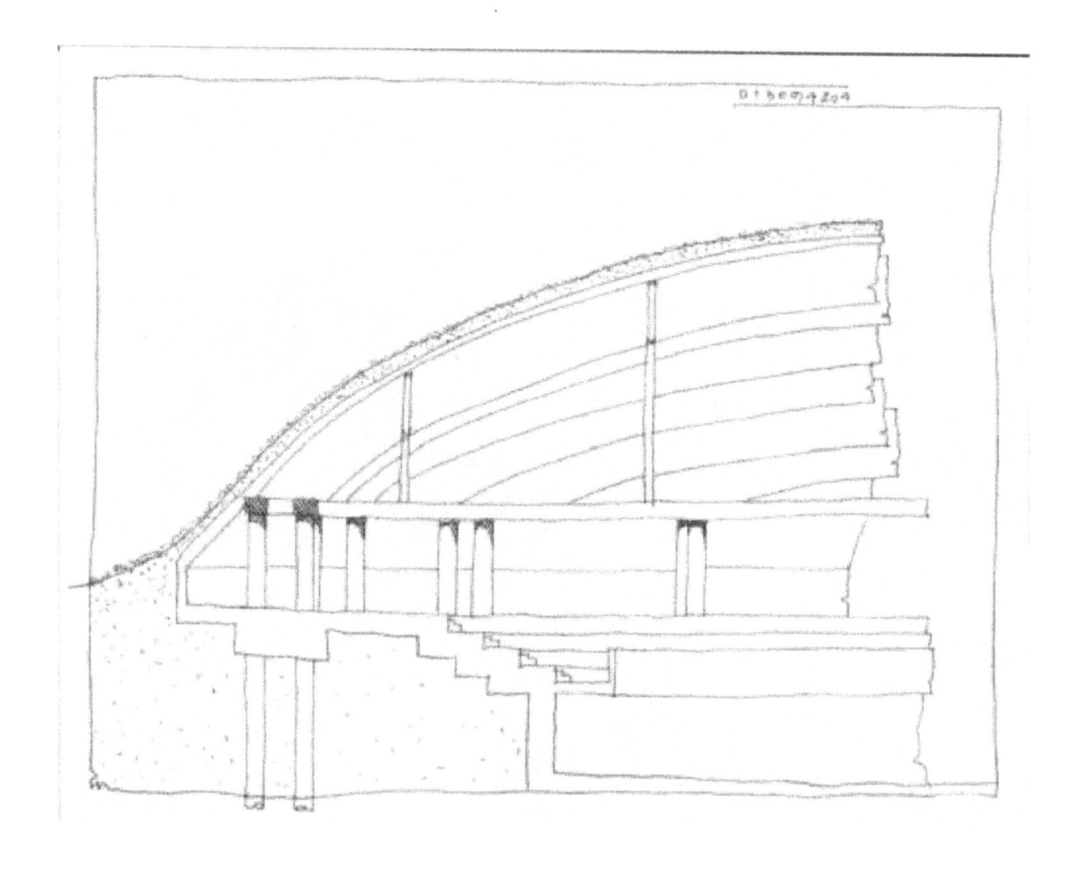

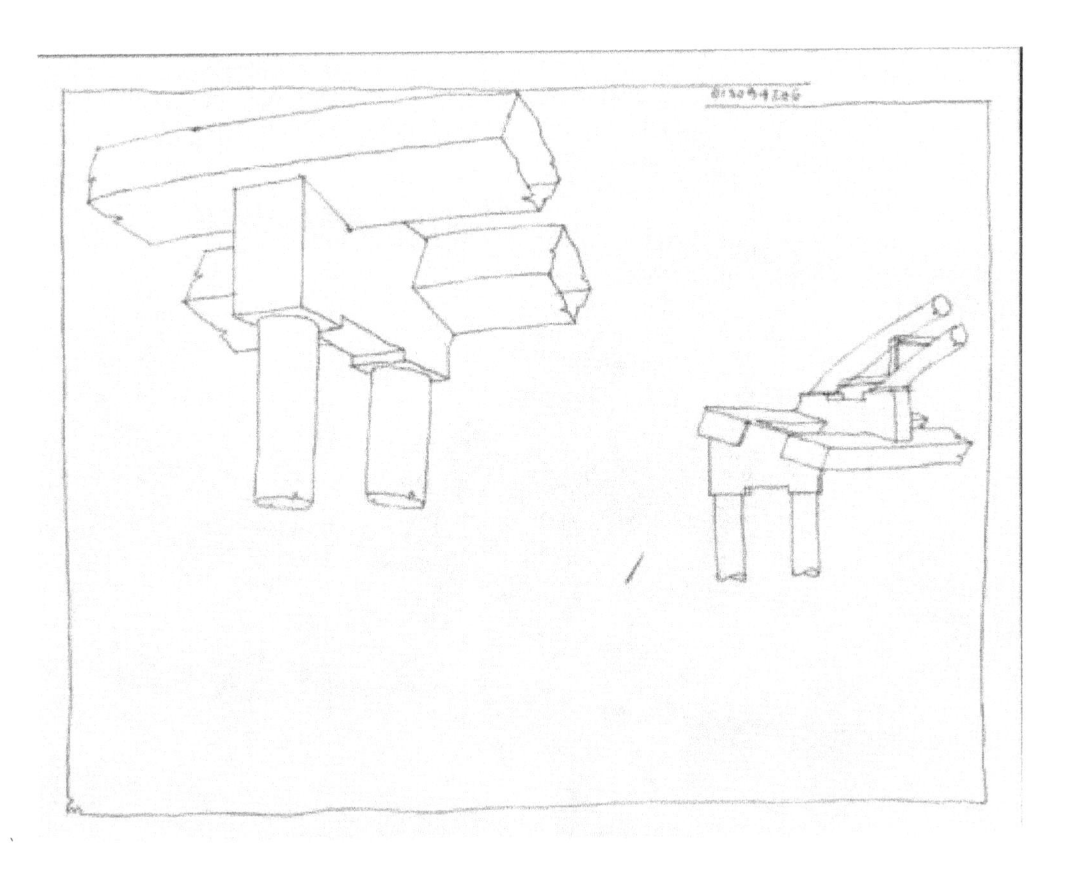

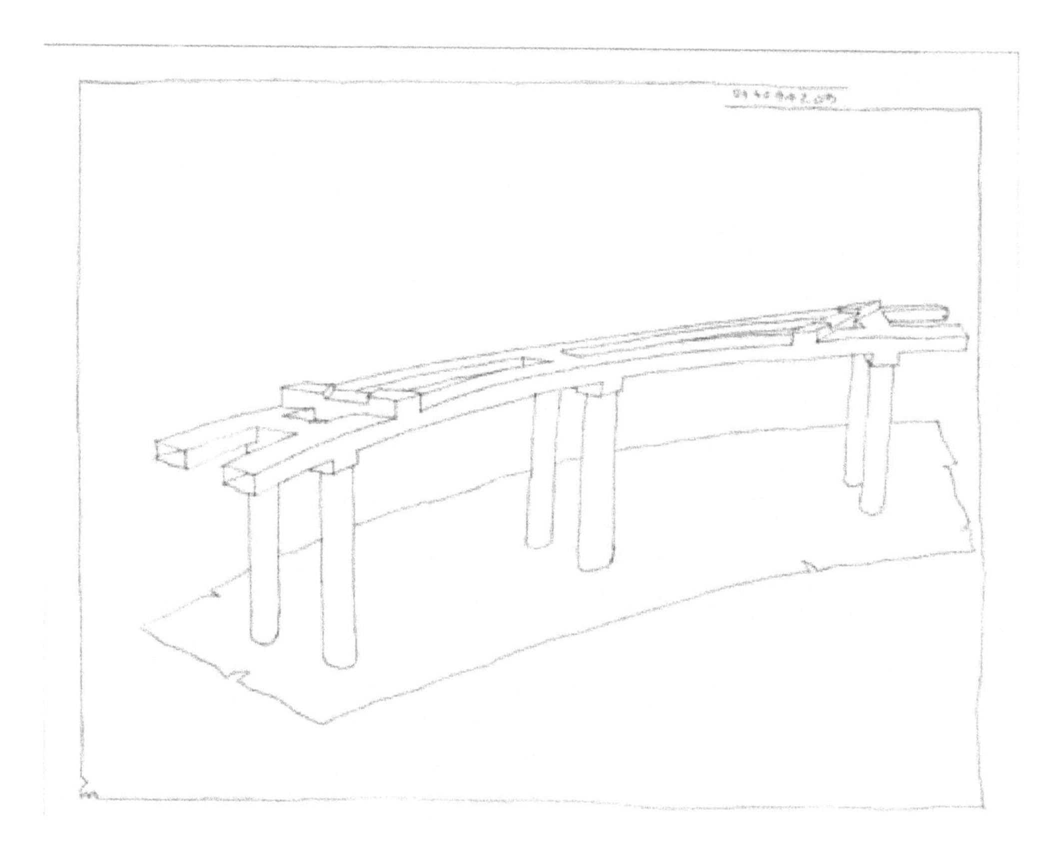

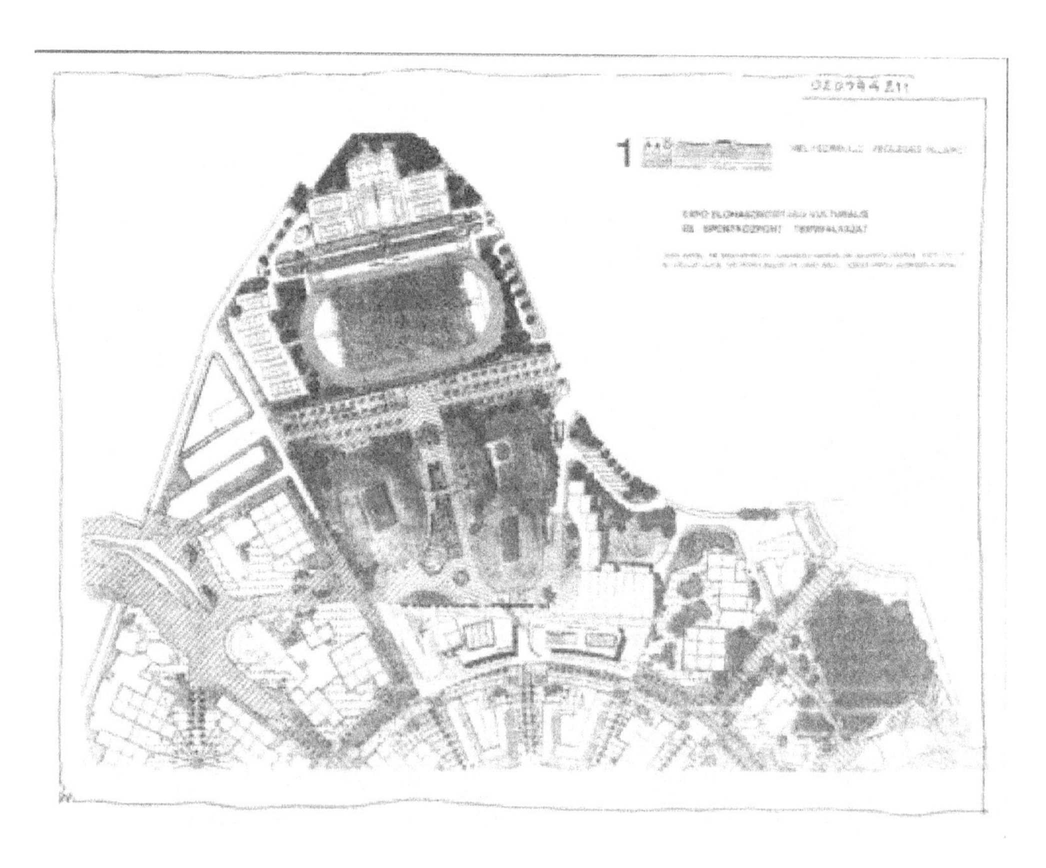

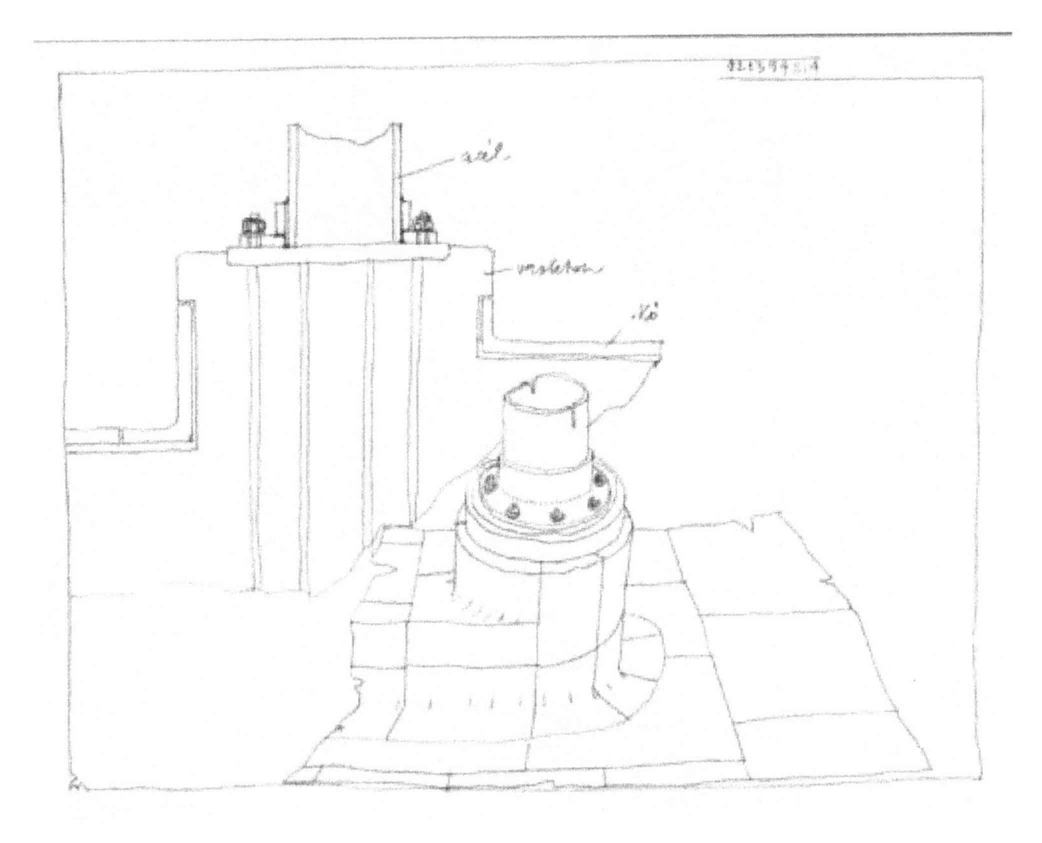

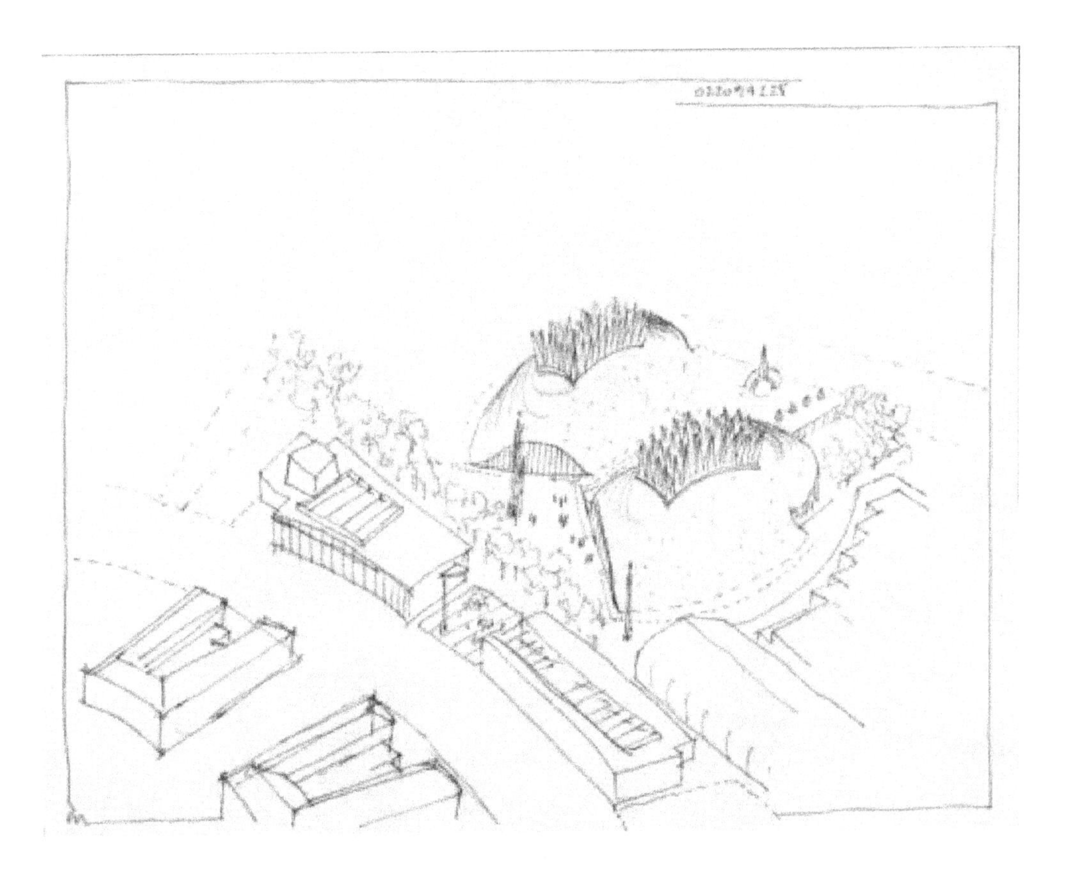

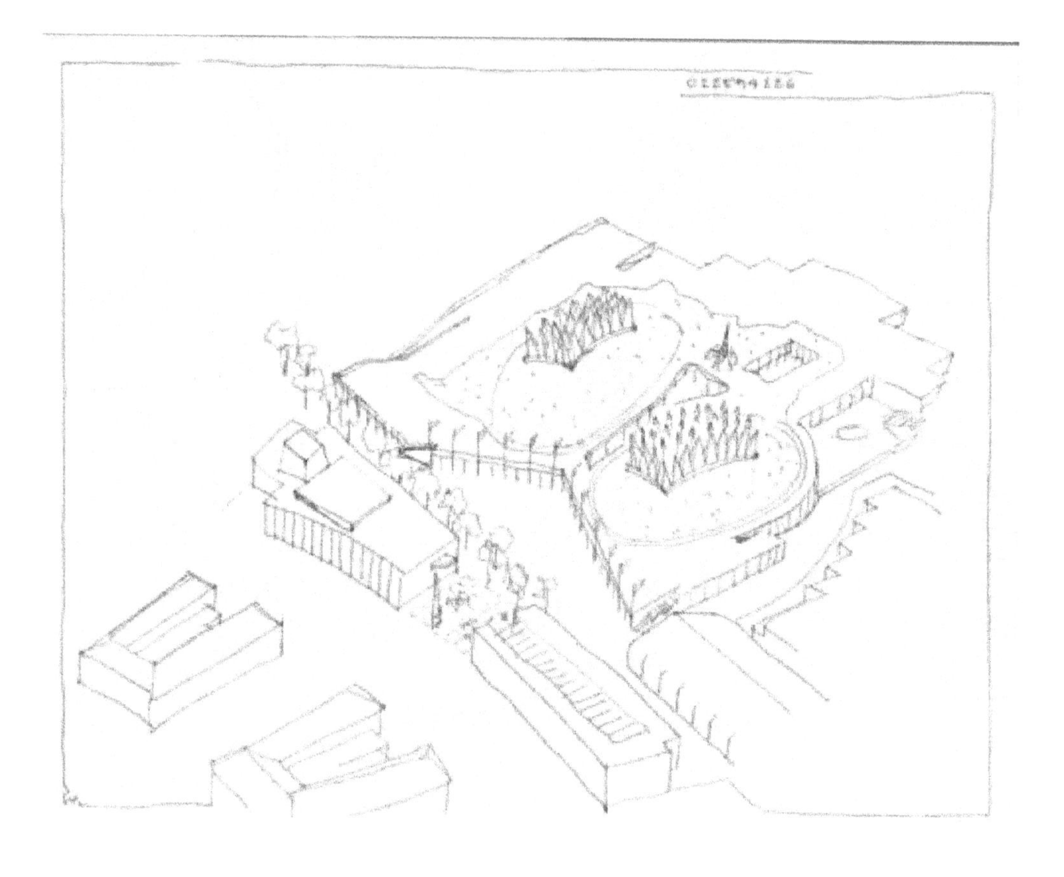

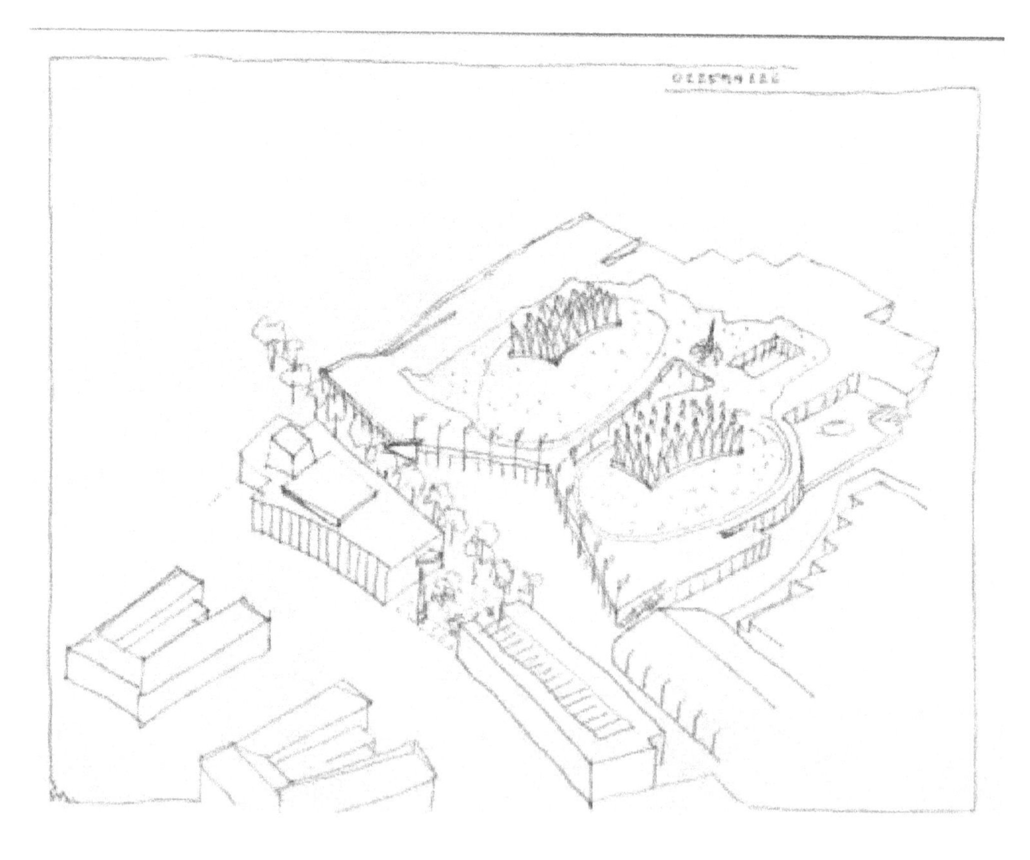

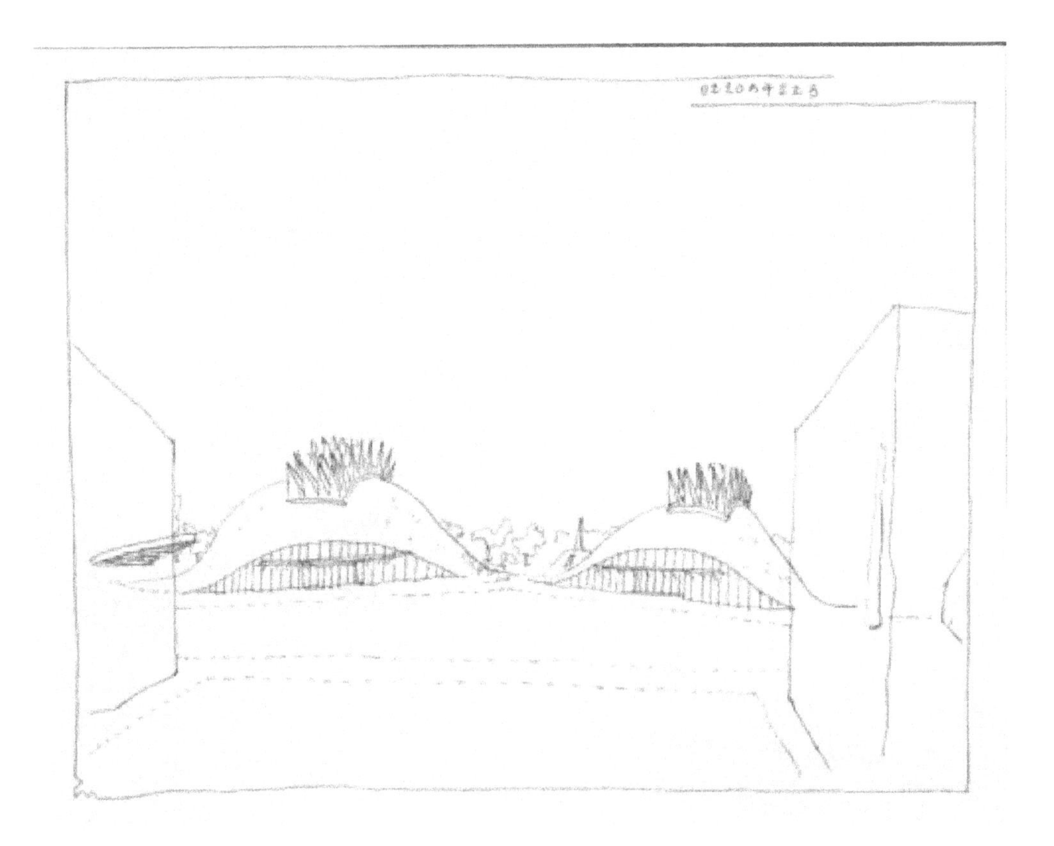

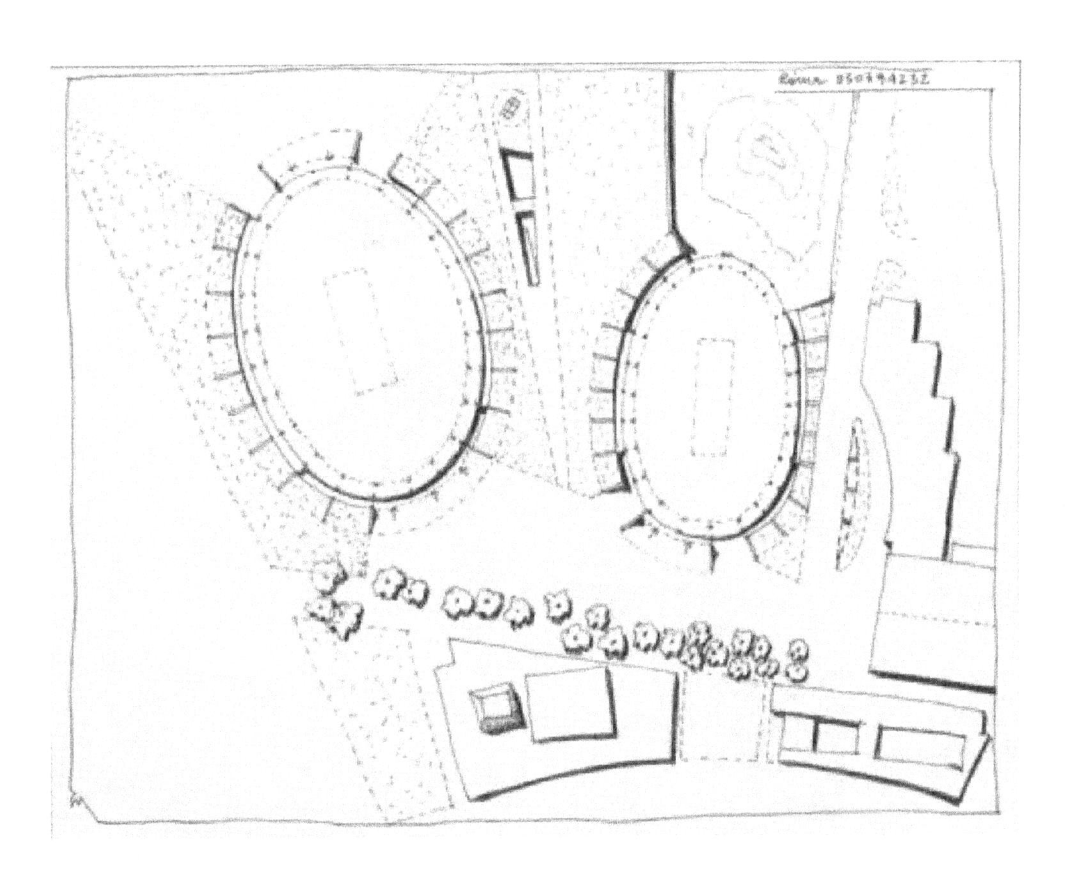

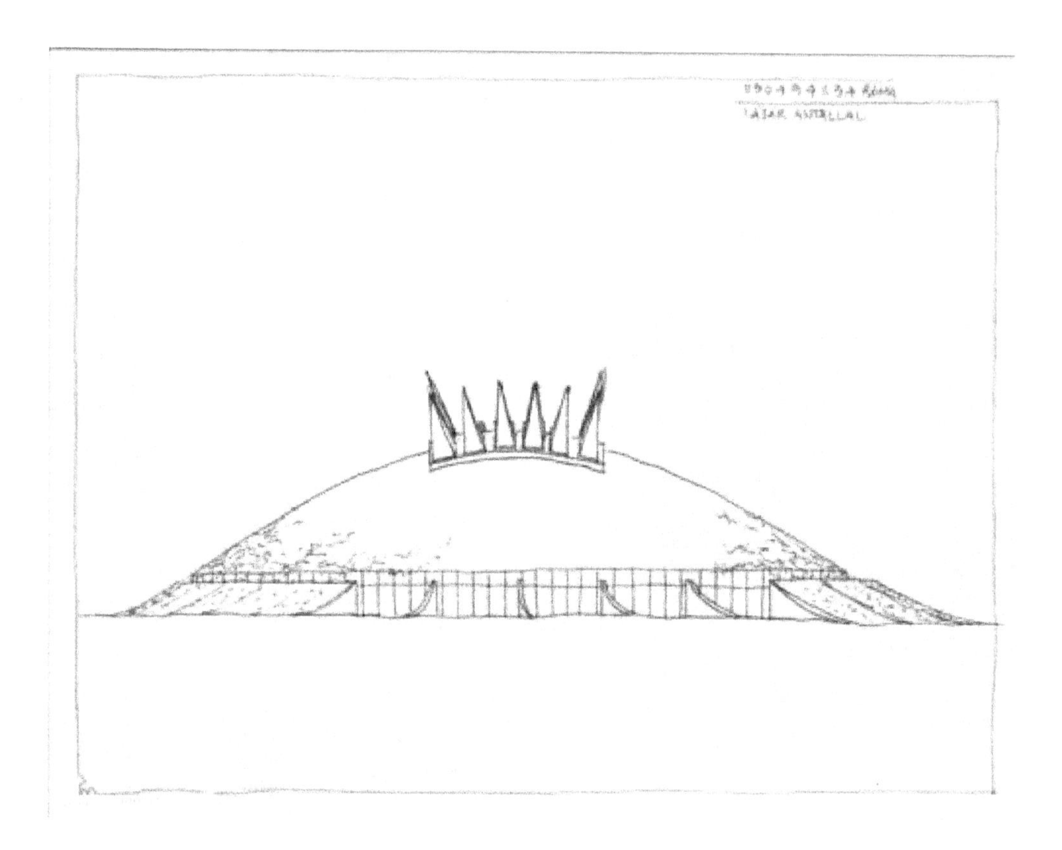

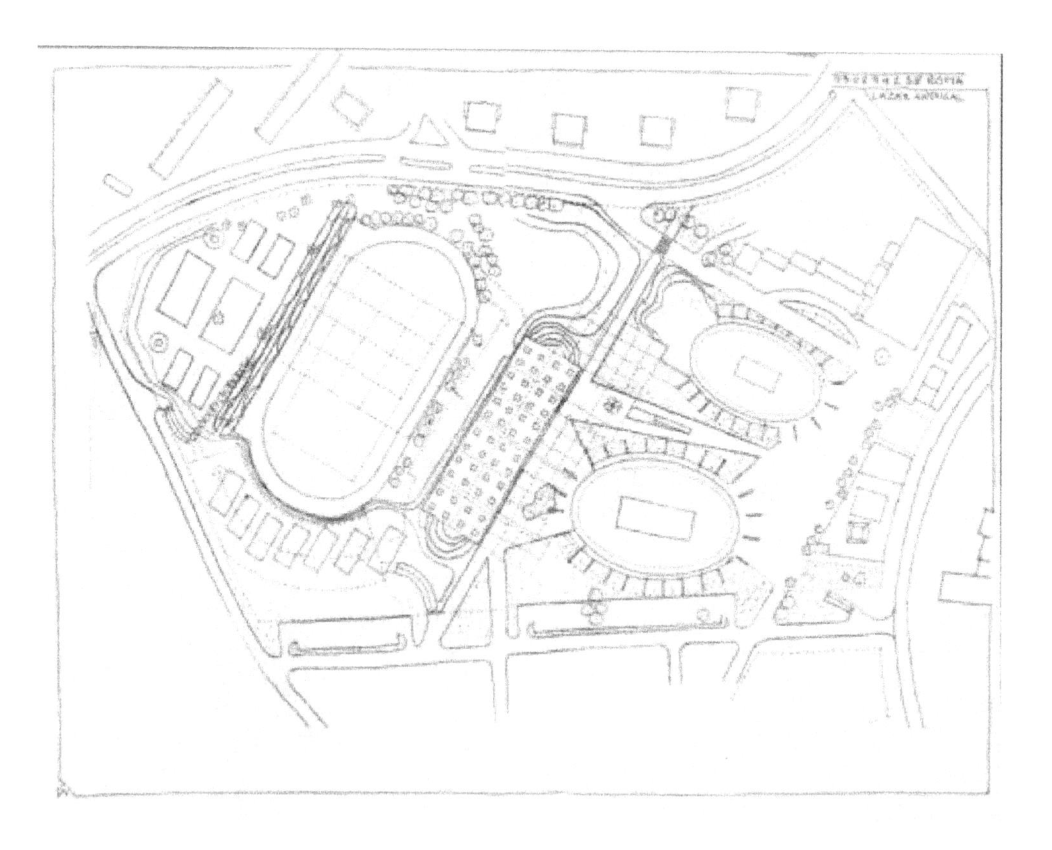

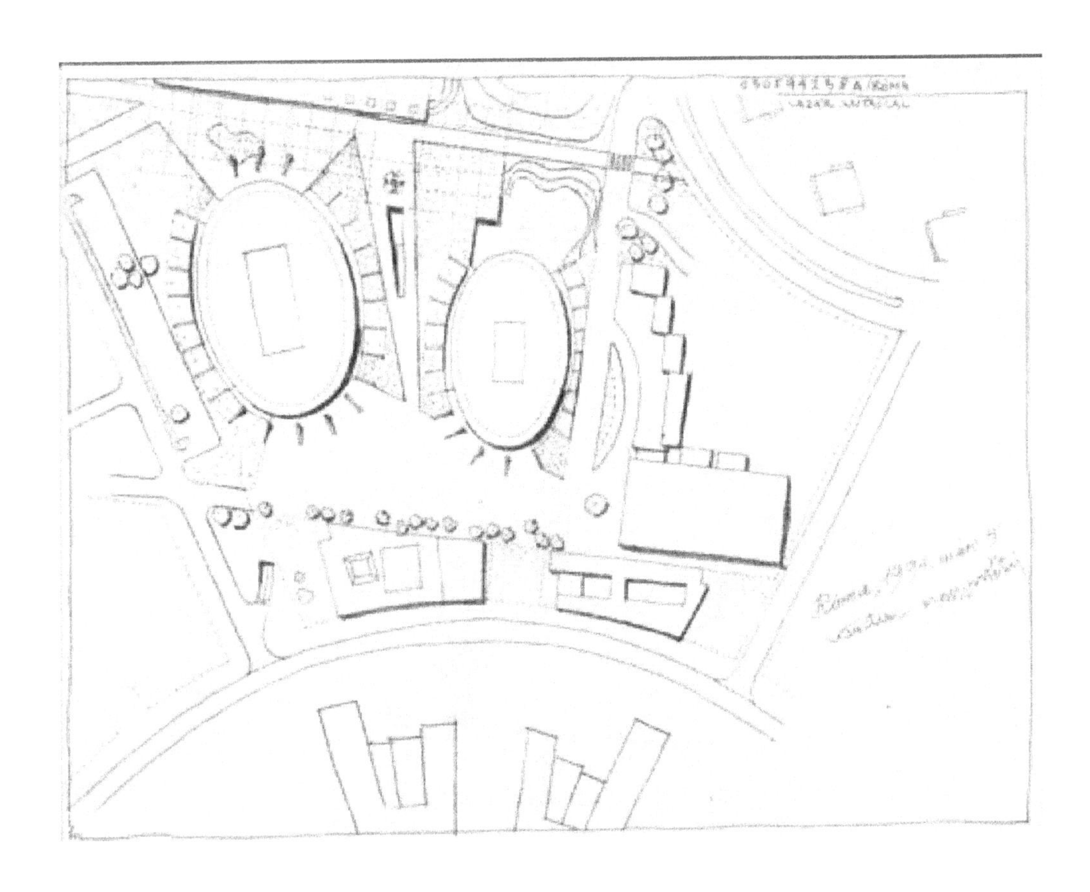

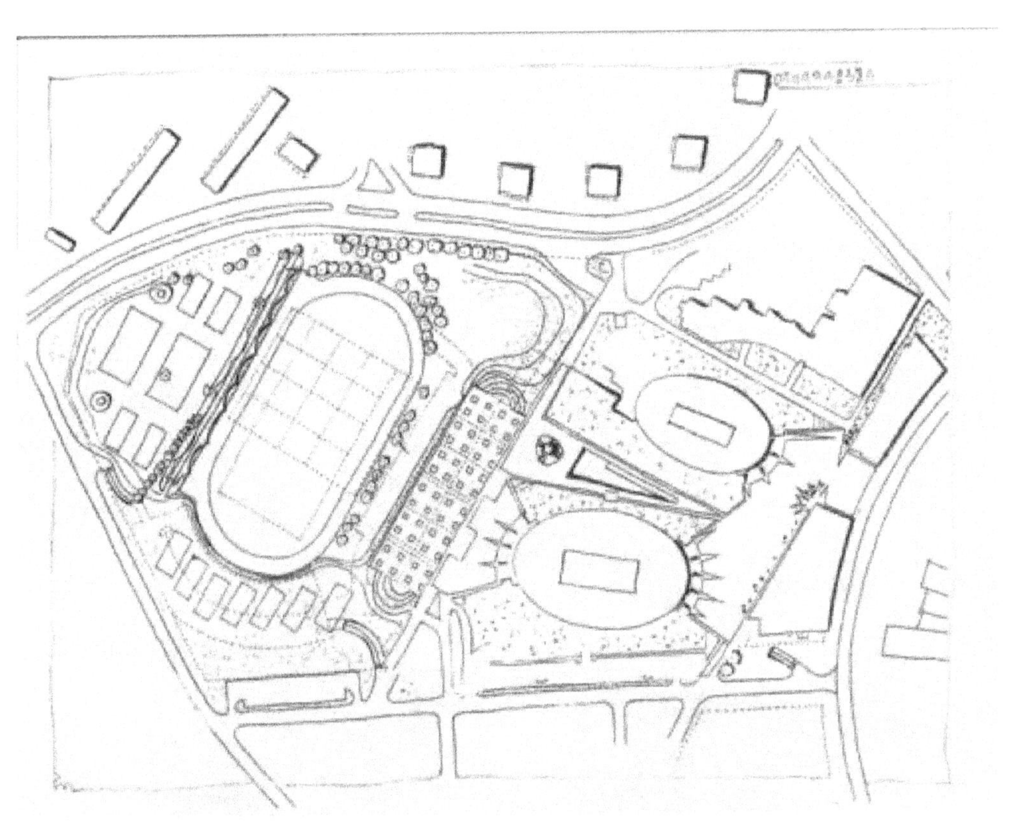

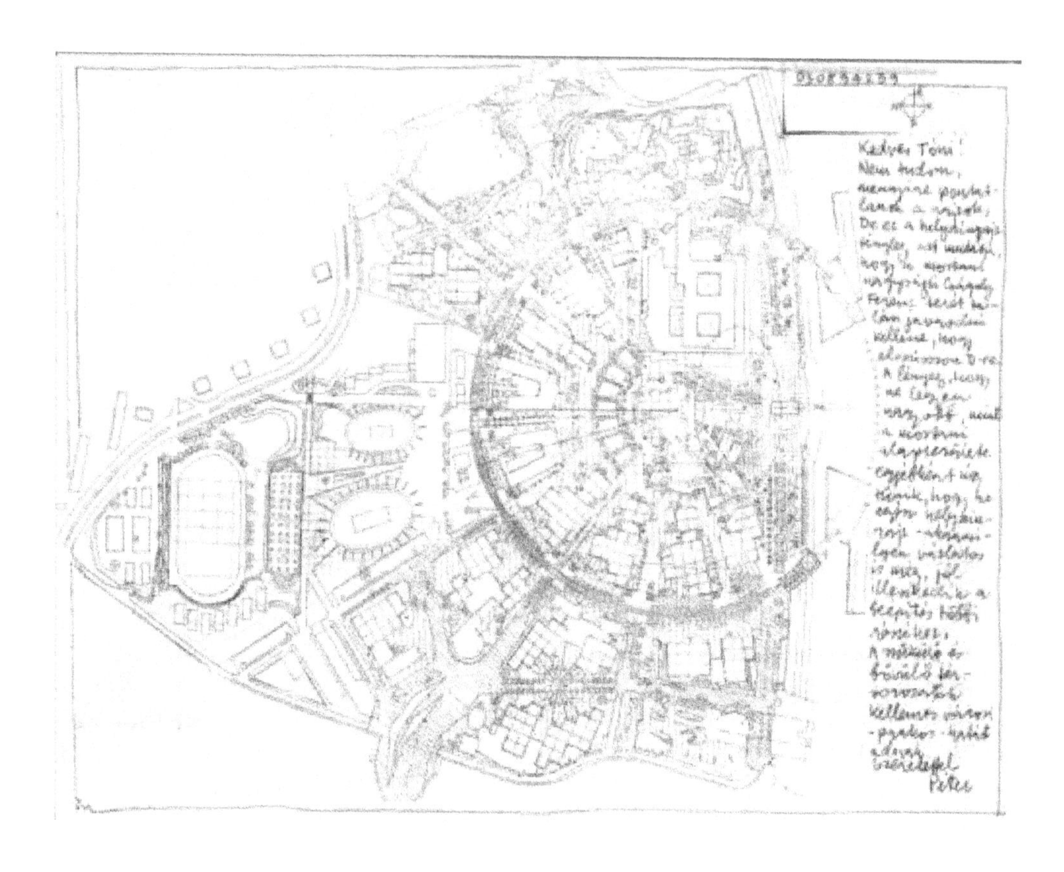
Kedves Tóni!
Nem tudom,
Péter

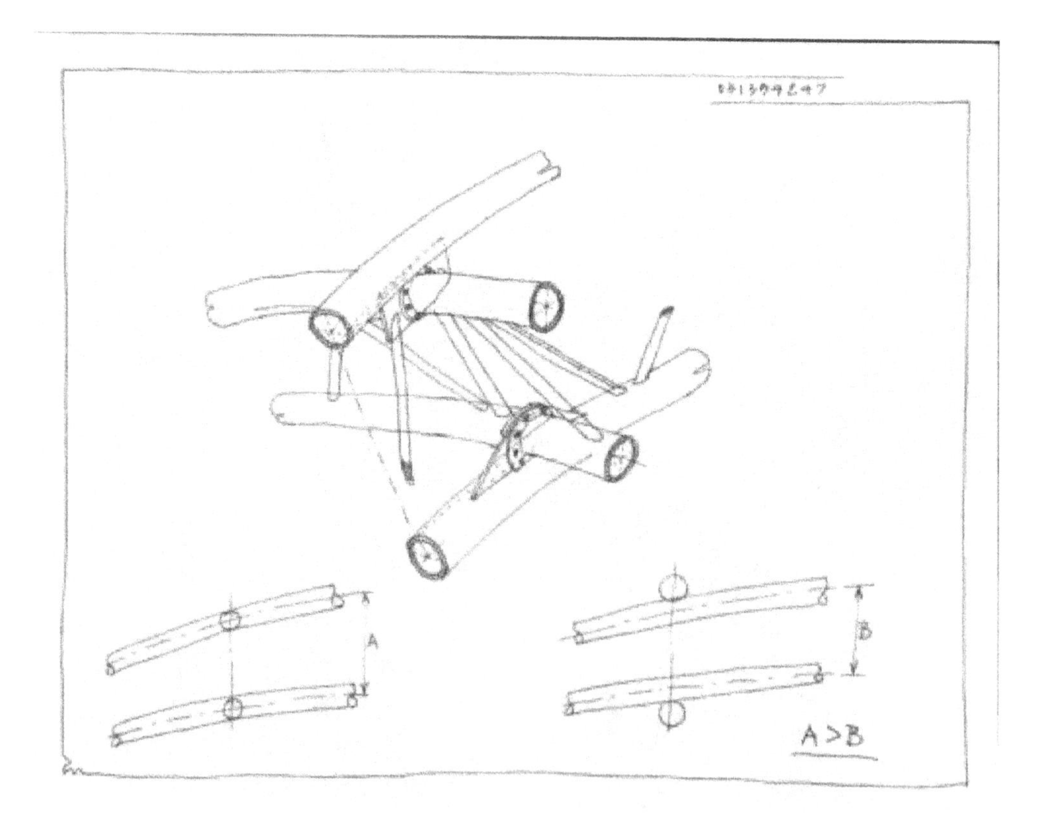
A
B
A>B

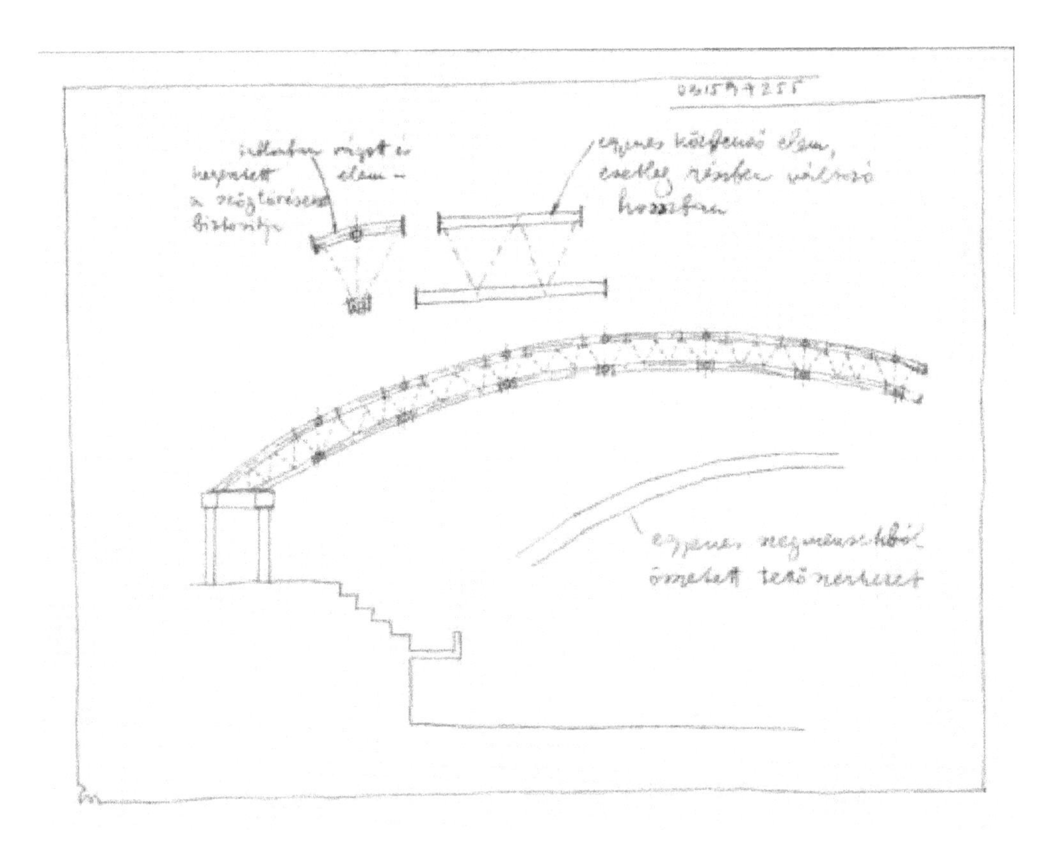

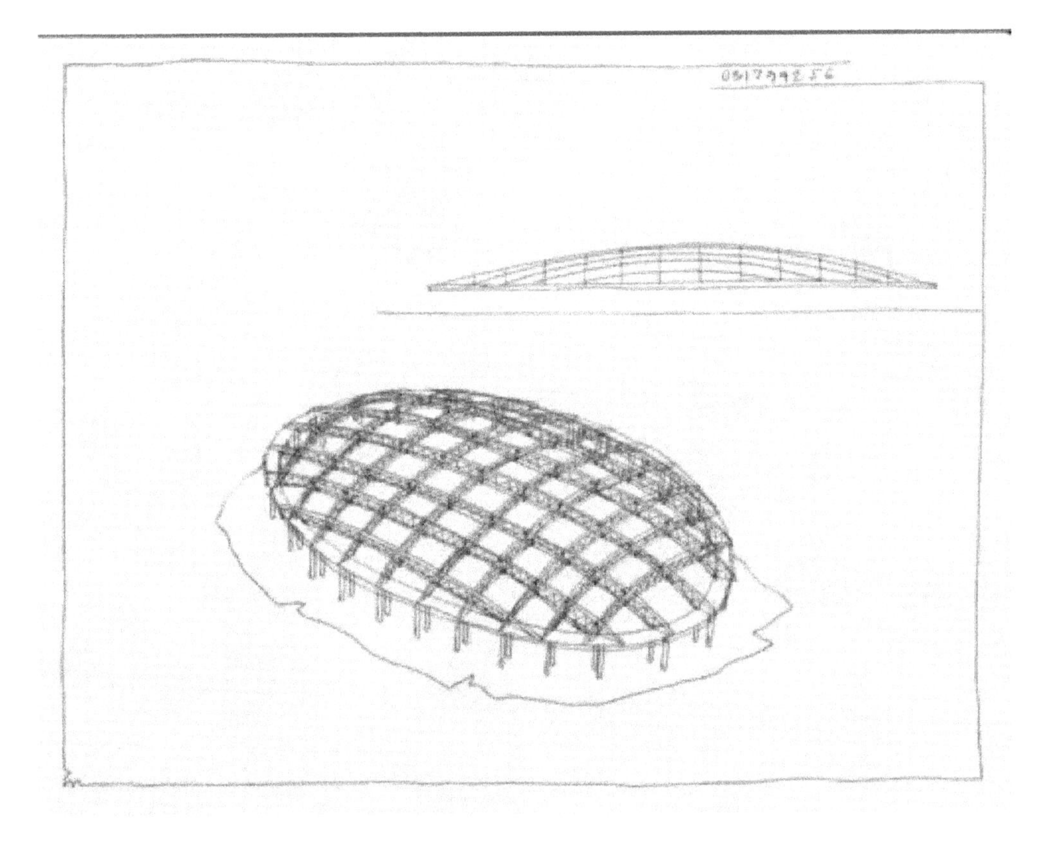

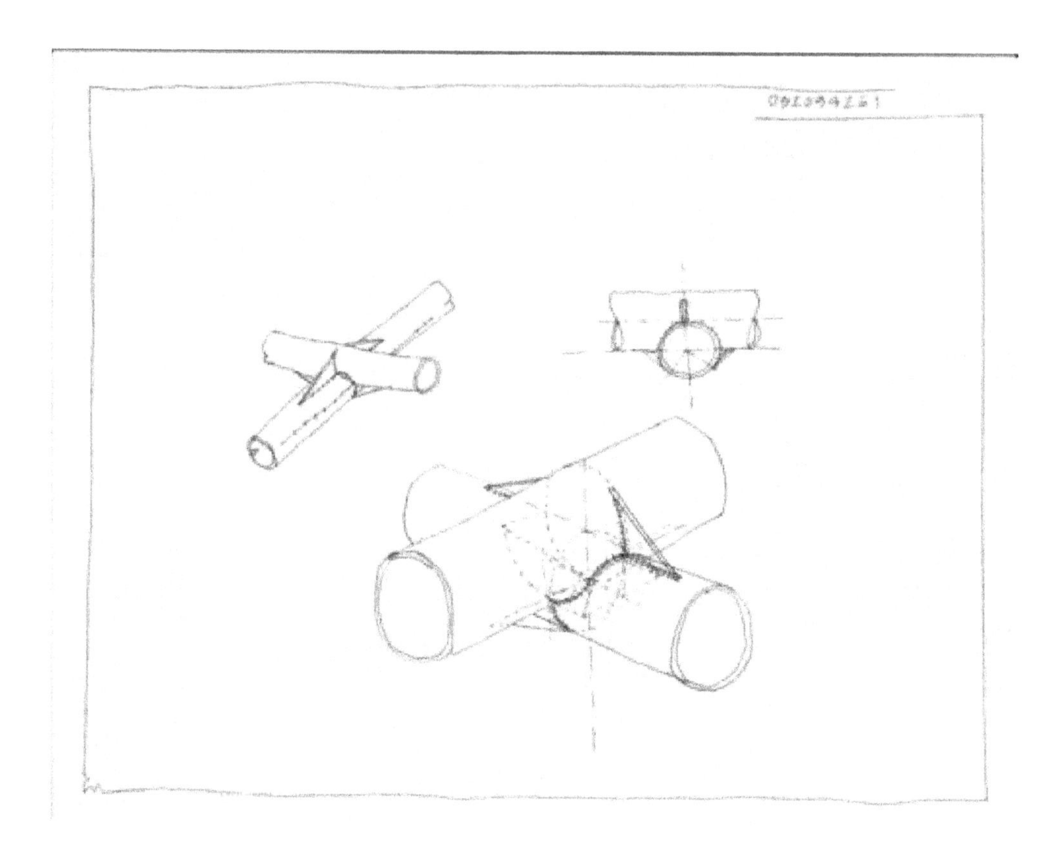

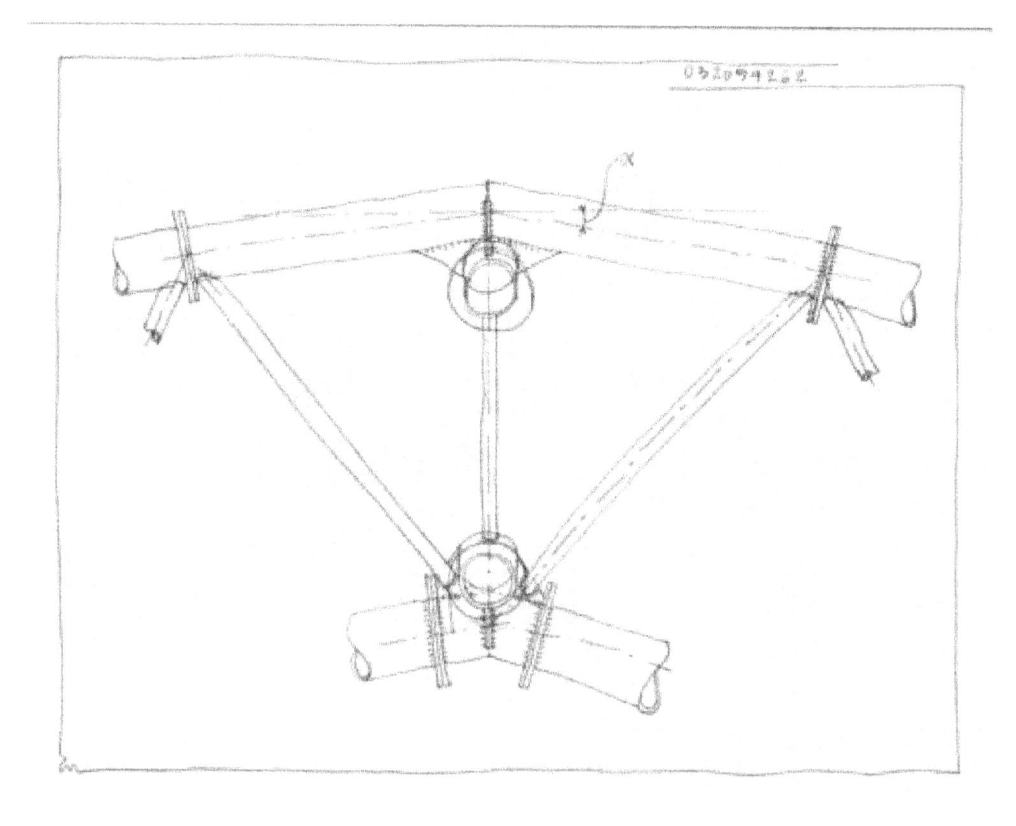

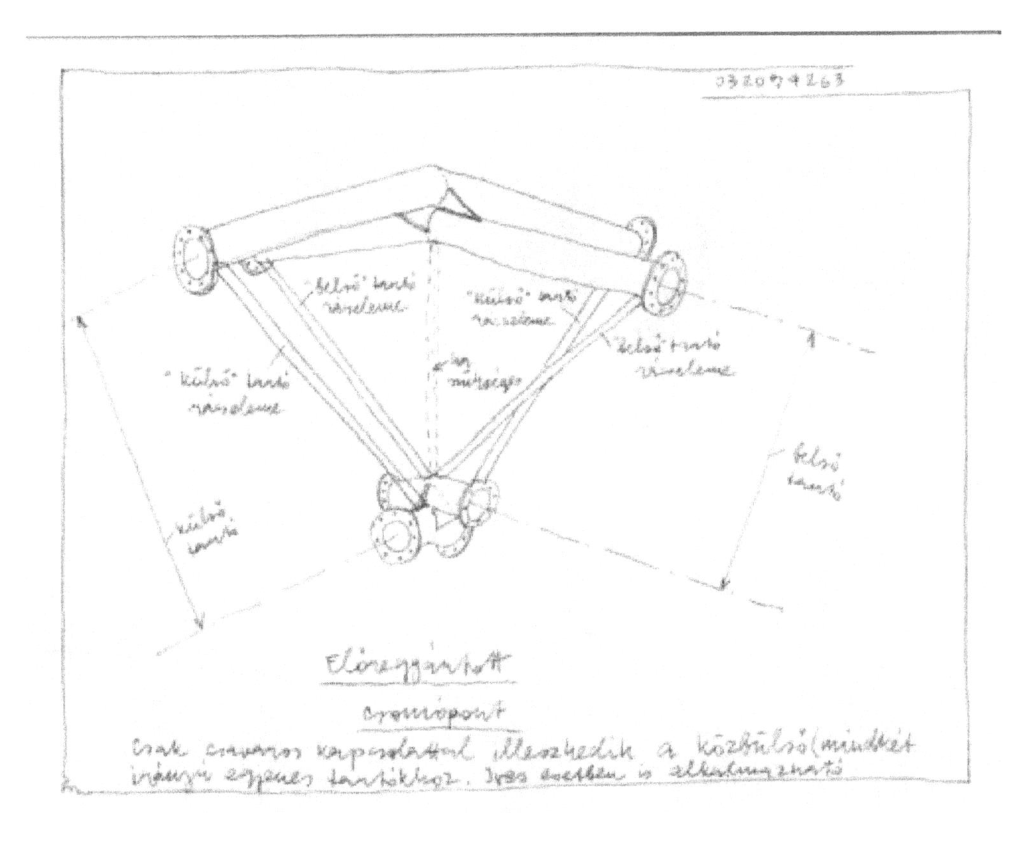
"belső" tartó rácseleme
"külső" tartó rácseleme
"külső" tartó rácseleme
"belső" tartó rácseleme
belső tartó
külső tartó
Előregyártott
csomópont
Csak csavaros kapcsolattal illeszkedik a közbülső (mindkét irányú egyenes tartókhoz. Íves esetben is alkalmazható

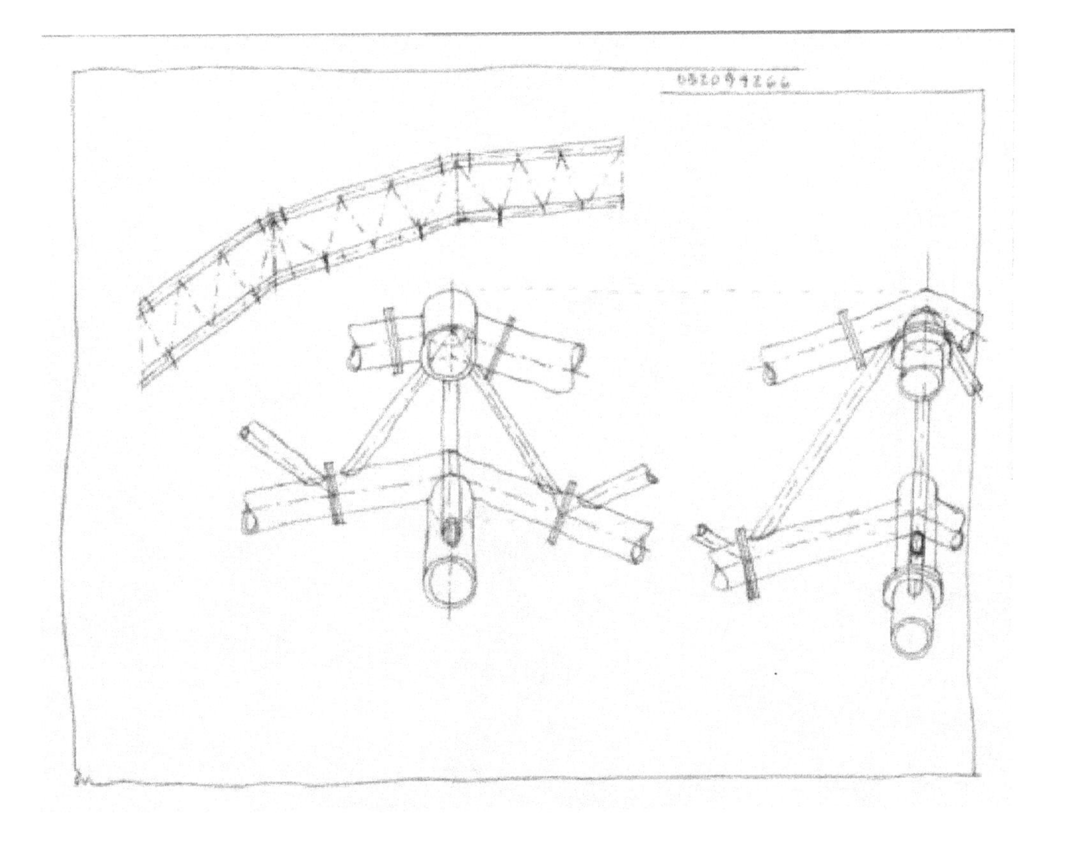

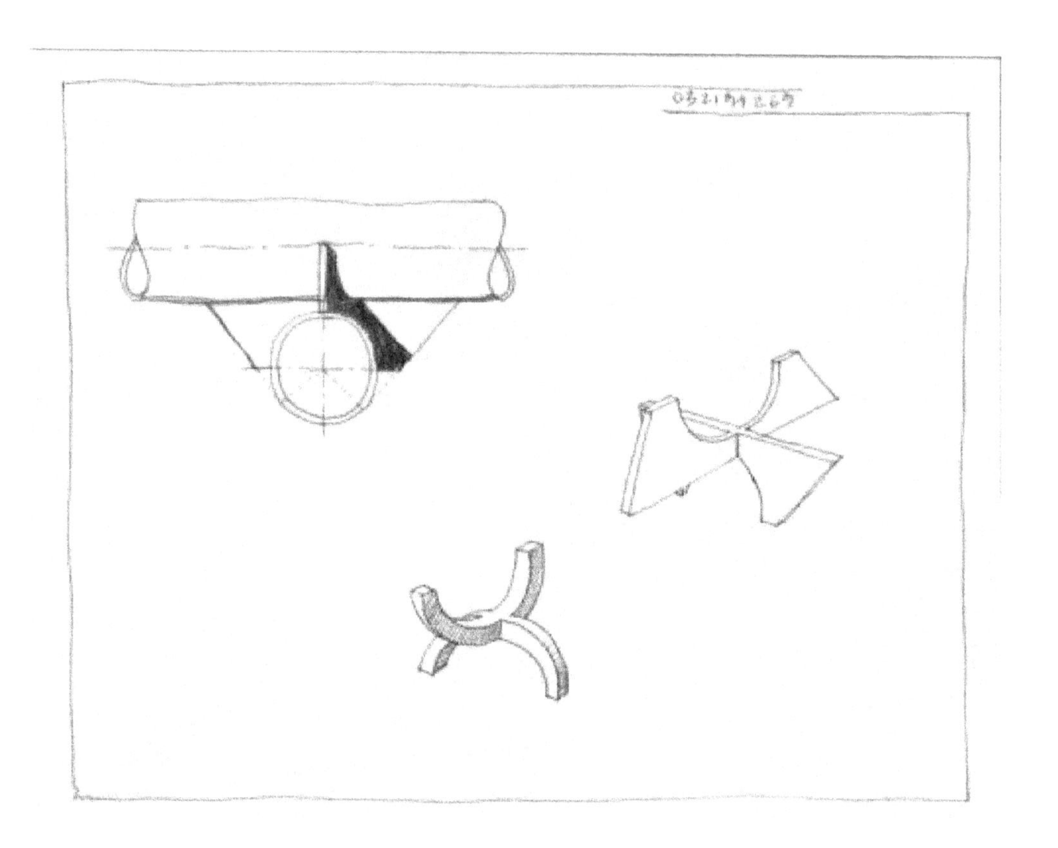

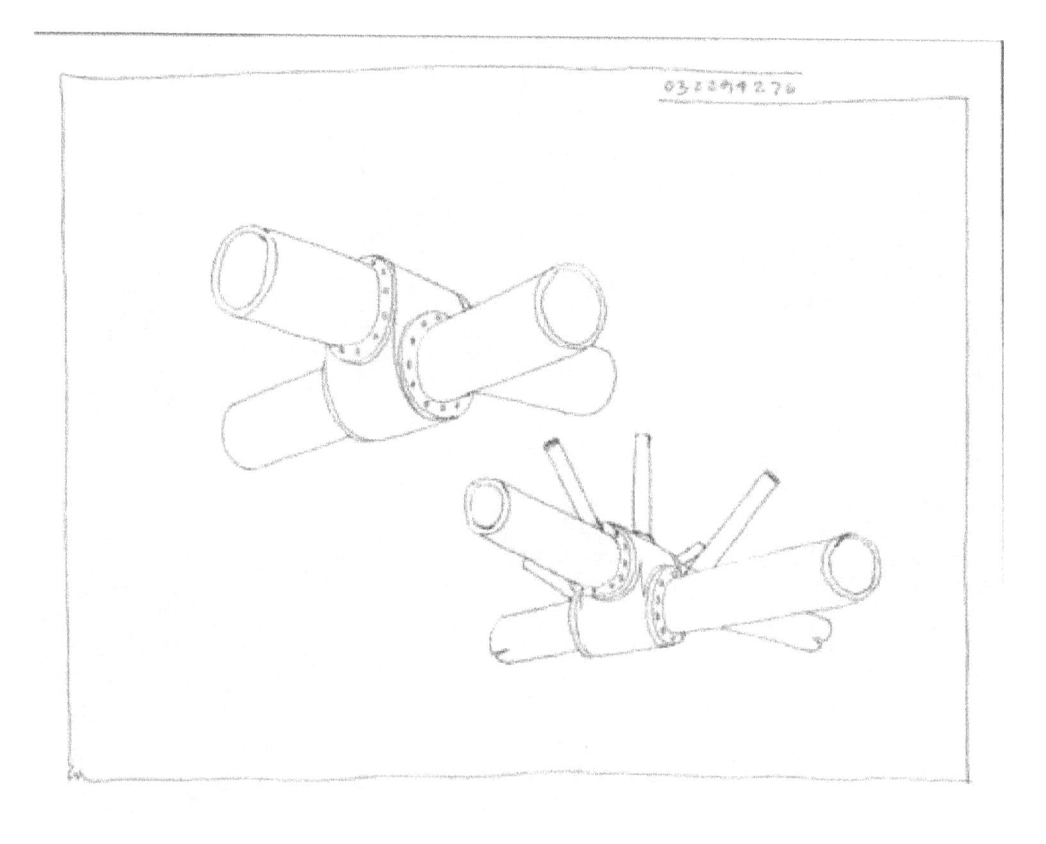

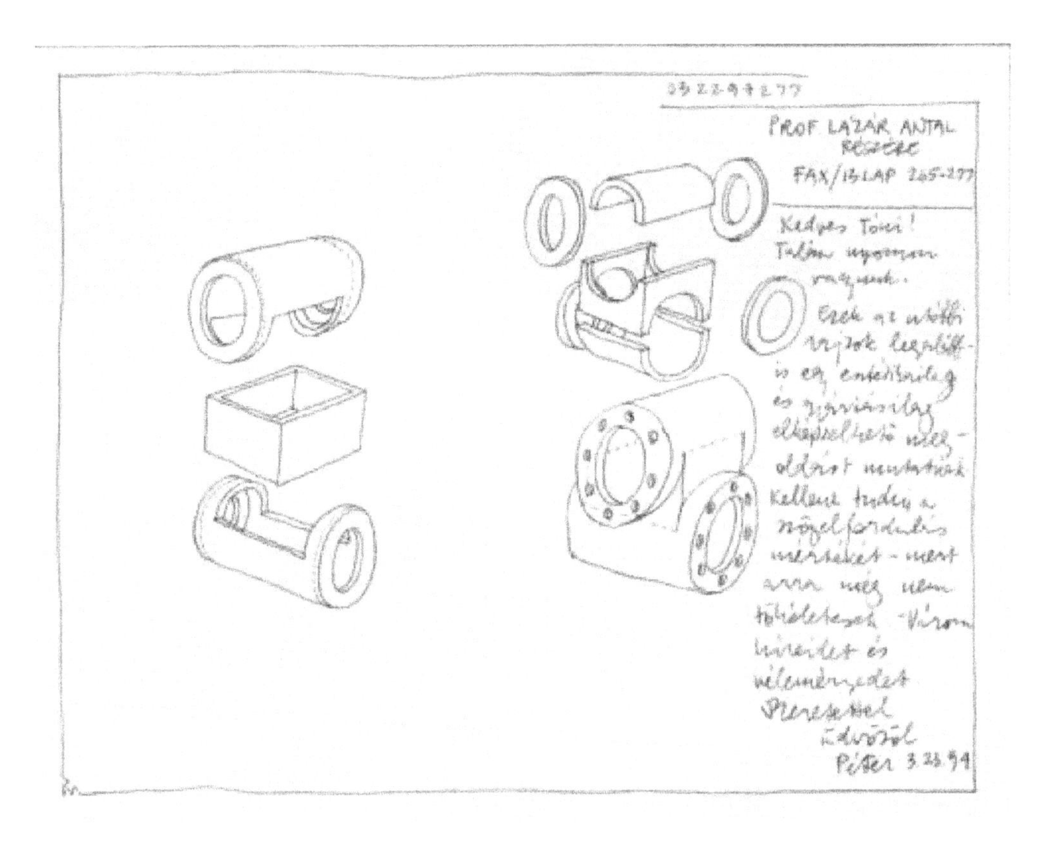
PROF. LÁZÁR ANTAL
RÉSZÉRE
Kedves Töni!

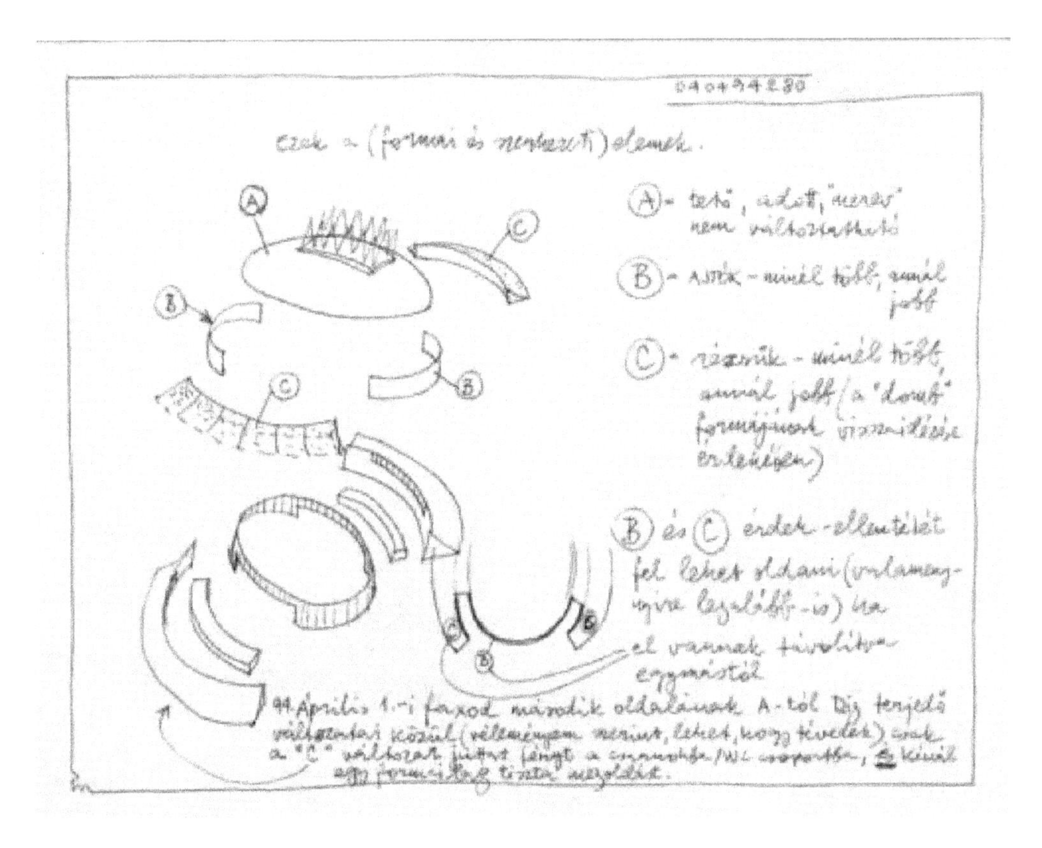
Ezek a (formai és szerkezeti) elemek.
A
B
C

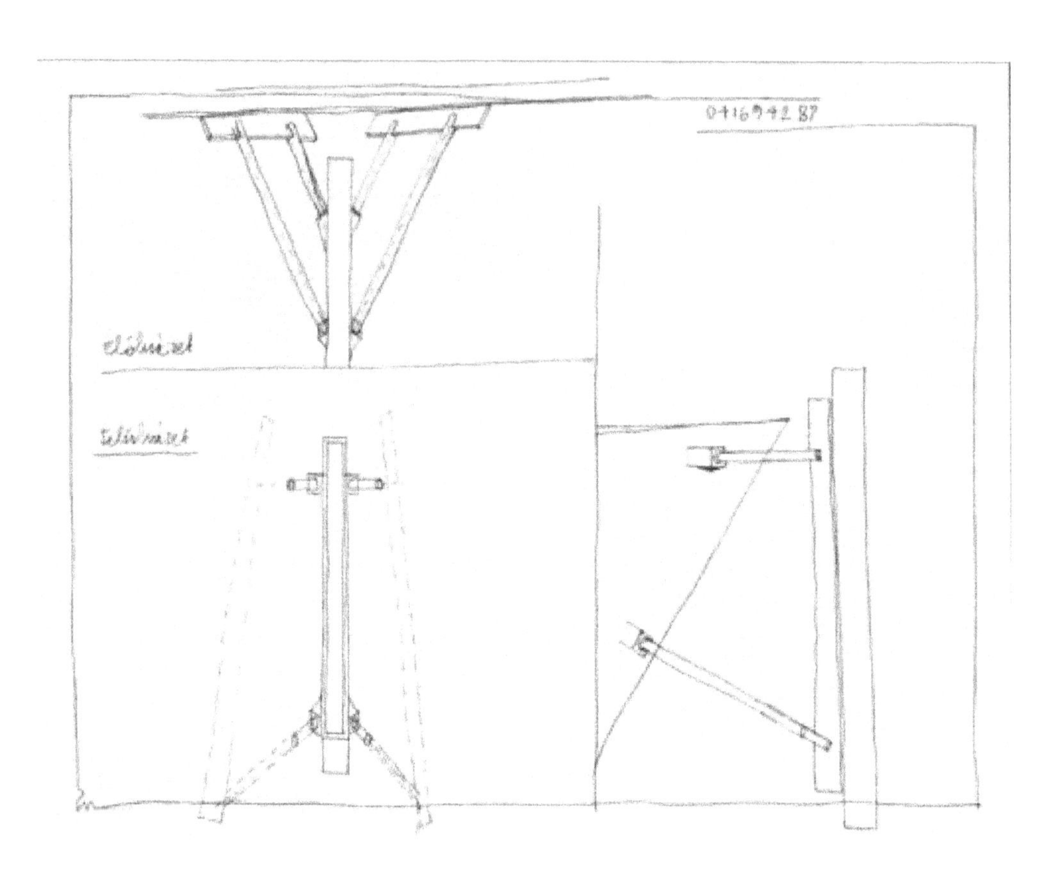
0416942 87
elölnézet

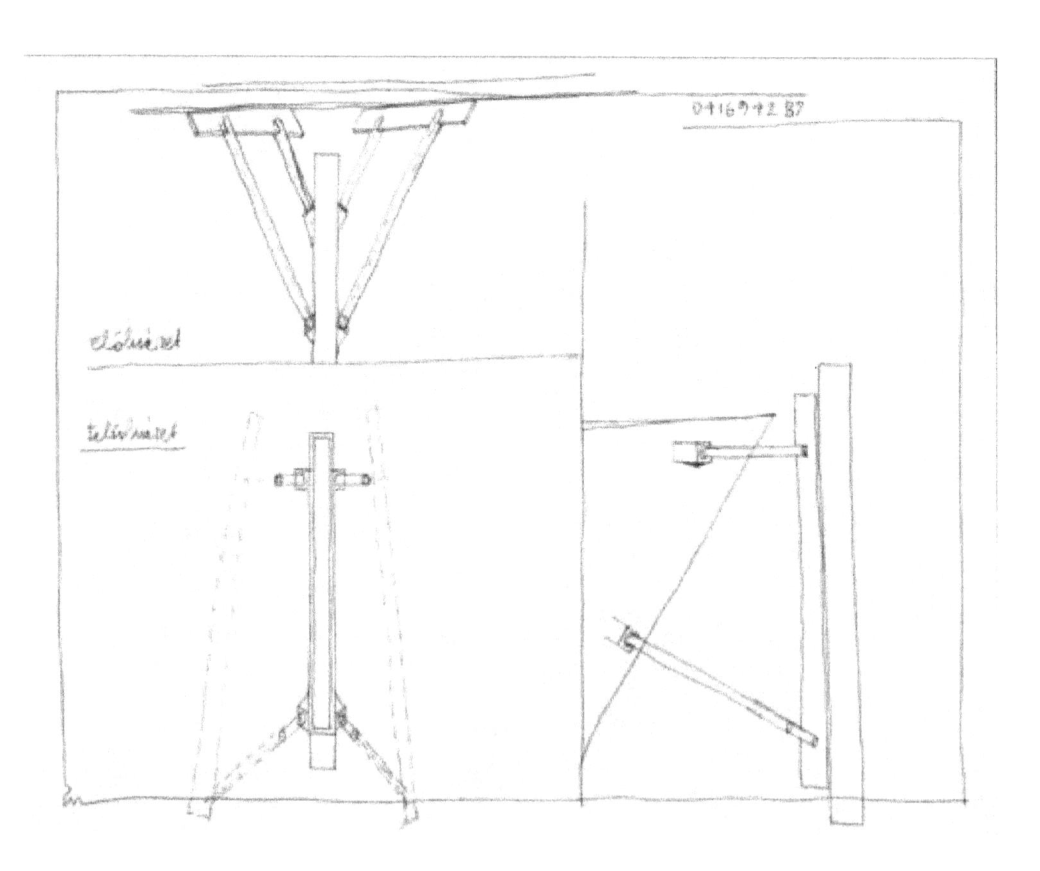
0416942 87
elölnézet

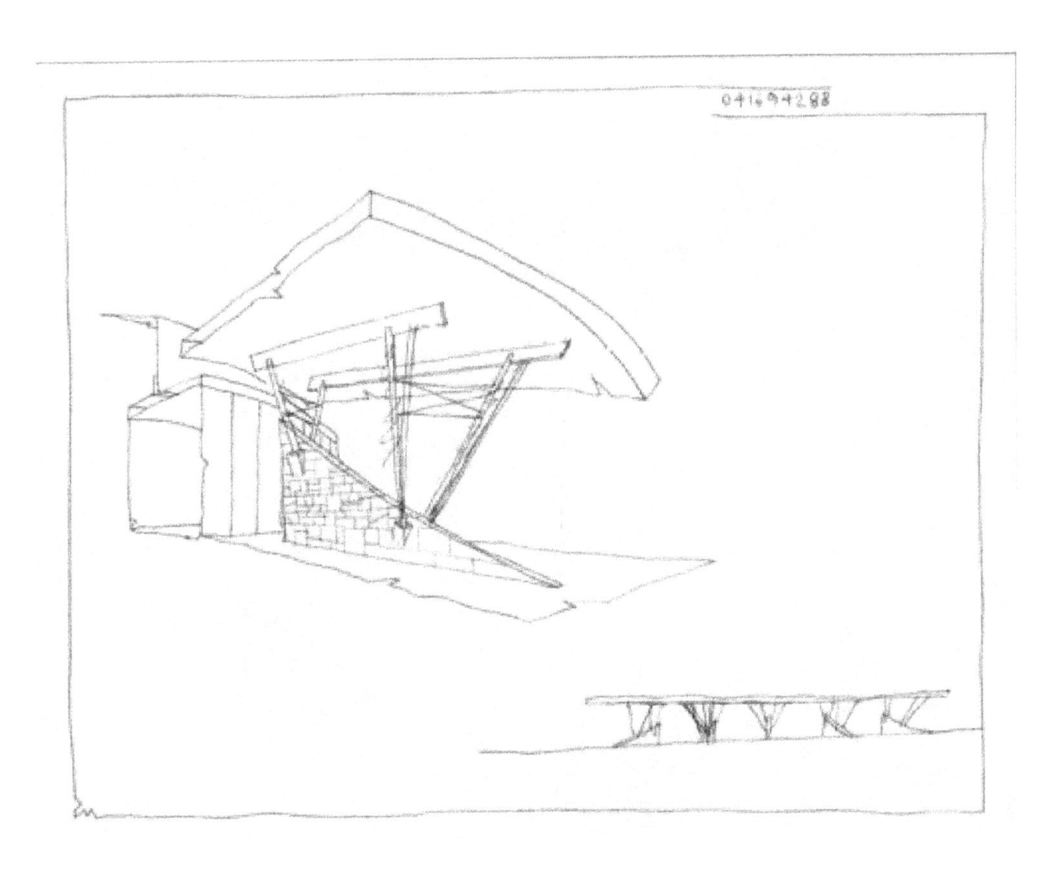
041694288

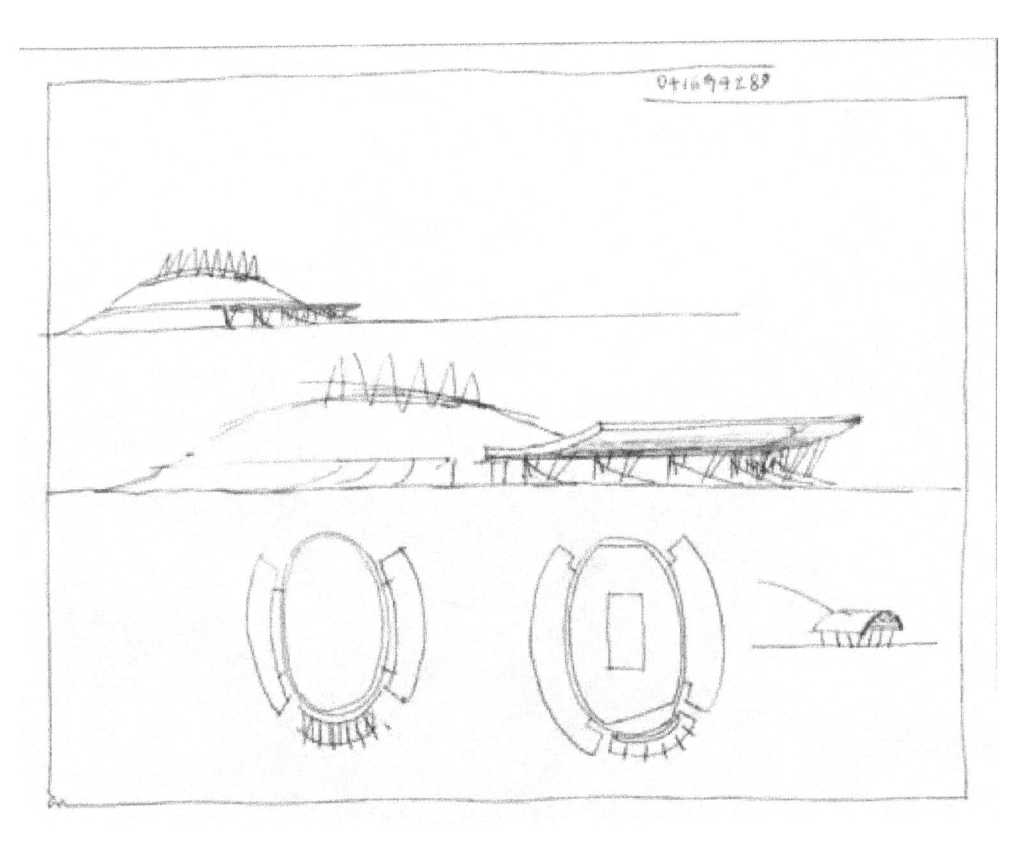
041694289

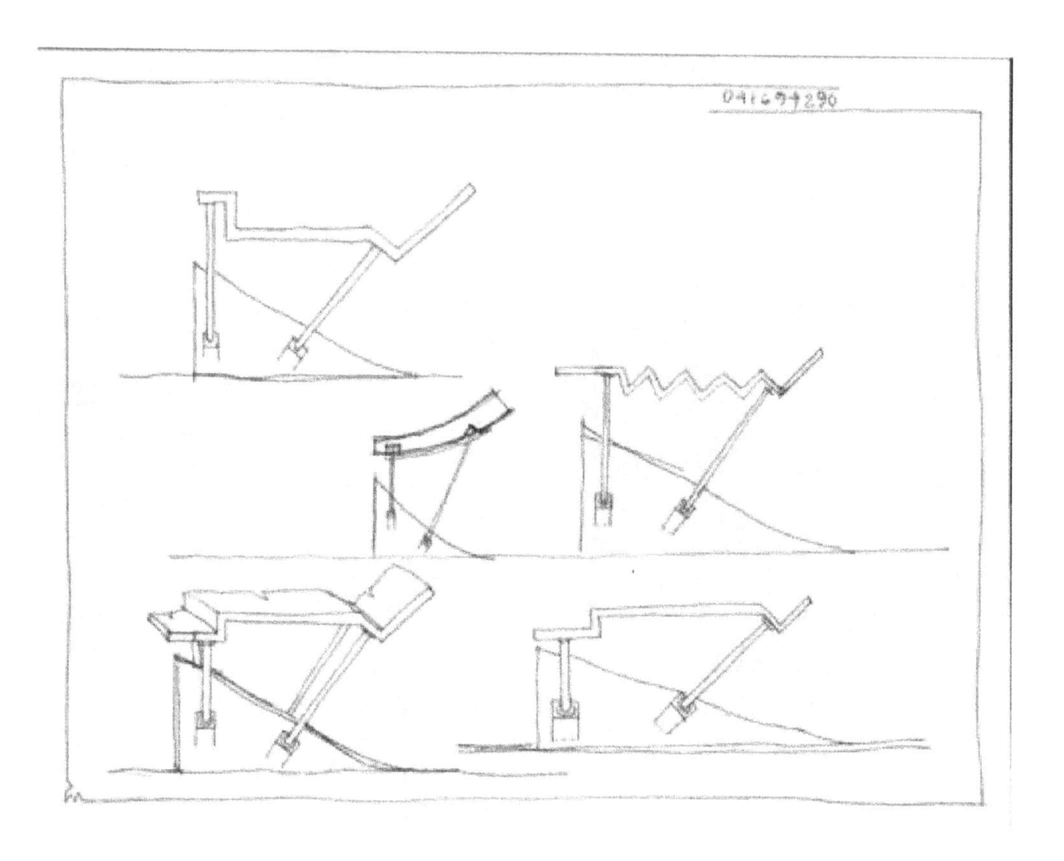
041694290

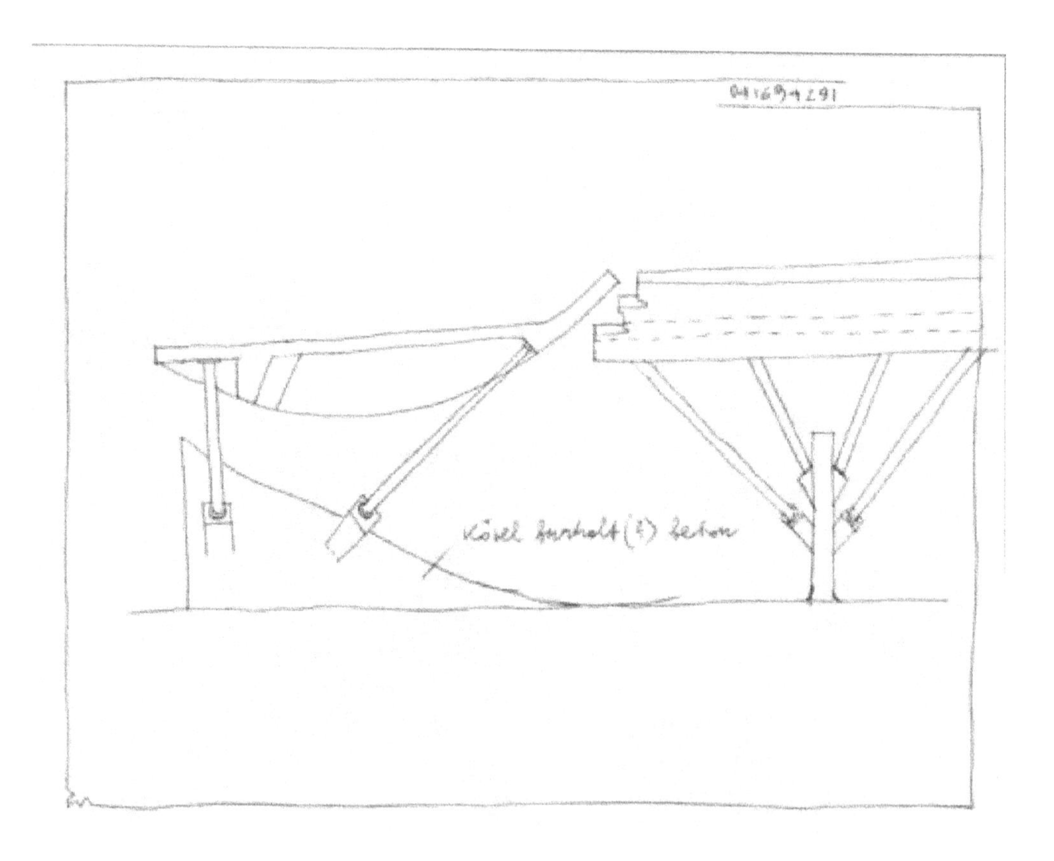
041694291

0417942.92

Kedves Tóni! Ezt a mai telefonunk után, vasárnap írom.
Sajnálom, hogy nem érkezett meg a tegnapi faxom, de így legalább volt időm gondolkozni a Te általad küldötteken. A Te rajzaidon az üveg donga boltozat nem volt kiépítve rajzolva, – ha az alapo [illegible] áll, akkor [illegible] kellene lenni. Hogy ezt kiküszöböljük, mit szólsz ehez a kombinációhoz?
Most még úgy gondolom, hogy jó lenne megőrizni az előző rajzokon feltüntetett háromszögű támfalak dinamizmusát, és valami térbeli alátámasztást – például amit rajzoltam – biztosítani.
Most még csak egy kérdésem van: a domb "púposságát" nem fogja-e zavarni befolyásolni az üvegtetők ívei ??

üveg donga
üveg donga
üveg donga
üveg donga

Úgy tűnik, hogy (saját kérdésemre válaszolva) nem lenne rossz.

Gondold [illegible] ezeket, én is gondolkozom a fenti alátámasztás részleteken. Szeretettel üdvözöl: Péter

nem párhuzamos tartó/vízelvezető részlet

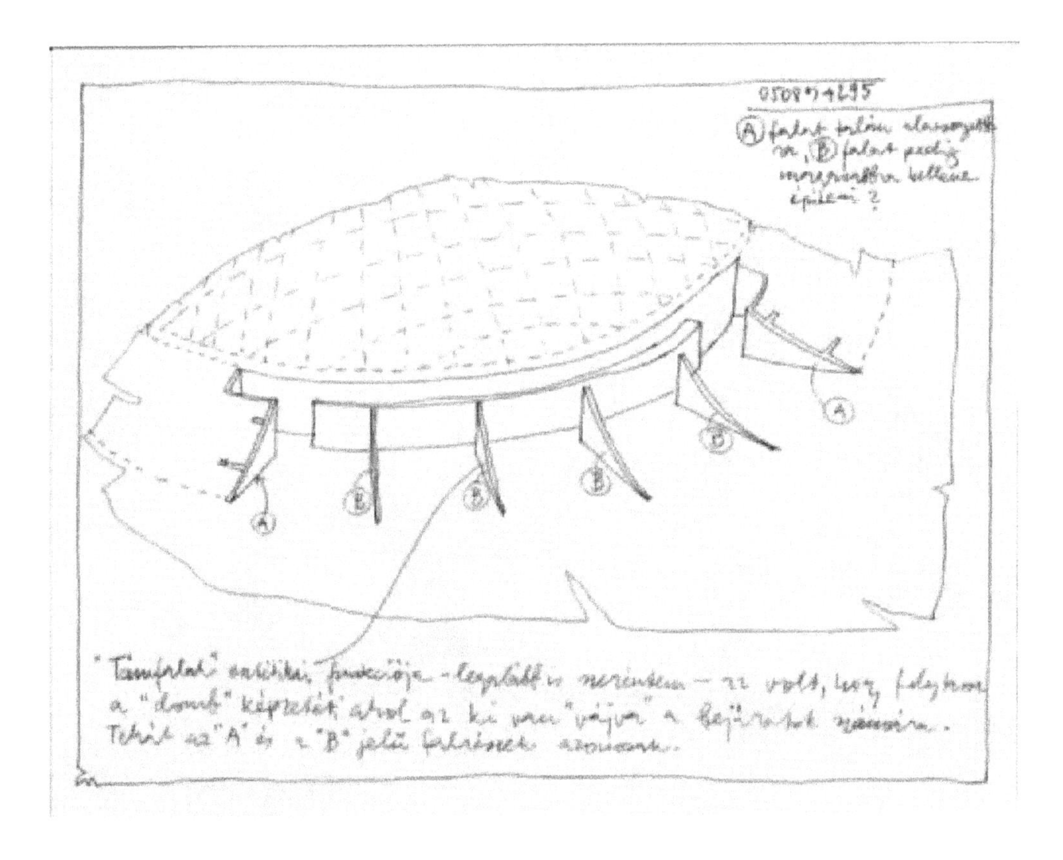

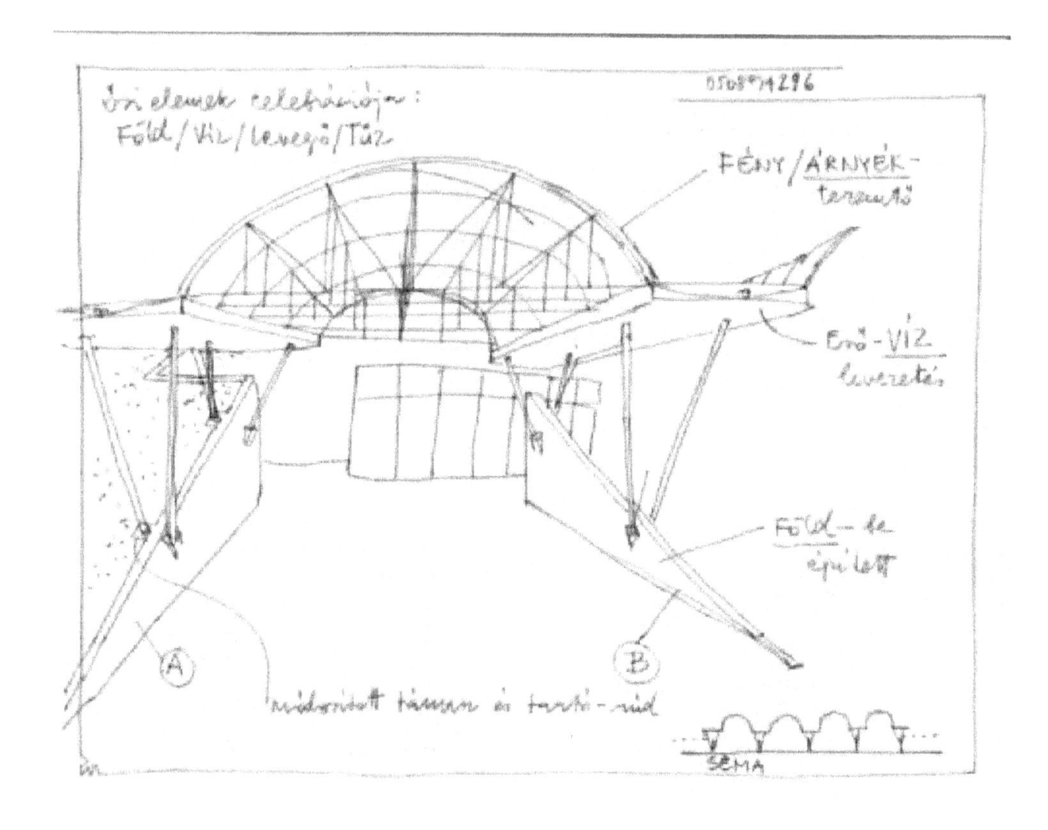
0508*14296
Föld/Víz/levegő/Tűz
FÉNY/ÁRNYÉK-teremtő
Erő-VÍZ levezetés
FÖLD-be épített
A
B
SÉMA

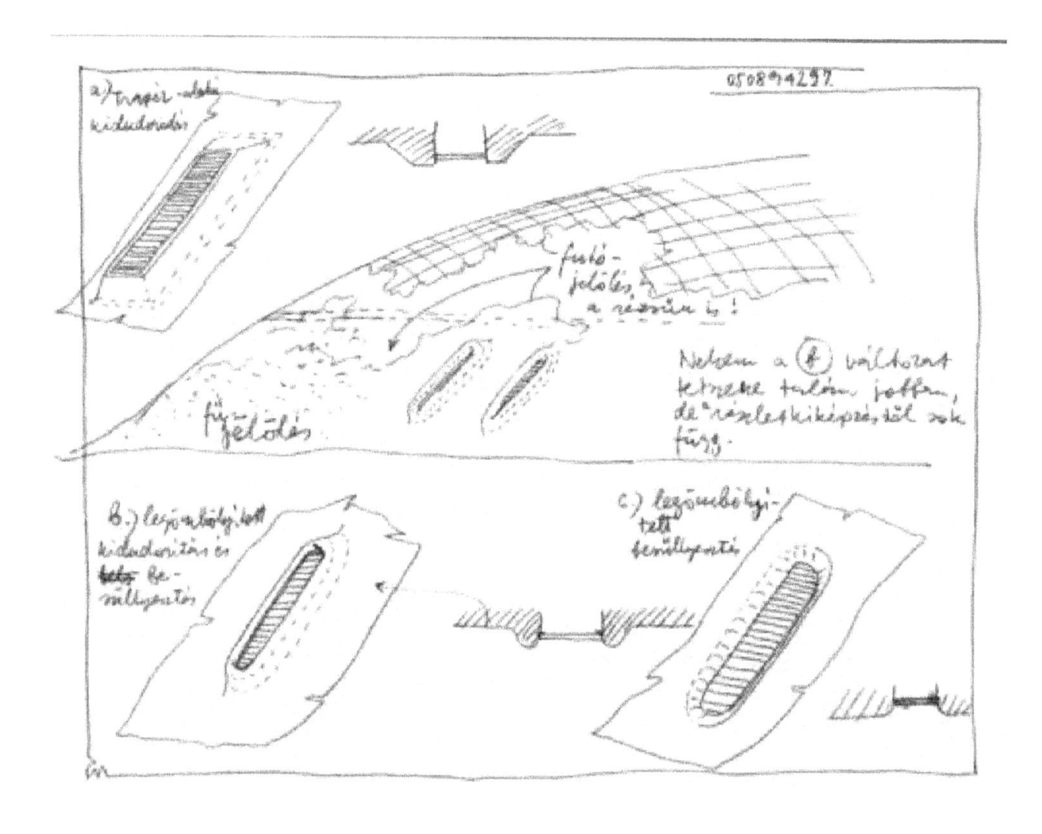
0508*14297
fű-jelölés
Nekem a (A) változat tetszene talán jobban, de részletkiképzéstől sok függ.

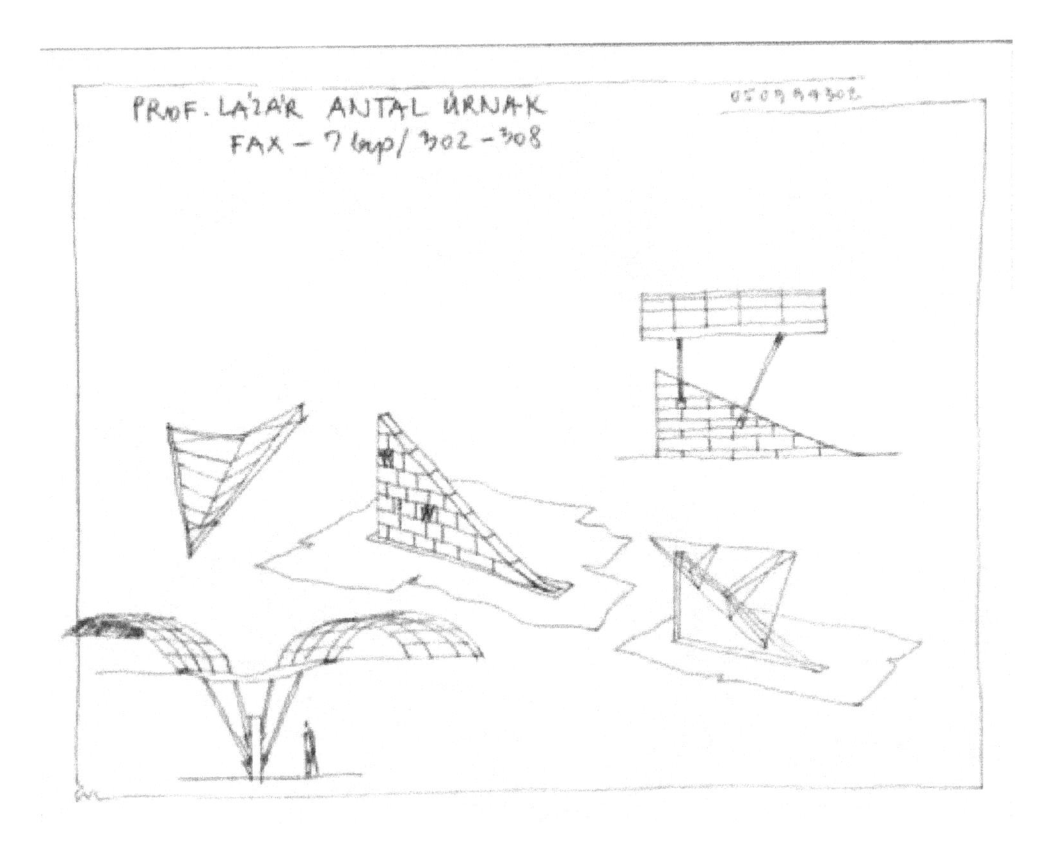
PROF. LÁZÁR ANTAL ÚRNAK
FAX – 7 lap/302-308

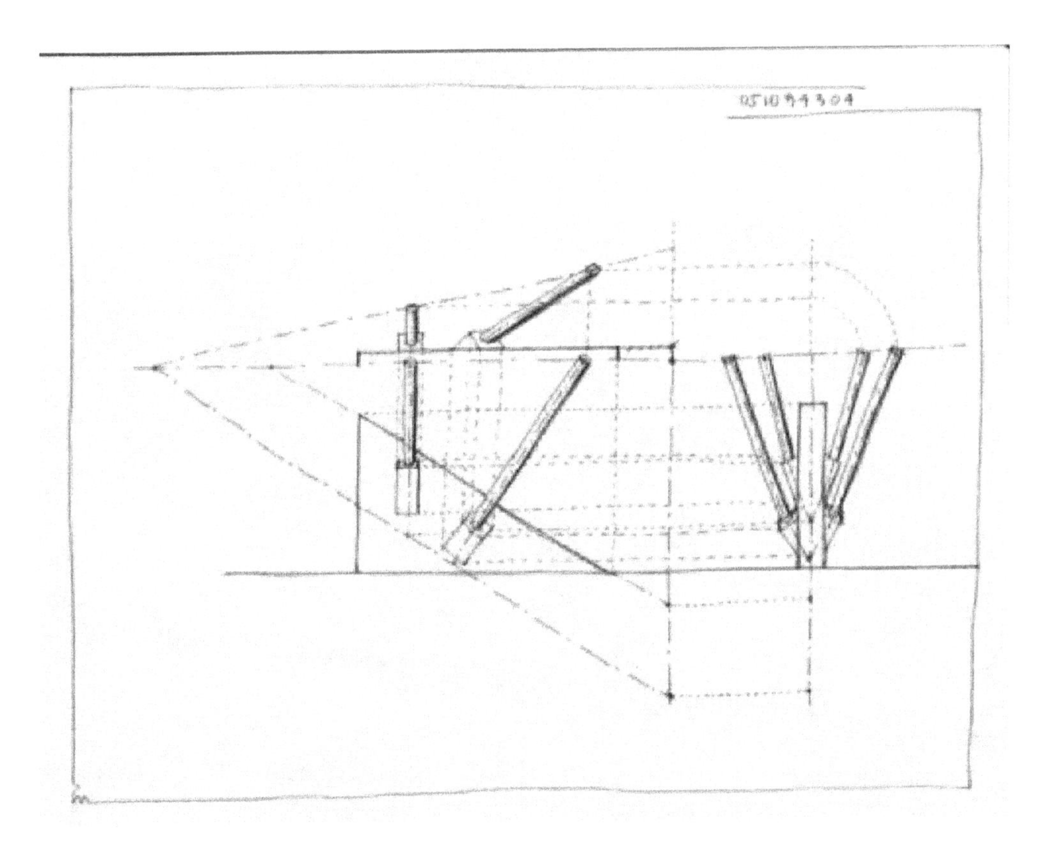

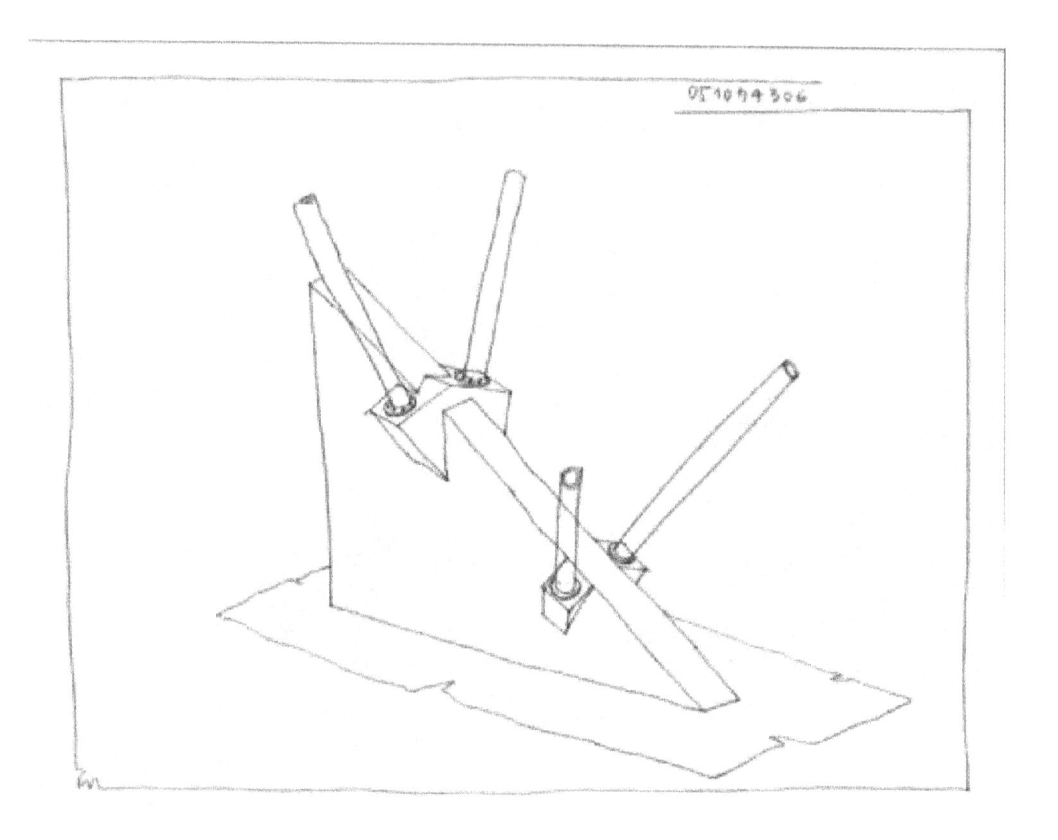

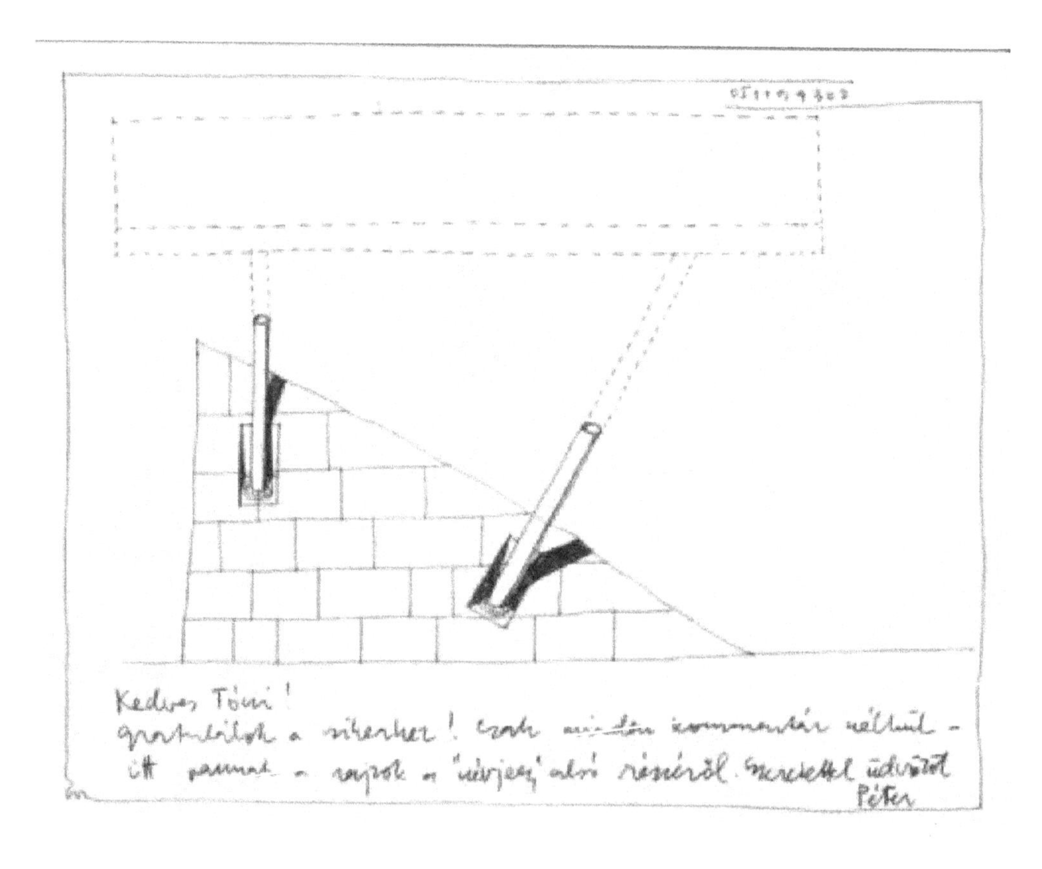
Kedves Tóni!
gratulálok a sikerhez! Csak kommentár nélkül –
itt vannak a rajzok a "névjegy" alsó részéről. Szeretettel üdvözöl
Péter

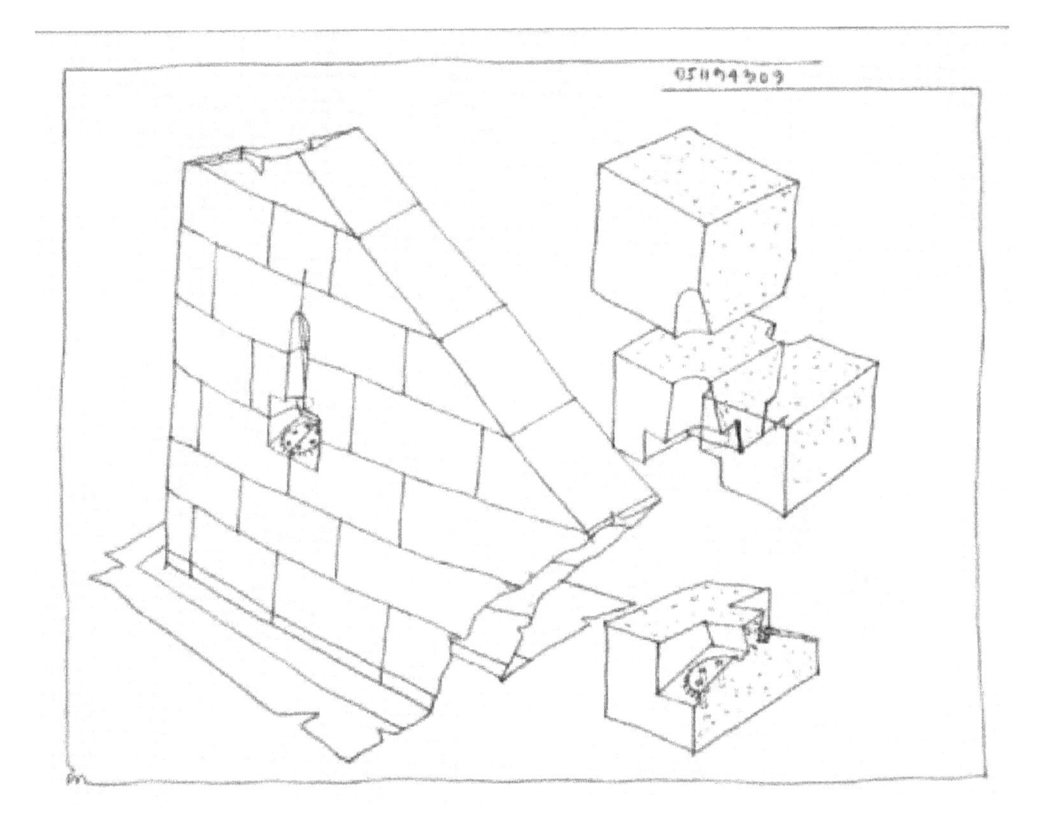

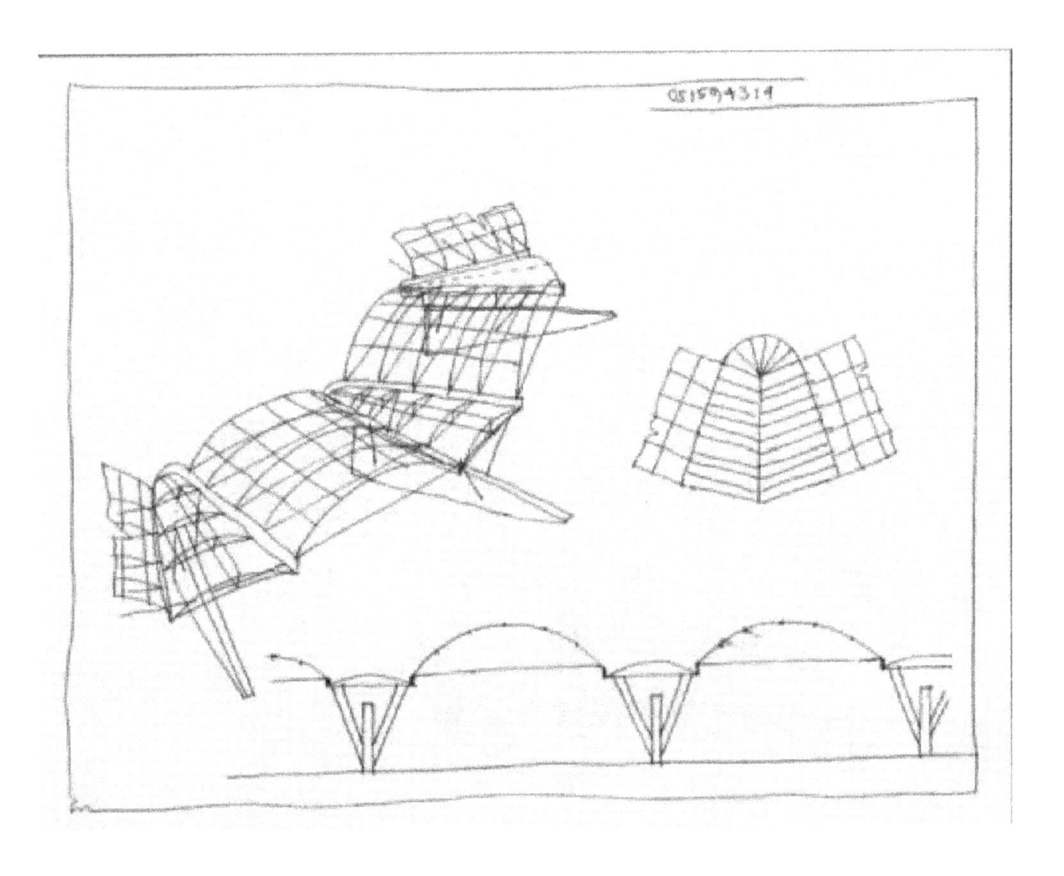

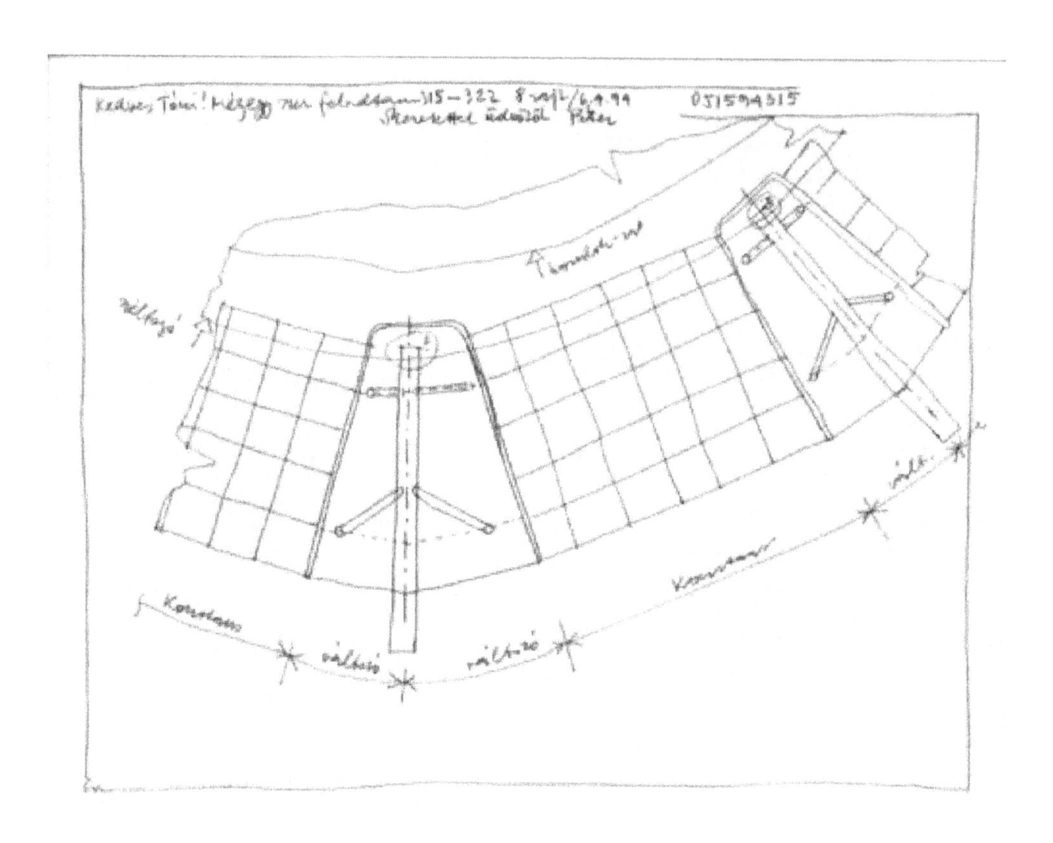
Kedves Tóni!
051594315

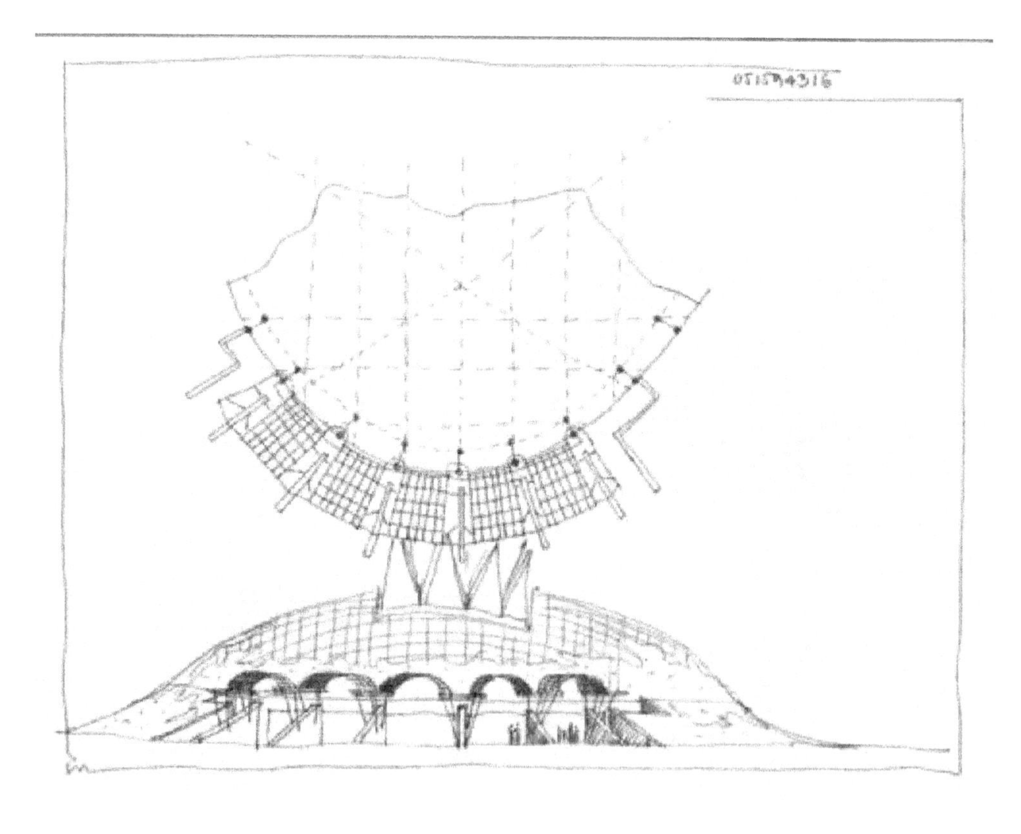
051594316

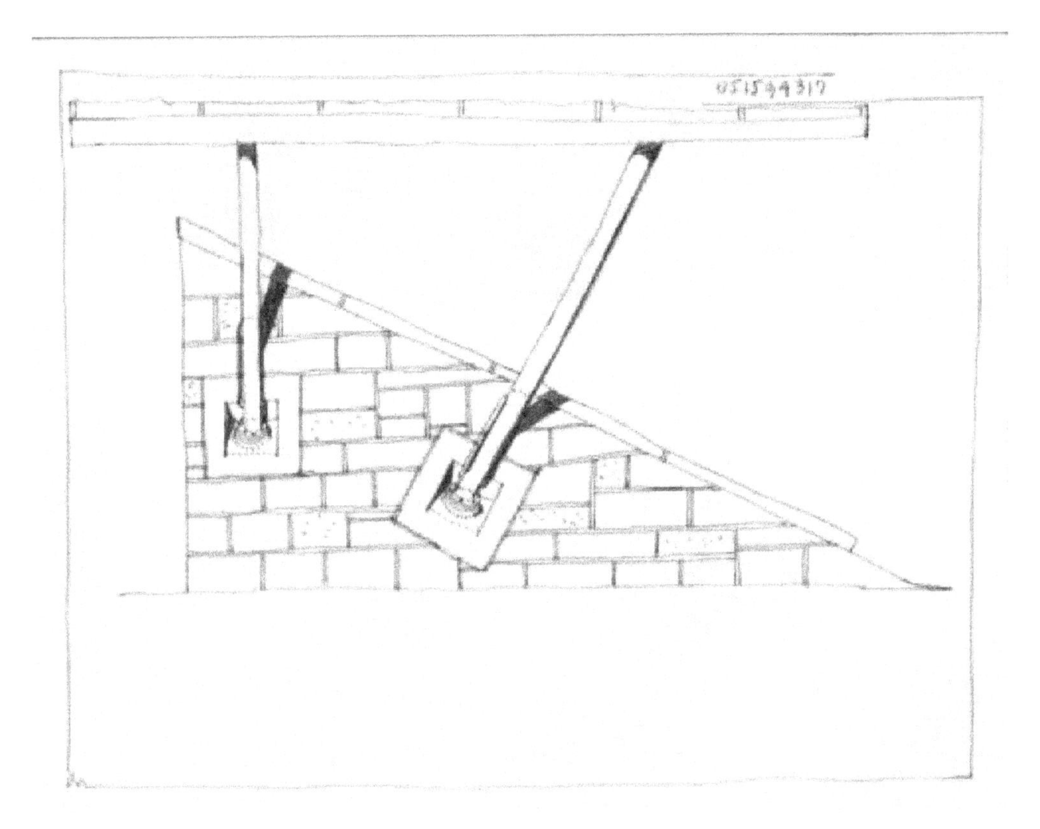
051594317

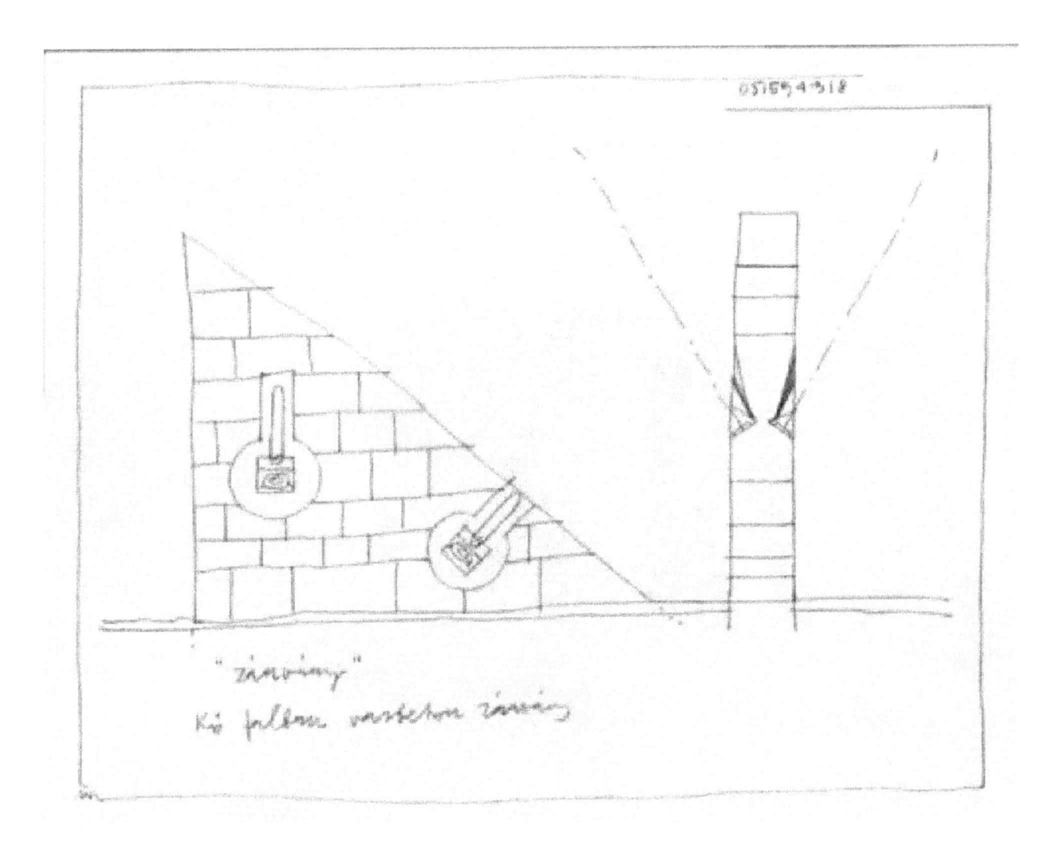
051594318
"zárvány"
Kő falban vasbeton zárvány

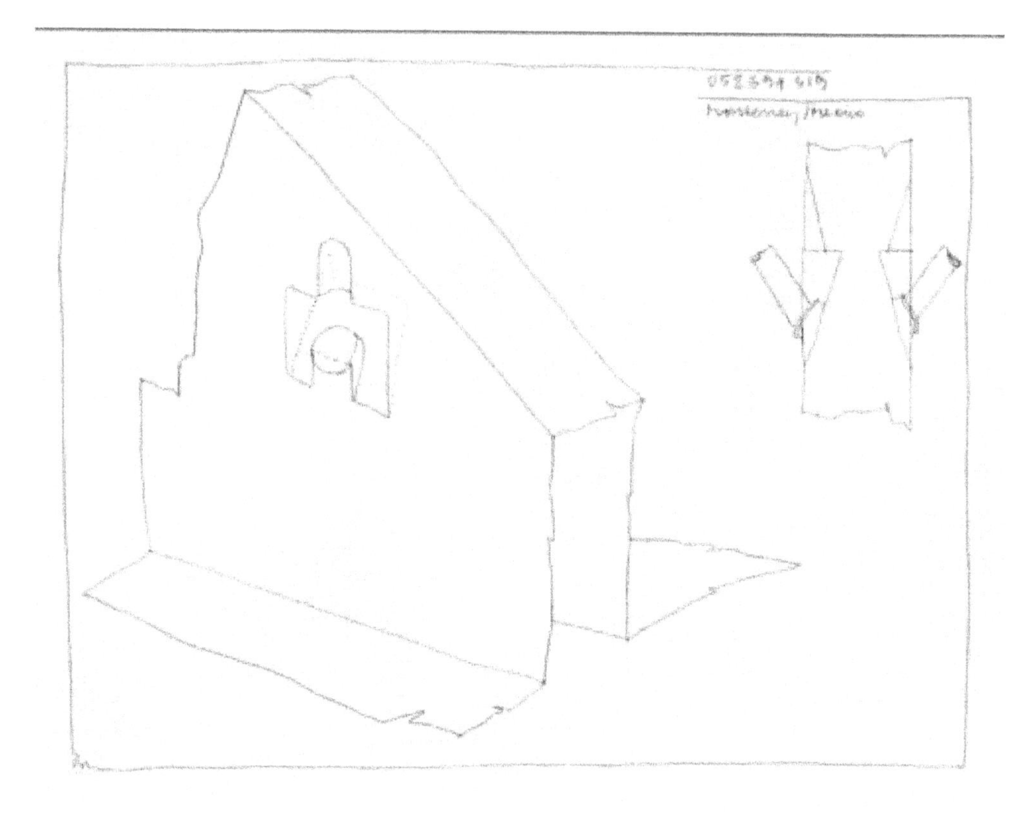
052394419

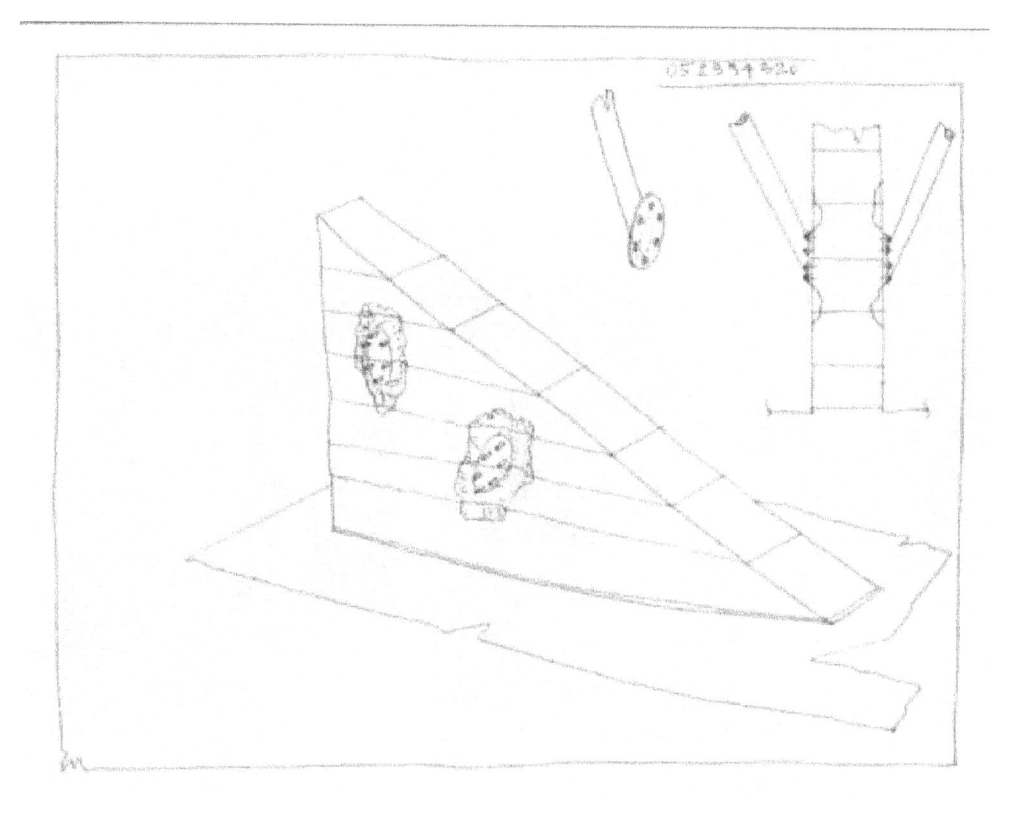
052394420

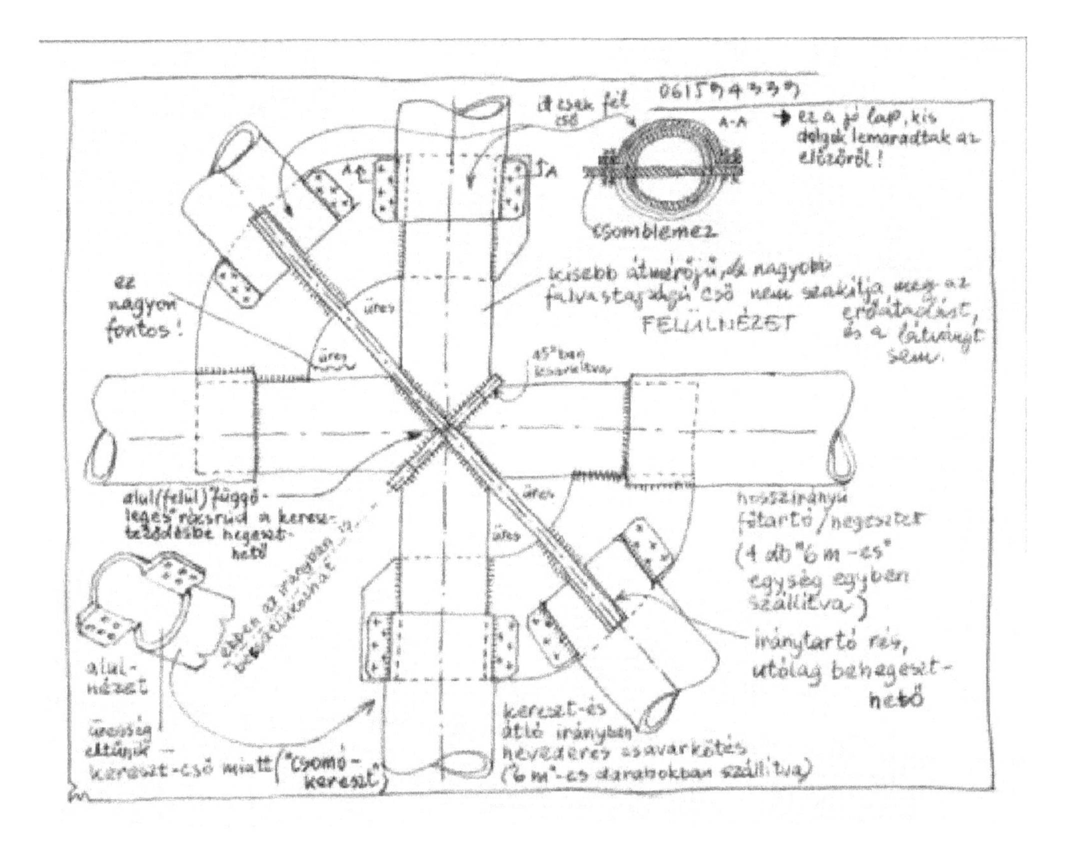
ez a jó lap, kis dolgok lemaradtak az előzőről!
A-A
csomblemez
kisebb átmérőjű, de nagyobb falvastagságú cső nem szakítja meg az erőátadást, és a látványt sem.
FELÜLNÉZET
ez nagyon fontos!
üres
45°-ban csavarítva
alul(felül) függőleges rácsrúd a kereszteződésbe hegeszthető
(4 db "6 m-es" egység egyben szállítva)
iránytartó rés, utólag behegeszthető
alul-nézet
kereszt-cső miatt ("csomó-kereszt")
kereszt-és átló irányban hevederes csavarkötés ("6 m"-es darabokban szállítva)

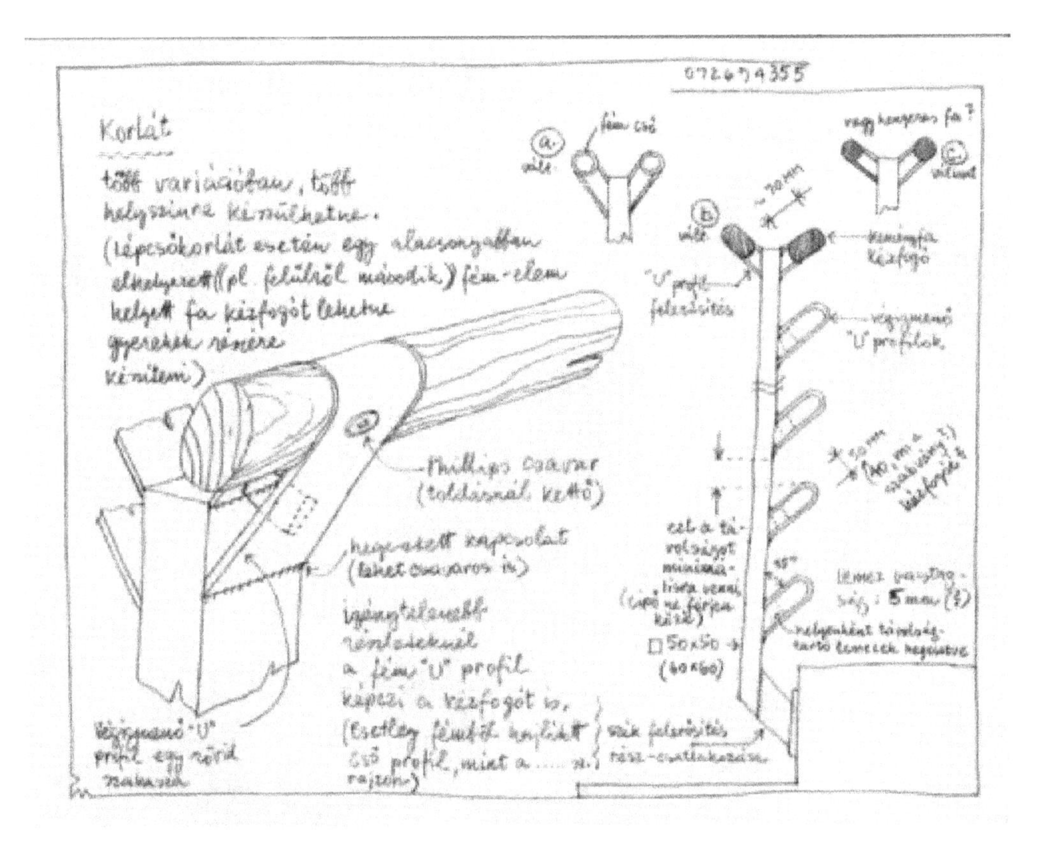
Korlát
több variációban, több helyszínre készülhetne.
(Lépcsőkorlát esetén egy alacsonyabban elhelyezett (pl. felülről második) fém-elem helyett fa kézfogót lehetne gyerekek részére készíteni)
Phillips csavar (toldásnál kettő)
hegesztett kapcsolat (lehet csavaros is)
a fém "U" profil képezi a kézfogót is,
végigmenő "U" profilok
□50x50 (60x60)
45°

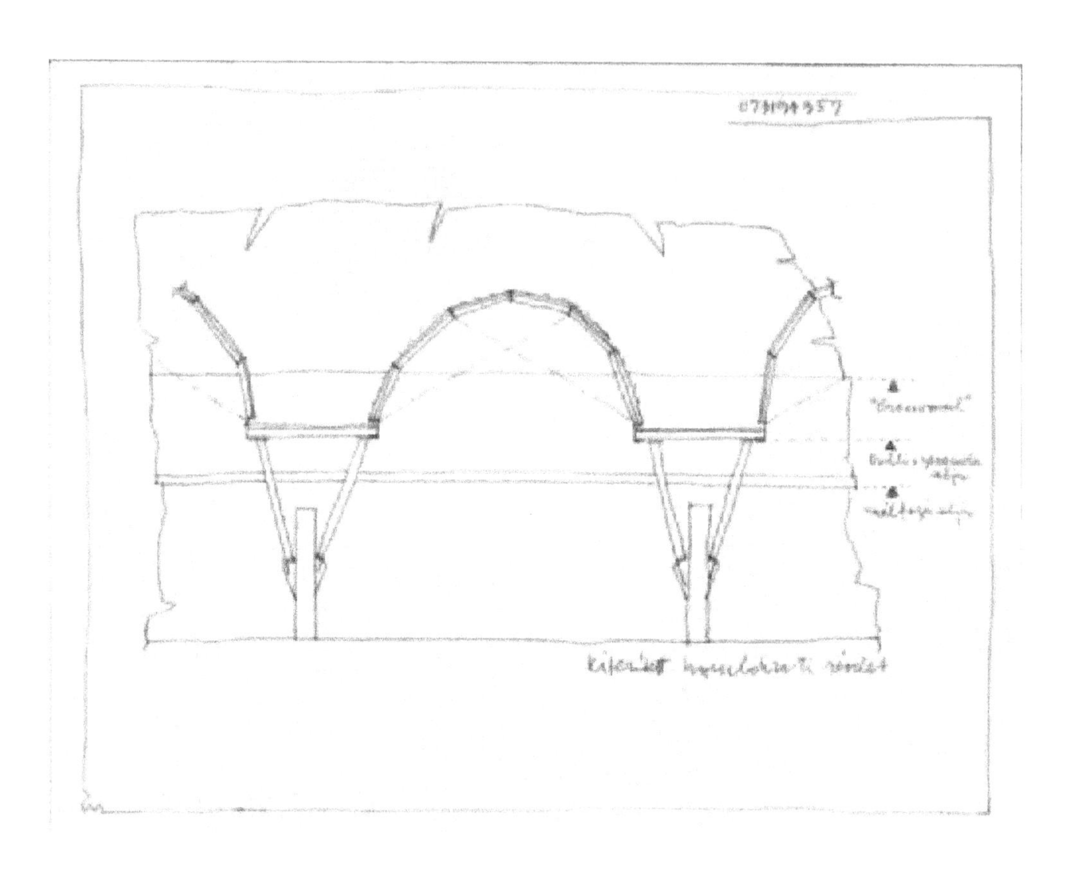

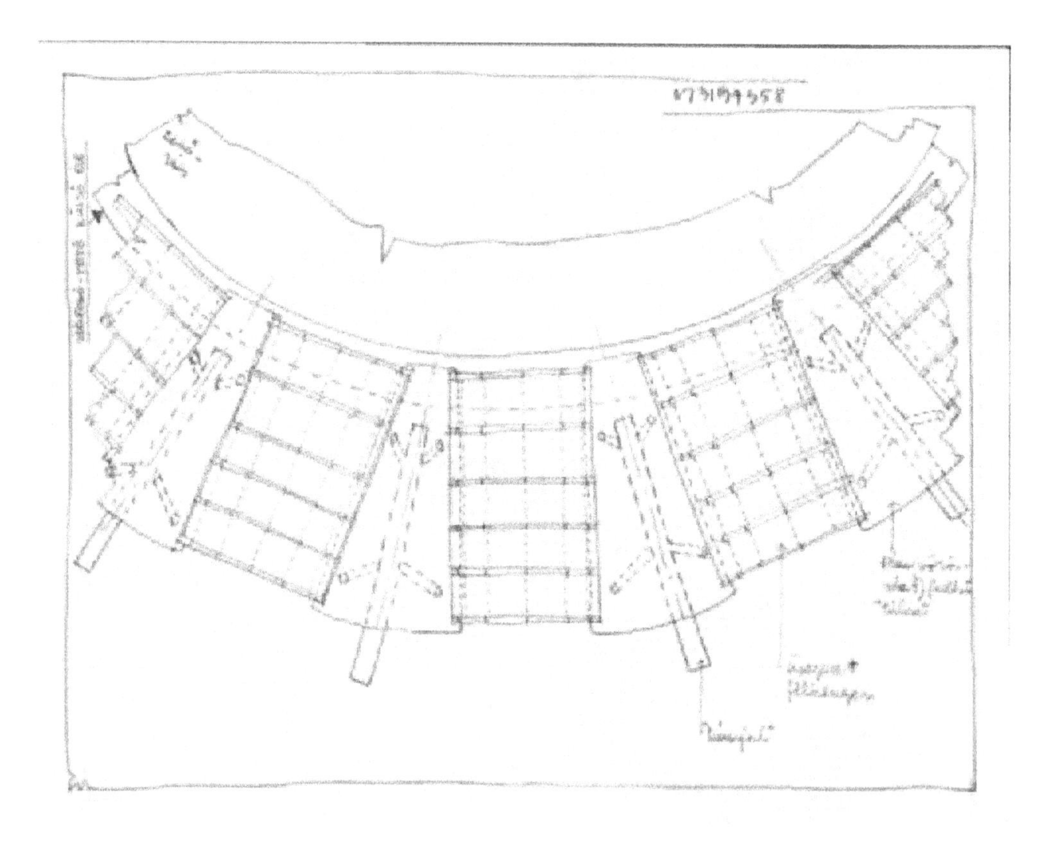

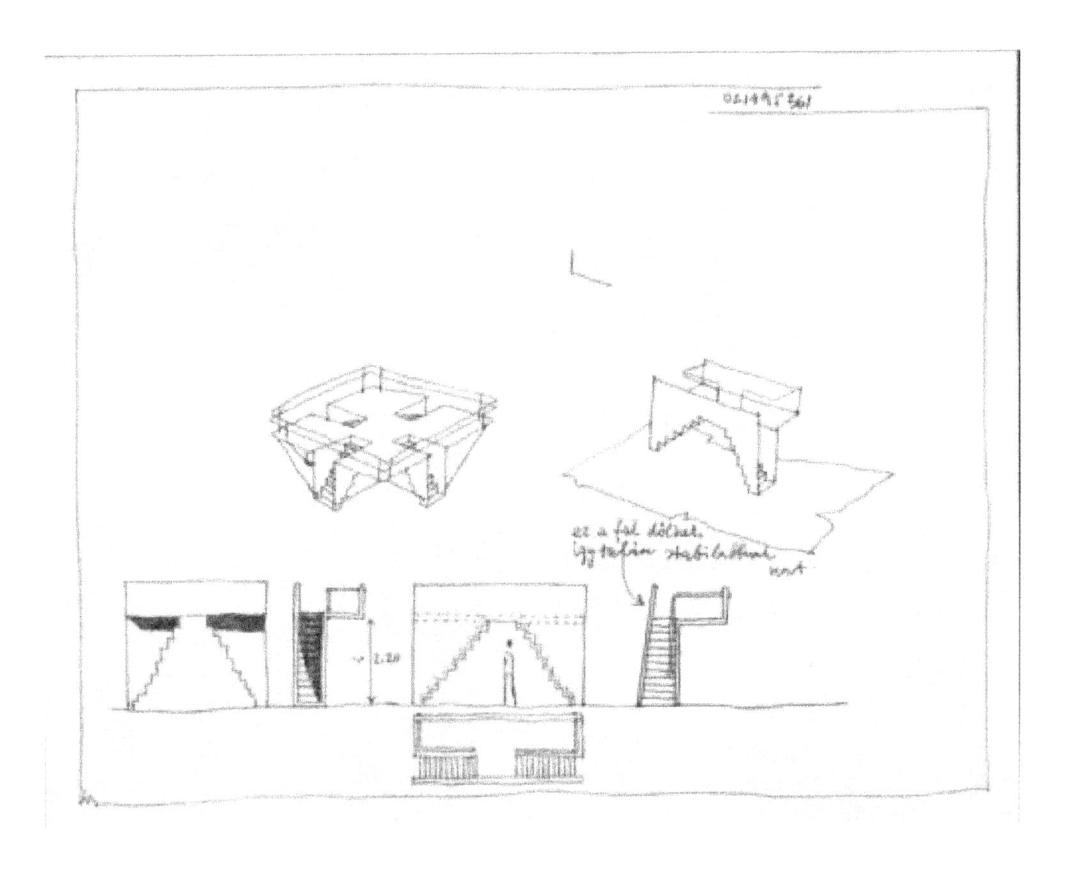

2.20

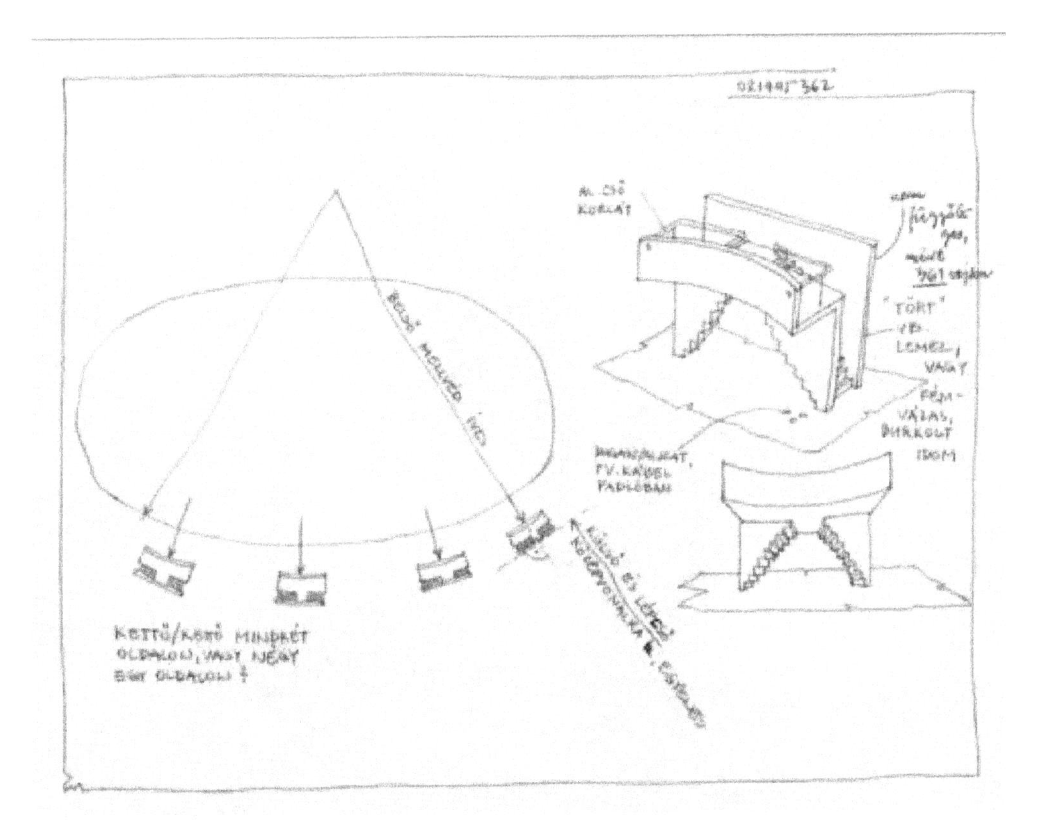

KORLÁT
"TÖRT"
LEMEZ,
VAGY
VÁZAS,
IDOM
PADLÓBAN

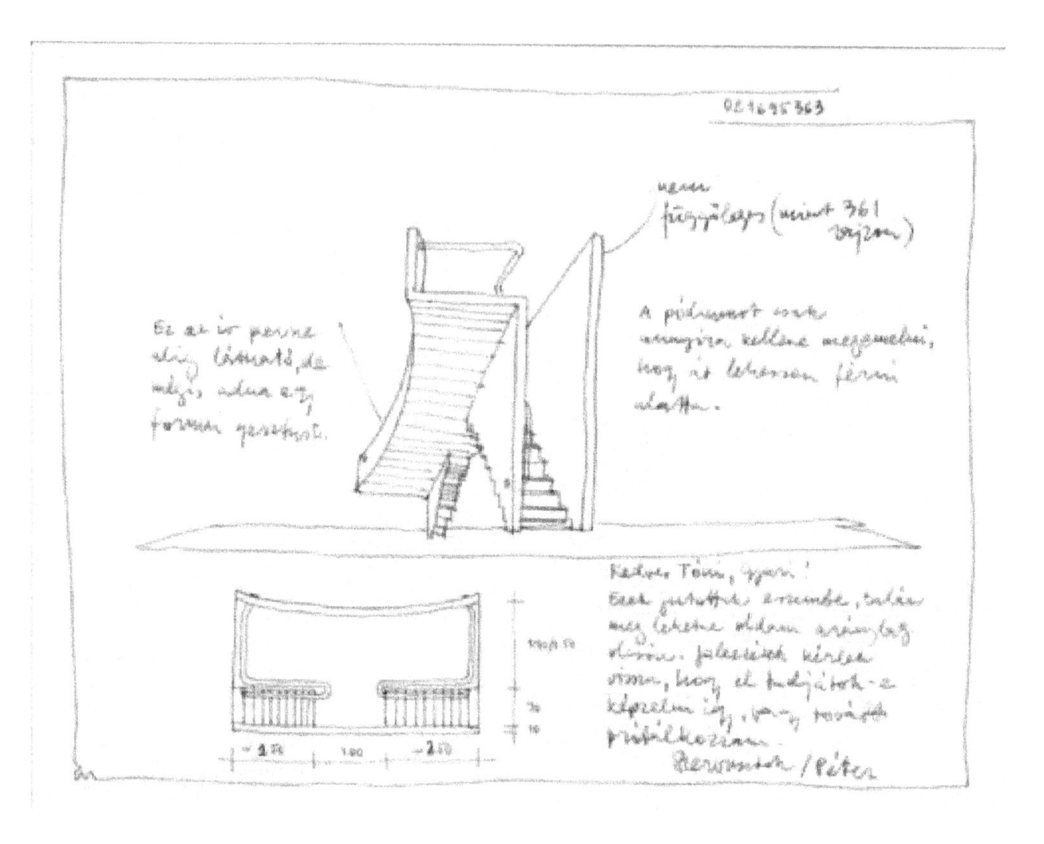
nem
függőleges
Ez az ív persze

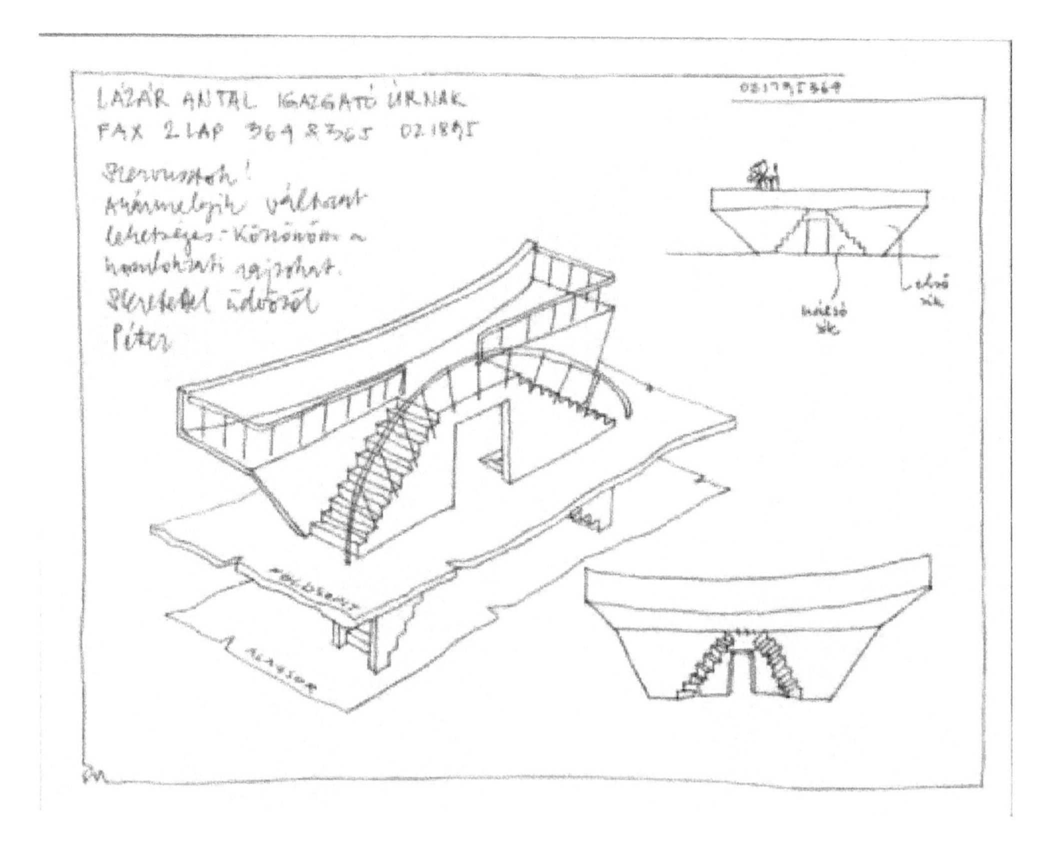
LÁZÁR ANTAL IGAZGATÓ ÚRNAK
FAX 2 LAP
Szervusztok!
Péter
FÖLDSZINT
ALAGSOR

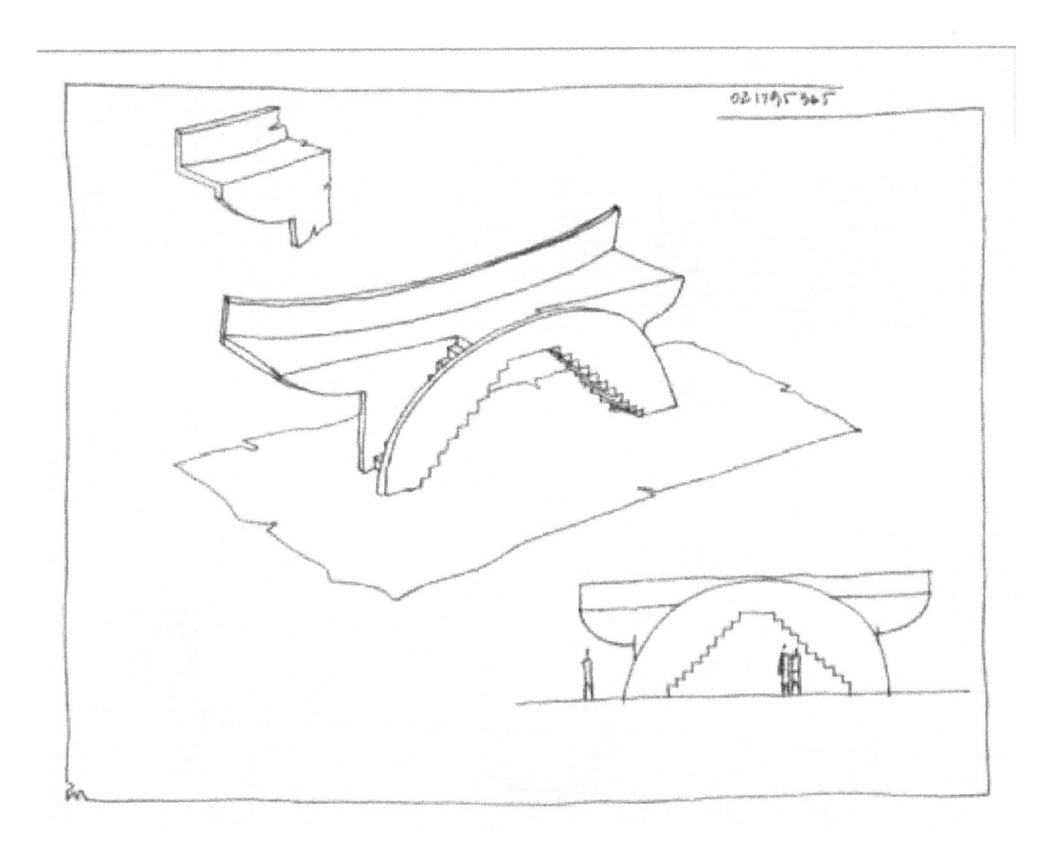

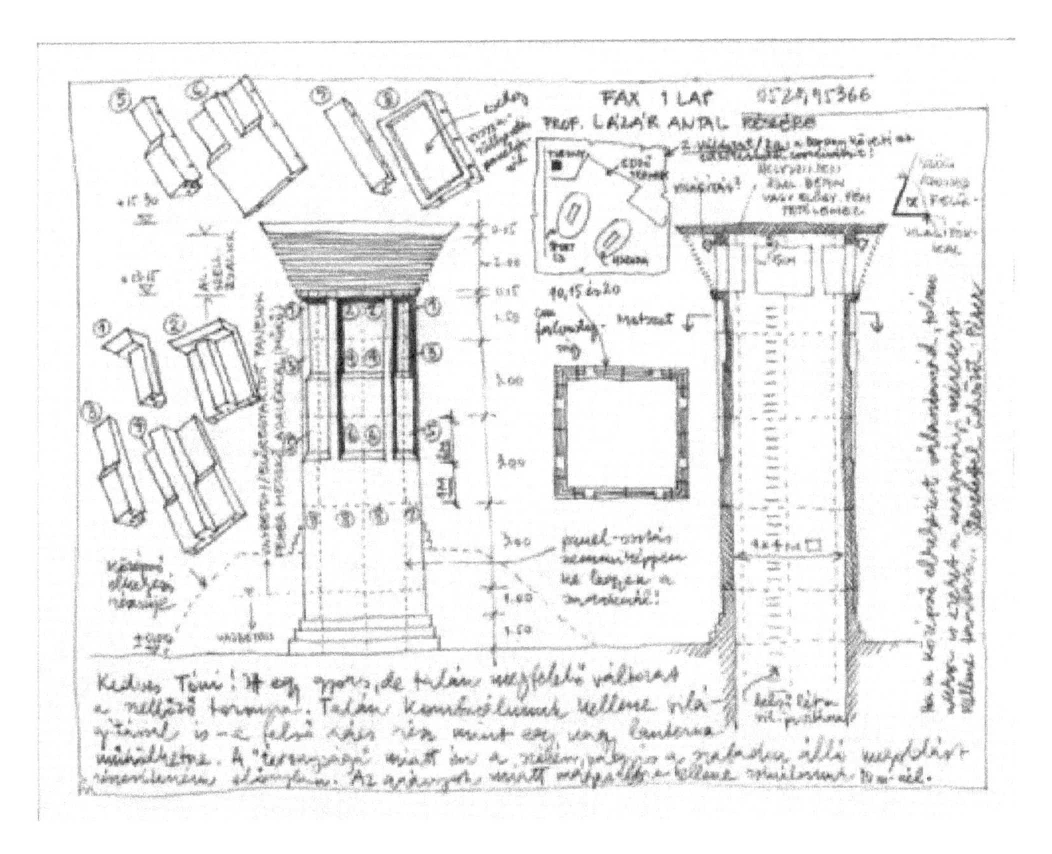

FAX 1 LAP
0524,95366
PROF. LÁZÁR ANTAL RÉSZÉRE
Metszet
Kedves Tóni!

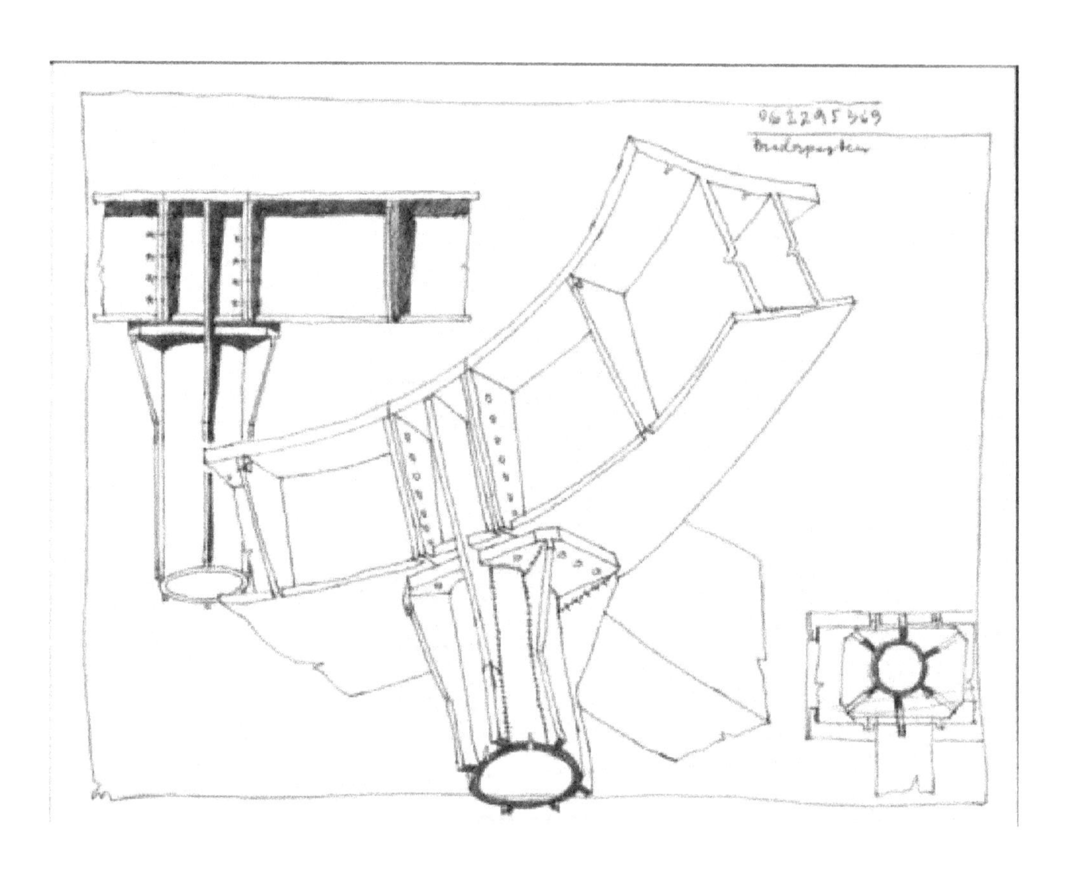

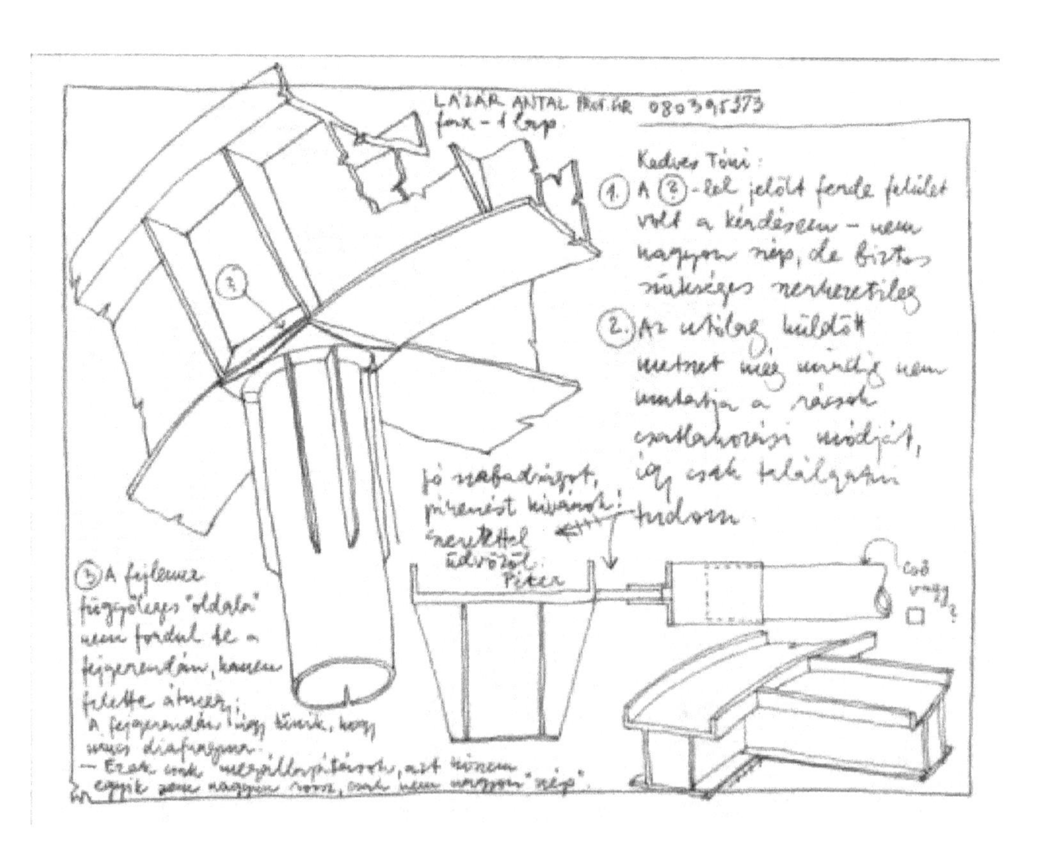

LÁZÁR ANTAL PROF. ÚR 080395373
fax - 1 lap
Kedves Tóni:
1. A 3-al jelölt ferde felület volt a kérdésem – nem nagyon szép, de biztos szükséges szerkezetileg
2. Az utólag küldött metszet még mindig nem mutatja a rácsok csatlakozási módját, így csak találgatni tudom
jó szabadságot, pihenést kívánok! szeretettel üdvözöl: Péter
3. A fejlemez függőleges "oldala" nem fordul le a fejgerendára, hanem felette átmegy;
A fejgerendán úgy tűnik, hogy nincs diafragma.
– Ezek csak megállapítások, azt hiszem egyik sem nagyon rossz, csak nem nagyon "szép".
Cső vagy □?

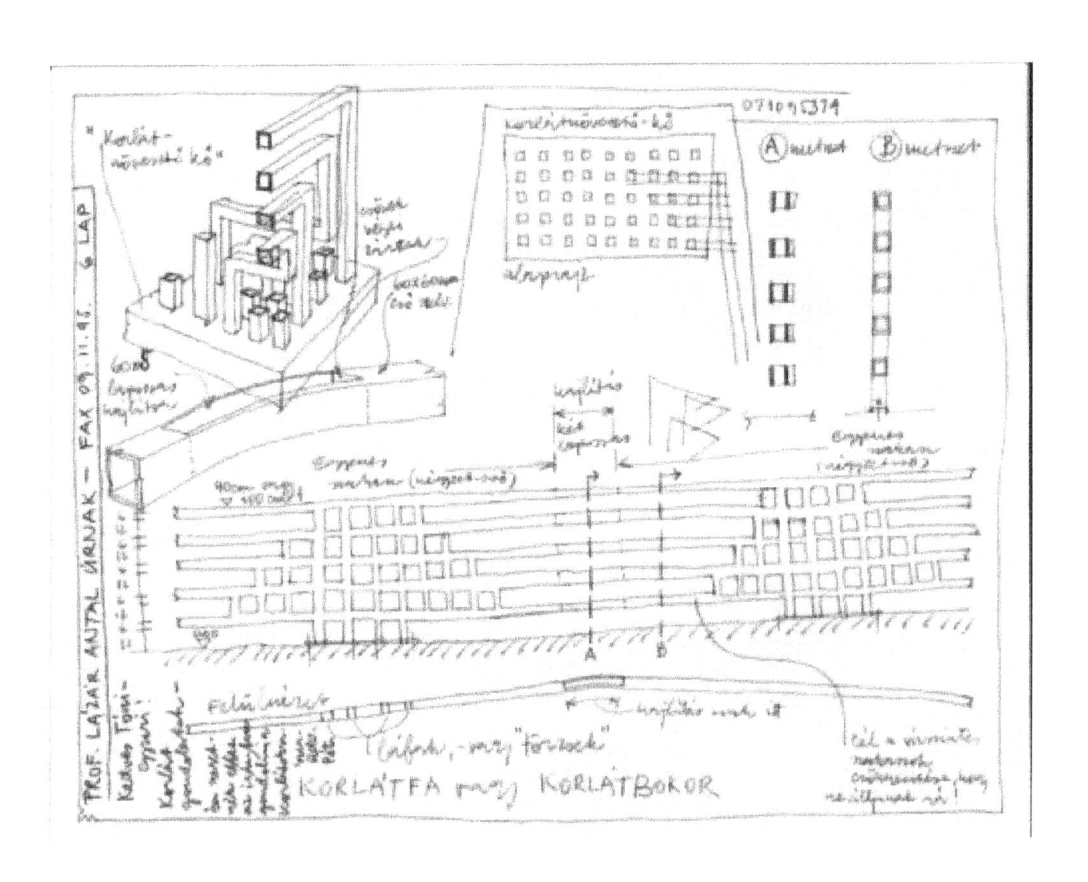
PROF. LÁZÁR ANTAL ÚRNAK – FAX 09. 11. 95. 6 LAP
0710953?4
A metszet
B metszet
Felülnézet
KORLÁTFA vagy KORLÁTBOKOR

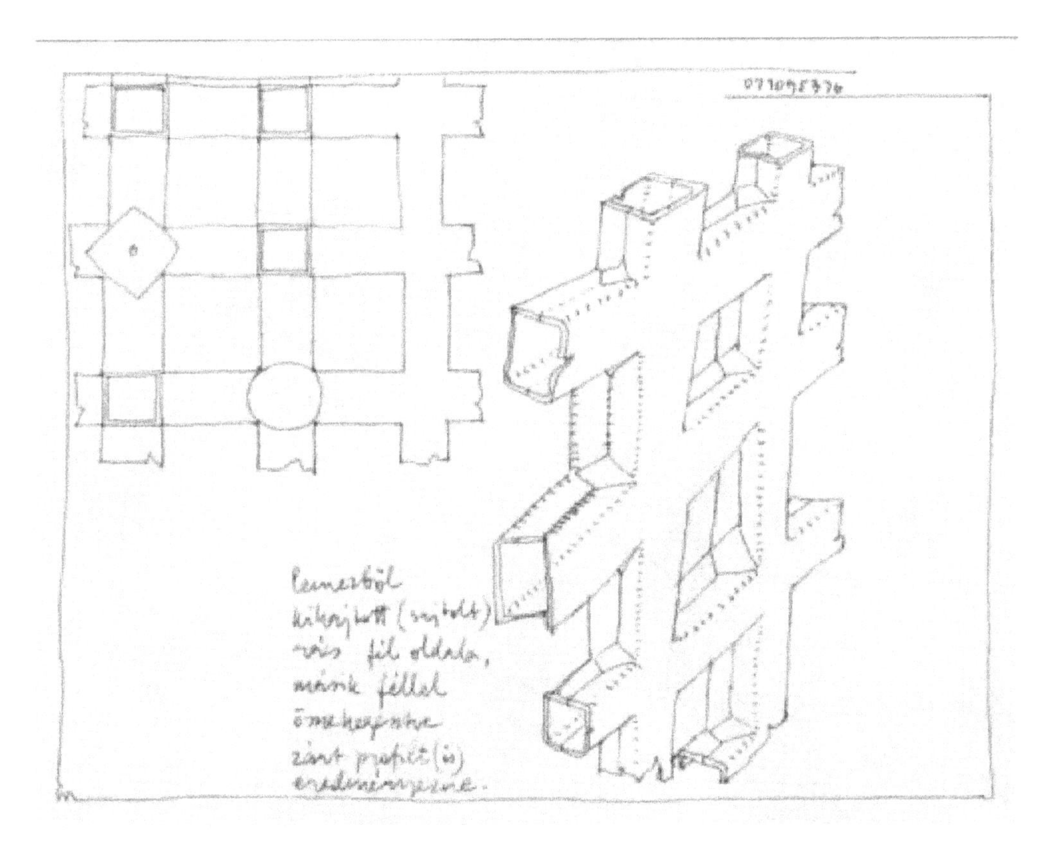
Lemezből
kihajtott
rács fél oldala,
másik féllel
összehajtva
zárt profilt (is)
eredményezne.

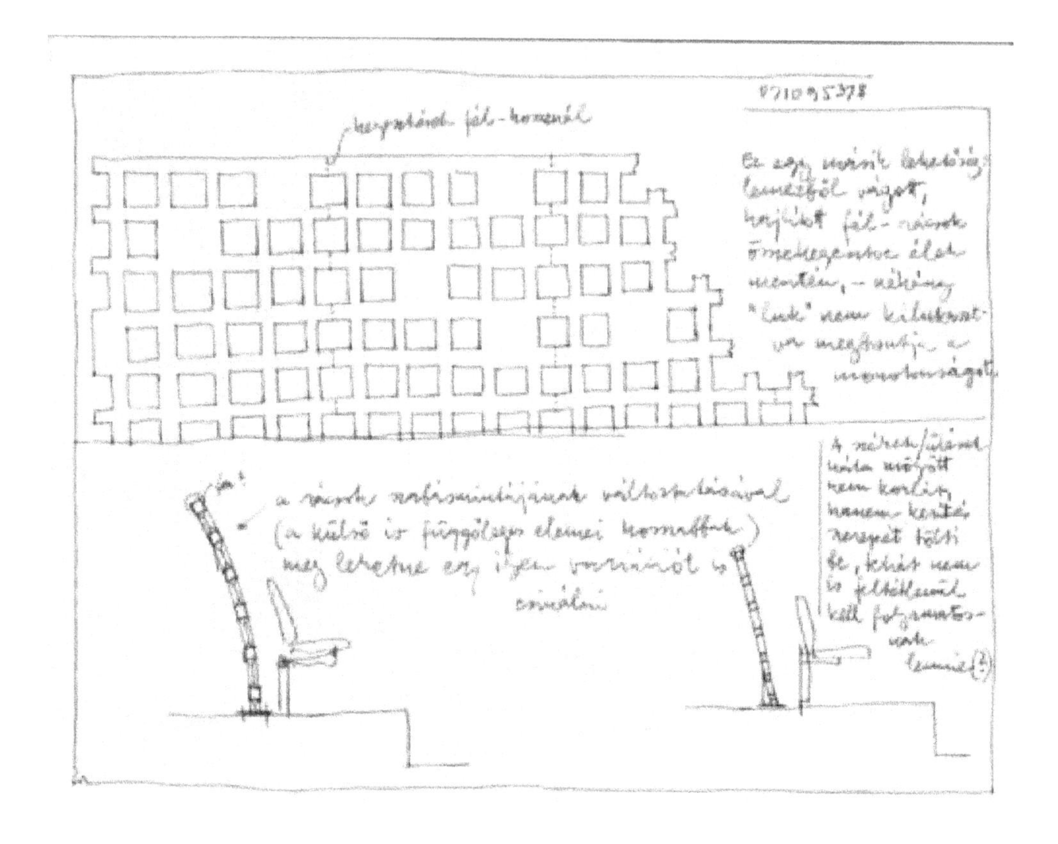

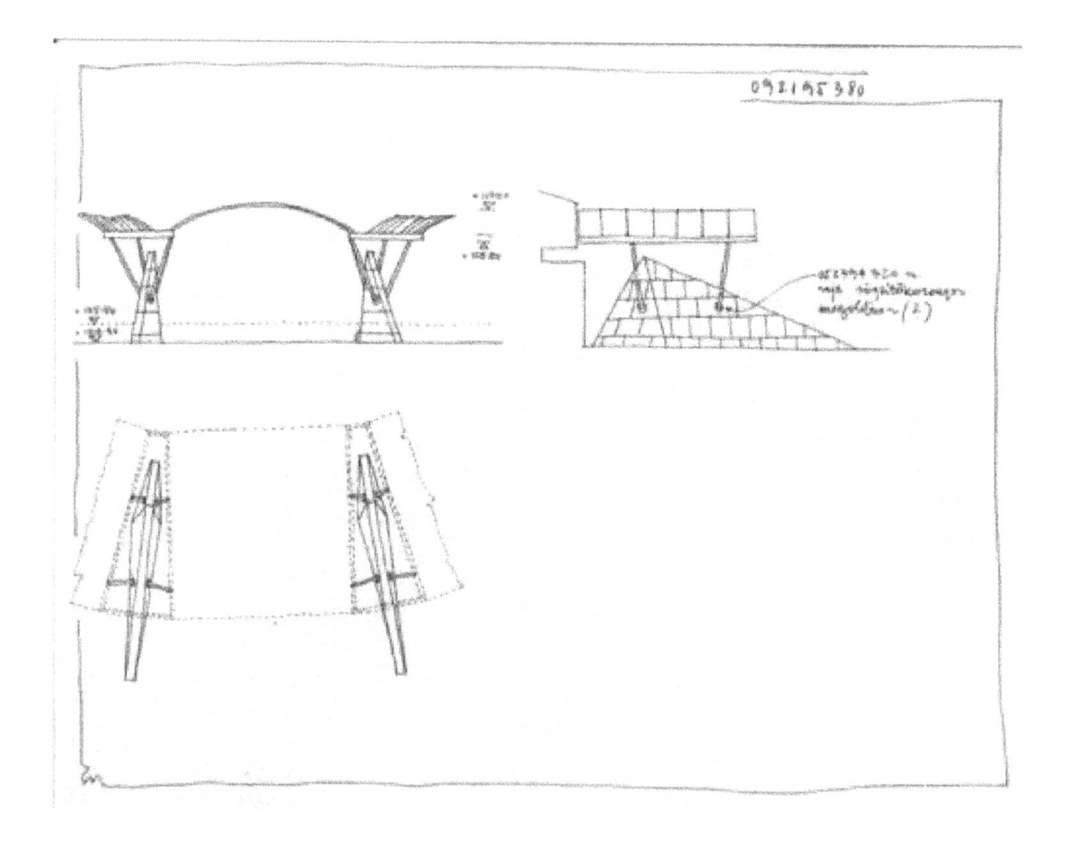

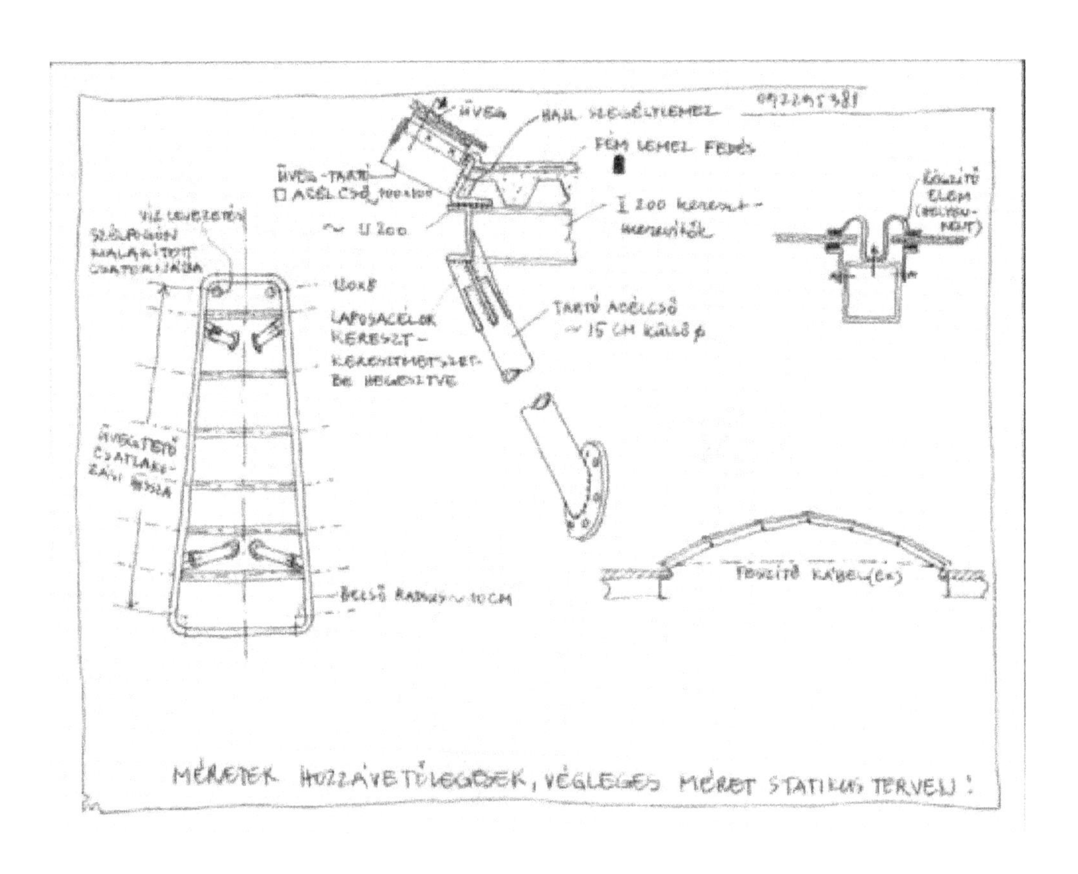
ÜVEG
FÉM LEMEZ FEDÉS
ÜVEG-TARTÓ
ACÉLCSŐ
~ U 200
I 200 kereszt-merevítők
LAPOSACÉLOK KERESZT-MEREVÍTMÉNYSZERŰEN HEGESZTVE
TARTÓ ACÉLCSŐ ~15 CM KÜLSŐ ⌀
RÖGZÍTŐ ELEM
ÜVEGTETŐ CSATLAKOZÁSI HOSSZA
BELSŐ RADIUS ~ 10CM
FESZÍTŐ KÁBEL (6x)
MÉRETEK HOZZÁVETŐLEGESEK, VÉGLEGES MÉRET STATIKUS TERVEN!

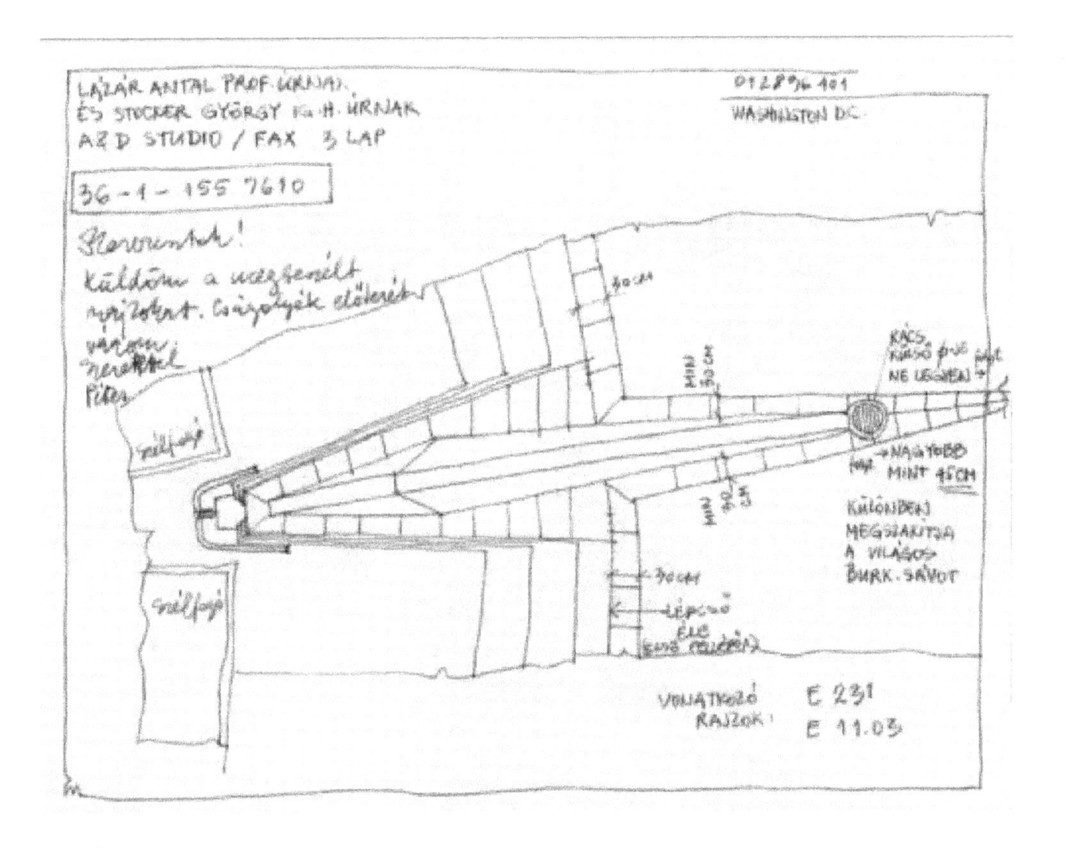
LÁZÁR ANTAL PROF. ÚRNAK
ÉS STOCKER GYÖRGY IG. H. ÚRNAK
AZD STUDIO / FAX 3 LAP
36-1-155 7610
WASHINGTON DC
MIN 30 CM
RÁCS KÜLSŐ ⌀-JE NE LEGYEN
NAGYOBB MINT 45 CM
KÜLÖNBEN MEGSZAKÍTJA A VILÁGOS BURK. SÁVOT
30CM
LÉPCSŐ ÉLE
szélfogó
VONATKOZÓ RAJZOK:
E 231
E 11.03

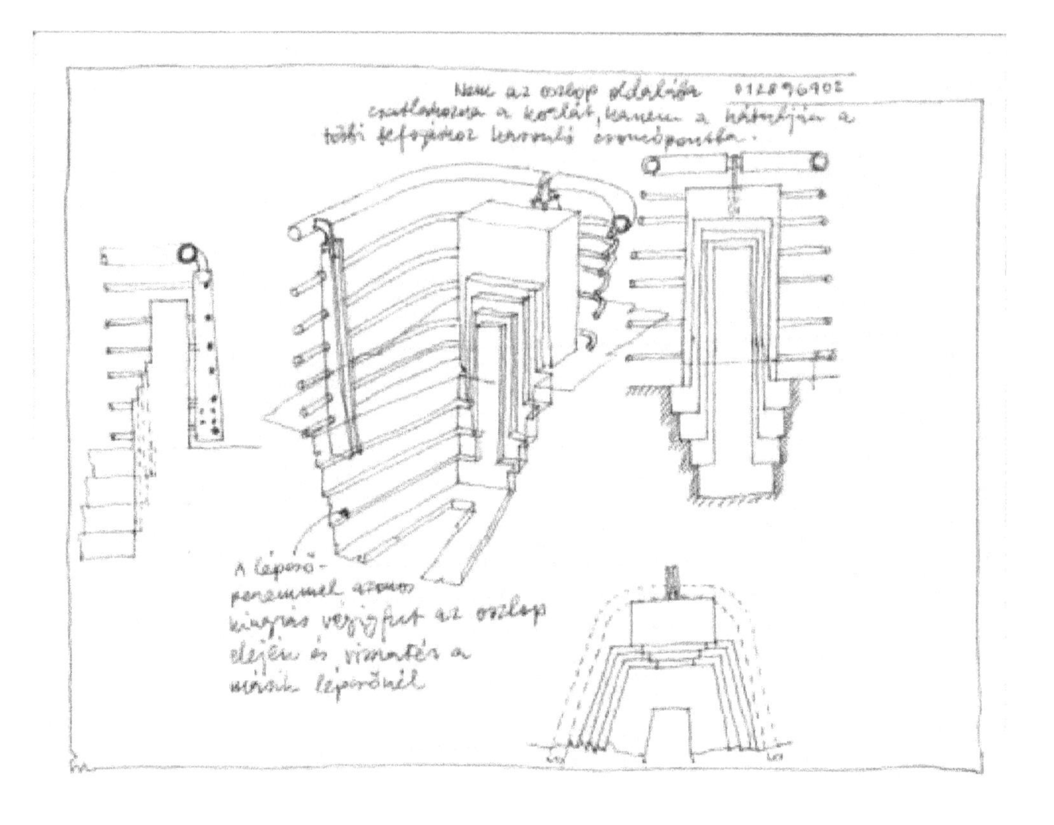

Peter Magyar

Dr. Peter Magyar, between 1989 and 2011, served as director of the Schools of Architecture in three American universities. He holds a Master of Architecture and a Doctor of Architecture degree, both issues by the Technical University of Budapest, Hungary. He was teaching, lecturing, and practicing internationally, and has designed large urban ensembles, some of them are constructed. He authored several booka about his projects, and in 2011 he won the Pro Architectura Hungarica Medal. In 2015 he became a member of the Hungarian (Szecheny) Academy of Arts and Letters. He was elected as a Fellow of the Royal Institute of British Architects in 2016. In 2017 in Berlin, and in 2018 in Amsterdam, his drawings and projects respectively were selected as finalist for the World Architecture Festival.

CPSIA information can be obtained
at www.ICGtesting.com
Printed in the USA
BVHW091332221222
654833BV00010B/248